SURVIVING THE CATACLYSM

SURVIVING THE CATACLYSM

Your Guide Through the Greatest Financial Crisis in Human History

by

WEBSTER GRIFFIN TARPLEY

SECOND EDITION, 2009

ProgRESSive

SURVIVING THE CATACLYSM

Your Guide Through the Greatest Financial Crisis in Human History

© 1999-2009 by

WEBSTER G. TARPLEY

WASHINGTON GROVE BOOKS

PO BOX 1486

WASHINGTON GROVE, MARYLAND 20880

USA

SECOND EDITION - ADVANCE REVIEW VERSION

Published June, 2009 by

Progressive Press, PO Box 126, Joshua Tree, Calif. 92252

ISBN 978-0930852-95-5

Length: 414,500 words on 664 pages.

Classification: Nonfiction, Politics, Economics

BISAC Subject Codes:

POL024000   Political Science / Economic Policy

POL023000   Political Science / Economic Conditions

BUS023000   Business & Economics / Economic History

BUS004000   Business & Economics / Banks & Banking

HIS036070   History / United States / 21st Century

Printed in the USA

TABLE OF CONTENTS

FOR LEAH AND CHLOE

PREFACE TO THE 2009 EDITION:

OVERCOMING THE ONGOING WORLD DEPRESSION

This book contains distinct two layers. The first group of chapters addresses the disintegration of the globalized international banking system based on derivatives during 2007-2008. This crisis represents an authentic world economic depression of unprecedented severity, posing a direct threat to the continued existence of human civilization as we have known it. It goes far beyond the mere collapses of speculative bubbles which we have known in such years as 1929 and 1987. This is now the disintegration of financial institutions in an unprecedented form, starting with the implosions of Countrywide Bank, Northern Rock, Bear Stearns, Lehman Brothers, Merrill Lynch, AIG, and other players in the world derivatives markets. Accordingly, the first group of chapters written in 2007-2008 is devoted to an analysis of these events, and above all to the delineation of an adequate economic program for fighting the depression, creating a world economic recovery, and thus preserving human civilization through the end of the 21st century. This material is most urgent, and it is therefore placed up front.

The second layer of the book reproduces in virtually unaltered form the text of a study prepared during 1998 during the time of the worldwide financial crisis variously called the Asian contagion, the Russian state bankruptcy, and the Long Term Capital Management derivatives hedge fund implosion. These chapters appear here for the first time in a printed book. This portion of the book offers a detailed snapshot of the trends existing 10 years ago which have brought us into the initial phase of the world economic depression. This study makes clear that a vast portion of the economic energies of the world were being devoted to staving off the overwhelming tendencies of the globalized financial system to destroy itself and disintegrate in an apocalyptic speculative orgy, meaning that virtually nothing was left over for world economic development. These chapters warned that what was then on the horizon was not a mere collapse, but rather a full-fledged disintegration and breakdown crisis of the world financial and economic arrangements which had been in place since the end of the Second World War. The causes of the coming depression were clearly identified in the form of the de-industrialization of the formerly advanced countries under the banner of the post-industrial society and the service-based economy which were clearly identified here as an impossible utopia ready to turn into hell on earth. In addition to de-industrialization, there was also the immiseration of the American middle class through a cut of at least one half (by 1998) in the prevailing standard of living as compared to what had been attained under the Lyndon B. Johnson administration in about 1966-67. Then came deregulation, in the form of the cancerous and speculative derivatives bubble fomented by such figures as Greenspan, Phil and Wendy Gramm, and the same Rubin-Summers forces within the Clinton administration which are running the Obama economic policy today. All of this was related to a worldwide age of oligarchy in which an extremely limited social stratum of financiers were the main beneficiaries of the system under which the entire world was being looted and robbed, as typified by some 40,000 deaths per day in the underdeveloped world due to starvation, malnutrition, and diseases like diarrhea or malaria which can be cured or prevented for a few pennies. This original book concluded with a detailed strategy for economic recovery based on policies to radically diminish the prevalence of speculation and fictitious capital in the economy as a whole, while returning to an emphasis and value system based on production, science, technology, industry, human progress, rising standards of living, full employment, and cultural optimism, thus rolling back a decidedly malevolent *Zeitgeist*.

Readers are invited to examine these 1998-1999 chapters and judge for themselves whether or not the method employed in this book as a whole is a reliable one. The author asserts that both the conclusions of the original *Surviving the Cataclysm* as well as the method which generated them have proven superior to all known competition. The point of stressing this at the outset is to invite the reader to consider most carefully the policy recommendations that are made in this book as a basis of action in the present and the future. An economist who successfully diagnosed with chronic maladies of the world economy in 1998-1999 is, it is argued here, also the economist whose advice ought to be seriously considered when it comes to finding ways to getting the world out of the current critical situation.

THE RAREST WISDOM: HOW TO GET OUT OF THIS DEPRESSION

The most precious knowledge which anyone can have at the present moment in world history is an understanding of how to deal successfully with the world economic depression so as to shift the direction of world events towards economic recovery and general prosperity. Despite what so many obscurantist and pessimistic schools of economics tell us, there is nothing inherently mysterious about organizing an economic recovery. Recovery is based on sweeping away speculative paper, meaning in today's world derivatives, and putting unemployed workers back into idle and shuttered factories so as to restart the production of hard commodity, tangible physical wealth. Money is not primary. Money is merely a way of mobilizing resources. Production is the central issue, and it is production which is today most universally neglected even as the world sinks deeper and deeper into depression. With this in mind, we must defeat the depression, outflank it, crush it. We did it before in the 1930s, and we can do it again now.

The immediate cause of the current breakdown crisis is the derivatives bubble, amounting to the fantastic sum of $1.5 quadrillion – that is to say, one thousand five hundred trillion dollars of notional value, with the "notional" referring to the value of the assets pledged. These instruments were illegal in the United States from 1936 until 1982, but since then they have grown exponentially and it is the presence of this kited mass of derivatives which makes the present situation so serious. The presence of these derivatives means that most comparisons between the current situation and anything before about 1992 are not valid, because of the profound changes brought by the derivatives bubble. Derivatives, meaning approximately financial paper based on other financial paper, often taking the form of mere bets on the fluctuations of other speculative values, claim to be a means for diminishing risk, whereas in reality they have multiplied risk to positively lethal levels. We must always think of the $1.5 quadrillion derivatives bubble as a tiered pyramid composed of credit default swaps, collateralized debt obligations, asset-backed securities, mortgage backed securities, structured investment vehicles, and all the other forms of this leveraged insanity. As long as the cash flow from the base of the pyramid towards its apex was positive, there was positive leverage, meaning absolutely astronomical hyper-profits at the top of the pyramid. The problem was that even a minor disturbance at the base of the pyramid would inevitably turn this entire mechanism into reverse, with negative cash flow and exponentially negative leverage for the financiers inhabiting the upper levels. This is what began to happen in 2005 and 2006, and which burst upon the world stage in 2007 and 2008.

Ruling class economists of all types try to say as little about derivatives as possible. The standard reactionary explanation for the present world depression is that poor people seeking to put a roof over their heads took out a series of subprime mortgages on slum properties and then defaulted on these loans. This phenomenon of mortgage default, in reality a small piece of the picture, has been portrayed as the cause of the collapse of the entire world banking and insurance system during 2008. Subprime mortgages are in themselves represent a minor slice of the world's speculative edifice. The only way they could ever impact large-scale financial phenomena is by virtue of their having been incorporated in asset-backed securities and mortgage backed securities, that is to say transformed into derivatives and incorporated into the very unstable derivatives bubble. It is the derivatives structure which has amplified and multiplied the subprime losses into an appreciable magnitude, thus calling into question the solvency of the entire derivatives bubble.

THIS IS A DERIVATIVES CRISIS

Imagine a world in which defaulting on subprime mortgages could in effect destroy the world system of globalized finance capital. We can imagine a modern Lenin telling his central committee: "Comrades, we have located the Achilles' heel of finance capital, We will now give up our revolutionary organizing and moved to American cities. Here we will take out loans which the capitalists call subprime mortgages, and then we will stop paying. A panic will break out and a leading Wall Street banks will go bankrupt. Capitalism will be over and we can then carry out the revolution." This ought to sound as absurd as it is, and illustrate how asinine it is to blame a breakdown crisis of the entire world banking system on a few penny-ante subprime mortgages. Notice, however, that this explanation blames poor people for the crisis and lets Wall Street financiers off with a whole coat.

A FIVE-POINT PROGRAM TO OVERCOME THE WORLD DEPRESSION

Let us now lay out the condensed essentials of a program to stop the depression and start a recovery towards prosperity. If any aspects of this program should not be clear, the reader is invited to plow through the entire book and then return to this page, since everything should be crystal clear by that point. Here is what must get done to unleash the tremendous potential productive forces of this country and the world.

1. Measures for re-regulation, nationalization, neutralization of fictitious capital, combating speculation, plus bankruptcy procedures and the preservation of labor, plant, and equipment.

This crisis has been caused by deregulation and privatization, as demanded of the Austrian and Chicago monetarists. Derivatives were long illegal, but they were then permitted and are now crushing the world. The prevalence of currency risk itself derives from the de-regulation of the international currency markets carried out in abortive fashion by Richard Nixon on August 15, 1971, which destroyed fixed parities and gold settlement. As for privatization, Fannie Mae and Freddie Mac were doing just fine as government agencies until they were privatized. It was the privatization which opened the door to speculative excesses and looting.

We must now proceed to re-institute a federal ban on derivatives contracts in securities of all types. This must extend to over-the-counter derivatives, exchange traded derivatives, counterparty derivatives, structured notes, design or derivatives and every other form this noxious plague has assumed. One way this can be done is along the lines of the Public Utility Holding Company Act, which allowed only one layer of holding companies above the actual generating facilities. In our case today, we can simply ban all layers of paper that had been piled on top of economic activity beyond the first degree. There must be no mercy for derivatives. Derivatives have no value. Like that dubious eastern European currency unit the rasbucknik in the Little Abner comic strip drawn by

Al Capp, derivatives have negative value because we have to pay some garbage men to come and take them away. Derivatives must be shredded, deleted, and otherwise annihilated. All of this can be done by legislative action if that is available, or else by executive order with reference to the Defense Production Act, the Trading with the Enemy Act, and other precedent-setting legislation. It would also be useful to declare the International Swaps and Derivatives Association to be an enemy alien waging economic warfare against the United States. Henceforth, derivatives contracts or derivatives transactions will become a federal crime as they should have been all along.

DELETE AND SHRED TOXIC DERIVATIVES

The cancellation and deletion of all existing derivatives instruments and contracts as a matter of overriding national survival will inevitably lead to the gutting of various Wall Street derivatives monsters, foremost among them J.P. Morgan Chase, Citibank, Bank of America, Goldman Sachs, Morgan Stanley, and a few others. In one way, we are fortunate that the top dozen or so Wall Street financial institutions represent the quasi-totality of the derivatives plague. These are the main zombie banks which have so far vainly absorbed a very high proportion of the TARP bailout money. We note that almost every Friday afternoon, Sheila Bair of the Federal Deposit Insurance Corporation seizes and shuts down certain insolvent local banks. These are generally small institutions in rural areas. Sheila Bair is guilty of malfeasance and nonfeasance in office because of her failure so far to seize control of J.P. Morgan Chase, Citibank, Bank of America, Wells Fargo, Goldman Sachs, Morgan Stanley, Bank of New York Mellon, and a few other money center institutions, all of which are manifestly bankrupt and insolvent. It is urgent that these institutions be put through Chapter 11 bankruptcy proceedings under federal judges who have been instructed to ruthlessly triage and obliterate all derivatives as the first step towards determining whether these banks can be saved at all. Because of the pervasive use of derivatives speculation by these money center banks, it is almost 100% certain that none of them can be saved. That will leave us with a local and regional banking system which may well salvageable, and with the inherent credit generating powers of the US federal government when it is acting, as it should, as its own bank. We will also need to return to a modern version of the Glass-Steagall Act, mandating the rigorous separation of commercial banks from stock brokerages and investment companies. This means that such monstrous hybrid combinations as J.P. Morgan and Chase Manhattan, or Bank of America with Merrill Lynch will have to be broken up, in the unlikely eventuality that they are still left standing.

STOP ADJUSTABLE RATE MORTGAGES AND HOME FORECLOSURES

Adjustable rate mortgages should never have been sold legally in this country. They must now be banned and outlawed. In order to maintain the fabric of human society itself, we must ban all foreclosures on primary residences for a minimum of five years or for the duration of the present world economic depression, which ever lasts longer. All arrangements concerning refinancing and other technical means of ameliorating the crisis will henceforth be conducted behind the protective screen of a blanket ban on throwing families out in the street to make them homeless or send them to the nearest Obamaville tent city. Some, like the disingenuous Senator Tester, will scream in horror that "a deal is a deal." We note with grim irony that the contracts of the United Auto Workers have been systematically shredded by Obama's auto task force under the leadership of the unsavory and incompetent New York Times reporter turned financier Stephen Rattner.

The financial institution which has so far done the most direct damage to the US taxpayer is of course AIG, an international insurance conglomerate. The astronomical losses have been centered in AIG Financial Products, a hedge fund set up in London to sell derivatives, especially credit default swaps, to the tune of $3 trillion, more than the gross national product of all of France. The US taxpayer has already bailed out AIG to the tune of $180 billion, and that figure is expected to rise beyond $400 billion in the near future. If children learn something from being burned by a hot stove, we should all learn that derivatives and hedge funds both need to be outlawed to prevent anything of the sort from ever happening again. We have already discussed the banning of derivatives. Hedge funds, the brainchild of Wall Street bandits like George Soros, are investment companies with limited numbers of high roller clients who "fly beneath the radar" of the Securities and Exchange Commission because they manage the assets of so few people. Once a hedge fund is regulated and transparent, it is no longer a hedge fund. We need to institute a regime of special surveillance for hedge funds, at which time hedge funds will by definition cease to exist, and if found solvent will join the ranks of normal investment companies.

The Securities and Exchange Commission must immediately reinstitute strong measures against short selling. There must be no naked shorts, and the uptick rule must be rigorously enforced. Margin requirements for stock speculators must be set at 100% for the duration of the crisis and beyond to discourage attempts at market manipulation.

The U.S. Treasury and the now moribund Commodity Futures Trading Commission must begin a vigorous offensive against the speculative manipulation of energy markets. That will require position limits, designed to prevent large financial institutions from attempting to dominate the oil or gasoline markets. It will include a systematic distinction between producers and hedgers on the one side, and mere speculators on the other, with the goal of protecting the producers and the hedgers from the sociopathic activities of the speculators. Here again, 100% margin requirements on speculative positions must be enforced.

2. Nationalize the Federal Reserve System and re-start lending and the credit system generally.

The US Federal Reserve System has always been an illegal and unconstitutional monstrosity by which control of credit creation, assigned by the U.S. Constitution to the executive and legislative branches of government, has been aggregated by cliques of unelected, unaccountable, and often unknown bankers working for private gain against the public interest. The long-term complaint against the Federal Reserve system is that it has kept interest rates much too high, actively conniving to prevent the sort of full employment in which the competition of employers for the available labor force would lead to an increase in wages and the standard of living. Using the bugaboo of inflation, the Federal Reserve has crippled every US economic recovery for decades, all in the name of surveying the interests of those who already have money and who want it to be worth more. In addition to this, the Federal Reserve System has repeatedly struck out in its basic mission of preventing panics and crashes. The Federal Reserve, expanding the money supply during the late 1920s in a vain effort to prop up the overvalued British pound, provided the speculative hot money that flowed into the Wall Street bubble of 1929, setting the stage for the crash of that year. Much more serious, the Federal Reserve was totally impotent in defending the US banking system from the banking panics which began to sweep this country after the Bank of England defaulted on gold payment and destroyed the only existing world monetary system in September 1931. During the 1990s, the Greenspan Fed was instrumental in fostering and fomenting the derivatives bubble which has now grown to represent a colossal threat to the survival of world civilization itself.

The Federal Reserve has thus struck out three times. The Federal Reserve must now be nationalized and set up as a bureau of the United States Treasury, most likely under the name of the Bank of the United States — looking back to the tradition of Alexander Hamilton, Henry Clay, and Daniel Webster. From that point onward, the size of the money supply, the prevailing interest rates, and the approved categories for federal lending and rediscount will be determined by public laws, debated and passed by the two houses of Congress and signed into law by the president — the only conceivable legal method under the prevailing system in this country. Economic decisions are not prevalently technical decisions. They are essentially political decisions, reflecting the interests of various groups in the society, and they ought to be openly addressed as the political matters they are. The nationalization of the Federal Reserve will revive some of the interest in politics which has flagged during recent decades, largely because the economic essence of politics has been put into the deep freeze of the Federal Reserve, far beyond the reach of the average voter.

ZERO INTEREST FEDERAL CREDIT FOR REAL PHYSICAL PRODUCTION

The newly created Bank of the United States will have the responsibility of issuing abundant credit for economic recovery. Obama's approach, by contrast, has been to pump $12.8 trillion into the zombie banking system of the derivatives monsters, and then somehow hope that these banks will begin to lend for commercial loans, plant and equipment. These are banks which have not extended credit for the productive economy for many decades. We must stop pouring trillions of dollars down Obama's derivatives wishing well, while hoping that the credit system revives. The United States government is more than powerful enough to create its own bank and then to reliably issue loans which will bring about economic recovery. At the beginning, we will need a series of trenches of $1 trillion each at 0% interest in order to get the recovery going. The maturities must be as long as necessary, according to the nature of the project involved. Some creditors short-term, but other maturities will be measured in decades and in some cases in centuries. The most important distinction to understand in regard to these loans is that they must go only for productive activity. Production means hard commodity manufacturing, the creation of tangible physical wealth in the form of food, clothing, shelter, housing, infrastructure, machine tools, scientific research, pharmaceuticals, energy production, transportation equipment, producer's goods of all sorts, and other technological objects which humanity requires for its survival. Production means mining, farming, light and heavy industry, steel, chemicals, plastics, housing and building construction, civil engineering, and many kinds of science and technology. If federal credit at 0% interest is extended in the form of loans to competent capitalist entrepreneurs for the purpose of putting productive labor to work in factories, construction sites, farms, and similar locations, we know that a sufficient real absolute profit will be generated so as to allow these loans to be fully repaid and become part of a revolving credit facility so that more loans can be more easily extended. At the same time, there must be a rigorous ban on the hijacking of this federal credit for anything that is not productive or socially necessary. This means that there will be no cheap federal credit for financial speculation, financial services, drug money laundering, organized crime, and the like. Those who wish to become active in these fields must take their chances in the free market which they claim to admire so much. They cannot and will not be subsidized by the public. This takes care of lending, and the generation of credit. But that will not be enough in itself, since it is only one side of the story. In order to start a recovery, we must also provide for the revival of borrowing, which has also been paralyzed by the panic.

3. Restart borrowing for production with a vast program of infrastructure development and science drivers for the modernization and recovery of the economy.

By now, we can estimate guess that the infrastructure deficit of the US economy must be approaching $10 trillion, at least as a rough ballpark figure or order of magnitude. The interstate highway system resembles a World War I battlefield pockmarked by shell holes. Bridges are now collapsing with alarming regularity. The freight rail system, the passenger rail system, and the commuter rail system, to the extent that they exist at all, are approaching the point of mechanical breakdown. Drinking water systems and sewage systems are more than a hundred years old in many parts of the United States, and are beginning to collapse, creating dangerous threats to the health and well-being of the American people. The building of canals, locks, water projects, and flood control facilities has stagnated since the time of Jimmy Carter. The electrical grid reaches the point of collapse every summer, and may soon undergo a catastrophic cascading breakdown. Over the past 30 years, the United States has lost about 500,000 hospital beds in about a thousand hospitals, many of them located in the economically disadvantaged inner-city areas, or else in such rural areas as Appalachia and the high plains, meaning that in many places a heart attack which might be survivable becomes a death sentence because there is no emergency room close enough to make a difference. The United States represents a society on the verge of thermodynamic breakdown, understood as a situation in which a series of vital systems fail simultaneously and there is no way to restart any of them amidst the cumulative breakdown.

Any serious program of economic recovery must begin with a massive national mobilization to deal with this c. $10 trillion infrastructure deficit which has been accumulated over many decades. This would include, for starters: an initial order of one hundred fourth generation, pebble bed, high temperature nuclear reactors to guarantee the viability of the continental electrical grid by providing economical and reliable base load capacity on the French model up to 90% of current overall electrical needs; 1,000 modern hospitals with an average of 500 beds each, largely located in the inner cities and in rural America, including especially Appalachia and the high plains; 100,000 miles of ultra modern high-speed magnetic levitation railways, including three transcontinental lines, two coastal lines, a north-south central line, provision for freight rail modernization, and attractive urban mass transit for the largest cities; a complete rebuilding of the entire interstate highway system; beginning the reconstruction of the fresh water and wastewater systems of the entire country; reconstruction and expansion of locks, canals, container shipping facilities, and the like; and adequate provision for new academic buildings for schools, high schools, colleges, and universities, plus public libraries and other public buildings. This program would begin to reverse the decades of rot which have overtaken US infrastructure over recent decades. We need present-day equivalents of the Tennessee Valley Authority, the St. Lawrence Seaway, the Apollo program, the transcontinental railway, the Erie canal, and the like. These projects spell tens of millions of modern productive jobs. Obama, by contrast, is offering bailouts for bankers.

At the same time, it is indispensable to cultivate science drivers from which we will derive the technological spinoffs of the future. We must launch a program on the scale of the Apollo moon shot for the exploration, permanent colonization, and industrialization of the Moon, Mars, and nearby interplanetary objects. We must spend as much for research into high-energy physics as our current limited scientific manpower will allow us to meaningfully spend. We must also pursue a Manhattan Project in the biomedical sciences with a view to developing cures for the principal dread diseases afflicting humanity, both for humanitarian purposes, and also to enable us to realize real economies in health care expenditure without resorting to triage, the rationing of care, or other morally abhorrent alternatives.

It is to be expected that the prime contractors for these projects will be agencies of the federal government, state governments, county and local governments, as well as regional consortiums among the states. These contractors will be priority recipients of long-term 0% federal lending from the Bank of the United States. Subcontractors requiring lines of credit to carry out their tasks within this overall program will also be eligible on a priority basis for 0% federal loans of the maturities they require. The impact of this infrastructure and science driver program will stimulate capital goods production, provide capital-intensive and energy-intensive high-wage jobs for modern productive labor, and reflate a credit system through the local and regional banks and will be involved in administering the relevant lines of credit ultimately deriving from the Bank of the United States. As the recovery begins to build, private capital will come out of its panic bunkers and begin to join in, leading to an open-ended economic boom based on full employment and high rates of productive capital formation.

Under no circumstances must public credit be channeled into the so-called alternative energy or "green jobs" boondoggles pushed by the Obama regime. As of today, solar panels and windmills, however modern, represent technologies which are inherently anti-economical and unworkable when it comes to generating base load electrical power. Solar panels are fine for space satellites or to power communications facilities far from the grid in the middle of nowhere, but it makes no sense to use them in an attempt to generate base load electrical power. Solar panels and windmills need to be subsidized for the simple reason that they cannot compete at any price of oil less than about $200 a barrel. Even worse, solar panels and windmills require more energy inputs than will ever be derived from these contraptions over their entire life spans. Alternative energy is therefore not a power source, but rather a net energy sink. The more green jobs the Obama administration creates, the poorer this country will become. This entire misguided green jobs project has rightly earned the name of the gangrene economy, representing a potentially fatal misdirection of scarce resources. The rest of the world, starting with Russia, China, India and dozens of other countries, are not impressed by the foolish arguments against nuclear power purveyed by the rich elitist Malthusian dilettantes of the Friends of the Earth, the Wilderness Society, Earth First, and the Canoe Federation. If the United States insists on turning away from modern technology, this society will have pronounced the final verdict of decadence and degeneracy upon itself, in the future will belong to other more vigorous peoples, less afflicted by the Anglo-Saxon cultural pessimism of Malthus and his successors.

4. Emergency relief for the victims of the depression.

While the economic recovery is being organized, it is also indispensable that we protect working families from the ravaging and devastating effects of economic depression. We must make sure that unemployment insurance is open-ended and fully funded for the duration of the crisis, with no limitation in the number of weeks that an unemployed worker can receive benefits. We must see to it that the food stamp program (SNAP) is also available to all who need it (currently about 11% of the US population), and the current benefits of about $120 a month for an individual and $240 a month for a family be approximately quadrupled, since we do not want malnutrition to lead to cognitive disorders in the young children currently growing up on the program. WIC, the special nutrition program for mothers and their children must be fully funded at radically enhanced levels. The Head Start program needs to be expanded into a free universal day care program serving breakfast and lunch along with educational activities for the children of working families who need it. The Earned Income Tax Credit must be expanded. We will also need to institute a system of family allowances for expectant mothers, along with more than doubling the value of the standard deduction and personal exemption on IRS form 1040. Since many senior citizens have seen their 401(k) accounts destroyed by the recent stock market crash, it is time to triple or quadruple the average Social Security pension so that it becomes possible for recipients to live a dignified life with all necessities and some amenities covered.

During the New Deal it was Harry Hopkins who captured the public imagination as a leading figure in the area of federal emergency relief. Hopkins was famous for putting almost five million people to work in just a few weeks for agencies like FERA (Federal Emergency Relief Agency) and CWA (Civil Works Administration). The glacial pace of the Obama stimulus stands in sharp contrast to Hopkins' successful approach to activist government. The New Deal alphabet soup started with FERA and CWA, which were joined by PWA, WPA, and many more. These agencies saved lives and improved the national infrastructure. Obama's alphabet soup is a toxic brew of conduits for funding bankers like TARP, the Fed's TAF and TALF, and Geithner's sinister PPIP, by which the federal government is to become a derivatives hedge fund in its own right. Obama's alphabet soup is toxic and deadly, the opposite of the New Deal.

One possible source for the revenue required to finance some of these improvements is a Tobin tax or securities transfer tax (STT) of approximately 1% on all financial turnover in stock markets, bond markets, derivatives markets as long as they exist, foreign exchange markets, and the like. The average citizen is groaning under an increasingly regressive sales tax burden. It is high time that the Wall Street financiers paid their fair share into a securities transfer tax which would represent in reality simply a sales tax on all financial transactions, to be paid by the seller. The securities transfer tax would have the added benefit of providing another factor to discourage parasitical speculation and market volatility.

Fifty million people in the US are now suffering from the lack of health insurance. With much private health insurance on the verge of bankruptcy because of derivatives speculation, and top companies kept going from week to week only by massive infusions of TARP bailout money, it is high time to make available for every person under US jurisdiction the option of Medicare for all. Private health insurance comes with an overhead margin of 30 to 40% for executive compensation, advertising, marketing, and other excessive spending. The administrative expenses under Medicare are in the neighborhood of 2% to 3%. Rather than imposing a single-payer system from the top down, or attempting to coerce anyone to buy any insurance or to change the insurance that they have, we must take the authentic New Deal approach by offering health insurance to all persons at a very attractive price in full confidence that, as the relative advantages of Medicare for all versus private health insurance become widely known, more and more people will gravitate into the Medicare option, most likely leaving private health insurance to "wither on the vine," as Newt Gingrich once predicted for Medicare. But this is a process that may take many years or decades until one system or the other finally wins out as public opinion evolves.

5. International economics and a new world monetary system

Since August 15, 1971, we have been living amidst the ruins of the Bretton Woods system. The role of the US dollar as the sole international reserve currency is clearly no longer sustainable. We must move rapidly in cooperation with other leading economic powers towards a multi-polar reform of the world monetary system in which the yen, the euro, the dollar, a possible Latin American regional currency, a possible Middle East regional currency, and a possible Asian regional currency will participate on conditions of equality and mutual advantage. We need not create yet another supernational bureaucracy, but rely mainly on the multilateral cooperation of sovereign states who share a principled commitment to economic recovery not through financial manipulations were derivatives speculation, but rather through the production of the physical means of human existence on the highest possible scientific, technological, and industrial level. In this sense, every nation has an inalienable right to development under natural law and God's law. We will need to return to fixed parities among the participating currencies as a means of driving the demon of pervasive currency risk out of the world. To a very significant extent this will be a regulated system, in which the governments of the world tell the private sector what the acceptable range of currency fluctuations will be, and severely punish efforts by sociopathic private interests to sabotage such a system. The main principle of a new world monetary system is that its purpose is the most comprehensive possible development of the world economy, including modern technology, full employment, and rising standards of living for all. No obscurantist fables about free markets, laissez-faire, the limits to growth, global warming, the ozone hole, biodiversity of the fate of this or that exotic species must never again be used to strangle the development of human beings in the world economy. A new institution, possibly called the Multilateral Development Bank, will be capitalized with several trillion dollars from the participating industrialized powers and given the task of facilitating the great projects of infrastructure on the agenda of the developing countries. These include great projects of the magnitude of the Dakar to Djibouti maglev railway; the Cape to Cairo maglev railway, the Maghreb and West African maglev lines; the Nile — Congo in land waterway, canal, electrical generation, and flood control system; the Mekong River basin development project, the Ganges Brahmaputra River basin Authority; several new Panama canals; the Kra canal; the Bering Strait Bridge Tunnel; a north-south Pan-American maglev line; the European land bridge or silk road development project; the Tunisia-Sicily-Calabria bridge-tunnel; and the Straits of Gibraltar Bridge Tunnel. All of these projects will enjoy the benefits of 0% development credits over maturities ranging from 50 years on up.

POLICY OPTIONS: LAUTENBACH'S FOUR CHOICES OF 1931

As the German economist Wilhelm Lautenbach (himself a supporter of the American System of political economy, as discussed below) told a meeting of the Friedrich List Society in Berlin in September 1931 called to discuss ways of ending the depression and preventing Hitler's seizure of power, there are basically four policy courses which are open to a national state in a time of acute economic breakdown crisis. These policy options essentially exhaust the available choices for a modern economy and banking system. Whatever we think we may be choosing in the current depression, it is almost certain that we will in fact be choosing one of these four courses. Therefore, let us examine each one carefully, with all the diligence of a life and death decision.

Deflation and budget cutting, liquidationism. The first policy option consists of letting the depression take its course, with minimal government intervention. Since this means letting the entire banking system sink into insolvency, and letting the supply of credit dry up completely. This approach leads to massive deflation of the type experienced in the US between 1929 and 1933, with astronomical rates of unemployment, widespread bankruptcy of small business, factory closings, and general immiseration, including widespread death by malnutrition and starvation. Deflationary policies are often accompanied by budget cuts and austerity, explained by the alleged need to balance the budget. Special targets of these austerity measures are social programs like unemployment insurance, food stamps, old-age pensions, government health care programs, and the like. This entire package is often justified by propaganda about doing away with the excesses of the speculative boom, punishing incompetent management, teaching the population to live within its means, and generally purging excesses from the system. In reality, deflation and budget cutting represent a policy which appeals to wealthy plutocrats of the criminal type. These are people who have money, and who believe that they will continue to have money, no matter what happens to the rest of the economy. Because of their inhuman cruelty and greed, they imagine that they will be able to buy up valuable distressed assets for pennies on the dollar, and that they will be able to employ skilled labor for coolie wages. These wealthy sociopaths are especially keen to target government run unemployment, food, and health programs so that starving and desperate workers can be forced to work for almost nothing to avoid starvation. For such plutocrats, every depression is an opportunity to institutionalize the low-wage, sweatshop economy.

The high priest of liquidationism was the sinister Andrew Mellon, the ultra-reactionary Secretary of the Treasury who dictated many aspects of financial and economic policy in the interests of a tiny cabal in Wall Street to Presidents Harding, Coolidge, and Hoover during the 1920s. Andrew Mellon is almost identical with today's crackpot monetarists of the Austrian, Chicago, or supply side persuasion. Mellon's favorite litany was: "Liquidate labor, liquidate stocks, liquidate the farmers, liquidate real estate … It will purge the rottenness out of the system. High costs of living and high living will come down. People will work harder, live a more moral life. Values will be adjusted, and enterprising people will pick up the wrecks from less competent people …." Mellon demanded that the full fury of the world economic depression be visited upon a virtually defenseless US population. Don't interfere with the depression, Mellon argued, and the crisis would turn out to represent nothing more than "a bad quarter of an hour." Naturally, this approach gives no thought to the large numbers of persons who may lose their lives or their health during the crisis, nor to a generation of young people and working people who may be crushed into permanent despair by disastrous economic conditions. Indeed, liquidationists aim at the permanent lowering of the standard of living of the entire population as a positive good. Liquidationism is also prominent among the possible interpretations of the "creative destruction" slogan of another reactionary economist, Joseph Schumpeter. "Creative destruction" has generally been touted by those who did not expect to be destroyed.

Implicit in the demand by Austrians, Chicago Boys, and supply-siders that the depression be given free reign to do its disruptive work is a mystical notion of the so-called business cycle. For example, the Wall Street propagandist Miss Calamity Shlaes of the Council on Foreign Relations has developed a spurious argument, religiously repeated by right wing radical radio talk show hosts, to the effect that the Roosevelt New Deal "prolonged" the depression of the 1930s. Prolonged it in comparison to what? The Calamity Shlaes argument is evidently that the Great Depression of the 1930s would have ended automatically on its own at some point before the end of the decade if nothing whatever had been done to mitigate its devastating effects. It is notable first of all that Miss Shlaes does not ask anything about the human toll in terms of morbidity, mortality, ruined lives, despair or the permanent lowering of the living standard which her recipe of benign neglect would have entailed. She thinks that depressions are part of the business cycle and that they end up more or less automatically. In reality, there is no guarantee whatsoever that the descent into the trough of an economic depression will be followed by any kind of upswing or rebound. Quite the contrary. If we look at the 1930s, we see immediately that the root cause of the collapse of world trade was the bankruptcy and default of the Bank of England on gold payments for the British pound in September 1931. This was a moment not just of collapse but true disintegration, meaning that the only world monetary system for financing trade which the world possessed at that time had been totally destroyed. World trade could not and did not revive until a new world monetary system was created under New Deal aurpices at the Bretton Woods conference in New Hampshire in 1944. In order for that new world monetary system to be created, the Axis powers had to be defeated, and resistance from Great Britain and her satellites had to be drastically reduced by the de facto bankruptcy of the city of London. The new Bretton Woods world monetary system, certainly not perfect but the most effective in human history up to that point, was in fact the indispensable prerequisite for a world economic recovery. If the very reactionary Miss Shlaes wanted to prove an automatic laissez-faire recovery from world depression, she would have to cite some country where Austrian school monetarist methods of opening the door wide to depression had in fact brought about a recovery before the middle of 1941. In fact, no such country existed.

Miss Shlaes and her co-thinkers also argue that the Great Depression was not ended by the government spending involved in the New Deal, but rather by the outbreak of World War II. We should point out that unemployment in the United States had virtually disappeared before Pearl Harbor as a direct result of the Roosevelt's Lend-Lease program of finally harnessing the credit resources of the Federal Reserve and the banking system for defense production, with first Great Britain and then the Soviet Union as the main beneficiaries of Lend-Lease deliveries. The reactionary argument against the New Deal is like saying that the depression was not ended by government spending, but rather by government spending. What the reactionaries are trying to say is that the depression was not ended by federal emergency relief for wage earners and other individuals, nor by infrastructure investments like the Tennessee Valley Authority (all of which they opposed tooth and nail), but rather by military expenditure. The entire position of these reactionaries is hopelessly dishonest, or garbled, and contradictory, and the fact is that liquidationism by itself has never led to an economic recovery, although it has inflicted untold damage on numerous societies. In the real world, you do not get out of a world economic depression through the mystical operations of some ying and yang cyclce. You get out of the depression by producing your way out of it. For this to happen, it is generally necessary for the government to implement an adequate economic recovery program, since in a depression the private banking and financial sector by definition has completely struck out.

These monetarists and liquidationists demand today that the American people capitulate and surrender to the forces of economic and financial depression without any attempt at self defense. It is a doctrine of astounding impotence, callousness, and pessimism, and one which clashes most sharply with any traditional definition of American culture, which has always been founded on optimism and can-do spirit. We need to remember that, no matter how bad the economic policies of Herbert Hoover were in fact, Hoover never completely capitulated to the depression in the way that some Austrian monetarists are demanding today. During the depression, the Austrian monetarist Friedrich von Hayek produced articles demanding that all interference with the depression must immediately cease, while government spending should be cut. Hoover, despite the demands of some Republicans like Andrew Mellon, refused to fully embrace this course. As Hoover pointed out in his acceptance speech for the Republican presidential nomination in Washington, DC on August 11, 1932, he had tried to fight to the depression. Hoover claimed that if he had followed the ultra-reactionary advice, "we might have done nothing. That would have been utter ruin. Instead, we met the situation with proposals to provide business and the Congress with the most gigantic program of economic defense and counter attack ever evolve in the history of the republic we put it into action." At a speech at Des Moines, Iowa on October 4, 1932, Hoover pointed out that "some of the reactionary economists urged that we should allow the liquidation to take its course until we had found bottom." But Hoover stressed that his administration had "determined that we would not follow the advice of the bitter end liquidationists and see the whole body of debtors of the United States brought to bankruptcy and the savings of our people brought to destruction."[1] Deflation, budget cutting, and overall liquidationism in the spirit of Andrew Mellon lives on today among the followers of Milton Friedman and his Chicago school, von Hayek and von Mises of the Austrian school, and the various stripes of supply side doctrine. Liquidationism has generally been professed by the reactionary right wing of the Republican Party, especially when out of power, including such figures as Robert Taft, Barry Goldwater, Ronald Reagan, and Ron Paul today. This is the approach of Limbaugh, Hannity, Glenn Beck, and the other reactionary radio talk show hosts of our own time. One advantage of this form of argument is that it can be based on folksy comparisons to the kitchen-table discussion of the household budget, references to belt-tightening, thrift, and the like. This permits the blurring of certain dramatic differences between the situation of an individual household and that of a national government with resources including credit, currency, and sovereignty.

---

[1] Herbert Hoover and Calvin Coolidge, *Campaign Speeches of 1932* (Garden City NY: Doubleday, Doran, 1933), pp. 6, 42-43.

Historically, a notable exercise in the sustained and ruthless application of budget cuts was the regime of German Chancellor Heinrich Brüning. As German chancellor between March 1930 and May 1932, Brüning was unable to muster a majority of the parliament and therefore used presidential decree-laws signed by President von Hindenburg to reduce wages, reduce worker benefits, cut social welfare payments, and rob workers of the unemployment insurance which was due them. Taxes were increased, and the German living standard declined sharply. Unemployment increased disastrously from 5 million in the winter of 1930-31 to 6 million in the winter of 1931-32, which represented more than 20% and was the worst in Europe by far. By the time Brüning left office, Hitler's seizure of power was little more than a half year in the future. The application of Austrian-school monetarism under Brüning was a catastrophic failure in economic terms, and politically opened the door for fascist dictatorship. How strange that today persons calling themselves libertarians should recommend similar policies.

Increased government expenditures with the goal of producing a recovery based on consumer spending were a second option indicated by Lautenbach. This is the policy of stimulus checks for individual taxpayers as seen under the Bush-Paulson regime. The idea is that by putting some cash in the hands of consumers, their additional spending will somehow lead to an economic recovery — provided that they do spend every penny. Programs of this type undeniably do some good to the extent that they provide cash relief to strapped households who cannot otherwise make ends meet. But, unfortunately, no amount of consumer spending can buy itself produce an economic recovery, and the amounts contained in the Bush stimulus checks or the supposed Obama tax cuts for wage earners are very small indeed.

The economic recovery of a modern national economy which has been hit by depression depends primarily on investments in capital goods — nuclear reactors, steel mills, chemical plants, biotech facilities, research laboratories, locomotives, railroad systems, canals, water systems, aircraft, space equipment, commercial and industrial buildings, mines, etc. Consumer spending cannot by itself create these big-ticket durable capital goods. Automobiles, washing machines, consumer electronics, home appliances, and the like are certainly desirable, but they do not represent a permanent addition to the capital stock of the nation, and they do not directly increase the productivity of labor on the required scale. It is often said that two thirds of the modern United States economy is represented by consumer spending, and that stimulus checks will increase the turnover in this department. The problem is that if two thirds of an economy are devoted to consumer production, that is a very sick economy in urgent need of a massive expansion of capital goods production. In other words, the proportion of labor devoted to capital goods production needs to be increased, even as the absolute quantity and quality of the standard of living provided by consumer production also increases. An economy where consumer spending plays the preponderant role is a spendthrift monstrosity which is destroying the prospects for its own future. A successful economy with viable prospects for the future is one that devotes increasing proportions of labor to capital goods and new branches of modern industry and technology.

At the very most, a burst of consumer spending financed by government expenditure could lead to a weak and temporary upswing in the economic situation, but once the consumer spending has been completed, things will fall back into the same old depression rut. Much debt will have been generated in the process. The consumer-led recovery is generally what is understood under the heading of Keynesian economics. The British economist Lord Keynes wanted governments to engage in deficit spending so as to place purchasing power into the hands of individuals whose spending would then restart consumer production and help to end the depression. Keynes was even specific in demanding that this consumer spending not produce any permanent additions to the stock of capital goods — in other words, Keynes wanted non-productive consumer spending. It is important not to confuse the British doctrines of Keynes, which are based on Malthus, with the much more successful approaches of the Roosevelt New Deal. Another economist who imagined that economic recovery could come through consumer spending was the Soviet Communist Nikolai Bukharin, who had been indoctrinated in monetarism and who tried to use the slogan "increased commodity turnover" to bring prosperity in the early days of Soviet Russia.

A consumer-led recovery was tried by the French popular front regime of Léon Blum in 1936. According to the accords of the Palais Matignon in Paris signed among French government, labor, and industry after the general strikes of that year, wages were increased by about 12% for working people. Every worker got two weeks of paid vacation.. The work week was cut from 48 to 40 hours. A system of unemployment insurance was established. This all translated into a tremendous increase in consumer spending. But these important victories were not enough to end the depression in France, nor were they able to prevent the Léon Blum regime from being toppled by sinister figures like the pro-Nazi Daladier.

In the early months of the Obama regime, many Democratic politicians in Congress pressed for various forms of deficit spending to be included in Obama's so-called stimulus. Some of these appropriations had the merit of preventing the collapse of certain locally or regionally important economic activities but, once again, this cannot and will not translate into a general economic recovery, understood as progress towards increased capital goods production, rising standards of living, and full employment.

A general reflation with abundant cheap credit for financial borrowers, or hot money recovery, was the third possible policy option outlined by Lautenbach. In this variant, the central bank offers vast amounts of extremely cheap credit, often for interest rates as low as 0% or even for negative interest rates, meaning that the borrower is in effect being subsidized to take the loan. Most of the recipients are bankers or non-bank banks. Under this policy, there are no restrictions or guidelines as to the use to which these very cheap loans will be put. This policy runs afoul of the perverse dynamic of bubble economies according to which the rate of return for speculation, criminal activity, drug money laundering, and the like will always be significantly higher than the rates of return for farming, industrial commodity production, building construction, mining, scientific research, or infrastructure building. This means that, in the aftermath of a collapsed bubble economy, cheap credit will flow preferentially into activities which are sociopathic, parasitical, criminal, or at the very minimum not productive, while hard commodity production of tangible physical wealth will languish for lack of credit because of the inherently lower short-term rates of return for this sort of production. Another possibility which has occurred repeatedly in recent years under the conditions of a globalized economy with almost no limitations on speculative capital flows is that cheap credit will immediately flee to other countries in the form of a currency carry trade or flight capital, tending to collapse the national economy which is trying to produce a recovery by issuing the credit in the first place.

A good example of these tendencies is Japan from the 1990s to today. The Japanese domestic bubble economy of 1986-1990, encouraged by pressure from James Baker III under the Plaza Accords of 1985 which vastly increased the value of the yen and thus crippled Japanese exports, came to an end — as all bubbles do — with the stock market crash beginning in 1990. The astronomically inflated Tokyo real estate values had furnished one of the most dramatic aspects of this bubble economy. When real estate prices came down, many Japanese banks were in reality insolvent, but the Japanese political and financial system was incapable of publicly recognizing this embarrassing fact and acting on it by putting such bankrupt banks into liquidation proceedings. (Before we laugh too loud at the Japanese, we should recognize that this is similar to, although not as bad as, the situation in Wall Street today in regard to such insolvent proprietary trading and derivatives monsters as J.P. Morgan Chase, Bank of America, Citibank, Wells Fargo, Bank of New York Mellon, and several other money center derelicts.) It was in these years that the term "zombie bank" was coined to describe a bank which was unable to provide credit for commerce or productive investment, but which focused exclusively on trying to avoid bankruptcy through proprietary trading and speculation, while taking advantage of the extremely cheap credit offered by the Bank of Japan.

OBAMA'S GIFT TO THE BANKERS: $12.8 TRILLION AND COUNTING

The Bank of Japan kept interest rates at or near 0% from 1995 into 2007. This time frame largely overlaps with the so-called lost decade of stagnation of the Japanese economy. However, at the same time, Japan emerged as a colossal money machine for the speculative hot money economy of globalization. This was done under the heading of the "yen carry trade." This meant that international financial institutions would borrow money from the Bank of Japan at 0%, and then use these funds as hot money for speculation in other countries. The international asset booms of the globalization era, like the US stock bubble, the dot com bubble, the housing bubble, and related phenomena in other countries were largely stoked by 0% liquidity coming from Japan. The constant flight of hot money out of the yen tended to push the value of that currency down, which the Japanese considered to be an advantage because of the stimulus that a slightly cheaper yen gave to Japanese exports. The yen did not collapse completely, primarily because of the overwhelming weakness of the gutted US dollar, which was backed up by very little productive capacity of any kind. All in all, the policy of an attempted hot money recovery in the Japanese case was a resounding failure, but this does not stop the Summers-Geithner clique controlling Obama's economic policy from attempting to imitate it, on an even larger scale:

> The U.S. government and the Federal Reserve have spent, lent or committed $12.8 trillion, an amount that approaches the value of everything produced in the country last year, to stem the longest recession since the 1930s. New pledges from the Fed, the Treasury Department and the Federal Deposit Insurance Corp. include $1 trillion for the Public-Private Investment Program, designed to help investors buy distressed loans and other assets from U.S. banks. The money works out to $42,105 for every man, woman and child in the U.S. and 14 times the $899.8 billion of currency in circulation..[2]

The Bernanke Fed has now reduced US interest rates to zero per cent. This policy was implicit in Bernanke's own personal ideological pedigree. He is after all "Helicopter Ben," the academic charlatan who once gave a speech alleging that a new world depression could be stopped by simply dumping bales of money out of helicopters, presumably onto the lawns of leading bankers in posh gated communities. As this money got spent, Helicopter Ben imagined, economic recovery would be the result. As of this writing, it is already clear that the Federal Reserve's 0% interest rate policy will be a catastrophic failure. The policies championed by Bernanke with the full support of Obama, Summers, and Geithner are instead likely to do two related things. The first is to seriously undermine the international value of the battered US dollar, quite possibly initiating an uncontrollable slide of this currency into perdition. Once the dollar's slide gets going, many around the world who hold dollars will start a panic rush for the exits, seeking to dump their dollars in exchange for anything in sight. This had always been Volcker's recurring nightmare, as is discussed in a later chapter of this book. A world wide dollar panic would in turn be inextricably linked with the coming of dollar hyperinflation, since the international value of the currency is the

---

[2] Mark Pittman and Bob Ivry, "Financial Rescue Nears GDP as Pledges Top $12.8 Trillion," Bloomberg, March 31, 2009.

most important single factor by far in determining its worth. If hyperinflation comes, that will make the crisis much worse, but it also will not be the end of the world. We can use the successful launching of the German mark or D-Mark in 1948 by a group of New Deal economists working for the US High Commissioner for Germany as an excellent starting point for a currency reform in extremis. As long as factories are intact and the skilled labor force exists, it is relatively easy to rearrange the universe of paper so as to put people back to work and restart production, and that is the heart of the matter.

A subset of the generalized failed policy of hot money, low interest rates, and quantitative easing of the money supply can come in the form of slightly more targeted payments by national governments to attempt to bail out insolvent financial institutions. This policy was introduced into the current crisis by British Prime Minister Gordon Brown, Chancellor of the Exchequer Alistair darling, and Mervyn King of the Bank of England in response to the bankruptcy of Northern Rock in the second half of 2007. A similar bailout policy has become the centerpiece of the Obama regimes support operations for the derivatives bubble and the Wall Street zombie banking community. This policy is not new, but represents a somewhat more robust version of the Reconstruction Finance Corporation set up by Herbert Hoover. By the time Hoover left office, the Reconstruction Finance Corporation had been given public money on approximately the same scale as one year's federal budget of the United States. This money was used to bail out selected banking institutions in a vain attempt to prevent the collapse of the entire US national banking and credit system. These payments were politically targeted and led to the inevitable unjustified charges of corruption, favoritism, and conflict of interest. But the most important thing to remember about the Reconstruction Finance Corporation, the ancestor of today's Bush-Paulson-Obama-Summers-Geithner TARP (Troubled Assets Assistance Program, the October 2007 bailout of Wall Street and derivatives to the tune of $700 billion plus) is its absolute and utter futility. The RFC was absolutely unable to prevent the generalized banking panic which ripped the United States at the end of 1932 and the beginning of 1933, a banking panic which led to the shutdown of virtually every banking institution in the country. A very cogent criticism of the TARP is therefore that it represents a useless rathole into which public funds are being poured, impoverishing every other aspect of next the life, and also no rational purpose whatsoever.

The fourth policy option discussed by Lautenbach in 1931 was the idea of **mobilizing the credit resources of the government and the banking system for the purpose of launching an ambitious program of infrastructure construction and development**. Lautenbach was very clear on two points which absolutely differentiate him from the failed doctrines of Lord Keynes. First, he was talking about central government lending, not primarily central government spending. Lord Keynes talked about deficit spending as a means of dealing with the depression, but Lautenbach saw that there was a better way. Why not force the central bank or the national bank to issue credit for large-scale projects of infrastructural development which were clearly in the public interest? In other words, cheap credit would be channeled on a preferential and indeed exclusive basis into the construction of transportation systems, railroads, canals, ports and docks, energy production, water systems, sewage treatment, and the like. Such cheap public credit would not be available for speculative, sociopathic, or criminal activity, thus reestablishing the bias in favor of productive and socially necessary economic activity which is indispensable for a healthy economy. This represented a second aspect in which Lautenbach diverged from Keynes. Keynes famously insisted that deficit spending to stimulate an economy stricken by depression had to be by definition nonproductive, so that it would not compete with existing productive capacity and thus lower the rate of profit. What is obviously missing in Keynes is any idea of technological modernization and improvement. Keynes thought it was fine for ditch diggers to dig ditches and then fill them up as a way of earning their daily wage from the government, but he was hostile to the idea of building new and more modern rail lines among the cities of Great Britain. Here, Keynes is showing his own Malthusian pedigree, since for Malthus the question of technology does not and cannot exist.

Lautenbach proposed that the German government launch a very ambitious and large-scale program of infrastructure construction and modernization in a way that would represent a permanent addition to the productive capital stock of the entire nation, while at the same time creating large numbers of modern productive jobs paying decent wages. This expenditure would of course exert a multiplier effect of the entire German economy, tending to revive industries like steel, chemicals, timber, locomotive construction, rolling stock, and a whole range of others. The net effect of these improvements would be to substantially increase the productivity of labor in the entire economy, thus setting the stage for a revival of export industry as soon as international economic conditions permitted. The key to this new policy, argued Lautenbach, was to force the central bank to honor a rediscount guarantee. This simply meant that any contract or a subcontractor who was engaged in carrying out the national infrastructure program could be guaranteed that all his or her commercial paper and bills of exchange would be turned into cash by local banks, because these local bankers could then turn around and automatically rediscount such paper with the central bank and receive cash for it themselves. In this way, the engine of credit would be preferentially put to work for the revival of the productive and socially necessary parts of the economy, without allowing hot money to flow into speculative and parasitical activities.

Today, we could add to Lautenbach's infrastructure program the equally imperative need for science drivers to get an economy moving through technological spinoffs capable of modernizing the productive process in the workplace. The classic examples include the US space program of the 1960s, which has led to the information technology and Internet of the present day. At present, we can distinguish a minimum of three science drivers that would qualify for cheap Federal credit: these are a revival of the space program, biomedical research to vanquish the diseases, and efforts in high-energy physics to perfect thermonuclear fusion power and then even more advanced forms of energy technology.

This idea of a rediscount guarantee was built into the New Deal program which finally and definitively ended the Great Depression in the United States during 1941 by reducing unemployment to normal levels. This was Lend-Lease, which harnessed the Federal Reserve and the banking system to provide credit for defense production. Each contractor and subcontractor was guaranteed that relevant commercial paper and bills of exchange would be automatically be discounted by local bankers and turned into cash, since each local banker could be sure of commanding the support of the Federal Reserve system. This amounted to a de facto nationalization during wartime of the Federal Reserve system for national goals, not the whims of cliques of unelected and unaccountable bankers. It is clear that Lautenbach fourth option is the one we need to implement today.

It is this fourth variant which we must fight for in the form of a second New Deal as the means of overcoming the world economic depression of today.

Webster Griffin Tarpley, Ph.D.

Washington DC

May 17, 2009

OBAMANOMICS, CASH FOR TRASH:
$12.8 TRILLION FOR WALL STREET

WALL STREET'S OBAMA GIVES THE LION'S SHARE TO THE ZOMBIE DERIVATIVES BANKERS; $12.8 TRILLION IN BAILOUTS DOOMED TO FAILURE

In its overall economic policy, the Obama regime is doing the exact opposite of what would be needed to pull the US economy out of depression and start an actual economic recovery. We have during 2007-8 gone through the initial phase of a financial panic accompanied by panic runs on banks, leading to the insolvency of the main money center institutions. The centerpiece of this panic has been a shift of the $1.5 quadrillion derivatives bubble from positive leverage into negative leverage, meaning that it is now losses which are being astronomically multiplied. A reasonable policy at this point would concentrate on restarting the stricken US manufacturing and industrial sectors, while rebuilding the nation's infrastructure and channeling funds into science drivers to create the technological spin-offs that will allow economic modernization. At the same time, draconian measures would be introduced to prevent a recurrence of the globalized speculative casino or bubble economy which flourished under Clinton and Bush the younger.

Obama is doing the opposite, in virtually every way. The Obama regime is pouring almost $13 trillion of bailout funds into zombie banks and derivatives houses, along with insurance companies like AIG, with the specific intent of restarting the cancerous, bloated, fictitious, and sociopathic growth of the derivatives bubble — known as "securitization" in the jargon of the Obama regime. (A special Fed program, the "TALF," is explicitly designed to re-start this toxic process of bundling and securitization.) Anyone who represents this world of parasitical speculation has a good chance of jumping on the Obama gravy train: this includes banks, hedge funds, insurance companies, credit card companies, money market mutual funds, and even well-heeled foreign bankers. The main criterion appears to be that, in order to qualify for a slice of the Obama bailout, the recipient must be contributing nothing whatsoever in the way of tangible, physical, hard commodity production of the manufactured goods which are the basis of modern human existence. Only derivatives jackals, hedge fund hyenas, zombie bankers, derivatives monsters, and other financiers need step forward to claim their piece of Obama's "cash for trash" approach to the economic crisis. General Motors and Chrysler, representing hundreds of thousands of the dwindling US stock of productive industrial jobs, have been driven into bankruptcy by being cynically denied a small part of the emergency financial assistance which has been showered on J.P. Morgan Chase, Goldman Sachs, Morgan Stanley, AIG, and their foreign partners — without any preconditions or standards whatsoever. As of this writing, most Chrysler factories have shut down for a period of months, and no one knows if they will ever reopen. General Motors will be closing down all its plants for an unprecedented seven weeks during the summer of 2009, and then again it is anybody's guess if these plants will reopen. The formerly industrial Midwest deeply distrusted Obama during the 2008 primaries, and events prove that their class instinct was correct: Obama is indeed the gravedigger of the US industrial economy, mercilessly and pitilessly carrying out the austerity dictates coming from his Wall Street backers as the few wretched remaining factories in this country are shut down. If a reactionary Republican like Bush had attempted to carry out this demolition job, it might have led to all-out resistance by the United Auto Workers and other unions in the form of an open-ended general strike, or of a developing mass strike process across the entire economy. Obama, by contrast, cynically uses the accumulated left cover with which he has been endowed by the controlled media so that his victims scarcely know what is happening until they find themselves homeless and destitute. Obama is truly one of the most brutal and cynical demagogues of recent world history.

HERBERT HOOVER SOMEWHAT BETTER THAN OBAMA

If we compare Obama with Herbert Hoover, who has up to now represented in the minds of many the most heartless and cynical response to the ravages of the world economic depression, we will find first that the similarities between these two figures are notable, and secondly that Herbert Hoover unquestionably had more positive features than Obama does today. Herbert Hoover kept promising that prosperity was just around the corner. The mantra of the Obama regime in the late spring of 2009 is that the "green shoots" of economic recovery are everywhere to be seen. Even an economic illiterate like Obama (who thinks that a price-earnings ratio is called a profits-earnings ratio) knows that this is demagogic nonsense. Secretary of the Treasury Tim Geithner, one of Obama's main economic handlers, has acknowledged that there is no recovery of the real economy, as distinct from the various speculative aggregates. As Geithner told a journalist, "Unemployment's going to keep increasing for a while... It's not going to feel better for a long time for millions of Americans." Geithner stressed that the immediate imperative is to re-start the bubble economy, meaning multi-trillion dollar bailouts for Wall Street, and then shift gears into "living within our own means" so as to reduce deficits over the medium term to avoid inflation and higher interest rates — meaning the systematic looting of the American people through health-care rationing, artificial measures to keep the price of energy impossibly high, and the chiseling of Social Security, Medicare, and Medicaid. Once the bubble economy is re-started after 18 months or two years, Geithner said in effect, the Obama regime will then withdraw the stimulus, and shift economic priorities to fight inflation and bring down the astronomical deficits created by the bailouts. Geithner conceded that dealing with such a large deficit would be a defining political challenge, since Obama would be demanding that Americans "give up things we don't want to give up," including by the gouging of Medicare and Medicaid — a policy with clearly genocidal implications. "We need to make it sustainable," concluded Geithner in the fashionable Malthusian jargon of the Obama clique. (Geithner to *Newsweek*, May 18, 2009)[3]

Obama's almost $13 trillion in bailouts are replaying on a larger scale of Herbert Hoover's Reconstruction Finance Corporation, which specialized in bailing out insolvent banks, but which could not prevent the closing of virtually every bank in the United States in March 1933. In other words, the main common feature in the economic policies of Hoover and Obama is a commitment of the vast majority of available resources to the bailout of the financial speculators who were responsible for the crisis. This was an immoral policy in each case, and above all a policy of total abject futility, since no power is sufficient to prevent a financial panic collapse from playing out once it has started. But Herbert Hoover also had positive features which Obama absolutely does not offer. Herbert Hoover was a strong supporter of a protective tariff to shield US farms and factories against overseas competition from what Hoover referred to as sweatshop and peasant labor working on cheap land, and therefore able to produce agricultural commodities for one quarter to one third less than the US internal price. Herbert Hoover was, in short, a protectionist in the same way that

---

[3] Geithner's father, Peter F. Geithner, oversaw a Ford Foundation program that Obama's mother, Stanley Ann Dunham Soetoro, worked in — probably microloans. Obama's mother may have met Geithner's father in Jakarta, Indonesia. Obama, say insiders, ''fell in love'' with Mr. Geithner, in the words of one, while a Geithner associate said Mr. Geithner reported being ''smitten'' with Mr. Obama — a lurid story indeed. ''They both have that kind of quiet confidence in their demeanor,'' this associate said. *Seattle Times*, January 18, 2009.

the Republican Party had advocated protectionism since the days of Lincoln and William McKinley. This already makes Hoover much better than Obama. In addition, Herbert Hoover had some idea of great projects of infrastructure as a means to deal with unemployment and economic collapse. Hoover was a strong supporter of the St. Lawrence seaway project, a large scale and ambitious program of canals and related water projects to allow oceangoing vessels to come into the Great Lakes. As journalists have noted, Obama has no notion of great projects or science drivers. Obama has no St. Lawrence seaway, no Apollo program, no transcontinental railroad, no Erie Canal, no Panama Canal, no Tennessee Valley Authority, no Manhattan Project. In short, Obama is totally alien to the optimistic US tradition of internal improvements at federal expense and the fostering of scientific research and development, which has been a hallmark of the American system of political economy since the days of Alexander Hamilton and Henry Clay. As William Greider put it, Obama "is putting himself on the wrong side of history by trying to restore Wall Street. It's clear that he and his advisers think that if you just pump enough capital into that handful of financial firms and banks, we can return to normal. I think every element of that is false." (*Princeton Alumni Weekly*, May 13, 2009)

By the end of the first hundred days of the Obama regime, the nature of Obama's economic policies had thus become clear. This was not the new deal of Franklin D. Roosevelt, but rather a strange mixture of Herbert Hoover's *laissez-faire* with the corporate state which emerged in Italy during the 1920s and 1930s. As long as Obama's current policy direction continues, the United States is condemned to lurch further and further into the abyss of a bottomless world economic depression of incalculable proportions.

OBAMA'S METHOD OF DISSEMBLING

Before analyzing Obamanomics in detail, we need to make two points concerning method. The first is that Obama is genuinely different from Bush in one key respect. Bush was an open, brutal reactionary who spoke with cynical bluntness about his own policies. "Bring it on," "dead or alive," and similar crude slogans remind us of Bush's tendency to blurt out more or less what he was doing. Obama is a very different proposition. The essence of Obama's approach is cynical hypocrisy — deception, dissembling, bait and switch, duping the public. Obama is slimy, slippery, shifty. He claims to be concerned about poverty and exclusion, but his policies are overwhelmingly designed to serve Wall Street. By using this method, Obama gains the precious advantage of left cover, which he hopes will let him operate more freely than Bush ever could.

Obama has also learned from Jimmy Carter, his predecessor among puppet presidents fielded by the Trilateral Commission. Carter campaigned promising he would never lie, and that he would deal first of all with the problem of unemployment. But when Carter got to the White House, he announced that inflation and the legendary energy crisis were the real issues. Carter began babbling about the "moral equivalent of war" in the form of energy austerity, and about the malaise which he said was gripping the country. Carter started off with a better standing in the public opinion polls than Obama enjoys today, but his fall from grace was precipitous, and his regime imploded after about two and a half years in office. From this experience, Obama's handlers and controllers have learned that the whining and grating note of austerity and sacrifice by itself would quickly doom any president who has nothing else to offer. Obama therefore resorts to an elaborate system of deception and camouflage which is placed in the foreground to distract attention from the ongoing services being massively rendered to the bankers and derivatives merchants in the background.

Obama has also learned from Dick Morris and the Clintons.   Morris was famous for recommending a laundry list of small bore, relatively inexpensive token programs that could be dished up to prove that the president was feeling your pain. The banks got a massive bailout in the Mexico crisis, and FDR's social safety net was attacked, but Clinton scored points for attacking Sista Souljah and recommending school uniforms to undercut gang proliferation. Hillary Clinton famously promised to restore industry in upstate New York, but never delivered. She did, however, win the title of "the laundry lady" because of her endless succession of meritorious but ultimately insignificant token projects.

OBAMA'S PSYCHOLOGICAL WARFARE AGAINST THE PEOPLE

Obama operates by combining these two methods. Obama is attempting to employ methods of mass brainwashing which go far beyond anything ever attempted by Carter. One element is the rhetorical litany of doom which became Obama's staple during his first weeks in office: "crisis," "devastating," and "catastrophe" became the former hope Pope's stock in trade. The shock value of these expressions was then supplemented by Obama's quick flurry of giga-numbers: $500 billion for a new round of the derivatives bailout, $650 billion to be looted from the economy through the carbon tax, and a $1.5 trillion deficit as a baseline for the coming year. We are reminded of the confession of former Obama campaign operative Sarah P. published in *Hill Buzz* on October 31, 2008. Here the defecting Obamabot revealed that "the internal campaign idea of the Obama campaign, is to twist, distort, humiliate, and finally dispirit you…. We do this to stifle your motivation, to destroy your confidence. We did this the whole primary, and it worked. Sprinkle in mass vote confusion [and it] becomes bewildering, most people lose patience, they just give up." According to Sarah, Obama wanted to convince the US population "that the world has gone mad" and that resistance was useless. These same methods are now being used as a technique of governance, and for the suppression of opposition.

In the background, over $12.8 trillion of Federal Reserve and Treasury money is being delivered to banks, insurance companies, hedge funds, stock brokerages, credit card companies, money market mutual funds, and other totally non-productive and often parasitical financial operations. Obama talks very little about this astronomical transfer of resources. He is helped by his right-wing pseudo-critics of the Limbaugh, Hannity, and Glenn Beck reactionary school, who studiously ignore bank bailouts and rather accuse Obama of giving taxpayer money to the losers, deadbeats, and underachievers among the working poor, homeless, foreclosure victims, unemployed, and food stamp recipients. This demagogic farce, in which the reactionary talkers are fully conscious participants, has tended to obscure what is actually going on.

NEGATIVE CURVATURE OF ECONOMIC SPACE-TIME

The second point of methodology is that we are presently in a panic collapse and disintegration phase of a real world economic breakdown crisis and economic depression, caused above all by the implosion of the $1.5 quadrillion derivatives bubble. We are walking around on the inside of that collapsing bubble. We are experiencing the paradoxes and anomalies of the negative curvature of our political and economic space. In this negatively curved space that we inhabit, like that of a pseudosphere, the hackneyed common sense of traditional wisdom and received ideas does not apply. Normally the three angles of a triangle add up to 180°, but in a world of negative curvature they add up to less. Conventional commonsense ideas about inevitable economic recovery, the business cycle, rugged individualism, big government, the banking and credit system, the sanctity of debt, the private sector, balanced budgets, contracts, and so forth simply will not work in this terrible world of negative economic curvature, which is now our world.

No power in the universe is capable of stopping the collapse of a bubble of these proportions once the icy winds of panic have begun to blow. Under these circumstances, it is futile, even criminal to worry for one instant about the prices of stocks, bonds, derivatives, or any other form of paper. There is nothing we can do about the price of paper. Attempts to reflate a collapsing bubble only make matters much worse. The $1.5 quadrillion derivatives bubble is gone, doomed, and the quicker this is realized the better off we all will be. We need to worry about the lives of people, and the levels of production of the physical, material goods and hard commodities which are indispensable for human survival. People and production are the key, and not the price of financial instruments of any kind. The issue in the housing crisis is not the price of homes, but whether we will be able to put a roof over the heads of the existing population. In recent years, wealth has been measured by stock and bond indices, bloated statements of the gross domestic product, and other largely fictitious measures. We need to develop a new focus on the real measures of wealth and poverty. These must include industrial production, freight car loadings, truck loadings, housing starts, morbidity and mortality statistics, and human longevity. We need to look much more at megawatt hours, tons of steel, agricultural implements, and railway rolling stock produced per capita to get an idea of how things are going.

To shift gears metaphorically, we can say that the zombie bankers and derivatives monsters who control Obama can be compared to Count Dracula. The vampire, as we know from the movies, attacks a victim to suck blood. When Professor Van Helsing of Vienna comes on the scene, his first task is to pull Count Dracula off the victim and stop the process of bloodsucking. Count Dracula gets a stake through his heart, or is forced out into the sunshine where he cannot survive. Only then can blood transfusions and other procedures to save the victim be brought into play. Obama, Summers, Geithner, Volcker, and Orszag have a much different approach. They propose to allow Count Dracula to continue to suck the blood of the victim, the US economy. They propose to deliver a transfusion, not into the victim, but to Count Dracula himself. They then argue that the goal is to have the life-giving blood proceed through the Count into the victim. At this point, common sense rebels. We need to get rid of Count Dracula, through appropriate regulations and laws.

FROM HOPE AND CHANGE TO SACRIFICE, CHISELING, AND LOOTING

Several days before his inauguration, Obama met with the editorial board of the *Washington Post*, and made clear his commitment to imposing an austerity policy on the American people, in such a way as to procure the financial means necessary to finance bigger and better bailouts for his Wall Street patrons. According to this report, Obama "framed the economic recovery efforts more broadly, saying it is impossible to separate the country's financial ills from the long-term need to rein in health-care costs, stabilize Social Security and prevent the Medicare program from bankrupting the government. Obama then promised: "This, by the way, is where there are going to be very difficult choices and issues of sacrifice and responsibility and duty," he said. "You have to have a president who is willing to spend some political capital on this. And I intend to spend some." Specifically, Obama promised to convene a "fiscal responsibility summit" to marshal political forces for a coordinated assault on what remains of the US social safety net. (*Washington Post*, January 16, 2009) Notice that this terminology of political capital is exactly the same one used by George W. Bush in early 2005 when he launched his attempts to privatize and loot Social Security, for the same purpose of shifting resources into the hands of the Wall Street predators. Obama would be tackling the same task, but using demagogic left-wing rhetoric, and leaning on the mass movement of dupes and fanatics who swept him through the primaries and into office.

When Franklin Roosevelt became president in March of 1933, he left no doubt that the responsibility for the economic depression, mass immiseration, and crushing unemployment statistics of those years belonged to the bankers and financiers who had presided over the bubble, the stock market crash, and the banking panic. As FDR stated:

> ... the rulers of the exchange of mankind's goods have failed, through their own stubbornness and their own incompetence, have admitted their failure, and abdicated. Practices of the unscrupulous money changers stand indicted in the court of public opinion, rejected by the hearts and minds of men.... The money changers have fled from their high seats in the temple of our civilization. We may now restore that temple to the ancient truths. The measure of the restoration lies in the extent to which we apply social values more noble than mere monetary profit.

In other words, Roosevelt told the people that Wall Street was to blame for the depression. Obama says nothing of the kind. Obama and his financier backers love to pretend that the new tenant of the White House is the reincarnation of Franklin D. Roosevelt, seeking to give the American people a second edition of the New Deal. A comparative glance at Obama's inaugural address shows how false and hollow this demagogic lie really is. Obama's cliché-ridden inaugural speech was an insult to the hundreds of thousands of poor dupes who turned out that day in bitter cold to hear a president who believes in man-made global warming. Obama made a feint in the direction of Wall Street, but then quickly came down in favor of the collective guilt of the American people for the depression, because of their rejection of austerity and their outrageous demand for a decent middle-class standard of living:

> "Our economy is badly weakened, a consequence of greed and irresponsibility on the part of some, but also our collective failure to make hard choices and prepare the nation for a new age."

Notice: the depression is not the responsibility of the derivatives merchants in Wall Street, but rather the fault of all the people; it is a "collective failure." In Obama's fantasy of collective guilt, it is *"we"* who are now responsible, not the Wall Street gluttons of privilege, malefactors of great wealth and economic royalists. And now, Obama added ominously, the good times were over and the hour of sacrifice, austerity, and a brutal reduction of the already decimated American standard of living was at hand:

> "...our time of standing pat, of protecting narrow interests and putting off unpleasant decisions — that time has surely passed. What is required of us now is a new era of responsibility."

Reciting the radical environmentalist-Malthusian mantra of wind power and solar power, Obama warned that the US cannot "consume the world's resources without regard to effect." This, as a few noted, was a 2009 version of Carter's infamous July 1979 televised "malaise" tirade, in which he blamed the American people for the incompetence and failure of his own administration. Only this time, Obama's diagnosis of malaise was preemptive. It was a grim promise of austerity, and Obama doubtless reveled in the inability of many of his gullible supporters to understand the enormity of what he was proposing. We are reminded of Jimmy Carter's description of his own inauguration. Writing years after the fact. Carter says that he was pondering the foolishness of the public even as he made his own austerity speech in January 1977: "Watching the sea of approving faces [on Inauguration Day], I wondered how few of the happy celebrants would agree with my words if they analyzed them closely. At the time, it was not possible even for me to imagine the limits we would have to face. In some ways, dealing with limits would become the subliminal theme of the next four years and affect the outcome of the 1980 election."[4]

SQUEEZING SAVINGS OUT OF HEALTH PROGRAMS FOR OLD AND POOR

Obama's sociopathic austerity goals are, if anything, more ambitious than Carter's, mainly because of the infinitely more advanced breakdown crisis currently ravaging the US and world economies. In addition to the crushing energy austerity of a carbon tax-cap and trade regime, Obama is also committed to gouging trillions of dollars out of the Medicare system, which is also a favorite target of his resident Malthusian bean counter, Peter Orszag. By the end of February, Obama was using his weekly radio broadcast to promise that he would "get exploding deficits under control." On February 22, anonymous administration sources, doubtless close to OMB Director Orszag, were quoted in the *Washington Post* pledging the Obama regime "to address the nation's chronic budget in balance by squeezing savings from federal health programs for the elderly and the poor." This is the essence of Obama's austerity agenda in service to Wall Street.

On March 4, 2009, Obama convened a special White House "fiscal responsibility summit," a sinister gathering of deficit hawks and austerity ghouls to debate ways to demolish the economic rights of the American people. The key slogan, repeated as a mantra by Orszag and others, was that Social Security, Medicare, and existing social programs have become "unsustainable." Obama and Orszag talked of cutting the budget deficit in half over the next five years. This reckless and irresponsible commitment was sandwiched in between the first $700-plus billion bank bailout (the TARP), which Obama had warmly supported and helped to get through Congress, and the Geithner-Volcker-Summers-Obama bank bailout plan for an even larger amount, which was then still in the works. Pro-austerity reactionaries like George Will began demanding that Obama make good on his promises for "entitlement reform," which he wanted to come in the form of a "grand bargain. This Big Bang will aim to create a new universe of domestic policy by, among other things, making the entitlement menu — particularly Social Security, Medicare and Medicaid, which are more than 40 percent of federal spending — manageable." (*Washington Post*, January 25, 2009)

When the "fiscal responsibility summit" was convened on March 4, the prevailing argument was that a $1-$2 trillion bank bailout was a mere bagatelle, a passing conjunctural moment of little importance. The main issue, said the chorus of austerity ghouls, was the structural deficit due primarily to Medicare and secondarily to Social Security, along with the debt inherited from past administrations. A consensus emerged that the necessary austerity would involve getting Democrats to approve the looting of Medicare and Social Security, while getting Republicans to accept higher taxation across the board, plus the de facto carbon tax of a cap and trade system. This is what Will meant by a grand bargain. Since there was no way that such a draconian austerity package could pass the Congress under normal rules, Congressman Spratt of South Carolina and others demanded a special fast-track process for austerity, similar to that employed by the base realignment and closing commission (BRAC). A group of unelected and unaccountable Malthusian technocrats would meet behind closed doors at an undisclosed location, and work out their proposal for the definitive shredding of health, education, and welfare in this country. This proposal would then be rammed through Congress under a special take it or leave it process by which amendments would be forbidden, as in past instances of NAFTA, WTO, and the September-October 2008

---

[4] See William E. Leuchtenburg, "Jimmy Carter and the Post-New Deal Presidency," in Gary M. Fink and Hugh Davis Graham, eds., *The Carter Presidency: Policy Choices in the Post-New Deal Era* (Lawrence, Kansas: University Press of Kansas, 1998).

TARP. Congressional committees would presumably play no role, and the Congress would be reduced to a rubberstamp status worse than under the Bush regime.

OBAMA: NO HIP REPLACEMENTS FOR SICK OLD PEOPLE

One of Obama's biggest priorities will be to chisel trillions of dollars out of the highly successful Medicare program, which has saved millions of lives among older Americans since it was instituted by Lyndon B. Johnson during the late New Deal, four decades ago. Obama's own mentality is clearly that of the Malthusian bureaucrat looking for useless eaters who can be triaged for the benefit of the proverbial bottom line. Obama dropped his smiling mask in an interview with the *New York Times* in which he hinted broadly that it was time for older people to give up on life-saving operations, and accept death cheerfully to help out the insurance company executives like those of AIG, who had dabbled in trillions of dollars of worthless and toxic derivatives.

> President Barack Obama said his grandmother's hip-replacement surgery during the final weeks of her life made him wonder whether expensive procedures for the terminally ill reflect a "sustainable model" for health care. The president's grandmother, Madelyn Dunham, had a hip replaced after she was diagnosed with cancer, Obama said in an interview with the *New York Times Magazine* that was published today. Dunham, who lived in Honolulu, died at the age of 86 on Nov. 2, 2008, two days before her grandson's election victory. "I don't know how much that hip replacement cost," Obama said in the interview. "I would have paid out of pocket for that hip replacement just because she's my grandmother." Obama said "you just get into some very difficult moral issues" when considering whether "to give my grandmother, or everybody else's aging grandparents or parents, a hip replacement when they're terminally ill. "That's where I think you just get into some very difficult moral issues," he said in the April 14 interview. "The chronically ill and those toward the end of their lives are accounting for potentially 80 percent of the total health-care bill out here." (Hans Nichols, *Bloomberg*, April 29, 2009)

According to this remarkable statement, we can see that Obama considers getting a hip replacement operation for an elderly lady to represent a moral dilemma, even as he shovels more trillions across the room to make good the criminal handiwork of derivatives bandits and hedge fund operators. For the latter, he has no qualms. Obama, we can see, is not only economically incompetent, but also morally insane. We would have to remind Obama of the Nuremberg precedents, which specify that the deliberate denial of adequate medical care to a civilian population represents a high crime against humanity, which caused previous perpetrators to be punished in most unpleasant ways.

DASCHLE'S PROGRAM OF RATIONING AND DENYING HEALTH CARE

The American people are fortunate that former Senator Tom Daschle, the infamous Senator from Citibank, South Dakota, was prevented from becoming secretary of Health and Human Services in the new regime, when Daschle's massive tax evasions were discovered during his confirmation hearings. Daschle was the author of a 2008 book, *Critical: What We Can Do About the Health-Care Crisis*. Daschle was a miserable excuse for an opposition leader, capitulating to Bush and other reactionaries at every turn, but in the madhouse of Washington lobbyists he has somehow been anointed as an expert on public health policy. Daschle wants to gouge doctors as well as patients, warning the former that they must surrender their independent professional judgment as trained physicians and take orders from ignorant cost-cutting Malthusian bureaucrats, learning to "operate less like solo practitioners." Daschle's announced policy goal is to restrict and sabotage the development and introduction of new medications and new medical technologies because, in his cruel and stupid view, the senator from Citibank believes that it is these new technologies which are driving up costs. In reality, biomedical research and progress will cut costs to the extent that cures are found for previously fatal diseases. Sounding like a member of the Hemlock Society, Daschle in his screed praised European proponents of euthanasia for their willingness to accept "hopeless diagnoses" and "forgo experimental treatments," while criticizing Americans for expecting too many benefits from the health-care system. Daschle demanded that the elderly "accept that they are old and die because the state cannot afford to give them proper medical care. This is monstrous, and it will very likely become law with most Americans never hearing of this provision," as one commentator wrote.[5] It was also noted that Daschle, realizing how unpopular such a vote to pull the plug on old people would undoubtedly be, proposed to smuggle his entire genocidal project through the Congress in the dead of night, using illegal and dishonest stealth methods. Demanding immediate cuts in all forms of health care, Daschle added: "If that means attaching a health-care plan to the federal budget, so be it," he said. "The issue is too important to be stalled by Senate protocol." Daschle's mantra is that health-care reform "will not be pain-free." Old people, in Daschle's demonic view, should be more accepting of the conditions that come with age, foremost among them morbidity and mortality, instead of treating them.[6]

Ted Kennedy, it was widely noted, would already be dead under the kind of rationing of care that Daschle and Obama are demanding.

Daschle is fanatically committed to imitating the least successful features of the British national health service. Daschle advocates the creation of a "National Coordinator of Health Information Technology," to impose criteria of alleged cost-effectiveness in treatments recommended by individual physicians for their patients. Some $2 billion for the leading edge of this genocidal bureaucracy were included in Obama's $787 billion stimulus package passed in February 2009. The Obama regime, according to Daschle's plan, will limit treatment to what they consider appropriate and cost effective. This will imply a watershed shift in the criteria governing Medicare, which now pays for treatments which are considered safe and effective. Under the Daschle-Obama approach, this would be replaced by the accountants' notion of cost-effectiveness, and too bad if you die.

OBAMA HOSTILE TO SINGLE-PAYER HEALTH CARE

The Obama White House has been consistently hostile to advocates of a single-payer national health care plan, which would allow patients to choose their own doctors and hospitals while receiving financial assistance from the federal government. One of Obama's retainers on this issue, Senator Max Baucus, has also excluded single-payer advocates from his public hearings into this issue. In May 2009, Obama announced with much fanfare that a group of health insurance companies had miraculously volunteered to save several trillion dollars on a national health care bill over the years ahead, but this verbiage was about as credible as the many campaign promises which Obama was routinely trampling on from day to day. This supposedly generous gesture by the rapacious health insurance firms was simply another piece of demagogy, designed to head off a push coming from certain Democratic House members in favor of the one rational alternative to the current system of institutionalized waste and profiteering. The United States requires the option of Medicare for all, in the form of an extension of the very successful system for senior citizens over the age of 65, to anybody in the population who wants it or needs it. Private insurance has overhead expenditure of 30% to 40% for executive salaries, marketing, advertising, stock dividends, and

---

[5] http://www.newclarion.com/2009/02/stealth-tyranny/
[6] Betsy McCaughey, "Ruin Your Health With the Obama Stimulus Plan," Bloomberg, Feb. 9, 2009.

derivatives losses. The overhead ratio for Medicare is more like 2% to 3%. Rather than coercing anybody to buy outrageously overpriced private insurance as a way of bailing out the derivatives losses of the big insurance companies, the solution was clearly to offer the 50 million uninsured the possibility of joining Medicare at once, on demand. If the private insurance companies are so addicted to competition, they certainly should not fear a situation in which they will compete against Medicare, and the consumer will choose which program is better. This would mean a period of perhaps decades in which Medicare for all would coexist with private health insurance, leaving the consumer free to choose. This would be the new deal alternative, and Obama, Dorgan, Daschle, and HHS Secretary Sebelius want no part of it.

Joining in the effort was another resident austerity ghoul of the Obama White House, the sinister but comical Peter Orszag, who might be central casting's idea of a typical pointy-headed bureaucratic nerd. But Orszag is a very sinister figure indeed, since his specialty is to rail against life-giving medical tests like CAT scans, MRIs, nuclear stress tests (for heart patients), and the like. On the basis of no qualifications whatsoever, Orszag has now been promoted to the status of expert, seeking the power to deny these tests to people whose lives may depend on them. All once again in the service of the bottom line of some insurance company, which undoubtedly has a lucrative job waiting for Orszag when the abortive Obama interlude collapses into the inevitable chaos and defeat.

At Obama's health-care austerity summit, this mentality prevailed. Here the demagogic ploy was the idea of offering a minimal package of bare-bones benefits, vitiated by rationing of care and technology limitations under plans developed by Daschle. The trick was that this shoddy package would be offered to a broad proportion of the US population, including many who currently have no coverage. Prominent in the discussion where labor skates from the Service Employees International Union (SEIU), who are fast emerging as a new model of low-wage sellout company union, seeking to build their membership rolls and dues payments with the help of the depression. Based on Daschle's program, the over-aged, the overweight, smokers, and the very sick could expect to be triaged and denied care as useless eaters

AIG: TENS OF BILLIONS FOR FOREIGN DERIVATIVES BANKERS

As for Obama's ethical dilemmas, he ought to apply them to one insurance company in particular, AIG, before he demands the ultimate sacrifice from defenseless old people. The Federal Reserve struggled hysterically to prevent the public from knowing the names of the banks and other entities which had been on the receiving end of almost $200 billion pumped into the bankrupt insurer AIG. On January 13, Rep. Alan Grayson asked Fed Vice Chair Donald Kohn to provide the names of the banks that had received TARP funds via AIG since September 2008. Kohn flatly refused, as did Bernanke. AIG then announced $61 billion in losses for the last quarter of 2008 - a sum which could only have been caused by massive derivatives losses. AIG boss Edward Liddy, a Goldman Sachs alumnus, demanded more taxpayer money. Economist Nouriel Roubini called this "a nontransparent, opaque and shady bailout of the AIG counterparties." After acrimonious congressional hearings, it became known that the financial institutions which had cashed in on the TARP payments to AIG had included Goldman Sachs ($12.9 billion), Merrill Lynch ($6.8 billion), Bank of America ($5.2 billion), Citigroup ($2.3 billion) and Wachovia ($1.5 billion). Even worse, a huge slice of the bailout money that went to AIG had been paid to foreign banks, including Société Générale of France and Deutsche Bank of Germany (almost $12 billion each); Barclays of Britain ($8.5 billion); and UBS of Switzerland ($5 billion). AIG stated that the cash paid to these so-called derivatives counterparties was used to "cover collateral payments, cancel derivatives contracts and meet obligations at its securities lending business." Obama criticized AIG for paying a few hundred million dollars worth of bonuses to its resident derivatives speculators, but said nothing about the payments to a counting house like Goldman Sachs, quite possibly because Goldman Sachs has been the single biggest source of funding for Obama's 2008 seizure of power.

More ethical dilemmas will doubtless pop up for Obama when we look deeper into the Treasury's Troubled Asset Relief Program (TARP) bailout. The TARP was started by Bush and Paulson, but Obama was always a key supporter, arm-twisting members of the black caucus and other Democrats to vote for this astounding tribute to Wall St. greed. Citigroup raked in $50 billion in funds and then turned around and lent $8 billion in December 2008 to a Dubai public sector company, according to a memo by Rep. Dennis Kucinich (D-OH), chairman of the House Domestic Policy Subcommittee. Goldman Sachs Group, which received $10 billion in TARP funds at the end of October, used $2 billion earlier in the year to jack up its own stock price through the repurchase of company stock. The Kucinich memo noted that the increase in Goldman's stock price "would have constituted a significant benefit to top executives at Goldman Sachs, who typically own large amounts of company stock." Bank of America received $25 billion in TARP funds, and then in mid- November 2008 invested $7 billion in the China Construction Bank Corporation. J.P Morgan Chase & Co. received $25 billion in TARP funds, and its subsidiary J.P. Morgan Treasury Services in the following month invested $1 billion in cash management and trade finance speculations in India. (Rachel Oswald, *RawStory*, March 9, 2009)

OBAMA TO CONGRESS: "WHATEVER PROVES NECESSARY" — FOR THE BANKS!

If there were still any doubt about Obama's intentions, it was dissipated by his speech to a joint session of the U.S. Congress on February 24. Obama's commitment to the futile and suicidal project of harnessing the resources of the United States federal government to an attempted bailout of the $1.5 quadrillion world derivatives bubble could hardly have been more transparent. At the same time, Obama was aware that this Congress, with his own help, had already been burned once, namely by the Bush-Paulson TARP bailout of September-October 2008. Obama accordingly turned on all of his mesmerizing charm to recite his creed:

> …I know how unpopular it is to be seen as helping banks right now, especially when everyone is suffering in part from their bad decisions. I promise you — I get it. But I also know that in a time of crisis, we cannot afford to govern out of anger, or yield to the politics of the moment. My job — our job — is to solve the problem. Our job is to govern with a sense of responsibility. I will not spend a single penny for the purpose of rewarding a single Wall Street executive, but I will do whatever it takes to help the small business that can't pay its workers or the family that has saved and still can't get a mortgage. That's what this is about. It's not about helping banks — it's about helping people. Because when credit is available again, that young family can finally buy a new home. And then some company will hire workers to build it. And then those workers will have money to spend, and if they can get a loan too, maybe they'll finally buy that car, or open their own business. Investors will return to the market, and American families will see their retirement secured once more. Slowly, but surely, confidence will return, and our economy will recover.

> So I ask this Congress to join me in doing whatever proves necessary.

"Whatever proves necessary" — for the derivatives mongers!! Even as he was driving the auto industry, and much else, into bankruptcy. This was plainly an open-ended blank check to Wall Street for whatever sum or sums of money they might choose to demand in the future. It was an astounding documentation of how degraded American political life has become. It was national suicide. The next day, the *Washington Post* reported this apocalyptic speech under the headline of "Day of Reckoning" — Obama's *dies irae*.

BAILED OUT BANKS ARE NOT LENDING TO SAVE JOBS

The mantra of Obama and his gang is therefore that the bailout of Wall Street is not really the bailout of Wall Street, but rather the bailout of Main Street. Their goal, they argue, is to restart lending by the commercial banks for the benefit of the entire US economy, thus reflating the credit system and making loans available. The most obvious problem with this argument is that the main Wall Street banks stopped making loans for plant and equipment decades ago, so as to concentrate on proprietary trading of the type that bid up the price of gasoline in the summer of 2008, plus derivatives speculation, and gouging the consumer with credit card interest rates and fees. In any case, after six months of bailouts, it is clear that the Wall Street money center banks, despite the bailout bonanzas which they have received, are not lending for the purpose of reviving the economy. Where, for example, were J.P. Morgan Chase, at Citibank, and Bank of America when General Motors and Chrysler needed those bridge loans for modernization, and to maintain production and employment? These banks, joined by Goldman Sachs and Morgan Stanley, were evidently using their cash on hand to bid up the price of gasoline by about 35% on the London ICE market, as their way of saying thank you to taxpayers who are also motorists. Where were these Wall Street bankers when Circuit City, a large consumer electronics chain, desperately needed financing to arrange a prepackaged bankruptcy? Alas, these banks were nowhere to be found, and Circuit City was forced to shut down with a loss of 35,000 jobs. If we look closely, we will see that commercial bank loans for expanded plant, equipment, and jobs have become the specialty of a small number of local and regional banks of modest proportions, such as the few banks which have kept Silicon Valley going over recent years. These are the banks which a rational economic recovery policy would seek to save. Of course, the Obama regime is now conniving to destroy those critical local banks which still make commercial bank loans to create jobs and production, with Obama's goal being to feed these viable local and regional banks into the rapacious jaws of the Wall Street derivatives monsters, in the same way that Washington Mutual was fed into the derivatives black hole which is J.P. Morgan Chase.

GEITHNER-SUMMERS-VOLCKER-BERNANKE DERIVATIVES BAILOUT DEBACLE

Because of the prevalent propaganda offered by the mass media controlled by Wall Street, the average person is genuinely bewildered about the cause of the current world economic depression. The Limbaugh-Hannity school blames the depression on poor people who took out subprime mortgages on slum properties from predatory lenders, and then defaulted. This fantastic mythology attributes the fall of the entire world banking system to marginal loans of tertiary importance. As far as is known, the word derivative has never been mentioned by Rush Limbaugh or heard of on his radio program, except on one occasion when this term crept in by accident in the middle of a rant on government spending being delivered by Rick Santelli of CNBC, who makes his living as a reporter covering trading pits where derivatives change hands. Limbaugh's 20 million listeners have absolutely no idea that the central factor of the entire financial disintegration is the $1.5 quadrillion derivatives bubble. These derivatives were pyramided and kited into a structure which generated astronomical profits at the apex, as long as positive leverage prevailed. But as Greenspan's housing bubble began to run out of steam in 2005 and 2006, combined with the gathering collapse of the automobile sector as signaled by the Delphi bankruptcy, the leverage of the derivatives pyramid began to go negative, meaning that astronomical losses were now being generated at the top. It is this fateful switch from positive leverage to negative leverage in the derivatives pyramid which is now inexorably destroying the entire Anglo-American banking system. Because of the complexity of derivatives, and because of the determination of the Wall Street media not to discuss this problem, the average person does not understand the cause of the present world economic depression. Since the depression impacts everyone, everywhere, all the time, it is a phenomenon which cannot be ignored. This is therefore an area where the danger of the proliferation of irrational, magical, and mythological explanations is very great. The sense of the German people from 1923 and 1929 on that they were living in an inexplicable madhouse without rhyme or reason was, of course, one of the main factors facilitating the rise of fascism. The very existence of derivatives is for many commentators now a taboo of the most absurd kind. Economics reporters and elected officials talk about these "financial products," "complex instruments," "exotic securities," and "toxic assets." Whenever these terms, or related ones like "counterparties" are mentioned, we know that derivatives are in reality being talked about. Derivatives can be defined as financial instruments whose value depends on other financial instruments. They are, in short, paper based on paper, as described in a later chapter.

On October 14, 2008, Secretary of the Treasury Paulson and Bush announced a total re-direction of the TARP program. The Treasury announced their intention to abandon the original plan to buy up bankrupt derivatives, and rather buy senior preferred stock and warrants in the nine largest American banks, precisely the zombie banks or derivatives monsters. In Obama' s first press conference on February 9, he dodged questions about additional bank bailouts by passing the buck to Treasury Secretary Geithner, variously dismissed as "Tiny Tim" and "the tax cheat." "And so tomorrow my Treasury Secretary, Tim Geithner, will be announcing some very clear and specific plans for how we are going to start loosening up credit once again," said Obama — clearly fearful of being exposed as a Wall Street puppet — as he dodged questions on the bailout. (Obama press conference, February 9, 2009)

DERIVATIVES FROM BAD BANK TO PPIP

On the morning of Geithner's promised statement, the *Washington Post* headline reported leaks that the next phase of the derivatives bailout would cost more than $1.5 trillion, although it also held out the possibility that "private capital" would play a key role. But Geithner's public appearance was a debacle, marked by a confluence of stammering incompetence and evasion. There were hints that the total price tag for the proposed "bad bank" might be as much as $2 trillion. (The bad bank would be a receptacle for toxic derivatives unloaded by banks and hedge funds onto the backs of the hapless taxpayers.) But Geithner refused to offer any specific details of how the bad bank might work. "This is very complicated to get it right," he told Bloomberg Television. "We are going to try to get it right before we give the details so that we don't add further to uncertainty in these markets." He refused to say whether the administration might have to ask Congress for more money to fix the banks, restore credit and counter recession, but did not rule it out. "We're going to consult with the Congress carefully to try to make sure the world understands that the resources necessary to solve this will be available over time," Geithner assured CNBC, adding: "The important thing is that... we send a basic signal, working with the Congress, that we will do what's necessary to fix this."

Geithner's performance triggered a 5% collapse in the Dow Jones industrials and the Standard & Poor's 500 stock index that same day. Geithner's bungling reflected the very high degree of personal and administrative ineptitude and fecklessness in the higher reaches of the Obama regime, starting with the tenant of the White House himself. In addition, the blame for this wretched punting reflected the collective failure of Obama's new derivatives brain trust. Geithner was anything but a free agent; he was a product of the clique around former Secretary of the Treasury Lawrence

Summers, who was in turn a protégé of Bob Rubin of Goldman Sachs, the Clinton administration, and the charred hulk of Citibank. As various journalistic accounts made clear, Geithner was the front man for this team:

> Just days before Treasury Secretary Timothy F. Geithner was scheduled to lay out his much-anticipated plan to deal with the toxic assets imperiling the financial system, he and his team made a sudden about-face. At the center of the deliberations with Geithner were Lawrence H. Summers... Lee Sachs, a Clinton administration official.... and Gene Sperling, another former Clinton aide. The debates among them were long and vigorous as they thrashed countless proposals and variations. Sometimes, Fed Chairman Ben S. Bernanke, Federal Deposit Insurance Corp. Chairman Sheila C. Bair and Comptroller of the Currency John C. Dugan joined in.... (*Washington Post*, February 17, 2009)

The approach supported for a time by this gaggle of derivatives devotees was the "aggregator bank" or bad bank, with the massive derivatives losses and the future risk shifted to the taxpayers. "Senior economic officials had several approaches in mind, according to officials involved in the discussions. One would be to create an 'aggregator bank,' or bad bank, that would take government capital and use it to buy up the risky assets on banks' books. Another approach would be to offer banks a government guarantee against extreme losses on their assets, an approach already used to bolster Citigroup and Bank of America." (*Washington Post*, February 17, 2009)

HOW TO BAIL OUT $1.5 QUADRILLION OF DERIVATIVES WITH $12.8 TRILLION OF TAXPAYER MONEY

But, once again, pro-derivatives policymakers ran up against the woeful inadequacy of their paltry means, denominated in trillions though they be, to deal with the astronomical hyperdimensions of the world derivatives bubble. What good were even $12.8 trillion ($12,800,000,000,000) in the face of the world derivatives exposure in the neighborhood of $1.5 quadrillion — i.e., one thousand five hundred trillion dollars ($1,500,000,000,000,000) — three orders of magnitude more? This was the gigantic problem which made an intellectual Lilliputian like Geithner appear so insignificant.

The size of the derivatives bubble is being systematically underestimated even by those commentators who are willing to talk about it at all. Barrett Sheridan wrote in *Newsweek*: "If some banks are too big to fail, $600 trillion has become the number too big to question. That's $600,000,000,000,000—the rough figure cited in many news reports for the total size of the derivatives market, now blowing up to such alarming effect. Official figures haven't been released, but surveys reveal the market has now grown to at least $668 trillion. But the good news is that most of it is not real money...." ("The Case for Derivatives," *Newsweek*, Oct 27, 2008) This account totally underestimates both the size of the derivatives bubble, and the deadly threat which it poses to human civilization in North America and elsewhere. Economist Robert Shiller of Yale even went so far as to advance the absurd thesis that derivatives, in reality the biggest single cause of the crisis in the financial markets, could in fact help solve the crisis. (Zachary Karabell, *Newsweek*, Feb 2, 2009) The Bank for International Settlements (BIS) in Basel, Switzerland did somewhat better: The BIS reported in mid-2008 that global outstanding derivatives had reached 1.14 quadrillion dollars: $548 trillion in exchange-traded credit derivatives, plus $596 trillion in over-the-counter derivatives. This was almost twenty times the total GDP of the entire world. By May 2009, the BIS statistics showed that the derivatives bubble was deflating, at least for the moment. The total notional amount of over-the-counter (OTC) derivatives contracts outstanding, according to the BIS, was $592.0 trillion at the end of December 2008, 13.4% lower than six months earlier. (BIS, May 18, 2009) If true, this would be the first major shrinkage in the recent history of the derivatives cancer.

The US Treasury's Comptroller of the Currency estimated that US banks held about $200 trillion of derivatives at the end of 2008. JP Morgan Chase came in with $87 trillion of official derivatives, followed by Bank of America with $38 trillion, Citibank with $32 trillion, Goldman Sachs with $30 trillion, HSBC and Wells Fargo with just under $4 trillion each, and Bank of New York Mellon with $1.2 trillion. These are the zombie banks. But these are still low-ball estimates. Because derivatives in the US are totally unregulated and even non-reportable by non-bank entities like hedge funds, we are forced to estimate them.

A revealing article from the McClatchy news service left no doubt that the root cause of the banking crisis was derivatives losses. This article focused mainly on credit default swaps, one of the most dangerous subsets among derivatives, but only one part of the gigantic derivatives problem. As McClatchy reporters Greg Gordon and Kevin G. Hall wrote, "America's five largest banks, which already have received $145 billion in taxpayer bailout dollars, still face potentially catastrophic losses from exotic investments if economic conditions substantially worsen, their latest financial reports show. Citibank, Bank of America, HSBC Bank USA, Wells Fargo Bank and J.P. Morgan Chase reported that their "current" net loss risks from derivatives — insurance-like bets tied to a loan or other underlying asset — surged to $587 billion as of Dec. 31 [2008]. Buried in end-of-the-year regulatory reports that McClatchy has reviewed, the figures reflect a jump of 49 percent in just 90 days." One expert "noted that Citibank now lists 60 percent of its $301 billion in potential losses from its wheeling and dealing in derivatives in the highest-risk category, up from 40 percent in early 2007." ("Too big to fail? 5 biggest banks are 'dead men walking,'" Greg Gordon and Kevin G. Hall, McClatchy Newspapers, March 9, 2009)

ZOMBIE BANKS DEVASTATED BY LOSSES

According to the McClatchy summary, "In their reports, the banks said that their net current risks and potential future losses from derivatives surpass $1.2 trillion":

Four of the banks' reserves already have been augmented by taxpayer bailout money, topped by Citibank — $50 billion — and Bank of America — $45 billion, plus a $100 billion loan guarantee.

The banks' quarterly financial reports show that as of Dec. 31:

— J.P. Morgan had potential current derivatives losses of $241.2 billion, outstripping its $144 billion in reserves, and future exposure of $299 billion.

— Citibank had potential current losses of $140.3 billion, exceeding its $108 billion in reserves, and future losses of $161.2 billion.

— Bank of America reported $80.4 billion in current exposure, below its is the $122.4 billion reserve, but $218 billion in total exposure.

— HSBC Bank USA had current potential losses of $62 billion, more than triple its reserves, and potential total exposure of $95 billion.

— San Francisco-based Wells Fargo, which agreed to take over Charlotte-based Wachovia in October, reported current potential losses totaling nearly $64 billion, below the banks' combined reserves of $104 billion, but total future risks of about $109 billion.

[A] bank shareholders' expert said that several of the big banks' risks are so large that they are "dead men walking."[7]

As soon as Obama's whiz kids begin thinking concretely about how a bad bank would have to operate, they were repeatedly paralyzed by the obvious absurdity of the fool's errand they were on. Even the act of talking about additional trillions for the Wall Street jackals would be politically damaging in the extreme. And nevertheless, Soros, Rockefeller, and Goldman Sachs were all demanding action. The result was Geithner's failure to deliver the assurances the financiers were demanding. According to one account, "As the first week of February progressed…the problems with both approaches were becoming clearer to Geithner, said people involved in the talks. For one thing, the government would likely have to put trillions of dollars in taxpayer money at risk, a sum so huge it would anger members of Congress. Officials were also concerned that the program would be criticized as a pure giveaway to bank shareholders. And, finally, there continued to be the problem that had bedeviled the Bush administration's efforts to tackle toxic assets: There was little reason to believe government officials would be able to price these assets in a way that gave taxpayers a good deal." (*Washington Post*, February 17, 2009)

THE GREAT FEAR OF CREDIT DEFAULT SWAPS

The *hoi polloi* could be kept in the dark, but generating an elite consensus on the need to spend 2 trillion additional dollars on toxic derivatives proved impossible without using the dreaded D-word. One op-ed writer charily approached the matter in this fashion: "Today's true market value of the U.S. banks' toxic assets (that ugly stuff that needs to be removed from bank balance sheets before the economy can recover) amounts to between 5 and 30 cents on the dollar. To remain solvent, however, the banks say they need a valuation of 50 to 60 cents on the dollar. Translation: as much as another $2 trillion taxpayer bailout. That kind of expensive solution could send the president's approval rating into a nose dive. Consider: $2 trillion is about two-thirds of the tax revenue the federal government collects each year. All the big banks are connected to a potentially lethal web of paper insurance instruments called credit default swaps. These paper derivatives have become our financial system's new master. The theory holds that dismantling a big bank could unravel this paper market, with catastrophic global financial and consequences. Or not. Nobody knows, because the market for these unregulated financial derivatives, amounting potentially to over $40 trillion (by comparison, global gross domestic product is now not much more than $60 trillion), is the financial equivalent of uncharted waters." (David M. Smick, "Tim Geithner's Black Hole," *Washington Post*, March 10, 2009) These were overwhelmingly lowball estimates, but the metaphor of derivatives as a black hole was accurate, as the present writer has continuously argued for many years.

French President Jacques Chirac once referred to derivatives as "financial AIDS." Berkshire Hathaway Chairman Warren Buffett, a notorious financial predator, had warned in 2002 that derivatives represented financial weapons of mass destruction. Then it transpired that Buffett had been long in derivatives during the 2008 panic, and had taken a major hit. In February 2009, Buffett warned that "Derivatives are dangerous" in his annual letter to shareholders. He revealed that he had lost hundreds of millions of dollars for Berkshire Hathaway when he foolishly scarfed up a re-insurance company loaded with toxic derivatives. (Greg Gordon and Kevin G. Hall, McClatchy Newspapers, March 9, 2009) By May 2009, Buffett had reversed his field once more, this time announcing that he was "doubling down" on his derivatives bets with the hope of recouping his losses and then some. Since Buffett had served as an informal financial advisor to Obama, we may

---

[7] "Too big to fail? 5 biggest banks are 'dead men walking,'" Greg Gordon and Kevin G. Hall, McClatchy Newspapers, March 9, 2009.

well wonder whether corruption and conflict of interest were not at work in this case. Was Buffett now guilty of insider trading based on his privileged knowledge of the extraordinary lengths to which the Obama regime was prepared to go in order to prop up the speculative, fictitious, cancerous derivatives racket?

SCHOLES: "BLOW UP OR BURN OUT DERIVATIVES"

Even Myron Scholes, the University of Chicago monetarist economist who helped to inflict the derivatives plague on the world, appears now to have recognized that his creation is a Frankenstein monster. In a March 2009 conference at New York University's Stern School in the presence of Obama's gray eminence, Paul Adolph Volcker, Scholes recanted some of the work which won him the part of the Nobel prize. Scholes said: "My belief is that the Fred Adair solution is to blow up or burn the OTC market in credit default swaps," Scholes said, adding that regulators should "try to close all contracts at mid-market prices" and then start up the market anew with clearer rules and shorter-duration contracts. Geithner also says that he wanted to "regulate" derivatives. The only regulation of derivatives which makes any sense is the "bright line prohibition," which was mentioned by Virginia Senator Mark Warner in regard to credit default swaps in a question to Fed boss Ben Bernanke a few weeks ago.

Geithner's approach to bailing out US banks and investment companies depends on identifying certain top institutions as being too big to fail, and then putting unlimited government resources at the service of these insolvent entities. This method is uncannily similar to the corporate state (meaning, strictly speaking, a guild organization of society) as practiced in Italy under the Mussolini regime in the 1920s and 1930s. The essence of the fascist corporate state is a state sponsored compulsory cartel designed to reduce wages, reduce production, and prop up and maintain the bloated speculative values of certain securities and paper promises to pay. In this system, government, management, and labor (generally in the form of a pliable company union like the SEIU) are practically merged, with the regime picking winners and losers.

PPIP: ANOTHER TRILLION FOR THE ZOMBIE BANKERS

Geithner's latest version of the corporate state is the Public-Private Investment Program (PPIP), fully equipped with $1 trillion in additional bailout funds for the zombie banks. The PPIP essentially puts the US federal government into business as a hedge fund, in cahoots with the big banks under a system rigged by Geithner to send the profits into private hands, while the losses remain with the government. The leading beneficiaries of PPIP are the usual Wall Street suspects, including J.P. Morgan Chase, Citigroup, Wells Fargo, PNC, and Bank of America. What these top zombies all have in common is huge derivatives and securities holdings, plus other mark-to-market assets.[8] If Goldman Sachs and J.P. Morgan Chase are, as expected, among the first institutions to be chosen to partner with Geithner's Treasury, this will confirm the privileged status of these two predatory institutions as the chosen winners in Obama's new fascist corporate state.

Another of Geithner's tricks has been the so-called stress tests, which purport to be in-depth analyses of the capital positions and financial health of the 19 top banks, almost all of which would be considered thoroughly insolvent by traditionally-accepted accounting methods. Sheila Bair of the Federal Deposit Insurance Corporation, a Bush holdover, is blatantly violating the law by not immediately seizing these bankrupt institutions and putting them through bankruptcy reorganization or, much more likely, Chapter Seven liquidation. Sheila Bair routinely seizes small rural banks

---

[8] http://online.barrons.com/article/SB123822921763064821.html

every Friday afternoon, but so far the Wall Street giants have been immune, even though they are far deeper in bankruptcy. This reflects once again the rule of Geithner's fascist corporate state, which is that smaller and less bankrupt institutions are to be fed into the larger and more insolvent ones, to prop up the money center titans at the expense of the shareholders and depositors of the smaller local and regional institutions. Once again, Sheila Bair's delivery of Washington Mutual to J.P. Morgan Chase for the purpose of propping up the latter is exemplary. The stress tests appear to be designed as a demagogic propaganda exercise pre-programmed to show that the Wall Street derivatives monsters are doing just fine, while the much healthier local and regional banks will show up as fatally undercapitalized, so that they can be forced to merge on very unfavorable terms with Goldman Sachs, J.P. Morgan Chase, and the other chosen winners of Geithner's corporatist cartel.

GEITHNER STRESS TESTS "A POTEMKIN MODEL"

The former bank regulator William Black has characterized Geithner's stress tests as "a complete sham... a Potemkin model. Built to fool people." Like many analysts, Black believes the "worst case scenario" used in the stress test does not go far enough. Black added: "There is no real purpose [of the stress test] other than to fool us. To make us chumps." Black noted Geithner's claim that the only real problem is a lack of confidence. Geithner is therefore arguing, "'If we lie and they believe us, all will be well.' It's Orwellian." Black described Geithner as a "failed regulator" who is now "adding to failed policy" by not allowing "banks that really need desperately to be closed" to fail. Black located Geithner's stress test charade in the context of the Treasury Secretary's toxic debt plan, which amounts in his words to "an enormous taxpayer subsidy for people who caused the problem." Bank stocks have been rising since Geithner unveiled his plan, and this is "bad news for taxpayers," says Black. "It's the subsidy of all history," Black summed up.

CNBC financial commentator John Browne, a former member of the British Parliament, called special attention to the incredible fact that the stress tests have been conducted without reference to the off-balance-sheet derivatives exposure of the banks in question, even though it is these derivatives which unquestionably represent the greatest threat of insolvency to most of the 19 top zombies being tested. Browne observed:

> The government announced its stress tests results 10 days ago. Seeing possible worst-case bank losses of $599 billion, the Fed ordered 10 out of 19 major banks to raise a total of $75 billion additional capital by November. The remaining nine banks were found to be healthy..... Sixteen of the 19 tested banks were believed by many analysts to be technically insolvent.... To realistic observers, the Treasury tests showed an alarming absence of stress. The Treasury assumed a worst-case unemployment rate of 10 percent, just 1.3 percentage points above today's official rate. With 13.7 million Americans without jobs, it is already the worst in 25 years. But there are 2.1 million more who wanted jobs but had not reapplied in the past four weeks. There are also those who, unable to secure full-time jobs, have been forced to accept part-time employment. If these so-called "marginally attached" are included, the unemployment rate is 15.9 percent. Additionally, if the pre-Clintonian computation method is used, unemployment is already over 20 percent, the official definition of depression — or double the worst rate assumed in the stress tests. *Most alarmingly, the stress tests made no mention of the banks' capital exposure to the vast derivatives market. Some major banks have exposure totaling several hundred percent of their capital....* Despite this massive citizens'

rescue, the top management of the money-center banks, with their reckless core ethics, are still in charge. The stress test made no demands for management changes.[9]

The stress tests are therefore totally worthless, and a transparent cloak for the further consolidation of Geithner's corporate state cartel of bankrupt financial institutions. The rest of the world is unlikely to be fooled by these machinations. To make the stress tests even softer, the Obama regime conveniently arranged for the banks to be released from the discipline of "mark to market," meaning that their toxic derivatives no longer had to be valued at mere pennies on the dollar, which in many cases was already a very optimistic overstatement of what this paper could bring. In advance of the stress tests, the banks were told to abandon mark-to-market, and presumably go back to their older and discredited "mark to model" valuations, which allowed them to arbitrarily assign any value they wanted to their bankrupt derivatives, by alleging the new and higher value had been generated by a proprietary computer model, as typified by the Black-Scholes model, which was implicated in the bankruptcy of the Long-Term Capital Management hedge fund in 1998.

OBAMA'S LEFT COVER APPROACH TO UNION BUSTING: THE UAW

No account of Obama's economic policies would be complete without establishing the central role of union busting and draconian cuts in wages, benefits, and the US standard of living in general. The most obvious target is the United Auto Workers, long considered to be one of the most militant and successful of all US unions. Right wing reactionary radio commentators, lost in their mythological dream world, allege that Obama has been handling the auto crisis so as to strengthen the hand of the UAW. Obama has done just the opposite in reality. If Obama had wanted to save the automobile industry and protect the interests of the UAW, he needed only to treat the Detroit automakers in the same way he treated AIG, giving them all the credit they needed with no preconditions and virtually no questions asked. Instead, Obama is cynically driving the auto makers into bankruptcy.

First, the UAW was required to accept concessions in wages and benefits that would degrade the situation of the average Midwest autoworker and union member, to the same shoddy level which has been inflicted on non-unionized workers working for foreign employers, in those low-wage southern states which have taken advantage of the notorious loophole in the Taft-Hartley Act known as "right to work," meaning simply that unions are virtually impossible to organize. These concessions attack the very reason for having a union in the first place: if the UAW cannot give something to its members which non-unionized southern workers do not receive, then what is the point of having a union? In the case of Chrysler, the UAW has agreed to accept a 45% share of the common stock of whatever company is left standing, and in exchange for this, the UAW has freed the Chrysler management (meaning in effect the hedge fund hyenas of Cerberus private capital) of all future liability for the healthcare benefits for UAW retirees, which have been written into union contracts over the years. (After these crimes, it will be hard to talk about the sanctity of contracts in this country for a good long time.) As the Limbaughs and Hannities rant on about the limitless power of the UAW, the hapless Gettlefinger leadership of that union has in effect accepted common stock, which by all odds will soon be worth absolutely nothing, as Chrysler continues to wallow in bankruptcy. The UAW will only get one meager seat on the Chrysler Board of Directors, which is far less than its worthless shares would have suggested. All in all, the UAW has been robbed blind by Obama and his sinister asset-stripping car czar, the former *New York Times*, Morgan Stanley, and Lazard Freres financier Steven Rattner, who knows absolutely nothing about the automobile

---

[9] John Browne, "'Stress tests' no test," *Pittsburgh Tribune-Review*, May 17, 2009, emphasis added.

industry and is officially listed as Counselor to Secretary of the Treasury Geithner. This is the same Rattner who threatened Perella Weinberg Partners' Xerion Fund, Stairway, and Oppenheimer that he would sic the White House press corps on these hedge funds if they did not knuckle under to the demands of the regime. Joseph Perella and Peter Weinberg had tried to get the same terms as the larger, Geithner-endorsed creditors, including JP Morgan Chase, Citigroup, Morgan Stanley, and Goldman Sachs. Rattner was acting to impose discipline on the emerging cartel.

Embarrassingly for Obama, car czar Rattner soon figured prominently in a blossoming New York State retirement fund kickback scandal. Rattner's hedge fund, Quadrangle, paid a finder's fee to one of the defendants in the kickback scheme in exchange for a $100 million investment by the state retirement fund in one of Quadrangle's funds. The Obama regime was already more corrupt than the Bush gang, which was a tall order.

RECONVERT DETROIT FOR TRACTORS, MAGLEV, NUCLEAR, AND SPACE

The answer for the automobile industry was immediate nationalization, removing the hedge fund profiteers and their derivatives from the picture. The new executives for the big three automakers needed to be drawn from the ranks of competent industrial engineers. After World War II, the UAW under Walter Reuther studied the problem of reconverting war plants for civilian production, and the method used in these studies would be relevant today. Since it is unlikely that the demand for private cars will be sufficient to maintain the existing auto plants, a significant part of these ought to be reconverted to the production of agricultural tractors for the Third World, equipment for the space program, rolling stock and other equipment for high-speed maglev rail, and components for turnkey nuclear reactors for the domestic and export markets. This reconversion can be easily carried out using 0% long-term federal loans from the Nationalized Bank of the United States. If the Detroit-Midwest automobile complex is permitted to collapse, the United States will be finished as an industrial power, and will exist only as a ravaged hulk or battered derelict, adrift before the hurricane of world depression. The tool and die and machine tool capabilities associated with the automobile industry are one of the most precious resources of humanity as a whole, and to allow these capabilities to be destroyed would be a gargantuan crime. If the United States is unable to retain a full set economy, this country will soon be classed as a banana republic, and anthropologists from China and other places will come to study the resulting ethnographic material, perhaps with a view to determining the stultifying clinical effects of Malthusian and monetarist decadence and degeneracy on a political and economic system.

OBAMA AND DUNCAN TARGET THE AFT

If the UAW is clearly Obama's number one target among industrial unions coming from the old CIO, the American Federation of Teachers is first among his targets in the area of public employee unions, which is the one area where the labor movement has been able to hold on to its gains, and even manage some modest growth. Given Obama's background as the son of a Ford Foundation operative, we can say that busting the teachers' unions is to some extent his family business. When Obama boasts that he was a community organizer, he is telling us in fact that he was a foundation-funded strike breaker or scab, a poverty pimp working for the Gamaliel Foundation, the Joyce Foundation, the Woods Fund, and the Annenberg Foundation. He showed his hostile intent towards the teachers' unions during the election campaign by his stubborn endorsement of "merit pay," one of the methods used to blame teachers for the collapse of the entire society which is mirrored in the disappointing performance of many students on standardized tests. Obama's approach to busting the teachers' union is centered on the idea of charter schools. In the hands of foundation operatives like the District of Columbia education czarina Michelle Rhee, charter schools represent a way to create an entire parallel education system, but with no union contract, no tenure and no guarantees of any kind for teachers. Today, the teachers' union represents the main organized force which is willing to fight for the continuation of free, universal, compulsory, public education in this country. Once the teachers union has been destroyed, the finance oligarchs will feel free to shut down most of the public education system, which they no longer want to pay for. Children of the oligarchy can attend expensive private schools. This is the program of foundations like the Gates, the Broad, and others, and this is Obama's program.

Obama has been especially ominous in his veiled threats to teachers and their unions. A recent sample: "For decades, Washington has been trapped in the same stale debates that have paralyzed progress and perpetuated our educational decline … If a teacher is given a chance but still does not improve, there is no excuse for that person to continue teaching," he said. "I reject a system that rewards failure and protects a person from its consequences." Obama only wants that for Wall Street, as we have seen. (*Washington Post*, March 11, 2009) Obama wants merit pay and charter schools, which have been resisted by the teachers unions, which constitute an important segment of the Democratic Party. Obama's glib comeback: "Too many supporters of my party have resisted the idea of rewarding excellence in teaching with extra pay, even though we know it can make a difference in the classroom." (AP, March 9, 2009) The response of the labor skates at the AFT has been both treacherous and pathetic. AFT president Randi Weingarten, who knows better, commented: "We finally have an education president…. We really embrace the fact that he's talked about both shared responsibility and making sure there is a voice for teachers, something that was totally lacking in the last eight years." The president of the less militant 3.2 million-member National Education Association, Dennis van Roekel, added: "President Obama always says he will do it with educators, not to them." But Obama's pick of Education Secretary Arne Duncan, who has distinguished himself by shutting down large numbers of schools in Chicago while constantly picking fights with the teachers' union, shows clearly enough where we are headed. Once again, Obama's spurious left cover is what allows him to carry out attacks on labor which would have caused riots under the Bush regime. This illustrates once again the reason why the US financier ruling class lined up behind Obama, and also why they will dump him once his abortive and catastrophic presidency has outlived its usefulness.

Obama's approach to the foreclosure crisis replicates the basics of his characteristic method, as we have seen it in other areas of the crisis. The rhetoric suggests that he wants to help the little guy, but the flow of funds makes it obvious that his main concern is the transfer of public wealth into the coffers of his Wall Street backers and controllers. The answer to the foreclosure crisis is simple: use the Defense Production Act to ban all foreclosures on primary residences for five years or the duration of the crisis, whichever takes longer. The same powers need to be used to prevent the shutdown of any farm, business, factory, airline, railroad, ferry, taxi company, trucking firm, restaurant, dry cleaner, or any other economic unit engaged in production or socially necessary services. Since this would not be popular on Wall Street, Obama has given it no consideration whatsoever.

DURBIN: THE BANKS "FRANKLY OWN THE PLACE"

Obama's foreclosure program involves $75 billion in incentives given to predatory mortgage companies, who have followed in the footsteps of the notorious Angelo Mozillo of the now defunct Countrywide, whose insolvency kicked off the world banking panic in August 2007. The program is purely voluntary for these predatory mortgage lenders, who are free to continue peddling their highly destructive Adjustable Rate Mortgages, which need to be outlawed. These firms are offered money to help homeowners avoid foreclosure, but the evidence suggests that foreclosures are increasing in the face of Obama's program, although it still may be slightly too early to tell. We do know that the leading beneficiary of Obama's alleged anti-foreclosure program has been the mortgage unit of J.P. Morgan Chase. The program is administered by Obama's Housing and Urban Development appointee, Shaun Donovan, a product of the Prudential insurance company mortgage operation.

The following report captures the present situation, which is surely deteriorating rapidly, despite the messianic and utopian promises issued by the Obama campaign and the Obama White House:

> Foreclosures "came back with a vengeance" last month and are likely to keep rising, said Rick Sharga, RealtyTrac's senior vice president for marketing. The Treasury Department has signed contracts with six big loan servicing companies — including Citigroup, Wells Fargo and JP Morgan Chase. Many have already started processing loans as part of the government's "Making Home Affordable" plan. "We need to get the long-term solutions for these folks," Shaun Donovan, Obama's housing secretary, said in an interview. In the coming months, Donovan said, there are still likely to be increased foreclosures, especially from vacant houses, second homes and those owned by speculators. None of those properties will qualify for a loan modification. However, he remained optimistic that overall foreclosures could start to decrease this summer. Alan Zibel, "Foreclosures up 24 percent in first quarter as temporary halts expire," AP, April 16, 2009.

Another measure was the so-called "cramdown," under which bankruptcy judges would be allowed to reduce the interest and principal on existing mortgages if they were headed towards default. This measure was sponsored by Sen. Richard Durbin (D-Ill.), one of Obama's original backers. Durbin told Illinois radio station WJJG: "And the banks — hard to believe in a time when we're facing a banking crisis that many of the banks created — are still the most powerful lobby on Capitol Hill. And they frankly own the place." The American Bankers Association, representing many of the zombie recipients of the TARP, pulled out all the stops to defeat Durbin's cramdown bill, with some help from Senate Majority Leader Harry Reid (D-Nev.). When the friend then came up for a vote in the Senate, it was voted down with the help of the following Democrats: Baucus, Bennett, Byrd, Carper, Dorgan, Johnson, Landrieu, Lincoln, Nelson, Pryor, Specter, and Tester. The Obama White House did nothing to get the cramdown passed. There were no phone calls, no address to the nation, no special news conference, no investment of political capital. Obama could care less about foreclosure victims.

OBAMA FAVORS BANKERS OVER PEOPLE BY ABOUT 35:1

Right-wing commentators, as part of their imbecilic campaign to portray Obama as some kind of a socialist who wants to transfer wealth to the poor, are already doing everything possible to blur the distinction between the $700 billion bailout or TARP, originally demanded in September-October 2008 by Bush and Paulson with the support of Obama and McCain, and the $787 billion stimulus passed by the Congress in mid-February 2009. There has to be a very clear distinction between these. The bailout is simply money poured down a rat hole, or better yet poured into the $1.5 quadrillion derivatives black hole. The stimulus, by contrast, is a very mixed bag, including elements that will prove highly beneficial and which needed to be much bigger, alongside other elements which are totally wasteful and counterproductive, or even dangerous.

In terms of the stimulus, we can immediately identify $27.5 billion for highway construction, $20.6 billion for other transportation programs, $22.4 billion for modernizing the electricity grid, $4.6 billion for the Army Corps of Engineers, $5.8 billion for state grants for water infrastructure projects, $5.4 billion for the construction and repair of federal buildings, $4.7 billion for capital improvements to national parks, $2.5 billion to expand broadband Internet in rural areas, $4.2 billion for military construction (provided that it is inside the US), and $4.5 billion for defense facility repair and energy projects, as representing about $102 billion of generally useful infrastructure expenditure, which can mainly be criticized because the amounts involved are so pitifully small in comparison with a US accumulated infrastructure deficit in the ballpark of $10 trillion. The $3 billion for basic scientific research and the billion or two for NASA are a wretched pittance, a tiny fraction of what would have been necessary to bring the science drivers up to speed. In any case, here are over $102 billion well spent; it should have been at least $500 billion in these categories alone, in many cases preferably 0% federal lending rather than on-budget federal spending.

In terms of emergency relief and assistance to hard-pressed working families, we can certainly count $20 billion for the Supplemental Nutrition Assistance Program (food stamps), $39.2 billion to extend emergency unemployment benefits, $25.1 billion for health insurance assistance for the unemployed, $18 billion for child support and other family assistance, $90 billion for a temporary increase in federal medical assistance to Medicaid, $9.7 billion for the National Institutes of Health, and probably $9.8 billion in other health expenditures. The $18 billion for child support and other family assistance, part of it under TANF, does something to roll back Bill Clinton's appalling abolition of the Aid to Families with Dependent Children provisions of the Social Security Act of 1935, known as welfare. An appropriation of $16.6 billion for student financial assistance means that the Pell Grant program will continue to allow poor students to attend college. The $54 billion granted to the states to fund their education budgets is also probably on the whole a good thing, as are the $12.2 billion for special education, the $13 billion for education for the disadvantaged, and $4.3 billion for various employment and training programs. These items, totaling about $330 billion, represent part of the pent-up demand for social justice which has been building during the nightmare of the Bush administration, and many of them have been imposed on Obama by House Democrats, who are responding to the needs of working people in their constituencies. The main criticism of most of these items is that they needed to be much larger, as they might have been but for the treacherous role played by the remnants of the Rockefeller liberal Republicans around Collins, Spector, and Snowe.

Some items are a mixed bag in themselves. When we, for example, see $13 billion for housing assistance programs, we can conclude that a significant part of this money will go to the likes of ACORN and profiteers of the Tony Rezko-Valerie Jarrett ilk. But some of this money might eventually find its way into some forms of housing construction or repair. $2.8 billion in grants for state and local law enforcement assistance is a bad thing if the money goes for more totalitarian police state surveillance, but on the whole a good thing if the cops get better radios and related equipment.

Other appropriations must be condemned as wasteful. This applies in particular to all of the appropriations earmarked for Obama's gangrene economy, and including the $16.8 billion for "energy efficiency and renewable energy" programs, and the $6 billion in federal loan guarantees for "renewable energy systems and electricity transmission."

Some expenditures mandated by the stimulus represent an absolute public menace. The leading example is the $2 billion assigned to the national coordinator for health information technology, which appears to be a combination of surveillance measures to intimidate honest humanitarian doctors who want to treat their patients properly, plus the institutionalization of Daschle's infamous plan for the rationing of care and the denial of high-tech modern treatment.

The $212 billion tax provisions of the stimulus are again a mixed bag. Some of this money would have been better spent on infrastructure and science drivers, since these are critical for ending the depression, not just mitigating its effects. Many of these tax reductions can be justified as welcome if limited assistance to cash-strapped working families, as long as it is clear that these are essentially relief measures which will not in themselves bring about a resolution of the depression crisis. Increases in the Earned Income Tax Credit are long overdue. Making Work Pay represents a tax break of $400 per year for individuals and $800 per year for low and moderate income families over the next two years, but these amounts are too small to be meaningful. The increase of the tuition tax credit to $2500 for non-wealthy families is another tiny step in the right direction, as is the expansion of the child tax credit to $1000 per child for low-income families. There is also nothing wrong with the $8,000 tax credit for non-wealthy home purchasers who act before the end of this year.

The overall problem with the stimulus is that it risks becoming a kind of propaganda screen or window-dressing to prevent the public from focusing on the immense transfer of public funds into the coffers of Wall Street, which is the real essence of Obama's economic policy. In any case, the $432 billion of infrastructure, health care, jobless benefits, food stamps and other spending in the stimulus are on the whole a positive if limited appropriation. These numbers needed to be much larger, but most of the money had already been siphoned off by the zombie bankers for a totally futile derivatives bailout.

Bloomberg News has provided an ongoing tally of the vast sums presently being convoyed by the Obama regime into the pockets of the assorted Wall Street parasites. Here is their most recent summary:

> The U.S. government and the Federal Reserve have spent, lent or committed $12.8 trillion, an amount that approaches the value of everything produced in the country last year, to stem the longest recession since the 1930s. New pledges from the Fed, the Treasury Department and the Federal Deposit Insurance Corp. include $1 trillion for the Public-Private Investment Program, designed to help investors buy distressed loans and other assets from U.S. banks. The money works out to $42,105 for every man, woman and child in the U.S., and 14 times the $899.8 billion of currency in circulation. The nation's gross domestic product was $14.2 trillion in 2008..... Commitments include a $500 billion line of credit to the FDIC from the government's coffers that will enable the agency to guarantee as much as $2 trillion worth of debt for participants in the Term Asset-Backed Lending Facility (TALF) and the Public-Private Investment Program (PPIP). FDIC Chairman Sheila Bair warned that the insurance fund to protect customer deposits at U.S. banks could dry up because of bank failures. The combined commitment has increased by 73 percent since November, when Bloomberg first estimated the funding, loans and guarantees at $7.4 trillion. Mark Pittman and Bob Ivry, "Financial Rescue Nears GDP as Pledges Top $12.8 Trillion" (Update1), Bloomberg, March 31, 2009.

If the Obama stimulus includes about $432 billion for infrastructure, modernization, and human needs, this must be compared to the $12.8 trillion of largesse for the banks.

The result is that, under Obama, the bankers win out over the people by about 35 to 1. Here is an overview of the many bailouts:

	Amounts (Billions)	
	Limit	Current
Total	$12,798.14	$4,169.71
Federal Reserve Total	$7,765.64	$1,678.71
Primary Credit Discount	$110.74	$61.31
Secondary Credit	$0.19	$1.00
Primary dealer and others	$147.00	$20.18
ABCP Liquidity	$152.11	$6.85
AIG Credit	$60.00	$43.19
Net Portfolio CP Funding	$1,800.00	$241.31
Maiden Lane (Bear Stearns)	$29.50	$28.82
Maiden Lane II (AIG)	$22.50	$18.54
Maiden Lane III (AIG)	$30.00	$24.04
Term Securities Lending	$250.00	$88.55
Term Auction Facility	$900.00	$468.59
Securities lending overnight	$10.00	$4.41
Term Asset-Backed Loan Facility	$900.00	$4.71
Currency Swaps/Other Assets	$606.00	$377.87
MMIFF	$540.00	$0.00
GSE Debt Purchases	$600.00	$50.39
GSE Mortgage-Backed Securities	$1,000.00	$236.16
Citigroup Bailout Fed Portion	$220.40	$0.00
Bank of America Bailout	$87.20	$0.00
Commitment to Buy Treasuries	$300.00	$7.50
FDIC Total	$2,038.50	$357.50
Public-Private Investment*	$500.00	$0.00
FDIC Liquidity Guarantees	$1,400.00	$316.50
GE	$126.00	$41.00
Citigroup Bailout FDIC	$10.00	$0.00
Bank of America Bailout FDIC	$2.50	$0.00
Treasury Total	$2,694.00	$1,833.50
TARP	$700.00	$599.50
Tax Break for Banks	$29.00	$29.00
Stimulus Package (Bush)	$168.00	$168.00
Stimulus II (Obama)	$787.00	$787.00
Treasury Exchange Stabilization	$50.00	$50.00
Student Loan Purchases	$60.00	$0.00
Support for Fannie/Freddie	$400.00	$200.00

Line of Credit for FDIC*	$500.00	$0.00

HUD Total	$300.00	$300.00
Hope for Homeowners FHA	$300.00	$300.00

The FDIC's commitment to guarantee lending under the Legacy Loan Program and the Legacy Asset Program includes a $500 billion line of credit from the U.S. Treasury.[10]

In conclusion, the spending priorities of the Obama regime can only be described as grotesque and obscene. A $20 billion increase in the funding for the food stamp program still leaves an individual trying to survive on less than $150 a month worth of food. Obama has metaphysical doubts about whether old people should get hip replacement operations if this is not deemed cost-effective. But all the criteria of restraint, prudence, and cost-effectiveness fly out the window as soon as the Wall Street bankers appear on the scene with outstretched palms. $1 trillion is suddenly available for the species of derivatives known as mortgage-backed securities. $500 billion appears like magic as seed money for Geithner's PPIP, designed to prop up the prices and credibility of those toxic derivatives.

As of April 2009, US manufacturing jobs were down to a mere 12.2 million out of 144 million total jobs, down 1.5 million jobs in a single year. Back in 2000, there had been 18.9 million jobs in manufacturing. In 2006, that had shrunk to 15.6 million, and then to 15.3 million in 2007. It is a breathtaking collapse. We must recall that, once certain green pieces of paper are no longer automatically accepted around the world, over 300 million people will have to live using the products of these 12.2 million manufacturing workers — obviously not an easy proposition. Obama is doing everything to accelerate this fatal collapse, and nothing to turn it around.

All of this means that there will be no economic recovery under the Obama regime as far as the real economy of working people, wages, factories, and production is concerned. The implications for the existing political system are ominous indeed. New bubbles may certainly emerge, with or without the help of the hyperinflationary fires. Unless the lunatic policies of the Wall Street puppet Obama are reversed soon, the United States will face a fate similar to that of the Spanish Empire in the first half of the 17th century, when pervasive economic decadence and decline reduced the formerly leading military power of Europe to a shell of its former self, and soon to a shattered relic.

---

[10] Source: Mark Pittman and Bob Ivry, "Financial Rescue Nears GDP as Pledges Top $12.8 Trillion" (Update1), Bloomberg, March 31, 2009.

PROLOGUE TO THE 2009 EDITION

1. EMERGENCY ECONOMIC RECOVERY PROGRAM

TO STOP THE BUSH DEPRESSION

1. Stop all foreclosures immediately for at least five years and for the duration of the depression by means of a compulsory federal law carrying criminal penalties. No foreclosures on homes, family farms, factories, public utilities, hospitals, transportation and other infrastructure. Outlaw adjustable rate mortgages.

2. Raise the federal minimum wage immediately to a living wage of at least $15 per hour, with the short-term goal of attaining a federal minimum wage of at least $20 per hour.

3. Immediate enactment of a securities transfer tax (STT) or Tobin tax of 1% to be imposed on all financial turnover in all financial markets to include the New York Stock Exchange, the NASDAQ, the Amex, the Chicago Board of Trade, the Chicago Board Options Exchange, the Chicago Mercantile Exchange, the market in federal securities, the foreign exchange market, the New York Mercantile Exchange, and all other financial markets. This tax will be paid by the seller. This tax will be extended to the notional value of all derivatives, including over-the-counter derivatives, exchange traded derivatives, structured notes, designer derivatives and all other financial paper. Derivatives will become reportable under penalty of law. It is conservatively estimated that the securities transfer tax will yield approximately $5 trillion of new revenue in its first year of application. This new revenue will permit a stabilization and consolidation of Social Security, Medicare, and Medicaid, and will permit the expansion of Head Start, the Food Stamps program, WIC, the Veterans Administration hospitals, while extending unemployment insurance up to an initial total of at least 52 weeks, to be prolonged as needed. Provide revenue sharing to deal with the looming deficits of states, counties, and municipalities.

4. Using the new revenue obtained from the securities transfer tax on Wall Street financiers, provide comprehensive tax relief for all small businesses, thus permitting them to pay the new living wage. Small business will also be aided by the provision of national single-payer health care, as described below.

5. Implement Medicare for all in the form of a single payer, universal coverage, publicly administered system to provide healthcare for all. No rationing of care will be permitted under any circumstances. Cost-cutting will be achieved through eliminating exorbitant corporate profits, through administrative reform, and above all through a federally-funded crash program, on the scale of the Manhattan Project, of biomedical research designed to discover new and more effective treatments and cures for the principal diseases currently afflicting humanity.

6. Simultaneously, enact comprehensive income tax relief for working families, raising the standard deduction for married filing jointly and the personal exemption to at least $25,000 each. This would mean that a family of four would pay no federal income tax on their first $125,000 of income. Expand the earned income tax credit (EITC) to approximately 4 times its current level, with at least $150 billion paid out. Increase EITC payments to persons living alone as well as to families with children. Make all college tuition and fees expenses

deductible, and remove the limits on the Hope and Lifetime Learning tax credits. Return to the FDR-Ike-JFK 90% top marginal rate for *unearned* income – capital gains, interest, dividends, royalties, etc., not wages or self-employment – of taxpayers with federal adjusted gross income over $25 million. Roll back the scandalous Bush tax cuts for the rich. Favor progressive taxation over proportional and regressive taxation at every level. Phase out the most regressive taxes, like the poll tax and the sales tax. Estate tax of 60% on all estates over $75 million to recapture the looted gains of the Reagan-Bush era.

7. Nationalize the Federal Reserve System and establish it as a bureau of the United States Treasury. The current privatized status of the Federal Reserve System constitutes a violation of the United States Constitution. The size of the money supply and interest rates will henceforward be decided not by cliques of private bankers meeting in secret, but rather by public laws passed by the House and Senate, and signed by the president. Use this authority to immediately issue an initial tranche of $1 trillion of new federal credits at 1% yearly interest rates and maturities up to 30 years, to be repeated as needed. Consider credit as a public utility. Make this initial credit issue available on a priority basis to states, counties and local governments for the purpose of infrastructure modernization. Distribute credit to the private sector for high-technology re-industrialization in plant, equipment and jobs, manufacturing, mining, farming, construction, and other production of tangible physical wealth and commodities only. Aim at the creation of 5 to 7 million new productive jobs at union pay scales per year to achieve full employment for the first time in decades.

8. Federally-sponsored infrastructure projects will include a new nationwide network of magnetic levitation railways, as well as light rail systems to facilitate commuting in all urban centers. These economical and attractive light rail systems will allow a large portion of the vehicle miles by private automobile using internal combustion engines to be phased out of use in daily commuting. Launch a public works program of highway and bridge reconstruction, water management systems, electrical grids, hospitals, schools, cultural facilities, and public libraries.

9. Comprehensive re-regulation of the entire financial and banking system. Regulate the current non-bank banks. Bring all the hedge funds under the oversight of the Securities and Exchange Commission, thus effectively ending their special outlaw status as hedge funds. Begin aggressive enforcement of all applicable antitrust and securities fraud laws, as well as all existing labor legislation, including child labor, wages and hours, etc. Minimum two week yearly paid vacation for all those employed in interstate commerce, rising to three weeks after one years' service. Mandatory paid sick leave. Free high quality all day and evening federal day care for all working families under Head Start. Repeal the Taft-Hartley law with its anti-union "right to work" provisions, re-affirm the inalienable right to collective bargaining, and revive the National Labor Relations Board as an effective ally of working people. Full Davis-Bacon Act enforcement for all federal contracts, without exception. Tax leveraged buyouts and private capital deals, including all profits deriving from them, in whatever form. End corporate welfare, and establish consumer protection. Revive Glass-Steagall to prevent nationwide banking oligopolies combining commercial banking with investment banking.

10. Free college for all qualified students. Any student earning a high school diploma will be entitled to free tuition and fees at a community college or state university. High quality remedial courses to give high-school dropouts a second chance, no matter what their age. Without investment in the human capital of a highly trained work force, there can be no

economic survival in the 21st century. Federal aid to raise teacher salaries through revenue sharing.

11.   Announce the intention of the United States to abrogate NAFTA, WTO, and all other international free trade agreements which have destroyed employment in this country, while increasing the poverty levels of the third world. Introduce a low protective tariff, starting at 10% *ad valorem* on manufactured commodities to prevent reckless dumping.

12.   Investment tax credit for purchase modern technology in the form of new physical tangible capital goods. Tax breaks for the creation of new jobs in physical commodity production. Severe tax penalties for the export of jobs to third world sweatshops.

13.   Immediately impeach and remove from office both Bush and Cheney, since otherwise all effective measures to deal with the Bush economic depression will be crippled by presidential vetoes. Prepare the impeachment of the RATS (Roberts-Alito-Thomas-Scalia) cabal of the Supreme Court, if they should attempt to sabotage this emergency economic recovery program under the color of judicial review.

14.   Protect the family farm by a program of debt moratorium for farmers, no foreclosures, 1% long-term federal credit for spring planting needs and capital improvements, Restore parity prices at 125% of parity. Rebuild farm surpluses and food stockpiles. Food for Peace for famine relief abroad.

15.   Hedge funds and investment banks becoming insolvent will be speedily liquidated, with no public funds whatsoever being used to bail out stocks, bonds, derivatives, or any other financial paper. Commercial banks facing bankruptcy will be seized by the government and put through orderly Chapter 11 bankruptcy proceedings, with compensation for bondholder, stockholder, and derivatives counterparties always the lowest priority, a provision to be enforced by law. Potentially viable commercial banks can re-open under government supervision with new capital to be lent out to businesses under the criteria outlined under (7) – low-interest, long-term loans for purposes of infrastructure modernization, high-technology re-industrialization in plant, equipment and jobs, manufacturing, mining, farming, scientific research, and hard-commodity trade, No assisted lending for financial speculation, narcotics, gambling, or criminal activity. The federal government should be prepared to assume control of the Clearing House Interbank Payment System (CHIPS) in case it becomes unviable.

16.   Keep open the options of capital controls and exchange controls if required by further deterioration of the crisis. Prepare to freeze most categories of financial debt (debt moratorium) for the duration of the crisis. Revive Defense Production Act powers to mandate production of needed commodities by private sector, as needed.

17.   End all embargoes, blockades, economic sanctions and any other economic warfare or limitations on non-military goods. Free flow of food, medicine, modern technology, and capital goods guaranteed for all nations. Freedom of the seas for the commerce of all nations. Equal access to internet and telecommunications. World net neutrality.

18.   New G.I. Bill of Rights for all military veterans, providing guaranteed tuition, fees, room, board, books and other expenses for four years of college, technological certification, and

transition to the civilian workforce. .Special assistance for home ownership. Massive upgrade of military hospitals and Veterans' Administration hospitals.

19.   Call an international economic conference of sovereign states to deal with this unprecedented world economic depression. The United States should take the lead in proposing a new world monetary system based on the alienable right of all nations and peoples to modern economic development and to the enjoyment of the fullest fruits of science, technology, industry, progress, and rising standards of living. The new monetary system should be based on fixed parities with narrow bands of fluctuation among the euro, the dollar, the yen, the ruble, and other world currencies, including emerging Latin American and Middle East regional currencies, with periodic settlement of balance of payments discrepancies in gold among national authorities. The goal of the new system is to promote world economic recovery through large-scale export of the most modern high-technology capital goods from the US, EU, and Japan to the developing countries. Create a Multilateral Development Bank with an initial capital of 1 trillion euros from US, UK, Japan, and other exporters to finance investment in the poorest countries with 1%, revolving loans with maturities up to thirty years. Immediate, permanent, and unconditional cancellation of all international financial debts of the poorest countries.

20. Revive international humanitarian, scientific and technological cooperation for the benefit of all nations. Roll back epidemic, tropical, and endemic diseases with an international program of biomedical research. Join with all interested nations in a joint international effort to develop new energy resources in the field of high-energy physics. Fund and expand an international cooperative commitment to the exploration, permanent colonization, and economic development of the moon and nearby planets. The spin-offs from these three science drivers will provide the new technologies for the next wave of economic modernization.

21.   Revive the Franklin D. Roosevelt "freedom from want" provision of the Atlantic Charter as elaborated in the Economic Bill of Rights from the State of the Union Address of January 1944 and incorporate these economic rights of all persons as amendments to the US Constitution: "The right to a useful and remunerative job in the industries or shops or farms or mines of the nation; the right to earn enough to provide adequate food and clothing and recreation; the right of every farmer to raise and sell his products at a return which will give him and his family a decent living; the right of every businessman, large and small, to trade in an atmosphere of freedom from unfair competition and domination by monopolies at home or abroad; the right of every family to a decent home; the right to adequate medical care and the opportunity to achieve and enjoy good health; the right to adequate protection from the economic fears of old age, sickness, accident, and unemployment; the right to a good education."

Webster G. Tarpley,

21 January 2008

Washington DC, USA

2. NO TO THE PAULSON-BERNANKE DERIVATIVES BAILOUT

BAIL OUT THE AMERICAN PEOPLE, NOT WALL STREET!
AN ECONOMIC RECOVERY STRATEGY FOR PROTECTIONISTS, DIRIGISTS, MERCANTILISTS, AND POPULISTS

by Webster G. Tarpley

Washington, DC, September 23, 2008 – The grand theft bailout now being rammed through Congress by Treasury Secretary Paulson, Federal Reserve Chairman Bernanke, and other officials of the Bush regime with the help of accomplices Pelosi, Majority Leader Harry Reid, and other parliamentarians is a monstrosity for the ages, combining every hideous feature of monetarism, elitism, oligarchism, and sheer feckless incompetence. It is to all intents and purposes a national suicide note of the United States of America, a contract with the devil that absolutely guarantees irrevocable national decline. For any person of goodwill there can be only one impulse at the present moment, and that is to stop this bailout – to block it, to sabotage it, to bottle it up, to load it with killer amendments, and to do everything legally possible to stop this insane design from going through.

IF MCCAIN VOTES AGAINST THE BAILOUT, HE WILL WIN THE PRESIDENCY

In political terms, McCain is now running well to the left of Obama on this issue, with a much stronger populist profile. McCain has attacked the outrageous greed and corruption of Wall Street. Obama does not dare attack Wall Street, since these are his masters. Obama, sounding like Milton Friedman, only attacks Washington. Obama has said that he will support whatever Paulson demands. That is not a surprise, since Paulson represents Goldman Sachs, and Obama is a wholly owned property of Goldman Sachs, which is his single biggest source of campaign contributions. Obama is a creature of Brzezinski, Soros, and Rockefeller, and without them he has no existence; Obama is an abject Wall Street puppet, an agent of finance capital. This week, both senators will have to decide how they vote on the odious derivatives bailout. Obama will surely vote in favor of it, since this is what Wall Street demands. If McCain votes against it, he will most probably propel himself into the White House on the model of Give 'Em Hell Harry in 1948. Filthy corrupt Democrats like Schumer are already attacking McCain as the new Huey Long. Huey Long, the Louisiana populist of the 1930s, had many positive features, and we could certainly use a good dose of Huey Long in this country to counteract the elitism, oligarchism, condescension, and arrogant snobbery of foundation operatives like Obama. The bailout is already very unpopular – 72% of all voters are opposed to it – and it will become more and more hated when it becomes clear that it is also a failure. McCain's course is clear. Will he have the brains and guts to cross Obama's T on this vital issue?

PAULSON OF GOLDMAN SACHS, WOULD-BE FINANCE DICTATOR

Paulson is a ruthless and brutal eco-freak usurer who learned his trade at the Goldman Sachs stock-jobbing operation. He is now the leading member of the committee of public safety which rules in Washington, and which includes Gates, Rice, and Mullen. He now demands the astronomical sum of 700 billion dollars for the bailout of mortgage-backed derivatives, collateralized debt obligations, credit default swaps, and other poisonous derivatives. Make no mistake – this is not a bailout of homeowners who are threatened with foreclosure; it is a bailout of the lunatic house of cards which desperate bankers have built on these mortgages using derivatives. The entire crisis is not a crisis of subprime mortgages, it is a crisis of the derivatives bubble which was launched by Wendy Gramm of the Commodities Futures Trading Commission and Greenspan of the Fed with the connivance of Robert Rubin of Goldman Sachs and Citibank, and others in the Clinton administration, some 15 years ago. These derivatives now amount to a total worldwide notional value that can be estimated between 1 quadrillion and two quadrillion US dollars. This sum is so large that it dwarfs the total value of the entire planet earth and all those who live here. Compared to the cancerous, bloated, and fictitious mass of derivatives which is at the root of this crisis, the $700 billion demanded by politicians, large as this may seem, is nothing but a drop in the bucket. And a drop in the bailout bucket is what it will be. The mass of world derivatives between $1 and $2 quadrillion represents an insatiable black hole which is capable of putting an end, not just to civilization, but the human life itself. The moral choice could not be clearer: humanity will either destroy the derivatives bubble in our time, or the derivatives bubble will surely destroy humanity. Those are the stakes in the current exercise.

Paulson and Bernanke, both lawyers for the Wall Street jackals, lampreys, vultures and hyenas, argue that the public interest demands a bailout of their cronies at Goldman Sachs, Morgan Stanley, J.P. Morgan Chase, Citibank, Bank of America, Wachovia, and the other large money center institutions. Before the American public antes up $700 billion just for openers in the game of genocidal poker which run by the infernal croupiers Paulson and Bernanke, we would be very well advised to examine the veracity of this premise.

COMMERCIAL BANKS ARE INDISPENSABLE

It is of course true that the healthy functioning of the United States economy requires a viable and flexible system of commercial banks. No one should doubt the necessity of commercial banks. Andrew Jackson was clinically insane on this point, and he still has not a few followers around today. But it ought to be clear that without the services of a well developed commercial banking system, it is impossible to organize business activities as essential as payments, deposits, checking, payrolls, and the discounting of short-term commercial paper, bills of exchange, bills of lading, and all the credit instruments that are intimately connected with real productive activity. Without a functioning commercial banking system, the economic heart of the United States would stop beating, as it briefly did at the end of the Hoover administration in March of 1933. Without commercial banks, no wheel of a factory or railroad can turn, and no commodities can move to show up in supermarkets.

JPM, CITI, BoA ARE DERIVATIVES MONSTERS, NOT COMMERCIAL BANKS

But when we look at institutions like J.P. Morgan Chase, Citibank, and Bank of America, we become aware that these large money center institutions have become detached from any conceivable connection to the world of production, wages, transportation, and all other useful and productive activities. These institutions are not commercial banks any more in any meaningful sense of the term. Ten years ago, in the midst of the Asian financial crisis and the aftermath of the Russian GKO state bankruptcy collapse, the boss of JP Morgan Chase went on television to announce that his bank was specialized in the "risk business." The risk business meant that JP Morgan Chase, had simply given up on the traditional activity of commercial banks, which was primarily to provide loans to corporations for productive investment in plant and equipment that would also create well-paid industrial jobs. J.P. Morgan Chase decided long ago that that activity was nowhere near profitable enough to be continued. Instead, J.P. Morgan Chase devoted itself more and more to the issuance, sale, and purchase of derivatives. As early as 1992, the best definition of J.P. Morgan Chase was that it was no longer a commercial bank but rather a derivatives monster. In 2002, the J.P. Morgan Chase derivatives monster came very close to imploding, collapsing in on itself like the hopeless black hole that it still remains to the present day. According to the most recent report of the Comptroller of the Currency of the US Treasury dated September 30, 2007, JP Morgan Chase today has between $90 trillion and $100 trillion of derivatives. In reality this is a very low-ball estimate, and the real derivatives exposure is some multiple of this figure – perhaps $300 or $400 trillion, especially now that Bear Stearns, a smaller black hole of derivatives has been absorbed. But even a mere $90 trillion is already six times the US GDP (currently estimated between $14 and $15 trillion).

DERIVATIVES ARE A FINANCIAL AIDS VIRUS

The question of the derivatives is once again the central issue of the crisis. Most people may not even know what derivatives are, although by now many have some idea that they are dangerous and toxic. French President Jacques Chirac once defined derivatives as financial aids, and he was right. A share of stock supposedly represents part ownership in a corporation. A corporate bond is a debt instrument issued by a corporation, with some claim to a part of the assets in case of bankruptcy liquidation. That means that the stocks and bonds are paper, but paper that is at only one remove from the real world of production, consumption, employment, and wages. The derivative is something radically different. A derivative represents paper based on paper, no longer a stock or bond, but a future, option, or index that is based on some stock, bond, or other form of paper. Derivatives are therefore at least one step further removed from the world of tangible physical commodity production of useful items which humanity requires in order to survive and to conduct civilization as we know it. In addition to the options, futures, and indices, we have all the possible permutations and combinations of the above, with new variations that are almost infinite. Even to catalogue these would take a book. In addition to these exchange traded derivatives, there is a much larger class of derivative which does not appear on the Chicago Board Options Exchange or analogous institutions in all the money centers of the world. The second and larger class represents the counterparty derivatives, including such things as collateralized debt obligations, mortgage backed securities, structured notes, credit default swaps, and the myriad of other derivative products. These derivatives were originally supposed to be used as a hedge against risk, but before too long they began to represent the biggest single source of risk and the entire lunatic edifice would finance. By now, to repeat this point yet again, the total world derivatives of in excess of one quadrillion dollars – that is to say, 1000 billion dollars, and may be already approaching the neighborhood of $1.5 quadrillion or even more. One of the inherent problems of derivatives is that nobody knows this exact figure, since derivatives are not reportable in many countries and tend to escape regulation by the proper financial authorities.

DERIVATIVES ARE USELESS AND A THREAT TO CIVILIZATION

You cannot eat derivatives. You cannot live in a derivative. You cannot wear derivatives as clothing, nor can you drive a derivative work. You cannot sail in them or fly in them. They cannot be used as tools of any useful trade. They are not computers, not machine tools, not pharmaceutical equipment, not agricultural implements. Derivatives are therefore totally outside the realm of capital goods production needs, no matter how these may be defined.

FOR RECOVERY, WIPE OUT, SHRED, DELETE ALL DERIVATIVES

J.P. Morgan Chase, therefore, performs no useful or productive social function, and there is absolutely no reason in the world why the people of the United States should want to bail out this pernicious and socially destructive institution. It has probably been several decades since J.P. Morgan Chase created a single modern productive job. J.P. Morgan Chase's strategic commitment in favor of the derivatives bubble means essentially that we can easily dispense with most of the functions of this self-styled "bank," really a casino. Instead of being bailed out, J.P. Morgan Chase ought therefore to be seized by the Federal Deposit Insurance Corporation, and put through chapter 11 bankruptcy. In the course of that bankruptcy reorganization, the entire derivatives book of J.P. Morgan Chase must be deleted, shredded, used as a Yule log, or employed to stoke a festive bonfire of the derivatives. The world did much better when there were no derivatives, and will get along just fine without them. Derivatives were of very dubious legality in general and were illegal in some of their specific forms until the mid-1990s.

INSTRUMENTS MEANS DERIVATIVES

According to Paulson's pact with the devil published in the *New York Times* on September 20, 2008, the Secretary of the Treasury is supposed to be empowered by Congress to spend $700 billion on mortgage related securities, obligations, and instruments. That last word *instruments* is the favorite euphemism of television commentators and journalists who want to propose a derivatives bailout without using this word, which has now become to some degree unmentionable and taboo, presumably because of its highly negative connotations left over from the crises of more than a decade ago. Accordingly, one very good killer amendment that ought to be added to this pact with the devil should state that not one penny of taxpayer money should ever be used to finance the purchase of derivatives, no matter how they may be euphemistically referred to.

WHY BUY MORTGAGE BACKED SECURITIES THAT HAVE NO PRICE BID?

Paulson wants to buy up derivatives. But at what price? Derivatives have no intrinsic value. Like the rasbucknik in the old *L'il Abner* comic strip, derivatives have negative value, since somebody has to be paid to cart them away. Counterparty derivatives currently have no price, since there is no market where they are trading, and nobody would want to buy them if there were such a market. Collateralized debt obligations were selling at 5 cents on the dollar a few weeks ago, but that was well before the current crisis broke in its full fury. So how will Paulson know how much to pay for the derivatives he wants to purchase? Will he use the discredited Black-Scholes model, which led to the bankruptcy of the Long Term Capital Management hedge fund ten years ago? Given all this, the only price which can be assigned to the mass of derivatives is not their notional value, but rather a big fat ZERO. Anything else is stealing from the government.

"INVESTMENT BANKS" DRIVE UP THE PUMP PRICE OF GASOLINE

Let us now leave behind the category of the commercial banks and move on to institutions like Goldman Sachs and Morgan Stanley, the stock jobbing operations or counting houses that like to call themselves investment banks these days, even though they do not have the status of a commercial bank and are not members of the Federal Reserve. Why should any public money at all be used to prolong the noxious lives of these sociopathic and pernicious institutions? A short examination of what these so-called investment banks do will reveal that there is no public interest in keeping these creatures alive, and that, once again, touch better off without them.

Investment banks used to assist corporations and floating issues of stocks or bonds on the financial markets. Investment banks were supposed to function as the advisers of industrial corporations and other corporations as they sought to raise capital needed for new plant, equipment, and jobs. But today, these functions have virtually disappeared. The investment banks do a certain amount of work in initial public offerings for IPO's of new securities, but these are almost always of a financially speculative nature. The main thing is that investment banks now place bets on certain classes of assets in the hope of turning a purely speculative profit for themselves. Goldman Sachs and Morgan Stanley maintain trading desks and engage in purely speculative trading of assets which they themselves own, and most of the time these assets represent derivatives of one kind or another. In recent times, the most important asset class which Goldman Sachs and Morgan Stanley have been trading is probably future indices on commodities, especially oil. Goldman Sachs and Morgan Stanley between them have in the past year by various estimates accounted for about half of the speculative activity in the commodities markets of London, New York, and other money centers which brought about the doubling of the per barrel price of oil between July 2007 and July 2008, increasing the cost of gasoline to almost five dollars per gallon.

GOLDMAN SACHS, MORGAN STANLEY CREATE I.C.E. TO FLAY AMERICANS

In a very real sense, American motorists filling their gas tanks at the pump at exorbitant prices have been involuntarily subsidizing the speculative derivatives activity of Goldman Sachs and Morgan Stanley. How bitterly ironic that the same American motorists should now be taxed in order to permit their tormentors to live on and to continue to mercilessly loot them. Goldman Sachs and Morgan Stanley found that even the very weak regulatory regime maintained here in the United States under the auspices of the Commodity Futures Trading Commission was too onerous for them because it slightly constrained their rapacious quest for speculative profits at the expense of the American people. These two investment banks therefore created a new speculative commodity exchange, the ICE or Intercontinental Exchange located in London, with a regulatory regime is virtually nonexistent. The ICE or Intercontinental Exchange in London is where about half of the world futures contracts in oil have been trading in recent months.

Goldman Sachs and Morgan Stanley, like their now-defunct brethren Bear Stearns, Lehman Brothers, and Merrill Lynch, have also made many speculative investments in the area of mortgage backed securities based on predatory subprime mortgages. The adjustable rate mortgages that underlie these derivatives should have been declared illegal long ago. But now let us imagine what will happen if a hapless victim of these predatory lending practices is forced into foreclosure in the current world economic great depression. Goldman Sachs will send the bailiff to your door to throw you, your family, and your belongings out on the street, even though you have been taxed to permit Goldman Sachs to continue its sociopathic existence. You will in effect be robbed out of one pocket even as you are being pushed out the door and made homeless by the same institution which has been the beneficiary of your forced charity. Surely any politician daring to come forward to suggest the public bailout of Goldman Sachs so that it can continue to enforce foreclosures against the American citizens who are paying the bill for the financial excesses of this bandit institution ought to be tarred and feathered and run out of town on a rail. Yet this is exactly what Pelosi, Reid, Dodd, and Frank are proposing to force through the U.S. Congress in the coming week. This represents a new low in public morality.

With Fannie Mae and Freddie Mac, the situation is slightly different, but the same criteria ought to apply. Fanny and Freddie worked very well during the three decades after the formation of Fannie Mae in 1938 as an agency of the federal government – a hillbilly cousin of the US treasury, as it used to be called. Things began to go wrong in 1968 when Fannie Mae was privatized, under the pernicious influence of the doctrines of the monetarist Milton Friedman of the infamous Chicago school of pseudo-economics and obscurantism. Fanny and Freddie have now been placed under the control of conservators, but they ought to be nationalized as part of a permanent state sector of the US economy, and operated as the public utility that they were intended to be. The salaries of their officials ought to be determined by the government-wide GSA schedule. Fannie and Freddie have guaranteed mortgages, and ought to continue to do so. But they have no obligation to guarantee mortgage backed securities or any other form of newfangled derivatives which were never mentioned in their charter. Accordingly, Fannie and Freddie thought to strip away the mortgage backed securities that have been used to package or bundle the mortgages that they now hold. The mortgages represent a valuable asset for the future, under conditions of economic recovery which we intend to organize. But that extra layer of derivatives paper represents a useless additional tax on the public treasury, which the US government has no obligation to maintain. In short, it is time to separate the socially useful core of actual mortgages representing residential and commercial properties from the harmful and speculative overlay of the mortgage-backed security. By this kind of financial engineering, speculators can receive condign punishment, even as the public treasury is believed of an extra layer useless payment which would only reward speculative crimes.

If anyone should inquire as to the ultimate philosophical causes of the current George Bush world economic depression, the answer is simple: this depression is a direct result of the influence of Milton Friedman and the Chicago school, who are themselves to kind of come down American version of the Viennese school of Friedrich von Hayek. Ludwig von Mises, and other charlatans masquerading as economists. The common denominator of the Chicago school is the Vienna school which is represented by the right-wing anarchist thesis that government is always bad and the private sector, especially speculators, are always good. This absurd thesis is now being consigned to the dustbin of history. Friedman and von Hayek, if they were alive today, would doubtless demand the full fury of the free market the unleashed against the American people. This would lead, not to a recovery, but merely to death on a large scale. The implications of the Chicago school and the Vienna school under current circumstances are nothing short of genocidal, and even the financiers are hastily dumping the discredited doctrines of Friedman and from Hayek as they rush to get their hands into the public till through bigger and better bailouts in an endless series. There is nothing anywhere in the world left today that might resemble a free market, only an endless list of cartels, trusts, monopolies, oligopolies, duopolies, and other conspiracies in restraint of trade. In fact, there has been nothing even vaguely resembling a free market in most of the world in the past several centuries. What is collapsing today in September 2008 is the delusion that such a thing as a free market might exist in the modern world.

The same negative judgment applies to the lunatic doctrines of Joseph Schumpeter, who preached the madness of creative destruction as a way out of the world economic depression of the 1930s. Schumpeter's doctrines today are nothing less than a public menace, and persons who demand a deflationary crash of the world economy by preaching the Andrew Mellon formula of liquidating labor, liquidating stocks, liquidating bonds, liquidating real estate, etc., are to be put in a padded cell. This is even worse than Herbert Hoover. It was tried in 1932-33, and it turned out to be a bottomless pit already then, so it does not need to be tried again.

BACK TO THE NEW DEAL: RESTORE THE GLASS-STEAGALL FIREWALL

Scribblers like Friedman and von Hayek were paid by finance oligarchs to wage a relentless war against that heritage of the Franklin D. Roosevelt New Deal, the set of policies which allowed humanity to survive the Great Depression of the 1930s. The current crisis would not have been possible in the present form if the institutional safeguards enacted during the New Deal had been left in place, as they should have been. These safeguards represent permanent features of civilization, and they need to be restored. The best example is the repeal of the Glass-Steagall Act under the Clinton administration in 1999. The Glass-Steagall Act was a classic piece of New Deal legislation which established that being a commercial bank and being a stockbroker are mutually exclusive activities that could not be legally combined in the same company. Commercial banking was one thing, and stock brokerage was something completely separate. Naturally, the greedy financiers and their spokesmen clamored for the repeal of Glass-Steagall, and they finally got their wish. Now less than 10 years later all of the Wall Street banks, seemingly without notable exceptions, are bankrupt and insolvent institutions that cannot not survive without a massive infusion of taxpayer money. We need to restore Glass-Steagall, which will mean among other things that Goldman Sachs and Morgan Stanley will not be eligible to become bank holding companies after all. If you don't like your tax bill next year, you should thank Newt Gingrich and others who made it their business to destroy and roll back the achievements of the New Deal in the name of the despicable ideology of monetarism as preached by Friedman and von Hayek. Newt, by the way, is now calling for an immediate deflationary crash to find out what the real prices of housing might be. This is like doing experiments on your own flesh, and Newt should go to the funny farm.

BACK TO THE NEW DEAL: RESTORE THE UPTICK RULE

Another example is the uptick rule. This New Deal measure meant that it was illegal to sell a stock short if it were continuously in decline. The speculator had to wait until there was an uptick, meaning a trade in which the stock in question increased in price; only then could a short sale be carried out. Another piece of bitter irony inherent in the present crisis is that this uptick rule was abolished by the feckless and incompetent Chairman Cox of the Securities and Exchange Commission at the beginning of last summer, just in time for the explosion of the world credit crisis which has led to the current world economic depression. Incredibly enough, Chairman Cox of the SEC has been unable to pull himself together long enough to permanently re-impose the uptick rule. Instead, he has drawn up a list of 799 financial institutions and banks whose stock will now be illegal to sell short for at least 10 days, although one suspects that this prohibition will be prolonged indefinitely. This crackpot expedient reveals the true nature of the current monetarist regime. Shorting and destroying General Motors, which actually produces something useful, is fine, but no shorting of JP Morgan Chase, which is a public menace that produces nothing but toxic paper. The long-term roots of the current crisis go back to August 15, 1971, when Nixon, Kissinger, Arthur Burns and George Shultz wantonly destroyed the Bretton Woods system of fixed currency parities, ushering in the new world of financial risk which is now collapsing around us.

NATIONALIZE THE FEDERAL RESERVE AS A BUREAU OF THE TREASURY

The present crisis ought to provide the death warrant for the failed Federal Reserve System. When the Fed was created back under Woodrow Wilson, its Rockefeller and Morgan sponsors promised that the Fed would protect us against all future financial panics. The Fed failed once in 1929-1933, and now it is failing again for a second time. The Fed is worthless as a firewall against depression. We must therefore seize the Fed, audit it, nationalize it, and operate it in the future as a bureau of the US Treasury. From now on, we must go back to the Constitution, meaning that the size of the money supply and short-term interest rates will have to be determined by public laws of the United States, passed by the House and the Senate and signed by the president. Using this method, we can mandate new initial credit issues of $1 to $2 trillion to be used exclusively as low interest (.5% to 1%) and long-term (30 to 40 year maturities) credit for productive purposes only – manufacturing, farming, mining, commerce, energy production, infrastructure, and the other things we need. We should stop having the Fed lend money to Citibank at 2% and then having the Treasury borrow that same money back for 4% to 5% in the form of Treasury paper. Nationalize the Fed, and let the Treasury finance itself, cutting out the parasitical middlemen like JP Morgan Chase, Goldman, Citibank, and the rest. The taxpayers will be the big winners.

HOOVER'S RECONSTRUCTION FINANCE CORPORATION WAS A FAILURE

The Paulson-Bernanke $700 billion is roughly comparable (factoring in about 2000% inflation from 1932 to 2008) to the Herbert Hoover Reconstruction Finance Corporation, which started with $2 billion real 1932 dollars, but failed because it tried to prop up insolvent banks and shore up collapsing financial values. Under FDR, the RFC was put under Jesse Jones, who used it to create real plant and equipment with great success. Under Jones, the RFC contributed decisively to US economic recovery by building up the Metals Reserve Company, the Rubber Reserve Company, the Defense Plant Corporation, the Defense Supplies Corporation, the War Damage Corporation, the U.S. Commercial Company, the Rubber Development Corporation, and the Petroleum Reserve Corporation. In other words, the RFC under Jones rebuilt the industrial infrastructure which we have been using down to the present day. Most of these investments represented added physical commodity production. Today, this could be repeated to produce infrastructure and energy plants for civilian use.

CLEARING THE DECKS FOR WORLD ECONOMIC RECOVERY

It is time to forget about paper and the price of paper, and to concentrate on production – securing the tangible physical commodities and hard commodity production which are necessary for human life and civilization. It is impossible to prop up financial values in a panic, and it is foolish to try. To secure a decent future, we must now enact the following measures. Any of these points, all of which seek to defend the general welfare and the public interest, can and should be used as killer amendments to be attached to the current bailout monstrosity as a means of bringing it down.

1. Stop all foreclosures on homes, farms, businesses, factories, mines, transport systems, for a period of at least five years or for the duration of the present world economic depression, whichever takes longer. If you throw a family out of their home or shut down a family farm, taxicab company, trucking firm, ferry, airline, railroad, or factory of any kind because of debt, you will be on your way to Leavenworth. All politicians now say that we have to keep families in their homes. Excellent! A uniform federal law with real teeth is the way to do it.

2. Seize bankrupt banks and financial institutions. Put them through Chapter XI bankruptcy, and cancel the hopelessly unpayable parts of their debts, starting with their derivatives book.

3. Wipe out all derivatives, whether exchange traded or counterparty, without compensation. They have always been illegal. They are now a threat to all of our lives. Not one penny of public money must go to buy derivatives.

4. Securities transfer tax or Tobin tax on all financial transactions, including stocks, bonds, foreign exchange, etc. This is a sales tax on finance oligarchs who need to start paying their fair share. This will take the life out of the booze for many speculators.

5. Stop oil, food and commodity speculation with comprehensive re-regulation including position limits, 50 to 100% margin requirements depending on market conditions, and by distinguishing between legitimate hedgers and predatory speculators.

6. No tax increases on households. Surtax for foundations like the Ford, Rockefeller, Carnegie, Annenberg, and Gates Foundations, who use their funds not for charity but for subversion and divide and conquer social engineering to divide and weaken the American people in defense of the financier interest.

7. Restore business confidence and credit with new credit issue through the nationalized Federal Reserve, operating under the legal auspices of the US Treasury. Use credit as a public utility. Provide cheap, long-term credit for productive purposes only, not parasitical speculation or financial services.

8. Institute an absolute guarantee for Social Security, Medicare, Medicaid, Head Start, WIC, food stamps, unemployment insurance, and the other remaining elements of the social safety net. No "entitlement reform" under any circumstances. Austerity for bankers, not people. Use the proceeds from the Securities Transfer Tax to replenish the Social Security Trust Fund and preserve the other vital programs through the end of the twenty-first century.

Using New Deal methods, it is possible to stop a depression cold in a single day. We did it before, and we can do it again. Only 28% of the American people now support the monstrous derivatives bailout, with 37% opposed and 35% unsure, according to Rasmussen on Sept. 22. This is an issue powerful enough to crystallize the current party re-alignment in the same way that slavery in the territories did in 1860, or the last depression did in 1932. Within a month, the current empty husks of the gutted Democratic and Republican Parties could collapse, and be replaced by the pro-Wall Street Bailout Party led by Obama and his phalanx of rich elitists and Malthusian fanatics from both parties, and the pro-middle class and pro-worker Anti-Bailout Party with support from right-wing Republicans, libertarians, and working class Democrats. Who will have the brains and guts needed to assert leadership over the Anti-Bailout Party? Will it be McCain? Or Hillary Clinton? Or someone else? We will soon find out.

3. FORCE THE FED TO OPEN A MAIN STREET LENDING FACILITY

FOR PRODUCERS, NOT WALL STREET PARASITES.

$1 TRILLION IN CHEAP FEDERAL CREDIT FOR DOMESTIC PRODUCTION AND HUMAN NEEDS

Nobody has been creating any special lending facilities for Main Street.
– Rick Santelli, CNBC, Sept. 30, 2008

By Webster G. Tarpley

Washington DC, Oct. 2, 2008 – To stop the derivatives bailout monstrosity, we need to be able to answer and defeat the demonic propaganda line coming from the various Wall Street mouthpieces alleging that, unless the Congress capitulates to the Bernanke-Paulson-Bush blackmail (supported by Obama and Pelosi), a credit crunch will soon destroy the American economy. The New Deal answer to this credit crunch blackmail is to recall that the Federal Reserve System is supposed to be the credit engine of the US economy, and that it can and must be coerced and forced into serving the needs of the US economy, rather than catering to the whims of anonymous cliques of unelected and unaccountable parasitical financiers and bankers. We must move immediately to provide abundant credit for production and commerce and all the other vital needs of the American people, while preserving the vital system of regional and local banks, by forcing the Fed to open a Main Street Lending Facility, where producers of all kinds, including small business, local merchants, small, medium and heavy industry, energy producers, the Detroit automakers and all their subcontractors, salesmen, and dealers can received immediate credit at between .5% and 1% interest to keep the US economy going. Up to now, that kind of deal has been reserved exclusively for the hyenas, jackals, and vultures of Wall Street. To keep this economy going, it is time to de-emphasize cheap federal credit to the parasites, and let them take their chances on the "free market" they claim to admire so much. We need a modern equivalent of FDR's Lend-Lease program – not for war production this time, but to re-start the collapsing domestic economy and get a genuine economic recovery going as we move towards full employment for the first time in many decades.

REFUTE THE DEMAGOGIC CLAIM THAT WALL STREET INTERESTS AND MAIN STREET ISSUES ARE IDENTICAL

Since Monday's defeat of the universally hated $700 billion Wall Street derivatives bailout in the House, the desperate financiers' party line has shifted: the Wall Street hedge fund hyenas and stockjobbing jackals have re-discovered their tender love for Main Street, small business, and the needs of blue-collar American workers. Wall Street and Main Street are in the same boat, they now assure us. The reason they wanted to take the $700 billion and run was out of their touching concern for the welfare of working families. According to the current Wall Street argument, the great danger now is that, because of the refusal of JP Morgan Chase, Citibank, and Bank of America to make loans, the US credit system will be deprived of the liquidity necessary to provide loans for consumers, small business, and commerce in general. "Unless we get our $700 billion," say the Wall Street vultures in unison, "the credit system will freeze up, and there will be no loans for car purchasers, businessmen needing credit to make payroll, department store and supermarket inventory, student loans, new credit cards, and new mortgages for home buyers. If stocks crash, then the little people will lose their IRAs and 401 (k) accounts. So give us the $700 billion pronto, or Main Street will be the big loser." This hysterical propaganda is now pouring out of the media outlets, who are all espousing a strange new version of trickle-down economics by proclaiming, "It's not a bailout of Wall Street! It's really a bailout of Main Street!" But this assertion is untenable, as is the related claim that anything short of full Wall Street access to the checkbook of the American taxpayer will lead to a systemic financial crisis in which chain-reaction bankruptcies force all banks and brokerages into insolvency and closure. The Bush economic depression is real enough, but there is no need for Main Street to share in the terrible fate which Wall Street has prepared for itself, provided that classic New Deal methods are applied.

The leading demagogue making this argument is, of course, Sen. Obama.

WALL STREET DERIVATIVES MONSTER: $1 QUADRILLION-PLUS OF JUNK

In reality, Wall Street is nothing but a derivatives monster, a black hole of hundreds of trillions of dollars of poisonous derivatives. Total world derivatives are now between $1 QUADRILLION (i.e., one thousand trillion) and $1.5 quadrillion, and Wall Street represents the lion's share of this. (We are forced to use estimates because most derivatives are not just unregulated, they are also unreported, so literally nobody knows the exact size of the derivatives bubble.) No money that is put into Wall Street will ever pass through it to benefit anyone else. The Wall Street derivatives black hole is so powerful that it could easily eat the whole earth and the entire solar system, and still be just as bankrupt as it was to start with. Banks like JP Morgan Chase, Citibank, and the Bank of America long ago gave up providing commercial bank services in the form of loans to companies seeking to purchase new plant and equipment for capital investment and job creation. The banks do not discount commercial paper any more. They deal in derivatives and speculation, and little else. A year ago, JP Morgan Chase alone officially had $93 TRILLION in derivatives of certain types – more than six times the total Gross Domestic Product of the United States, and this is a very low-ball estimate indeed. When they were still investment banks, Goldman Sachs and Morgan Stanley created the Inter-continental Exchange (ICE) in London to facilitate their oil futures speculation; there are indications that Goldman and Morgan between them accounted for almost half of the run-up in the world oil price, meaning in effect that these two criminal organizations were responsible for almost 25% of the total price of oil. This means that about a quarter out of every dollar paid at the gas pump by commuters, cab drivers, and truckers was going to subsidize Goldman Sachs and Morgan Stanley.

WHY HELP HEDGE FUND HYENAS, ASSET STRIPPERS, AND DOWNSIZERS?

As for the hedge fund hyenas, their game is to buy companies, break them up, and sell the pieces, destroying countless jobs in the process. Chrysler Corp. is being destroyed by the Cerberus hedge fund in this way right now (and should be saved by immediate nationalization). The hedge funds are also past masters of the art of the runaway shop, sending formerly well-paid industrial jobs overseas to low-wage third world sweatshops. Otherwise, the hedge funds are occupied with speculation of all types.

From this brief summary, it should be clear that Wall Street, by choosing the path of derivatives, high-leverage speculation, and asset stripping, has severed any previous relation with the world of production, wages, employment, and capital investment. If Wall Street were to suddenly cease to exist, the immediate direct impact on commercial bank lending to industrial corporations, construction firms, mining companies, transportation firms like airlines, truckers, and railroads, small and medium industry, and small business in general would be minimal, with one exception. The exception is simply that, if the top ten money center banks succumb to the crushing weight of their derivatives, there will ensue a banking panic and general collapse of business confidence which will tend to paralyze the banking and discounting roles of local and regional banks in a way similar to the Herbert Hoover banking panic of 1932-1933. So far we have had panic runs on Countrywide Bank, Northern Rock in the UK and Ireland, Bear Stearns brokerage accounts, Lehman Brothers, Washington Mutual, Wachovia, and the Singapore branch of bankrupt insurance giant AIG. If this wave goes on to engulf local and regional banks and credit unions, the economic heart of the United States will stop beating in the same way as it did in March of 1933, when every commercial bank in the country was closed on the eve of FDR's inauguration.

The answer to providing credit in the crisis requires us to look very critically at the Federal Reserve. This institution was sold to congress under Woodrow Wilson with the argument that a private central bank would prevent any future panics like those of 1893 and 1907. In this, the Fed has clearly failed to deliver. The Fed contributed to the Wall Street bubble of 1929, and, much worse, did nothing to stop the banking panic of 1932-33. During the 1990s, Greenspan did everything to prevent limits or regulations on the $1 quadrillion-plus derivatives bubble which is the main cause of the present crisis. Greenspan was also responsible for the dot com bubble and the housing bubble, with the collapse of the latter functioning today as the firecracker which sets off an avalanche. The Fed has long been recognized as illegal, unconstitutional, elitist, oligarchical, and more concerned with inflation than in job creation – indeed, as being hostile to full employment. Now we can add that the Fed has struck out three times (1929, 1932-33, and the derivatives crisis of 2007-8), and needs to be replaced. Obviously, the demand of immediate nationalization of the Fed as a bureau of the US Treasury is fully justified. We will quite soon need to get to a system where the money supply and short-term lending rates are established by an act of congress, passed by the House and the Senate and signed by the president. This is the only permanent way to get out of the current world depression, but the issues involved are widely misunderstood. We therefore require a transitional program to move from the bankrupt private Fed of today to the future Fourth Bank of the United States (fourth after those of Hamilton, Madison, and the attempted one of Daniel Webster), which will be the world's greatest engine of economic development and progress in human civilization.

NATIONALIZING THE FED ON THE INSTALLMENT PLAN

Let us consider ways to nationalize the Fed step by step, to nationalize the Fed on the installment plan, to help deal with the crisis, even as we educate our fellow citizens as to why this process must be pursued and accelerated. Rather than starting with the maximalist ideological demand of nationalization (although this is fully justified), let us move towards full nationalization through a series of graduated intermediate steps that will allow New Deal methods to prove themselves in the crucible of the world economic crisis, even as all the blather about deregulation, privatization, "free markets," etc., falls by the wayside in impotence and failure. Let us bridle the lawlessness of Bernanke and his gang through a series of practical demands which grow organically out of the unfolding events of the present crisis, and not based on an abstract ideological approach. Let it also be clear that we have no time or patience for those crazed exponents of the Chicago or Austrian schools who want to abolish the Fed altogether to gratify the shade of crackpot Andrew Jackson, so that we can go back to wampum, clam shells, or barter. Those who are so bewildered by the complexity of modern life as to entertain such ideas as serious public policy should address themselves to issues more easily grasped than international finance and development economics.

Under the current system the Fed controls the money supply and the issuance of credit. What is the Fed doing right now? Since the derivatives crisis exploded in June-July 2007, the Fed has been injecting hundreds of billions of dollars of liquidity (money) into the banking system in a desperate bid to shore up collapsing paper values. The policy of liquidity injections was the Fed's main emphasis from August to December of 2007, when its failure was recognized.

BERNANKE'S ORGY OF EASY FED LENDING TO BANKS, BROKERS, STOCKJOBBERS

After that, the Bernanke Fed began creating a series of special lending facilities where bankers, stockbrokers, insurance companies, foreign central banks, and other financial operators could get cheap credit at special subsidized rates, generally well below the Fed's discount rate (currently 2.25%), and even below the Fed's target rate for interbank lending known as the Fed funds rate (currently 2% in theory, but in reality oscillating between 1% and 1.5%). Here are the main special windows that the Fed has opened up. Notice that in each case the cheap federal credit is primarily for financial, banking, brokerage, insurance, and mutual fund companies, meaning that most of its goes to the parasitical interests who have created the present crisis and are now demanding an taxpayer-funded bailout.

TERM AUCTION FACILITY (TAF)

Created in December 2007, the TAF is a way to allow troubled banks to avoid the public opprobrium of going to the Fed discount window. The TAF allows depository institutions of take part in periodic credit auctions set up by the flagship New York Fed branch, where banks buy 84-day loans with special low interest rates. As of Sept. 29, the TAF amounts to $75 billion in loans at the October 7 monthly auction, with an extra $150 billion added before the end of the year. The Fed appears on track to lend at least $375 billion – exclusively to banks – through the TAF before the end of the year.

TERM SECURITIES LENDING FACILITY (TSLF)

Under this program, the firms that are listed as primary dealers of Treasury securities are allowed to exchange certain types of collateral for Treasury bills and bonds, which are (so far) extremely liquid and easy to sell. The collateral these dealers can offer appears to include securities which can be very volatile. The program is operated together with the Bank of England, the European Central Bank, the Bank of Japan, the Swiss National Bank, and other foreign central banks. Here is an early 2008 list of the primary dealers who work with the New York Fed. Note the presence of many foreign banks, who thus qualify for special privileges where American producers and small businessmen do not:

ABN AMRO Incorporated
BNP Paribas Securities Corp
Banc of America Securities LLC
Banc One Capital Markets, Inc.
Barclays Capital Inc.
Bear, Stearns & Co., Inc.
Cantor Fitzgerald
CIBC World Markets Corp.
Credit Suisse First Boston Corporation
Daiwa Securities America Inc.
Deutsche Banc Alex. Brown Inc.
Dresdner Kleinwort Benson North America LLC

Fuji Securities Inc.
Goldman, Sachs & Co.
Greenwich Capital Markets, Inc.
HSBC Securities (USA) Inc.
J. P. Morgan Securities, Inc./Chase Securities Inc.
Lehman Brothers Inc.
Merrill Lynch Government Securities Inc.
Morgan Stanley & Co. Incorporated
Nesbitt Burns Securities Inc.
Nomura Securities International, Inc.
SG Cowen Securities Corporation
Salomon Smith Barney Inc.

UBS Warburg LLC.   Zion's First National Bank

Under the TSLF, the Fed intends to lend about $400 billion up to the end of October 2008, with much more coming before the end of the year.

PRIMARY DEALER CREDIT FACILITY (PDCF)

This new Fed window provides overnight loans to these same primary dealers in exchange for very dubious collateral, including all investment-grade securities, meaning bonds that are subject to going to junk level within days in the current climate. As of Sept. 15, shares of common stock will be accepted for the first time. What if the stock turns out to be that of Bear Stearns, Lehman, AIG, Wachovia, or other bankrupt banks, and the stock value goes to zero? The taxpayers will be left holding the bag. This means that, for the first time in history, primary dealers can borrow directly from the Fed, while industrial corporations and farms still cannot. The interest rate here is the Fed's bank discount rate, meaning a very low 2.25%, far less than the prevailing prime rate from commercial banks, which is 5%, a rate none of these quasi-bankrupt brokers could ever qualify for anyway. Compare that to the interest rate on your credit card and you will see what a precious service the Fed is providing – now to banks and brokers who are not Fed member banks and not even banks at all. The Fed has not announced any limit in the dollar amounts that could be lent out under this program, meaning that the lending may be literally unlimited.

ASSET-BACKED COMMERCIAL PAPER MONEY MARKET
MUTUAL FUND LIQUIDITY FACILITY (ABCPMMMFLF)

This is part of the Fed's attempt to bail out these money market mutual funds after the Reserve Fund Primary Fund broke the buck by falling below $1 per share, and the exclusive Putnam Prime Money Market Fund was liquidated to avoid bankruptcy, threatening to push $3.4 trillion in similar funds into panic liquidation. The Fed effectively guaranteeing all of this, with an initial lending program of $50 billion. Collateral includes asset-backed commercial paper, but only from these dubious mutual funds, not from businessmen who need credit for production, payroll, or commerce.

CURRENCY SWAP LINES WITH FOREIGN CENTRAL BANKS

These are dollar loans to foreign central banks, with an upper limit of $620 billion. They are allegedly used to protect the value of the US dollar and the other currencies against selling pressure in the foreign exchange markets.

In addition to these immense programs, the Fed has lent $85 billion to the bankrupt insurance company AIG, plus $35 billion to JP Morgan Chase to cover possible losses from the takeover of Bear Stearns back in March. By launching this stunning array of lending programs, the Fed oligarchs have thoroughly blurred the line between their member banks and the rest of the economic and business world, destroying their favorite earlier basis for denying credit for production. If the Fed serves only its member banks, that is one thing. But if a mutual fund company or an insurer or even foreigners can get cheap credit, why not a steel mill, a car wash, or a trucking company? After all, humanity does not live by financial paper alone, and real production and real services are the key to human survival.

RESULT: OVER $1.5 TRILLION OF CHEAP CREDIT FOR FINANCIERS, PARASITES, AND EUROGARCHS, BUT NOT ONE RED CENT FOR PRODUCERS AND THE PUBLIC

From this summary, we can see that the Fed has in recent months provided more than $1.5 trillion in lending for bankers, brokers, insurance companies, and mutual fund investment companies. Many of these lucky recipients of cheap US government credit are foreign commercial bankers, especially in the euro zone and Japan, to whom the US government is not obligated in any way. In effect, this means that the vast majority of these cheap federal loans are going to shore up the cancerous mass of kited derivatives which is crushing humanity. Incredibly, we have generously subsidized federal lending to support the bloated, fictitious, and usurious asset bubble which the derivatives represent. The Fed has been working overtime to support this mass of mortgage backed securities, structured investment vehicles, collateralized debt obligations, credit default swamps, and other over the counter, counterparty, and structured note derivatives. All of this is hidden behind the blather about poor people and subprime mortgages being responsible for the crisis, an absurdity. At the same time, there have been no special federal facilities for Main Street, for small business, for department stores, for small and medium industry, or even for the largest industrial corporations. (The same prejudice against real production has been shown by the Securities and Exchange Commission, which has temporarily banned short selling, but only against banks and financial companies, and not against industrial, pharmaceutical, transportation, or utility corporations!) It is time to redress this unbelievable situation.

A $1 TRILLION, .5% MAIN STREET LENDING FACILITY FOR PRODUCERS

The Fed must now be forced, through a federal law or presidential executive order using emergency powers, to open a special window to provide cheap federal credit for those forgotten people, the producers. A Federal Reserve line of credit of (initially) $1 trillion must be made available for productive activities of all kinds. In practice, this means that any businessperson or entrepreneur must be able to get credit for production through his or her local commercial bank. In technical terms, the local and regional banks must be directed to accept for discount purposes the commercial paper, bills of lading, bills of exchange, and promissory notes of productive businesses to establish lines of credit for said businesses at a rate of interest varying between .5% (one half of one per cent) and 1%. Maturities will be flexible, from 90 days for ordinary retail merchandise lending to 30-40 years for certain classes of capital and infrastructure investment. This will be done within the framework of the new Fed Main Street Lending Facility which will obligate and commit the Fed and its several regional branches to automatically and reliably accept for rediscount such commercial paper, bills of lading, bills of exchange, promissory notes, and related instruments generated out of production and hard-commodity commerce.

If the local bankers judge that productive investments in plant and equipment proposed by local entrepreneurs, whose reliability is known to them, are credit-worthy under these circumstances, they will be able to set up lines of credit for productive businesses and have these lines of credit automatically backed up by the guaranteed full lending power of the entire Federal Reserve System and all its branches, without exception. If state and local governments need capital to rebuild infrastructure in the form of bridges, roads, water systems, mass transit lines, bus fleets, libraries, schools, hospitals, public buildings, parks, recreation areas, and other socially useful installations, these state and local governments will also be guaranteed lines of credit for such contractors and subcontractors as they designate. No "privatization" of such facilities will be permitted at any time now or in the future. In other words, a significant part of the Fed will pressed into service for commodity production, socially necessary and useful services, and infrastructure development. The exclusive dedication of the central bank to financier interests to the detriment of business and labor will be finally broken.

MSLF WILL SAVE REGIONAL AND LOCAL BANKS, NOT WALL STREET

Local and regional banks participating in credit issuance under the MSLF will be kept in business by the Federal Deposit Insurance Corporation and given loan assistance as needed, on condition that they write off 100% of their derivatives book and refrain from making these dangerous investments at any time in the future. Banks which insist on maintaining their useless and socially destructive derivatives exposure will be seized as soon as they become technically insolvent, and bankruptcy judges overseeing Chapter XI proceedings will be given binding instructions by statute that all derivatives are to be wiped out in the course of bankruptcy re-organization as part of the effort to restore the viability of these banks. Shareholders who will be wiped out in this process should voice their concerns to bank management and directors at once, and thus help these banks to escape the deadly derivatives contagion, and survive.

Politically, this program addresses the urgent needs of small, medium, and large industry, small business, organized labor, working people in general, students, the working poor, and retirees. This proposal will tend to polarize the country between the overwhelming majority represented by these groups and others on the one hand, and a minority made up of Wall Street, its clients, hangers-on, and rent-seekers, and a few other groups – such as the foreign bankers the Fed is currently subsidizing – on the other.

THE DERIVATIVES BAILOUT RESEMBLES HOOVER'S 1931 RFC, A FAILURE

The lesson of the Great Depression of the 1930s is that all attempts to shore up bloated speculative values in the midst of a panic are doomed to failure, and must make the entire situation still worse. The Reconstruction Finance Corporation was created by Herbert Hoover in January 1931 with $3.5 billion of capital, a large sum at that time. But under Hoover, the RFC wasted its efforts in fruitless attempts to prop up bankrupt banks, and in attempting to support the speculative bubble which was inexorably collapsing. Thus, the RFC was able to save a few banks here and there temporarily, but was totally impotent to stop the banking panic of 1932-33, which led to the shutdown of every bank in the United States on March 4, 1932 in the early hours of FDR's inauguration day. The success of the RFC began under the New Deal when Jesse Jones of Texas used $50 billion for productive investment in plant, equipment, and jobs, many of them for defense purposes. The lesson is clear: in a depression, we must ignore the fate of speculative and fictitious paper and the price of that paper, and concentrate everything on helping people, especially by providing the forms of useful production upon which human life and human civilization depend.

CHEAP GUARANTEED FEDERAL CREDIT FOR PRODUCTION, NOT SPECULATION OR DERIVATIVES

We know what is productive. Production means physical production, the manufacture of real physical wealth in the form of hard commodities. Productive activities include farming, mining, construction, scientific research, transportation (trucking, taxicabs, urban mass transit, ferries, airlines) infrastructure (including railroads, highways, power grids), commerce of merchandise and commodities, defense production, nuclear reactors, electric power, water projects, mechanical repairs, garment industry, food and canning, machine tools, capital goods, pharmaceuticals, health care and hospitals. By contrast, you cannot eat, wear, live in, ride in, or drive a derivative, and you cannot use a derivative as a tool of means of production of any kind.

So much has already been done for the greedy bankers and brokers that we can fairly say that this new lending facility should be strictly off limits to Wall Street, to hedge funds, to stock brokers, and to money center banks. Regional and local bankers, as we have seen, have a key role in administering these loans to local business in their capacity as local lending agents of the Federal Reserve. But no money under the new program should go for financial services, finance companies, insurance, or speculation of any kind.

Our definition of Main Street is thus as inclusive as possible. It includes the Detroit auto makers, California's Silicon Valley, the Maryland genome corridor, the Texas-Oklahoma-Louisiana oil patch, the Boston high-tech complex, the farmers of the upper Midwest and high plains, Chicago light industry, and southern rice and cotton farmers. It includes any auto repair shop, dry cleaners, restaurant, or plumber. Main Street as used here means any business that provides production or a socially necessary service, and these are precisely the interests that have been scorned, despised, and neglected by the banker-controlled private central bank known as the Federal Reserve. Apart from that narrow enclave known as Wall Street and the money center banks, Main Street means virtually the entire US economy. The MSLF is also the best way to support reasonable valuations, once the present tempests have passed, of the common stock of industrial corporations which many persons hold in their IRAs and 401(k) accounts.

NEW LEND-LEASE FOR ECONOMIC RECOVERY FROM THE BUSH DEPRESSION

In January 1941, Franklin D. Roosevelt secured congressional approval for Lend-Lease, the program which finally harnessed the US system of credit and production to provide the necessary equipment for the defense of the United States and its British, Soviet, and other allies. It was Lend-Lease which, by guaranteeing that the banking system and the Federal Reserve would be mobilized to provide abundant, cheap, long-term credit for defense production, which finally ended the Great Depression entirely and allowed the US to attain full employment during the months before Pearl Harbor. Lend-Lease made this country the arsenal of democracy. Today, our task is not to mobilize against any foreign enemies, but rather to defeat the world economic and financial depression. The credit we need must serve to turn this country away from the perilous path of financial speculation followed during recent decades, most especially since the collapse of the Bretton Woods system August 15, 1971. We must respond to the disintegration of the globalized world finance system with a concerted campaign for the re-industrialization of the United States using the most modern available technology, along with a rebuilding and massive upgrading of the national infrastructure.

The ultimate goal remains the complete nationalization of the Fed, and a return to constitutional legality. The power to create money belongs to Congress, which cannot transfer or alienate that prerogative by a mere statute like the Federal Reserve Act. There is also the little matter of saving the taxpayers hundreds of billions of dollars, year in and year out. Under the current system, the JP Morgan Chase borrows Fed-regulated Fed funds at 2%, and JP Morgan Chase then turns around and lends the same money back to the Treasury for 4% to 5%. This spread is often even wider, and the difference between the Fed funds rate and the interest rates on Treasury bonds is an outright subsidy to the Wall Street banks for doing nothing, pure gravy for the financiers. If the Fed's currency issuance function were brought back into the Treasury, the taxpayers could save an average of between two and six per cent on Treasury borrowing compared to the current system, which would save hundreds of billions of dollars on the bloated US national debt. The US federal government, if only it is properly managed, is the most powerful institution in the known universe, and it surely does not require the services of bankrupt derivatives sinkholes like Chase, Citibank, and Bank of America. Those banks, as corporations, are mere creatures of the government, and we can easily dispense with their services. Once the Federal Reserve has been nationalized, we will save literally trillions by having the government lend to itself without these parasitical Wall Street middlemen getting in the way.

AFTER SEPTEMBER 2008, ONLY NEW DEAL ECONOMICS IS LEFT STANDING

With this crisis, all existing schools of economic thought save one have fallen into discredit. The fascist corporate state, supported by Obama and many Democrats, has failed. Communism and Marxism have failed. The deregulation and privatization demanded by Milton Friedman's monetarist Chicago school and Von Hayek's Austrian school (both branches of the Mount Pelerin society) as applied to derivatives have created the present crisis, so they are also finished. Only the methods of the FDR New Deal are left standing, and it is to the vigorous application of New Deal that we must now turn without delay.

4. END THE FED –
END WALL STREET BANKSTER RULE

END THE DERIVATIVES DEPRESSION

The "End the Fed" rallies of November 22, 2008 raise a vital issue: it is past time to abolish the unconstitutional, illegal, and failed institution known as the Federal Reserve System, the privately owned central bank which has been looting and wrecking the US economy for almost a hundred years. We must end a system where unelected, unaccountable cliques of bankers and financiers loyal to names like Morgan, Rockefeller, and Mellon set interest rates and money supply behind closed doors, leading to de-industrialization, mass impoverishment, and a world economic and financial depression of incalculable severity. The Fed helped cause the crash of 1929, did nothing to stop the banking panic of 1932-33, and is the main cause of the $1.5 QUADRILLION derivatives crisis which is devastating the world. The Federal Reserve System is Wall Street's murder weapon against the United States, and the Fed must be stopped.

The purpose of abolishing the Fed is to get re-industrialization, economic modernization, full employment, and rising standards of living for all the people. Contrary to monetarist fetishes, the value and soundness of currency in the modern world are determined by the ability of a national economy to produce physical commodities that the rest of the world wants to buy. The decline of the dollar has its roots in the wanton destruction of the US industrial base initiated by the Trilateral administration of Jimmy Carter and Fed boss Paul Adolph Volcker with his 22% prime rate. Over the past forty years, the US standard of living has declined by two thirds, and the country has become a post-industrial rubble field, a moonscape monument to the folly of a post-industrial service economy. If you want to go back to sound money, you must gear up modern industrial production so that the world will need dollars to buy goods manufactured in this country. No amount of gold will do the trick.

Gold has a critical role to play in a new international currency system, but returning to a gold coin standard would create the most ferocious deflation of all time. Got any credit card debt? If you do, a gold coin standard would make it infinitely harder to ever pay it off. You would be slaving for the rest of your life to pay off a $5,000 credit card balance, or less.

The United States is blessed by the world's greatest tradition of economics, the American System of political and national economy. Contrary to monetarist mythology, the American System never had anything to do with free trade or "free markets." It is a tradition of protectionism, mercantilism, and dirigism. It starts with Governor Winthrop of Massachusetts Bay in the 1600s, who promoted industry and launched a sovereign currency. Benjamin Franklin, the founder of the post office, was another dirigist. George Washington was always devoted to infrastructure projects, and Alexander Hamilton created the First Bank of the United States, without which the new nation would have collapsed into poverty, chaos, and a return of British monetarist rule. The Second BUS was created by James Madison, again to ward off chaos. Henry Clay coined the term of The American System, and it meant a national bank, a protective tariff, and national infrastructure financed by the federal government. Daniel Webster tried to create a third BUS, and when he fell short the slide into slave power and civil war resulted. Friedrich List, Matthew Carey, Henry Carey, and Justin Morrill were American System economists who influenced or advised Lincoln. The rise of the US as the world's greatest industrial power came thanks to a protective tariff and a controlled currency, the greenbacks. When Wall Street imposed the Cross of Gold, the American System tradition was continued by the Populist Party. The New Deal, the fruit of mass struggles and the rise of the labor movement, provided a way out of the Herbert Hoover depression by forcing the Morgan-controlled Fed to knuckle under to the FDR presidency. JFK tried to revive the New Deal and break the power of the Fed, and was assassinated by the financiers with the help of the CIA.

Monetarists pretend that this history does not exist. Their hero is Andrew Jackson, whose hare-brained meddling caused the Panic of 1837 and shut down US economic development, putting the country firmly on course for the Civil War two decades later. When they talk about the constitution, monetarists seem to be working off the Confederate constitution of 1861, which eliminated the General Welfare clause, and ruled out a protective tariff. During the 19th century, the free trade party was the pro-British slavery party. Monetarist dogma is a mix of Herbert Hoover, Robert Taft (of the Skull & Bones family), Barry Goldwater, Ronald Reagan, and other reactionary Republicans. Monetarism is based on the von Hayek-von Mises Austrian school, which started when a bunch of rent-gouging Viennese landlords wanted to abolish rent control and hired some scribblers to prove that "the market" was always infallible and government is always the enemy. Von Hayek got his chance under the reactionary old battle axe Margaret Thatcher, who brought back rickets, scurvy and pellagra for British working people. The dumbed-down US version of the same doctrine is Milton Friedman and his Rockefeller-funded Chicago School, which got its big road test under the fascist Pinochet regime in Chile.

MONETARISM CAUSED TODAY'S WORLD ECONOMIC DEPRESSION

Today's depression has been caused by 40 years of monetarist-inspired deregulation. Derivatives were illegal from 1936 until Reagan legalized them in 1982. Then Wendy Gramm, Greenspan, Bob Rubin, and Larry Summers teamed up to start the derivatives bubble during the Clinton years. Now there are $1.5 quadrillion of derivatives strangling the world economy. Derivatives, not subprime mortgages, are the reason for today's crisis. Today's depression also comes from privatization – like the privatization of Fannie Mae, which worked fine for thirty years as a government agency, but was then privatized, opening the door to the looting excesses which are now well known. The oil market is deregulated, and Goldman Sachs and Morgan Stanley were quick to exploit this situation. This past summer, when you were paying over $4 a gallon for gas, more than half of that was going directly to Wall Street hedge fund hyenas, with a full $1 per gallon for Goldman Sachs and Morgan Stanley alone, the backers of the deregulated offshore ICE exchange.

The real enemies of economic progress are the Wall Street bankers, financiers, and finance oligarchs. If you let them control the government, the results are catastrophic. We must therefore fight to take government out of the hands of the bankers. Any other strategy amounts to surrender to Obama and his fascist corporate state.

HOW TO END THE DEPRESSION WITH A RETURN TO THE AMERICAN SYSTEM

1. Wipe out derivatives, destroying the largest mass of fictitious capital the world has ever known. This includes credit default swaps, mortgage backed securities, structured investment vehicles, collateralized debt obligations, repo agreements, and other toxic paper. Outlaw hedge funds. Outlaw adjustable rate mortgages. Stop all foreclosures. Seize bankrupt banks, brokerages, and insurance companies and put them through debt triage under Chapter 11 bankruptcy proceedings. Re-establish the uptick rule against short sellers. Stop speculators with position limits and margin requirements for oil and other energy markets. Stop exporting jobs to third world sweatshops under NAFTA , CAFTA, and WTO.

2. Seize control of the Federal Reserve System and nationalize it as a bureau of the US Treasury. Decisions about money supply and interest rates must be made by public laws, passed by the House and the Senate and signed by the President. Re-start the US economy by issuing an initial tranche of $1 trillion in cheap 0.5% to 1% federal credit – federal lending, not spending – to state and local governments as well as to private companies engaged physical production. Production means infrastructure, manufacturing, mining, construction, farming, forestry, transportation, and commerce in tangible goods. Productive activities qualify for 1% or less federal credit. Gambling, narcotics, prostitution, financial speculation, speculation, and money laundering are not productive, so they must take their chances in the free market they claim to admire so much. A centerpiece of a recovery program would be the rebuilding of rail systems, water systems, electrical grids, and the interstate highways, all of which are approaching the point of physical breakdown. Nationalize the Big Three auto companies and reconvert them for mass transit.

3. We must keep Social Security, Medicare, Medicaid, unemployment insurance, food stamps, Head Start, WIC, and the remaining parts of the social safety net fully funded, since IRA/401k accounts and private insurance will increasingly be wiped out. Federal emergency relief on the model of FERA, CWA, and WPA will soon be needed. Any cuts in these programs will lead to death on a vast scale, especially among the old, the sick, and the very young. Monetarist ideologues who sneer at the nanny state should tell us where they stand when it comes to the very real threat of genocide against the American people.

4. Abolish the International Monetary Fund and the World Bank, and set up a new world monetary system based on full employment through the revival of industrial production.

Webster G. Tarpley for ACT INDEPENDENT.ORG

5. STATEMENT TO G-20 SUMMIT, LONDON, APRIL 2, 2009

FROM ACT-INDEPENDENT.ORG: FREEZE THE $1.5 QUADRILLION DERIVATIVES BUBBLE AS THE FIRST STEP TO WORLD ECONOMIC RECOVERY

Washington DC, March 22 – On the eve of the long-awaited London conference of the G-20 nations, we are rapidly descending into the chaos of a Second World Economic Depression of catastrophic proportions. In the year since the collapse of Bear Stearns, we have moved toward the disintegration of the entire globalized world financial system, based on the residual status of the US dollar as a reserve currency, and expressed through the banking hegemony of London, New York, and the US-UK controlled international lending institutions like the International Monetary fund and the World Bank. This is a breakdown crisis of world civilization, prepared over decades by the folly of de-industrialization and the illusions of a postindustrial society, and further complicated by the deregulation and privatization of the leading economies based on the Washington Consensus, itself a distillation of the economic misconceptions of the Austrian and Chicago monetarist schools. If current policies are maintained, we face the acute danger of a terminal dollar disintegration and world hyperinflation.

The G-20 leaders are must deliberate a new set of policies capable of leading humanity out of the current crisis. We must first identify the immediate cause which has detonated the present unprecedented turbulence. That cause is unquestionably the $1.5 quadrillion derivatives bubble. Derivatives have provoked the downfall of Bear Stearns, Countrywide, Northern Rock, Lehman Brothers, AIG, Merrill Lynch, and Wachovia, and most other institutions which have succumbed. Derivatives have made J.P. Morgan Chase, Bank of America, Citibank, Wells Fargo, Bank of New York Mellon, Deutsche Bank, Société Générale, Barclays, RBS, and money center banks of the world into Zombie Banks.

Derivatives are financial instruments based on other financial instruments – paper based on paper. Derivatives are one giant step away from the world of production and consumption, plant and equipment, wages and employment in the production of tangible physical wealth or hard commodities. In the present hysteria of the globalized financial oligarchy, the very term of "derivative" has become taboo: commentators prefer to speak of toxic assets, complex securities, exotic instruments, and counterparty arrangements. At the time of the Bear Stearns bankruptcy, Bernanke warned against "chaotic unwinding." All of these code words are signals that derivatives are being talked about. Derivatives include such exchange traded speculative instruments as options and futures; beyond these are the over-the-counter derivatives, structured notes, and designer derivatives. Derivatives include the credit default swaps so prominent in the fall of AIG, collateralized debt obligations, structured investment vehicles, asset-backed securities, mortgage backed securities, auction rate securities, and a myriad of other toxic variations. These derivatives, in turn, are pyramided one on top of the other, thus creating a house of cards reaching into interplanetary space.

As long as this huge mass of kited derivatives was experiencing positive cash flow and positive leverage, the profits generated at the apex of the pyramid were astronomical. But disturbances at the base of the pyramid turned the cash flow and exponential leverage negative, and the losses at the top of the pyramid became immense and uncontrollable. By 2005-6, the disturbances were visible in the form of a looming crisis of the automobile sector, plus the slowing of the housing bubble cynically and deliberately created by the Federal Reserve in the wake of the collapse of the dot com bubble, the third world debt bubble, and the other asset bubbles favored by Greenspan. Financiers are trying to blame the current depression on poor people who acquired properties with the help of subprime mortgages, and then defaulted, thus – it is alleged – bringing down the entire world banking system! This is a fantastic and reactionary myth. The cause of the depression is derivatives, and this means that the perpetrators to be held responsible are not poor mortgage holders, but rather globalized investment bankers and hedge fund operators, the derivatives merchants. We are now in the throes of a world wide derivatives panic. This panic has been gathering momentum for at least a year, since the fall of Bear Stearns. There is no power on earth which can prevent this panic from destroying most of the current mass of toxic derivatives. It is however possible that the ongoing attempts to bail out, shore up, and otherwise preserve the deadly mass of derivatives will destroy human civilization as we have known it. We must choose between the continued existence of derivatives speculation on the one hand, and the survival of human society worldwide on the other. If this be crude populism, make the most of it.

FREEZE DERIVATIVES FOR THE DURATION OF THE CRISIS

The G-20 must remove the crushing mass of derivatives which is now dragging down the world economy. Derivatives must be banned going forward, but this by itself will not be sufficient. The ultimate goal must be to wipe out and neutralize the existing mass of $1.5 quadrillion in notional values of toxic derivative instruments. Some governments may be able simply to decree that derivatives be shredded, deleted, and otherwise liquidated, and they should do so at once. Virtually all governments should be able to use their emergency economic powers to freeze derivatives and set them aside for at least five years or for the duration of the crisis, whichever lasts longer. Legal issues can be settled over the coming decades in the courts. Humanity is in agony, and we must act against derivatives now. Going forward, we must ban the paper pyramids of derivatives in the same way that the Public Utility Holding Company Act of 1935 banned the pyramiding of holding companies.

Derivatives were illegal in the United States between 1936 and 1983. In 1933, an attempt was made to corner the wheat futures market using options, and the resulting outcry led to a 1936 federal law banning such options on farm commodity markets. This ban was repealed by the Futures Trading Act of 1982, signed by President Reagan in January 1983. During the G.H.W. Bush administration, Wendy Gramm of the Commodity Future Trading Commission went further, promising a "safe harbor" for derivatives. Despite the key role of derivatives in the Orange County disaster during the Clinton years, a valiant attempt by Brooksley Born of the CFTC to make derivatives reportable and subject to regulation was defeated by a united front of Robert Rubin, Larry Summers (today running US economic policy), and Greenspan. Despite the central role of $1 trillion of derivatives in the Long Term Capital Management debacle of 1998, Phil Gramm's Commodity Futures Modernization Act of 2000 guaranteed that derivatives, notably credit default swaps, would remain totally unregulated. These pro-derivatives forces must bear responsibility for the current depression, and those still in power must be ousted.

The Bernanke-Bush-Paulson-Obama-Geithner policy pursued by the United States, which amounts to a $10 trillion (Fed and Treasury) effort to bail out the world derivatives bubble on the backs of taxpayers, can only make the depression worse, will never lead to an economic recovery, and must therefore he rejected. Krugman is right: "zombie ideas" rule Obama's Washington. The Fed's TALF amounts to subsidies for securitization, meaning more derivatives. The derivatives bailout was pioneered by Gordon Brown, Alistair Darling, and Mervyn King in the case of Northern Rock. These efforts are doomed to costly futility. The $1.5 quadrillion derivatives bubble is comparable to the black holes of astrophysics, those artifacts of gravity collapse which will irresistibly suck in all matter that comes near them. It compares to a world GDP of a mere $55 trillion, itself a figure inflated by financial speculation. The derivatives are the black holes of financial engineering, and can easily consume all the physical wealth and all the money in the world, and still be bankrupt. Gordon Brown's demand of $500 billion for the IMF is enough to bankrupt several nations, but pitifully inadequate to deal with the derivatives. They can only be dealt with by re-regulation – a quick freeze, leading to extinction and permanent illegality. We reject Brown's IMF world derivatives dictatorship.

Derivatives pose the question of fictitious capital – financial instruments created outside of the realm of production, and which destroy production. After WWI, fictitious capital appeared as tens of billions of dollars of reparations imposed on Germany, plus the war debts owed by Britain and France to the United States. These debts strangled world production and world trade, while bankers and statesmen tried desperately to maintain these debt structures. They become totally unpayable in the collapse of 1931, and US President Herbert Hoover proposed the Hoover Moratorium of 1931-1932, a temporary freeze on all these payments. The Lausanne Conference of June 1932 was the last chance to wipe out the debt permanently. But the Lausanne Conference failed to act decisively, and passed the buck. By the end of 1932, there was near-universal default on reparations and war debts anyway. And by January 1933, Hitler had seized power. We urge the London G-20 to defend world civilization against derivatives. The G-20 must not repeat the mistakes of Lausanne. It is time to lift the crushing weight of derivatives from the backs of humanity, before the world economy and the major nations collapse into irreversible chaos and war, as seen during the 1930s.

TO THE READER (1999)

> I have not found among my belongings anything as dear to me or that I value as much as my understanding of the deeds of great men, won by me from a long acquaintance with contemporary affairs and a continuous study of the ancient world; these matters I have very diligently analyzed and pondered for a long time, and now, having summarized them in a little book, I am sending them to Your Magnificence. – Machiavelli, *The Prince*.

This book has been written in the shadow of the greatest financial crash of all human history. The idea of writing it came to me when I was speaking at a conference in Melbourne, Australia in July 1995, when I heard the news that Japan's Cosmo Credit Union had gone bankrupt. "That is the beginning of the end," I told my very kind Australian host when we heard this news on television. That event could already have triggered an immediate world-wide banking panic, and it prompted me to consider what I could do to issue a warning to persons of good will. The text was well advanced by October 1997, when the wave of panic from the Hong Kong virus was hitting the American and European markets. The last phases were completed in August-October 1998, against the background of the Russian, Brazilian, and Long Term Capital Management debacles, and on the eve of the sinister false dawn of the euro.

It has been my aim to offer an overview of the collapse and disintegration of the world financial system before the breakdown had been completed. My goal was to provide something more than an instant book which appears shortly after the fact. I wanted if possible to write a pre-emptive book, a forecast that would help people to survive as individuals, and which, more importantly, would give them the concepts needed for the United States and the other modern nations to withstand the crisis. By the time you read this, the central political issue of the day may well be whether the International Monetary Fund will put the United States into receivership, or whether the United States should put the IMF into bankruptcy liquidation. In my view, it is the IMF, along with the entire globaloney system of world finance, which has to go.

I considered it important to present this analysis in the form of a book. Newspaper and magazine articles are valuable, but ephemeral. Because they are written for the moment, they always tend to express the political or financial hopes and fears of the moment. In other words, their common failing is that they can easily become propaganda. Anyone who believes as I do that the world financial system is indeed well advanced on the path leading to collapse and disintegration has the responsibility of making the case for that view in the systematic, inclusive and permanent form which a book-length study affords. Anyone who declines to assemble in book form an overview of the disintegration, while offering piecemeal a program of measures to deal with it, hardly lay claim to the mantle of historical or economic prescience. Agencies with far greater manpower and resources than I possess could have produced a book of this type, but have not done so. I therefore offer my own work to fulfill a vital need emerging in the world.

But why should anybody care about the opinions of Webster G. Tarpley about the world economy? The comprehensive answer is represented by this book as a whole. But in terms of an immediate and ponderable credential, I offer the following. This analysis was written for a private client in one of the three top Swiss banks, and was issued on November 15, 1993.

IS THE DERIVATIVES CRASH AT HAND?

It has of course become a commonplace in the world financial press that the very possible defeat of NAFTA on Nov. 17 could collapse the Mexican and other third world stock exchanges, thus precipitating a world-wide financial and banking panic that could bring down the US dollar and the American banking system. This "NAFTA 1929" scenario is eminently plausible, especially because possible warning tremors of the long-awaited derivatives panic have already been observed.

The Dow Jones Industrial Average continues to trade near its record highs in the neighborhood of 3700. But during the first two weeks of October, an alarming decline has taken place in the Dow Jones Utilities Average, and this appears to be associated with a reversal in the overall direction of the market for long term US Treasury bonds.

On October 29, [1993] the Dow Jones Utilities closed at 240.18. On Monday, November 15, the Dow Jones Utilities closed at 222.52. This represents a decline of more than seven per cent during a relatively short period, a significant correction in a sector of the market that is likely to be easily upset by volatility. Utility companies include electric power companies and similar firms that tend to appeal to conservative investors who are averse to risk but want stable prices and safe returns. Wall Street observers stress that the utilities average is prediscounting a rise in the rate of inflation that is now widely reputed to be on the horizon, including such basic sectors as food.

The decline in utilities was then quickly reflected in the prices of long-term US Treasury bonds. Interest rates on the 30-year reached their lowest point on October 15, with yields hovering around 5.75%. This corresponded to the highest price on these bonds in recent history. By Friday, October 29, the last trading day in the month, the interest rate on 30-year bonds had backed up to 5.96. During the following week the interest rate on these long bonds rose a startling one quarter of one per cent, bringing the yield up to 6.20%. This was accompanied by a downward slide in prices and above all by markedly increased volatility, with the long bond price jumping around from hour to hour like the quotation of a highly speculative stock. The *New York Times* noted on November 5 that the sell-off was a "little like the fires in California. Selling has swept the market like wind-driven flames while traders and investors watched, stunned and unable to stop it." On Nov. 15, with long bond yields only slightly better at about 6.15%, the same paper discussed the skittishness of the bond market under the headline "Signs of Investor Nervousness Grow." Many of the Wall Street crowd now think that the long rally in bonds, which had its beginnings back in 1991, is now definitively over. If so, the resulting instabilities could prove profoundly unsettling to the world of finance.

This turned out to be a highly accurate forecast. The bond rally was indeed over, and interest rates were turning sharply upward. What followed was the great bond market crisis of 1994, the worst since the period after World War I. This was the turning point which Soros, Orange County, Barings, Goldman Sachs, and other powers of the financial world guessed wrong. By their miscalculation, they variously incurred bankruptcy, liquidation, default, grievous loss, and personal ruin. Based on this track record, it is worth reading this book, even if its analysis contradicts the allegedly authoritative insider opinion being offered by brokers, bankers, and economics professors. If Robert Citron and Nick Leeson – to name just two – had heeded my advice at the end of 1993, they would have avoided the kind of notoriety which they achieved in 1994 and 1995.

It is the author's hope that the programmatic ideas in this book may be used to facilitate the immense task of world economic recovery and reconstruction in a post-oligarchical twenty-first century. Ideally, it might be employed as a sourcebook by candidates preparing to run for office in the aftermath of the cataclysm, or by government officials around the world. The basic ideas of economics are universals, and their essence does not vary much from place to place.

Today, some economic authorities deny that there is any crisis, and thus maintain that nothing needs to be done about it. Others admit that there is a crisis, but deny that anything can be done – this is a group which is destined to grow. Some others have been predicting the crisis for a long time, and claim that only they know how it can be solved. The author indignantly rejects the idea that economic recovery is some kind of book sealed with seven seals, which only a certain individual or party has been mysteriously empowered to open. No mortal human being, or group of them, has any monopoly on the ideas and programs which can produce economic recovery. The notion that they do represents an obscurantism worthy of Simon Magus, the founder of gnosticism. There is nothing esoteric, nothing secret at all about economic recovery. There is only the blindness generated by vast and stubborn ignorance, hardened by greed, pride, envy, and the other cardinal sins. Valid economic theory has developed historically over many centuries, and it is no one's private property.

The author's hope is that the considerations contained here may contribute to the rise of a new school of thought in economics, history, philosophy, sociology, and other areas of inquiry. This might be called the anti-oligarchical school, and the contention here is that it is the typical American outlook. Oligarchy is the social reality behind globalization and usury. An anti-oligarchical current in modern thought would provide the needed antidote to the oligarchical assumptions which now pervade the *Zeitgeist*, and which make the task of dealing with the looming breakdown crisis of world civilization much more difficult than it really needs to be. Every nation on earth would profit from promoting an enlightened and tolerant nationalism as against the presently dominant oligarchical modes of thinking. For the United States, the effective countering of oligarchical axioms would necessitate a revival of the ideas of Franklin, Hamilton, Lincoln, and Franklin Roosevelt, whose eclipse has made our intellectual tradition insipid.

This book aims at intellectual as well as economic reconstruction. In the late twentieth century, people think of education and learning as questions of *information*. This notion of information silently accepts empiricism and pragmatism as the inevitable ways of looking at the world. This boom rejects empiricism and pragmatism as philosophical schools, and rather attempts to exemplify the historical-philosophical method associated with Plato and his successors. Readers are therefore encouraged to concentrate on the philosophical method which the information is meant to convey.

The great need of the current moment is for a regroupment of anti-oligarchical and anti-globaloney forces worldwide. This needs to be done on a civil basis, without abuse or vituperation, and carefully respecting the human dignity of each and every participant. Methods inherited from the Protestant sectarians of the seventeenth century, from the Inquisition or counter-Reformation, or from the Third and Fourth Communist internationals will surely be counter-productive. Rigidly organized formations have often turned out to be their own worst enemies, and in any case belong to the past. Instead, there are two relevant models for the type of discussion which the author of this book hopes to stimulate. One model goes back to the gardens of the Rucellai mansion in Florence in the years just after 1515-1516. Here in the so-called *Orti Oricellari* a group of Florentine and Italian patriots gathered in the midst of a very difficult age to discuss strategy. Machiavelli was one of the participants, and one of the lasting fruits of these discussions is Machiavelli's masterpiece, the *Discorsi*, a book which perhaps more than any other influenced the American Constitution of 1787, and thus the entire concept of the modern state. The other model is the network of correspondents maintained by G. W. Leibniz during the years before and after 1700, which provided the impulse for many of the scientific innovations which have made the modern world possible. A modern equivalent for the *Orti Oricellari* or the Leibniz network might be found today on the Internet. In this spirit, the author invites comments and criticisms of his work, and will attempt, within the ever-present financial constraints, to find a way to expand his web site so as to promote a many-sided dialogue among serious participants. Others should do the same.

Parts of Chapters VI, VII, and X have previously appeared in different form in various publications and at my website.

Webster G. Tarpley
December 1998

Webster G. Tarpley was born in Pittsfield, Massachusetts in 1946. In 1966 he graduated *summa cum laude* from Princeton University, where he was elected to Phi Beta Kappa. He was a Fulbright scholar at the University of Turin, Italy. He later taught English at Cornell University and the University of Milan, Italy. From 1974 to 1984, he was a correspondent in central Europe, during which time he co-authored *Chi ha ucciso Aldo Moro* (Who Killed Aldo Moro, 1978) a study of international terrorism. In 1979-80, he appeared as commentator for *Teleradiosole*, a television station in Rome. From 1984 to 1996, he was a correspondent in Washington DC. He is the co-author of *George Bush: The Unauthorized Biography* (1992), which sold 25,000 copies and remains the only critical biography of the former President. In 1997 he published an anthology entitled *Against Oligarchy: Essays and Speeches 1970-1996*. These books can be consulted on the internet at www.tarpley.net. Tarpley has appeared with CNN Crossfire, Charley Rose, and numerous television and radio programs. He has lectured in numerous colleges and universities around the world. In 1995 Tarpley was named a consultant to the Universal Ecological Academy of Moscow. He holds an MA from Skidmore College and a Ph.D. in history from the Catholic University of America. He can be reached at tarpley@radix.net, or by mail at PO Box 1486, Washington Grove, Maryland 20880-1486 USA.

CHAPTER

I. THE ONCOMING CATACLYSM

You remember the closed banks and the breadlines and the starvation wages; the foreclosures of homes and farms, and the bankruptcies of business; the "Hoovervilles," and the young men and women of the nation facing a hopeless, jobless future; the closed factories and mines and mills; the ruined and abandoned farms; the stalled railroads and the empty docks; the blank despair of a whole nation – and the utter impotence of the federal government. - Franklin D. Roosevelt, September 23, 1944.

Around the turn the third millennium, the world is poised to experience the final disintegration of the current international financial system. If the present policy consensus among the Group of 7 nations persists, virtually all of the leading financial institutions of the planet will be wiped out in a panic of awesome scale and rapidity. The International Monetary Fund, the World Bank, the Bank for International Settlements, the Federal Reserve System, the Bank of England, the Bundesbank, the Banque de France, the Bank of Japan - all will be at high risk of default, bankruptcy, liquidation, and final demolition. Not just the United States dollar, but all currencies and all paper financial instruments risk becoming virtually worthless and non-negotiable - inevitably so, if the current policies are not urgently reformed. Entire types of markets, such as many stock markets and derivatives markets for futures and options on paper instruments, will almost certainly cease to exist.

The approaching cataclysm must not be confused with a mere collapse in these markets. A collapse is a decline in prices. Today the Dow Jones Industrial Average hovers above 8000 points. Within a day or two it could descend to 1000, to 50, or to 10. That is a collapse, the same type of event which we saw in 1929 or, in a milder form, in 1987. But what happens when the Dow Industrials approach zero? What happens when the New York Stock Exchange suspends trading, as it came close to doing in the worst moments of the 1929 and 1987 crashes? What happens if the New York Stock Exchange shuts down and stays shut, the market for Dow stocks becomes so illiquid as to disappear? If the stocks in question become non-negotiable paper, in the same class with the bonds of Tsarist Russia, the Confederate States of America, and other lost causes, then this kind of instrument can be said to have disintegrated. If something similar happens in bonds, futures, options, indices, and other paper instruments, and if we also have a panic run on banks and a currency crisis, then we begin to see what a disintegration might look like.

Decades ago, Al Capp's comic strip *L'il Abner* featured the rasbucknik, a communist-bloc currency unit. The peculiarity of the rasbucknik was that it not only had no exchange value, but actually had negative value. How can a currency have negative value? Because, if you had a mass of rasbuckniks, you had to pay someone to take them away. A great deal of the $200 trillion or so in financial paper which oppresses the world towards the close of the twentieth century will soon be found to be in the same category with the rasbucknik.

Disintegration is much worse than 1929 or 1987, or the Panics of 1837, 1873, or 1893. Disintegration is worse than the Tulip bubble, the Mississippi bubble, or the South Seas bubble. The classic modern example of financial disintegration is the German hyperinflation of 1923, when the German mark fell from 4.2 to a US dollar in 1914 to 10-12 trillion marks to a dollar by mid-November 1923. That meant that the value of all existing paper instruments had been wiped out, and order had to be restored from outside of the country. Collapse is a bear market, followed by severe economic slowdown and high unemployment. Disintegration is no market – and, what's worse, no job, no food, no electricity, no clothing and other merchandise - unless and until an anti-depression program is proposed by the President and validated by the Congress.

In the era of credit cards, debit cards, and electronic fund transfers, the concept of disintegration has acquired new and ominous overtones. A meltdown of the interbank settlement systems, followed by a shutdown of most banks, would lead to a freeze on most plastic money, checks, automated teller machines, and the like. Ask yourself how much cash you have in your pocket right now, and how many days you and your family could live with food bought with that cash. Then recall that the entire world System (as Henry Kissinger reverently refers to it) could be shut down in 3 to 5 business days, or even sooner.

Ponder the food shelves of your local supermarket. Note that apart from bread and grains, a rising proportion of that food is now imported, including meat, fish, fruits, vegetables, and other items. What will happen if the US dollar is no longer routinely accepted in world trade, as could very easily happen in the kind of crisis that now looms? Many varieties of food that are now available will no longer be there. If food supplies are cut off for several days, food riots with the looting of supermarkets are likely to follow. A scenario like this one gets much uglier as the days go on. Ask the residents of Moscow or Jakarta, who have been living through it. And of course, it *can* happen here.

Disintegration implies no mere financial blowout, however inconvenient. Disintegration threatens the breakdown crisis of a whole mode of civilization, as in the collapse of the Roman Empire after Diocletian and Constantine, or as in the combination of war, bankruptcy, and plague which wrecked the civilization of Medieval Europe. The fourteenth century breakdown crisis in Europe reduced the population by about one third. Given the more demanding thermodynamic prerequisites of the late twentieth-century world economy, a full-fledged breakdown crisis now might reduce today's world population from almost six billion to less than a billion, possibly over a period of several decades. Demographic collapse can already be observed in Russia, to cite only one example.

This is the cataclysm which is now rapidly approaching. The handwriting is on the wall: since the fall of 1994, we have experienced an unprecedented series of financial and economic crises. After the fateful turn upward in US Treasury bond interest rates in October, 1993, we had first of all the great bond market crisis of 1994, which was the worst since World War II. Then, around Thanksgiving 1994, came the Orange County bankruptcy - the biggest municipal bankruptcy in American history. Popular legend blamed Robert Citron, the man in charge of Orange County's investments. But Citron's practices were absolutely typical, and the insolvency of this once-rich county had been caused by derivative investments sold to Orange County by Merrill Lynch.

It was through the Orange County debacle that many ordinary people first heard of derivatives. They were surprised to find that these extremely volatile "financial products" had already inflicted grievous losses on Procter & Gamble, Gibson Greeting Cards, Ferruzzi, and Cayuhoga County, Ohio. Pay attention to these derivatives, since they are destined to play a key role in the coming collapse, much as brokers' margin loans did in 1929, or as portfolio insurance did in 1987. In early December 1994 there began the crisis of the Mexican peso and the Mexican stock market. The Mexican crisis revealed the foolishness of those who had touted the so-called "emerging markets" around the world, promising windfall profits in the looting of underdeveloped nations which had turned away from protectionism, communism, or statist models. From Brazil to India, from Poland to Argentina, all emerging markets were touched by panic.

By the last Sunday in January 1995, the Mexican crisis had brought the world to the edge of panic and collapse. On that day Georgia Senator Sam Nunn told one of the Sunday morning television interview programs that a US bailout package for Mexico could not pass the Senate. On Monday, January 30 the Mexican stock and currency markets panicked. That evening President Clinton decided to use emergency powers and Executive Orders to halt the Mexican panic with a US bailout package. When Clinton acted, other lending institutions joined in, and the result was a $50 billion bailout package. Clinton's action on Tuesday prevented the fall of the Mexican banking system on Wednesday, which would have been followed by panic runs and bankruptcies for the main Wall Street banks on Thursday. By Friday, the European, Japanese, and world banking systems would have been in ruins. Clinton had solved nothing, although he had bought some time. As for Mexico, it began to undergo a violent contraction in real economic activity along the lines of the US experience in 1930-33.

At the end of February 1995, Barings Bank went bankrupt. A previous crisis at Barings had detonated the Panic of 1893 in Wall Street. This time Barings ceased to exist. Attempts by Barings to blame its bankruptcy on a rogue broker are an insult to the intelligence of the public. It is now an institutionalized practice to scapegoat a "rogue trader" if a large financial institution is bankrupted or decimated by derivatives losses. This is about as ridiculous as the kindred practice of blaming every political murder or act of terrorism on a deranged "lone assassin." But in May 1995, another venerable British merchant bank, S.G. Warburg, had to be saved from bankruptcy through a takeover by the Union Bank of Switzerland.

By March 1995, the crisis of the United States dollar occupied center stage. It was natural that a worldwide financial crisis should envelop the world's leading currency. Some suggested making the German mark or the Japanese yen into worldwide reserve currencies, but these are even less capable than the dollar of discharging such functions. The dollar's wild roller-coaster of instability during the rest of the spring calmed somewhat during the summer, but started up again in September.

In June, in the midst of the financial equivalent of a category V hurricane, the heads of state and government of the Group of Seven - the leading economic powers of the world - met at Halifax for another of their yearly consultations in the series started at Rambouillet in 1975. Although the US delegation was able to at least place crisis symptoms like Mexico and Barings on the agenda, no serious measures were ordered to deal with the reality of the crisis. Rather, the G-7 consensus called for "reflationary crisis management," pumping up money supplies in order to stave off liquidity crisis and bankruptcy. Much of the new liquidity was to come from Japan, which had embarked on attempted reflation with a 0.5% prime rate. The world continued to drift into the maelstrom.

During the summer months of 1995, it became evident that the colossal family fortunes of the titled European nobility, especially the British, were aware that the bubble of paper investments was about to explode. They began shifting their assets into gold, silver, other precious metals, basic metals, strategic metals, oil, grain, and other foods. They were buying in the cash market, and they were demanding immediate delivery to their own warehouses. They did not want options or futures; they insisted on taking physical possession. These oligarchical families were thus preparing for the cataclysm, going short on paper instruments and long on commodities. Their policy was no longer paper speculation; it was speculative hoarding of tangible, physical raw materials. This move by the leading oligarchical *fondi* was studiously ignored by the leading financial commentators.

As July 1995 turned into August, the icy breath of banking panic was felt in Japan and Taiwan. This was the run on Tokyo's Cosmo Credit Union. Cosmo was soon followed by Hyogo Bank, the first bank failure in postwar Japanese history. During the following weeks it emerged that the leading Japanese banks had built up more than $1 trillion in bad loans in their real estate lending portfolios. Soon the ratings of the Japanese banks in question, which include the very biggest in the world, went past F to FFFF or 4-F, unfit for service. In the last week of September 1995, a new and unexpected ingredient was added to the panic: Speaker of the House Newt Gingrich, Chairman Pete Dominici of the Senate Budget Committee, and more than 154 Republican House members began to agitate for a Treasury default on the public debt of the United States. Such a default had never occurred in recorded history so far, but Newt and his fellow enthusiasts of the Conservative Revolution were threatening to use the need to raise the $4.9 billion ceiling on the public debt to force Clinton to accept a reconciliation bill that would include a capital gains tax cut plus savage cuts in Medicare, Medicaid, Social Security (in Title 4A, aid to families with dependent children, commonly known as welfare), farm support payments, student loans, and other entitlements. Dominici was claiming that ten market insiders like Soros's man Druckenmiller had told him that balancing the budget would far outweigh the problems inherent in a default. On the day that Gingrich made his threats, the US dollar fell by about 5% against world currencies. It was clear that a default by the US Treasury, which had become a distinct possibility for October-November 1995, had the potential to detonate the final phase of the ongoing collapse, and perhaps thus to usher in disintegration itself.

The situation of the Japanese banks and the desperate measures undertaken by the Tokyo government to bail them out dominated the financial news during late 1995 and 1996. Japanese hot money dished out by the Bank of Japan to keep Japanese commercial banks above water was the key to price gains in US stocks. In the fall of 1995, the US branch of Daiwa Bank reported over a billion in losses, and this was blamed once again on a rogue trader. In June 1996, it was allegedly another Japanese "rogue trader" who racked up astronomical losses for Sumitomo and its copper trading operations. How long could Japanese interest rates at 0.5%, providing liquidity to pump up the world bubble? These were the questions the speculators asked each other in 1997.

1997 saw one of the greatest monetary crises of the postwar period. In 1992 and 1993 the monetary crisis was centered in Europe. In 1994 the epicenter was the Mexican peso; in 1995 the US dollar was collapsing for a time. In 1997 it was the turn of Thailand, the Philippines, Malaysia, Indonesia, Singapore, and finally Hong Kong. The danger emerged that a financial debacle in one or more of these countries could administer a lethal blow to the Japanese banking system, and magnify a regional currency crisis into the beginning of world disintegration. This potential began to turn into reality with the explosion of the Asian regional crisis in the summer and autumn of 1997. The regional crisis was immediately as systemic one, involving Russia, Latin America, and all the so-called merging markets. Russia began to fall apart in May 1998, and by August Russia had defaulted. In the meantime, Brazil was in the tempest as well. In the midst of it all, the Japanese banking system continued to deteriorate, and the world was moving deeper into economic depression, towards final financial disintegration.

THE FAILURE OF PROFESSIONAL ECONOMICS IN THE AGE OF GLOBALONEY

The implication of these recent events is that this is not a time of financial stability, and that we do not have a stable world financial system. Risk is pervasive, and the danger of default is never absent. We see the empirical fact of a series of crises. But behind them there is the larger issue that combines practical survival with theoretical economics: what about a new world depression on the scale of the 1930s, or even worse? What about a worldwide financial meltdown? What about, to use the bankers' own code word, the threat of "systemic crisis"? Academic economists are usually found cheerleading for some new rip-off of the public interest in the name of "competitiveness in the global economy" (hereinafter "globaloney" for short). But a few of these older academics, in their lucid moments, are willing to admit that economic theory is in total crisis. The Keynesian synthesis was overturned by the monetarists, they will say, and the monetarists have been overturned by the unexpected consequences of monetarism as practiced by governments from

Nixon to Carter to Thatcher and Reagan. There is no theory left standing, concede the academics, as they leave for their next board meeting. Economics as a science in search of truth is long since dead. All that is left is chaos theory and "fuzzy engineering," the specialty of the quantitative analysts employed by hedge funds and securities firms.

THE INGREDIENTS OF GLOBALONEY

Most economists are only too happy to repeat the absurd litany of globaloney. But everyone should remember the warning that sausage-eaters should stay out of the sausage factory, since they are sure to be shocked when they see how their favorite snacks are really made. So it is with that most dubious sausage, globaloney. Here are some essential components of this new creed:

1. Floating exchange rates among currencies, with wild gyrations and no gold convertibility.
2. Hot money speculation, stockjobbing, and usury, culminating in hedge funds and the $150+ trillion worldwide bucket shop of financial derivatives.
3. Privately owned and privately controlled central banks, with the private Bank for International Settlements as the flagship, the Federal Reserve, the Bank of England, etc.
4. Free trade, dumping, and the runaway shop, as in NAFTA, GATT, the European single market, etc.
5. Secular deflation; depression as cure for inflation (Keynes in reverse), with high interest rates expressing the political ascendancy of the bondholders.
6. Deregulation, especially of financial markets, with growing domination by oligopolies and cartels.
7. Stagnating and declining world production, especially in basic industry and especially in per capita terms.
8. Casino society, frantically seeking monetary wealth under the constant threat of systemic crisis.
9. Permanently high unemployment and declining standards of living, with weak labor unions, union-busting, a shrinking middle class, and fabulous wealth for a tiny, parasitic oligarchy of financiers of about 500,000 persons worldwide.
10. Anti-statism, with the withering away of the national state, its infrastructure, and its social safety net, except when the insolvency of financial institutions threatens systemic crisis (Bush S&L bailout, Greenspan's backdoor bailout of US banks at Treasury expense, $50 billion Mexican bailout fund, $500 billion Japanese bailout fund, and IMF bailouts funded by taxpayers of IMF member states).
11. A race to the bottom among nations (and even among states and provinces) to gut health, environmental, safety, and other regulations, while offering tax incentives to venture capitalists.
12. Oligarchy, more often referred to under such terms as "the establishment," "the elites," "the market, " "market forces," or "market democracy."
13.   *Class war* of the tiny finance oligarchy against the vast majority of humanity.

Such are the principal axioms of the way things are done at the moment. Many a career has been made with these crude slogans. Each of these points is a shibboleth of the globalized economy, and each one is at the time an affront both to God's natural law as well as to the practical needs of developing human society. That leaves the question of whether these arrangements are headed for systemic crisis. Reagan, with the help of Volcker, had been the harbinger of a serious recession in 1982. Bush had also presided over a pronounced downturn. But these had been contained. What about the possibility of a collapse or even of a disintegration, accompanied by bottomless depression?

During the collective insanity of a dying financial bubble, almost nobody wants to hear anything about economic crisis. But this remains the great issue of our time, and the evidence looks worse and worse the more one looks. For example: economic depression itself is not a theoretical possibility; in terms of declining industrial production and infrastructural decay, depression is already a practical reality and has been with us since the height of Volckerism in 1982-83. By postwar historical standards, economic depression is already a given. The only question is when this state of affairs begins to impact the consciousness of the hedge-fund operators and mutual fund speculators who dominate "the market."

In the past, economists were capable of frankly discussing the possibility of a new world economic depression. Let us hear once more the comforting words of Paul Samuelson, the MIT professor whose textbook, *Economics*, was the standard college introduction to economics for several decades. Samuelson for many years reassured everyone that a new depression was impossible because of the "built-in stabilizers" of the modern US economy. (In the meantime, one of the last of his stabilizers, the cold-war military economy, has been dismantled.) Samuelson was also sure that the government would never permit a new depression. We cite from Samuelson's 11th edition, published in 1980:

> Banks are much safer than they used to be before the depression.... Banks are safe today because everyone realizes that it is a vital function of government to stand behind them (and behind its Federal Deposit Insurance Corporation, set up to protect depositors) should a depression come and panicky 'runs' on the banking system ever recur.
>
> No banking system with fractional reserves - i.e., none which keeps less than 100% of its deposits in cash - can ever turn all its deposits into cash on a moment's notice. So every fractional-reserve system would be a 'fair-weather system' if government did not stand ready to back it up. If panic ever came again, Congress, the President, and the Federal reserve Board would act, even using their constitutional powers over money to print the money needed in a national emergency! Had this been said and done back in the black days of the early 1930s, history might have been different. Our country might have been spared the epidemic of bank failures that destroyed the money supply, creating fear and crisis for the whole capitalist system.
>
> With the American people of both political parties realizing that the government stands behind the banking system, it is highly improbable that a panic could ever get started. Here is a case where being prepared to act heroically probably makes it unnecessary to do so. [Samuelson, 281-282]

Unfortunately, since the coming of global deregulation and globalization, and since the Republican Party's conservative revolution of November 1994, nothing remains of the factors cited by Samuelson to justify his optimism. An Executive Branch whose chief concern is to hold Kenneth Starr and the would-be impeachers at bay may not be able to act. The US Government has done much to make the economic crisis worse, and cannot be relied upon to fight the breakdown crisis, even when it is finally evident to all. Citizens must mobilize to secure a positive outcome.

WARNINGS

The coming of the final collapse phase has been to some degree an open secret. While publications that cater to the gullibility of the American middle classes have seldom devoted any systematic analysis to the possibility of a financial cataclysm, publications addressed to the international financial elite – that is to say, to the beneficiaries of globalization – have sometimes conducted a brutally cynical discussion of the dimensions and timing of the catastrophe over the period of the last several years. A number of popular writers have also pointed to the danger of depression. To bring the average American up to speed, we will provide a quick overview of this debate.

The popular author Douglas Casey has been predicting world economic depression since the time of the Carter administration. In his most recent book, published in 1993, he reaffirmed this perspective that what he calls a "Greater Depression" will soon be upon us: "In *Crisis Investing* (1979) and *Strategic Investing* (1982), I argued that a depression was inevitable. This prognosis still holds, and I believe this depression will dwarf the events of 1929. ...Why should a depression occur now? A depression could have materialized out of any of the credit crunches in the last three decades, including the financial squeezes of 1962, 1966, 1970, 1980, and 1982. With each episode inflation went higher, interest rates rose, unemployment increased, and the bankruptcies were bigger. Near bankruptcies (such as Lockheed, New York City, Chrysler, Continental Bank) became more numerous and dangerous and more likely to demand a government rescue. But each time we experienced just a recession that the government ended before the underlying distortions in the economy had been eliminated.... there likely will be a titanic struggle between the forces of inflation and the forces of deflation. Each will probably win, but in different areas of the economy." [Casey, 3, 9, 30] Notice that Casey believes that it is government which is ultimately responsible for depressions.

A MUTUAL FUND CRISIS

One specific feature of the coming crisis was singled out for attention in 1993-1994 by Donald Christensen, the publisher of the *Insider Outlook* newsletter. Christensen's focus is the mutual fund market, and the likelihood of a severe decline, caused in part by mutual fund managers engaging in high-risk speculative practices, including "weird instruments," as he calls derivatives. In his book *Surviving the Coming Mutual Fund Crisis*, Christensen warned of a coming "mutual fund crisis [that] will probably come to a head some time in 1996 or 1997." "If we are lucky," Christensen added, "- if for some reason the push to ease mutual fund investment limitations slows or if America's unquestioned love affair with the mutual fund idea cools - we might make it to the turn of the century." [Christensen, 177]

THE BIGGEST FINANCIAL CATASTROPHE SINCE 1776

A secular decline in stock and other asset prices based on analysis using the Elliott Wave Theory was offered by Robert R. Prechter, Jr., in his July 1995 book, *At the Crest of the Tidal Wave*. Prechter forecast a "slow-motion economic earth quake that will register 11 on the financial Richter scale." According to Prechter, "Markets that began declining early will continue their descent to depths currently inconceivable to conventional observers. The giant wash will take with it wholesale prices, consumer prices, employment, profits and tax receipts, as well as the fortunes of banks, manufacturers, insurance companies, and pension funds. Ultimately, the process will devastate the debt balloon, the welfare state, the solvency of municipal and federal governments, and the political status quo." [Prechter, 408] Specifically, Prechter predicts the following: "(1) the stock market is near the end of Cycle wave V from 1932; (2) the Dow Jones Industrial Average will fall back to at least 1000; and (3) when the stock market falls that far, we will have a depression." [Prechter, 409]

Prechter's view is derived from material published in the *Elliott Wave Theorist* going back to the early 1980s. At that time, Prechter was predicting about a dozen fat years of spectacular bull markets, followed by the "biggest financial catastrophe since the founding of the Republic" towards the middle of the 1990s. In this perspective, we are faced today with the end of a Grand Supercycle bear market; the result will be to wipe out all financial gains reaching back to the conclusion of the American Revolution. According to the Elliott Wave analysis, the coming crash will be so severe as to provoke a worldwide monetary and economic collapse, including "worldwide banking failures, government bankruptcy, and eventual destruction of the paper money system." [*Elliott Wave Theorist*, April 6, 1983 and April 3, 1984] Prechter's expectation is that the long-term low point in world markets will be reached between 1998 and 2004, and he recommends liquidating stocks and bonds, getting out of debt, putting cash in T-bills, and acquiring a gold hedge.

Another early warning came from economist Lyndon LaRouche. In the *Executive Intelligence Review* of June 24, 1994, LaRouche offered the following forecast:

> The presently existing global financial and monetary system will disintegrate during the near term. The collapse might occur this spring, or summer, or next autumn; it could come next year; it will almost certainly occur during President William Clinton's first term in office; it will occur soon. That collapse into disintegration is inevitable, because it could not be stopped now by anything but the politically improbable decision by leading governments to put the relevant financial and monetary institutions into bankruptcy reorganization." [*EIR*, June 24, 1994]

Possible financial collapse has also been widely discussed in the daily newspapers, especially in Europe. On August 2, 1995, the liberal German daily *Frankfurter Rundschau* used the occasion of the panic run on Japan's Cosmo Credit Union to analyze the relations of the Japanese banks to the rest of the financial world. According to this paper, "The fear is spreading outside of Japan that a much bigger bank than the troubled medium-sized Cosmo Credit Union could go under, thereby triggering a chain reaction in the international financial system." This soon happened.

On September 8, 1995 the German financial weekly magazine *Wirtschaftswoche* assembled various commentaries on the parlous state of world financial markets under the title "Selling in a Panic." Leading the Cassandras was Roland Leuschel of Banque Bruxelles Lambert (Lambert as in the late lamented Drexel Burnham Lambert) who predicted new market turbulence: "this time as well," said Leuschel, "there will be a crash at the stock exchange." Leuschel had stated earlier that "the countdown to the crash has begun. We are paying the price today for the creation, during the past two years, especially in the United States, of the biggest financial bubble in human history." To this were added the ruminations of hedge-fund magnate George Soros, to the effect that "at present, the market is in a boom phase, but exactly because of that, it has the potential for a crash." Soros quickly added that "something special has to happen in order to trigger a collapse." But a few weeks later Soros, for one, decided that he had been too bearish for his German readers. At this time, Soros was announcing profits of hundreds of millions of dollars raked in by selling the US currency short. On September 22, 1995 Leuschel repeated his analysis to the *Sueddeutsche Zeitung* of Stuttgart in an article entitled "Clouds Over Wall St." This time Leuschel focussed on the unrealistically high price/earnings ratios of the S&P 500 stocks. For Leuschel, these p/e ratios were comparable only to levels reached in Japan in 1989, before the Nikkei turned downwards, and in the US before the 1929 crash. Leuschel also characterized the German public debt and budget deficit as "a time bomb."

A PARASITIC PREDATOR

Another critical estimate of the perspectives of the global economy came in 1995 from David C. Korten, a disciple of Willis Harman who proceeds from New Age premises towards a utopian ecological and communitarian program, but offers numerous valid observations along the way. Korten sees first of all that the world financial system has separated itself from the productive economy, and is now attacking the latter. He describes graphically the life of the half-million or so persons who make up the world's financial elite, rising each morning to immerse themselves in tracking the market gyrations that flicker across their computer screens and at the same time to ignore the reality around them. "The global financial system," he finds, "has become a parasitic predator that lives off the flesh of its host – the productive economy." [Korten, 193] Korten sees derivatives as what they are, new and risky forms of leverage purchased using borrowed money. Derivatives create risk; they do not manage it, because it is becoming unmanageable. Financiers love volatility for its own sake, since it brings fees and profits. Korten portrays "corporate cannibalism," the practices of the raiders and leveraged buyout specialists. "A rogue financial system is actively cannibalizing the corporate sector," he stresses. [Korten, 214] Summing up recent financial explosions, Korten concludes that "this system is inherently unstable and is spiraling out of control – spreading economic, social, and environmental devastation and endangering the well-being of every person on the planet. Among its more specific sins, the transmogrified financial system is cannibalizing the corporations that once functioned as good local citizens, making socially responsible management virtually impossible and forcing the productive economy to discard people at every hand as costly impediments to economic efficiency." [Korten, 206]

"SHOCKPROOF"!

By contrast, one of the most absurd blanket denials of any current possibility of financial system meltdown came at the beginning of 1996 in *Foreign Affairs*, the organ of the New York Council on Foreign Relations (CFR), which is itself the American branch of the Royal Institute for International Affairs, the so-called Chatham House. The author was Ethan B. Kapstein, the director of studies at the CFR. Kapstein's line of argument might have made the most unscrupulous mutual fund salesman blush. As evidence of imperturbable stability, Kapstein cited the great financial debacles of 1995, including the Mexican crisis, the Barings bankruptcy, and the losses of Daiwa bank in New York. Kapstein was mightily encouraged by the ability of the System to survive these dramatic financial collapses: "...the markets responded to these financial crises with little more than a 'ho-hum.' In fact, the US stock market boomed, and interest rates around the world declined. The Bank of England allowed Barings to fold, and nothing happened. American regulators closed Daiwa Bank's New York office, and the markets did not squeal. Both inside and outside the US government and international organizations, analysts continue to debate whether the Mexican bailout was really necessary." So the idea is that the System has been able to deal with three potential catastrophes without batting an eye. The title of Kapstein's piece suggests his conclusions: "Shockproof: The End of the Financial Crisis."

Look at the difference – enthused Kapstein – between 1995 and the bad old days of 1974, at the dawn of the deregulated hot money era, when bank failures of the small to middling sort like Herstatt and Franklin National were capable of sending the entire System to the brink of insolvency! According to Kapstein, the sage central bankers, with their 1975 Basel Concordat and their 1987 Basel Accord on minimum capital standards, have guaranteed that the markets will continue unshakable. Kapstein's conclusion is that "Over the past 20 years the leading economic powers have created a regulatory structure that has permitted the financial markets to continue toward globalization without the threat of systemic collapse." No more depressions, assures Kapstein, who ends on a note of nostalgia for Schumpeter's theory that depressions brought "creative destruction" and kept the System dynamic. Kapstein chose to ignore the greater Japanese banking crisis of which the Daiwa shenanigans were but a facet. This Japanese crisis, as Kapstein surely knew, had in mid-1996 impelled the US government to ready a bailout fund of $500 billion, ten times as large as the

Mexican bailout fund which he does mention. From 1996 on, the Japanese banking crisis remained the most obvious menace of systemic breakdown.

The Basel Accord and its purported minimum capital adequacy standards have been rendered meaningless by the so-called off-balance sheet activities of the biggest banks, including derivatives. What use can these standards be if Chase Manhattan's derivative exposure amounted to 267 times its equity capital at the moment that Kapstein was writing? In reality, as we will show, the world financial System has been to the brink of meltdown and breakdown about three dozen times since the world monetary crisis began over 30 years ago with the November 1967 devaluation of the British pound sterling. By now, all the available energy of the System is devoted to preventing the wild speculative instability and volatility of the System from destroying it, as they constantly tend to do. The growth of the speculative bubble means that these recurring crises are more and more likely to initiate the downfall, and not less and less likely to do so.

THE END OF THE BUSINESS CYCLE?

Even the editors of *Foreign Affairs* must have been aware that Kapstein's crude argument, amounting to the classic "this time is different" or "new paradigm" often heard in the last stages of a speculative bubble, could hardly have been convincing. In their July-August 1997 issue, accordingly, they published another article in the same spirit, buttressed this time by a more detailed analysis, but arguing for a thesis just as absurd as Kapstein's: this time the assertion was that not just financial panics are relics of the past, but that periodic contractions of business activity are also passé. If Francis Fukayama could assert the "end of history" some years earlier, no one should be surprised if the CFR now tries to consign both financial panics and economic depressions to the dustbin of history.

The idea of the business cycle is mainly a mystification. Especially in modern American history, what are usually labeled as business cycles represent the results of British political-economic machinations occurring within the context of virtual economic warfare. As we will discuss at some length, severe panics and depressions generally take place because powerful forces want them to take place – and that someone is more often than not the City of London finance oligarchy. Another way of saying this is to point out that the depressions of the post-Napoleonic era have been crises either of a world monetary system centering on the British pound sterling and British debt structures, or (after 1944) of a world monetary system based on the dollar in which the British capacity to create mischief was still quite robust. So 1929 was not a cyclical crisis.

In "The End of the Business Cycle?" Professor Steven Weber, a political scientist at Berkeley asserts that, given the globaloney economy of the late twentieth century, "in the advanced industrial economies the waves of the business cycle may be becoming more like ripples." Even professional economists have commented on the weakness of what they call the current recovery, but for Weber this is a harbinger of a new historical pattern. From now on, he argues, the business cycle will be "dampened." Among the factors contributing to the new era Weber lists the service economy, which weakens trade unions, whose strength was anchored in manufacturing. "Declining union power," Weber points out, "contributes to the development of increasingly flexible labor markets, extending to downwardly flexible real wages in some OECD countries, notably the United States." This mirrors John J. Sweeney's point that of all the advanced industrial nations, the United States is currently experiencing the most extreme decline in real wages and growth of inequality in remuneration - a situation which itself constitutes a crisis, but which Weber sees as a factor of stability. Pausing to congratulate the Fortune 500 companies for reducing their full-time work force by more than 30% over the last 15 years, Weber celebrates the rise of the temps, whose numbers have grown by 19% over the last 3 years and who now constitute no less than one tenth of the entire American work force. In the fast-growing professional and technical fields, Weber asserts, "paradoxically, permanent status as a temporary worker is becoming an increasingly respectable career path."

It is under the subhead of "More Markets, More Money" that Professor Weber skates on the thinnest ice of all. He attempts to argue that the new, exotic, and very dangerous financial instruments called derivatives have increased the stability of the international financial system:

> The growth of other financial markets as well as mutual funds and similar products has been phenomenal – particularly, but not only in the United States. Concerns about derivatives trading reflect that enormous growth. In developed countries, trading in over-the-counter derivatives exceeded $8.5 trillion in 1993, along with more than $6 trillion in interest rate swaps outstanding. Activity in standard financial instruments traded on exchanges (currency futures, stock market index options, interest-rate futures) doubled between 1992 and 1994. These new financial products spread and diversify risk. And despite a few heavily publicized losses on derivatives contracts in the mid-1990's, these numbers will probably climb higher as corporate treasurers and fund managers become better at using these new tools to stabilize financial flows and protect themselves against shocks.

Were there any dark clouds on Weber's horizon? He sees a secular decline in world inflation, which he fears may bankrupt developing countries that borrow money on the expectation that the task of repaying it in dollars cheapened by inflation. Some countries, he feels, will have forced either to default or to renegotiate their debt. "Does this signal another international debt crisis?", he asks. Not to worry, replies Weber, the big banks have long since quit making loans to the third world, so private investors and mutual funds (which contain the life savings of the American middle class) will be left holding the bag. Weber's conclusion is that "...debt rescheduling need not spawn a systemic crisis as it did in the early 1980's."[11]

Weber's piece represents the apotheosis of the stateless, deregulated, hot money financial system: "Global capital markets, " he writes, "are increasingly efficient at linking capital to production, managing risk, and providing shock absorbers that cushion economic fluctuations." He describes the benefits of securitization of debt in glowing terms: "Investors can buy repackaged pieces of risk and spread their holdings across countries, industries, and time periods." He impatiently dismisses warnings of a possible systemic crisis, and seems to belittle the recent emergencies that have taken the world to the brink of meltdown: "The doomsday argument, advanced by writers like William Greider, that complex markets might act in synergy and come crashing down together is simply not supported by a compelling theoretical logic or empirical evidence. Two and a half years after the peso collapsed in Mexico, the striking aspect of that 'crisis' is how limited the feared 'Tequila

---

[11] Ironically, the same issue of *Foreign Affairs* that offered Professor Weber's desperate optimism also hosted the somewhat more sober view of MIT's Professor Paul Krugman. In a review critical of a book converging on the "end of the business cycle", Krugman covers his own flank more cannily than Weber, noting that "anyone who reads the business press knows that the mood these days is one of 'what, me worry?' optimism. After six years of fairly steady growth with surprisingly quiescent inflation, every major newspaper or magazine has either suggested or flatly declared that the business cycle is dead – that the recession of 1990-91 was the last such slump we will see for many years to come...near the end of another long recovery, in the late 1960's, pronouncements that the business cycle was dead were just as prevalent as they are today." Krugman believes that the business cycle will continue, simply because the economics problems of the future will be new, "and because the problems are new, we will handle them badly, and the business cycle will endure."

effect' turned out to be in both scope and longevity." There are a couple of million unemployed workers in Mexico who might want to take issue with that retrospective.

Weber's prose, like the 1920s irrational exuberance of Professor Irving Fisher of Yale and Professor Joseph Stagg Lawrence of Princeton cited with such consummate irony by Professor Galbraith in his celebrated book *The Great Crash*, appears destined to illustrate the stubborn persistence of human folly and vanity in some future account of the millennium crisis. We can only hope that policy makers are not guided by such a distorted and utopian outlook.

At the Federal Reserve, Greenspan, rather than consider reforming the system, was readying his printing presses for the eventuality of a total panic. On May 7, 1998, Greenspan attended a conference sponsored by the Federal Reserve Bank of Chicago: "With financial leveraging there will always exist a remote possibility of a chain reaction, a cascading sequence of defaults that will culminate in a financial implosion if it proceeds unchecked. Only a Central Bank, with unlimited powers to create money, can with a high probability thwart such a process before it becomes destructive." Others were less confused. On February 8, 1996, Senator Edward Kennedy told an audience at the Center for National Priorities that the United States and the world had entered a "quiet depression."

THE WORLD FINANCIAL SYSTEM IS IN PIECES

At the Group of Seven meeting in Lyons, France, held on June 27-29, 1996, International Monetary Fund (IMF) Managing Director Michel Camdessus gave a talk on world financial conditions to a seminar. Camdessus' remarks were summed up in an article written by journalist Clovis Rossi for the Brazilian newspaper *Folha de Sao Paulo*, June 28, 1996. The title of the article was "Next Crisis is in the Banks, says IMF." Rossi quoted Camdessus as saying that "the 'next earthquake' in the world after the Mexican crisis will be in the banking sector." "The world financial system is in pieces and it is urgent to tighten the screws."

IT WILL START WITH A BANKING CRISIS

A few months later, at a September 28, 1996 Washington press conference of the Inter-American Development Bank, Camdessus was asked where he thought that "financial lightning" might strike next. "I suspect it will start with a banking crisis," replied Camdessus. Camdessus also demanded the urgent reform of Latin American banks so as to prevent repeats of the Mexican banking crisis in other nations. "Ladies and gentlemen," croaked Camdessus like the proverbial raven of ill omen, "Nevermore! Nevermore! This just cannot be so!" At the 1996 annual meeting of the IMF in Washington, Camdessus elaborated on this warning. He told the IMF board on October 1 "to take urgent care of the Achilles' heel of the global economy today, the fragility of national banking systems." Camdessus added that "in many countries a banking crisis is an accident waiting to happen.... On the basis of recent experience, let me tell you that this is something we truly don't want to see repeated.... We must also avoid the systemic consequences such a crisis can entail."

RECIPE FOR A DEPRESSION

The issue of economic depression, which it was for a long time taboo even to mention, has belatedly begun to preoccupy elite opinion-makers of the US Eastern Anglophile Liberal Establishment. The July 1996 issue of the *Atlantic Monthly* ran a cover featuring a "Recipe for a Depression," with the legend "mix falling wages, a push for zero inflation, and a bipartisan drive to eliminate the budget deficit. Simmer." This cover called attention to a featured package of two articles, the first entitled "The Forces Making for an Economic Collapse," written by New School economist Thomas I. Palley. Palley discussed the slow and anemic recovery from the Bush recession of 1990-91, the chronic weakness of consumer demand as families struggle under massive accumulations of consumer debt, and the dangerously deflationary impact of deficit-reduction measures like the proposed balanced budget amendment. He also criticized the apparent deflationary obsession of Alan Greenspan and the Federal Reserve Board, which was insisting on combating the specter of cost-push inflation even when real unemployment and underemployment were at a minimum of 14%. Palley pointed to the impact of labor-market globalization under free trade and the declining power of trade unions.

According to Palley, under NAFTA (the North American Free Trade Accord, which includes the US, Canada, and Mexico), the US merchandise trade surplus with Mexico, which was $5.4 billion in 1992, has turned into a deficit of $15.4 billion. If, as NAFTA backers claimed, every billion dollars of US exports translates in to 19,000 jobs, then NAFTA has already destroyed 395,200 jobs, many of them in manufacturing. In an interesting twist, Palley also listed the world-wide guild of professional free-trade economists, with their deflationary bias, as a cause of the possibly looming depression. As Palley summed up the situation:

> The past twenty-five years have witnessed a persistent weakening of structural conditions within the US economy. This weakening has been predicated on changes in labor markets which have undermined the position of American workers, polarizing income distribution and increasing job insecurity. The effects of these changes have been obscured by a debt binge by households and government, and by favorable demographic factors. However, households now face increasing financial constraints, government faces political constraints, and the demographic situation is changing radically. At the same time, in the face of increased capital mobility, wages continue to decline and job insecurity widens. These are the grounds for believing that the next economic recession could spiral into a depression." [Palley, 58]

US BANKS ARE INSOLVENT

The British Tory Lord William Rees-Mogg is the former editor of the *London Times*; he was a publicity man for Sir Anthony Eden's imperialist policy in the Suez fiasco of 1956. His resentment against the United States for refusing to rescue the British Lion from the Suez humiliation marks him, like many of his British contemporaries, down to this very day. Lord Rees-Mogg and his American annex James Dale Davidson have theorized about the financial outlook in a recent book. They wrote in 1993:

> We said that the 1990's would be a decade of depression. To a greater extent than conventional wisdom would allow, this forecast too, has come true. Britain is clearly in depression. The *Financial Times* said on October 16, 1992, 'The British economy is like a battered car on a steepening descent. The same can be said of Scandinavia. New Zealand and Australia entered slumps years ago and have not recovered. Unemployment in Canada has reached 11.8% as we write, 30% higher than it stood at the end of 1930." [Rees-Mogg, 13]

In Lord Rees-Mogg's view, the depression was already upon us. He cited the crushing debt burden of the advanced sector:

> Running huge debts to postpone a further decline in living standards has been considered a policy success by the few observers, like David Levy of the Jerome Levy Institute, who acknowledge that the current environment is a depression. Indeed, Levy worries that the government deficit may be too small to offset the implosion of the private economy.... Those

who speak optimistically about a 'contained depression' beg the question." [Rees-Mogg, 390-391]

Lord Rees-Mogg made no bones about that fact that some of the largest US money center banks were unsound: "The lowest-rated American banks, including the 'too-big-to-fail' banks, have $600 billion in assets, of which only $500 billion appeared to be performing in 1992. The capital of these banks is far less than $100 billion. They are insolvent." [Rees-Mogg, 398]

In the summer of 1997 Lord Rees-Mogg, partly because of the fall of the Tory government and the ascent of a Labour Party regime (albeit a Thatcherized one), became thoroughly pessimistic, and began to see Tony Blair (despite his "Cool Britannia" image) as the new Ramsay MacDonald of the current world economic depression. Let us concentrate on the financial aspects of Rees-Mogg's forecast. He writes: "After 1929, everyone vowed that there must never again be so great a Wall Street crash, and there never has been. Yet such crashes have occurred in other advanced stock markets, notably in the Tokyo market after 1989, that fell by about 70 percent from the peak, about as large a fall as Wall Street suffered in the three years after the 1929 crash. There is nothing in the organization of late-20th century stock markets which makes a crash impossible; indeed, some people think that the growth of derivatives makes a crash more likely.... the values on Wall Street are now out of line with any historical precedent in the 125 years of Wall Street statistics. There probably will be a major correction, and there certainly could be a crash. If it happens on Wall Street, it will also happen in London, though the London values are more moderate." [*London Times*, June 26, 1997]

LIKE THE ROLLING CRISIS IN AUSTRIA, MAY 1931

Then we have the veteran economist Charles Kindleberger, Paul Samuelson's colleague at MIT during the 1960s. Kindleberger was also aware that something had gone wrong in world finance: "In 1994 especially, a number of Latin American countries encountered trouble, the worst of which was felt in Mexico.... the United States and Canada came to the rescue.... The crucial and unanswerable question is whether in stopping the crisis in Mexico, the financial authorities may have prevented a run on emerging markets more widely, in a perhaps-fanciful analogy with the rolling crisis that started in Austria in May 1931." [Kindleberger, 186-187] The historical analogy is not fanciful but valid. But Kindleberger, like Greenspan, seemed to think that as long as we have an international lender of last resort, like the IMF or the BIS, any depression can be kept under control. He pays no attention to the hyperinflation that can derive from the monetizing of debt.

A CONTAINED DEPRESSION

Financial journalist Steven Solomon is the author of a useful insider account of how central bankers have attempted to cope with recurring threats of systemic crisis in the world financial system, a subject on which he is more blunt than many of his colleagues. Solomon acknowledged the existence during the early 1990s of a "contained depression," but quickly added that the way out of this situation is a global economy administered by a cabal of unelected central bankers, and not by national governments: "Like the stock market boom and abrupt global crash on Black Monday [October, 1987], the [1982-83] (less developed country or third world) debt crisis was a manifestation of the dangerous debt explosions and revulsions unleashed by the global capital regime. So too were the real estate overlending booms and busts in Japan, the United States, and the United Kingdom, which made the 1990s 'contained depression' unique in the postwar era." [Solomon, 41] But for the end of the nineties, Solomon saw a recovery in the US, thanks primarily to the efforts of the Greenspan Fed. Solomon thought that the real danger might come from a "curtailment of central bank independence in a futile effort to boost growth through lower interest rates, or to trade protectionism. Either could abort the world recovery prematurely and possibly topple the faltering world economic and monetary order." [Solomon, 493]

What will be the outcome of the great speculative episode of the 1990s? Historically, every boom had led at length to a bust. Economist John Kenneth Galbraith responded in a recent book that "...one thing is certain: there will be another of these episodes, and more beyond. Fools, as it has long been said, are indeed separated, soon or eventually, from their money. So, alas, are those who, responding to a general mood of optimism, are captured by a sense of their own financial acumen. Thus it has been for centuries; thus in the long future it will be." [Galbraith 1990, 110]

One of the most perceptive economists in the world is doubtless the Frenchman Maurice Allais, the winner of the 1988 Nobel Prize in Economics, which is awarded by the Bank of Sweden. Maurice Allais has been a consistent voice for realism, and a critic of the global hot-money finance system and of its ideology, the so-called doctrine of globalization. Economists of the Anglo-American school like to present globalization as a process of metaphysical inevitability. Allais is wise enough to show that globalization does not have ontological status, but is rather the product of the greed and blindness of certain power groupings or financier factions. "A gigantic accumulation of debt is eating away at the core of the world economy," wrote Allais in *Le Figaro* on November 29, 1993. "The pursuit of global liberalization of the exchange markets ... [is] at minimum adventurous, and in reality very dangerous." In January 1994, Allais assailed the globaloney gospel propagated by the World Bank and OECD in their pamphlet "Trade Liberalization: Global Economy Implications," which he categorized as "pseudo-scientific" and "totally erroneous." Allais commented that "the same men at the World Bank, OECD, and GATT who hold out the prospect of an increase in wealth of $213 billion per year [through free trade] by the year 2002, remain absolutely silent about the financial flows amounting to an average $1.1 trillion per day, 40 times more than the amounts corresponding to trade payments. These financial flows totally destabilize foreign exchange markets and make it impossible to apply trade agreements in any reasonable way. The fact that experts from such leading institutions practice such disinformation, consciously or unconsciously, is unbelievable." Allais pointed out in the spring of 1996 that "the globalization of the economy is certainly profitable for a group of privileged persons. But the interests of these groups cannot be equated to the interests of humanity. Rapid globalization must produce general unemployment, injustice, confusion, and instability. This is disadvantageous for all nations and is neither unavoidable, nor necessary, nor desirable." [*Le Monde*, April 9, 1996]

MELTDOWN CAUSED BY AN UNCONTROLLED DOLLAR PLUNGE

The 1994-1995 dollar dive that saw the battered greenback lose about 17% of its value against the Japanese yen and about 13% against the German mark was ostentatiously ignored or downplayed in many quarters, but it was taken seriously by some. One was Paul Erdman, remembered by many as the author of that engaging novel, *The Crash of 1979*, who dedicated a short book to this latest season of shocking monetary instability. Erdman was able to discover the potential for a systemic breakdown in the combination of currency gyrations, derivative speculation, and the uncertainty of international interbank settlement. Erdman warned that the "Herstatt effect" of 1974 might now be repeated on a vast scale. With foreign exchange transactions worldwide over $1 trillion per day by 1990, the value of Japanese fund transfers alone had reached 100 times the country's official Gross Domestic Product. Erdman cited BIS figures showing that it took less than three days for Japan's interbank funds transfer systems to generate a turnover equal to Japan's total economic output for one year. The same process also took about three days in the US, and four days in stodgier Germany. Erdman described this "ballooning" of the value of world financial transactions, citing Peter Norman of the *Financial Times*, who wrote that "big UK clearing banks have at times found the equivalent of their entire capital committed in temporary overdrafts by mid-morning. This need not matter if business flows normally. But in the event of a failure the authorities *could be confronted with a chain reaction that could jeopardize the world financial system.* " [Erdman, 72-73] Certainly no one could deny that the ballooning of international financial transactions, which had reached an estimated $5 trillion per day by the summer of 1997, contained the obvious potential for a liquidity crisis and consequent panic.

As Erdman summed up this latter eventuality: "Simulations carried out on the CHIPS system, one of the two large interbank transfer systems in the United States, have suggested that an unexpected failure by a big participant could result in nearly half of all institutions being unable to settle transactions, with perhaps a third of them being left in limbo. And because the dollar is the currency in which the vast majority of global financial transactions are settled, if the American clearing system goes down, so does the world's. The risk of a meltdown caused by an uncontrolled plunge in the dollar, which could set off a chain reaction that would start in the foreign exchange market but then spread throughout all derivative markets, is definitely there." [Erdman 75] This was clearly one of several potential Achilles heels of the entire System.

VOLCKER: A SYSTEM IN DISARRAY

One of the most celebrated protagonists of postwar financial and monetary affairs is at the same time associated with an almost apocalyptic pessimism regarding the dollar. We refer to Paul A. Volcker, a former official of the US Treasury and the former Chairman of the Federal Reserve Board of Governors. Volcker was present at the destruction of Bretton Woods at Camp David on August 15, 1971, and must bear significant responsibility for today's world economic depression, as we demonstrate further on in this book. Volcker knows from personal experience that when a dollar fall acquires momentum, the decline can be extremely difficult to stop, even when other governments try very hard to be cooperative. After Volcker's Plaza currency deal in 1985, the dollar lost 41% of its value against the Japanese yen – rather more than the central bankers had wanted. [Volcker, 269] One of the by-products of braking that fall of the dollar was the October 1987 world stock market panic.

The lability of the dollar is amply chronicled in Volcker's memoir *Changing Fortunes*, a kind of monetarist duet sung together with Toyoo Gyohten, formerly of the Japanese Finance Ministry at the Woodrow Wilson School in Princeton. In this memoir, Volcker admits his deep "concern about an excessive depreciation of the dollar." [Volcker, 279] Volcker cites a 1984 Federal Reserve memo which, he says, summed up his great fear for the fate of the greenback. That memo commented that "we have reached a rather uncertain equilibrium with a large budget deficit and a large current account deficit, both financed in large part by borrowing overseas ...the capital inflow can shift very quickly if confidence in the dollar should diminish. Such a loss of confidence in the dollar could be triggered for example by fear of the re-emergence of US inflation or a shift in the preferences of fickle investors." But Nixon's capitulation of August 15, 1971, counseled by Volcker, had placed the country at the mercy of such "fickle" investors in the first place. These risk factors remain emphatically with us.

When he was at the Fed, Volcker was constantly haunted by the fear that the dollar would suddenly disintegrate. "Sooner or later," he writes, "I thought there would all too likely be a sickening fall in the dollar, undermining confidence...." [Volcker, 180] He laments that President Reagan did not care about a dollar dive. In this connection Volcker has supplied his own epitaph as a policy maker: "Increases of 50 percent and declines of 25 percent in the value of the dollar or any important currency over a relatively brief span of time raise fundamental questions about the functioning of the exchange rate system. What can an exchange rate really mean, in terms of everything a textbook teaches about rational decision making, when it changes by 30 percent or more in the space of twelve months only to reverse itself? ...The answer, to me, must be that such large swings are a symptom of a system in disarray." [Volcker, 246] The world financial system described by Volcker is clearly crisis-prone and ultimately unworkable. Volcker's colleague Gyohten calls the current arrangement a "non-system" and he stresses that it "was not the result of anyone's choice." Rather, the global economy "was inevitable when the Bretton Woods system became unsustainable. What is wrong with the current non-system is its lack of stability and predictability in exchange rates, which seems to hurt the stable growth of trade and investment." [Volcker, 303-304] So we have been living for thirty years amidst the ruins of Bretton Woods. It is surely time to restore a functioning world monetary mechanism.

MONETARY MELTDOWN

Another analysis involving systemic breakdown as a consequence of dollar and other monetary instability comes from Judy Shelton of the Hoover Institution at Stanford University in her 1994 book, *Monetary Meltdown*. Here the starting point is the post-1971 currency chaos, which the author contrives to present as a result of Keynesian theory, even though it was the arch-monetarist Milton Friedman who was the loudest advocate of the abolition of government-set currency exchange rates. Shelton surveys the "breakdown in orderly currency relations around the world" and wonders if we are "slated for a new round of beggar-thy-neighbor exchange rate policies" reminiscent of the competitive devaluations pioneered by the British during the 1930s. With governments now officially excluded from the exchange rate business, Shelton wants them to intervene anew, but only so as to exclude themselves once again, this time via the institution of "honest money" in the guise of fixed parities, but with a brutally deflationary gold coin standard, an idea she says is backed by Robert Mundell, Jack Kemp, Lewis Lehrman, and others.

Shelton asks: "...in this nuclear age ... shouldn't we take evasive actions to halt the process that begins with currency turmoil and protectionist exchange rate policies and ends with political confrontation and the possibility of military conflict? . . Can the syndrome be interrupted to prevent a catastrophic outcome?" [Shelton, 12] What Shelton seems to have in mind is less a catastrophic financial breakdown crisis per se than a process of international conflict which escalates through trade war and economic war into military hostilities. "Money meltdown," she says, "is a warning sign that nationalistic economic policies are threatening to dissolve the trade and financial relationships that undergird a peaceful world community." [Shelton, 12] During the world financial turbulence occasioned by the Russian default, Ms. Shelton appeared from Paris on CNBC to call for a new Bretton Woods monetary conference to be prepared by an international commission chaired by Greenspan. She also wanted the US to apply conditionalities to the $18 billion refunding being sought by the International Monetary Fund. One useful aspect of her remarks was the demand that the United States subject the IMF to conditionalities about the use of the funds; the cherished dream of the IMF bureaucrats has long been to subject the United States itself to the *Diktat* of monetarist conditionality.

EMERGING MARKETS A CASINO

In October 1996 the German economic paper *Handelsblatt* carried an analysis by Rimmer De Vries, the well-known former resident economist of J.P. Morgan & Co. in New York. De Vries observed that "this time, unlike two years ago with Mexico, if problem debtor countries like

Thailand or Turkey have a currency crisis, there will not be any billion-dollar rescue packages. The crisis will simply be allowed to happen." This underestimated the addiction of the IMF to the bailout approach to crisis management. But in a timely warning for holders of US global economy mutual funds, De Vries also warned that "what today is called 'emerging markets' by the international credit markets, can only be likened to a casino. And the time will come when the banks and investment funds responsible for this will simply pull the rip cord."

L'HORREUR ECONOMIQUE

As the anaconda of economic globalization slowly tightened its coils of speculation, downsizing, and marginalization around the struggling body of humanity, thinkers of all sorts grappled with the need to comprehend the incubus of the end of the twentieth century. One who attracted international attention in 1996 was Viviane Forrester, the author of a longer essay entitled *L'Horreur Economique*. Mme. Forrester became a celebrity as a prominent critic of the *bateau ivre* of the new economic order, revered by students and other protestors against the Balladur-Juppé-Chirac policy of sacrificing the welfare of France to the all-consuming Moloch of the Maastricht treaty, with its monomaniacal 3% limit for budget deficits. The title of her book is drawn from a verse by Arthur Rimbaud (1854-1891), the French late romantic poet. Mme. Forrester, who had previously been a novelist, believed that world civilization has entered a time in which most people are superfluous, simply no longer needed by the rapacious and profit-obsessed ruling caste of financiers with laptops who spend their time trading "options on options on options" in international financial markets: "Pour la premiere fois – she writes – la masse humaine n'est plus materiellement necessaire, et moins encore economiquement, au petit nombre qui detient les pouvoirs...." Employment, she feels, is historically over, and it is only because of the cowardice of politicians that society maintains the pretense that unemployed persons should be forced to find jobs, when there are no jobs. "On ne sait" – she writes --"s'il est risible ou bien sinistre, lors d'une perpetuelle, indéracinable et croissante penurie d'emplois, d'imposer à chacun des chômeurs decomptés par millions – et ce, chaque jour ouvrable de chaque semaine, chaque mois, chaque année – la recherche 'effective et permanente' de ce travail qu'il n'y a pas." Dismayed by permanent mass unemployment in Europe, Mme. Forrester is of course too fatalistic, since high jobless rates are the result of identifiable government and corporate policies, and not of any fatal laws of economics as such. In reality, there is an abundance of productive work that needs to be done, but which is blocked by the financial system. But Mme. Forrester performs a useful public service when she warns that if high unemployment persists, it will be only a question of time before fascist demagogues (she points to the racist Jean-Marie LePen) come forward proposing the Final Solution for this new surplus population. Permanently high unemployment levels may elicit calls from financiers for the elimination of the useless eaters. In the global economy, the value of human life has indeed been cheapened. Mme. Forrester also succeeds in expressing some of the mutilation and degradation of humanity during the *saison en enfer* called globaloney. Her chilling message is that the outcome of the post-industrial utopia is not likely to be leisure and comfort, but rather genocide.

ONE BILLION UNEMPLOYED

The reality of world unemployment and underemployment is most stark. According to a September 1998 report from the UN's International Labor Organization, world unemployment was headed for 150 million persons, reflecting 10 million who had lost their jobs as a result of the crises of 1997-98. The ILO also reported that the number of persons either lacking full-time jobs or earning less than the minimum necessary for survival was between 750 and 900 million, or about 30% of the world population. Here was another eloquent indictment of globaloney.

THE DEPRESSED WORLD ECONOMY OF THE MID-1990s

The so-called "global economy" of the 1990s turns out to be a euphemism for a new and more acute phase of a world depression which has been going on since 1982. Only a purblind ideologue could argue that the global economy (or a globaloney economy) has been successful or beneficial for the people of the world. Under globaloney, Europe has taken the prize for mass unemployment, while the United States leads in the decline of living standards; Japan has experienced permanent recession and banking crisis. The old Soviet economic sphere, the COMECON, has lost up to two thirds of its factory and farm production, while Latin America has undergone a sharp contraction in jobs and living standards. In Africa, life expectancy was spiking downward. Southeast Asia, after a phase of expansion, is now beginning to pay the piper. The winners, by contrast, are tiny cliques of financiers and oligarchs.

If we examine a data series as fundamental as world crude steel production, we find stagnation during most of the 1990s at levels inferior to 1989. World steel production reached 785.9 million tons in 1989, but then fell for several years, touching an interim 1990s low of 722.7 million tons in 1992. After that, steel output hovered around 750 million tons, with 752 million tons in 1996.

For a time after World War II, the world economy was supported by the forward momentum generated in the United States. For two decades after 1945, economic progress was maintained by the reconstruction of Europe and Japan. Now, as we look across the world, there are no positive factors left, and no factors of stability. The US has been in productive decline for almost 40 years, since the 1958 recession. Japan has a banking crisis. Germany is drowning in unemployment and debt. Eastern Europe and the former Soviet sphere are being decimated by IMF shock therapy. Latin America is experiencing a violent contraction. Southeast Asia is rapidly beginning to fall apart. Africa is chiefly the theater of famine, civil war, and genocide. There is nothing left. The world speculative bubble has no visible means of support. It is a vagrant world.

GERMANY: MORE JOBLESS THAN WHEN HITLER SEIZED POWER

All European countries have been in recession throughout the 1990s, with brief periods of weak and ephemeral recovery. The case of Germany is highly instructive, since it also provides a barometer for the state of the entire world economy. For many years in the recent past, Germany has been the world's largest exporter, often exporting more than Japan, a country with almost twice its population. Now Germany, with a national debt of about DM 1.5 trillion at the end of 1995, has one of the heaviest per capita debt loads in the world. In January 1997, it was officially announced that Germany had 4.66 million unemployed – or 12.2 percent. To this figure must be added 320,000 part-time workers, 260,000 participants in government make-work programs, 1 million trainees and re-trainees who have dubious job prospects, and almost 2 million who have dropped out of the official government unemployment system and are working in the black economy, drugs, crime, and so forth. This makes a grand total of 8.138 million Germans who do not have a normal full-time job. New jobless claims in January 1997 over December 1996 – about 510,000 – also constituted the biggest one-time increase since the government began keeping official jobless figures during the 1920s.

Compare today's 8.138 million to the unemployment figure when Adolf Hitler seized power in Germany: then it was 6.1 million. Today's German unemployment, with a comparable population, is one third greater than in the depths of the Great Depression. There are true pockets of despair in eastern Germany, where youth unemployment is between 40% and 50%. According to Wilhelm Noelling, the former governor of the central bank of the German federal state of Hamburg, Germany is already in a "Maastricht depression."

Since the German economy is central to the European economy as a whole, we see that all of Europe is in depression, with more than 16 million official unemployed in the EU countries. Under current policies, there will be no European economic recovery. The deflationary Maastricht Treaty for European monetary union prescribes that no country can join the new European currency, the so-called euro, if its yearly budget deficit is more than 3% of its "gross domestic product." Entrance to the euro is also barred to countries whose public debt is more than 60% of their yearly gross domestic product. The country's rate of inflation must not exceed 3.3% The country's long-term interest rate must not exceed 9.3%. The country must have managed to show its exchange rate stability by joining the Exchange Rate Mechanism and remaining there for a prescribed time. By contrast, the unemployment rate can be sky-high, and the standard of living can be falling at any velocity - the country can still join the euro.

THE GNOMES OF LONDON

The Maastricht Treaty also creates an unelected, unaccountable private central bank which is beyond the reach of national governments and beyond the reach of the elected European Parliament in Strasbourg. Maastricht expressly forbids the issuance of subsidized credit or low-interest credit, which happens to be the only way to get out of depression. In the autumn of 1995, the attempt of the French regime of the neo-Gaullist Prime Minister Alain Juppé to observe the Maastricht austerity criteria elicited resistance from many levels of society in the form of the most extensive general strikes since 1968. At the time, Juppé tried to deflect the blame to British finance. Speaking in Avignon in mid-October, Juppé announced that "I do not want to cut the deficit in order to please the market, those people I'll call...the gnomes of London." Juppé specified that the gnomes of London were "the modern version of the gnomes of Zürich...speculators who take surplus value out of the economy...earning their living by creating tensions and difficulties for others."[12]

In May 1997, German pro-austerity Finance Minister Theo Waigel announced that falling German tax revenues made it unlikely that Germany itself could meet the infamous Maastricht convergence criteria. A year later, the discrepancies were papered over by accounting tricks. The grim European panorama extends to reputed strongholds of banking like Switzerland. Remember the fabled soundness of the Swiss banks? Guess again. According to a 1997 official report released by the Swiss Banking Commission, between 1991-1996, Swiss banks lost a total of 42.2 billion Swiss francs, a sum approaching $30 billion. Most of the losses had come in Swiss real estate since the mid-1980s speculative bubble burst in 1991.

THE EX-USSR

In the larger countries of the ex-USSR, including Russia and Ukraine, the "transition to a market economy" promised by the IMF turned out to be one of the most colossal disasters in modern history. In Russia, "economic reforms" like price deregulation and the privatization or sell-off of state property were carried out by President Boris Yeltsin, Prime Ministers Yegor Gaidar and Viktor Chernomyrdin, privatization czar Anatoly Chubais, and outside advisers Anders Aslund and Jeffrey Sachs. The policy was called shock therapy, and it was fully backed by Camdessus and the IMF. In launching this folly in October 1991, Yeltsin promised that the worst would be over by the end of 1992. But even after the end of Yeltsin's catastrophic 5 year plan at the end of 1996, there was no end in sight to the unfolding disaster.

---

[12] For the gnomes of Zürich, see Chapter IV.

Over the initial five year period of shock therapy, Russia's Gross National Product went down by 52%. IMF shock therapy turned out to be worse than Hitler: during the 1941-1945 onslaught of the Wehrmacht, the Soviet economy lost only 24%. During the four worst years of the Great Depression in America, GNP sank by just over 30%. Russian industrial production was down by 55%. This is again worse than 1929-1933 in the United States, when industrial production went down by just under 54%. Most dramatic, and most fraught with evil portent for the future, was the decline in investment, which was down by 78% by 1995 and kept falling.

Russia experienced a bout of hyperinflation during the first year of shock therapy in 1992, with prices rising by a rate of 1,354% over the entire year, and touching a momentary yearly rate of 2,318% by the end of December. In that dark December, Moscow prices were rising by about one per cent per day, conjuring up the specter of Weimar. After that, average yearly inflation subsided somewhat to 896% for 1993, 302% for 1994, 190% for 1995, and 48% during 1996. But real incomes kept dropping. During 1996, it was estimated that real incomes in Russia were down by about 46%. Inflation may be back to 300% by early 1999.

In the chronically troubled Russian farm sector, the grain harvest dropped from 99.1 million tons in 1993 to 81.3 million tons in 1994 and a disastrous 63.5 million tons in 1995. This was the worst result for Russian grain production in thirty years. 1996 was not much better with a harvest of 69.3 million tons. The 1998 harvest was the worst in 40 years, with only 48.6 million tons of grain officially reported. This was about half of the level of 1997. By 1994, Russian production of all kinds of food was estimated to be about half of what it had been during the last years of the Soviet era. Tractor production was down by 87%. Textile production was down by 85%. By October 1998, 15 million Russians – one out of every ten – were officially unemployed. An estimated 40% of the entire Russian population was below the very austere official poverty line. Those who were getting the minimum wage were receiving the equivalent of $5.50 per month, and wages were many months in arrears.

This economic implosion produced an unmistakable demographic impact: between 1992 and 1995 the Russian population declined by 728,000 persons, with a rising death rate combining with a falling birth rate to do the damage. In 1996 alone the birth rate dropped by an additional 5%. Speaking at a Woodrow Wilson Center forum in Washington DC on December 9, 1997, Dr. Murray Feshbach reported that the population of Russian was declining at a rate of 1 million persons per year. As causes for the decline, Feshbach singled out communicable diseases – both infectious and parasitic – and the material and psychological toll exacted by the economic crisis. The further social effects of shock therapy, especially the formation of a criminal elite in politics and business, have been strikingly chronicled by Stanislav Govorukhin in his book, *The Great Criminal Revolution*.

In the case of Ukraine, the economist and member of the national parliament Dr. Natalya Vitrenko reported that the gross domestic product of the country had fallen by 58% between 1990 and the end of 1996. The decline was 10% during 1996, so there was no sign even that the collapse was slowing. The 58% loss of GDP turned out to be worse than the collapse of production in Nazi Germany at the end of World War II, which totaled minus 56%. Submitting to the IMF thus turned out to be worse than losing a world war. Dr. Vitrenko estimated that of the 22 million jobs existing in Ukraine at the end of the Soviet era, 8 million had been destroyed. 71% of the Ukrainian population had a real income of less than $1 per day or less than $25 per month. 27% had incomes between $25 and $50 per month. Only 2% of the population got an income over $50 per month. The IMF puppets responsible for this carnage were President Leonid Kuchma and Prime Minister Pavlo Lazarenko. Ukraine was also suffering from an acute demographic disaster: the total population of the country fell from 52.2 million in 1992 to 50.5 million in mid-1998, a decline of 1.7 million or 3.25%.

LATIN AMERICA

After the brush with national bankruptcy in 1994-1995, the Mexican government was required as a precondition for international lending to impose a very severe austerity regime. This austerity produced a violent contraction in the levels of production and employment in the entire Mexican economy. Over the 1995, the austerity program produced more than 1 million new unemployed. By the end of 1996, Mexico had reached almost 50% unemployment, up from 41% in 1991. Productive employment – as distinct from service employment – has declined by a third since the eve of the first Mexican debt crisis in 1981. The Mexican manufacturing sector had declined by about one half over the same 15-year period. Mexico had a real international indebtedness of $214 billion, much more than the official figure. Bailout funds borrowed from the United States early in 1995 were repaid, but only by taking out loans from other borrowers. To avoid the worst of the contraction, Mexico needed an open-ended debt moratorium, the nationalization of its central bank, and exchange controls to prevent the flight of domestic hot-money capital. But Mexico got none of that. Other Latin American countries have been battered since December 1994 in a way similar to Mexico.

El Financiero of Mexico City reported that between 1994 and 1998, the number of indigent persons suffering from malnutrition in Mexico had risen from 20 to 26 million. According to this report, another 40 million of Mexico's 96 million population were living in extreme poverty, while another 20 million were surviving on incomes insufficient to buy even a third of what the UN Economic Commission for Latin America identified as the rock-bottom market basket for labor. This would mean that 86 million of Mexico's 96 million people were living in poverty. [13]

ASIA

For a number of years, Japan has been in the throes of its worst postwar downturn. Between April and July 1997, Gross Domestic Product declined by a sickening 11%, indicating a severe contraction in domestic economic activity. The Hashimoto government, inspired by monetarist criteria, responded to its large budget deficit (now estimated at 7% of GDP) by sharply increasing the tax bite, an austerity policy that only made matters worse. The background for these events was provided by the ongoing Japanese banking crisis, which, as noted, centers on some $1.5 trillion in bad real estate loans left over from the 1980s bubble economy. Japanese banks reported aggregate losses of $17 billion for the first 6 months of their 1997 fiscal year.

In South Korea, the beginning of 1997 saw the bankruptcy of Hanbo Steel, the country's second-largest steel company and a leading chaebol or conglomerate. Hanbo succumbed to a debt burden of about $6 billion, which was 22 times the company's equity. The demise of Hanbo also undermined a number of South Korea's leading banks, who were left holding the bag for this large debt. The impacted banks included Korea First Bank, Cho Hung Bank, the Korea Exchange Bank, the Seoul Bank, and the government-run Korea Development Bank. The Hanbo debacle was the opening of a protracted financial-political crisis in South Korea which featured the bankruptcy of the largest of the leading industrial groups, including Kia and other giant firms. Kia was nationalized and Korea First Bank received a government bailout.

Then began the collapse of the myth of the so-called "Asian Tigers" or NICs - "newly industrialized countries" - featuring Hong Kong, Thailand, Singapore, and Malaysia. At the beginning of March 1997, the largest and most prestigious finance company in Thailand, the $3.8

---

[13] *El Financiero*, September 2, 1998.

billion Finance One PLC, went bankrupt. From this obscure event commenced the unraveling of the entire world, something only deregulated globaloney could have made possible. The Thai government implemented financial emergency measures to prevent a total national panic and crash. Trading in all bank and financial institution stock was halted by the central bank, the Bank of Thailand. Finance One was quickly merged with the country's twelfth largest commercial bank, and a government bailout was carried out. The stock market fell to one half of its 1996 peak, and $700 million fled the Thai finance companies. IMF Managing Director Michel Camdessus quickly appeared on the scene, and called on ASEAN, the association of southeast Asian nations, to save Thailand by bailing out the international hot-money speculators. Camdessus complacently told the Thais: "What you are doing is exactly what you must do to avoid the recurrence of a Mexico-like crisis." As we have seen, this was bad advice. The Bank of Thailand affirmed its readiness to act as a buyer of last resort for the commercial paper and promissory notes of all finance companies.

One barometer of an incipient new and sharper phase of world decline in real economic terms was that world steel production fell by 0.2% during 1996, reaching 750.8 million tons. The decrease in production was largely attributable to the European Union and second-place Japan, which was down almost 3%. China became the world leader in steel production, increasing its output by 10.1%, becoming the only country to exceed 100 million tons of yearly steel output. The US was the third largest steel producer with 94.4 million tons of output. Among the IMF shock therapy victims, central Europe was down almost 10%, while the USSR successor states were down 3.3%

"A WORLDWIDE FINANCIAL EXPLOSION - YOU HAVE BEEN WARNED"

A couple of days before Halloween 1996, the *London Times* carried a remarkable column by City of London writer Anatole Kaletsky. The column warned that a "worldwide financial explosion" is at hand. "The great bull market may not yet be over. But it is suddenly in mortal danger," wrote Kaletsky. "Bonds round the world and the Anglo-Saxon currencies have entered the kind of wild speculative period when even aggressive investors may be well advised to stand aside – and stock markets cannot ignore a shock in bonds and currencies." "You have been warned," was Kaletsky's conclusion. Well-known Deutsche Bank investment guru Kenneth S. Courtis later told the German business daily *Handelsblatt* that, because of the Japanese banking crisis, world financial markets were at "five minutes to twelve" already during the spring and summer of 1995. Courtis noted that "world markets are spectacularly leveraged around this yen-dollar deal.... When a market is this lopsided, and it suddenly starts to go the other way, everyone's going to rush to get out the door at once when it blows." [*Handelsblatt*, November 4, 1996]

IRRATIONAL EXUBERANCE

A singular warning against excessive speculation came from Alan Greenspan, the Chairman of the Federal Reserve. Speaking on December 5, 1996 at the American Enterprise Institute, a stronghold of free enterprise ideologues, Greenspan asked: "How do we know when irrational exuberance has unduly escalated asset values, which then become subject to unexpected and prolonged contractions as they have in Japan over the past decade?" Greenspan went on to admonish market operators that "a collapsing financial asset bubble" would necessarily harm the overall economy. Much attention was focussed in the aftermath of this speech on the "irrational exuberance" section. Much less attention was given to the question of the "prolonged contraction" on the Japanese model, which is of course much scarier. Greenspan's delphic language referred to the collapse of the Japanese bubble economy in 1990-91, followed by the present $1 trillion plus banking crisis.

Towards the end of February 1997, speaking before the Senate Banking Committee, Greenspan embroidered this warning with further comments: "There is no evidence...that the business cycle has been repealed. Another recession will doubtless occur some day.... We have had 15 years of economic expansion interrupted by only one recession – and that was six years ago. As the memory of such past events fades, it naturally seems ever less sensible to keep up one's guard against an adverse event in the future.... However, caution seems especially warranted with regard to the sharp rise in equity prices during the past two years. These gains have obviously raised the question of sustainability," especially because of "very high earnings growth and continued rising profit margins." But later in 1997 Greenspan began to toy with the "New Paradigm" argument, which claims that the globaloney world economy has freed itself of the depressing old baggage of recessions and what not. More seasoned observers noticed that the "New Paradigm" blather was simply a new edition of the eternal slogan of the speculator fearing the inevitable retribution of the crash: "This time it's different." In June of 1998, Greenspan hailed "the best economy in fifty years."

BLACK FRIDAY WARNING FROM BEIJING

In mid-December 1996 the Chinese government newspaper *People's Daily* suggested that a new world stock market panic might be imminent. Although markets were now at dizzy heights, wrote *People's Daily*, "a drastic rise is bound to lead to a drastic fall, and there is no exception to this in stock markets at home or abroad .... The overheated stock market in China reminds us of the 1929 stock crisis in the United States [when] people of all strata were talking about stocks." The article went on to discuss the Japanese bubble economy of 1986-1990, the New York crash of October 1987, and the Mexican panic of 1994-95. In November 1994 Chinese Premier Li Peng had been asked whether the Chinese currency would soon be made convertible. "If our currency is convertible, another Black Friday crash in the US would hurt China," Li had replied at that time. As the Asian currency crisis of 1997-98 unfolded, it became evident that China was well served by the residual protectionist measures left in place.

PESSIMISM IN DAVOS, 1997

Every year in February important leaders of world banking and industry gather at Davos, Switzerland, on top of the Magic Mountain known to readers of Thomas Mann. Fred Bergsten of the Institute for International Economics in Washington set the tone for the 1997 proceedings with his warning of "potential major shocks to the world economy; any of them could hit in 1997. The most immediate and urgent problem is Japan." The Pollyanna view was that the Japanese banking crisis had been last year (1996), but that a US banking crisis might be on the agenda for 1997. Still others were terrified of the effects of the January 1, 1999 European monetary union. The European Monetary Union "might crash," thought Ulrich Cartellieri of Deutsche Bank. Gone was the arrogant optimism of earlier years that the "System" would be able to deal with all challenges that might emerge.

The Davos elitists were disturbed by the appearance of John J. Sweeney, the new president of the revived AFL-CIO. Before an audience long inebriated by globaloney, Sweeney warned of the dangers of attempting to import the "highly costly, very toxic" American model of labor docility. The destructive trends in the global economy, argued Sweeney, derive from "corporate choices, not economic laws. Too many companies rewarded by government incentives have taken the low road in international competition. They are cutting their workforces, their wages, and benefits. They are fighting against working people and their unions. They scour the globe in search of places where working people have low wages and no rights. This road has been paved by conservative administrations that cut back on the protections afforded working people, consumers, and the environment. They joined the assault on unions and labor rights. They passed trade agreements designed to protect the rights of those who invest their money, while ignoring the concerns of those who invest their time and labor." But the finance oligarchs remained wedded to these methods.

DOMINO EFFECT ON INTERBANK SETTLEMENT

During the Davos proceedings, Onno Ruding of Citibank posed the question of systemic meltdown: "In their crisis of 1990 US banks took appropriate steps. Japanese banks and the Japanese government have yet to take such steps. There is a real danger that a bank or other failure could have a domino effect on the interbank settlement system. What happens if, say, a Japanese bank in New York or London has a liquidity crisis at a time of day when Tokyo is sleeping? Would the problem get out of control in the few hours before Tokyo opened its business day?" A good question; Citibank itself has been to the brink so often during the last ten years that the precipice must feel like home.

A CRISIS OF OVERPRODUCTION?

At the beginning of 1997, William Greider published his *One World, Ready or Not: The Manic Logic of Global Capitalism*, an attempt to survey the new world order of rentier economy and the universal runaway shop. [Greider 1997] Greider's book provides much information, but also significant confusion. An example is Greider's habit of treating the US Federal Reserve as if it were a part of the United States government. Greider has spent enough time with Paul Volcker to know that the Federal Reserve is a private owned and privately managed institution which attempts to control the elected and constitutional government, rather than being controlled by it. To his credit, Greider tries to offer an overall theory of why the globaloney capitalism of the 1990's is so crisis-ridden. Unfortunately, Greider concludes that the global system is subject to crises of overproduction, of a glut of things to buy on the world market relative to effective demand.

For Greider, the central contradiction of the prevalent system is "...the global revolution's inclination to create new productive supply faster than the available demand can consume the goods. Too many auto factories chasing too few car buyers." [Greider 1977, 233] "The wondrous new technologies and globalizing strategies are able to produce an abundance of goods, but fail to generate the consumer incomes sufficient to buy them." [Greider 1997, 220] Greider cites Clyde Prestowitz of the Economic Strategy Institute to the effect that the United States is losing ground today because this country plays the role of the "market of last resort," condemned to absorb the excess capacity of all other countries in order to prevent a breakdown of the entire world system. [Greider 1997, 206] This US role leads to a weak labor market and downward pressure on real wages here, while workers in other countries get to keep their export-dependent jobs. (Prestowitz and his institute, Greider explains, speak "for US multinational manufacturers.") In the opinion of Greider and Prestowitz, US trade deficits, US foreign indebtedness, and the socioeconomic impact of excessive imports absorbed by the world's "buyer of last resort" are the key factor in a coming crisis. Greider plays up Prestowitz's forecast that "The trade deficits will provoke a moment when you have to say stop...Nobody knows when the moment is, but the longer you postpone it, the more indebted we become. Sooner or later, we are going to have to stop importing. But the other countries are refusing to import more. That's the point of breakdown. Sometime in the next five or ten years, we are looking at some kind of crisis." [Greider 1997, 209] Another of Greider's authorities, Christopher Whalen, adds: " We are headed for an implosion. If you keep lowering and lowering wages in the advanced countries, who's going to buy all this stuff? You look around and all you can see is surplus labor and surplus goods. What we don't have is enough incomes. But the only way people find out there are too many factories is when they wake up one morning and their orders are falling. If this keeps up, we're going to face a lack of demand that's worse than the 1930's." [Greider 1997, 221]

The notion that capitalist crises are essentially crises of overproduction is an old one, which has been carried forward in British economics from Parson Malthus to Lord Keynes. Malthus, it will be remembered, warned the capitalists that no one would be able to buy their production if they did not support a state church with a well-paid clergy, and added that a "Church with a capacious maw is best." Keynesian make-work schemes had essentially the same inspiration. But the reality of today's world is not overproduction or a glut of commodities on the world market. Today's world is a world of underproduction and tragic underconsumption. Today's world is a world of hunger and want, far worse than the Bretton Woods world of 1944-1971. World per capita production of the vast range of industrial and agricultural commodities is stagnant or falling. The United States has perhaps the fastest-falling standard of living of the traditional OECD countries, but we have no monopoly on declining conditions of life. Living standards are falling like a rock in the old COMECON states, in Africa, and in Latin America. Europe and Japan are also in decline, while Southeast Asia is falling fastest of all.

From his mistaken idea of overproduction, overcapacity and the unsustainability of US trade deficits, Greider derives the threat of a systemic world financial crisis. Greider is better than many writers when it comes to recognizing the relative autonomy of financial markets to over-speculate and multiply paper IOUs, without reference to the underlying realities of production: he identifies a "basic elasticity in the value of financial assets that allows financial markets, in extreme circumstances, to become unhinged from the tangible realities of commerce... Financial prices, whether one thinks they are sound or illusory, are rising much faster than the economic activity upon which they are presumably based." [Greider 1997, 230, 232]

Overproduction and over-speculation combine for Greider to produce the threat of breakdown: "The evidence of recent years – recurring bubbles of private and public debt that go bad and abruptly collapse – strongly suggests that it is finance capital that is overreaching reality .... The growing imbalance of industrial overcapacity ultimately means that the capital investors must be disappointed too, since they are busy investing in more factories than the world really needs. Sooner or later the marketplace will discard many of those surplus factories. When that happens, the capital invested in them fails, too." [Greider 1997, 233] Greider is lucid enough to see that the Japanese banking crisis of summer 1995 had taken the entire world system to the brink of catastrophe. In those days, he says, "the world was, in fact, flirting with a large, historic crisis – the threat of a general deflation like the 1930's – and major governments were more nervous than they revealed. If Japanese banking collapsed, it would likely bring down the world system." [Greider 1997, 254] "Adhering to its own principles," he says, "the rentier regime was flirting visibly with catastrophe, a monetary disorder the world had not experienced in sixty years: a full-blown deflation of prices, collapsing values for both financial assets and for real goods and labor." [Greider 1997, 305] We should note in passing that those who approach the study of the global system from the point of view of production and the runaway shop are likely to be more impressed by the deflationary tendencies, while those who study the ballooning of the financial aggregates come away thinking of hyperinflation.

Greider's conclusion on the globaloney system is pessimistic, as he lets megaspeculator George Soros sum it up: "I cannot see the global system surviving. Political instability and financial instability are going to feed off each other in a self-reinforcing fashion. In my opinion, we have entered a period of global disintegration only we are not yet aware of it." [Greider 1997, 248] Greider's own final financial forecast sounds like this: "Alternatives to further deregulation of global finance are seldom discussed in the US press or politics and are automatically derided by influential economists and bankers. The orthodoxy reigns confidently despite gathering signs of systemic stress...The future will eventually reveal whether dire warnings such as mine are justified, whether the optimism of finance capital is well founded or another tragic episode of manic, misplaced hopes." [Greider 1997, 258]

As the crisis unfolded, Greider's Malthusian-Keynesian prejudice led to more serious consequences. In October 1998 he was still talking about "the fundamental problem of overcapacity that already exists worldwide," and demanding that "somebody somewhere must close lots of factories."[14] But this was what the globalized bankers themselves were demanding, and what the crisis was tending to accomplish. An executive of ING Barings told the *Far Eastern Economic Review* in October 1998 that "to achieve equilibrium, 78% of all manufacturing capacity in Indonesia, 77% of that in South Korea, and 64% of that in Malaysia and Thailand will have to shut down."[15] *Wall Street Journal* ideological overseer Robert Bartley (one of the clique around Kenneth Starr) wrote that China and the former Asian tigers all suffer from "overinvestment and overcapacity. Instead of taking its lumps and enduring some creative destruction, China is engaging in a huge round of state-financed investment." "The lesson for developing countries in Asia and elsewhere," Bartley added, "is that it's useless to try to dodge the bullet of creative destruction through capital controls or extravagant fiscal stimulus." Greider's Malthusian prejudice thus leads him to a deplorable convergence with some of the most ruthless spokesmen of the world finance oligarchy.

THE $55 TRILLION HORROR SHOW

Another alarm came from the Hollinger Corporation, the well-known British intelligence outlet, through one of its flagship newspapers, the London *Sunday Telegraph*. The occasion for this comment was the announcement of a $144 million derivatives loss by the National Westminster Bank, one of London's big clearing banks. On March 9, 1997, in Neil Bennett's City Editor's Comment, one could read the following:

> I had dinner with Tony Dye last week, the PDFM fund manager, who has famously taken a £ 7 billion bet on a market crash.... In the wake of NatWest's derivatives scare [a £ 90 million loss], he conjured up a scenario that would give small children nightmares. The total value of derivatives in the world today is $55 TRILLION. That is $55,000,000,000,000 to the layman - a tidy sum and twice as large as the world's gross domestic product.... Every bank has vast derivative liabilities. Barclay's, for example, admitted in its results that it had derivatives worth 922 BILLION pounds at the end of last year, up more than a quarter on 1995. If a domino effect rippled through the world's derivatives markets, it could knock over some very big institutions. This is where the nightmare turns nasty. Who would bail the banks out? Governments and central banks of course. But governments are already today's largest debtors, which does not make them the ideal candidates to rescue the financial system. They could only do it by printing money. That is the sure path to hyperinflation and sky-high interest rates. The value of money would be destroyed and savings and pensions along with it.

---

[14] William Greider, "The Global Crisis Deepens," *The Nation*, October 19, 1998.
[15] *Far Eastern Economic Review*, October 1, 1998.

The figure offered here for world derivatives exposure is much too low, but there is no doubt that a central bank bailout of worthless derivatives would indeed generate the greatest hyperinflation of all time.

DERIVATIVES MELTDOWN

Although Kindleberger ignores, and Rees-Mogg denies, any threat of hyperinflation, Neil Bennett is able to see it as a clear and present danger. To underline their concern, the editors of the London *Sunday Telegraph* repeated their warning on March 16, 1997: "The City's worst nightmare, a meltdown provoked by a crisis in derivatives markets, suddenly looks less like a lurid chapter from a paperback, and more like a future event... the financial world is asking whether this latest debacle is a NatWest problem, or a warning of a potential, systemic nightmare for the burgeoning world of derivatives." Around the same time, the London *Daily Telegraph* was warning that a market crash was inevitable. One article commented as follows: "It is almost certain – though bullish dealers in the City may wishfully deny it – that share prices will take a tumble some time this year.... A stock market crash? But surely things have never looked rosier on the rosy pages of the *Financial Times*. In the City, the mood has not been so euphoric since the mid-1980s. But nothing is more certain, in the world of financial markets, than this: what goes up must, sooner or later, come down.... The only question is when the crisis of the 1990s will come, and how big it will be."

DERIVATIVES NIGHTMARE SCENARIO

According to the Hollinger people, derivatives are the big factor of Anglo-American financial instability: "The nightmare scenario today, is that something similar could happen in New York and London. For now it is the British and American banks, their portfolios bulging with 'derivatives,' that look dangerously exposed. NatWest has just found out how perilous that market can be.... So don't be too confident that the bankers have learnt the lessons of history. And don't forget another reason for being uncheerful: many governments have been running unjustifiably large budget deficits. In the event of a downturn, that could mean a fiscal crisis to compound the monetary crisis." This analysis was on firm ground as far as it went.

Also during the late winter of 1997, Fed boss Greenspan addressed a meeting of the Atlanta Federal Reserve district officers, telling them "There have been occasions when we have been on the edge of a significant breakout," bankerspeak for a systemic crisis and meltdown. But, claimed Greenspan on this occasion, the Fed response has so far "turned out to be adequate to stem the atomic erosion."

Parts of American academia picked up the cudgels to defend derivatives. One was professor Burton G. Malkiel, the Chemical Bank Chairman's Professor of Economics at Princeton University. The most recent edition of Malkiel's book *A Random Walk Down Wall Street* was published in 1996, but the preface is dated March 1995, meaning that Professor Malkiel would have had an opportunity to ponder the Orange County and Barings bankruptcies, both of which he does mention. But even in the light of these experiences, he denies the potential for a systemic crisis triggered by a derivatives crash. Wrote Malkiel: "Hysteria seems especially out of place when people proclaim that the large losses triggered by derivatives could threaten the stability of the world financial system. While enormous leverage and extraordinary potential losses from derivatives will continue to receive banner headlines, a number of international study groups have concluded that a spreading world financial crisis caused by derivatives is highly unlikely. Speculators who take large risks will continue to risk ruin, and some financial institutions – even large ones – will continue to fail. But a systematic undermining of world financial stability caused by derivatives trading does not deserve to be on the top of anyone's worry list." [Malkiel, 305] Malkiel went on to advise the small investor to buy options to hedge index mutual funds, to use index options and futures for hedging, and even to write options as a part of portfolio management. But small investors need to be warned that any time you write an option, you risk infinite losses that can utterly wipe you out. They should beware of Professor Malkiel's advice, which appears destined to be inscribed on the walls of the same Princeton pantheon of punditry where we find the assurances of his illustrious predecessor, Professor Joseph Stagg Lawrence, one of the famous optimists of early October 1929.

A VERY DEEP DEPRESSION

Not everyone viewed Greenspan as infallible. The Fed boss thought full employment, rising wages and economic growth over 2.5% per year were all highly dangerous because they might interfere with speculation – a good summary of the outlook of those who command the System. One critic of Greenspan was Harvard economics professor and former Clinton administration Secretary of Labor Robert Reich. Some months after leaving office, Reich warned of a possible new depression in an interview with Martin Walker of the London *Guardian*. Reich suggested that all is not well with the much-admired US economy. "When the bottom half of the workforce gets low-wage and insecure jobs, and when you're not investing both publicly and privately, what do you have five years from now, but watered-down Republicanism?" In Reich's view, the villains are central bankers and financiers who push deflationary austerity at the expense of the common good. "Social inequality," Reich went on, "is widening fast, insecurity is rampant, and our savings are being invested all round the world, rather than here. Corporate chiefs got raises of 50 percent last year, but not ordinary people, and they are living in gated, guarded communities, in a divided society.... Nations are defined by their implicit social contracts, and to sacrifice that on the altar of central bankers, is in my view a great failure." Reich concluded with comments on Europe: "Joining the Euro may be fine in the long run. But to move so quickly, and impose so much fiscal austerity, risks turning a situation of high structural unemployment into an even worse crisis.... It is the very opposite of what one would want in policy right now. The recovery has not yet taken hold in Europe, and if Europe goes on an austerity binge, and then the U.S. follows suit for fear of inflation, then I would not be surprised if we all head into a very deep depression." [*Guardian*, April 22, 1997] Reich evoked the long-taboo specter of economic depression in another interview a few days later with the *London Observer*, warning that the Federal Reserve has "forgotten the specter of the Thirties depression." The Fed's policies have increased poverty in the U.S, said Reich.

FEDERAL RESERVE: UNELECTED AND UNACCOUNTABLE

Another recent somber prognosis for the US economy came from James Medoff, Reich's colleague in the Harvard economics department, and from co-author Andrew Harless. The Medoff-Harless analysis sees the United States as *The Indebted Society*, falling deeper and deeper into crisis, in a kind of deflationary spiral they described as follows:

> ... the lender-friendly policies of the Indebted Society push it deeper into debt. The power of lenders, and the economic ideas that have flowed from this power, produce policies designed to minimize the risk of increased inflation.... As a result, lenders become more important, and their power increases. As the Indebted Society goes deeper into debt, its interest burden increases, and it must borrow more to service its existing debt. Consequently, it goes even deeper into debt. The deeper the Indebted Society and its members go into debt, the less their resources can support that debt. As the debt increases relatively to those

resources, so does the risk that the debts cannot be repaid. Creditors therefore demand higher interest rates to compensate then for higher risk. The debts then become more difficult to service, and the cycle of debt upon debt is intensified. [Medoff and Harless, 159-160]

Although the authors do not spell it out, it is obvious enough that this cycle leads towards default and bankruptcy. Medoff and Harless look around for resources that might be mobilized to produce more, thus allowing for an end to borrowing and a reduction of debt. They recognize that these resources do exist, specifically in the form of the swelling ranks of the unemployed and underemployed. Their conclusion is that "...America does have slack resources, and the decision not to use those resources is deliberate. That decision is being made by unelected and unaccountable officials at the Federal Reserve and is being encouraged by the vast majority of economists at America's universities." But in the end our authors shy away from any direct political challenge to the Federal Reserve System, proposing instead such palliatives as cash bonuses to Fed directors if overall national economic performance, including unemployment, were to improve. But one suspects that the bondholders could always offer larger incentives than government ever could.

The Federal Reserve and its foreign opposite numbers in the world system of private central banks think that robust economic growth, full employment, and rising wages are all dangerous. The French economist Alain Parguez has coined phrases for this state of affairs, which he calls the "international rentier economy" and the "rentier welfare state." Parguez and Mario Seccareccia have argued that "governments are entering into debt and borrowing heavily from individuals or financial institutions just to pay interest income to what is largely the same class of high income earners or rentiers at usurious rates set by...the respective countries' central banks." [Parguez] This certainly applies to the United States, where the biggest component in federal budget deficit during most of the 1990s has been debt service on the national debt.

WHITE HOUSE WORKING GROUP ON FINANCIAL MARKETS

After the 1987 stock market crash, the US government assembled a special financial crisis pre-planning group consisting of the Secretary of the Treasury, the Chairman of the Federal Reserve Board, the Chairman of the Securities and Exchange Commission, and the Chairman of the Commodity Futures Trading Corporation (CFTC). This group has been occupied for a decade with the review of crisis scenarios (like the one at the beginning of the Appendix) and with the development of contingency plans. These contingency plans have been codified and placed in the hands of the top officers of stock markets across the country. The SEC emergency plan is officially titled Executive Directory for Market Contingencies, and is unofficially known as the "red book." The CFTC has an equivalent emergency handbook for the futures markets.

According to one account, "The Working Group's main goal...would be to keep the markets operating in the event of a sudden, stomach-turning plunge in stock prices – and to prevent a panicky run on banks, brokerage firms, and mutual funds. Officials worry that if investors all tried to head for the exit at the same time, there wouldn't be enough room – or in financial terms, liquidity – for them all to get through. In that event, the smoothly running global financial machine would begin to lock up ...worries about the financial strength of a major trader could cascade and cause other players to stop making payments to one another, in which case the system would seize up like an engine without oil." In plain English, they are looking at the question of CHIPS breakdown raised above. Fed boss Greenspan is said to have given his "irrational exuberance" speech to the White House Working Group behind closed doors at the end of 1995, a full year before he warned in public about excessive speculation.

Among the contingencies studied by the White House Working Group are "a panicky flight by mutual fund shareholders; chaos in the global payment, settlement, and clearance systems; and a breakdown in international coordination among central banks, finance ministries, and securities regulators...." [*Washington Post*, February 23, 1997] The White House group has extensive contact with the London financial community, and also with GLOBEX, the world-wide futures trading system owned by the Chicago Mercantile Exchange. At the very minimum, such extensive focus on possible financial calamities suggests that the US Government does not believe that world financial markets are "shockproof." But the approach suggested by press accounts may soon prove to be the opposite of what is needed, especially in the face of incipient banking panic.

BIS: "WE SIMPLY DO NOT KNOW"

On June 9, 1997 the private central bank of private central banks, the Bank for International Settlements (BIS) of Basel, Switzerland, issued a sibylline admission that the world financial system was careening out of control and toward crisis. The BIS first sheepishly admitted that many of the financial and economic events of 1996 had been "surprising" from the point of view of its theoretical forecasts. Can these surprises be explained? The BIS replied: "One part of an honest answer is that we simply do not know. Rapid technological change and deregulation, which today profoundly affect all aspects of the global economy, increasingly cloud our sense of what is possible and reasonable....There are many economic processes that we do not fully understand." The BIS offered a disconcerting survey of this "overbanked" world, where "rents from established franchises" are increasingly "threatened." There is the problem of "bank fragility in Asia," along with that of "restructuring" in Ibero-America. Underlying the whole picture is the "downside" that "liberated financial sectors are prone to more costly misadventures," including "the risk to 'gamble for resurrection' .... When the bubble bursts, banks and their customers will face major difficulties." The BIS repeated what is already well known: namely that the great threat of breakdown to the international financial system is located in the netting, settlement, and payments system, which today has to handle $5 trillion of daily turnover in the international currency, derivatives, and interbank clearing pipelines. "It has also been recognized for some time that failures in payment and settlement systems for large-value transactions constitute a potential source of systemic fragility," said the BIS. "While we have not yet experienced the economic losses that might be associated with a major failure in payments systems...a few close calls in recent years were wake-up calls." To avoid these pitfalls, the BIS wanted "a world with no barriers to universal banking" and a "framework which will preserve the financial system, regardless of the kinds of shocks or the degree of asset price inflation to which it might be subjected." The BIS, we see, was far less sanguine than Mr. Kapstein. The bewildered paralysis of the BIS reflected here is an encore performance of the BIS's inability to do anything to stop the central European banking crisis of 1931-33.

William H. Gross of the PIMCO funds, billed as "the Peter Lynch of bonds," brought out a new book entitled *Everything You've Heard About Investing Is Wrong!* in which he advised his readers to prepare emotionally for the "coming post-bull market," which the author predicted would become known as the "era of 6%." Investors, recommended Gross, would have to bite the bullet and learn to live with those modest yields. Soon this perspective might look like paradise.

Milton Friedman argued that the International Monetary Fund was obsolete and ought to be abolished on libertarian grounds. Former Treasury Secretary William Simon asserted logically enough (from his point of view) that since "the market" was now setting currency parities, there was no more need for the International Monetary Fund, which therefore ought to be abolished as a big-government dinosaur. Simon pointed out that his predecessor at Treasury, George Shultz, had already gone on record in 1995 in favor of liquidating the IMF. Back then, Shultz had told the American Economic Association that the IMF has "more money than mission." Shultz had wanted to "merge this outmoded institution with the World Bank, and create a charter for the new organization that encourages emphasis on private contributions to economic development."[16]

GROUP OF THIRTY: A ONE IN FIVE CHANCE OF SERIOUS DISRUPTION

A little more than a month after the BIS report was issued, the London *Financial Times* pondered the recent warnings on the lability of the world financial system that had come from Greenspan, from the BIS, and also from Gerald Corrigan, the man who had been the head of the New York Federal Reserve Bank during the late 1980s. (Corrigan, as the *Financial Times* editorial page noted, had "warned that the growing complexity and integration of financial flows would make it much harder to manage shocks such as the 1987 stock market crash.") As the *FT* saw it, the common note of these warnings was that "the frothiness of markets could have systemic consequences." To these three Cassandras the *Financial Times* added a fourth, the financial think tank that calls itself the Group of Thirty. This body had issued a report dealing with "limiting systemic risk in a world where the larger financial institutions and markets have outgrown national accounting, legal and supervisory arrangements." The finding of the Group of Thirty, which even the *Financial Times* must concede is too complacent, estimates "...the likelihood of a serious disruption of the international financial system at one in five over the next five years..." The "practitioners" surveyed were confident that they themselves and their counterparties would infallibly be spared. And they hastened to add that although disturbances were indeed possible, "any shock is not expected to spread far beyond the point of impact." [*Financial Times*, July 15, 1997] And in any case, opined the report, governments will be forced to bailout improvident speculators if they are big enough: "...since many global players are likely to be deemed too big to fail if threatened with insolvency, taxpayers of the world are heavily at risk." Even as this was being released, the 1997 Asian crisis, the biggest world economic and financial upheaval since 1931, was building towards its explosion.

ASIA BOILS OVER[17]

During the summer of 1997, a series of "emerging market" currencies which had pegged themselves to the dollar went into crisis. The currencies included the Czech crown, the Thai baht, the Malaysian ringgit, the Philippine peso, and the Indonesian rupiah. These currencies had gotten into severe difficulty because of the dollar's momentary appreciation against the yen and mark: the currencies in question had been carried so high by the dollar that they had priced themselves out of other export markets. After some years of export surpluses, they developed balance of payments problems. When this situation was noticed by Soros and the other hedge fund operators, the currencies came under heavy speculative attack through short selling and other techniques. The Prague authorities tried to defend the crown with interest rates of 75%. In July 1997, Thailand was unable to keep servicing its estimated $110 billion of foreign debt. Thailand was obliged to submit to the draconian monetarist dictates of the International Monetary Fund, which entailed a humiliating loss of national sovereignty for a people whose claim to fame has historically been that they never accepted subjection to foreign colonialists.

Soros' speculative offensive may have been motivated by political considerations as well as by his desire for windfall profits. By targeting the currencies with dollar pegs, he was in effect seeking

---

[16] William E. Simon, "Abolish the IMF," *Wall Street Journal*, October 23, 1997.
[17] This was the 30th post-war systemic crisis; see table in Chapter IV.

to undermine the economic links between the United States and its Asian partners and erode what was left of the formal dollar zone. Perhaps the beneficiary was to be the euro, whose backers clearly aspired to terminate the dollar's role as the world reserve currency. In addition, with Asia depressed and the Japanese yen in crisis, the euro would be more important, and would be able to buy up assets at fire-sale prices. In any case, a very large part of the hot money used to attack the Asian dollar pegs came from institutions based in Britain and the European Union.

MAHATIR INDICTS SOROS

The government of Malaysia formally protested the speculative attacks on the ringgit masterminded by Soros and his Quantum Fund. In August 1997, Malaysia was unable to make scheduled payments on its $50 billion in foreign debt. Foreign Minister Abdullah Ahmad Badawi complained to US Secretary of State Madeleine Albright that southeast Asian currencies "continue to be bedeviled by currency fluctuations caused by hostile elements bent on such unholy actions." "It is the height of international criminality that the fate of millions could be subject to the mercy of a few unscrupulous traders," said the Malaysian minister. In response to these charges, the US State Department reached a new low, with spokesman Nick Burns defending Soros as "an honorable individual who has done a lot of good things around the world" and sniffing that the Malaysian protests were "inappropriate." Soros is under investigation in Italy and Croatia, and has not been forgotten by the British widows and orphans whom he despoiled by helping to force a pound devaluation in September 1992. Soros is widely resented in eastern Europe, Ukraine, Russia, and related areas. By endorsing the most predatory international speculators of this type, the United States government was sowing a whirlwind of hatred which may be reaped through the needless suffering of individual Americans under future circumstances now impossible to predict, but easy to guess at.

Malaysian Prime Minister Dr. Mahatir Bin Mohamad renewed his indictment of Soros at the 1997 annual meeting of the International Monetary Fund, which was held in Hong Kong, a city which had recently been ceded back to China by the British. Addressing the annual meeting of the World Bank on September 20, 1997, Mahatir made the following remarks:

> We now know that even as Mexico's economy was manipulated and made to crash, the economies of other developing countries too can be suddenly manipulated and forced to bow to the great fund managers who have now come to be the people to decide who should prosper and who should not .... Everyone gains from 'prosper-thy-neighbor' policies, while only one side gains from 'beggar-thy-neighbor' mindsets ... . But the currency traders have become rich, very, very rich, through making other people poorer. These are billionaires who do not really need any more money. Even the people who invest in the funds they operate are rich. We are told that the average return is about 35% per annum. And we are told that we are not worldly if we do not appreciate the workings of the international financial market. Great countries tell us that we must accept being impoverished, because that is what international finance is all about. Obviously, we are not sophisticated enough to accept losing money so that the manipulators become richer. We are also warned that these are powerful people. If we make a noise or we act in any way to frustrate them, they would be annoyed. And when they are annoyed, they can destroy us altogether, they can reduce us to basket cases. We have to accept that they are around, that they will always be around, and that there is really nothing we can do about it. They will determine whether we prosper or we don't ... I mention all these, because society must be protected from unscrupulous profiteers. I know I am taking a big risk to suggest it, but I am saying that currency trading is unnecessary, unproductive and immoral. It should be stopped. It should be made illegal. We don't need currency trading. We

need to buy money only when we want to finance real trade. Otherwise we should not buy or sell currencies as we sell commodities ... We like to think big. We even have great ideas for bringing wealth to other developing countries. We proposed the development of the Mekong Valley, beginning with the railroad from Singapore to Kunming, because we know that transportation will stimulate economic development. It is a big project, but small projects make little impact on the economy .... But we are not going to be allowed to do this, because you don't like us to have big ideas. It is not proper. It is impudent for us to try, or even say we are going to do it. If we even say that when we have the money we will carry on with our big projects, you will make sure we won't have the money by forcing the devaluation of our currency.

This was the most courageous and far-reaching critique of the globaloney economy of the late twentieth century so far offered by a head of government. It was clear that Mahatir was acting as the spokesman for an informal group of developing countries and Asian countries, and that his critique enjoyed sympathy in certain quarters of the Chinese government, as well as in traditionalist circles in Japan. His speech had conjured up the long-overdue world revolt against the globaloney tyranny.

On the following day, September 21, 1997, the financial corsair George Soros attempted a reply to his persistent antagonist. It is significant that Soros was unable to answer without himself citing the immediate danger of a world financial "bust":

We do live in a global economy .... But global capitalism is not without its problems ...I have seen many ebbs and flows and booms and busts. I fully recognize that international capital markets have become much more institutional in character and demonstrate much greater resilience, but I cannot believe that the present boom will not be followed by a bust until history has proven me wrong. The risk of a breakdown is greatly increased by the fact that our theoretical understanding of how financial markets operate is fundamentally flawed .... Dr. Mahatir's suggestion yesterday to ban currency trading is so inappropriate that it does not deserve serious consideration. Interfering with the convertibility of capital at a moment like this is a recipe for disaster. Dr. Mahatir is a menace to his own country...If social services are cut when instability is on the rise, it may well engender popular resentment and lead to a new wave of protectionism both in the United States and in Europe, especially if and when the current boom is followed by a bust of some severity. This could lead to a breakdown in the global capitalist system, just as it did in the 1930's....

Soros' tirade is a clinical specimen of the globaloney mentality. The globalized system is headed for a breakdown, he says, but you must on no account attempt to head this off by regulating it. Greenspan's response to the Long Term Capital implosion (discussed below) had the same irrational quality.

SELL STOCK NOW!

As the Dow Jones Industrial average passed the 8000 mark in July 1997, a number of America's mass-circulation magazines began to express their nervousness over whether stocks were overpriced and might soon be subjected to a "correction." In mid-1996, *Business Week* had celebrated "Our Love Affairs with Stocks" on its front cover, proclaiming "Never before have so many people had so much riding on the market," although hedging its hype with the question, "Should we worry?" [18] A year later, it was time to worry. *Money* magazine's August 1997 issue showed on its cover an average investor sitting perilously at the crest of what looked like Prechter's tidal wave. The

---

[18] "Our Love Affairs with Stocks," *Business Week*, June 3, 1996.

headline read: "Don't Just Sit There... SELL STOCK NOW!" Further reading revealed that the magazine's recommended tactic involved the liquidation of only a modest 20% of stock portfolios in favor of bonds and cash.

During the same week, *Time* offered its readers an account of "Wall Street's Doomsday Scenario," detailing the preparations afoot among brokers, mutual fund managers, and government agencies for dealing with an approaching meltdown or other event marking the end of the bull market. Despite the trading curbs and pauses instituted by the New York Stock Exchange, warned *Time*, "another meltdown is quite possible. And that hasn't been lost on a number of institutions quietly preparing for the worst. Some of the nation's largest mutual-fund companies, like Vanguard and Fidelity, have detailed battle plans should the market fall apart." *Time* feared mutual fund redemptions, but placed great stock in the Fed's ability to lower interest rates, and stressed the need to keep market functioning in an orderly way. Merrill Lynch's energency plan included setting up a crisis staff on the 32nd floor of its Manhattan headquarters. Vanguard planned to mobilize a "Swiss army" of 1,000 brokerage temps who would try to prevent panic among shareholders. At Fidelity, phone jacks were poised to fall from the ceiling of the cafeteria to service phones manned by temps ready to urge shareholders not to sell.[19]

SYSTEMIC RISK THROUGH SETTLEMENT RISK

One obvious vulnerability of the present world financial system which has emerged from the discussion so far is the high potential for liquidity crisis, especially in case of gridlock in the interbank netting, settlement, and payment system. By the fall of 1997, it was a member of the Board of Directors of the Swiss National Bank, the central bank of the nation whose official title is *Confœderatio Helvetica*, who was pointing to this explosive potential. Speaking on October 14, 1997, Professor Bruno Gehrig stressed the danger of a "chain reaction" because of the heightened "settlement risk" in today's interbank payment systems. Gehrig cited the 1974 bankruptcy of West Germany's Herstatt Bank (see Chapter IV), noting that "the core of the problem is still the same." The problem, according to Prof. Gehrig, is the time lapse between the settlement of the first leg of a foreign exchange transaction, and the settlement of the second leg, which may come after an interval of hours or even days. What happens if a counterparty goes bankrupt during this interval? Prof. Gehrig prudently points out that this implies "a credit risk for the bank amounting to the full value of its payments," and "a liquidity risk" as well. This means that there is also the threat of a general banking panic: "These already worrisome risks, as seen from the perspective of a single bank, in the meantime pose a systemic risk and therefore a danger for the functioning of the financial markets." Referring to a more recent cataclysm of the world banking system, Gehrig also recalled the "severe clearing problems" which had been created by the collapse of Baring Brothers bank in 1995. Gehrig summed up his argument saying that "many banks are completely unaware that they are routinely being exposed to risks in foreign exchange trading which are bigger in value than their transactions of several days. The amount of risk, even with respect to only one counter-party, can therefore surpass the stock capital of the bank." Banks are not doing enough to shield themselves and efforts "effectively to contain the systemic risks are...not sufficient;" "here is the danger of a chain reaction and collapse of payment systems.... The systemic risks have reached an intolerable level." Many banks, concluded Gehrig, seem to be relying mainly on "the erroneous belief" that they are "too big to fail." [20]

---

[19] *Time*, August 4, 1997.
[20] *Neue Zuericher Zeitung*, October 15, 1997.

The liquidity risk that is closely linked to settlement risk was emphasized around the same time by London *Sunday Times* columnist Paul Durman, who interviewed the bearish British hedge fund manager Tony Dye, whom we have already met as the financier who had issued a warning of a derivatives crisis in the late winter. Dye was again worried about a derivatives panic, especially regarding index future contracts on the FTSE, the *Financial Times* Stock Exchange Index which is the principal blue-chip barometer of the London market. Dye once again saw a derivatives shock endangering the entire system: "The scale of derivatives trading hints at the extent of leverage in financial markets – large economic interests underpinned by only small down payments. When markets turn, many over-leveraged investors will have to raise cash quickly in order to meet their commitments. The wave of forced selling that ensues is the classic way in which financial markets become unstable and crash."[21]

During the weeks and months leading up to the Hong Kong crisis, a mood of fey frivolity had crept over financial circles. The editors of *Euromoney* magazine devised a game based on an imaginary future financial meltdown, and invited "50 experienced financial professionals" from the City of London to come and spend a few days playing simulated crisis set at the eve of the euro era. *Euromoney* felt that in the exercise, "that was meant to show a way out of a global meltdown.. the surprise outcome was the fierce rivalry between financial centres." Notably, wrote *Euromoney*, "'those bloody Germans' ...formed a united front for self-preservation in the crisis.[22] Earlier in the month the same magazine had run another euro-crash scenario by David Lascelles, who was also the author of "The Crash of 2003, an Emu fairy tale." By now many establishment publications were talking openly about the risk of a crash – in somebody else's stock market. One was the London *Financial Times*, which noted on October 11, 1997 that "by almost every measure, such as price earnings ratios and dividend yields, US stocks are very highly valued by historic standards. And the 'Q' ratio, of companies' share prices to their underlying assets is now well above its peak in 1929 just before the crash." On August 9, the London *Economist* had run a cover showing a high-flying kite labeled "Dow" with the words "Lovely while it lasts."

But the finance oligarchy was also taking steps to secure its control of those assets which would represent wealth in the post-disintegration world. The gold price was pushed down towards $300 by the scandalous decisions of governments to sell off large parts of their gold stocks. These stocks were in effect being privatized, sold to venture capitalists for a fraction of what they would fetch on a non-rigged market. In July 1997 the Australian central bank announced that it would sell 167 tons (5.4 million ounces) of its bullion reserves. In October the Swiss central bank, famous for maintaining a de facto gold standard, said that it would also begin liquidating its gold stocks. It was an outrageous scandal. Why sell public property at severely depressed prices? And why now? The gold sales had some of the flavor of Russia's distressed-merchandise privatization under the IMF's shock therapy. Now the Swiss were also going to be shocked.

OCTOBER 27, 1997: ASSAULT ON THE HONG KONG DOLLAR

During the second half of October 1997, the hedge funds and currency speculators turned their attention once again to the Hong Kong dollar, which by that time was the only southeast Asian currency still capable of defending a "peg," or relatively stable exchange rate, with the US dollar. During the week ending October 24, 1997 the Hang Seng index of leading Hong Kong stocks collapsed by 25%. The monetary instability which had plagued Thailand, the Philippines, Indonesia,

---

[21] London *Sunday Times*, October 12, 1997.
[22] *Euromoney*, September 26, 1997.

South Korea, and Malaysia was now focussed on Hong Kong. When the British had returned Hong Kong to China in the previous summer, they had left behind a bloated speculative bubble economy and a dangerously overvalued real estate market, which in turn had weakened the local banks. The speculative attack was timed to coincide with the visit of Chinese President Jiang Zemin to the United States; the speculators were happy to embarrass Jiang and make him lose face.

Interest rates in Hong Kong ratcheted up to 300% per day as automatic defense mechanisms kicked in. Certain Asian currencies like the Taiwan dollar were also hit hard. On October 23 the Brazilian stock market fell by more than 8%, confirming widespread fears that this immense country was in a crisis of its own. $10 billion in hot money fled Brazil, where the government responded by raising interest rates to 43%, strangling the domestic economy; big ticket purchases immediately fell by more than a third. By the end of this week, Wall Street was also beginning a decline. On Monday, October 27, the Dow Jones Industrials lost almost 555 points, the biggest point drop ever, but at 7.18% only the twelfth worst day in the history of the DJIA. The so-called circuit breakers designed by the 1988 Brady committee were activated for the first time, with a 30 minute trading halt when the Dow reached minus 350 at 2:35 PM, and a 60 minute timeout when the Dow crashed through minus 550 at about half past three. Luckily for the stockjobbers, the second pause meant that the trading day came to an early halt. This crash came just a few days after the tenth anniversary of the all-time record crash of the Reagan market on October 19, 1987. Strictly speaking, this time the market break was more comparable to the 190-point mini-crash of Friday, October 13, 1989, which had pared almost 7% from the Dow in the last two hours of trading. That had also been the twelfth worst day when it occurred. But back then, the world economy could still count on the propulsive effect of intact economies in Germany and Japan, and financiers could look forward to penetrating the Soviet sphere. This time it was different; this time the strength of the world economy had been mortally sapped by years of globaloney.

At the close of the trading day, Treasury Secretary Rubin came out on the steps of his office to attempt a reassuring statement. His comment revealed the area which we have identified as the greatest concern: "Our consultations," he said, "indicate that the payment and settlement systems and other market mechanisms are working effectively." In an interview with *Newsweek*, Rubin again mentioned the financial "infrastructure." The great fear was that some important institution would become insolvent, and that its default would cause the interbank netting and payment systems to jam up, resulting in chain-reaction bankruptcy all around. That, Rubin hastened to tell the public, had been avoided.

On the following day, the Brady system of drugged markets (discussed in Chapter II) proved its mettle. Colossal amounts of liquidity were pumped into the markets by the Federal Reserve, especially through the Chicago S&P 500 contract. IBM led a number of firms in announcing that they would buy back large quantities of their own stock, a trick that had been popularized during the crash of a decade earlier by then-White House chief of staff Howard Baker. The Fed, remembering that a prime cause of the 1987 crash had been selling of stock by Fidelity and other mutual funds to procure cash that might be needed for a wave of mutual fund redemptions, this time pre-emptively offered unlimited borrowing to mutual funds so they could keep their stock positions and still pay off whatever little people might want to take their money off the table. Financier Warren Buffett, who had announced some time before that he was pulling cash out of stocks and putting it into Treasury securities, now made a well-publicized move back into the market. Out in Hong Kong, the Hong Kong and Shanghai bank helped to stabilize the bourse by buying up its own shares. All of this generated a significant updraft, and helped the Dow on Tuesday, October 29, 1997 to recoup 337 points or 4.7% on all-time record volume of almost 1.2 billion shares. This shameless exercise in market-rigging was presented for the edification of a gullible public as the result of a bold stand by America's small investors, who refused to panic. After all, assured the commentators, Hong Kong was a hole in the wall, and Wall Street remained the center of the universe.

After the fall of October 27 and the rebound of October 28, there remained for some time the question of whether any of the world's important banks or brokerage houses had succumbed. The prices of US Treasury securities had risen during the late October turbulence as a result of the so-called "flight to quality": a number of financiers, sensing that a stock market crash was in the cards, bought bonds. One of them, it appears, had been Soros, whose bond profits were reported to have partially offset his very large losses on stocks. The threat to US government bonds was also clear enough: it came from forced liquidations of US Treasury paper by cash-strapped Asian central banks and financial institutions. All in all, it was estimated that Asian central banks had sold off $14 billion worth of US Treasury bonds in late October and early November. (It was estimated that a total $621 billion in Treasuries were held abroad, prevalently in Asia, with the Bank of Japan holding $210 billion, the Bank of Korea $30 billion, and the Hong Kong Monetary Authority $88 billion.)

NOVEMBER 1997: JAPAN[23]

Japanese banks traditionally hold large portions of their assets in the form of stock in Japanese corporations. If the Tokyo stock market goes too low, dropping below the 16,000-17,000 range, some Japanese banks begin to be threatened by insolvency because of the erosion in the current value of their stock holdings, which must be periodically marked to market. The workings of this Japanese link between stock prices and banking crisis were illustrated in the wake of the Hong Kong panic, when the Nikkei average reached a 28-month low on Friday, November 14, 1997. Between August 1997 and the middle of November of the same year, the Nikkei average of 225 stocks had lost about one quarter of its total value, and even more in dollar terms.

During the second week of November, Japan's Sanyo Securities went bankrupt. Sanyo had been the seventh largest financial broker in Japan. The Sanyo bankruptcy was the first time that a brokerage house had gone belly up in Japan during the entire post-1945 era. Sanyo had boasted the largest trading floor in Asia, but it succumbed to its more than $3 billion in debts. Then the 1997 market break claimed another important victim. On Friday November 14, the *Financial Times* hinted that a big Japanese bank was moribund: "Brokers allege that one of Japan's biggest banks has already fallen below the minimum set by the Bank of International Settlements." On November 17, 1997 it was announced that the tenth largest commercial bank in Japan, the Hokkaido Takushoku Bank, was going out of business. This bank, known as Hokutaku for short, was brought down by bad real estate loans left over from the 1990 collapse of the bubble economy. "We had to reach a judgment that we would not be able to continue our operations," said a communiqué from the bank. Hokutaku had assets of $76 billion. The non-performing loans were almost $7.5 billion, or 13% of the bank's total of outstanding loans. Rubin wrote a letter to his Japanese counterpart Mitsuzuka in which he expressed serious concern about the viability of the Japanese banking system.

The liquidation of Hokutaku focussed attention on the parlous financial situation of Yamaichi Securities, one of Japan's leading brokerages. During the second week in November 1997, the bond rating agency Standard & Poors downgraded Yamaichi's bonded debt to BBB, citing the brokerage for "inability to counteract unfavorable market conditions." For a time Yamaichi struggled to survive by shutting down its operations in Europe and America, while cutting its payroll by 26%,

---

[23] This was the 31st post-war systemic crisis; see table in Chapter IV.

from 7,484 to about 5000. But financial analysts complained that this was too little too late. Yamaichi was one of the Big Four Japanese brokerages, the others being Nomura, Daiwa, and Nikko. When Yamaichi finally went bankrupt in late November 1997, it was the biggest bankruptcy in Japan's postwar history. After its demise had been announced, Yamaichi was the belated target of the biggest panic run in the postwar history of Japan, as investors pulled out $93 billion, or just over half of Yamaichi's total accounts, in a week or two. Brokerage houses of the middle rank, including Kankaku and New Japan, announced downsizing plans of their own. Nippon Credit Bank said it was cutting its staff by a third.

At this point, the Japanese stock market rallied on reports that Prime Minister Hashimoto had raised the possibility of using public funds to bail out the Japanese banking system, perhaps along the lines of what Bush did for the bankrupt American S&Ls. This news propelled the Japanese market up by 8%. But when Hashimoto denied that he was about to undertake such a politically risky operation, the Tokyo market began falling again. By early 1998, the "risk premium" paid by the Japanese banks in the interbank market (meaning higher interest rates paid to counterparties because of the uncertainty of dealing with Japanese banks groaning under bad debts) had risen from 5 basis points to 35 and then to 116 basis points – 1.16%. This was a terrible handicap for these banks. The danger now was that Japanese banks would begin to liquidate their portfolios of US Treasury securities, leading to a panic crash of the Treasury bond market. By mid-November, the Russian stock market was down 40% from its August peak. The Bovespa index of Sao Paolo showed the Brazilian market down by 38% since October 22, 1997.

SOUTH KOREA: #11 GOES UNDER[24]

In South Korea, the world's eleventh largest economy, the central bank gave up its attempt to keep the won within a band of fluctuation in relation to the US dollar. The depreciating won broke through the "Maginot line" of 1000 to the greenback. After declaring that capitulation to the IMF was unthinkable, the Seoul government announced on November 21, 1997 that it was obliged to submit to the IMF conditions in order to obtain a loan. "Let's...share the pain and turn this misfortune into a blessing," said South Korean President Kim Young Sam.[25] An intelligent Korean civil engineering student quoted in the same report commented, "We'll have to sacrifice our economic sovereignty in return for an IMF bailout."

And so it came to pass. The IMF, the central bankers, and the finance ministers saw clearly enough that South Korea was unquestionably big enough to bring down Japan, and that Japan in turn was more than big enough to bring down the United States and Europe. South Korea was not capable of meeting the scheduled debt service payments on its $170 billion of foreign debt. So South Korea was granted a bailout package of $55 billion, the biggest in IMF history. But to obtain this money, Seoul was forced to pledge to junk all the procedures that had permitted the reconstruction and development of the country after the Korean War. As the *Financial Times* noted with some satisfaction, "the rescue plan was finally agreed when the Korean government gave up a dogged struggle to preserve the main elements of its dirigist economic structure." Henceforth the Republic of Korea would be subjected to "market principles instead of state directives" and would be compelled to "yield to investor discipline," meaning submit to the depredations of well-connected predators like Soros. South Korea was going to be opened up to foreign financial operators – as if the crisis had not been caused by an overdose of precisely that! One investment

---

[24] This was the 32nd post-war systemic crisis; see table in Chapter IV.
[25] *Washington Post*, November 22, 1997.

banker gloated that "South Korea is one of the last transitional economies to market capitalism."[26] One of the very last national economies capable of sustained economic dynamism was being scuttled by the greedy monetarist ideologues of the fast buck.

The IMF announced a $57 billion bailout package for South Korea on December 3, 1997. But the IMF standby loan was made contingent on what the IMF termed a "stabilization program." The globaloney economists had a special rage against South Korea, and they clearly wanted to subject that country to the classic Andrew Mellon treatment of mass liquidations and insolvency. When the South Korean authorities nationalized two insolvent banks instead of letting them go bankrupt, and when Seoul provided funds for Daewoo to take over troubled Sangyong Motors, the international financiers were incensed at what they seemed to think was South Korea's refusal to abandon dirigism. The financiers also claimed that South Korea had concealed the true extent of its debt problem. Things were complicated by the fact that South Korea was in the midst of a presidential election campaign, in which the IMF was under attack. IMF director Camdessus had tried to get all the presidential candidates to sign an oath of fealty to the IMF conditionalities, but Kim Dae-jung declined, and was rewarded with an improvement of his poll numbers as a result. But after Kim Dae-jung had won the election, he began intoning the IMF litany of "sweat and tears" in his inaugural address of Feb. 25, making a self-fulfilling prophecy that "consumer prices and unemployment will rise. Incomes will drop, and an increasing number of companies will go bankrupt." This equation of economic reform with immiseration and insolvency amounted to a concession of defeat before the race had even started; such economic pessimism, as the Russian experience suggests, is the hallmark of the IMF's stubborn incompetence and inability to produce positive results.

Spokesmen for the financiers demanded the most drastic measures against Korea. Peter Kenen, a Princeton professor of international monetarism, called for the IMF to renege on the entire bailout package and force Seoul into chaotic national bankruptcy. "At this stage, frankly, I think it would be better to say we'll put up $50 billion for troubled countries that are the victims of Korean default and make an object lesson of the Koreans for their cavalier way of handling all this," raved Kenen, who had apparently forgotten that the true beneficiaries of this bailout were, as always, the US banks and the US Treasury. Deflation prophet Edward Yardeni offered his view that "the truth of the matter is that Korea Inc. is already bankrupt. All that's left to do is file the papers. This is a zombie economy."

In early December, as later become known, South Korea had $6 billion cash on hand, as against $150 billion in international obligations coming due over the short term. South Korea was set to default within the space of five business days – despite the fact that its industrial plant was among the most modern, and its work force among the most skilled, in the entire world. What counted under globaloney was not the fundamentals, but the deregulated panic. If South Korea had defaulted, the country's ability to continue to import oil might soon have been terminated, leading to a general blackout for a nation which relied on oil-fired plants for 90% of its electricity. South Korea was thus just a few weeks away from chaos; if this scenario had been consummated, as it still might be, Korea might even have been unified under North Korean auspices – a nightmare for that country, and the world. But since the Cold War was over, the financiers no longer cared about such issues.

A quick fix was therefore imperative. The haggling over the South Korean bailout was still going on when Christmas Eve arrived in Washington. Treasury Secretary Rubin, announcing an interim,

---

[26] *Financial Times*, November 4, 1997.

preliminary $10 billion quick fix for South Korea to stave off default and world panic over the days ahead, remarked that he "wouldn't spend a nickel to help private investors or private creditors," a sound bite he liked so well that he repeated it on several subsequent occasions. Rubin assembled the package, and South Korea moved back slightly from the brink. Some observers, perhaps grasping for straws, were mightily impressed by the "not a nickel" rhetoric, but it was eyewash. As Erik Hoffmeyer, the former governor of the Danish central bank, told the Copenhagen newspaper *Politiken* on January 7, "there is a very great risk that the money which flows to South Korea will only be used to pay the loans of the most nervous creditors. Now, does that make sense?"

If South Korea had succumbed, this financial shock might have proven sufficient to set off a stock market and banking panic in Japan. And if Japan were to fall, the next domino would be the US Treasury market and with it the entire US financial edifice. That might restore London as the undisputed financial capital of the world. And surely London knew that, even if ideologues like Kenen did not. South Korea was an Asian domino big enough to detonate an immediate systemic crisis. Despite all this, gold was at a 12-year low, due largely to announced and rumored gold sales by central banks. These maneuvers amounted to support operations for all sorts of dubious financial paper.

YARDENI: DEFLATION AND OVERPRODUCTION CRISIS

In the wake of the October-November 1997 turbulence, a number of observers finally began to see the threat of all-out world economic depression, although they often attempted to avoid such terminology. *Business Week* wrote about the "threat of deflation." The starting point of this argument was once again the Malthusian thesis of a crisis of overproduction, along the lines developed by Greider. "Today, for the first time in years," wrote *Business Week*, "there is worldwide overcapacity in industries, from semiconductors to autos...production everywhere is running ahead of consumption." The main inspiration for this view seemed to come from Edward E. Yardeni, the chief economist at Deutsche Morgan Grenfell, who was telling Wall Street that deflation, and not inflation, was now the danger. *Business Week* observed that because of deflation, "in the worst case, a wave of business and personal bankruptcies sets off a chain of failures throughout the entire financial system. Investment and growth collapse." The threat was especially acute for highly leveraged companies which had taken on too much debt, and would end up trying to pay back that debt with more expensive dollars than those they had borrowed. "The Great Depression of the 1930s was exactly this sort of deflationary spiral. From 1929 to 1933, prices fell by 10% annually. Even moderately leveraged companies went under, the banking system was devastated, unemployment soared, and the economy and the stock market went into a deep swoon that was only ended by World War II. The biggest danger for the global economy today may be the prospect of a sustained deflationary downturn in East Asia." [27]

The editors of *Business Week* may not know it, but they are acting out the old vulgar Marxist cliché that the capitalists always deny that a crisis is coming, but when the crisis finally arrives, they parrot the Malthusian thesis of a crisis of overproduction, citing the empirical evidence of warehouses filled with goods that cannot be sold. The capitalists then cancel investment plans and cut production in order to raise the falling prices they think are causing the problem. ("In today's age, you cannot get price increases," complained CEO John Smith of General Motors.) In doing this, they exacerbate the depression. *Business Week* wanted President Suharto of Indonesia to cancel "huge, money-wasting investments, including a national car project." Taking this advice would make the future far worse for Indonesia. This article was scary enough to attract the attention of the

---

[27] *Business Week*, November 10, 1997, p. 55.

London *Economist*, in its "Will the world slump?" issue, which countered that "inflation, not deflation, remains the bigger risk." [28] Robert J. Samuelson, for his part, finally conceded that there might be "a gathering storm." [29] Better late than never.

The cause of a world economic depression like the current one is always insufficient production and insufficient consumption, along with the unbridled expansion of speculation and debt. The *Financial Times* began citing "The Second Coming" by William Butler Yeats, which reflects a cultist prophecy that the end of the millennium will be marked by a paroxysm of chaos and evil, opening a dark age. From Yeats came the following satanic verses:

> The darkness drops again; but now I know
> That twenty centuries of stony sleep
> were vexed to nightmare by a rocking cradle,
> And what rough beast, its hour come round at last,
> Slouches towards Bethlehem to be born?

CNBC, the financial news network that broadcasts on American cable television, featured an interview a few days after the crash with Mr. Arch Crawford, the publisher of the *Crawford Perspectives* newsletter. Mr. Crawford attributed the financial turbulence to two main groups of factors. The first was the unfavorable alignment of the moon and the planets, which was impelling investor sentiment in the wrong direction. He also advanced an explanation based on Seasonal Affective Disorder (SADS), which induces a depressive mentality during those weeks of the year when the daylight hours are the shortest. According to Mr. Crawford, studies have shown that a preponderant proportion of stock market declines have taken place within 2 months of the autumnal equinox, and this market break was also a creature of such twilight. The danger was that it was the twilight of civilization itself.

INFLATION OR DEFLATION?

In addition to the warnings of deflation that began to appear in the autumn of 1997, there were also emphatic warnings of immediate world-wide hyperinflation caused by the combined impact of the IMF bailouts along with the money-printing activities of central banks, especially the Japanese one but also the Fed, who were seeking to play the role of lender of last resort for otherwise insolvent banks, insurance companies, and brokerages. In reality, the interval from October 1997 to October 1998 has turned out to be a period of very marked worldwide deflation, in the sense that the dollar prices of most basic commodities as measured by barometers like the Commodity Research Bureau index have declined by about 20%. On the other hand, a number of currencies, most notably the Indonesia rupiah, have exceeded the 50% yearly inflation rate which seems to be the academic economists' yardstick for hyperinflation. The Russian ruble was also headed in the same direction. After October 1997, asset price inflation continued in the United States for some months, in some cases until July 1998. This tendency was advertised by the London *Economist*, whose front cover of April 18, 1998 read "America's Bubble Economy." "But it is asset-price inflation, especially in the United States, that now poses a potentially bigger and more imminent threat to the global economy," the *Economist* elaborated, suggesting that the US was really sicker than Japan.

Those warnings of hyperinflation would have been well advised to specify precisely which currencies were likely to hyperinflate. When hyperinflation destroyed the German mark in 1923, the

---

[28] *Economist*, November 15, 1997.
[29] *Washington Post*, November 19, 1997.

British pound sterling was the obvious beneficiary, since pounds could purchase German assets, production, and labor at severely depressed prices. Similarly, the incipient hyperinflation in Indonesia provided an opportunity for foreign venture capital using dollars.

ASIAN MONETARY FUND

As the Asian currency and banking crisis gathered momentum, Japan proposed what would have been (and might still become) an important step towards world monetary reform. This was the Japanese idea for an Asian Monetary Fund, a regional financial cooperation organization to offer protection to currencies under speculative assault. This would have been at minimum a regional monetary agency operating outside of the control of the IMF. It might have quickly become a regional alternative to, and even adversary of, the IMF. When the idea of an Asian Monetary Fund was first suggested by the Japanese government, US Treasury Secretary Rubin was vaguely supportive. Then the IMF began flexing its muscles, and Rubin was eclipsed at the Treasury by Undersecretary Larry Summers, an exponent of the brutal IMF line. Summers sharply attacked the Asian Monetary Fund and Japanese Ministry of Finance official Sakakibara, who was arguing for this idea. When South Korea appealed to its traditional allies, the United States and Japan, for emergency financial assistance, Seoul was told that it had to submit to the IMF first, accepting whatever disastrous and meddling conditionalities that might entail. By the time the 18 heads of state of the Asia-Pacific Economic Cooperation (APEC) group met in Vancouver, Canada on November 23-24, the Asian Monetary Fund had gone a-glimmering. Instead, the proceedings were dominated by endorsements of the so-called Manila Framework, a crisis management scheme hatched by finance ministers in the Philippine capital on November 18; this scheme provided only for a "cooperative financing mechanism" to provide money to supplement IMF loan packages, and called for all efforts to be subservient to the IMF.

January 1998 began with the bankruptcy of Peregrine Investments of Hong Kong, one of the largest investment houses in Asia. The bottom-fishers at Zürich Investment Group had considered buying a stake in Peregrine, but concluded that the firm was already in desperate condition. Peregrine said that the final blow to its survival had come from the fall of the Indonesian rupiah, which was already severely depressed, and which fell a breathtaking 48% on just one day, January 22, 1998. Henry Kaufman, the "Dr. Doom" of the 1970s who was now the head of his own Wall Street bond firm, was making a comeback, and warned in Toronto on January 13 that the IMF was incapable of braking the slide into a "financial holocaust." Under these auspices, the Davos Conference of January 29-February 3, 1998 was, apart from the Chinese and AFL-CIO interventions, more of a magic mountain than ever. The 1998 Davos theme was copied from the November 1987 ads placed in newspapers by stockbrokers who sought to anesthetize their jumpy customers by announcing: "The Worst Is Over!" Unfortunately, these finance oligarchs should have known better, and the worst was only beginning.

SPRING 1998: NO CONFIDENCE IN THE IMF

The IMF bailout packages for the Asian countries proved quite controversial, and opened a phase of unprecedented criticism of that organization. Eisuke Sakakibara (the Mr. Yen of the Japanese Finance Ministry) in a March 2 interview with *Mainichi Shimbun* of Tokyo, called for a new world monetary conference: "I believe that many world leaders may well be starting to contemplate the idea of a financial agreement along the lines of the Bretton Woods agreement." He added that "many people are now realizing that both the International Monetary Fund's checks and its solutions are insufficient."

The London *Economist* of January 10, 1998 ran a cover story showed pills inscribed "IMF" bubbling like Alka-Seltzer in a glass of water, with legend: "Kill or Cure?" The article noted that the ongoing crisis had mightily energized critics of the IMF: "The Fund's many critics are once again in good voice. They are a motley chorus: right-wingers in the United States who cannot bear to see tax-dollars spent on foreigners (whose only thanks, after all, will be to steal more American jobs); surviving left-wingers everywhere, who regard capitalism as evil and the IMF as its instrument; other clever types who feel it is insanely stringent." Were the $57 billion bailout of South Korea and the $43 billion bailout of Indonesia justified? The *Economist* was skeptical, perhaps because the bailouts in question were to a large extent bailouts of Japanese and American, rather than London, banks: "Invoking the risk of 'systemic' breakdown is the most obvious way to justify the IMF's intervention. Without an emergency injection of dollars, it is argued, companies in South Korea and the rest would default on their debts. This would cause distress elsewhere, especially in Japan, where stagnation could turn into outright depression. From there the crisis could spread to the United States, Europe, and the rest of the world, as banks fail, credit disappears, stock markets crash, and economies collapse. This is the nightmare that has driven governments, notably America's, to support and indeed insist upon the Fund's course of action." The *Economist* judged that these dangers were all exaggerated, and preferred to focus on the "moral hazard" problem, which occurs when the presence of a lender of last resort encourages risky and irresponsible practices by banks, lenders, and companies: the *Economist* insisted on "the hidden costs of bail-outs. In a market-based system of finance, the risk of losing your money is not an avoidable nuisance but a fundamental requirement."

More realistic was *Business Week*, which is read by American businessmen, and which quoted Sakakibara's comment that "This isn't an Asian crisis. It's a crisis of global capitalism." The *Business Week* line took the systemic crisis quite seriously, and recommended increased government activism to stave off disintegration: "...another round of deep devaluations in Asia could force Latin American to follow suit. That would deliver a second whammy to US exports, corporate profits, and stocks. Capital investment would drop, and consumers – seeing much of their mutual-fund wealth disappear – would spend less. The West could slip into economic stagnation, Asia into a long recession. With 'globalization' no longer delivering the goods and social turmoil breaking out, big developing countries such as China might postpone free-market reforms for years."[30] One subhead noted: "One more big shock – a Chinese devaluation, another Nikkei plunge – could clobber world trade for years." *Business Week* wanted an emergency task force of global leaders to solve the regional crisis, possibly with a world summit meeting, the exposure of all bad debt, and fast currency stabilization "before hyperinflation hits" the Asian region.

THE CFR CRITIQUE OF THE IMF

The position of the Wall Street/State Department interface on these matters was articulated by Martin Feldstein.[31] Feldstein's thesis: "The IMF's recent emphasis on imposing major structural and institutional reforms as opposed to focusing on balance-of-payments adjustments will have adverse consequences in both the short term and the more distant future. The IMF should stick to its traditional task of helping countries cope with temporary shortages of foreign exchange and with more sustained trade deficits." Feldstein faulted the IMF for wanting to give Asia the Russian-style shock therapy treatment. The main accusation was that the IMF was going wrong by treating Indonesia and especially South Korea in the same way that the IMF had treated Russia – violating

---

[30] *Business Week,* January 26, 1998.
[31] "Refocusing the IMF," *Foreign Affairs*, March/April 1998, pp. 20-33.

sovereignty by dictating a total transformation of all economic policy down to minute details. For Feldstein, the IMF's excesses grew out of its recent history, especially in dealing with the post-communist countries. He saw the IMF as "acting in Southeast Asia and Korea in much the same way that it did in Eastern Europe and the Soviet Union" while "applying the traditional mix of fiscal policies (higher taxes, less government spending) and credit tightening (implying higher interest rates) that were successful in Latin America." But these may not be what is needed in Asia. The IMF was now going too far: "...the IMF's role in Thailand and Indonesia went far beyond the role that it played in Latin America. Instead of relying on private banks and serving primarily as a monitor of performance, the IMF took the lead in providing credit .... The conditions imposed on Thailand and Indonesia were more like the comprehensive reforms imposed on Russia, including the recent emphasis on reducing Russian corruption, than like the macroeconomic changes that were required in Latin America."[32] For South Korea, wrote Feldstein, a quick fix to provide cash to meet short-term foreign debt payments would have been enough, rather than the IMF's attack on the entire *chaebol* structure.

One senses that Feldstein was genuinely worried that if the South Korean bailout failed, then Japan would go down and the US would be next. It was in this context that he discovered such notions as sovereignty and moral rights, concepts that were not much talked about during Russian shock therapy. Feldstein observed that much of what the IMF wanted to wipe out in South Korea represented institutions and practices that were alive and well in western Europe. In other words, the Russian experience had made the IMF so addicted to the most extreme laissez-faire, unbridled *capitalisme sauvage* that the IMF now needed to be reminded that it simply will not do to treat South Koreans etc. as if they were in the same category with the defenseless Russians. That was no doubt be interesting news for Russians, who had been put through the IMF meatgrinder with no regard whatever for their sovereignty or moral rights. Feldstein's comments were political dynamite for the Russian front. The owl of Minerva was taking flight at dusk, revealing much of the real essence of the system at the very moment that the system was crashing down.

CHINA: A NEW DEAL TO FIGHT THE WORLD DEPRESSION

By far the most rational response to the severe world-wide turbulence of late 1997 came from the People's Republic of China. The Chinese leaders, turning away from the myths and tragedies of the Mao period, were now pursuing an economic policy inspired by Confucius and Dr. Sun Yat-sen. With Zhu Rongji's replacement of Li Peng as Prime Minister, the aftermath of the 1989 Tien An Men repressions had been relegated to the past. Speaking at the 1998 Davos Forum, Chinese Deputy Prime Minister Li Lanquing affirmed China's commitment to internal improvements, infrastructure, public works, and great projects as part of a comprehensive program totaling $750 billion. This was to include the Three Gorges Dam, other water projects, railroads, highways, steel plants, housing, and much more. The Chinese press was full of calls for a policy in the spirit of Franklin D. Roosevelt. "China's reforms and development need a Chinese-style New Deal," wrote the influential *Outlook* magazine of March 13, 1998. A few days later, *China Daily* reported that new Prime Minister "Zhu Rongji, the man who stemmed China's inflation without stifling growth, is poised to launch the Chinese version of Roosevelt's New Deal this year .... Zhu has made it clear that massive investment will be channeled into infrastructure, echoing Roosevelt's bid to revive the American economy in the 1930s." Zhu had five areas for economic reform, including grain storage and delivery, investment and funding, housing, medical care, and science and technology. This campaign was a central point in President Jiang Zemin's address to the Ninth National People's

---

[32] Martin Feldstein, "Refocusing the IMF," *Foreign Affairs*, March/April 1998, pp. 20-33.

Congress in Beijing on March 19; although Jiang was still using the long-standing formula about "socialism with Chinese characteristics," it appeared that what was meant was a New Deal with Chinese characteristics. According to some Chinese officials quoted in the Western press, the Chinese program actually carried a price tag of $1 trillion; it was evidently the greatest business opportunity of all time. All that was missing was the diplomatic effort towards a New Bretton Woods conference, in which point China evidently had decided to defer to the United States.

While the rest of the world violently contracted, China hewed to a growth target of 8%, especially impressive since most of this was real physical growth. For the first half of 1998, China reported 7% growth, but President Jiang Zemin and Prime Minister Zhu Rongji kept repeating that, with an improved second half, 8% yearly growth was still within reach. This was the year of disastrous flooding in China, with an estimated $20 billion in damage, and the response of the government was to increase credit by about 1 trillion ren min bi (RMB) during the closing months of 1998. On August 31, *People's Daily* featured an article endorsing the American New Deal in more detail than previously. The piece was entitled "Background on Franklin Roosevelt's New Deal," and focused on FDR's response to the banking crisis of 1933 (see Chapters VI, VII, and XI below), and on his dirigiste policies in the various spheres of the economy. Chinese readers were being prepared to understand the crisis gripping the entire world.

THE G-22 AND THE NEW ARCHITECTURE

During late 1997 and early 1998, US Treasury Secretary Rubin called repeatedly for a "new financial architecture," although the exact content of this phrase was not defined. Hopes for reform came to be attached to the Group of 22, a hybrid group made up of G-7 wealthy nations along with some emerging markets countries. The G-22 was called for a time the Willard Group, after the Washington hotel where in had been meeting in early 1998. The G-22 met in Washington at the Madison Hotel on April 16. Rubin's speech portrayed the Asian crisis as a global crisis, and he repeated his "not one nickel" for the private banks policy. He made modest proposals for greater transparency and oversight on derivatives. He criticized hedge funds and speculators for having torpedoed the economies of the Asian tiger nations. But the British were hostile to any attempt to curb the speculators or re-introduce exchange controls, and Germany and France were not interested in any new architecture, since these countries imagined that they already had their future blueprint in the form of the euro, which once again proved its remarkable capability for hog-tying the European states in the midst of the crisis. There was no specific talk of a new Bretton Woods. Three task forces were told to come back in October with reports on various aspects of the crisis. The G-22 subcommittee meeting in Tokyo on July 29 began developing early warning mechanisms for national financial distress – somewhat late in the day.

PARALYSIS OF THE BIS

Just as it had during the world monetary crisis of 1931, the Bank for International Settlements continued to punt. On June 8, this private central bank of private central banks published the consensus line of the central bank governors on the unfolding world breakdown. BIS Managing Director Andrew Crockett, writing in the BIS *Annual Report*, threw up his hands, conceding that the Asian contagion represented "the first crisis in the postwar period featuring the combination of banks as the principal international creditors, and private sector entities as the principal debtors. Principles of how to manage and resolve a crisis of this sort were not known in advance and, indeed, are still under discussion." Although thus temporizing himself, Crockett attacked the Japanese for their "decade of temporizing." Not to be outdone, the IMF refused to call for any curbs on the hedge funds, which had manifestly detonated the worst crisis since 1931. The IMF's *World Economic Outlook*, issued on April 13, asked the pertinent question, "Should hedge funds be subjected to greater regulatory and disclosure requirements?" The answer was, of course, a resounding no. Just as in the 1930s, the central banks would prove capable only of recriminations, but impotent when it came to putting forward a solution.

THE SOUTH KOREAN CONTRACTION

As a result of the Soros-led speculative attack, South Korea was soon experiencing a capital flight in excess of $1 billion per day. George Soros was putting out the watchword, "Sell Korea," and the stock market was now down 60% and the won down 40% from their pre-crash levels. South Korea was in the midst of a violent contraction of production, employment, and living standards, similar to the American experience of 1929-31. In the spring of 1997, South Korean companies were going bankrupt at the rate of 2,000 per month. James Wolfensohn of the World Bank tried a *Diktat* of his own, telling South Korea "no public funds for bailing out industry." On May 27, 300,000 South Korean workers staged a strike against the mass layoffs dictated by the IMF. Since the crisis began, household consumption in the country had declined by 10.5%, the worst collapse in the history of this data series going back to the end of the Korean War.

THE PHILIPPINE GOVERNMENT BANKRUPT

The new Philippine president Joseph Estrada bluntly stated in his State of the Nation address on July 27, "Our economy is in bad shape, and the national coffers are almost empty. The government cannot fulfill the needs of the economy. In short, the government is bankrupt. He cited a foreign debt of $51 billion and a budget deficit of $2.1 billion, frankly lamenting: "I thought we had a lot of money. They were saying we were economically stable, the new economic tiger of Asia. It turned out we're not a tiger, but a puppy."

INDONESIA: THE IMF TOPPLES SUHARTO[33]

Indonesia owed the international bankers $150 billion. As part of the price enacted for the initial aid package of October 1997, the IMF had specified that 16 banks had to be shut down, including one owned by Suharto's son. This was a micro-managed *Diktat* with a clear political overtone, and it set off a nation-wide banking panic, with depositors running to get cash out of their accounts, and withdrawing $2 billion in just a few hours. By the end of November, two thirds of all Indonesian banks had experienced panic runs. The central bank responded by printing money as best it could, leading in turn to an international attack on the rupiah at the end of December, with capital fleeing to safe havens abroad. The *Economist* of February 21, 1998 focused on "Asia's Coming Explosion," highlighting the situation in Indonesia, the fourth largest in the world. "There is now at least an even chance that this nation of 200m people will shortly erupt in murderous violence ... the chief victims of the violence will be the ethnic Chinese who make up 3% of the population but own much of the wealth, and ...this will put pressure on them and, most important of all, on China itself, to respond in some way... an explosion in Indonesia will bring on a new, darker phase of Asia's economic crisis – which could in turn bring political change elsewhere. "President Suharto was seen by the *Economist* as "gripped by self-delusion." His main crime seemed to be a desire to peg the rupiah to the dollar.

---

[33] This was the 33rd post-war systemic crisis; see table in Chapter IV.

THE SPECTER OF STAND-STILL AGREEMENTS

In February, President Suharto informed President Clinton that "the current IMF program has not been a roaring success... Where is the alternative? Because what you've got here now isn't working." Suharto was calling the fall of the Indonesia rupiah "insane." Steve Hanke, the *Wall Street Journal*, and others wanted Indonesia to imitate Argentina by instituting a currency board, a committee of foreign bankers who would dictate the dimensions of the country's money supply. Indonesia, through whose archipelagoes one third of all world maritime trade passes, was approaching internal anarchy. In early April, IMF official Stanley Fischer was in Jakarta to supervise the IMF's 117 points of oversight. Indonesian Economics Minister Ginandjar spoke of the status of Indonesia's foreign debts. He said that Indonesia's policy was "not a moratorium. But it's often called a stand-still." With that we were back to 1931 and the stand-still agreements, amounting to temporary forbearance by foreign creditors, arranged by Schacht when the banks of central Europe blew out.

The overthrow of Suharto was a replay of a scenario which the IMF has frequently played out in third world nations: the IMF demands the abolition of subsidized prices on basic consumer goods - typically the price of staples like bread or rice. Riots break out at once, and the government is overthrown. In the case of Indonesia, the removal of subsidies was dictated by the IMF in an agreement signed with the Indonesia government on April 13. In that deal, the IMF exacted a pledge to end virtually all remaining state subsidies by October 1, 1998. The state sector, including the state oil company Pertamin, were to get no further investment. Instead, the entire state sector was to be placed on the auction block under distressed merchandise conditions. The government rice import and provisioning board, BULOG for short, was marked for extinction. The austerity measures were extorted by the IMF as the price for continued disbursements of $40 billion in still-pending aid. The government reluctantly announced that it would terminate government price subsidies on rice, palm oil, gasoline, public transportation, and some other basics. Prices on these items went up between 25% and 71%, and electricity rates jumped by 20%. At this point, middle-class college students protesting the Suharto regime were joined in the streets by aggressive gangs of looters, and repression of the riots by the army left 500 dead. Although the mass discontent occasioned by the price increases was real, the timing of the riots had the choreographed appearance of a typical CIA "people power" insurrection of the type seen in the Philippines in 1985, or the MI6 "rent-a-mob" toppling of the Shah of Iran. Despite the fact that he had just been re-elected for another term in office, Suharto the tendered his resignation; he was succeeded by his running mate in the recent election, B.J. Habibie, who promised to work with the IMF. By the time of the political crisis, the rupiah had fallen from the June 1997 rate of 2,500 to a dollar to almost 13,000 – a devaluation of about 85%. Malaysia's Mahatir, speaking at a forum in Tokyo on June 2, demanded to know, "Can it be that all the assets of that huge country, with 220 million hard-working people, are suddenly worth only one-sixth of its previous value? What, indeed, is the worth of a nation, if someone can devalue and even bankrupt it?"

"WE ARE DYING"

Before the fall of Suharto, the price of rice and other foods had increased by up to 300% in many parts of Indonesia. A wage freeze had been imposed in 1997, and overall inflation was running at 50% per year. During the first hundred days after the fall of Suharto, the price of rice more than doubled, while inflation exceeded a 70% yearly rate. The looting of rice stocks by desperate people became one of the key factors in the breakdown of public order. An August 31, 1998 report of the UN's International Labor Organization forecast that 66% of Indonesians would fall below the poverty line in 1999, a level of immiseration the country had left behind during the 1960s. 37% were already below the poverty line as of the first half of 1998, and 48% would enter poverty before the end of 1998. Indonesia's poverty measurement a diet providing fewer than 2,100 calories per day. The report said that 5.4 million Indonesians would lose their jobs during 1998, with official unemployment rising to 7%, or 6.7 million persons. One member of the research team blurted out that 20% of the 92 million person workforce were already unemployed.[34] By August 1998, Indonesia had inflation of 100%, and had suffered a 30% contraction in economic output. US Secretary of State Madeleine Albright certified on July 30 that "no nation has been hit harder by the financial crisis than Indonesia, traditionally a source of stability and growth within the region." According to orthodox monetarist economics, a devaluation of 85% should have made Indonesia the world's export superstar and returned it swiftly to prosperity. Instead, Indonesia was collapsing, too broke to buy the components and semi-finished commodities needed for its exports. On August 11, the Banque Indosuez of Paris told Bloomberg Financial News that Indonesia had "defaulted on a foreign debt payment falling due that week. Even though the report was instantly denied by the Indonesia government, this blip was enough to restart panic selling of Indonesian assets in many quarters.

The tragic situation of Indonesia was starkly depicted in the report of Indonesian Finance Minister Bambang Subianto the International Institute of Finance on October 4, 1997. The minister said, "We are dying."

A FINANCIAL MOUNT ETNA

Other countries were also writhing under IMF conditionalities. In Thailand, the newspaper *The Nation* was forced to pose the desperate question of whether Thailand could be saved or not. Among the 50 economists who participated in the debate, more than one wanted to revive great projects of infrastructure, such as the project promoted during the 1980s by Pakdee Tanapura and others for a canal across the Isthmus of Kra, to relieve pressure on the Straits of Malacca and create a development corridor in Thailand itself. On July 31, Ukraine obtained a loan of $2.2 billion from the IMF, accepting conditionalities for money which would go to pay August debt service requirements. The *Straits Times* of Singapore informed its readers that, back in January, it had invited in a group of economists to evaluate the IMF's performance in dealing with the "Asian contagion." The initial question posed was whether the IMF were "the amputating god or angel of mercy. Six months later, the paper had concluded that the IMF was indeed an "amputating god." On July 20 Malaysian Special Functions Minister Tun Daim Zainuddin told a seminar that the IMF has "failed, and failed miserably" in dealing with the Asian crisis. For Mexico City's *Excelsior*, Indonesia was the "cruel mirror" in which the emerging market victims of the IMF could contemplate their own future destiny; columnist Neme Salum expatiated on the "Hitlerian nature of the IMF." Italian economist Paolo Savona compared the post-1971 monetary arrangements to Sicily's famous volcano "Mount Etna, where once in a while a crack opens and swallows a gorgeous slice of land." Among the Asian states there was a wave of barter deals, in which jets, cars, rice, electronics and other commodities were exchanged among Thailand, Indonesia, Malaysia, and South Korea outside of the financial system – a sure sign that the world monetary arrangements were failing in the most basic way.

---

[34] Kompas/*Straits Times*, September 1, 1998.

THE SPRINGTIME OF WALL STREET AND BELTWAY EUPHORIA

Despite this grim world situation, the springtime of 1998 was marked by the gloating of the Clinton administration over the first US budget surplus in three decades, an unemployment rate of 4.1%, and the new highs of the stock market. Stoked by flight capital exiting the stricken markets of Asia and Latin America, the Dow peaked on July 17. For the lesser fry, the party had ended earlier: the Russell 2000 index of small-cap stocks reached its peak back in April. According to Salomon Smith Barney, the average NYSE stock fell 24% in the 11 days after the July 17 top, while the average NASDAQ issue fell 35% and small cap stocks fell 43%. The Dow was maintained with the help of the Brady drugged market system described in the following chapter.

> World Bank official Jean-Michel Severino told a conference in Melbourne, Australia on June 16, "We are probably at the end of the first cycle of the crisis and we are entering into a deep recession, or you could even use the term depression. This depression could be very long-lasting."

Then true global panic began to clutch the human heart in its icy claws.

SOROS SINKS THE RUBLE

During the month of May, the Russian stock market took a 44% dive. On June 3, a billion-dollar GKO auction produced a 54% coupon yield, and even this was considered a moral victory. The putrid Russian banking system also began to generate concern. The Toko Bank failed, and the stock price of the Sberbank, which was the centerpiece of the national savings mechanism and the largest holder of GKOs, was mercilessly hammered. The Moscow interbank market was approaching breakdown, with the potential for chain-reaction bankruptcy for all Russian banks. US Deputy Treasury Secretary Larry Summers, one of the svengalis of shock therapy, was forced to admit that "Russia's problem has the potential to become.... central Europe's and the world's." Treasury Secretary Rubin seconded this analysis, telling CNN: "There is also the risk once again of contagion if Russia really has substantial instability and difficulties that can spread to central Europe and that they can spread further." Contagion was now the euphemism for panic. The terminology was reminiscent of the Vienna banking crisis of spring 1931, with the GKOs in the role of the "mass of kited bills" against which President Hoover inveighed at that time (see Chapter VII).

Part of the difficulty was that the only visible means of support for post-1991 Russia was the sale of oil and raw materials on the world market. The prices for oil and metals were now at two-decade lows, meaning that Russia's foreign exchange was becoming very scarce. The fall in the world oil price in 1986 had helped to doom Gorbachev; a repeat of the oil price collapse now threatened to finish off his successor. "What's the issue?" asked shock therapist Boris Nemtsov on June 29. "Will we succeed in avoiding a bankruptcy of the Russian Federation or not? That is the issue." The answer soon proved to be default. On July 13, the IMF announced an emergency 2-year loan package of $22.6 billion, supposedly designed to stabilize the ruble. $11.2 of this was the IMF's own money, with much of the rest from Japan and the World Bank. The Russian stock market rose by 28% between July 13 and July 15, but it proved to be a mugs' rally.

On August 13, the *banquerotteur à la baisse* George Soros opined in the London *Financial Times* that Russian finances were "in a terminal state," and demanded a devaluation of the ruble by 15-25%. Holders of GKOs started to panic, and the yields on GKOs, which move in the opposite direction to their prices, rose from the previous day's close of 137% to 210%, a high rate for the government paper. The Moscow business journal *Kommersant* described this ploy by Soros as "the trigger, but certainly not the cause" of the catastrophe which now ensued for Russia. Foreign banks issued urgent margin calls to Russian banks, since foreign loans to the Russians secured by Russian securities as collateral were now insufficient to cover the value of these loans. Ironically, it was just a month after the IMF bailout package for Russia, which had been touted as a solution for all such problems. Thanks in large part to Soros, August 13, 1998 became Moscow's Black Thursday, the day when Moscow's interbank clearing system, the local equivalent of CHIPS, CHAPS or BOJ-Net, jammed up and froze completely. Just before Black Thursday, Prime Minister Kiriyenko had started talking about the need to stimulate production – in itself a departure from the shock therapy litany, according to which production would always take care of itself. On August 19, Central Bank Chairman Dubinin was obliged to confirm that the entire $4.8 billion initial IMF *tranche*, which had been transferred to Russia in July, had already been spent in fruitless currency support operations and in a $1 billion buyback of GKOs.

MOSCOW, AUGUST 17, 1998: BEGINNING OF THE END FOR GLOBALONEY[35]

On August 17, 1998 the Russian government imposed long overdue capital controls and exchange controls. Prime Minister Kiriyenko announced that the government would attempt to defend a ruble parity of about 9.5 to the dollar with the help of the new measures; this amounted to a devaluation of 34%. Principal payments on $40 billion in foreign loans to Russian banks and other firms were banned for 90 days, meaning that Russia was officially in default. Soon the default covered Russia's $180 billion in foreign obligations. GKOs and OFZs reaching maturity between August 17 and December 31, 1999 were restructured by *ukaz* into long-term obligations.

Payments by Russian banks to foreign creditors were banned for 90 days. The dozen top Russian banks were ordered to form a payments pool to ensure the liquidity of the interbank market. There was no immediate formal default on scheduled debt payments pledged specifically by the Russian government to foreign entities, but this followed *de facto* within less than two weeks. The default on GKOs meant that State debt instruments were to be converted: Russian holders of GKO government bonds might get 31 kopeks for every ruble, while foreign holders would get only 11 kopeks on the ruble. For Russia and the world, it was a great watershed, the end of an era. According to press reports, foreign investors had signed forward currency contracts with Russian banks in the amount of some $100 billion. This mass of kited derivatives was used by foreign holders of GKOs and OFZ state securities to hedge against changes in the value of the ruble. If the Russian banks had been forced to honor these contracts (stipulated before the August ruble collapse), these banks would have been bankrupted. But the controls instituted on August 17 blocked payment on these futures contracts.

The IMF-Sachs-Aslund Russian shock therapy of 1991-92 had marked the worldwide victory of predatory financier capitalism. But now the ascendancy of globaloney was finished; *laissez-faire* was over in Russia, and protectionist forces around the world were recovering enough to contemplate re-regulation as an antidote to the nightmare of speculation. Credit Suisse First Boston, J. P. Morgan, and Deutsche Bank and other big losers howled, threatening various reprisals. Visa International froze the credit cards issued by Russian banks. But if they wanted to treat Russia like a banana republic, they had to remember that Russia had nuclear bananas. A return to regulated currency markets had been advocated by economists like Leonid Abalkin and Sergei Glazyev, a former minister was currently an advisor to Yegor Stroyev, a leader of the Federation Council, the upper house of the Russian parliament. Another leading Russian protectionist was Taras Muranivsky of the Moscow State University for the Humanities.

---

[35] This was the 34th post-war systemic crisis; see the table in Chapter IV.

On August 17, Prime Minister Kiriyenko had stated "The deteriorated situation forced us to retreat to the second line of defense in order to fulfill the program that we adopted. It is this that will be discussed with the international finance organizations." On that same day, Camdessus arrived with an IMF delegation. But this time there was no new bailout. The IMF bailout strategy was in a shambles. "There is nobody left who can play fireman; central banks cannot do it any longer," lamented Bundesbank board member Reimut Joachimsen, the representative of Rheinland-Westfalia on the Bundesbank Council.[36]

STALINGRAD FOR THE IMF

On Friday, August 21, Prime Minister Kiriyenko told the Duma that Russia was about to enter a new and very serious financial crisis. On August 26, German Finance Minister Theo Waigel angrily declared that no help for the stricken Russian Federation would be forthcoming from the IMF, the G-7, or the European Union. "Russia must do it by herself," snapped Waigel. If Russia had no hope of Western largesse, reasoned the speculators, she would have no incentive to remain solvent, so they started to take what money they could and run. First they sought dollars, and the ruble rate declined by 12% compared to the greenback, but soon this department of currency trading was shut down. Then they sought German marks, and here the trading pits stayed open, declining by 41% on that one, fateful day. On August 27, 1998, the automatic convertibility of the Russian ruble, the bedrock of all shock therapy and free market reform, was suspended. On September 12, Russia failed to make a scheduled payment on restructured debt arrears dating back to the Soviet era and owed to the Paris Club of creditors. Russia was supposed to pay $462 million, but managed to scrape together only $115 million. The new Prime Minister, Yevgeny Primakov, stressed that his government "will pay all our debts.... Russia does not refuse to carry out its obligations." But Russian default was now complete all along the line.

Anti-nomenklatura Russian economist Tatyana Koryagina observed around this time that "the world economy has reached the point where – if economic liberalism is a dead-end street, it has hit the concrete wall at the end of the street. This liberalism will explode the entire economy and then there will be global chaos, which will be economic fascism. A 'New World Order' is economic fascism, when a huge number of people are thrown into desperate poverty, and only the speculators make any profit. We are on the verge of a particular sort of anti-financier revolution – a revolution against financial speculators."

Angry depositors were lined up outside Russian banks for weeks. One of the banks hardest hit was the SBS-Agro, the largest commercial retail bank with 2,200 branches, 5.7 million depositors, and 1,500 corporate clients. The boss of SBS-Agro was Aleksandr Smolensky, who had gone from petty hustling under the Communist regime to elbow his way into the restricted clique of self-styled oligarchs who were the power behind the Yeltsin regime. Now, with irate savers besieging Smolensky's posh offices, his insolvent bank was on the verge of being seized by the Russian government. "Things are warped. It's a catastrophe," said Smolensky. The Communist Party was demanding the re-nationalization of key industries.

HEDGE FUNDS AND BANKS MAULED ON RUSSIAN FRONT

Among the big losers was Credit Suisse First Boston, which had long been one of the most important participants in the market for Russian state securities, the so-called GKOs. Now CSFB had to confess to trading losses of $500 million on the Russian front, although rumors put the losses

---

[36] *Corriere della Sera*, August 27, 1998.

as $2-$3 billion, enough to prove fatal, and perhaps enough to activate the fabled system of Swiss financial self-defense, which aims above all at saving the three largest banks in the Zürich Bahnhofstraße, of which Credit Suisse is one.

American banks and hedge funds suffered heavy losses of their own on Russian Treasury debt. The face value of the Russian Treasury debt was about $40 billion, and was been written down to about $7 billion, for a loss of $33 billion. Of that $33 billion loss, about one-quarter-- or $8 billion-- was sustained by foreign holders of Russian GKOs. Then there were losses on investments in Russian stocks, losses on about $100 billion in Russian derivatives, and losses on direct loans by Western financial institutions of loans to Russian banks and industry. According to a late August report by Morningstar, which monitors mutual funds, three emerging-market funds which had between 10 and 20% of their investments invested in Russian debt and bonds, had lost close to 30% for the year to date. The three were Morgan Stanley Institutional Emerging Markets Debt A, Morgan Grenfell Emerging Markets Debt, and the T. Rowe Price Emerging Markets Bond Fund. Edmond Safra's Republic National Bank of New York announced a $110-million charge in the third quarter, wiping out its earnings for the period. Chase Manhattan was vulnerable to the Russian events because of its $500 million in exposure; J.P. Morgan had slightly under $400 million; BankAmerica, with $412 million; Citicorp checked in with $500 million; and Bankers Trust had $1 billion. Goldman Sachs was reported to have incurred losses. The Quantum Fund of George Soros, based in the Netherlands Antilles, had lost $2 billion in Russia, some in bonds, but mostly in stocks, according to chief investment officer Stanley Druckenmiller. The Julian Robertson Tiger Fund later posted a $3.4 billion loss, a hit equal to 17% of the fund's value – despite the presence on the Tiger board of directors of Lady Margaret Thatcher. Everest Capital, a $2.7-billion hedge fund based in Bermuda, lost about $500 million. Omega Fund, a $4.5 billion hedge fund run by Leon Cooperman, had a Russian debt position of $135 million, most of which was lost. The High Risk Opportunity Fund, a $450-million fund run by III Offshore Advisors, a West Palm Beach, Florida hedge fund, held ruble-denominated debt of $850 million, and was reportedly wiped out. Estimates began to circulate in the world press according to which Western investors in Russia could hope to get 17-20 cents on the dollar out of their investments, at most. German banks, whose exposure was know to be great, attempted to cultivate the impression that their lending to Russia was covered by the Hermes system of government-backed export credit insurance, named for the deputy minister who designed it back during the Helmut Schmidt era. In this case, a large part of the $56 billion in German bank loans to Russia would have to be made good by the German taxpayer. But the exposure of German banks included trade financing of Gazprom and other firms, and also excludes German bank holdings of Russian GKOs, which were now worthless outside of Russia. The *Frankfurter Allgemeine* commented on August 29 that "the developments in Russia rather are, as is often the case in stock market history," the "forceful prick with the needle, which will make the balloon of illusions blow apart." On the following Monday, just as Clinton was flying to Moscow to meet with Yeltsin and the Russian government, the Dow tumbled 517 points in New York, the second worst daily point loss on record. The very heavy selling was attributed to hedge funds liquidating US assets to cover the huge losses they had sustained on the Russian front. The hedge funds were the carriers of the contagion.

WORSE THAN 1917

Part of the Russian tragedy was that, under shock therapy, the country had become dependent on imported food. Butter imports to Russia were likely to fall by 20% and more in 1998, according to spokesman for the New Zealand Dairy Board, which was demanding cash up front for all shipments. Fruit imports to Russia, especially from the USA, were dropping by 30% to 50%.

Shortages of fruit, sugar, pasta, and flour were quickly emerging. Cargoes bound for Russia were piling up on the docks in German and Baltic ports, while Russian importers figured out whether and how they should pay. Some types of raw materials exports accelerated, due to the 50% devaluation of the ruble.[37] A society to which Raisa Gorbacheva belonged published an appeal for the homeless children of Russia, who numbered over 2 million. During Clinton's visit to Moscow, he met with opposition leaders, including General Aleksandr Lebed, the military man turned politician. Lebed said after the meeting, "I told him today that the situation in Russia is catastrophic. The situation is worse than 1917... Now we have stockpiles of poorly-guarded nuclear weapons." The business newspaper *Kommersant-vlast* of August 18 had predicted conditions comparable to those of the 1918-1921 civil war of the red and white armies, when millions of Russians were killed. The obvious failing of the Russian program was that it did nothing specifically to re-start domestic production, put people back to work, defend living standards, or promote world trade. Without these components, the ghost of Hjalmar Schacht might soon haunt the Kremlin.

August-September 1998 was the moment when a rational US government would have declared a comprehensive debt moratorium on all of Russia's international payment obligations, and would have launched a New Lend-Lease program of the type described at the conclusion of this book. Instead, when President Clinton went to Moscow in the first week of September, he demanded that the Russians stick to the IMF's Herbert Hoover economics, the monetarist folly which had landed Russia in the crisis in the first place. Clinton's refusal to face reality was very ominous for the future of humankind.

In neighboring Poland, the immiseration became aggravated to the point that the post-communist elite became concerned that the impoverished but unbowed Polish working people, with their strong revolutionary traditions, might be goaded into insurrection. The decline in standards of living was specifically attributable to the so-called "Plan II," a new brainchild of Finance Minister and Deputy Prime Minister Leszek Balcerowicz, an annex of the IMF and the resident enforcer of Poland's first round of shock therapy back in the 1980s. Balcerowicz wanted to fire 120,000 miners and 40,000 steel workers. Despite 30% short-term interest rates, venture capital began to flee the country, with $8 billion vanishing during just a few months.

The world depression was deepening: India, although somewhat insulated from the currency dramas of 1997 by the fact that the rupee was already floating, found that her exports had declined 8% during the first quarter of 1998. In May alone, exports had collapsed by 17.4%. By June, exports were down 11% from the year-ago level. At this point India had about $25 billion in foreign exchange, and the rupee was sliding inexorably lower. India had been wise enough to resist some of the key points in the globalization program: the rupee remained not fully convertible, the main commercial banks remained in the state sector, there had been little privatization of government-owned companies, labor laws still protected jobs, farmers still received subsidies, and imports of consumer goods were discouraged. As a result of this vestigial protectionism, India fared better than many other Asian countries in 1998.

$18 BILLION FOR THE IMF?

After having earmarked $20 billion for Thailand, $45 billion for Indonesia, $57 billion for South Korea, $23 billion for Russia, and $2 billion for Ukraine, the IMF's coffers were severely depleted. The Russian bailout of July 13, as we have seen, left the IMF – with between $3 and $8 billion left in its depleted till – strapped for cash and highly vulnerable to new outbreaks of panic. As

---

[37] *Journal of Commerce*, August 31, 1998.

Greenspan frequently stressed, the world finance oligarchy saw a replenishing of the IMF as an immediate imperative. But late in the evening of July 21, House Speaker Newt Gingrich decided not to bring to the floor the funding authorization bill which would have given the IMF $18 billion in taxpayers' money for new bailouts. GOP circles offered verbiage about the need for delay to allow an evaluation of the effectiveness IMF policies in treating the Asian and Russian crisis, but it was clear that many Republicans were frightened of voting for a handout to the international banker shortly before the November 1998 Congressional elections. At this time, polls were giving the Democratic Party a fighting chance to win the dozen seats needed to re-assume control of the House, putting a certain end to Gingrich's career. Gingrich as tax collector for the IMF made an inviting target. Gingrich undoubtedly thought that it would be much safer politically to punt for the moment, and then to force Clinton to assume the opprobrium of calling the Congress back after the November election for a lame duck session to approve the IMF funding. But this time, the bear blew first....

The IMF funding had been held up primarily by Rep. Dick Armey of Texas, the Republican Majority leader. Armey was an obscure economics professor from Texas and an obsessive monetarist ideologue; he opposed the IMF for all the wrong reasons, but may nevertheless go down in history as one of its gravediggers. On July 17 and 18, press reports had told of Armey, for one, giving up his efforts to block the IMF refunding. But opposition to the IMF bailout went far beyond Armey as an individual. Gingrich's tenure as Speaker must appear as extremely unsatisfactory from the point of view of the international financiers. He had been expected to get legislation passed to prop up the stock market by investing Social Security contributions in common stocks, or even in mutual funds, but he had failed to do so. Now, he had failed to rescue the IMF *in extremis*. On September 1, House Appropriations Committee Chairman Robert Livingston reportedly reversed his earlier position and decided to oppose the $18 billion for the IMF.[38] The $18 billion for the IMF was finally contained in the appropriations bills passed towards the end of October 1998. Giving this money to Camdessus after the IMF had certified its own uselessness by way of the Russian debacle was a sign that the US ruling elite had a very tenuous hold on the real world.

These days, an $18 billion bailout fund can be consumed by just a week or two of hedge-fund attack against a medium-sized country. The United States government would have been much better advised to outlaw hedge funds, while using the $18 billion as an economic development fund for Israel, Jordan, Lebanon, and the Palestinian state. The Wye River talks between Arafat and Netanyahu, which were held just as this appropriation was going through, showed that the Israeli-Palestinian negotiations had reached the extreme outer limits of what could be accomplished without a US-sponsored Marshal Plan for the Middle East. Giving $18 billion to the IMF was like throwing it down a rat hole – worse, since it permitted the IMF to exacerbate the world depression with its Herbert Hoover economic prescriptions in the face of imminent disintegration.

JAPAN: THE PARALYSIS OF AN OLIGARCHY

Japan remained the epicenter of the world financial and monetary crisis. By the beginning of 1998, the country was reeling from the bankruptcies of Hokutaku Bank and Yamaichi Securities, and business confidence was at a new nadir. The Japanese government was promising world central bankers and finance ministers that Tokyo would permit "no more defaults" – a wholly impossible task. The proper approach would have been a law imposing a uniform and orderly freeze on all real estate and financial debt associated with the Japanese bubble, with all this paper remaining in

---

[38] *Congressional Quarterly Monitor*, September 1, 1998.

suspended animation for the duration of the crisis. But with Hashimoto came the spell of Britain's Tony Blair, who was lionized on his visit to Japan, where he preached breakneck liberalization at all costs. On January 12, with Blair still in the country, a receptive Prime Minister Hashimoto appeared before the Diet with a $500 billion bailout package for the insolvent Japanese banking system. Hashimoto stated specifically that the purpose of his measures was to prevent Japan from becoming the detonator of a "world financial crisis" and a "world recession." Hashimoto wanted to add $130 billion to the Japanese deposit insurance fund, allegedly to protect savers, but more likely to bail out stockholders and bond holders of the banks. A new fund with the significant name "Special Budget for Crisis Management in the Financial System" was created with an endowment of $100 billion. The government-operated Postal Savings Bank, where many Japanese now preferred to leave their money for safe-keeping, was instructed to make new loans quickly to expand credit. $45 billion was earmarked for tax cuts for households. It soon turned out that the Japanese banks felt that they would lose face if they were to activate these arrangements for their own benefit; perhaps they also feared panic runs sparked by hedge funds if they announced that they needed government help. In any case, scant use was made of the government bailout facility during the following months. Hashimoto had proposed the biggest financial bailout in history, but it was still a financial bailout, and it failed to save Hashimoto, much less the banks.

By strict accounting standards, Japan Inc. would have been insolvent at midnight on March 31, 1998, but the word had gone out from the ministries that "accounting leniency" was now in order, and so the banks were able to survive. It was a replay of the forbearance enjoyed by the US banks during the Bush years. Hashimoto insisted with going ahead with his "Big Bang" liberalization of financial markets at the beginning of the new Japanese fiscal year on April 1, 1998. Hashimoto would have been better advised to re-regulate, instituting capital controls and currency controls to protect the falling yen. The Japanese Central Bank became virtually independent of government control, in a move that imitated recent changes at the Bank of England. Financial markets were deregulated. The immediate effect of these changes was to facilitate the flight of speculative capital out of the country.

On April 25, the Hashimoto government proposed a stimulus package of $128 billion in government spending and related measures in the hope of stopping deflation and pulling the country out of its slump. The money supply was 51% larger than it had been twelve months earlier, but deflation continued unabated. Certain circles tried to exploit the international financial tension to engineer a break between the US and Japan. Eric Lincoln of the Brookings Institution seriously proposed a campaign of petty affronts and insults to Japanese diplomats to telegraph that the US "no longer regards Japan as a global partner."

In May, Eisuke Sakakibara repeated that a New Bretton Woods approach might be needed to reform the current world monetary arrangements. Soon, Mita copiers went bankrupt, while Mazda and Mitsubishi were in trouble in the auto sector. Kobe Steel and NKK were also in dire straits. Tao Steel announced liquidation in early September, and Hitachi said that, with losses of $1.8 billion projected for the current year, it was facing its worst financial crisis since the war. The falling yen caused widespread consternation among the other Asian nations especially. On June 11, Thailand's Deputy Prime Minister Panitchpakdi warned that the skidding yen "might trigger a second crisis" in Asia that would be worse than anything seen so far. Such a crisis, he warned, "would pull the whole world into it. It would be like a black hole. The second Asian crisis would mean the first worldwide depression."

On June 18, the United States and Japan joined in a half-hearted and episodic support operation for the very weak yen. The New York Federal reserve, acting for the Treasury, bought about $4 billion worth of yen, raising the yen rate of exchange from 147 to 137 to the dollar. This was a Rubin-Sakakibara co-production arranged in telephone conversations between Clinton and Hashimoto. But it soon developed that there was no comprehensive strategy.

HASHIMOTO HOOVERIZED BY THE CRISIS

The Japanese were referring to their predicament as the "Hesei depression," meaning the depression of the reign of Emperor Akahito. Norio Ohga, the chairman of Sony, on April 2 derided Prime Minister Hashimoto as "'worse than Herbert Hoover." By June, Hashimoto's popularity was down to 30%. He was under attack from the City of London: on June 16, Anatole Kaletsky of the London *Times*, picked up the line that he was "Herbert Hoover of Japan," while claiming that Japan's "economic problems are so trivial and the solutions are so obvious." Kaletsky wanted to activate the yen printing presses. On July 12, Japanese voters massively repudiated the Liberal Democratic Party and the Hashimoto government at the polls. In voting for the Upper House of the Diet, the LDP lost 17 seats, while opposition parties made large gains.

In August, a new government was formed under Prime Minister Keizo Obuchi, a veteran wheelhorse of the Takeshita faction of the Japanese Liberal Democratic Party. By this time, the mass of non-performing debt burdening the Japanese banking system was widely estimated to have climbed to about $1.5 trillion – more than enough to scuttle the entire world system, to which the Japanese banks were joined by a myriad of derivatives contracts. At a time when decisive measures of debt moratorium and debt reorganization were urgently required, Obuchi attempted to continue along the accustomed path of the Japanese political-financial oligarchy. As Finance Minister he appointed another senior LDP baron, the former Prime Minister Kiichi Miyazawa. Miyazawa, as Finance Minister in an earlier government, had presided over the launching of the notorious Japanese bubble of 1986-1991. Miyazawa was associated with the so-called bridge bank scheme, which was based on a plan drawn up by marplot economist Jeffrey Sachs – the wrecker of Bolivia, Poland, and Russia, who now had Dai Nippon as his quarry. The bridge bank (or "total") was a warmed-over version of the Bush administration's Resolution Trust Corporation (RTC), which bailed out US S&Ls and real estate interests after the orgy of real estate speculation during the Reagan years. The first chairman of the RTC was William Seidman (known these days for his weekly pontification sessions as the senior commentator of the cable financial news network CNBC), who hastened to Tokyo to share the secret of his "success story." But the RTC had never been a success story: it was an outrageous bailout of speculators funded by the American wage earner, with a bill to taxpayers that was already somewhere between $100 billion and $200 billion, a figure destined to increase at compound interest over many years to come. The RTC had been a significant factor in the stagnation of US living standards during the alleged Clinton recovery after 1993.

The special adviser to the Obuchi cabinet on financial strategy was Toyoo Gyohten, the alter ego and partner of Paul Volcker, whom we have already encountered. Gyohten, like Volcker, could be counted upon to act as a "financial institutions conservative" – attempting to save the banks and their mass of bad debts at the expense of factories, living standards and the real economy. Gyohten is associated with the "internationalization of the yen," something that might lead to currency blocs under the present circumstances.

The mentality of the Obuchi regime was a stubborn attempt to deny the gravity of the crisis, and to avoid a radical break with established routine. From the standpoint of traditional Japanese ethics, failure to pay one's debts is incompatible with personal dignity – it represents a loss of face. It is considered unethical for bankers to announce that they are writing off bad debts, even if they have the loan loss provisions to be able to do so. To save the bank and the debtor from both losing face, new low-interest loans are extended, and the illusion of solvency and respectability all around is preserved. The almost hysterical resistance to owning up to the enormity of the insolvency led to a situation in which Japanese banks routinely hid the extent of their bad debts, opening a vulnerable flanks for hedge funds, who were free to spread wild rumors about imminent bank failures and to short the stock of the banks they targeted. The Long Term Credit Bank (LTCB), struggling to survive with its immense portfolio of non-performing loans, was a prime example. On August 25, Finance Minister Miyazawa told the Diet that a derivatives default by the LTCB alone "could lead to a Japan-triggered global financial depression." (By mid-September, the LTCB was about to be nationalized; its good loans were slated to be sold to Sumitomo, while its bad loans would be taken over by the long-suffering Japanese taxpayers. Yasuda Trust, Daiwa Bank, and Fuji Bank were not far behind.) This was the transparency issue so widely touted by Wall Street – although Wall Street, needless to say, was far from ready to practice the Saran-wrap accounting that it was preaching for the Japanese. On September 10, the *Kochi Shimbun* reported that 19 of Japan's largest banks had potential derivatives losses of ¥24 trillion – about $180 billion. Denials of this highly plausible report failed to restore confidence.

Japan was prodded in a more constructive direction by China, which felt strains because the yen – having fallen 20% since the New Year as a result of the Japanese strategy of competitive devaluation – was now far too low. On June 25, the Chinese Foreign Ministry stated that "Japan, as a major economic power, should assume greater responsibility at a time of Asian economic difficulties. The yen should play a role of stabilizing Asian economies and not become a destabilizing factor," which it clearly already was. In the absence of a policy change, Japan was heading towards a short-term deflationary collapse, perhaps triggered by the default of a large bank or banks on derivatives contract with overseas institutions.

THE COLLAPSE OF FREE MARKET IDEOLOGY

By September, Krugman of MIT was proposing "the drastic step of imposing currency controls" as a fall-back option for saving the System.[39] Intelligent European opinion had never forgotten that capital controls are an indispensable part of the modern state's armory of self defense. During the second wave of the hedge funds' speculative attack on the European Monetary System (EMS) in 1993 (see Chapter IV), Maurice Allais had talked about the obvious necessity of stopping this new piracy: "The entire West is now in a fundamentally unstable financial situation," Allais told a Paris newspaper. "Poorly considered decisions could the whole world into a collapse, compared to which the stock market crisis of 1987 will seem negligible, and which could be comparable to the Great Depression." In that discussion, Allais warned that the "perverse effects of unrestricted currency exchanges are very much underestimated." Allais cited the obvious remedy: "In the immediate term, only European Community exchange controls would give us the means temporarily to deal with the situation.... In fact, no measure that would permit the speculators to succeed, and to enrich themselves, is acceptable.... The current attack against the EMS, the only coherent monetary organization in the world, is based on gigantic disinformation. It is animated, supported, and orchestrated in an incredible way by financial interests, whose origin governments should investigate."

Back in 1993, Jacques Delors – who was at that time the President of the European Commission – had intervened in a debate on monetary issues in the European Parliament to state: "I don't see why, on the international level, we should not be studying ways to limit capital movements."

---

[39] Paul Krugman, "Saving Asia: It's Time To Get Radical," *Fortune,* September 7, 1998.

[September 13, 1993] Delors spoke of the possibility of European Community regulations to prevent wild speculation by means of controls on the movements of capital. The monetarist side reacted to these moderate proposals with hysteria. Delors was demonized by British finance officials as a leading figure in the sinister "eurocrat" clique of Brussels. When Delors left office in June 1994, he attacked the "brutal and purist neo-liberal ideology" for disregarding "the idea of the public good." Delors' monetary and infrastructure policies were thereupon branded by Rees-Mogg as "insane" and liable to "cause a panic in the European bond markets." But even in Britain, re-regulation has not died out completely. Former Labour Party Chancellor of the Exchequer Dennis Healy has proposed a tax on financial derivatives. Healy pointed to the "systemic risk" posed to the world financial system by the new instruments.

ZURICH GNOMES: BETTER POISON THAN *GAU*

The *Neue Zürcher Zeitung* felt desperate enough to sacrifice the purity of monetarist ideology in the interests of staying out of bankruptcy court. "With the ruble collapse and the de facto state bankruptcy of Russia, the crisis which has been boiling for a year is now threatening to turn into a global *GAU*-- *Größten aller Unfälle*, or worst possible calamity, wrote this paper. "Like dominoes, one currency after the other, one financial market after the other, is falling throughout the globe. The specter of a worldwide recession is spreading." The editorial singled out the Chinese RMB, the only stable currency in Asia. The reason for this stability was in the Swiss view not only China's $140 billion in foreign exchange reserves, but also the fact that the RMB is not fully convertible. Quoting Krugman on the need for "temporary foreign exchange controls," the *NZZ* hastened to add that this proposal comes straight from the "poison cabinet;" although these were "disgusting perspectives for a world which was just about to remove the last remnants of capital controls in the age of globalization," the Swiss finance paper concluded that there was no alternative to a quick trip to the poison cabinet.[40]

HANKE BLAMES PLATO

Ultra-monetarist ideologue Steve Hanke of Johns Hopkins responded by claiming that "The idea of exchange controls can be traced back to Plato, the father of statism. Inspired by Sparta, Plato embraced the idea of an inconvertible currency as a means to preserve the autonomy of the state from outside interference. It's no wonder that the so-called Red-Brown (Communist-fascist) coalition in the Russian Duma has, in recent weeks, rallied around the idea of exchange controls and an inconvertible ruble. This also explains why the leadership of Beijing finds the idea so user-friendly. The temptation to turn to exchange controls in the face of disruption caused by 'hot money' flows is hardly new. Tsar Nicholas II first pioneered limitations on convertibility in modern times, ordering the State Bank of Russia to introduce in 1905-06 a limited form of exchange control to discourage speculative purchases of foreign exchange." Hanke also cited Friedrich von Hayek's 1944 anti-New Deal tirade, *The Road to Serfdom*, in an attempt to show that foreign exchange controls represented "decisive advance on the path to totalitarianism and the suppression of individual liberty" and "the complete delivery of the individual to the tyranny of the state, the final suppression of all means of escape not merely for the rich, but for everybody."[41] The United States, of course, had imposed exchange controls during most of the 1960s, but the ultra-monetarists tried to associate them only with the bloodiest dictatorships.

---

[40] "Monetary Policy Out of the Poison Cabinet," *Neue Zürcher Zeitung*, August 29, 1998.
[41] "The Siren Song of Exchange Controls," *Wall Street Journal* European edition, September 1, 1998.

DEBTOR IN POSSESSION

Business Week showed a dose of realism in a call for a "New Deal" on global debt: it was "time for a global write-down" in the form of "debtor-in-possession financing. Debtor In Possession (DIP) involves segregating the defaulted loans of a bankrupt company, wiping the slate clean, and starting the borrowing process all over. A restructured company gets new credit, the bank gets a small percentage of its old unwise loans back over time, and everyone starts to play the all-important growth game again. DIP is a desperation strategy used only when corporations face ruin and banks stand to lose everything. This is increasingly the plight of Russia, Asia, and parts of Latin America, where de facto default may be the best choice among evils .... Ask any Kansas farmer or CEO of a multinational in Chicago. World demand for their products is plummeting, along with prices paid and profits made." Noting that many banks face write-offs ranging from 30% in Hong Kong to up to 80% in Indonesia and 90% in Russia, the magazine suggested that even these banks would be better off exchanging bad debt for new long-term paper. Japan would be a prime beneficiary of such an approach. "Only a dramatic write-down can get the country moving again and pull Asia with it." [42]

Jacques Sapir of the Paris School of Higher Studies in the Social Sciences, provided some sound advice for Russian policy makers in particular. "The only reasonable solution," he wrote, "is for the Russian economy to distance itself from the markets ...the Russian government should install extremely strict exchange controls, reserving the buying and sales of currency only to exporters and importers. Then, a limited convertibility must be installed via an administrated exchange rate. This was, by the way, the situation in France in the fifties." Sapir proposed to provide an injection of liquidity to end the barter economy and ward off the emergence of local currencies in the Russian regions. Sapir sensibly pointed out that "the Russian economy cannot survive on raw material exports alone." The long-term Russian interest was a "relaunching of industry," including consumer goods and heavy industrial equipment for the public sector. Sapir was on firm ground when he called for a change in overall economic doctrine for Russia: "The moral discrediting of liberalism in Russia is today a key problem to the social stability, or, on the contrary, the instability of the country...Russian officials could well inspire themselves by what was done in Europe and in particular in France, especially during the post-Second World War period of reconstruction." [43] Laurent Joffrin of *Liberation* called for Russia to break with the "market fundamentalists" and return to the path of statist guidance of the economy.[44] On the floor of the European Parliament in Strasbourg, the German Christian Democrat Elmar Brok deplored the German and European negligence which had allowed "Harvard professors" to "preach unfettered liberalism" to the Russians, with European taxpayers now left holding the bag.

Even British newspapers were suddenly open to the once-taboo topic of monetary reform. On March 8, 1998, the London *Observer* had ridiculed the notion of a New Bretton Woods conference. By Friday, August 28, the leftish *Guardian* was publishing a commentary advocating the immediate convening of a "new Bretton Woods" conference. The *Guardian*'s Dan Atkinson called for a return to the New Deal in response to the crisis: "The money-changers are fleeing the temple of civilization.... With the 1990s 'triumph of capitalism' going up in flames, what would [Roosevelt] have done today?" "Roosevelt, we can be confident, would have had little time for bond dealers or derivatives traders .... He would have understood that, as in the 1920s, banking and speculation are the problem, not the solution. Roosevelt would have pressed for an international version of the

---

[42] "Needed: a New Deal on Global Debt," *Business Week*, September 7, 1998.

[43] *Le Figaro*, September 1, 1998.

[44] *Liberation,* September 1, 1998.

Glass-Steagall Act, limiting each bank to one country and forcing them to divest their investment arms and other activities. No `global' banks for him.... as the deflationary gale hit with full force, Roosevelt would have mobilized the public sector to stand ready as employer of last resort. There would have been no question of ordinary workers bearing the pain of `adjustment.'" "He would have beefed up the financial regulators as he did 60 years ago, and unleashed them on the guilty men: the rogue traders and insider dealers. Lengthy prison terms could have been expected." Above all, FDR would "have convened an international summit to reshape the institutions (World Bank, IMF) that helped us into this mess in the first place, purging them of their obsession with sound money and balanced budgets."

THE END OF FREE MARKET UTOPIA

Robert Kuttner, who had toiled over the years to salvage something of the spirit of the New Deal in the Democratic Party, attributed the financial turbulence to "the great illusion of our era – the utopian worship of free markets." After the collapse of communism, the world had been afflicted by "an almost lunatic credulity in pure markets and a messianic urge to spread them worldwide." The current wreckage was due to the depredation of international speculators, but the "IMF perversely demands exposure to speculators as a precondition of assistance. Kuttner warned that the protectionist measures of Russian and Malaysia were not part of "a coherent system of stabilization and development" and might therefore become "isolationist and destabilizing." But surely the creation of a rational New World Economic Order was the task of the United States, and not of the smaller countries. Kuttner called upon "the economic priesthood of the West" to revise its "ultra free-market" litany: "What we need is a program of stabilization and reconstruction in the spirit of the post-World War II years, with limits on speculative money flows and more development aid.... Let's hope conventional wisdom shifts before crisis turns to catastrophe."

ALLAIS AFTER THE LTCM DEBACLE

Nobel laureate Maurice Allais responded to the August-September acceleration of the crisis by calling for "deep and radical reforms" to deal with the present crisis. Allais saw the two main problems of the financial system as "the *ex-nihilo* creation of money, and short-term borrowing used to finance long-term loans." He demanded that "monetary creation must be relegated to the State and only to the State" and that "all monetary creation other than that of basic currency by the central bank must be rendered impossible." Allais condemned existing stock markets as "true casinos" whose fluctuations "considerably influence the real economy." Allais proposed to fight margin buying, program trading and index arbitrage, suggesting that "the financing of stock exchange operations by the creation of *ex-nihilo* means of payment by the banking system be rendered impossible." He further recommended that the continuous intra-day quotation of stocks-prices be eliminated, and replaced in each financial market by a single quotation or fixing per day for each stock or bond, as a way of suppressing the day-trading activity of hedge funds and others. He urged that "the automatic programs of buying and selling be eliminated; and speculation on indexes and on derivative products be ended." Allais noted that the "international monetary structure" is characterized by "major perversions," among which he enumerated "the instability of floating exchange rates; the imbalances in current account balance of payments; competitive devaluations; the development of a massive speculation on the exchange markets; the worldwide utilization, as unit of value, of the dollar, whose real value on the international level is extraordinarily unstable and unpredictable; the fundamental contradiction between a total liberalization of short-term capital movements and the autonomy of national monetary policies."

Allais proposed "a New Bretton Woods system," which he saw as mandatory because "institutions which generate in themselves the germs of their own destruction" must be reformed. Such a reform would have to include: "the total abandonment of a system of floating exchange rates and its replacement by a system of fixed, although eventually revisable, exchange rates; exchange rates ensuring an effective equilibrium of balances of payments; the prohibition of any competitive devaluation; the complete abandonment of the dollar as currency of account, exchange and reserve at the international level; the fusion in one body of the World Trade Organization and of the International Monetary Fund; the creation of regional organizations; prohibition of the large banks' speculating for their own account on foreign exchange, stocks and derivative products; and finally, the progressive establishment of a common accounting unit at the international level with an appropriate system of indexation." [45] These reforms were far more vigorous and comprehensive than anything proposed by mainstream Anglo-American academics.

CHINA'S DEFENSE OF THE REN MIN BI

China was committed neither to devalue the ren min bi (RMB), nor to sever its link with the US dollar. During 1998, the official Chinese line changed from determination to keep the present value of the RMB fixed at least through the present year to "maintaining the ren min bi's value through the year 2000 and beyond." But, also during 1998, the available reserves of the Bank of China declined by about $40 billion, indicating that China was paying an immense price for currency stability, and might soon have to have recourse to new methods. A great advantage for the Beijing government was that the RMB was not fully convertible in the way that the Hong Kong dollar was. The Chinese motivated their policy during the summer of 1998 with statements like this one by central banker Liu Mingkang, Vice Director of the People's Bank of China: "China is a responsible member of the international community, and her policy must be to take into account other nations' interests. A big devaluation of the RMB would be a blow to other nations' economies, while a small devaluation would have no advantage.... Imports [of semi-finished commodities and export industry equipment] make up over 50% of the price of China's export of manufactured products. Devaluing by 10% would yield a price cut of less than 5%, but would immediately lead to increases in domestic prices and a negative foreign reaction, and in the end would just cause sever damage to market confidence. Thus, for China, devaluation is not a good measure."

The Chinese also argued that even if the Japanese yen fell further, this would create no problems for China that needed to be solved by Chinese devaluation. Japanese high-tech exports and Chinese foodstuffs and light industry products did not directly compete, and cheaper Japanese capital goods were a boon for the Chinese development strategy. During August, the Chinese State Administration of Foreign Exchange (SAFE) issued a circular banning the widespread practice of hedging against a devaluation of the RMB, a practice that had been undermining the currency. Foreign companies frequently borrowed RMB to pay off foreign currency loans before they matured, but no more.

THE HONG KONG BEAR TRAP

The autonomous Chinese administration in Hong Kong was also determined to protect its own dollar peg. On August 14, 1998 the monetary authorities of the Hong King region used a portion of their $96.4 billion exchange reserves (the world's third largest after those of Japan and the Chinese central government) to engineer a very effective short squeeze against the international hedge fund

---

[45] *Le Figaro*, October 26, 1998.

operators, intervening in currency, stock, and stock index futures markets at the same time. The short squeeze took place on a Friday before a long three-day weekend. According to Hong Kong Financial Secretary Tsang Yam-kuen said that his government had evidence that the hedge funds were mounting a complex "double play" across the currency, stock, and stock index future markets.

The double play started from the hedge funds' perception of Hong Kong as a city-state, small enough to be pushed around. First, the hedge funds established very large short positions against Hong Kong stocks. Then, the hedge funds dumped large amounts of Hong Kong dollars by going short in the futures markets, driving the currency down. This forced Hong Kong Hong Kong to defend its dollar by raising its discount rate and other interest rates. Higher interest rates lowered prices in the Hong Kong stock market, so the hedge funds could cover their short positions and pocket a handsome profit. Officials surprised the hedge funds with massive buying of both HK dollars and Hong Kong stock. "I am certain that if anyone is speculating against the Hong Kong dollar peg, we have the skill and strategies to handle it easily," asserted Tsang. "If speculators want to attack the Hong Kong dollar, they will be punished as usual."

The Hang Seng stock index, which had fallen by over 60% during the past twelve months, managed an 8.5% rise, the biggest percentage gain in 23 years. Hong Kong thus was refusing to imitate the follies of Britain's 1931 "Singapore Defense" of the pound sterling (see Chapter VII). Hong Kong temporarily banned short selling, and readied both criminal penalties for unreported short selling and stiffer sentences for short selling in violation of existing law. Behind Hong Kong stood the Chinese government in Beijing. On the day before the Hong Kong operation, People's Bank of China Deputy Governor had issued a clear warning to the hedge funds, reiterating that "devaluation is not a good policy for China," and pointedly stating: "I would like to tell speculators that China is a big player, and they had best not miscalculate." A few days earlier, on August 8, a dispatch of the New China News Agency datelined Hong Kong and redolent of Hsun Tzu's *Art of War* had dismissed rumors spread by hedge funds about a coming devaluation of the Chinese RMB as the "trick of 'making noise in the east while attacking from the west' being attempted by speculators whose real target was to generate panic in Hong Kong." The hedge funds had also launched a whispering campaign about bank failures in the hopes of starting a panic run on the Hong Kong banks.

Hong Kong Monetary Authority Chief executive Joseph Yam wrote to the *Financial Times* that his goal had been "to tackle currency manipulation by those who have built up large short positions in the stock index futures... we do object to people manipulating our currency to engineer extreme conditions in the interbank market and high interest rates to make profits in the short positions in stock index futures. We have reason to believe there has been such manipulation.... to deter currency manipulation, we took action to tackle the matter at the source, and that meant making sure that those engaging in this activity lose money." Anson Chan, the Hong Kong Chief Secretary for Administration, stressed that the goal of Hong King's measures was to defend its link to the US dollar against the speculators, arguing that "cutting it would set off another wave of currency instability in Asia.... Businesses engaged in those export activities need certainty in exchange rates," he added. In Chan's view, when the British departed Hong Kong in 1997, they left behind a bubble economy in real estate, but the Asian panic had now collapsed real estate also with Hong Kong stocks. Hong Kong had its own $30 billion infrastructure program to fight the depression.

Hong Kong's envoy to the United States, Kenneth Pang, replied to the many critics by protesting that "Hong Kong had "the freest market in the world" where "Adam Smith is as revered as Mother Teresa." But Pang added that "not all speculation is equal," and the hedge fund operators besieging Hong Kong were "the kind of financial gamblers whose cold-bloodedness could freeze mercury at

10 paces.... there comes a time when national governments must defend the public good and their economies. Our actions had nothing to do with Adam Smith and everything to do with responsible economic stewardship. Governments cannot sit idly by while speculators take delight in economic ruin."

The *Financial Times* menacingly headlined, "Hong Kong plays with Fire in Attempt to Hit Speculators." Milton Friedman labeled Hong Kong's measures as "insane." Hong Kong anti-government agitator Martin Lee wailed that 'the invisible hand of Adam Smith has been replaced by the invincible hand of the government." Interestingly, the City of London was divided over the issue. The London *Times* broke ranks with the monetarist purists and commented:

> Titanic struggles are being waged between speculators and the international financial order.... In Hong Kong, self-help is being tried. The authorities detected a speculative plot by hedge funds, and Joseph Yam, sparky head of the Hong Kong Monetary Fund, was allowed to use exchange reserves to buy stocks and share index futures as well as the currency, putting a treble squeeze on hedge funds. More than 45 minutes ahead of a long weekend, this tactic was sensationally successful.... Many Asian currencies, with the exception of China and Hong Kong, have also been driven too low by speculation and the withdrawal of capital.... The IMF...[is not effective because it] does not allow for speculative raids aimed purely at destabilizing markets. Hong Kong could offer a better second-stage response. If it works, it should provide a model for cost-effective international intervention in countries that lack the reserves to do it themselves. If the hedge funds win, world recession looks increasingly likely.

The Achilles heel of Hong Kong was that its banking system, like the British banks which created it, was based on real estate loans. This was the time bomb left ticking when the British departed in 1997. When property prices fell in Britain, there was always a danger that the value of the land and buildings held as collateral by the bank would no longer be enough to cover the value of the loan, so the bank would demand more margin or else call in the loan, bankrupting the borrower. The problem was that by July 1998, property prices in Hong Kong were down 40% from a year before, and their fall had not been arrested by a government freeze on all land sales until March 1999. The outlook was for a further decline of 30 to 40% in late 1998 and early 1999. Falling real estate prices thus threatened to wipe out Hong Kong's banks and capital at the same time.

A pitched battle between the hedge funds (including the Quantum Fund, Tiger Fund, and Moore Capital) and the Hong Kong authorities developed on August 28, with record turnover on the Hong Kong stock exchange; the Hang Seng index ended the day down just over 1%, but there were signs that the speculators had been severely punished by the government's $10 billion war chest operations. "D-day in Hong Kong," was the headline of the *Hong Kong Standard* the next day. The Hong Kong authorities were trying to drive up the forward prices of stocks and Hong Kong dollars, putting the squeeze on speculators trying to roll over into September and December contracts.

The Confucian world was defending itself. In Taiwan, the government issued a directive to banks not to sell shares of stock. On August 30, Taipei newspapers reported that Taiwan had barred all securities and investment trust companies from selling or buying hedge funds linked to Soros. "Authorities have not approved sales of [Soros'] Quantum Group's funds in Taiwan and anyone found illegally doing so will be severely punished," wrote the *China Times*. [46] The foreign exchange director of the Taiwan central bank also hinted at a Hong Kong-style ambush against speculators shorting the Taiwan currency and Taiwanese stocks.

---

[46] "Taiwan bars deals linked to Soros's funds," Reuters, August 30, 1998.

MALAYSIA: EXCHANGE CONTROLS

Repeating his view that "the free market system has failed and failed disastrously," Malaysian Prime Minister Mahatir Mohammed ordered exchange controls in defense of the ringgit on September 1, 1998. Mahatir cited the financial self-defense measures already being applied by world governments including Hong Kong, Taiwan, and Russia. According to the new regulations, approval was required for transfer of funds between External Accounts. Transfers to residents' accounts were permitted only until September 30, 1998; thereafter, approval would be required. Withdrawal of ringgit from External Accounts required approval, except for the purchase of ringgit assets. All purchases and sales of ringgit financial assets could only be transacted through authorized depositary institutions. All settlements of exports and imports had to be made in foreign currency. With effect from October 1, 1998, travelers were allowed to import or export ringgit currency of not more than 1,000 ringgit per person. There were no limits on the import of foreign currencies by resident and non-resident travelers. The export of foreign currencies by resident travelers was permitted, but only up to a maximum of 10,000 ringgit equivalent. The export of foreign currencies by non-resident travelers was permitted, up to the amount of foreign exchange brought into Malaysia. Mahatir said that ringgit in circulation outside of his country (offshore ringgit) had reached a value of "100 million outside the country and that we can repatriate within one month. If they don't of course the money is just waste paper. It's worth nothing at all. If they try to bring it in, we will stop them and we will confiscate such money." He put the larger offshore ringgit account at "more than 20 billion certainly, maybe even 25 billion. But that money ...has got no value. In order to give it value they must hold a parallel account in a Malaysian bank." Mahatir quickly got the attention of every "emerging market" in the world. And at a September 5 press conference in Tokyo, just before he left for talks with US Treasury Secretary Rubin, Japan Finance Minister Miyazawa said that he had asked Toyoo Gyohten, the special adviser to Prime Minister Keizo Obuchi, "to study the issue." Sakakibara later endorsed what Malaysia had done.

At the November APEC summit in Kuala Lumpur, Vice President Gore (subbing for Clinton) caused a diplomatic incident by praising the often violent protest movements of Southeast Asia. Gore sounded like a spokesman for some phantomatic Hedge Fund Liberation Front. Was the goal of US foreign policy now to make the world safe for hedge funds? (Gore also showed himself to be exceedingly maladroit: his own 1996 election campaign had been largely financed by hot money from Asia. He was now insulting and offending his own fund-raising base. The politician George Bush had called "Ozone Man" had committed a grievous blunder.)

Mahatir had assumed the position once occupied by President Nasser of Egypt: he was the leading statesman of the progressive Moslem countries. The result of exchange controls was that Malaysia was not forced to join its neighbors in groveling before the IMF. The Arab world, by contrast, was unable to act as a protagonist in the crisis. Iraq was struggling to be free of a murderous UN embargo, Algeria was in virtual civil war, Syria was a French client state, and Egypt was immobile. Back in the 1970s and early 1980s, the recycling of Arab petrodollars represented the world's main liquidity pump. But as Arab surpluses declined through the late 1980s and 1990s, this role had been assumed more and more by Japan, which became the world's leading financial surplus power. Now even states like Saudi Arabia were more likely to be borrowing money than lending it. The Saudi oligarchy had been making bad business decisions for more than a quarter of a century. At the November 1998 Jakarta summit of the Organization of Petroleum Exporting Countries, the Saudi delegation had foolishly maintained, against all the evidence, that world demand for oil was destined to rise despite the impact of the Asian economic collapse, and forced production quotas to be set accordingly. By mid-1998, depressed demand left the world market glutted with oil, despite attempts by the Saudis and others to cut back production by 800,000 barrels per day.

LONDON FACTIONS

By early September, City of London insiders were reporting that the British financial community was verging on civil war over the question of going back to exchange controls and protectionism. The *Times* and the *Daily Mail* were advocating currency controls and were supporting the Hong Kong defense measures. The *Financial Times* and the *Independent* were fanatically committed to the free market. The Swiss *NZZ* proposal to impose currency controls in all the merging markets was seen in London as an index of Swiss desperation. The German bankers' chorus of support for exchange controls in Russia was seen as specific to Russia alone, although the German banks were also very nervous. Some saw a revival by Germany of the 1989 Herrhausen plan for development investments in Poland and Russia, reflecting Germany's post-1945 experience.

During the summer of 1998, John Grey of the London School of Economics had gained world attention through his book *False Dawn: The Delusions of Global Capitalism*. Grey depicted the carnage wrought by the free market in Russia, Mexico, and also in the erstwhile *laissez-faire* paradise of New Zealand. Grey attributed these policies to the "Anglo-American style free market" doctrine, but made clear that within this the "Washington consensus" was the dominant force. The responsibilities of Washington are grave indeed, but the world cannot forget the central role played by the British finance oligarchy in the demolition of the Bretton Woods system and in the introduction of the chaotic non-system which has evolved into globalism, which is depicted in Chapter IV. We also cannot forget that the pestilence of post-1979 Thatcherism – a project to which Prof. Grey was not wholly alien – was an indispensable component in the current global brew. However, Prof. Grey was certainly on firm ground in forecasting that the current global panic will be more damaging than 1929-32. [47]

OUTLAW HEDGE FUNDS

The Dow losses of 517 points on Monday, August 31, and losses of the following days were widely attributed to panic selling by hedge funds who were seeking to recoup, by fair means or foul, at least a part of the massive losses they had suffered when the convertibility of the Russian ruble was been suspended. Late on the afternoon of Friday, September 4 Ron Insana of CNBC reported rumors that a large sell program had hit the stock index futures market with about one hour of trading left in the afternoon, driving the Dow down from -50 to about -150 during the last minutes before the official beginning of the long Labor Day holiday. The bond market had shut down some hours earlier. Insana reported that some on Wall Street thought that this was a surprise attack by a hedge fund desperately seeking some day-trading profits. When hedge funds begin sabotaging the functioning of the Federal Reserve-Treasury Brady System of drugged markets (described in Chapter II), we might expect the authorities to get very upset, and to begin considering sanctions against hedge funds in general. It was high time for the Fed and the Treasury to shut down the hedge funds.

But as summer 1998 turned to autumn along the Potomac, the US government did absolutely nothing. Muriel Siebert, the first woman to found a Wall Street firm, former New York State Banking Commissioner, and now a leading discount broker and *grande dame* of the financial world, made a sensible call for a minimal reform measure: speaking on CNBC, she called for the Securities

---

[47] *Guardian*, September 8, 1998.

and Exchange Commission or the Commodity Futures Trading Commission to impose margin requirements on foreign currency futures, which were still operating in a pre-1929 world of no margin requirements whatsoever. Seconding her call, the DeHaan Foundation of Naples, Florida pointed out that typical currency futures routinely involve $65 or more of leverage for every $1 actually invested by the speculator. In a sample case, "a hedge fund with $1 million invested could make $32 million on a 50% price drop in a currency with currency futures." [48] But even this was too much for the Washington set, who only had eyes for Monica Lewinsky.

THE ARMAGEDDON SCENARIO SPREADS

Although the London *Financial Times* did not like exchange controls, it demanded that the central banks stand ready to pump unlimited liquidity into failing banks and brokerages to preserve the speculative bubble. The *FT* wanted Greenspan to stop dithering and lower interest rates, pronto. To add urgency to its call, the paper cited "an Armageddon scenario" by David

Zervos, chief strategist with Greenwich NatWest in London. According to the nervous Mr. Zervos, "the value of international debt securities totaled $3,600 billion at the end of March, much of it used as collateral (for example by hedge funds) on further loans worth around $30,000 billion. In addition, the Bank for International Settlements believes that by the end of last year there was another $30,000 billion in credit market exposure outstanding in interest rate swap agreements. These provide another source of leverage by allowing investors to swap fixed for floating interest-rate payments without owning the underlying debt. This implies that on a conservative estimate

there is $60,000 billion in global credit market exposure." These figures are low, as we demonstrate below. "Historically plausible increases in risk, argued Mr. Zervos, "could suddenly reduce the value of these assets by $1,500 billion. That could cause banks accepting debt as collateral to put out margin calls. And, says Mr. Zervos, 'if there were a failure of one or more large counterparties to meet the margin call, the resulting sale of collateral and liquidation of swap positions could easily drive spreads further and induce even more widening, more margin calls and a complete collapse in the credit market.'" This outcome could be closer than you think, suggested the paper, citing "rumors that one US investment bank had failed" – this was widely though to be the venerable Lehman Brothers. The spreads, meaning the difference between the interest rates on Treasury bonds and other bonds were indeed gaping wide, and the *Financial Times* wanted Greenspan to open the cash spigot. Then, Armageddon arrived with the 1998 autumnal equinox for Long Term Capital Management LP.

37. LONG TERM CAPITAL: OPAQUE CRONY CAPITALISM[49]

Just before the Labor Day weekend, the US stock markets were in a rolling crash, in which a 50 to 100 point loss was beginning to look like a relatively good day. By the time the Dow had fallen almost 20% from its July top, Greenspan began to perceive that his usual pro-rentier anti-inflation litany (which he had repeated in July) was no longer enough to keep the evil spirits at bay. In a September 4, 1998 speech at Berkeley, he now pronounced deflation to be just as noxious as inflation: "In the spring and early summer," he revealed, the unelected FOMC "was concerned that a rise in inflation was the primary threat to the continued expansion of the economy. By the time of the committee's August meeting, the risks had become balanced, and the committee will need to consider carefully the potential ramifications of ongoing developments since that meeting" at its

---

[48] *Washington Post*, September 20, 1998.
[49] The numbering of the crises refers to the table in Chapter IV.

next session of September 29. " The Commodity Research Bureau index, in which raw materials are heavily represented, was at its lowest level in 21 years. Gold was at $273 per ounce, also a 20-year low. Oil prices were at their lowest level since their historic 1986-87 bottom. (A day earlier, Robert T. Parry, President of the San Francisco Federal Reserve Bank, had told an audience in Boise, Idaho that "falling US and foreign stock markets, as well as possible effects of problems abroad on US corporate profits, could restrain consumer and business spending in this country.") Greenspan offered reassurances that the US economy was strong, without the "imbalances" that often mark economic expansions. Greenspan was ignoring, among other things, the $200 billion record US trade deficit of 1997, and with it the threat of an early dollar crisis. The US, Greenspan conceded, "cannot remain an oasis of prosperity unaffected by a world that is experiencing greatly increased stress." On the Monday after Greenspan's speech, US markets were closed for the Labor Day holiday, Tokyo saw a 5.3% Nikkei jump, up to 14,790, the second best day of the year. Kuala Lumpur, prospering behind Mahatir's protective shield, was up almost 23%. But the dollar ominously fell to 131.45 against the yen. It was the classic central bank predicament of the Scylla of dollar collapse and the Charybdis of stock market and banking panic.

During the next few days, the Bank of Japan lowered its overnight funds rate target from one half of one per cent to one quarter of one per cent, citing the need "to prevent the economy from falling into a deflationary spiral," meaning an all-out economic depression. There were rumors that Fuji Bank, Japan's fifth largest, had taken a massive $15 or even $22 billion hit in derivatives speculation. The immediate result was to boost the dollar by more than 5 yen, the biggest one-day increase since 1982. On September 10, the Bank of Japan lowered its discount rate from 0.50% to 0.25%. On September 23, Greenspan told the Senate Budget Committee that the world crisis had entered a "more virulent phase," with the implication that deflation was more threatening than inflation; the Dow managed at 3.3% pop that day.

Even as Greenspan spoke that afternoon, the Fed – in the person of President William McDonough of the New York branch – was acting as lender of last resort for the syndicate of big banks that were scrambling to save themselves by taking over Long Term Capital, the Merton-Scholes high-leverage hedge fund, which was bankrupt with a reported $1 trillion in derivatives outstanding. (Long Term Capital was leveraged at 500:1, but what of that? J.P. Morgan was leveraged at over 600:1, with $6.2 trillion in derivatives as against just $11 billion in equity capital.) The story was broken by David Faber of CNBC on the afternoon of Wednesday, September 23, 1998 As Roger Altman pointed out the following day on CNBC, the Fed was setting a very ominous precedent: by promoting Long Term Capital as too big to fail, the Fed was taking a principle which had since May 1984 been applied only to banks (meaning big ones, like Conti Illinois), and was now applying it to a very highly leveraged hedge fund which had no FDIC-insured accounts. Within a few days, Union Bank of Switzerland announced a $685 million loss, and Dresdner Bank said it was $144 million to the downside. LCTM's total loss was about $4 billion.

If US banks went under, the FDIC would have to pay depositors, and the taxpayers would soon have to bail out the FDIC. Would Soros' Quantum Fund qualify for a taxpayer-funded bailout under this precedent? Was Soros also too big to fail? If the precedent meant what Altman suggested, the fires of hyperinflation would soon be burning, and it was time to buy gold. LCTM had come close to shredding the 401 (k) accounts of a generation of Americans by collapsing stocks and mutual funds: was Greenspan ready to bail out those small investors as well? Between August 29 and October 19, currency in circulation grew at an annual rate of 16.4%, and the M3 money supply grew at 17% annually. Greenspan was using system repurchase agreements, coupon passes, and open market operations to churn out liquidity. The dollar softened and the gold price spiked upward: there were reports that central banks were replenishing their gold stocks in the face of the hurricane. Between late September and early October, the dollar managed to fall ¥ 10 (or, in forex jargon, "ten big figures") in just 10 days.

The Fed's bailout of Long Term Capital once again raised the issue of crony capitalism in America. One of LTCM's partners was David Mullins, the former vice chairman of the Federal reserve Board, and thus a member of the Greenspan monetarist clique. According to some accounts, Mullins had been LTCM's point man in arranging the bailout by his former colleagues at the New York Fed. Under the Fed bailout, LCTM's management were rewarded by getting to keep their posts and their generous compensation packages. This was the kind of sleazy transaction which American economists loved to condemn when it took place in Third World countries, but most of them were silent now. And since the entire bailout remained cloaked in secrecy, Greenspan's and Rubin's repeated demands for transparency on the part of the poorer countries were exposed as hypocrisy: the hedge funds still had no reporting requirements whatsoever, and no institution is as opaque as the New York Fed.

Greenspan had long pontificated that derivatives were under control; in the spring of 1998 he had beaten back a proposal by Brooksley Born of the Commodity Futures Trading Commission to study the threat posed to bank solvency by derivatives. As for hedge funds, Greenspan had intoned that they were already strictly regulated by their own investors. If Greenspan were ready to debase the currency in order to bail out the likes of Long Term Capital, he was violating the Federal Reserve Act (which mandates that the Fed maintain sound monetary conditions), and could therefore be impeached or otherwise ousted. A Fed-generated hyperinflation would surely provide the political basis for a future nationalization of the Fed. In the meantime Greenspan, who had in the past endorsed the S&L practices of Charles Keating, was becoming a true Duke of Moral Hazard.

As for Brooksley Born, she had emerged during 1998 as the most competent US official working on financial and economic questions. Her proposal to draw up a report on the explosive destructive potential of derivatives elicited hysterical opposition from many quarters Congressional backers of the derivatives bubble even inserted a special provision into the budget late one night which specifically banned Ms. Born from preparing such a report over the first six months of FY 1999. Senator Lugar (R-Indiana) was indignant that Ms. Born wanted to examine these "healthy and productive markets." Without personal backing from Hillary Clinton, Ms. Born might not have been able to resist the power of the derivatives lobby. The much-touted transparency was for export only.

The Long Term Capital bailout ended the scandalous immunity from criticism enjoyed by the incompetent, pro-speculator Greenspan Fed. Former Fed official Lawrence Lindsay called attention to the international blowback: the US had been demanding that Japan bite the bullet and let its big banks go bankrupt (so that, of course, the hedge funds could bid 10 cents on the dollar for Japanese assets at the bankruptcy auction, thus making Japan pay for an entire phase of the depression.) Now, at the first sign that the US banks might blow, the Fed was moving in with a massive bailout. [50] The hypocrisy and duplicity of Greenspan's line would not be lost on the Japanese. Domestically, as columnist Robert Novak wrote, Greenspan's moves "looked like the Fed caricature painted by populists for much of the past century: impervious to the woes of businessmen and farmers in the real economy, but ready for quick-action when high-flying investors are imperiled. A former Fed vice chairman sitting as a principal of Long Term Capital adds to the perception that the buddy system is at work." [51] And how could it be otherwise, with the money power in the hands of the Federal Reserve Board, an unelected and unaccountable oligarchy?

---

[50] *Wall Street Journal*, September 28, 1998.
[51] *Washington Post*, September 28, 1998.

Greenspan lowered the US federal funds rate by a quarter point at the Federal Open Market Committee meeting of September 29, and acted on his own to lower it by another quarter point on October 15, 1998. The immediate goal of these rate cuts was to revive the junk bond market, which had dried up because of the risk aversion of many speculators after the Russian default and the LCTM collapse. Greenspan's stewardship was open to harsh critique: fully 43% of American households had invested in the stock market, often by way of mutual funds that were falling faster than the underlying stocks. (see Chapter III). Many had bought their stocks *de facto* on margin, using high-interest credit cards. Another way to buy on margin was to use the credit card to pay for the groceries, while using the paycheck to buy stocks – with a broker call loan if you could get one, or without. This entire castle of debt was now beginning to cave in.

US REAL ECONOMIC IMPACT

It was time to watch the world trade figures as they documented a violent contraction of the goods-producing sectors of the entire world economy, since it was this decline which threatened the lives of millions. Statistics released by the US Commerce Department on September 20 showed that US exports to South Korea, Taiwan, Singapore, Hong Kong, Malaysia, the Philippines, Thailand and Indonesia had declined by a striking 27.7% between December 1997 and July of 1998. Exports to Japan were down 5.6%, and shipments to China were off an ominous 9.6%. July 1998 exports were down by 1.3%, and were at a 17-month low. The US merchandise trade deficit, as distinct from overall balance of payments, was headed in 1998 for an all-time record of about $250 billion, far worse than the $150 billion range which had been associated with the dollar crisis of 1987, and also worse than the $200 billion ballpark levels of 1996 and 1997. A violent 1930-style contraction was on. The goods-producing sectors hit hardest were the farm sector, industrial raw materials, and West Coast sectors which relied on exports to the Far East. Much of the impact was in agriculture. By mid-1998, it was estimated that net US farm income was falling from the $60 billion of 1996 to about $45 billion for 1998, a drop of 25%. With half of all US grain usually destined for export, the fall in Chinese and Japanese demand was causing a 30% decline in US farm exports to Asia. According to Senator Daschle, "In 1998, the average net farm income for Great Plains farm family of four was approaching the poverty level."

Boeing was also suffering, since 40% of its orders for 747 jumbo jets usually came from Asia. Layoffs were in the cards, and the stock price was hammered. The same was true for Motorola, which relied on Asian markets to sell its mobile phones; Motorola announced that it was letting go 15,000 workers worldwide – 10% of its workforce. Motorola also cancelled plans to build a $3 billion computer chip plant near Richmond, Virginia. The company cited "the worst global downturn in semiconductor history." Toys R Us began closing 90 stores, 40 in the US and the rest overseas, while laying off 3,000 employee and taking a half-billion restructuring hit.

THE LATIN TIME BOMB

Brazil was a great power of the debt world. With almost $500 billion in foreign debt, Brazil's debt was as big as South Korea, Indonesia, and Russia put together. Could the System survive default on a cool half trillion? We might soon find out. In May, Brazilian bonds were "stuck like glue to Russians bonds" in a predictable linkage. August 21, 1998 was Black Friday in the São Paulo financial markets; the falling stock market activated circuit breakers for the first time since the previous October. When the decline reached 10%, the Brazilian government ordered the National Bank of Economic and Social Development to buy up stocks, and thanks to these support operations, the damage for that day was limited to a mere 2.9% But for August, the Bovespa index registered a loss of almost 30%, and capital flight was an estimated $7 billion. By the end of the month, capital was flowing out of Brazil at an average rate of $1 billion a day, and this accelerated when Moody's cut the rating of Brazilian bonds. The central bank under Gustavo Franco had about $70 billion on hand to defend the *real*, but this was unlikely to deter the hedge fund onslaught. According to *Folha de Sao Paulo*, the "markets" viewed $50 billion in reserves as the magic number at which the currency would implode.

Brazil's president Henrique Cardoso, an Anglophile who professed total fealty to the IMF, was trying to win another term in an election to be held on October 4. This was a reminder that the Mexican crisis of 1994-95 had been partly occasioned by reflation measures laid on to influence the outcome of the presidential contest in that country. In mid-September, the cash-strapped IMF tried to reassure investors by announcing that it was ready to help Brazil. After the South Korea, Indonesian, and Russian debacles, it was not clear how such reassurances could be effective. In mid-September, there was an attempt to circle the wagons around Brazil with organized support. Brazil doubled its interest rates to 49.75%, and Brazil and the IMF began talking about a bailout; stock prices in São Paulo rebounded mightily for a few days in another mugs' rally.

After Cardoso had been re-elected, the IMF began to assemble a bailout of $42 billion, which was less than South Korea's, for a country with almost three times more foreign exposure. Even as crisis management, it was hardly an impressive gesture. Nevertheless, at the end of October, Cardoso announced yet another round of murderous austerity in an attempt to fulfill the IMF conditions.

In Mexico, a key focus of crisis was the Fund for savings Bank Protection (Fobaproa). Fobaproa had been created with $65 billion in funds, but it now faced insolvency and needed a bailout. The implosion of Fobaproa threatened to trigger the disintegration of the Mexican banking system, especially since Fobaproa bonds represented 30% of the assets of Mexican banks. After the Russian default, the notion that Mexico was too big to fail was open to question.

US BANK STOCKS DOWN 50%

The stock market decline of August and September 1998 overtook the stocks of the US money center banks with remarkable ferocity: many quickly lost half of their value or more. The largest of these, Citibank, which was exposed to Latin America to the tune of about 21% of its alleged net worth, was down about 50% from its recent highs. Bankers Trust and J.P. Morgan were battered in a similar fashion. The Dow as a whole was down about 20% from the July 17 peak at this time. The world financial community, ignoring the experience summed up in later chapters of this book, expected the central banks to act decisively to stop the crisis. But Greenspan testified to the House Banking Committee's LCTM hearings on September 16 that the alleged plan for coordinated interest rate cuts by the central banks of the leading countries did not exist. Hans Tietmeyer, the leader of the deflationary brotherhood at the Bundesbank, had already announced that he saw no need for a rate cut. Japanese stocks promptly reverted to a 12-year low. Speaking one day earlier at the same hearings, corsair George Soros had cynically and frankly listed the ways in which world finance was already undergoing "disintegration." The markets were not acting like a pendulum, said Soros, but rather like "a wrecking ball." Unlike George Shultz and others, Soros wanted to keep the IMF fully funded.

Things were made worse with the mid-September 1998 leaking of a report by the Comptroller of the Currency, which pointed to the danger of a new epidemic of non-performing debt and loan defaults looming for US banks. "Projecting risk over the next 12 months, credit risk is expected to further increase in all commercial portfolios," said the report. "Banks are leaving themselves with fewer options to control the risks associated with commercial lending should the economy falter." Regulators said that the banks had been lowering their credit standards, and making too many questionable loans: "For the fourth consecutive year," said the report, "underwriting standards for commercial loans have eased." The report singled out "home equity products," meaning the ubiquitous second mortgages peddled on television by sports figures and dancing girls, as a special problem area. The report had been ready in June, but had not been disclosed until it was leaked. After loading their credit cards with high-interest debt, American homeowners had refinanced that debt by pledging their homes as collateral for home equity loans, which were extended even when they had no equity. Now, with installment debt at $1.26 trillion, they had filled up their credit cards a second time, and were approaching default all along the line.

The gravity of the crisis was beginning to sink in. Newspaper ran stories to reassure their jumpy readers. *Forbes* magazine tried to reassure the public that this was not 1929, but merely 1987 – an index of how bad things already were. The *Neue Zürcher Zeitung* consoled the Bahnhofstraße that "1998 Is Not 1929."[52] Much of this was an elaborate apology for that fact that the central banks had done absolutely nothing to stop the crisis. Alan Greenspan so far "has kept his powder dry" – a nice way of describing total immobility. If "systemic risk" were to emerge, argued this paper, not only the Fed but even the Eurogarchs would turn to reflation before it were too late. [53] James Galbraith had noted in the *Washington Post* a few days earlier that the Fed had done nothing for 18 months in spite of an obvious crisis, and called for interest rate cuts to keep the US out of recession for another year. (He was not to be confused with John Kenneth Galbraith, who had also been issuing repeated calls for lower interest rates.) James Galbraith did not call for a new Bretton Woods, but rather voiced the hope that regional institutions like the European Monetary Union or the Asian Monetary Fund might replaced the failed IMF. After the failure of so-called reform in Russia, capitalism was a dead duck in Russia, he recognized. Congress could force the Fed to cut interest rates, but Galbraith was pessimistic that they would, so prospects were "bleak." This book argues that it was neither 1929 nor 1987, but rather 1931 – meaning that the world faced, not with a stock market decline, but rather with the disintegration of the big banks and other existing financial structures.

CLINTON ADDRESSES THE CFR ON THE WORLD CRISIS

The existence of a world financial crisis of unprecedented severity was clear for all to see no later than the end of October 1997. But this basic reality had been recognized neither by the Clinton White House nor by the rest of the US government. As late as November 1997, Clinton had fatuously called the Asian panic "a few little glitches on the road." Between October 1997 and October 1998, the United States government had taken absolutely no serious measures of any kind to fight the depression. Rubin had produced a few good lines, while Greenspan had spouted restrictive, then expansive, rhetoric, but nothing had been done. The President needed to propose legislation to outlaw hedge funds. He needed to call for derivatives to be declared illegal and be phased out in an orderly way. It was time to compel Greenspan to increase margin requirements for stock purchases. Above all, the United States had to invite the nations of the world to Bretton Woods II. But nothing, absolutely nothing, had been done in one full year. (The Republican Congress, it is true, had been considering the final tearing down of the Glass-Steagall firewall between banks and brokerages just when such safeguards were needed most. And they had tried to make bankruptcy more difficult for working families, just when they should have been enacting a series of domestic debt cancellations and debt moratoria.)

---

[52] *Neue Zürcher Zeitung,* September 19, 1998.
[53] *Neue Zürcher Zeitung*, September 19, 1998.

The Asian Monetary Fund had been allowed to die stillborn. The G-22 had gone nowhere. To be like FDR, one had to be an activist, and activity was here nowhere to be seen. The US government record contrasted not at all favorably with that of Herbert Hoover, who had at least called for a 1-year international debt moratorium under similar circumstances. All of the conclusions drawn at the end of Chapter VII of this book were unfortunately applicable to the Clinton Administration, and even more to the Federal Reserve. Even the Japanese government, mocked by US commentators because of its paralysis, was a by comparison with the US a whirlwind of activity with its stimulus packages, bank bailouts, and Asian Monetary Fund ideas. If the term for Japan were paralysis, the term for Washington and especially the Federal Reserve might be *rigor mortis*.

On September 14, Clinton finally told the New York Council on Foreign Relations that the United States had to provide leadership for the world in dealing with what he now acknowledged to be "the biggest financial challenge facing the world in a half-century." "The United States has an absolutely inescapable obligation to lead," said Clinton. A quarter of the world's population now faced declining or negative economic growth, he said. Clinton was worried about Russia, and had been reading the Washington Post series on the new Asian misery. Clinton directed Rubin and Greenspan to convene a meeting of the G-7 finance ministers and central bankers within 30 days to discuss anti-crisis moves to recommend ways to adapt the international financial architecture to the 21st century," and also spoke about the work of the G-22; in this connection he mentioned cooperation with Romano Prodi of Italy.

What was missing was still the indispensable call for a New Bretton Woods. On the same day, the G-7 finance ministers and central bankers had issued cryptic boiler-plate in which they noted that "inflation is low or falling in many parts of the world" and that their countries would coordinate their actions "to preserve or create conditions for sustainable domestic growth and financial stability in their own economies." Was this a promise of reflation, or merely a reflation of promises?

Published reports later indicated that Clinton had indeed been considering something along the lines of a New Bretton Woods. But over the Labor Day weekend, he had been in contact with Britain's Tony Blair – the worst possible choice for a discussion partner; White House Chief of Staff Erskine Bowles was later reported to have been talking about a "New Bretton Woods." There followed a rush to define what a New Bretton Woods might mean: Tony Blair, advised by his ideological salad chef Anthony Giddens of the London School of Economics, came out with his own delphic "Third Way" version at a Commonwealth meeting in Ottawa on September 29.

Jacques Chirac also wanted to appropriate this slogan, and his intent to muddy the waters was immediately evident: Chirac called for a "New Bretton Woods" on September 25. What Chirac meant was a kind of IMF world dictatorship, exercised through a strengthened IMF Interim Committee, with the finance ministers meeting frequently to act as a kind of world directorate or world financial control board for the bondholders – in effect, a universal oligarchy of financiers. As of September 1998, the head of the IMF Interim Committee was Carlo d'Azeglio Ciampi, an arch-monetarist former official of the Bank of Italy and former Italian prime minister. French Finance Minister Strauss-Kahn made this intent painfully clear when he specified that Chirac was calling for "a true IMF government," whose goals would include financial transparency and other favorite concerns of the Paris and London creditors' clubs.

Camdessus was calling for greater transparency and strengthened IMF surveillance, and was also contemplating the IMF Interim Committee as a kind of world-wide committee of public safety. He was adamant that controls were inadmissible.[54] For Camdessus, the 24 finance ministers of the

---

[54] Michel Camdessus, Before the Next Crisis Begins, *Washington Post*, September 27, 1998.

Interim Committee would take over hands-on decisional control of the IMF. They would become the new ephors of the System.

NEW BRETTON WOODS

Many policy makers, responsible persons, and intellectuals around the world are aware that what is needed is a new world monetary system, although there are many divergences about what its features might be. On April 7, Italian prime Minister Romano Prodi told a press conference at the Willard Hotel in Washington DC, "I personally believe we must move towards a new Bretton Woods." On June 2, Prime Minister Mahatir Mohammed of Malaysia said at a policy symposium in Tokyo: "I believe the time has come to deal with the entire issue of reform of the international financial system to ensure currency stability and contain the activities of those who buy and sell money for no other purpose than to make profits." On August 30, Taichi Sakaiya, the director of Japan's Economic Planning Agency, called for an urgent meeting of world leaders to avert global financial crisis. Sakaiya suggested that the G-7 nations, together with Russia, should meet to try to calm markets. [55] The adequate answer to the unprecedented world crisis was to convoke a second Bretton Woods, a world monetary conference to re-establish a regime of fixed parities and eventual gold convertibility of the most important trading currencies. The whole world was waiting for the United States government to issue the call for Bretton Woods II. What a real Bretton Woods II would like is discussed in detail in the final chapter of this book.

True to form, the BIS clique of central bankers blindly opposed meaningful monetary reform. On November 20, 1998 Fed boss Greenspan, Bank of England chief Eddie George, European Central Bank head Wim Duisenberg, and Hans Tietmeyer of the Bundesbank all spoke out in opposition to fixed exchange rates. Here were the Four Horsemen of the coming financial Apocalypse.

THE WORLD THE USURERS MADE

Much of the world was now undergoing a violent economic contraction. A September *Washington Post* series summed up the tragic dimensions of the damage. Clinton had been impressed by the account he found here of the nurses, pharmacists, and medical aides of the bankrupt Seoul Christian Hospital who, fired with no back wages when the hospital closed, were now homeless and camping out in the lobby of the facility. In Indonesia, unemployment had gone from 5 million to 20 million, and was headed higher. South Korea had lost 1 million jobs during 1998, and was posting 100 bankruptcies each day; it was the worst crisis since the Korean War of 1950-53. Thais were being fired at the rate of 2,000 per day. The Indonesian government now reported its revised estimate that 100 million of its people would fall below 2,100 calories per day by the end of 1998. Malnutrition was severe enough among children in many areas as to cause the severe emaciation called marasmus, which is often accompanied by irreversible brain damage. "Many of the problems being seen in Indonesia – hunger and malnutrition, rising dropout rates, increasing child labor, crime and prostitution, family disintegration – are also increasing in Thailand, South Korea, and other Asian nations," wrote the *Washington Post*.

Social progress was also being rolled back. Divorces, separations, and family violence had spiked upward across Southeast Asia. In Indonesia, government officials were estimating that 2.7 million children would drop out of school this year because of the crisis. In Thailand, child prostitution was increasing, and 12-year old girls were selling for $800 to $1,600 in some rural districts. South Korea was still wealthy enough to afford orphanages for the economic orphans whom parents could no

---

[55] BBC, August 30, 1998.

longer care for. The parks of Seoul were rapidly filling up with homeless men. If America had Cleveland Cafes during the bust of the 1890s, and Hoovervilles and apple sellers during the Great Depression, Seoul now had the IMF Hope Wagon, a food stand staffed by a dozen homeless men who had lost their jobs in the crisis and who were now dishing up boiled noodles. The men named their pathetic project the IMF Hope Wagon, but they were not making money. It was an epiphany, a defining moment in the depression.

Regional immigration patterns were being reversed. Thailand, with 2 million jobless, had deported a quarter million Burmese migrant laborers. Laotians coming to Bangkok in search of jobs were being arrested; news of the crash had not yet reached the villages of rural Laos. Malaysia deported 50,000 Indonesians, and South Korea sent home a similar number of foreign workers. Filipinos were being expelled from many countries.

"Go back to your village!" the nervous Thai government told peasants out of work in the larger cities. "No One Told You to Come to Jakarta!" was the Indonesian government's variation on the same theme.

The middle class was being crushed even more rapidly here than elsewhere in the world. "The greatest success story of East Asia – the emergence of a broadening middle class – is evaporating like the steam from a cup of tea," commented the *Washington Post*. The president of a Seoul shipping container plant lamented: "For the past 30 years, it was growth, growth, new jobs, new jobs, so people all became middle class. Now, it is really miserable. There is no middle class. These people are all lower class." It was a "class plunge." While it would be misleading to exaggerate the prosperity attained by these countries under globalization, it was clear that the progress achieved during an entire generation had been wiped out in just a few months, for purely financial reasons.

In Russia, hoarding foodstuffs and other necessary commodities was the order of the day. The period from September 4 through September 9 saw a wave of panic buying. Shoppers were desperately stocking up on rice, buckwheat, sugar, noodles, tea, coffee, laundry detergent, soap, pasta, and other staples. One man told an American reporter that he had seen the price of sugar go up three times while he was waiting in line in a supermarket with his shopping cart. A researcher said all the eggs had disappeared from the supermarket where she shopped, and when a new stock of eggs appeared later in the day, the price had gone up 50%. "Political turmoil means hunger, so we begin to store food," she observed. Chicken was selling for 90 rubles per kilogram, while the official minimum wage was 84 rubles per month.[56]

STANDSTILLS: THE WORLD IN SCHACHTIAN GRIDLOCK

"The best medicine would be for the Western world to accept the fact that you have to give them breathing space – let's say, 6-9 months – in which these countries wouldn't pay the interest on their debts," said Asian fund manager and economist Marc Faber in an interview with *Barron's*.[57] It became clear during September that the dangerous half-measure of standstills was beginning to attract supporters among those who chose to forget the lessons of the 1930s. On the occasion of releasing its *Trade and Development Report 1998* on September 16, the United Nations Trade and Development agency (UNCTAD) issued a communiqué advocating a "financial safeguard mechanism for currencies under speculative attack." UNCTAD noted that "Turning a blind eye to the systemic nature of financial instability is neither responsible nor acceptable. Global surveillance and regulation have lagged behind the integration of financial markets – with increasingly costly

---

[56] *Washington Post*, September 6, 7, 8, 1998.
[57] *Barron's*, August 31, 1998.

consequences. Crisis management requires a mix of old and new techniques in order to reduce the volatile movements of international capital ... debtor developing countries facing a speculative attack on their currencies should have the right to impose unilateral standstills on capital transactions like the trade safeguard actions permitted under WTO rules." An UNCTAD survey had concluded that countries which "had undergone across-the-board financial deregulation and liberalization" were prone to "speculative bubbles" and "excessive capital flows." UNCTAD scored the "exaggerated faith in markets" on the part of policy makers."

The Report listed "Essential tools: debt standstills and capital controls," including "the application of insolvency principles to currency attacks." UNCTAD proposed "a standstill on debt servicing to ward off predatory investors and give a country the breathing space needed to design a debt reorganization plan, thereby helping to prevent the liquidity crisis from escalating into a solvency crisis." But it added that "a full-fledged procedure, analogous to Chapter 11 of the United States Bankruptcy Code, is neither practical nor necessary. Article VIII of the IMF's Articles of association could provide a legal base for the imposition of a debt standstill." "The decision to impose a standstill could be taken unilaterally by the country experiencing a currency attack; and evaluation of its justification could be the responsibility of an independent international panel established for this purpose." The Report praised capital controls as "a proven technique for dealing with volatile capital flows" and an "indispensable part of developing countries' armory of measures for the purpose of protection against international financial instability." Contrary to the United Nations view, American Chapter XI was an absolutely indispensable tool for fighting the world depression. Rumors swirled during the same week that Camdessus was seeking authority from the IMF member governments to set himself up as Standstill Czar, empowered to tell governments in regard to which debts they could declare standstills, and for how long.

One of the few points of agreement at the disastrous IMF conference of the first week of October 1998 was the revival of standstill. Camdessus wrote in his report that "in extreme conditions, countries may find it necessary to put in place a moratorium on ...debt service payments" while they try to reschedule their debt. The IMF wanted to preserve the sanctity of debt, but also to head off unilateral debt moratoria and defaults of the type declared by Russia on August 17, 1998.

Jacques Rueff recorded in his memoirs how horrified he was by US envoy Henry Stimson's support for standstill agreements during the summer of 1931. Standstill agreements are by nature dangerous half-measures which leave all important questions suspended without a final answer, and thus tend to consign the economies in question to limbo. A standstill agreement boils down to a mutual pledge not to rock the boat in the midst of a category V financial hurricane. Standstills mean extended gridlock, an intolerable situation in human affairs. Standstills by their very nature prevent the issuance of new credit, and do nothing to restore confidence. All of this should have been clear from the German experience of 1931 and thereafter. Even a partial and temporary debt moratorium is insufficient, as the one-year Hoover Moratorium of June 1931 taught the world. Hoover proposed a moratorium because he was opposed to debt cancellation, not because he was trying to bring it closer. In order to be effective, a moratorium on international financial debt had to be general and open-ended – it had to freeze all principal and interest payments *for the duration of the crisis*. Those who were proposing standstills in 1998 needed to be reminded that they were in fact much less radical than Herbert Hoover. Those who thought that capital controls plus standstill agreements would do the trick needed to be reminded that they were endorsing the failed policies of Hjalmar Schacht in 1931 (see Chapter VII). A far more vigorous approach was needed, as shown in the final chapter of this book.

OCTOBER 1998: THE WORLD FINANCE OLIGARCHY PARALYZED

In August and September 1998, the world finance oligarchy had been forced to look into the glowing bowels of Hell. The half-million bankers and fund managers who are the chief beneficiaries of the globaloney system had felt the icy breath of panic on their necks. Had the near-death experience impelled them to consider any serious reforms?

The IMF and World Bank annual meetings held in Washington at the beginning of October 1998, including the G-22 session on which reform hopes had been pinned, underlined that they had not. *Laissez-faire* orthodoxy prevailed up and down the line. As for President Clinton, the promise he had shown in his mid-September speech to the CFR turned out to be empty verbiage. Clinton refused to lift a finger against hedge funds or derivatives, and made no move to re-instate gold convertibility, fixed parity, or pro-industrial economic dirigism. William Greider accurately summed up Clinton's failure of nerve:

> American politics is about to be transformed by [the world crisis], especially if it remains so passive. President Clinton, other troubles aside, stands a fair risk of becoming a "New Democrat" version of Herbert Hoover. Like Hoover, Clinton entrusted his economic policy to conservative financial experts (in his case, Robert Rubin and Alan Greenspan). Now he is captive to their narrow, cautious view of what's unfolding.[58]

But Greider's proposal to fight the depression domestically seemed to be to "flood the streets with money," which was ironically the direction in which Greenspan was also leaning. It was high time to understand that there was no monetarist solution for the crisis. To his credit, Greider also called for a new Bretton Woods, leading to a "more stable system of currency relationships."

Delusions of "relative stabilization" were rife in Washington by the end of October 1998. That month proved to be the Dow's best since early 1987. But was this pleasant reprieve being purchased at the price of incipient hyperinflation stoked by the Greenspan Federal Reserve?

HALLOWEEN 1998 AT THE EDGE OF THE ABYSS

On the day before Halloween 1998, the heads of state and heads of government of the Group of 7 issued an unusual statement, claiming in effect that the worst was over. Their finance ministers spoke of the success of crisis management, and repeated their mantra about transparency, while professing eternal fealty to the IMF. The G-7 created the structure of an emergency lending fund, under which troubled economies which had placed themselves under IMF dictation could draw at will on lines of credit when they needed a quick fix. The IMF quick fix facility was the product of consultations among the emerging levy of Third Way politicians, including Clinton, Germany's Gerhard Schröder, Britain's Tony Blair, Canada's Jean Chrétien, and Italy's Massimo D'Alema. The nervous new optimism of the Third Way leaders in late October 1998 was based on a number of factors. The Dow was up some 13% from its late August lows. Greenspan had lowered US interest rates twice, and seemed ready to keep on doing so. The Congress had approved $18 billion for the IMF. The Japanese taxpayer was going to be dunned half a trillion dollars to bail out the Japanese banks. The IMF was putting up at least $40 billion for a financial Maginot line around Brazil.

Thailand's stock market was up 50% from its August lows. Hong Kong had also gained back 50%, and was back over the 10,000 level. The US dollar had fallen from ¥ 145 in August to ¥ 117, which relieved much of the devaluation pressure on the Chinese ren min bi. Market insiders now

---

[58] William Greider, "Breakdown of Free-Market Orthodoxy," *Washington Post*, October 7, 1998.

thought that Long Term Capital Management had not mortally wounded Lehman Brothers, Bankers Trust or any other big banks. A wave of large takeovers was in the offing: Daimler was buying Chrysler, Deutsche Bank acquired Bankers Trust, America Online purchased Netscape, Exxon merged with Mobil, British Petroleum had bought Amoco, Total was acquiring Petrofina, and Rhone Poulenc and Hoechst were merging. All this helped pump up stocks. But each of these mergers meant thousands of lost jobs. The late 1998 flurry of mergers and acquisitions guaranteed that 1998 would be the worst year for layoffs during the entire 1990s globaloney decade. And, just beyond the Christmas holidays and the hoped-for Santa Claus rally, there loomed the brave new world of the euro. A more fatuous fool's paradise could hardly be imagined, but it was an illusion that might last for weeks or months. Thanks to crony financing by Greenspan and the other central bankers, money center banks had simply rolled over their mass of kited derivatives from end of the third quarter 1998 into the first and second quarters of 1999, when the tight money likely to be associated with the euro will make them even harder to finance.

Not everything was serene. There was trouble for the bankers in unexpected quarters. Pakistan's Prime Minister Nawaz Sharif, with his country almost three months in arrears on debt payments, declared that it could simply not fulfill the conditions being demanded by the IMF, and there were signs that Iran, its oil income reduced by the low world market price, might be on the verge of default.

The impact on the Japanese oligarchy of the Russian default caused by the IMF's doctrinaire monetarism, and the LCTM bailout organized by Greenspan, was very ominous for the future prospects of the Anglo-American free market creed. For the men behind screens in Tokyo, these events had underlined the incompetence and the duplicity of the IMF and Federal Reserve chieftains who had been tormenting and insulting them for many long months. By late October 1998 the Japanese oligarchy was thoroughly disenchanted with globaloney, and was pondering a return to the highly successful dirigist methods long associated with the Japanese Ministry of Finance and Ministry of International Trade and Industry: these included window guidance of firms by the government, directed lending to provide credit for production, and a strategic industrial policy. At the time the $550 billion bank bailout was approved by the Diet, Finance Minister Miyazawa announced a separate $30 billion fund to defend East Asian currencies and economies, starting with Indonesia. This was a new unilateral form of the Asian Monetary Fund which the IMF and the US Treasury had blocked a year earlier. Japanese thinking was once more oriented towards an Asian economic sphere, possibly including China, Malaysia, and Indonesia; this kind of combination could be impervious to IMF assault, even if backed by the Anglo-Americans. The Japanese were impressed by Mahatir's success with exchange controls, and were happy to leave their money in Malaysia. The big issue would be the Japanese ability to withstand the IMF-Wall Street-City of London wrecking operation which was sure to follow.

THE BRITISH LIBOR PARTY

In the background, the Tony Blair regime, called by some the British LIBOR Party (after the London Interbank Offered Rate, which appeared to have replaced the old Marxism of the Trades Union Congress as the main article of faith) was still trying to collect on the City of London's Russian derivative contracts, which were already in the same category as the bonds of the Czarist era. Once again the mangy British lion was attempting to bait the Russian bear – always a perilous exercise for the world. The intellectual bankruptcy of the political leaders of the wealthy countries could not have been more complete, making the next wave of the crisis merely a question of time.

EUROPE IS NEXT

The euro was launched in January 1999. After the Russian default, the 11 European Union currencies which were candidates for merger into the EMU monetary union were subjected to varying levels of pressure, and stresses and strains began to appear in the European currency grid, which had last been reviewed by the finance eurogarchs during their May consultations. One key to the divergence was in widening bond yield spreads between weak sisters Italy and Spain on the one hand, and Germany on the other, where the government bonds called Bunds were in demand for reasons largely related to Germany's past reputation as an economic power. The question was raised, could the euro be launched on schedule?

By early September, voices were raised in favor of stopping the implacable euro austerity. Hannes Swoboda, Socialist Party deputy in the Austrian parliament, called for a suspension of the EMU convergence criteria for the duration of the impact of the Asian and Russian crises on Europe. He said that this would provide an emergency instrument to prevent the European Union from sliding into a real recession. As it was, the hands of the eurocrats were tied by the Maastricht straitjacket at precisely the moment when anti-cyclical measures, including protectionist steps, were most imperative. The Maastricht treaty was turning out to be a Nessus shirt for the European financial Hercules.

The enterprise of launching a new world currency in the midst of a financial hurricane was evidently a parlous one. The euro would necessarily appear as something of an unknown quantity, to the average person if not to the financial eurogarchs. As Bundesbank President Hans Tietmeyer once remarked, "A failure of the monetary union might be a drama, but its success under unstable conditions might be a tragedy." French Interior Minister Jean-Pierre Chevènement had commented about the euro, "I believe it is like the Titanic," and called for the band to play "Nearer My God to Thee." There appeared to be two alternatives: if Duisenberg & Co. at the European Central Bank decided to prove their anti-inflation mettle to the satisfaction of the bond-holders, their policy might well prove so restrictive and deflationary as to provoke a violent and possible fatal contraction in European levels of production and employment – an all-out depression. Given the monetarist peer pressure on the bankers' camarilla running the European Central Bank, demanding that they show themselves the worthy heirs of the sturdy anti-inflation fighters at the German Bundesbank, this was by far the more likely alternative. If so, Wim Duisenberg might turn out to be one of the great villains of the world breakdown.

If, on the other hand, the ECB tried to provide credit sufficient to maintain current levels of economic activity, it was likely that it would come under attack by the hedge funds and the banks that follow them in for the kill, leading to a new edition of September 1992 on a grand scale. There was also the question of what would happen to the vestigial francs, lira, and gulden during the last phase of their existence, when they might be rapidly depleted by panic flights into the dollar or even into gold.

DOLLAR CRASH

The Long Term Capital affair should have served as a reminder to Americans that the United States was the derivatives capital of the world, with 90% of the known US share of the weird instruments concentrated in the hands of the money center banks. It was in the wake of LTCM that the idea of a general US banking panic began to dawn on certain mainstream observers: Jim Hoagland wrote in the *Washington Post* that a Wall Street insider friend had told him in mid-September that "for the first time in my professional life I hear serious people worrying about the survival of their banks." [59] A few more Merton-Scholes capers, and the entire edifice could come crashing down. The Federal Reserve response to Long Term Capital emphatically raised the specter of hyperinflation in the dollar zone, with astronomical hyperliquidity being pumped into the banks to prevent bankruptcy all around. Greenspan's largesse to the derivative banks, if continued for long, would guarantee hyperinflation in the dollar. (By late 1998, Russia was lurching towards its second bout of hyperinflation in the globaloney era, with a 300% yearly rate expected. What hyperinflation looked like in Germany in 1922-23 is portrayed in Chapter VII) The aftermath of the first airing of Long Term Capital's debacle included a decidedly weaker dollar, and a sharp rise in the price of gold, so these lessons were not being lost on the investment world.

Looking forward, we must ask the painful question of what the effect on the US banking system would be if we were to have a few more Long Term Capital cases, plus insolvencies by Brazil, Mexico, and Argentina. We must also factor in the reality that US banks act more like hedge funds than banks in most of their operations. Such a scenario would doom the US banking system, although Greenspan might preserve the illusion of vitality with the formaldehyde of Fed loans. Hyperinflation would be one way to take care of the mortgage debt, credit card debt, and all other debt of American households – unless corrupt politicians manage to sneak through legislation indexing existing debt to the inflation rate, in which case the most timid members of the middle class will soon be parading with pitchforks. But in the larger picture, hyperinflation would doom the US dollar as a reserve currency.

The universal and virtually automatic acceptance of a US dollar not convertible into gold which has prevailed after 1971-73 has been an historical anomaly. The post-1973 regime, as we show in Chapter IV, has been far less successful than the original Bretton Woods system of 1944-1971. If Greenspan begins to redline the dollar presses, it is simply a question of time until the dollar will cease to be acceptable in international trade. The time is coming when we will either have a new world monetary system, or the US will have to pay for imports in gold. The endgame of the dollar hyperinflation scenario would involve a free fall of the dollar, a move out of all paper and into gold, commodities, and real estate by the finance oligarchs, and a collapse in the secondary market of US Treasury securities. It is fervently to be hoped that Greenspan and the Fed will be dumped, and New Deal policies re-instated, before we reach that point.

The waning months of 1998 gave every indication that the worldwide contraction of production and employment was gathering momentum. The United States lost 193,000 jobs in manufacturing between January and October 1998. In November, a wave of mass layoffs in the petrochemical sector continued, with Monsanto wiping out 2,500 jobs and Texaco terminating 1,000 workers. US steel shipments fell by 9.3% in September 1998. China reported exports down 17.3% compared to a year before. Chinese steel exports for the first 9 months of 1998 were down 38% in comparison with the same period of 1997. Industrial production in Brazil was down 2.9% in the third quarter of 1998, and declined by 3% in Argentina during the same period. Farm prices worldwide were at their lowest levels in 20 years, despite severe mass starvation in a number of parts of the globe.

World crude steel production had reached an all-time peak in 1997, with total output of 794.5 million tons exceeding the previous 1989 peak for the first time. But, according to figures from the International Iron and Steel Institute in Brussels, output was declining during 1998. World steel output in September 1998 was down 6.3% compared with September 1997, and 1998 production was down by 0.5% on a year-to-date basis. Russian production was down 21.4% compared with the year ago month, and the NAFTA zone was down 4.7%. China, by contrast, remained the world's

---

[59] Jim Hoagland, "Storm off the Coast," *Washington Post*, September 27, 1998.

biggest steel producer with a robust 4.9% increase over the year-ago month. Japan was down 8.8% on the same basis.

One who denied the reality of the contraction was Tony Blair. On October 11, 998 Labor Party Chancellor of the Exchequer Gordon Brown pontificated that the British economy was "a rock of stability in these troubled times." Unfortunately for the Blair regime, the London *Observer* reported that same day that Britain faced over 400,000 layoffs in manufacturing by the end of 1999, which would bring industrial employment in the former workshop of the world down to the levels of 150 years ago. British farm incomes are experiencing their worst decline since the 1930s. According to the *Guardian* of October 28, "activity in the manufacturing sector has collapsed." But on October 21, Blair told the British Parliament that it was time to stop the "idiotic hysteria" about the prospects for the British economy, and described the minds of the Conservative opposition as "black holes." Blair's friend Eddie George, the Governor of the Bank of England, caused a furore of his own when he stated that is was fine for unemployment to rise in the devastated north of England, if this were necessary to protect better-off Kent and Surrey from inflation. George is not likely to venture into Yorkshire any time soon without an armed escort.

Between mid-October 1998 and early January 1999, the pace of the crisis slowed. But the first business days of January brought a flurry of renewed crisis symptoms: with the euro launched, the dollar showed alarming weakness, falling 5% against the yen, fast enough that the Bank of Japan launched support operations for the US greenback – a rarity since 1995 – on January 12. The dollar's weakness was partly attributable to Clinton's impeachment and trial in the Senate, and partly to the collapse of the IMF bailout of Brazil, where the state of Minas Gerais on January 6 defaulted on payments to the central government. Soon Brazil was losing $1 billion per day of flight capital despite the high interest rates which had been strangling its economy for more than a year. On January 13, Brazil devalued its currency amidst a world stock market downturn, and two days later announced that it would abandon any currency peg in favor of unmoored floating. These events were sure to increase the pressure on Argentina, Mexico, and other Latin American debtor nations. Jeffrey Sachs took the occasion to gloat that all of the IMF's 1997-98 bailouts – including Thailand, Indonesia, South Korea, Russia, and Brazil – were now all certifiable fiascos.

THE BUBBLE

The attempt to estimate the approximate dimensions of the world financial bubble of the late 1990s is necessarily a parlous enterprise. But we must get some idea of the size of the bubble, how fast the bubble is turning over, and its growth rate, in order to appreciate fully the desperation of the human predicament at the close of the century and of the millennium. Such an attempt must be articulated on two levels. The first is the attempt to determine the total monetary value of all outstanding financial paper, including derivatives, stocks, bonds, mortgages, debentures, promissory notes, commercial paper, credit card accounts, mutual funds, certificates of deposit, securitized assets of all types, etc. Such a world total is indispensable, since it implies a rate of return on the bubble, whether in the form of fixed interest, or variable dividends, or other returns. But the bubble is not a static magnitude. All of these assets are traded every day, be it in markets or over the counter. The second important feature of the bubble is its rate of turnover. How fast are these derivatives, stocks, bonds, mortgages, debentures, commercial paper, acceptances, promissory notes, etc., changing hands? The total amount of world financial turnover implies a series of costs connected with trading profits, commissions, fees, and related costs. Finally, both the bubble and the turnover were rapidly growing, at least until a possible turning point between October 1997 and October 1998.

US BUBBLE, 1997-98

The biggest component of the bubble is represented by derivatives, which are discussed in more detail in the following chapter. Derivatives include exchange-traded futures and options on financial assets and commodities, plus over-the-counter currency and interest rate swaps, and the more complex derivatives known as structured notes. In 1990, according to the Federal Deposit Insurance Corporation, US commercial banks held $6.8 trillion of off-balance sheet derivatives. Since then, these derivatives holdings of banks have been expanding at an average 20% yearly rate, reaching $20.3 trillion by the end of 1996. In the first quarter of 1997 alone, off-balance sheet derivatives held by all US banks grew by 10%, bringing US derivatives reported by banks to $32 trillion as of March 31, 1997. If we include the derivatives holdings of American investment banks and insurance companies along with the derivatives held by commercial banks covered by the FDIC, then the total US derivatives figure rose to about $40 trillion as of the end of the first quarter of 1998. (This still leaves out derivatives held by hedge funds, non-bank corporations, institutions, endowments, individuals, and state and local governments. It would also leave out derivatives that are simply not reported by any of the above.)

At the end of 1996, the US Securities and Exchange Commission estimated that the total equity capitalization of all US corporations attained $9.2 trillion. As of the July 1997 interim market top, the total market value of all US stocks trading on exchanges undoubtedly exceeded $10 trillion.

Bonded debt is another large category. The Public Debt of the United States topped out at just short of $5.57 trillion during the first week of September 1998, and towards the end of the month was just over $5.5 trillion. Corporate bonds, junkified or not, are a separate category. In 1997 alone, some $119 billion worth of junk bonds were floated. The total market value of the US bond and credit market was estimated at about $21 trillion as of the end of the third quarter of 1997. Smaller components of the bubble also add up. US mutual funds are about $4 trillion. US installment debt in another $1.5 trillion. US mortgage debt is about $3.4 trillion.

THE US BUBBLE AT ITS PEAK, 1997-98

DERIVATIVES	$40 TRILLION
STOCKS	$15 TRILLION
CREDIT MARKETS	$21 TRILLION
MUTUAL FUNDS	$5 TRILLION
MORTGAGES	$3.5 TRILLION
INSTALLMENT DEBT	$1.5 TRILLION

TOTAL US BUBBLE	$85 TRILLION

Financial paper of all types is thus more than one full order of magnitude greater than the so-called Gross Domestic Product, which is itself a figure heavily larded with financial and other services.

THE WORLD BUBBLE

The size of the US bubble is an important part of the story, but it is far from being the whole story. The world total of derivatives approached a probable historical top at no less than $130 trillion in notional value of outstanding contracts during early 1998. It is thought that derivatives held by American banks represent about one third to one fourth of derivatives held worldwide. We incline towards the one fourth estimate, especially because of the very rapid growth rates for derivatives in the most recent years in the United Kingdom, Germany, and other European countries, plus derivative growth in Japan, where there were no legal derivatives at all until a few years ago. To get a round figure, let us therefore say that derivatives holdings by all the world's banks, insurance companies, corporations, brokers, governments, individuals, and other owners must now be at least $130 trillion.

This estimate is buttressed by the mid-1997 "Public Disclosure of the Trading and Derivatives Activities of Banks and Securities Firms", a report issued jointly by the Basel Committee on Banking Supervision and the Technical Committee of the International Organization of Securities Commissions. According to this study, world derivatives held by banks and brokers grew from $62.6 trillion at the end of 1994 to $69.35 trillion at the end of 1995, a growth rate of almost 11%. The great powers of the derivatives world were led in 1995 by the United States ($23.1 trillion), Japan ($11.5), France ($9.4), Great Britain ($7.4), Switzerland ($6.3), Germany ($4.3), and Canada ($3.3). Switzerland was the per capita leader, with $877,673 in derivatives for each Swiss.

If this accounting of world derivatives is adjusted upward in line with the $32 trillion for US derivatives at the end of March 1997 cited above, we would have gotten a snapshot of world derivatives holdings at the end of the first quarter of 1997 in the amount of just under $100 trillion. And this figure surely understated the reality, due to non-reported derivatives, and because of the holdings of hedge funds, non-bank corporations, institutions, endowments, individuals, and governments, which were generally omitted.

The great question mark is represented by the derivatives holdings of hedge funds. Hedge funds, by present definition, report nothing. The most recent window on the hedge fund world was opened by the collapse of Long Term Capital Management, which turned out to have more than $1 trillion of derivatives exposure. Long Term Capital Management was a medium-sized hedge fund, not comparable in size to the giants like the Soros Quantum Fund or the Robertson Tiger Fund, which were five to eight times as big. If one hedge fund of the middling sort can generate $1 trillion in derivatives, what might be the value of the unreported derivatives of the 5,500 hedge funds operating in this world? World derivatives may amount to $150 trillion, $200 trillion, or even more. As long as hedge funds are allowed to operate in complete secrecy, there is no reliable way of knowing the notional value of their derivatives contracts.

In 1993 the International Monetary Fund estimated the total of the world's publicly traded financial assets as about $24 trillion, and further estimated that this entire total was being bought and sold every 24 days. This would imply a yearly turnover figure of $250 trillion in stocks and bonds alone six years ago, and a daily turnover of $1 trillion already back then. One year earlier, in 1992, the Organization for Economic Cooperation and Development (OECD) had estimated the financial assets of its member states at $35 trillion. A November, 1994 study by the McKinsey Company consulting firm forecast that total world financial assets would reach $53 trillion in constant dollars or $83 trillion in nominal dollars by the year 2000. But this falls far short, especially because of derivatives growth.

By 1993, the IMF thought that the yearly trade in US Treasury securities amounted to a little over $80 trillion. According to the McKinsey study, global bond trading amounted to more than $500 billion per day, for a yearly total of $125 trillion. All in all the McKinsey study, taken together with more recent data suggested a mid-1990s daily world turnover of about $1.5 trillion for stocks, and about $.7 trillion for bonds for a daily total certainly in the neighborhood of $2.2 trillion, with a yearly turnover of about $0.55 quadrillion.

The SEC thought that the market value of all the world's stocks had totaled $22.4 trillion at the end of December 1996. The world-wide price increase for stocks during the first half of 1997 certainly brought the world's equity capital to $25 trillion by July 1997, which may have represented the pre-Asian crisis top. This entire mass of stocks must be turning over about once a month, or perhaps even more rapidly. A monthly turnover would bring yearly stock transactions to about $315 trillion during the latter half of 1997.

A rough estimate of the world bubble might therefore look something like this. We set world derivatives at $130 trillion, world stocks at $25 trillion, and world credit markets of all sorts at perhaps $40 trillion, adding in bonds, money markets, etc. Other financial instruments would then represent all mortgages, real estate trusts, mutual funds, consumer and credit card debt, etc. The US bubble would represent about one third of the total world bubble.

THE WORLD BUBBLE, 1997-98

DERIVATIVES	>$130 TRILLION
STOCKS	$25 TRILLION
CREDIT MARKETS	$40 TRILLION?
OTHER INSTRUMENTS	$5 TRILLION?

TOTAL WORLD BUBBLE	>$200 TRILLION

If this is roughly the size of the bubble, let us attempt to put it in motion. How fast do derivatives turn over? Not all of them do. There is no instant market for structured notes, which must be carefully evaluated using the recondite Black-Scholes equations to figure out what they might be worth. Complex designer derivatives or over-the-counter derivatives do not readily trade on exchanges. These are the privately negotiated contracts that exist in the virtual space between the laptop computers of two or more yuppy quants. As for the futures and options, we must recall that they have definite dates of expiration and do not last through the year. Options, in particular, are wasting assets that become worthless if they are not used by a certain date.

The International Swaps and Derivatives Association publishes statistics on certain types of over-the-counter derivatives, especially currency and interest rate swaps. According to this source, the total world notional value of privately negotiated derivatives contracts was $17.7 trillion in December, 1995. One year later, at the end of December 1996, the total of these non-exchange derivatives was set by the ISDA at $24.292 trillion. This implies a growth rate of a stunning 37% per year. Such derivatives growth, if continued, would bring this total to over $33 trillion by the beginning of 1998. Again, there is every reason to believe that any attempted summary of privately negotiated contracts which are not reportable to governments will tend to understate the real dimensions of the phenomenon.

According to the IMF's *International Capital Markets* study issued in August, 1995, during the year 1994 world options, futures, index futures and index options markets traded 1.14 billion contracts worldwide, with slightly more than half changing hands in the United States. The Chicago Mercantile Exchange billed itself as "the world's largest market." Yearly turnover on the CME reached a new all-time record in 1994, with a total of $183 trillion in this single exchange. In 1995, the CME saw 203.2 million options and futures contracts change hands, for a total turnover of $169 trillion. In 1996, CME trading amounted to 198 million contracts. The Chicago Board of Trade, another center of futures trading, saw the buying and selling of 222.4 million contracts in 1996. At the Chicago Board Options Exchange, 176 million options contracts changed hands during that same year.

Europe's biggest market for exchange-traded futures, options, and other derivatives is LIFFE, the London International Financial Futures and Options Exchange. The action at LIFFE amounts to £160 billion a day, for a yearly total of 168 million derivatives contracts with a total yearly value of £40 trillion (roughly $64 trillion) in 1996, the current record. LIFFE says it is larger than its two closest European competitors combined. But Germany's Deutsche Terminbörse, plus France's MATIF, plus Switzerland's Soffex, have a bigger combined turnover than LIFFE. So this suggests a yearly European derivatives turnover of somewhat more than $125 trillion. LIFFE's busiest day was March 2, 1994, when 1.6 million contracts changed hands, and its biggest month was October 1996, when the volume was 18.4 million contracts.

If, out of the first-quarter 1997 world total of $100 trillion in derivatives reported by banks, $25 trillion were privately negotiated swaps and structured notes, and $75 trillion were traded on exchanges and turned over every 20 business days, we might expect a yearly turnover of about $940 trillion on the world's derivatives exchanges - somewhat more than recently observed. But derivatives are like an iceberg, with the visible transactions above the water and the structured notes and privately negotiated transactions and hedge fund operations out of sight. There is every reason to believe that total buying and selling of exchange-trade derivatives plus over-the-counter derivatives is in excess of $1 quadrillion per year.

Commodity trading, no matter how speculative, tends to be dwarfed by the turnover in paper instruments. The New York Mercantile Exchange (NYMEX) bills itself as the world's largest market for energy and metals, including futures and options on commodities. NYMEX includes COMEX, the New York commodity exchange. During 1996, the turnover on NYMEX amounted to 80 million contracts for a total value of over $2 trillion. NYMEX sees its main world competitor in the London Metals Exchange (LME), which seems to be of roughly comparable dimensions.

THE BALLOONING OF FINANCIAL AGGREGATES: A CASINO SOCIETY

A breathtaking and even chilling feature of the global economy is the endless proliferation and hypertrophy of financial transactions. The Bank for International Settlements estimated, for example, that international bank loans amounted to $3.6 trillion in 1991, already a tidy sum. But bank lending, as we will see, is in no way the characteristic feature of the modern global economy. The global economy deals in financial aggregates that are whole orders of magnitude greater than this modest figure.

Many observers of the contemporary scene have called attention to the "casino economy" or "casino society" of the late twentieth century. The term appears to have been coined by the British economist Susan Strange with her book *The Casino Society*. This notion reached a larger audience when it was taken up in by *Business Week* with the article "Playing With Fire: Games the Casino Society Plays" in the issue of September 16, 1985. In those days people were shocked to notice that between 1973 and 1985, the volume of futures trading in stocks and bonds had increased ninefold, while total national output had increased only threefold. But that, it was discovered later, was just a small sample of what was to come.

By 1998, foreign exchange transactions amounted to more than $1.5 trillion per day, dwarfing the $20 billion per day that used to be the norm as recently as the 1960s and the $640 billion level which had impressed Treasury Secretary Brady in 1989. As of mid-1995, London still lead the world in foreign exchange transactions with $460 billion in turnover each day, followed by New York with $250 billion, Tokyo with $160 billion, Singapore with $100 billion, and Hong Kong,

Zürich and Frankfurt with $80 to $90 billion each, for the 1995 grand total of $1.2 trillion daily. [60] Since there are about 250 business days each year, $1.5 trillion per day adds up to a yearly turnover of $375 trillion in currency markets - as of October 1998.

World yearly financial turnover in mid-1998 could therefore be roughly estimated in the following terms, which we offer with a caveat about inevitable duplication:

Currency trading	$0.4	quadrillion
Stocks and bonds	$0.55	quadrillion
Derivatives	$1.0	quadrillion

This would suggest that the total turnover of world financial markets of all sorts is between $1.5 and $2 quadrillion. One way to see if these figures are in the ballpark is to compare them with the figures for interbank payment transfers going through the interbank payment systems of the world.

INTERBANK TRANSFERS

A good place to start is CHIPS, the New York Clearinghouse Interbank Payments System, with is a netting and settlement system for the largest New York money center banks and other member banks, and which can be fairly described as the cash aorta of the current world financial system, especially as regards international payments in the dollar sector. In 1997, the CHIPS home page on the Internet was telling the public that the average CHIPS daily transfer value was "well over $1 trillion." The total cash throughput of the CHIPS system in 1996 was about $331.5 trillion. This meant that the average daily throughput of CHIPS in 1996 was about $1.33 trillion (That was more than the yearly throughput for 1971, the first full year of a computerized CHIPS, which was only $1.13 trillion.) During 1997, CHIPS turnover reached a colossal of **$362 trillion** on almost 59 million transactions. This was an average rate of **$1.44 trillion per day**. The biggest day so far on CHIPS has been November 28, 1997, when **$2.24 trillion** surged through the cyber-plumbing.

CHIPS Yearly Volume Statistics

Year	Business Days	Banks	Total Dollar Volume in $1000's	Total Transaction Volume
1970*	180	9	$547,615,444	531,778
1971	250	15	$1,131,043,459	801,725
1972	250	15	$4,766,919,981	2,029,312
1973	250	15	$9,184,508,815	2,710,927
1974	250	56	$10,704,349,972	3,474,194
1975	250	63	$10,984,093,108	6,035,347
1976	250	69	$13,138,412,336	7,123,203
1977	250	77	$16,190,636,464	8,247,530
1978	250	80	$20,357,618,638	9,587,874
1979	250	92	$26,844,745,422	10,939,641
1980	251	100	$37,121,139,871	13,244,426
1981	250	99	$40,090,491,736	15,865,423
1982	251	99	$52,971,279,272	18,642,034
1983	251	117	$60,307,620,949	20,187,976

---

[60] *Financial Times*, September 20, 1995.

1984	250	138	$69,134,986,179	22,822,230
1985	250	142	$78,401,027,605	24,850,426
1986	251	140	$106,583,481,092	28,527,878
1987	252	139	$139,808,593,176	31,900,251
1988	251	139	$165,388,378,741	33,962,623
1989	251	140	$190,212,347,368	36,520,215
1990	251	131	$222,107,644,171	37,324,466
1991	251	126	$217,312,321,589	37,564,127
1992	253	122	$238,255,498,155	39,073,091
1993	252	121	$265,745,211,884	42,162,247
1994	251	115	$295,443,759,600	45,598,359
1995	251	111	$310,021,249,560	51,032,782
1996	252	104	$331,541,104,158	53,489,396
1997	251	95	$362,186,525,130	58,971,837
1998**	169	90	$229,960,580,221	39,393,238
TOTAL			$3,526,443,184,096	702,614,556

* First Day On Line was April 6, 1970.

** Year-To-Date as of August 31, 1998.

All Dollar Amounts are Expressed   in Thousands.

[Source: www.chips.org]

It is thought that CHIPS handles about 95% of all international dollar transactions. We might therefore raise the official CHIPS annual throughput by about 5% to get an approximation of the total of all international dollar interbank transactions, which by 1998 had to be almost **$380 trillion** each year.

Then we have Fedwire, the computerized system for money transfers among the Federal Reserve System's member banks. In 1995, Fedwire carried a total of about **$223 trillion** in payments. Are these the same sums that are reflected in the CHIPS statistics? Probably, sometimes. If we simply add the CHIPS and Fedwire turnover, we get about **$600 trillion** per year of interbank transfers for the US alone, which may need to be adjusted downward for duplication of some transfers to get a national total, but which does not seem to be exorbitant when compared to Japanese and European statistics.

The Bank of Japan has created its own settlement system, the BOJ-NET. BOJ-NET in 1996 carried a daily average traffic of 157.4 trillion yen per day, which at 118 yen to the dollar represented the equivalent of $1.33 trillion of interbank transfers each day, for a yearly total of about **$335 trillion**. The City of London operated its Clearinghouse Automated Payments System (CHAPS), which in 1992 handled almost $38 trillion. Various German payment systems moved just over $100 trillion in 1992. Then there is the case of Switzerland, a small country with a highly developed banking system. The Swiss Interbank Clearing System in 1992 carried the equivalent of $93.6 billion each day, for a yearly throughout of $23.4 trillion. The new Trans-European Automated Real Time Gross Settlement Express Transfer (TARGET) is scheduled to be ready for euro transactions starting on January 1, 1999.

By 1992, bank transfer figures were already large enough to make IMF analysts nervous. In their study entitled "Large-Value Transfer Systems" [61] issued by the International Monetary Fund in 1994, Bruce J. Summers and Akinari Horii commented that "the daily flows of funds over these systems is huge in relative terms as well, on average equaling the value of annual GDP every 2.6 and 2.8 days in Switzerland and Japan, respectively, and every 3.4 days in the United States for Fedwire and CHIPS combined." [Summers and Horii 74] This means that bank transactions which have something to do with all forms of production and services can be thought by now of as being finished up in the first two or three days of January, with the rest of the 250 business days of a calendar year being devoted to financial speculation only.

$1.5 QUADRILLION IN TOTAL WORLD YEARLY TURNOVER

If US yearly interbank turnover came in at $600 trillion and Japan generated $335 trillion, for a combined total of $935 trillion, let us estimate the rest of the world, including the European Union with the United Kingdom, plus Switzerland, at $400 trillion in yearly interbank turnover. This would give us a yearly figure of almost $1.4 quadrillion for interbank transactions in the world economy. Updating and adjusting out figures for growth in the bubble and for the countries not included in the tabulation, we come to the conclusion is thus that by the late spring of 1998, the total volume of world interbank transfers was indeed likely to be approaching the colossal sum of **$1.5 quadrillion**. This estimate is broadly coherent with the following detailed figures for interbank transfers during 1992, six years in the past.

DAILY INTERBANK TRANSFERS, 1992

1992 figures; daily payments in billions of US dollars.

FRANCE

Paris Clearing House	97.0
SAGITTAIRE	44.7
Banque de France credit transfer system	32.1

GERMANY

Elektronische Abrechnung mit Filetransfer (daily electronic clearing)	212.9
Daily local clearing	142.0
EIL-ZV (intercity credit transfer system) (Eiliger Zahlungsverkehr)	34.9
local credit transfer system	21.6

ITALY

SIPS (Sistema Interbancario di Pagamenti)	38.9
Electronic Memoranda	33.9
BISS (Banca d'Italia continuous Settlement System)	9.3

JAPAN

bill and check clearing systems	112.6
Zengin Data Communications	54.5

---

[61] See Bruce J. Summers ed., *The Payment System: Design, Management, and Supervision,* (Washington: International Monetary Fund, 1994).

FEYCS   196.1
(Foreign Exchange Yen Clearing System)
BOJ-NET   1133.8

SWITZERLAND
SIC   95.1
(Swiss Interbank Clearing System)

UNITED KINGDOM
Town clearing   9.8
CHAPS   147.9
(Clearing House Automated Payment System)

UNITED STATES
Fedwire (funds)   796.8
[Fedwire (securities)   558.8]
CHIPS   953.2
(Clearing House Interbank Payment System)

[Source: *Payment Systems in the Group of Ten Countries* (Basel: Bank for International Settlements, 1993).[62]]

TOTAL 1992 DAILY FUNDS TURNOVER $4.167 trillion

TOTAL 1992 YEARLY FUNDS TURNOVER $1.042 quadrillion

The 1992 result was thus a daily turnover of $4.167 trillion and a yearly turnover of $1.04 quadrillion in the interbank payment systems of these six countries alone. If we factor in the securities that are transferred over Fedwire (about $558.8 billion a day in 1992), the daily turnover rises to $4.726 trillion and the yearly turnover to about $1.18 quadrillion, but this may represent duplication. Note that CHIPS average daily volume jumped from $953.2 billion per day in 1992 to $1,440 billion per day in 1997, an increase of about 51%. BOJ net went from $1.13 trillion per day in 1992 to $1.33 trillion in 1996, for an increase of about 18%. So we again converge on the conclusion that, by 1998, yearly interbank transfers must indeed have been in the neighborhood of $1.5 quadrillion or more.

LIQUIDITY CRISIS

The ballooning of financial transactions poses the problem of a potential liquidity crisis. The figures just developed suggest that a more than $5 trillion is passing each day through the payment systems, markets, and cash registers of the world. Now, $5 to $6 trillion is a lot of money. Just how much can be hinted at through a comparison of this hefty sum with the total US money supply in its various guises.

The Federal Reserve System regularly publishes a figure which it calls M-1. M-1 represents the total of US currency circulating outside of banks, plus checking accounts (or demand deposits), plus travelers checks not issued by banks, plus some other checkable deposits like NOW accounts. In October 1998 the M-1 money supply was hovering around a mere $1.1 trillion. This is the cash instantly available for the needs of the financial system.

---

[62] See also David Folkerts-Landau, Peter Garber, and Dirk Schoenmaker, "The Reform of Wholesale Payment Systems" (online).

The Federal Reserve also publishes figures for something called M-2, which is a slightly broader definition of the money supply. M-2 represents M-1 with the addition of savings accounts, money market accounts, Individual Retirement Accounts, and Keogh plans. In October 1998 M-2 was about $4.3 trillion.

The Fed also tracks a data series it calls M-3, which lumps together M-2 plus large bank deposits over $100,000 that cannot be withdrawn on demand, such as jumbo certificates of deposit. In M-3 the Fed also includes Eurodollars held in US, UK, and Canadian banks by US residents, although other Eurodollars are not included. In October 1998, M-3 came to about $5.8 trillion.

Finally, the Fed also publishes statistics regarding what it calls "liquid assets". These include the M-3 money supply plus savings bonds, short-term Treasury bills, and bankers' acceptances. In September 1997 the Fed's figure for liquid assets was about $6.3 trillion.

Banks used to guard against panic runs by setting aside reserves in the form of cash kept in their vaults against the eventuality that large numbers of depositors might suddenly demand that their savings be paid out to them in greenbacks. But under globalism, reserve requirements have been dwarfed by the tremendous magnitude of the banks' speculative business. Reserve requirements are thus unlikely to be of much help, as a group of recent commentators have observed: "Although some central banks consider reserves important, reserve requirements – expressed as a percentage of banks' eligible liabilities – are rapidly declining while payment flows are increasing. Non-interest-bearing reserve requirements are increasingly difficult to enforce in today's global financial markets, as banks find ways around them." [63] The potential difficulty ought therefore to be obvious: the amount of money churning through the electronic plumbing of the banking system every day is exceedingly large in comparison with the total money supply. If the plumbing were to freeze, it would be impossible to turn even a small fraction of the outstanding paper instruments into cash, and this realization would rapidly lead to panic.

THE QUADRILLION-DOLLAR BUBBLE

The deadly sickness of the world economy of the late twentieth century can be summed up in the following global analysis: the System is currently attempting to maintain some $200 trillion worth of paper instruments and well over $1 quadrillion in turnover on the basis of industrial, agricultural, and related commodity production which we must now estimate as below $10 trillion per year This estimate of $10 trillion in combined world agro-industrial commodity production is a very generous one, and may overstate current levels by as much as a third. This figure has been drastically lowered over the past decade by such events as the 60% decline in commodity production in the entire former Soviet sphere of influence, and is now falling as a result of the Asian crisis. But let us use $10 trillion for purposes of argument.

The problem of the world economic and financial system thus boils down to how to maintain the circulation of $200 trillion in paper promises to pay on the back of a mere $10 trillion in tangible physical wealth:

$$\frac{\$200 \text{ trillion}}{\$10 \text{ trillion}} = \frac{\$200,000,000,000,000}{\$10,000,000,000,000} = \frac{20}{1}$$

[63] David Folkerts-Landau, Peter Garber, and Dirk Schoenmaker, "The Reform of Wholesale Payment Systems" (online).

For every dollar of production, there are 20 dollars of paper claims. (The situation is actually much worse, since speculative profit on trading the assets in question is being omitted for purposes of simplification.)

At this point a yuppy quant investment banker from Wall Street may observe: "The problem is not as serious as you make it look. After all, we don't need to pay back the whole debt every year. We merely need to pay the interest and roll over the principal."

And of course, the yuppy quant is right, up to a point. What has to be paid every year is a rate of return on the $200 trillion. For purposes of illustration, let us assume that the rate of return is a very modest 5%. As of this writing, the yield on 30-year Treasury bonds is just above 5%, which is an all-time-low. All other Treasury securities yield less. But many other investments yield far more. To our investment banker, a 5% return is a bad joke. He likes returns of 35% per year and up. But let us settle on 5% for purposes of illustration here. 5% of $200 trillion = $10 trillion. This is the total of debt service and dividends that has to be paid each year. The yearly debt service and dividend requirement is thus roughly equal to the total value of world production.

"See," says our investment banker. "You only have to come up with $10 trillion in interest and dividends out of your $10 trillion of production."

But this will not be easy. The money that can be used to pay the $10 trillion in debt service is not our whole $10 trillion in real production. We can only use the world PROFIT on the $10 trillion of production. A very good rate of profit for farms and factories in this post-industrial world is about 5%. A 5% profit on $10 trillion gives us a worldwide profit of $500 billion.

$$\frac{\$10 \text{ trillion}}{\$500 \text{ billion}} = \frac{20}{1}$$

How can we stretch $500 billion of world profit so as to cover the $10 trillion of world debt service? In other words, how can we stretch each $1 of real profit from world commodity production to pay $20 of world debt service?

The yuppy investment banker is undaunted. "We can arrange financing for the missing $9.5 trillion, but it will cost you at least 15%. Of course, the bankers will want to see collateral. And naturally, we will want to cut costs, junk low-profit departments, and downsize your work force." So what the investment banker proposes as a solution is first of all to add to the debt and increase the interest rate on much of it. He wants to cut productive employment, reduce production, and increase the burden of debt service that has to be borne by each dollar of remaining real production.

Our $10 trillion in worldwide real physical production is already shrinking. Since about 1971, we have witnessed a 2% to 3% decline in real per capita commodity production (as distinct from services, etc.) each year in the United States. The decline is attributable to hostile takeovers, downsizing, and to the other aspects of globaloney. So we have the worst of all possible worlds: the paper demands for income are growing, even as the real-production levels and real absolute profits are disappearing.

Notice that a system with $20 of debt service for every $1 of real profit cannot be described as a liquid system. It is a very illiquid system. If everyone demands to collect their debt service at the same time, and nobody is willing to extend new loans, then it is clear that the debt service cannot be paid. Indeed, if the bond holders in general realize how unlikely they are to be paid, then a general panic is almost certain to ensue. Up to now, one of the main factors which has delayed the panic has been naive monetarist blindness of people like our yuppy quant investment banker.

Notice also that even a lender of last resort cannot help the System to avoid panic. Such a lender can at most finance one or two more rounds of ballooning debt and falling production. Every delay in the panic comes at the price of making the panic more serious and destructive when it finally does arrive. Notice finally that the bubble of paper promises to pay has been growing at a hyperbolic rate, while world agricultural and industrial production is declining. The divergence between debt-service requirements on the one hand and the means to service the debt, on the other, is increasing every minute.

Two outcomes are possible within the framework of globalist/monetarist ideology: the first is a liquidity crisis and panic that destroys financial institutions immediately and thus brings down the System. Some might describe this variant as hyperdeflation. The other outcome is an attempt by governments to churn out enough cash to permit the debt to be serviced. But that leads to a period of hyperinflation, followed by chaos and ending up in the destruction of the System. And this sums up why a collapse and disintegration of this system are unavoidable, and why a breakdown crisis of world civilization is an immediate threat for the end of the twentieth century. The only alternative is represented by the policies outlined in the final chapter, to which the reader is invited to turn at any time.

HOW THIS BOOK CAN HELP YOU

This quick recap of the worsening world financial and economic crisis ought at least to convince any rational human being that an epoch-making crash is now a distinct possibility. If you read further, you will learn more about why the crash is inevitable - unless current policies are urgently reformed - and why it will tend to destroy paper financial instruments of all kinds.

The author has no illusions about the tenacity of human folly; he is well aware that his advice will be dismissed with scorn by many, and that he will be vilified by those who have a vested interested in maintaining popular illusions until the very last moment, for the advantage of a few insiders. But the author is also convinced that there are still many who will respond to a timely warning. Woe to those who are caught unprepared by the crash! The cataclysm that is coming will threaten all of us with a breakdown of the normal activity of production and distribution of the most basic products - of food, of clothing, of electrical power. If allowed to continue very long, the cataclysm will attack the very fabric of human society in ways that most people now alive in the United States can hardly imagine, but which residents of South Korea, Indonesia, and Russia may have less difficulty in envisioning, based on their recent tragic experience.

The people blind-sided by the coming cataclysm will know all the gut-wrenching horrors of seeing every prop of their imagined financial assets and holdings swept away in days, if not in hours. It will be the worst financial and economic disaster in all of human history. But that does not mean that there is nothing that you as an individual can do. As a human being you have the right to life, liberty, and the pursuit of happiness. You have the right to survive. This book can help you to survive in four ways:

1. First, this book can help you to understand what is happening. You can only make sense of your own individual life if you can situate personal experience within the context of broader historical reality. That reality is not what Rush Limbaugh says it is. The stock market and mutual fund boom of the 1990s has been a very dangerous form of collective insanity. This book can insulate you from mass hysteria and irrationality in the crash by showing in advance that the panic was lawful and predictable, that it was inevitable under prevalent policies and standards of public morality. The Titanic is about to collide with the iceberg, and you must recognize what is now going to happen.

2. This book can help you to turn away from the mentality of usury, the axioms of greed and parasitism, which have flourished over recent decades. If your expectations remain those of greed and usury, you will be unable to make the decisions which you must make in order to survive the crash. Up to now, for example, you have probably been concerned with obtaining high rates of appreciation or return on your stocks and mutual funds. If you continue to operate on these expectations, you risk being wiped out in the coming crash. If, by contrast, you prioritize providing shelter, food, and clothing for your family, your chances of survival will be greatly enhanced. The Titanic is listing, and you must put aside your preoccupation with social life on board.

3. This book provides specific ideas on how you can reorganize whatever assets you may now have to increase your ability to survive the cataclysm. These recommendations are for the average person who may have some stocks, an insurance policy, a few bucks in a money market or mutual fund, savings bonds or just a bank account. Even if you have only debt, a clear understanding of what is happening may enable you to fare better. The Titanic is sinking, and your must find a life jacket.

4. This book asserts that there are no real solutions to the crisis to be found for individuals. The gravity of the cataclysm means that the current economic and financial policies of the United States and the other leading countries of the world must be junked as soon as possible. We are already in a worldwide economic depression of unprecedented severity, worse than the 1930s if we take the entire world situation into account. Therefore, we need new policies, policies of economic recovery. This book will help you to understand what the President and Congress must do to get out of the depression, since you the citizen are going to have to make sure that the needed measures be carried out. We will need Chapter 11 bankruptcy reorganization for the entire US economy, a world debt moratorium, a nationalization of the Federal Reserve System, cheap federal credit for production, and an infrastructure program. We will need an emergency world monetary conference to set up a new world monetary system. Your life jacket can save you from drowning for some time after the Titanic disappears beneath the waves, but what you need most is a Coast Guard cutter to take you on board and get you back to dry land. What the public can learn from the oncoming cataclysm about national and international economic policy may represent the most important factor in the survival of the United States and the world into the twenty-first century.

CHAPTER
II. DERIVATIVE MADNESS

These guys have no right threatening our system. – Broker, September 1998.

On October 14, 1997 the Royal Swedish Academy of Sciences announced the awarding of the 1997 Nobel Prize in Economics to Robert C. Merton, a professor of business administration at the Harvard Business School, and to Myron S. Scholes, professor emeritus of finance at Stanford University and research fellow at the Hoover Institution. The Royal Swedish Academy hailed Merton and Scholes, along with their late associate, the economist Fischer Black, for their work in developing the mathematical formula which is widely used today to determine the value of options. This is called the Black-Scholes equation, which the two worked on during their time at the Massachusetts Institute for Technology in the early 1970s, and which they published in the *Journal of Political Economy* in 1973. Merton and Scholes were active as speculators in their capacity as partners in Long-Term Capital Management, a hedge fund based in Greenwich, Connecticut, where they worked with John Meriwether, the former head of bond trading at Salomon Brothers who had himself become something of a legendary figure on Wall Street.[64] Merton and Scholes, like Steve Hanke and many others, were academics and speculators at the same time, a combination that boded ill for the disinterested search for truth. During the month of September 1997, this firm had attracted attention by paying $6 billion of its capital back to its investors, with the comment that "the fund has excess capital." This may have reflected the estimate that it was dangerous to remain fully invested, or else that keeping this money in the company might have resulted in a rate of return on assets that money-hungry investors might have seen as too low.

According to the Royal Swedish Academy, the Black-Scholes equation, which was itself based partly on earlier work by Merton, is "among the foremost contributions to economic sciences over the last 25 years." The 1997 Nobel Prize was thus devoted to the apotheosis of the yuppy quant, or quantitative analyst. The Black-Scholes equation is the equivalent of Einstein's $e = mc^2$ for the derivatives world. In presenting the Black-Scholes equation to its readers, the *Washington Post* – perhaps fearful of lawsuits – displayed some wisdom by affixing the warning, "Don't try this at home." The American press hailed Merton and Scholes as the scientists who had taken the value of options out of the realm of mere opinion, and elevated this issue into the serene climate of pure science. The Black-Scholes equation and its numerous variations are a staple on the laptops of yuppy quants and traders from London's LIFFE to Paris's MATIF to Singapore's SIMEX, and the Chicago markets. According to one account, "the main insight of the Black-Scholes model is that the value of an option has nothing to do with investor expectations about the future price of the asset on which it is based. In other words, the option to buy an asset should not be regarded as more attractive simply because investors expect the price of that asset to rise." [65]

Long Term Capital Management LP was considered "the Cadillac of hedge funds," said an investor, since it was "very speculative, but low-risk." In addition to Merton, Scholes, and Meriwether, Long Term Capital also featured the presence of David Mullins, the former vice

---

[64] Mr. Meriwether, a Salomon bond trader, had been tainted by that company's illegal manipulation of the Treasury securities market of 1991. According to Michael Lewis' Wall Street memoir *Liar's Poker*, Mr. Meriwether, when challenged by Salomon chairman John Gutfreund to bet $1 million on a hand of poker, had tried to up the ante to $10 million, prompting Gutfreund to leave the table.

[65] *Washington Post*, October 15, 1997.

chairman of the Federal Reserve Board. During the first two years of operations, the Black-Scholes equation was applied through a strategy of quantitative arbitrage, and reportedly worked well enough to permit investors to triple their money.

Two weeks later after the Royal Swedish Academy had announced the awarding of the year's Nobel Prize in economics to Merton and Scholes, the financial markets of the world were swept by a tempest of selling which originated in Hong Kong, and which represented the extension of the southeast Asian currency crisis which had been in progress during the entire summer of 1997. One of the main causes of this instability was derivatives speculation of the type encouraged by the Black-Scholes calculations. Reality once again was located outside of the mathematical equations that purported to determine value. Reality was that derivatives speculation had no value for world civilization as a whole, or rather, had a negative value. Derivatives speculation added absolutely nothing to the ability of humanity to feed, clothe, house, educate, and heal itself, or to provide capital goods and infrastructure for future existence. Derivatives speculation tended strongly to disrupt and destroy productive activity. Ask the citizens of Orange County, California. By late 1998, it was clear that the combination of unregulated derivatives speculation and unregulated hedge funds added up to a time bomb under the IRAs and 401 (k) accounts of tens of millions of Americans.

MERTON AND SCHOLES CREATE A TRILLION-DOLLAR BLACK HOLE

Less than a year after Merton and Scholes had received the accolades of the Royal Swedish Academy, the financial world was shocked by the news that their firm, Long-Term Capital Management, was struggling to avoid bankruptcy with the help of a consortium of two dozens of the world's largest banks. It seemed that the magical powers of the fabled Black-Scholes equation had somehow backfired, and had produced catastrophic losses on $1 trillion in derivatives contracts. It was a possible new Hatry case (See Chapter VI).

Earlier in September, the genial polymaths at Long Term Capital had made known losses of $2.5 billion, reportedly equal to more than half of the firm's equity capital. Merton, Scholes & Co. had guessed wrong on Russian GKOs, Danish mortgages, and the pound sterling/dollar cross. They had reportedly shorted gold futures. Incredibly, they had even bet that the volatility in US financial markets would subside; instead, volatility was at one of its highest levels in the century, inferior only to the 1929, 1974, and 1987 market episodes. (If ever proof of the inherent superiority of the historical-philosophical method over reductionist Newtonian social science were wanted, here it was.) On August 1, 1998, Long Term Capital had $4.1 billion in equity, and over the next 54 days it had lost $3.5 billion of that. Some in Wall Street were indignant about the LTCM bailout. "These guys have no right threatening our system," said a broker at T. Rowe Price. "You just can't take a few billion dollars in capital and turn it into a trillion." [66]

Long Term Capital had tried to procure a quick capital infusion from Soros' Quantum Fund, in August, but had been rebuffed. The bailout committee for Long Term Capital included Goldman Sachs, Merrill Lynch, Morgan Stanley Dean Witter, Travelers, and UBS Securities, all acting with the full backing of the New York Federal Reserve. According to news reports, these institutions were preparing to buy 90% of Long Term Capital for $3.5. Since these are not charitable institutions, it must be assumed that they were acting for self-preservation, fearing the effect on their own solvency of the imminent bankruptcy of Long Term Capital, and the subsequent unwinding of the $1 trillion in derivatives. According to CNBC's Ron Insana, Long Term Capital

---

[66] *Washington Post*, September 26, 1998.

habitually employed leverage ranging between 50:1 and 200:1.[67] In retrospect, it turned out that LTCM was leveraged at 500:1, but that was still more conservative than the 600:1 leverage employed by J.P. Morgan in its derivatives portfolio as of December 31, 1997. The stocks of the bailout sponsors were mercilessly pounded on September 24; a few more like this and the New York Federal Reserve might experience runs of its own.

Even in its own terms, the Black-Scholes equation had always been based on at least one crucial fallacy. The Black-Scholes equation assumes that market volatility and turbulence will proceed on a constant level, and that these can be measured through standard deviations from historical prices. This means that the Black-Scholes equation, no matter how it may be souped up, will break down precisely when it is most needed: in the moment of panic crash and financial meltdown calamity, the boundary condition which is and deserves to be in the center of theoretical and practical interest. The Black-Scholes formula is of no use when collapse turns into disintegration, and this is the central issue of this book. The total inability to predict or allow for future events is of course common to all formal-mathematical expressions. This would appear to have been the fatal defect which overtook Merton and Scholes during the financial typhoon of summer 1998.

Former Federal Reserve official Lawrence Lindsay, speaking on CNBC, noted that the Black-Scholes formula has been imitated by most money-center banks in their own risk calculation methods. Lindsay summed up the constant-risk feature of Black-Scholes as another way of saying that "the world does not come to an end." Readers should consult Chapter VII for evidence that, on the contrary, some leading bankers did indeed experience July-September 1931 as the end of their pound sterling-centered world.

Scholes personally had apparently experienced some difficult moments in the course of his career as a speculator. He told journalists that during the 1970s "I was sailing in deep waters. At one time I was in a very weak position....I had to go back to the banker and ask for mercy. But in the end, I guess it turned out fine." Those who have no reason to expect disinterested acts of mercy from their bankers should stay away from the Black-Scholes equation and from derivatives in general. Before the month of October 1997 was over, the southeast Asian currency crisis was lashing stock markets all around the world. The main vehicle of the speculation that was causing this crisis were derivatives. What had the Swedish Academy been thinking? There had been numerous signs over recent years that this august body had gone off the deep end. During the same month, for example, they gave the Nobel Prize for Literature to Dario Fo. Dario Fo was a clown, but at least he was an entertaining one, and not a public menace.

THE BUCKET SHOPS OF THE LATE TWENTIETH CENTURY

The classic American bucket shop of the nineteenth century is a very close ancestor of the modern financial derivatives. The bucket shop was a kind of gambling den, often sleazy and disreputable. With its stock ticker and seating for clients, the bucket shop closely resembled the trading room of a stock brokerage, but there was a crucial difference: in the bucket shop, no shares of stock were actually bought or sold. No phone calls were exchanged with stock exchanges or other trading rooms. The patrons of the bucket shop were there to place bets on whether the next transaction of a given stock reported on the stock ticker would be represent a gain, a loss, or unchanged; sometimes they also wagered on how much the stock would go up or down. If they

---

[67] See "Wall Street Struggles to Save Big Fund" and "At Huge Hedge Fund, A Magic Touch Is Lost," *Washington Post*, September 24, 1998 and CNBC, September 24, 1998.

guessed right, they won; if they guessed wrong, they lost their money. But they never became owners of any stock. Theirs was a classical side bet placed from afar.

Bucket shops came to be regarded as what they were, a form of gambling and therefore illegal in a healthy and growing industrial society. Bucket shops came to be seen as a social evil, and were suppressed by new laws and by the more vigorous enforcement of old ones. Laws prohibiting bucket shops remain on the books in almost all states. These ordinances can and should be used in an emergency to close down the derivatives trading pits, starting from the three big Chicago bucket shops - the Chicago Board of Trade (CBOT), the Chicago Mercantile Exchange (the Chicago Merc), and the Chicago Board Options Exchange (CBOE).

The old bucket shops were also less harmful than the derivatives markets of today. The betting that went on in each individual bucket shop had virtually no impact on the behavior of the actual stocks being traded on the real exchanges. But today, the volume of cash dedicated to placing the side bets is colossal, and the derivatives markets are intimately linked to the buying and selling of the underlying stocks, commodities, and other instruments through a complex series of circuits and feedback mechanisms, especially in the form of index arbitrage, which will be revealed in some detail below.

FINANCIAL AIDS

"Financial AIDS" - that is the short and effective definition of derivatives offered by French President Jacques Chirac at a recent yearly G-7 meeting. The then Japanese Finance Minister Hashimoto had used exactly the same term several years earlier. Derivatives are variously defined in today's popular literature as financial contracts whose values and returns are linked to, or derived from, the performance of some underlying asset. Derivatives thus can be seen to include futures, options, currency and interest rate swaps, mortgage-backed and other securitized instruments, stock indices, options indices, futures options, and futures options indices. A better way to define derivatives is that they are financial paper based on other financial paper which involve a wager on the future behavior of the underlying financial paper. This broader and more accurate definition allows us to see that mutual funds are very close to derivatives. Derivatives are side bets, intrinsically identical to forms of gambling that were illegal in happier eras than our own. An exhaustive list of derivatives is included towards the end of this chapter.

Derivatives exposures in selected countries, 1994-95

(currencies in billions)

Country	Amounts outstanding		1995 Growth
	1994	1995	
United States	$20,301	$23,129	13.9%
Japan	9,867	11,532	16.9%
France	11,695	9,374	-19.8%
United Kingdom	6,655	7,367	10.7%
Switzerland	5,327	6,321	18.7%
Germany	3,117	4,258	36.6%
Canada	2,460	3,321	35.0%
Netherlands	1,250	1,596	27.7%

Sweden	1,026	1,278	24.6%
Belgium	508	689	35.6%
Italy	432	483	11.8%
Grand Total	**$62,638**	**$69,348**	**10.7%**

[Source: Basel Committee on Banking Supervision, International Organization of Securities Commissions.]

DERIVATIVES IN ANTIQUITY: FUTURES

A futures contract binds the buyer of the contract with the obligation to buy a specified asset at a specific price at a future time. Derivatives devotees are anxious to find a Biblical justification for their current mania if they can. Some attempt to go back to the Book of Genesis and the episode in which the Pharaoh of Egypt called upon Joseph to interpret his dream in which seven fat cows and seven ears of corn were followed by seven emaciated cows and seven blighted ears of corn. Joseph replied that this meant that seven years of crop failure and famine would follow seven years of prosperity. Joseph also recommended a policy to avoid mass starvation during the lean years, which was to create a government agency charged with maintaining food stocks:

> Let Pharaoh do this, and let him appoint officers over the land, and take up the fifth part of the land of Egypt in the seven plenteous years. And let them gather all the food of those good years that come, and lay up corn under the hand of Pharaoh, and let them keep food in the cities. And the food shall be for store to the land against the seven years of famine, which shall be in the land of Egypt; that the land perish not through the famine. [*Genesis*, 34-36]

A modern economist paraphrases Joseph's advice as a recommendation that "Egypt should initiate future-buy contracts during the seven-year period of oversupply to avoid famine during the period of undersupply that would follow. [Malkiel, 281] But this is projecting derivatives where Joseph was suggesting government requisition under emergency powers – an issue that will preoccupy us once again at the end of this book. Other authors have found evidence of futures trading in India around 2000 BC. Some have found futures contracts in the grain-purchasing practices of Roman Emperors. The direct ancestor of the modern futures contract would appear to be the "to arrive" grain contract that was commonly used by European grain traders during the 1700s. These were contracts that bound the buyer to purchase the grain cargo of ships as soon as they arrived in port.

OPTIONS: AS OLD AS ARISTOTLE

The options contract gives the buyer the right, but not the obligation, to purchase a specific asset at a specific price at some time in the future. Anxious once again to find a Biblical justification for their activities, pro-derivatives commentators have tried to find an option back in chapter 29 of the Book of Genesis, where Jacob contracted with Laban to carry out seven years of labor in order to acquire the option of marrying Rachel. Derivatives apologists are on much firmer ground when they argue, as the *Wall Street Journal* is fond of doing, that derivatives are as old as Aristotle. In his *Politics*, Aristotle tells the story of the Ionian philosopher Thales, who was able to predict one winter that the olive harvest of the coming autumn would be especially abundant. Thales therefore took his entire savings and invested it in what we today might call time-sharing options on all the olive presses in the region where he lived. He went to the owner of each olive press and paid relatively modest amounts for the option of using the press for the habitual price during the time when the olive harvest would be brought in. The harvest was indeed a bumper crop, and the options purchased by Thales were all in the money. Later, Aristotle recounts, "...when the season came for making oil, many persons wanting [oil presses], he all at once let them upon what terms he pleased; and raising a large sum of money by that means, convinced [the public] that it was easy for philosophers to be rich if they chose it, but that that was not what they aimed at; in this manner Thales is said to have shown his wisdom." [Aristotle, *Politics*, 1259a[68]]

DUTCH TULIP OPTIONS C. 1635

A recent heyday of options came in Holland during the seventeenth century, when that country was the financial center of the world. In the days of the tulip bubble, tulip options were all the rage. Call options on tulip bulbs were written and bought. During the time that the price of tulip bulbs was rising, speculators noted that greater profits could be realized by buying tulip call options than by buying the bulbs themselves. This is because of the leverage inherent in options: the same amount of cash could command more call options than actual bulbs for immediate delivery in the cash or spot market. But when the tulip bubble collapsed, it was found that those who had written options and sold them faced astronomical losses. The writers of put options were wiped out with a vengeance.

Interesting insights on the Amsterdam options market can be found in the work entitled *Confusion de Confusiones*, published in 1688 and written by Joseph de la Vega, a player on the Amsterdam market. Amsterdam was for a time the financial center of the world, but its ascendancy lasted little more than a century. Amsterdam took over pre-eminence from declining Italian banking centers like Venice and Genoa during the late 1500s, and was superseded in its turn by London. Derivatives, specifically options, played an important role in the decline of Amsterdam. We should remember that New York has been the financial center of the world only since 1931 or since 1945, depending on how this is calculated. (Some experts might deny that New York has ever been the financial center of the world, and that London has held first place all along.) Today all signs suggest that New York's world dominance as a financial center may be significantly shorter than that of Amsterdam, and that derivatives will be a leading factor in New York's collapse.

After the collapse of the Dutch tulip craze, options were widely execrated and distrusted. In England, there was even a law which prohibited options. This was Barnard's Act of 1733, which remained in force with few interruptions until 1860. Stock options were prominent in the speculative orgy that preceded the Great Crash of 1929, and stock options came close to being outlawed in the US at the federal level in 1934.

DERIVATIVES AND POST-1971 CHAOS

Chroniclers of the recent hypertrophic growth of derivatives cannot get around the fact that they are the by-products of the degeneration of the world financial system after the dismantling of Bretton Woods. The link is conceded by Malkiel, who writes that "the demise of the Bretton Woods system of fixed international exchange rates and the change to a floating or flexible exchange rate regime drastically increased the variability in foreign currency values. Leo Melamed of the Chicago Mercantile Exchange recognized that this new system, where markets rather than governments determined the prices of currencies, created the opportunity for the inception of futures trading." [Malkiel, 284-285] In 1975, the Chicago Board of Trade began trading in the futures of Ginnie Maes, the bonds issued by the Government National Mortgage Association (GNMA). In January 1976, a futures contract on the 90 day bills of the US Treasury was offered. In August 1977, a

---

[68] Aristotle, *The Politics*, trans. William Ellis (Buffalo: Prometheus, 1986), p. 20-21.

futures contract on the 30-year bellwether US Treasury long bond was introduced. In 1982, the Kansas City Board of Trade began selling a futures contract based on the Value Line Stock Index. This was the first index futures contract of the recent era. Soon after, investors could buy futures contracts based on the Standard & Poor's index of 500 stocks, as well as other S&P stock indexes. Then came the Major Market Index, an index future that roughly corresponded to the 30 stocks that also made up the Dow Jones Industrial Average. Another index futures contract emerged which was based on the broader New York Stock Exchange Index.

For a long time, the Dow Jones Corporation resisted attempts to create a futures contract based directly, explicitly, and by name on the Dow Jones Industrial Average and the 30 stocks that are its components. But in June 1997, it was announced that the Dow Jones Industrial Average would be available first a stock index, an index future, and as index futures options. These contracts were made available in denominations suitable for large institutional investors, and at the same time in smaller version which individual investors could buy. Those who bought these when they came out were just in time to lose their shirts in the Hong Kong shock at the end of October 1997.

SWAPS

Swaps are different from the futures and options contracts which trade on public exchanges. Swaps exist as contracts between companies or individuals, and may or may not be known to the public at large. A recent treatise on swaps defines this derivative instrument as "a contractual agreement evidenced by a single document in which two parties, called counterparties, agree to make periodic payments to each other. Contained in the swap agreement is a specification of the currencies to be exchanged (which may or may not be the same), the rate of interest applicable to each (which may be fixed or floating), the timetable by which the payments are to be made, and any other provisions bearing on the relationship between the parties." [Marshall and Kapner, 3] Swaps often involve the pledge of one counterparty to pay a fixed rate of interest, while the other contracts to pay a floating rate. The underlying assets involved are called notional values or notionals. Here again, exchange rate swaps came into use after the 1971 collapse of the Bretton Woods system of fixed exchange parities. Originally swaps were called back-to-back loans, and they were used to evade the postwar foreign exchange controls imposed by the British government to defend the sickly pound sterling. An early landmark in the development of swaps came in 1981, with a currency swap contract between the World Bank and IBM, brokered by Salomon Brothers. Here the attempt was no longer to evade exchange controls, but to obtain the use of foreign currency without the expense of actually changing money. Interest rate swaps began to appear in London in the early 1980s. The first American interest swap was probably the fixed-for-floating swap offered by the Student Loan Marketing Association in 1982. You have a friend at Chase Manhattan who was responsible for the first commodity swap in 1986. The legality of commodity swaps under US law was called into question soon after, so commodity swaps tended to migrate to London. In 1989 the CFTC rescinded its own earlier opinion, now finding that commodity swaps were legal. But doubts still persisted that swaps would stand up to a determined legal challenge.

EXOTIC DERIVATIVES

Collateralized mortgaged obligations have been in vogue since about 1986. The recent fad for structured notes got started in Japan during the late 1980s, and became world-wide after about 1991. Structured notes can be anything – literally anything that a pair of yuppy quants sitting at laptops can dream up between them with the help of fuzzy engineering and manic axioms. Recent structured notes have included:

• The Swedish krona interest rate minus the Paris interbank lending rate cubed (i.e., raised to the third power);

• 19,000% minus the London Interbank Offered Rate (LIBOR) multiplied by 1900;

• Twelve times the difference between LIBOR for German marks and LIBOR for US dollars, expressed as yen;

• The average currency swaps spreads in Japan, Spain, and Italy multiplied by functions of the 10-year constant maturity rate for US Treasury securities. [Beder in Lederman-Klein, 174]

Market-traded derivatives have also become more and more exotic. In a *reductio ad absurdum* of this tendency, the Chicago Mercantile Exchange in November 1998 began offering a derivative "product" keyed to the Quarterly Bankruptcy Index. It was marketed as a way to hedge against bad times.

RISK MANAGEMENT?

Proponents of derivatives argue that they are tools for risk management, useful for distributing and apportioning existing risk in ways that actually add to the overall stability of the financial system. The argument here is often that derivatives are useful for hedging. The economics textbooks of the 1950s often gave examples of the economically useful function of certain types of hedging. Take the miller who buys a large quantity of wheat for the purpose of grinding it into flour. The process of milling takes a certain number of days or weeks. What happens to the miller if the price of wheat goes up or down sharply during the time that the wheat is going through his mill? He may stand to collect a windfall, or he may suffer losses large enough to force him to raise the price of his product, or perhaps even large enough as to drive him into bankruptcy. The miller therefore protected himself with the help of a futures contract. At the same time that he bought his wheat for immediate physical delivery in the cash market, he also sold the same quantity of wheat short for future delivery at today's price, at about the same time that the lot of wheat in question would be leaving the mill. The miller would pocket the cash proceeds of the sale at once. In order to fulfill the short contract, the miller would buy wheat at the future date. If the price of wheat went up in the interim, the wheat in the mill would rise in value, but the miller would have to pay more when he entered the market to cover his short contract. The gain and the loss would cancel each other out, leaving the miller at break even, impervious to the ups and downs of the market. Similarly, if the price of wheat went down, the wheat in the mill would be worth less, but the miller would recoup that loss when he bought the wheat to cover the futures contract. In this case also, the miller would break even and would free to pursue his business insulated from market fluctuations. Textbooks accounts of this process stressed that the speculators who were often the counterparties in these deals performed a socially useful role by accepting the risk involved in the hope of obtaining a profit.

Proponents of derivatives would have us believe that derivatives today are being used in this way, to absorb, distribute, and dampen risk. They tell stories of companies that take in large amounts of foreign currencies from the sale of industrial goods protecting themselves against fluctuations in the foreign exchange market by selling futures contracts in the same currencies they are taking in. They regale us with tales of small investors who buy put options on stocks they own as a way of insuring themselves against sharp declines. Such hedging, they aver, is prudent, safe, and tends to reduce risks for those involved.

Such an analysis appeals to those who want to prevent derivatives from being regulated, or even measured. These are the free-enterprise ideologues who assert that "the notion that an expansion in the use of OTC derivatives has somehow increased systemic risk, and that additional regulation is needed to reduce this risk, has no obvious factual basis." [Edwards, 36] But the heavy losses incurred in derivatives transactions show that this is simply not the way that derivatives are being used. If Soros, Druckenmiller and Julian Robertson were using derivatives for portfolio insurance and for protection against foreign exchange fluctuations, they would not be reporting gains and losses in the range of half a billion to several billion dollars. Hedge funds in general, and the *de facto* hedge fund that lurks inside every large bank, are using derivatives for high-risk speculation. Post-1987 derivatives exposure overwhelmingly lacks the carefully matched symmetrical structure of put and call options, long and short futures that would be typical of hedging. Derivative positions tend to be one-sided and univocal all-or-nothing bets that take a definite view of future events. Whatever else Nick Leeson, Robert Citron, Joseph Jett and their confreres were doing or not doing, it is clear that they were not hedging anything. That is why the profits and losses turn out to be so large. This increases risk for the individual counterparties, and immensely increases the systemic risk for world finance.

There is also plenty of important anecdotal evidence that derivatives are being used for risky gambling, not prudent risk management. Gary Gastineau, the head of derivatives research at the S.G. Warburg investment bank, told a magazine reporter some years ago that "given long enough, he might be able to think of a risk management reason for entering into a wedding band swap. 'But that's not really their purpose. These things are done by people who think they know better than the market where interest rates are headed." [69]

Another comment on this issue of how derivatives are actually being used appeared in the London *Sunday Telegraph* of March 9, 1997, in Neil Bennett's article on "The $55 Trillion Horror Show." This came in the wake of the derivatives losses by NatWest. Bennett wrote: "Every ban has vast derivatives liabilities. Barclays, for example, admitted in its results that it had derivatives worth 922 million pounds at the end of last year, up more than a quarter on 1995. Barclays and its peers say the risk of these vast positions is minimal, because they are all matched and hedged. If the financial markets crash, the losses from one set of contracts will be offset by the profits on another. The trouble is that not every operator in financial markets is so prudent. Some are running very risky positions indeed. If and when world stock markets fall, some wouldn't be able to pay their losses. That would mean that all those prudent, hedged banks were not hedged because their counterparties were going bust. Suddenly, even large banks could be starting at vast losses." [London *Sunday Telegraph*, March 9, 1997]

DERIVATIVES = LEVERAGE

The key to speculation is leverage, and derivatives make possible a dimension of leverage which could hitherto only be imagined. Options and futures contracts allow a speculator to control the ownership of financial instruments at a future time using far less cash up front than would be necessary to buy them. We must also add that stock markets (the purview of the Securities and Exchange Commission, with margin requirements set by the Federal Reserve) are much more stringently supervised than futures markets (the domain of the weaker Commodity Futures Trading Commission) or options markets. It is in short much easier to speculate in derivatives using borrowed money than it is to carry out the same type of maneuvers in the cash market for stocks.

---

[69] Carol J. Loomis, "Cracking the Derivatives case," *Fortune*, March 20, 1995, p. 54. See also Carol J. Loomis, "The Risk That Won't Go Away," *Fortune*, March 7, 1994.

Fortune magazine took stock of derivatives risks in the late winter of 1995, in the wake of the Orange County and Barings bankruptcies. This article concluded of derivatives that "in the hands of speculators, bumblers, or unscrupulous peddlers, they are a powerful leveraged mechanism for **creating** risk." [*Fortune*, Loomis, 51] Fortune found that the fact that derivatives contracts are not specified on the balance sheets of banks and corporations "tends to obscure the leverage and financial might they bring to the party." In the case of Gibson Greeting cards, another firm that lost big on derivatives, "many of the [derivatives] contracts, usually because they contained options, incorporated leverage that caused Gibson's losses to increase dramatically in response to small changes in interest rates." [Loomis, 54] As always, the leverage that makes the value go up faster than the market when conditions are favorable is the same leverage that will generate exponential losses when conditions turn unfavorable, as they always eventually do.

INFINITE LOSSES

If you buy stocks for cash in the stock market, you can lose everything if they crash. In the worst case, you can lose 100% of your investment, plus commissions and fees. If you buy on margin, you can be left owing money to your broker up to the total cost of the stocks, plus interest. For most people, this should already be bad enough. But with derivatives, we enter into a new dimension of risk. Here you can suddenly lose more than everything. Any party to any futures contract, whether buyer or seller, faces unlimited losses if the market moves in the wrong direction. This also means that any contract you sign which has a futures contract embedded in it can saddle you with unlimited losses. This is because you are legally obligated to buy or sell the underlying asset. The best advice we can give is therefore to stay away from futures trading in any form. If you buy put options or call options, you can lose 100% of your investment, plus commissions, fees, interest, and margin. If you think you will be protected by stop loss orders, remember that stop loss orders will work very well, except when you really need them, in the moment of total panic and market meltdown.

But if your write or sell options, be they put options or call options, your potential losses are once again unlimited. You are legally obliged to deliver or to acquire the asset in question if the owner of the option you have written decides to exercise the option. Any small investor who writes options or sells options (the same thing) should receive an urgent psychiatric examination. Beware also when signing financial contracts, since these often contain options embedded in them. Under certain circumstances, those embedded options can inflict infinite losses on you. Have you not seen the news reports of shocked and bewildered little people who have let themselves get talked into selling an option on heating oil or orange juice with many assurances that it was a sure winner, and who now find that their losses far exceed their modest personal net worth? Do not join the ranks of these pathetic victims!

To drive home this lesson, let me quote from the advice offered by the experienced investor Morton Shulman in his 1981 book *How to Invest Your Money and Profit from Inflation*. Shulman's chapter on options is subtitled "Strictly for Fools." Shulman tells the story of a firm where he worked which studied 150 option buyers and 38 option sellers. The option buyers lost money three out of four times, and the habitual options buyers always lost money. Each and every one of the options sellers lost money. The options sellers who were trying to protect their stock portfolios did especially badly: "...holders of stock portfolios who sell options get the worst of both worlds. As their stocks go down in falling markets, they take massive losses cushioned only slightly by the option premium, but in rising markets when they should be making huge profits, the options are exercised and they end up only making a 5 of 10% profit on their investment. They limit their profits, but have unlimited losses. The option seller who attempts to trade his stock against the option can be murdered by a whip-sawing market...It's a mug's game! And don't listen to any broker who tells you different. He's making too much out of you to give you honest and disinterested advice." [Shulman 144]

Lest any reader take away the impression that the stock market is safer than the derivatives markets, we must recall here that any short selling in the stock market also brings with it the risk of unlimited losses. As we will argue later in this chapter, the stock market is too risky for the individual investor precisely because it is now a dog being wagged by its overgrown derivatives tail.

Derivatives in the form of interest rate swaps, currency swaps, and similar deals often assume the form of extremely complicated contracts. Sometimes as many as 250 different cash flows are being exchanged. The small investor should reflect here on the experience of Procter & Gamble, one of the largest corporations in the United States, which has alleged that it was fleeced on two swaps contracts that carried what P&G called "huge, concealed risks." The first problem is that these contracts are often incomprehensible not just for the small investor, but even for sophisticated corporate financial officers. The second problem is that the bank that is selling the swap may refuse to let the derivatives customer see the full details of what the customer has signed and is going to pay for. This is what happened to P&G, which complained that Bankers Trust was using "a secret, proprietary, complex, multivariable pricing model" that Bankers Trust simply would not divulge, even when P&G was losing big money and was trying to figure out what it might do to cut its losses. [Loomis, 62] What the average person needs to know about derivatives boils down to how to avoid them, and how to support legislation to make them illegal once and for all.

$150+ TRILLION IN WORLD DERIVATIVES

More than any other single factor, derivatives are responsible for the ballooning of the money throughput of world financial markets, which in turn causes most of the risk of liquidity crisis and financial disintegration. We should remember how impressed many investors were back in 1972 when Henry Kaufman estimated that the non-communist countries had a total debt of about $3.6 trillion, or when he raised that estimate to $14.3 trillion in 1981. Back in the 1980s, it was estimated that the total debt burden of the US economy was growing at the rate of about $1 trillion per year. At the dawn of the derivatives era, back in early September 1989, Chris White of EIR attempted to develop an aggregate figure for the entire debt burden on the productive activity of the American economy. The total paper claims included federal government debt, state debt, city and county debt, business debt of all financial and non-financial corporations, plus consumer, mortgage and household debt of individuals. The total debt plus other forms of income-bearing paper amounted to about $20 trillion. It was estimated that the money needed to pay the debt service on this debt and roll it over as it came due amounted to between $4.5 to $5 trillion.

But these sums, once so imposing, are now chicken feed. The New York Clearinghouse Interbank Payment System (CHIPS) announced that on January 21, 1997 it had set a new all-time turnover record, processing interbank payments in the amount of more than $2.178 trillion. (In 1971, the first full YEAR of computerized operations, CHIPS processed a total of $1.131 trillion, which seemed like a good chunk of cash back then.) While it is difficult to determine the exact amount, it is clear that a very large portion of these funds go into buying and selling derivatives. (If the public wants to know how much, the remedy would be to pass laws making all derivatives reportable to the government, something they presently are not.)

DERIVATIVES LOSSES, 1987-97

(in millions of US dollars)

Year	Entity	Losses
1987	British local municipal authorities	$500
1987	Merrill Lynch	335
1987	Volkswagen	260
1988	Kloeckner-Humboldt-Deutz	380
1989	Chemical Bank	33
1990	Hedged Securities Associates, Inc.	100
1991	Allied Lyons	275
1992	J.P. Morgan	50
1992	Louisiana State Retirement Fund	43
1992	Nippon Steel	130
1992	Central Bank of Malaysia	2,660
1993	Showa Shell Sekiyu	1,580
1993	Ohio counties (Putnam, Portage, Sandusky)	11
1993	Kashima Oil	1,450
1993	Metallgesellschaft	2,000
1994	Codelco, Chile	206
1994	Quantum Fund (Soros)	600
1994	Proctor & Gamble	157
1994	Glaxo	150
1994	Orange County, California	2,000
1995	Barings	1,500
1995	Wisconsin State Retirement Fund	100
1995	Daiwa	1,100
1996	Sumitomo	2,600
1997	Belgian government	1,232
1997	NatWest Markets	146
1997	Volkswagen	850
1997	Chase Manhattan	160

[source: *EIR*, news reports]

By late 1997, the Asian collapse had made derivatives losses so pervasive that it would be impossible to begin to list them.

NUCLEAR MINES

The fine print in standard derivatives contracts may hide any number of surprises, especially in combination with the derivatives laws of various countries. During a bout of intense international anxiety about the derivatives exposure of Fuji Bank and other Japanese institutions in the late summer of 1998, wire services pointed to the following Catch -22. Banks use a standard derivatives contract drawn up by the International Swaps and Derivatives Association (ISDA) in most over-the-counter derivatives transactions, including interest-rate swaps, foreign currency swaps, and bond options. The standard ISDA form contains a cross-default clause which specifies that default on any single derivative transaction with any counterparty would automatically permit all the other derivative transactions with all counterparties involved to be deemed in default. The trick is that the Japanese legislation establishing the bridge bank bailout agency foresees placing insolvent banks under a bankruptcy administrator or receiver to run that bank. This might mean default for derivatives market players, since the ISDA standard agreement says that when a receiver is appointed to take over the running of a bank, the master agreement is terminated. This is called the cross-default clause, and a single disgruntled counterparty would be enough to trigger it. This would produce the financial equivalent of the nuclear chain-reaction inside a fission bomb. [70]

DERIVATIVES ARE ILLEGAL

Derivatives are in reality nothing but a form of gambling - gambling which transpires in trading pits, in electronic markets, or in the cyberspace that joins the laptop computers of those yuppy "quants" or quantitative analysts who are the "gnomes of Zürich" in the current financial turbulence. Until recently many types of derivatives were simply illegal. In the United States, trading of options on agricultural commodities had come under wide attack by farmers during the 1920s. In 1933, an attempt was made to corner the wheat futures market using options, and the resulting outcry led to a 1936 federal law banning such options on farm commodity markets. This ban was repealed by the Futures Trading Act of 1982, which was signed by President Reagan in early January, 1983. From that time on, options trading on US agro-markets has been legal once again. The US farm economy did much better between 1936 and 1983, when farm market options were illegal, than it has done after 1983.

WENDY GRAMM

Through the early 1990s, certain kinds of swap agreements were still illegal according to some, and of very dubious legality according to others. Under the provisions of the Commodity Exchange Act, it is still illegal to buy and sell futures contracts outside of the trading floors of the commodity exchanges. An over-the-counter derivative like an interest rate swap often constitutes a binding contract to buy or sell a futures contract, and thus constitutes an illegal transfer of the futures contract outside of the exchanges. In 1989, the CFTC issued a policy statement which created a "safe harbor" for swap transactions meeting certain criteria. That meant that the CFTC promised not to prosecute or otherwise restrain anyone dealing with these swaps contracts. But there was still a lingering doubt over whether these swaps contracts would stand up to challenge in the federal courts. As the CFTC later conceded, "the legal status of swaps activity has been questioned in recent years because of uncertainty over the applicability of the Commodities Exchange Act."

But in mid-January, 1993, during the waning days of the disastrous Bush Administration, Wendy Gramm, then the chair of the Commodity Futures Trading Commission (which regulates commodities exchanges) helped the derivatives brokers out by declaring their products legal. The Wendy Gramm in question was none the than the wife of Senator Phil Gramm (R-Texas), who later, in 1996, ran for the GOP presidential nomination. And how could Wendy Gramm and the other CFTC commissioners legislate for the United States of America? Under the Futures Trading Practices Act of 1992, the CFTC was granted general exemptive authority in certain of these matters. In January, 1993 Wendy Gramm and her colleagues jointly exercised this exemptive

---

[70] *Reuters*, September 2, 1998.

authority and declared that the swaps were legal. Not only were they legal, but they were legal when entered into with offshore institutions beyond US law.

Wendy Gramm touted her decision as one which "eliminates legal and regulatory uncertainties that could have become a major deterrent to the growth of US financial markets. Today's action will help the US remain the world leader in financial innovation.... Legal certainty for swaps,' crowed Wendy, "will help US markets continue to innovate ad grow. This certainty will also aid in reducing financial risk in our markets. Exchanges and over-the-counter markets will have the freedom to be more creative in meeting the competitive challenges of the global marketplace." Within less than two years, the school children of Orange County, California had reason to bless the foresight of Wendy Gramm and her cohorts.

Derivatives holdings of selected major international banks

(currencies in billions)

Country	Amounts outstanding 1994 U.S. dollars	1995 U.S. dollars	Growth during 1995 $USD Percent
Chase Manhattan	$1,367	$4,834	253.6%
JP Morgan	2,471	3,447	39.5%
Bank of Tokyo Mitsubishi	1,197	3,869	139.7%
Citicorp	2,665	2,590	-2.8%
Swiss Bank Corp.	2,009	2,581	28.5%
Société Générale	3,274	2,543	-22.3%
Industrial Bank of Japan	1,880	2,071	10.2%
Credit Suisse	1,600	1,959	22.4%
Fuji Bank	1,971	1,891	-4.1%
Paribas	2,142	1,877	-12.4%
National Westminster	1,394	1,869	34.1%
Banque Nationale de Paris	1,919	1,814	-5.5%
Union Bank of Switzerland	1,718	1,781	3.7%
Bankers Trust NY	1,982	1,702	-14.1%
Salomon Inc.	1,470	1,659	12.9%
Deutsche Bank	1,410	1,651	17.1%
Sumitomo Bank		1,644	
Merrill Lynch	1,169	1,610	37.7%
BankAmerica	1,376	1,581	14.9%
Barclays	1,490	1,569	5.3%
HSBC	1,638	1,527	-6.8%
Sanwa Bank	1,248	1,495	19.8%
Lloyds	1,154	1,435	24.4%
Lehman Brothers Holdings	1,086	1,209	11.3%
Goldman Sachs	995	1,091	9.6%
Credit Lyonnais	1,827	1,053	-42.4%

NationsBank	511	1,007	97.1%
Morgan Stanley	835	985	18.0%
Royal Bank of Canada	703	929	32.1%
ABN-AMRO Bank	706	924	30.9%
Canadian Imperial Bank of Commerce	569	880	54.7%
First Chicago	622	815	31.0%
Indosuez	935	787	-15.8%
CommerzBank	392	776	98.0%
Tokai Bank	854	671	-21.4%
Long-Term Credit Bank of Japan	863	651	-24.6%
Dresdner Bank	473	641	35.5%
Skandinavska Enskilden Banken	416	557	33.9%
Credit Agricole	704	524	-25.6%
Bank of Montreal	403	498	23.6%
Bank of Nova Scotia	372	488	31.2%
Toronto Dominion	353	460	30.3%
Bayerische Vereinsbamk AG	288	454	57.6%
Svenska Handelsbanken	306	410	34.0%
Union Européene de CIC	290	409	41.0%
Rabobank	330	397	20.3%
Credit Commerciale de France	604	367	-39.2%
Westdeutsche Landesbank	345	356	3.2%

[Source: Basel Committee on Banking Supervision, International Organization of Securities Commissions.]

GREENSPAN'S LOVE AFFAIR WITH DERIVATIVES

On May 1, 1997 Greenspan visited Chicago, but she was not there to celebrate international labor day in the city where the holiday started more than a century ago. Today, of course, Chicago is the world capital of derivatives. Greenspan spoke at the Chicago Federal Reserve Bank's Conference on Bank Structure and Competition, and praised the new innovations in the derivatives field, such as the "bundling" of mortgages and loans for securitization purposes. But, having mentioned derivatives, he was also forced to refer the question of financial meltdown that derivatives always raise. Greenspan conceded that it was also necessary to keep some form of centralized overview over banks and derivatives.

Greenspan's approach was to acknowledge potential dangers, but to insist that nothing be done. He commented: "A purely decentralized regulatory approach would... greatly diminish our ability to evaluate and contain potential systemic disruptions in the financial system, since no regulator would be responsible for monitoring the consolidated banking organization. We should remember that one of the primary motivations of a society having a central bank and a safety net is precisely to limit systemic risk." This was pure doubletalk, since Greenspan had been the person most responsible for the June 1994 failure of the Clinton Administration's attempt to merge the regulatory functions of the Federal Reserve (responsible currently for bank holding companies and Fed member banks), the Treasury's Office of the Comptroller of the Currency (responsible for national banks), the Office of Thrift Supervision (responsible for savings and loan institutions) and the Federal Deposit Insurance Corporation (responsible for banks chartered by states). This was a last forlorn hope that someone might do something about derivatives. But the Federal Reserve had rejected any encroachment on its prerogatives. In ending his speech, Greenspan articulated his own creed of de-regulation in financial affairs: "Over the last three decades, the folly of attempting to legislate or regulate against the primal forces of the market is one of the most fundamental lessons learned by banking regulators." At a later Congressional appearance, Greenspan pontificated that derivatives were already strictly regulated – by the wealthy investors who were putting up the money!

During 1997, a controversy developed about how derivatives exposure should be reported on the books of banks and corporations. The Financial Accounting Standards Board of Norwalk, Connecticut came forward with a reasonable and rational proposal to require the 15,000 US corporations whose stock is traded on public markets to report their derivatives exposure to the public, and to mark the value of this paper to market at "fair market value." The FASB is the national body responsible for setting standards for accounting, a kind of steering committee for the green eyeshade set. At the time this recommendation was made, corporations were either not reporting their derivatives holdings at all, or else were noting them "off balance sheet," meaning that explosive derivatives risks were being relegated to the fine print of the annual reports of these firms. After such debacles as Orange County, Barings, and many others, it was time to make derivatives reportable to the public in the same way that tuberculosis, for example, is reportable to the public health authorities. Part of the impact of the new rules would be to make it harder for corporations to cover up losses incurred through wheeling and dealing in derivatives.

The FASB's proposals were summed up in a 134-page booklet released on September 2, 1997 under the title *Accounting for Derivatives Instruments and Hedging Activities*. The idea was merely to let some sunshine in on the dank chambers where the derivatives fungus grows. Nothing more than disclosure was being mandated. Greenspan obviously regarded this fairly anodyne measure as a mortal threat to the System over which he presides, a System of which derivatives are now the life-blood. He sent three letters to Edmund Jenkins, Chairman of the FASB, boisterously demanding that the changes in accounting standards be dropped at once. "We understand that the [FASB] Board intends to adopt a new approach as a final standard without exposing it for public comment and debate," Greenspan wrote. This was a red herring, since the FASB had been holding public hearings on the changes for almost a year by the time Greenspan wrote his letter. If anything, the FASB itself was finally getting around to action rather late in the day. Greenspan then went on to state that "major companies in a number of industries that use derivatives have expressed serious concerns" about the new rules. This was true, since the usual list of suspects had indeed sent their own letter to the FASB complaining that they did not want to have to come clean about their derivatives dabbling.

This list was led by the commercial banks that have transformed themselves into hedge funds, including Bankers Trust, Chase Manhattan, J.P. Morgan, NationsBank, Wells Fargo, BankAmerica, First Chicago NBD, who were joined by Goldman Sachs, American International Group Insurance, and others. Republican Senators Al D'Amato and Phil Gramm also signed. One unnamed Republican Senator told the *Washington Post* "Why is the FASB so immune to all this criticism? It seems as if they're pushing generally rejected accounting practices." But, even according to the laissez-faire ideologues, how can markets work efficiently if vital information is kept secret from the public?

The following is an educated guess on how this matter will finally be resolved. In the spring of 1933 the Senate Banking and Currency Committee, chaired by Democratic Senator Peter Norbeck, held a series of public hearings to examine the stockjobbing practices which the leading New York banks had engaged in during the years leading up to the crash of 1929. These hearings are often referred to as the Pecora hearings after Ferdinand Pecora, the chief counsel of the committee. (The impact of these hearings is assessed in another part of this book.) One of the main witnesses called before the committee was Charles E. Mitchell, who had been one of the great powers in Wall Street as head of National City Bank, the country's largest. Mitchell was forced to acknowledge before the committee that he and his bank had been guilty of a scandalous repertoire of practices. Public indignation over these practices was very great, and contributed to the creation of the Securities and Exchange Commission. Mitchell himself was personally ruined, and became, along with other bankers and stockbrokers, the object of widespread opprobrium.

One does not have to be a prophet to forecast that, in the wake of the coming derivatives catastrophe, public hatred will tend to become focussed on these exotically poisonous financial instruments. The public will demand an accounting of which regulators did what and when to help visit the derivatives plague on the country and the world. The choreography of those hearings will doubtless assign a leading role to the nondescript figure of Alan Greenspan, who by that time will hopefully be the former chairman of the defunct Federal Reserve System, which by that point should have been long since placed in receivership by the US Treasury. Perhaps Greenspan will be joined by Wendy Gramm, and other derivatives malefactors. As for derivatives, they should be declared illegal once again, as they were for many years. The best vehicle for a ban on derivatives might well turn out to be a constitutional amendment, perhaps the same one that bans the reconstitution of a private central bank like the Federal Reserve. If the ban on derivatives and the private central banking system that made them possible is anchored in the Constitution, there will be more hope that the derivatives cancer will not recur in some future epoch of speculative frenzy.

Derivatives holdings of major U.S. banks, as of Sept. 30, 1996, with derivatives as a multiple of equity.

(billions $)

Holding company	Equity	Assets	Derivatives	Multiple
Chase Manhattan	21	323	5,660	268
JP Morgan	11	212	4,509	407
Citicorp	20	272	2,557	125
Bankers Trust NY	5	121	1,906	358
BankAmerica	21	243	1,808	88
NationsBank	13	188	1,325	100
First Chicago NBD	9	107	1,024	113
Republic NY	3	51	289	90
First Union	9	134	147	17
Bank of New York	5	52	119	23
Top ten banks	118	1,701	19,344	164
All U.S. banks	**370**	**4,458**	**20,385**	**55**

[source: US Comptroller of Currency]

CONGRESS WON'T SAVE YOU

One of the further consequences of Wendy Gramm's folly is that swaps and most over-the-counter derivatives remain free from any reporting requirement. Ask the CFTC and they will tell you that they have no idea of the total notional value of US OTC swaps contracts. By 1997, the world had witnessed Orange County, Barings and so many other derivatives disasters. The response of demented elements of the US Congress was to propose further deregulation of derivatives markets! This was the proposal contained in the bill S. 257, sponsored by Sen. Richard Lugar (R-Ill.) of the Senate Agriculture Committee and co-sponsored by Sen. Patrick Leahy (D-Vt.), the ranking minority member of that same committee. The Lugar-Leahy proposal amounted to the complete and final deregulation of US commodity exchanges and futures markets. Lugar and Leahy wanted to create what they call "professional markets" open only to large institutions and very wealthy individuals. These professional markets would become the real markets, where the prices are really set. Any other market functioning outside of the professional one would be a mere appendage, a kind of junior or kiddie market, which would inevitably follow the lead of the professionals. The prices and related behavior of the deregulated professional market would be determining for the rest of the market.

BACK TO THE STAMP TAX

Another thing to remember about derivatives is that they are untaxed. Even the many states that exact a sales tax on food purchases in a supermarket do not call upon George Soros and his ilk to pay a sales tax on their derivatives transactions. Until 1965, the United States levied a small tax, often called the stamp tax, on the sale or purchase of stocks and debt instruments. There were attempts starting in the late 1980s to revive such a transfer tax. In 1987, Speaker of the House Jim Wright (D-Texas) called for the restoration of a transfer tax on financial markets. Wright proposed that buyer and seller each pay the Treasury one half of one per cent of the total value of the transaction, which would have added up to 1% – less than the sales tax paid often by the ordinary citizen on groceries, but apparently too much for Wall Street. Wright was blamed for the October 1987 crash of the New York Stock Exchange, and was later hounded from office by Bush and Gingrich over spurious accusations of an illegal book deal. A little later, Sen. Lloyd Bentsen (D-Texas), then the chairman of the Senate Finance Committee, also proposed a transfer tax on certain types of financial paper. In 1990, this idea also surfaced in a report of the Congressional Budget Office entitled "Reducing the Deficit: Spending and Revenue Options." Under the heading "Impose a 0.5% Tax on the Transfer of Securities," the CBO opined that "the tax would have to be broad-based, applying to stocks, debt, options, and trades by American on foreign exchanges."[71]

The London derivatives market is called LIFFE, and it is the biggest in Europe. Parisian derivatives traders go to MATIF, the *marché à terme*. In Germany, derivatives trading, including sale of German bond futures, was held to be illegal under the gambling laws until laws were changed in 1989, opening the way for the opening of the Deutsche Terminbörse in 1990.

There were no financial futures markets in Japan until 1988. Until that year the only way to buy a stock index future based on the Nikkei 225 stock index was to go offshore, specifically to the Singapore International Monetary Exchange (SIMEX) - later the playground for Nick Leeson - where a Nikkei 225 stock index futures contract was launched in September, 1986. Japan finally succumbed to this species of derivatives madness in September 1988, when a Nikkei 225 futures contract was offered for the first time on the Osaka Securities Exchange; the Tokyo market soon offered futures contracts of its own.

The American academic world has come forward in defense of derivatives. Professor Burton G. Malkiel, for example, is the Chemical Bank Chairman's Professor of Economics at Princeton University. Chemical Bank is now a part of Chase Manhattan, and constitutes one of the superpowers of the derivatives world. So Professor Malkiel knows where his bread is buttered. He offers a common defense of derivatives, arguing that derivatives are a response to the chaotic

---

[71] " Pp. 388-389.

fluctuations in currencies and therefore of all financial values – fluctuations which began to escalate when international speculators had forced the abandonment of the fixed currency parities and the rest of the Bretton Woods system. Malkiel especially wants to defend program trading and index arbitrage, which is often based on price differentials between the New York Stock Exchange and the Chicago S&P 500 futures contract or some other stock index future. In his book, *A Random Walk Down Wall Street*, Malkiel takes the floor in favor of derivatives: "Futures markets arose to cope with underlying volatility. Blaming futures and related program trading for the volatility in the stock market is as illogical as blaming the thermometer for measuring uncomfortable temperatures. By making the market more quickly responsive to changes in underlying conditions or the sentiment of large institutions, program trading increases the efficiency of the stock market. To eliminate new instruments and techniques would be to make our markets less efficient. And because of the increasing integration of world financial markets, traders abroad would be sure to utilize any opportunities we discard." [Malkiel, 304]

This argument contains many of the fallacies of globaloney. Malkiel is ready to concede that volatility and instability are big problems, but he insists on trying to deal through these public problems with the means of the private sector, which means the attempt to make money off of volatility while ostensibly trying to treat it. Instead of using derivatives, why not neutralize volatility through fixed parities, re-regulation of markets, securities transactions taxes, exchange and capital controls, and the other basic tools of government regulation? All of this is taboo, because it contradicts the lunatic logic of globalization. Malkiel also suggests that national states are too weak to do anything anyway. Malkiel, like numerous other modern economic writers, is a devotee of the "random walk" notion, which posits that a purely random selection of stocks for one's portfolio will do as well as the most expensive expert advice. Malkiel and his numerous co-thinkers are thus like Dante's Democritus, who ascribed the entire world to chance ("Quivi vid'io...Democrito, che'l mondo a caso pone." [*Inferno*, iv.136]) Malkiel appears as an iconoclast in relation to the reputations of the celebrated stockjobbers of the recent era in Wall Street, but his insights do not help in solving the problems of public policy.

DERIVATIVES AND BANKING PANIC

As the chart shows, American bankers by 1996 were collectively dealing derivatives in a notional amount 55 times greater than their equity capital, according to government statistics. Some money center banks had gone much further: JP Morgan, for example, had entered into derivatives dealings which carried a notional value that is 407 times the equity capital of the bank. The bankers would doubtless argue that their derivatives contracts involved the exchange of payments which are far smaller, and that the notional values involved represented underlying assets which are not, formally speaking, being exchanged. But the Orange County, Barings, and other negative experiences with derivatives must still impel us to contemplate the consequences of the default of one or more of the large derivatives counterparties. Certainly the potential exists here for a chain-reaction crisis which could raise doubts about the solvency of banks in general, tie the banking system in knots, leaving institutional investors and the general public in doubt as to the solvency of many banks, and thus generate a banking panic at least on the scale of 1932-33.

Here in the United States, the most recent experience we have had with the insolvency of a large bank with a large derivatives exposure came with the failure of the Bank of New England, a derivatives pioneer which was partly done in by this type of pioneering. The General Accounting Office 1994 report on derivatives commented upon the problems encountered in wrapping up the Bank of New England, especially in regard to the unwinding of the bank's extensive derivatives portfolio: "Should a crisis arise, federal regulators are likely to be involved in containing and resolving financial problems at banks and thrifts because of the potential risk to the financial system and the potential government liability for losses incurred by the federal deposit insurance funds – the Bank Insurance Fund and the Savings Association Fund. In the past, resolving problems or crises in the financial system has been expensive....the failure of the Bank of New England in 1991...cost the Bank Insurance Fund about $1.2 billion. The bank also had a portfolio of derivatives with an notional value of $30 billion that had to be carefully closed out, unwound, or transferred to other counterparties under federal supervision to avoid market disruptions." [GAO, 42-43]

There is now a clear and present danger that derivatives speculation will lead to the bankruptcy of one or more leading American banks, and perhaps to a general run on all banks. If derivatives lead to a nationwide banking panic of the 1932-33 type, all depositors as well as all bank stockholders and bondholders and all bank employees will be the losers. We must also pay careful attention to the danger that the US government and the taxpayers will be called upon to make good the losses on insured bank deposits which such a derivatives-detonated banking panic might generate. This would occur if bank failures were to overwhelm the Bank Insurance Fund of the Federal Deposit Insurance Corporation, the federal agency which provides insurance on bank deposits up to $100,000 per person. The Bank Insurance Fund exists to pay off the depositors of banks that fail. The money in the fund is paid in by the banks themselves, although it is also clear that the banks pass this fee along to their depositors in the form of lower rates of interest and pervasively higher fees. But once the money in the Bank Insurance Fund is gone, the United States government is left holding the bag. Any further cash to compensate depositors for their lost savings will have to come from the US Treasury, and thus, from the taxpayers.

As pro-derivatives spokesman Franklin R. Edwards told a November 1994 conference on derivatives at the American Enterprise Institute in Washington, DC, "The issue comes down to whether or not prudential regulation of banks' derivative activities can adequately protect the federal deposit insurance fund and taxpayers...." [Edwards, 21] A bit of simply arithmetic will show how grim the outlook is. The following chart shows the evolution of the FDIC's Bank Insurance Fund, and its new cousin, the Savings and Loan Fund, over recent years. One need only compare the Bank Insurance Fund with its $25 billion dollars to the $2 trillion in total deposits to begin to see the problems that the bankruptcy of one large institution might pose, to say nothing of what a general banking panic would do.

Fund Balance and Insured Deposits * ($ Millions)

	BIF Fund Balance	BIF-Insured Deposits	SAIF Fund Balance	SAIF-Insured Deposits
12/89	13,210	1,873,837	0	882,920
12/90	4,045	1,929,612	18	830,028
12/91	-7,028	1,957,722	101	776,351
12/92	-101	1,945,550	279	732,159
12/93	13,122	1,905,245	1,157	697,885
12/94	21,848	1,895,258	1,937	693,610
12/95	25,454	1,951,963	3,358	711,897
3/96	25,748	1,959,270	3,650	715,834
6/96	25,828	1,957,949	3,914	713,179
9/96	26,106	1,981,488	8,722	687,932
12/96	26,854	2,007,447	8,888	683,090

* Insured deposit amounts are estimates. 12/96 fund balances are unaudited. [source: FDIC]

SYSTEMIC CRISIS

The main concern raised by the proliferation of derivatives is the danger that derivatives will cause the disintegration of the entire world financial system, or at least play a prominent role in that disintegration. This is the issue of systemic crisis. Systemic crisis is of course the overarching theme of this book, and is referred to in one form or another in virtually every chapter. To anchor this analysis, let us here note the official definition of systemic crisis as offered by the Bank for International Settlements, the private central bank of private central banks which forms the apex of the current doomed world financial system. According to the BIS, systemic crisis denotes "a disturbance that severely impairs the working of the financial system and, at the extreme, causes a complete breakdown in it. Systemic risks are those risks that have the potential to cause such a crisis. Systemic risks can originate in a variety of ways, but ultimately they will impair at least one of these key functions of the financial system: credit allocation, payments, and pricing of financial assets. A given financial disturbance may grow into a systemic crisis at one point in time and not another, depending on the financial and economic circumstances prevailing when the shock occurs." [BIS, 1992]

The United States government, through the General Accounting Office, has recognized the potential for a derivatives panic to generate a financial conflagration on a planetary scale. The GAO noted in its 1994 report: "The concentration of OTC derivative activities among a relatively few dealers could also heighten the risk of liquidity problems in the OTC derivatives markets, which could in turn pose risks to the financial system....the abrupt failure or withdrawal from trading of one of these dealers could undermine stability in several markets simultaneously, which could lead to a chain of market withdrawals, possible firm failures, and a systemic crisis." [GAO, 12]

Journalists writing for financial insiders can sometimes speak more bluntly about these dangers than can timid government bureaucrats. In addition to the warnings that appear in the previous chapter, let us take the following one: "The worry about derivatives lies less in the nature of the risks being run, than the wider context which is dangerously opaque. The Bank of England concluded last year that the unsupervised status of some of the large players in the system 'does represent a supervisory hole at the very heart of the derivatives market.' ...Most central bankers claim that the probability that the mispricing of derivatives could lead to a systemic shock is low, but cannot be ignored. They also worry that...complex derivative linkages across global markets could then make the contagion hard to contain." [John Plender, "Through a market, darkly" in *Financial Times,* Erdman, 75] The veteran financier Felix Rohatyn of Lazard Freres & Co. of New York City offered the following evaluation of the role of derivatives in complicating and multiplying systemic shocks in 1994, a few months before the Orange County/Mexico/Barings episodes: "In many cases hedge funds, and speculative activity in general, may now be more responsible for foreign exchange and interest-rate movements than interventions by the central banks. ...Derivatives...create a chain of risks linking financial institutions and corporations throughout the world; any weakness or break in that chain (such as the failure of a large institution heavily invested in derivatives) could create a problem of serious proportions for the international financial system." [*New York Review of Books*, July 14, 1994, pp. 51-52] Since nothing has been done to regulate derivatives, or even to determine their extent, all these caveats remain emphatically operative.

DERIVATIVES AND SYSTEMIC CRISIS

If derivatives can create a panic in the United States banking system, then there is no doubt that they can create a systemic crisis, the feared meltdown and disintegration of the entire world financial system. By the early to middle 1990s this issue had become so obvious as to become unavoidable. In fact, it was so obvious that it began to compel even the tight-lipped central bankers to attempt to reassure the investing public. Brian Quinn, Executive Director of the Bank of England, was offering rationales for derivatives: "No officer charged with managing other people's money can afford to ignore the benefits that can come from a judicious use of the current range of derivative products; and business and finance courses at universities and colleges already see derivatives as a subject that must be covered in the curriculum....Derivatives are not only here to stay, but probably also to grow, albeit perhaps at a less hectic pace....Derivatives do not entail any new risks. If the presence of derivatives makes prices of financial assets more volatile, does this necessarily mean the financial system is inherently less stable? The instinctive answer to this seems to be 'yes'. However, academic work – while inconclusive – suggests that, if anything, the opposite is the case....More generally, the markets seem to be developing their own safeguards and sanctions, not least in the form of losses to shareholders." This kind of doubletalk was in vogue in 1993 and early 1994.

But soon the Bank of England could no longer afford to appear so complacent about derivatives. John Footman, the Bank of England press spokesman, said on June 13, 1994: "We are concerned about the derivatives transactions done by subsidiaries and securities firms. The generation of a speculative bubble would concern us if we saw that, but we see the risk being laid off in various directions, in an extremely complex way. What we need to be sure of, is that traders are not suffering undue risk...." Even as Footman spoke, Nick Leeson and Barings were well launched on the campaign of derivatives speculation that would lead to the Barings bankruptcy of February 26, 1995. The activities of Barings and Leeson were the direct responsibility of the Bank of England and of its erratic governor, Eddie George. Later, the June 1996 Sumitomo copper futures crisis was centered on the London Metals Exchange, right under the nose of the Bank of England, and British regulators proved singularly uncooperative with the US and Japan even after the crisis had become public knowledge. Still later, in 1997, it would be the turn of NatWest Markets to post a hefty loss of almost $150 million. Reassuring statements from central banks, especially the Bank of England, were clearly worthless. Although the leading governments are at least vaguely aware of the colossal dangers inherent in the current unbridled derivatives speculation, not one of them has proven able to muster the political will necessary seriously to regulate derivatives, much less to ban them. Rather, as we will see, governments and central banks have tended to use derivatives to manipulate financial markets, thus making themselves complicit in the great derivatives scandal of the end of the millennium.

The coming systemic crisis might therefore look something like this. The stage is set by depressed real production, pervasive speculation, deregulated financial markets, and impotent governments. A shock to the system, perhaps an international monetary crisis or a political event, causes a precipitous fall in stock markets or bond markets in one or more parts of the globe. Stock and/or bond losses bring on the bankruptcy of important brokerage houses and banks. These failures cause the momentary jamming of the interbank clearing and payment systems of the world. The large derivatives exposure of the bankrupt counterparties, because of the very concentrated forms of leverage involved, creates the fear that a limited number of bankruptcies will be multiplied into a very large number of insolvencies through the chain reaction of derivatives default. Because of the very large total value of financial instruments, and very large servicing requirements on derivatives and debt, a liquidity crisis and currency crisis is added to the already explosive mixture. A general panic ensues in which exchanges and markets are shut down indefinitely and virtually all banks close, while other financial institutions are forced to suspend their operations and are unable to resume business over the short term because of the net of complicated derivatives contracts in which most institutions are caught. Confidence cannot be restored unless and until governments re-emerge and take charge of the situation by wiping the slate clean of all derivatives wagers.

MONETIZING DERIVATIVES: SURE PATH TO HYPERINFLATION

Supporters of derivatives will argue the old Kindleberger thesis that as long the Fed is there as a lender of last resort, there will be no wave of universal bankruptcy, and therefore no deflationary depression on the model of 1929-1933. Conceding that point only for the sake of argument, we then find that the extraordinarily large sums involved in the derivatives bubble would force the lender of last resort to disburse liquidity in such astronomical quantities as to make hyperinflation inevitable. A derivatives bailout might in fact subject the United States dollar to the greatest depreciation in the history of economics, a hyperinflation that would do to the United States in a short time what the hyperinflation of the late Roman Empire did to that power over a number of centuries.

By virtue of the Monetary Control Act of 1980 and other legislation, the Federal Reserve System has the legal capability of monetizing the financial debt of any person or institution. This has always been an open door for unthinkable abuses by the Federal Reserve. But now, in the derivatives era, the values to be monetized have gone into intergalactic space. One of the relevant provisions from the United States Code is as follows:

> In unusual and exigent circumstances, the Board of Governors of the Federal Reserve System, by affirmative vote of not less than five members, may authorize any Federal Reserve bank, during such periods as the said board may determine, at rates established in accordance with section 357 of this title, to discount for any individual, partnership, or corporation, notes, drafts, and bills of exchange of the kinds and maturities made eligible for discount for member banks under other provisions of this chapter when such notes, drafts, and bills of exchange are indorsed or otherwise secured to the satisfaction of the Federal Reserve bank: Provided, That before discounting any such note, draft, or bill of exchange for an individual or a partnership or corporation the Federal reserve bank shall obtain evidence that such individual, partnership, or corporation is unable to secure adequate credit accommodations from other banking institutions. All such discounts for individuals, partnerships, or corporations shall be subject to such limitations, restrictions, and regulations as the Board of Governors of the Federal Reserve System may prescribe." [12 US 343]

This means that the unelected and unaccountable Federal Reserve can take in all sorts of financial paper and hand the bearer a large percentage of the face value of that paper in cash. With US banks currently holding upwards of $40 trillion in derivatives, the threat is that the Federal Reserve could decide to buy up all this bankrupt paper and turn it into cash. Such an act of lunacy, of which the current Fed is fully capable, would start the greatest hyperinflation of all time. That hyperinflation would hopefully the absurd notion that central bankers have any principled commitment to oppose inflation, if hyperinflation turns out to be the only way momentarily to salvage the Wall Street bankers who control the Federal Reserve board.

HYPERINFLATION OR HYPERDEFLATION? THE WORST OF BOTH!

We are left with the fundamental certainty that collapse and disintegration are coming. What is not certain is whether the disintegration will be of a hyperinflationary or hyperdeflationary type. We must also be cautious here about the confusion inherent in this terminology. Inflation and deflation are both terms that became widely used during the years of acute financial crisis that followed World War I. Before the German events of 1922-23, for example, what has been known as inflation was often described simply as the depreciation of a currency. The idea that inflation and deflation exist as two separate economic syndromes with clearly differentiated symptoms may not be tenable. One hint in this direction came during the 1970s, when the term stagflation had to be coined to describe a combination of high unemployment (previously thought to be typical of deflation) along with high inflation. This stagflation was the key to the "misery index" of the Carter years, which was designed to measure economic malaise by adding the unemployment rate to the inflation rate.

The stagflation observed in the formative years of the globaloney economy points ominously to the conclusion that the disintegration expected around the year 2000 may succeed in combining the worst features of the two phenomena which the economists of the interwar years called inflation and deflation. The everyday reality of the late 1990s, as observed by millions of struggling American families, is one of wage deflation combined with price inflation especially in services, with high levels of real (as distinct from officially admitted) unemployment and underemployment. There is every reason to believe that panic collapse and disintegration will make all of these phenomena worse. We must stand in awe before the globaloney economy, which has the potential of uniting the scourges of inflation and deflation, once considered polar opposites, but now brought together by *laissez-faire*.

HEDGE FUNDS

One of the earliest hedge fund operators was the legendary Jesse L. Livermore, the bear who made millions by selling stocks short before, during, and after the crash of 1929. After World War II, the exclusive private banks of Geneva, Switzerland sometimes engaged in some of the practices now typical of the modern hedge fund, but this was on a much smaller scale. A pioneer of modern hedge funds was the Soros Quantum fund, which made money on the European monetary crisis of September 1992, lost in early 1994 on the dollar-yen, and won by shorting the dollar in spring 1995. Quantum was a so-called macro-fund. "Hedge funds pool monies of wealthy investors, who generally put up a minimum of $1 million, and take positions in stocks, bonds, real estate, foreign exchange, derivative positions such as futures and options on the foregoing and on interest rates. Managers of hedge funds work not for a percentage of the assets but for a share of the profits, ranging up to 20%. The Quantum Fund of George Soros was reported to work with about $10 billion, most of it his own money, rather than borrowed." [Kindleberger, 243] Another famed hedge fund operator of recent years was Michael Steinhart, who wisely decided to quit while he was still ahead in the early autumn of 1995.

The hedge funds are the piranhas, sharks, and killer whales of the investment world. Using their contacts to intelligence agencies, finance ministries, and central banks, they map targets for speculative attack around the world, often combining subversive political objectives with their more basic avidity for windfall profits. Some of these practices amount to insider trading with information which governments and central banks should keep secret. Others amount to illegitimate interference in the domestic affairs of sovereign countries. The hedge funds attack currencies like a submarine wolf-pack in the North Atlantic during World War II. The hedge funds, no matter how well-funded, are really only the pilot fish for the banks, insurance companies, capital corporations, and other large institutions which play the role of killer leviathans and behemoths of the financial seas. The hedge fund attack is often the signal for the feeding frenzy of these larger predators. Every large American bank contains hedge fund operations within it, and in many cases these are the most lucrative sector of the bank. When the resulting school of predators attacks the currency of a small or medium country, then can frequently use leverage and derivatives to out-match the financial resources of the country's central bank, including whatever swap or currency support agreement the country may have. In this sense, the speculative oligopolies of banks and hedge funds are more powerful than entire countries, even big ones.

As Kindleberger observed, "In the fall of 1995 ...the G-7 – finance ministers of Britain, Canada, France, Italy, Japan, and the United States – agreed to assemble a kitty of $50 billion to come to the aid of currencies in crisis. Whether that will be enough to cope with exchange markets that trade $1 trillion a day, and with hedge funds, such as the Quantum Fund of George Soros, which reportedly made a profit of $1 billion in the attacks on the pound and the lira (and lost another $600 million by going short of the yen at a time when it was rising) is something that history may reveal." [Kindleberger, 164]

What history revealed was that Long Term Capital Management LP of Greenwich, Connecticut was capable of $1 trillion in derivatives exposure, and that its implosion threatened to open a hole large enough to sink the entire world banking system under the conditions prevailing in the early autumn of 1998. The details could be relegated to some future Pecora hearings. The urgent and immediate task was to outlaw hedge funds. During the late 1980s, junk bond dealers and insider traders had been led in handcuffs through Wall Street at lunch hour by federal marshals. It was now high time for some hedge fund operators to provide a similar public spectacle on the way to the hoosegow. The name "hedge fund" is in any case a dangerous misnomer. These operations do not hedge their bets – they bet the ranch on a specific outcome, and then try to bring it about with every weapon they can bring to bear.

By 1998, there were 5,500 hedge funds worldwide, and they reportedly managed a total of almost $300 billion in assets. To repeat, these were investment companies that escape regulation by having fewer than 100 investors, which allowed them to fly below the SEC radar, such as it is. Many of them made themselves even harder to track by locating offshore, in such exotic locations as the Cayman Islands or the Netherlands Antilles. Hedge funds made an average return of 20% in 1995. In 1996, hedge funds lost 1% of their investors' money – and 1996 was not a bad year for hedge funds.

George Soros remained the most famous hedge fund operator, and possibly the largest. The Soros group included the Quantum Fund, the Quota Fund, the Quasar Fund, and others. In October 1998, in the hedge fund shakeout occasioned by the veiled bankruptcy of Long Term Capital Management, Soros reduced his funds from 8 to 6. At this point the Quantum Fund reportedly had about $20 billion in assets. Queen Elizabeth II, by all odds the richest person in the world, was reputed to be among Soros' preferred clients. One of Soros' leading competitors was Julian Robertson, who ran the Tiger Fund, which was also thought to be worth about $20 billion. Each of these hedge funds was probably about 5 or 6 times bigger than the Merriwether/Merton/Scholes Long Term Capital Management operation. So if LCTM controlled derivatives for a total notion value of about $1 trillion, we can guess that Soros and Robertson might each move derivatives to the tune of $5 trillion or more, if they wanted to.

In many ways, the hedge fund represents (along with the leveraged derivatives in which they trade) the archetypal degenerative phenomenon of the 1990s globaloney era. When Soros and his cohorts attacked Thailand in the spring of 1997, they were in effect pulling the thread which would before long cause the entire international speculative money racket to unravel. They initiated the downfall of their own system. The hedge funds have been variously described as the glue or the connecting links in the globalized system. But it would be folly to think of them as shock absorbers are as some other mechanism of equilibrium. The hedge funds create shocks, magnify them, and transmit them from the provincial plantations of the system in towards the center. During 1997, the hedge funds were indispensable in transforming the crisis of a fourth-rate currency like the Thai baht into a panic in Tokyo and Wall Street. In 1998, Long Term Capital Management came very close to transforming the Russian default into a chain reaction bankruptcy of the biggest Wall Street and Zürich banks. At every critical turn in the 1997-98 crises, the hedge funds have been on hand to exacerbate whatever problems already existed anywhere in the world. For hundreds of millions of people, hedge funds and their managers are the objects of violent execration. Since many around the world associate hedge funds with the United States, here again is a harvest of hate which may be slaked in blood at some future time.

The specialty of the hedge fund is of course its very high leverage, which in the case of Long Term Capital may have reached 500 to 1, or even higher. Leverage of this type makes it possible for a small gyration in a currency cross to turn into a multi-megaton, thermonuclear explosion on Wall Street, which is exactly what happened with LTCM, when wrong guesses on the ruble, the yen, and Danish mortgages almost sank the Wall Street banks.

The hedge fund phenomenon is more extensive than it might seem. The Long Term Capital Management episode showed conclusively that large money-center banks, both in the United States and Europe, were acting far more like hedge funds than like traditional commercial banks. This included not just notorious cases like Bankers Trust, but also Union Bank of Switzerland and many others. Each of these large banks has a proprietary trading operation which is indistinguishable from a very large hedge fund, and relies on the Black-Scholes and similar mumbo-jumbo to guide its speculative strategies.

Some banks also farm out some of their derivatives business to hedge funds. This brings us to the sad case of BankAmerica, which relied heavily on the hedge fund operations run by D. E. Shaw, the so-called "King of Quants." BankAmerica (the merger of NationsBank and the Bank of America) had lent $1.3 billion to Shaw, and had to absorb a loss of $372 million on the transaction. BankAmerica's own in-house hedge fund-type activities generated a loss of $529 million during the third quarter of 1998. These reverses caused the bank's president to resign. On some days in the late summer of 1998, D. E. Shaw's trading operations were said to have accounted for 5% of the overall volume on the NYSE – which ought to make small investors ask if they really want to take the chance of being run over by the stampede when such gorillas run for the exit. Other hedge funds which were hit hard by the third quarter 1998 crises included Michael Vranos' $1 billion Ellington Management Group, and the $118 million Eagle Global Value Fund of Minneapolis. Blackstone Alternative Capital Management offers a hedge fund of hedge funds, in which certain corporate pension funds have reportedly invested.

Even what appear to be old-line industrial companies can turn out to be the mere shells within which hedge funds lurk. Take the case of General Electric. GE no longer relies on refrigerators or turbines for its profits. The heart of GE is today GE Capital Management, a speculative trading operation which exploits the full range of highly leveraged finance techniques. By 1998, GE Capital was providing 42% of GE's overall profit. (Much of the rest came from the NBC television network and such ventures as CNBC.) The word on the Street is that GE Capital is "a hedge fund in drag."

At the Leach committee's October 1, 1998 hearings, New York Federal Reserve Bank Chairman William McDonough helpfully offered the following detailed description of precisely how the fall of Long Term Capital Management could have triggered the End of the World:

Had Long Term Capital been suddenly put into default, its counterparties would have immediately 'closed out' their positions. If counterparties would have been able to close out their positions at existing market prices, losses, if any, would have been minimal. However, if many firms rush to close out hundreds of billions of dollars in transactions simultaneously, they would be unable to liquidate collateral or establish offsetting positions at the previously existing prices. Markets would move sharply and losses would be exaggerated. Several billion dollars of losses might have been experienced by some of Long Term Capital's more than 75 counterparties.... as losses spread to other market participants and Long-Term Capital's counterparties, this would lead to tremendous uncertainty about how far prices would move. Under these circumstances, there was a likelihood that a number of credit and interest rate markets would experience extreme price moves and possibly cease to function for a period of one or more days or even longer. This would have caused a vicious cycle: a loss of investor confidence, leading to a rush out of private credits, leading to a further widening of credit spreads, leading to further liquidations of positions, and so on.

McDonough had, in effect, given the Leach committee a scenario for a panic collapse of the entire System. Greenspan, however, remained determined to defend hedge funds to the last. On that October 1, 1998, after the Long Term Capital Management debacle, Greenspan did not attempt to hide the fact that LCTM had posed the immediate risk of systemic crisis, of a panic crash of the entire system, obviously including panic runs on leading banks and chain-reaction insolvencies among those banks. Greenspan referred to J.P. Morgan's legendary 1907 meeting with Wall Street financiers, when old Jupiter had told the assembled stockjobbers that the panic had to be stopped here and now. Greenspan told the Congressmen: "Had the failure of LCTM triggered the seizing up of markets, substantial damage could have been inflicted on many market participants, including some not directly involved with the firm, and could have potentially impaired the economies of many nations, including our own." There it was: LCTM could have triggered a world depression, but it would be a terrible mistake enact some laws and regulations to make sure that this could not happen again in the near future. For although Greenspan was not afraid to portray himself as the new J.P. Morgan, he declined to suggest any regulatory policies whatsoever for hedge funds, even when the Congressmen asked for something other than the usual Federal Reserve "obfuscation and deflection," as moderate Republican Michael Castle put it. . Instead, the oracle intoned:

> If, somehow, hedge funds were barred worldwide, the American financial system would lose the benefits conveyed by their efforts, including arbitraging price differentials away. The resulting loss in efficiency and contribution to value added and the nation's standard of living would be a high price to pay – to my mind, too high a price.

Most Americans, who are not Ayn Rand fans like the Fed chairman, would have a hard time thinking of how their living standards had been enhanced by hedge funds. The unelected and unaccountable Greenspan his rejection of regulation with the pronouncement that the present decline of the US economy under the domination of "highly leveraged financial institutions, has been a conscious choice of the American people since the 1930s." This may also come as a surprise to the many Americans, who have never been asked by the Federal Reserve for their opinions on this matter. Now that the Supreme Court has made it possible for even Presidents to be hit with civil suits, Greenspan's defense of hedge funds and derivatives may lay the basis of a new and thriving field of action for lawyers – suing Greenspan and other Federal Reserve officials for their malfeasance and nonfeasance by the victims of the colossal financial panic they have refused to avoid.

Hedge funds are intelligence fronts as well as financial institutions. Like Rothschild making a killing in London by being the first to learn the result of the battle of Waterloo, modern hedge funds require the latest political and financial intelligence to know how to move. Soros is widely rumored to receive confidential intelligence from British sources, as well as from his contacts at the New York Federal Reserve. Hedge funds actively connive to create situations from which they can profit. This may involve backing certain pro-globaloney political leaders against their opposition in the third world. It may involve covert operations, like Soros' funding of efforts to legalize mind-destroying narcotics in the United States. It has even involved conniving to trigger a default by the United States Treasury, something which had never happened in all of US history.

In September 1995, Newt Gingrich told a meeting of government bond traders that "I, the Speaker" would not schedule a vote on the budget until Clinton had accepted the GOP's budget dictates. "I don't care what the price is. I don't care if we have no executive offices and no bonds for 60 days – not this time," raved Newt. Senator Pete Domenici (R-NM), the chairman of the Senate budget committee, was equally fanatical, telling the Joint House-Senate Economic Committee that, if the Congress were to give in to Clinton on the issue of mandatory entitlement payments, "the impact on Treasury bills will be worse than if we have a 40- or 50-day hiatus... " By hiatus, Domenici meant a default of the United States Treasury on bonded debt, something which Jefferson David, Kaiser Wilhelm II, Hitler, and Stalin were all unable to bring about, but which the Republican Party was evidently trying to provoke. Had the Senator lost his mind? No, no, he seemed to protest, "I didn't dream this up. I went out and talked to a bunch of people that work in this area. I had 10 of them last night in a room and they actually said, "We're not at all sure that there will be a black mark on T-bills if, in fact, we don't do anything for a while [i.e., after a US default], and we're certain it won't be as black and bleak on the cost of T-bills in the future as it will be if we don't solve the ever-growing problem of mandatory expenditures." Domenici confessed that a member of his 10-person camarilla had been none other than Stanley Druckenmiller, a fund manager for Soros. Druckenmiller later confirmed that he had offered this advice. All of this raised the obvious question: had Soros and Druckenmiller sold US Treasury paper short in the expectation that the price of such paper would collapse in the event of a US default? Had they then urged the Republican anti-government fanatics to bring about precisely such a default? Had promises of PAC money and soft money contributions played any role in these proceedings? Here, if ever, was matter worthy of a special prosecutor.

In the meantime, one thing was clear: hedge funds had to be outlawed, once and for all.

NAME YOUR POISON

The following is probably the most detailed list of derivatives available to the general public. Such a list can never be complete, since new types of derivatives are being developed every day by yuppy quants all over the planet. Knowing the names of the main types of derivatives may help the average person to avoid them. Never buy any of the items named below. Never sign a contract in which any of these items is mentioned, implied, embedded, or otherwise included. Never purchase insurance, annuities, or any other financial instrument in which any of these derivatives are present. Do not deal with banks, brokers, insurance companies, investment companies, financial advisers, or financial companies of any kind who will not certify in writing that they are free of all the derivatives named below. Demand that your state and local governments, and any private or public pension fund in which you have an interest, certify that they do not own and do not intend to own any of these derivatives. Tell your Congressman you want all of these instruments outlawed. Flee derivatives like the plague that that they are.

DICTIONARY OF DERIVATIVES FROM A TO Z

ACCRETING SWAPS
ACCRUAL TRANCHES
AGAINST ACTUALS (AAS)
AMORTIZING SWAPS
ASIAN OPTIONS
ASSET ALLOCATION SWAPS
ASSET-BASED SWAPS
ASSET SWAPS
AT-THE-MONEYS
AVERAGE RATE OPTIONS
BACK SPREADS
BACKS
BACKWARDATIONS
BARRIER OPTIONS
BASIS SWAPS
BASIS TRADES
BEAR SPREADS
BEARS
BINARIES
BLENDED INDEXES
BOOTSTRAPS
BOX SPREADS
BOXES
BREAK FORWARDS
BREAKS
BULL SPREADS
BULLS
BUSTED PACS
BUTTERFLIES
BUTTERFLY SPREADS
BUY/WRITES
CALENDAR SPREADS
CALLABLE SWAPS
CALL OPTIONS
CALLS
CAPLETS
CAPS
CARS
CASH FLOW BONDS
CHRISTMAS TREES
CIRCUS SWAPS
CMOS (COLLATERALIZED MORTGAGE
    OBLIGATIONS)
CMO STRIPS
CMO PAC BONDS
CMO RESIDUALS

CMO TAC BONDS
CMTS (CONSTANT-MATURITY
    TREASURIES)
CMT CAPS
COLLARS
COLLATERALIZED MORTGAGE
    OBLIGATIONS (CMOS)
COMBINATIONS
COMMODITY CURVES
COMMODITY FUTURES CURVES
COMMODITY SWAPS
COMPANION TRANCHES
COMPOUND OPTIONS
CONDORS
CONSTANT MATURITY TREASURY
    DERIVATIVES
CONTANGOES
CONTINGENT PREMIUM OPTIONS
CONTRACTS
CONVERTIBLE SECURITIES
CURRENCY SWAPS
DEEP-OUT-OF-THE-MONEY OPTIONS
DEFERRED SWAPS
DELAYED PREMIUM OPTIONS
DELTA HEDGES
DELTA NEUTRAL SPREADS
DESIGNER DERIVATIVES
DIAGONAL SPREADS
DIFF SWAPS
DIFFERENTIAL SWAPS
DIFFS
EUROPEAN OPTIONS
EQUITY DERIVATIVES
EQUITY INDEX SWAPS
EQUITY-LINKED BONDS
EQUITY PARTICIPATION NOTES
EQUITY SWAPS
EURODOLLAR FUTURES CONTRACTS
EURODOLLAR FUTURES STRIPS
EUROSTRIPS
EXCHANGE-TRADED FUTURES
EXCHANGE-TRADED OPTIONS
EXCHANGES FOR PHYSICALS (EFPS)
EXOTIC OPTIONS
EXTENDABLE SWAPS
FENCES

FIXED-FOR-FLOATING SWAPS
FLOATERS
FLOATING RATE CMOS
FLOATING RATE NOTES
FLOATING RATE TRANCHES
FLOORS
FORWARD CONTRACTS
FORWARD EXCHANGE AGREEMENTS
  (FXAS)
FORWARD EXCHANGES
FORWARD INTEREST RATES
FORWARD RATE AGREEMENTS
FORWARD SWAPS
FRONT SPREADS
FROWNS
FRAS
FUTURES CONTRACTS
FUTURES
FX (FOREX) CONTRACTS
FX OPTIONS
FX SWAPS
FXAS
FUTURES STRIPS
GAMMA HEDGES
GENERIC PACS
GENERIC SWAPS
HAIRCUTS
HALF-CMT FLOATERS
HEDGES
HORIZONTAL SPREADS
HYBRID SECURITIES
INDEX AMORTIZING NOTES
INDEX AMORTIZATION SWAP
INDEX OPTIONS
INTERBANK SWAPS
INTEREST RATE SWAPS
INTERMARKET SPREADS
INVERSE FLOATERS
INVERSE FLOATING RATE CMOS
IOS (INDEX OPTIONS)
KITCHEN SINK BONDS
KNOCK-IN LIBOR CAPS
KNOCK-INS
KNOCKOUT CALL OPTIONS
KNOCKOUTS
KNOCKOUT OPTIONS
LADDERS
LEAPS

LEVERAGED DERIVATIVES
LIBOR-LINKED PAYOUTS
LIBOR-IN-ARREARS SWAPS
LIMITED PAC IOS
LONG CALLS
LONG-DATED SWAPS
LONG PUTS
LOOKBACKS
LOOKBACK OPTIONS
LOOKFORWARDS
M-CATS
MACRO OPTIONS
MACROECONOMIC SWAPS
MACROHEDGES
MASTER SWAP AGREEMENTS
MICROHEDGES
MORTGAGE-BACKED DERIVATIVES
MORTGAGE-BACKED SECURITIES
MORTGAGE HEDGES
MORTGAGE SWAPS
MOTO OPTIONS (MORTGAGE OVER
  TREASURY)
MULTIPERIOD OPTIONS
MUNI SWAPS
MUNICIPAL SWAPS
MUTUAL FUNDS
NOTIONALS
OFF-MARKET SWAPS
OFFSETS
OPTIONS
OTC COMMODITY DERIVATIVES
OTC OPTIONS
OVER-THE-COUNTER DERIVATIVES
PAR SWAPS
PARALLEL LOANS
PARTIAL ACCRUAL IOS
PERCENTAGE CHANGE OPTIONS
PERIODIC CAPS
PERIODIC FLOORS
PERIODIC INTEREST RATE CAPS
PLAIN VANILLA SWAPS
PLAIN VANILLA DERIVATIVES
PROPRIETARY DERIVATIVES
PUTABLE SWAPS
PUTS
PUT OPTIONS
QUANTO OPTIONS
RAINBOW OPTIONS

RAINBOWS
RANGE FORWARDS
RATE-CAPPED SWAPS
RATIO SPREADS
RATIO SWAPS
REMICS
REPLACEMENT SWAPS
REPOS
REVERSE FLOATERS
REVERSIBLE SWAPS
REPURCHASE AGREEMENTS
ROLLER COASTER SWAPS
SEASONAL SWAPS
SECOND GENERATION OPTIONS
SHORT CALLS
SHORT-DATED SWAPS
SHORT PUTS
SHORT HEDGES
SKEWS
SMBS
SMILES
SPREAD LOCKS
SPREAD-LOCK INTEREST SWAPS
SPREAD OPTIONS
SPREADS
STEP-UP RECOVERY FLOATERS (SURFS)
STEP-UPS
STOCK INDEX FUTURES
STRADDLES
STRANGLES
STRIPPED MORTGAGE-BACKED
  SECURITIES (SMBS)

STRIPS
STRUCTURED NOTES
SUPER PACS
SUPER POS
SUPERFLOATERS
SURFS
SWAPS
SWAPTIONS
SYNTHETIC CALLS
SYNTHETIC INSTRUMENTS
SYNTHETIC OPTIONS
SYNTHETIC PUTS
SYNTHETIC SECURITIES
SYNTHETIC UNDERLYINGS
TAC POS
TENORS
THETA HEDGES
TIGRS
TIME SPREADS
TIME SWAPS
TOGGLE ZS
TOPS
TREASURY-LINKED SWAPS
VEGAS
VERTICAL SPREADS
WEDDING BANDS
YIELD CURVE SWAPS
ZERO COUPON SWAPS
ZERO PREMIUM OPTIONS
Z BONDS

QUANTS

The exponential growth in derivatives over the past decade has produced a new figure in Wall Street, the quant or quantitative analyst. These are very often yuppies toting laptop computers and using exotic forms of mathematical and quantitative analysis to try to predict the behavior of markets, or to determine what a complex derivative might be worth to a buyer or a seller. The fundamental belief of the quant is that there exists no lawfulness or rational order in the world. The quant sees the universe as a darkling plain, the reign of chaos. Modern science and modern civilization, by contrast, have been based on contrary ideas, typified by Gottfried Wilhelm Leibniz. For Leibniz, the universe is lawful, and mankind can use reason to understand the laws with ever-increasing degrees of accuracy. For Leibniz, the universe we live in is a least-action universe, in which natural processes characteristically "choose" the least-action path to accomplish what they do. Things happen because there is sufficient reason to make them happen. And so we live in the best of all possible worlds – not the best world we might imagine, but the best possible world, given the demands of freedom and responsibility for good and evil. Thanks to this outlook, we have achieved progress in civilization and increased the population of the world to almost 6 billion people. Leibniz and his school were interested in advancing the General Welfare, not in filling the pockets of parasitical speculators.

GIAMMARIA ORTES: FOUNDER OF GAME THEORY

Today's quant, whether he knows it or not, hearkens back to eighteenth-century Venetian economists like Giammaria Ortes. Ortes (1713-1790) was part of a general Venetian effort in those days to build up the credibility of social sciences based on statistical analysis. Ortes produced a calculus on the value of opinions, a calculus of the pleasures and pains of human life, a calculus of the truth of history. In this way Ortes became the model for Bentham's hedonistic or felicific calculus with its slogan, the greatest good for the greatest number.

The British parson Thomas Malthus is a diluted version of Ortes. Ortes posited an absolute upper limit for the human population of the earth, which he set at 3 billion. This is the first appearance of the notion of carrying capacity. Ortes also insisted that there never had been and never could be a real improvement in the standard of living for the earth's human population. Government action, Ortes asserted in polemic with such figures as his contemporary Benjamin Franklin, could never do any good. As befits his status as the first modern quant, Ortes was also addicted to card playing, especially to the popular game of *faro*. In 1757 Ortes published his mathematical study of card playing. Here Ortes made the following observation on the essence of gambling and human nature: "The fact that a passion for gambling is a superstition will not seem strange to anyone who considers that any human passion is just as much a passion as an error, precisely because it is a persuasion for which no reason can be furnished... since in human affairs everything depends on passion, everything depends on superstition, and one superstition does nothing but fight another, so that the man who is considered the most important is the most superstitious." [72] Ortes believed that increasing the standard of living of some would inevitably lower it for others, and that no nation had ever been able substantially to raise the standard of living of its entire population. Economists of today prattle that the notion of economics as a zero-sum game was developed by John von Neumann. But Ortes had made the argument for a zero-sum game before the American Revolution:

> The good therefore, understood as the possession of goods in excess of what is needed, can only be expressed between the individual and the commonality as the number zero, and since there is an inevitable lack of goods for some if these are to be abundant for others, this good can only appear as a mixture of economic good and evil, which tends neither to one nor to the other, or as the vector sum of forces which, operating with equal energy in different and opposite directions, destroy each other and resolve themselves into nothing. (Ortes, *Della Economia Nazionale*, 1774)

Ortes would have had no difficulty in recognizing derivatives as a form of gambling, or in applying his gambling method to futures, options, and swaps. So the quant is nothing new.

THE WOODSTOCK OF CHAOS

During the 1990s, the Society of Quantitative Analysts (SQA) sponsored a yearly Wall Street event called Fuzzy Day. This purpose of this gathering was to acquaint the SQA membership – the quants – with the latest in chaos theory, fractals, fuzzy engineering, genetic algorithms, Lyapunov analysis, Lorenz attractors, stochastics, swarm simulation, and other demented mathematical

---

[72] Giammaria Ortes, *Calcolo sopra i giuochi della bassetta e del faraone.*

formalisms which might be brought to bear on making money in the markets. Fuzzy engineering and fuzzy analysis are supposed to represent new types of mathematical procedure that allow greater insight because they are more flexible. In reality, they represent what used to be called fuzzy thinking, and the flexibility they promise is what older statisticians would call a bigger fudge factor. [Vaga, 53 ff.] An article of faith for chaos theorists is that the passage of time, even a very short time, brings an exponential increase in uncertainty and unpredictability. So for a chaos theorist, there can be no long-term forecasting. For the chaos buffs, even your familiar five-day weather forecast is a flying leap into the abyss.

Chaos theory became respectable after one of its recent proponents, the far-out Ilya Prigogine, received a Nobel Prize in 1977 for work done in this field. Another term for chaos theory is the study of non-linear dynamic systems. The quant regards chaos theory as a branch of speculative philosophy – meaning not metaphysics, but rather a philosophy of speculation on the markets for the purpose of making money. According to the quants, there are two types of chaos. Type A chaos is low-dimensional, low-information chaos, where there is still some hope of discovering an ordering pattern. Type B chaos is high-dimensional, high-information chaos, and finding any ordering principle is simply hopeless. The chaos theorists have studied the fluid dynamics of Prandtl and others. They focus on the moment when the flow of a fluid or a gas around a cylinder or a wing ceases to be laminar (smooth) and becomes turbulent. They know about Reynolds numbers, which identify the point where the flow changes from smooth to turbulent.

The topic of the May 1992 Fuzzy Day, held at the Marriott Twin Towers in lower Manhattan, was "Chaos and Nonlinear Prediction: Financial Market Applications." The event was attended by over 200 analysts and money managers from the financial district. Although these quants were convinced that chaos rules the universe, they always hope to salvage a brief and limited predictability in the financial markets which they can then use to make money. Even if a few stocks can be made predictable over a few days or even a few hours, then big bucks may be in the offing for the quants. The same thing goes for a pattern that might be detected in the very large – like a momentary tendency of very large numbers of stocks or derivatives.

The quants are fascinated by the forms of structures that emerge in extremely turbulent, rapidly fluctuating high-energy plasmas, like solitons. They love to contemplate what are called Mandelbrot fractals, examples of patterns which seem simple at first but then reveal greater and greater complexity as they are studied more and more. The quants have been frequently burned by conniving chaos theorists offering their systems as sure-fire tools for discovering those tiny insights into market predictability that can be so lucrative. So the quants were skeptical and very demanding, and quickly became brutal when they felt that the wool was being pulled over their eyes. So hypercritical were the quants that, during their Fuzzy Day proceedings, they drove a speaker from the podium with hoots and shouted obscenities.

One of the speakers at the 1992 Fuzzy Day was Doyne Farmer, who enjoyed a reputation as the "dean of chaos theory." Doyne Farmer was the president of the Prediction Company, which had been hired by a Wall Street firm for the development of investment applications. Farmer's main thesis was that a non-linear system like the stock market was probably 95% random chaos, but with 5% predictable dynamics of what he described as a "low-dimensional" type. Low-dimensional chaos is still chaos, but it has fewer degrees of freedom and less 'noise'. The low-dimensional realm is they key for the speculator, argued Farmer, since you "don't need much low-dimensional stuff to get rich." [Vaga, 53-56]

THE TWO KOLMOGOROVS

Another speaker at Fuzzy Day 1992 was Cornell University Professor John Hubbard, who told the quants about work currently being done at the Cornell Supercomputer Facility and the Fractal Research Center. Professor Hubbard's central idea was to invite the quants to contemplate the information density of the Dow Jones Industrial Average. Hubbard told the quants that, for his own part, he had no idea whatsoever of how to answer that question. Interestingly, the main mathematical authority cited by Hubbard was Andrei Nikolaevich Kolmogorov, possibly the greatest Russian mathematician of the twentieth century. In Hubbard's view, the true meaning of the Kolmogorov theorem boils down to "Hey, it's worthwhile being smart." If you insist on applying dumb procedures you will not be able to discover the pattern that underlies the Dow.

Kolmogorov (1903-1987) was for many years professor at the Moscow University. He was one of the most universal of mathematicians, leaving virtually no field untouched: Kolmogorov studied the theory of trigonometric series, measure theory, set theory, the theory of integration, constructive logic (intuitionism), topology, approximation theory, probability theory, the theory of random processes, information theory, mathematical statistics, dynamical systems, automata theory, theory of algorithms, mathematical linguistics, turbulence theory, celestial mechanics, differential equations, Hilbert's 13th problem, ballistics, and applications of mathematics to problems of biology, geology, and the crystallization of metals. Kolmogorov wrote over 300 research papers, textbooks and monographs, covering almost every branch of mathematics.

The quants were interested in Kolmogorov the statistician and expert on probability theory, in the Kolmogorov who developed what is today called Kolmogorov complexity. Unfortunately for the chaos buffs and quants, the phenomenon studied by Kolmogorov that was likely to impact them in the near future is *turbulence*, including the physics of thermonuclear and chemical explosions. Many systems dissipate energy. But some systems conserve energy, and some of these will develop a singularity in a finite time, or a finite-time blow-up. Kolmogorov addressed some of these problems in his 1941 paper entitled "Dissipation of energy in locally isotropic turbulence," and returned to the same topic a number of times during his long career. One of the applications of Kolmogorov's work was the Soviet hydrogen bomb.

By the close of the 1990s, the world economic and financial environment was already very dense with crisis events. Under normal circumstances ("normal" meaning not real normalcy, but rather the typical day-to-day routine amidst the post-1971 wreckage of the Bretton Woods system), crisis events, even those that momentarily threaten the meltdown of the financial institutions, tend to dissipate against the background of the humdrum everyday world. But as the crisis events become more and more frequent and concentrated in time, the danger increases that several crisis events may detonate at more or less the same time. A quick flurry of almost simultaneous crisis events may do the opposite of merely dissipating and subsiding into the everyday routine of banks and markets. Simultaneous crisis events may begin to resonate, and reverberate, re-enforcing each other as they do so to the point of forming a singularity. From such a singularity we may expect a shock wave to radiate outwards into the surrounding financial and economic space, detonating further crisis events and new singularities as it goes. The resulting multiple shock waves of panic and insolvency provoke an implosion, which will represent the breakdown and disintegration of the entire financial system. The model for such an implosion is provided by chemical and thermonuclear explosions.

THE BRADY SYSTEM OF DRUGGED MARKETS

The survival of Wall Street in the years after the October 1987 collapse was made possible by a system of rigged markets which is associated with Secretary of the Treasury Nicholas Brady of the Dillon Reed investment house in Wall Street. Brady was by family tradition a close ally of George Bush, and his role in rigging the markets got him the job of Secretary of the Treasury in the disastrous Bush administration. In the autumn of 1987, in the wake of the crash, Brady was asked by President Reagan to assemble a task force for the purpose of studying the causes of the market panic, and how a repeat might be prevented. Staff came from James Baker's Treasury Department, but most of the work was done by denizens of Wall Street itself. That included the New York branch of the Federal Reserve, J.P. Morgan, Kidder Peabody (since liquidated), Merrill Lynch, E.F. Hutton, First Boston, Morgan Stanley, Salomon Brothers, and Shearson Lehman - the usual bunch of suspects.

By January 1988, the Presidential Task Force on Market Mechanisms delivered its findings. Brady held a press conference after the close of the markets. The atmosphere was gloomy: that very day, January 8, the Dow industrials had taken a new 140 point dive (the twelfth worst percentage decline since October, 1928) and were back at the immediate post-crash levels of October 1987. The conclusions that Brady announced to the public were vague truisms, including that "from an economic viewpoint, what have been traditionally seen as separate markets - the markets for stocks, stock index futures, and stock options - are in fact one market." [Brady, p. vi]

The Brady commission made very few suggestions for increased regulation. One timid proposal was that "one agency must have the authority to coordinate a few critical intermarket issues cutting across market segments and affecting the entire financial system...." [Brady, ibid.] These included clearing and credit mechanisms, margin requirements, and "circuit breaker mechanisms," such as price limits and trading halts." As far as the general public knows, next to nothing was done to implement the recommendations of the Brady bunch. But the Brady commission was like an iceberg: the most interesting part remained invisible.

To understand the machinations of the Brady commission, we must recall that in 1929 there was one dominant stock market, the NYSE. In those old days, you could buy a stock for cash, or you could buy it long with a call or sell it short with a put. These were more or less the only transactions practiced. But in recent years, as we have seen, markets have been created in Chicago and other centers where stock index futures and stock options are traded. Since 1982, the Chicago Mercantile Exchange has listed a futures contract on the 500 stocks that make up the Standard & Poor's 500 Stock Index. In theory you are buying each stock on this 500-stock list for future delivery. In practice, if you hold the futures contract to maturity, you receive a cash settlement of $500 times the currently quoted price. You do not receive any stock certificates. Notice once again that stock index futures are a species of the deadly derivative instruments.

The S&P 500 Stock Index lists stocks which, taken together, make up about 80% of the market value of all stocks listed on the NYSE. It can therefore be thought of as roughly representing the entire market. For some years there was also the Major Market Index, or MMI, which was traded on the Chicago Board of Trade. Many of the 20 stocks in the MMI were also among the 30 stocks which make up the Dow Jones Industrial Average. The MMI could also be thought of as roughly corresponding to "the Dow." As of 1997, there were stock index futures which directly mirrored of the 30 stocks of the Dow Jones Industrials.

Once these new derivatives, the stock index futures, began to trade, many Wall Street hucksters began to look for ways to make a fast buck by taking advantage of the momentary differences between the Chicago and New York markets. One of the most elementary was called "index arbitrage," or, more accurately, "garbitrage." The typical garbitrageur hired a computer nerd to set up a computer program capable of rapidly comparing the current price of the S&P 500 index future in Chicago with the prices of the corresponding stocks in New York. If the stock price went up and the index future price went down, it was time to sell the stock and buy the future, "locking in" a nifty profit simply by virtue of this transaction, which had to be carried out by computerized sell and buy orders so as to seize the momentary advantage. Other variations on this theme included "portfolio insurance," which figured prominently in the 1987 panic. This entire complex is often referred to as "program trading."

The Brady commission studied the events of the "market break" of October 14 to October 20, 1987, and especially the interplay of the cash markets for stocks on the New York Stock Exchange, on the one hand, with the market for stock index futures on the Chicago Mercantile Exchange and the Chicago Board of Trade. Brady's staff noticed that the greatest losses for stocks on the NYSE occurred when the price of the stock index futures listed in Chicago dipped below the level implied by the current price of the underlying stock or stocks in New York. When the stock index futures in Chicago do down in this way, they are said to be trading at a discount to the respective stocks.

The Brady bunch found that when the price of the stock index future in Chicago dipped below a certain level, cascades of sell orders for the corresponding stocks were dumped on the New York Stock Exchange. This had been the case during the first hour of trading on Monday, October 19, 1987, when "an apparent record discount of the futures relative to the stocks" had obtained. That motivated the index arbitrageurs and others to enter an avalanche of sell-at-market orders, causing a 100-point drop in the Dow Industrials during the first hour, generating an initial panic. But on that same day, during the next hour or so, purchases of index futures in Chicago increased the price of the S&P 500 in Chicago. The futures were at a premium, and the NYSE started an upward rally that lasted until almost noon until it, too, was engulfed by panic.

"Eureka !" shouted the Brady bunch in unison. If we can find a way to keep the price of the index future in Chicago above the implied equivalent price of the underlying stocks in New York, program traders will always tend to sell the index future and buy the stocks, thus shoring up the NYSE. The Brady bunch then set to work designing a system according to this principle. They knew that although the cash that actually changes hands in the S&P 500 futures pit of the CME is far less than the daily cash turnover in New York, the vale of the stocks represented by the index futures contracts traded on the CME is much larger than the value of the stocks actually traded each day in New York. In other words, the notional value of the CME index futures contracts is greater than the cash value of the NYSE trades. This means in effect that market movements generated by smaller sums of money in Chicago can generate market movements implying far more money in New York. There is a multiplier effect, and this is the basis of the phenomena known as "downdrafting" and "updrafting."

The other advantage of Chicago is that the Chicago Mercantile Exchange, the Chicago Board of Trade and the Chicago Board Options Exchange are not supervised by the Securities and Exchange Commission. Because of laws passed in the aftermath of the Crash of 1929, the SEC enforces margin requirements for the NYSE and other stock markets; the margin levels are set by the Federal Reserve Board. But the CME, CBOT, and CBOE all function under the oversight of the Commodity Future Trading Commission, which has no legal power to set margin requirements in these markets. In Chicago, exchanges set their own margin requirements. For established day traders, those who buy a futures contract and sell it the same day, there are no margin requirements at all. This means that those wishing to use the Chicago derivatives pits as a means to steering the NYSE can do so either totally or in large part with borrowed money.

Under the Brady system, a few tens of millions of dollars used to buy futures contracts in Chicago can generate hundreds of millions of dollars of buying updraft in New York. Where does the money come from ? There should be no mystery. At 8:15 AM on the morning of Tuesday, October 20, 1987, Federal Reserve boss Alan Greenspan issued the following laconic communiqué:

The Federal Reserve Bank affirms its readiness to serve as a source of liquidity to support the economic and financial system.

Which is to say that the monetary resources which really belong to the people of the United States will be dissipated in the foolish and doomed attempt to support a speculative financial bubble. Greenspan is still at his post, and his commitment to the garbitrageurs has never lapsed. In practice, much of the cash that is pumped into Chicago under the Brady system appears to come from the New York Federal Reserve Bank, the heart of the privately owned and privately directed Fed system. The Brady system of drugged markets amounts to a hijacking of the public interest by a network of bureaucrats in the Federal Reserve in cahoots with Wall Street speculators. It is amazing that their racket has lasted as long as it has. But the end is now at hand.

Needless to say, political calculations loomed very large in the rigging of the Brady bunch system. For the average person, the Dow industrials represent the stock market and the financial world in general. With the Brady system, the DJIA could be kept up even when the overall market is much weaker, by the simple expedient of buying the S&P 500. Brady was partly motivated by his desire to keep the stock market from blowing up during 1988, so that George Bush could get elected. After that it was a matter of saving Bush's presidency, and giving him a chance for re-election.

Because of very lucky circumstances, the Brady system survived the test of the "mini-crash" of Friday, October 13, 1989. That was the day financing for the leveraged buy-out of United Airlines collapsed at about 2:40 PM EDT, leading to a plunge in UAL stock and a trading halt for UAL on the NYSE. By 3:07 PM, the CME declared that the S&P 500 futures contract was limit down - it had lost 12 points (the equivalent of about 100 Dow points) and trading was automatically halted for 30 minutes. This was an attempt at "circuit breaking" in the manner suggested by Brady. Two minutes later, the NYSE began collecting program trading orders into a special computer file known as the "sidecar," which allows the NYSE to compare and match buy orders and sell orders before they hit the trading floor.

At about the same time, a hot line conference call was set up among the CME, the CBOE, the Amex and the NYSE. At 3:30 PM EDT, the S&P 500 contract resumed trading in Chicago, and by 3:45 EDT it had fallen an additional 30 points - the equivalent 250 Dow points. At that point the S&P futures contract was once again declared limit down by the CME, and trading was halted again, this time for 60 minutes. Luckily for Brady and Bush, the CME was scheduled to close for the weekend at 4:15 EDT, and silence descended on the pits for the day. In New York, stock exchange officials watched the Dow's losses near 200 and prepared to close the NYSE if the collapse were to reach minus 250 on the Dow, which would have been limit down under the rules prevailing at the time. Luckily again for Brady and Bush, the NYSE closed before that level could be reached. Feverish efforts during the weekend concentrated on buying stock index futures contracts in Chicago, and by Monday the situation was essentially under control - for the moment.

In the 1987 crash, the most dramatic losses on the afternoon of October 19 had been booked with both stocks and index futures in free fall. In 1989, the trading halts on CME and CBOE had not stopped the collapse of stocks. As one broker told the *New York Times*, "When the futures and options markets stopped trading, the only vehicle left was the equity market."[73] The Brady system's most essential function, the buying of index futures to support the NYSE, had proven itself unable to stem the tide of an incipient panic. The weekend saved the day, for it allowed the Brady bunch to arrange a flood of buy orders for index futures in Chicago for Monday morning. Luckily for Brady, by Monday morning the panic seems to have dissipated.

The more basic purpose of the Brady bunch mechanisms is a support operation for financial paper in general. A panic in the NYSE tends to bring down bloated paper values everywhere. Keep the DJIA up, and you have made an important contribution to stabilizing what Sir Henry Kissinger calls "The System." By the late spring of 1997, a City of London operator was commenting on the new highs beyond the 7000 mark registered on the New York Stock Exchange after the 9% decline of the Dow in late March and early April 1997. "Right now what is going on in the New York stock markets is pure manipulation using derivatives. No one is buying actual stocks or selling. The market moves up, like it did yesterday, purely in a manipulation by hedge funds and stock index funds. Hedge funds take some 'good' piece of data that day and immediately drive the futures market up the equivalent of 100 points or so on the Dow. That forces the index funds to re-adjust their positions to reflect the shift in the index futures. Then, as that rises, the hedge funds push it even higher and take a profit on the play. But in the real market almost no one dares to do anything."

SIGNPOSTS FOR DISINTEGRATION

The special characteristic of the coming financial panic is that it will involve not just a radical decline in values in financial markets, but will also be marked by a disintegration of the markets themselves. The "financial products" that are traded on the markets will decline sharply in price, in many cases becoming virtually worthless, like the Imperial Russian bonds after they were repudiated by the Bolshevik government, or the bank notes of the Confederate States of America after Appomattox. Even more important, the markets themselves where these ephemeral "financial products" are now traded will themselves cease to exist, or will live on only in truncated form.

Orderly markets in futures, options, indexes, futures options, and other derivative paper all depend on buyers and sellers who are present in sufficient numbers to allow relatively liquid markets and who share enough of a common outlook to be able to allow the price bid and asked to meet on the graph. The growing derivatives panic threatens to undermine all of these assumptions, which are all utopian in the context of today's markets. The impact of complicated over-the-counter derivative instruments has been to introduce the most massive uncertainty into markets as soon as regularly scheduled payments on derivative contracts break down. At that point, no one knows even approximately what a derivative contract might be worth. The bankruptcy a few years ago of the Bank of New England, where the "unwinding" of derivatives contracts was a process that took many months, suggests that once panic sets in, months will be required to determine what some of the more complicated swaps and hedges might be worth. And long before the accountants can produce these figures, it will have become an open secret that most derivatives are so uncertain as to be worth nothing.

* The more exotic the "financial products" dispensed on a market, the quicker that market will tend to freeze when the investors and traders feel the icy breath of panic on their necks. In the world

---

[73] *New York Times*, October 14, 1989.

that lies before us, would anyone care to estimate the forward value of a futures option on the Standard and Poor's 500 stock index as quoted on the Chicago Mercantile Exchange? What will be the value of a futures option on the Value Line stock index, trading at the Kansas City Board of Trade? Or of a futures option on the NYSE composite, quoted on the New York Futures Exchange, a subdivision of the NYSE? Who will dare to hazard a bid on a US Treasury bond future on the Chicago Board of Trade? Or of an option on the NASDAQ 100 stocks quoted on the Chicago Board Options Exchange? Almost all of these wildly speculative instruments are historically very new. With very few exceptions, they are all phenomena of the speculative orgy of the past 20 years, and they may well be approaching the end of the line. When the coming panic makes the value of the underlying instruments either zero or unknowable, it will become impossible and remain impossible to make a market in the various kinds of derivative paper.

* As we will show in detail in a later chapter, there are now more mutual funds in the United States than there are stocks listed on the NYSE. These instruments have been around since about 1929, a little longer than the other types of derivatives. These mutual funds offer collections of stocks, bonds, or foreign securities assembled by professional money managers. Whatever the plight of stock and bond owners, those investors holding mutual funds will find themselves at one further remove when the companies involved go on the bankruptcy auction block. The mutual fund era is also coming rapidly to an end. In the panic, massive panic redemptions would tend quickly to wipe out this "industry."

* One of the most important components of the coming panic will be the moment when the US dollar becomes widely unacceptable in international transactions. Once the dollar has been deprived of its political-military ability to command goods and services worldwide, even its domestic value will be very difficult to determine. Since August 15, 1971, the US dollar has become beyond a doubt the most overvalued currency on this planet. Given the colossal overhang of overseas or "xenodollars," the insolvency of the dollar will mean the end of many of the world's largest financial institutions who continue to hold them. A currency reform for the United States is now unavoidable if a functioning economy is to survive until the end of the century.

* According to its own histories, the New York Stock Exchange originated in 1792 when the representatives of a number of counting houses began meeting under a tree in lower Manhattan during certain hours each day to buy and sell various securities. After the 1987 crash, the NYSE instituted rules 80 A and 80 B, which aimed at preventing the panic free-fall of stock market prices. Adopted on October 19, 1988, circuit breakers originally halted trading for one hour with a 250-point drop and two hours with a 400-point decline. These circuit breakers were triggered in their original form for the first and only time on October 27, 1997, when the DJIA fell 350 points by 2:35 p.m. and 550 points by 3:30 p.m. That reflected an approximate 7% overall decline and shut the market for the remainder of the day. These rules are likely to be invoked more frequently in the near future as milestones on the path to disintegration.

NYSE CIRCUIT BREAKERS

According to the original 1988 circuit breakers, if the Dow Jones industrial average rose or fell 50 points, the NYSE instituted limitations on index arbitrage carried out by computer programs. These so-called program trading curbs allowed computer transactions only against the current direction of the market. If the market was falling, the limitations permitted sell orders only if the price of the individual stock had risen on the previous transaction. If the market was rising, program buys are permitted only if the stock price has declined on the previous transaction. Once the Dow Jones industrials had reverted to a rise or fall of no more than 25 points, the program trading curbs were generally lifted. If the market then went back to a gain or loss greater than 50 points (measured against the previous day's close), the program trading curbs were automatically re-imposed. There was no limit to the number of times these curbs could be switched on and off during a day. Program trading curbs were imposed innumerable times through 1998, as volatility increased and interday large point swings became the rule rather than the exception. Rule 80A was triggered 23 times on 22 days in 1990, 20 times in 1991, 16 times in 1992, 9 times in 1993, 30 times on 28 days in 1994, 29 times in 28 days in 1995, 119 times in 101 days in 1996, and 303 times in 219 days in 1997. Here is an excellent barometer of rising volatility.

The second level of "circuit breakers" originally took effect if the Standard and Poor's 500 stock index traded on the Chicago Mercantile Exchange (CME) went "limit down," currently a decline of 15 CME points approximately equivalent to 100-plus DJIA points. At this point the NYSE activated its so-called "sidecar," which fed all program trading orders into a special computer bank. This computer bank is the "blind file." After five minutes, the officers of the NYSE opened the blind file and, on the basis of what they found, took measures. These included trading halts for one or more stocks. They could also ban stop-loss orders by institutional investors and even by individual investors if their trades are larger than a certain limit.

If, in spite of the program trading curbs and the sidecar, the Dow Jones industrials fell more than 350 points below the previous close, the entire market was shut down for a 30 minute mandatory cooling off period. If, after this first interval of forced shutdown, the DJIA continued to fall to a level of 550 points below the previous close, NYSE rule 80 B mandated a cooling off period of 1 hour during which the stock market must remain closed.

After these safeguards were triggered in the Hong Kong typhoon of October 27, 1997, the stockjobbers decided to modernize their system. On April 14, 1998, the New York Stock Exchange made known that it would implement new circuit-breaker regulations to increase and widen the thresholds at which trading is halted for single-day declines in the Dow Jones Industrial Average. These revisions to NYSE Rule 80B were approved by the Securities and Exchange Commission. The point levels were now to be set quarterly at 10, 20, and 30 percent of the DJIA by using the DJIA average closing values of the previous month, rounded to the nearest 50 points. Point levels were henceforth to be adjusted on Jan. 1, April 1, July 1 and Oct. 1. In accordance with these new rules, on June 30, 1998, the New York Stock Exchange announced new circuit breaker trigger levels for third-quarter 1998, effective Wednesday, July 1. The points represented the thresholds at which trading was to be halted market wide for single-day declines in the Dow Jones Industrial Average.

For the turbulent months of July, August, and September 1998, the 10, 20 and 30 percent decline levels, respectively, in the DJIA were set as follows:

* A 900-point drop in the DJIA would halt trading for one hour if the decline occurred before 2 p.m.; for 30 minutes if before 2:30 p.m.; and have no effect between 2:30 p.m. and 4 p.m.

* A 1,750-point drop would halt trading for two hours if the decline occurred before 1 p.m.; for one hour if before 2 p.m.; and for the remainder of the day if between 2 p.m. and 4 p.m.

* A 2,650-point drop would halt trading for the remainder of the day regardless of when the decline occurred.

The other way in which the NYSE could grind to a standstill is by way of trading halts in individual stocks. These are currently of two forms. The first is the regulatory halt, in which a company asks one of the 16 floor governors of the NYSE to stop trading in its stocks because of pending important news or for some other reason. If a floor governor agrees, the trading in the stock can be halted for a minimum of 30 minutes.

Then there is the non-regulatory halt. When the market specialist who oversees trading in a stock finds that he can no longer maintain an orderly market in a stock in the face of overwhelming volatility, the specialist (who is himself a broker and a member of the NYSE) can halt trading, provided he can secure the approval of one floor governor or of two of 100 floor officials of the NYSE. The cumulative effect of a large number of non-regulatory trading halts would thus translate into a virtual shutdown of the NYSE. Something in this direction took place on October 19-20, 1987.

Finally, all US stock markets can be closed if the President so orders. This kind of closure could be indefinite. A fascinating episode in the history of the NYSE, much ignored by researchers, is the closing of the market for several months at the beginning of World War I in the summer and fall of 1914. This would appear to have been a favor to the British and to the Morgan interests.

It is quite possible that the most extreme moments of crisis which occurred during the market panic of October 19-20, 1987 can provide us with some hints for the coming breakdown. During the moments of greatest tension on October 20, many individual stocks opened late, never opened, or were shut down, sometimes repeatedly, by their specialists. On that day, there were repeated reports that the financial clearinghouse of the Chicago Mercantile Exchange was approaching bankruptcy. There were also rumors of the bankruptcy of important market participants, including banks, brokerages, and institutional investors. But the Federal Reserve was able to mobilize enough liquidity to stave off these insolvencies. Now, in the derivatives era, that is a feat that the Fed would have greater difficulty in duplicating, given the colossal sums involved. In 1987, "the result was sell-side order imbalances in [stock and futures] markets, leading to the near disintegration of market pricing."

The Chicago Board Options Exchange suspended trading at 11:45 AM on Tuesday, October 20, because of its rule that trading on the NYSE had to be open in at least 80% of the stocks which constitute the options index it was trading. At 12:15 PM, the Chicago Mercantile Exchange also shut down for almost an hour because of the large number of individual stock closings on the NYSE, and perhaps also because of reports that the NYSE as a whole was about to shut down. On that Tuesday, October 20, a government investigation later found, "the securities markets and the financial system approached breakdown.... a widespread credit breakdown seemed for a period of time quite possible. Amid rumors, subsequently revealed to be unfounded, of financial failures by some clearinghouses and several major market participants, and exacerbated by the fragmentation and complexity of the clearing process, the financial system came close to gridlock. Intermarket transactions required funds transfers and made demands for bank credit almost beyond the capacity of the system to provide."[74]

In retrospect, October 1987 emerges as a close call, but not the real thing. Back in October 1987 it was "near disintegration", "approached breakdown," "almost beyond the capacity of the system" and "close to gridlock." To begin to create an adequate conceptual model of what is now to come, we must assume that the worst of 1987 will be surpassed at a very early stage of the imminent meltdown, not merely in stock markets and derivatives markets, but in all financial markets. This time it will be breakdown, failures, gridlock and disintegration very early in the game. After this prelude, the financial markets will sink into an uncharted financial Orcus presided over by the shades of the Bardi, Peruzzi, and Fugger.

---

[74] Brady Commission, *Report of the Presidential Task Force on Market Mechanisms*, Washington DC, January, 1988.

STOCKS AS AN APPENDAGE OF DERIVATIVES

The average person who dabbles in investing generally sees the New York Stock Exchange and its Dow Jones Industrial Average as primary, and the Chicago options and futures markets as an accessory to the underlying stock exchanges. That is an outmoded view, and has been since the late 1980s at the latest. Today's stock market could not function without the help of derivatives. Derivatives provide the adrenaline or, if you will, the formaldehyde of the Dow Jones Industrials. So it is now the derivatives tail wagging the stock market dog.

THE 1966 PEAK OF THE CONSTANT-DOLLAR DOW

All the hype about a great bull market in stocks during the 1990s can be put in perspective if we employ the simple expedient of adjusting nominal gains for the loss of buying power due to inflation. If the Dow Jones figures are adjusted for inflation as expressed by the Consumer Price Index, we find that the Dow peaked in 1966, and fell sharply thereafter until Volcker relaxed interest rates in 1982. After that, the constant-dollar Dow tended to rise (although it fell back during 1987), and surpassed its 1966 peak only in with the doubling of the Dow between 1995 and 1997. Recent Dow gains are considerably pared down once they have been adjusted for inflation. The result is a constant-dollar Dow Jones Industrial Average which went nowhere over almost 30 years (1966-1995), but which qualifies as overpriced and overbought today. That is a very ominous combination. [See Prechter, 51, 119; Christiansen, 224]

There is another level of bleakness which available figures do not allow us to calculate with any exactitude, but which can at least be hinted at here. Nominal dollars are one thing, and constant dollars, adjusted for inflation, bring us closer to reality. But what about the devaluation and international depreciation of the dollar during the same period? The dollar was formally devalued in 1971 and 1973, and the general direction of its wild roller-coaster ride since 1973 has been down. Currency markets are dominated by derivatives trading, and certainly not by the purchasing power of the dollar when it comes to consumer goods or producer's goods.

For example, the first half of 1995 was a time of rising US stock prices, but it was clear enough that these were largely erased by the fall of the dollar on world markets at the same time. That fall is reflected only partially and belatedly in the Consumer Price Index and Producer Price Index. This suggests that the downward adjustment of the Dow gains of the 1990s needs to be much more radical than even bearish theorists might be willing to admit. In the last analysis, it is likely that the vast majority of small spectators who may consider themselves quite successful have simply been running hard to stay in place, or even lose ground.

For the broader market of secondary and small-capitalization stocks, the picture is at least equally grim. One index that tracks these stocks is the Value Line Composite, which in 1982 provided the basis for the first stock index futures contract. The Value Line Composite, like many other indices, reached a high in 1987. But after that, the VLC did not surpass its 1987 high until the middle 1990s. This means that during the years 1987-1995, the price of the average stock was flat.

PUMPING UP THE STOCK MARKET

Great efforts are presently being made to pump up the stock market by artificially channeling new cash flows into share purchases. The Brady system of drugged markets already does this, but the Brady system by itself is no longer enough. Among the cash flows on the planet that still remain to be looted, the Social Security tax and the Social Security Trust Fund (including the proceeds from what the public knows as FICA, the payroll tax, the self-employment tax, etc.) represent one of the largest. Corporate raiders have already looted private pension funds. They have now set their sights on Social Security, the biggest pension fund of them all. Many Wall Street influentials have further realized that the post-1995 era of virtually interest-free Japanese hot money cannot prop up bloated speculative stock prices forever. They have accordingly turned the attention to the large amounts of cash going into the Social Security Administration.

Social Security (technically, Old Age and Survivors and Disability Insurance Trust Funds or OASDI) provides old age pensions for those who spent a sufficient number of years during their working lives in occupations which are covered by the law. The system operates on a pay-as-you go basis, with any momentary surplus being aside to a trust fund where it is invested in Treasury securities, which represent the most secure paper available in this turbulent age. But now forces in Congress proposed that Social Security be "privatized". At minimum, privatization would mean that Social Security tax proceeds in amounts up to $10 trillion, would be invested on Wall Street.

The Social Security tax (indicated as FICA on paycheck stubs) consists of 6.2% of the employee's wages paid by the employer, plus an equal amount paid in by the employer, for a total of 12.4% of most wages earned in the entire country. This is the money that the Wall Street brokers want to get their hands on. In the process, the entire risk of providing pension payments in the future will be transferred to the hapless individual working person, who will pay through the nose for the wonderful benefit of vastly increased risk.

For brokers, this would mean an unprecedented bonanza not just in stock prices, but especially in commissions, fees, etc. The inflow of funds into the stock market would also mean a period of further capital gains for speculators. This would be true whether a government agency bought the stocks in large blocs, or whether individuals were allowed to establish Social Security "accounts" for which they would make their own investment decisions. When the stock bubble induced by the infusion of Social Security funds started to show signs of fading, the speculators who had hopped aboard for the ride could collect their capital gains and head for the exit. But the unsuspecting elderly would remain trapped inside for the duration, and the inevitable puncturing of the stock market bubble would wipe out the hope of pensions from the federal government. Thus, a stock market panic that brought down both stocks and mutual funds would leave many retirees with absolutely no way to finance a dignified old age, or even survival.

Many might have expected the 20-25% stock market decline of July-September 1998 to have taken the wind out of the sails of the Social Security privatizers. But their enthusiasm was unabated in mid-September. "I don't think any economists will have changed their minds based on what's happened over the last few weeks," Kevin Hassett of the American Enterprise Institute told a reporter. Congressman Mark Sanford (R-S.C), a ringleader of the privateers, conceded that "the politics will be tough, real tough, if the market sinks," but still intended to push ahead with his bid to gamble the pension money of the middle class on stocks. [75]

---

[75] *Washington Post*, September 12, 1998.

CHAPTER

III. THE $6 TRILLION MUTUAL FUND GAMBLE

Exit, pursued by a bear.
-Shakespeare, *The Winter's Tale*, IV.i

According to the Investment Company Institute, the trade association of the mutual funds, by the end of September 1998 there were 7,271 US open-end mutual funds, and these funds held a total of $4.9 trillion in assets. Also according to the ICI, in December 1997, there were over 500 closed-end funds, with a total market value of almost $150 billion. The total assets of all kind of investment company funds were therefore in excess of $5 trillion, and would soon attain $6 trillion. Over recent years, these funds have been growing at about $20 billion per month. In addition to mutual funds and closed-end funds, there were also hedge funds, highly speculative investment companies which catered to limited numbers of super-rich clients. By 1996, there were 2,400 hedge funds operating in the United States. By the end of 1997, there were 5,500 hedge funds operating worldwide.

The growth of mutual fund assets during the 1990s constituted a genuine mania on the part of the American middle class. Mutual fund assets were $94 billion at the beginning of 1980; by the beginning of 1993, this figure had grown to $1.6 trillion. By the spring of 1997, that had tripled. By April, 1997 the top 50 mutual fund groups had assets of over $2 trillion. According to the Internet's Mutual Fund Cafe, Fidelity was in first place with $308 billion, followed by Vanguard with $218 billion. Vanguard, whose assets had grown by 36% during the previous twelve months, was gaining on Fidelity, whose growth over the same period had been 19%. But Fidelity's share of the mutual fund market was still 13%.

MUTUAL FUND MANIA

All this means, in the broadest terms, that the life savings and retirement money of the middle class postwar generation has been wagered on mutual funds. Is this a safe bet? The vast majority of commentators take for granted that it is. Here is one example of the prevalent optimism:

> Behind the hype, out of earshot of bells and whistles, and beneath the sexy sales talk, a mutual fund is really an entity that lets a small investor behave like a big investor. By putting money into a mutual fund, you are hiring experts to invest your money and try to keep it on top of market ups and downs. For as little as $1,000 (and in some cases, as little as $20), you buy access to some of the best investments available today. [Gould]

There are few statistics available, but we venture to doubt whether mutual funds, as this author seems to suggest, are the most popular investment vehicles for really large investors.

The history of mutual funds is, if anything, even more turbulent than the story of the stocks that many mutual funds buy. Mutual funds and their ancestors, the investment trusts, have experienced crashes in 1890, 1929, 1937, and 1969-1974. Experience shows that mutual funds are very volatile, speculative paper. The 1990s have seen the biggest mutual fund mania ever. Under the virtual sponsorship of federal and state governments, mutual funds are today raking in the life savings and retirement nest eggs of a new and gullible generation. Anyone who knows the track record of mutual funds will be very likely to stay away from them.

Beyond this, mutual funds pose a deadly risk for the future of civilization in north America. A whole generation of credulous persons have entrusted their life savings to mutual funds, and the coming crash is very likely to cut this down to small change. In the twentieth century, middle class people who have been financially ruined and whose governments have been unable to provide a remedy have reacted very badly, as we learned in the case of Weimar Germany. Imagine mass riots by the middle-aged victims of a mutual fund blowout. This is no mere theorizing: look at Albania, where a large part of the population was fleeced by an investment scam. And then look at Russia, where the damage done by investment companies like the now-bankrupt MMM is a key ingredient in the ongoing social explosion.

Today's 7271 mutual funds are almost twice as numerous as the stocks listed on the New York Stock Exchange. The mutual fund "industry" currently employs almost half a million people, each one with his or her hand out for loads, commissions, 12b-1 fees, charges, and the like.

Everything that has been said about the dangers of derivatives applies with equal force to mutual funds. Remember the definition of a derivative security – financial instruments whose returns are linked to, or derived from, the performance of some underlying paper asset, or paper based on paper for short. Mutual funds, as represented by fund shares that are based on stocks, bonds, mortgages, futures, options, commercial paper and other paper assets, exactly fulfill this definition of a derivative. Mutual fund shares might be better called equity derivatives. An intelligent and well-informed person will accordingly avoid mutual funds and investment funds (open-end funds as well as closed-end funds).

OPEN END AND CLOSED END

In order to discuss mutual funds, a few simple issues must be defined. A mutual fund is an open-end investment company as defined by the Investment Company Act of 1940 with its numerous amendments over the years. An open-end investment company is a management company which is offering for sale or has outstanding any redeemable security of which it is the issuer. A redeemable security is one which the company is required to cash in on demand. Most open-end companies are constantly in the process of creating and selling new shares of their own capital stock. The buying and selling price is determined by a twice-daily calculation of the value of the assets of the company. An open-end investment company is what the average person thinks of when they hear the term "mutual fund." The open-end funds are by far the prevalent type. From the point of view of the investor, the open-end company is one that sells you fund shares directly, at most through a broker or salesman, but not through stock purchase on an exchange. An open-end company is one that claims to stand ready to buy back any amount of its own stock, at the price determined by the per-share value of its portfolio, without forcing the investor to find a buyer on the stock exchange.

A closed-end company is any other kind of investment company. The closed-end company normally has a fixed number of shares which can be bought and sold on a stock exchange. The company is not obligated to buy back its own stock. The current owner who wants to sell closed-end shares must find a buyer on the stock exchange where the closed-end fund is listed. Closed-end funds were in eclipse for a long time after 1929, but they have seen something of a resurgence during the 1990s. Closed-end funds have been especially active in emerging markets and other stocks from foreign countries. Insiders see closed-end funds as riskier than mutual funds.

It is interesting to note that the term "mutual fund" was unknown before the crash of 1929. Before the crash, closed-end funds were known as investment trusts, and the few open-end companies called themselves Boston-style or Massachusetts-style investment trusts. But nobody called themselves a mutual fund. Who invented the term "mutual fund"? One writer replies: "The term 'mutual fund' seems to have emerged in the late 1930s, though its precise origin is hard to pin down. One credible theory is that it was invented in order to give fund salespeople a friendly new name for their product. Terms such as 'investment trust' and 'investment pool' reminded too many Americans of the fortunes they'd lost in the crash." [Daugherty, 11]

The ploy has worked marvelously. Who today identifies the benevolent and judicious connotations of "mutual fund" with the crash of 1929? Almost nobody. And thus a new generation of Americans, the hapless Baby Boomers, are risking their nest eggs, retirement funds, and life savings, much of which they have invested in mutual funds. Over 40% of all US households now hold stocks or mutual funds of some type, meaning that over 37 million households are exposed to the vagaries of the stock/mutual fund nexus.

Until the end of World War II, there were less than $2 billion invested in investment companies of all types. The great leap forward for mutual funds came in 1958, when the value of all investment companies jumped from around $10 billion to around $5 billion. 1958, not by coincidence, marks the approximate end of the postwar period of net productive investment in the US economy. With the 1958 recession, more and more funds began to build up which were unable to find investment in the production of tangible physical wealth in the domestic economy. Part of this surplus streamed into mutual funds. Other, more volatile funds, aptly called hot money, streamed into the Eurodollar market being created in London at that time.

INVESTMENT TRUSTS AND BARINGS, 1890

Investment trusts are thought to have originated in Dundee, Scotland around 1873, with the founding of the first investment trust by young Robert Fleming. Small investors in Scotland wanted a better return on their savings than was readily available from banks or British government bonds. Fleming sold shares to these modest savers and invested in various American railroad ventures. He touted the advantages of simplicity, diversification, and of experienced full-time professional investment managers like himself. Fleming also offered higher returns. By 1890 there were more than thirty investment trusts. Many trusts were now investing not only in the British Empire (Australia, New Zealand, South Africa), but in Latin American countries as well, where even higher returns could be obtained. The trusts also bought the stock of English beer companies. Then the government of Argentina, a favorite of the investment trusts, defaulted on bond payments. Barings Bank (which was finally wiped out in the Nick Leeson caper of 1995) thereupon went bankrupt for the first time. Shares in investment trusts collapsed.

The London *Economist* wrote in February, 1893: "Of many of the trust companies which were formed in such rapid succession a few years ago, when the mania for this form of joint-stock enterprise was rampant, it may be said with truth that, having sown the wind, they are now reaping the whirlwind." The investment trusts had revealed their strong tendency to collapse – faster than stocks – in the face of panics and market declines. The 1890's debacle presents the pattern we will see again and again and again.

THE ROARING TWENTIES

The next great investment trust mania started during the Coolidge administration. The creation of the Coolidge bubble by Montagu Norman of the Bank of England and Benjamin Strong of the New York Federal Reserve Bank is told in another chapter. One of the most important ingredients in the heady brew of speculation during those years was the investment trust.

The most notable piece of speculative architecture of the late twenties, and the one by which, more than any other device, the public demand for stocks was satisfied, was the investment trust or company. The investment trust did not promote new enterprises or enlarge old ones. It merely arranged that people could own stock in old enterprises through the medium of new ones....The virtue of the investment trust was that it brought about an almost complete divorce of the volume of corporate securities outstanding from the value of corporate assets in existence. The former could be twice, thrice, or any multiple of the latter. The volume of underwriting business and of securities available for trading on the exchanges all expanded accordingly. So did the securities to own, for the investment trusts sold more securities than they bought. The difference went into the call market, real estate, or the pockets of the promoters.

So wrote John Kenneth Galbraith in his study of *The Great Crash*. [Galbraith, 46-47] Most investment trusts or investment companies of the 1920s would today fall under the heading of closed-end funds. The growth in the number of investment trusts and in the dollar value of their assets rose to a crescendo during the Coolidge bubble, and peaked at the eve of the October 1929 crash. It was estimated that in 1921, there were only about 40 investment trusts operating in the United States. By the beginning of 1927 this had risen to 160 investment trusts. During 1927, 140 new investment trusts were launched. During 1928, the figure grew by 186. During 1929, investment trusts were formed at the rate of about one every business day, for a yearly total of 265. That gave us 751 investment trusts operating by the last days of 1929. Between 1927 and the autumn of 1929, the assets held by the investment trusts expanded by a factor of 1100%. By the autumn of 1929, these assets were estimated to have exceeded $8 billion. One in ten American households had invested money in an investment trust.

Many of these investment trusts refused to make public what kinds of shares they were buying; they claimed that this would mean giving away their most important proprietary expertise. In practice, many investment trusts were buying worthless stock the trust promoters wanted to unload from their own accounts; they were also engaged in wildly speculative practices. The investment trusts were in effect blind pools.

LEVERAGE

Leverage is that financial technique by which it is possible to obtain the use and earnings of large amounts of capital by committing a relatively smaller amount of one's own funds. A mortgage where the down payment is 20% of the value of the home to be bought is an example of leverage. In this case you put down $20,000, let us say, to get the use of $80,000. In a rising market, borrowing money to buy assets with a fractional down payment of one's own money can produce a very handsome profit, especially as expressed as a percentage of one's own original stake. The problem is that while leverage can generate enhanced returns in a rising market, the fall in value of the underlying assets rapidly leads to reverse leverage, with percentage losses being multiplied until one's own capital is wiped out.

Leverage has been compared to the effect of a bull whip: the energy applied to one end is magnified so as to make the other end of the whip break the sound barrier, producing the characteristic cracking of the whip. But leverage, unfortunately for the speculators, works both ways.

Galbraith offers the example of a hypothetical investment trust organized in early 1929 with a capital of $150 million. In this example, one third the capital of the trust was derived from the sale of bonds, one third from the sale of preferred stock, and one third from the sale of common stock. The bonds and the preferred stock are in essence fixed income securities paying an invariable return. With the 50% rise of the stock market during the first half of 1929, the $150 million of assets of the hypothetical trust would have also increased by 50% or $75 million to a value of $225 million. The bonds and preferred stock of this trust would not increase in price, since their fixed earnings would not be enhanced. The entire impact of the increased share value of the trust's holdings would be concentrated on its common stock, which would tend to rise in value by 150%, from $50 to $125 million. That was a very gratifying gain, to be sure, and an example of how beneficial positive leverage can be.

But now let us assume that this same leveraged investment trust was launched with exactly the same capital structure just before the October 1929 crash. By the end of October, the average value of the blue-chip stocks in the trust's portfolio would have declined by about one third. This time, by the implacable workings of reverse leverage, the 33.3% decline among blue chips as a whole would have translated into the reduction of the common stock of the trust by 100%, to about zero.

If the original portfolio of the late-starting investment trust had been worth $150 million, the one third fall in the Dow left that net worth at $100 million. But this would have been enough to cover only the value of the preferred stock ($50 million) and of the bonds ($50 million), a total of $100 million. There was nothing left to shore up the $50 million value of the common stock, which was accordingly virtually worthless.

Thus, the stock of the investment trusts of 1929 fell on the average much, much faster than the common stock of industrial corporations. By early November 1929, the stock of most investment trusts had become virtually unsalable. Investment trust stock was, in practice, non-negotiable paper. If holders of such stock needed cash urgently, they were forced to sell common stock in corporations like RCA, ATT, GM, or US Steel, if they were lucky enough to have any. This demonstrates the main lesson to be learned: that in a crash, investment company stock will always be even more dangerous than the common stock of companies in which the investment trust has invested. Of course, the investment trusts of yore and the mutual funds of today will argue that they offer the advantage of expert judgment in picking stock. How many geniuses bloom during a bull market! How easy it is to profile oneself as long as the Dow is rising! But how bitter the disillusionment when prices collapse!

WARNINGS BEFORE THE CRASH

Paul Cabot of State Street Investment Corporation of Boston, delivered the following admonition in the *Atlantic Monthly* for March 1929:

> In my opinion there is today in this country a large and well-known investment trust whose shares are selling for far more than their intrinsic or liquidating value, which has continually managed its portfolio so that it can show the greatest possible profits and thereby obtain the greatest market value for its shares, regardless of their real worth. Generally speaking, in this trust during the past year the good securities that have appreciated in value have been sold and the poorer ones retained or increased, simply to show profits. Some months ago, in testifying before the New York Stock Exchange, I was asked to state briefly what were, in my opinion, the present abuses in the investment-trust movement. My reply was (1) dishonesty; (2) inattention and inability; (3) greed.

Have things really changed since 1929? Is it really different this time? We shall see. Here is further comment on the role of leverage in the 1929 investment companies:

By 1927, the leverage concept in corporate structure led to the creation of highly leveraged investment trusts. Generally speaking, the pre-World War trusts sold common stocks, but no bonds, and so were unleveraged. The new trusts of the late 1920s were highly leveraged. United States & Foreign Securities, for example, had three classes of stock (one common and two preferred) as well as a bond issue. Founded in 1924, U.S. & Foreign became the prototype for many of the 265 trusts formed in 1929 alone. The new trust companies of that year sold some 3 billion in securities to the public, and this money was almost immediately reinvested through stock purchases, many of them on margin. In mid-1929, an investor might purchase shares in an investment trust on margin, while the trust itself was using margin. It was conceivable that a buyer would put down $10 for $100 worth of stock, which itself represented $10 in equity and $90 in debt! In the early autumn of 1929, leveraged trusts were purchasing other leveraged trusts, compounding the situation still further. [Sobel, 358-359]

And the leverage did not stop there. Years after the crash, the Securities and Exchange Commission issued a monumental report on stock market and investment company abuses. According to that report, "Investment companies employed their publicly contributed funds in a wide variety of ways: participation in underwritings of securities; trading in securities and commodities; dealing in puts and calls, foreign exchange, bankers' acceptances and commercial paper, and oil and gas royalties; short selling; loans to brokers, dealers, and others on securities; granting of options on securities issued by others, dealing in real estate; reorganization of industrial companies, and rendering investment advisory service." [SEC, Part Three, chapter VII, p. 2501] Compare this with the activities of any aggressive growth mutual fund of today, and you will see how little has changed.

As we see, investment trusts before 1929 acted very much like George Soros's Quantum Fund or other speculative hedge funds of today. (The Soros Quantum Fund and other hedge funds escape from regulation under the Investment Company Act of 1940 by virtue of having fewer that 100 investors. Having fewer than 100 investors allows his hedge fund to "fly below the radar" of the Securities and Exchange Commission.)

As the bubble inflated, some investment trusts decided that they could make more money by lending their cash as broker call loans to finance margin purchases. Persons taking a plunge in the market by buying stock in an investment trust were often buying a piece of the companies that were furnishing the credit the plungers needed to speculate in the first place. Many investment trusts invested in each other, often in a pyramid scheme but sometimes not. Compare this to the modern phenomenon of "multifund" or "fund of funds" mutual funds that invest their money exclusively in other mutual funds, allegedly for purposes of diversification.

THE CARNAGE

United Founders, an investment company that was part of the American Founders Group family of trusts, reached a high of $75 per share in 1929 but declined to about 75 cents during the early 1930s, for a loss of 99%, compared to a 90% decline in the Dow industrials over the same period. During the last months of the boom the Wall Street investment bank of Goldman, Sachs and Company had created the Goldman Sachs Trading Corporation, which then proceeded to launch high-profile leveraged investment trusts like Shenandoah Corp. and Blue Ridge Corp., even as it expanded by merging with still other investment companies. The three corporations formed a holding company pyramid, with Goldman Sachs Trading at the top, Shenandoah one level below, and Blue Ridge a further step down. This pyramid structure accentuated the whip-lash effects produced by market movements upon the shares of Goldman Sachs Trading.

The shares of Goldman Sachs Trading Corporation were issued in December 1928 at $104 per share and reached $222.50 by February 7, 1929. The Goldman Sachs Trading stock split for two for one, but by 1932 it was selling for $1.75 per share. Goldman Sachs Trading Corp. was one of the most prodigal of all the investment trusts. As investment trust critic John T. Flynn wrote, "...the palm for losses must go to the Goldman Sachs Trading Corporation. This investment trust was set up by Goldman, Sachs and Company, bankers, and is presided over by Mr. Waddill Catchings, the gentleman who last year [1929] wrote a book called *The Road to Plenty*, explaining to the people and the government just how to get prosperous and stay that way. With prospective profits of $30,000,000 from its security holdings and sales, the Goldman Sachs Trading Corporation certainly seemed on the road to plenty in October. But the road turned out to be a two-way street. And after the market went to pieces the trust reversed its direction and marched back along the road to plenty until it had canceled its $30,000,000 profits and, from the shrinkage of its investments, accumulated a deficit of $90,000,000. The actual shrinkage in investments was $121,404,839." [Flynn, 110] Shares of the Shenandoah Corp. were issued at $17.50, but opened at $30 and closed that same day at $36. By the end of 1929, Shenandoah stock was down to a little over $8, and later reached 50 cents.

Ten dollars invested in the average investment trust at the beginning of the Coolidge bubble in 1925 reached a high of $105 before the crash, and then declined to less than 25 cents by 1932. Out of 751 investment trusts active at the time of the crash, only 200 were left by the time the markets had touched bottom in 1932.

POST-CRASH CRITIQUES

The memory of the investment trust debacle of 1929 was the subject of a muckraking attack by John T. Flynn, who was active in radio broadcasting until the early 1960s. Flynn authored a series of exposes of investment trust malpractice that appeared in the *New Republic* starting in April of 1930. This series was quickly made into a book entitled *Investment Trusts Gone Wrong!* (New York, 1930). Flynn was indignant about the failure of investment companies to provide transparency:

> In spite of many criticisms which have seeped into the press, no adequate statement of the abuses to which the investment trust has been put in this country has yet been made. As a matter of fact, no adequate statement can be made until these institutions are compelled to come out of the dark corners in which most of them do their work. The information about their operations is meager. But there is enough to give us a picture of bad management and losses little short of amazing. [Flynn, 33]

When the Senate Banking and Currency Committee held its celebrated Pecora hearings into Wall Street banking and stockjobbing malfeasance during the spring of 1933 (before the background of banking panic), John T. Flynn assisted the committee chief counsel, Ferdinand Pecora, in making the case against the malefactors of great wealth and economic royalists. But no regulation of the investment companies was enacted.

THE CRASH OF 1937

With the coming of the Roosevelt administration, the US stock market began slowly to clamber up out of the depths of depression. But on March 19, 1937, the market crashed again in the context of a second decline sometimes known as the "New Deal depression." The surviving investment trusts again declined faster than the rest of the market, once more attracting government scrutiny. It was revealed that the trust managers were once again up to their necks in dangerous, speculative and corrupt practices. For a while, there was a serious possibility that the Congress would conclude that investment companies of all types were incorrigible and simply outlaw them once and for all. But the lobbyists for the investment trusts prevailed, and the Congress passed the Investment Company Act of 1940, which provided a small measure of regulation.

THE GO-GO ERA

For many Americans it took almost twenty years after the end of World War II to satisfy the pent-up consumer demand of the war years. By the beginning of the 1960s the luckier middle class families had paid off some of their consumer debt and began to think about investing. Once again mutual fund promoters were there. This became the go-go era, with go-go connoting a return to speculative practices which had been frowned on since 1929. This was the era of Gerald Tsai (pronounced "sigh"), manager of the Fidelity Capital Fund, and later of his own Manhattan Fund. Tsai used aggressive trading to rack up annual percentage returns that were much higher than the progress of the Dow, to say nothing of savings accounts. Tsai became the 1960s archetype of the "gunslinger," the aggressively speculative fund manager who became a celebrity by virtue of the high returns he delivered for a time. One of Tsai's tricks was to concentrate his assets in small and obscure stocks, with the effect of bidding up the price. This recalled the artificial churning developed by the pre-1929 stock pool. There might be a year or two of high capital gains on the stock price. But in most cases subsequent lack of performance by the company would deflate the stock, by which time Tsai hoped he had cashed in and moved on. But often he was not quick enough.

In December 1968, the Mates Fund, managed by the then-celebrated Fred Mates, defaulted on redemptions. Mates had invested a large portion of the fund's assets in non-negotiable "letter stock" which could not be traded on public stock exchanges. Now one of Tsai's favorite letter stock companies filed for bankruptcy, and 40% of Tsais's fund portfolio turned out to be non-negotiable paper.

Another famous gunslinger of the go-go era was Fred Carr, the manager of the Enterprise Fund and one of the high-fliers of that era, but later one of the big losers of the 1970s. Fred Carr made a timely exit from the Enterprise Fund. Carr later joined First Executive Life Insurance Company of California, where he began offering "guaranteed investment contracts" (GICs), which were purchased in large numbers by small investors through 401 (k) company retirement plans. Fred Carr was also one of Michael Milken's biggest junk bond customers. When the junk bond market collapsed, First Executive Life went bankrupt on April 11, 1991. Liabilities were $49 billion, making this the largest insurance bankruptcy in US history. With that suddenly nothing was guaranteed, and pensioners who depended on First Executive stood to lose one third of their holdings. Most made out better later through a support operation mounted by other insurance companies for cosmetic and political reasons.

BERNIE CORNFELD AND IOS

Then there was the notorious case of Bernie Cornfeld, the mutual fund salesman who blossomed into a thief on a grand scale. Cornfeld was a pioneer of country funds, multifunds (his "Fund of Funds" scam) and offshore money laundering in general. Cornfeld, operating from Switzerland,

Panama, and the Caribbean, founded Investors Overseas Services, which later spawned the Fund of Funds. Cornfeld's offshore vehicle to mount attempted hostile takeovers of US mutual funds. Cornfeld recruited new customers for the high-risk go-go funds. For a time, Cornfeld's IOS was the largest mutual find organization outside of the US. Many of Cornfeld's clients were wealthy Americans seeking to stash their money away in offshore tax shelters. At various times Cornfeld rubbed elbows with names that are household words among mutual fund initiates today. Early in his career Cornfeld got a $26,000 loan from the Dreyfus Corporation. In the early 1960s Cornfeld acted as super salesman for Tsai's Fidelity Capital Fund, leading many hapless small investors across the bridge of Tsais. John Templeton and his management corporation helped finance Cornfeld's insurance company in Luxemburg. Later, Cornfeld defied the SEC by acquiring a controlling stake in the Value Line Special Situations Fund. At another time, the SEC came after Cornfeld and banished IOS from doing business in the United States. In response, Cornfeld set up an elaborate system of routing US orders through London. This was done with the help of Arthur Lipper III, Cornfeld's London broker. Michael Lipper worked as director of research in his brother Arthur's firm until 1973. Michael Lipper is today the owner of the well-known Lipper Analytical Services, which tracks the performance of mutual funds.

Cornfeld's empire collapsed during the first months of 1970. IOS became strapped for cash and was forced to dump shares. IOS' distressed merchandise liquidations were an important factor in the stock market decline of April-May 1970 otherwise associated with the Penn Central bankruptcy. "Investors Overseas Services ran out of money in the week of the worst stock-market panic since World War Two," was a press comment at the end of the first week of April 1970. During the spring and summer of 1970 a number of Wall Street firms were forced into liquidation. Cornfeld was ousted by the IOS board in June 1970, and his successor was an organized crime figure named Robert Vesco. Vesco promptly gathered up whatever funds remained in the IOS treasury and launched himself into the life of an independently wealthy international fugitive. By 1973 Cornfeld was in jail in Switzerland. The IOS shareholders were left with nothing.

There was another important mutual fund called Equity Funding, whose manager, Mike Riordan, wanted to emulate Bernie Cornfeld. In this case, the mutual fund salesmen would sell a customer some mutual fund shares, and then convince the customer to use these shares as collateral to borrow the money needed to pay premiums on an insurance policy that the salesman also was selling. But by April 1973, investigations had disclosed that $2 billion in insurance policies that the customers thought they owned simply did not exist. In 1968, the stock market embarked on a period of generally falling prices - a bear market, which continued until the beginning of the Reagan bubble in 1982. Here are some of the fund net asset value losses over the period September 1969 to September 1974:

Manhattan Fund – lost 73%

Fidelity Capital Fund – lost 43%

Fidelity Trend Fund – lost 42%

Channing Growth Fund – lost 48%

Invest Fund – lost 50%

Enterprise Fund – lost 51%

Neuwirth Fund – lost 52%

Eaton & Howard Fund – lost 62%

American Investors Fund – lost 63%

Keystone S-4 Fund – lost 63%

Value Line Special Situations Fund – lost 74%

[see Christensen, p. 62]

These grim statistics provide a timely warning for the mutual fund investors of today. The years 1969-1974 represent the opening phase of the last bear market in recent historical experience. Mutual fund advocates might like to explain why their funds might do better in the NEXT bear market. Given the pervasive turn to derivatives, leverage, short selling, and the like during the 1990s, there is every reason to believe that mutual fund performance in the next bear market will be worse than these figures might suggest.

MILKEN AND THE JUNK BOND ERA

During the junk bond era of the 1980s, many mutual fund companies entered into close relations with Michael Milken, the notorious junk bond king. Milken operated from Drexel Burnham Lambert in Los Angeles. Milken himself was the junk bond marketer for Kohlberg Kravis Roberts, the firm which carried out the junk-bond assisted takeovers of companies like RJR Nabisco. Milken marketed the junk bonds with the help of his friend Ivan Boesky. But he also had help from some of the big names in mutual funds today. One was Fidelity: "...Fidelity – where Ned Johnson was thought to be willing to back any investment lead as long as it would sell – was present at the creation of the junk-bond mutual fund market." [Henriques, 240] Fidelity was one of the four or five biggest purchasers of junk bonds. One of the Fidelity buyers was Milken's friend William Pike, the head of the Fidelity High Income Fund. On March 5, 1992 the SEC announced its official finding that Pike had violated the mutual fund laws by failing to keep proper records of his bond repurchase (repo) deals with Drexel Burnham Lambert. Pike was suspended from the investment advisory business for three months.

Patsy Ostrander was the manager of the bond sectors of Fidelity's Puritan Fund and Equity Income Fund. Ostrander also worked closely with Michael Milken and took kickbacks from him. In October 1991, after she had departed Fidelity, Ostrander was indicted for accepting illegal compensation, and for failing to disclose her personal investments to her employer. After a 1992 Manhattan trial in which Michael Milken testified, Ostrander was convicted of accepting an illegal gratuity and was sentenced to two months in jail. [Henriques, 337 ff.]

When Fidelity sued Ostrander to recover certain profits, she replied with a proffer in a Suffolk County (New York) court which alleged the following: "During the period of Mrs. Ostrander's employment Fidelity allowed firm professionals flagrantly to manipulate the Fidelity mutual funds under their control in order to generate profits in personal trading....despite the prevalence of trading abuses, Fidelity took no action to prevent, discourage, or discipline the perpetrators, but rather maintained a compliance system that was manifestly inadequate." [Henriques, 344-345] When the junk bond market collapsed during the late summer of 1989, the value of the assets held by all US junk bond mutual funds fell by a full 30%. But even this stern lesson was soon unlearned, and junk bonds bounced back to have their best year ever in 1993.

THE CRASH OF 1962

One of the oldest arguments in favor of mutual funds was that they help stabilize the stock market by buying stocks they already have in their portfolios during downturns, when less experienced investors may lose their nerve and panic. The mutual funds were expected to buy into weakness. But as a matter of historical fact, mutual funds have shown a marked tendency to sell shares during market plunges, thereby adding to the selling pressure. Mutual funds sell stock at those times because they fear that their own customers will demand their money back through redemptions.

On Monday, May 28, 1962, the Dow Jones average of 30 industrials dropped by 34.95 points to close at 537, thus racking up the then-biggest decline in history except for October 28, 1929, when the loss had been 38.33 points. This decline took place on a volume of 9.35 million shares, at that time the seventh largest turnover in history. On Tuesday, May 29, stocks declined during the morning but then rose through the afternoon, ending up with a gain of 27 points on volume exceeded only by that of October 29, 1929.

On these days there was much worry in Wall Street that mutual funds, which had experienced five years of rapid growth, might dump shares on the market and add momentum to the decline. One Wall Street historian recalls the situation:

> If the danger to the market from the consequences of margin selling was much less in 1962 than it had been in 1929, the danger from another quarter – selling by mutual funds – was immeasurably greater. Indeed, many Wall Street professionals now say that at the height of the May excitement the mere thought of the mutual-fund situation was enough to make them shudder.... In a serious stock-market decline, the reasoning went, small investors would want to get their money out of the stock market and would therefore ask for the redemption of their shares; in order to raise the cash necessary to meet the redemption demands, the mutual funds would have to sell some of their stocks; these sales would lead to a further stock-market decline, causing more holders of fund shares to demand redemption - and so on into a more up-to-date version of the bottomless pit...the mutual funds' power to magnify a market decline had never been seriously tested...the funds had built up the staggering total of twenty-three billion dollars in assets by the spring of 1962, and never in the interim had the market declined with anything like its present force. Clearly, if twenty-three billion dollars in assets, or any substantial fraction of that figure, were to be tossed onto the market now, it could generate a crash that would make 1929 look like a stumble. [Brooks, 10]

John Brooks, the chronicler of these events, recalls one market observer who told him that the threat of a downward cycle induced by mutual fund redemptions was "so terrifying you didn't even mention the subject." [Brooks, 11] In the event, the market break of 1962 was brought under control within a few days, and the market had returned to normalcy within a week. That was in the era when mutual funds controlled $23 billion in assets. But the story was much different in 1987, when mutual funds had increased their numbers to over 2,000 and their assets to the level of $233 billion, and a single fund, Peter Lynch's Fidelity Magellan, had $9 billion in assets. This time mutual fund selling, especially by Fidelity, was a very important factor in the crash.

THE QUEST FOR REDEMPTION: THE CRASH OF OCTOBER 1987

On Friday, October 16, 1987, the Dow Jones 30 declined by 108 points, then an all-time record loss. 50 points of that decline had come during the last half-hour of the trading day. The prices of stock index futures in Chicago were pounded that afternoon until the trading pits were almost completely deserted by buyers. On Sunday afternoon, October 18, 1987, the top executives of the Fidelity family of funds met in their Boston offices. The Fidelity managers feared that small investors, realizing over the weekend that a panic crash was in progress, would begin to redeem their Fidelity shares in large amounts. They also feared that it would prove impossible in the midst of the panic for Fidelity to secure bank loans to pay off these redemptions. They anticipated chaotic market conditions, with an absence of buyers, at the opening of American markets on Monday morning. So Fidelity managers scoured their portfolios for about $90 million in stocks that could be sold on the London Stock Exchange starting at approximately 3 AM New York time. They also prepared a second, and much larger, sell order composed of stocks that could only be sold in New York.

As one expert on Fidelity observes:

> In that vast wave of [London] sell orders, the $90 million worth contributed by Fidelity was actually quite small. But anyone who saw those wee-hour sell orders from Boston must have wondered, with a sinking feeling: How much would Fidelity be trying to sell in New York? And if Fidelity - the biggest, the smartest, the richest, the most successful of all the mutual fund companies - if Fidelity was selling into this panic, what on earth would the rest of the mutual fund industry do? [Henriques, 283]

On the morning of the crash, October 19, 1987, selling by mutual funds was a decisive component in the panic on the New York exchange. Part of what happened is documented in the January, 1988 *Report of the Presidential Task Force on Market Mechanisms*. This post-mortem of the crash is known as the Brady report in honor of the task force chairman, Nicholas F. Brady of Dillon, Reed, who later became Secretary of the Treasury in the Bush Administration. In its Study IV entitled "The Effect of the October Stock Market Decline on the Mutual Funds Industry," the Brady report concluded that "On October 19, three [mutual fund] companies alone sold $913 million of stocks, while the rest of the industry was a net buyer of $134 million. Given the high level of redemptions and the uncertainty about the near future, the group of three mutual fund companies sold heavily in the stock market on October 16, 19, and 20." [Brady, IV-1]

Mutual fund buying generally represented bargain hunting and bottom fishing later in the day. According to Brady, "before 10 AM on Monday, October 19, the three mutual fund companies had sold $570 million of stocks on the NYSE alone. This accounted for approximately one quarter of all trading on the NYSE for the first 30 minutes that the Exchange was open. The three companies sold in large volume in all US markets at the opening on Monday, but focussed their selling on the NYSE. The three mutual fund companies were heavy net sellers because of very high levels of redemptions on Friday, Saturday, and Sunday (October 16, 17 and 18) and the expectation that a significant amount of redemptions would continue throughout the early part of the week. After the $570 million of sales were executed during the first half hour on Monday, selling by the equity mutual funds of the three companies trailed off for the rest of the day. Nonetheless, the volume of early morning selling had a significant impact on the downward direction of the market." [Brady, Part IV, pp. 1-2]

$500 million of the selling that day is thought to have come from Fidelity alone. Total net stock sales by mutual funds amounted to $3.6 billion between October 16 and October 26. [Henriques, 284-286] As one of Fidelity's executives later told the *Washington Post*, "By Monday morning redemptions that had accumulated through the weekend were ten times the experience we'd ever had....Frankly, we hadn't anticipated a series of events like October 16 through 19." So much for the advantages of prescient professional fund managers. The name of this Fidelity official was Gary

Burkhead, who was rewarded for his foresight and diligence by being made the president of Fidelity's management company. Fidelity did experience the large liquidations that its managers had feared. Assets under management by Fidelity dropped from $81 billion as of October 1 to $69 billion after the crash. But the bloodletting among the mutual funds was soon mitigated by the Federal Reserve's support operations and the drugged markets later codified as the Brady system.

By 1993, institutional investors, including mutual funds, pension funds, foundations and endowments controlled 60% of all stock listed on public exchanges. A few thousand money managers are thus collectively majority stockholders of almost all US corporations. These are now other-directed yuppies, very much oriented to peer opinion and susceptible to be stampeded by market adversity. A panic among these few thousand could thus mean a general collapse of stock prices and of mutual fund net asset values.

The mutual fund boom of the 1980s and 1990s grew out of the inflationary mass psychology of the Carter era. During that time of high inflation, people became accustomed to investment returns that were much higher than the postwar average. When inflation declined somewhat under Reagan, savers felt that the interest rates on their bank certificates of deposit were too low. So they readily turned to mutual funds, which seemed to promise a higher return. When bankers observed this phenomenon, they also began to offer mutual funds. If a depositor turned in a certificate of deposit and complained of low returns, he or she was invited to walk across the bank lobby to another desk where they found a mutual fund salesperson. Mellon bank, for example, seems less and less interested in retail banking per se, and more and more interested in mutual funds, as documented by its 1993 acquisition of Dreyfus Corporation. Chemical Bank and Nationsbank have also made deals to market mutual funds.

Many of the buyers of bank-sponsored mutual funds and of mutual funds in general believe that the instrument they have bought is somehow government insured. Very often the name of the fund sounds very much like the name of the bank. Tragically for small investors, mutual funds are not insured by the government. According to a 1993 survey by the Securities and Exchange Commission, 28% of bank customers mistakenly believe that mutual funds offered by banks were insured by the US government. In addition, 49% of mutual fund shareowners thought that their shares were guaranteed by the US government.

NOW AND THEN

The central question thus becomes: can the modern mutual fund be expected to perform better in a stock market panic than its predecessor, the leveraged investment trust of 1929? The New Deal and the 1930s produced many sensible pieces of legislation designed to protect the public from some of the worst abuses which had contributed to the severity of the crash. One was the regulation of margin accounts by the Federal Reserve. Another was the Glass-Steagall law, with its prohibitions of interstate banking and its fire-wall between banking and stock underwriting. The Investment Company Act of 1940 belongs to this group of laws. Our problem today is that just when we would need these protective measures the most, the forces of the Republican Conservative Revolution in the Congress are vehemently demanding that the last of them be done away with. The proposed merger of Travelers Insurance with Citibank, if it were allowed to go through, would be the last nail in the coffin of Glass-Steagall, which has already been made a dead letter by the deliberate failure of the regulators to enforce it.

The Investment Company Act of 1940 had wisely outlawed pyramids, in which there were several layers of investment companies, each one holding the shares of the investment company below it; only the lowest investment company on the totem pole held a portfolio of stocks and bonds. In addition, at about the time this law was passed, investment companies developed inhibitions about certain notorious speculative practices like selling short, lending stocks to short sellers, using margin, using extreme leverage, and the like. Most of this involved a kind of self-policing of the investment companies. But now the self-policing has melted away in most cases, and the bad old ways are back in extreme form.

During the age of anti-government demagogy and de-regulation, and especially during the Reagan-Bush era, the oversight and enforcement activities of agencies like the Securities and Exchange Commission have atrophied down to almost nothing. In the nineteenth century it was *caveat emptor* – let the buyer beware. Then, especially with the New Deal, we got a modest dose of *caveat vendor* – let the seller beware. But now we are back to *caveat emptor* again, with a vengeance. The historical memory of the pathetic losers of 1929 and 1968-1982 has been completely erased.

FUNDAMENTAL INVESTMENT LIMITATIONS

Until the end of the 1980s, many investment company funds voluntarily renounced risky trading practices like margin buying, leverage, selling short, and writing options and other derivatives. These limitations were sometimes reflected in the fund prospectus. During 1990 and 1991, most mutual funds reversed these policies and informed their shareholders that they were setting out once again on these risky paths. In August of 1991, for example, the Fidelity New York Tax-Free Money Market Portfolio changed its ground rules so as to be able henceforth to "lend any security or make any other loan" up to one third of its assets. This meant that the fund stood ready to lend shares for a fee to short sellers who contracted to give the same shares back later. But if the shorts were wiped out, as sometimes happens, the fund might face serious losses. Here was a new risk added to that inherent in the securities the fund bought.

The process culminated on February 19, 1992, when a last group of nine Fidelity mutual funds instituted drastic changes in their by-laws. In practice, the changes meant that these Fidelity funds were lifting their own previous regulations banning margin buying, selling short, investing in the stocks of uncertain newly launched companies, and buying shares in mutual funds owned by other companies. These "fundamental investment limitations" were now formally discarded. Fidelity presented these changes as a matter of adjusting Fidelity's own methods to the methods that had become standard practice in the mutual fund "industry." [Christensen, vii] In a narrow sense, that was true.

DERIVATIVES

Having been forewarned about the deadly danger of derivatives, the first thing a prospective mutual fund buyer will want to know is if the mutual fund in question trades or holds derivatives. One brokerage house in the Washington, DC, area has already realized that intelligent investors fear derivatives like the plague. Their radio advertising for their proprietary mutual funds features a promise of "no derivatives." But this is not enough. What is their definition of a derivative? Does it include repos, as well as structured notes? Naturally you will want carefully to read the fund prospectus, the additional statement of information, and the most recent annual report. But, by the late 1990s, the prevarication of some fund managers mean that you may not be able to trust what you read. One of the most experienced and realistic writers on the mutual fund mania is Donald Christensen, the author of *Surviving the Coming Mutual Fund Crisis*. Christensen sees clearly that the "weird instruments" of the derivatives world have added an incalculable new dimension of risk for mutual fund investors. He also points out how mutual fund managers are now attempting to conceal the presence of derivatives in their portfolios: "Actually, mutual fund promoters' games for hiding involvement with derivatives had already been perfected by 1993. Some fund managers who used the securities simply unloaded them just before the date when they were required by law to disclose holdings of the funds' portfolios. Then, as soon as the reporting date had passed, the managers went right back into the derivatives fracas." [Christensen, 127]

Writers on derivatives also point out that mutual funds have been dabbling heavily in the new high-risk derivative products: "According to a recent study performed by the Investment Company Institute, the most common derivatives owned by mutual funds are forward foreign exchange contracts, inverse floating-rate securities (mortgage and non-mortgage based), interest-only mortgage derivatives, principal-only mortgage derivatives, and structured notes." [Tanya Styblo Beder in Lederman and Klein, 174]

Among the worst offenders on the derivatives front are the so-called personality funds or superstar funds. These usually employ as their icon some investment guru whose acumen is a Wall Street legend. Personality funds can and do use such derivative techniques as options and futures, thus opening the pandora's box which we reviewed in the previous chapter. We need merely recall here that writing options always entails the possibility of unlimited risk. Some personality funds also use leverage, meaning that they borrow money to speculate on stocks, and thus incur debt service on the money they borrow, which increases the expense ratio or costs of running the fund.

SECURITIZATION AND JUNKIFICATION

For about a quarter of a century the Government National Mortgage Association, commonly known as Ginnie Mae, has been packaging home mortgages together into interest-bearing bonds that can be bought and sold. The Federal Home Loan Mortgage Association, the Federal National Mortgage Association, Student Loan Marketing Association, better known as Freddie Mac, Fanny Mae and Sallie Mae, do the same with their paper. Now the same process is being repeated with car loans, equipment leases, promissory notes, and the like. Sears securitizes receivables for its Discover card. General Motors Acceptance Corporation, which finances car purchases, makes its auto loans into bonds. This produces a bond that may seem remarkably safe until something goes wrong. Such dubious paper is now pervasive in the world of mutual funds.

In September-October of 1998, when the Long Term Capital Management hedge fund imploded, the market for securitized debt of all sorts became highly illiquid, greatly alarming the Greenspan cabal at the Fed. The interest rate spreads between Treasury bills and securitized debt gaped to enormous proportions, indicating that "the market" considered the securitized instruments very risky indeed. The interest rate cuts of September-October 1998 were undertaken to some degree in order to avoid the possible collapse and disintegration of these junkified markets. Within a few weeks, federally-backed Fannie Mae and Freddie Mac securitized debt instruments had bounced back somewhat, but securitized mortgage and credit card debt that lacked the federal guarantee remained nearly impossible to sell.

Let us now review the various types of mutual funds, and the peculiar risks inherent in each.

AGGRESSIVE GROWTH, GROWTH, GROWTH AND INCOME, CAPITAL APPRECIATION, MAXIMUM CAPITAL APPRECIATION

An early example was the Dreyfus Leverage Fund, which started in 1968. This is now called the Dreyfus Capital Growth Fund. During the 1974-75 stock slump, growth and income funds declined by 39.3%, growth funds by 48%, and aggressive growth funds by 46%. One widely-read handbook on mutual funds has this to say about aggressive growth funds: "The object of aggressive-growth funds is maximum capital gains. For that reason, they tend to invest in promising new companies or in old companies whose stock prices have been beaten down but seem poised for a comeback. The managers of these funds don't concern themselves with dividend income. They may also use riskier trading techniques than more conservative funds do, such as option writing, short selling, and buying on margin." [Daugherty, 18] At this point, alarm bells should be sounding.

During the late winter of 1997, a prominent newspaper carried a description of the strategy of a well-known aggressive mutual fund, specifying that "The fund can also make bets against companies by 'short-selling' their stocks, or selling borrowed shares it doesn't own. In this strategy the fund makes a profit if it pays less to replace the borrowed shares than it received when it sold them. About 2% of the fund's assets are invested in this way." [*Washington Post*, February 23, 1997] It is our duty to point out once again that short selling exposes the short seller to a risk which is theoretically without limit.

The same article in the *Washington Post* revealed that the American public was shifting more and more money into stock funds, traditionally thought to be more volatile than bond funds. An official of MFS Fund Distributor Inc. commented that "There's been a real shift away from conservatively managed accounts to equity over the past five years, and it's really accelerated with the bull market," said this official, who added that almost 60% of all contributions to 401 (k) retirement plans are going into stock funds, up from 45% in 1990. More and more retirement money is flowing into riskier mutual funds. The *Washington Post* offered the following comment: "Buying highflying stocks pays off in a market like today's, when the best returns can be found in equities. The concern is that when the stock market rally ends, retirement plans may be vulnerable." Indeed.

Another problem with Aggressive Growth Funds is the tax consequences of the way gunslinger managers may tend to react to a market decline. They may begin to sell their best holdings to maintain their "beat-the-market" performance statistics. This creates capital gains for which you will be taxed. But at the same time more dubious stocks remain in the fund, so the net asset value declines. If you stay in, you will be paying capital gains on an asset that is declining in price. Need we say more? This became a prominent issue during the market decline of the third quarter of 1998, as we describe below.

Then there are balanced funds, which are theoretically half invested in stocks and the other half invested in bonds or preferred stocks. It sounds like a good defensive strategy: the stocks go up with the stock market, but if the stock market declines the bonds will be more stable and may benefit from flight to quality buying. But balanced funds still declined by 29.3% in during the 1973-74 stock market dip. Equity income funds concentrate on stocks that offer current income through the dividends they pay. Normally, their holdings should include the stocks of older, better-known, and established companies, such as those on the Fortune 500 list. But that guarantees precisely nothing in a crash, and equity income funds were down 30% in 1973-74.

TREASURY BOND FUNDS

As we will explain in a later chapter, if you are going to hold any paper at all, make sure that it is United States Government paper backed by the full faith and credit of the most powerful government on the planet. Treasury securities are very convenient to own directly. Why incur the leverage and derivatives risk and extra expense of working through mutual fund managers and lawyers? If you want Treasuries, own them yourself. Treasury funds sometimes contain zero-coupon strips, which represent the face value of Treasury securities from which the periodic interest payments have been separated. The face value will be paid at maturity by the Treasury, but in the meantime the zero-coupon strip can fluctuate wildly, depending on the expectations of inflation.

BOND FUNDS ,CORPORATE BOND FUNDS

Bonds are supposed to be more conservative, less speculative, and more reliable than stocks. Bond fund prospectuses throw around terms like "fixed income." But this does not mean that the investor is guaranteed a fixed income. "Fixed income" is merely a Wall Street jargon term for bonds, often junk bonds. So read the label carefully, and beware.

Truth in labeling never arrived in the land of corporate bond funds. Under current law a bond fund can advertise itself as holding only investment grade bonds, while in reality its holdings include 35% of junk bonds. Junk bonds are high-risk bonds that have last call among bondholders on the assets of a company when they are sold off on the bankruptcy auctioneer's block. Junk bonds pay higher interest than investment grade securities, but that higher interest comes nowhere near recompensing the holder for the astronomical risk of default. Nobody in their right mind wants to hold junk bonds in the even of a panic. Other funds may advertise themselves as holding only bonds of the highest investment grade. But even in this case 20% of the bonds could be pure junk or derivatives. Junk bond funds, we recall, tanked by almost one third during the junk bond crisis at the end of the 1980s; some junk bond funds were down by one half. Many bond funds have entered into derivative contracts of the "inverse floater" type. Recall that these are derivatives in which the value of the contract goes down when interest rates go up, and vice versa. Inverse floaters were a favorite ploy of Orange County Treasurer Robert Citron. As derivatives, they are poison. Other bond funds buy interest-only strips (IO's), another volatile instrument.

Another example of bond fund risk emerged in July 1994 when the Paine Webber Short-Term U.S. Government Securities Fund sustained heavy losses from its "structured notes," derivatives based ultimately on home mortgages. The structured notes crashed because of Greenspan's interest rate hikes after February 1994. The fund managers found that the structured notes were highly illiquid and could not be sold. Paine Webber bailed out the fund to avoid a flight from its other funds. In 1989-1990, the Putnam High Income Government Trust experienced a wave of redemptions related to the options that had been used to enhance the yield of this fund.

MUNICIPAL BOND FUNDS

Municipal bonds funds confront you with the risk that a major American city or county will default. New York City underwent a serious financial crisis in 1975. In 1994, Orange County California provided the biggest municipal bankruptcy in US history. Other jurisdictions have suffered horrendous losses from dabbling in derivatives, hurting their bondholders severely. Washington DC would already be bankrupt except for its draconian Financial Control Board and the hope of a federal bailout. Such losses will be multiplied through the effects of leverage and derivatives. But, even more disturbing, municipal bond funds often buy more exotic types of instruments including "demand notes," which entitle the holder to receive the principal on demand at any time. They also buy "put bonds" which entitle the holder to receive the principal sum of the underlying security at specified times. These bonds are more risky than bonds without these features. Need we say more?

INDEX FUNDS

Index funds are supposedly mutual funds that mimic stock averages like the Standard and Poor's 500 stock index. But fund managers often cannot resist the temptation of souping up their fund so that it will do better than the average and thus beat the market. The usual means of souping up such a fund are derivatives.

MORTGAGE-BACKED BOND FUNDS

As with all securitized paper, when you buy these you are assuming the risk that the seller of the bonds does not wish to face. Ginnie Mae prices went down by 6% in 1987 and 2% more in 1988. Mortgage-backed securities also experienced a severe decline in 1992-1993, when Greenspan lowered interest rates. Many homeowners who were sick and tired of mortgage usury re-financed their home mortgages at the new lower rates, so the price of mortgage-backed securities went down. To prevent this, some mortgages now actually impose a penalty for early repayment, but this "prepayment risk" remains. These instruments are paper based on paper, and thus qualify as derivatives. Flee them.

INTERNATIONAL AND GLOBAL FUNDS

International and global funds face two very severe risks. One is the tremendous volatility of international exchange rates, which can easily gyrate by 50% in a year or two. Such fluctuations will heavily impact the results. The other problem is the emerging markets mania, leading to investments on the Mexico model. These investments have once again fared poorly during the Asian and Russian crisis if 1997-98.

MONEY-MARKET FUNDS

These are supposed to invest in commercial paper, short-term government and agency securities, and certificates of deposit. A money market mutual fund is not the same thing as a money market checking account in a bank. The bank money market account is insured by the Federal Deposit Insurance Corporation, but the money market mutual fund is not. In these times, this makes the risk far too great. But suppose a money market mutual fund advertises that it invests solely in United States Treasury securities. This can also turn out to be deception. Many of these funds enter into repurchase agreements or "repos." A repo is a contract between two parties under which one party will sell a security to a counterparty and then buy it back on a set date at a set price. The seller is paid for the sale. The buy-back price is usually higher than the original sale price, which can be thought of as interest on the money which the seller gets to use. Repos were one of the obsessions of Robert Citron of Orange County, California. They are derivatives, and must be avoided like the plague. So if your money market mutual fund engages in repo deals with banks and brokerages, you assume the risk that the bankruptcy of these latter will blow out your fund, even though the US Treasury itself may still survive intact.

Other money market mutual funds may concentrate on Ginnie Mae, Sallie Mae, and Freddie Mac bonds, which the US Government guarantees slightly less emphatically. But again, all bets are off if these securities are used in repo operations, which bring in all the risk implied by bankrupt brokerages and insolvent banks. In 1989, Integrated Resources defaulted on about $1 billion of commercial paper, $23 million of which was held by money market funds of the Value Line group; Value Line ate the losses to maintain confidence in its funds. In March 1990 the Mortgage and Realty Trust defaulted and soon went bankrupt. Ten money market funds were left with an exposure of $75 million to the bankrupt firm. T. Rowe Price, which had invested the largest portion of this, paid $65 million to buy back the bankrupt paper from the individual funds involved.

FUNDS OF FUNDS, MULTIFUNDS

A mutual fund that does not hold stocks or bonds, but rather buys the shares of other mutual funds, is an idea that goes back to that picaresque plunderer, Bernie Cornfeld. A fund of funds brings the investor the worst of all possible worlds, especially if one multifund holds shares in other multifunds. As soon as two levels of mutual funds are involved, you have a pyramid of a certain type. You no longer have paper based on paper. You have paper based on paper based on paper. The impact of leverage, derivatives, short selling, margin buying, and all the rest are multiplied. That may be good when the market is rising, but it spells woe to the vanquished when the market is falling. If you buy such shares on margin, then the loaded gun of reverse leverage in several forms will be pointed at your head.

CLOSED-END FUNDS

Closed-end funds were revived during the Reagan bubble of the 1980s, although they still represent a small minority of investment companies doing business. Open-end funds supposedly enjoy a greater stability of capital, since their investment capital does not increase when their shares are bought, and does not shrink when shares are sold. Closed-end funds generally do not redeem their own shares; these are bought and sold on the NYSE, the Amex, or the NASDAQ. Like other stocks, most closed-end funds can be bought on margin, which further multiplies the risks faced by the investor in a crash. The manager of a closed-end fund can supposedly plan more effectively because it is certain how much capital there will be to invest through the year.

Because of this feature, the closed-end funds do not grow to the gigantic size of the open-end mutual funds like Fidelity Magellan or the others. Closed-end funds generally trade at a discount to the net asset value of the stocks, bonds or other assets they own. This means that if the assets of a closed-end fund are $100 million, the total value of the shares of the closed-end fund may amount to $85 million or to $90 million, but very seldom to the full $100 million. Very rarely, a closed end fund's total stock may be worth more than the net asset value of its holdings. In that case it is said to be trading at a premium. The fact that closed-end funds typically trade at a discount is an insoluble conundrum for fund technicians, but it plainly reflects doubt about the stability of investment trusts, doubt which has never evaporated after 1929. The underlying shares are worth less, and not more, when they are packaged as a closed-end fund. The closed-end fund is riskier than the stocks themselves. Mutual funds avoid this embarrassing moment of truth by redeeming their own shares themselves according to their calculation of net asset value. So they support their own shares by buying them back. A number of closed-end funds use options and futures to try to enhance the risk/reward characteristics of their holdings. The use of derivatives should be reflected in the fund prospectus, but here there is room for many ugly surprises since derivatives are pervasive in today's world of finance.

CLOSED-END LEVERAGE

By 1993, about half of all closed-end funds were employing some type of leverage. Another kind of closed-end fund is the dual-purpose fund, which bears an uncanny resemblance to many pre-1929 investment trusts. The dual-purpose fund is supposed to provide both capital gains and current income. In order to do this, the dual fund issues two kinds of stock. The capital shares, otherwise called common stock, receive the results of any capital appreciation or depreciation. The dual purpose fund also issues preferred stock. Probably to avoid the cathexis of 1929, the dual purpose funds like to call their preferred stock "income shares." These income shares are entitled to receive the dividend income earned by the entire portfolio, but do not get any benefit from capital gains. The preferred share income pool must also support the entire expense of running the fund. These income shares often have a fixed date of expiration at which time they will be paid off and redeemed. The rate of return on the income shares is often very attractive, since they are getting most of the dividends produced by the entire portfolio. [See Fredman and Scott, passim]

TARPLEY'S LAW

This is our old nemesis from the 1920s – leverage. Although closed-end mutual funds are small potatoes, their structure lets us restate and re-stress some points about leverage which are valid for today's global house of cards. The leverage of such a dual purpose fund can be calculated by dividing the total value of the fund (income shares plus capital shares) by the value of the capital shares alone.

Thus:

$$\text{leverage} = \frac{\text{value of capital shares plus income shares}}{\text{value of capital shares}}$$

Taking the case of Joe Blow's Closed End-Fund, which has equal amounts of income shares and capital shares for a total of $200 million:

$$\text{leverage} = \frac{\$200 \text{ million}}{\$100 \text{ million}} = 2$$

Taking the reciprocal of 2, we get 1/2, which is the amount the market must decline to make the capital shares worthless. Let us call this Tarpley's law. Tarpley's law applies to mutual funds as well. We are expounding it under the heading of closed-ends funds because the income shares of the closed-end funds make it possible accurately to quantify at least part of the leverage used in the fund, and this makes the illustration of the law more understandable. The income shares have a fixed value at redemption. When quants look at a dual purpose fund, they see the purchase of a capital share as the purchase of an option to buy the entire portfolio of the fund by redeeming and paying off the income shares. The dual purpose fund is thus a derivative not just by being a stock certificate based on stock certificates, but by being itself an option. It is a derivative two times over, and that spells big trouble. The leverage embodied in such a fund will multiply the capital gains for the capital stockholders if the securities in the fund portfolio go up. But with falling values for those securities, reverse leverage will set in. If the dual purpose fund has equal amounts of income shares and capital shares, then if the market goes down by one half, the capital shares will be approximately worthless. So dual purpose funds are not a good idea if a crash looms on the horizon.

LEVERAGED MUNICIPAL BOND FUNDS

Municipal bond funds have been popular in the past because of their manifold tax advantages. The Orange County bankruptcy of December 1994 now casts these bonds in a less favorable light. There are also closed-end funds that invest in municipal bonds, and these are often leveraged. Many muni bonds closed-end funds issue preferred stock equal to 30% or 40% of the total capital of the fund. If the preferred stock equals 40% of the fund value, then according to Tarpley's law a market decline of 60% will devalue the common shares by 100%, thus making them worthless. (If the fund has dabbled in other financial tricks, they will be worthless even sooner.) And there are other ways that these leveraged muni bond funds can be eroded. If both long term interest rates and short term interest rates rise, then the payments to the preferred shareholders would rise, but the net asset value of the common shares would fall by an amount reflecting the leverage.

EMERGING MARKET CLOSED-END FUNDS

Some of the most visible of the closed-end funds trading over the last few years on the stock exchanges have been the country funds, which tend to invest in the securities of a single foreign nation. Some of these funds were able to obtain spectacular returns for a year or two by investing in countries like Mexico, Brazil, Argentina, Indonesia, India, Hungary, Poland, and other developing countries. The greatest successes came in the so-called merging markets, generally formerly communist or protectionist countries. Given the lessons of 1997-98, it ought to be evident that these emerging markets are extremely risky, and must be avoided.

REDUCTIO AD ABSURDUM

One of the original selling points of mutual funds was that they offered simplicity. You chose a mutual fund in order to avoid having to find your way in the bewildering labyrinth of the stock market, where thousands of issues were bought and sold. But now there are over 7000 investment funds – actually 12,771 if you are rich enough to be able to include hedge funds in the selection. This is almost three times the number of stocks that trade on the New York Stock Exchange. For the small investor, mutual funds are now more confusing than stocks. And remember that if you buy mutual fund shares, you will be charged an average of almost 1.5% per year of your entire investment for the privilege of being thus confused. It makes one nostalgic for the days when banks were willing to pay you interest on your money.

REDEMPTION RISK

All of the factors mentioned so far combine to establish a palpable risk that if you attempt to cash in your mutual fund shares during the coming financial crisis, your fund may be in default. Notice also that many mutual funds have the right to delay giving you your money back for seven full days. In addition, many funds now have provisions written into the fine print allowing them to repay you "in kind." This means that you may not get cash, but shares of stock or some other paper asset that is allegedly equal in value to your shares at the time of redemption. Put these two practices together and you have a chilling combination. Suppose a panic breaks out and prices begin to collapse. You demand redemption of your shares, but your fund invokes the seven-day waiting period. During the seven days, stock prices are decimated. At the end of the waiting period you are presented with shares of stock that were equal in value to your fund shares on the day you redeemed them, but which are now worthless. This is yet another reason to conclude that mutual funds are not a good bet for the very stormy weather that is now headed our way.

SAVINGS AND RETIREMENT

There are plenty of books designed to help individuals manage their 401 (k) retirement plans, which are IRS-qualified, defined contribution retirement plans designed to provide employees with some retirement income. The amount of contributions is pre-established, and the risk of the final payoff is borne exclusively by the employee. Contributions to the plan are tax-deductible in the year they are made, and no tax need be paid until the future time when the benefits are received. Sometimes the money that you put into the plan is your money only. Sometimes the employer also makes a contribution to your plan, such as matching half of your contribution.

One critical issue we need to examine here is HOW the 401 (k) money is to be invested. Some plans allow you to invest only in the stock of the company you work for. Sometimes only money market mutual funds can be bought. More often you are offered a choice, typically by the mutual fund company or other asset management company that your employer has designated to manage the plan. Usually there are three or four choices, often including a Guaranteed Investment Contract (GIC), mutual funds of various kinds, money market funds, and perhaps other stocks or bonds.

Take, as a sample, the 401 (k) plans being offered to the employees of a medium-sized eastern state. This plan offers only variable options, meaning that you are required to choose among mutual funds and mutual funds only, with the only variation being aggressive, moderate, and conservative risk. This is far too narrow and far too risky, even in the allegedly conservative variant. Why not offer US Treasury bonds? Why not offer the bonds of the state in question, which will at least be free of state and local taxes? The reason is clearly that it is more lucrative for the company which manages the state's 401 (k) operations to limit the choice to mutual funds, even though these may be far more risky for the employees hoping for retirement income.

Another option offered in many 401 (k) company retirement plans is a guaranteed investment contract. These are inherently unacceptable. Remember the worries of pensioners who depended on checks from First Executive Life Insurance Company of California and Mutual Benefit Life Insurance Company of New Jersey when these two firms went bankrupt in 1991.

When Mutual Benefit failed in the summer of 1991, it caused a whiff of panic among the holders of tax-exempt mutual funds. Mutual Benefit was also the insurer of John Nuveen & Company's Nuveen Tax Exempt Money Market Fund. Mutual Benefit was supposed to guarantee that the Nuveen shareholders could redeem their shares. This threat soon receded, but insurance companies today are loaded with derivatives, so things will be much worse in a future crash.

The asset management company that runs the 401 (k) program in our medium-sized eastern state may also dun you each year for their services. Now this sounds like a mere bagatelle, but it could mean more than one-half of one per cent of your total assets in the plan will be skimmed off, year after year after year. If you get to $10,000, they will be taking $55 every year, or rather $66, since the state board of trustees also have an annual asset fee. Add in a $12 flat fee and shell out $88 - not a sum to throw out of the window for no reason. If you work for 20 years and keep contributing, this bite could climb into the thousands of dollars. At the end of a few decades, such fees will make a very noticeable difference in your final asset total. Magnanimously, the asset management company promises not to demand more than $1,000 per year for its services, however large your account. The issue of mutual funds fees has been little discussed as long as the market was rising.

As mutual funds began reporting losses in 1998, many mutual fund holders began to wonder why they were paying fees for managers who are losing money.

Even a humble certificate of deposit has the advantage that the bank still pays you interest on money that you in effect lend the bank. The bank is not yet brazen enough to demand a fee from you for the bother of taking your money – for savings, at least. And, the CD is FDIC-insured, which may mean less than it once did, but is still a whole lot better than the mutual funds, where you are out in the cold and on your own if the funds default. Your problem is that most of the time the instruments offered by 401 (k) plans are inherently extremely risky in a time of convulsions like the present and future. Forget about mutual funds, GICs, stocks, and corporate bonds, be they junk or investment-grade. In the wake of a collapse and disintegration, if you are left holding paper from Joe Blow's Highly Leveraged Mutual Fund, you are going to be out of luck. The only paper that can even be considered are United States Treasury securities that engage the full faith and credit of the United States government – Treasury bonds and notes, and United States Savings Bonds. In the coming environment even these are a form of speculation – a bet that the US government will muster the will to come up with the money to honor its own solemn promises. Since the autumn of 1995, when Rep. Gingrich and Sen. Dominici flirted with US government default in their failed bid to ram through their budget, the faith and credit of the United States have been somewhat tarnished. But United States bonds remain the only kind of interest-bearing paper that you could even dream of holding as we go towards the twenty-first century. Everything else is just fluff.

The managers of the 401 (k) plan engaged by the boss are likely to be instinctively hostile to US Treasury securities. That is because there are far fewer commissions, fees, and other extra charges for them here. But if you opt out of the boss's 401 (k) plan, then you may be losing whatever money he was willing to put into your retirement plan. That is obviously a painful choice, but opting out completely may be preferable to pouring your own good money down the sinkhole of soon-to-be-worthless paper investments. Tell the boss you want to be a saver, not an investor. Demand the obvious: include US Treasury and US Savings bonds in the company plan, including the new inflation-indexed Treasury bonds and US Savings bonds. State bonds may also make good sense, especially for tax purposes in high-tax states.

Finally, recall that as of 1993, your employer has no liability whatsoever for the activities of the management company which runs your 401 (k) plan. Your employer also has no liability for what happens to the hard-earned money you have entrusted to the mutual fund which are offered under the plan. The mutual fund sales pitch may sound convincing, but when the bottom falls out of the market you and you alone will be left holding the bag. All of this has obvious implications for your personal Individual Retirement Account (IRA). Here at least you are the one who makes the choices. Confine yourself to US government instruments; they are already risky enough.

The terrible third quarter of 1998 provided a better late than never object lesson in the dangers of mutual funds. Investors who had not paid attention to a whole battery of fees and charges when the funds were increasing in value began to find them intolerable when values were going down. Mutual funds also showed they could do what a stock or bond generally could not: inflict a capital gains tax liability despite falling share prices. This is because the tax liability of the owner of mutual fund shares is determined not by the fund's Net Asset Valuation, but rather by the capital gains which are realized by the fund's asset manager during the year. James Glassman cited the example of the Oakmark Small Cap Fund, which by the end of October 1998 was trading at $13.32, down 22% on the year. This fund showed a capital gains distribution of $2.86 per share in the year to date. This meant that the fund manager had been compelled to sell stock which had realized gains in order to provide cash for redemptions at a time when many other stocks were falling. Glassman calculated that a small investor in the 20% tax bracket who owned 1000 shares of Oakmark would end up owing $582 in capital gains taxes on an investment on which they had lost about $3,350. This was truly a double whammy.[76]

MUTUAL FUNDS AND HEDGE FUNDS

In the mid-1990s there was a flurry of attention to the issue of whether mutual funds ought to be allowed to invest in hedge funds. The answer is a thousand times no, since hedge funds routinely engage in the riskiest of all financial behaviors. There is also the question of whether hedge funds should be eligible to become part of their array of choices for individual 401 (k) plans. This is more insanity: make sure your retirement assets are safely invested directly in US government paper. The only thing to do with hedge funds is to ban them, under the most draconian criminal sanctions. As of 1998, the hedge funds are a ballistic missile that is poised to blow the 401 (k) and IRA accounts of millions of Americans sky high.

---

[76] *Washington Post*, October 29, 1998.

CHAPTER

IV. DESCENT INTO THE MÆLSTROM
THIRTY YEARS OF WORLD FINANCIAL CRISIS

"… I think the financial system we have today is inherently unstable. We need to set up a new system to stabilize financial markets. Otherwise, the repetition of crisis after crisis … is going to result in a major meltdown of the world financial system." – Eisuke Sakakibara, Japanese Finance Ministry, January 22, 1999.

The present breakdown crisis of the world economy is the outcome of the half-century that separates us from the end of the Second World War. Anyone who wants to understand what is happening today must be conversant with this history. If, for example, you are puzzled by the fact that the US dollar currently has the purchasing power of less than 8 cents of the Eisenhower-Kennedy era, it is certainly relevant to know that since the 1960s the greenback has been officially devalued not once, but twice, in addition to the many unofficial reverses inflicted by "the market." It is certainly relevant to know that the beginning of the rapid decline in US standards of living coincides with Richard Nixon's decisions of August 15, 1971, which signaled the beginning of the end of an international monetary system worthy of the name, and that these decisions were precipitated by anti-American actions by the British government.

In September 1939, the US was still mired in depression, with the New Deal depression of 1937 compounding the previous collapse of 1929-33. Official statistics indicated 10 million jobless, but the real figure, as the war showed, was over 20 million. As FDR admitted in 1937, over a third of the nation was ill-fed, ill-clothed, ill-housed. Lend Lease, beginning months before Pearl Harbor, was the turning point.[77] By 1944, unemployment had been virtually eliminated, with ten million men and women entering the labor force. Eleven million were in the armed forces, and twenty million in war production. Five million new civilian jobs had been created.

Between 1941 and 1945, the gross national product more than doubled. By 1944, US war production was equal to about double the total war production of the Rome-Berlin-Tokyo axis. In 1945, the US possessed about half of the war production in the world. This included production for US forces, plus war materials given outright to the USSR and the UK under the Lend-Lease Act.

By one estimate, the materials given away were enough to equip 588 armored divisions, or 2,000 infantry divisions, according to US standards. This included 28,000 jeeps, 219,000 trucks, and 12,000 tanks given to the Soviet Union. A new synthetic rubber industry was created to replace the natural rubber lost in the Pacific. The war effort also included the multi-billion dollar Manhattan Project, which was the high-technology leading edge of the war effort, and which produced, not only the atomic bomb, but also the celebrated atomic pile built under Stagg Field at the University of Chicago by Enrico Fermi, the first development of peaceful uses of nuclear energy, the key to the economic development of the post-war world, and a source of new production that could pay for the war many times over, if it were universally implemented.

---

[77] See Chapter XI.

US LIVING STANDARDS ROSE IN FDR'S WAR MOBILIZATION

In the midst of all this, the civilian standard of living improved, apart from certain wartime shortages, with real weekly wages in manufacturing up 53% from 1939 to 1945. Farmers enjoyed federal price supports which Roosevelt set at 110% of parity, with a 23% increase in farm production, increased yields per acre, and a much bigger output per man hour because of increased mechanization.

The first key to this tremendous accomplishment was the dirigistic nature of wartime credit policy. The most typical form of this was the Emergency Plant Facilities Contract. Companies wanting to finance the expansion of war plants were guaranteed the repayment of their expenditure by the War Department in a series of five yearly payments. By an Act of Congress of October 9, 1940, war contractors were authorized to borrow money at once on the basis of these contracts from banks and from the Reconstruction Finance Corporation. All war contracts were guaranteed by government agencies and given the right to instant guaranteed credit. Each war production contract had a vendor number, by which the contractor could secure immediately the needed working capital from a local bank. The Federal Reserve was required to honor this contract for rediscount, if necessary. This privilege extended not only to the primary contractor, but also to sub-contractors and sub-sub-contractors. The credit needed to finance all war production was thus guaranteed down to the level of the last washer, of the most humble component part. In the case of contracts to buy from foreign vendors, as for example in the realm of strategic metals or other production, the procedure was the same. Anyone, anywhere in the world, who wanted to sell something that the US Federal government wanted to buy, was sure to find the financing he needed, by virtue of that federal government decision. In addition, the tax laws were altered so that investments in wartime plant and equipment made by plant owners would be written off through depreciation in just five years – the equivalent of a federal mandate for technological progress so rapid that the plant would be considered obsolete in slightly more than that amount of time.

The Defense Plant Corporation, a branch of the Reconstruction Finance Corporation, spent more than $8 billion directly on building new plants, which were then leased to private companies who operated them, and in many cases later bought them. By virtue of that $8 billion spent, the Defense Plant Corporation by 1945 was the direct owner of about 10 per cent of total US industrial capacity. In total, $23 billion was spent during the war on new plants, with $17 billion spent by the federal government directly. The US machine tool park has never looked so good in the years since, and in a very real sense the country has continued all along to live on that wartime investment in plant and equipment. This work was all supervised by federal agencies like the War Production Board, which had final authority to assign all US production. Thus, in times of crisis, when survival was at stake, the ideological ballast of free enterprise and free trade was jettisoned.

Was the federal defense program inflationary? Inflation was kept within acceptable bounds by price controls, but the astounding aspect is the low level and stability of interest rates, despite government borrowings to pay about half the cost of the war, which could not be paid even from the increased tax revenues and the expanding tax base. By the end of the war, the US public debt was at the all-time high of $257 billion dollars as a result of necessary wartime borrowing. Yet, the average interest rate on this debt was at 1.94%, less than two per cent and less than the average interest rate on the public debt in 1929, which was 2.53%, or in 1919, when it was at 4.2%. This was accomplished by Roosevelt's *de facto* nationalization of the Federal Reserve, making the Fed a support agency of the Treasury for marketing US government bonds. The Treasury was interested in a cheap supply of abundant lending to market its war bond issues, and a deal imposed on the Fed before the war started forced the Fed to toe this line.

THE NEW DEAL STATE

The prewar New Deal had introduced lasting changes into the structure of US society and government. One advocate of a return to the New deal ethos recently described the New Deal as "progressive-populist." In this view, the New Deal "defined the modern mixed economy. It added the idea of macroeconomic management by the federal government, as well as direct federal spending in a variety of areas dedicated to the betterment of the common American. It included a social-democratic welfare state, and a dose of economic planning. It contained a salutary whiff of class warfare whenever 'economic royalists' sought to resist its forward momentum. The political genius of the New Deal and of subsequent approaches that carried forward the 'progressive-populist' tradition was that it provided redistribution and social justice *via inclusion.* Social security and medicare, public schools and college loans, starter homes for families and low-rent housing for the elderly were never programs described as taking from the haves to give to the have-nots, though they have sometimes had that result. They defined needs – secure retirement, decent medical care, opportunity for home ownership or for good education – that applied to a substantial majority of the electorate. They made very clear that there was more to civic life than a giant marketplace in which buyers and sellers were free to choose and free to loose. It was this conception of the society, market, state, and polity that made Democrats the majority party." [Kuttner 7] There is surely no need to give the British any credit for these accomplishments, as Wallace Peterson does. Keynes sneered at Roosevelt's grasp of economics, and at Bretton Woods did everything possible to cut short American postwar prosperity by putting London usury back in control.

FDR'S DE FACTO NATIONALIZATION OF THE FED

A vital part of the New Deal mix was FDR's control over the Federal Reserve. The nationalization of the Fed embraced the three areas of its activity: open market operations, the discount rate, and reserve ratios. All were set to maximize productive efficiency for winning the war, not for maximizing the opulence of a narrow class of wealthy investors. In its Open Market operations with government securities, the Fed was obliged to buy enough of each issue to guarantee that it be sold at full par value, with an interest rate structure as determined in advance by the Treasury. A typical wartime yield pattern was:

0.38%	for 3 month Treasury bills
0.88%	for 12 month Treasury bills
2%	for ten-year Treasury bonds
2 1/2%	for twenty-year Treasury bonds

A LOW YIELD GOVERNMENT SECURITIES STANDARD

The long term bonds, with a higher interest rate, were just as liquid as the three-month bills, so banks tended to buy more and more of the long-term government securities, resulting in a very stable, long-term debt structure. The liquidity of all Federal securities was guaranteed by the Fed policy of standing ready to buy any and every US Treasury security at full face value at all times, from any customer whatsoever. These securities were funded at par. As one discontented monetarist remarked about this arrangement:

> The Federal Reserve became in effect a slot machine that would always pay off; anyone could insert into it an unwanted government obligation and receive in return an amount of money equal to the support price. Such a policy put us on a type of monetary standard that might accurately be called a 'low yield government security standard,' for the central bank stood ready to monetize unlimited amounts of these obligations at virtually fixed prices.

Since FDR's system was so successful, what could be the basis of this objection? Perhaps that the general welfare, and not private greed, was the main criterion followed. Interest rates were kept pegged at their desired levels by the Fed Open Market Committee. As just noted, the net effect was the monetization of the public debt, the turning of government bonds into a completely liquid new form of money. The discount rate was kept at one percent, although the rate in practice was at one half of one percent for discount transactions involving short-term government obligations. The reserve ratio of the Fed in terms of gold required for issuing Federal reserve notes - paper money - was lowered by Congress in June 1945 from 40% gold to 25% gold.

FDR'S ECONOMIC BILL OF RIGHTS, 1941-44

The great President Franklin D. Roosevelt, in the waning days of World War II, sought to make his legacy of economic recovery and human dignity irreversible with an Economic Bill of Rights, which he fully intended to anchor in the Constitution. FDR had begun to consider a codification of the economic rights of the American people in his State of the Union address delivered on January 6, 1941, in which he proclaimed the celebrated Four Freedoms. The Four Freedoms were later partially included in the US-UK Atlantic Charter signed by Roosevelt and British Prime Minister Churchill on warships off the coast of Newfoundland in August 1941.[78] The Four Freedoms, to all intents and purposes, constituted the political platform for which the US was about wage war. For Roosevelt, the economic rights were an elaboration of the Four Freedoms, which he enumerated as follows in the State of the Union Address of January 6, 1941:

> In future days, which we seek to make secure, we look forward to a world founded upon four essential human freedoms.
> The first is freedom of speech and expression – everywhere in the world.
> The second is freedom of every person to worship God in his own way – everywhere in the world.
> The third is freedom from want – which, translated into world terms, means economic understandings which will secure to every nation a healthy peacetime life for its inhabitants – everywhere in the world.
> The fourth is freedom from fear – which, translated into world terms, means a world-wide reduction in armaments to such a point and in such a thorough fashion that no nation will be in a position to commit an act of physical aggression against any neighbor – anywhere in the world.

Roosevelt then proceeded from the concept of the Four Freedoms to then begin an enumeration of specifically economic rights, which can also be considered as part of the program for which US servicemen were shortly to fight and die. This part of the 1941 State of the Union speech is worth citing at length:

> Certainly this is no time to stop thinking about the social and economic problems which are the root cause of the social revolution which is today a supreme factor in the world.
> There is nothing mysterious about the foundations of a healthy and strong democracy. The basic things expected by our people from their political and economic systems are simple. They are:
> Equality of opportunity for youth and for others.
> Jobs for those who can work.
> Security for those who need it.

---

[78] Churchill later refused to respect the Four Freedoms in India and in other parts of the British Empire.

The ending of special privilege for the few.

The preservation of civil liberties for all.

The enjoyment of the fruits of scientific progress in a wider and constantly rising standard of living.

These are the simple and basic things that must never be lost sight of in the turmoil and unbelievable complexity of our modern world. The inner and abiding strength of our economic and political systems is dependent upon the degree to which they fulfill these expectations.

Many subjects connected with our social economy call for immediate improvement.

As examples:

We should bring more citizens under the coverage of old age pensions and unemployment insurance.

We should widen the opportunities for adequate medical care.

We should plan a better system by which persons deserving or needing gainful employment may obtain it. [*New York Times*, January 7, 1941]

In his State of the Union message of early 1944 FDR called for an economic Bill of Rights which would have made full employment for all, and not the wealth of a few, the lodestar for postwar American economic policy. FDR proposed to recognize that Americans had the "right to a useful and remunerative job." They also had, as FDR stated, "the right to earn enough to provide adequate food and clothing and recreation." For FDR, the rights of Americans included the right of every family to a decent home, to adequate medical care, to a good education, and to protection against fears of economic insecurity as a result of old age, sickness, injury, or unemployment. The State of the Union Address of January 1944 is cited at the conclusion of this book as the towering matter of unfinished business facing this nation, stressed and repeated by Roosevelt in 1941 and again in more detail in 1944, but which so many professors and pundits have mysteriously chosen to forget.

Because the moral and intellectual giant FDR was followed by dwarves like Truman, none of this ever made it into the US Constitution. This turned out to be an embarrassment for the US in the Cold War against the USSR, since Stalin's prewar Soviet constitution was more progressive in spelling out and enumerating – at on paper – the economic rights of the individual, without which political rights are reduced to hollow shells.

THE GI BILL OF RIGHTS

In 1944, Congress enacted the GI Bill of Rights, which provided benefits for some 15 million returning veterans. The veteran was guaranteed federal unemployment compensation of $20 per week for as long as one year if needed to make demobilization smoother. The government would guarantee the veteran a loan of $2,000 for the purpose of buying a home or starting a business. There were payments for job training and college education for up to four years, with reasonable allowances for tuition, books, and living expenses. The GI Bill did for the veteran, and to some degree for the entire American middle class, what the Homestead Act of 1862 had done for the farmer and for the West in general. Home ownership and a college education for the first time became hallmarks of middle class status. After the death of FDR, the best that could be accomplished was to get the US government committed to the "maximum feasible" level of employment in the Employment Act of 1946. The White House Council of Economic Advisors was first created by this bill in order to help the President pursue the goal of full employment, and the Joint Economic Committee of the Congress was constituted to assist the Congress in the same effort.

MARCH 1951: THE FED DEFIES TRUMAN AND WINS

There was precious little the monetarists of the Fed could do to assert their pernicious ideas as long as Roosevelt was alive. At the end of the war, only 4.7% of the Federal budget was allocated for debt service. As long as FDR lived, the Fed was brought to heel under these arrangements. At the outbreak of the Korean War in 1950, Secretary of the Treasury Snyder attempted to re-impose the wartime arrangements on the Fed for the duration of the conflict. The Fed revolted in the name of fighting inflation, "sound money," respect of market forces and of the need to "execute monetary and credit policy," all in conformity with the ambitions of Wall Street and London, who desired a return to massive usury. Snyder and Truman announced that the Fed had agreed to continue to maintain the stability of prices and yields on government securities, but this understanding was promptly repudiated by Chairman McCabe of the Fed with the support of Marriner S. Eccles, the outgoing chairman. Eccles appealed for the respect of the independent status of the Fed, which he argued ought not to be degraded to the status of a "Treasury bureau." The media flayed Truman and Snyder, who promptly caved in. Despite the declaration of a state of national emergency over Chinese entry into the Korean War, the Fed let the interest rates on government securities rise, and refused to subordinate itself to the needs of the Treasury. The capitulation to the bankers of the Truman Administration, as deleterious in its own way as the cashiering of General Douglas MacArthur about one month later, was formalized in the so-called Accord of March 4, 1951, more appropriately described as an outrageous Wall Street stab in the back in time of war.   The implacable march of monetarism at the Fed had resumed.

THE FED SENDS INTEREST RATES INTO ORBIT

Maverick Texas Democratic Congressman Wright Patman proposed a law to force the Federal Reserve Open Market Committee to keep government securities at par value, thus keeping interest rates down, but he was unable to secure passage. McCabe soon quit and was replaced by William McChesney Martin, a friend of the City of London and of the Bank for International Settlements. Patman complained in retrospect that "the Federal Reserve would spend the next ten years sending interest rates in orbit." But even then, the monetarists did not get their way completely. The landmark Defense Production Act of 1950 imposed very specific obligations on the Fed in the generating of credit for defense industry. The following is a quote from the 1963 *The Federal Reserve System Purposes and Functions*, issued by the Fed itself:

> Another part of the fiscal agency activities of the Federal Reserve Banks is their work in connection with the so-called 'V-loan program.' This program, authorized by the Defense Production Act of 1950 and implemented by Regulation V of the Board of Governors, is an arrangement to assist competent contractors and sub-contractors who lack sufficient working capital to undertake defense contracts for the production of essential goods and materials. For this purpose the Departments of the Army, Navy, Air Force, Commerce, Interior, and Agriculture, the Defense Supply Agency of the Department of Defense, the General Services Administration, the National Aeronautics and Space Administration, and the Atomic Energy Commission are authorized to guarantee loans made by commercial banks and other private financing institutions. The Reserve Banks act as fiscal agents for the guaranteeing agencies in connection with such loans. (275)

Only with the end of the Cold War at the beginning of the 1990s did the fed succeed in breaking totally free of all latent obligations to use monetary policy for the national interest.

BRETTON WOODS: LORD KEYNES AGAINST THE USA

The main features of the postwar economic system were established at Bretton Woods, New Hampshire, in 1944. The US delegation was led by Harry Dexter White of the Treasury Department, who was later accused of being the Alger Hiss of the Treasury; perhaps he had rubbed the British the wrong way. Keynes attempted to make the centerpiece of the new order his so-called bancor, a wholly artificial currency unit to be created under supernational, one-world auspices. Bancor would have in practice enhanced the power of the British in the new system, while reducing that of the United States.

Keynes also wanted countermeasures to limit US exports and to reduce the demand for dollars, which were needed by all countries for postwar reconstruction. Creditor countries that ran a surplus were to be subjected, according to Keynes, to various sanctions and penalties. Of course, there was really only one creditor country likely to run a surplus: the United States. Debtor and deficit countries were to be treated much more gently. Great Britain was the leading member of this category. Keynes wanted provisions to force countries with strong currencies to weaken them with inflation, speculation, domestic consumerism, and tariff cuts. He thus wanted to codify what Lord Norman had gotten Benjamin Strong of the Fed to do for the British during the 1920s. He wanted the US to bail out the rotten finances of the British Empire, while the British kept their Imperial Preference trade war system intact. But US ascendancy proved too great for Keynes to realize his scheme. The dollar was to become the main reserve currency for the world. The best the British could obtain was to keep the pound sterling in the role of a kind of secondary reserve currency, preserving the institution of sterling balances – pound deposits kept in London by the British Empire and later Commonwealth states. However, Lord Keynes' poisonous prescriptions for depleting the too-robust US economy and relieving pressure on the pound have remained in force as the long-term and ultimately successful British approach to cutting the bloody Yanks down to size and for transforming a world economy based on progress through production into the speculative madhouse of today.

Under Bretton Woods, the price of gold as expressed in US dollars was for decades set at $35 per ounce. Only the dollar had a direct gold parity. The gold content of the other currencies was established indirectly, by means of their fixed parities with the dollar. The fixed parities that gradually emerged were intended to be relatively permanent: a pound sterling was to be worth $2.80. The dollar was to be the equivalent of 357 yen, 625 lire, and so on. American tourists learned that there were about four German marks to a dollar, and five of De Gaulle's new French francs. Fluctuations were to be confined to a plus or minus 1 % band. These fixed parities provided the inestimable benefit of price predictability: they meant that international traders would know that dollar-denominated bills of exchange used in international import-export transactions could be expected to vary no more than plus or minus 1% over their three month or six month lifetimes. This feature of Bretton Woods was an important plus for the restoration of world trade, which had been sapped by a chaos of floating rates and hot money after the British default on gold payment of September 1931.

Under Bretton Woods, the United States was expected to buy and sell gold in settlement of international transactions. If the United States ran a payments deficit with the rest of the world, then the rest of the world might ask for settlement in gold at the rate of $35 per ounce. When Roosevelt sent the Bretton Woods Treaty to the Senate for consideration in February 1945, he repeated his prophecy that "this generation of Americans has a rendezvous with destiny." Roosevelt told the Congress that the Bretton Woods pacts "spell the difference between a world caught again in the maelstrom of panic and economic warfare or a world in which nations strive for a better life through mutual trust, cooperation, and assistance." In retrospect, the new world monetary system constituted one of the most important positive results of World War II. Bretton Woods, flawed as it was, proved indeed to be one of the turning points of modern history.

The Bretton Woods treaty passed the United States Senate on July 19, 1945 by a vote of 61 to 16. One of the isolated band of nay-sayers was the isolationist "Mr. Republican," Senator Robert Taft of Ohio, who denied that twentieth-century wars have economic causes, and who warned that Bretton Woods would make the US into an international Santa Claus.

THE ANGLO-AMERICAN LOAN OF 1946

The end of World War II revealed the catastrophic weakness of the British imperial position, despite the exertions of Anglophiles in the US government to shore up London with largesse from American taxpayers' pockets. For several decades, Britain was the Sick Man of Europe. When Lend-Lease was terminated in September 1945, the British were "plunged into an immediate financial catastrophe." [James, 63] London sent Lord Keynes across the Atlantic again in hopes of putting the touch on Uncle Sam. The British were treated with great generosity: first of all, they were relieved of their theoretical obligation to make payments for the Lend-Lease assistance they had received during the war. In addition, the British were given an immediate postwar loan of $3.75 billion, probably the largest sum ever lent at one time in world history up to then. (If the same money had been offered to the USSR for purposes of economic reconstruction, there would have been no Cold War. There also would have been no postwar US economic decline, since the Soviets would have used the funds to place orders for capital goods with American factories, something the British had no intention of doing on the same scale. But, with Truman in the White House, no postwar loan was every extended to Moscow.) This loan was repayable over 50 years at 2% interest. But there were some conditions attached: the British had to promise to stop stalling on the ratification of Bretton Woods, and they had to agree to make pound sterling convertible one year after they got their money. The British were expected to abandon the policies of imperial preference, which had been keeping out US exports and strangling growth in India, Australia, and the smaller colonies. Of course, the British had promised to do most of this in order to receive Lend-Lease deliveries in the first place. Now they extorted a second round of US payments to repeat the same pledges.

THE BANK OF ENGLAND TARGETS BRETTON WOODS

The British took the American money, which was used to finance a series of imperialist financial political-military measures aimed at keeping the Empire intact. But opposition to Bretton Woods remained loud. C. F. Cobbold, the deputy governor of the Bank of England, urged the government to "snap our fingers at the Americans and develop the sterling area," meaning the Empire. Right-wing Tories joined with liberal imperialists and with anti-American left-wing Laborites (then in power in the Clement Attlee government) in opposing the new monetary system.

In July 1947, the British attempted to restore the convertibility of the pound sterling by lifting all exchange controls. This proved to be a fiasco. Sterling reserves turned into flight capital and fled the country. After just six weeks, London was forced to re-impose exchange controls. The Bank of England was happy, because they had wanted all along to keep exchange controls in place. Thanks to this debacle, the British were able further to postpone restoring the convertibility of the pound. Part of the game was to maintain the so-called sterling balances kept in the City of London. These sterling reserve accounts were nominally set up in the name of the various British colonies around the world. Of course, India and Jamaica would have been glad to use these sterling balances to buy capital goods from the United States. But that would have produced a pound glut on world currency markets, sinking the pound. So to avoid this and to keep the vaunted status of the pound as a reserve currency, the British were determined to keep the sterling balances in London.

The summer of 1947 marked the beginnings of the Marshall Plan, a program of US credit to promote European economic recovery, reduce unemployment, and prevent Western Europe from being ingested by Stalin. The British received the lion's share ($3.16 billion) of the Marshall Plan credit, which they once again wasted on measures to shore up the Empire, plus old-fashioned illegal flight capital. France received $2.8 billion, and had mediocre results. $1.53 billion went to the Benelux states. Other countries, like Germany ($1.41 billion) and Italy ($1.52 billion), used their much smaller credit facilities together with technological investment and hard work (in which the British ruling class had no interest) far more wisely to promote industrial recovery. Germany developed was called a "social market economy" (*soziale Marktwirtschaft*), in which continued private ownership of the means of production was combined with collective bargaining guarantees and an eventual institutionalization of the role of labor unions in plants. Much inspiration was drawn from the social doctrines of the Roman Catholic church, which had stressed since Pope Leo XIII that property rights are not absolute, but are accompanied by social responsibility. West German recovery was assisted by dirigistic, government-backed revolving development financing provided by the state-owned Kreditanstalt für Wiederaufbau, while Germany, contrary to popular belief, retained a considerable state-owned sector.

In 1947, Soviet Foreign Minister V.M. Molotov stormed out of the Paris founding conference of the Marshall Plan. Eight Soviet satellites – Albania, Bulgaria, Czechoslovakia, Finland, Hungary, Poland, Romania, and Yugoslavia – joined Moscow in rejecting an Anglo-French invitation to take part in the plan. Together with these eight nations, Moscow also opposed the Marshall Plan by means of the Communist Information Bureau (Cominform), a warmed over communist international based in Prague. The satellite economies were bound to the USSR through the Molotov Plan, and the Soviet bloc effectively dropped out of the Bretton Woods system. In 1948, the US, UK, and French zones of occupied Germany implemented the currency reform which gave birth to the D-Mark, the highly successful postwar German mark. Although the credit for this new currency was often attributed to Ludwig Ehrhardt, the D-mark had actually been designed by some unsung US occupation administrators.

ANGLO-AMERICAN RELATIONS DIVERGE

The American Executive Director of the IMF, Frank Southard, asserted that the British should be considered ineligible to draw dollars from the IMF because they were still using exchange controls. British representatives snarled that "we were not prepared to tolerate interference by the Fund in our affairs. This exercise would therefore probably end in a stalemate... [with] Anglo-American relations continuing to diverge." [James, 94] Cobbold threatened that the British would consider pulling out of the IMF if the pound were undermined by leaks to the press. On September 19, 1949, the British devalued the pound sterling by 30% after a period of running a trade deficit. Many of the British elite saw this as just one more competitive devaluation of the pound designed to continue the beggar-my-neighbor policies of the 1930s. The British devaluation was copied by the sterling area and by Norway, Sweden, and Denmark, with France, Germany, Belgium and Portugal devaluing by lesser amounts.

1950-1962: THE FLOATING CANADIAN DOLLAR

At the same time that the British devalued, they tightened their exchange controls and trade restrictions. The British financiers also used their Canadian Commonwealth government in order to signal their fundamental hostility to fixed parities. The Canadian dollar cut loose from its Bretton Woods parity and began to float in 1950. This float was to continue until 1962. According to the official IMF history of the Bretton Woods system, the Canadian float "constituted a rather powerful advertisement for the attractions of floating." [James, 99]

LONDON WEAKENS BRETTON WOODS

During the 1950s, the British - despite their devaluation - were still unwilling to lift exchange controls on the pound and accept responsibility for keeping their currency within the Bretton Woods fluctuation bands. In other words, the British still rejected convertibility at fixed parities. They were given aid and comfort by Milton Friedman, who wrote his opening attack on fixed parities (including the European Payments Union, the ancestor of the European currency snake) in 1953.[79] One genial British idea for avoiding fixed parities was called the ROBOT Plan, which appeared in 1952. ROBOT proposed a wider band of fluctuation than Bretton Woods did: the British wanted to fluctuate between $2.40 and $3.20, equivalent to plus or minus 33% ! This was a mockery of fixed parities and bands of fluctuation. One commentator noted that with ROBOT, the British "proposed to subvert the one aspect of Bretton Woods – mutually fixed exchange rates – which had not remained a dead letter." [James, 99] ROBOT was also an attempt to subvert the fixed parities of the European Payments Union.

In 1958 no less a personage than the Governor of the Bank of England spoke as follows: "It would be prudent to organize monetary policy both at home and abroad, on the probability that something like a unified floating-rate policy is inevitable but to make no attempt to force the pace until it becomes more acceptable to the Western world as a whole." [James, 99-100] This remarkable statement makes plain the policy of subverting the Bretton Woods system which the British were relentlessly to pursue for many years, and which finally allowed them to bring down the system in 1971. Why did the British do these things? The official IMF history of Bretton Woods comments that "floating attracted the Bank of England because it would allow greater room for interest rates as an instrument for the control of the domestic UK economy." [James, 100]

The British refused to agree to convertibility at a fixed exchange rate until after the Suez crisis of 1956 had brought the Empire to the verge of collapse. At this point, the British needed US support to get their hands on some $738.5 million which they wanted to withdraw from the IMF. Getting British troops out of the Suez canal region of Egypt and finally accepting convertibility at a fixed rate were the two pre-conditions for obtaining the support of US Treasury Secretary George Humphrey.

In the case of France, the politicians of the Fourth Republic were forced to suspend convertibility in 1946, and were never able to re-establish it. These politicians borrowed $262.5 million from the IMF in connection with the 1956 Suez crisis. But restoring convertibility at par value was left to President Charles De Gaulle. After De Gaulle assumed power, he and his economic adviser Jacques Rueff were able to reset the parity for the French franc on December 27, 1958. In other words, the French had been unable to fulfill the Bretton Woods requirements until the European Economic Community had already started to function, which it did in January, 1958.

---

[79] See Milton Friedman, "The Case for Flexible Exchange Rates," in *Essays in Positive Economics* (1953).

THE IMF AND THE ROOTS OF IMMISERATION

A sinister aspect of the Bretton Woods Treaty was the creation of an International Monetary Fund, originally thought of by many as a lending facility for countries experiencing currency instability. The IMF took its place as a key part of the supernational bureaucracy of the United Nations. When the IMF was created, a large part of its staff came directly from the British Colonial Office in London, and these new supernational functionaries brought along their characteristic monetarist and anti-development mentality. The IMF was empowered to demand a letter of intent from countries seeking to borrow money from the Fund. That letter of intent was supposed to contain the country's plan for putting its financial house in order. In order to get the loan approved, the letter of intent had in practice to contain the "conditionality" demanded by the IMF, which was generally based on monetarist domestic austerity, and later (in the era of structural adjustment) came to include the litany of economic globalization and privatization. France was humiliated by having to submit to IMF conditionalities to get a standby IMF loan in 1956. Over the years, most developing countries have been through the IMF mill several times.

It is important to note that there are no known cases of a "happy ending," in which the IMF's conditions actually led to economic progress. Italy and the British themselves went through this same mortifying process during the mid-1970s, and IMF officials have made clear that they do not regard the United States as immune from surveillance and conditionalities. All in all, the IMF has been one of the institutions most destructive of world economic development. Towards the end of the 1980s, Egyptian President Hosni Mubarak estimated that fully half a billion persons had lost their lives as a direct result of IMF conditionality; he cited the fact that the IMF's recipes consistently depleted levels of expenditure for public health, hospitals, clean water, sewage treatment, and related items. According to Mubarak, these forms of IMF austerity had claimed about 50 million lives each year over the previous decade.

There was also an International Bank for Reconstruction and Development, called the World Bank for short. Here the lending was supposedly for specific development projects rather than for currency stabilization. Before too long the World Bank was preaching a strange gospel of "small is beautiful", and "appropriate technology", meaning that large-scale infrastructure had to be shunned in favor of projects based on obsolete technology, deemed more becoming for backward nations. By 1990 the World Bank was being accused of "technological apartheid" by spokesmen for the developing sector.

THE BIS AND NAZI FINANCE

An international network of private central banks acted in close cooperation with the IMF. The focus of this network was the Bank for International Settlements in Switzerland, originally founded under the Young Plan to facilitate reparations payments by Germany to the Allies after World War I. After Hitler had illegally conquered Czechoslovakia, the BIS had agreed to deliver Czechoslovak gold deposits into the hands of the Hitler regime. The BIS during the 1930s had been a hotbed of pro-Nazi sentiment, but this did not prevent the BIS from resuming its role as the (privately owned) central bank of central banks – although, for political reasons of plausible denial, the New York Federal Reserve district and not the Fed Board of Governors in Washington purchased the United States seat at the BIS. The BIS monthly meetings in Basel have represented an important coordination point of international high finance, always in a monetarist key.

The resulting system appeared to express the hegemony of the US dollar, with an appropriate niche being provided for the sickly British pound sterling. In reality, Anglophile sentiment was very strong among central bankers, whose occult fraternity had been founded during the 1920s by Sir

Montagu Norman of the Bank of England. The center of gravity of the US Federal Reserve was its New York branch, from time immemorial a bastion of the House of Morgan, itself the *longa manus* of London. The dominant mentality of the entire postwar system was thus very much tinged with British oligarchical ideology.

The evolution of the US economy under the Bretton Woods-Federal Reserve arrangements was never idyllic. In 1945, Stalin had assumed that when the war ended, the capitalist world would sink back into the depression that had been ended by the Lend-Lease program and its related credit apparatus instituted early in 1941. Stalin accordingly thought that it would be in the US interest to maintain full employment by granting the USSR a generous economic reconstruction loan, which would translate into capital goods orders to US factories. Stalin was dismayed when the new Truman administration, under the influence of W. Averell Harriman, a member of the Churchill inner circle, not only refused to provide such a reconstruction loan, but even ordered an early cut off of Lend-Lease deliveries (which FDR had been using to bootleg reconstruction goods into Russia, circumventing Congressional prohibitions).

The result was approximately what Stalin had expected: with war production winding down, and with the demobilization of millions of GIs glutting the labor market, the US went into an ugly downturn during 1945-46. In 1949 there was another slump. Economists, afraid that even pronouncing the word "depression" might bring back the horrors of the 1930s, coined the term "recession" to denote these periodic valleys in the postwar business cycle. During these years Truman's Harrimanite advisers, like Clark Clifford, maneuvered Truman into attacking labor unions as a way of beginning to break up the FDR - New Deal coalition, which was the possible basis of a nationalist consensus in favor of the economic development which the bankers did not want. Truman's role as willing saboteur of the New Deal national constituency coalition explains the high regard in which this venomous little man is held today by establishment academics.

THE GREAT STRIKE WAVE OF 1946: TRUMAN ASSAILS THE FDR COALITION

During World War II, American labor unions had generally honored a wartime no strike pledge. When the war ended, the unions were stronger than ever before, with substantial memberships and cash on hand to pay strike benefits. The mood among demobilized GIs was an angry and radical intolerance for the plutocratic special privilege which had remained pervasive on the home front. The leading financiers were anxious to organize a wave of anti-union reaction, as they had after World War I. A key part of this offensive aimed at breaking the close ties between the Democratic administration and the labor unions. Roosevelt advisor and labor leader Sidney Hillman had been so influential in the defense production mobilization that "Clear it with Sidney" had become a byword in the federal bureaucracy.

By the end of January 1946, 1 million American workers were out on strike. There were strikes in coal, oil, and steel, and railroads. During 1946 there were over 5,000 strikes. British social democrat Roy Jenkins describes Truman's response to the great strike wave of 1946 as a "fairly wild programme of temporary seizure of the industries by the federal government." [Jenkins 84] According to Robert Donovan, "In one year [Truman] had seized the coal mines twice; he had seized the railroads, he had seized 134 meat-packing plants; he had seized ninety-one tugboats; he had seized the facilities of twenty-six oil producing and refining companies; he had seized the Great Lakes Towing Company. And all he had on his hands now was disaster." Truman, who was given to transports of great rage that were played on by his handlers, in May 1946 composed a raving speech in which he called for the breaking of the labor movement and even executing some of its leaders. "The effete union leaders receive from five to ten times the net salary of your President,"

Truman wrote. "Every single one of the strikers and their demagogue leaders have been living in luxury, working when they pleased. I am tired of government's being flouted, vilified.... Let's give the country back to the people. Let's put transportation and production back to work, hang a few traitors, make our country safe for democracy, tell Russia where to get off and make the United Nations work." This amounts to a chilling recipe for American fascism, and it is closer to what Truman really thought than what he said in his public speeches. "Big money has too much power and so have big unions," he wrote to his mother and sister on January 23, 1946. "Both are riding for a fall because I like neither."

The turning point came when Truman openly assumed the role of strikebreaker in May 1946. The 400,000 members of the United Mineworkers' Union went on strike on March 31, 1946. Many miners went back to work when Truman seized control of the mines, but 164,000 defied him. On May 23, 1946 the locomotive engineers and trainmen walked off their jobs. Shutting down the national rail transportation system. On Saturday, May 25, Truman called on Congress to give him the authority to draft the striking railroad workers into the army and force them to work under military discipline. Truman wanted to seize industries, and to slap labor leaders with injunctions and contempt proceedings if they resisted. He wanted criminal penalties for those who refused what amounted to slave labor. It would have been the most draconian labor law in American history. Truman delivered his speech in the House chamber before a Congress gripped by anti-union frenzy. He got the greatest ovation of his entire term in office when, after reading a note from his handler Clark Clifford, he announced that the railroad union leaders had capitulated. Reagan's breaking of the PATCO strike was in this great tradition. In December 1946 Truman broke a strike by John L. Lewis' mineworkers, hurling US labor into headlong retreat. None of this, it is safe to say, would have happened if Roosevelt had been alive.

Truman's status as a puppet president was widely known during his time in office, and was an object of public derision. In foreign affairs, Truman did what he was told to do by Averell Harriman and his cronies, including Dean Acheson, Robert Lovett, and John J. McCloy. In domestic matters, he listened to Harrimanite Clark Clifford and his self-styled Monday-night group. Clifford recounts in his memoirs that at the annual dinner of the Washington Gridiron Club in 1947, "with President Truman watching, one of the skits showed him as a ventriloquist's dummy sitting on the lap of a smug, heavily made-up Clark Clifford. I was profoundly upset...." [Clifford, 96] The Harriman bank had supported Hitler, and it was now making labor policy for the United States. The FDR-New Deal coalition was fatally weakened. The 1946 takeover of the Congress by resurgent reactionary Republicans was only possible because of Truman's wild and flailing attacks on the labor movement. This was the GOP Congress that overrode Truman's veto to pass the Taft-Hartley law, which rolled back many gains made by labor under the New Deal.

EUROPEAN RECOVERY AND THE MARSHALL PLAN

The Marshall Plan of 1947 provided the minimal credit mechanisms necessary to re-start production in war-shattered Europe. The currency parities were rigged in such a way as to permit the victorious dollar to buy up plants and labor at depressed prices, and then realize a handsome profit on the resulting new production. By 1949, the industrial and agricultural production of western Europe again exceeded the 1938-39 prewar levels. But German labor was slow to realize improvements in its standards of living: it was only at the end of the 1950s that the German standard of living surpassed the prewar level of 1938-39, which itself reflected more than a decade of downward pressure on wages by Bruening and then by the Nazi regime. Many of the improvements associated with the Marshall Plan were in fact due to initiatives by clever economic nationalists who achieved much with limited means, such as the certain West German circles and the Italian group around Enrico Mattei. In terms of funding, the British always got the lion's share of Marshall Plan dollars. In any case, the ability of the dollar to command the wealth of western Europe by means of favorable currency parities was one of the essential features of the postwar years.

The origins of the Korean War of 1950-53 are a complicated story of British-sponsored geopolitical intrigue (see www. tarpley.net for details), but the economic impact of this conflict was clearly to establish a large-scale, permanent defense production sector which managed to hold on until the early 1990's. The wave of inflation that swept through western Europe, followed closely by German re-armament, provided a powerful stimulus to further European recovery.

1953 RECESSION: US EXPORTS STAGNATE

Back in the US, the winding down of the Korean War was accompanied by another recession in 1953. The way in which the economy recovered from that downturn showed that the seeds of future disasters were now present. Eisenhower thought that he could avoid mass unemployment through useful initiatives like his federal highway program, which built the network of interstate parkways. But Ike and his liberal Republican administration did not realize that in order to be lasting, the US recovery needed to be export-led, with capital goods shipments into the developing sector or "Third World." During the 1950s, the tendency of US business as influenced by Federal Reserve policies was to focus on the US internal market while abandoning third world markets to the recovering Western Europeans and Japanese. The end of Marshall Plan assistance to western Europe in 1952 accentuated this inward orientation of US business, which came to regard the US domestic market as its exclusive preserve. The Big Three auto makers arrogantly assumed that they could produce inferior motor vehicles with "built-in obsolescence," and oblige American consumers to go on buying them indefinitely. The folly of this policy began to become evident by the end of the 1950s, when Volkswagen and other foreign producers began to penetrate the US domestic car market by offering sturdy and economical cars, without the trendy yearly model changes pioneered between the wars by General Motors.

The Wall Street elite, not the government, were the ones who had decided that with the end of Marshall Plan exports to Europe, the US would de-emphasize capital goods exports to the outside world. The Wall Street financiers were willing to build up western Europe and Japan as a barrier against Stalin and the Red Army, but they were not willing to promote real scientific, technological, and economic development in the countries now merging from the colonial yoke. The Wall Street elite tended to agree with the British imperialists on these matters, and the British were attempting to perpetuate colonialism and underdevelopment with all means at their disposal. The decision to apply the brakes to US capital goods exports after about 1953 was one of the most important strategic turning points in the postwar history of the United States, since it did much to determine the shape of the entire postwar world by guaranteeing the eventual collapse of the Bretton Woods system, thus prefiguring the trends which produced the globaloney era of the 1990s.

The partial recovery of the US economy after 1953 was based on the revival of consumer demand, sustained above all by installment-plan debt. This made things look relatively prosperous on the home front: many families were now able to afford to own a car – at least for some months, until the impossibly large balloon note used to finance the purchase came due and the finance company repossessed. More ominously, the failure of the United States aggressively to market its capital goods to the rest of the world limited third world development. The stagnation of US hard-commodity exports to the rest of the world meant that demand for dollars was much weaker than it might have been. The third world was anxious to buy, but unable to do so. A credit facility along the lines of a super Export-Import Bank would have been the solution.

DOLLAR OVERHANG AND EURODOLLAR MARKET

In most of the 1950s and 1960s, the US continued to run a trade surplus with the rest of the world, but US foreign investment plus US foreign aid and military activities were so large that the US balance of payments was veering into red ink by the end of the Eisenhower years. Some of these dollars were redeemed for US gold, but others accumulated in London in the form of a permanent Eurodollar market which was set up in 1959 with the help of monetarist Guido Carli of the Bank of Italy. This Eurodollar hot money market revived London (which had been dead as a doornail during the early 1950s) as a financial center. For the US, it was a grave loss of national sovereignty, since the US government had no control over the Eurodollar banks that were dealing in US currency. One effect was to speed up US inflation.

Economist Robert Triffin was preaching during these years about what he claimed was the main internal contradiction of Bretton Woods. The world, Triffin said, was anxious to possess US dollars to use as reserves for generating new credit. These US dollar balances abroad (xenodollars, we would say today) were likely to increase relative to US assets. This xenodollar overhang would then lead to instability, with the foreign holders of dollars fearing a devaluation of the dollars relative to gold. In other words, Triffin foresaw that the US liquidity ratio, understood as the relation between US gold stocks and outstanding dollar liabilities, would decline. Triffin's answer to this so-called "Triffin dilemma" was to go back to Keynes and his supernational "bancor" currency unit proposed at the Bretton Woods conference of 1944. As we have argued, the real answer to Triffin's dilemma would have been high-technology US capital exports to the developing sector, which would have created a new and massive demand for dollars, repatriating more and more of them. But Wall Street had already rejected this alternative.

THE 1957 RECESSION: END OF US POSTWAR EXPANSION

The expansion of US domestic consumer credit proved impossible to sustain. By 1957, a severe economic recession had taken hold. Some thought that a new depression was at hand. A more realistic view was that the US recession, while serious, would remain within limits. US banks and corporations would survive, thanks in part to their earnings in western Europe and Japan, where the surge of postwar economic reconstruction still had several more years to go. Western Europe would eventually run out of steam during the middle sixties, as signaled by the Italian recession of late 1964 and the German recession and labor troubles of 1966-67.

The Italian recession of autumn 1964 marked the beginning of the end of the *miracolo economico*, which had been enhanced by the nationalist economic policies of Enrico Mattei, a former leader of the anti-fascist resistance. Mattei's Ente Nazionale Idrocarburi (ENI) provided the methane that fueled the early stages of the Italian recovery, and then set out to make Italy independent of the British-dominated Seven Sisters oil cartel. Mattei offered Arab countries like Egypt and Tunisia one half of the profits of oil development on their territory according to his celebrated "fifty-fifty" formula. Third world nations were comfortable with an Italian presence which was unlikely to turn into neocolonialism, as it might with some of the stronger European states. Mattei also sought similar opportunities for ENI in the Soviet sphere. In all this Mattei was challenging the designs of London, and MI6 remains the chief suspect in his October, 1962 assassination.

In West Germany, the downturn had been preceded by the overthrow of Christian Democratic Chancellor Konrad Adenauer by a coterie of his CDU party which included Helmut Kohl. This "regicide" faction was taking advantage of the aftermath of the *Spiegel* affair of 1963. A report published in the newsmagazine *Der Spiegel* claimed that the West German armed forces – the new

Bundeswehr were only partially capable of defending the country. Defense Minister Franz Josef Strauss ordered the *Spiegel* offices to be raided, and the blowback forced Strauss's resignation. After the fall of Strauss, it was only a matter of time until Adenauer followed, to be succeeded for a time by the monetarist ideologue Ludwig Ehrhardt. By 1966-67, German postwar upswing, the so-called *Wirtschaftswunder*, had lost considerable momentum. By 1967, German influentials like Theo Sommer and others were of the opinion that West Germany could no longer maintain high levels of economic growth by exporting automobiles, but needed to begin exporting nuclear energy plants and other capital goods to the developing countries .Monetary crisis and the lack of a suitable credit mechanism prevented this highly realistic perspective from being pursued.

THE GOLD DRAIN HITS FORT KNOX

During 1960, $2 billion of US gold stocks were purchased by foreign monetary authorities. A large part of that money was invested by US banks in Germany, which was running a large trade surplus; German reserves rose by $2.2 billion during the year, much of which was short-term hot money attracted by a possible revaluation (up-valuation) of the German mark. At the same time, the price of gold in London, which had hovered near the US Treasury selling price of $35.0875, jumped up into the $38-40 range. Late in 1960, the US and seven other nations launched the gold pool, a consortium of central banks that stood ready to support the dollar by selling gold on the open market.

The economic deterioration of the United States was slowed and even partially reversed by the Kennedy Administration, despite the presence of monetarists like C. Douglas Dillon at the Treasury. Kennedy was fundamentally a dirigist, dedicated to using the powers of the Presidency forcefully to advance the economic progress of all the people. His investment tax credit helped to accelerate new capital investments in plant and equipment. His NASA moon program provided a science driver which, by producing new technologies like the silicon chip and innumerable others, created $10 of new economic activity for every dollar spent on the program. Kennedy was distrustful of the Federal Reserve attempt to a secure a monopoly on the printing of US currency notes, and was interested in the potentialities of the United States Notes (the descendants of Lincoln's greenbacks), as well as of the Treasury Silver Certificates (which went back to FDR). Kennedy wanted to promote strategic defense against Soviet missile attack, while at the same time offering the Kremlin an olive branch with a policy of peace through strength. Kennedy was striving for a *modus vivendi* with Castro. Kennedy's policies brought the promise of a rebirth of the visibly dwindling American power. Certain aspects of Kennedy's pro-growth policies are illuminated in Donald Gibson's *Battling Wall Street: The Kennedy Presidency*. During his entire term in office, Kennedy was forced to function under the burden of the gold drain – the diminishing US stock of monetary gold which resulted from the more aggressive demands of the foreign central banks to turn in their paper dollars for bullion. Before being elected, Kennedy promised that he would not devalue the dollar in relation to gold.

1965: DE GAULLE URGES A NEW ROLE FOR GOLD

In early 1965, the French Government announced that it intended to convert some of the $300 million it then held into gold. On February 4, President Charles De Gaulle spoke at length about the question of reforming the international monetary system. De Gaulle advocated basing trade relations "on an unquestionable monetary basis that does not bear the stamp of any one country in particular. On what basis? Truly it is hard to imagine that it could be any other standard other than gold, yes, gold, whose nature does not alter, which may be formed equally well into ingots, bars, or coins, which has no nationality, and which has, eternally and universally, been regarded as the unalterable currency *par excellence*.... Certainly the terminating of the gold exchange standard without causing a hard jolt and the restoration of the gold standard as well as the supplementary and transitional measures which will be essential, particularly the organization of international trade on this new basis – all that must be examined calmly." [Solomon, 55]

De Gaulle and his economic adviser Jacques Rueff were correct in asserting that the international monetary system required gold as a means of settling international accounts at the end of each trading period. As De Gaulle said, "The supreme law, the golden rule, is the duty to balance, from one monetary area to another, by effective inflows and outflows of gold, the balance of payments resulting from their exchanges." That much was incontrovertible. The United States needed to liquidate its international balance of payments deficit by gold deliveries. If US gold stocks ran low, then it was time to undertake changes in economic policy, such as a campaign to increase exports. Rueff's goal was to force the US to export enough to remain solvent, rather than flooding the world with paper, and in this Rueff had reality on his side. Finite gold stocks were a way of establishing a reality principle for monetarist officials, of which the US had far too many. For if the US monetarists continued to dominate American policy, the dollar price of gold would have to be increased, or, in other words, the dollar would have to be devalued. (It should be added that if what the French were aiming at was a pre-1914 gold coin standard, in which the money supply is rigidly limited by gold stocks, this would have proven a deflationary and growth-hampering mistake.) During the middle 1960s, various study groups contemplated the problem of the US balance of payments and the Eurodollar overhang, but to no avail.

1. 1967: THE BRITISH POUND STARTS A WORLD MONETARY CRISIS

The breakup of the Bretton Woods system began in earnest in 1967 with the devaluation of the British pound. Despite the postwar devaluation of 1949, the pound sterling had remained the sick man of the entire system, and the currency whose postwar recovery had been the most halting and uncertain. Nevertheless, the British insisted on keeping the institution of the sterling balances – the reserve accounts of their colonies and "former" colonies. In 1964, the era of Tory domination was ended by a new Labour Party government under Harold Wilson, a former pro-communist activist of the 1930s who owed much to Lord Victor Rothschild of the notorious banking family. Wilson's regime applied policies of de-industrialization with the rationale that the quality of life was more important than production or material progress. This was coded language for de-industrialization, which the British were undergoing in any case. The Wilson regime was an important precursor to Lyndon B. Johnson's "Great Society," which had similar premises.

Wilson's focus on the "quality of life" was accompanied by an upward spike in the British balance of payments deficit. Chancellor of the Exchequer James Callaghan promised the United States that the British would not devalue the pound, and the whole issue of devaluation was for a time a taboo in Number Ten Downing Street, where it was labeled "The Unmentionable." During the pound crisis of 1964, George Brown of the British cabinet claimed that there was an international conspiracy by Swiss bankers – the "gnomes of Zürich" – to bring down the pound sterling. Lord Cromer, the head of the Bank of England (and one of the patrons of Henry Kissinger) kept in close touch with William McChesney Martin of the Federal Reserve – the man whom the cartoonist Herblock delighted in depicting wearing a Herbert Hoover style collar.

In September 1965, a group of central banks tried to ambush speculators with a "bear squeeze" designed to punish the smaller fish who had sold the pound short. In the next year, Wilson tried a domestic austerity program, which had no impact on the City of London financiers who were avidly speculating against their own currency. The Bank Rate of the Bank of England, the main line of defense of the pound, was raised by a mere one per cent between October and November. There was no real defense of the pound, only some window dressing.

In November 1967 it was announced that Britain had incurred the largest monthly trade deficit in its history. The British talked about borrowing $3 billion from the IMF, but Managing Director Pierre-Paul Schweitzer turned them down. Schweitzer was notoriously close to London, so it looked like an elaborate charade. The British failed utterly to mount a serious defense of the pound, which would have included raising the Bank of England bank rate to a much higher level to attract funds. On November 17, 1967 the Bank of England made a show of stiff upper lip, spending $1 billion of reserves to keep the pound at its existing parity. The next day, the pound was devalued by 14.3%, dropping its parity from $2.80 to $2.40.

The pound devaluation of 1967 has to be compared to that of 1931. The latter inaugurated a world monetary crisis characterized by competitive devaluations and beggar-my-neighbor policies of cutthroat competition among currency blocs. 1967 had a similar, though less powerful, effect. The pound devaluation focused all attention on the probability of a dollar devaluation. The speculators – many of them British – who had been shorting the pound now turned to shorting the dollar and taking long positions on gold. The Federal Reserve immediately raised its discount rate from 4 to 4.5%.

The British were mimicked in their devaluation by a group of countries in the sterling zone, including Denmark, Iceland, Ireland, Israel, New Zealand, Spain, and others. The notion that the Bretton Woods edifice was ripe for an upheaval thus gained widespread acceptance. 1967 also marks the point at which the postwar growth in American real wages, according to certain measures, began to grind to a halt. Early in 1968, the Johnson Administration imposed mandatory capital controls to reduce the growing gold outflow.

**THIRTY YEARS OF CRISIS, 35 TIMES TO THE BRINK;
THE THREAT OF SYSTEMIC CRISIS EVERY 10-11 MONTHS ON AVERAGE**

Monetary, financial, and economic crises of systemic potential, 1967-1998.

1. Devaluation of the British pound sterling, November 1967, ushering in the world monetary crisis and the final agony of the Bretton Woods system.
2. Run on US Treasury gold stocks, March 1968. This "gold and dollar" crisis occurred because of fears the dollar would follow the pound into devaluation.
3. US default on gold convertibility of the dollar and breakdown of fixed parities, August 15, 1971, ordered by Nixon in response to British demands for $3 billion in US gold stocks.
4. Second devaluation of US dollar, followed by final breakdown of the Smithsonian currency parities, March 1973.
5. First world oil crisis and British domestic collapse, October 1973 - March 1974.
6. Bankruptcies of the Herstatt Bank of West Germany and the Franklin National Bank of New York, June-July 1974.
7. British pound crisis, March-December, 1976.
8. Carter dollar crisis, October-November, 1978.
9. Second world oil crisis, January 1979.
10. Volcker's 21% prime rate and US de-industrialization crisis, 1979-1982; German Chancellor Helmut Schmidt's depression warning and possible brush with US banking collapse, June 2, 1981.

11. Silver Thursday, March 27, 1980: collapse of Hunt Brothers' attempted corner on world silver market, near-bankruptcy of Bache Halsey Stuart Shields.

12. Drysdale Government Securities default, May 17, 1982, Penn Square Bank insolvency, July 4, 982; failure of Ambrosiano Holding, Luxemburg, July 1982.

13. Mexican debt crisis, July-October, 1982 (Volcker's Mexican weekend, August 13, 1982; brush with world banking panic and interbank clearing gridlock, September 7, 1982).

14. Brazilian debt crisis, December 1982 – November 1983.

15. Panic run on Continental Illinois Bank, May - July 1984.

16. Volcker "Superdollar" deflation and final destruction of US export industry, July 1984 – March 1985.

17. Ohio and Maryland bank and S&L panic, March-May 1985.

18. Collapse of oil prices and Mexican debt crisis under De La Madrid, June – September 1986.

19. January-February 1987: Brazil default and debt moratorium, with dollar crisis.

20. American stock market and futures market crash, October 1987.

21. Greenspan dollar crisis, December 1987 – January 1988.

22. Bankruptcy of Drexel-Burnham-Lambert, RJR-Nabisco default threat, Campeau bankruptcy, junk bond collapse, January - February, 1990.

23. Failure of Bank of New England, threatened insolvency of Citibank, Chase, and other US banks, 1990-1991.

24. European Rate Mechanism crisis, September 1992.

25. Second speculative assault on European Rate Mechanism, leading to permanent loosening of fixed parities, August 1993.

26. World bond market crisis, Orange County-Mexico-Barings, February 1994 - February 1995.

27. Japanese banking crisis, August - September 1995; $1 trillion in bad loans.

28. Daiwa Bank threatened by insolvency in wake of $1.1 billion bond trading losses, November 1995.

29. Sumitomo copper futures trading crisis; 31% decline in world copper price, June 1996.
(Crises 30 and following are discussed in Chapter I.)

30. Southeast Asia currency and stock market crisis, featuring Thailand, Philippines, Malaysia, Hong Kong, Singapore, Indonesia, South Korea, with world stock market panic, July - November, 1997.

31. Japanese banking crisis, November 1997.

32. South Korean insolvency crisis, December 1997.

33. Indonesian crisis, November 1997 April 1998.

34. Russian monetary, stock market, and interbank crisis starting in May 1998. Failure of IMF bailout attempt, July-August 1998. Russian default.

35. Long Term Capital Management insolvency with bailout by New York Federal Reserve, starting September 23, 1998. Threat of world banking panic and interbank plumbing freeze.

Based on this record, we can also project the following future crises now on the horizon. Under existing IMF and Federal Reserve policies, these crises may be delayed, but they cannot be avoided. Taken together, the following events constitute the final disintegration of the New World Order dollar-based globalized system of the 1990s:

36. *Latin American stock, banking, and currency crisis, featuring Brazil, Argentina, and Mexico, with US banking crisis, 1999-2001.*

37. *Japanese banking panic.*

38. *European currency crisis with euro collapse.*

39. *Hyperinflationary-hyperdeflationary collapse of the US dollar and of all world paper values; flight to gold and commodities, barter regime, IMF-Fed-BIS insolvency, and disruption of world trade and commodity flows.*

40. *Breakdown crisis of world civilization, with threat of widespread depopulation.*

---

2. MARCH 1968: THE RUN ON US TREASURY GOLD

The pound was no longer the linchpin of the international monetary order, but it was still important enough to bring on the worst international monetary crisis since 1931. When the British defaulted on gold payments in September 1931, the most dramatic immediate consequence of their decision was to start a massive run on US gold stocks, which led to the banking crisis of 1933. In 1967 something remarkably similar happened. Between November 1967 and March 1968, the US lost a staggering $3.2 billion in gold, equal to about 20% of total American gold stocks. International speculators – the New York and London money center banks – began to buy gold, betting that the price of bullion would go up. During 1967 the London gold pool (the US and its seven allies) was forced to sell more and more gold to support the $35 per ounce price. The buying of gold reached a climax in March 1968, and brought the entire international monetary system to the brink of breakdown. The last giant wave of selling started on March 1, 1968, and on March 10 an estimated 900 tons of gold was sold by the pool for about $1 billion. Normal trading in the London market had been about 3 to 5 tons per day. The price of gold in Paris, where the gold pool did not operate, rose to $44.36, well above the $35 Bretton Woods benchmark.

The gold drain was so intense that Washington asked the British to close their gold market on March 15, which they did, although the Paris gold market stayed open. The London market stayed closed until April 1. In the meantime the US and its seven gold partners agreed that their central banks would stop buying and selling gold in the open markets of the world. Instead, they would limit gold dealings to buying and selling among central banks, at an obligatory $35 per ounce. This created a two-tier gold market: one open to all comers, with fluctuating prices, and a second for central bank settlements, at the official $35 parity. US Undersecretary of the Treasury Frederic Deming vowed that this two-tiered system would last "till hell freezes over."

During this crisis, the British pushed the US to devalue the dollar by raising the price of gold. Arch-monetarist Milton Friedman, backed by First National City Bank of New York, was calling for floating exchange rates. The US Congress took emergency action to eliminate the requirement that the Federal Reserve maintain a 25% gold backing for all Federal Reserve notes. Wilbur Mills (D-Ark), the chairman of the House Ways and Means Committee, warned that rejection of this measure "could create the greatest run on our gold stocks that has ever occurred." Senate Republican leader Everett Dirksen (R-Ill) was less agitated, intoning that he did not believe "that the sky is falling, as Chicken Little said." Voices were raised calling for the end of the convertibility of the dollar into gold. One was Senator Jacob Javits (R-NY), who recommended on February 28 that Washington suspend convertibility and shut down the gold pool. The outcome of the "somber and tense" talks among the central bankers was dominated by the fear that a suspension of dollar's gold convertibility would bring back the chaos that followed the British default of 1931.

Robert Solomon of the Federal Reserve seemed pleased that this crisis had contributed to ending the role of gold as an international money. He told the Federal Open Market Committee that the outcome "can be interpreted as constituting a demonetization of gold at the margin.... the monetary authorities of the world...are not dependent on an increasing stock of gold." [Solomon, 123] At the IMF, discussions began about "paper gold" (the later Special Drawing Rights) and measures to make the Bretton Woods bands of fluctuation broader. Among these were the crawling peg, the clean and dirty floats of the 1930s, and other worthless expedients. In the meantime, the final agony of Bretton Woods was approaching.

No sooner had the ink dried on the March 1968 agreements than a dual monetary crisis broke out: international speculators in London and New York bank board rooms perceived that the French franc was too weak for its current parity, while the German mark was too strong for its current exchange rate. Part of this was connected to the destabilization of France experienced in the May 1968 mass upheaval. President De Gaulle called a French devaluation "the worst form of absurdity" and denounced "odious speculation." But the old lion had lost his vim, and he was forced to resign in April 28, 1969. The fall of De Gaulle removed an important obstacle to the plans of certain Anglo-American groups for an end to both fixed parities and gold convertibility.

1969: FIRST D-MARK FLOAT

Currency speculation continued into the spring of 1969. On April 29, 1969 German Finance Minister Strauss talked to journalists about a possible multilateral realignment of currencies, and – since that meant the up-valuing of the D-Mark – set off "the heaviest flow in international financial history," as Robert Solomon put it. Germany was obliged to take in $4.1 billion in foreign currency, especially Eurodollars. The Bonn cabinet loudly announced that they would not revalue the mark, and that this decision was "final, unequivocal, and for eternity." Some dollars began to flow out, but others were holding out for eternity. The new French President Pompidou, a former Rothschild employee, waited until most Frenchmen were at the beach before carrying out a stealth devaluation of the French franc by 11% on August 8, 1969. By the end of the summer, the German cabinet had to revise their "eternal" rejection of revaluation. In an important innovation, they floated the D-mark upward for almost a month before setting a new parity reflecting a revaluation of 9.3%.

During 1970, a new element of chaos was introduced by the British dominion of Canada, which in May launched a permanent, open-ended float of the Canadian dollar. Recall that the Canadian dollar had also floated between 1950 and 1962. Thus, Canadian compliance with the fixed parities made mandatory at Bretton Woods had lasted a grudging 8 years - a good barometer of the hostility of the London oligarchy to government regulation of currency rates. The Canadian dollar has continued to float until this writing. The IMF inaugurated its new Special Drawing Rights, originally billed as "paper gold," and later valued according to the quotations of a basket of 14 currencies. The SDR was reminiscent of Keynes' bancor. (Later, in 1975, the IMF would abolish an official price of gold altogether, leaving only the dubious SDR as an international standard of value. Needless to say, no stable monetary order could be built on a paper chimera like the SDR.)

Inside the US, there was a whiff of panic in the stock market in May 1970 when the Penn Central Railroad expired in bankruptcy and Chrysler seemed about to follow. These events coincided with Nixon's invasion of Cambodia, which detonated an upheaval on university campuses. The May 1970 stock market dip and the subsequent world monetary crises eventually led to the near bankruptcy of duPont Glore Forgan, at that time one of America's leading retail stock brokerages. In later years, the establishment-backed Wall Street financier Ross Perot would tell the story of how he received urgent phone calls in the night from government officials imploring him to save duPont Glore Forgan in order to stop a general panic crash. Perot did agree to undertake the bailout. At the September 1970 IMF meeting in Copenhagen, Pierre-Paul Schweitzer demanded that the US use its gold to finance its deficits so as to head off a further buildup of dollars in foreign hands. This was an unkind cut from the IMF against its ostensible master and set the stage for 1971, the year of the terminal crisis of Bretton Woods.

3. AUGUST 15, 1971: NIXON DISMANTLES BRETTON WOODS

Every great historical event requires two components: it has an objective side and subjective side. Two decades of dollar weakness and US economic stagnation had now created the objective potential for the terminal crisis of Bretton Woods. But the collapse of the old Bretton Woods order also required a subjective ingredient, some considerable force on the historical stage that saw an advantage for itself in pulling down the weakened structure. This subjective ingredient was provided by the British oligarchy and their fellow travelers.

The demolition of Bretton Woods – like the crisis of 1931 – was a deliberate British project which required the joint effort of the British and Commonwealth governments (especially Canada), the Bank of England and its assets in the US Federal Reserve System, and a pro-British clique in the US Treasury around Paul Volcker. Even all this would not have been enough without the pathological folly of Richard Nixon, John Connally, and other generally non-witting US officials.

During 1970, the British held a general election that ousted the Wilson Labour Party regime and brought in Edward Heath and his Conservatives. Heath personally looked more modern and less like a Colonel Blimp than his Tory predecessor, Harold MacMillan. Heath's job as a thespian was to act the part of a good European and thus get the British into the Common Market, which they had been trying to enter since 1963. General De Gaulle of France, who had blocked their entry, had resigned in 1969 and died in 1970. The British were certain they could get their way with the unsavory Pompidou, the Rothschild banker.

Heath brought with him Lord Home of the Hirsel as Foreign Secretary, Lord Carrington as Defense Minister, and Anthony Barber as Chancellor of the Exchequer. (Margaret Thatcher was Education Minister.) In order to attach himself to the EEC, Heath had to distance himself from both the US and the British Commonwealth. Heath began busily posturing in these directions. "The long-cherished 'special relationship' with the United States was declared to be abruptly ended, and sentimental allegiance to the Commonwealth was briskly shelved." Naturally, it was all a deception posture. To distance himself from Washington, Heath declined to visit Nixon, seldom called him, and even insisted that direct bilateral consultations between London and Washington be phased out, since the British wanted to negotiate as part of Common Market delegations. Kissinger later wrote that Heath had made Nixon feel like "a jilted lover."

Heath expressed thinly veiled hostility for the US. He referred with contempt to the pro-American pose assumed by other British leaders: "Now, there are some people who always want to nestle on the shoulder of an American president. That's no future for Britain." Heath was also contemptuous of the Nixon-Kissinger proclamation of 1973 as the "Year of Europe." He said to Kissinger, "Who are you to propose that there should be a Year of Europe? You're not part of Europe." [Campbell, 344-345] This was the British Prime Minister who would administer the *coup de grace* to the Bretton Woods system, even as he attached the British financial parasite to the European Community to ride out the storm. Ultimately, Heath was destroyed as a politician by his own scheming; after the oil shock of 1973, he faced massive labor agitation. He put Britain on a three-day week and was defeated at the polls in early 1974. But Heath had fulfilled his two basic missions for the British oligarchy: pull down the dollar and intrude into Europe.

PAUL VOLCKER: LONDON'S MAN AT THE US TREASURY

Inside the Treasury Department in Washington was a group of officials that constituted an important British asset. This was an alleged "study group" called the Volcker Group, after the then Undersecretary for Monetary Affairs. Volcker owed his career to the New York Federal Reserve

Bank, the great bastion of Morgan and British power on Wall Street. The Volcker group was a pro-British cell in the Treasury. The Volcker group was the successor of the so-called Deming Group, which had been created by Lyndon Johnson in June 1965 to study how the US could help the British. The Deming Group's mission had been (in LBJ's words) to "consider what steps the United States could take to arrange for a relief of pressure on sterling, so as to give the United Kingdom the four- or five-year breathing space it needs to get its economy into shape, and thereby sharply reduce the danger of sterling devaluation or exchange controls or British military disengagement East of Suez or on the Rhine." [Solomon, 82] The Volcker Group continued this mandate of elaborating a pro-British monetary policy in a way that would inflict grave damage on the United States for the benefit of the London finance oligarchs.

CONNALLY LETS THE BRITISH OFF THE HOOK

In December 1970, Nixon named former Texas Democratic Governor John Connally as Secretary of the Treasury. Connally portrayed himself as a fighting US nationalist, anxious to end "Marshall Plan psychology" and fight for the best possible deal for US exporters by forcing the others to upvalue their currencies. He talked coercion and unilateralism, while demanding that other nations remove trade barriers and pay their share of the common anti-Soviet defense. During a cabinet-level meeting with Nixon, according to one source, Connally presented "an unbelievable diatribe" against the European Community and Japan, implying that these were the real enemies of America. [Odell, 248] Just after August 15, Connally met with economics professors, and wrapped up the discussion by saying: "My basic approach is that the foreigners are out to screw us. Our job is to screw them first." But despite this tough talk, Big Jawn let the British off the hook every time.

It is clear that the Volcker Group quickly captured the boisterous Connally, who was not well-versed in international monetary affairs. As one source relates, "during one of Connally's first Treasury staff briefings in late 1970, an adviser told him that over the next six months the country was going to face its gravest financial crisis since the depression. Interest rates were starting to fall; the payments deficit would grow. The suspension of convertibility was inevitable, he declared. The only choice was between picking the time and waiting for a crisis to force America's hand. This adviser pressed for closing the gold window and adopting a supporting domestic policy of restraint." [Odell, 250] The anonymous official who gave Odell this story appears to have been Volcker or one of his minions. Connally immediately ordered planning to begin for the suspension of dollar convertibility. Volcker claimed he wanted to suspend gold convertibility as a means of forcing the other nations to revalue their currencies, supposedly to help the US trade position. This was sold to Connally as a tough nationalist line. Volcker, in reality, was already looking ahead to the "controlled disintegration" which he would later openly embrace. Ironically, wrecking the old system was the worst thing that could have happened to the US.

Speculation against the dollar in the spring of 1971 was fueled by hot money, much of which was flowing out of London and New York and into Frankfurt and Tokyo. These flows were mightily stimulated by the actions of the Federal Reserve. During 1969, the Fed had raised interest rates to levels not seen since the American Civil War. The crunch peaked with a 7.9% rate on three-month Treasury bills in January 1970. This was the fabled "credit crunch" of 1969 and early 1970. During the credit crunch, the Nixon White House cited the authority of monetarist Milton Friedman as a theoretical justification for policy. Early in 1970, the Federal Reserve began lowering interest rates and easing monetary policy. Since interest rates in Europe were higher, bankers and brokers directed their hot money to Europe, where it was used for leverage to short the dollar. At about this time, the Nixon administration dumped Friedman, and began to profess Keynesianism.

The dollar also came under pressure during the first half of 1971 because of an outflow of gold from the Treasury. Between January 1971 and August 15, total gold outflow came to $845 million. But fully half of this sum was accounted for by US gold payments to the International Monetary Fund, which was presenting its claims when they hurt most.

NIXON'S "BENIGN NEGLECT" OF THE DOLLAR

Back in 1968, the Johnson administration had imposed stringent capital outflow restrictions, which mainly impacted US banks and corporations that wanted to invest in Europe and Japan. These controls included the mandatory requirement that no dollars be shifted out of the US for purposes of corporate investment in western Europe and the developing sector. These controls afforded some protection for the dollar against speculation by US banks and corporations themselves. But the new Nixon administration, with its Friedmanite creed of "benign neglect" of the dollar, had relaxed these controls in April 1969.

During April and May of 1971, the German Bundesbank was obliged on a number of days to deal with hot money inflows in the range of $1 to $3 billion. German Superminister Karl Schiller attempted to convince the other EEC countries to accept a joint European float against the dollar, but failed to secure agreement. By May 10 the German mark and the Dutch gulden were floating separately, while Austria and Switzerland revalued. Connally was adamant that the US would not devalue the dollar, even as currency chaos spread.

AUGUST 1971: THE BRITISH DEMAND $3 BILLION IN GOLD

The climactic crisis of the Bretton Woods system was precipitated by the British. As President Nixon recounts this dramatic episode in his memoirs:

> In the second week of August the British Ambassador appeared at the Treasury Department to ask that $3 billion be converted into gold. [Nixon 518]

At this point, the entire gold reserves of the US Treasury were about $10.1 billion. The British were in effect demanding that almost one third of the entire US gold stock be handed over to them. Decades of anti-US resentment and retribution for such humiliations as two pound sterling devaluations, the postwar US loan, the Suez debacle, the pullback from east of Suez and the nominal loss of the Empire were rolled up in this venomous ploy. Bretton Woods was a flawed system, but it was the only monetary system the world had, and wantonly to destroy it was a crime against humanity. Because of decades of wrong policies, the US was trapped in a position of pathetic weakness, and even Nixon knew it:

> Whether we honored or denied this request, the consequences of our action would be fraught with danger: if we gave the British the gold they wanted, then other countries might rush to get theirs. If we refused, then that would be an admission of our concern that we could not meet every potential demand for conversion into gold. Connally deferred giving his answer, but we knew that we would very soon have to confront a major crisis concerning the international economic position of the United States. [Nixon 518]

This was an attempt to bring down the entire international monetary system, and it succeeded fully. On Friday, August 13, 1971 Nixon and his advisers retired to Camp David in Maryland's Catoctin Mountains for one of the most fateful sessions in monetary and financial history. Unfortunately for the United States and the world, Nixon's team was dominated by the incompetents who had presided over the monetary ruin of the dollar, and who in many cases would continue so to preside. These included: Federal Reserve boss Arthur Burns; Peter Peterson, the head of the Council of International Economic Policy; Undersecretary of the Treasury for Monetary Affairs Paul Volcker; George Shultz; Caspar Weinberger; plus Nixon advisers Paul McCracken, Herbert Stein, and speechwriter William Safire. Kissinger was in Paris for a secret meeting with Le Duc Tho of North Vietnam.

Although by this time Nixon professed to be a Keynesian, the dominant spirit in that infamous Camp David group was once again that of Friedmanite *laissez-faire*, free-market monetarism in the critical arena of international monetary affairs. Arthur Burns had been Milton Friedman's teacher, and George Shultz was his friend, student, and admirer. Volcker would later motivate his 21% prime rate with Friedmanite arguments on the money supply.

THE BRITISH SCUTTLED BRETTON WOODS

The French government the same week had asked for a mere $191 million in gold, and the rage of the media focussed on Paris, not London. William Safire's account of this fateful meeting coheres with that left by Nixon. William Safire, a participant at the critical Camp David meetings of August 13-15 who took extensive notes on the discussions, has Connally explaining the crisis thus:

> Connally: What's our immediate problem? We are meeting here because we are in trouble overseas. The British came in today to ask us to cover $3 billion, all their dollar reserves. Anybody can topple us – anytime they want – we have left ourselves completely exposed. [Safire, 666]

The decisive role of the British in forcing the hand of the US government is still a matter of dispute, with the Anglophiles attempting to cover up for London's act of economic warfare. The attempted British raid on Fort Knox was not widely known at the time these events took place. But on November 22, 1971 Hendrik S. Houthakker, a well-known economist and former member of Nixon's Economic Advisory Council, referred to the British role in a speech at DePaul University, noting that "There is as yet little public knowledge of what exactly led to the President's decision to suspend the convertibility of the dollar into gold.... One clue to the developments that precipitated the decision of August 15 may well be the recent disclosure that two days earlier the United Kingdom drew the entire amount of its so-called swap line with the United States, amounting to $750 million.... If the British action was indeed the immediate reason for our August 15 decision, it will be interesting to know Britain's motives for thus bringing down the Bretton Woods system of which it had been one of the principal architects." [Brandon, 225]

According to journalist Henry Brandon, "British officials in London angrily denied the accusation. Questioned as to the exact facts, they replied that they had asked the Federal Reserve Bank of New York shortly before August 12 to activate a reverse 'swap' (guaranteeing dollar holdings against devaluation) and then questioned over the transatlantic telephone as to how much they were asking for, replied that they wanted as much as possible, which meant in effect up to the full amount of the facility they had with them - $2 billion. When the Fed declined to go along with that request and limited the amount to $750 million...the British did not press for more. The reverse swap was carried out on August 13." Charles Coombs, the Senior Vice President of the Federal Reserve Bank of New York, also denied that the British asked for $3 billion. [Brandon, 223-224]

A SMOKESCREEN FOR LONDON

In January 1972, *Fortune* magazine published an article by Juan Cameron that revealed more about the causes of August 15. Cameron wrote that Nixon's moves were "dictated by the largest money run in history which culminated in a panicked request from the Bank of England for a guarantee against devaluation of its dollar holdings totaling some $3 billion. The British request, viewed as tantamount to a to a demand for gold, was relayed to the White House on the morning of August 13." Cameron also reported that the British demand was "considered a distinctly foul blow; after all, the United States had helped rescue sterling at least three times during the 1960s. An outraged Treasury abruptly turned down the request." [Brandon, 224-225]

Arthur Burns later put out the pro-British line of the cabal of private central bankers on this issue, minimizing the British move as an "irritant" that "did not play a role in the decision to close the gold window and, as far as I can remember, and I participated in all the important discussions at the Camp David meeting, the British action was never mentioned." [Brandon, 225] But Safire's minutes of the Camp David meetings, backed up by the memoirs of Nixon and Connally, show that Arthur Burns was lacking in candor.

Robert Solomon of Burns' staff at the Fed also hews to the central bank line in his standard work on postwar monetary affairs, *The International Monetary System, 1945-1981*: "Some observers have suggested that the weekend meeting was triggered by a British request for coverage of its dollar holdings by means of a Federal reserve swap drawing on the Bank of England. It is true that such a drawing was agreed to on August 13, in the amount of $750 million. There was confusion in the communication between the British and American authorities as to just how large a drawing was being requested; the swap line would have permitted a drawing of $2 billion. The amount of $750 million, agreed to on Friday, August 13, was about equal to the Bank of England's dollar accruals in August. But, as Henry Brandon points out, the British request was no more than an irritant." [Solomon, 185] Solomon is also fibbing.

The Fed officials were deliberately confusing two separate transactions. Swap agreements were short to medium term agreements among central banks for mutual lending of each other's currency for use in support operations that were supposed to benefit currency stability. If the British were asking for coverage on dollars they held under a swap agreement, they were asking that sufficient pounds be lent to them to cover the value of those dollars. In effect, coverage meant insurance against losses on dollar holdings if those dollars were to be devalued. But the British were not attacking along a single axis; they were mounting a many-pronged attack on the dollar. The British Ambassador showing up at the Treasury with a demand for $3 billion in gold was a government to government demarche that ran parallel to and additional to whatever amount of dollars the Bank of England was demanding from the New York Fed. In other words, the British were using the gold demand to force a devaluation crisis that would shake the monetary order, while at the same time seeking to indemnify themselves against dollar losses that they might otherwise absorb in the process.

Even Paul Volcker is more honest in his memoirs than Burns and Solomon. Volcker, then at the Treasury, was in touch at the time with Charles Coombs of the international desk of the New York Federal Reserve Bank. Volcker recounts that "the foreign exchange desk in New York had called to inform [Coombs] that the British had just asked for 'gold' for their dollar holdings of about $3 billion. If the British, who had founded the system with us, and who had fought so hard to defend their own currency, were going to take gold for their dollars, it was clear the game was indeed over." That is clear enough. But Volcker adds two other elements. First, he attempts to blur the nature of the British request: "The message to Coombs apparently had gotten a bit garbled; I was told later that the request was for some combination of 'cover' to guarantee the value of their dollars, but not necessarily for gold." [Volcker, 77] We have already cleared up this confusion.

Volcker also hurries to deny that the British caused the crisis, suggesting indeed that their demand was beneficial: "One story later circulated that the British request precipitated our decision to go off gold. That was not true. Demands for gold had been building from other, smaller, countries. The momentum toward the decision was by that time, in my judgment, unstoppable. There was, however, a sense in which those last requests for gold and guarantees were helpful: no one could argue that the United States had reached its decision frivolously." [Volcker, 77] We were covered, says Volcker.

Treasury Secretary John Connally wrote in his memoirs about a call he received in Texas from Volcker on Friday, August 6: Volcker "...said that we had received word that on Monday...that the United States would be asked by Great Britain to convert three billion dollars into gold. In the past, we had converted small amounts of dollars into gold for various countries, primarily third world countries, and usually in the amounts of five, ten or fifteen million. This was the first time we had been advised we would be asked to convert a large amount into gold...For every dollar in gold that we had at Fort Knox...$7 were being held in official hands by governments around the world. We knew if we converted three billion dollars for one country, it would set off a chain reaction among other nations to get their dollars converted while we had gold left." [Connally, 237-238]

George Shultz, who would later supersede Connally at the Treasury, and who was present at Camp David in his capacity as Director of OMB, admits that Nixon's decisions were precipitated by a British demand for gold, although he does not specify the amount: "A British demand for conversion of dollars into gold (or its equivalent in guarantees) was made in the course of the preceding week and forced final decisions to be made by the weekend. If the British demand had been honored, it surely would have started a 'run' on the Fort." [Shultz and Dam, 110]

Finally, we have the younger James Reston's biography of Connally. The younger Reston has no trouble revealing the main facts in the case: "...Great Britain, contemplating its future entry into the Common Market, demanded $3 billion - all its dollar reserves. If Britain's demand were honored, the gold stock at Fort Knox would drop below its statutory bottom of $10 billion, and a run on American gold was sure to follow." Reston also points out that it was Connally, in his famous tough-talking and posturing press briefing of Monday, August 16, who "covered up the fact that the British demand for gold had prompted the decision." [Reston, 408, 411]

DOLLAR DEVALUATION AND US EXPORTS WERE NEEDED

By now, the necessary US policy would have been to devalue the dollar against gold by about 15%, while negotiating an upvaluing of the other currencies so as to maintain fixed parities. Foreign central banks could have been persuaded to exercise temporary restraint on siphoning off US gold stocks. The US would have required capital controls, exchange controls, and credit controls to fight hot money flows by US banks and corporations. The one good measure that Nixon did implement on August 15 was a momentary return to a Kennedy-style investment tax credit for purchases of capital equipment and machinery. Dirigistic elements in the tax code needed to be increased, and permanently. But no combination of measures could have worked without addressing the need for a US and world economic recovery, led by exports of high-technology capital goods and infrastructure components into the developing sector and other poorer countries. This could have been done unilaterally by a boxcar increase in the funding of the Export-Import Bank, making it the powerhouse of an export-led recovery. The Federal Reserve needed to be nationalized to fight usury and to provide cheap long-term credit for agricultural and industrial production. None of this was seriously considered by the Nixon regime.

The dollar was illiquid because there was an insufficient world demand for dollars; the way to increase demand for dollars was to begin selling and financing capital goods the world wanted to buy, but did not have the credit mechanism to pay for. Instead, Nixon foolishly pulled the plug on the entire system by suspending the convertibility of the dollar into gold – he closed the Treasury gold window. Burns argued in favor of keeping the gold window open – meaning, in practice, letting the British cart off their loot. Nixon's act of folly unleashed a monetary firestorm that has lasted for almost three decades. The tragic news was released in Nixon's television speech on Sunday, August 15, 1971:

> In recent weeks, the speculators have been waging an all-out war on the American dollar...Accordingly, I have directed the Secretary of the Treasury to take the action necessary to defend the dollar against the speculators. I have directed Secretary Connally to suspend temporarily the convertibility of the dollar into gold or other reserve assets, except in amounts and conditions determined to be in the interest of monetary stability and in the best interests of the United States.

Using Presidential emergency powers, Nixon also imposed a 10% surtax on all imports, which caused a loud outcry in Europe and Japan. On the domestic front, Nixon further announced a 90-day wage and price freeze that amounted in practice to a wage freeze. The wage freeze was denounced by George Meany of the AFL-CIO and other union leaders, but they soon wilted. For the labor movement, this – perhaps even more than Reagan's breaking of the PATCO air traffic controllers – was the turning point which led into decades of declining membership and bargaining power. It soon turned out that the prices of stocks and bonds were not among those fixed by the freeze. Interest rates, including those on consumer debt, were not affected. Nixon asked corporations to freeze their dividends, but this was voluntary. Phase II of Nixon's program began in November 1971; this still featured many mandatory controls, but these were less comprehensive. The beginning of Phase III in January 1973 removed most price controls, and many prices rose sharply. Nixon responded by re-imposing a temporary, limited freeze. All controls were finally lifted in the spring of 1974, a few months before the Watergate affair forced Nixon's resignation. The aftermath of the controls was the double-digit inflation during the outset of the Ford administration. Nixon's "Phases" were a key factor in the dilapidation of his political capital that made him vulnerable to Watergate.

ON THE BRINK OF TRADE WAR AND DEPRESSION

In London, Ted Heath could now act the part of the outraged European. His biographer says that Nixon's "unilateral action evoked shock and outrage in Europe and Japan, where it was seen almost as an act of economic war. Heath, despite his deliberate refusal of a special relationship, was furious at what he regarded as an act of international irresponsibility on the part of Washington." Heath attacked especially the feckless Connally, referring to the wound the Texan had received when President Kennedy was assassinated. "I knew they killed the wrong man in Dallas," remarked Heath. [Campbell, 343]

Milton Friedman of the monetarist Chicago school attacked Nixon's wage and price freeze as "pure window dressing which will do harm rather than good." But on the broader issue of fixed parities, Friedman was well pleased. No fixed parities meant the de-regulation of monetary affairs, getting the governments out and letting the "market" decide what a currency is worth. Monetarists were interested above all in the domestic money supply.

Nixon's August 15 statement recognized, as we have seen, that "the speculators have been waging an all-out war on the American dollar," but there were no specific measures to hobble or to punish these speculators, who were of course the Wall Street and City of London banks. Instead, the speculators were rewarded. These bankers cashed in their chips with a huge profit, and began to look for new targets. Most European exchanges closed during the mid-August dollar crisis. During

August, the Bank of Japan waged a costly but futile battle to defend its old parity with the dollar at 357.37 yen to the dollar. Japan capitulated and began its own float upwards on August 27, after taking in more than $4 billion. Shultz later commented that "US officials had formed an alliance with the market itself to force a change in the behavior of foreign officials." [Shultz and Dam, 115] All major currencies were now floating.

In the wake of August 15, 1971, a group of cabinet-level finance ministers met in the White House Library in an attempt to coordinate policies. Present were Schultz, Volcker, Helmut Schmidt, Karl Otto Poehl (the future head of the Bundesbank), and Valery Giscard d'Estaing. This was the Library Club, whose members would remain as protagonists of the ongoing financial fiasco well into the 1980s.

From August 15 until almost Christmas, monetary chaos threatened to disrupt world trade. The Europeans wanted a return to fixed parities, but could not agree on the specific numbers. The US made no proposal, but refused to devalue the dollar. Meanwhile, chaotic floating went forward. Dollar-denominated bills of exchange maturing in between 30 and 90 days were the basis, not just of oil sales, but of most world commodity flows, and no one now knew even approximately what such bills might be worth by the time they matured, because all parities were now floating in various degrees of chaos. Who would dare to discount such bills? And if the bills could not be discounted, how could trade continue? As the weeks went by and "Typhoon" Connally (as he was called in the Japanese press) jawboned and bullied the Europeans and Japanese, the dangers increased. Schweitzer and the IMF were demanding that the US devalue the dollar by raising the official price of gold. Henry Kissinger and Arthur Burns demanded an official devaluation and a quick deal on new fixed parities. Ted Heath postured that he would not meet Nixon at all until such time as the US had begun serious monetary bargaining. This was evidently a tactic suggested to Heath by Kissinger as a way to box in Connally. [Odell, 284]

During November 1971, Nixon became convinced that the strong-arm approach with the Europeans had yielded all it ever would. Burns and Kissinger scared Nixon with a list of retaliatory measures that the other countries were preparing. Former Treasury official Francis Bator was mobilized by Kissinger to warn that if "Connally does not change course soon, the other side will start shooting back. Control over events will shift to the war parties in all the capitals, and August 15 will be a turning point in postwar Atlantic and US-Japan history." [Odell, 281]

THE AZORES: POMPIDOU DUMPS THE GOLD STANDARD

In Rome at the end of November, Connally and Volcker surprised the squabbling Europeans, who were unable to agree among themselves on anything. British Chancellor of the Exchequer Anthony Barber demanded to know whether the US were willing to devalue the dollar. Connally said audibly to his aides, "I'll take his pants off." Connally then offered a 10% dollar devaluation, which shocked the Europeans because it was much more than they wanted. There was a silence of about one hour, broken by German Finance Minister Karl Schiller, who stated the maximum upvaluing of the mark that the Bonn government was prepared to accept. As Connally later noted, "Tony Barber wanted to do whatever he could do to ingratiate himself with France. So he became the spokesman against whatever proposal we offered." However, the deadlock was now broken.

In December, 1971 Nixon met with French President Pompidou met in the Azores. Nixon was accompanied by Kissinger, Connally, and Volcker. Here Nixon finally agreed to devalue. This squalid affair was an exercise in absurdity, since it merely involved an adjustment of the price at which the United States would NOT buy and sell gold. In exchange for a return to fixed parities, Pompidou agreed not to insist on the restoration of dollar convertibility into gold. France thus dropped its historic Gaullist pro-gold position, and acquiesced in the Anglo-Americans' attempted demonetization of gold. Nixon and Pompidou agreed that the US dollar would be devalued by 8.6% from $35 per ounce to $38 per ounce and that the gold window would remained closed. The basis for monetary clearing would continue to be absent.

DOLLAR DEVALUATION AND SMITHSONIAN PARITIES, DECEMBER 1971

This deal formed the basis of the next meeting of the Group of Ten, held in the great hall of the old Smithsonian Institution building in Washington, which convened on December 17, 1971. The dollar was formally and officially devalued in respect to gold by 8.57%, while Germany upvalued the mark by 13.57% and Japan upvalued the yen by 16.9%. Sweden and Italy each devalued by 1% in respect to gold. New bands of fluctuation of plus or minus 2.25% were applied to all countries. In a bombastic ceremony, Nixon called this "the most significant monetary agreement in the history of the world."

But the Smithsonian parities would be swept away by international hot money flows within less than fourteen months, despite a second devaluation of the dollar. Canada declined to join in the new parities and continued to float, thus signaling the bedrock British hostility towards a new system of fixed parities. Because of the high level of economic integration that had been attained in western Europe, the EEC countries were eager to restore for their intra-European commerce the advantages of fixed parities. In early March, 1972, the six EEC countries decided to re-establish fixed parities among themselves and to limit fluctuations to a band that was only 2.25%, one half as wide as the 4.5% provided for at the Smithsonian. This was the European snake. The EEC snake was said to be crawling along the slightly more capacious Smithsonian tunnel. Later, Belgium and the Netherlands tried to keep their parities within a 1.5% band, this was referred to as the worm in the snake.

4. SECOND DOLLAR DEVALUATION AND THE END OF THE SMITHSONIAN PARITIES

On May 1, 1972 the British, with their candidacy for EEC membership now progressing, decided to join the EEC snake. The holders of hot money began to sell the pound short. Would the British government defend the new Smithsonian parity of the pound? The speculators studied the collected speeches of Chancellor of the Exchequer Anthony Barber. They found that he said in his March budget speech that "the lesson of the international balance-of-payments upsets of the last few years is that it is neither necessary nor desirable to distort domestic economies to an unacceptable extent in order to maintain unrealistic exchange rates, whether they are too high or too low." That was a clear signal that the Heath government was eager to deep-six the Smithsonian parities. The speculators, meaning above all the City of London, started shorting the pound with a vengeance. And all this time the Canadian dollar continued its float, showcasing London's ultimate intentions.

THE BRITISH TORPEDO THE SMITHSONIAN DEAL

During the six days before June 23, 1972, the Bank of England was forced to sell $2.6 billion to maintain the sterling parity. No serious use was made of the bank rate, the traditional weapon for sterling defense. On June 23, the British announced that they were cutting free from both the European snake and the Smithsonian parities, and letting the pound float. The first major breach had been opened in the new Smithsonian system. Once again the perpetrators were the duplicitous British. Denmark left the snake but not the Smithsonian, while Italy remained in the snake only with the help of special concessions.

Nixon's secret White House taping system, the existence of which was revealed during the Watergate scandal, shows how little Nixon understood of the significance of these events. On June

23, 1972 Chief of Staff H.R. Haldeman told Nixon that Britain had just floated the pound. "That's devaluation ?" Nixon asked. Haldeman tried to present a report from the White House staff on the British decision, but Nixon would not listen. "I don't care about it. Nothing we can do about it," Nixon said. Haldeman told Nixon that Burns of the Fed expected a 5% to 8% decline of the pound against the dollar. "Yeah. OK. Fine," replied Nixon. Haldeman added that Burns was concerned about speculation against the Italian lira." "Nixon: "Well, I don't give a [expletive deleted] about the lira. [Unintelligible.]" Nixon seems to have been unaware that these events represented the beginning of the end of the Smithsonian arrangement, and the prelude to a second devaluation of the dollar. [Odell, 186]

With their solo float, the British had spurred on the forces tending to blow up the labile Smithsonian parities. By January 1973, Italy had adopted a two-tier currency system, with a floating financial lira and a fixed-parity trade lira. In late January, Switzerland cut loose from its parity and began its own float. By February 10, more than $6 billion in hot money had rushed into Germany, speculating on yet another upvaluation. European currency exchanges had to close yet again.

UNIVERSAL FLOATING AND MONETARY CHAOS

At this time Paul Volcker of the Treasury flew to Tokyo, Bonn, London, Paris, Rome and back to Paris with the Italian Finance Minister Malagodi in tow for a ministerial meeting at the home of Giscard d'Estaing, and then back to Bonn. On the same evening that Volcker returned to Washington, Treasury Secretary Shultz announced the second devaluation of the dollar, this time by 10%. An ounce of gold now was officially equal to $42.22 in US money. Shultz expressed this new relation in terms of SDR's in a polemical gesture against pro-gold forces. Shultz claimed that the dollar devaluation had "no practical significance," which was true only to the extent that the US gold window stayed firmly closed. Shultz announced that the Japanese yen would now begin to float, and that the US would abolish capital controls by the end of the year. By now the yen, lira, Swiss franc, pound and Canadian dollar were all floating.

Germany was the only major currency holding on to its Smithsonian parity. On March 1, European central banks, especially the Bundesbank, took in $3.6 billion in hot money. The exchanges closed another time. Negotiations began among the Europeans as to what to do. The British demanded, as their price for joining a common float, a guarantee of unlimited financial support without guarantee or collateral, and with no specific obligation to repay. This was politely but firmly declined. On March 11 the EEC ministers met in Brussels, where Germany, France, Belgium, the Netherlands, Denmark, and Luxembourg agreed to form a currency snake that would float jointly against the dollar. In the process Germany revalued by 3%. Sweden and Norway soon joined this new snake without a tunnel. And since the rest of the world was floating, for all practical purposes the US was floating too, as metaphysicians were not slow to point out. The Smithsonian regime was dead, and the world was plunged into the chaos and anarchy of permanent floating rates, which has continued down to this very day. Helmut Schmidt marked the event by formally proclaiming the "end of Bretton Woods."

From the US side, a very significant and laconic commentary on the demise of the system came from Treasury Secretary Shultz, an ideological opponent of both fixed parities and of gold. "Santa Claus is dead," quipped Shultz, signaling that the United States, in an attitude of deplorable irresponsibility, would not make any serious exertions or commit serious resources for the purpose of preserving the most effective international monetary system the world has yet known.

SPECULATORS RULE THE GLOBAL VILLAGE

Gazing back at the proud edifice of the classical Bretton Woods system from amidst the ruins of the chaotic non-system that has replaced it, economic writers have often agreed that the pre-1971 years were "the golden age of capitalism," "the most successful international monetary system the world has ever seen," and "the best overall macro performance of any regime." Economists like Simon Kuznets have noted that under Bretton Woods "material returns [had] grown, per capita, at a rate higher than that ever observed in the past." [James, 148] Those who think that the growth of US budget deficits and public debt is caused primarily by government overspending should contemplate the following sequence. 1974 was the first full year of floating rates. Fiscal year 1976 began on September 1, 1975, and this is when the fall of Bretton Woods began to show up in the US budget deficit. So it was just after the last gasp of the fixed parities that the US deficit first ballooned to an all-time record in peace or war, the $66.4 registered in FY 1976. The rate of growth of the international debt bubble had begun noticeably to accelerate.

Governments had created a monetary system in 1944, and this monetary system had now been destroyed by international hot-money speculators. The speculators had proven that they were more powerful than the governments; the bandits had taken over the global village. Only chaos had resulted. The speculators and bankers had no interest in a new gold-related system of fixed parities. They were rather triumphant that they had forced the deregulation of the key feature of international financial life. The universal prevalence of floating rates meant greater risk, especially in forward currency markets. As the great currency floater Paul Volcker delicately expressed it in his memoirs, "at the start of the 1970s, there began to be just a germ of a vested private interest in instability in the exchange markets....when exchange rates were freed, bank traders soon found out they were very good at making money from the fluctuations." [Volcker, 230] Only the demented supporters of chaos theory could imagine that this had been a gain. Part of the impetus for the creation of today's surrealistic world of derivative instruments has come from post-1973 monetary risk. The world would have been far better off with an orderly, regulated world of fixed parities which would have obviated part of this rationale for derivatives in the first place.

With the return of floating rates, some observers once again feared the return of all-out world economic depression of the post-1931 variety. To understand these fears, we should recall the then-traditional view of the floating rates of the early interwar years as expressed by Melchior Palyi in his *Twilight of Gold*, referring to the floating rate period of 1918 - 1924: "Throughout the early postwar years, international trade had been distorted, disorganized and even disrupted by fluctuations in foreign exchange rates. They obliterated business and investment calculations ....Maintaining a balance of payments came to depend on speculative capital movements in large volumes..., their direction hinging on guesses and rumors about the positive or negative stabilization prospects of individual currencies....Under a regime of 'floating' exchange rates...rational monetary policy was severely handicapped by foreign exchange fluctuations. The crucial aspect of broadly fluctuating exchange rates was the fact that they failed to fulfill the function assigned to them in monetary theory - to bring about an automatic adjustment of the respective countries' international accounts." [Palyi, 42-43] In the 1970s also, there would no automatic adjustment in international accounts, but greater and greater distortions.

In 1994, a quarter century after these fateful events, a retrospective analysis of the floating exchange rate system was offered by the 47 influential establishment-oriented bankers and economists of a group calling itself the Bretton Woods Commission. The chairman of this blue-ribbon panel was none other than Volcker himself, who had been, in practice, one of the leading gravediggers of the old fixed-rate system. Here is the verdict of the Bretton Woods Commission on the impact of currency deregulation:

> Since the early 1970s, long-term growth in the major industrial countries has been cut in half, from about 5 percent a year to about 2.5 percent a year. Although many factors contributed to this decline in different countries at different times, low growth has been an international problem, and the loss of exchange rate discipline has played a part. [Greider 1997, 250]

Volcker's own commission found that in addition to the braking of world growth, unemployment has been higher and capital investment has been more anemic in the post-1971 world of floating rates than in the regulated currency world of Bretton Woods: "When current exchange rates are misaligned, resources are misallocated; when exchange rates are unduly volatile, it creates uncertainty and productive investments are inhibited," wrote the same group.

Japan is a country that must export in order to live, but the relation between the Japanese yen and the US dollar has been one of the most unpredictable of the post-1971 era. The Japanese have thus had ample opportunity to study the deleterious impact of exchange rate gyrations on commodity production for export. Here are the observations of Kenichi Ohno of Tsukuba University, a Japanese economist: "A sharp appreciation of the home currency throws tradable industries into disarray...A sudden loss of international price competitiveness, amounting to 10-40 percent in real terms, is much larger than the typical profit margins in these industries....To survive, these industries are forced to make costly downsizing adjustments. These include operating below capacity, implementing cost-cutting measures, scaling down investment plans, and even scrapping existing facilities, laying off workers...outsourcing, shifting manufacturing bases abroad, joint ventures with foreigners, and so on." [Ohno, see also Greider 1997, 249] American exporters would be largely wiped out by these effects during the 1984-85 era of the Volcker superdollar.

In the event, it took another decade and several more deliberate shocks administered to the world economy to precipitate the world into pervasive economic depression. In 1973, the German and Japanese economies were still reasonably vigorous, and the US, though stagnant, still possessed an intact industrial base. But in terms of a qualitative-quantitative world composite of wages, living standards, employment, investment, growth rates, and world trade volume, the period 1965-1971 represents the overall high water-mark of postwar economic development on this planet.

When the dust had settled on the ruin of the Smithsonian system, Volcker submitted the Treasury's plan for rebuilding world monetary relations. This turned out to be very similar of Lord Keynes' 1944 draft, with great stress on the supremacy of supernational institutions. Instead of bancor, Volcker relied on the SDR as the instrument for creating new reserves. Under Volcker's system, countries that persisted in running deficits or surpluses would have been subjected to supernational IMF coercion in the form of "sanctions" and "graduated pressures." But the Volcker-Keynes scheme was never implemented.

1973 AS WORLD-HISTORICAL WATERSHED

In his useful book, *The Myth of Free Trade*, economist Ravi Batra stresses that 1973 constituted a turning point in American history, marking the transition from rising real wages to a falling standard of living. However, he fails to relate this to the leading empirical facts of world history in those years, which chiefly involve the collapse of the Bretton Woods system. About this Batra has nothing to say. Instead, he asserts that 1973 marked the transition from protectionism to free trade in American tariff policy. While this is broadly true, the events which marked this shift were initially not so much changes in the tariff *per se* as they were entropic changes in the world monetary and financial system, which Batra fails to see. He stresses that *"in 1973, for the first time in its three-century history, the United States became a free-trade economy, and has remained so ever since.* Thus 1973 was also a watershed year as far as America's foreign commerce is concerned... *Never in pre-1973 history did American wages fall while productivity rose... Not until 1973 was America a free trade economy, and not until 1973 was the generally positive link between wages and productivity – expected and preached by economists for decades – severed... Free trade has done to America what even the Great Depression could not do.*" [Batra 1993, 41, 47, 51, 53] These valuable insights need to be supplemented by an awareness that, in the absence of a satisfactory world monetary system, trade will suffer no matter what else individual countries may do or not do about their tariffs.

5. FIRST WORLD OIL CRISIS, OCTOBER 1973

The dominant clique of Anglo-American financiers was not relying merely on technical adjustments in monetary structures. Rather, they now turned to political-military means: they asserted their predominance with the first great oil shock of 1973. In October 1973, the Kippur war between Israel and the Arab states broke out. This war was the handiwork of Henry Kissinger, David Rockefeller of the Chase Manhattan Bank and the British Foreign Office, all of whom were interested in adjusting the balance of power in the Middle East and the balance of financial power on a world scale. The plan for the entire exercise had been provided by Lord Victor Rothschild, the sometime head of a think tank attached to Royal Dutch Shell, the dominant force within the Seven Sisters oil cartel. The operation had been discussed at a meeting of the self-styled Bilderberg Group of finance oligarchs held at Saltsjöbaden, Sweden on May 11-13, 1973.

After the hostilities began, the Organization of Petroleum Exporting Countries announced an oil boycott. In late December 1973, the OPEC moves had become the pretext for a 400% increase in the price of oil. But OPEC was never the real cartel. OPEC was largely a Potemkin cartel. The real cartel were the Seven Sisters. Without the connivance of the Seven Sisters and their Royal Dutch Shell/British Petroleum leadership, none of OPEC's antics could have been made to stick. In December 1973, the *New York Times* reported that oil-bearing supertankers of the leading oil companies had been put into a holding pattern on the high seas because storage facilities were already full to bursting with crude. In spite of this, the price of oil was bid up on the commodities markets. The Seven Sisters thus took advantage of the OPEC theatrics to increase the price of oil four times over. In doing so they administered a stunning blow to the productive economy of the world. This was doubtless the greatest shock to the real economy since 1945. Petroleum products are used not only for transportation and heating, but also, in the form of fertilizers and tractor fuels, represent a decisive input into agriculture. Prices in all these areas skyrocketed, and much existing plant and equipment, based on the premise of cheap fuels, was rendered extravagantly obsolete.

THE DEEPEST RECESSION SINCE WORLD WAR II

As a result of the monetary and oil crises, the world during 1974-75 experienced the deepest recession it had known since World War II. Inflation surged upward. European countries and Japan, all heavy importers of oil, went from surplus to deficit in their balance of payments accounts: the impact was the equivalent of a 2% across the board tax on all their economic activity. Because the oil price was always posted in dollars, an unprecedented demand for the US currency temporarily silenced the European critics of the Eurodollar glut. The oil shock temporarily stabilized the dollar.

The dollar balances that built up in Saudi Arabia, Iran, and the other OPEC states had to be invested somewhere. Overwhelmingly, they were sent to Chase Manhattan, Citibank, and the other US money center banks: this was called the recycling of petrodollars. Europeans and Japanese now had to pay interest to get back temporarily the money that had been filched from their coffers. Developing countries like Brazil were especially hard hit by the rising energy prices, which ruined their balance of payments positions and made debt installments even more onerous.

An included feature of this downturn was constituted by one of the scariest bear markets in Wall Street's recent history. Between January 1973 and October 1974, the Dow Jones Industrials declined by 44%. The news commentators who in the late 1990s fawned on Alan Greenspan as an oracle needed to recall the foolish analysis Greenspan was offering just as this sickening slide began. On January 17, 1973 Alan Greenspan, then working as a private economist, was already well launched in the doubletalk business. "The danger, said Greenspan, "is that business may get too good too soon. Up to now there has been a strong element of business and consumer caution that has helped to keep the recovery under control. There are signs, though, that the caution is diminishing." Very soon the "Nifty Fifty" glamour stocks, the darlings of the 1960s "go-go" phase on Wall Street, were being mercilessly hammered. Even Ross Perot gave up his posturing and sold his controlling stake in duPont Glore Forgan, at that time the number two US retail broker behind Merrill Lynch, after losing a considerable amount of his own personal *fondo*. An interim bottom was reached in October 1974, when Ford had taken over the presidency after Nixon's forced resignation.

HEATH PUTS BRITAIN ON THE THREE-DAY WEEK

Nowhere did the economic and monetary crisis of the early 1970s reach a more acute pitch than in Great Britain, the sick man of Europe. In 1973, the Tory Heath regime attempted to impose an incomes policy – doublespeak for a government program to keep union wage settlements low. In those days, Britain still had a militant and well-organized labor movement, and strikes began to multiply. Engineers, metalworkers, and other workers went on strike, shutting down factories, power plants, shipyards, and newspapers. The coal miners' union demanded a 31% wage increase. Old people were soon in danger of freezing in their unheated homes. With the 1973 oil crisis looming, Heath declared a state of emergency and launched the slogan "SOS" - "Shut Off Something," so as to cut energy consumption. Electric signs were ordered shut off, and Piccadilly Circus in the heart of London was left in darkness. Another decree set all thermostats at a maximum of 63 degrees. Train engineers instituted a ban on overtime. Heath put Britain on a three-day work week. By Christmas 1973 half a million workers had lost their jobs; by January 1974 official unemployment was 2.2 million, the highest since the Great Depression. The unions proved capable of great disruption, but incapable of imposing or even of suggesting anti-depression policies adequate for starting an economic recovery in Great Britain.

In February 1974 Heath called a general election with the slogan "Who Governs?" He evidently thought he would be the beneficiary of an anti-labor backlash, as De Gaulle had been in 1968. But the election failed to give anybody a clear majority. Heath tried a coalition with the Liberals, but Wilson and Labour soon returned to power with a minority government. The British domestic crisis was long-lasting; as we will see, in 1976 the British were forced to grovel before the IMF.

6. FLOATING TO THE BRINK: HERSTATT AND FRANKLIN NATIONAL GO BROKE

Some stability was provided by the maintenance of fixed parities among the European countries, but the EEC snake also had a wild ride. During the first half of 1973, before the oil shock, the US dollar fell about 7.7%. French President Pompidou observed: "We are witnessing the third devaluation of the dollar." But Pompidou was scarcely better off: after a few months in the snake, France had used up $3 billion in reserves in support operations for the franc and had to drop out.

After OPEC raised prices, the dollar climbed rapidly, and by January 1974 the greenback had bounced back some 17% from its 1973 lows. But then the roller-coaster of floating rates took the dollar down 9% between January and May of 1974. This pervasive chaos claimed some important victims: the Herstatt Bank of Cologne, Germany, which went under in June, and Michele Sindona's Franklin National Bank of New York, in July.

The Herstatt episode provided the first brush with worldwide financial meltdown under the conditions now prevailing in the new, deregulated, post-Bretton Woods world. This small bank almost reduced the entire world financial system to a pile of rubble, not primarily because of the size of the crisis, but because the complacent central bank gurus were taken completely by surprise, and had not prepared any of the crisis management mechanisms to which they would devote most of their time over the following decades.

The private bank of I. D. Herstatt had rushed into the new forms of currency speculation – especially speculation on the Eurodollar market – made possible by the chaotic floating-rate regime. But I. D. Herstatt's traders soon made some catastrophic bets. German bank regulators acted with old-fashioned German thoroughness, and revoked Herstatt's banking license on June 26, 1974. The Bundesbank, Germany's central bank, ordered a halt in the clearing of payments for Herstatt's accounts for the end of that business day, 4 PM Central European time. Herstatt had been wrapped up under the German domestic banking rules.

CHIPS IN DANGER OF GRIDLOCK

But Herstatt's business was not just German or even European; it had become thoroughly globalized, as the bankers would say today. 4 PM in central Europe was 10 AM in New York, and the closing of Herstatt left $620 billion of Herstatt's foreign exchange transactions in the international pipeline. All of Herstatt's outstanding dollar transactions had been left dangling unsettled in the New York clearinghouse system. Who would pay?

Herstatt's US correspondent bank was Chase Manhattan, but Chase refused to pay claims against Herstatt. This posed an immediate threat to CHIPS, the Clearinghouse Interbank Payment System, the computer system for dollar payments and settlements among banks. Then as now, CHIPS was the world's main "private plumbing artery" – the aorta of cash liquidity. "A panicked chain reaction of nonpayments backed up throughout CHIPS, threatening global plumbing gridlock. For several months international lending fell drastically, maturities shortened, and interest rate risk premiums were demanded from some banks. It took a year for counterparties to disentangle who owed what to whom." [S. Solomon, 116-117]

Over the years, Herstatt has been cited repeatedly as a classic prototype of systemic meltdown. This was not because of the size of the losses, but because of the alarming way the interbank settlement system seized up. As Paul Erdman wrote, "...Bankhaus Herstatt of Cologne...was not that big a bank and hardly a key player in the global banking system, [but] it did have a large-scale foreign exchange business. Its closure took place after the settlement of the deutsche mark leg of foreign exchange transactions but before settlement of the dollar leg. In other words, the US banks doing business with Herstatt did not get the dollars they were due after they had already paid the marks they owed the German bank. Some of Herstatt's trading partners, faced with nonpayment, then refused to make payments on their own account or for customers. The result was a chain reaction that, in essence, froze transfers between banks and brought the whole financial system to a halt, a result that subsequently became known as 'the Herstatt effect.'" [Erdman, 71-72]

By the time the unelected and unaccountable central bankers assembled behind closed doors for their next monthly meeting in Basel in July 1974, Michele Sindona's Franklin National Bank on

New York's Long Island had also failed. The central bankers put out a delphic communiqué suggesting that they would be lenders of last resort for banks in their own country, providing temporary liquidity for banks in trouble. At the end of 1975, the central bankers approved the secret Basel Concordat, which purported to establish that supervision of bank solvency was the main responsibility of the host country in the case of foreign bank subsidiaries, and of the parent country in the case of bank branches. This secret Basel Concordat was made public only much later, in March 1981.

The dollar was up in September 1974, and then fell by 8% by January 1975. France rejoined the European snake in July 1975, but had to drop out again in March 1976. By the end of 1975, third world debt had surpassed $200 billion.

Monetary crisis and oil shock seemed remote to some, but their impact on the daily lives of Americans was very real: unemployment remained quite high in 1974-75. Dr. M. Harvey Brenner of Johns Hopkins University studied the impact upon individual human beings of the recession of these years. Brenner found a 2.3% increase in the overall mortality rate of the US population, a 2.8% increase in the rate of cardiovascular disease, a 1.4% increase in deaths from cirrhosis of the liver, and a 1% increase in suicides. There was a 6% jump in both arrests and in admissions to state mental hospitals. Brenner concluded that 45,000 people had died before they otherwise would have – about as many deaths in two years as in either the Korean or Vietnam wars.

FORD TO NEW YORK CITY: DROP DEAD

The reality of approaching depression hit the center of the world financial system, New York City, in March 1975. The city government had no money left and was unable to borrow. America's greatest city was bankrupt. Despite austerity that had begun under Mayor Lindsay, New York City's debt had reached $13.6 billion, and no bank was willing to provide credit for a bailout or a rollover. The collusion among bankers eager to force a crisis and attain a new level of austerity was clear enough. President Gerald Ford declined to do anything to help the city with words that one large tabloid and many New Yorkers interpreted as "Drop Dead." The city was put into receivership and its financial affairs, meaning almost all important government decisions, were placed in the hands of a Mutual Assistance Corporation (Big MAC) dominated by monetarist Felix Rohatyn of the Lazard Frères investment bank. Rohatyn served as austerity enforcer for Wall Street, and New York City went into irreversible decline. Poor Abe Beame, the elected mayor, "had all the power of the mayor of Paris during the [Nazi] occupation", as the Richmond Borough President noted. [Delamaide 159] The gutting of New York City's transportation, health, education, and other infrastructure in order to guarantee payments to the bondholders and banks was a pilot project which since has been repeated all over America. During the 1990s, Washington DC was subjected to a bankers' austerity dictatorship under a financial control board that looks and acts very much like Big MAC. Indeed, the Big MAC model is pretty much exemplary for the way the Federal Reserve runs the country.

In the midst of this madhouse, the top leaders of the leading industrial nations met at Rambouillet in the summer of 1975, inaugurating the series of largely empty yearly meetings that has continued ever since. Schmidt, Giscard, Callaghan, Ford, Miki and Moro took no action to restore an international monetary system. They were now resigned to life amidst the ruins of Bretton Woods, with floating rates and no dollar convertibility. The US policy was summed up as the "benign neglect" of the dollar. The French, now under the blueblood horseman President Giscard d'Estaing, gave up their long-standing Gaullist critique of the dominant Anglo-American line in international finance, and began their quick reversion to the status of *entente cordiale* junior partner of London.

France stopped mentioning the fact that gold was indispensable for a functioning world monetary system. The Rambouillet summit spawned nothing but the yearly confabs of the G-7 leaders, which merely showcased the impotence of the world leaders even to identify, much less to tackle, the great and urgent issues of monetary reform which only a Bretton Woods II could have resolved. This gathering was the prelude to a new series of capitulations by sovereign governments to the gaggle of cartels and oligopolies masquerading as "the market."

7. BRITISH POUND CRISIS, MARCH-DECEMBER 1976

In the meantime, the Sick Man of Europe appeared destined to sink beneath the waters of the North Sea, with journalists asking front-page questions like "Is Britain Dying?" In the wake of the oil the shock, the British had borrowed more than $2 billion from the IMF, exhausting the credit lines to which they had automatic access. In March 1976 the government of Nigeria gave the pound a downward push by liquidating part of its sterling balances kept in London. At the same time, a group of schemers inside the British Treasury rigged a round of sterling sales by the Bank of England to coincide with a reduction in the Bank of England's prime lending rate. The schemers may have been courting yet another competitive devaluation of the pound in the honored British tradition of beggar-my-neighbor. But soon the pound sterling was in free fall. As Volcker later was to discover, it is easy to start a sick currency on the downward track, but much harder to apply the brakes. The British hurried to procure means to support the pound, initially through swap agreements for $5.3 billion negotiated with the G-10 central banks. The US Secretary of the Treasury at that time was William Simon, a doctrinaire monetarist ideologue if there ever was one. Simon insisted that the British undergo the full IMF austerity treatment. Simon summed up his handiwork in informing US President Ford that "in agreeing to this the British Government has accepted the strict conditionality which the IMF would require." [James 280]

At this point Prime Minister Harold Wilson of the Labor Party resigned, and was replaced by James Callaghan, whose expertise in currency devaluations had been displayed in the pound crisis of November 1967. Wilson had been a protegé of Lord Victor Rothschild of the banking family, but Lord Rothschild was now looking ahead to the Thatcher era. Wilson had accordingly been undermined by a series of operations which had featured the participation of then-CIA Director and Thatcher ally George Bush. Callaghan was destined in fact to preside over nothing more than an interlude on the way to Thatcherism. A second tidal wave of selling hit the pound in September 1976.

Denis Healey, the right-wing Labour Party Chancellor of the Exchequer, attempted to extract more loans from the IMF, but the conditionalities demanded by the Fund were severe, including a £3 billion cut in the British budget. The Labour Party and the Callaghan cabinet were deeply divided, with left wing trade unionists opposing the IMF's austerity. Some ministers wanted protectionist measures. On November 23, 1976, Foreign Secretary Anthony Crosland cynically told the cabinet that "The Government should then say to the IMF, the Americans, and the Germans: if you demand any more of us we shall put up the shutters, wind down our defense commitments, introduce a siege economy. As the IMF was even more passionately opposed to protectionism than it was attached to monetarism, this threat would be sufficient to persuade the Fund to lend the money without unacceptable conditions." Indeed, some international finance officials were scared that the pound would now actually collapse. US Undersecretary of the Treasury for Monetary Affairs Edwin Yeo III later recalled: "We feared that if a country like Britain blew up, defaulted on its loans, and froze convertibility, we could have a real world depression." [James, 281]

The British finally signed their IMF letter of intent on December 15, 1976, pledging to maintain their incomes policy, cut their budget by £1.5 billion right away and then by £2 billion more in the following year, cut their deficit by £1.8 billion, and slow the rate of credit expansion over 3 years. The British also decided finally to liquidate the sterling balances with the help of the IMF, a task which was made less dangerous for them by the foreign exchange advantages inherent in their new North Sea oil wells, which began to come on line at this time. But despite North Sea oil, British inflation was still running at 18% during 1977.

In many ways this exercise was a dress rehearsal for the Volcker monetarist austerity in the United States three years later. The British began extensive reliance on their monetary growth rate targets for judging policy. More broadly, this crisis is associated with the abandonment of Keynesian economics by the British Labour Party, and by extension by leftists around the world. At the Labour Party conference of September 1976, Callaghan remarked that "we used to think that you could just spend your way out of a recession...I tell you, in all candor, that the option no longer exists and that in so far as it ever did exist, it only worked...by injecting bigger doses of inflation into the economy, followed by higher levels of unemployment." [James, 282] According to one British commentator, these were the "words which effectively buried Keynes." The liquidation of Keynes left the field dominated by the primitive Viennese monetarism of von Hayek and the even more primitive monetarism of Milton Friedman and his Chicago School. Callaghan himself would soon be supplanted by Thatcher.

Britain was not the only country that had a close encounter with monetary and financial collapse during late 1976. Italy was also hit during that year by a precipitous decline in the lira, and turned to the IMF and the European Community for loans. In December 1976, the Christian Democratic Prime Minister Giulio Andreotti, heading a minority cabinet that depended on the votes of the Italian Communist Party for its survival, warned the great financial powers that "were Italy to collapse both politically and economically, Italy would not be the only loser." [James, 284]

NORTH-SOUTH DIALOGUE: LOST CHANCE FOR MONETARY REFORM

In 1967, Pope Paul VI had issued the encyclical *Populorum Progressio*, a landmark call for world economic development as the primary means for securing world peace. Here the Pope had suggested the creation of an international development fund ("erarium") to issue grants and loans to poor countries. This encyclical, with its watchword that "development is the new name for peace," had energized the Catholic left in Latin America and elsewhere, and had kept alive the idea of a change in development policy. The United Nations had sponsored Development Decades, and had debated (but rejected) a Special United Nations Fund for Economic Development. These efforts had some effect, but by the 1970s the third world was clearly losing ground economically. In August 1976, government representatives from the 85 nations of the Non-Aligned Movement convened in Colombo, Sri Lanka for their Fifth Conference. This was the movement which had been founded at Bandung in 1955, and which had featured such leaders as Nehru, Nkrumah, Tito, Nasser, Sukarno, and others. The conference centered on the question of a new world economic order, which at this time was at the top of the world agenda. The Colombo meeting was preparatory for a North-South Conference of delegates from advanced industrial nations and third world developing states which was scheduled for Paris about a month later.

The consensus at Colombo, as summed up in the speech of Prime Minister Indira Gandhi of India, favored an immediate debt moratorium on the international financial obligations of the poorest third world countries, and also those which were "subjected to imperialist pressures." The Non-Aligned wanted a new world monetary system to replace the damaged Bretton Woods institutions, including the IMF. There was a call for the creation of new credit and cash liquidity for real economic development purposes. The Non-Aligned advocated triangular trade agreements involving OPEC oil producers, members of the Comecon bloc, and third world states, with OPEC providing financing and oil, the third world providing labor, markets, and natural resources, and the socialist bloc furnishing capital goods. There was a tacit consensus among the delegates that, if the rich OECD countries of the Rambouillet (western Europe, Japan, and the US) were to reject the third world demands, the Non-Aligned states should declare a unilateral debt moratorium. The Vietnamese suggested a third world economic bloc. The Italian government, chaired by Christian Democrat Giulio Andreotti (who stayed in office thanks to the continued support of Enrico Berlinguer's Italian Communist Party) was invited to represent the Non-Aligned in the councils of the G-7 and OECD; he was pleased to accept. Italian Foreign Minister Arnaldo Forlani, advised by the present writer in a number of meetings involving his *chef de cabinet*, Prefetto Semprini, at the Palazzo della Farnesina in Rome, proposed on August 20, 1976 the formation of an Organization for Technical Cooperation with the Developing Countries. Gerald Ford, attending the Republican National Convention in Kansas City, seemed unconcerned with the evident prospect of a moratorium on financial debt. The Miki government in Japan was also inclined to keep and expand its third world markets if possible, whatever happened to the New York and London banks.

On September 27, 1976, Guyana Foreign Minister Dr. Fred Wills addressed the 31st session of the UN General Assembly in New York and stated: "The crippling problem of debt and the servicing of debt has assumed a special urgency. Developing countries cannot afford to depart from their basic and fundamental demand made in Manila and Colombo earlier this year calling for measures of cancellation, rescheduling, and the declaration of moratoria. We must eschew all attempts to deal with this problem by the divisive tactics of a case-by-case approach. We cannot afford to mortgage the future of unborn generations to the obligations of burdensome capital repayments and crushing debt servicing. The time has come for a debt moratorium." On October 1, 1976 Italian Foreign Minister Forlani addressed the General Assembly, and stressed the traditional readiness of Italy to cooperate with the developing states. "Italy," he said, "is persuaded of the necessity, also emphasized at Colombo, to establish a new international economic order ("nuovo ordinamento economico internazionale"), which will open to each country a path to development.... This goal can only be achieved in an economic system which has solved the fundamental problems of raw materials, trade, the debt of developing countries, and technology transfer." Forlani pledged that Italy would work within the European Community and also bilaterally to pursue these goals. At the Paris North-South Conference in mid-September, it appeared that an agreement on monetary reform and a world development strategy might be found, since Andreotti's Italy, Miki's Japan, and even the France of Giscard d'Estaing were open to the third world demands, and were especially anxious not to alienate the oil-producing nations who appeared to be parties to the Colombo effort. But the conference was torpedoed by US Secretary of State Henry Kissinger with the help of the British Foreign Office, and one of the few chances for world monetary reform was quickly lost. The unity of the Non-Aligned was broken by the case-by-case (or divide and conquer) methods of Kissinger and the British.

8. THE CARTER DOLLAR CRISIS OF OCTOBER-NOVEMBER 1978

The election of Jimmy Carter was the harbinger of much economic woe. Carter was the former governor of Georgia, and had suffered a nervous breakdown after being defeated in a bid for re-election. (He later described this as his "born again" experience.) He had been groomed for the US Presidency by the Rockefeller-dominated Trilateral Commission: at the 1974 Trilateral meeting in Kyoto, Japan, Carter had reportedly been introduced by Gianni Agnelli as the next president of the

United States. The Carter cabinet was a hotbed of ineptitude, and the US government was reeling from the combined impact of Watergate and the ignominious 1975 termination of the Vietnam War. The Great U-turn of the US economy was to a very large extent the work of Carter, who promoted deregulation, appointed Volcker to the Federal Reserve, sabotaged nuclear energy development, made possible the rise of Khomeini, and played hob with the Atlantic alliance. Helmut Schmidt in particular went ballistic over Carter's unpredictability. Soon after the election, Carter and Mondale began talking about a "locomotive theory," according to which Germany and Japan were expected deliberately to inflate and weaken their currencies in order to relieve pressure on the very sick US dollar. Germany and Japan, not suprisingly, demurred.

If we examine the time span between September 1977 and October 1978, the fall of the dollar in relation to the yen was 40%, and in relation to the mark, 13%. With top US officials like Treasury Secretary Werner Michael Blumenthal demonstratively "talking down" the dollar with the idea they were helping US exports, the dollar continued to fall with unprecedented speed, losing about a quarter of its value between January 1978 and the end of October 1978. By the fall of 1978, US inflation was running at about 9% annually. The *Wall Street Journal* accused Carter of "wrecking the international monetary system for the second time in a decade." On October 24, 1978 the Carter administration imposed voluntary wage and price controls, with a 7% limit which would be enforced through guidelines for preference in the distribution of government contracts.

In November 1978, Carter announced that he had assembled a Dollar Defense Package, an intervention fund of $30 billion with which to defend the dollar against speculation. The dollar was to get concerted support from Japan, Germany, and Switzerland in what Volcker called "a good old-fashioned rescue program." [Volcker 150] These gigantic and costly exertions were only enough to procure a few months of stability, and a modest 7% lift for the dollar. During this period the US Treasury was also conducting support operations for the dollar by selling off gold bullion to the amount of 750,000 ounces per month. Another grim novelty were the "Carter bonds," US Treasury securities denominated in foreign currencies like yen and marks; this was the first time in a long time that the US had been forced to borrow directly from private investors in overseas capital markets. There was also a full 1% hike in the Federal Reserve's discount rate, which was engineered by Paul Volcker, at that time still operating as President of the New York Federal Reserve Bank. The discount rate, which had been at 6.5% in January 1978, had risen to 9.5% by November 1, 1978.

Volcker comments in his memoirs that "all pretense of insouciance was gone" when it came to the Carter Administration's view of the dollar. He describes top Treasury official Anthony Solomon as "nervous" about the need for continuous dollar purchases by the Treasury to avoid a new dollar decline. Indeed, there is reason to think that the dollar might have undergone a catastrophic collapse if the US currency had not been saved by a new oil shock, which multiplied world demand for dollars by increasing the dollar-denominated price of oil. It is thus clear that the dollar collapse of the latter part of 1978 represented another systemic crisis with the potential to blow apart the entire world financial system.

9. KHOMEINI AND THE SECOND WORLD OIL CRISIS, 1979

Demand for dollars received a powerful boost from the second oil shock of 1979. The Carter Administration, with Zbigniew Brzezinski and Cyrus Vance at the controls, had activated the Bernard Lewis-British intelligence "arc of crisis" plan for the Middle East. In the mind of Brzezinski, this was a gambit to threaten the southern flank of the USSR with militant Islamic fundamentalism. The British goals were of a longer-term nature. In any case, it was now the specter of the venerable MI-6 asset Ayatollah Khomeini which was agitated to raise the price of gas. The oil price began to rise in December 1978, as reports arrived from Iran about the final phases of the revolution against the Shah. The fall of the Shah's regime in January 1979 provided a plausible cover for reports that Iran's oil production was decreasing sharply. This report stampeded oil consumers to top off their storage facilities. The Seven Sisters and their OPEC cat's paw were able once again to jack up the oil price, which more than doubled during the year. By the first quarter of 1979, Japan's current accounts had been thrown once again into substantial deficit, and the yen weakened. The Bank of Japan was forced to raise interest rates four times in three months to support its own currency. When 1979 was over, it emerged that world oil production had not fallen, but the prices stayed up anyway. The 1979 doubling had more dramatic economic effects than the 1973 quadrupling, since the world economy was much weaker by 1979.

The 1979 second oil shock left the economic centers of the world with simultaneously high rates of unemployment and inflation. A new term, stagflation, was coined to describe this condition, and a "misery index" was devised by Carter to measure its severity. To calculate the misery index, you simply added the percentage of unemployed to the annual rate of inflation. By 1980 the misery index was 20%, more than three times its average level under Kennedy and Johnson. By now the British had brought their North Sea oil production on line, and were benefiting from oil shocks as befitted a net exporter of oil.

In the summer of 1979, the dollar was softening again. After attending the Tokyo economic summit of the G-7, Carter retired to Camp David to contemplate the panorama of the admittedly dismal US economic and political situation. The latest Seven Sisters extravaganza had engendered long lines of cars at gas stations across America, and while irate motorists blamed Khomeini, they also blamed Carter. US hostages were also being held in Teheran. Carter addressed the nation on July 15 with a mentally dissociated oration in which he evoked the national "malaise" and the "crisis of the American spirit." He seemed to be berating the American people for the incompetence of his own administration. This performance, which probably sealed Carter's political doom, documented to some degree the historical and cultural pessimism that had spread among elites and bureaucracies as a result of the economic and political traumas of the decade.

Part of the malaise was due to Carter's policy of wholesale deregulation. Oil and natural gas prices, airlines, trucking, and numerous other aspects of the US economy were being exempted from the regulations under which they and the country had prospered during the entire postwar era. The parity system of farm price supports also began to decay. Safety standards in the air and on the nation's highways deteriorated, and many smaller urban centers were deprived of air and trucking service. As we will see, even usury was deregulated.

Carter had also profiled himself as an active opponent of nuclear energy, both in the United States and abroad. A trifling incident occurred at the Three Mile Island nuclear plant near Harrisburg, Pennsylvania in the fall of 1979, most probably as the result of willful sabotage by pro-environmentalist extremists infiltrated among the workers in the plant. No one was killed, but the television networks had a field day. Carter's hostility to the nuclear option plus the hysteria developed by the mass media after Three Mile Island effectively sealed the doom of the American nuclear industry: after this time not one new nuclear reactor has been ordered for construction in the United States, and virtually all of those that had been ordered were cancelled.

THATCHER MILK SNATCHER

In addition to the second oil shock, the world economy was also assailed during 1979 by the pestilence of monetarism in a new and acute form: the new Tory regime of Margaret Thatcher.

Thatcher was a greengrocer's daughter who owed her political career to Lord Victor Rothschild, the patron of the pocket borough or rotten borough which Thatcher represented in the House of Commons. Thatcher had acquired the nickname of "Thatcher milk snatcher" when, as Minister of Education in the 1970 Ted Heath regime, she championed a looting measure that deprived British elementary school children aged between seven and eleven of their daily free container of milk. Free milk meant the risk of socialism, Thatcher averred. (But the outgoing Wilson Labour government had already deprived secondary school kids of their milk ration.) Methyr Tydfil, an impoverished Welsh coal mining town, protested that they had enough of malnutrition and rickets, and wanted to continue free distributions. Thatcher used threats to make them give up. Stealing milk from poverty-stricken little children to balance the budget so as to stabilize the market in gilts (British government securities) accurately encapsulates the savage cruelty of the policies of Thatcher and her crew. Thatcher seemed a caricature from a Dickens novel, but here she was exercising great power in the modern world.

The Thatcher ruling clique included Sir Keith Joseph, Sir Alfred Sherman, Nicholas Ridley, and Sir Allen Walters. The idol of 10 Downing Street became Friedrich von Hayek, the theoretician of rent-gouging and a barbarous relic of the Austrian reactionary circles of the 1920s. Even more than Friedman, von Hayek was the guiding spirit of the infamous Mount Pelerin Society, which had set itself up above Vevey on Lake Geneva, Switzerland (the home of the sinister Nestlé international food conglomerate). The Mont Pelerin group had started back in those postwar days when the FDR New Deal was being hailed around the world as the model for the successful modern state. The Mount Pelerin litany was less taxation of the rich, deregulation, privatization, weak government, budget cutting, austerity for the masses, and the various excesses of oligarchic libertarianism. In more general matters of scientific method, Thatcher was guided by Sir Karl Popper, a plodding and arid empiricist who had succeeded Lord Bertrand Russell as the president of the Aristotelian Society.

THE PLAGUE OF THATCHERISM

With the pound depreciating at 18% per year, Thatcher pledged to "drive inflation out of the economy." She did not spell out so clearly that she intended to do this on the backs of British working people and the long-suffering middle class of the tight little island. In June 1979, British Treasury Secretary Sir Geoffrey Howe quickly raised British interest rates from 12% to 17%, delivering a stunning blow to Britain's economy in the process. Those who objected to such much misery were told of the need to "be staunch," "stay the course," and "keep a stiff upper lip" – the litany of phlegmatic British ruling-class stoicism. By the time Thatcher had been in power for 18 months, British unemployment had doubled from 1.5 million to 3 million. This maneuver preceded the activities of Volcker at the US Federal Reserve; Volcker was in effect reading from a British script.

Between 1979 and 1990, Thatcher wildly deregulated and privatized, while letting Britain's infrastructure rot. She sold off publicly owned companies like North Sea oil, British Aerospace, Cable and Wireless, Rolls-Royce, British Leyland, British Steel, British Telecom and many more at prices which were a steal for the buyers and a rip-off for the British ratepayer. Because of Thatcher's example, the privatization of state-owned industry and even of basic infrastructure became an integral part of the "structural adjustment" measures dictated to would-be borrowers by the IMF. Thatcher's deregulation of animal feed standards set the stage for the Mad Cow disease epidemic and crisis of 1996. Thatcher's privatizations of local water services have caused permanent water shortages in many parts of Britain, quite part from any drought. Britain's "socialized medicine" National Health Care System has simply been ruined by Thatcher's cost-cutting, efficiency, and competition gimmicks. By the mid-1990s, rats were more numerous in merry England than people, with an increase in the rodents of 39% between 1970 and 1993.

Up until this time, the main international showcase of Milton Friedman's Chicago school monetarism had been the dictatorial regime of Chilean strongman Gen. Pinochet, who had placed the control room of his national economy in the hands of doctrinaire Chicago boys in 1976. Chile is of course one of the most Anglophile nations of Latin America, but was hardly a telegenic showcase for the new-look ultra-monetarism of the 1980s. Thatcher was a more effective demagogue: she exercised a quasi-hypnotic domination over Reagan, who hastened to repeat the Iron Lady's worn out clichés. British cabinet officials reportedly dreaded Thatcher, whose verbal tirades were supposed to be the equivalent of a thrashing with her oversized pocketbook. Her psychological ascendancy over the Anglophilic George Bush was, if anything, even stronger.

Thatcherism had an economic impact, and it induced a long-lasting political transformation when it was imitated by the US Republican Party. As Robert Kuttner wrote towards the end of the Reagan era, "...the ultra-*laissez-faire* internationalism of the Republican 1980s cherishes turbulence and makes domestic economic stabilization all but impossible." [Kuttner 21] The importance of national political decisions was diminished: "An integrated global market economy leaves little if any room for national *policy*. It serves as a relentless engine of *laissez-faire*. It also creates the image as well as the reality of government paralysis and government incompetence – which is very handy if you happen to be the conservative party whose doctrine is that governments are seldom competent anyway. This is why conservative parties are now [1987] ascendant throughout the western democracies." [Kuttner 23] On the American scene, "global laissez-faire drives a wedge between the Democratic Party and its ability to deliver populist remedies to its natural base of non-rich wage earners who are vulnerable to the vagaries of the market.... Many aspects of the Democratic Party's confusion today can be understood as a refusal to consider or define the limits of laissez-faire capitalism, as it operates globally." [Kuttner, 24]

10. VOLCKER'S 21% PRIME RATE BRINGS ON US DEPRESSION

After his malaise speech, Carter had demanded that every member of his cabinet submit a signed resignation. From the Treasury Carter ousted the inept W. Michael Blumenthal, known mainly for wanting to jaw-bone the dollar down. Blumenthal was replaced by G. William Miller, up to then the Fed Chairman. But now Carter introduced a truly disastrous innovation: he appointed as Federal Reserve Chairman Paul Adolph Volcker, soon to become one of the truly great usurers of modern times. At the time he was named by Carter, Volcker was the President of the Federal Reserve Bank of New York, that bastion of British and Morgan power. If the Soviet invasion of Afghanistan in December 1979 was the beginning of the end of the Soviet Empire, then the appointment of Volcker some months earlier was a harbinger of the industrial collapse of the United States. The Soviet aggression in Afghanistan, by increasing east-west military tensions, would normally have scared hot money out of Europe and into the safe haven of the US dollar. But by this time the dollar was so discredited that much of the hot money turned its back on all paper currencies and went into gold, which hit $875 on January 21, 1980.

Volcker was a monetarist and "financial institutions conservative," meaning that he cared little for the economic fate of the American people as a whole, but only reacted to threats to the big banks and to the Federal Reserve System. During the Carter years, a special task force of the New York Council on Foreign Relations developed a new US strategy for the 1980s which was summed up as the "controlled disintegration of the world economy." Volcker had been a member of that CFR team, and thus stood behind books like the Fred Hirsch's *Alternatives to Monetary Disorder* (1977), a product of the CFR's 1980s Project, in which controlled disintegration was openly discussed. We cite from the essay included in this book and entitled "Politicization in the World Economy: Necessary Conditions for an International Economic Order," by Fred Hirsch and Michael W. Doyle:

> The international economy in the 1980s is therefore likely to be a considerably looser regime than the international order established on paper (and at least substantially in reality) in the original articles of the IMF and in the provisions of the GATT. The system is likely to be loose in a variety of ways: replete with exceptions on aspects such as the monetary regime, customs unions, free-trade areas and association agreements, and containing special provisions for developing countries and domestic producers facing injury.
>
> The obvious danger in such a regime resides in its potential instability. Some limited loosening is by no means unequivocally undesirable. It can be seen as a rational response to the earlier tendency, which was most manifest in the 1960s, for economic integration to run far ahead of both actual and desired political integration, thereby forcing countries into sub-optimal policy choices. *A degree of controlled dis-integration in the world economy is a legitimate objective for the 1980s and may be the most realistic one for a moderate international economic order.* A central normative problem for the international economic order in the years ahead is how to ensure that the dis-integration indeed occurs in a controlled way and does not rather spiral into damaging restrictionism." [80]

This quote comes from the sub-section entitled "Prerequisites of a Controlled Loosening." Speaking in Leeds, Yorkshire, England in 1978, Volcker had overtly repeated the finding of this study that "controlled disintegration is a legitimate objective of the 1980's." This objective Volcker now proceeded to pursue with a vengeance.

Volcker immediately began to imitate the London policy by raising US interest rates – in order, he claimed, to respond to the soaring 14% inflation rate and to the weakness of the dollar. Volcker posed as a disciple of Milton Friedman. He argued that the only important variable was the M1 money supply. If this could be gotten under control, Volcker claimed, a golden age of prosperity would follow. During the late summer of 1979, the Fed and the Treasury sold off $4.6 billion of foreign currencies to support the dollar.

Volcker launched his program with a theatrical gesture: he flew home from the IMF annual meeting in Belgrade and convened unusual weekend meetings of the Federal Reserve and the Open Market Committee. On October 6, 1979 an increase of the discount rate from an already steep 11% to 12% was announced. Volcker also revamped the Fed's system for guiding the federal funds rate, the amount of interest paid by banks for their overnight borrowings among themselves. Volcker's new methods meant that the federal funds rate would fluctuate more over the short term. The dollar got a 5% pop out of Volcker's new line.

THE HIGHEST INTEREST RATES SINCE BEFORE JESUS CHRIST

Volcker pushed US interest rates inexorably higher. In March of 1980, Carter and Volcker added a patchwork of credit controls, and Carter attacked the population for using credit cards too much. By April 1980, the prime rate charged by US money center banks to their most reputable customers had reached 20%. In the second quarter of 1980, the government's estimate of real Gross National Product was plummeting at a yearly rate of 10%; it was the sharpest single-quarter drop in postwar US history. (Congressman Henry Reuss later complained that "for the first time in history, a Democratic President put the economy into recession.") After fluctuating downward to 11% in July,

---

[80] Hirsch 55, emphasis in original.

the US prime rate levitated upward again and reached 21.5% a few days before Christmas 1980. US rates stayed high, hovering at 20.5% in May 1981. These were, as German Chancellor Helmut Schmidt and others complained, the "highest real interest rates since the birth of Christ."

Although Helmut Schmidt was never the prophet he thought he was, he was correct in his warning of June 2, 1981 that Volcker's high interest rate policy was very close to precipitating world depression. There were rumors on Wall Street that same day that total US banks reserves were so low that many banks were not able to meet their reserve requirements; the entire US banking system was said to be only hours from total collapse.

Volcker's usury made 1980 one of the worst years since World War II for the average weekly earnings of American working people. These earnings fell 5.8% during 1980 alone. Between 1979 and 1982, the Volcker high interest rate regime cut the average weekly wages of American production workers by 11.2%, or almost $34 in 1982 dollars. This was the biggest short-term drop in living standards in the postwar period – up to that point.

As Volcker's interest rates rose, they collided with the anti-usury laws that were on the books in many states. As Volcker ratcheted interest rates higher and higher, the legal usury ceiling shut down local lending in state after state. In Arkansas, an interest rate limit of 10% was anchored in the anti-usury article of the state constitution itself. Voters twice rejected attempts to repeal this provision, even though home mortgages and auto loans were impossible to obtain within the state. Ultimately this resistance collapsed. In an incredible act of folly, the US Congress voted to abolish all these usury laws. This was part of the Banking Act of 1980, under which all banks were obliged to keep their reserves at the Fed. With this law, the Fed gave up its famous Regulation Q, which had been used to regulate the interest rates that banks could pay on savings accounts. Banks could now pay any interest they wanted, including on checking accounts. Savings and loan institutions were soon deregulated, and allowed to lend money not just to home buyers, but to a whole range of high-risk activities as well. This set the stage for the S&L debacle of the mid-1980s, the bill for which is now pushing above one trillion dollars.

The assertion here that Volcker and his policies pitched the United States into a new great economic depression must not be seen as some kind of rhetorical flourish or hyperbole. At least one authoritative writer dates the beginning of the depression back to the early 1970s, when real wages began to decline. This is Wallace Peterson's argument in his 1994 *Silent Depression,* where he identifies the *"silent depression"* as "two decades of sluggish economic health, a time when, by most of the accepted measuring rods, the economy's performance was subnormal. The word 'depression' ...is the appropriate label for our condition because, first, the downturn has continued for such a long period of time – twenty years – and also because from three-fourths to four fifths of Americans saw the American Dream slipping from their grasp at one time or another during these years." Why is this depression not generally recognized? Peterson replies that "this depression is *silent* because there is none of the sound and fury that come with a major crash such as the one in 1929; much of the public, the press, and the people in the government sense that something has indeed gone wrong, but they are sure of exactly what it is." [W. Peterson, 9-10] The key to the distinction is the difference between an economic depression and a financial panic. After 1971-73, the real economy has been increasingly thrown into depression as a means of staving off financial panic.

11. COLLAPSE OF THE HUNT BROTHERS' SILVER CORNER, 1980

On January 21, 1980 the price of gold in London reached a peak of $875 per troy ounce; fear of Carter's erratic behavior and of more inflation had stimulated demand. In the same month, the attempt by the Hunt brothers to corner the world silver market lifted silver to $52 per ounce before this bubble was deflated. The wealthy Hunt brothers of Texas had begun buying silver in 1973. By early 1980, the Hunts controlled more than two thirds of the silver in the United States. In January 1980, an ounce of silver was selling for $52.50, compared to $6 in early 1979. The Hunts had borrowed more than $1.8 billion to buy silver futures contracts on very low cash margins – sometimes as little as 5%, due to lack of action by the ineffective Commodity Futures Trading Commission. In February and March of 1980, the Hunts were absorbing almost 10% of all the bank credit generated in the United States. They also drew financial resources from the Eurodollar market, from Saudi Arabia, and from others.

When Volcker's interest rates pushed the prime rate to 20%, the Hunts were faced with more debt service on their silver holdings than they could afford to pay. On Silver Thursday, March 27, 1980, the price of silver crashed down to $10.40. This threatened to bankrupt not only the Hunts, but also their broker, Bache Halsey Stuart Shields, along with the First National Bank of Chicago, and who knows what other institutions. Volcker appears to have conducted support operations for silver to prevent Bache, which was liquidating silver contracts to recoup part of its losses, from going belly up. Volcker personally helped to broker a deal between the Hunts and Engelhard Mineral and Chemicals Corporation which allowed the Hunts to pay a off debt of $650 million using silver rather than cash.

But because of the gravity of the threat to the banking system, Volcker went even further: he sponsored a consortium of 13 banks which floated a $1.1-billion, ten-year loan to permit the Hunts to pay off their short-term obligations. The buccaneering Hunts lost more than $2 billion to their own megalomania and greed. Overall it had been another brush with meltdown, the first of several facilitated by Volcker's usury.

Volcker's 21.5% prime rate vastly accelerated the de-industrialization on the battered US economy; it was compared by some to a Soviet thermonuclear attack. As a result of the unprecedented interest rates, the traditional industrial areas of the Great Lakes and the north Atlantic seaboard collapsed into a rust bowl. Steel mills, chemical plants, plus small and medium concerns that had been weakened by the oil shocks now had no strength left, and succumbed. The same thing happened in home building. In Kentucky, the home builders' association printed wanted posters with mug shots of the seven governors of the Federal Reserve who were accused of "premeditated and calculated cold-blooded murder of millions of small businesses." Middle class businessmen sported lapel stickers with a hangman's noose and the inscription: "Hang Tall, Paul." By 1982, Volcker had created the worst recession since World War II. Hatred of Volcker was probably the most important single factor in Carter's 1980 election defeat. But Reagan kept Volcker at the Fed for all but the last year of his two terms in the White House.

THE GREAT U-TURN

The pro-labor research team of Bennett Harrison and Barry Bluestone later chronicled the profound anti-labor shift in American national policy that set in with Carter and was continued under Reagan in their 1988 book, *The Great U-Turn*. They are unquestionably right in pointing out that the decision to repudiate the social contract which had governed labor relations during the entire postwar period was made under Carter, the Democrat. They also stress the importance of ideologues like Jude Wanniski, Arthur Laffer, and David Stockman in the development of supply-side economics, the eclectic mass of slogans which was used to justify such pieces of folly as the Kemp-Roth tax cuts, which benefited a tiny layer of parasites at the expense of the common weal.

Harrison and Bluestone show that the 4.5 million people thrown on the streets as unemployed during the 1979-1982 interval, even as US GNP fell by 4.9% in the last quarter of 1981 and by an additional 5.5% in the first quarter of 1982, were the precondition for historic defeats of the labor movement whose effects are still being suffered. They also note how the great industrial cities of the Great Lakes and Middle West, including Youngstown, Detroit, Buffalo, and Akron were brought to their knees.

SENATOR BYRD TAKES ON THE VOLCKER FED

In March 1982 Volcker was hauled before a Senate committee by Minority Leader Robert Byrd (D-W. Va.) and other Democrats. They demanded that the astronomical rates come down. Volcker said "Look, I can't affect interest rates," disingenuously claiming that only the market could do that. Byrd threatened that if Volcker failed to act, the Congress might pass a law forcing interest rates down. That would have been an important step toward the necessary policy, the nationalization of the privately owned, privately managed and runaway central bank.

"To whom are you accountable?" Byrd asked Volcker at one point.

"Well, the Congress created us and the Congress can uncreate us," was Volcker's reply. [Greider 1987, 473] But the doughty Byrd soon found that only 15 of his 46 Democrats would support a bill directing the Fed to lower interest rates.

There were very few forms of productive activity that could have sustained a 21.5% prime rate. In fact, there were very few legal businesses of any type that could have kept going at this rate. The only way to remain solvent was now to speculate – or worse. Drug money laundering, organized crime, and other manifestations of the black or submerged economy were now among the few viable areas of investment. It was the reverse of the traditional American pro-industrial dirigism. By the middle of 1982, Volcker and his interest rates had brought about a violent contraction of the real economy of the US and the world. Volcker had started a severe world economic depression. Benjamin Strong and the New York Fed had provoked the First Great Depression of twentieth-century America during the 1920s; Volcker's Fed had now precipitated the Second Great Depression.

With the Drysdale and Penn Square debacles and the Mexican bankruptcy looming on the near horizon, it was clear that further pursuit of the monetarist high interest rate regime would generate more than a depression collapse of the real economy: the next step would have been a disintegration of the banking and financial system worldwide. It was at this point, in July-August 1982, that Volcker threw overboard the Friedmanite theories that had guided his 33-month orgy of usury. Volcker now reversed his field and began to lower the Fed funds rate and ease credit. Outright lunatics like Milton Friedman, and Beryl Sprinkel at the White House, protested that Volcker had gone soft.

As Reagan administration official and "deficit hawk" David Stockman explained at the time: "Volcker is a financial-institutions conservative and that's how he thinks." Volcker didn't care how high the jobless rate might be, Stockman added, "but, if there's fragility in the financial system, then he moves." One Federal Reserve Bank vice president commented: "We have a very crude steering mechanism. In retrospect, I wouldn't have steered so close to the edge." [Greider 1987, 530] But many Americans are still on the edge.

On August 3, 1982, the valiant Sen. Byrd had introduced his Balanced Monetary Policy Act of 1982, which ordered the Fed to bring interest rates down. "It is time for Congress to wrest control of monetary policy from the hands of a tiny band of monetary ideologues in the White House, the Administration, and the Federal Reserve," said Byrd. "It is time for basic economic policy once more to be set by those elected officials who must bear the final responsibility." [Greider 1987, 513]

This remains an excellent argument for repealing the Federal Reserve Act of 1913. Byrd's bill alarmed Volcker and the rest of the Fed clique. The Byrd measure would have been the first time that the legal, constitutional, and elected government had formally brought the Fed to heel. It would probably not have been the last time, and it might have proven the antechamber to nationalization.

EMS: THE SECOND PHASE THAT NEVER WAS

Certain circles in western Europe still cultivated a spirit of economic realism, and had not yet reached the level of collective dementia exhibited by the wildly monetarist Anglo-Americans. Among these were two clever freemasons, French President Giscard d'Estaing and German Chancellor Helmut Schmidt. These two had become friendly during the monetary tempests of the 1960s, when they both attended numerous conferences as finance ministers for their respective countries. Schmidt in particular was horrified by the "unpredictable" and erratic Carter. As the Belgian economist Robert Triffin put it, Schmidt and Giscard wanted to create "an oasis of stability less at the mercy of the backwash effects of US policies and policy failures." [James, 298] Volcker's economic policies alarmed German bankers, and impelled Schmidt and Giscard to take measures of economic self-defense which otherwise might not have come about.

The high point of the Schmidt-Giscard cooperation was the Bremen EEC summit of July 1978, which upgraded the European currency snake into the European Monetary System, which had the potential to become more than a useful grid of fixed parities and a "zone of monetary stability." Plans were drawn up for a "second phase " of the EMS, which would have included lending at preferential rates to third world customers who would use the credit thus extended for capital goods purchases pertaining to their economic development projects. In September of 1978, Giscard d'Estaing's UDF party issued a proposal for a $100 billion development program to be sponsored by Europe and carried out in Africa. This approach was built on the earlier efforts of Jürgen Ponto, the chairman of Dresdner Bank, who had been assassinated by the Baader-Meinhof group (a reputed British intelligence asset) in the summer of 1977. Unfortunately, the plans for the second phase of the EMS remained on the shelf and were never realized. The British boycotted the early phase of the EMS, but later joined it, causing even greater trouble on the inside.

During this same period, former Prime Minister Aldo Moro of Italy attempted to provide his country with a stable government by securing the cooperation of the Italian Communist Party for a nationalist coalition headed by Giulio Andreotti. Moro was kidnapped and assassinated by the Red Brigades during the spring of 1978, and his widow later accused Henry Kissinger of having made death threats to her late husband.[81] Italian magistrates wanted Kissinger to answer questions on the matter, but he abruptly departed the country and has never testified. By the early 1980s, the power of the older European nationalists and industrialists was fading.

$12 TRILLION IN LOST PRODUCTION

Let us pause for a moment during the second year of the Reagan presidency to survey the impact on the real economy of the monetary crises, the dollar devaluations, the two oil shocks, and the Volcker orgy of usury. Many believe that the great conflagrations of international high finance have little relevance to economic conditions on Main Street. Reality is otherwise. During the fixed-parity, well-regulated years of the 1960s, officially measured overall US economic growth averaged 4.1% per year. The official GNP expanded by more than 50% during the decade. During the floating-rate

---

[81] See W. Tarpley et al., *Chi ha ucciso Aldo Moro* (Milano: Bollettino Internazionale, 1978).

and increasingly deregulated 1970s official economic growth was an anemic 2.9% per year, and more and more of this was financial fluff.

Viewed from a longer historical perspective: yearly US economic growth after the Civil War averaged 3.4%. The secular downturn in this figure came in 1973, the year when the parities finally collapsed and the floating rates came to stay. Between 1973 and 1993, US economic growth averaged 2.3% By 1993, the total production lost by the US economy in the floating rate era added up to an estimated $12 trillion in 1973 constant dollars. This means a loss of $40,000 per person, enough to pay off the national debt AND restore the entire infrastructure to its 1973 level, according to the calculations of Jeffrey Madrick in his *End of Affluence*. Madrick forecast that "by the year 2013 the total shortfall, assuming the economy grows at 1 percent a year less than our historical norm, will amount to more than $35 trillion of lost production since 1973."

32 MILLION JOBS WIPED OUT

In 1982 Bluestone and Harrison set out to examine the ongoing de-industrialization of America, including such phenomena as the runaway shop, plant closings, flight capital, and disinvestment. Their conclusion was that "it is evident that somewhere between 32 and 38 million jobs were lost during the 1970s as the direct result of private disinvestment in American business." [Bluestone 1982, 8] Many of these job losses were concentrated in the period after Volcker's appointment to head the Federal Reserve, when the 20% prime rates (and even higher borrowing rates for less preferred customers) provoked a hecatomb of businesses. The losses were heavily concentrated in the basics – auto, steel, and tires. Between January 1979 and December 1980, US automobile producers announced the shutdown of twenty plants employing over 50,000 workers. Because of the loss of business to suppliers of auto parts, materials, and components, these twenty plant closures forced the shutdown of 80 additional plants upstream. Job losses in the subcontractor and supplier network were estimated at 350,000 by the Congressional Budget Office, and at 650,000 by the AFL-CIO.

YOUNGSTOWN STEEL PLANTS DESTROYED BY DYNAMITE

On Thanksgiving Day, 1979, when the Volcker interest rate escalation was already in full swing, the US Steel Corporation placed an ad in the *New York Times*:

> The United States Steel Corporation announced yesterday that it was closing 14 plants and mills in eight states. About 13,000 production and white collar workers will loose their jobs. The cutback represents about 8 per cent of the company's work force. The retrenchment was one of the most sweeping in the industry's history....

A fourteenth shutdown hit the US Steel plant in Youngstown, Ohio, where an additional 3,500 jobs were lost. Youngstown at that time was still attempting to recover from the closure of the Campbell Works, owned by the Youngstown Sheet and Tube Company, which had obliterated 4100 jobs. In Youngstown, the steelworkers' union local and area businessmen tried to buy the plants which had been operated by Youngstown Sheet and Tube. The US Steel management fought implacably to prevent the plants from being put back into production. On April 28, 1982, the US Steel managers used high explosives to blow up four blast furnaces at a Youngstown plant. Television crews were present. Neither Nazi Germany nor Tojo's Japan nor Stalin's USSR had ever succeeded in blowing up an American steel mill, but Volcker had succeeded. It was in many ways the defining moment of the Volcker era. No fewer than 15 steel plants closed in the spring of 1985, and many of them were also blown up.

All told, plant closures in the American steel industry reduced the nation's steel producing capacity by a hefty 11%. According to the United Rubber Workers of America, between mid-1975 and early 1981 there were 24 shutdowns of US tire and rubber plants, wiping out 20,000 jobs. It was during this dismal period that the distinction between "sunrise" and "sunset" industries, and among "rust belt", "frost belt" and "sun belt" economic regions were coined. But almost half the jobs lost to plant closings during the 1970s were lost in the so-called sunbelt states of the south and west. Despite popular delusions, the proportion of pre-1970 plants that were closed by 1976 was higher in the southern states than elsewhere. Corporate managers and the bankers whom they served began to demand a friendly business climate, meaning no unions, low wages, low corporate income taxes, and most of all low payroll taxes, unemployment benefits, and welfare contributions. From all of these points of view, poverty-stricken Mississippi was the model state. A bidding war or "new war between the states" emerged as states competed to offer tax breaks, cost-free infrastructure, and other inducements to get plants relocated within their borders. The dominant theme in trade union negotiations became the "give back", the surrender of gains in wages, pensions, working conditions, and grievance procedures dearly won in past years. It was a race to the bottom, with working families as the losers.

TAKING DOWN THE AMERICAN WAY OF LIFE

Living standards and real wages, which had come to a full stop in their progress and gone into reverse around 1970, were now in full retreat. *Business Week* published a celebrated and very sinister editorial calling for the dismantling of the standard of living of American working people. *Business Week* pontificated that "some people will obviously have to do with less, or with substitutes, so that the economy as a whole can get the most mileage out of available capital.... Indeed, cities and states, the home mortgage market, small business and the consumer, will all get less than they want because the basic health of the US is based on the basic health of its corporations and banks: the biggest borrowers and the biggest lenders. Compromises, in terms of who gets and who does without, that would have been unthinkable only a few years ago, will be made in the coming years because the economic future not only of the US but also of the whole world is on the line today."[82] Here we have a foreshadowing of the mass austerity of the late 1990s global economy. Globaloney was introduced as a desperate expedient to meet the strains of a crisis-ridden world economy in which monetary and price structures had undergone catastrophic disruption. Not much later, the very same nostrums were being touted as a model that developing and newly independent countries should embrace because of its own intrinsic merit.

1982: START OF THE WORLD ECONOMIC DEPRESSION

In reality, it is misleading to classify the plant closings of the late 1970s and early 1980s merely under the heading of de-industrialization, although this is certainly true as far as it goes. These plant closures represented the shock front of a *world economic depression*, which engulfed many parts of the world in 1981-1982. A total of 66,000 US firms filed for bankruptcy protection in 1982, the highest level since 1932. According to Dun and Bradstreet, 24,900 firms ceased operating completely and were liquidated. In December 1982 12 million Americans were officially out of work, while another 5 million had given up in despair.

Since 1982 the entire world, formally speaking, has been in depression, in the way the United States was in the late 1930s. Germany had been the most successful economy of the postwar period.

---

[82] *Business Week*, October 12, 1974.

Until 1981-2, Germany had a chronic labor shortage, with more jobs offered than workers unemployed. It was in 1981-82 that the jobless rate shot up to the neighborhood of 2 to 3 million and stayed there year after year. It was also in 1981-82 that the physical volume of world trade, which had been rising steadily for decades, turned downwards and never again regained its previous rate of growth.

According to the OECD's study *Maritime Transport*, the total annual tonnage of world trade carried by ships reached a 1979 high of 3.714 billion metric tons. By 1983, seaborne trade was down to 3,090 billion metric tons. The 1979 level was not again exceeded until 1989. (If the total volume of world seaborne trade tonnage is calculated on a per capita basis, then the high reached in 1979-80 has never been matched since.)

1982 worldwide bankruptcies in business and commercial banking were at the highest level since World War II. International Harvester ($4.22 billion in debt), in the US, Dome Petroleum ($6 billion in debt) and Massey-Ferguson ($1.2 billion in debt) in Canada, and AEG Telefunken ($2 billion in debt, 160,000 employees) in West Germany all went bankrupt during 1982. Chrysler would have joined the list, had it no been for the histrionic abilities of Mr. Iacocca, who put aside free market slogans to plead for and secure a US government bailout, which Chrysler workers (if not "Iacuckoo" and the company's top management) fully deserved.

12. DRYSDALE, PENN SQUARE, AMBROSIANO ALL BANKRUPT

Another sign of the times was the bankruptcy of Drysdale Government Securities, a creature of the Chase Manhattan Bank. With Reagan's big deficits, the Treasury securities market was up to $30 billion a day in turnover, more than ever before. Here a certain David Heuwetter began using a capital of about $10 million to leverage positions of as much as $10 billion in the Treasury securities market. One of his favorite procedures was repos – repurchase agreements, sales of securities with a promise to repurchase at a specified price or, in other words, getting a loan using the securities as collateral. When the loan was paid back, the securities would be returned. Heuwetter also liked reverse repos, paying a price to get securities into his own hands. Heuwetter would obtain the securities and then sell them, thus selling short what he had borrowed, hoping to buy them later for less.

Heuwetter was playing a shell game that depended on more and more new repo deals. After a while, other securities dealers saw that Heuwetter with his 1000:1 leverage was dramatically overextended, and stopped dealing with him. Heuwetter's friends at Chase Manhattan helped Drysdale by borrowing securities from Merrill Lynch when Heuwetter needed them for short covering. Then Merrill Lynch got cold feet and demanded repayment. Chase was evasive until Merrill Lynch threatened to dump on the market hundreds of millions of dollars' worth of Chase certificates of deposit it was holding, which would have collapsed their value. Heuwetter finally defaulted on May 17, 1982. Anthony Solomon, the President of the New York Fed, pumped in billions of liquidity to prevent panic. Chase ended up losing $117 million, and its CEO Willard Butcher had egg all over his face.

Interestingly, when Orange County, California went bankrupt in 1994, it turned out that the favorite plaything of its manager Robert Citron had been the repo, and that Citron had been encouraged by Merrill Lynch. The 1982 blather about improving internal controls had proven meaningless. Solomon of the New York Fed had promised more monitoring of securities trading, but that did not prevent Salomon Brothers under John Gutfreund from illegally attempting to corner the Treasury securities market in 1991.

Panic was in the air during 1982. In February 1982, a newspaper report of problems at the Hartford Federal Savings and Loan in Hartford, Connecticut triggered a panic run by depositors. This S&L was soon merged into another bank, but it is worth remembering that the infamous S&L crisis of the middle 1980s was a direct result of the Volcker policies: S&L institutions always faced the problem of borrowing short-term to lend long-term on home mortgages. Volcker jacked the short-term interest rates up so high that no traditional S&L could stay in business.

In July 5, 1982 the smallish Penn Square Bank of Oklahoma City, based at a shopping center and with capital of just $39 million, was seized by the Comptroller of the Currency, the top Treasury official charged with oversight of national banks. Penn Square had bad loans of more than $47 million to oil entrepreneurs. But that was just the tip of the iceberg. Penn Square had developed an extensive off balance-sheet portfolio of letters of credit and loan participations. Penn Square had taken the lead in organizing $2 billion of participation loans to Oklahoma oil interests which had involved much bigger banks. Chase Manhattan was into these participation loans for $200 million, Conti Illinois for $1 billion, and Seattle-First National (called Seafirst) for $400 million. Penn Square itself had outstanding claims of $506 million. When it folded, depositors lost their money in excess of the insurance limit for the first – although not the last – time in the history of the Federal Deposit Insurance Corporation.

Seafirst was mortally wounded by the Penn Square fiasco, and for a time a banking panic was imminent in the Pacific Northwest. Thirteen big money center banks had to come up with $1.5 billion in loans to prevent a run on Seafirst in early 1983. But foreign and out of state depositors then panicked anyway, and Seafirst had to seek a takeover by the Bank of America, an operation that would also have blown up without even more loans from the San Francisco Fed. Seafirst had been the twenty-sixth largest bank in the United States and the largest in Washington state.

Continental Illinois, the seventh largest bank in the US, was also mortally wounded by the Penn Square collapse, although the death agony lasted longer than for Seafirst. Conti chalked up quarterly losses of $61 million and then $99 million in the wake of the Penn Square debacle, and never recovered. Confidence was not helped when the Banco Ambrosiano, Italy's largest private bank, failed in July, 1982. Both Italy, the home of the parent company, and the government of Luxembourg, where much of the bank's business took place, declined to rush in with cash because technically Ambrosiano Holding SA (Luxembourg) was a holding company, and not a bank.

Related to the fall of the Banco Ambrosiano was also the murder of Roberto Calvi, the man who had controlled that bank. Calvi was found hanging under the Blackfriars Bridge in London. British courts ruled that his death was a suicide, despite the physical impossibility of suicide in such a location and despite evidence that Calvi had been murdered according to the ritual of certain British Freemasons.

13. FRIDAY, AUGUST 13, 1982: VOLCKER'S MEXICAN WEEKEND

"My Latin loans are as good as a T-bill." Walter Wriston, boss of Citibank, c. 1981.

"The idea was that if their [Mexican] banks didn't open Monday morning, then our banks wouldn't open on Tuesday." – Tim McNamar, Undersecretary of the Treasury. [S. Solomon, 194]

During Reagan's first two years in office, the United States remained gripped by the very severe Volcker recession. In the developing countries, Volcker's interest rates detonated a debt crisis. Harbingers had included debt crises in places like Zaire, Peru, and Turkey during the 1970s. By 1980 India was in trouble, but the British secured their own interests preemptively by getting India a $5.3

billion bailout, the biggest in IMF history, in 1981, before the big debt crisis got rolling. The beneficiaries were the London banks whose exposure to India had been the greatest.

Mexico was one of the leading developing countries, and, with about $80 billion owed, one of the superpowers of debt. With India already safely taken care of, British intelligence had stoked the crisis with a summer 1982 BBC "Money Programme" documentary loudly warning that Mexico was rapidly running out of cash. Volcker tells us in his memoirs that he was fishing in Wyoming on August 9, 1982 when he was visited by the chairman of the Continental Illinois Bank, "who flew out to tell me the bank was in so much trouble that it would need Federal Reserve support." [Volcker, 200] The next day, August 10, "my office called to tell me Mexico was about out of money, so I headed back to Washington almost fishless." [Volcker, 200]

The bankruptcy of Mexico became impossible to conceal by August 13, 1982, when the monetarist finance minister of that much-exploited country, Jesus Silva Herzog, arrived in Washington to report that Mexico was insolvent and would require a bailout package of several billion dollars. If sufficient aid were not forthcoming, added Silva, Mexican President Lopez Portillo was ready to go into a speed-dialing mode to contact world heads of state and announce a formal Mexican default on $80 billion of international financial debt.

That would have spelled the end of the System.

Volcker and IMF Managing Director Jacques de la Rosière scrambled frantically for 48 hours in a desperate bid to stave off world meltdown with a plausible-looking emergency bailout package. Treasury Secretary Don Regan and his subaltern Tim McNamar joined in. Volcker got $1.5 from the IMF and the Group of 10. Another $1 billion came from the Commodity Credit Corporation, and the last billion was provided by US purchases of Mexican oil. Even as Hades gaped below their feet, US Energy Department bureaucrats wanted to haggle about the price of that oil. Volcker directed their attention to the big picture, saying: "I don't give a damn what you pay for oil! If you *don't* do it, the whole thing is going to come crashing down – and it'll be your fault!" [S. Solomon, 203]

On August 20, 1982 Mexico announced a suspension of payments on its foreign debt. On September 1, 1982 Mexican President Jose Lopez Portillo decreed the nationalization of the Mexican banking system, while denouncing "parasitical bankers who are destroying the nation." He also began to track down Mexican flight capital in the United States. He imposed comprehensive exchange controls to curtail future capital flight, and limited repatriation of dividends to a yearly 15% of the net worth of the Mexican subsidiary. Soon the Mexican government made clear that it would not make principal payments until 1984. Speaking at United Nations headquarters on October 1, 1982, Lopez Portillo deplored the combination of high interest rates and collapsing raw materials prices, while warning of a "New Dark Age."

The Mexican bank nationalization coincided with the 1982 IMF-World Bank annual meeting in Toronto. There was considerable hysteria among the crowd of 150 finance ministers, 50 central bankers, 1000 commercial bankers, and 1000 reporters. Four horsemen of usury attempted to impose a common strategy on this unruly mass. They were Volcker, Bank of England Governor Gordon Richardson, Swiss central bank chief Fritz Leutwiler, and de la Rosière of the IMF. According to Leutwiler, all were "worried" and "depressed."

Foremost in the minds of the four champions of usury was not the life or death of millions of Mexican campesinos. They were concerned about a rupture of the world's interbank plumbing system. At this point Chemical Bank and Manufacturers Hanover Trust were acting as Mexico's representatives in CHIPS, the Clearinghouse Interbank Payment System. Now a panic run on Mexican banks developed, and on September 7, 1982 Mexican banks directed Chemical and Manny Hanny to pay out $70 million more than Mexico could cover.

ANOTHER THREAT OF CHIPS MELTDOWN

Immediately the following situation developed: "CHIPS was run by America's biggest banks, which executed payment transfers on behalf of correspondent banks around the world. At the end of the day they netted out the transactions to be settled between them. Each bank collected what it was owed from its correspondents. But if all the netted CHIPS transactions could not be settled, then no CHIPS payments were made. Thus if Manufacturers and Chemical refused to cover the Mexicans' $70 million shortfall, all CHIPS transactions would unwind. In short order the world's dollar payment system would freeze up. The international interbank market was already quaking from the teetering of Continental Illinois and other US banks and the June 1982 collapse of Italy's Banco Ambrosiano.... On September 7 in Toronto, a tragic end grew nigh. 'I'm convinced the international payments system was on the brink,' says Leutwiler. 'New York interbank clearing would have broken down and after that spilled over to London and Switzerland. So we were all on the spot together. It was an unthinkable disaster if it happened.'" [S. Solomon, 209-210] Volcker, Richardson, and Leutwiler decided to keep CHIPS functioning by pumping in the needed $70 million, and then by repeating that operation every day over the next few weeks.

The other result of the Toronto IMF annual meeting was the firm commitment of the central bankers to a creditors' cartel – a lockstep of the world's big commercial banks. Volcker repeatedly warned the bankers that if they did not remain united, the debtor countries would come together in a debtors' cartel powerful enough to dictate reforms in the world financial system. "Get your act together or they will," was Volcker's repeated admonition. [S. Solomon, 249] Later, in the summer of 1985, Treasury Secretary Baker was alarmed by the possibility of political actions by the Latin Americans along the lines of a debtors' cartel. [S. Solomon, 253] In order to keep the Latin Americans paying, the Treasury promoted a cosmetic Baker Plan for Latin American debt.

James Baker III, Bush's idea man and the Secretary of the Treasury in Reagan II, must rank as one of the founding fathers of the globaloney system of the 1990s. In October 1985, Baker sponsored a meeting of finance officials and central bankers in Washington under the explicit watchword of "globalization." This gathering reached a consensus to designate the IMF and World Bank as the lead agencies for the process of globalization, including the abolition of capital and exchange controls to ensure the free flow of speculative capital, and the abolition of all limits on the quick repatriation of profits by investors.

By the mid-1980s, many features of the globaloney era had already emerged. In 1986, Professor Susan Strange of the London School of Economics in her book, *Casino Capitalism*, could offer the now-familiar image of the world as a trading floor populated by quants:

> The Western financial system is rapidly coming to resemble nothing as much as a vast casino. Every day games are played in this casino that involve sums of money so large that they cannot be imagined. At night the games go on at the other side of the world. In the towering office blocks that dominate the great cities of the world, rooms are full of chain-smoking young men all playing these games. Their eyes are fixed on computer screens flickering with changing prices. [Strange 1986, 1]

Strange recognized the instability of this system. But, despite the massive evidence adduced in this book that the British finance oligarchy was an important catalyst in the decomposition of the Bretton Woods arrangements, Professor Strange preferred to blame the United States. She esteemed Ernest Mandel, the Belgian Trotskyist economist. The institutional changes recommended by Professor Strange tended to enhance the power of the international finance oligarchy. She thought, for example that the American "division of authority over financial policy and monetary management gives the

White House and the Administration too much power, and leaves the chairman of the Federal Reserve Board at the mercy of any President with a political axe to grind." Professor Strange breathed a sigh of relief that the formidable Paul Volcker was at the Federal Reserve, making this "not so acute an issue." But in the longer run, she sternly added, the United States could not get along without a central bank even more independent of the elected government, like the German Bundesbank. Her other alternative was a US constitutional amendment similar to the British Bank Charter Act requiring two-thirds supermajorities in Congress "before certain credit-creating and spending limits could be breached." [Strange 1986, 175-6]

THE DEBT BOMB

Morgan Guaranty economist Rimmer de Vries commented that the Mexican suspension was "like an atom bomb being dropped on the world financial system." The *Sunday Times* of London headlined, "The Day the World Ran Out of Credit." The London *Economist*, notoriously the mouthpiece of the Rothschild interests, went with cover stories on "The Crash of 198?" and "the Nightmare of Debt," complete with images from Hieronymus Bosch. *Time* magazine's cover read: "The Debt Bomb." This formulation had been popularized by *Executive Intelligence Review* during the spring 1982 Falkland Islands war, in the context of a discussion of the possibility of a cartel or common front of the debtor nations.

Volcker's colossal usury had brought grim recession to the industrialized countries. The recession meant lower demand and lower prices for raw materials, which cut the earnings of the third world. Many of the developing sector countries, for example Brazil, had loaded on new debt to keep their economies going in the face of the two oil shocks of the 1970s. Now, the debt service due on these loans began to skyrocket as floating rate rollover loans began to charge the full Volcker interest rates. Most of this debt was in the form of medium-term syndicated Eurodollar loans made on a rollover basis. When the rollover time came, the loans had to be re-financed, and the interest rates went up into the Volcker stratosphere. Also in hock were now Soviet-bloc nations like Poland and Romania, who had been borrowing in western capital markets to finance their development plans. Volcker's measures meant that repaying what they owed had become impossible. The third world debt bills more than doubled. For Latin America, it was the beginning of a Lost Decade, with protracted hard times and stagnant or falling standards of living.

KAUFMAN: THREAT OF DEPRESSION VIA DEBT DEFLATION

Total debt of third world and eastern European countries had amounted to $90 billion in 1971, but reached an official $626 billion by 1982. A great deal of this debt came from the Eurodollar market, that wholly unregulated floating crap game with its center of gravity in the City of London. By the end of 1982, about 40 countries were substantially in arrears on their debt service payments. Henry Kaufman of Salomon Brothers, known to reporters as "Dr. Doom" because he often reflected the humors of bearish bond traders, estimated that total world debt outside of the Soviet bloc had by 1981 attained the figure of $14.3 trillion, up from $3.6 trillion a decade before. Kaufman feared that this "awesome" debt burden might bring on world economic depression through what he called "debt deflation." By 1983, the index of US industrial production was still stagnant at the level of 1976.

Mexico was forced to endure the humiliating ritual of submitting a letter of intent to the IMF, requesting loan assistance. The country was supposed to reduce its public deficit, moderate wage increases, and lift exchange controls soon. The new government of President de la Madrid soon emerged as subservient to the IMF. At this time Mexican unemployment was about 40%. True to form, the IMF began demanding that Mexico fire more public sector workers. In order to stave off the world banking crisis, the IMF lent Mexico $3.9 billion over three years. The BIS and other agencies also joined in, bringing the package to almost $6 billion. The IMF strong-armed banks across the world to get them to join the bailout, since a failure would have sparked universal panic. This yielded another $5 billion.

Naturally, the problem with this bailout was that while Mexico's problem was too much debt, the bailout massively increased debt and debt service. At the same time, Mexico was plagued by too much unemployment and insufficient production. But the IMF conditionalities meant that employment and production, especially in the state sector, would be further reduced. So the momentary crisis was papered over in a way that guaranteed another and more serious crisis a little further down the road. This is the common denominator of all IMF interventions bar none, and the reason they have tended to block recovery in the country in question and in the world at large.

One avid supporter of IMF conditionality as a pre-condition for bailouts of third world debtors was Michel Camdessus, a French civil service bureaucrat. During the debt crisis years of 1982-83, Camdessus was the chairman of the Paris Club, the coordination center for governments and other official lenders. Camdessus described himself as "impassioned" on the subject of developing-country debt. Later, debt-collecting bureaucrat Camdessus would become the Managing Director of the International Monetary Fund.

1981: THE POLISH CRISIS

The threat was clearly that of a world-wide banking panic. If substantial chunks of debt had been declared non-performing, as they were in reality, a chain reaction of bank failures would have gone around the world in 40 minutes. Poland went through a political upheaval around the Solidarnosc agitation of 1981, and by the end of the year Poland's $24 billion in foreign debt was in default. Bankers Trust and the American banks, who had less exposure, wanted a hard line; the German and other European banks, more heavily involved, wanted to be conciliatory. Felix Rohatyn of Lazard Frères, the head of New York City's Big MAC austerity enforcement agency, demanded that Poland be declared in formal default, which would have wiped out the capital of numerous European banks. Rohatyn hinted that this would be a way of forcing the USSR to bail out Poland. But the implicit Soviet guarantee for Soviet-bloc satellite borrowers which had been taken for granted in previous years was now a dead letter. Romania, Hungary, and Bulgaria all had to negotiate bailout packages with the west. In August 1982 Yugoslavia submitted to IMF conditionalities and embarked upon the rounds of austerity that destroyed the economic basis for the continued existence of the country, which dissolved into civil war a decade later. The austerity conditions accepted by the Ceauşescu regime of Romania in the early 1980s were also the first step on the road that led to the collapse of that regime in December 1989.

Argentina, with $40 billion of foreign debt, was in crisis after losing the 1982 Falkland Islands war. There were calls for the ouster of the Harvard-trained MBAs working in government agencies; these persons were labeled as "Trojan horses." There was discussion in the Peronist and Radical parties of Argentina's forming a common front with Mexico and other South American states in dealing with the Club of Paris, the united front of the creditors. This discussion reflected a campaign by *EIR* magazine for "Operation Juarez," a strategy for a Latin American debtors' cartel capable of asserting the developing countries' interests by confronting the Wall Street and London banks with a potential debt bomb. Argentinean opposition leaders continued to eye a debtors' cartel as a way to secure a debt moratorium, fresh development credit, and a shift to pro-development export policies by the OECD nations. Argentina finally got nothing more than a bridge loan, which was scarcely enough to keep its interest payments current.

14. BRAZILIAN DEBT CRISIS, DECEMBER 1982-NOVEMBER 1983

Brazil had the biggest foreign debt of all the developing countries, $87 billion. Brazil's financial czar Delfim Neto had always been willing to pay interest rates two percentage points above the markets. By 1982, Brazil was paying 86% of its export earnings in the form of debt service on foreign borrowings. In his October 1982 speech to the UN General Assembly, Brazilian President João Figueiredo signaled some support for the stance assumed by Mexico. For a time there was a real possibility that a Latin American debt cartel led by Mexico and Brazil might emerge as a counterweight to the Paris Club and the IMF, but this option became unrealistic because of the attitude of the Brazilian government, which resented being placed in the same boat with Mexico, Argentina, and Poland. "I think we could sue Mexico in the courts for what they have done to us," was the cynical remark of one Brazilian diplomat [Delamaide 119]. Delfim Neto convinced the Brazilian government to reject the feelers extended by Lopez Portillo, With this attitude, Brazil could do nothing but capitulate to the IMF.

In December 1982 Carlos Langoni of the Brazilian central bank announced that his country was at the end of its tether and needed more loans. After a couple of days, Brazil declared a two-month suspension of debt payments. Capital had been fleeing from Brazil since September, and the crisis had been detonated by Société Générale of France, which cut off credit to Brazil altogether in mid-December. The Saudi Arabian Monetary Authority was also swift to grab its money and run. Banco do Brasil, one of the country's biggest banks, appeared to be unable to settle its obligations to CHIPS. US money center banks (no doubt assisted by the New York Fed) poured half a billion dollars into CHIPS over several weeks to ward off chronic end-of-the-day crises that would have meant gridlock for the entire system.

Brazil's IMF package totaled $6 billion, the biggest ever. In addition, 169 banks lent Brazil $4.4 billion for 8 years and rolled over $4 billion in principal repayments scheduled for 1983. The IMF dragooned the individual commercial banks into taking part; the Fund used the debt crisis to increase its hegemony over the big banks. Even Fritz Leutwiler, the head of the Swiss central bank and the president of the BIS, complained in public about the IMF's extortionist tendencies. Paltry concessions were extended to the Latin Americans by the banks: Mexico got a 2/3% interest discount, and Brazil was granted a grace period before resuming repayment.

On one critical New York evening in the spring of 1983, bankers were on tenterhooks as they awaited a key Brazilian interest payment. Langoni claimed that the payment had been made, but the Americans did not believe him. Then he claimed to have technical problems. In Washington, Volcker and the Treasury were gripped by fear that the entire System might come down. Volcker, with the help of J.P. Morgan, kept CHIPS open beyond the usual east coast closing time. The Treasury alerted the Reagan White House that a very serious world crisis might be about to explode. The White House did not understand, and Reagan's slumber was not interrupted.

CHIPS: THE LONGEST DAY

One of the worriers that evening was McNamar of the Treasury, who later reminisced about the threat to CHIPS: "If you can't close all interbank transactions, you can't close any interbank transaction. It meant if we weren't going to close the New York clearing banks that night, what the hell were they going to do when they opened in Tokyo or London? What positions did they have? It would be absolute chaos. That CHIPS system was one of the greatest Achilles' heels of the world financial system, and few people understood it." [S. Solomon, 242] Dawn was breaking over Tokyo when the Brazilian payment finally arrived. Had it come from Brazil, or had it come from Volcker at the Fed?

By the time of the 1984 Cartagena conference, it was clear than there was no immediate prospect for militancy on the debt question on the part of Brazil, Mexico, and Argentina. The bankers had won the day. But Brazil once again became insolvent in January 1987, and finally declared a formal unilateral debt moratorium on private bank debt against the Paris Club of creditors on February 20, 1987, one day before the Louvre meeting of central bankers and finance ministers. Brazil's unstable finances contributed mightily to dollar jitters from 1983 until 1987 and beyond.

Denmark, Sweden, Ireland, Italy, and France all instituted austerity programs to pay the debt service on their growing obligations. Finance Minister Jacques Delors of the new Mitterrand regime secured numerous loans to roll over France's $45 billion in foreign debt. But by now, the country with the biggest foreign debt was the United States. By the end of 1982 foreigners owned Treasury obligations amounting to $140 billion. The US budget deficit reached a record $111 billion in 1982, and then doubled in 1983.

As hedge fund corsair George Soros commented at the time: "If it takes the threat of a breakdown to induce collective action, while collective action is necessary to avoid a breakdown, it follows that we shall hover on the verge of disaster for the indefinite future." [Delamaide, 26] Thanks to the efforts of Mr. Soros and his friends and colleagues, we have indeed hovered on the verge of disaster ever since.

A last gasp in the Latin American anti-debt agitation of the mid-1980s came from the Peruvian government of President Alan Garcia. Peru was on the verge of insolvency by August 1986, and after acrimonious exchanges the IMF declared Peru ineligible for further international loans. On July 14, 1987, the Peruvian currency was hit by a wave of capital flight. On July 28, Garcia announced exchange controls and the nationalization of the banking system. Garcia, playing a weak hand from an isolated position, told the banks that he intended to limit interest payments on Peru's international debt to no more than 10% of Peru's export earnings. The implication was that if the banks wanted more interest, they needed to help Peru export more and earn more abroad. Garcia had assumed that Peru's creditors would back off from declaring Peruvian debt non-performing and the country officially in default, and in that he was right. But Peru was placed in an effective financial quarantine, which caused a marked slowdown in the domestic economy, so that by the time Garcia ended his term in 1990, his domestic and international support had largely dissolved into indifference or outright hostility. Garcia found no emulators.

Volcker later congratulated himself in his memoirs that there had been no Latin American debtors' cartel during the 1980s: "The borrowers themselves never resorted to organizing a debtors' cartel, threatening to bring down the financial house by collective default if demands for debt relief were not met. There was, to be sure, enormous sensitivity toward obtaining concessions provided another country, but the Latin American countries always rejected the idea of forming themselves into a hard negotiating bloc. I think they saw it in their individual interest, looking toward the future, to cooperate with their creditors as far as possible. No doubt mutual suspicions and rivalries among many of the Latin American countries also worked against their coordinating positions. Moreover, by good fortune or otherwise, there always seemed to be one important country that was doing fairly well and sensed it had a lot to lose from joining others in a strong confrontation with their creditors." [Volcker, 210] Volcker's exercise in classic divide-and-conquer imperialism turned out to be a success, avoiding a debtors' cartel, although not important defaults. In retrospect, these events may have represented one of the last chances for an equitable and rational reform of the international monetary system before its final end-of-millennium cataclysm, and this chance was utterly lost.

IMF ECONOMIC GENOCIDE

The failure of third world resistance to the IMF during the first half of the 1980s condemned the developing countries to undergo the Structural Adjustment Policies dictated by the IMF. These were severe austerity measures based on Thatcher-Volcker economics, which often triggered bloody civil disorders and political instability. An IMF favorite was to force the termination of public subsidies or price controls on staple food items; riots generally followed. When the IMF dictated a 200% increase in the price of bread to its puppet Carlos Andres Perez of Venezuela in 1989, riots followed which left over 1000 people dead. In Tunis in January 1984, the IMF dictated food price increases, triggering riots by jobless youth. In Nigeria in 1989, universities were closed by student protests. In Morocco in 1990, IMF nostrums caused a general strike and a popular upsurge against the regime. When the IMF repeated this procedure in Indonesia in 1997-98, it knew exactly what it was doing. Michael Chossudovsky, a recent student of the IMF, remarked:

> Structural adjustment is conducive to a form of 'economic genocide' which is carried out through the conscious and deliberate manipulation of market forces. When compared to genocide at various periods of colonial history (e.g. forced labor and slavery), its social impact is devastating. Structural adjustment programs affect directly the livelihood of more than four billion people. The application of the structural adjustment program in a large number of individual debtor countries favors the 'internationalization' of macro-economic policy under the direct control of the IMF and World Bank acting on behalf of powerful financial interests (e.g. the Paris and London Clubs, the G-7). This new form of economic and political domination – a form of 'market colonialism' – subordinates people and governments through the seemingly 'neutral' interplay of market forces. The Washington-based international bureaucracy has been entrusted by international creditors and multinational corporations with the execution of a global economic design which affects the livelihood of more than 80% of the world's population. At no time in history has the 'free' market – operating in the world through the instruments of market economics – played such an important role in shaping the destiny of 'sovereign' nations .... The application of the IMF's 'economic medicine' tends to further depress world commodity prices because it forces individual countries simultaneously to gear their national economies towards a shrinking world market. [Chossudovsky 37]

By 1998, the total debt of the third world was about $2 trillion. For supporters of debt moratoria for the developing countries, it was easy to show that most of this debt was a political pretext used for looting. Part of the debt could be attributed to the lasting effects of the oil shocks. Another significant part could be traced back to the Volcker period of astronomical interest rates. A great deal of debt had been generated by manifestly unfair terms of trade, meaning a world trade system which valued manufactured goods over agricultural products, much to the detriment of underdeveloped exporters. There was also flight capital, by which third world finance oligarchs illegally smuggled vast fortunes to Miami, London, or Switzerland. Finally, the debt burden was further increased by compound interest on all these factors, inexorably accruing year after year after year. So it was that after paying exorbitant debt service for decades, most countries found themselves with far more indebtedness than in the early 1980s. They had been running hard, only to lose more and more ground. It was a murderous treadmill. Only debt moratoria could break the vicious cycle, but these would have to be followed by new credit issuance. Something more sophisticated than Calvin Coolidge economics was plainly required to implement such a reform. In the meantime, there was a massive net transfer of wealth from the underdeveloped countries to the wealthy ones, exactly the reverse of what was necessary for economic and political stability.

15. PANIC RUN ON CONTINENTAL ILLINOIS BANK, MAY-JULY 1984

In early May 1984, the British news agency Reuters reported rumors of the imminent bankruptcy of the Continental Illinois Bank of Chicago. The Reuters story was reported by Commodity News Service, by JiJi Press, and then by the Japanese financial newspaper *Nihon Kezai Shimbun*. Japanese money managers concluded that Conti Illinois was about to fail, and began dumping Conti certificates of deposit while wiring electronic withdrawal orders. This panic began in Tokyo during the morning of Thursday, May 9, 1984 – which was the late evening of Wednesday, May 8 in Chicago.

It was 2 AM in Chicago when European markets opened, and the panic run on Conti escalated. When Conti finally opened for business, bank executives found that the flight of funds was already so severe that Conti risked being driven into default and bankruptcy that very day. Conti needed to roll over loans totaling about $8 billion each day in order to survive. The Reuters story had scared off half of this cash, and also forced Conti to pay a risk premium of 1% on what it was able to borrow. Conti rushed to the discount window of the Chicago Federal Reserve, and increased its borrowing from $850 million to $3.6 billion, and then to $4.7 billion by May 16.

At the Treasury in Washington, the Comptroller of the Currency tried to quell the panic by issuing a formal denial of the Reuters story, but nobody believed him. At that time, the US government and the Fed had an off-the-shelf plan for dealing with incipient banking panic, worth quoting here because it is still pretty much in effect: "The FDIC would infuse capital into the bank on an interim basis until a lasting rescue could be fashioned. All depositors, not just those covered by the FDIC insurance ceiling, would be protected. If things got really bad, the Fed would flood the markets with money. The FDIC even had the documents prepared. The names simply had to be filled in." [S. Solomon, 170]

On May 14, sixteen leading US banks announced the creation of a $4.5 billion credit line for Conti Illinois. But the global panic run on Conti continued around the clock. On May 17, Volcker and the Treasury announced the largest banking bailout in US history, with a $2 billion capital infusion and FDIC coverage for all depositors and even creditors. But these unprecedented measures were unsuccessful, and the hemorrhaging on Conti deposits went on apace.

A RUN ON MANUFACTURERS TRUST COMPANY

On May 24, 1984 rumors swept the bourses of Europe that Manufacturers Hanover Trust, America's fourth largest, was about to succumb to third world loan losses. Manny Hanny stock lost 10% of its value in a single day. Then all stock and bond prices turned downward. The dollar was slipping. The biggest us banks were forced to increase their interest rates by a *de facto* risk premium of 1% to keep their deposits from fleeing. A panic run soon broke out against the Financial Corporation of America, the holding company for the largest US thrift, the American Savings and Loan Association. The Conti crisis had given a decisive push to the S&L crisis that would rage through the rest of the decade.

With the horrible specter of nationwide and international banking panic at the door, the doctrinaire free marketeers of the *laissez-faire* Reagan Administration, facing a general election in the fall, opted for the nationalization of Conti Illinois through the Federal Deposit Insurance Corporation, which acquired 80% of Conti stock in return for buying $4.5 billion of Conti's bad loans; the taxpayers would foot the bill for Conti's losses. Once Conti had recovered, it could be privatized at bargain prices to parasitic venture capitalists. Reagan's Comptroller of the Currency, Todd Donovan, soon telegraphed to the markets that big banks like Continental enjoyed a free insurance policy from the Fed and the FDIC. The concept of **"too big to fail"** had become official.

THE REAGAN BULL MARKET

Instantly as Volcker brought down interest rates in August 1982, a colossal speculative bubble began in the stock market. Momentum gathered on October 5, when the Federal Open Market Committee endorsed Volcker's change of course. The news leaked out quickly. In four days of trading, the Dow Jones industrials rose 115 points to a new high of 1021. The upward motion was to continue with periodic bumps into October 1987. This stock market boom had a sinister and artificial quality. It was based first of all on easy money and low interest rates, as the Benjamin Strong bubble of 1929 had been. But this time around, demand for stocks was not generated by any hopes of future increases in production and earnings, but rather by the prospects of a buy-out of a company's shares. Mergers and acquisitions became the order of the day. These included special techniques like the hostile takeover. The shares of the target company were bought up, and its management ousted. This might be done by means of a tender offer.

Soon it became common to carry out a hostile takeover with billions of dollars of borrowed money: the leveraged buyout. The money to accomplish the takeover was raised by selling high-interest but below-investment grade bonds – junk bonds. After the hostile, junk-bond assisted leveraged buyout was complete, the junk bond holders had to be paid off. Parts of the target company were then sold off through a process of asset stripping; other parts of the target company were simply shut down, and their employees fired. The entire work force was "downsized" or "right-sized", as monetarist jargon put it, meaning mass layoffs. Sometimes the whole target company was broken up and sold off to other companies, yielding a sum that allowed the junk bondholders to be paid off (if they were lucky) while the corporate raiders, takeover artists, and their retinue of parasitical "investment bankers" and lawyers walked away with handsome profits and commissions, leaving the employees on the sidewalk.

HOSTILE TAKEOVERS AND POISON PILLS

There were also "poison pill" strategies designed to ward off corporate raiders. If the raider seized control of the company, the poison pill would detonate like a doomsday machine and destroy the booty. One poison pill was devised to ward off T. Boone Pickens' assault on Unocal; it included a provision in company by-laws that if a hostile takeover occurred, the company would make a self-tender offer for its own stock at an astronomical price – high enough to guarantee that Unocal could not survive. The company's workers, office staffs and customers were never consulted about these measures. This strategy was devised by none other than Nicholas Brady – George Bush's close friend and later Secretary of the Treasury – back in 1985, when he was with Dillon Reed. Thanks to Brady, Unocal came out of the fight burdened with a crushing $3.6 billion of high-interest debt.

The hostile leveraged buyout was uncannily designed to make the twin problems of the US economy worse. On the one hand, it vastly increased the amount of paper claims that had to be met out of the profits of production – the junk bond dividends most especially. On the other hand, levels of employment and production were steadily reduced. The result was an indebted economy with a reduced productive and tax base, deeper in depression and drifting closer to outright disintegration. As Adam Smith once observed, there is a lot of ruin in a nation. To make the outrageous scandal complete, the junk bonds were subsidized by struggling taxpayers. Since the tax code allowed firms to deduct interest payments made to their bondholders, the IRS was the indispensable backer of this secular shift from equity to debt.

GETTY OIL

The first of the great hostile takeovers was attempted during the first week of January, 1983 by J. Hugh "Chairman Mao" Liedke, the chairman of Pennzoil and a former business partner of then-Vice President George Bush. Liedke wanted to take over Getty Oil, which he coveted because of its large reserves of oil in the ground within US borders. Liedke made a series of tender offers to Gordon Getty's Getty Trust and the Getty Museum, between them the holders of a majority of Getty Oil's stock. Liedke was seeking to oust the management group around chairman Sidney Petersen. But Petersen, the Getty Trust and the Getty Museum found a "white knight" in the form of Texaco, which bettered Liedke's tender offer and ended up buying Getty Oil. Liedke later sued Texaco, and obtained an outrageous $11 billion damage settlement with the help of a Houston judge loyal to the Bush machine. This settlement would have been enough to destroy Texaco along with all its jobs and production for the sake of restoring the gains of a corporate bandit like Chairman Mao Liedke. The federal and state judiciary were in general the pliable servants of the leveraged buyout raiders. Texaco underwent bankruptcy reorganization some years later and emerged in severely truncated form. [See Tarpley and Chaitkin, 443 ff.]

The theory of the leveraged buyout had been launched years before by the Italian-American economist Franco Modigliani of MIT, with the help of Merton Miller; these two thought that loading a corporation with debt need not undermine its value. This daring leap into the void was published as "The Cost of Capital, Corporation Finance, and the Theory of Investment" in *American Economic Review* in 1958. Given the US tax laws, they concluded, debt was better than stock when it came to financing a company.

The hostile takeover had been imported into the United States from Britain. A Scotsman named James Gammell had been convinced by George Herbert Walker (George Bush's maternal uncle) to finance the oil-drilling ventures of the future President. Gammell had joined the board of Zapata Petroleum, and had stayed on when this company was acquired by Pennzoil. In the mid-sixties, Gammell suggested to Pennzoil boss Bill Liedke that he use a cash tender offer to take over United Gas Pipeline Company of Shreveport, Louisiana. At the time this was common practice among British stockjobbers, but virtually unheard of in America. The tender offer to the public was for only a portion of United Gas's shares; but stockholders were afraid that the price would collapse once the tender offer had closed, so they rushed to tender as many shares as they could. Liedke went deep into hock to buy $240 million in United Gas shares, and Pennzoil absorbed United Gas, a company five times its size. [Tarpley and Chaitkin, 145-149]

The Reagan Administration provided all the necessary ingredients for the orgy of mergers and acquisitions: tax write-offs of leveraged buyout debt, plus financial deregulation, and the most lax enforcement possible of antitrust laws, were all the order of the day. In December 1981 the official who was supposed to function as Reagan's antitrust chief, William Baxter, told Washington reporters, "There is nothing written in the sky that says the world would not be a perfectly happy place if there were only 100 companies." Harold William, then the Chairman of the Securities and Exchange Commission, complained to a House subcommittee: "It has become acceptable to assume that corporate control may change hands with no greater concern about the consequences than accompanies an exchange of property deeds in a game of Monopoly." [Bluestone, 158]

THE BIGGEST BUYOUT: $26.4 BILLION FOR RJR NABISCO

The most massive perpetrators of leveraged buyouts were the boys at Kohlberg, Kravis, Roberts, who spent more than $60.3 billion in acquiring a corporate empire bigger than that of J.P. Morgan when old Jupiter was at his zenith. But Kohlberg, Kravis, and Roberts, as far as is known, never made a net investment in productive plant and equipment or new productive jobs. They carried out highly-leveraged hostile takeovers and financed them with junk-bond debt. Kohlberg, Kravis, Roberts bought up Safeway supermarkets, Duracell, Motel 6, Stop & Shop Supermarkets, Tropicana, and Playtex. In 1988 KKR carried out the largest leveraged buyout in world history, paying $26.4 billion in borrowed money for RJR Nabisco, a company that manufactured cookies, crackers, and cigarettes but which possessed a cash flow that the raiders coveted. Involved in the RJR caper in 1988 were such Wall Street stalwarts as Robert Rubin of Goldman Sachs (now Secretary of the Treasury) and Felix Rohatyn of Lazard Frères, at one point Clinton's unsuccessful candidate for Chairman of the Federal Reserve.

MILKEN'S MOBSTERS

KKR's ascendancy owed much to Henry Kravis' close ties to the George Bush machine, to which he was a leading contributor. KKR started off in 1976 with just $120,000 of its partners' capital. The vast bulk of the money was borrowed, at first from the yearly buyout funds into which KKR enticed not just banks like Bankers Trust, but also mutual bond houses like Fidelity Investments of Boston and state employee pension funds and other institutional investors who had no business taking such risks. As the demands for buyout cash increased, KKR turned more and more to Drexel Burnham Lambert and its aggressive junk bond operator, Michael Milken. Milken and his friend Ivan Boesky were fixtures at the annual High Yield Bond Conferences organized by Drexel at Boesky's Beverly Hills Hotel during the middle 1980s. These were the legendary Predators' Balls, with T. Boone Pickens, Carl Icahn, Irwin Jacobs, Sir James Goldsmith, Meshulam Riklis, Oscar Wyatt, Saul Steinberg, Ivan Boesky, Carl Lindner, the Canadian Belzberg family, Nelson Peltz, Ronald Perelman, and William Farley among those present. These were the investors who bought Milken's junk bonds, whose proceeds were used in turn to finance KKR's hostile takeover operations. The Predators' Balls were interfaces of high finance with money laundering. "Milken's Monsters" were in reality "Milken's Mobsters."

In 1982, the US Congress passed one of its landmark deregulation bills - the Garn-St. Germain Depository Institutions Act, which deregulated what was now called the S&L "industry". Congressman St. Germain, the Democratic Chairman of the House Banking Committee, enjoyed S&L contributions to his campaign PAC and liked to be entertained by thrift officials with lavish parties and party girls. Republican Jake Garn of Utah was a free-market ideologue. The Garn-St. Germain law was a piece of folly which now bids fair to cost the taxpayers more than $1 trillion by the time the books are closed sometime late in the twenty-first century. S&Ls could now invest not just in home mortgages in their local area, but also put up to 90% of their money in business loans, consumer loans, commercial real estate, and even riskier and more exotic projects. Minimum down payments for consumer home loans were eliminated in favor of 100% financing. It was made harder for the Federal Home Loan Bank Board and its insuring arm, the Federal Savings and Loan Insurance Corporation, to throw out corrupt or incompetent S&L managers. A lonely voice of opposition was that of Rep. Henry Gonzalez (D-Texas), a protegé of Fed critic Wright Patman, who thought that the S&Ls should stick to their original mission of providing financing for homes.

At a late 1982 Rose Garden signing ceremony for the Garn-St. Germain law, President Reagan quipped "I think we've hit the jackpot." [Day, 124] At around the same time, states like California, Texas, Florida, Maryland and Ohio also removed most of their state regulations on the thrifts. In many cases these state de-regulations were more aggressive than the federal measures, and opened up investments by S&Ls in wind farms, junk bonds, restaurants, and brothels in Nevada. The Texas S&Ls were the most imaginative in invading new territory; one Austin thrift chief applied to open a branch of his S&L on the moon.

16. VOLCKER'S SUPERDOLLAR AND US DEFLATION

Owing to the high Volcker interest rates, the US became a haven for international speculative hot money and flight capital flows. The dollar began to rise against other currencies during 1980, and kept increasing in value until its peak in February 1985. The appreciation of the dollar during this time added up to a whopping 40% in trade-weighted terms. According to IMF calculations, the 263 yen/3.44 DM US dollar of February 1985 was up 67% over its level of 1980. The hot money was an important factor in the booming Reagan market on Wall Street, and also pumped up prices in US real estate.

But the expensive dollar priced US exporters out of the world market. Tragically, some of these businesses that had been able to survive the Volcker interest rates up to 1982 succumbed now to the soaring dollar. The devastation of the former US industrial base was complete, and the country was now totally dependent on imported goods. The export companies and the good industrial jobs they had provided were now gone, and lowering the dollar would no longer revive them. From now on everything you could buy in a department store was going to bear the tags of Hong Kong, Thailand, Guatemala, or some other paradise of the runaway sweatshop. US imports grew rapidly, and the inevitable balance of payments crisis began to brew up.

During the Reagan years, the US merchandise trade deficit remained alarmingly high. In 1982 the merchandise trade deficit stood at $36 billion; in 1984 the trade deficit exceeded $100 billion for the first time: by 1985 it had reached $122 billion. A couple of years later, data on a shockingly large monthly US trade deficit were to become one of the atmospheric factors detonating the October 1987 Wall Street crash. By the mid-1980s, the Reagan Administration and others finally became alarmed about the expensive dollar. Margaret Thatcher of Great Britain called the White House to plead with Reagan to spare her the excruciating historical embarrassment of seeing the battered British pound sterling, worth almost $5 dollars when this century began, fall below $1.00.

SEPTEMBER 1985: THE PLAZA DEAL TO BRING THE DOLLAR DOWN

There was surprise when the dollar continued to strengthen during 1983 and 1984, despite the fact that US interest rates had begun to subside from their historic peaks. One reason for the superdollar was clearly enough that the US economy was in the throes of bankruptcy and deflation. Large numbers of banks and corporations were in deep trouble and fighting to stave off bankruptcy; they were scrounging for every dollar they could get to keep current on their debts. Every bankruptcy that did occur, and there were plenty, wiped out a mass of dollars. So the collapsing US economy ironically generated a soaring superdollar.

The Superdollar caused great strain in the world economy as well. The Bundesbank began intervening against the dollar in early 1985. The finance ministers of the G-5 countries met at the Plaza Hotel in New York City on September 22, 1985 to coordinate measures to bring the dollar down. The operative language in the communiqué was "that in view of the present and prospective changes in fundamentals, some further orderly appreciation of the main non-dollar currencies against the dollar is desirable. They stand ready to cooperate more closely to encourage this when to do so would be helpful." Volcker, who was physically pushed before the television cameras by Baker, was afraid that once the dollar started down, foreign hot money would flee the US and the dollar fall would become unstoppable, leading to a crash. On this, Volcker was eventually proven right.

According to the orthodoxy of the economists, a cheaper dollar should have resulted in more US exports and a smaller US trade deficit. But that assumed that the US was still an economy based on agro-industrial production, something it had finally ceased to be under Volcker. The exporters who could have benefited from a lower dollar had closed their doors. By early 1986, the US was once again in recession, although the economists conceded this reality only after the fact. The trade deficit stayed high. And the federal budget deficit rose from $185 billion in 1984 to $212 in 1985 and $221 in 1986.

As soon as the dollar began to fall, Volcker became correctly obsessed with the idea that it might be impossible to stop it from accelerating into a catastrophic fall. This note is sounded repeatedly by S. Solomon, Greider, and others in their memoirs of Volcker's heady days of usury. Volcker himself, in his memoirs, recurs repeatedly to worries about a precipitous decline in the dollar, a "sickening fall" with a very hard landing. [Volcker 180]

17. OHIO BANK HOLIDAY AND MARYLAND S&L PANIC, MARCH-MAY 1985

In March 1985 the Home State Savings Bank of Cincinnati, Ohio was accurately rumored to be on the verge of insolvency. This set off a panic run not just at Home State, but at 70 other Ohio thrifts that were insured by the Ohio Deposit Guaranty Fund, a state-chartered insurance fund that was operated by S&L officials. With memories fresh of the Conti Illinois disaster one year earlier, foreign depositors were beginning to doubt the integrity of the entire US banking system, and this fear was sending the dollar down. Ohio Governor Richard Celeste turned in desperation to Volcker, who thought that if more than one bank were to fail, the shock might bring down his entire System.

Even so, Volcker was not generous with his help. Volcker asked one favor: when Celeste closed the Ohio thrifts, could he please avoid the expression "bank holiday," since this would remind the public of the 1933 banking panic, and of the close linkage between depositor lines and breadlines. Celeste shortly signed an executive order closing most of he Ohio thrifts. It was indeed the first partial bank holiday declared by an American state since the fateful 1932-33 banking panic. For a few days the entire US banking system – commercial banks and S&Ls in the same boat – was on the brink of panic collapse. There were rumors that Bank One and other Ohio commercial banks were also in trouble. But the Ohio legislature promised to pay the thrift depositors. Volcker readied his Federal Reserve air force of cargo planes and his Federal Reserve panzer divisions of Brinks armored cars to carry cash to banks experiencing panic runs. A currency crisis was avoided by a whisker. President Reagan acted to reassure the public, intoning: "This is not a major threat to the banking system. There is no other problem of that kind anyplace else in the country that we're aware of."

But the Great Communicator had his index cards out of order that day. Less than a month later, stealth panic runs were hitting thrifts in Maryland. Volcker called Governor Harry Hughes to tell him that the Old Court Savings and Loan of Baltimore was borrowing heavily at the Fed discount window, signaling that the Old Court depositors were pulling out. Volcker offered help in order to avoid publicity. So far the run was largely invisible, confined to ATM machines and wire withdrawals, but if the news broke on television an old-fashioned panic would materialize, and it might spread around the country. Old Court was owned by yuppy embezzler Jeffrey Levitt, who was soon arrested. In May 1985, Maryland shut down Old Court. This finally started the much-feared panic runs at other Maryland thrifts. On Monday, May 13, 1985 depositors were withdrawing cash from Maryland thrifts at the rate of $4 million per hour. Gov. Hughes cut short a trip to Israel and arrived home the next day to proclaim "a state of public crisis." Hughes imposed a limit on withdrawals of $1000 per person per month at more than 100 Maryland thrifts.

18. 1986: FALLING OIL PRICE DRIVES MEXICO TO BRINK OF DEFAULT - AGAIN

Despite Volcker's earlier exertions in the case of Mexico, that country had another brush with bankruptcy in early 1986 – an event which once more put financial meltdown at the top of the world agenda. In September 1985, Mexico City was hit by an earthquake. During the winter of 1985-86, the price of oil, Mexico's leading source of foreign exchange, fell by 40%. Deprived of $6 billion in income, or almost half of its oil revenue, Mexico was impelled towards default. On February 21, 1986, President Miguel de la Madrid Hurtado, a former central banker generally inclined to play the role of a pliant IMF asset, signaled that Mexican default was near. De la Madrid was visibly in trouble: when he tried to make the opening speech of the 1986 World Cup soccer championship, he was roundly whistled and booed by 100,000 spectators in the Azteca Stadium. Among the 300,000,000 television viewers that day were the central bankers, who recognized that de la Madrid and his post-1982 austerity regime were wildly unpopular among Mexicans. The peso crashed by 30%. The Mexicans had concluded that default was cheaper than continuing to pay the IMF and the banks. Volcker flew to Mexico City in June 1986 to warn de la Madrid against defaulting. De la Madrid proved willing to compromise. By September, Volcker was close to completing the loan package needed as bait to prevent Mexican default. But John Reed of Citibank insisted on squabbling over 1/16 of a point in the interest rate to be paid. Volcker rode roughshod over Reed, who left that final meeting "purple in the face" and "foaming at the mouth". [S. Solomon, 263] This is the same labile Reed who raved in July 1990 that countries like "Bolivia and Peru will disappear" from the map.

GREENSPAN ENDORSES KEATING'S LINCOLN SAVINGS AND LOAN

Back in the US, the speculative excesses of the deregulated S&Ls were being undercut by the deepening economic depression, and many of these banks were on their way to early insolvency. The oil-driven real estate boom in Texas, Colorado, Oklahoma and the other oil states began to collapse when the price of oil started its decline in 1985. In 1986 oil went below $20 a barrel. Shortly the price of a barrel of oil was in single digits, and the S&Ls that had ridden the crest of the speculative wave were under water. After the 1987 stock market crash, real estate prices also went into decline, bankrupting still more S&Ls. A famous S&L bankruptcy was that of Charles Keating's Lincoln Savings and Loan, which Alan Greenspan had praised in glowing terms in a letter to a Federal Home Loan Bank office when Greenspan was working as a Wall Street consultant and influence peddler in February 1985 [Mayer 324].

A fawning biography of Greenspan published recently attempts to paper over this embarrassing episode, but it deserves to be remembered. [Beckner, 160] Greenspan (the former head of Ford's Council of Economic Advisors) was working at that time in his own firm, Townsend-Greenspan & Company, which was put on retainer by the picaresque Keating, who was closely allied with Milken and his mobsters. Keating met personally with Greenspan on December 17, 1985, when he was in Washington to issue marching orders to his pet US Senators Cranston, Glenn, Riegle, McCain, and DeConcini, who later became notorious as the Keating Five or the Lincoln Brigade. Greenspan eventually received some $40,000 in compensation from Keating [*Inside Job*, 351] Somehow, Greenspan was able to escape the opprobrium he deserved.

In 1984-85, Ed Gray, then the chief of the Federal Savings and Loan Insurance Corporation, was trying to limit the amount of money which S&Ls could invest directly into junk bonds, shopping centers, racehorses, and commercial real estate. Keating was adamantly opposed to such limitations, since he was heavily invested in all manner of dubious ventures, as later came out at his trial. Keating got Greenspan to write directly to Gray in opposition to the limits on so-called direct investment. Limits on direct investment, intoned Greenspan, were a violation of free market principles. It was the same argument Greenspan would use in arguing against limits on derivatives a decade and more later. Greenspan argued that Gray was too concerned about possible dangers. In the course of his argument, Greenspan cited 17 S&Ls which, he claimed, were exemplary of how well deregulation of the thrifts was working. One of those Greenspan praised was Lincoln Savings and Loan, Keating's S&L, which would shortly go bankrupt.

In fact, 16 of the 17 S&Ls which Greenspan had singled out for commendation had gone out of business four years later. Lincoln Savings and Loan, wrote Greenspan, was a "strong institution that poses no risk to the FSLIC." [Day 262] In February 1985, Greenspan wrote a letter to the San Francisco federal Home Loan Bank board, asking that Lincoln Savings and Loan be exempted from the direct investment limits. In that same month, Greenspan testified before a House subcommittee that direct investments were just the ticket for S&Ls. Lincoln Savings and Loan was seized by the FSLIC on April 14, 1989. Just before the end, Greenspan's Federal Reserve Board had taken the unusual step of extending a loan of $98 million to Lincoln Savings and Loan, which was not a commercial bank and not a member of the Federal Reserve System. Chairman Henry Gonzalez of the House Banking Committee suspected that Greenspan was bailing out some well-heeled clients who had deposits in excess of the $100,000 insured level, making sure they got away with their money before Lincoln blew sky high. [Day 393] The initial cost to taxpayers of the Lincoln insolvency was more than two billion dollars – almost enough to fund the Head Start program for a year. Keating was indicted and later convicted on charges of $1.1 billion in bank fraud. [Day 342-3] The bill to taxpayers for the practices Greenspan touted is now approaching $1 trillion. Keating later went to jail for his financial handiwork.. Greenspan was made chief of the Federal Reserve, and his myopia in regard to looming mega-losses has become even more severe.

After 1987, many commentators agreed that Texas was in what they called a regional economic depression. In 1987 Republic Bank, a large Texas commercial bank, was in trouble and had to be merged with InterFirst Corporation to form First RepublicBank Corporation, which itself went belly up less than fourteen months later, right in the middle of George Bush's 1988 presidential campaign. In early 1989, Mcorp, another of the biggest banks in Texas, was seized by regulators when it too was clearly about to blow.

George Bush's marplot son Neil was a key player in the multi-billion dollar Silverado Savings and Loan bankruptcy. During Reagan's last days in office, the Federal Home Loan Bank Board under Danny Wall signed dozens of sweetheart deals with corporate raiders and profiteers like Ron Perelman, Robert Bass, and their ilk. In winding up 200 S&Ls, Wall signed away tens of billions of Treasury funds in transactions and tax breaks that Rep. Gonzalez criticized as "probably illegal." As soon as Bush entered office as President in 1989, he proposed the comprehensive bailout of the S&Ls that Reagan had avoided. Bush promised a bailout that would cost $90 billion plus interest, with the taxpayers getting stuck for no more than $40 billion. This turned out to be a tiny fraction of the ultimate price tag. Bush's plan included a new Office of Thrift Supervision and Resolution Trust Corporation, which would become for a time the nation's biggest owner of real estate and junk bonds.

A $25 TRIGGER PRICE TARIFF ON OIL?

In 1988, there were proposals to create a government supported $25 a barrel parity price for oil using an import tax that would trigger if the world market price of oil went below $25 a barrel. This would have restored the depressed economy of the oil states, but it was rejected by the free marketeers and bureaucrats of the Bush administration. There were also proposals to shift the burden of the S&L bailout onto the backs of those who had participated in the 1980s bubble of junk bonds, stocks, real estate, and the like. This could have been done with a 10% surtax on unearned income, including interest, dividends, and capital gains. But the country club Bushmen insisted on forcing the middle class to pay through the nose. Stanford University economists concluded that the total bill for the S&L bailout might reach $1.3 trillion, with $900 billion representing interest payments. The Congressional Budget Office used its own computer model to estimate the economic impact of capital resources consumed by the S&L bailout, and found that $40 billion a year would be siphoned off during the early 1990s. This was clearly a cause of the 1990-92 downturn, and also one reason why the upturn after 1992 has been so weak. The extinction of S&Ls as we once knew them has also contributed to the difficulty many middle-rank wage earners experience when they try to purchase their own home. The loss of the S&Ls in their traditional form has been a factor in the permanent lowering of the American standard of living.

A strange support operation for the dollar was mounted during these years by the Gorbachev regime of the moribund Soviet Union. Under Gorbachev's half-baked reforms, the stagnation of the Brezhnev era had turned into the beginnings of collapse, in economic as well as in political terms. Gorbachev's perestroika and acceleration resulted in the USSR's growing inability to pay its foreign debts. In order to procure foreign exchange, the Soviet government organized regular shipments of Moscow's gold reserves by cargo plane to Switzerland, where they were discretely sold on the world market. This process was kept up until the Soviet gold stocks had been dramatically reduced. The Soviets needed the western currencies, but an important side effect was to mask the weakness of the dollar in relation to gold.

GANG OF FOUR BUSHMEN AT THE FED

Small wonder that Volcker during these years feared an abrupt and uncontrollable collapse of the US dollar. Volcker was afraid to lower US domestic interest rates, even though another severe recession was building up. In February 1986, Volcker was outvoted by his own Federal Reserve Board of Governors, where a pro-Bush Gang of Four (Manuel Johnson, Wayne Angell, Preston Martin and Martha Seeger) demanded a pre-emptive cut in the discount rate to help Bush get elected president in 1988. But if the US rates declined, Volcker reasoned, hot money entering the US might prove insufficient to finance the staggering US budget deficit and trade deficit.

After the 1985 Plaza Accord, Japan had raised its discount rate. That would strangle the Japanese industrial economy, but it would also attract hot money to Japan, and thus help bring the dollar down as hot money rushed from New York to Tokyo. But this shift was no longer enough for Treasury Secretary Baker, since it kept the yen high. Baker wanted a low dollar AND high demand for US exports. Baker therefore pressured Japan to stimulate domestic demand for services and consumer goods. In other words, Baker wanted to weaken the Japanese economy so as to make it resemble the US, quite apart from interest rate levels. As a result of this US pressure, a weakened Japanese government capitulated and inaugurated the Great Japanese Bubble Economy during the middle of 1986. The birth of the Japanese Bubble was signaled by the two cuts in Japanese interest rates which Volcker and Baker were able to extort during 1986. Easy money available at lower interest rates was channeled into Japanese speculative markets, where traders from US and UK banks and brokerages, operating under increased financial deregulation, joined in pumping up the bubble.

JAPAN GETS SEVEN-ELEVEN BANKRUPTCY, NOT WORLD DEVELOPMENT

The rational course for Japan in the mid-1980s would have been to launch a new round of capital-intensive infrastructure and producers' goods exports into the developing sector. The Japanese had a plan to do just that: the Global Infrastructure Fund developed by the Mitsubishi Research Institute, which called for $500 billion of Japanese investments in rail, water, and energy infrastructure in third world nations. Zbigniew Brzezinski was especially pugnacious in warning the Japanese that the US establishment would wreck Japanese attempts to export economic development to the Third World. Because of US and British pressure, the resources that could have been used to carry out this splendid plan were poured into such idiotic investments as trophies in US real estate (including pathetic losers like Rockefeller Center) and US entertainment companies. Later, under this same policy, a group of Japanese investors bought the Southland Corporation, owner of the Seven-Eleven convenience stores in the USA. Despite the large cash flow of these stores, Southland carried crushing junk bond debt from a leveraged buyout, and soon went bankrupt.

Baker, for his part, was helped along by the collapse of the world price of oil. The economic depression was now in full swing, and demand for all raw materials used by industry was weakening. The case of oil was especially dramatic. In contrast to 1973, the US was now the great debtor country, laboring under a crushing load of Treasury commitments. Under these circumstances, the low oil price made the oil imports and the merchandise trade deficit easier to handle, and thus constituted a subsidy to the decadent dollar. Although a low oil price helped the dollar, it did not help George Bush's immediate social circle, and he could not remain deaf to the demands of potential campaign contributors for higher oil prices. Bush was for a time conflicted by this dilemma.

19. DOLLAR CRISIS AND BRAZILIAN DEFAULT, JANUARY-FEBRUARY 1987

Despite Volcker's fears of a hard landing for the dollar, the Fed Governors, led by the pro-Bush Vice-Chairman Preston Martin, lowered the discount rate again in July 1986 and yet again in August, coming down to 5.5% Reagan wanted the Congressional Republicans to win the November 1986 elections. GOP Senate leader Bob Dole wrote Volcker a letter appealing for lower rates. During the summer of 1986, Volcker hysterically churned out his line that "the world economy is in danger!" The Fed's easy money policy was helping to fuel the final stages of the Wall Street speculative psychosis. The fall of the dollar was slowed in November 1986, when Baker successfully arm-twisted Japanese Finance Minister Miyazawa to lower his discount rate to 3%, the lowest in postwar history. A month later, in January 1987, Germany reduced its own discount rate to 3% under crushing US pressure.

1987 was a year of prolonged crisis for the dollar and the rest of the world financial system. One point of crisis was certainly the collapse of the New York Stock Exchange and of other world equity markets in October. But it is vital to see that the 1987 stock collapse and threat of systemic crisis, grave as they were, were sandwiched in between two distinct dollar crises whose implications were even more sweeping in terms of world financial and monetary disintegration. Indeed, the stock market debacle was in many ways the by-product of the interest rate measures taken to save the dollar.

JANUARY 1987: THE DOLLAR IN FREE FALL

By the beginning of 1987, signs of catastrophic dollar weakness were everywhere. 1986 had brought the second worst current account deficit in American history ($152 billion); 1987 was destined to be even more disastrous ($167 billion). The Bank of Japan spent $10 billion on dollar support operations. But then the *New York Times* published a leak that the Reaganauts wanted the dollar to fall further. The dollar declined by 3% within a few hours. The dollar broke below 160 yen, then below 150 yen. The Japanese had expected the US to support the dollar at these levels. On January 23, the Dow pulled a quick 115-point dive, allegedly over worries over an impasse in US bank deregulation. On February 3, 1987, the dollar took another rapid downward slide on world markets. That day the Saudi Arabian Finance Minister Mohammed Ali Abalkhail got so nervous that Baker was forced to offer him a formal reassurance that the dollar was not in free fall.

The Group of Five finance ministers met to deal with the dollar crisis at the Louvre Palace in Paris on February 22, 1987. This time, the announced goal was not to drive the dollar down, but to stabilize it. The dollar had been falling since the time of the 1985 Plaza agreement, and Volcker was becoming alarmed that the greenback's downward acceleration was too great. He wanted concerted action to stop the decline of the US currency.

On February 21, 1987, one day before the Louvre meeting, Brazilian President José Sarney had finally and formally defied the IMF by declaring a unilateral debt moratorium on interest repayments.

The bankers had been preparing for this eventuality for some time, and Brazil remained isolated and especially vulnerable because it had no oil reserves and thus could not withstand an Anglo-American trade embargo. On April 14, 1987, Brazilian Finance Minister Dilson Funaro, the leading proponent of the debt moratorium, was forced out of office. In March 1989, Bush's new Secretary of the Treasury, James Brady, announced his Brady Plan, an allegedly comprehensive re-organization of Latin American debt. Part of the necessary cash was extorted from Japan in exchange for the face-saving shuck of enhanced status within the councils of the IMF. New obligations called Brady bonds were issued. Under the Brady Plan, the Latin American states were obliged to carry out radical liberalization and globalization of their economies and financial systems, in exchange for the IMF seal of approval on new bonds and other debt instruments. Drifting even further away from its nationalist traditions, Mexico accepted the Brady Plan in February 1990, and the rest of the Latin American nations followed. But in the meantime, the Brazilian debt moratorium was another life and death menace to the US banks. Would entire sectors of the US banking system disintegrate? Or could the Louvre session provide a support operation for the battered dollar? Once again, the world financial system moved to the brink.

THE LOUVRE PLAN TO PROP UP THE DOLLAR

After nearly 15 years of chaotic floating rates, the G-5 communiqué now came out for exchange rate stability, warning that "further substantial exchange rate shifts among their currencies could damage growth and adjustment prospects in their country" and pledging "to cooperate closely to foster stability of exchange rates around current levels." [Nau 278] The dollar was supposed to be pegged to the yen at 150 yen to a dollar, but this target collapsed after less than 2 months. Volcker was more and more hysterical about the decline of the dollar, which he "absolutely and fundamentally," "cross my heart and hope to die" wanted kept where it was. In an exercise in central bank paranoia worthy of Montagu Norman and Benjamin Strong, the exchange rates supposedly fixed at the Louvre were initially all kept secret.

In April 1987, there was yet another brush with dollar free-fall. Towards the end of that month the greenback hit 137 yen and DM 1.77. "The spring was one of those white-knuckle periods," recalls Robert Heller, then a member of Volcker's Federal Reserve Board. [S. Solomon, 352] Some Japanese investors began to pull their money out of the US, and Treasury bonds began to fall. But the Japanese Ministry of Finance window-guidance officials arm-twisted most of their countrymen to keep their cash in dollars. So from May to August, the dollar stayed on an even keel. The dollar calm was purchased by $70 billion in dollar support operations by the Louvre partners, especially Japan.

20. THE OCTOBER 1987 NEW YORK STOCK MARKET CRASH

To support the US currency in the face of the twin deficits, the US resorted to strangling the growth of the money supply during 1987. After May, the growth in the M1 money supply was a negative 1.1 %, the tightest money of the entire Volcker era. This was another major factor in popping the Wall Street stock bubble in October. At the same time, Japanese holders of US Treasury bonds lost confidence in the dollar and began to repatriate their money, and the US bond market tanked. On August 14, 1987 the US merchandise trade deficit came in at a whopping $15.7 billion. This triggered a new stampede of global hot money, especially Japanese, out of the dollar. The dollar began to fall again. The 30-year US Treasury long bond, which had been yielding 8.4% in August, was paying a sky-high 10.4% by the time of the crash. In other words, the long bond price, which moves in the opposite direction to yield, had collapsed. The price of gold, always a good reflection of fears about the dollar, went from $400 to $475 on the eve of the crash. Too add to the mirth of the overall situation, the monetarist anti-inflation robots of Karl-Otto Pöhl's Bundesbank insisted on raising their interest rates.

The inexorable decline of the long bond leading up to the October 1987 crash was the sure symptom that something was going very wrong. Volcker resigned in July 1987, after two full terms as Fed boss. Volcker, we see, knew when it was time to head for the exit. His successor was the sleazy Keating fan, Ayn Rand cultist and jazz connoisseur Alan Greenspan, who on September 3, 1987 raised the Federal Reserve discount rate by one half point in a desperate bid to attract hot money back into the dollar. High interest rates might help the dollar, but they set the stage for the panic crash in Wall Street which was to follow. A more immediate trigger for the Great Crash of 1987 was provided by Secretary of the Treasury Baker. On the weekend of October 17-18, with Wall Street already thoroughly destabilized, Baker threatened to drive the dollar through the floor unless the Bundesbank lowered its interest rates. This was viewed by many as a "public trashing of the Louvre accord" by Baker. Many foreign investors concluded that the Bushmen were mentally disturbed, and that this was the last chance to get their funds out of the dollar before Baker could carry out his threat of competitive devaluation. The final panic ensued with the opening of business on Monday.

On October 19, 1987 the Dow Jones Industrials declined by 508 points, in both absolute and relative terms the biggest one-day debacle in the market's history.

On the crash Monday, rumors swirled that E. F. Hutton and L.F. Rothschild were about to fail. Soon Rothschild did fail. Hutton had been denied further credit by its banker, Bankers Trust. Hutton had been the target of check-kiting charges by the SEC in 1984. But when E.F. Hutton talked, people listened – especially if its talk was an announcement of bankruptcy. The New York Fed made sure Hutton was bailed out in the short term, and six weeks later Hutton sold itself to Shearson Lehman. Stock trading specialist A. B. Tompane, which had weathered the hurricane in 1929, sold itself to Merrill Lynch at 3 AM in the night after the crash to dodge bankruptcy.

GREENSPAN AS LENDER OF LAST RESORT

At 8:41 AM the next day, October 20 – Terrible Tuesday – Greenspan signalled his intention to bail out everybody by flooding the banking system with cash liquidity and new bank reserves: "The Federal Reserve, consistent with its responsibilities as the nation's central bank, affirmed today its readiness to serve as a source of liquidity to support the economic and financial system." This was another way of saying that the Fed was more than willing to act as the lender of last resort to otherwise bankrupt speculators, provided they were big enough. The Greenspan Fed threw its monetary policy goals and dollar support out the window and promised to bail out banks, brokerages, and NYSE floor specialists with as much liquid cash as might be required to keep them going. This was something the Fed had never done for farmers, or steel mills, or tire plants - or the owners of mortgaged homes.

One of the first to need a bailout was First Options of Chicago, the largest of the nineteen members of the Options Clearing Corporation, which had suffered heavy losses in the crash. First Options was owned by Conti Illinois, which by now had been re-privatized. However, Conti Illinois was still under government strictures that included maximum limits on lending to First Options. The problem was that First Options needed more cash than Conti was allowed to lend it. A run on First Options developed, posing yet again the issue of a jam-up of the interbank clearing system and thus of a worldwide meltdown.

21. RETURN TO DOLLAR CRISIS, DECEMBER 1987-JANUARY 1988

As Greenspan's spate of Federal Reserve dollars began to slosh around in the gutters of Wall Street, the US dollar began to fall again. The stock market crash appeared as a mere episode in a year-long dollar crisis. On December 3, acting under immense US pressure, the Bundesbank cut their discount rate once again, this time to 2.5%, yet another new low in their postwar history. This was designed to support the dollar, but the dollar continued to fall. By the end of 1987, the dollar had lost fully 55% of its value as compared to its peak in February 1985!

A piece of meaningless boilerplate that was soon named the "Son of Louvre" deal was cobbled together with conference calls on December 22, appealing once again for dollar stability. But the dollar continued to collapse. A by-product of the fall of the dollar was a great fear among the Japanese that the end of the world was at hand, which set off a near-crash of Tokyo stocks.

On the first business day of 1988, unprecedented central bank intervention began to put a squeeze on the banks that had shorted the dollar. On January 4-5, the Bank of Japan and the Bundesbank bought about $1 billion each, with about $685 million in purchases by the Fed. Many speculators had large uncovered short positions against the dollar, which they now scurried to cover. The psychological impact was enough to halt hot-money attacks on the dollar for the short run. The dollar was also helped by the Baker-Miyazawa deal, an accord designed to advance the fortunes of Bush on the one hand, and of Miyazawa on the other. Japanese Prime Minister Takeshita publicly announced that Japan would not raise interest rates, and thus would assist the dollar to recover.

Greenspan kept jacking up US interest rates into 1989 to prevent a collapse of the currency. During 1988, short-term US interest rates increased by three full percentage points. The need to avoid a collapse of the dollar was the overriding priority. But these high interest rates once again strangled domestic economic activity. Between 1987 and 1993, Greenspan was able to reduce the average weekly earnings of the American worker by about 6.2%. [*Economic Report of the President 1997*, 352]

REAGAN'S LEGACY: AMERICA AS A DEBTOR NATION

The United States had become a net creditor nation for the first time in 1918, when the European Allies, including the British, found their own financial positions decimated by the debts they had contracted in the course of the Great War against the Central Powers. But during the Reagan-Volcker era, the net creditor status of this country was gradually eroded by the trade deficits, which had started in 1971, but which had grown implacably through the Reagan years. By the middle 1980s, the United States was borrowing more money each year than it lent out to the rest of the world. By 1988-89, just as the Great Communicator was leaving office, the United States reached an overall negative net asset position vis-à-vis the rest of the world: the combined total of what foreigners owned in America, plus what Americans owed to foreigners, had come to exceed in worth the combined total of what Americans owned abroad plus what foreigners owed to Americans.

According to figures provided by the Bureau of Economic Analysis of the Department of Commerce, the net international investment position of the United States was still positive in 1988, if direct investment were counted at its current market value. By 1989, the US net international investment position was negative irrespective of whether the investments were counted at current cost or market value. By 1995 the US was a net debtor nation to the tune about $800 billion, with foreigners owning about $500 billion in US government securities. [*Economic Report of the President 1996*, 419] In 1970, the United States had held net foreign assets equal in value to 30% of US annual output. By 1994, Professor Wynne Godley of Bard College estimated, America owed the rest of the world assets equal to 8.5% of its yearly output.

In late 1993, the United States crossed a related watershed when the net balance of the financial payments paid on these assets also turned negative. This meant that the total profits, dividends and interest paid to foreigners by Americans had exceeded the profits, dividends, and interest paid to Americans by foreigners. 1994 then became the first full year of negative net financial returns for the United States since 1914, with a $30 billion net outflow. America, in short, was losing money on globaloney. [Greider 1997, 202-204]

Rising foreign indebtedness combined with stagnant domestic productivity add up to a grim long-range perspective, as Harrison and Bluestone also recognize. They note that "if the United States continues to lag behind the rest of the world in productivity, it will be necessary for the dollar to fall steadily against foreign currencies in order for us to pay off foreign debt. If this goes on very long, the standard of living in America will gradually, but surely, fall further behind that of our trading partners. We will fall prey to the notorious 'British disease'." [Bluestone 1988, 155] In 1998, this is still what was happening.

22. DREXEL-BURNHAM-LAMBERT AND CAMPEAU GO BELLY UP

The stock crash of 1987 was the beginning of the end for KKR, Drexel Burnham Lambert, Milken, and the junk bond orgy. The mergers and acquisitions boom of the 1980s had added $1 trillion of debt to the balance sheets of corporate America. In December 1988, Comptroller of the Currency Robert Clarke warned the banks that buyout and merger loans should be carefully considered, and added that higher loan loss provisions should be imposed on such loans. In December 1988, Drexel plead guilty to six felony violations of the securities laws, mainly in the junk bond and mergers & acquisitions arena. Then Milken was arrested and indicted for securities fraud in early 1989, a sure sign that the Anglo-American finance oligarchy had momentarily satiated its appetite for junk bonds. In the fall of 1990 Milken, was allowed to cop a guilty plea and receive a short prison sentence which he never completed serving. According to the sentencing guidelines applied to other felons, Milken should have remained in durance vile well into the fourth millennium. (Soon he was using his substantial residual wealth to purchase the status of a philanthropist.) A provision of the S&L bailout that passed in August 1989 required federally insured thrifts to sell their junk bond inventories by 1994, but many had started early. The junk bond market was heading down.

THE LAST DAYS OF JUNK-BOND POMPEII

The last days of junk-bond Pompeii included the debt-ridden acquisition of Time Inc. by Warner Communications, which required $11 billion. In the twilight of the junk bond era, Drexel Burnham Lambert had invented the "reset" bond, a junk bond that would have its interest rate automatically adjusted upward in order to compensate the bondholder if the price of the bond were to fall. The interest rate was supposed to rise to whatever level proved necessary to jack the bond price up to its $1.01 on the dollar par value. If the bonds were not reset, then the bondholders had to be paid off at once, which would bankrupt the company that had issued them. On September 15, 1989 Robert Campeau defaulted on $450 million in interest payments. Campeau, himself a straw man, was the nominal head of the Canadian Campeau Corporation, which had carried out the leveraged buyouts of Allied Department Stores for $3.3 billion in 1986 and Federated Department Stores for $6.7 billion in 1988. In the week of Campeau's default, the junk bond market went though a debacle comparable to October 1987 for stocks. On September 15, an anonymous bureaucrat spoke off the record from behind an opaque screen at the Federal Reserve, intoning the mantra "No banks will fail because of Leveraged Buyouts." During 1988 and 1989, as better-informed US banks were reducing their exposure to Campeau, the Dai Ichi Kangyo Bank had increased their loans to the fey Canadian magnate. With pathetic naiveté, Dai Ichi Kangyo had been attracted by Brooks Brothers, Bonwit Teller, Bloomingdales and other glamorous gems in Campeau's doomed empire. A month after Campeau's demise, general nervousness was increased when the Dow Jones Industrials plummeted 200 points in an hour in the October 1989 mini-crash.

On December 27, 1989 one of KKR's largest buyouts, now operating under the name of Hillsborough Holdings, was forced to declare bankruptcy. For a short time, this was the biggest bankruptcy in the wake of a leveraged buyout. Then, on January 15, 1990, the Campeau empire finally went bankrupt under a burden of $6 billion in debt. The junk bond market was momentarily moribund, although, in a tribute to the gullibility of investors, it would be resuscitated in grand style in 1993, and reached new peaks in the years thereafter.

On February 12, 1990, Drexel Burnham Lambert was unable to secure loan assistance from its former allies, and collapsed into bankruptcy and subsequent liquidation. Not even the New York Fed was willing to provide Drexel with emergency financing. It was a political decision. So Drexel went down, but it took the entire system very close to interbank plumbing meltdown for the twenty-second time in the post-1968 era.

FINANCIAL SYSTEM GRIDLOCK

According to the GAO's derivative report of four years later, "when Drexel Burnham Lambert failed in 1990, federal involvement was necessary to keep payments flowing among Drexel's various debtors and creditors and to avoid financial system gridlock." [GAO 1994, 43] The extreme danger of this crisis was later confirmed by Alexandre Lamfalussy of the BIS in Basel: "Without the intervention of the US authorities, the failure of Drexel Burnham Lambert might have blocked the [international] payments mechanism, with widespread repercussions." [Lamfalussy, 11] Another aspect of the profound impact of the Drexel-Burnham-Lambert bankruptcy was that "clearing and settlement in the $1 trillion mortgage-backed securities market narrowly averted a major disruption." [S. Solomon, 458] The dangers were multiplied because Drexel's buccaneering management were engaged in a chicken game with the Fed and the Treasury, in effect daring the regulators not to bail them out by pointing to the catastrophic potential of Drexel's demise. But the Feds were determined to make an example of Drexel for the sake of disciplining the System.

On January 26, 1990, Moody's Investors' Service downgraded the junk bond debt of RJR Nabisco. That afternoon junk bonds crashed again, this time falling by 10% in twenty minutes. Within a few days RJR bonds were trading at 56 cents on the dollar. The problem was that RJR had issued reset bonds, and might soon have to increase the coupon yield on those bonds to bring their price back to $1.01 on the dollar. That would have drained even RJR's cash flow and brought about the biggest bankruptcy in US corporate history, probably taking some big banks down as well. KKR and RJR executives came within 48 hours of such default in early February 1990. KKR was now a symbol of megalomania and greed, not sure-fire profits. In the end, KKR was able to save their RJR reset bonds only by buying out RJR a second time, and injecting more than $5 billion in new funds, including even some of KKR's own money.

THE END OF THE GREAT JAPANESE BUBBLE

In December 1989 the Japanese Bubble Economy reached its apex. The Nikkei Dow stock index (as it was then called) topped out above 39,000 points, the all-time record. The zenith of the speculative frenzy in real estate was attained somewhat later: The average price of residential, commercial, and industrial land prices in the six largest cities of Japan rose from $7000 per square meter in 1970 to an astronomical $62,100 per square meter in 1990, a rate of growth unmatched anywhere in the world. In Tokyo, the commercial real estate rose from $7,400 per square meter in 1980 to an incredible $100,000 per square meter in 1990. New York City real estate at that same time peaked at a shabby $1,200 per square meter, while in London's West End theater district the top price of the day was a modest $13,400 per square meter. At one point it was estimated that the paper value of real estate in greater Tokyo alone exceeded that of all the land in the United States.

During the 1920s, British high finance had deliberately stimulated the growth of a speculative bubble in stocks and real estate in the United States. The Anglo-American strategy towards Japan from

1985-86 on amounted to a similar approach, which can only be described as economic warfare. In September-October 1929, the British had used a sharp hike in the Bank of England discount rate to explode the Wall Street bubble. In the case of Japan around 1990, it was the Japanese government itself which realized the need to deal with the bubble as best it could. In the fall of 1990 Finance Minister Hashimoto warned that the further financial deregulation demanded by Wall Street and London would infect Japan with "foreign financial AIDS." Under its new governor Yasushi Mieno, the Bank of Japan raised its discount rate from 2.5% in May, 1989 to 6% by the end of 1990. This was an effort to deflate the bubble gradually and control the inevitable damage. But the Japanese had waited until it was too late.

The only really effective way to treat a bubble is to prevent it in the first place. All other therapies are extremely painful. Financial panic broke out in Japan during the week ending March 18, 1990 when the Japanese stock market, by then the largest in the world, declined by about 4% of its value. On Monday March 21, the Nikkei average lost another four per cent in the third largest one-day decline ever registered. That was followed by a decline of about one per cent, and then a brief respite granted by the Vernal Equinox Day holiday. On Thursday March 22, the Nikkei ended the day with a loss of 963 points, equal to about 3% of overall value. On this day, the Nikkei lost about 1600 points in a single hour, and had declined more than 1800 points, or 6%, at the end of the morning trading session. By this point the Nikkei average had lost almost 24% on the year, which was more than the decline that took place in Tokyo after the October 1987 crash.

The yen had also become very weak. On March 20, the Bank of Japan raised its Official Discount rate, the keystone of entire interest rate structure, by one full percentage point to 5.25%. Despite this increase, the yen continued to decline against the dollar, and even more against the D-mark. Observers said that the increase was too small and came too late. According to published reports, the Bank of Japan was forced to delay raising interest rates because of pressure from Bush, who told Japanese Prime Minister Kaifu during their meeting in California not to start another world-wide round of interest rate increases.

23. BANK OF NEW ENGLAND, CITIBANK AND CHASE BANKRUPT

During the Great Depression between the two world wars, the collapse of 1929 had been followed by a US banking disintegration that reached critical mass during the fall and winter of 1932-33. About 3 to 4 years had separated the collapse phase from the banking panic. By a remarkable coincidence, the stock market and dollar crashes of 1987 were followed 3 to 4 years later by the threatened disintegration of the US banking system.

Federal Reserve officials were aware that they were presiding over a possible re-run of the banking panic of 1932-33. The Fed was filled with "continual conversations about this period and the 1930s", especially when "all the main money supply indicators suddenly collapsed in autumn 1930." [S. Solomon, 465] Eliot Janeway and others were warning in the press of a deflationary crisis in full swing.

Greenspan acknowledged the peril of banking panic on September 13, 1990, noting that there were "all too many problems in the banking system, problems that have been growing of late as many banks, including many larger banks, have been experiencing a deterioration in the quality of their loan portfolios...." [*Financial Times*, September 14, 1990] A student of this period sums up: "Just how close the US banking system came to collapsing in 1990-91 was necessarily conjectural, since it depended much on developments in the economy. But there was little doubt that the wildfire spread of market fear of major bank collapses nearly became a self-fulfilling disaster...." [S. Solomon, 464]

It was noticeable that the banks had stopped making loans. The reason was simply that these banks feared panic runs and, like their predecessors of 1932-33, thought that had to conserve their own cash to cover demand deposits. Bank bonds were downgraded by Moody's and the other agencies until many had reached BB, which was hardly reassuring. Many customers found that they themselves were more credit-worthy and could borrow more cheaply than the banks they were unsuccessfully trying to borrow from. As Greenspan later admitted, bank "fragility...in fact was the cause of the credit crunch." [S. Solomon, 463]

The Bush administration railed against this new credit crunch and even indirectly blamed the Fed. The Bushmen claimed that "overzealous bank regulators" were responsible for the halt in lending, having become too strict now after their anything goes attitude of the 1980s bubble. Bush even used his triumphalistic post-Gulf war State of the Union speech of January 29, 1991 to call on the Fed to lower interest rates and on the banks to make "more sound loans now." Greenspan responded with a critique of the 1980s, primly remarking that "it is now clear that a significant fraction of the credit extended during those years should not have been extended." [S. Solomon, 458]

In the waning days of the Reagan Administration, the White House still claimed to have presided over the longest peacetime economic expansion since the 1960s, or even in all of US history. By the end of 1988, the foreign debt of the United States, now the greatest debtor on the planet, had attained $500 billion, equal to 10% of GDP. According to the National Bureau of Economic Research, the US went into recession in July 1990 – just before Iraq took possession of Kuwait. Economic activity had been weaker under Bush than under any American president since Herbert Hoover in 1929-1933. The Bush recession in the US was accompanied by a deep economic downturn in western Europe, which for most countries was the worst since World War II. Against this background, the US banking system started to blow, starting in January 1990 with the Bank of New England.

The Bank of New England had been among the ten largest bank holding companies in the United States, with $30 billion in assets. But BNE had also built up $36 billion if off-balance sheet activity, mainly in derivatives. The came the collapse of the Boston real estate market. The Boston Federal Reserve pumped $18 billion in loans into BNE to keep it alive between January 1990 and January 1991, when it was finally seized and shut down. The huge covert bailout by the Fed was designed to allow BNE to unwind the vast majority of its derivatives positions, thus avoiding a likely short-term worldwide derivatives panic during 1990. William Seidman, the chairman of the FDIC, estimated that BNE would cost his agency $2.3 billion, the second most costly bank failure in US history after First RepublicBank Corp. of Dallas. It took the best part of a year to unwind BNE's derivative exposure. In early 1991 the buyout artists of KKR, now converted to bottom-fishing, trained their sights on the insolvent BNE. KKR was joined in this venture by Fleet/Norstar. This acquisition was approved by federal regulators in April 1991.

THE FORBEARANCE OF THE REGULATORS

By Bush's second year in office, most US money center banks were technically bankrupt, and were being kept going by what federal regulators call "forbearance" – leaving those tottering banks alone, while lending them money under the table. This is a form of mercy that banks do not ordinarily extend to homeowners fighting foreclosure, but it was emphatically Bush's policy. On December 7, 1990, the Bush White House convened an emergency meeting, with Baker present, to figure out what to do about the US banks. Before them the Bushmen saw six big, insolvent banks: Citicorp, Chase Manhattan, Manufacturers Hanover, Security Pacific, Chemical Bank, and the Bank of New England.

Most dramatic was the case of Citibank. While Bush was attempting to whip up hysteria and focus it on Saddam Hussein, a "silent, slow-motion, global wholesale money market flight from America's largest bank" was taking place day by day. [S. Solomon, 464] In April 1990, IBCA Banking Analysis of London declared that Citicorp was "undercapitalized and under-reserved." Standard and Poor's and then Moody's downgraded Citibank. In July 1990, bank analyst Dan Brumbaugh stated on the ABC network program *Nightline* that not only Citicorp, but also Chase Manhattan, Chemical Bank, Manufacturers Hanover and Bankers Trust were all already insolvent. During September 1990, there was a near electronic panic run on Citibank, while Chase Manhattan, and other New York money center banks were also under increasing pressure.

THANKSGIVING 1990: CITIBANK SILENTLY SEIZED BY FEDERAL REGULATORS

For Citibank, the biggest US bank with an alleged $213 billion in assets, survival entailed a period of two and one half years during which mighty Citicorp was silently seized and put into receivership by federal regulators who began operating the bank using its nominal officers, like the incompetent John Reed, as ventriloquists' dummies. Citicorp was now a secret ward of the Fed and the Comptroller of the Currency. [*EIR*, November 1, 1991] In October 1990, an auction of Citicorp money-market commercial paper attracted no buyers; it was saved only by purchases arranged by Goldman Sachs, and by a 13% interest rate. On the day before Thanksgiving, 1990, Citicorp Chairman John Reed and President Richard Braddock were summoned to the New York Federal Reserve on Wall Street. Awaiting Reed and Braddock were E. Gerald Corrigan, the President of the New York Federal Reserve, and William Taylor, the director of bank supervision for the Federal Reserve Board in Washington.

The Citibank crisis was a product of the collapse in US commercial real estate prices during 1989-1990. A shock wave of real estate collapse had wiped out 9 of the 10 largest banks in Texas over previous years, and that shock wave had now engulfed New York City. Reed, anxious to re-orient Citibank away from Walter Wriston's Latin American loan racket, had loaded up with real estate loans in the northeast states. Citibank had thought that only 1% of these loans would turn out to be unsound. Corrigan and Taylor had now concluded that 20% or more of the $30 billion loan portfolio would not perform, and that Citibank had to brace itself for a minimum of $5 billion in losses. Corrigan and Taylor were worried that Citibank, which had one of the lowest capital-to-asset ratios among major banks, didn't have sufficient capital to survive those losses.

Citibank had lent money to Campeau, Donald Trump, Olympia & York, John Portman, and Moutleigh and Randsworth Trust. When the New York department store Alexander's failed, Citibank was the big loser. Citibank also had to liquidate its London subsidiary of Citicorp Scrimgeour Vickers. At the end of 1990, Citicorp announced an addition of $340 million to its loan loss provisions, but this was grossly inadequate window-dressing. During 1990, Citicorp's non-performing real estate loans were up 120% to $2.6 billion, while the bank's portfolio of foreclosed real estate was up 78% to $1.3 billion, and the market value of these properties had fallen by 55%.

The New York Fed was in effect seizing control of Citibank, and would retain that control for a reported two and one half years. A small army of 300 federal bank regulators occupied Citibank's headquarters. Reed was obliged to cut Citicorp's dividend and then suspend it entirely, More than 11,000 Citicorp employees were fired. From November 1990 on, Reed traveled every month to Washington to report to the Fed and to the Treasury's Comptroller of the Currency.. The regulators cleared every major decision he made – which implicates them in the firings, in Citibank's derivatives exposure, which was built up in those years, and in Citibank's private banking and money laundering services that assisted the graft and embezzlement carried out by the family of then-Mexican President Carlos Salinas de Gortari.

THE THREAT OF FUNDING CRISIS

According to a recent journalistic account, "The stakes for the regulators in this case were enormous. 'We were running fire drills in case they had a problem that required government attention,' one top former official recalled. A run on Citibank would have required intervention by the Federal Reserve and help from the central banks of other nations, another key insider said." "What regulators feared most ... was a 'funding crisis' like the one that took down Continental Illinois National Bank a decade ago. Much of Citi's funds are big corporate deposits, many from overseas, that are not protected by federal deposit insurance. If those depositors got nervous and decided to withdraw their funds, even a healthy bank could not survive." In other words, the issue was a Systemic meltdown. [83]

The Citibank crisis remained acute all during 1991. In December 1991, Citibank was officially placed on the government's secret watch list of banks in critical condition. In August 1992 the Office of the Comptroller of the Currency required Citibank to sign a Memorandum of Understanding, a public reprimand whose exact terms remain secret. But Citibank was the biggest beneficiary ever of regulatory forbearance, the bending of the law. Some respite came in February 1991, when Saudi Prince Waleed bin Talal, already a 4.5% stockholder in Citibank, agreed to plough an additional $590 million back into the foundering concern. $600 million more soon flowed in from Middle East and domestic sources. Fidelity Investments also put some money into Citibank.

In the third quarter of 1991, Citibank posted a quarterly loss of $885 million, with non-performing loans at $6 billion and non-performing real estate loans at $3 billion. For the first time since 1813, no dividend was paid to the stockholders.

CITIBANK TECHNICALLY INSOLVENT AND STRUGGLING TO SURVIVE

In August 1991, Rep. John Dingell (D-Mich.) observed that Citicorp was "technically insolvent" and "struggling to survive." This comment triggered panic runs on Citicorp in Hong Kong and Australia, where the FDIC does not operate. During that same week, the New York Fed lent out $3.4 billion, with almost all of it reportedly going to Citicorp. Perhaps this was the money needed to make up for the loss of deposit base in the Far East. Certainly Citicorp had to fear panic runs in the US as well. During the summer of 1992, the former Wall Street broker turned austerity candidate for the presidency, Ross Perot, announced in delphic language that he was selling Citibank stock short, because he expected it to crash soon. In Perot's opinion, Citibank was insolvent.

Bankrupt banks were reorganized through mergers, which promised bigger bankrupt banks in the future. Chemical Bank took over Manufacturers Hanover, while the Bank of America absorbed Security Pacific. Citibank and Chase remained more or less in their original form. During these months there were significant bank failures in Norway and in Sweden.

On April 11, 1991, First Executive Life had been seized by California regulators; its $49 billion in liabilities made it the largest insurance failure in US history. Mutual Benefit Life Insurance Company of New Jersey was also bankrupt. 1991 also saw the demise of BCCI - the Banque de Credit et Commerce Internationale - allegedly because of a $1.2 billion fraud carried out by shipping tycoon Abbas Gokal. BCCI had been the owner of First American Bank, which employed former Defense Secretary and Truman controller Clark Clifford.

---

[83] *Washington Post*, May 16, 1993, Brett D. Fromson and Jerry Knight, "The Saving of Citibank".

GREENSPAN'S BACKDOOR BAILOUT

The Fed funds rate peaked at 9 7/8% between February and June of 1989, when the Fed began lowering, reaching 8.25% by the end of 1989. Then there was an interlude of paralysis before rates started slowly down again, touching 7.75% on October 29, 1990. Making up for lost time, Greenspan brought the Fed funds rate and the discount rate to 4.5% by early December 1991. Afraid of a banking collapse, and attempting to help Bush get re-elected the following year, Greenspan lowered the discount rate from 4.5% to 3.5% on December 19, 1991. Greenspan then took the Fed funds rate to 3%, and kept it there during late 1992 and during all of 1993. The direction of these interest rate reductions would not be reversed until February 1994.

Greenspan was providing a massive public bailout to US commercial banks at taxpayers' expense and without Congressional authority. It was a backdoor bailout. He helped the banks to steer away from short-term bankruptcy: by mid-1992 the Fed was keeping the overnight rate for federal funds in the neighborhood of 3%. At the same time, the thirty-year long bond was paying 7%. This meant that a Federal reserve member bank could borrow money at 3%, and use it to buy Treasury securities paying 7%, thus locking in a nearly four-point spread which represented pure risk-free profit to the bank. This was soon the biggest racket in town. Naturally, it would have been more convenient for US taxpayers if the Treasury had been able to borrow directly from the Fed at 3% rates, eliminating the banks as middlemen. That would have shrunk the debt-service burden imposed on the Federal budget much more effectively than the austerity nostrums proposed around this time by Perot and other demagogues. But Greenspan would have been horrified by such a proposal - for the Fed to have bought the Treasury issues at such low rates would have gone back to the bad old days before 1952 when the Fed was de facto forced to do the bidding of the elected government. It would have been a violation of the sacred laws of the free market !

LLOYD'S OF LONDON BANKRUPT

In 1990, the ancient and celebrated international insurance firm Lloyd's of London announced a loss of £ 2.319 billion. This was but part of a string of Lloyd's losses which would amount to almost £ 10 billion by 1993. Attempts by Lloyd's sleazy management to unload these catastrophic losses on gullible, status-seeking American investors who became partners (or "Names") with Lloyd's have led to lawsuits which are still making their way through the courts. The one clear fact was that Lloyd's, a crown jewel of British finance, was hopelessly bankrupt.

The same decline in real estate prices that had undermined the Wall Street banks also took its toll in Canada, where the giant real estate holding company, Olympia & York, defaulted and had most of its assets seized. Corrupt Canadian courts prevented Olympia & York from going into bankruptcy for several months while Canadian creditors got first pick of Olympia & York assets. Olympia & York represented powerful blackmail against Wall Street: its owners, the Reichmans, owned a large piece of Manhattan. If these properties had gone on the auction block as a result of bankruptcy liquidation, the bottom would surely have fallen out of New York City real estate, and none of the money center banks located there, including Citibank, could have survived. The New York Fed made sure that Olympia & York was handled with kid gloves.

OLYMPIA & YORK BANKRUPT

Olympia & York finally went into chapter 11 bankruptcy in May 1992 in Toronto, New York, and London. Olympia & York was controlled by the Reichman family, allies of Edgar Bronfman and his cohorts. The Reichmans had been bankrollers of Campeau on his takeover binge. One of

Olympia & York's development projects had been Canary Warf in the London docklands, a typical office building gentrification of a former productive site that had been encouraged by the Thatcher regime.

IMF SHOCK THERAPY: A NECKTIE FOR A CORPSE

The 1989 fall of the East German communist regime and the other eastern European communist governments, followed by the breakup of the USSR during 1991, should have imparted a new impulse towards economic expansion in world jobs and production. This should have been the occasion for the new eastern European, Russian, and Newly Independent State governments to become the recipients of a new and better Marshall Plan for their economic reconstruction and modernization. These were exactly the countries and peoples that had been robbed of their chance to participate in the first Marshall Plan by the cold war machinations of London. Such a Marshall Plan would have generated hundreds of thousands of new jobs in the US. But, with Bush in the White House, there was to be no Marshall Plan this time; Polish President Lech Walesa remarked sadly that the western aid offered to his country amounted to a "necktie for a corpse."

Instead, the eastern European and former Soviet economies were treated as passive objects for looting and exploitation, which was conducted under the cover of extreme monetarist theories. At the Houston G-7 economic summit in July 1990, the entire USSR and its successor states were consigned to the tender mercies of the International Monetary Fund, which soon issued a report providing the basis for shock therapy in that entire vast area. In Poland and later in Russia, the speculator and profiteer George Soros brought in the baby-faced Harvard economics professor Jeffrey Sachs. Sachs was the son of a trade union bureaucrat working for the Michigan state AFL-CIO in Lansing. Sachs' past exploits had included the reorganization of the Bolivian economy to sharply reduce employment in the tin mines, while Bolivia became one of the world's largest producers of cocaine. In Poland, Sachs was called in by the first non-communist government, that of Prime Minister Tadeusz Mazowiecki, in September 1989. Sach's Polish alter ego was Finance Minister Leszek Balcerowicz. Sachs came forward with extremist demands for the removal of all price controls and state subsidies on basic consumer items, such as bread and apartment rents. Currencies of the former communist bloc had their official parities abolished; they were made convertible and cast into the maelstrom of floating exchange rates. In Russia, Sachs worked with Yeltsin's prime minister, Yegor Gaidar. Then came the centerpiece of the Sachs shock therapy: the selling off to private venture capitalists of the state property of the successor states of the USSR. Plant, equipment, and infrastructure that had cost the blood, bones, and lives of millions of workers under Stalin and during World War II was suddenly opened up to local *nomenklatura* oligarchs and western raiders whose archetype was George Soros. The Russian government issued vouchers so that the average person might finally receive a pittance from this vast sell-off of state property. These vouchers were bought up by highly-leveraged gangster concerns like MMM, which soon succumbed to bankruptcy.

THE IMF TREATMENT: A TWO-THIRDS DECLINE IN PRODUCTION

The net effect of IMF shock therapy has been to reduce the overall level of industrial and agricultural production in the former communist states by about two thirds. These nations are now left with one third of the farm and factory production they had when they were still under communist auspices. Poland lost somewhat less than two thirds, Russia about two thirds, Ukraine somewhat more than two thirds. The losses are no longer due to Karl Marx or the Stalinist command economy; they are due to the looting carried out by the City of London and Wall Street under IMF conditionalities. Because of shock therapy, east Europe and the USSR successor states are themselves now deep in economic depression.

The collapse of the Communist regimes, the Warsaw Pact, and the Comecon set the stage for the so-called European Monetary Union. According to documents made public in the spring of 1998 by a German newsmagazine, Chancellor Kohl of Germany had been reluctant to accept the monetary union and the new currency it would make mandatory, since Germany was reluctant to give up the relatively stable German mark. But Kohl's agreement to dump the D-mark in favor of the euro was extorted by French President Mitterrand and British Prime Minister Thatcher as the price for allowing the re-unification of Germany after the Berlin wall came down. As the Chancellor recalled in a speech on April 30, 1998, Thatcher had told Kohl in December 1989, "We beat you twice, and here you are again." Kohl finally caved in to Mitterrand and Thatcher and accepted the European Monetary Union at a meeting in Strasbourg on December 9, 1989. Kohl later described this as "the darkest hour of my life" and an outcome "contrary to German interests." [84] Kohl had become prominent as part of the oligarchical opposition to Konrad Adenauer, a strong and successful nationalist leader who was willing to defy both the United States and the Soviet Union if necessary, to say nothing of Great Britain.

As the Soviet bloc came to an end, Pope John Paul II issued a penetrating analysis of the convergence between financiers and commissars made possible by the free market platform. In his encyclical *Centesimus Annus* (1991), Pope Woityla wrote of the "affluent society or consumer society" as a response to communism. Such a society, he pointed out, "seeks to defeat Marxism on the level of pure materialism by showing how a free-market society can achieve a greater satisfaction of material human needs than Communism, while equally excluding spiritual values. In reality, while on the one hand it is true that this model shows the failure Marxism to contribute to a humane and better society, on the other hand, in so far as it denies autonomous existence and value to morality, law, culture, and religion, it agrees with Marxism, in the sense that it totally reduces man to the sphere of economics and the satisfaction of material needs." In other statements, the Pope criticized utilitarianism, and showed that Marx and Adam Smith (representing "capitalisme sauvage" or unbridled capitalism) essentially agreed in their deterministic denial of human freedom and human responsibility.

24. EUROPEAN RATE MECHANISM CRISIS, SEPTEMBER 1992

After 1990, apart from a boomlet in pent-up consumer spending by East Germans, the European economies remained depressed even relative to their performance of the 1980s. By 1991 France was in a downturn journalistically billed as its "deepest postwar recession." The key to the crisis was an alliance of British City of London monetarists like John Major and Norman Lamont, French Cartesian chauvinist officials like François Mitterrand, and deflation-minded central bankers at the German Bundesbank. These are the cooks responsible for the superdeflationary Maastricht Treaty of December 1991, designed to bring the twelve European member states to a single European currency, supposedly by 1999. This Maastricht Treaty established so-called convergence criteria, ostensibly for the purpose of getting the various national economies ready for the transition to the single currency. These alleged convergence criteria are clinical examples of monetarist and deflationary extremism. One criterion is the reduction of national budget deficits to 3% of GDP. Money supply and inflation must also be brought under control. National currencies must attain stability before they are merged into the new Euro-ducat, finally called the euro.

---

[84] *Der Spiegel*, April 27, 1998.

MAASTRICHT CONVERGENCE

As part of the alleged "convergence" called for under the European Single Market of 1992, the British pound in October 1990 finally rejoined the European Monetary System, which the British preferred to call the European Rate Mechanism in order to minimize its importance. The heart of this arrangement was still the old European snake of the 1970s, with bands that allowed most of the currencies to fluctuate by 2.25% around their central parity. Exceptions were made for the British pound, Spanish peseta, and Portuguese escudo, which were granted leeway to move 6% above or below the target parity.

By September, 1992 the forces of international speculation – again meaning the City of London and Wall Street banks, brokerages, and hedge funds – decided to test the resolve of the European central bankers to maintain these parities, which were an essential condition for avoiding an even greater deterioration in the European economies. The speculators were led by George Soros, the operator of the Quantum Fund, one of the most aggressive of the highly-leveraged hedge funds. The Quantum Fund was reputed to contain capital contributed by the British Royal Family. Soros was also notorious for his close relations to the New York Federal Reserve Bank, which reportedly fed him the sensitive intelligence which made his trading strategies possible.

Other US banks openly joined in the speculative orgy against the European Rate Mechanism (ERM) and afterwards boasted of their handsome winnings. Citicorp, still a ward of federal regulators, speculated heavily, leading to the conclusion that the federal regulators involved, especially those from the New York Fed, thought that derivative betting on the breakup of the ERM was a legitimate economic activity worthy even of official Fed sponsorship.

The central target of the speculators was the core of the ERM, the relation between the French franc and the German mark. The glaring weakness of the ERM was that France was in a deep downturn and needed cheaper credit in order to avoid more job losses. But French interest rates had to be kept high in order to attract foreign hot money deposits. The German Bundesbank was pursuing its usual monomaniacal deflation, with high interest rates maintained throughout. The Bundesbank claimed that because of the extra expenditures incurred by the German government in the newly added eastern states, it was doubly important to fight inflationary tendencies with stringent tight money. The basic hedge fund approach was thus to use borrowed money in the futures markets to short the franc, pound, lira, and all the other ERM members except the D-mark.

The political occasion for the speculation was given on June 2, 1992 when Danish voters rejected the Maastricht Treaty and the common European currency in a referendum. A similar referendum was scheduled to be held in France on September 20. Bankers realized that the French population might also reject Maastricht, in which case that carefully crafted monetarist house of cards might be blown away. This uncertainty meant that the way was open to speculate against Maastricht in the long run by speculating on the breakup of the ERM in the short run. This was a world-wide upheaval that included a dollar crisis; during August, the Tokyo Nikkei average reached a new low of 14,309 yen, while on September 1 the US dollar hit a new low of 1.3977 to the mark in Frankfurt.

European central banks began struggling to keep their currencies within their assigned bands when large speculative movements began in July 1992. Finland had become a de facto member of the ERM in June 1991, and had devalued its markka in November 1991. On August 26 Finland had raised its base interest rate from 15.5% to 17%. By September 3, the Bank of Finland's convertible reserves had fallen from the July 31 figure of 31 billion markka to 23.07 billion. The base interest rate was then raised to 18%. On Sept. 8 Finland decided to surrender to the speculators allow the markka to float, and it quickly depreciated by 13%.

SWEDISH INTEREST RATES AT 500%

Then came the turn of Sweden, Another country aligned with the ERM, whose internal downturn was already the worst since the 1920s. On August 13 the Swedish Riksbank began raising the interest rate on the Swedish crown, which then stood at 13%. By September 9, the discount rate was 75% On September 14, after Germany had slightly reduced interest rates, the Swedish rate was reduced to 20%. Then, on September 16, the Swedish crown came under the most extreme short pressure because of events in Britain, where the pound had dropped out of the ERM. On that day the Swedish discount rate was raised to 75%, and a few hours later to 500%.

On September 14, the Bundesbank deflationists relented a little and lowered their discount rate to 8.25% from 8.75%. The Lombard rate, which acts as a ceiling on short-term interest rates, was notched downward by a quarter point to 9.5% These were the first interest rate cuts by the Bundesbank in almost 5 years. In return for these cuts, the Bundesbank demanded and got a 7% devaluation of the Italian lira, which the Bundesbank had asserted was highly overvalued in the ERM currency grid.

On September 14, speculation targeted the British pound. Prime Minister John Major loudly proclaimed that another pound devaluation would constitute a "betrayal." But Major's Chancellor of the Exchequer, Norman Lamont, considered the ERM a straitjacket from which he could not wait to escape. On September 14-16, the Bank of England claimed to have spent 15 billion pounds out of its total reserves of 44 billion pounds in useless support operations, buying pounds in exchange for other currencies. On September 16, the Bank of England raised the bank rate from 10% to 12%, and then to 15% three hours later. The Bank of England then cancelled the second bank rate hike and allowed the pound to float at 7:30 PM local time. The bank rate was lowered to 10% the next day.

On the fifth anniversary of these events, the *Financial Times* concluded that they had broken Major's "authority and split the Tory party," leading to Major's election defeat in the spring of 1997. For the *FT*, the 1992 Black Wednesday can be "seen as one of the great national defeats in British postwar history – comparable to, say, the Suez debacle, Harold Wilson's devaluation in 1967 or James Callaghan's humiliation by the International Monetary Fund...." [85]

Corriere della Sera later revealed that the 30% devaluation of the lira had been orchestrated at a meeting on board Queen Elizabeth II's Royal Yacht Britannia in Italian waters on June 2, 1992. The purpose of this maneuver was to devalue the Italian currency so as to cheapen the purchase price for Italian assets being bought by British and other financiers when the large Italian state-owned sector (including IRI, ENI, SNAM, Finsider, and other large holding companies and firms controlled by the Ministry for State Participations) were put on the auction block of privatization. This meeting was reportedly attended by bankers from S.G. Warburg and Barings of London, along with officials of the Italian Treasury and Finance Ministry. Soros was thought to have been the leading edge of this operation. Romano Prodi, the Italian prime minister after the breakup of the post-1945 party system, was widely regarded as a close associate of speculator Soros. Italy was further shaken in early 1993 when its second largest group of companies, Ferruzzi, went bankrupt as a result of derivatives losses.

THE FOURTH (OR FIFTH) DEVALUATION OF THE BRITISH POUND

This was at least the fourth devaluation of the British pound in the twentieth century. 1992 came in the tradition of 1931, 1949, and 1967. (Some might also count 1972, when the British were the

---

[85] *Financial Times*, September 17, 1997.

first in the world to drop out of the Smithsonian parities.) In 1992 as in 1931, it was British-based financial institutions and their US minions that took the lead in shorting the pound. In 1992 as in 1931 and 1967, the British pound was used less as a national currency and far more as a speculative vehicle that also could be used to cause havoc among for sturdier currencies. The result of the 1931 British devaluation and default was to wreck the only system of currency relations then available – the gold standard which rotated around the pound. In 1992, the fall of the pound partially wrecked the EMS fixed parity arrangement, and helped to make sure that the ongoing European downturn would be a long and deep one.

On September 17, speculative pressure on the lira became so strong that the Italian currency followed the pound in quitting the EMS altogether and embarking on a solo float. Also on September 17, Spain announced that it would devalue the peseta in the EMS by 5%. This left an EMS composed of the German mark, the French franc, the Dutch guilder, the Belgian franc, the Danish crown, the Irish punt, the Spanish peseta and the Portuguese escudo. The mark-franc relation had to withstand several more weeks of speculative pressure. On September 22-23 a run developed against the French franc, which obliged the Bundesbank to dump the equivalent of more than $65 billion on the market in selling marks and buying francs.

In the weeks that followed, US banks and hedge funds proudly announced how much they had made by shorting the pound and the lira. Soros was one of the biggest winners; his profits on the fall of the pound were the equivalent of having personally stolen something like a ten-pound note from every man, woman and child in the United Kingdom. In the wake of the debacle, many European countries announced austerity programs: Italy pledged $75 billion in tax hikes and budget cuts; Sweden was not far behind. The Bundesbank had squandered one third of its foreign exchange in support operations; the Banque de France had about 10% of its foreign currency reserves left. Italy and Ireland were cleaned out. British losses were also heavy.

The war of the hedge funds against the ERM had terrible economic consequences for the average European worker. European industrial production is wholly integrated, with products crossing borders numerous times before they reach the consumer as finished commodities. Without true fixed parities, every border crossing brings additional foreign exchange risk, and corresponding needless expense. This is the destructive handiwork of the speculators. In May 1993, German Finance Minister Theo Waigel announced that Germany was suffering "the sharpest economic crisis" since its founding as the Bundesrepublik Deutschland in 1949. During the French election campaign of spring 1993 the politician Edouard Balladur asserted that the French economy was in its "worst state since the Second World War."

25. FINAL DESTRUCTION OF ERM FIXED PARITIES, JULY-AUGUST 1993

A sequel to these events developed in July 1993, when Soros and other speculators provoked a crisis in the European Rate Mechanism (ERM) by unleashing a heavy speculative attack against the French franc, the Belgian franc, the Danish crown, the Portuguese escudo, and the Spanish peseta. The central banks offered some resistance, spending some $8.7 billion in support operations during just a few hours, but the European governments soon capitulated to the speculators by widening the fluctuation bands for the ERM – a destructive concession that made the ERM much less effective in guaranteeing stable exchange rates among the European trading partners.

The starting point for this crisis was once again the high interest rate policy of the German Bundesbank, combined with severe downturns in the other European countries, which had unemployment rates ranging between 10% and 13%. These countries needed cheaper credit, but cheaper credit would have weakened their currencies even further in relation to the German mark, forcing them out of the ERM. French Prime Minister Balladur said he wanted a *franc fort* (a strong franc) but what he got was *Francfort* (the German banking center in Frankfurt am Main, where the Bundesbank is located). On August 1, 1993 the finance ministers of Europe gathered to declare the impotence of their governments by "widening" the fluctuation bands of the ERM from the earlier 2.25%, which was already rather elastic, to 15%, which was so wide that the whole exercise had become virtually meaningless.

During this crisis there were numerous attacks against currency speculators in the French and other European newspapers. Hedge fund operators were described as "parasites" and "terrorists." French Finance Minister Michel Sapin threatened the hedge-funds with retribution, reminding them that "during the French revolution such speculators were known as *agioteurs*, and they were beheaded." On August 12, 1993 French Prime Minister Edouard Balladur stated on television:

> We must reform our world monetary, financial, and credit system, and act to protect the prosperity of nations from purely speculative activities. This is an economic and moral duty of all civilized nations. There are, all over the world, a group of speculators who would like a situation in which all the currencies of the world float as much as possible.... We cannot agree to have billions and billions change direction in a quarter of a second and threaten the prosperity of a country.

There were calls from a number of quarters for capital controls and exchange controls. The French papers singled out "Anglo-Saxon speculators" for much-deserved criticism. The fact that Soros was closely linked to both the New York Federal Reserve Bank and the Queen's Royal Household did nothing to dispel the Gallic allegations that an "Anglo-Saxon conspiracy" was at work. But Gallic rage turned out to be impotent: after all the invective, France did nothing to outlaw hedge funds, derivatives, and other destructive activities. Later, the *New York Times* admitted that the six leading American banks had made 40% of their second quarter 1993 profits from currency speculation. The wrecking of the ERM permanently damaged Europe's capacity for economic survival, with the result that the old continent would continue its high unemployment and economic decline for as far as the eye could see.

BRADY: $1 TRILLION A DAY IN CURRENCY SPECULATION

The EMS crisis of September 1992 signaled that the derivatives era was in full swing. US Treasury Secretary Nicholas Brady told the late September annual meeting of the IMF that the daily turnover in world currency markets had attained $1 trillion per business day. (Compared to that, as the cynical Deutsche Bank speculator Hilmar Kopper said, the Bundesbank's losses were "peanuts.") Trading of US Treasury securities had reached $300 billion per day. That $300 billion was just $37 billion less than the total reserves of the US Fed. The monetarist central bankers had encouraged the derivatives in which many of these transactions were carried out. Now the derivatives were turning to devour their creators like a Frankenstein's monster. In late December 1993, the large German firm Metallgesellschaft announced derivatives losses of over $2 billion. At the end of 1993, Spain's fourth-largest bank, Banco Español de Credito (called Banesto) was seized by the Spanish central bank. Economics Minister Pedro Solbes told the Cortes that the seizure of Banesto had been imperative in order to prevent a collapse of "the entire banking sector." Derivatives speculation was once again the culprit. A few days later, Banco Latino, the second largest in Venezuela, was placed in receivership by the government after derivatives losses.

In addition to the partial smashing of their monetary parities and the draining of their central bank reserves, the medium-sized powers of western Europe had other troubles. When the old Soviet-dominated German Democratic Republic (DDR) was re-unified with the German Federal Republic

(BRD), Chancellor Helmut Kohl made the fatal error of allowing the existing debts of the DDR to be carried forward on the books at full value. Debt was respected even if it was wholly illegitimate, communist debt. When Alfred Herrhausen of Deutsche Bank was assassinated in 1989, he was succeeded by the just-cited Hilmar Kopper, a horse of a different color who believed in "Anglo-Saxon management culture." In today's world, that is a euphemism for usury. The Trusteeship Agency (Treuhand), set up to manage the state property of the absorbed East German state, was operated according to Wall Street and City of London criteria after the Easter, 1991 assassination of Detlev Rohwedder, its founding chief executive. This meant that much of the DDR's industrial production, geared to the vanished Comecon market, was not maintained. The DDR's high quality industrial workers went on the dole. These factors combined to produce a public debt of the Bonn government that passed $1.4 trillion late in 1995. German per capita public debt was already by that time one of the highest in the world.

On the eve of the 1992 US presidential election, the International Monetary Fund carried out a blunt and arrogant interference into US internal affairs by attempting to dictate the policies that Washington should adopt. At a session of the IMF executive board meeting on September 9 to prepare for the Fund's annual conference, IMF Managing Director Michel Camdessus used unusually blunt language to criticize the conduct of the United States. The IMF had never been truly happy with George Bush, who was thought to be insufficiently austere and too interested in his own re-election prospects; even Bush's repudiation of his own "read my lips – no new taxes" pledge was not enough for the IMF. At a press briefing in Washington on September 11, a senior IMF official called on the US to implement revenue increases and spending cuts totaling between $240 and $300 billion. The IMF additionally demanded from the US a carbon tax on gasoline, coal, and other fossil fuels, as well as a nation-wide sales tax or value-added tax of 5% on almost all goods and services. The IMF also decreed cuts in the already frayed US social safety net.

In Russia, the IMF shock treatment was ruining the country from the start. During March 1993, when the Clinton administration thought that Yeltsin was in danger of losing power by a defeat in a spring referendum, Secretary of the Treasury Lloyd Bentsen warned the IMF that they could not treat Russia like a banana republic. But this positive impulse was soon smothered by the entrenched Washington bureaucracy with the help of counter-moves by the Anglo-American finance oligarchy. The Zhirinovsky shock of December 1993 reminded Washington once again that the current Russian policy is bankrupt and suicidal. In a statement Clinton referred to the "immiseration" suffered by the Russian population. Russia was much too important to be left to the IMF, but nothing was done.

CAMDESSUS: KILL THE SCAPEGOAT

Clinton's man at the State Department, the superficial Strobe Talbott, stated the US goal as "less shock and more therapy for the Russian people." But the permanent bureaucracy of the IMF was defiant. Michel Camdessus became hysterical because of the wave of criticism of the IMF. In a rare public defense, Camdessus raved on February 1 1994: "From time to time I ask myself: 'Which will be the next one in order to kill the scapegoat?' This is just unfactual. Full stop." Camdessus said that the Russian government was to blame for the crisis there. "We will move as rapidly as we can. But if it means signing off on a bad program that will make things worse, that we will not do," said Ernesto Hernandez-Cata, IMF deputy director in charge of Russia. Many IMF and State Department bureaucrats argued that Russia had actually turned away from the true rigors of shock therapy in March 1992.

GREENSPAN'S PREVENTIVE STRIKES

On February 4, 1994 Alan Greenspan and the Federal Reserve Open Market Committee conducted their self-styled "preemptive strike" against alleged inflationary tendencies with the first increase in five years in the federal funds rate. During the ensuing three weeks, the Treasury's 30-year bond was hammered mercilessly, losing four and one half points or 4.5% of its value. At the same time, bond markets in western Europe also experienced severe selling pressure. By mid-year, it was already the worst year for British government bonds, the celebrated gilts, since 1914. The structure of world leverage was built around a 3% Fed funds rate; Greenspan proceeded to knock down this house of cards, and big derivatives bets began to go bad.

The roots of this situation went back to the October 15, 1993 historic top of the long bond and its subsequent decline along with the battered Dow Jones utilities. George Soros, presumably acting to quell rumors that his financial empire had become completely insolvent, told the *London Times* that he had indeed lost $600 million on February 14, 1994 by shorting the Japanese yen, but insisted that he would survive. Soros and his chief trader Stanley Druckenmiller had assumed that the trend of the yen against the dollar was down, but in the wake of the breakdown of US-Japanese talks on February 11, the yen rose by 5% on the expectation that the US would seek a higher yen as a way to cut Japan's trade surplus with the US. That was the tale told by Soros.

A WORLDWIDE BOND MARKET MELTDOWN

If misery loves company, Soros was comforted. Goldman Sachs was reported to have lost a cool $640 million in its Japanese bond trading during January. This firm had ignored the long bond's mid-October top and insisted that long bond yields were headed towards 5.5% in January. A CNN commentator spoke of a "worldwide bond market meltdown." It was in fact the worst bond market crisis since the 1930s. It was soon revealed that Procter & Gamble, fundamentally a soap company, had incurred huge losses through derivatives. This was the company which was once so conservative that it used to be called Procter & Safe. A Cargill investment fund called Minnetonka announced losses of $100 million on derivatives.

ENTER THE "ROGUE TRADERS"

A new archetype for the alleged "rogue trader" emerged in the person of one Joseph Jett, once the boss of the government securities trading desk of Kidder, Peabody in Wall Street. Joseph Jett had been the personal protege of Kidder tycoon Edward A. Cerullo, the center of a coterie of yuppy quants. Jett, an Afro-American in his early thirties, had allegedly developed a system for recombining US Treasury strips (government securities that have been separated into two parts, the principal and the interest flow). Kidder claimed that Jett had tricked the firm's computers and built up $600 million in phony trading positions, recording 60,000 transactions Kidder said never took place. Kidder said Jett covered up trading losses of $100 million, reported $350 million in profits which never existed, and wrongly received a 1993 bonus of $9 million. General Electric, the parent company of Kidder, Peabody, was obliged to reduce its earnings estimate for the quarter by $210 million, a heavy blow. Jett denied all wrongdoing; Cerullo soon quit the company. Before long Kidder, Peabody had ceased to exist. The *Wall Street Journal* saw no need for regulatory action, commenting that derivative securities are as old as Aristotle.

DERIVATIVES AS COLLATERAL FOR THE FED

At this time Comptroller of the Currency Ludwig was most worried about "exotic and especially complex derivative instruments," which he said might prove incomprehensible to senior bank managers who had been trained in the long-gone world of corporate lending. And worry he might: the Federal Deposit Insurance Corporation Improvement Act of 1991, a piece of legislation occasioned by the de facto insolvency of the FDIC bailout fund, gave non-bank banks the right to borrow from the Fed, and to use **derivatives** as eligible collateral.

GREENSPAN'S DOLLAR CRISIS DEEPENS

Normally rising interest rates should have helped the dollar, but Greenspan's Chinese water torture had the opposite effect. During the spring of 1994, the dollar fall became pronounced. This crisis was triggered by the financial warfare waged by the City of London. The British were in effect organizing a bear raid against the highly vulnerable dollar in the same way that they might organize a run on the currency of a central American banana republic, possibly as part of the preparation for a coup d'etat.

At the end of April 1994, Treasury Secretary Bentsen had asked the Federal Reserve to carry out support operations in favor of the dollar, but that quickly proved to be completely inadequate. Since the beginning of 1994, the dollar had fallen by about ten per cent in relation to the Japanese yen, and about six per cent in relation to the German mark. On May 4, it was announced that the Fed had been joined by 16 other central banks to carry out a coordinated intervention in support of the dollar, the first of these exercises since August 1992. An estimated $3 to $5 billion was expended, and the dollar acquired a short breathing space. Bentsen recited his *mea culpa*: "This administration sees no advantage in an undervalued currency." The German Bundesbank's half-point reduction in its discount and Lombard rates reflected a desire there to avoid a precipitous drop by the dollar.

Together with the interventions came yet another collapse in the market for US Treasury securities. On May 6, 1994 the Treasury's 30-year bond recorded its biggest one-day decline since the Kuwait crisis, a fall of 2 3/16 points, raising the yield .21 % to 7.54, the highest level in 18 months. On the following Monday, the long bond fell almost another full point, bringing the yield to 7.65. This was a decline measured in boxcar numbers. Traders said the long bond's fall since early February was the most severe since 1987, when T-bond weakness had been a harbinger of market panic. (The Dow Jones utility average, which often moves in sync with bonds, was then down about 30% from the highs reached in September 1993 – the equivalent of 1500 Dow Jones industrials points. The utilities had fallen 10% in just two weeks during the spring of 1994.)

Wall Street insiders stressed the anti-Clinton political nature of the dollar/T-bond crisis. The *New York Times* summed up Wall Street's view as a "more general loss of confidence in President Clinton's handling of foreign policy, the months of distraction over his and his wife's personal finances, coupled with widespread uncertainties about the fate of health care and the ability of the Federal Reserve to continue raising interest rates despite mounting political pressures against the moves from the White House." Another commentator claimed that Clinton was "Jimmy Carter II economically." There was also an element of mistrust against the Federal Reserve and Greenspan personally.

According to the hackneyed proverbs of Economics 101, higher interest rates should have promoted a stronger dollar. But in this case sharply falling prices on Treasury bonds were causing investors to sell those bonds and often dump the dollars they received on the market. The laws of Adam Smith were seemingly abrogated; the *New York Times* wrote that such a "perverse reaction is another indication of the truly massive speculation that had been going on regarding American interest rates."

Bond ratings for Bankers Trust reflected the fact that this institution was really no longer mainly a bank, but more like a hedge fund (and an increasingly shaky one at that) which had abandoned corporate lending in favor of the interest rate arbitrage just described. Greenspan's politically inspired, anti-Clinton moves to raise interest rates blew out the cornerstone of the derivative edifice. The derivative dollar responded to these changes in ways that the old cash markets never would have.

GREENSPAN'S CHINESE WATER TORTURE

The rate of collapse of the international finance markets slowed somewhat during May 1994, and the denizens of lower Manhattan and their political clerks were quick to congratulate themselves that the worst was probably over. There was talk of having weathered "the February to April turmoil in global stock, bond, and foreign exchange markets," as columnist Hobart Rowen put it. But on May 17, 1994 Greenspan led the Federal Open Market Committee and the Federal Reserve Board of Governors in the fourth installment of their "preventive strike" against inflation: after quarter-point increases in February, March, and April in Fed funds, this time it was a half-point hike in Fed funds to 4.25% plus an increase in the discount rate from 3 to 3.5%. Wall Street concluded that this would be the last interest rate increase for the time being, basing this on the passage in the Federal Reserve communiqué which concluded that the rate increases so far "substantially remove the degree of monetary accommodation which prevailed through 1993." Treasury Secretary Bentsen said that he had convinced Greenspan during a tennis match to act with apparent finality in order to avoid "a Chinese water torture on interest rates." German interest rates were now lower, so the stock market and bond market gained ground for a couple of days after the Fed's action, but continued dollar weakness soon evoked fears that Greenspan would raise interest rates yet again, in order to convince investors not to dump the US dollar.

DERIVATIVES: THE THREAT OF SYSTEMIC CRISIS

One day after Greenspan's move, the General Accounting Office (GAO) issued the result of a 2-year study of derivative securities. The release of this study was timed with a morning session of Congressman Edward J. Markey's (D-Massachusetts) Subcommittee on Telecommunications and Finance of the House Energy and Commerce Committee, and an afternoon hearing of the Senate Banking Committee. According to the GAO, the notional value of derivatives contracts outstanding at the end of 1992 was at least $12.1 trillion worldwide. (The fine print of the report included an estimate from *Swaps Monitor* magazine that the derivatives issued by the 50 largest global dealers amounted to almost $26 trillion at the end of 1992.) But the GAO claimed that notional amount "is not a meaningful measure of the actual risk involved." In the view of this report, the gross credit risk for 14 large US financial institutions was a mere $114 billion, equal to only 1.8% of the $6.5 trillion notional amount of their derivatives exposure. For the GAO, derivatives credit risk was thus reduced to "loss resulting from a counterparty's failure to meet its financial obligations."

Even so, anxiety did flicker through the stultified bureaucratic prose of the report: "... the abrupt failure or withdrawal from trading of [a major over-the-counter derivatives dealer] could undermine stability in several markets simultaneously, which could lead to a chain of market withdrawals, possible firm failures, and a systemic crisis. The federal government would not necessarily intervene just to keep a major OTC derivatives dealer from failing, but to avert a crisis, the Federal Reserve may be required to serve as lender of last resort to any major US OTC derivatives dealer, whether regulated or unregulated. " The report listed 4 US money center banks with derivative contracts already over one trillion dollars: Chemical Bank ($1.621 trillion); Citicorp ($1.521 trillion); J.P. Morgan ($1.252 trillion); and Bankers Trust ($1.166 trillion. The GAO was clearly worried that a derivatives panic would rip away the last facade of solvency these bankrupt institutions still maintain, and force the Federal Deposit Insurance Corporation to make good on its commitment to reimburse hundreds of billions of dollars in insured deposits, exposing in turn the bankruptcy of the FDIC. If a large over-the-counter derivatives dealer failed, says the GAO, "the failure could pose risks to other firms - including federally insured depository institutions - and the financial system as a whole. Financial linkages among firms and markets could heighten this risk."

So what did the GAO propose to do about this threat of a final coup de grace to the agonizing US banking system? Outlaw derivatives? Tax them to the point of extinction? Hardly; the GAO merely wished to place derivatives within the bureaucratic purview of US regulators, who had shown themselves totally complaisant. The pious wishes of the GAO came down to the following: "...that Congress require federal regulation of the safety and soundness of all major US OTC derivatives dealers. Regulators should attempt to prevent financial disruptions from turning into crises and resolve crises to minimize risks to the financial system. Thus, firms that become insolvent should be allowed to fail but to do so in an orderly fashion." Even these minimal requests led to no action.

A FINANCIAL NUCLEAR CHAIN REACTION

The collective anxiety of certain Wall Street circles about the explosive potential of the derivatives crisis was expressed at the end of May by Felix Rohatyn, senior partner of the Lazard Frères investment bank, and the former financial dictator of New York City. Rohatyn said he was nervous about the derivatives crisis "because the genie is out of the bottle and could touch off a financial nuclear chain reaction, spreading around the world with the speed of light." But what of the argument that derivatives help to manage and thus mitigate risk? "My gut tells me," says Rohatyn, that "the big players too often are on the same side. They may be long on the dollar or short on interest rates. Then, something can happen that triggers a huge stampede: They all try to get out at the same time." This was at least more realistic than the usual pro-derivatives pabulum.

Even timid moves to regulate derivatives were roundly condemned by Greenspan, who told the Markey subcommittee "There is no presumption that the major thrust of derivatives activities is any riskier, indeed it may well be less risky, than commercial lending." According to Greenspan, there was no need for any additional government regulation; everything necessary was already being taken care of by the magic of the marketplace: "...today's markets and firms, especially those firms that deal in derivatives, are heavily regulated by private counterparties who, for self-protection, insist that dealers maintain adequate capital and liquidity.... As far as the Federal Reserve Board is concerned, we feel we are ahead of the curve on this issue." Words which were destined to return to haunt the Fed chairman in the inevitable post-cataclysm Pecora-style investigations of what went wrong.

Congressman Markey compared such regulators who "have to rely on the kindness of strangers" to the pathetic Blanche DuBois in Tennessee Williams's *A Streetcar Named Desire*. House Banking Committee Chairman Congressman Henry Gonzalez (D-Texas) on May 26 made public a bill to increase derivatives regulation with an emphasis on avoiding a taxpayer bailout of banks which might go under because of their derivatives activities. Gonzalez talked of imposing a 1/10 of 1% tax on the notional value of derivatives contracts. (Later, in the spring of 1995 and with the Democrats in the minority, Gonzalez would offer the Derivatives Safety and Soundness Supervision Act of 1995, with provisions for both the reporting and the taxation of derivatives.)

Despite days of attempted jawboning by Clinton, Secretary of the Treasury Bentsen and other officials, the dollar soon fell to a new all-time postwar low of less than 99 yen. The relation of the dollar to the D-mark also deteriorated markedly. Soros was in action against the dollar this time as well. The *Washington Post* of June 25, 1994 quoted a source close to Soros gloating that during the ineffective central bank dollar support operations of the previous day "we could buy dollars in the market for 1.582 [D-marks] and sell them to the Bundesbank, which was standing there buying dollars for 1.608 marks.... We could make a 1 percent to 2 percent gain on our money in a matter of three hours."

During the last days of June 1994 there were reports that the principal British banks had joined in an offensive strategy designed to bring down the dollar. On June 28, a *Neue Zürcher Zeitung* "Eurobonds" column datelined London reflected the commitment of the S.G. Warburg banking house against the US currency. S.G. Warburg's president, George Magnus, had told *Le Figaro* on June 23 that "whatever decision is taken by the US Federal Reserve, the interpretations will be bad." BBC reports also hyped the drama of the dollar crisis. Pressure on US Treasury securities continued: by the first day of July, 1994 the 30-year Treasury bond was yielding 7.71%, up almost 2% from its mid-October low of 5.75%.

THE DERIVATIVES CRASH: PAINE WEBBER IN TROUBLE

On Friday July 23, 1994 the Paine Webber investment group announced a new dimension in its bailout of one of its mutual funds. The fund in question was the Paine Webber Short-Term U.S. Government Securities Fund. Investors who bought into this fund may have concluded from its name that they were getting the alleged security of Treasury bills and perhaps medium-term notes. But it turned out that managers of this fund had tried to jack up their yield by buying "structured notes," or designer derivatives, based ultimately on home mortgages. The prices for these mortgage-backed derivatives began to collapse when in February, when the Federal Reserve began its campaign to raise interest rates. By April, the share prices of Paine Webber's mutual fund were also in free fall. When fund managers tried to sell some of their mortgage-backed derivatives, they found that there was no market for the structured notes. Investors soon launched a class-action lawsuit, which Paine Webber paid $33 million to settle in June. Then Paine Webber spent $55 million to buy certain derivatives from the fund, seeking to stabilize its value. The firm said it would spend an additional $180 million to bail out the Short-Term U.S. Government Fund. This made a grand total of $268 million spent on this mutual fund alone. Because Paine Webber, under US tax laws, wrote off part of this expenditure as a capital loss - in effect shifting part of the loss the taxpayers - the bailout ended up costing the firm just $34 million. This was still enough to wipe out Paine Webber's second-quarter earnings, leaving the firm with a loss of $25 million. As a mid-1980s advertising campaign had stressed: Thank you, Paine Webber.

26. ORANGE COUNTY, MEXICO, AND BARINGS

During the first days of December 1994, when many Wall Street stockjobbers were awaiting the arrival of a "Santa Claus rally" in share values, US financial markets were rocked by the crisis of the Orange County investment fund, managed by County Treasurer Robert L. Citron. The first public word on the Orange County crisis came on December 1, the same day that the US Senate followed the lead of the House and passed the deplorable GATT free-trade accord and its accompanying supernational World Trade Organization.

Citron was the custodian of funds deposited by about 180 cities, towns, and agencies within Orange County. The Treasury contained about $8 billion in such deposits. About 40% of the money came from towns or agencies who did so voluntarily, presumably attracted by Citron's past record as something of a financial wizard capable of bringing in investment yields of 10% per year, somewhat above the average. Citron pursued a leveraged investment strategy along the following lines: he took his original pot of $8 billion to the brokers as an ante, and was able to borrow $12 billion more, which he invested in derivatives and in the four-year notes of US government agencies. (This seems like high leverage, but it was rather conservative in comparison with the methods of George Soros and some other big betters.) Citron's favorite plays included floating-rate derivatives and reverse repurchase agreements. The floating-rate contracts included the species known as inverse floaters, which go down in value when interest rates go up. Citron also put large amounts into the designer derivatives called structured notes, favoring a type also designed to increase in value when interest rates go down. As is usual with margin transactions, the securities bought by Citron remained in the hands of the brokers as collateral.

The kind of operation Citron was running was something of an open secret, both in Orange County and on Wall Street. A year before the fall, an Orange County internal audit had cited Citron's "risky and unusual transactions." When Citron sought re-election to his job in June 1994, his opponent, an accountant named John Moorlach, attacked him for investing in "junk." The breaking point came in the last days of November, just as Mellon Bank was announcing that it had taken a $130 million hit in its own derivatives dealing. In Citron's December 1 official statement on the crisis, he estimated that the damage would be kept to a "paper loss" of $1.4 billion. Wall Street began to feel nervous. The same papers that carried this news also reported Chemical Bank's announcement that it would liquidate 3,700 jobs, almost 10% of its entire work force.

As the new business week began, Citron failed to make scheduled payments to the brokers on the reverse repurchase agreements. These initial defaults involved Nomura Securities, Smith Barney, and CS First Boston (a branch of Credit Suisse). Nomura and Smith Barney agreed to roll over the loans Citron had contracted, but CS First Boston demanded immediate payment in full of the $2.1 billion Citron owed them.

CITRON'S BROKERS SELL HIM OUT

On December 5, Citron, who had become the target of an investigation by the Securities and Exchange Commission, resigned his post. By this time the semi-official press estimate of the losses had risen to $1.5 billion. The brokers who had been Citron's collaborators began a massive dumping of the securities they still held as collateral. CS First Boston led the charge, dumping $2.6 billion of securities on December 6. On the following day, Nomura dumped $900 million, while Kidder Peabody, already burned by hundreds of millions of derivatives losses in the Jett affair, was able to unload $900 million out of $1 billion it had been holding as collateral. Prudential jettisoned $1 billion. Smith Barney tried to unload $800 million on December 8, but did not complete the process until the next day, when Morgan Stanley for its part was able to dump $1.6 billion. Merrill Lynch, citing its long-standing link to Orange County, said it was still holding on to $2 billion in collateral.

The day that Citron quit, the financial world was greeted with the perplexing news that the Fidelity Magellan Mutual Fund, the largest mutual fund in the US, would not make a year-end distribution of taxable income to its 3 million shareholders. With 500 million shares outstanding, the distribution had been announced at $4.32 per share, for a grand total of $2.38 billion. Normally plus or minus a few pennies from the pre-announced figure for such a distribution would be the maximum divergence expected. "It was really an error in the calculation of the estimate," said a Fidelity official with a straight face, arousing widespread suspicion that there was a link to Orange

County. It later turned out that Fidelity Investments had been left holding $3 billion in Orange County paper. Had Fidelity's dubious management decided to procure some loan-loss reserves on the sly?

Also on the day that Citron quit, the Federal Reserve Board announced that it had compelled Bankers Trust, one of the most aggressive dealers in derivative securities, to sign an unusual written agreement – public, and enforceable in court – pledging to inform its customers about the immense risks of derivatives before closing any deals. Bankers Trust had been sued by Procter & Gamble, the soap manufacturer, and by the Gibson Greeting Card Co. when they both lost big on derivatives sold by Bankers Trust.

ORANGE COUNTY BANKRUPT

On December 6, Orange County filed for bankruptcy and protection from its creditors under chapter 9 of the federal bankruptcy law, which is the part that governs cities and towns. Orange County officials had assumed that this filing would put a stop to the panic sale of their assets by the brokerage houses. But they were mistaken. The brokers who dumped Orange County collateral after the bankruptcy was filed cited an obscure passage from the bankruptcy law which allows brokers to sell securities that are in their hands as collateral in reverse repurchase transactions. Orange County sued Merrill Lynch for selling the derivatives in the first place, and also sued Nomura Securities and other brokers for selling the collateral. In a separate action, investors who held Orange County bonds started a class action lawsuit against Merrill Lynch, Smith Barney and Citron. On December 8, Orange County went from bankruptcy to default by failing to make a $110 million payment that was due on a bond issue.

These events unsettled Wall Street profoundly. On the day of the default, and in the midst of the collateral dumping, the Dow Industrials fell by about 50 points. The municipal bond market, which has never been very liquid, became as arid as the Sahara desert. In the Treasury securities market, the bills and notes with short maturities fell sharply, while bonds with maturities of about 20 years or more went up. On December 3, the day after the Orange County crisis became public knowledge, the long bond price had risen by one and one-quarter points, despite a positive jobs report for November which normally would have been a negative for the fixed-income markets. The reason offered for this curious phenomenon was that holders of short-term bills and notes were fleeing them because they thought that these securities were being dumped by the brokers who held them as collateral for Orange County.

In any case, the next several days witnessed a so-called flattening of the yield curve on Treasury securities: by December 13, the yield on a 30-year Treasury bond was 7.85%, only 5 basis points (0.05%) more than the yield on a five-year note and four basis points more than the yield on a 10-year note - an anomaly. The securities of federal agencies, which were even more prominent among the collateral held by brokers, were battered. Their prices went down and their yields went up, and the spread between Treasury securities and the agency paper (for which the guarantee of the full faith and credit of the US government is somewhat less emphatic) increased by 30 basis points.

A TWO BILLION DOLLAR LOSS

And all that was before the December 12 announcement that Orange County would now liquidate its holdings. The *New York Times* estimated the losses at just over $2 billion, representing a 27% loss on the county's initial capital of slightly more than $8 billion. That is an example, although a relatively mild one, of what reverse leverage can do. The *Wall Street Journal* gave a figure of $2.5 billion for the loss, and some analysts were soon saying $3 billion. J.P. Morgan paid $4.4 billion in cash to take over Orange County's unencumbered notes. Morgan drove a hard bargain: its profit on this operation was eventually over $100 million. On December 12, San Diego County, Orange County's neighbor to the south, reported a "paper" loss of $358 million on its investment fund of $3.3 billion, an 11% hit. San Diego claimed that its fund was not leveraged, so things would not get as bad as in Orange County, but it did concede that almost half of the loss came from derivatives.

In Texas, the investment fund run by the state treasury, called Texpool, was hit by panic withdrawals by its participants, which included 1,300 towns, school districts, and other agencies. On December 9 and December 12 (a Friday and the following Monday), Texpool investors pulled out about $1 billion or 19% of the fund's total assets. This was occasioned by a story in the *Wall Street Journal* which suggested that Texpool had followed a Citron strategy, and had bought $75 billion in derivatives. A New York City official was quick to reassure the markets that New York was not exposed to derivatives "in that way," and Maryland and Virginia officials also denied playing the Citron gambit, but skepticism was spreading.

On December 13, Orange County suspended all "non-essential payments." A county official specified that this meant no more money for "anything not directly related to health, welfare, or public safety." The victims were the average citizens and taxpayers. In Ohio, Cuyahoga County, which includes the city of Cleveland, had earlier reported losses of $115 million on leveraged investments. Now Orange County cut all its budgets by 11% and froze spending for four years. Drastic cuts crippled social services for children. Later, Orange Country voters sturdily refused in a referendum to increase their own taxes to facilitate debt payments to the Wall Street crowd. Financiers deplored their lack of civic responsibility.

Washington DC was the next candidate for municipal bankruptcy. After the newly re-elected Mayor Marion Barry announced a shortfall in tax revenues of half a billion dollars, the now-Republican Congress (which oversaw the district) moved quickly toward the naming of a financial control board on the model of the 1975 New York City Big MAC. This board, acting in the name of banks and bondholders, proceeded to dictate murderous austerity to capital of the United States. The school system was especially hard hit.

THE MEXICAN BANKRUPTCY: 48 HOURS FROM A WORLD-WIDE MELTDOWN

The Mexican crisis began in the *bolsa* and the currency markets on December 20, 1994, before the smoke from the Orange County explosion had cleared. This was initially the crisis of a single "emerging market" economy, albeit an important one. Soon Mexico had become the epicenter of the crisis of all the "emerging" economies, from India to China to Russia to the Philippines and Indonesia. By the end of January, the Mexican crisis had brought the entire world financial system to the brink of panic. At stake was implicitly the huge mass of debt owed by the developing countries, which had reached $1.6 trillion.

The Clinton administration had responded to the Mexican crisis first with a commitment of about $18 billion to stabilize the Mexican currency. It soon became clear that this would not be enough, so Clinton began to talk about a $40 billion program of loan guarantees for Mexico, to be funded by the US Treasury. This was announced by Clinton on the evening of Thursday, January 12, 1995, after a meeting with Congressional leaders. At the beginning, this plan had strong bipartisan support in Congress. But soon this support began to erode. Gingrich was for the plan, then backed away from it, and then jumped back to support it again. By January 19, a Republican supporter of aid to Mexico told the press: "it has fallen apart ... It's all politics now." The newly elected Republicans of the House, known for their free-market fanaticism, were refusing to support what they saw as another big government, foreign aid giveaway to bankrupt socialists. By January 22, 1995 Bob Dole was telling a Sunday morning interview show that there was not enough support to pass the package, which was fast acquiring the reputation of a bailout of the Wall Street high rollers who had guessed wrong on the peso with their derivatives contracts. Dole talked of the need to increase the collateral pledged to the US Treasury in case of non-payment, including a lien on Mexican oil. Dole wanted a currency board, like that imposed on post-Versailles Germany, in which foreign bankers would dictate how much currency Mexico could issue. Another week went by.

Then came Sunday January 29, 1995 with the same Sunday morning interview shows. First was Sen. Sam Nunn, the moderate Democrat, saying that the Mexican package could not pass. Nunn thought that this impasse might presage a financial debacle. A few minutes later, it was Texas GOP Sen. Phil Gramm popping off, stating categorically that no loan guarantee package of the type envisaged by Clinton could ever pass. Gramm ridiculed the president for having designed measures that would make any country banker laugh. One commentator noted that there was even resentment in the Congress against the British government. After all, some Congressmen were saying, the British were the number two international investors in Mexico. Why should they not take a major part in the bailout? Why should it be left to the United States? After the interventions of Gramm and especially Nunn, it was clear that Monday would bring panic.

On Monday, the Mexican peso reached a new all-time low, losing about 10% of its value. The stock market, or Bolsa, was down about 3%. The Brazilian stock market reacted in sympathy by falling about 8%. The US dollar, now viewed as part of the peso zone, was pulled into the maelstrom, losing 1 pfennig against the D-Mark and flirting with a three-month low. Jitters hit "emerging market" stock markets all over Latin America and in eastern Europe: had they gone from emerging to submerging in a cybersecond? This was the much-feared tequila effect. Senator Moynihan estimated that Mexico was about two days from defaulting on its international payments obligations, which increased the panic among the holders of the *tesobonos*, Mexican government securities which have to be paid off in US dollars. During the morning, American Express refused to sell US dollars to holders of Mexican pesos at any price. The Mexican peso was thus approaching the *de facto* suspension of its convertibility. By nightfall there was more than a whiff of world financial panic in the air.

TEQUILA HANGOVER: A $50 BILLION BAILOUT OF THE SYSTEM

On Monday, Clinton bitterly denied that he was pushing a bailout for Wall Street in the form of aid for Mexico. He was in contact with the leaders of Congress, who all assured them that the legislative branch would be impotent to act in useful time. The votes, they all assured him, were not there. If Congress was unwilling to act, the Mexican markets were also unwilling to wait, and default was imminent. Then Undersecretary of the Treasury Summers came in with news that he had convinced the IMF to add $10 billion to their previous Mexican bailout offer, raising the IMF offer to $17.8 billion in medium-term loans. In addition, said Summers, the Bank for International Settlements had doubled its offer, going from $5 billion to $10 billion. Canada was ready to ante up $1 billion, and a group of other Latin American countries was offering $1 billion. With $20 billion from the US Treasury, almost $50 billion could be assembled for Mexico under the President's emergency powers, without the need for fighting a bill through the Congress. Slightly before midnight, Clinton decided that he would take this path.

At 8:45 AM on Tuesday morning, Clinton called in the leaders of Congress to tell them that since the legislative process was not working, he was going to launch an aid package for Mexico using his executive powers. The US funds would come from the Exchange Stabilization Fund, a mechanism created more than a half-century ago, which contained $25 billion. Speculators were quick to notice that if $20 billion were granted to Mexico, then only $5 billion would remain specifically earmarked for the defense of the dollar. Rubin knew about Mexico, since his former firm, Goldman Sachs, had been one of the leaders in the "emerging markets" ripoffs. Gingrich, Dole, Gebhardt, and Daschle all announced support for Clinton.

In explaining these moves to reporters later, Secretary Christopher said several times that Clinton had faced "a dire situation," with the very real danger of Mexican default and thence of unspecified but serious "problems" for the world economy. Rubin agreed that the Mexican crisis had been "grave" and "dire." He groped for other terms to describe Mexican "distress," but broke off, saying "there are some words that a Secretary of the Treasury should never use." Camdessus of the IMF noted with much alarm that "Mexico was in imminent danger of having to resort to exchange controls. Had that happened, it would have triggered a true world catastrophe." [86] Of course, exchange controls had been applied in many countries during the great postwar era of world prosperity. Why should they now mean the end of the world was not at all clear. (Camdessus maintained a list of countries about to explode on an index card he kept with him at all times. French Marshal Joffre during World War I had done the same for his ammunition reserves. French peasants use such methods for keeping track of their grain stocks.[87] At this point there were 10 countries on Camdessus' index card.)

Christopher, Rubin and Summers stressed that the conditionalities to be applied to Mexico were "stringent." That included an oil facility by which Mexican oil income would go directly to Washington in case of default. Rubin also stressed that the IMF and the US would demand limitations of domestic credit, restrictions on the growth of the money supply, restraint on the state deficit, increased independence of the central bank from the government, and total transparency of Mexican government financial dealings.

To save the Mexican economy in the real world, a minimum program would have included exchange controls to stop the flight of capital, the nationalization of the central bank, and a total moratorium on international debt service and principal payments. The real current international debt of Mexico was estimated at about $185 billion. The treatment jury-rigged by Rubin prescribed healing the patient by another massive increase in that debt, which could not be paid in the first place. Nothing was solved for Mexico, but Clinton did deserve credit for recognizing a genuine systemic crisis, which none of the GOP parliamentary cretins on Capitol Hill had been able to do, given their obsessive ideological preoccupations. By 1998, Mexico's foreign debt was about $238 billion; Brazil had $466 billion. However, Clinton at the same time became responsible for the first of the great international bailouts of the 1990s.

THE THINKING THAT MADE THE DEPRESSION GREAT

Summers indirectly conceded that the overriding issue had been to avoid a world financial panic. Debating former FDIC head William Seidman, Summers countered Seidman's charge that the bailout was a violation of the free market with the quip that "your kind of thinking was what made the Depression great."

BARINGS LIQUIDATED

Just a few weeks after the climax of the Mexican crisis, the System was faced with yet another acute threat of systemic crisis and financial meltdown. It was on Sunday, February 26, 1995 that the

---

[86] Remarks made February 2, 1995.

[87] Alistair Horne. *The Price of Glory* (New York: St. Martin's, 1962), p. 22.

world became aware of the bankruptcy of Baring's Bank, one of Britain's oldest and clubbiest merchant banks. If anything represented the heart of the British establishment, it was Barings. Barings had financed the British Empire war effort against Napoleon. During the nineteenth century, Barings was referred to as the sixth great power of Europe. When Barings had run into trouble in 1890, it had provoked the worst British financial crisis since the South Sea Bubble of 1720. The Barings failure of 1890 had been a contributing factor in the Panic of 1893 in the United States.

The cause of the Barings bankruptcy this time involved Barings Futures Singapore, which was engaged in high-stakes derivatives speculation on the Singapore International Monetary Exchange (SIMEX), the great deregulated derivatives trading pit of Asia. Most of the derivatives positions taken up by Barings were put and call options on the Tokyo Nikkei 225 stock index. The pattern of these put and call options was the one called a strangle or a straddle. With this pattern, Barings stood to win money if the Nikkei index stayed between 21,000 on the upside and 19,000 on the downside. If the Nikkei were to go above or below that range, Barings would lose.

On January 17, 1995 a sharp fall in the Nikkei was occasioned by the Kobe-Osaka earthquake, a great natural disaster which claimed 5,000 lives. Just after the earthquake, the Nikkei declined by over 1,000 points, finishing up at 17,785. Now facing heavy losses, Barings traders nevertheless increased their Nikkei exposure until they had bought futures contracts priced at about $7 billion. This was the well-known *va banque* technique familiar to anyone who has ever seen the inside of a gambling casino. When the SIMEX authorities began to investigate this huge futures exposure, one of the traders involved, a certain Nick Leeson, fled Singapore and was later arrested in Germany, whence he was finally extradited back to trial and conviction in draconian Singapore. Leeson had vainly begged to go on trial in London.

The loss to Barings was about $1.4 billion. Since that more than wiped out Barings' capital, the erratic Eddie George, the Governor of the Bank of England, arranged for Barings to be taken over by a white knight, which turned out to be the ING bank of the Netherlands, ING paid just one pound sterling for Barings, but also committed to a cash injection of about 700 million pounds. Here, if ever, was opaque crony capitalism at work.

YET ANOTHER ROGUE TRADER

Nick Leeson became the most famous of that rapidly-multiplying breed, the "rogue trader." (Other rogue traders had included the now-familiar Joseph Jett and Antoine Moreb of Citibank, the latter accused of opening a $1.4 hole in John Reed's bookkeeping at Citibank some years earlier.) Top management was always quick to repudiate the actions of these rogue traders when losses became too big to hide. But the same managers had always fostered the work of the Leesons as long as they were winning money. One must conclude that these desperate men were kept around by financial executives to rack up profits, but also to be used as scapegoats whenever losses mounted. As the financial system breaks up, the rogue traders will doubtless number in the thousands.

27. $1 TRILLION IN BAD REAL ESTATE DEBT: THE JAPANESE BANKING CRISIS

In August 1995, Japan's Cosmo Credit Union (Kizu Shinyo Kumai) went bankrupt. Two of the smaller Japanese banks also went belly up: first, also in August, the Hyogo Bank of Kobe with $36 billion in assets failed; it was a landmark - the first Japanese bank failure since World War II. Then, in March 1996, the end came for Taiheiyo Bank, a smaller bank in the Tokyo region. The total of bankrupt credit unions soon rose to four. Just as in the US, Japanese banks risking insolvency were merging to keep the wolf away from their door: in the spring of 1996 the Bank of Tokyo merged with the Mitsubishi Bank, creating (for the nonce) the world's largest bank with assets of $679 billion. But many Japanese depositors sought the greater safety of Japan's government-owned Postal Savings Bank, whose privatization was soon being demanded by the hedge funds, who wanted to loot its deposits.

During the second half of 1995, the world financial and banking system was once again moving towards collapse and disintegration. On August 21, the IMF, along with plus bond rating agencies Moody's and Standard and Poor's, issued warnings calling attention to the dangerous weakness of the Japanese banks. The six largest Japanese banks, it is worth remembering, were also still among the six largest in the world. In October there were signs of a slow run on Japanese banks on the part of the London Eurodollar market. The Japanese banks were losing their deposit base. They were also being subjected to a risk premium or "Japan premium" of around 0.40% on the deposits they kept. This risk premium was wiping out the earnings of the Japanese banks in the Euromarket. So the British bankers were making the Japanese crisis worse, perhaps hoping that if things got bad enough in Japan, the crisis would spill over into the US. The word was that the US Fed expected a Japanese banking crisis before the end of 1995. There were reports that Fuji Bank had lost $3 billion in currency speculation.

The Japanese banking crisis was a result of the 1986-1990 Japanese Bubble Economy, and especially of wild speculation in real estate in real estate. During July and August 1995, it had emerged that non-performing real estate loans held by the large Japanese banks totaled $1 trillion to $1.5 trillion and up, out of a total of $7 trillion of Japanese bank lending for all purposes. The reserves of the Japanese banks had also been gutted as the Nikkei stock index declined from its 1990 high of nearly 40,000 points to its 1995 levels of about 14,000 points. Japanese banks traditionally held large blocks of stock as part of their asset base. In December 1996, the Hanwa Bank of Osaka, with $5.9 billion in assets, failed and was shut down by Japanese regulators.

On September 7, 1995 the Bank of Japan reduced its Official Discount Rate, the interest rate for lending to Japanese member banks, to a very low 0.5%. The Bank of Japan was attempting to mimic the backdoor bailout of US banks by the Greenspan Fed of 1992-1993, when Fed funds lent to member banks at a little more than 3% could easily be invested in Treasury securities with a 7% coupon, allowing the bank a risk-free profit that could be used to restore the illusion of solvency. But this time, there was a difference: the Bank of Japan was encouraging its commercial banks to borrow money for almost nothing and then quickly invest that money, not in lowly Japanese government securities, which generally pay only 2%, but rather in lucrative foreign speculation, especially in the US. The Japanese Ministry of Finance had also liberalized the rules for Japanese financial institutions investing abroad. The Japanese were at this point the holders of about $600 billion in US Treasury bonds, and Japan Inc. intended that figure to rise. It was also clear that a great deal of the money which pumped up the US stock market by about one third during 1995 and by another third during 1996 represented virtually interest-free loans to Japanese banks that were being put to work on Wall Street. Such were the workings of the Byzantine backdoor bailout being attempted by the Japanese government. The entire world leverage structure soon depended on Japanese hot money in fantastic quantities.

At the same time, it was clear that a chaotic default by one of the big Japanese banks would represent an incalculable catastrophe for the world financial and banking system. If a Japanese bank were desperate for short-term liquidity to meet a panic run, it would be forced to liquidate a significant part of the $600 billion plus in US Treasury paper held in Japan. That could lead to a panic in the US Treasury market, supposedly the safest in the world. If T-bonds were to tank, every bank in the world would begin repatriating its Treasury assets. In all, about $1 trillion of the US public debt was thought at this point to be held by foreigners – one of the disadvantages of being the world's largest debtor country. A Treasury market crash would lead to a collapse of the US dollar and to a widespread refusal to accept dollars at any price. That would propel us all beyond mere collapse, and into the giddy hyperspace of financial disintegration.

A $500 BILLION BAILOUT FUND

Precisely this kind of scenario was prominent in the minds of US bankers and their political minions. On October 16, 1995 House Banking Committee Chairman Jim Leach (R-Iowa) declared during hearings of his committee that the US government was "prepared to cooperate fully with Japanese authorities to facilitate, in any emergency, liquidity for Japanese banks operating in the United States." Behind this pledge was the creation of a $500 billion fund by the US government and the Fed to bail out the US Treasury by bailing out the bankrupt Japanese banks. Featured in this action were Greenspan, Rubin, and Larry Summers of the Treasury. If a Japanese bank or banks had their backs to the wall, the Federal Reserve System would privately buy that bank's T-bonds. The Japanese banks would thus not have to dump their Treasury securities on the market. Panic would be avoided. The Japanese banks could sell their Treasury bonds under the table directly to the Fed.

The Federal Reserve, one insider privately observed, was "very fearful of a major fall in the US Treasury debt market. This is an agreement to bail out the Treasury – not to bail out Japan." If the London run on Japanese banks continued, "Japanese banks will have to dump Treasury paper to get cash. The bottom could fall out, not to mention crash the dollar." The Treasury claimed for its part that this was nothing new: "If a foreign central bank ever wants to buy back US Treasury bills, we are always happy to buy back our paper with dollars, just so that foreigners don't go into the open market and depress the price" of Treasury bonds. The extent of potential US instability was confirmed on June 23, 1997 when Japanese Prime Minister Hashimoto told a New York luncheon audience that Japan might have to sell off some of its holdings in US Treasury bonds. This statement, which Hashimoto later found it politic to deny, instantly triggered the biggest decline of New York stocks since October 1987.

28. STILL ANOTHER ROGUE TRADER: DAIWA BANK

In early November 1995, a Manhattan grand jury indicted Daiwa Bank on charges of covering up a scheme to hide $1.1 billion in bond trading losses by its New York branch; Daiwa claimed that Toshihide Iguchi, the executive vice president of its New York branch, was in reality a rogue trader in the Nick Leeson tradition. As Citron and Leeson of Barings had taught the world, derivatives trading was out of control at virtually every bank in the world. At $1.1 billion, Daiwa's losses were large enough to represent another threat of meltdown of the entire System. But this affair was wrapped up with little publicity and great speed, probably because of the US-Japanese anti-crisis arrangements in force at this time, including the $500 billion bailout fund.

SPECULATIVE HOARDING OF COMMODITIES

With the world financial system patently approaching the brink, the great family fortunes controlled by wealthy European aristocrats began to go short on paper of all types. The best informed and most unscrupulous money in the world was certainly not buying mutual funds. The summer of 1995 saw a large movement by these family fortunes towards a strategy of speculative hoarding of precious metals and strategic raw materials and other commodities. These family fortunes began to buy gold, silver, platinum, nickel, oil, and food commodities. Their calculation was that these minerals especially would represent wealth in the aftermath of a panic collapse of paper values. There was also a tendency for British, Swiss, and Dutch cartel interests to seize control over parts of the word which produced one or more of the 35-40 commodities upon which human existence most immediately depends. Many of these vital commodities offered the speculators the enticement of very low purchase prices, since most commodities had been depressed by low demand due to industrial stagnation, mass impoverishment, and other effects of world economic depression. During the first six months of 1995, buying by Japanese and other Asian investors helped raise Japan's gold imports to 165 tons, about twice the rate for the same six months of 1994. Around the middle of April, 1995 an unidentified purchaser - identified by some as international fugitive financier Marc Rich - bought between 25 and 75 million troy ounces of silver (equal to between 777 and 2331 tons) of silver at the New York Commodity Exchange (COMEX). The silver in question was picked up by trucks at the COMEX loading dock and delivered to bank vaults in Delaware and Rhode Island. On August 21 of the same year, the London *Financial Times* suggested that one or two financial institutions were attempting to corner the silver market.

Most speculative hoarders took immediate physical delivery of their purchases. Futures and options they considered as too risky, because of the high probability of clearing house insolvency. Storing metals with brokers would also be foolhardy, since the metals would be tied up for months in court proceedings if the brokers went belly up in a panic. So the speculative hoarders uniformly preferred to place their holdings in their own private bank vaults and fortress-like warehouses.

International factors were all too starkly reflected in the precipitous fall of the US dollar. In April 1995, the greenback finally hit its new historic lows of 79.75 Japanese yen and 1.3675 German marks. The Japanese yen rose during 1994-1995 because Japan was gripped by severe deflation. Japanese banks were facing bankruptcy and were desperately trying to increase their stocks of cash yen. Again a collapsing economy was propping up a national currency. Then the yen began to fall and the dollar started to rise. Part of it was huge flows of hot money pumped out by the Bank of Japan. But part of it was that the US was now deflating faster than Japan, so dollars were now in greater demand than yen.

THE WARNINGS OF 1996

1996 stands out as a year of warnings from international financial and monetary authorities. At the yearly economic summit of the Group of 7 at Lyon, France, IMF Managing Director Camdessus opined that "the world financial system is in pieces and it is extremely urgent to tighten the screws [*Folha de Sao Paolo*, June 28, 1996] Later in the year, on October 1, at the IMF's annual meeting in Washington DC, Camdessus was asked where he though financial lightning would strike next. Camdessus replied, "I suspect that it will start with a banking crisis."

On December 5, 1996 Greenspan warned investors of the "irrational exuberance of speculation" that threatened US markets with a "prolonged contraction" on the Japanese model. This declaration ought to be compared to the statement warning of speculative excess made by Paul Warburg, the founder of the Federal Reserve System, in March of 1929. Greenspan's pronouncements can also be compared to an anti-speculation warning made by the Federal Reserve Board in the spring of 1929. These statements amount to pro-forma exercises in the covering of one's own bureaucratic posteriors in the face of impending disaster.

Greenspan had it within his power to raise the margin requirements for stock purchases, which at the time were set at 50%. He could have ordered them up to 60%, 70%, of higher. The Fed was given this power in the wake of the crash of 1929. A hike in margin requirements would have been an interest rate increase targeted exclusively at speculative stock purchases. Greenspan did nothing on this front. His warning merely caused the Dow to pause in its relentless trek towards the ionosphere.

In mid-1996, Chemical Bank acquired Chase Manhattan, thereby creating the biggest bank in the United States. The new giant was to have a capital of $32 billion, but derivatives holdings of $4.7 trillion. During the same week, Wells Fargo carried out a hostile takeover of the larger First Interstate Bancorp. Normally the merger of two technically bankrupt institutions was enough to purchase at least a year or two of survival for the resulting monster bank. At the same time, it became known that Bankers Trust had been silently seized (perhaps as early as 1994, according to some accounts) by federal regulators in a repeat of the November 1990 seizure of Citibank by the New York Fed. The New York Fed reportedly then began partially unwinding the BT derivatives portfolio, which had been one of the very largest of any bank in proportion to capital.

29. SUMITOMO DERIVATIVES COLLAPSE THE WORLD COPPER MARKET

A small example of the explosive potential of the Japanese banking crisis was delivered in June 1996, when the chief copper trader for Sumitomo Corporation, Yasuo Hamanaka, joined the vilified but rapidly growing ranks of the alleged rogue traders. Hamanaka was accused of having tried to corner the world copper market at the London Metals Exchange, between 1993 and 1996. Sumitomo announced a loss of almost $2 billion on copper futures - derivatives - traded on the London Metals Exchange. Sumitomo is the world's leading copper supplier. The world copper price collapsed by one third in the wake of these revelations, spelling disaster for countries like Chile which rely on copper for foreign exchange.

A special emergency effort on the part of the Bank of England, the Bank of Japan, and the Federal Reserve was necessary to prevent this crisis from expanding into a global meltdown. The Sumitomo affair was surrounded with suspicion that the crisis announced was merely an aspect of a larger crisis that was being kept hidden. Suppressing the real news was thought to have been a part of the damage control by the always secretive central banks. With Sumitomo, the world had been to the brink once again. In the wake of the Sumitomo debacle, there were several weeks of pronounced summer jitters on the New York stock market.

THE BANK OF ENGLAND RAISES INTEREST RATES

On October 29, 1996, under the cover of the final phase of the US election campaign, the Bank of England reversed a world trend by raising its interest rates. A few days later, on November 7, the influential director of the Finance Ministry's International Finance Bureau, Mr. Eisuke Sakakibara of the Japanese Ministry of Finance – the now-famous "Mr. Yen" – opined that it was "time for the yen to end its fall against the dollar." But the yen kept falling for the moment. It was also clear that higher Japanese interest rates would tear to pieces the entire structure of world leverage created since 1995 on the basis of Japanese hot money.

Deutsche Bank economist Kenneth Courtis warned that the British and Dutch interest rate increases of early November 1996 might presage a global tightening, which might set off "a massive fall in the dollar, and in global stock and bond markets." In somewhat the same spirit, Anatole Kaletsky, the financial editor of the *London Times*, told his readers about a looming "worldwide financial explosion" of which "you have been warned." [*London Times*, October 29, 1996.]

In early December 1996, Japanese bank shares fell 15% during a four-day period. The Tokyo stock market became even more unstable during the week ending January 10, 1997 with losses of more than 10% – the approximate equivalent of 700 Dow points. This was the worst week for the Tokyo bourse since the week ending September 28, 1990, during the deflation of the Japanese bubble economy. On January 10 alone the Nikkei was off 4.26% or 770.22 points for the day, the equivalent of about 300 Dow points. There was a danger that these stock market losses could drive important banks into bankruptcy, since Japanese banks still keep large portions of their reserves in industrial stock. This stock has to be marked to market every year on March 31, when the Japanese fiscal year ends. If the Nikkei fell much further, some of the banks might become insolvent.

A January 1997 announcement by Moody's Investors Service informed the markets of a lowered ratings outlook for Nippon Credit Bank Ltd., Hokkaido Takushoku Bank Ltd., Yasuda Trust & Banking, and Chuo Trust & Banking, which were all downgraded to negative from stable. Moody's said the downgraded banks had been having serious asset quality problems and their respective earnings, existing capital and reserves might not provide a sufficient cushion to absorb required loan-loss provisions. Shares in Mitsubishi Trust & Banking Corp were also pounded. Sakakibara said Japan's financial sector, especially banks, must be ready for major ``bloodletting'' after the planned "Big Bang" British-style deregulation of Japanese markets to which the Hashimoto government was committed. These events were the immediate harbingers of the great Asian Crisis of 1997-98.

The deadly hangover from the Japanese bubble economy threatened not only banks, but also Japanese insurance companies. Late in April 1997, the Ministry of Finance shut down Nissan Mutual Life. This was the first forced liquidation of a Japanese insurance company by the government since 1945. At the time it was terminated, Nissan Mutual Life was sporting a capital deficit of $1.5 billion, which came from losses on stocks and on real estate. Nissan Mutual was thought to be the first in a long line of Japanese insurance companies about to succumb. But Finance Minister Mitsuzuka pledged that policy-holders would not be hurt by the demise of Nissan Mutual. Prime Minister Hashimoto found it politic to reassure the Japanese nation that he would not permit the country's largest banks to fail. Given a world debt structure now leveraged with assumptions of a rising dollar and a falling yen, any reversal in that pattern brought with it the danger of upheaval, perhaps of definitive upheaval. It was, however, equally true that if the yen continued to fall and the dollar continues to rise, that would also destroy the System although in a different way. By May 1997, the dollar had reached a top of 127 yen. By the end of May, the dollar had fallen by 10%, reaching about 112 yen. This set the stage for the southeast Asia crisis which is described in detail in chapter 1.

RESULT: A DOOMED SYSTEM

In historical retrospect, the post-1973 rubble of monetary chaos criss-crossed by lightning-fast international hot money flows does not merit the title of "monetary system" at all. It is a ship of speculative fools constantly lurching between the Scylla of dollar free-fall and the Charybdis of domestic market meltdown. It is a form of institutionalized, chronic crisis whose attention is focussed not on economic development, but rather on counteracting its own fragility. The purpose of the System, in other words, is to guarantee the future of speculation by warding off the more and more frequent threats of collapse and disintegration that the market goddess Fortuna continues to brandish. Available resources are wasted in increasingly expensive crisis management, looting the world in the process.

This financial System has ruined the world, and now threatens the very fabric of human civilization. And remember: if, at any time over the past thirty years, anybody told you that this System was on the brink of collapse and doomed to crash, they were absolutely right. The utter failure of the System is real, and its apparent speculative successes are the grand illusion. So give thanks for the Cassandras; they have been closer to the truth all along. The prattle of yesteryear about north-south conferences, oil for technology, development decades, technology transfer, and so forth is extinct. Globaloney and free-market brutality are the order of the day. "Fend for yourself," intone the television commentators, "you're on your own." The financiers, hedge fund operators, central bankers and free-market ideologues have led humanity into a blind alley, and at the end of that blind alley we have found a nightmare.

In a speech before the Philadelphia World Affairs Council on November 6, 1998, IMF Managing Director Michel Camdessus underlined that, during the last 15 years of globalization, fully 75% of the countries of the world have experienced what he defined as "severe banking crises." He recalled some of these episodes, such as the banking crisis in Chile in the beginning of the 1980s. The United States, Japan, France, Italy, and Russia have been among the leading victims of banking crisis, although Camdessus mentioned none of them. Camdessus further specified that each of these severe banking crises had inflicted economic damage on the country in question equal to between 20% and 30% of the country's yearly GDP. This remarkable statement adds to our awareness of the immense and tragic cost which is inseparable from the current globalized form of the System.

During the early Cold War, madmen like John Foster Dulles used to talk knowingly about "going to the brink" of thermonuclear war against the Soviets. Today, at the close of the twentieth century, brinksmanship is the specialty of a different breed of madmen, the central bankers and their entourage of finance ministers and technocrats. After a quarter of a century spent at or near the brink, these new brinksmen are confident that their crisis-management will be able to deal with any eventuality. They should ponder the case of the deranged empiricist who leapt from the top of the Empire State Building in New York City. At first he was worried, but as he fell past floor after floor on his way down he became more and more convinced that nothing was going to happen to him. Finally, after having fallen a hundred floors, when he was approaching the sidewalk at terminal velocity, his confidence in his own safety was at its maximum. But then....

This is the predicament of those empiricists who argue today that this labile non-system is "fundamentally sound" (as Herbert Hoover might have said) or, in today's insider jargon, ***shockproof***.

CHAPTER
V. THE IMMISERATION OF AMERICA
THIRTY YEARS OF PHYSICAL ECONOMIC DECLINE

During the late 1950s, various writers at universities and think tanks began to spin out the chimerical vision of a "post-industrial society". This slogan was launched in 1958 by David Riesman in his essay, "Leisure and Work in Post-Industrial Society."[88]The idea was that modern industry was so productive that there was no longer enough work to keep the entire population busy; accordingly, decisions about what to do with leisure time were now more important than how to organize and advance production of physical goods. Backward, low-technology work was onerous and should be exported to the developing countries, said the post-industrialists. All that remained for the US was advancing high technology towards perfection while devoting more and more time to leisure.

By 1967, French journalist Jean-Jacques Servan-Schreiber was predicting the withering away of the working day in his influential book, *The American Challenge*. In his breathless chapter on "The Post-Industrial Society," he leaned on Herman Kahn's forecasts for the year 2000 to prophesy that "In 30 years America should be a post-industrial society with a per capita income of $7,500. There will be only four work days a week of seven hours per day. The year will be comprised of 39 work weeks and 13 weeks of vacation. With weekends and holidays this makes 147 work days a year and 218 days off. All this within a single generation." [Servan-Schreiber, 58] For the overworked and stressed-out American working families of today, this utopian rhetoric appears as a grim joke.

These ideas were reworked by the Ad Hoc Committee on the Triple Revolution and by ideologues like Robert Theobald and Daniel Bell, who by 1973 was able to celebrate the post-industrial world as an accomplished fact in his *The Coming of the Post-Industrial Society.*[89] Post-industrialism had been helped along by none other than President Lyndon B. Johnson, who copied it from the British regime of Labour Party politician Harold Wilson. Johnson argued that the "quality of life" was more important than production (and in the same breath suggested that the US switch to a British-style parliamentary form of government). During the late 1960s, de-industrialization appeared as a radical, anti-establishment rhetorical posture. Nothing could have been further from the truth. Anti-industrialization was and is the program of profoundly reactionary forces, including international bankers and the titled European aristocracy. De-industrialization promptly became the action program of the bureaucracy of the supernational institutions, above all of the IMF.

THE FOLLY OF POST-INDUSTRIALISM

Thirty years after the Triple Revolution manifesto, in the spring of 1997, the International Monetary Fund released a working paper in preparation for the spring meeting of the IMF-World Bank Interim Committee meeting. The substance of the paper is a sweeping praise of de-industrialization and a catalogue of how far the world has declined towards the extinction of industry. This IMF "Working Paper" states, "All advanced economies have experienced a secular decline in the share of manufacturing employment – a phenomenon referred to as de-industrialization. This paper argues that contrary to popular perceptions, de-industrialization is not a

---

[88] In *Mass Leisure* (The Free Press, 1958).
[89] (Basic Books, 1973).

negative phenomenon .... de-industrialization [is the result of] ... economic dynamism." The IMF paper prefers to call the industrial economies, "advanced economies", because manufacturing and industry no longer predominate in them. In the advanced economies as a whole, "the share of manufacturing employment declined from about 28 percent in 1970 to about 18 percent in 1994," with the sharpest fall occurring in the United States, which went from a level of 28 percent of the labor force engaged in manufacturing in 1965, to 16 percent in 1994. By contrast, between 1970 and 1994, the share of the European labor force engaged in manufacturing fell from 30 to 20%, while the decline in manufacturing employment in Japan was less steep.

The IMF heralds the United States as the model de-industrialized country: while "all advanced economies have witnessed virtually continuous increases in the share of service employment since 1960, the United States has been one of the pioneers in this context...," going from 56% of the labor force employed in services in 1960, to 73% in 1994, "a higher share of employment in services than any other advanced economy...." The report concludes that "de-industrialization implies that the role of trade unions is likely to change over time in the advanced economies." No American worker can doubt what that means.[90]

The response of New York financial circles to folly by the IMF showed how deeply the axioms of de-industrialization and the post-industrial society have been imbibed by the stockjobbing community. In a front page article, the *Wall Street Journal* endorsed the IMF's glorification of industrial shut-down. "Viewed from the sweep of history," opined Jacob Schlesinger of the Dow Jones paper, "the IMF is right. The disappearance of manufacturing jobs isn't necessarily a symptom of an economy's demise, but could be a symptom of success."[91] In New York City during the 1950s, a clothing store chain called Robert Hall promised its customers the lowest price on a suit because of their chain's "low overhead." In the real world of economics, the service sector has to be classed as the overhead that must be carried by the manufacturing sector. A service economy thus comes down to an economy in which overhead is much larger than actual production. A service economy means "high overhead," which in turn greatly increases the unit cost for the buyer. That is what has happened to the US economy over the past 30 years, and that is why the ability of the US dollar to command manufactured goods in the real world has diminished so radically.

The post-industrial ideology with its accompanying stress on the service economy over hard-commodity production has proven to be the royal road to Hell. Today we have a post-industrial economy, and it is a ruin. We have achieved a service economy, and it is hopelessly bankrupt. The only hope of survival lies in rolling back post-industrialism, radical environmentalism, deregulation, and every other disastrous innovation that has triumphed after the Kennedy assassination of November 1963.

THE GOVERNMENT LIES WITH STATISTICS

A very serious initial difficulty in analyzing the decline of the US economy over the past three decades arises as soon as we seek a statistical overview the facts in the case. Unfortunately, we cannot trust the data issued by official government bureaus that ought to be the raw material for our research. Official US government statistics have been hopelessly unreliable since the beginning of the Volcker era in 1979. The deliberate fudging of government numbers has become more and more of an open scandal over the years. Some readers may be aware of the controversies about the Census, which center on the desire of powerful forces, especially in the Republican Party, to destroy

---

[90] IMF Rowthorn report, 1997.
[91] *Wall Street Journal*, April 28, 1997.

the possibility of accurately knowing how many persons live in this country. There has also been an attack on the government's ability to know the rate of inflation. The desire to keep the public in the dark about these and other issues is predicated on the desire to gouge and chisel the American people. Today, proposals to falsify government statistics in order to reduce entitlements (meaning the hard-won economic rights of Americans) are brought forward by blue-ribbon commissions packed with the failed economic experts of previous administrations.

Government bureaucracies charged with collecting statistics had become seriously under-funded, obsolete in their equipment, and demoralized during the free market fetishism of the Reagan-Bush era. It was also clear that under Reagan-Bush, the statistics were getting more and more of a massage to serve the political needs of the regime. In 1991, the US Department of Commerce admitted that it had miscalculated the nation's merchandise trade deficit accounts by $73 billion. In 1992 the Commerce and Labor Departments jointly acknowledged that their estimates of growth in US manufacturing between 1977 and 1989 had been one third too high. In 1992, the Census Bureau certainly delayed and sought to suppress a study showing that almost 20% of Americans working full time were not earning enough to support a family of four above the poverty line.

There is also the question of flawed methodologies. As political commentator Kevin Phillips remarks: "In contrast to many European countries, the United States in compiling jobless data excluded persons without employment who had stopped looking for work, while art-time workers who wanted full-time jobs were nevertheless counted as entirely employed." [Phillips, 98] According to a spring 1991 estimate from the Economic Policy Institute, the official unemployment rate of 6.8% masked real unemployment and underemployment rate of 12.4%. After she had stepped down as Commissioner of Labor Statistics for the Labor Department, Janet Norwood pointed out the manifold inaccuracies of the statistics put out by the BLS.

The Labor Department systematically ignores the more and more numerous legions of despair. In order to be counted as unemployed under the current system, you have to report periodically to your state unemployment office. As long as you are collecting your unemployment insurance check, there is a clear incentive to show up. After your jobless benefits are exhausted, there is far less of an incentive. Once you have concluded that there is little hope that the unemployment office can help you to find a job, there is no incentive to report, and every reason to drop out of the system. The dropouts can either work at odd jobs or become a part of the extra-legal submerged economy. But the result is that they disappear from the official unemployment statistics. During the Bush downturn of 1990-92, officials of the California Department of Finance estimated that federal statistics were understating layoffs across the country by more than 2 million jobs.[92] In 1992, the Labor Department stated that it had understated job losses in 1991 by about 600,000 jobs.

The year 1990 offered an opportunity that comes only every ten years: the chance to compare the Labor Department Bureau of Labor Statistics estimate of unemployment (which is based on a more or less biased sample of households) with the figures developed by the US Census Bureau, which tries to deliver an exhaustive profile of the population. In Detroit, the BLS found 9.8% out of work, but the Census put the figure at 19.7%; in New York it was 9.8% jobless according to the BLS vs. 9% with the Census; in Los Angeles 6.1% BLS vs. 8.4% Census; and in Chicago, 7.9% BLS vs. 11.3% Census. And we should recall that the 1990 Census, conducted under the supervision of Bush machine wheelhorse Robert Mossbacher, was itself notorious for undercounting the inner-city poor; indeed, Mossbacher had officially and publicly refused to do anything to address concerns

---

[92] *Los Angeles Times*, February 3, 1992.

that urban poverty was being left out of the Census picture. So our only certainty is that real unemployment is much higher than the BLS says it is.

Federal statistics are just as unreal when it comes to inflation. In 1991, consumer pollster Albert Sindlinger reported that his monthly sample of 3,000 US consumers were reporting that they were convinced that inflation, including tax increases, was advancing at a double-digit yearly rate. Later that year, when the Labor Department was still claiming that inflation was under control at between 3% and 4%, Sindlinger's poll said that average people estimated the inflation around them at 14%.

The BLS understates inflation in many ways. During the Volcker era, BLS statisticians cooked up an adjustment they called the "Quality Adjustment Factor." This was based on the claim that, even though the product you were buying today was more expensive than the similar product you were buying five years before, the current product was better. This then allowed the BLS to reduce the current price of the item before factoring it into the Consumer Price Index, since part of the price increase was not really inflation, but a price increase justified by improved quality. Using this sleight of hand, the BLS was able to cut the inflation rate about in half on many items during the Volcker era.

The BLS consumer market basket furthermore does not take due account of expenses like health insurance, auto liability insurance, lawyers' retainers, bank service charges, and the costs of a college education. The BLS also neglects many quasi-essential amenities that might be bought at a drugstore. From the point of view of understanding inflation as a factor in the erosion of real incomes and standards of living, the biggest problem with the BLS is that almost no consideration is given to the impact of income taxes, Social Security taxes, real estate taxes, state taxes, sales taxes, and other taxes at all levels of government. Some of these problems were treated in an article in the *Wall Street Journal* of May 10, 1990, entitled "Inflation May Be Worse than Data Show." There is no doubt that BLS statistics continue to underestimate inflation, contrary to the baseless assertions of Michael Boskin and others who have arbitrarily reduced the Social Security cost of living adjustment as a means of gouging millions of elderly Social Security recipients.

INCOMPETENT EXECUTIVES AND PAPER ENTREPRENEURS

Writing at the end of the Volcker era of astronomical interest rates, the veteran industrial engineer Seymour Melman described the deterioration in the productive talents of the average American corporate executive. "Until recently," Melman found, "the managers of US industry were the world's best organizers of industrial work," but in the mid-1960s the production competence of US industry and its corporate executives had been visibly deteriorating. Corporate executives had long since ceased to be true 'captains of industry' on the nineteenth- or early twentieth-century model. By the 1960's the dominant type was no longer interested in production per se, but rather in getting the highest rate of return on capital, irrespective of where on the globe or in what kind of activity it could be procured." Melman cited the new boss of a large shipyard who arrived with a phalanx of aides, each one equipped with a Master's Degree in business administration (MBA). The new management sent a letter to administrators and technicians of the shipyard which read in part: "I remind you all that we are not here to make ships. We are here to make money." [Melman 1983, 54]

Melman suggested that modern managers' neglect of physical production in favor of speculation was destroying a social contract on which the privileged position of the company executive was based: "Management has been expected to organize work, and in exchange has been permitted to control production, and to take a large share of the profits and power. But managerialism, oriented with primacy to profits/power, has developed a trained incapacity to organize work. The traditional basis for legitimacy of managerial power is being destroyed by the controlled deterioration of the

US production system and the parallel efforts of management to sustain its money-making in the presence of a growing workless population." [Melman 1983, 291]

Robert B. Reich, the Harvard professor who worked for the Federal Trade Commission before becoming Clinton's Secretary of Labor, described the new executives as paper entrepreneurs rather than product entrepreneurs: "Paper entrepreneurs - trained in law, finance, accountancy - manipulate complex systems of rules and numbers. They innovate by using the systems in novel ways: establishing joint ventures, consortiums, holding companies, mutual funds; finding companies to acquire, 'white knights' to be acquired by, commodity futures to invest in, tax shelters to hide in; engaging in proxy fights, tender offers, antitrust suits, stock splits, spinoffs, divestitures; buying and selling notes, bonds, convertible debentures, sinking-fund debentures; obtaining Government subsidies, loan guarantees, tax breaks, contracts, licenses, quotas, price supports, bail-outs; going private, going public, going bankrupt." [93]

The new executives are motivated by gains in their personal income and power, and disregard the medium or long-term interests of their companies. The criteria for success are short-term and monetarist. What counts is the bottom line of a short-term balance sheet, since that is what the Wall Street financiers look at, and it is they who control capital and personal advancement. Not to be forgotten is the ascendancy of the extended House of Morgan in the corporate boardrooms which choose the CEOs. The ideal of the new managers is the sweat-shop or the NAFTA-GATT runaway shop, which allows them to cut worker compensation to the lowest levels; their demon is an active trade union. Wage-gouging and union-busting are thus the two first points in their MBA catechism. Even better is to make money in financial markets, without workers and without reference to any system of production.

The modern Federal Reserve has encouraged these tendencies with its interest rate policy. Most obviously during the Volcker years, but in reality during the entire postwar period, the Fed has kept interest rates much too high for the needs of an industrial economy. By the mid-1990s, Wall Street and the Fed were publicly visible as a moneyed power that was separate from, and in many ways opposed to, whatever productive economy remained. The much-watched Greenspan statements of 1996-97 left not doubt that the Federal Reserve regarded a growing economy and full employment as evils that had to be avoided, lest even the mildest inflation erode the profit margins of the bondholders who had the power to collapse the dollar by sending their hot money abroad into other currencies. Statistics – however doctored – that reflected well on production and consumption were considered bad for Wall Street, since they might induce the Fed to raise interest rates, and thus the price of money, the commodity with which Wall Street was concerned.

The result was a caricature of the declining British rentier economy of the 1890s, leading toward the same disastrous outcome. Like American hot money today, British overseas investment "contained a fatal weakness .... The British exported immense amounts of capital and, in the short term, they made a lot of money. But this led to the atrophy of the British industrial base." [94] Two decades ago the president of Bulova Watch boasted that "We are able to beat the foreign competition because we ARE the foreign competition." [Melman 1983, 27] This is even more true today.

THE DECLINE OF US MACHINE TOOLS

Machine tools are the heart of an industrial economy. They are the metal-cutting and metal-forming machines that produce other machines; machine tools shape and stamp metal, and include

---

[93] *New York Times*, May 23, 1980.
[94] *AFL-CIO Viewpoint*, vol. 5 no. 4, (1975).

the robot machine that do much of the work along the modern assembly line. Machine tools include machines for boring, drilling, gear-cutting, grinding, turning, and milling of metal or of ceramics. Machine tools have historically been produced by a large number of advanced-technology small and medium companies, and they may be considered as the point where a scientific discovery turns into production technology. This happens in the process of machine tool design. Traditional machine tools include the drill press and the lathe. Modern machine tools increasingly use lasers, electron beams, and plasmas for welding and cutting.

One of the best gauges of the health of a modern economy is to look at the state of its machine tool production and inventory. No nation which lacks machine tool production on a large scale can even be considered fully industrialized. During World War II, US strategic planners found that the availability of machine tools constituted the single most critical bottleneck for defense production of all kinds. During FDR's defense buildup, US machine tool production went from 34,000 units in 1938 to 307,000 in 1942. During the first half of the twentieth century, the United States machine tool producing industry was the dominant one on the planet. Companies like Cincinnati Milacron were proverbial for their quality and reliability, which translated into lasting market leadership.

But in 1978, the US became a net importer of machine tools, and soon thereafter American machine tool executives began to see themselves more as importers and marketers of imported machine tools, than as producers in their own right. By 1978, only 31% of the total US machine tool stock was less than 10 years old, compared to 37% in Germany and 61% in Japan, according to 1980 statistics from the National Machine Tool Builders' Association. The average age of a US machine tool was the same as it had been in 1940, after the ravages of a ten-year depression. Ten years is a reasonable working lifetime for a machine tool, after which it can be considered obsolete.

The failure to modernize the machine tool park was an important factor in declining productivity by the late 1970s. Machine tool executives tried to explain their wretched track record by complaining about the relatively higher wages enjoyed by US workers. But that begged the question, since in the more successful past, US machine tool workers' wages had outpaced those of foreign workers by an even larger percentage. From 1939 to 1947, average hourly earnings in the US increased by 95%, while the prices of machine tools increased only 39%. [Melman 1983, 4] The secret was the application of technological advances to the production process, making possible increased quality, higher wages, and growing profits all at the same time. That is what industrial capitalism means.

US MACHINE TOOL OUTPUT PER CAPITA COLLAPSES

In 1981, the US produced 301,313 machine tools. By 1983, under the impact of Volcker, output had declined to 150,837 units, a drop-off of 50%. In 1967, there were 158.4 machine tools produced in the US for every 100,000 persons in the population. By 1995 that number had fallen to 37.6, meaning a per capita decline of almost two thirds over slightly less than three decades. The obsolescence of the machine tool park also increased. By 1989, 62% of US machine tools were more than ten years old. This is inevitably reflected in technological backwardness. Back in the 1950s, the US Air Force took the lead in promoting the development of numerically controlled machine tools, meaning machine tools whose functioning is directed by computers of various kinds. But the US machine tool industry has always been slower than the foreign competition in adapting this American innovation to their own production. By the early 1990s, only 10% of the US machine tool stock was made up of numerically controlled units.

In 1967, the production workers of the US machine tool industry numbered about 80,000. By 1995, about half that number were still on the job. Even more alarming, the average machine tool worker of the mid-1990s was between 50 and 55 years old, and was thus a candidate for retirement.

When this age group left the shop floor, certain vital skills were likely to be permanently lost unless this industry could be quickly revived. According to a 1994 RAND Corporation Study, US machine tool makers were highly competitive in areas such as layered manufacturing, net shape manufacturing, flexible machining systems, laser welding and cutting, waterjet machining, and some other applications. But to develop these further would have necessitated credit at reasonable interest rates, and machine tool rates of profit could never hope to compete with derivatives when it came to ripping off a fast buck.

INFRASTRUCTURE: A TEN TRILLION DOLLAR DEFICIT

As of 1996, the accumulated deficit in all forms of US infrastructure had reached the gigantic figure of $10 trillion. Anyone who has taken a bumpy ride on an interstate highway, or who has made a train trip, who has experienced a blackout or brownout, who has been flooded out, who has required an hour or more to reach a hospital for treatment of a life-threatening emergency, who has commuted through daily traffic jams, or who has lived under water rationing, should be aware of the crisis of American infrastructure. In 1958, John Kenneth Galbraith's *The Affluent Society* argued that although the postwar US economy had succeeded in providing a certain number of people with a degree of prosperity, public services and public investments were suffering from an increased impoverishment. This tendency has only been exacerbated in subsequent decades, even after the illusion of affluence was long gone.

The decline of US infrastructure has been going on for a long time. In 1981 the Council of State Planning Agencies, an organization supported by the nation's governors, reported a shocking pattern of depletion of the national public works inventory, an important part of the fixed capital stock of the entire US economy. This survey was significantly titled *America in Ruins*. The finding of this report was that "America's public facilities are wearing out faster than they are being replaced. The deteriorated condition of the basic public facilities that underpin the economy presents a major structural barrier to the renewal of our national economy. In hundreds of communities, deteriorated public facilities threaten the continuation of basic community services." This 1981 report found that one fifth of American bridges needed replacement. New York City alone had an infrastructure deficit of over $40 billion, and was replacing streets designed to last 25 years at an average rate of every 700 years. By the year 2000, the report forecast, the aquifer providing irrigation water for Texas, Oklahoma, and the surrounding states would be totally exhausted. According to the Army Corps of Engineers, 9,000 of the 43,500 dams needed repairs and improvements. But in the face of all this, public works spending measured in allegedly constant dollars had fallen from $38.6 billion in 1965 to less than $31 billion in 1977. Per capita spending on public works dropped from $198 per person in 1965 to $140 in 1977, a 29% decline. Pat Choate, the co-author of this report, calculated about the same time that increased wear and tear on private cars because of potholes and abysmal road surfaces makes it 30% more expensive to own a car in the US. Interestingly, Pat Choate later ran for vice-president in 1996 on the Ross Perot ticket. He had found in the meantime that blaming it all on Japan, which had not neglected its infrastructure to the same degree, was more salable than the bitter truth of America's wanton self-neglect.

HIGHWAYS

Even a modest fellow like President Eisenhower appears as a titan of wisdom and foresight with his 1953 policy of building the interstate highways system to provide necessary infrastructure, along with extra insurance against a relapse into high unemployment and economic depression. By 1981, the interstate highway system had reached 42,500 miles, and it was already deteriorating at a rate that required the replacement of 2,000 miles per year. At that time 8,000 miles and 13% of the system's bridges were already in need of replacement. Just the upkeep of the interstates would have required $700 billion dollars during the 1980s, but virtually none of that money was ever spent. In 1991, it was estimated that $3.2 trillion in repair work would be required to restore our dilapidated system of interstate highways alone. [Vranich 353]

The decline of the American highway system has eroded the productivity of labor in some very serious ways. In 1986, the Federal Highway Administration concluded that traffic jams cost the US $9 billion per year, and 750 million man-hours. [Phillips, 138] In 1991, a study by the state of California estimated that highway congestion and gridlock were forcing the average motorist to spend 10.5 workdays per year sitting in traffic. The cost per motorist was put at $1,200, and the total man-hours lost per year were estimated at 1.2 billion. By the late 1990s, things were much worse. According to a November 1998 study by Tim Lomax and David Schrank of the Texas Transportation Institute at Texas A&M University, in 1996 traffic jams caused Americans 4.6 billion hours of needless delays, wasted 6 billion gallons of fuel (the equivalent of 134 supertankers), and cost the country $74 billion in lost time and gasoline (about twice the yearly federal highway budget). 88% of the costs were the result of wasted man-hours, and 12% of wasted fuel. The most congested areas were listed as Los Angeles, Washington DC, Miami, Chicago, and San Francisco-Oakland. The time lost by commuting drivers in small and medium cities rose 400% between 1982 and 1996, meaning that rush-hour traffic conditions were deteriorating even faster in these areas than in the larger ones. In a touch of poetic justice for the government planners who had failed to act against this growing problem, Washington DC had the highest annual congestion cost per driver – $1,290. Washington DC commuters were spending 82 hours – more than two whole working weeks per year – sitting in traffic, up from 70 hours in 1994. Many commuters in larger metropolitan areas had to spend a total of 3 hours per day driving – and sometimes even more. Long daily commutes mean increased stress and exhaustion, and a decline in job performance. One obvious way to improve the productivity of labor is to build modern urban mass transit and restore existing highways with more infrastructure investment.

Another dimension of the obsolescence of the US highway system is the cost of repairs caused by the deteriorated condition of urban highways used for commuting. According to the Environmental Protection Agency's *Politics and Potholes, 1998* study, the bad roads are costing US drivers $6 billion in extra repair costs. In Detroit, the average driver will pay an extra $1,400 for repairs over the life of each car because of the bad state of the roads. In Washington DC, the extra cost will be $1,071 over the life of each car, which has to be added to the $1,290 in yearly congestion costs cited above. Top federal bureaucrats please take note. Overall, 57% of US urban highways were in less than good condition in 1998.

BRIDGES

By the mid-1990s, America had 574,671 bridges used for highway and railroad purposes that were more than 20 feet long. Fully one third of these bridges (32.5%) were rated as deficient, meaning that they needed either extensive repair or emergency replacement. According to the Federal Highway Administration, 18.7 per cent of these substandard bridges were structurally deficient, while 13.8% were functionally obsolete, or unable to bear up under current traffic volume. An example of the structurally deficient was the Williamsburg Bridge in New York City, which was shut down for a time during the early 1990s, interrupting both motor vehicle traffic and subways. Functionally obsolete was the Woodrow Wilson Bridge on Washington DC's Capital Beltway. In some parts of upstate New York, it was impossible to go from one town to another without executing multiple detours because of bridges that have been closed down. By 1995 the Federal Highway Administration was saying that $53 billion per year would have been needed simply to preserve roads and bridges in their current condition, and that $72 billion would be needed yearly for necessary improvements. But during the first half of the 1990s, current state *and* federal spending for bridge and highway maintenance was only $35 billion per year, not even enough to maintain the status quo.

Looking ahead, there are no signs of improvement. By 1998 the Federal Highway Administration had doctored its estimates and now asserted that we would have to spend about $50 billion per year for twenty years to repair and rebuild the US highway system, which comes out to an unrealistically low $1 trillion figure. Evidently the new low estimates were required to conceal the woeful inadequacy of the much-touted Transportation Efficiency Act for the 21st Century, passed by the Congress and signed by the President in the summer of 1998, which provided $217 billion per year over six years for roads and highways. This came out to just over $36 billion per year in federal money, an increase of $10 billion per year over the previous highway bill, but still only slightly more than the $30 billion the Federal Highway Administration said in 1998 would be needed to maintain the current deplorable conditions. And if we go by the older and more realistic FHA estimates, $36 billion per year in federal construction was unlikely to maintain present conditions, even when state spending is added in. Ironically, most criticism of this bill focused not on its manifest inadequacy, but rather on its alleged pork-barrel implications.

Part of the problem was the way US roads were built. Because of decades of inadequate budgets, highway commissioners and other contractors had to stress how many miles they had built or repaired each year. In order to make their meager dollars go further, they were using building techniques which gave US roads a life expectancy of 10 to 20 years. In western Europe, highways are routinely built to last almost 50 years. The European methods, whose superior quality is evident to those who have experienced the German *Autobahn*, could be easily duplicated or even surpassed here, but only if we were willing to pay the increased initial costs per mile, which turn out to be far more economical in the long run. But the short-range US frame of reference perpetuates construction methods which guarantee that drivers will be facing washboard roads within about a decade after the ribbon has been cut.

RAILROADS

The US rail grid is now at the point of systemic breakdown. In 1929, the US had 229,530 miles of track in operation. By 1995, we had only 109,332 miles. Fatal accidents involving passenger trains were a regular occurrence. Between 1950 and 1995, track miles per household had declined by 73%. Rail employment had also collapsed, thanks in part to a reckless management campaign against union-supported work rules, which were vilified as "featherbedding." In 1980, there were 458,000 railroad workers of all types; by 1994, railroad jobs had been cut to 190,000, a net decline of 59%. Rolling stock had also been decimated. In 1980, there were 28,094 locomotives; by 1996 there were only 18,505, a falloff of 34%. In 1980, there were 1,068,114 class I freight cars on the rails. By 1996 only 590,930 remained, meaning 45% fewer. Despite these staggering cuts in the rail system, the railroad system must still bear the largest share of tons and ton-miles of freight in this country. The decline in bulk-carrier capacity means that the US faced the classic problem of the old USSR, which never had enough rail cars to move the harvest to the consumers in the cities. After the Carter-era deregulation, the US had been left with six main freight carriers, including Union Pacific, Southern Pacific, CSX, Norfolk Southern, Burlington Northern Santa Fe, and Conrail. By 1998, Conrail was being absorbed by its competition. The executives of these companies have exhibited an unusual preoccupation with short-term bonanzas and have practiced primitive accumulation against their fixed capital.

AIR TRANSPORT

In 1970, the average age of a US passenger aircraft was four years. By 1995, the average age of a passenger airliner was 14 years. This figure was destined to increase sharply. These older airliners would need more mechanical attention than newer planes, but in fact they were getting less. Between 1979 and 1995, the number of aircraft mechanics employed per plane declined by 20%. During the last quarter of the century, the US had built just two modern airports of the first magnitude – Atlanta and Denver. The new Denver airport had to withstand a barrage of carping media criticism. Meanwhile airports like Washington National, New York's LaGuardia, and Boston's Logan were fully obsolete. Washington National was adding parking spaces, but no additional runway space. Washington National got a new terminal and new parking garages, but nothing was done to modernize the radar equipment, which began to fail shortly after the new terminal was opened. Even more ominously, nothing was done to improve the obsolescent runways of DCA. The total deficit in new airport construction was about $50 billion according to some estimates, or more according to others. But even with new airports, there were structural limits to expansion of air traffic in areas like the Richmond to Boston northeast corridor or the Los Angeles-San Francisco route. Airplanes could be built, and perhaps also new airports. But there was no way to add to existing, overcrowded airspace. This pointed towards modern high-speed rail as a solution for trips up to 300-400 miles across densely populated urban areas, above all the Boston to Richmond corridor.

Flying is also more dangerous. Carter deregulated the airlines, leading eventually to the disappearance or bankruptcy of names like People Express, New York Air, Pan Am, Braniff, Eastern, Midway, TWA, Ozark, Capitol, Republic, and others. Raiders like George Bush's friend Frank Lorenzo took a heavy toll. Reagan broke the air traffic controllers' union, and flight safety standards have never recovered. By the mid-1990s, there were new primitive accumulation airlines like ValuJet, which bought up the outdated equipment of bankrupt airlines and flew them with crews of laid-off pilots and flight attendants. The results included numerous fatalities, as with the 110 who died in 1996 when a 27-year-old Valujet aircraft crashed in the Florida everglades. For many destinations, fares were higher than they were before deregulation, with massive price gouging in markets where there is only one carrier.

For the impact of airline deregulation on flight safety, it is enough to consult the 1996 *Flying Blind, Flying Safe*, by Mary Schiavo, the former Inspector General of the US Department of Transportation. This book is filled with chilling tales of bogus parts, substandard air traffic control, perfunctory inspections, and airliners actually held together by duct tape. Schiavo focused on start-up airlines like Valujet, which used shoddy aircraft that had been subjected to maintenance by uncertified repair shops. She also targeted the "cost-benefit analysis" mentality of the Federal Aeronautics Administration, which rejected a plan to install smoke detectors in cargo holds at an industry-wide cost of $350 million because this was allegedly not cost-effective at an implied cost of human life equal to $2.6 million per fatality. In practice, the FAA acted only after the victims were already dead. Ms. Schiavo's forecast for US air travel if these trends are not urgently reversed was one crash per week in the years ahead.

WATER PROJECTS

During 1996-1997, a series of highly destructive floods underlined the wretched state of US flood control and related water projects. In 1996 came a series of floods in northern California. In the spring of 1997 came flooding along the Ohio River. Then, an abrupt melting of heavy snows threw the upper Mississippi-Missouri complex into a flood emergency. In April 1997, there followed an unprecedented flood stage of the Red River of the North, a river which rises in Minnesota and eventually flows north across the Canadian border. The flood surge of the Red River of the North inundated and partially destroyed Grand Forks, North Dakota, and its sister city of East Grand Forks, Minnesota. As the crest of the Red River moved north towards Winnipeg, Manitoba, it turned out that the Canadian flood control measures were far superior to the American ones; the Canadians had dikes around some of their smaller towns, plus a spillway to take the river through the city of Winnipeg and into Lake Winnipeg.

At the height of the flood crisis, the *Minneapolis Star-Tribune* reported that representatives from Congressional offices from the region were discussing a "Marshall Plan" approach to dealing with the damage toll. The same day, the governors of the two stricken northern states (Ed Schafer of North Dakota and Arne Carlson of Minnesota) held a joint news conference, stating their intention to form a joint Red River management authority.

Another aspect of the same water management question regards the water supply and sewage systems of large cities. By the mid-1990s, American cities had a total of some 436,000 miles of water pipes. Every year a water main break occurred once for every 3.7 miles of this system. At the then-current overall rate of replacement and modernization of 2% of the existing mileage per year, it would take more than 50 years to modernize the system. Replacing the cast iron pipes in the nation's water system would have cost an estimated $210 billion. In many large cities where budget problems were most acute, at current rates of replacement it would take 200 years to replace today's century-old pipes. The system will collapse well before that.

Water pipes in many cities of the northeastern and midwestern United States are made of cast iron produced between 100 and 140 years ago. During the severe cold wave of January 1994, a water main burst in Brooklyn, New York and closed down the Brooklyn Battery tunnel. The Boston water system loses almost as much water by leakage as it delivers to consumers. Washington DC residents and visitors were routinely warned about the danger of cryptosporidium microbes which had infested the water system of the capital of the United States. Presumably the President, whichever party he represents, is drinking bottled water.

ELECTRICITY

In 1996, the Republican National Convention that nominated Bob Dole for President was held in San Diego, California. The city attempted to capitalize on this event by touting its many modern and forward-looking features. But on August 10, during the convention, the electric power grid serving a number of western states experienced a partial shutdown, which cut off the electric current in many parts of downtown San Diego. Some delegates and reporters were trapped in elevators when the electricity went off. But since the television networks still had electricity to run their cameras, they treated this crisis as a minor distraction, and certainly not as a political issue. But in reality, the instability of electric power supply in the United States was an issue that would soon explode into the public consciousness.

Until 1978, the US per capita electrical generating capacity had grown by least 2% per year for a number of years. In 1978, a 2% increase was not attained. 1988's decline in generating capacity of 0.46% inaugurated the era of net reductions in potential electricity production. By 1991-1993, the shrinkage in generating capacity was about 1% per year. As a result of this accelerating decline, the safety margin of reserve generating capacity, which ideally ought to represent one fourth or at least one fifth of demand above and beyond the average, has been reduced to 10% or even less. In the Northeast and the Midwest, every winter brings the threat of a blackout. In most parts of the country, the peak of summer air conditioner use also brings the threat of a collapse of supply grids, or at least of rolling brownouts neighborhood by neighborhood.

Since the probable sabotage of the Three Mile Island reactor in 1979, the orders for about 100 nuclear power plants have simply been cancelled. But environmental fanaticism has also blocked the construction of 80 large coal-fired (or "dirt-burner") plants which had been designed to assume a share of the basic burden of providing electricity, and not just for intermittent use in special situations. The Long Island Lighting Company's multi-billion dollar Shoreham Nuclear Plant tragically qualifies as human history's most expensive public works project to have been licensed as safe and ready to function, only to be dismantled before producing a single kilowatt-hour of electricity. Long Island now suffers from the highest electric rates anywhere in the United States, and this entire episode could never have happened without the active complicity of Gov. Mario Cuomo, considered by some as the leading progressive politician in the United States around 1990.[95]

THERMODYNAMIC DEVOLUTION – THE POINT OF NO RETURN

More than a decade ago, the rate of decline of US infrastructure raised the question of a possible point of no return, after which the United States would no longer have the capability of rebuilding its infrastructure with its own skills and resources. This point would represent the thermodynamic devolution of the economy into a collapse unstoppable without adding new resources from outside. By 1998, this point appears to have been passed in rail technologies, and perhaps also in power generation.

HEALTH CARE

During the 1993-1994 debate about health care reform, critics and defenders alike of the deeply flawed Clinton reforms felt obliged to preface every exchange of views with a litany of "We all know that the US has the best health care system in the world...." The problem is that this generalization is increasingly untrue. The quality and availability of US health care has been declining for many years, and the decline has accelerated with the ascendancy of "managed care" schemes after the defeat of the Clinton plan. The most obvious precondition for good health care is the availability of hospitals. It is also imperative that these hospitals be geographically located so that they can be quickly and readily reached by patients who are experiencing medical emergencies. If you cannot get to the hospital in less than 20 to 30 minutes at the very most, and if you are a heart attack patient, accident victim, or stroke patient, the effect is often the same as having no hospital at all – the patient risks being pronounced dead on arrival.

Between 1980 and 1993, 675 US hospitals were shut down, and their technology, staffs, and services were lost or dispersed. Hospital closings continue apace, and take their toll especially in rural areas like the farm belt, and in low-income urban areas like the inner cities. The decline of US health care is clearest when compared with the standards established by Congress just after the Second World War. In 1946 the Hill-Burton Act became law, calling for an extensive survey of hospitals and hospital bed availability, with a view to establishing a minimum standard for access to hospital care. For many good reasons, one key parameter that was studied under the Hill-Burton law was the number of hospital beds per 1,000 of population. Under Hill Burton, 4.5 to 5.5 beds per thousand of population was set as the optimum availability ratio. Remember that this was more than fifty years ago, before AIDS and drug-resistant TB had ever been heard of. Over the quarter-century

---

[95] See *License to Kill* (New York, 1998).

after the passage of Hill-Burton, this country made significant progress towards fulfilling the criteria set up by this law.

But today, this country's performance is a failure as measured by the standards of a half-century ago. As of 1994, America as a whole has just 3.46 hospital beds for 1000 population. Some states do even worse. California has a scandalous 2.5 beds per 1000 of population. Did you think that Seattle has a good quality of life? Guess again, since Washington state has just 2.17 hospital beds per 1000 citizens, quite apart from where these hospitals are located. That was after shutting down almost 15% of all hospitals and 13% of all hospital beds during the decade 1985-1994. Large states like New York, Texas, Illinois, and Michigan are all well below the Hill-Burton minimum of 4.5. An instructive case is that of New York City. In 1960, the borough of Manhattan had 78 hospitals, but by 1995 that number had been reduced to 33 hospitals. During the same period Brooklyn went from 56 hospitals to 28. The city as a whole dropped from 154 hospitals in 1960 to 79 in 1990. In their annual report for 1991, the New York City Hospital Visiting Committee characterized the care being offered in city hospitals as the worst "in recent memory."

Much of this destruction has been wrought with the help of for-profit managed care companies and health maintenance organizations (HMOs). A good example is the case of Columbia/HCA Corp., which resulted from the 1994 merger of the Columbia Hospital Corp. with Hospital Corporation of America. HCA was founded in 1968 by Thomas Frist and his son Thomas Frist, Jr., now US Senator from Tennessee, both in partnership with Jack Massey, the founder of Kentucky Fried Chicken. HCA was the subject of a $5.1 billion leveraged buy-out in 1989. A strategy of Columbia/HCA has sometimes been to buy up the hospitals in a given area and then shut some of them down, thus obtaining a greater return on capital invested. This amounts to asset stripping designed to create a local monopoly, and it can be very lucrative for financiers. But those who died on the way to the hospital were out of luck. Columbia/HCA investor Richard Rainwater has called this strategy the "Wal-Mart approach to health care." Those who need treatment for the cholesterol buildup they are suffering after eating Massey's chicken are going to be in trouble.

For-profit, managed care health businesses operating in a largely deregulated environment inherently lower the quality of health care below the levels that are acceptable for a civilized community. Recently publicity has been given to drive-by deliveries (mothers forced to leave the hospital 24 hours after giving birth) and drive-by mastectomies. Gag rules have prevented doctors from acquainting patients with the full range of treatment choices for their complaints because the more expensive ones were not paid for by the plan. In other cases, doctors were given secret financial incentives for not sending their patients to specialists. In the Washington, DC area, a top official of MAMSI-Optimum Choice issued a letter to doctors working as primary care physicians in his plan, warning them to reduce their referrals of patients to such specialists. This amounted to practicing medicine without a license, and led to calls for stern legal retribution or re-regulation.

To increase their profit margins, managed-care hospitals were attempting to replace trained Registered Nurses with so-called health technicians, meaning unskilled workers who have been given two to four weeks of training in some of the functions of the Registered Nurse. The obvious problem is that "techs" with no understanding of medicine become extremely risky when life-and-death situations arise in which the judgment and training of the experienced nurse are required. All of these approaches reflect the "paper entrepreneur" or cost-accountant obsession with the bottom line. The only way to save real money in medical care is to fund a crash program attack on heart disease, cancer, AIDS, TB, and other diseases so as to find effective prevention, cures, and treatment. If it costs $100,000 per year to treat a cancer patient, the answer is discover a cure that will neutralize the cancer for a fraction of that sum.

Worst off are those who do not even make it to the doctor or the hospital because they have no means of payment. About 40 million Americans, including some 10 million children, have no medical insurance whatever. The real bottom line for the average person is that while in 1965, it required 3.3 weekly paychecks to pay for the average in-patient hospital stay, the average hospitalization by the mid-1990s cost the equivalent of 16.2 weekly paychecks. The additional 13 paychecks meant that the average working person's ability to afford hospitalization had declined by 79.6%, one of the sharpest deteriorations in the entire consumer market basket. It may be objected that "only" 40 million people – the uninsured – were obliged to pay their own hospital bills directly, but these costs were also quickly passed on by insurance companies to the insured in the form of premium increases.

Whatever Americans pay for health care, the dividends paid to the stockholders of for-profit HMOs represent money that is being drained out of the health care system. It is clearly impossible to continue with for-profit health plans making life and death decisions about the fate of patients in an almost totally deregulated environment. This led to the agitation for a modest Patients' Bill of Rights during 1998, but the measure was killed by the Republican leadership, who wanted to subvert it in favor of their latest privatization rip-off, the so-called medical savings accounts.

EDUCATION

American education by the mid-1990s was in crisis. US illiteracy rate was one of the worst among the wealthier countries. According to the National Adult Literacy Survey, 20% of US adults read at or below a fifth grade level, meaning that they were virtually unemployable in today's world. An estimated 40 million Americans over 16 had "significant literacy needs" – meaning that they were, in many cases, functionally illiterate. The same study noted that American adults who did not have a high school diploma could expect to earn a mean monthly wage of $452. Federal spending dedicated specifically to adult literacy was about $470 million per year, a drop in the bucket compared to the $18 billion poured down the IMF rat-hole in 1998 alone.

According to an April 1995 survey by the General Accounting Office, the United States had about 80,000 schools. Of these, 60% had a physical plant in which one major building needed "to be extensively repaired, overhauled, or replaced". About one third of all schools required "extensive repair or replacement of one or more buildings." An immediate investment of $112 billion would be required just to get American school buildings up to par. In cities like Washington, DC, the closure of schools because of crumbling schoolhouses with leaky roofs had become a dramatic public issue.

The physical degeneration of educational plant had gathered momentum despite increase in government funding to education. In 1960, government at all levels invested $135 billion in education; by 1990, it was $1,837 billion. But this 13.5-fold increase in spending was largely cancelled out by a 12-fold depreciation in the purchasing power of the dollar, so in the real world our schools spending had stagnated. The wages of teachers had risen modestly, but the yearly construction of new school floor space per capita had declined by about 60% compared to 1967.

The 1995 General Accounting Office report also pointed to numerous qualitative shortfalls in education. 40% of US schools lacked laboratory facilities adequate to support science classes. One quarter of all schools were short on computers, and 61% did not have modems to make the most of the computers they did have by communicating with other computers and with the Internet. As for the content of education, US standards have declined radically during the last two decades. Phonics have been replaced by "whole language" and other incompetent approaches, with the result that Johnny still can't read. Notions of scientific truth and of truth in general have been undermined by the "self-esteem" school of pedagogy, which thought that consoling oneself with myths and legends about ones alleged ethnic group was more important than being able to master real problems in the real world. The classics of world literature and the English language itself were under attack by multicultural hoaxsters. Scientific curricula were undermined by radical environmentalist hoaxes about global warming, and history has been distorted by ignorant and opinionated teachers reducing history to mechanistic determinism based on race, gender, class, ethnicity, and other factors.

THE PROHIBITIVE COST OF COLLEGE

In 1965, 24 average weekly paychecks were enough to pay for a year's tuition plus room and board (but not books and incidentals) at a 4-year private college in the United States. Today a year of college at a 4-year private college will require the family to shell out 43 paychecks. That means an additional 19 paychecks, a 79% decrease in affordability. The average working person's ability to send a child to college, one of the hallmarks of the American middle class, has declined by 44.2%, and this is coherent with a halving of the standard of living.

According to a 1996 *Newsweek* study, the cost of keeping a student in the most prestigious private colleges was about $1,000 a week, out of reach of most families: "divide the annual cost of a school like Brandeis [$28,827] by the number of weeks (28) in the college year, and you get $1,000 a week – which is more than the weekly income of about 70% of American households." [96] The average cost of tuition, room and board for a year at a private college was $17,631, as compared with $6,823 at public universities.

In the past, less wealthy young persons were assisted by scholarships and fellowships in their higher education. These have declined, and the remaining ones have become more overtly political than they were. The great landmark legislation of the late New Deal-Fair Deal was the GI Bill of Rights, which made it possible for returning veterans to go to college. It was the GI Bill which institutionalized the right of the American middle class to a four-year higher education, often at a residential college or university. The subsidy for college tuition built into the GI Bill of Rights was worth at least $26,400 in 1995 dollars.

Beyond schools and universities, there is another important factor in educating citizens: the public library. Public libraries are a tradition thought up by Petrarch, realized for the first time by Cardinal Bessarion, and brought to the United States by Benjamin Franklin. A well-stocked and well-staffed fabric of local public libraries is a necessity for any civilization worthy of the name, and is even more imperative today. In July 1991 the American Library Association sounded the alarm that US public libraries were worse off than they were back in the Great Depression. Part of the problem was that public officials cared less and less about libraries; the Bush administration's budget for 1992 proposed cutting spending on public libraries by 73%.

DECLINING REAL INCOMES AND STANDARDS OF LIVING

These results can also be corroborated by other approaches, including a reading of certain government statistics. The following data make a first important point by showing that the rapid improvement of the American standard of living which marked the quarter-century after World War II has long since ceased:

---

[96] "Those Scary College Costs," *Newsweek*, April 29, 1996.

MEDIAN FAMILY INCOME, 1950-1995

YEAR	INCOME	% CHANGE
1950	$18,305	
1960	$25,220	+37.8%
1970	$34,523	+36.9%
1980	$36,912	+6.9%
1990	$39, 086	+5.9%

[1993 dollars]

[*Money Income of Households, Families, and Persons in the United States*, Income Branch, Bureau of the Census]

We see that the once robust improvement in family income has, at first glance, slowed to a crawl. The more recent story is told by the following figures, which diverge slightly from those above because of a change in the base year on which they are calculated. Here is median family income from 1970 to 1995:

Year	Income	Year	Income
1970	$32,229	1983	$32,160
1971	$31,923	1984	$32,878
1972	$33,284	1985	$33,452
1973	$33,941	1986	$34,620
1974	$32,879	1987	$34,962
1975	$31,999	1988	$35,073
1976	$32,548	1989	$35,526
1977	$32,727	1990	$34,914
1978	$34,011	1991	$33,709
1979	$33,901	1992	$33,278
1980	$32,795	1993	$32,949
1981	$32,263	1994	$33,178
1982	$32,155	1995	$34,076

[1995 dollars]

[source: US Department of Commerce, Bureau of the Census, Current Population Reports, Consumer Income, "Money Income in the United States," P-60 193.]

These statistics leave us with a disheartening first impression of stagnation, the appearance of a quarter century on the road to nowhere. But reality is much worse than stagnation, as we realize when we recall that these are median *household* incomes. They do not specify how many jobs are being worked, or by how many people, whether the wife and children are working, and so on. As these issues are factored in, our perception of stagnation turns into a sickening awareness of decline. We must also realize that minority groups are much worse off than the average. 1997 figures, which showed an overall family income of $37,005 also showed black households earning $25,050, Hispanic households earning $26,628, white households earning $38,972, and Asian households earning $45,249. [97]

To be more specific: Median income means the income of that hypothetical family which in income terms finds itself exactly halfway down the list of all families. Half of all American families earn more, and half earn less. These figures from the Census Bureau are supposedly expressed in constant dollars, meaning that they are adjusted for inflation. Pro-financier economists falsely claim

---

[97] *Washington Post*, September 25, 1998.

that government statistic overestimate   inflation. In reality, government statistics substantially *underestimate* the ravages of inflation. Inflation has always been *greater* than the government has been willing to admit. It is also very important to notice that the figures just cited do not even pretend to take increased taxation into account. These figure show gross income before taxes, not the earnings that you are actually able to keep. In these figures, no allowance whatever is made for federal tax increases, including the FICA payroll tax, for increased state and local taxation, bracket creep, and the diminished power of exemptions and standard deductions to protect part of earnings. All of these factors represent a very serious erosion of nominal income, and taken together, have cut the real median family income by 50%, as we discuss elsewhere in this chapter.

Even taking these numbers at face value, they represent a sweeping indictment of the globaloney economy: whereas median family income rose by about 37% per decade during the regulated 1950s and 1960s, in the deregulated world an entire quarter century has passed with only a miniscule 6% improvement. The average family might have been reasonably comfortable with an income of $32,229 in 1970, during Nixon's first term. But that family was certainly a lot worse off on $74 less money a dozen years later, with Ron dozing in the White House and Paul Adolph Volcker running the country from the Federal Reserve. And 11 years after that, in 1993, when Bush was handing a ruined economy off to Clinton, the same family was theoretically just about $800 better off than it had been at the start, having progressed just 2% in 23 years, despite the fact that mom was now working and dad was moonlighting as well.

AVERAGE WEEKLY EARNINGS

Median family income has stagnated, but that is only the beginning of the story. Median family income means income from all sources, including the wages of wives and mothers who are now typically forced to enter the work force. When we get to the average weekly earnings provided by the average job, we are a little closer to the truth. As the following graph shows, average weekly earnings rose through the 1950s and 1960s and reached a small plateau in 1972-1973. Then they were quickly dragged down by the collapse of Bretton Woods, the oil shocks, inflation, and Volcker. By 1991, average weekly earnings were down almost 19% in comparison with the 1972-1973 peak. And they have stayed down during Clinton's first term and into his second term, according to the government's own figures. In 1996, the average wage for all private-sector employees in the Unites States was $400.14 per week, or $20,007 per year. This is about $5000 more than the poverty level for a family of four.

AVERAGE WEEKLY EARNINGS IN PRIVATE SECTOR, 1959-1996

Year	1982 Dollars	
1959	$260.86	(McChesney Martin at Fed; recession)
1960	261.92	
1961	265.59	(Ike departs; JFK in White House)
1962	273.60	
1963	278.18	(JFK assassinated; LBJ
1964	283.63	president)
1965	291.90	
1966	294.11	(Vietnam war)
1967	293.49	(£ crisis)
1968	298.42	(gold and dollar crisis)
1969	300.81	(Nixon)

1970	298.08	
1971	303.12	(end of gold convertibility, end of Bretton Woods)
1972	315.44	
1973	315.38	(end of fixed parities)
1974	302.27	(Ford; recession)
1975	293.06	(End of Bretton Woods,
1976	297.37	7% pay cut, 73-75)
1977	300.96	(Carter *malaise*)
1978	300.89	
1979	291.66	(Volcker 22% prime, 11%
1980	274.65	pay cut, 79-82)
1981	270.63	(Reagan; magic of the marketplace rules)
1982	267.26	(Reaganomics recession)
1983	272.52	
1984	274.73	
1985	271.16	
1986	271.94	(stealth recession)
1987	269.16	(Greenspan-Bush, 6% pay cut, 87-93)
1988	266.79	
1989	264.22	(Bush; deep recession)
1990	259.47	
1991	255.40	
1992	254.99	
1993	254.87	(Clinton 'recovery,' 74 cent
1994	256.73	pay hike, 93-96)
1995	255.29	
1996	255.73	
1997	260.89	(a statistical aberration?)

[1982 Dollars: current dollars divided by the consumer price index for urban wage earners and clerical workers on a 1982=100 base.]

[source: *Economic Report of the President 1997*]

We see that, during the post-1973 floating rate era, the average American wage worker has taken a 19% pay cut. The real wages of an average job have been falling at almost 1% per year, year after year. In the thirty-nine years between 1959 and 1996, average weekly earnings had risen exactly three cents.

As the government notes, these data "are based on reports from employing establishments and relate to full- and part-time wage and salary workers in nonagricultural establishments." These figures thus comprehend transportation, public utilities, wholesale and retail sales, finance, insurance, real estate, and services in general. They cover about 80% of the persons who are employed. The advantage here is that we are looking at the money that can be earned each week from a single job.

Ravi Batra is one of the few American economists who has called attention to the Average Weekly Earnings data series, which the monetarists studiously avoid. Batra comments: "Nineteen seventy-three marked a turning point in US history, because the legendary American living standard, which had begun its long upward march after the revolution of 1776, peaked that year. Ever since then, average real earnings of as much as 80 percent of the work force have been on the decline. Such a protracted fall is unique not only in the postwar period but in the entire history of the nation. That is why 1973 is a watershed year. It initiated something the United States had never faced before." [Batra 1993, 31-2] Batra also points out that if rising Social Security and other taxes are taken into account, the fall in average weekly take-home pay from the average job is even greater. Wallace C. Peterson also highlights this data series in his *Silent Depression*, stressing that these data mean that "for large numbers of working Americans, dreams of home ownership, better cars and appliances, vacations, and college for the kids gradually slipped away." [W. Peterson 37] Neither Batra nor Peterson identifies the collapse of Bretton Woods as the principal cause of the decline.

These statistics for average weekly earnings ought to suggest a new criterion for evaluating American presidents. If a candidate wants to be elected, he should be expected to specify the rate of improvement in average weekly earnings he or she proposes to bring about, describing in detail how this is to be done. If a President wants to be re-elected, the first the public should want to know is the change in average weekly earnings in that President's first term. A President who has not been able to raise average weekly earnings by 10% could hardly argue that his first term had been a success; Wage growth during the period 1959-1965 averaged just under 2.25% per year. With the policies described at the end of this book, it would be possible to raise the level of average weekly earnings by at least 20% during four years.

REGRESSIVE TAXATION ON THE MARCH

In this age of barbarism, it is important to recall certain humanitarian principles of taxation which have fallen out of favor because they contradict the greed of the new plutocrats. There are three kinds of taxes: regressive, progressive, and proportional. Regressive taxes fall most heavily on the poor. If everyone were taxed a lump sum like $5000, this would be an unbearable hardship for the poor, but would hardly be noticed by the very rich. Regressive taxes must be condemned because they contribute to the destruction of poor families. In America over the past 30 years, the institution of the family has become weaker and weaker, and the orgy of regressive taxation has played a central role. Payroll taxes, user fees, sales taxes, and the like are all examples of regressive taxes.

Progressive taxation starts from the correct principle that those who have more can afford to pay more. In order to promote family formation and family stability among those of modest means, the income used to provide vital necessities like food, clothing, shelter, medical care and education should be shielded from taxation. The very poor should obviously pay no tax at all. But the rich family can very well give up part of its luxuries through taxation. Back when the US economy was well managed, tax rates increased gradually as we went from the upper middle class to those who were frankly rich. Even so, rich people sought help from their accountants and lawyers, and still found ways to avoid paying their fair share. A decisive turning point came when the former Hollywood actor Ronald Reagan assumed the presidency. Reagan had worked in the movies in Hollywood during the 1950s, when the top marginal tax rate was 91% on earned income over $200,000. Reagan whined that his ambition to make more money left him once he had amassed $200,000 (at that time a fabulous sum) in any given year, and he concluded that this slackening of greed under the impact of high marginal tax rates was the leading economic and social problem of the United States in the 1980s. And Reagan solved it: with the help of Dan Rostenkowski, he cut the top rate from 70% to 28%. Whatever progressivity there was in the US tax code went out the window.

There is supposed to be a third category - proportional taxation. This is what the so-called flat tax is supposed to represent. For purposes of argument we will leave aside the most glaring inequity of the proposed flat tax, which is the fact that it is levied only on earned income, including wages, and not at all on unearned income, like interest, dividends, and capital gains. Proportional taxation proves to be a mirage, a subterfuge used by supporters of regressive taxation to challenge the fairness of a progressive tax schedule.

Taxing everyone equally sounds very fine and egalitarian, but reality looks different. The problem is that if you take 15% of a rich man's income, you force him at most to give up 15% of his extravagant luxuries, while leaving the rest of his luxuries, his amenities, and his necessities intact. If you hit the middle class with the same 15% tax, you begin to undermine their ability to pay for college education and home ownership. And if you take 15% of the income of poor families, you are slicing into food, clothing, shelter, medical care, and the basic necessities of life. So the only rational conclusion for tax policy is that proportional taxation in practice turns out to be regressive, and therefore anti-human and unacceptable. This is even before we get back to the fact that the Steve Forbes flat tax of 1996 is not even a proportional tax, since does not tax the most wealthy categories at all. The Steve Forbes flat tax is nakedly regressive, even more so than a formally proportional tax would be.

GREENSPAN'S GREAT PAYROLL TAX STING OF 1983

In order to finance a tax bonanza for parasitical plutocrats under conditions of Volcker-induced depression, the Reagan White House was inclined to gouge the American middle class by means of the Social Security payroll tax, the withholding category which appears as FICA on the paychecks of wage-earners. In December 1981, Reagan appointed Dr. Alan Greenspan of the economic consulting firm of Townsend-Greenspan & Co. to head a blue-ribbon National Commission on Social Security Reforms. More than a year later Greenspan delivered the commission's report, which claimed that there had been no time to hold public hearings. Greenspan also claimed that Social Security faced a cumulative deficit of $1.6 trillion over the next 75 years. What was the answer? Greenspan told the Senate Finance Committee:

> The 75-year deficit to be addressed and eliminated is judged by the Commission to be 1.8 percent of taxable payroll. We recognized, as a commission, that making judgments about the size of the deficit over such an extended period of time is subject to a rather substantial margin of error. Nevertheless, I suspect that most, if not all, of us concur that the probability that the deficit could in fact be zero and, hence, need not be addressed in exceptionally small. Hence, the commission agreed to a set of recommendations which would eliminate a deficit amounting to 1.8 percent of taxable payrolls through 2056."

As of 1997-98, Social Security is financed through a payroll tax levied on earned income. The employer pays 7.65% and the employee pays 6.2% for a total of 13.85% of gross wages. It is common knowledge that in reality the employee is the one who pays the entire tax, since the employer adjusts the pay scale to lower the wages by an amount equal to the employer's share of the tax. But the employee's weekly withholding statements and yearly W-2 forms show only the 6.2% paid by the employee, who therefore tends to underestimate the tax that is actually being subtracted from each paycheck. FICA is implacable: there is no escape for wage earners. There are no shelters or exemptions or deductions or refunds; every dollar of income is subject to the full force of the tax. FICA is silent: the tax manuals do not talk about it because there is nothing you can do to avoid it. Those who clip coupons and live on their investments do not have to pay Social Security tax. In addition, there is an upper limit to how much money is subject to this payroll tax. Only income up to about $65,000 is taxed.

These factors combine to make the FICA or Social Security payroll tax a very regressive and onerous tax. So it was typical that Reagan, while cutting the income tax on the fat cats of the upper brackets, shifted the burden of taxation so heavily to an impost which falls disproportionately on poorer and working Americans. The other important impact of a payroll tax is that it increases the reluctance of businessmen to hire anybody in the first place. No matter how adept they may be at shifting the burden of the payroll tax onto the employees, small businesspeople are nevertheless deterred from hiring new personnel, since on paper it is they who are paying the tax: the threshold for making a profit out of the new hire has been raised.

By the mid-1990s, the Social Security payroll tax was providing a larger and larger part of the general revenue of government. In 1948 it brought in 5.9%. In 1965 FICA gave the government 15.6% of tax revenue; in 1975 it was 27.5%, in 1984 33.1% and in 1990 an estimated 36.8% of all government revenue. Under Johnson, accounting rules were changed so that FICA. revenue could be counted against a possible deficit; without this trick, the much-touted 1998 surplus would have been revealed as the deficit it really was. Greenspan was rewarded for his role as payroll tax hatchet man with his current post as head of the Federal Reserve: here was an economic functionary who had proven his loyalty to the finance oligarchs and their strategies. But although the proceeds from the FICA payroll tax increase of 1983 were supposedly needed to guarantee the solvency of the Social Security trust fund, the additional money collected (about $250 billion) was not set aside for future pension payments. It was rather treated as current general revenue and thus used to pay for current expenses. At most it was invested in Treasury bonds.

This tragedy was played out as farce in 1991, when Senator Moynihan (D-NY) proposed putting the entire Social Security system back on a pay-as-you-go basis, with no trust fund whatever. That, argued Moynihan, would allow a FICA tax cut of some $50 billion per year. Moynihan called the current arrangement "fraud," "thievery," "embezzlement," and "abuse of trust." President Bush replied that Moynihan's proposal would drive Social Security "to the brink of insolvency," and would "threaten to bankrupt the system." It was a clash of demagogues in which the people were the big loser. In April 1991, Moynihan's Quixotic campaign was defeated, 60-38.

THE GROWING TAX BITE

We must stress once again that United States government figures on average family income and average weekly earnings are fundamentally misleading because they do not take the tax bite into account. The following graphic presentation gives at least a general notion of the degree to which income statistics must be discounted to reflect the reality of growing taxation:

COMPARISON - 1948 AND 1990

PERCENTAGE OF FAMILY INCOME TAKEN BY FEDERAL TAXES AND SOCIAL SECURITY

	MEDIAN INCOME, FAMILY OF 4	PERSONAL EXEMPTIONS & STANDARD DEDUCTION ($600, $267)	PERCENTAGE OF INCOME SUBJECT TO TAX	FED. TAX AND SOC. SEC.	FED. TAX AND SOC. SEC. AS % OF INCOME
1948	$3,468	$2,667	23%	$197	6%
1990	$29,184	$8,763	70%	$5,484	19%

[Source: Schlosstein, 356; Quirk and Bridwell, 117]

Another calculation shows the increase of the federal tax bite on the median family's income, even as the tax bill for the top 1% of millionaires and multi-millionaires declined:

YEAR	MEDIAN FAMILY'S FEDERAL TAXES INCOME + SOC. SEC.	EFFECTIVE RATE PAID BY TOP 1% INCOME + SOC. SEC.
1948	5.30%	76.9%
1955	9.06%	85.5%
1960	12.35%	85.5%
1965	11.55%	66.9%
1970	16.06%	68.6%
1980	23.68%	31.7%
1985	24.44%	24.9%
1990	24.63%	

[source: Phillips, 110]

Note that this calculation does not reflect state income tax, homeowner's property tax, personal property tax, or sales tax. Many states, for example, had highly regressive sales taxes of between 5% and 7%. This growing burden must still be added. This table gives some idea of the impact of state and local taxes.

STATE AND LOCAL TAX BURDEN AS A PERCENTAGE OF INCOME, 1990

TOP 1%	7.6%
UPPER MIDDLE 20%	9.5%
MIDDLE 20%	10.0%
LOWER MIDDLE 20%	10.9%
BOTTOM 20%	13.8%

[source: *A Far Cry from Fair*, Citizens for Tax Justice, April 1991.]

From these tables it can readily be seen that the combined federal and state tax bite on a wage-earning family around median levels can easily range between 29% and 35%. Note also the regressive character of state and local taxation, which often relies on the highly regressive sales tax as its main source of revenue.

The bottom line is that a 1960 average wage earner who rented a home in a low-tax state might have grossed $261.92 in 1982 constant dollars, but might have been able to keep about $230. By 1995, a person grossing the average weekly income of $255.73 (again in 1982 constant dollars) and living in Michigan or Massachusetts or New York might have been taking home just under $160 with which to meet skyrocketing insurance fees, HMO bills, college tuition costs, bank service charges, and credit card interest, none of which are sufficiently reflected in the government's cost of living figures that underlie the constant dollars. Which brings us back to our main point: the American standard of living has been cut in half.

The other shortcoming of these government figures is that they do not take into account the need of the productive individual for a higher standard of living as technological progress goes forward. During the Eisenhower years, a high school education was often enough to prepare a worker to handle the technology that prevailed in those days. As we approach the year 2,000, it is clear that two to four years of college represent the bare minimum of training required to get a worker ready to be seriously productive. Today we also require more complicated and expensive scientific and cultural equipment in the home, including whole classes of technology which were not available in 1955. Computers and software are only the most obvious example. So as time goes by, a standard of living which does not expand and improve becomes a more and more inadequate standard of living. Progress requires a higher and higher standard of living to keep pace with the science, technology, and culture of tomorrow. A viable standard of living cannot stand still, but must improve in order to avoid deterioration. Government figures have no inkling of this obvious need. Government economists simply divide current dollar figures by the Consumer Price Index (which understates even simple price inflation) and call the result constant dollars. This is a cruel hoax.

THE DECLINE OF THE CORPORATE INCOME TAX

During the Truman and Eisenhower years, the federal government derived upwards of 30% of its total income from the corporate income tax, which was a tax on corporate profits. By Reagan's second term, the corporate income tax was providing a mere 6.2% of government revenue, and when Bush left the White House that figure was only 8.3%. This means simply that corporations have avoided or evaded most of their federal tax liability, leaving a shortfall of between one fifth and one fourth of the entire federal pie to be made up by the soaking of the middle class and the poor. Notice also that these same corporations often extort deep tax cuts from state and local governments with the threat of moving their operations elsewhere in the great race to the bottom. The result is that many corporations purely and simply pay no tax, neither federal nor state, and use the proceeds for speculation in derivatives, real estate, and the like. The celebrated case is that of General Electric, Reagan's ideological home (and the fortress of the union-busting doctrine known as Bullwerism after a former anti-labor CEO). In 1983-1985, GE earned $5 billion, but paid not a penny in federal tax. Much of the proceeds were used for stockjobbing, including buying up the company's own stock. GE's chairman indignantly rejected any attempt to plough the proceeds back into technological research.

The free ride enjoyed by the paper entrepreneurs placed by the Wall Street interests in the CEO's chairs of US corporations has been another big factor in the regressive revamping of the US tax system. As one student of the subject notes, "Individual income taxes have, since 1955, averaged in the 44-48 percent range of all federal tax receipts. On the other hand, the corporate income tax which in 1955 made up 27.3 percent of federal tax receipts, has steadily eroded its contribution to the government. In 1983 – two years after the initial Reagan tax reform (the Economic Recovery Act of 1981) with personal income taxes near their highest share of all federal income tax receipts over the period covered – the corporate income tax fell to its lowest percentage contribution: 6.2 percent of all federal receipts." [Strobel 92]

ESTATE TAX, GIFT TAX, EXCISE TAX

These are all taxes which hit the wealthier brackets rather harder than they do those with more modest incomes. In 1948, this trio of taxes accounted for just over one fifth of total federal revenue – 20.6%. By 1990, these taxes were providing just 6.6% of federal revenue. The estate tax has been largely circumvented by such expedients as transforming large private fortunes into foundations and allegedly charitable trusts. More loopholes for avoiding estate tax were built into the 1997 tax changes. The gift tax has also been frustrated as wealthy persons found clever ways to transfer assets to their close relatives without paying the tax. Excise taxes are still with us, and remain regressive, although it is far better to tax luxury goods than basic food staples. Here is another 15% of total federal revenue which has been shifted largely to the backs of the middle class. As a result of all these changes, by the end of the Reagan era personal income tax plus FICA payroll tax made up 67.2% of federal revenue, up from 53.5% during the Eisenhower years.

RESULT: THE STANDARD OF LIVING CUT BY 50%

Back in the days of the US-USSR cold war, it was common to hear politicians orate that the American standard of living was the highest in the world, and that the would-be aggressors in the Kremlin had better realize that we were willing and able to fight and win World War III in order to protect the American way of life, and especially our standard of living. Well, don't look now, but the American standard of living that we were prepared to fight for has been cut in half from its Kennedy-Johnson level, and the crime has been perpetrated not by the Kremlin, but by Wall Street and the City of London. In other words, the US population is now producing and consuming about half as much as it did per capita in the days before the world monetary crisis. This finding was confirmed in 1996 by a group of economists led by Christopher White in the September 27, 1996 issue of *EIR* magazine.

White and his co-workers Richard Freeman, Marcia Merry Baker, John Hoefle, and Anthony Wikrent came to these conclusions thanks in part to their use of the elementary but very powerful analytical tool of counting paychecks.[98] In their analysis of the decline of the typical market basket representing the standard of living of the average American consumer, they calculated how many weekly paychecks of a typical wage-earner were required to pay for a house, a car, a year of college, and the like. The results converged on the notion that the US standard of living has been cut by one half over the past three decades. Surely AFL-CIO President John J. Sweeney is right when he argues that "although every advanced industrialized nation is part of the global economy, the United States is experiencing the most extreme declines in wages and increases in inequality." [Sweeney, 68]

In 1967, before the world monetary crisis, the average US worker needed 35 weekly paychecks to pay for a new car. By 1996, it took 58 average weekly paychecks to buy a car. (Each of these figures is inclusive of financing costs.) Already by 1980, the average hourly wage of US auto workers ($15.02) was less than the hourly wage of their counterparts in Germany ($15.46) and Belgium ($15.30). Consumption is the flip-side of production. If per-capita production falls by half, then per-capita consumption will tend to follow it down, perhaps with a certain time lag. And sure enough: between 1967 and 1995, the US per-household production of cars had dropped by 54%. Furthermore, the 1995 car was lighter and likely to fare less well in a serious accident. Between 1967 and 1990, the per-household production of steel dropped by more than 50%. These very basic figures are exactly in line with the halving of the overall US living standard.

FOOD

Since the late Eisenhower administration, the dollar prices of food have increased by about 400%, although the percentage spent for food in the average paycheck has declined by about 1.5% over that same time. But food scarcity has nevertheless been very real for millions of Americans. By 1993, fully 10% of the population was receiving food stamps. Now many of these same people still need help, but have had their food stamps cut off by Gingrich's 104th Congress. Thanks to the family farm, America was for a time a land of plenty. Much of that abundance has been looted by Cargill, Continental Grain, Dreyfus, and "Supermarket to the World" Archer Daniels Midland,

---

[98] See also *EIR*, January 1, 1996.

where the boss's son, Dwayne Andreas Jr., was convicted of illegal price fixing. But during the 1990s, farm commodity prices, long in decline, sank to less than 50% of parity – meaning that the market price is less than half of what it actually takes to produce the commodity on a sustained basis. The ABC television program *Nightline* on June 19, 1998 discussed the question of whether the farm economy of High Plains states like the Dakotas were moribund. This points to very serious problems of food supply during the years ahead.

HOUSING

In 1963, the United States produced 0.029 new housing units for every existing household. Housing starts per household peaked near 0.035 during the early 1970s. By the mid-1990s, the figure was 0.013 new housing starts for every existing household. This is a decline of more than 55% over three decades, and of almost two thirds from the best level achieved during this time. The proportion of multi-family housing construction (typical of urban areas) among all new units has declined sharply. Part of the reason for the decline is the greater cost of financing. In the Volcker and post-Volcker era of exorbitant interest rates, the mortgage debt burden that must be carried by a family wishing to own a home has increased astronomically. Single family mortgage debt was about $21 billion in 1945. By the mid-1990s, that mortgage debt was $3.4 trillion, an increase of 16,200%

The vast increase in mortgage usury means that the total cost of buying a home has gone up out of all proportion. In 1963, when Kennedy was in the White House, the average salary or wage earner needed the total proceeds from 399 paychecks in order fully to pay for the average home. That meant working for almost eight years just to own the home. By 1996, it took 877 full paychecks (almost seventeen years of work) to pay for the average home. This adds up to a 55 % decline in the average working person's ability to buy a new home.

The majority of newer homes are built with materials and methods which are inferior to those of thirty or forty years ago. Brick makes up a smaller and smaller part of new construction. Sheathing made of aluminum foil and foam is unable to withstand high winds and may disintegrate if the siding is blown off. These new homes fare poorly in hurricanes and severe storms.

As of the mid-1990s, 18.4% of all US dwelling units were built before 1939 and thus qualified as old. Big-city apartment units in this older group had often received little or no maintenance, but have been treated as speculative properties by generations of rent-gouging landlords. In New York City, 60% of all rental apartments had serious defects. In 1993 there were 33.472 million American households which rented their family dwelling. Of these, a HUD study conducted by Dr. Bruce Link found that 17.6 million fell into the "extremely precarious" category. These were the aged, the unemployed, and others who were one or two paychecks away from being evicted. They made up 53% of all renters, up from 41% in 1978.

At the bottom of the ladder are the homeless. In 1993 it was estimated that about 7 million Americans had experienced homelessness during the late 1980s, which amounted to a submerged nation of homeless Americans and families almost the size of Belgium. Government help in acquiring a home has become exceedingly scarce. After World War II, the GI Bill of Rights made it possible for returning veterans to buy a home with little or no money down by virtue of a government-guaranteed 30 year mortgage with a government-assisted fixed interest rate of just 4%. This was one of the keys to establishing home ownership as an economic right of the American middle class. Clinton touted reports that home ownership had reached an all-time high during his second term, but much of this had been made possible by mortgage financing so onerous that mass foreclosures would be inevitable in case of a serious downturn. All in all, the housing component of the average American standard of living has deteriorated by almost 60%.

Some localities used to protect low-income tenants with rent control laws. But by 1998, only New York, New Jersey, Maryland, California, and the District of Columbia had rent control laws on the books in some areas. Landlord lobbies had succeeded in outlawing any form of rent control in 31 states. One locality which recently removed rent controls was Cambridge, Massachusetts, the home of Harvard and MIT. In 1994, the average rent in Cambridge was about $500, but after rent controls were lifted, this had increased to $1,050, and 3,500 working families were forced to find someplace else to live. Rick Hill, a black pipefitter, was forced to leave Cambridge for a rodent-infested home in a tough neighborhood where he has to worry about his children's safety. Hill told a *Washington Post* reporter that what bothered him most about being driven from his previous home was "that I helped build the [subway], I helped build Harvard, I helped build the roads, and all these yuppies just take over like it's nothing." With the end of rent control, Cambridge was on track to become an island of gentrified privilege for the mandarins of the Harvard-MIT boutique.

UNEMPLOYMENT

As everyone conversant with the real world knows, the alleged Reagan Recovery of the post-1982 period was built on dead-end, low-skilled, low-paid jobs with few or no benefits – like hamburger salesman, pizza home delivery boy, or croupier. Reagan had a resident ideologue on his Council of Economic Advisers, Beryl Sprinkel by name, who from time to time released imposing studies to prove that the jobs created under Reagan were in reality highly paid and most desirable. Under the influence of people like the foot fetishist Dick Morris, the 1996 Clinton campaign tried to carry out some of the same sleight of hand, arguing that Clinton had created 8.5 million new jobs in the private sector of which 68% allegedly paid "above-median wages." In reality, only half of Clinton's new jobs were above the median wage, and we have now seen what the median looked like.

In April 1997, the Clinton Administration claimed that unemployment had fallen to 5.1% In reality, the Labor Department's own figures make clear that the jobless, plus part-time workers who would work full-time if they could, combined at that time to give us an unemployment rate of 13.3%. To this must be added those who had exhausted their unemployment benefits and who despaired of finding a job, and thus did not report to their state unemployment offices. When these legions of despair are factored in, we find that the actual rate of unemployment under Clinton II rose to somewhere between 15% and 20%.

DOWNSIZING

By now everyone is aware of the job-destroying practice called "downsizing" or even "rightsizing" by corporate executives, but viewed by most Americans as plain old mass firings, just what you would expect in a depression. Mass layoffs are nothing new per se. One important qualitative change during the 1990s is that the layoffs generally hit white-collar salaried workers with the same virulence that used to be limited to the blue-collar hourly workers on the production line. This new dimension in layoffs was a key factor in the defeat of George Bush in the 1992 election. By that time the Great Fear of joblessness and home foreclosure was abroad in the normally Republican suburbs of the country, and frightened voters shifted into the Democratic column. Clinton was able to capture these voters because they were so worried about being fired.

Many executives were GOP sympathizers and appear to have delayed their layoff announcements until after the election was over. The turn of the year 1992-1993 turned out to be a moment of truth of sorts. Within about a month about 120,000 layoffs were announced. The biggest of these was Sears, Roebuck, which made public its plan to fire 16,000 full-time workers and eliminate 34,000 part-time jobs; 6,000 jobs at Sears suppliers were lost in the process. IBM and Boeing also announced staggering layoffs at the same time. Wall Street was generally delighted by these firings.

Certain business executives became famous for their hecatombs of layoffs. Here are some recent examples of the handiwork of these highly paid **Corporate Killers**, as they were described by a leading national newsmagazine. [99]

Robert Allen	AT&T	January 1996	40,000 Layoffs
Walter Shipley	Chase/ Chemical Bank	August 1995	12,000
Charles Lee	GTE	January 1994	17,000
Lou Gerstner	IBM	July 1993	60,000
Ronald Allen	Delta	April 1994	15,000
John McDonnell	McDonnell- Douglas	April 1994	17,000
Michael Miles	Philip Morris	Nov. 1993	14,000
Frank Shrontz	Boeing	February 1993	28,000
William Ferguson	Nynex	January 1994	16,800
Albert Dunlap	Scott Paper	1994	11,000
Robert Stempel	GM	December 1991	74,000
Robert Palmer	Digital	May 1994	20,000
Edward Brennan	Sears	January 1993	50,000

More recently, the *New York Times* published a seven-part series on "The Downsizing of America". Here the central quantitative finding was that corporate downsizings had wiped out more than 43,000,000 jobs in the United States from 1979 through 1995. [100] Even before the end of the year, it was clear that 1998 would become the worst year for mass layoffs in the entire globaloney decade of the 1990s. Tens of thousands of jobs were lost in the late 1998 spate of mergers and acquisitions. Even more ominous was that Boeing's announced 1998 layoffs had climbed to almost 50,000, representing about 70% of the company's work force.

AN EXTRA MONTH OF WORK, 1969-1987

In her book *The Overworked American*, Juliet Schor established that, in contradiction with the Triple Revolution committee and others who predicted the massive growth of leisure time and the withering away of labor, the hours spent working by the average American relentlessly increased between 1969 and 1987 – essentially, during the floating rate era. She believed her estimates to be the first comprehensive calculations of working time in two decades. Her findings: "According to my estimates, the average employed person is now on the job an additional 163 hours, or the equivalent of an extra month a year... Men are working nearly one hundred (98) more hours per year, or two and a half extra weeks. Women are doing about three hundred (305) additional hours, which translates to seven and a half weeks, or 38 added days of work each year." The increased work load was across the board, shared by low, middle and high income categories. It also burdened family patterns of all types – people with children, without children, married, single – all were working longer. [Schor 1991, 29] In more recent research, Schor found a tendency to attempt an escape from the rat race by certain groups through what she called "downshifting" – a voluntary reduction of wages and hours. Voluntary downshifters seek to obtain more free time and less stress. [Schor 1998, 114-5] If we add the extra hours of work to the impact of moonlighting, plus the

---

[99] "The Hit Men," and "Corporate Killers," by Allan Sloan, *Newsweek* cover story, February 26, 1996.
[100] New York Times, March 3-9, 1996.

increased time consumed by commuting owing to the deterioration of roads and bridges, we begin to see how few hours remain for family life.

AMERICANS LITERALLY WORK THEMSELVES TO DEATH

Schor also found a pattern of stress in the lives of working people. Thirty percent of adults reported experiencing high stress almost every day. A third of the population report that they are more rushed in their everyday activities, an increase of 25% over 1965. Workers' compensation claims related to stress tripled during the first half of the 1980s. "According to a recent review of existing findings, Americans are literally working themselves to death – as jobs contribute to heart disease, hypertension, gastric problems, depression, exhaustion, and a variety of other ailments. Suprisingly, the high-powered jobs are not the most dangerous. The most stressful work-places are the 'electronic sweatshops' and assembly lines where a demanding pace is coupled with virtually no individual discretion." [Schor 1991, 11] The average American is now suffering from a sleep deficit of 60 to 90 minutes per night below the optimal level. Europeans make out somewhat better, since they enjoy much longer yearly vacations, and limits on overtime work are often established by law. In Switzerland, for example, inspectors sometimes make spot checks on office workers to see if they are still at their desks after hours, since this practice is prohibited. In France and Italy, the trade unions have pressed for a shortening of the work week to 35 hours. When Harvard President Neil Rudenstine recently collapsed from exhaustion, the event triggered a spate of solicitous commentaries in news magazines about the high stress suffered by top executives. But the implacable depletion of American working people got far less fanfare.

THE PRODUCTIVITY OF INDUSTRIAL LABOR

The most important overall measure of the wealth of any society is the productivity of its industrial workers. Measuring this productivity brings together the effects of improved infrastructure, the realized rate of scientific discovery as new technology, the impact of better organization and management, standard of living, education, health, morale, longevity, and many other factors.

Productive labor involves the creation of tangible physical wealth. Productive labor is hard-commodity production in farming, manufacturing, mining, construction, transportation, scientific research, and the like. Retail sales, service, administrative, clerical, advertising, legal and financial personnel are not productive and can only be justified by the backup they can provide in to those who actually are productive. But the story of postwar America is the atrophy of productive occupations accompanied by the exorbitant growth of the service, sales, administrative, advertising, marketing, and financial overhead.

A steelworker, a farmer, a scientist, and an industrial engineer are productive. Doctors, teachers, and nurses are socially necessary. But occupations like hamburger sales, pizza home delivery, gambling croupier, financial services analyst, mutual fund salesman, image consultant, and so forth are not productive and seldom socially necessary. And in case you've been wondering: lawyers, paralegals, and jury consultants are never productive and not socially necessary beyond an irreducible minimum. Right now, there are far too many of them. Criminal activities like narcotics smuggling and gambling are socially destructive, even if the legislature decides to legalize them. Sociopathic activities now loom very large in international capital flows, as well as in most calculations of Gross Domestic Product. In 1977, it was estimated that the total sales of the world's drug pushers amounted to some $175 billion. By the mid-1980s, drugs sales had risen to about $260 billion. By the mid-1990s, the total international narcotics trade exceeded $520 billion per year. The total turnover of the international crime syndicate which organizes this trade is thought to be approaching $1 trillion.

By 1997, there were 75 riverboat gambling operations in the United States, along with 30 state lotteries. In addition, some $88 billion was thought to be spent on illegal sports betting. These activities produce nothing, but the costs they generate represent a parasitical net detraction from actual national wealth.

RETAIL SALES

By April 1997 retail giant Wal-Mart had outdistanced General Motors, Macdonald's, and Manpower Associates as the largest private business employer in America, according to *Fortune* magazine. This is an ominous symptom of the devolution of the U.S. economy into a post-industrial economy. In 1996, Wal-Mart employed 675,000 workers worldwide, as compared to 647,000 for General Motors. With $106.1 billion in sales, Wal-Mart is now the fourth largest company in America. The implications for a further fall in the standard of living are most stark. According to the Bureau of Labor Statistics, in December 1996, the average worker engaged in motor vehicle production earned $847.19 per week, plus health and dental benefits. In December 1996, the average retail worker earned $237.69 per week, only 28% of what an auto worker earned. Wal-Mart employees received either partial health benefits, or none at all.

Ravi Batra has shown that the declining real wages of retail trade employees, when combined with growing taxation, have left these persons in a desperate situation. "When such sharp tax rises are taken into account,: he writes, "the living standard of retail employees by the 1992 election had dropped more than 20 percent below the 1950 low. In fact, it is now approaching the 1939 level, when the country, with an unemployment rate of 15 percent, was still reeling under the Depression." [Batra 1993, 27]

Not only are jobs disappearing. The jobs that are destroyed are often those directly involved with the production of tangible physical commodities. The jobs that remain are often non-productive, socially unnecessary or even pathogenic occupations. In 1945, 60% of the US work force was engaged in productive labor, including farming, manufacturing, and infrastructure. By the mid-1990s, this figure had fallen to 17% productive, and was continuing rapidly to decline. According to other figures, in 1947 there were 60.9 million people in the US work force. Of these, 47.2% were employed in productive jobs. By 1996, there were 133.7 million Americans in the work force, but the percentage of productive workers had declined to 26%, a little more than half of the postwar level. The absolute number of manufacturing and farming workers had declined by 400,000, while the workers in infrastructure had grown by 6.4 million. The result is that each productive worker must provide the tangible, physical commodities needed by not only by his own household, but also by the households of three non-productive overhead workers. This is a key to the declining US standard of living, and also the basic reason for inflationary tendencies in the US economy.

Manufacturing workers, a narrower category than productive workers, have been drastically reduced in their proportion of the overall work force. The following chart shows the decline in the part of the US labor force which is engaged in manufacturing. These BLS statistics include both white collar and blue collar manufacturing workers.

Year	Labor Force (millions)	Mfg Workers (millions)	Mfg Workers as % of Labor Force
1943	55.45	17.60	31.7%
1950	62.21	15.24	24.5
1960	69.63	16.80	24.1
1966	75.77	19.21	25.4
1970	82.77	19.38	23.4
1979	104.96	21.04	20.0
1980	106.94	20.29	19.0
1990	125.84	19.08	15.2

[source: Bureau of Labor Statistics, US Department of Labor]

Even these grim statistics do not tell the whole story. As a result of the Asian contraction of 1997-98, US manufacturing employment declined by some 193,000 jobs between January and October of 1998, going from just over 18.8 million workers to just over 18.63 million. This represented an anemic 13.5% of the US labor force.

In the decade after World War II, it was possible for the average manufacturing worker to provide for a family of four with a single paycheck from a full-time job. By 1995, it took three paychecks to support a family of four. The family that gets by on a single paycheck is now a rarity; currently only about 10% of all families are of this type; in 1950 80% of families were. Related to this is the presence of large numbers of women in the work force. This trend has positive and negative features. As long as employment represents an autonomous choice, it may be highly beneficial. But when a woman's employment is coerced by economic duress, it is a negative. Women's employment becomes a social evil when it interferes with child development during the first few months and years of a child's life. There are no adequate studies determining how many women genuinely want to be in the labor force, and how many are coerced into being there by the threat of economic privation.

During the Bush downturn, the market research firm of Yankelovich, Clancy, and Shulman surveyed the attitudes of working women, and found that many of them were not working because they wanted to, but simply to make ends meet. Among married women with children under age six, 60% were working in 1991, as against only 19% in 1960 – the percentage had tripled in 30 years. Data from the US Census Bureau and Eurostat suggest that the number of American women with school-aged children who were working in the mid-1990s was one of the highest in the industrialized world: 78% of American working women had children between 5 and 16 years of age. This put the United States well ahead of 13 European countries in this category. Second in line was Portugal with 69% of working women having children between 5 and 16, followed by such countries as France with 63%, Britain with 59%, Germany with 57%, and Italy with 43%. In the related department of the proportion of working women with children under the age of 5, the US ranked third on the same list of 14 countries with 63%. This list was topped by Austria with 69% and Portugal with 67%. France checked in with 55%, Britain with 47%, Germany with 44%, and Italy with 43%. The very high proportion of American women with children, including those with infants, toddlers, and pre-schoolers, suggests that grinding economic necessity, and not the quest for personal fulfillment, is coercing women to enter the labor market in such large numbers. Quite apart from individual motivation, it should also be clear that many infants and toddlers who are deprived of contact with their own mothers will be permanently disadvantaged in their emotional and intellectual development, leaving society as a whole disadvantaged in decades to come.

MANUFACTURING PRODUCTIVITY IN DECLINE

Between 1899 and 1950, the average hourly output per American production worker increased by almost 400%, with an average annual increase of 5%. To the extent that these gains did not represent speed-up, they represented increased labor productivity. But under the impact of the world monetary crisis, there came an unprecedented decline in manufacturing productivity:

1965-1970	2.1%
1970-1975	1.8%
1975-1980	1.7%

In 1980, US manufacturing productivity shifted into reverse and actually declined by 0.5%, putting this country in last place in the industrialized world. After 1980, the data series on manufacturing productivity became virtually meaningless. On paper, the average annual rise in manufacturing productivity between 1980 and 1987 was a very healthy 4.1%. But this growth did not reflect the real productivity growth that comes from technological improvement. This growth was mostly from the combination of layoffs plus speedup – wringing more production from a diminished labor force. In 1979, 21 million Americans had manufacturing jobs. By 1983, in the midst of the Volcker downturn, only 18.4 million manufacturing jobs were left. More than a million and a half of these manufacturing jobs had been permanently eliminated. Increasing productivity by layoffs and speedup was a one-time quick fix which could not be repeated, but rather led to a degradation of the labor force and, further down the road, to an inevitable decline in productivity. But try telling that to a bottom-lining Harvard MBA.

The decline in industrial productivity is an important part of the decline in overall economic growth. Economic growth figures are inherently unreliable because they lump commodity production together with services and finance. Even so, a trend is visible here as well. US economic growth averaged 3.4% per year from 1865 onwards. But in 1973, economic growth slowed to about 2.3% In twenty years of this slower growth, about $12 trillion in production was lost, compared to what total economic output would have been if the earlier historical rate of growth had simply been continued. As Jeffrey Madrick points out, "The enormity of the $12 trillion shortfall since 1973 can be envisioned in many ways. Twelve trillion dollars is more than enough to have bought each of America's homeowners a new house, or paid off all of our government, mortgage, and credit-card debt, or replaced all of our nation's factories, including capital equipment, with new ones....by the year 2013, the total shortfall, assuming the economy grows at about 1 percent a year less than our historical norm, will amount to more than $35 trillion of lost production since 1973."

Seen from another point of view, the productivity gains of American workers can be considered as one of the pillars of the entire society. If productivity stagnates, the social order is at risk. Here is the view of social observer Max Lerner, writing in the mid-1950s: "...there has been a steady increase in the productivity of American workers, unequaled in world history. The role that was formerly played by continued access to free land, in cutting down a sense of class inferiority and class bitterness of the worker, was later played by the continuing rise of the productivity curve due to technological advance." [Lerner, 501] If productivity and real wages continue to stagnate, new flare-ups of class bitterness may be on the agenda.

CREEPING DOLLAR HYPERINFLATION: 1,200%

As a result of the secular tendency for unreported inflation, we find a constant erosion of the US dollar to command physical commodities in the real world. If we take an Eisenhower-Kennedy era dollar as our benchmark, today's dollar is worth only about 8 cents. By the same token, all dollar figures for the supposed value of production must be deflated by a factor of just over 12. It now takes over $12 to command the hard commodities in the real physical world that $1 commanded around 1961. Prove it for yourself with prices you can remember for a gallon of gasoline, a hamburger, a quart of milk, a loaf of bread, transit fares, a newspaper, and a haircut. Inflation "only" 500%, you think? Then factor in a visit to the doctor's office, a day in a hospital, a pair of glasses, a new car, and a year of college for junior. Look at your car insurance, your health insurance, and your homeowner's policy. You will soon reach a figure of 1200% inflation with no trouble at all.

REAGANOMICS: THE BREAKING OF THE SOCIAL CONTRACT

During the Eisenhower years, companies offered trade unions a kind of *de facto* social contract or labor relations truce. This truce was violated more and more during the 1970s, especially under Carter, and was ended by Reagan's first term in the White House. In the post-1971 floating rate environment, companies demand flexibility in the labor market, as well as mobility, and "the only way for capital to achieve this degree of flexibility – that is, to produce the necessary amount of insecurity – was to attack the social wage itself." [Bluestone 1988, 180] Financiers, bankers, and business interests decided that American workers had to be made much more desperate than they were, in order to coerce them into taking the lousy jobs and pay scales that were increasingly offered. One thrust was the systematic dismantling of any social safety net that might allow a working family to survive during a time of unemployment, or to bargain for higher wages: "It appears that companies also have in mind the whole panoply of government policies that provide social insurance, welfare and food stamps, and minimum wages. These shelters from the insecurity that comes with being totally dependent on the demands of capital represent the spoils of past political victories by workers and their unions. The social wage is costly to business, and increasingly they want out. **That** is what the corporate demand for good business climate is mainly about." [Bluestone 1988, 181]

State politicians in southern states during the 1970s and 1980s opposed increases in federal welfare payments, even though their states would get more money back from Washington without any increase in the taxes they paid. Bluestone and Harrison offered the following rationale for such moves: "The reason for southern opposition goes to the very heart of the social-wage issue. While low-wage states do not wish to raise taxes and therefore signal a worsening business climate, their legislators are even more concerned about the possibility of providing grants so large that they might **compete** with the minimum-wage levels in their local labor markets, now being trumpeted as an inducement to employers. They fear that the supply of low-wage labor will be reduced by higher welfare benefits, and so they vote to keep welfare families at below-subsistence levels." [Bluestone 1988, 188] As we show in Chapter IX, these short-sighted, low-wage attitudes have historically been typical of the Southern oligarchy. During the 1970s, they appear to have become typical of vast areas of the US business and finance elite. Reaganomics thus amounted to a unilateral declaration of class warfare in the United States, although many union leaders and working people refused to see it that way at the time. Under the avuncular Great Communicator, "capital has unilaterally ended even giving lip service to the great postwar social contract. The Reagan victory of 1980 was thus a real watershed in American history; the Reagan regime was profoundly committed to 'disciplining' labor by fundamentally undermining the social wage." [Bluestone 1988, 188]

WELFARE

The welfare system had already been eroded during the Carter-Reagan-Bush administrations. If measured in 1991 dollars, the median Aid to Families with Dependent Children payment declined from $669 per month to $451 per month between 1975 and 1990, a reduction of about one third. The draconian welfare reform bill written by Rep. E. Clay Shaw (R-Fla.) passed by Congress, and signed by Clinton in 1996 was on the surface a direct frontal attack on the poorest and most defenseless groups in the American population. But the secondary impact and medium-term potentials of this misbegotten law also made it a sneak attack against the American middle class. In blunt terms, international finance capital appeared to be preparing a reserve army of homeless, unemployed, and destitute with the intention of hurling them at against the living standards of suburbia. Middle class voters who supported such a welfare reform, because they had been blinded by their propaganda-stoked resentment against the inner-city and rural poor, might soon come to regret their own gullibility.

Peter Edelman was the former assistant secretary for planning and evaluation at the US Department of Health and Human Services who in 1996 resigned in protest over what was then still the welfare bill. Edelman had been an advisor to Robert Kennedy in 1967, and was proud that he has spent 30 years trying to fight poverty in America. Edelman kept silent until after Clinton had been re-elected in 1996, but then spoke out in an article entitled "The Worst Thing Clinton Has Done," which was published in the *Atlantic Monthly*. In Edelman's judgment, "the bill that President Clinton signed is not welfare reform. It does not promote work effectively, and it will hurt millions of poor children by the time it is fully implemented. What's more, it bars hundreds of thousands of legal immigrants – including many who have worked in the United States for decades and paid a considerable amount in Social Security and income taxes – from receiving disability and old-age assistance and food stamps, and reduces food-stamp assistance for millions of children in working families." The bill, he pointed out, was stigmatized by Senator Kennedy as "legislative child abuse."

Edelman cited data from the Urban Institute showing that even under the unrealistically optimistic assumption that two thirds of long-term welfare recipients would find jobs, the current welfare law would move 2.6 million people, including 1.1 million children, into poverty. Further, the 1996 law reduced the incomes of 11 million low-income families, fully 10% of all the families in America. Of the families thus impacted, 8 million families with children would suffer losses of an average $1,300 per family as a result of food stamp cuts. Many working families slightly above the official federal poverty line of $12,158 for a family of three would lose income. [101]

But these statistics turn out to understate this vast problem. The fact is that jobs were not available in sufficient numbers to accommodate the welfare recipients that were going to have their benefits terminated in 1999, when the welfare law's draconian two-year limit on welfare payments to many current recipients would expire. This was the point stressed by the US Conference of Mayors in late November 1997, with a warning that unless there were increased investments in job-creation, transport, child care, and health coverage, huge numbers of Americans risked abject poverty in 1999. These were the conclusions of a 34-city survey commissioned by the mayors.

Philadelphia Mayor Ed Rendell, the chairman of the mayors' task force on the welfare-to-work issue, stated that "By the summer of 1999, for the first time since the great depression, there will be large numbers of Americans in American cities without any subsidies at all, without any cash payments. We cannot let that happen." Rendell pointed to a "serious mismatch" between the large numbers of welfare recipients seeking employment and the jobs available to them. "Regardless of

---

[101] See Peter Edelman, "The Worst Thing Clinton Has Done," *Atlantic Monthly*, March 1997.

the training and child-care available, it is too much to expect that these numbers of welfare recipients are going to find jobs in this market, " said Mayor Rendell. [*Financial Times*, November 22, 1997] One key problem was that inner city welfare victims had no cars and could not reach jobs at shopping malls and industrial parks in the suburbs, given the lack of any serious urban mass transit system in many metropolitan areas where welfare was most common.

56 MILLION FORGOTTEN PERSONS AT THE BOTTOM OF THE ECONOMIC PYRAMID

According to Schwartz and Volgy, in 1989 – at the high point of the "Reagan recovery" and before the onset of the Bush recession – 56 million Americans (or 22.8% of the entire population) resided in household with income insufficient to provide the basic necessities of life. (This research assumed that any household with an income below 155% of the official poverty standard would not be able to afford these basic necessities. Their figure for those suffering from privation was about double the government's estimate of Americans living in poverty.) According to the same study, there were 5.9 million workers who worked full time and still failed to attain a level of economic self-sufficiency, and in their households lived 18 million Americans, a number equal to the total inhabitants of the eleven largest US cities at that time. [Schwartz and Volgy, 61-71]

Recovery from the Bush recession was so slow that it was 1997 before the government could claim that the official (understated) poverty rate had subsided to 13.3%, or about the level of 1989. Even so, the Children's Defense Fund noted that there were still almost 10 million children with a working parent who were in poverty.[102] By the time the figures were announced, the world financial panic left little doubt that a massive downturn was at hand. How many more decades before the poor could get out of poverty? Or how many generations?

BALANCING THE BUDGET

The notion of balancing the US federal budget has been a theme of hysterical demagogy on the part of such figures as Ross Perot, the Concord Coalition, and the dominant "Contract on America" faction of the mid-1990s Republican Party. But in reality, all attempts to balance the federal budget by means of austerity budget cuts, increased taxes (or "revenue enhancement"), or by some combination of these, was doomed to something worse than failure. The US budget deficit became a problem during the Ford Administration in the wake of the collapse of the Bretton Woods world monetary system. The problem became more alarming around 1985 after the destructive impact of the Volcker interest rates, which destroyed agricultural and industrial companies of all types, and after the "superdollar" period, which wiped out many of the remaining exporting industries. The effect of Volcker was to destroy the nation's tax base, since the thousands of companies that succumbed to Volcker's interest rates represented a large part of the high-wage, high value-added capital-intensive and energy-intensive companies in the country. Steel mills and steelworkers pay more in taxes than pizza parlors and pizza delivery boys. Interest on the public debt skyrocketed even more after Greenspan's 1990-1993 back-door bailout of the insolvent US banking system, when banks were given the chance to borrow Fed funds at about 3% and then invest them in 30-year Treasury bonds paying about 7%, thus locking in a risk-free 4% profit at taxpayer expense.

The inherent fallacy of trying to balance a budget by means of budget cuts and/or tax increases lies in the central role played by government expenditure in today's depressed economy. The typical federal budget of the early 1990s added up to about $750 billion in discretionary spending plus $750 billion of entitlements (Social Security, Medicare, Medicaid, farm programs, etc.) for a total

---

[102] *Washington Post*, September 25, 1998.

federal outlay in the neighborhood of $1.5 trillion. This federal outlay in turn represented almost one fifth of the entire American economy. Under these circumstances, federal budget cuts had the effect of reducing overall economic activity and further destroying the tax base. Many of our remaining high technology production lines were dependent on Pentagon contracts. Cut the defense budget, and this precious economic component is decimated. Cut Social Security and Medicare/Medicaid, and whole areas of medical and consumer sending became depressed. The lesson of the past 20 years is that budget cuts have the effect of cutting the economy and the tax base, and result in reduced tax receipts after the cuts have been carried out. Reduced tax receipts mean a bigger deficit. So the effect of budget cuts has been to *increase* the deficit every time. Austerity does not work; increased production and consumption work. It is far better to do nothing and live with the existing deficit than to undertake destructive austerity campaigns that leave things much worse than the simple status quo.

In 1985, the Gramm-Rudman-Hollings Act was signed into law by Reagan. This law featured the "planned train-wreck", or automatic sequestering of spending if the budget deficit did not meet certain pre-established targets. The backers of the Gramm-Rudman-Hollings guillotine wrote into law that the federal budget would be balanced by the year 1990. In order to reach this goal, the budget cutters were willing to sacrifice US defense spending for purely monetary goals whatever the USSR might be doing – at a time when the cold war was very much alive. By the time fiscal year 1991 ended, the US budget deficit was not zero, as prescribed by this law, but $386.4 billion. After dumping his own "Read-my-lips-no-new-taxes" pledge amidst much conflict with Congressional Republicans, Bush signed the budget deal of October, 1990 with its "son of Gramm-Rudman" feature, the triple rolling sequester that meant that any spending increases within the three main categories of federal expenditure had to be immediately covered by corresponding cuts within that category, or else by new taxes. Within a mere 2 years, this ingenious mechanism had raised the deficit to just short of $400 billion. Despite this experience, Sen. Phil Gramm started his bid for the 1996 GOP presidential nomination with yet another fiscal austerity pitch, promising that "as President, I will balance the federal budget the way you balance the family budget." Of course, the federal budget involves controlling money supply, interest rates, tax policy, the international value of the dollar, and a few other things that most families are unable to decide at the proverbial kitchen table. The failure of Sen. Gramm's candidacy indicates that more than a few voters rejected his oversimplifications.

By the end of the fiscal year on September 30, 1998, the Clinton Administration was claiming a balanced budget. This claim was made possible by a number of accounting tricks, including counting the Social Security payroll tax as a part of current income. Otherwise, the budget would have shown a deficit of some $60-70 billion, much better than Reagan/Bush, but a long way from the prosperity and recovery being alleged. The immense social cost of reaching even this superficial and cosmetic result have been hinted at above.

ENTITLEMENTS ARE YOUR ECONOMIC RIGHTS

The budget-balancers often proclaim that fiscal responsibility requires us to strip the American people of their entitlements. An entitlement, in current budget parlance, refers to Social Security, Medicaid, Medicare, and certain kinds of farm payments. An entitlement is usually an economic right under natural law which the US government has finally recognized, frequently under the influence of Franklin D. Roosevelt or his political heirs. These rights include the right not to be destitute, especially in one's old age, the right to comprehensive medical care at any age irrespective of income, and other rights. Welfare is an economic right that was recognized under Roosevelt and stripped away by Clinton's signature on the 1996 welfare law. Politicians like Perot and writers like Peter Peterson and Phillip Longman are examples of the attempt to make entitlement a dirty word. Their goal is simply to strip away the economic rights of the US population, starting with the weakest. Their moralistic posturings cloak the logic of Treasury bond holders, who want federal revenue channeled preferentially into their own pockets. They are impatient with those who recall that Social Security payments are a restitution of your own money, the money you paid in during your working years.

Longman writes that "today every American – rich, poor, middle class – knows he or she is entitled to a plethora of social benefits as a matter of 'right.'" [Longman, 2] "Today just over 50 percent of all US households contain at least one member who is receiving a direct entitlement benefit from the government, such as a veteran's or Social Security pension, unemployment compensation check, or disability payment....At any given time, 30 percent of the US population is receiving another form of entitlement: indirect benefits, expressly designed to subsidize some favored group such as home owners, farmers, or senior citizens, that government delivers through loopholes in the tax code. A prime example is the home mortgage deduction." [Longman, 3] "Reform of the US entitlement system means reform of the middle class and well-to-do." [Longman, 5] To paraphrase a popular discount broker, who do these guys think they're kidding? This kind of plutocratic sophistry is now widely discredited.

See for example Michael Lind, who comments that "conventional political journalists and think-tank experts bemoan the greed of 'the middle class'; we cannot blame the economic elite, they solemnly say, we are all to blame for the deficit." [Lind, 190] Longman for his part makes no secret of the fact that he wants to roll back what is left of the FDR New Deal and head off any residual possibility of a "Suburban New Deal" coming from the Carville-Greenberg wing of the Clinton camp or from the Gephardt forces. The kind of austerity being demanded would decimate the American middle class, which in its modern form is a direct product of the FDR New Deal. The basis for the existence of the modern American middle class is precisely the FDR-era entitlements: "When one analyzes the New Deal...one finds, particularly in the case of the [post-June 1933] second New Deal, a program to elevate the labor-dependent classes in society, that is, the small farmers, the small businesspersons, and labor, unionized or not – all of whom were dependent upon employment and not capital income for their livelihood." [Strobel, 16] Abolish the entitlements, and you have gone far towards abolishing the middle class.

In a related polemic, the stagnation of American median family income has been whitewashed recently in public print by the economic columnist of *Newsweek* and the *Washington Post*, Robert J. Samuelson. Samuelson's shtick is berating his middle-class readers for complaining about their declining standards of living. If middle America shared the wisdom of Samuelson, he suggests, they would realize that they are better off after all. For Samuelson, the US middle class must simply abandon its exaggerated expectations and exorbitant pretensions in order to realize that they've never had it so good. Your problem, says Samuelson, is that you feel entitled in the first place. Statistics showing stagnation and decline are buried by Samuelson under an avalanche of "VCRs, personal computers, cable TV, microwave ovens." After all, you can't argue with an appliance. In attempting to propagate such gadget-based euphoria, Samuelson has done his best to confuse the reasonably clear picture offered by the official data. In his 1995 book *The Good Life and its Discontents*, he refused to publish even the government's own most recent (massaged) data for 1991-1993.[103] Samuelson decided that these data were "unduly distorted" by too many low-wage Hispanics and also by the "lingering effect from the 1990-1991 recession."

---

[103] See Robert J. Samuelson, *The Good Life and its Discontents: The American Dream in the Age of Entitlement 1945-1995* (New York: Times Books, 1996). See also the *Newsweek* cover story, "It's Not as Bad as You Think," January 8, 1996.

The real reason, of course, was that Samuelson was embarrassed by what he admits was a "sharp drop" in median family income over 1990-1993. This represented a problem for Samuelson because the goal of his book is to convince middle Americans that their daily experience of slow economic strangulation is just a figment of their imaginations. Samuelson did not refer to the figures for average weekly earnings cited above, which present the reality of decline more starkly because they are not supplemented by second and third jobs.

Samuelson also used his *Newsweek* column to attack anybody who even vaguely approaches telling the truth about the falling American standard of living. On September 23, 1996 he wrote a shabby piece called "Confederacy of Dunces" to attack as "junk journalism" a series of articles then being published in the *Philadelphia Enquirer* on the very timely theme of "America: Who Stole the Dream?" As usual, Samuelson cited statistics on how many American homes have hairdryers, toasters, dishwashers, etc. to claim that "statistics implying lower living standards are contradicted by what people buy or own." This is propaganda, not economic science.

HOUSEHOLD DEBT

Household debt, including mortgage debt and consumer debt, was a mere $1,632 per household in 1950. By 1995, the average household was in hock to the tune of $49,248. The average family would have need more than 120 weekly paychecks to pay off this debt. Another by-product of inadequate wages is credit-card debt, which is only partially reflected in the overall household debt figure just cited. By the spring of 1997, Americans' credit cards were groaning under $1.21 trillion of high-interest debt. By September 1998, the installment figure had climbed to $1.26 trillion. That came to more than twelve thousand dollars per household. During the Bush Administration, it was calculated that one average paycheck was no longer enough to pay the median household expenditure of mortgage payment, and car payment, plus health, homeowners, and liability insurance costs. That left nothing at all for food, clothing, utilities, or anything else. Small wonder that the single-paycheck family is now the exceptional case.

PERSONAL BANKRUPTCIES: THE NIGHT OF THE LIVING DEBT

Another measure of the desperation of individuals and families is the pace of personal bankruptcies. In 1986, hardly a good year, there were 500,000 personal bankruptcy filings. 1996 saw more than a million personal bankruptcies, a record. But in the twelve months ending on June 30, 1997, personal bankruptcy filings totaled more than 1.3 million, showing that things were getting rapidly worse, and not better. And during the period April 1 to June 30, 1997, fully 367,168 persons, families and businesses (13,991) went under – the largest quarterly total ever, according to the Administrative Office of the US Courts in Washington. (*Washington Post*, August 31, 1997] In the year ending June 30, 1998, there was a new all-time record of **1.4 million personal bankruptcies**. One out of every 70 American households was now going bankrupt every year.

In the summer of 1998, Congressional Republicans were promoting a new measure to make the clean slate and fresh start of a chapter 7 bankruptcy more difficult for the average person to obtain. Supporters of this bill, including the lobbyists of VISA, MasterCard, and American Express, outdid each other in posturing about the decline in moral fiber which allowed so many Americans to take what had once been considered the shameful route of personal bankruptcy. The rampant usury of the credit card companies and declining standards of living were not discussed; the message was Just Say No to filing for Chapter 7. A few Democrats responded by citing the blank checks and incitements to spend freely being sent through the mail to minors with no job and no income. Democratic Rep. Nadler of New York pointed out that the so-called reform gave banks the right to collect from debtors before child support or federal back taxes had been paid. Nadler noted that under the new regime, many Americans who were in fact insolvent would be viewed by the law as too rich for Chapter 7, and too poor for Chapter 13, and would thus be denied relief. In the meantime, credit card companies, sometimes dangling the promise of restored credit, were attempting to trick or coerce unwary borrowers into paying the old debts they had expunged through bankruptcy. Said San Jose bankruptcy attorney Ike Shulman of the bill collectors' tactics: "It's like the night of the living dead."[104]

THE CRUSHING OF THE MIDDLE CLASS

The middle class has not been around very long, historically speaking, as the most numerous and most important component of human society. The origin of a numerous, urban middle class engaged in trade, small and medium industry, and the free professions within European civilization goes back to the Medici of Florence and their international textile production, commercial, and banking operations. In the dark ages in Europe, there had been no middle class to speak of: there were the wretched serfs on the land, the lords in the castle, and very little in between, since a town of any size was a genuine rarity in the landscape. In France, towns and cities grew up under the Medici influence and provided the political constituency for the first modern nation state, the one created by Louis XI, who reigned from 1461 to 1483. Louis XI used the middle class of the towns as a base for attacks against the unruly barons and oligarchs of the French nobility. King Henry VII of England, the first of the Tudor line and the founder of the New Monarchy, did something very similar. So the modern state and the middle class have always gone hand in hand.

In post-1945 America, political conditions and union organization permitted a very large portion of prosperous blue-collar factory workers to own homes, send their children to college, and to otherwise acquire a middle-class standard of living. The middle class is the indispensable social stratum for a democratic republic. The small industrial concern with its middle-class owner is typically the interface between the scientific laboratory and the production line, the point where an invention becomes a machine tool. Old Karl Marx, that British-backed slanderer of industrial capitalism, saved his most bitter contempt for the middle class (what he called the petty bourgeoisie) because he sensed that this group was really the key to modern society. Machiavelli's famous *Discorsi* show that he viewed a large middle class as a precondition for the stable government of a republic.

Historically, the hallmark of the middle class has been its independence. A small or medium industrialist, a doctor or lawyer in private practice, a small businessman, or a family farmer often owed their livelihood to no single power center, and were accordingly not easy to order around and oppress. As the family farm has been wiped out as a matter of government policy in the service of the food cartels, as the small and medium industrialist has been eliminated by conglomerates and leveraged buy-outs, as the independent doctor and lawyer have been swallowed up by the large law firm and HMO, and with expansion of low-level white collar jobs in corporate and government bureaucracies, the independence of the middle class has been eroded. As C. Wright Mills noted, the American middle class was structurally weakened after 1945. If you crush the American middle class, you are left with a vast and impoverished underclass and a tiny but opulent overclass making up about 1% of the population or less. Societies of this form cannot realize scientific and industrial progress, since too few people are sufficiently educated to be productive. Societies of this form

---

[104] *Washington Post*, September 13, 1998.

cannot escape the destruction of class warfare and cannot be stable. All this explains why the statistics suggesting the rapid erosion of the American middle class compel our attention.

The *New Yorker* magazine recently profiled the Iowa working family of Bonita and Kenny Merton of Des Moines. This is a family which is going deeper and deeper into debt in a desperate struggle to maintain a standard of living. Kenny Merton's comment surpasses reams of sociological analysis: "There ain't no middle class any more. There's only rich and poor." [105]

Another hallmark of the American middle class was the possession of a savings account at the local bank. Today, there are almost no savers left, but more and more self-styled investors who turn out to be day traders and speculators in a crapshoot they cannot understand. A watershed in regard to America's savings came when the Commerce Department announced that the savings rate had turned negative, with savings declining by 0.2% in September 1998. The savings rate measures the share of disposable personal income which remains after all purchases have been made. In that September, disposable personal income was $6.055 trillion, while spending hit $6.067 trillion, leaving $12 billion in red ink for American families. These were the families who filled up their credit cards to maintain their standard of living, and then re-financed the credit card balances with home equity loans, a fancy name for second mortgages. Now, the credit cards were fully loaded once again. Something had to give, and that produced what some accounts termed the first decline in the savings rate since 1959, when the government first began publishing this monthly data series. But that was deliberately misleading, since nobody believes the savings rate was ever negative during the late 1950s, despite the severe recession of those years. The *Wall Street Journal* reported with brutal cynicism that, in reality, this was thought to be the first decline in the savings rate since 1933, the year in which the Great Depression touched bottom for American wage workers. In short, the American standard of living was headed back toward 1933.

Insights into the political reflection of this same basic problem came from Stan Greenberg, Clinton's sometime pollster. During the middle 1980s, Greenberg carried out a series of interviews in Macomb County, Michigan, the suburban area north of Detroit that includes cities like Warren and Centerline. This is an area of neat single-family homes, and represents one of the classic manifestations of American suburbia. Greenberg found what he later described as "A New Middle-Class Consciousness:" He chronicled "a middle-class consciousness built out of the wreckage of Democratic and Republican economic failures: First, the middle class, while the center of this new world, is poised for extinction. Second, the middle class is being crushed by growing bills, taxes, and the cost of basic necessities. Third, husbands and wives are working harder and longer hours, sacrificing family life, and putting children at risk, but only to pay for basics, not to really get ahead. And fourth, the wealthy are making out just fine." When asked what they thought was happening to the middle class, people used words like "endangered," "overtaxed," "shrinking," "fading away," "declining," and "there is none." The dominant idea was that the middle class was disappearing, and that before too long there would be the millionaires on one side and the poor or the other, with nothing in between. "Everybody is going to be either very rich or very poor. There's going to be the rich in their little towers, and there's going to be everybody else floundering around trying to survive." [Greenberg, 165] This was clearly realistic, but at the same time it was no future for America.

---

[105] Susan Sheehan, "Ain't No Middle Class," *The New Yorker*, December 11, 1995.

CHAPTER
VI. MODELS OF COLLAPSE

Well, they hired the money, didn't they?
– Calvin Coolidge, *Literary Digest*, March 24, 1923.

We need to emphasize once again a fundamental concept of this book: the financial and economic cataclysm that is now at the gates will be fundamentally different from what most people associate with the crash of 1929. The crash of 1929, strictly speaking, was an example of financial collapse. Stock values plummeted and unemployment skyrocketed, but the New York Stock Exchange remained open and an orderly market for shares of stock re-emerged, although prices kept declining. Only in 1931 did disintegration set in, and this was not because of stock market events in New York, but rather because of the British pound sterling default on gold payment. 1932-3 brought the disintegration to America in the form of a banking panic.

COLLAPSE VS. DISINTEGRATION

The coming cataclysm will include events of a fundamentally different type. This time, to repeat, entire chunks of the world financial system will be simply annihilated, possibly within the course of a few days, just as Barings Bank was. This class may well include the International Monetary Fund, the World Bank, the Federal Reserve, the Bank for International Settlements, the Bank of England and the other central banks of the G-7 nations. If current policies are continued, the US dollar is a likely goner, along with every sort of paper promise to pay anything. Our thesis is that we are currently – in the winter of 1998 – experiencing the final collapse phases of a crisis without precedent. We will experience collapse, but the crisis will not end there. After the collapse phase, some time during the next year or two or three, we will enter into the terrifying maelstrom of financial disintegration.

In this chapter we will look back at the crash of 1929 as a case study in financial collapse. In the next chapter we will examine the German hyperinflation of 1923 and the British default of 1931 (among other examples) for clues as to the nature of the disintegration which awaits us beyond the waves of collapse.

HOW THE CITY OF LONDON CREATED THE CRASH OF 1929

The events leading to the Great Depression are all related to British economic warfare against the rest of the world, which initially took the form of the attempt to restore a London-centered world monetary system incorporating the gold standard. The efforts of the British oligarchy in this regard were carried out by a clique of international central bankers dominated by Lord Montagu Norman of the Bank of England, assisted by Benjamin Strong of the New York Federal Reserve Bank and Hjalmar Schacht of the German Reichsbank. This British-controlled gold standard proved to be a straightjacket for world economic development, somewhat along the lines of the deflationary Maastricht "convergence criteria" for Europe in the late 1990s. The parallel extends to Britain's opting out of the European Monetary Union while watching its victims writhe in a deflationary straightjacket tailored between Threadneedle Street and Saville Row.

The New York stock exchange speculation of the Coolidge-Hoover era was not a spontaneous phenomenon, but was rather deliberately encouraged by Norman and Strong under the pretext of relieving pressure on the overvalued British pound sterling after its gold convertibility had been restored. In practice, the pro-speculation policies of the US Federal Reserve were promoted by Montagu Norman and his satellites for the express purpose of fomenting a Bubble Economy in the United States, just as later central bankers fostered a Bubble Economy in Japan after 1986.

When this Wall Street Bubble had reached gargantuan proportions in the autumn of 1929, Montagu Norman manipulated the British bank rate sharply upwards, repatriating British hot money, and pulling the rug out from under the Wall Street speculators, thus deliberately and consciously imploding the US markets. This caused a violent depression in the United States and some other countries, with the collapse of financial markets and the contraction of production and employment. In 1929, Norman engineered a collapse. As we have already hinted, we consider that these matters are not merely of historical interest. The repertoire of central bank intrigue, speculative bubbles, defaults, devaluations, bank rate manipulations, deflations and inflations constitute the essential arsenal being used by British and other European oligarchical economic warfare planners today.

Lord Montagu Norman was always obsessed with secrecy, but the British financial press has often practiced an arrogant and cynical bluntness in its self-congratulatory accounts of its own exploits. Therefore, wherever possible we will let the British, especially the London *Economist* magazine and Lord Keynes, speak for themselves and indict themselves. We have also drawn on the memoirs of US President Herbert Hoover, who had moments of surprising lucidity even as he, for the sake of absurd free-market, *laissez-faire* ideology, allowed his country to drift into the abyss. As we will see, Hoover had everything he needed to base his 1932 campaign for re-election on blaming the Federal Reserve, especially its New York branch, for the 1929 calamity. Hoover could have assailed the British for their September 1931, self-inflicted devaluation. Hoover would have been doing the country a permanent service, and he might have done somewhat better in the electoral college. But Hoover was not psychologically capable of attacking the New York Fed and its master, Lord Montagu Norman.

ECONOMIC DECLINE AFTER WORLD WAR I

The roots of the crash of 1929 are to be sought in the economic consequences of World War I, which was itself a product of the British geopolitical machinations of King Edward VII and his circles. The physical impact of World War I was absolutely devastating in terms of human losses and material damage. This destruction was then greatly magnified by the insistence of London and Paris on reparations to be paid by defeated and prostrate Germany. After a few years of haggling, these reparations were fixed at the then-astronomical sum of 32 billion gold-backed US dollars, to be paid over 62 years at an interest rate of 5%. According to this plan, Germany would have been paying reparations well into the 1980s. Even Lord Keynes, in his "Economic Consequences of the Peace," compared this to the imposition of slavery on Germany and her defeated allies, or to squeezing a lemon so hard that the pits squeak.

The reparations issue was complicated by the inter-allied war debts, owed especially by France and Britain to the United States. For a time, a system emerged in which Wall Street made loans to Germany so that Germany could pay reparations to France, which could then pay war debts to Britain and the US. But this system was based on usury, not production, and was therefore doomed. The most dramatic evidence available on economic stagnation during the 1920s is the fact that during this decade world trade never attained the pre-war level of 1913.

LORD MONTAGU NORMAN'S CABAL OF CENTRAL BANKERS

A dominant personality of the City of London during these years was Sir Montagu Norman, the Governor of the Bank of England during the period 1920-1944. Norman came from a line of bankers. His grandfather was Sir Mark Wilks Collet, who had himself been Governor of the Bank of England during the 1880s. Collet had also been a partner in the London firm of Brown, Shipley & Co., and also in the New York bank of Brown Brothers & Co., later Brown Brothers, Harriman and in that guise one of the most politically potent banks on the wrong side of modern American history. The dominant figure of this bank was W. Averell Harriman, who – as we have shown in other locations – had much to do with the Cold War, the Korean War, and the Vietnam War.[106] The managing partner of Brown Brothers, Harriman during the 1930s was Prescott Bush, father of the later President George Herbert Walker Bush.[107]

Acting by himself and relying only on his own British resources, Montagu Norman could hardly have aspired to play the role of currency dictator of Europe. Norman's trump card was his ability to manipulate the policies of the United States Federal Reserve System through a series of Morgan-linked collaborators.

As Governor of the Bank of England, Montagu Norman was the central figure in an international cabal of central bankers which included most importantly Fed co-founder Benjamin Strong of the New York Federal Reserve Bank, then as now the flagship of the entire system. Strong was Governor of the New York Federal Reserve Bank between 1914 and his death in 1929. Strong was an operative of the House of Morgan who had worked at Bankers Trust and helped to found the corporate culture of that bank. Montagu Norman also owned a large piece of Hjalmar Schacht, Governor of the German Reichsbank and later Finance Minister in governments in which Adolf Hitler was chancellor. Montagu Norman himself, along with King Edward VIII, Lady Astor and Sir Neville Chamberlain, was one of the strongest supporters of Hitler in the British aristocracy. Norman put his personal prestige on the line in September 1933 to support the Hitler regime in its first attempt to float a loan in London.

THE FEDERAL RESERVE: CAUSE OF DEPRESSION

One of the main causes for the Great Depression of the 1930s, and also for the financial cataclysm which is now upon us, is the Federal Reserve System of the United States. Many naive persons think of the Federal Reserve System as a part of the United States government, which it emphatically is not. Probably this is because the only money we have nowadays is marked "Federal Reserve Note." The Federal Reserve is a privately owned and privately managed institution. Those who can remember the 1960s can recall that there were once dollar silver certificates as well as United States Notes, the descendants of Lincoln's greenbacks, in several denominations. But after the Kennedy assassination, the private Federal Reserve established a monopoly on printing money.

In this way the Federal Reserve System violates the letter and spirit of the United States Constitution. There, in Article I, Section 8, Clause 5 we read that the Congress shall have the power "to coin money, regulate the value thereof, and of foreign coin, and fix the standard of weights and measures." This indicates that the only legal way we have to direct US monetary and interest rate policy is by way of an act of Congress which has been signed into law by the President. This disposition cannot be altered by statute; to depart from it would require a full-fledged constitutional amendment.

---

[106] See W. Tarpley, *Against Oligarchy* online at www.tarpley.net.
[107] See *George Bush: The Unauthorized Biography*, online at www.tarpley.net.

The Federal Reserve was created in December 1913 when Woodrow Wilson signed the Glass-Owen bill into law as the Federal Reserve Act. That bill had been the product of cloak-and-dagger machinations by Wall Street financiers and their political mouthpieces, many of them in league with the City of London. Wall Streeter Frank A. Vanderlip, the president of the National City Bank (at that time the largest bank in America), in his autobiography *From Farm Boy to Financier* narrates that the secret conference which planned the Federal Reserve was "as secret - indeed, as furtive - as any conspirator." Vanderlip was one of the insiders invited to the Jekyll Island Club on the coast of Georgia in the autumn of 1910 by the Senator Nelson Aldrich, the father-in-law of John D. Rockefeller Jr. Aldrich also invited Henry Davison of J.P. Morgan & Co., and Benjamin Strong, the future Governor of the New York Federal Reserve Bank. Also on hand was Paul Warburg of the notorious international banking family, descended from the Del Banco clan of Venice. "We were instructed to come one at a time and as unobtrusively as possible to the railway terminal on the New Jersey littoral of the Hudson, where Senator Aldrich's private car would be in readiness, attached to the rear end of a train for the South," wrote Vanderlip.

JEKYLL ISLAND

On Jekyll Island this crew began to decide the main features of the central bank of the United States: "We worked morning, noon, and night.... As we dealt with questions I recorded our agreements...If it was to be a central bank, how was it to be owned - by the banks, by the Government or jointly? When we had fixed upon bank ownership and joint control, we took up the political problem of whether it should be a number of institutions or only one." In the end, says Vanderlip, "there can be no question about it: Aldrich undoubtedly laid the essential, fundamental lines which finally took the form of the Federal reserve law." [Vanderlip]

Today each of the twelve Federal Reserve Banks - Boston, New York, Chicago, San Francisco, and so forth - is a private corporation. The shares are held by the member banks of the Federal Reserve System. The Class A and Class B Directors of each Federal Reserve Bank are elected by the shareholders from among bankers and the business community, and other Directors are appointed by the Federal Reserve Board in Washington. Members of the Board of Governors of the Federal Reserve System in Washington are chosen by the President and must be approved by the Senate, for what that is worth. But when we come to the vital Federal Reserve Open Market Committee, which sets short-term interest rates and influences the size of the money supply by buying or selling government securities, the picture is even worse. The FOMC comprises 7 Fed Governors from Washington plus 5 presidents of Federal Reserve Banks appointed by the respective Directors of these banks. The New York Federal Reserve is always represented. In practice, 5 Federal Reserve district presidents who have never been seen by the President or voted on by the Congress have a vote on setting the credit policy and money supply of the United States. Public policy is made by a private cabal of self-appointed and self-coopting plutocrats.

How was this sleazy product marketed to the Congress? Interestingly, the Congressmen were told that the Federal Reserve System would prevent panics and depressions like those of the 1870s and 1890s. Here is a sampling compiled by Herbert Hoover of selling points used by lobbyists seeking votes for the Federal Reserve Act:

> We shall have no more financial panics.... Panics are impossible....Business men can now proceed in perfect confidence that they will no longer put their property in peril.... Now the business man may work out his destiny without living in terror of panic and hard times.... Panics in the future are unthinkable.... Never again can panic come to the American people. [Hoover, 7]

The verdict of history must be that the Federal Reserve has utterly failed to deliver on these promises. The most potent political argument against this arrangement is that it has been a resounding failure. Far from making financial crises impossible, the Fed has brought us one Great Depression, and it is about to bring us a super-depression, a worldwide disintegration.

THE BRITISH RECORD OF STARTING WALL STREET PANICS

It is time to put away all the nonsense about waves, cycles, and epicycles which has been peddled by the economists of the world. The simple fact is that American financial panics have generally been deliberately manufactured by the London finance oligarchy with the help of American financiers, for political and strategic, as well as economic, reasons.

- In the Panic of 1837, the stage had been set for depression by outgoing President Andrew Jackson's and Secretary of the Treasury Roger Taney's abolition of the Second Bank of the United States, by their cultivation of the state "pet" banks, by their imbecilic Specie Circular of 1836, which demanded gold payment to the federal government for the purchase of public lands, and by their improvident distribution of the Treasury surplus to the states. London's ultimate weapon turned out to be the Bank of England bank rate. With all the American defenses sabotaged, the Bank of England sharply raised its discount rates, and gold specie and hot money liquidity fled back across the Atlantic, while British merchants and trading houses cut off their lines of credit to their American customers. In the resulting chaos, not only did private banks and businesses go bankrupt, but also the states of Mississippi, Louisiana, Maryland, Pennsylvania, Indiana, and Michigan repudiated their debts, permanently impairing US credit in the world. Internal improvements came to a halt, and the drift towards secession and civil war became more pronounced.

- The Panic of 1873 resulted from a British-directed effort to ruin the banking house of Jay Cooke and Company, which had served Lincoln and his successors as a quasi-governmental agency for the marketing of United States Treasury securities and railroad bonds during and after the Civil War. During the Civil War, Cooke had financed the Union cause with a precursor of the savings bond, which he sold to the American people in small denominations. The Cooke insolvency had been preceded by a massive dumping of US stocks and bonds in London and the rest of Europe. This was London's way of shutting down the Civil War boom that Lincoln's dirigist and protectionist policies had made possible. Instead, a long depression followed.

- The Panic of 1893 was prepared by the 1890 "Baring panic" in London, caused by the insolvency of Barings Bank, the same bank which again went bankrupt and was sold off in the spring of 1995. In the resulting depression, the US Treasury surplus was reduced to almost nothing, and a budget deficit loomed. Using this situation as a pretext, British speculators drove the exchange rate of the dollar down to the point where owners of gold began exporting their gold to London. Treasury gold stocks dipped below $100,000,000, and then kept falling to $68,000,000; US national bankruptcy threatened. In response to this crisis, the feckless President Grover Cleveland gave control of the US public debt to the New York banking houses and Morgan and Belmont, themselves British agents of influence. Cleveland capitulated to Wall Street by selling US gold bonds to Morgan and Belmont at reduced prices, with the taxpayers picking up the tab; Morgan and Belmont promised to "use their influence" in London to prevent further British bear raids against the US dollar and gold stocks. All of this caused another long depression.

The economics profession is largely bankrupt today, with virtually every recent Nobel Prize winner in economics with the sole clear exception of Maurice Allais a likely candidate for admission to a psychiatric institution. One of the reasons for the depravity of the economists is that their assigned task has always been one of mystification, especially the job of covering up the simple and brutal fact that American depressions have generally been caused by Bank of England and City of London bankers. All the mystical mumbo-jumbo of curves and business cycles and creative destruction (Joseph Schumpeter is a good example) has always had the purpose of camouflaging the fact that the Bank of England bank rate was the nineteenth century's closest equivalent to the hydrogen bomb.

DEFLATION CRISIS OF 1920-21

The New York panic of 1920-21 represents yet another example of British economic warfare. The illusion that the existence of the Federal Reserve System might serve as a barrier against new financial panics and depressions received a nasty knock with the immediate postwar depression of 1920, which was a co-production of the Bank of England and the New York Federal Reserve. The British deliberately provoked this Wall Street panic and severe depression during a period of grave military tension between London and Washington occasioned by the naval rivalry of these two powers.[108] The British Bank Rate had been at 6% from November 1919 until April 15, 1920, when it was raised to 7%. The bust in Wall Street began in the late summer of 1920. The UK bank rate was lowered to 6.5% in April 1922, and it went all the way to 3% by July 1922.

The Federal Reserve, as usual, followed London's lead, gradually escalating the discount rate to 7% in June 1920, and descending to 6.5% about a year later. The argument used by the central bankers' cabal to justify their extreme tight money policy was the need to fight the climate of postwar inflation, speculation, expansion and freeing of consumer demand that had been pent up in wartime. This depression lasted about two years and was quite sharp, with a New York composite index of transaction indices falling 13.7% – the sharpest contraction since 1879. In many other countries this was the fiercest depression on record. As Keynes later complained, the US recovered much more rapidly than the British, who scarcely recovered at all.

The fact that this depression was brought on deliberately by the Norman-Strong duo is amply documented in their private correspondence. In December 1920, Strong and Norman agreed that "the policy of making money dearer had been successful, though it would have been better six months earlier. They agreed, too, that deflation must be gradual; it was becoming now too rapid and they favored a small reduction in rates both in London and New York." [Clay 132]

THE CRASH OF 1929

The panic of 1929 is a prime example of a financial collapse which was not prevented by the Federal Reserve. In fact, the 1920s speculative bubble and subsequent crash of 1929 were directly caused by Federal Reserve policies. Those policies in turn had been dictated by the world of British finance, which had been decisive in shaping the Federal Reserve to begin with.

During World War I, all the industrialized nations except the United States had left the gold standard. Only the United States had been able to stay on gold, albeit with protective exchange controls. During the 1920s, about two thirds of the world's supply of monetary gold, apart from Soviet holdings, was concentrated in two countries – the United States and France. The British, who were fighting to preserve their dominance of the world financial system, had very little gold. The British were determined to pursue their traditional economic imperialism, but they had emerged from the war economically devastated and, for the first time, as a debtor nation owing war debts to

---

[108] See discussion of War Plan Red in *Against Oligarchy*, online at www.tarpley.net.

the United States. At the same time, the British were fighting to keep their precious world naval supremacy, which was threatened by the growth of the United States Navy. If the US had merely built the ships that were called for in laws passed in 1916, or had carried out General Billy Mitchell's policy of naval supremacy from the air, the slogan of "Britannia Rules the Waves" would have gone into the dust-bin of history during the 1920s. In the event, British naval domination lasted well into World War II.

The pre-war gold parity had given a dollar to pound relation of $4.86 per pound sterling. As an avid imperialist, Montagu Norman was insisting by the mid-1920s that the pound return to the gold standard at the pre-war rate. A high pound was a disaster for British exports, but gave the British great advantages when it came to buying American and other foreign real estate, stocks, minerals, food, and all other external commodities. A high pound also maximized British earnings on insurance, shipping, and financial services.

THE GOLD EXCHANGE STANDARD, 1925-1931

The nineteenth century gold standard had always been an instrument of British world domination. The best economic growth achieved by the United States during the century had been registered between 1861 and the implementation of the Specie Resumption Act, which took effect in 1879. During that time the United States enjoyed the advantage of its own nationally controlled currency, Lincoln's greenbacks. Specie resumption meant re-opening the Treasury window where holders of paper dollars could have these dollars exchanged for gold coins. The United States in 1879 thus returned to a gold coin standard, under which paper money circulated side by side with $20 and $50 gold pieces. This practice proved to be deflationary and detrimental to economic development, while it increased American vulnerability to British currency manipulations. Some of these disadvantages were pointed out by the Populists of the 1890s. (See Chapter IX)

The post-1918 gold standard de-emphasized the circulation of gold coins. It was rather a gold exchange standard, under which smaller countries could hold some of their reserves in the leading gold-backed currencies like the pound sterling or the dollar. These currencies were counted as theoretically as good as gold. The advantage to the smaller countries was that they could keep their reserves on deposit in London and earn interest according to the British bank rate. As one London commentator noted at the time, "...many countries returning to gold" have had such confidence in the stability of the system, and in particular in the security of the dollar and of sterling, that they have been content to leave part of the reserves of their currencies in London." [*Economist*, September 26, 1931, p. 549]

The post-1918 gold exchange standard included the workings of the so-called gold points. This had to do with the relation of currency quotations to the established gold parity. Norman wanted the pound sterling to be worth $4.86. If the pound strengthened so as to trade for $5, let us say, then the pound was said to have exceeded the gold import point. American and other gold would be shipped to London by those who owned gold. If, as later happened, the pound went down to 4.50 dollars to the pound, then the pound was said to have passed the gold export point, and British gold would be physically shipped to New York to take advantage of the superior earnings there. This meant that if Norman wanted to keep a strong pound, he needed to weaken the dollar, since with a strong dollar the British gold would flee from London, forcing Norman to devalue the pound sterling by lowering the gold parity. Notice that gold movements were to some degree based on the decisions of individual banks and investors.

(During the later 1930s, after the a period in which the dollar floated downward in terms of gold, the United States under Franklin D. Roosevelt established a gold reserve standard, called by FDR's critics a "qualified external bullion standard," in which gold transactions were limited to settlements with foreign central banks, while private citizens were barred from holding gold. This qualified external bullion standard was similar to the gold reserve provisions of the Bretton Woods system of 1944-1971, and would today represent the appropriate centerpiece of a new world monetary system for the 21st century.)

Norman's problem was that his return to the pre-1914 pound rate was much too high for the ravaged post-1918 British economy to support. Both the US and the British had undergone an economic downturn in the early 1920s, but while the US soon bounced back, the British were never able to recover. British manufactures were now considered low-quality and obsolete.

CHURCHILL: THE GOLDEN CHANCELLOR

Nevertheless, Norman insisted on a gold pound at $4.86. He had to convince Winston Churchill, the Chancellor of the Exchequer. Norman whispered into Churchill's ear: "I will make you the golden chancellor." Great Britain and the rest of the Empire returned to the gold standard in April 1925. Norman himself craved the title of "currency dictator of Europe." And indeed, many of the continental central banks were in his pocket. Nevertheless, it was much easier to return to the gold standard than it was to stay there. British industrial exports, including coal, were priced out of the world market, and unemployment rose to 1.2 million, the highest since Britain had become an industrial country. Emile Moreau, the governor of the Bank of France, commented that Norman's gold standard had "provoked unemployment without precedent in world history." British coal miners were especially hard hit, and Britain experienced a general strike, which was defeated with Winston Churchill as chief strike-breaker.

But Norman did not care. He was a supporter of the post-industrial society based on the service sector, especially financial services. The high pound meant that British oligarchs could buy up the world's assets at bargain basement prices. They could buy US and European real estate, banks, and firms. Norman's goal was British financial supremacy:

> ...his sights remained stubbornly fixed on the main target: that of restoring the City to its coveted place at the heart of the financial and banking universe. Here was the best and most direct means, as he saw it, of earning as much for Britain in a year as could be earned in a decade by plaintive industrialists who refused to move with the times. The City could do more for the country by concentrating on the harvest of invisible exports to be reaped from banking, shipping, and insurance than could all the backward industrialists combined. [Boyle 222]

Montagu Norman's golden pound would have been unthinkable without the puppet role of Benjamin Strong of the New York Federal Reserve Bank. Since the pound was grotesquely overvalued, the British were running a balance of payments deficit because of their excess of imports over exports. That meant that Norman had to ship gold from the Bank of England across the Atlantic. The British gold started to flow towards New York, where most of the world's gold already was.

The only way to stop the flow of gold from London to New York, Norman reasoned, was to get the United States to launch a policy of easy money, low interest rates, reflation, more consumer goods, fewer capital goods for export, and a weak dollar - in short, a policy of inflation. The key to obtaining this was Benjamin Strong, who dominated the New York Fed, and was in a position to dominate the entire Federal Reserve system which was, of course, independent of the political control of the elected US government which these oligarchs so much resented.

NORMAN CREATES THE AMERICAN BUBBLE ECONOMY

In essence, Norman's demand was that the US should launch a bubble economy. The newly-generated credit could be used for American loans to Germany or Latin America. Or, it could be used to leverage speculative purchases of stocks. Very soon, most of the new credit was flowing into broker call loans for margin buying of stocks. There are many parallels between the measures urged for the US by Norman in 1925 and the policies urged on Japan by London and Wall Street in 1986, leading to the Japanese bubble and the subsequent banking crisis, which ushered in the millennium meltdown.

In 1925, as the pound was returning to gold, Montagu Norman, Hjalmar Schacht and Charles Rist (the deputy governor of the Banque de France) visited Benjamin Strong in New York to mobilize their network of influential insiders for easy money and low interest rates in the US. Strong was able to obtain the policies requested by Norman. Norman & Co. made a second pilgrimage to Wall Street between 28 June and 1 July 1927 to promote American speculation and inflation. On this second lobbying trip, Norman was frantic because the first half of 1927 had witnessed a large movement of gold into New York. Strong and his cabal immediately went into action.

The second coming of Norman and Schacht in 1927 motivated Strong to force through a new reflation of the money supply in July and a further cut in the US discount rate in August of that same year. The rediscount rate of the New York Fed was cut from 4% to 3.5%. This was the cheap credit which stoked the culminating phase of the Coolidge Bull Market during 1928 and 1929. Strong also got the FOMC to begin buying US Treasury securities in open market operations, leaving the banks flush with cash. This cash soon wandered into the broker call loan market, where it was borrowed by stock speculators to buy stock on margin, fueling a growing stock speculation. Interest rates in London were supposed, according to Norman, to be kept above those in New York - although Norman later deviated from this when it suited him.

In his essay "The Economic Consequences of Mr. Churchill," Lord Keynes noted that the British had returned to gold at a rate that was at least 10% too high; Keynes showed that the British government had also chosen a policy of deliberately increasing unemployment, especially in the export industries, in order to drive down wages. In order to stem the flow of gold out of London, Keynes observed, the Bank of England's policy was to "encourage the United States to lend us money by maintaining the unprecedented situation of a bill rate 1 per cent higher in London than in New York." [Keynes, 254]

THE FEDERAL RESERVE FOMENTS INFLATION

One alarmed observer of these events was, ironically, Secretary of Commerce Herbert Hoover of the Coolidge administration, who condemned the Fed policies as "direct inflation." "In November, 1925," recounted Hoover later, "it was confirmed to me by Adolph Miller, a member of the Reserve Board, that Strong and his European allies proposed still more 'easy money policies,' which included continued manipulation of the discount rates and open market operations - more inflation." Hoover says he protested to Fed chairman Daniel Crissinger, a political appointee left over from the Harding era, and a man who was in over his head. "The other members of the board," says Hoover, "except Adolph Miller, were mediocrities, and Governor Strong was a mental annex of Europe." [Hoover, 9-10]

Hoover had to some extent struggled behind the scenes in 1925 against Norman's demands, but by 1927 he had begun to defer in matters of high finance to Coolidge's Secretary of the Treasury,

Ogden Mills, who was willing to go along with the Bank of England program. After the crash, Hoover's friend Adolph Miller of the Fed Board of Governors told a committee of the US Senate:

> In the year 1927...you will note the pronounced increase in these holdings [US Treasury securities held by the Fed] in the second half of the year. Coupled with the heavy purchases of acceptances it was the greatest and boldest operation every undertaken by the Federal Reserve System, and, in my judgment, resulted in one of the most costly errors committed by it or any other banking system in the last 75 years....What was the object of the Federal Reserve Policy in 1927? It was to bring down money rates, the call rate among them, because of the international importance the call rate had come to acquire. The purpose was to start an outflow of gold – to reverse the previous inflow of gold into this country.[109]

A few years later the British economist Lionel Robbins offered the following commentary on Miller's testimony: "The policy succeeded.... The London position was eased. The reflation succeeded. But from that date, the situation got completely out of control. By 1928 the authorities were thoroughly frightened. But now the forces they had released were too strong for them. In vain they issued secret warnings. In vain they pushed up their own rates of discount. Velocity of circulation, the frenzied anticipation of speculators and company promoters, had now taken control. With resignation the best men in the system looked forward to the inevitable smash." [Robbins, 53-54]

CENTRAL BANKS DELIBERATELY PRODUCED STUPENDOUS INFLATION

Robbins contends that the Wall Street bubble of 1925-1929 was built on top of an economy that was sinking into recession in 1925. The Norman-Strong bubble masked that recession until the panic exploded in 1929. Robbins places the responsibility for the crash at the door of the Federal Reserve and its European counterparts: "Thus, in the last analysis, it was deliberate co-operation between Central bankers, deliberate 'reflation' on the part of the Federal Reserve authorities, which produced the worst phase of this stupendous inflation." [Robbins, 54] The evolution of Norman's tactics shows clearly enough that he did not provoke a crash in New York out of self-defense, to protect the Bank of England's gold from being exported to Manhattan. Norman was willing to sacrifice massive quantities of gold in order to feed the New York bubble and thus be sure that when panic finally came, it would be as devastating as possible. Between July 1928 and February, 1929, the New York Fed lending rate was 5%, half a point higher than the 4.5% that was the going rate at the Bank of England. As the London *Economist* commented, "two years ago [in early 1927] no one would have believed New York could remain half a point above London for more than a few weeks without London being forced to follow suit." [*Economist*, February 9, 1929, 275] All during the autumn of 1928 the Bank of England hemorrhaged gold to Manhattan, as British pounds hurried to cash in on the 12% annual interest rates to be had in the Wall Street brokers' call loan market. Even in January and February of 1929, months when the Bank of England could normally expect to take in gold, the gold outflow continued.

During the first week of February, 1929, Norman raised the London bank rate to 5.5%. The *Economist* snidely commented:

> Finally, the 5.5 per cent. rate comes as a definite signal to America. It must not be supposed that Continental centres will remain indifferent to London's lead, and its cumulative effect may well be a definite pronouncement that Europe is not prepared to stand idly by and see the world's stocks sucked into a maelstrom. Wall Street can scarcely

---

[109] Senate Hearings pursuant to S.R. 71, 1931, p. 134 in Robbins, 53.

remain indifferent to such a pronouncement, especially if the New York Reserve Bank follows by a sharp increase in its own rate. In any case, the establishment of European interest rates upon a new and higher level may well draw gold back from New York before long; and if so the 5.5 per cent. rate will have done its work. [*Economist*, February 9, 1929, 275]

The higher British bank rate scared a number of Wall Street speculators. During the same week the Federal Reserve Board issued a statement that seemed to threaten measures "to restrain the use...of Federal Reserve facilities in aid of the growth of speculative credit." [Galbraith, *Great Crash*, 39] The effect of this communiqué was similar to the Greenspan "irrational exuberance" warning of December 1996. In two days the Dow Jones average declined by about 15 points to 301. On the day Norman hiked the rates, the volume went over 5 million shares. But within a few days the momentum of speculation reasserted itself.

The signal sent by the higher London Bank Rate was underlined in March 1929 by the Anglophile banker Paul Warburg. This was once again the scion of the Venetian Del Banco family who had been the main architect of the Federal Reserve System. Warburg now warned that the upward movement of stock prices was "quite unrelated to respective increases in plant, property, or earning power." In Warburg's view, unless the "colossal volume of loans" and the "orgy of unrestrained speculation" could be checked, stocks would ultimately crash, causing "a general depression involving the entire country." [Noyes, 324]

Between February and April 1929, the Bank of England was able slightly to improve its gold stocks. By late April the pound began to weaken, and the Banque de France, true to Moreau's hard line policy, siphoned off more of Norman's gold. July 1929 was a bad month for Threadneedle Street. By August 21, 1929, the Bank of England had paid out 24 million pounds' worth of gold since the start of the year. In August and September, however, the gold outflow slowed.

On the morning of 4 September 1929 the New York hedge fund operator Jesse Livermore received a confidential message from a source in London according to which a "high official" of the Bank of England – either Montagu Norman or one of his minions – had told a luncheon group of City of London men that "the American bubble has burst." The same official was also quoted as saying that Norman was looking for an excuse to raise the discount rate before the end of the month. The message concluded by noting that a financier by the name of Clarence Hatry was in big financial trouble. [Thomas and Morgan-Witts, 279-280]

THE PROPHET OF LOSS

The New York Federal Reserve Bank had raised its discount rate to 6% on August 8. Soon thereafter, the market began to run out of steam. The peak of the Coolidge bull market was attained on September 3, 1929, when many leading stocks reached their highest price quotations. On September 5, the market broke downward on bearish predictions from economic forecaster Roger Babson, who on this day won his nickname as "the Prophet of Loss." During the following weeks, the market drifted sideways and downward.

On September 20, 1929, it became known in the City of London that the Clarence Hatry group, which supposedly had been worth about 24 million pounds, was hopelessly insolvent. On that day Hatry and his leading associates confessed to fraud and forgery in the office of Sir Archibald Bodkin, the Director of Public Prosecutions, had lunch at the Charing Cross Hotel, and were jailed. Hatry later asserted that in late August, he had made a secret visit to the Bank of England to appeal to Montagu Norman for financing to allow him to complete a merger with United Steel Company, a UK firm. Norman had adamantly refused Hatry's bid for a bridge loan. By 17 September when

Hatry stock began to fall on the London exchange, Hatry had liabilities of 19 million pounds and assets of 4 million pounds.

When, on 19 September, Hatry approached Lloyd's Bank in last a desperate bid for financing, the wayward financier had told his story to Sir Gilbert Garnsey, a chartered accountant. Garnsey had made a second approach to Norman for emergency financing, and had also been rebuffed. At this point Norman had informed the chairman of the London Stock Exchange that the Hatry group was bankrupt; in this conversation it was agreed that trading in Hatry shares would be suspended on September 20.

Norman thus wanted the Hatry bankruptcy; he could have prevented it if he had wanted to. How many times did Norman, who had a free hand to make loans and who operated totally in the dark as far as the British government and public were concerned, bail out other tycoons who happened to be his friends and allies? The Hatry affair was useful to Norman first of all because it caused a rapid fall in the London stock market. London stockjobbers who were caught short on cash were forced to liquidate their New York holdings, and the *Economist* spoke of "forced sales" on Wall Street occasioned by the "Hatry disclosures." [*Economist*, November 23, 1929, 955] More important, Norman could now pretend that since confidence in London had been rudely shaken, he needed to raise the bank rate to prevent a further flight of funds.

SEPTEMBER 27, 1929: NORMAN RAISES THE BANK RATE

Less than a week after the Hatry group's debacle, Norman made his final and decisive bid to explode the New York bubble. He once again raised the Bank of England discount rate, this time by a full point. As the *New York Times* reported from London, "the atmosphere was tense in the financial district and exciting scenes were witnessed outside the Royal Exchange. Ten minutes before noon a uniformed messenger rushed into the corridor of the Bank carrying a framed notice over his head. The notice read: "'Bank rate 6 1/2 per cent.' A wild scramble ensued as messengers and brokers dashed back to their offices with the news." One of the subtitles of the article was "BUSINESS FEARS RESULTS". [*New York Times*, September 27, 1929] And well they might have. 6.5% was a very high discount rate for London in those days. The London rate had not been so high since 1921, during the so-called deflation panic of 1920-21.

The British move towards higher rates was imitated within two days by the central banks of smaller continental states where British influence was high: Austria, Denmark, Norway, Sweden, and the Irish Republic all hiked their discount rate. On October 10 the British monetary authorities in India also raised the discount rate there by a full point. Added to the steps already taken by the Bank of England, these actions generated a giant sucking sound as money was pulled out of New York and across the Atlantic.

The *Economist* approved Norman's maneuver, while blaming the high bank rate on "the continuance of Stock Exchange speculation in America, with its concomitant high call rates." Such a high rate would of course be highly destructive to British factories and farms, but this, as we have already seen, counted for nothing in Norman's machinations. The *Economist*'s commentary ended with a very sinister prophecy:

> Still, on the whole, few will doubt that the Bank was right this week to change over to its ... alternative of imposing dearer money rates at home. It has decided to do so at a moment when the fates are becoming propitious to an early success, which should permit of a relaxation of the present tension before too long a period has elapsed. [*Economist*, September 28, 1929, 557]

What the *Economist* meant by success, as we will see, was the detonation of a colossal panic in New York. By abruptly pulling millions of pounds out of New York, Norman turned the sagging Coolidge bull market into the biggest rout in stock market history up to that time. Then, as the *Economist* suggested, the British bank rate would come down again.

John Kenneth Galbraith, in his much-quoted study *The Great Crash*, curiously manages to avoid mentioning the raise in the British Bank Rate as the immediate detonator of the Crash of 1929. Perhaps Galbraith, who was born in Canada, has a soft spot for the City of London; he is certainly a close friend of Lord Eric Roll.

Various London outlets now began feverishly signaling that it was time to pull the rug out from under the New York market. A prominent signaler was Philip Snowdon, the Chancellor of the Exchequer in the Labour Party government of Ramsay MacDonald, which had come into power in the spring of 1929 on a platform which had included the need for better relations with the United States after the era of severe naval rivalry. On October 3, 1929, Snowdon addressed the Labour Party's annual conference in Brighton. Snowdon's audience was understandably not happy with a higher bank rate, since they would be the main victims of unemployment.

BRITISH CHANCELLOR SCORES NEW YORK "ORGY OF SPECULATION"

Snowdon, while stressing that Norman's actions were independent of the Exchequer, genially told the delegates that "there was no other recourse." Why not? Snowdon first repeated the argument about defending London's gold stocks: "Monetary conditions in America, Germany, and France have been such as to create a great demand for the currencies of those countries, dollars, marks, and francs, and a consequent selling of sterling, with the result that the rates of exchange have gone against us recently, reaching points where payments were taken in gold." The US, in particular, was the culprit: "In New York, with America's plethora of liquid capital and high rates, there has been an unusual year's orgy of speculation, draining money away from England." "There has been a raid on the financial resources of this country which the increased bank rate is now intended to check" Snowdon ranted. "The object of the increased rate is to draw money back to England," Snowdon stressed. The hardship of high rates must be blamed on the US: "...there must be something wrong and requiring our attention when such an orgy 3,000 miles away can so dislocate the financial system of this country and inflict injury on our workers and employers." It was time to bail out of New York and come home to London, Snowdon urged: "British credit is the best in the world. The British market is the safest in the world for those who are satisfied with reasonable investments and not lured into wild speculations." [*New York Times*, October 4, 1929]

When J.P. Morgan read this speech, he was reportedly apoplectic that Snowdon had repeated his catchphrase of "orgy of speculation" so many times. But J. P. Morgan was also in the process of going short. Snowdon's speech was widely applauded in the City of London, the *New York Times* reported the next day, and his "reference to the effect of the American speculation on the international situation was also approved...the feeling is that such movements must be allowed to bring their own correction." [*New York Times*, October 6, 1929] The "correction" was now only a few weeks away.

On October 21, 1929 the Great Crash began. On October 24, at the height of that day's panic, Winston Churchill appeared briefly in the visitors' gallery of the New York Stock Exchange to view the boiling trading floor and savor the chaos his policy had wrought. On October 29, the principal market index lost 40 points on a volume of almost 12.9 million shares, an all-time record in that epoch.

OCTOBER 29, 1929: LONDON LEADS FOREIGN SELLING ON WALL STREET

One of the remarkable features of October 29 was the large number of immense block lots of stock that were dumped on the market, in contrast to the previous days when the panic had mainly involved smaller margin-leveraged investors. In those days the financial editor of the *New York Times* was the veteran journalist Alexander Dana Noyes, who had played the role of Anglophile Cassandra of the Coolidge market: at every periodic convulsion in the speculative fever, Noyes had proclaimed that the day of reckoning had finally come. In his later autobiography, *The Market Place: Reminiscences of a Financial Editor*, Noyes admitted in passing that the British had played a key role in the dumping of these large blocks of stock: "Afterward, it came to be known that the forced selling was not only stock which had been bought for the rise by the hundreds of thousands of outside speculators, but represented also the closing-out of professional speculators who had been individually 'carrying' immense lines of stock. Possibly London, which after its habit had been joining in the American speculation...started indiscriminate foreign selling." [Noyes 330]

By the end of October, the total value of stocks listed on the New York Exchange had declined by 37%. That, it turned out, was only the beginning. By the time the bottom was finally reached in March 1933, stocks had declined in price by more than 80%. By 1932 commodity prices had fallen by 30 to 40%. World manufacturing production was down by 30 to 50%. World trade declined by two thirds. The International Labor Office in 1933 said that approximately 33 million persons were out of work.

THE LONDON *ECONOMIST* GLOATS

By Halloween, Norman was able to reduce the London rate from 6.5% to 6%. The *Economist* gloated:

> Seldom has the country received a more agreeable surprise than that sprung upon it by the Bank of England when at, twelve o'clock on Thursday morning, it announced that its rate had been reduced from 6 1/2 to 6 per cent. Five weeks ago, when Bank rate was raised from 5 1/2 to 6 1/2 per cent., doubts were freely expressed lest the new rate might not prove effective in correcting the exchanges and stemming the flow of gold from this country; and voices were heard foreboding that 6 1/2 per cent. might have to be followed by 7 1/2 per cent. in a few weeks' time. Less than three weeks sufficed to confound the school of extreme pessimists, for by the middle of October [when the New York panic began] it was plain that all danger of a higher Bank rate had passed. The dollar was nearer the import than the export gold point, the mark was back to par, and London and the sterling was proving a magnet for the world's floating balances.

> The final collapse of the Wall Street boom under the avalanche of selling which began on Thursday of last week, and which must be regarded as the main factor in the Bank's decision, has confounded optimists and pessimists alike. ...it must be borne in mind that the Bank rate was raised to 6 1/2 per cent. last September solely to make London an attractive centre for short money. ...the crux of the situation lay in the attraction of the New York market both for floating balances to be lent at call, and for the funds of private investors anxious to participate in the profits of a boom which appeared to have no end. Steps had to be taken by the Bank of England to counter a situation which threatened to become critical for its own reserves.

> Even before Wall Street's 'Black Thursday,' events showed that the new Bank rate was achieving its objects to an extent surpassing expectations.... With the final collapse of the Wall Street boom, and the definite end of a critical phase in the world's monetary history, in which New York had been an inconveniently overwhelming competitor for international funds, the

Bank of England decided...to lose no time in allowing Bank rate to drop to the level of the market rate....

...it would be premature to jump to the conclusion that the Wall Street break has cleared the world's monetary and commercial horizon of every cloud...there is warrant for hoping that the deflation of the exaggerated balloon of American stock values will ultimately be for the good of the world....we look for a gradual improvement in the international monetary situation as the huge balances hitherto concentrated in New York redistribute themselves over the rest of the world - thus greatly easing the strain on the British banking system and opening possibilities for a further reduction in Bank rate in the not very distant future....

The cessation of the westward flow of funds, even if the reversal of the process does not lead to the early recovery by London of all, or nearly all, her lost gold, should greatly ease the difficulties presented by the problems of international debt payments and the interrelated Reparations issue...The 6 1/2 per cent. rate *has done its work and done it well*. [London *Economist*, November 2, 1929, 805-806, emphasis added]

On November 23, when the smoke had cleared on Wall Street and the wreckage there was more clearly visible, the *Economist* catalogued "Reactions to the Wall Street Slump." Again they recurred to Montagu Norman's interest rate hike of September 26: "That advance...was a by no means negligible factor in turning into the opposite direction the tide of funds which had been flowing so strongly toward New York, and in causing the edifice of the American speculation to totter." [*Economist*, 23 November 1929, p. 955]

By mid-December the London discount rate was down to 5%. The *Economist* in its year-end review of 1929, repeated its praise for Norman's bank rate stratagem: "In the financial world we faced and met a crisis which, in the opinion of the doubters, threatened even to endanger the gold standard in this country. But after enduring a long-continued drain of gold...the Bank at a critical moment took a course as bold as it was successful, and in the event it proved necessary only to put up with acutely dear money for a matter of weeks." In that holiday season of 1929 the *Economist* saw "a depression from across the Atlantic of cyclonic force" but since "Great Britain's monetary position in regard to gold need give rise to no anxiety" and British "industry starts a New Year ...on more even terms with our competitors than for many years past," Norman had scored a "success."

Norman had succeeded in torpedoing the US economy, but he had also unleashed a world depression. The British had been in a depression since 1920 anyway, so from their standpoint getting the rest of the world to join them in their misery was a positive development.

Benjamin Strong had died in October 1928. Montagu Norman lived to see the dawn of the Bretton Woods era. Norman's stepson is Peregrine Worthshorne, the stridently anti-American columnist of the London *Sunday Telegraph*.

VII. MODELS OF DISINTEGRATION

"Liquidate labor, liquidate stocks, liquidate real estate." – Andrew Mellon

Beyond financial collapse, however serious, there lies the dimension of disintegration. Now it is not just that prices are falling. Now the market itself is closed, and the avidly traded scraps of paper are worthless. More serious, the vital functions of civilization itself are failing. We now face the breakdown crisis of an entire society.

Germany between 1921 and 1923, during the years of the so-called Weimar Republic (the regime between the fall of the Kaiser in 1918 and the coming of Hitler in 1933) affords us an opportunity to study the impact of financial disintegration on a large and highly industrialized twentieth-century nation. The disintegration at the onset of the third millennium will potentially be just such a breakdown crisis of a whole mode of human existence. It can further be compared to the fall of the Roman Empire during the first millennium, and to the fourteenth-century breakdown crisis in Europe (which will be discussed in the following chapter).

THE HYPERINFLATION OF THE LATE ROMAN EMPIRE

It has not been sufficiently recognized that the final fall of the Roman Empire in the west around 476 AD involved an economic crisis, more precisely a crisis of hyperinflation. The fall of the Roman Empire was greatly accelerated by the reforms of the Emperor Diocletian, who ruled around the year 300 AD. The Roman Empire had already partially disintegrated during the period 200-300 AD, with frequent coups and assassinations of emperors. The borders of Rome along the Rhein and the Danube were under heavy attack by the barbarian tribes. From modest beginnings as the son of a slave, Diocletian had worked his way up through the ranks of the Roman legions, and had fully assimilated the Roman oligarchical outlook.

Diocletian's reforms aimed at stabilizing the finances, social structure, and military power of the Roman Empire. In order to maintain the production of basic commodities, which was then largely carried out through guilds, Diocletian decreed laws that made it impossible to change, sell, or alter the property of any of these guilds. This meant that the methods of production could be neither changed nor improved. If your father was in the bakers' guild, you had to join it too. You were legally precluded from aspiring to get a better job. Some guilds were strategically important but understaffed. Diocletian often made it obligatory for any man marrying the daughter of a member of these guilds to join the guild himself, however he may have been apprenticed. In effect, Diocletian outlawed scientific and technological progress, which would have had to be carried out by modernizing the production methods and property of the guilds. Diocletian, like the Environmental Protection Agency of today, wanted such technological progress halted in the name of what was stable, appropriate, and sustainable. But as a result, productivity stagnated and the Roman Empire was doomed. Diocletian had institutionalized the limits to growth.

DIOCLETIAN'S BALANCED BUDGET PLAN

Diocletian was a great fan of the balanced budget. To get more revenue, he increased the tax bite on farmers, who often became the debt slaves later called serfs. He held towns accountable for the taxes owed by the surrounding countryside, a policy which tended to depopulate the towns, undermining urban life in general. He also tried to bill public officials for unpaid taxes, which made it hard to find responsible public officials. Diocletian also issued the famous decree on prices in 301 AD. This fixed the maximum price for hundreds of commodities, including gold, and also set maximum wages for artisans, lawyers, and other trades and professions. Many features of Diocletian's totalitarian state found their way via the Byzantine Empire into Soviet communist practice.

Diocletian's prices are expressed in denarii; by this time the denarius was a copper coin. You could hire a teacher for a month for 200 denarii, pay a tailor 20 denarii to sew a pair of pants, or retain a lawyer for a case in court for 1,000 denarii. In those days wheat in Rome was sold by the modius, which equaled nine tenths of a peck. Diocletian's maximum price decree set the price of wheat at 100 denarii for each modius. Since wheat had been sold at Rome for one-half a denarius during the second century AD, this was already a very steep price. Records of how this and other prices later evolved are available for Egypt. In Egypt the standard measure for grain and other foods was the artaba, which was equal to 3.3 modii. In the years right after 301, the price of wheat in Egypt was 330 denarii per artaba, just as the proportions would suggest. But by 335 AD, wheat had reached 21,000 denarii per artaba, and by 338 AD the figure was 36,000 denarii. Prices had gone up over one thousandfold on this most basic commodity, the staff of life. [Shapiro, 44]

By 342 AD wheat was going for 75,000 denarii per artaba, and by 350 AD it took 500,000 denarii to buy the same amount. That fulfills any definition of hyperinflation. Under Caesar Augustus, pork sold for 10 denarii per pound. By 362 AD a pound of pork was 14,400 denarii, which rose to 30,000 denarii by 390 AD.

Diocletian's successor Constantine created a pure gold coin called the solidus. The name of this coin survives in modern Italian as "un soldo" and "i soldi," which are the most common generic expressions for money. The solidus was something like a European Currency Unit or the IMF's Special Drawing Rights in that it was used for government accounts and calculations. In 350 AD, we find, a solidus was worth 576,000 denarii. A manuscript dating from a few years later contains the passage, "The solidus now stands at 2,020,000 denarii; it has gone down!" By 390 AD, there is evidence that it took 4.5 million denarii to buy a solidus. [Shapiro, 45]

Monetarists might attribute all this solely to the debasement of the coinage, but it ought to be clear that the principal cause of the Roman inflation was the rapid decline of farm and artisan production as a result of Diocletian's reforms. The Diocletian hyperinflation was a central factor in a breakdown crisis of civilization in the Mediterranean basin and related areas which was marked by the disintegration of human civilization and the coming of the Dark Ages, a disaster which it took humanity almost 1,000 years fully to overcome.

The worst cases of modern inflation have often involved the depreciation of paper money under the impact of war, economic warfare, or some other crisis. We in America had our continental money, which was issued by Congress during the Revolutionary War. The continentals depreciated by a factor of about 1000 during their life span. Then there were the paper *assignats* of the French revolution, which fell by 1796 to 533 *assignat* francs to one metal franc. Until the twentieth century, these were considered extreme models of runaway inflation or hyperinflation.

THE FALL OF THE HUNGARIAN PENGO

Other currencies suffered when many countries abandoned the gold standard during World War I. This was especially true of the losers, and of countries impacted by revolutions. After 1918 the Austrian paper crown depreciated by a factor of 14,300. For the Hungarian paper crown, the decline was by a factor of 16,600. After World War I it took 1.8 million Polish paper marks to buy one gold zloty. In the Soviet Union, the value of a gold ruble was fixed in 1924 at 50 billion paper Soviet rubles.

The all-time champion of depreciation appears to be the Hungarian pengo. By 1946 it took 1.4 nonillion pengoes to purchase the goods that were obtained for 1 pengo in 1938. The pengo had thus depreciated by a factor of

$$1,000,000,000,000,000,000,000,000,000,000.$$

A currency reform was required in order to restore confidence in the Hungarian currency, which was renamed the forint or florin.

Before any Americans of the late twentieth century try to have too much fun at the expense of the hapless pengo, we should recall that the forces of depreciation converging on the US dollar in the current cataclysm are at least as virulent as those which brought down the Hungarian currency. So far as is know, there were few derivatives in Hungary in those days, and there was scarcely a Euro-pengo or xeno-pengo market of the type which saps the strength of the dollar. There is no guarantee that some of us will not have to mark down our assets by a cool nonillion or two.

WEIMAR HYPERINFLATION: A TRILLION TO ONE

During the years and months leading up to November 1923, the German mark underwent a monetary inflation without precedent in all of history. In 1914 a US dollar had been the equivalent of 4.2 German marks. By the culmination of the hyperinflation the spot rates for the gold-backed US dollar in Berlin were as follows, expressed in trillions of paper marks to a dollar:

November 13, 1923	.84
November 14, 1923	1.26
November 15, 1923	2.52
November 20, 1923	4.2

[Source: Bresciani-Turroni]

Thus, by the time the Weimar hyperinflation reached its peak, the mark had depreciated by a factor of one trillion. But reality at street level was even worse than these figures convey. As the leading student of the Weimar inflation, Bresciani-Turroni, writes: "...these were the official quotations. Actually in the open foreign market the dollar reached much higher rates. According to the figures referred to by Schacht in his book on the stabilization of the mark the dollar was quoted at 3.9 trillion paper marks at Cologne on November 13th, 1923; 5.8 trillion on the 15th; 6.7 trillion on the 17th, and 11.7 trillion on November 20th. This was the highest quotation." [Bresciani-Turroni, 24]

ZWEIG: THE WITCHES' SABBATH OF HYPERINFLATION

The Austrian man of letters Stefan Zweig wrote about the beginnings of the hyperinflation in his memoir of Europe between the wars, *The World of Yesterday*. He recalls the idyllic scene at an ocean resort on June 24, 1922 being shattered by the news that the nationalist political leader Walter Rathenau had been murdered. This assassination triggered the attack on the German mark by the British currency dealers which started the hyperinflation. Zweig writes:

'Walter Rathenau assassinated!' A panic broke out, and shook all of Germany. The mark collapsed with a jolt, and from then on it fell non-stop, until it was quoted in the fantastic, crazy trillions. Now began the true Witches' Sabbath of inflation.... I have experienced days when I had to pay 50,000 marks for a morning paper, and 100,000 marks for an evening paper. Anyone who had foreign money to exchange delayed the transaction for several hours, since at 4 o'clock he received several times as much as he would have gotten at 3, and at five he got a multiple of what he would have gotten 60 minutes earlier.... On street cars, one paid in millions.... A pair of shoe laces cost more than a shoe had once cost, no – more than a fashionable shoe store with 2,000 pairs of shoes had cost before; to repair a broken window, more than the whole house had formerly cost--a book more than the printer's shop with a hundred presses. For $100 one could buy rows of six-story houses on Kurfuerstendamm....

Some aspects of the situation were comparable to the effects of IMF shock therapy and "liberal reforms" in Poland, Russia, and Ukraine in the 1990s:

Messenger boys established foreign exchange business and speculated in currencies of all lands.... All values were changed...the laws of the State were flouted....Berlin was transformed into the Babylon of the world. Bars, amusement parks, honky-tonks sprang up like mushrooms...the Germans pursued perversion in their vehement and methodical way. Even the Rome of Suetonius had never known such orgies as the pervert balls of Berlin, where hundreds of men costumed as women, and hundreds of women, as men, danced under the benevolent eyes of the police....

The cause of the German hyperinflation was a campaign of economic warfare against this defeated country by the victorious and vindictive British and French. The great factor weighing down the future value of the mark were the reparations, which were about equal to half of the total value of real estate, factories and other property existing in Germany before 1914. The British knew that the value of any currency is determined by its value as measured against other world currencies on international exchanges. For a country like Germany, which had to import raw materials and export finished industrial commodities, this was especially true. So the London banks drove down the international value of the mark, knowing that a collapse in its domestic buying power would soon follow. This process was accelerated by political destabilization in the form of separatist or secessionist movements, and by private armies or militias- called Freikorps - of disgruntled war veterans and malcontents. There was also a wave of terrorism, especially of political assassinations, which claimed hundreds of victims, among them Rathenau.

In January 1923, French and Belgian armies occupied the coal-producing Ruhr region, citing as a pretext that Germany had failed to deliver 125,000 telephone poles that had been pledged as reparations in kind. When 1923 came in, the dollar could buy 18,000 marks. By September the dollar could buy 100 million marks, and the worst was yet to come.

ASH WEDNESDAY FOR THE GERMAN MARK

Every day at noon a new exchange rate between dollar and mark was fixed in Berlin. Except for a few brief interludes, this always meant a new, lower value for the mark. Usually it was double-digit inflation, often enough triple digit-inflation - per day! Paper money became a wasting asset. Any bank notes which you had on hand in the morning had to be spent at all costs before the fateful noon whistle, because at that time they would loose most of their value. People were therefore desperate to convert their paper money into tangible, physical commodities - what the Germans called *Sachwerte*. It was better to buy any physical commodity that hold on to paper. A commodity one did not need could be bartered later to obtain something one did need. The main thing was to unload the paper as fast as possible.

Before 1914, the largest German banknote in circulation had been the 1,000 mark note, which was originally worth about $250 of those days. But during 1922-23, 5 million mark notes were printed, followed by 500 billion mark notes, and, in the last days of the hyperinflation, a one trillion mark note. By the end even a postage stamp could cost 10 billion marks. When one of the largest Berlin banks added two floors of new office space to its main headquarters, a member of the board of directors was asked why the expansion was taking place. With typical "Berliner lip" humor he answered that the extra room was needed to store all the extra zeroes.

Those who lived on fixed incomes were quickly wiped out. That included rentiers who thought they could finance their retirement by clipping the interest coupons on bonds. Those who bought annuities saw their value dissolve to nothing. Patriotic citizens who had bought war bonds and savings bonds from the German government were soon using those bonds for wallpaper. Insurance policies, especially life insurance, turned out to be one of the very worst of investments.

Public officials, civil servants and government workers at all levels lost everything. Teachers were big losers, as were professors. The ranks of German scientists were decimated by immiseration. Doctors fared very poorly because the government health care plan paid them for their services after days or weeks had gone by, so the money they got was worthless. Lawyers also suffered, especially those who specialized in civil cases. Lawsuits demanding millions of marks in damages became rare when the litigants realized that even if they won their case, the damages would be worthless by the time they were collected. Landlords found that they could not increase rents to keep up with depreciation because of rent control laws. By the end of 1922 rents made up less than one half of one per cent of average household expenses. This meant that evictions and homelessness were not on the scale that they otherwise might have been, providing a key political shock absorber.

THE DESTRUCTION OF THE GERMAN MIDDLE CLASS

Military officers, whether they were retired or still on active duty, were reduced to paupers, with predictable political results. These desperate men rallied around reactionary leaders like General Ludendorff, the former army commander who was Hitler's superior officer in the Munich beerhall putsch of November 1923.

In Germany during those years owner-managers of small and medium sized industries and other businesses would sometimes sell their companies when they wanted to retire, since they intended to put the proceeds in a bank account, or perhaps buy bonds and live off the interest. Such persons were often getting on in years, and were slow to understand the ruthless dynamics of the hyperinflation that was swirling around them. Once they had exchanged their plant and equipment for paper money, they generally discovered the folly of their actions, but by then it was too late.

Savings accounts were also hit by the full fury of the hyperinflation. A woman who had 600,000 marks in the bank in 1919 still had the equivalent of $70,000 gold-backed dollars of that period - quite a substantial sum. By the fall of 1923 her bank sent her a letter announcing that her account was being terminated because it was so small. The bank told her that since it could no longer make change for a sum so small as 600,000 marks, they were sending her a bank note for 1 million marks. She began to understand her situation when she noticed that the stamp on the letter that brought her all this was also for 1 million marks.

The hyperinflation thus destroyed the German middle class - the small and medium industrialists, the owners of other small businesses, the civil service officials, office workers, and the independent professionals like doctors, lawyers, and professors. These strata were generally annihilated in one of the biggest forced transfers of wealth that had ever been seen in history. But the impoverished members of the middle class in their rage and confusion often became the advocates of the totalitarian political parties that soon began to grow.

A student recalled that at one point in 1922 he sat down at a cafe to drink a cup of coffee, which according to the menu was supposed to cost 5,000 marks. He sat and read the newspaper for an hour. When he asked the waiter how much he owed him, he was told that the bill would be 8,000 marks. The waiter explained that the cause for the discrepancy was the depreciation of the mark during the intervening hour; the dollar had gone up against the mark by 60% in 60 minutes, or one per cent per minute. [Guttman 61]

INFLATION ONE PERCENT PER MINUTE

The consequences for a leisurely lunch in a first-class restaurant can easily be imagined, especially if the dreaded noon fixing intervened. Many restaurants were shut down because of the effects of this problem. In Pearl Buck's *How It Happens*, an eyewitness to the inflation tells of how she saw the price of rolls go up from 20 to 25 marks during her lunch hour.

German employees and workers had traditionally been paid at the end of the month. They soon wanted to be paid every day, and then twice a day, so as to be able to convert their paper earnings into tangible commodities. Workers' wives would typically come to the factory gate at lunch time to pick up their husbands' pay envelopes. Teachers tried to get the same procedure established. The wives would then run to the shops and buy something, anything, in order to unload the paper marks before the stroke of noon and the next round of depreciation of their money.

The Reichsbank made enormous exertions to provide cash for payrolls and other purposes. The capacity to print paper marks was expanded. The payroll of the average small business often necessitated large baskets to carry the bills. Wallets soon became obsolete and were replaced by cigar boxes, then by briefcases. Cash registers were too small, and shopkeepers soon started to use packing crates to hold their income.

Cash was a wasting asset, so barter exchange became extremely popular. People got their pay in the form of a new suit or a pair of shoes at the end of the month. One lucky man arranged to get paid in grain and was able to maintain his standard of living. Large chocolate bars were a favorite barter item, as were matches. For the humble, a brick of bituminous coal often became the coin of the realm. The story was told of two women who were carrying a shopping basket full of money. While looking at dresses in a store window they put the basket down and walked away. When they came back the cash was still there, but the basket had been stolen.

William Guttman, a writer on the subject, gives the following estimate of price inflation for food items:

Item & Quantity	Pre-War Price	Summer 1923	November 1923
1 kilo rye bread	0.29 marks	1,200 marks	428 billion marks
1 egg	0.08 marks	5,000 marks	80 billion marks
1 kilo butter	2.7 marks	26,000 marks	6 trillion marks
1 kilo beef	1.75 marks	18,800 marks	5.6 trillion marks

[source: Guttman 62]

Hyperinflation generated some winners. Companies who earned foreign currency found that they were well advised to keep it for as long as possible before reconverting it into marks at a windfall profit. Many were the bankrupt doctors and professors who opened up a small foreign exchange office in an attempt to rebuild their fortunes. Porters, waiters and taxi drivers in places frequented by foreigners did well because they got tips in hard currency.

LARGE DEBTS WERE ESSENTIAL

A certain class of industrialist who had contracted large debts now found that these debts had been virtually wiped out. As this process accelerated, a number of devil-may-care entrepreneurs with the right connections began to assemble vast business empires based on contracting debts in paper marks, and paying off those debts when paper marks sums had dwindled down to virtually nothing. Hugo Stinnes is the most celebrated figure of this type. Another such operator, Friedrich Minoux, commented, "It was absolutely essential to have a large debt...Really, you did not have to be clever in those days to make a fortune; all you had to do is borrow and put the money into solid things." They key to success was the ability to have credit and to obtain the necessary bank loans. Once a bank had approved your loan, you had it made. Debt became the royal road to taking over company after company. Otto Wolf the elder, at that time the up-and-coming chief of a conglomerate, commented: "I am not yet quite as big as Herr Stinnes - but I am already in debt to the tune of several billion!" [Guttman, 108]

Stockholders did better than bondholders, but not by much. The bondholders lost everything. Stock prices increased enormously, but not enough to keep up with hyperinflation. There were also periodic crashes in the stock market. By November 1923, it was calculated that those who had held their stocks until the bitter end of the hyperinflation had lost five sixths of the pre-inflation value of their money. As Bresciani-Turroni sums up the case:

> Expressed in paper marks the prices of shares seemed high. This exercised a psychological influence on the great mass of the shareholders. Deluded by the apparently high prices, even the most cautious shareholders were induced to sell their securities; and only much later when the veil of inflation had been torn aside, did they realize that they had made a very bad bargain.

Buying gold watches or gold bullion proved to be a much better investment than stocks.

The other great class of winners included the sleazy demi-monde of pimps, prostitutes, gangsters, embezzlers, smugglers, small-time currency speculators and the owners of bars, gin mills and cabarets. The typical *nouveau-riche* was often a common criminal or other sociopathic element who had become the proprietor of a chain of bars or brothels. The gangsters were anxious to put on cultural airs, so there was a great speculative market in art objects.

Again we see eerie parallels between the Weimar tragedy of 1923 and the IMF shock therapy of the 1990s, which had similar effects in Russia, Poland, Ukraine, and the other formerly communist states. During late 1992 and early 1993, Russia underwent an incipient hyperinflation. In that cruel winter of IMF shock therapy, Russian inflation was for a time more than 1% per day, more than 10% per week, more than 50% per month. The inflation rate for December 1992, if calculated on a yearly basis, was 2,318%. Inflation for all of 1992 was 1,354%, and in 1993 subsided to 896%. This wiped out the Russian middle class, and quite possibly created a harvest of hatred and despair that will torment the world for many years to come.

In the German hyperinflation, no matter how fast one's income might rise, no matter how cunning one's personal investment policy in tangible commodities, one was always the loser in a world in which important prices were rising hour by hour. Industrial workers fared better than most others because of their well-organized unions, but even they found that by January, 1923 their real wages were only about 48% of the pre-1914 level. This erosion was further increased during the culminating days of the inflation. White-collar employees in 1914 had incomes about one third higher than their blue-collar counterparts. By late 1923 white-collar pay had declined to about the same level as blue-collar, meaning that the white-collar strata were even bigger losers than the factory losers.

HYPERINFLATION MADE GERMANS RIPE FOR HITLER

Any kind of real production was inevitably and inexorably depleted by the hyperinflation. At some point the goods produced had to be sold for paper marks, and no matter how fast the proceeds were turned into raw materials, production and transactions cannot be instantaneous. Machinery became obsolete, maintenance was neglected, and capital investment stagnated. Some industrialists seemed rich, but their wealth was inevitably the result of asset-stripping the firms they controlled.

The inflation quieted down in late 1923. This involved a currency reform carried out under the direction of Hjalmar Schacht, the veteran member of the Montagu Norman-Benjamin Strong central banking clique. It was on the basis of his 1923 performance that Schacht advanced his claim to the status of financial wizard. Schacht's wizardry was the least of it. The main reason why it proved possible to bring the runaway hyperinflation to a halt was because of outside aid, specifically from the United States. The key role was played by General Charles G. Dawes, a colorful Chicago banker who developed a plan to get Germany back on her feet through debt organization for the reparations bill and a loan of $200 million from the US. This stabilized Germany for the rest of the decade, until the Crash of 1929 destroyed the American ability to lend to Germany and the rest of central Europe. Dawes was by no stretch of the imagination a philanthropist, but the loans he engineered ushered in the 1924-1929 "relative stabilization" of the German economy.

But the psychological and political consequences of the hyperinflation proved even more difficult to master. It is significant that the Munich beerhall putsch, the species of coup d'etat attempted by Field Marshal Ludendorff and Hitler, came just weeks after the peak of the hyperinflation. The middle class white collar workers who had lost everything became a key recruiting ground for Hitler. As Zweig wrote, "We must always remember that nothing made the German people so embittered, so full of rage, so ripe for Hitler as the inflation."

1931: BANKING PANIC IN CENTRAL EUROPE
AS PRELUDE TO WORLD DISINTEGRATION

In late 1929 and 1930, the British noticed very little change in their usual depression routine. But the October 1929 explosion in New York cut off loans and wrecked the banking system in central Europe, as signaled by the Kreditanstalt bankruptcy in Vienna in May 1931, and the fall of the Danatbank and the rest of the German banks in July of the same year. Vienna had been chronically troubled because of its status as the full-sized head of a truncated body after the breakup of the Austro-Hungarian Empire. The Kreditanstalt, a Rothschild property, was the survivor among the Vienna banking houses, which had succumbed one by one in the postwar slump. As a result, Kreditanstalt owed $76 million abroad, mainly to UK and US investors. An international effort to bail out the Kreditanstalt with the help of the Rothschilds, the Bank for International Settlements, the Bank of England, and others availed nothing.

Failure of the Kreditanstalt meant the bankruptcy of much of central Europe. The crisis of the German banks took center stage. Even more than in Austria, the drying up of New York as a source of lending was the main culprit here. It was estimated that Germany had to meet yearly foreign payments of $800 million, including the onerous reparations. A run on the Berlin banks developed. Within a short time Germany was forced to export two fifths of her gold reserves for a total of $230 million.

The crisis in Berlin inevitably had immediate and serious repercussions in London. Some believed that British financial houses had been too slow to pull their money out of Berlin, and that large sums owned by the British had been frozen in Berlin when the banks there were shut down. Part of the panic traveled to London by way of Amsterdam: the Dutch banks had loaned heavily in Germany, and the Dutch withdrew their assets from London to stay afloat. By mow the tremors unleashed by the Crash of 1929 had undermined the entire banking system in Germany, Austria, Romania, Hungary, and the rest of central Europe.

It was at this point, with a cynical reversal of their entire policy, that the British decided to scuttle the sterling-centered international monetary system which they had re-assembled after World War I. Their gesture was similar to the speculative attacks on the pound mounted by George Soros and other British-backed hedge-fund operators in September 1992, attacks which aimed at destroying the European Exchange Rate Mechanism, the grid of relatively fixed parities among the continental currencies.

THE HOOVER MORATORIUM OF JUNE 1931

In the midst of the German crisis, the fact that German reparations and inter-allied war debts could not be paid was finally recognized by US President Herbert Hoover, who was realistic enough to proclaim the debt moratorium which bears his name - the Hoover moratorium of June 1931, which froze all reparations and war debt payments for 1 year. This moratorium was approved by the US Congress with sweeping majorities in December 1931. But the Hoover moratorium was too little and too late. One year was not enough: to be effective: a debt moratorium must last for the duration of the crisis, however long it takes until economic normalcy has been fully and completely restored. By the time Hoover had made up his mind to act, Schacht's Reichsbank was just a few weeks away from defaulting on gold payment and imposing strict controls on all currency transfers to the outside world. The Hoover Moratorium also contained a domestic political trick: if the European governments were not required to pay their debt to the United States government, then those same Europeans might still have enough liquidity to pay back their loans to American privately owned banks and businesses. So the US Treasury would have suffered, for the benefit of Wall Street. In December 1932, when the Hoover moratorium year had come to an end, France, Belgium and other debtors defaulted, and the Hoover Moratorium became permanent in practice.

Under the guidance of Schacht and Montagu Norman, the Germany of Chancellor Heinrich Bruening rapidly evolved into the prototype of the autarkic currency blocs of the 1930s. Most of the classical Schachtian apparatus later employed by Hitler was already in place before Hitler ever came to power.

There had been a better alternative for Germany in 1931. This might have been the strategy proposed by *Oberregierungsrat* Dr. Wilhelm Lautenbach (1891-1948) and the Friedrich List Society, which met behind closed doors on September 16-17, 1931 to consider possible solutions to the banking crisis. This discussion had been occasioned by a paper prepared by Undersecretary Schäffer (1886-1967) of the Finance Ministry and entitled "Gedanken zur Krisenbekämpfung" - ideas for fighting the crisis. Reichsbank president Hans Luther was part of the seminar, along with other leaders of business, finance, and industry. In his keynote speech, Lautenbach reviewed the alternatives offered by monetarism in a depression. On the one hand was deflation, with budget cuts, falling wages and prices, factory closures, and increasing unemployment. Lautenbach saw this policy as untenable, in contrast to the IMF economists who dealt with Asia in 1997-98. The only other alternative seemed to be attempted stimulation by way of low interest rates and easy money, but if this were all that was done, hot money would have fled the country and collapsed the exchange rate. This would have turned out to be a path to hyperinflation. But, noted Lautenbach, Germany had masses of merchandise in the form of unsold inventories, millions of unemployed, and hundreds of idle factories. Recovery was a matter of reorganizing these resources. But, with the government coffers empty, how could state action bring this about? The Reichsbank, Lautenbach pointed out, could generate as much liquidity as was needed. Bond issues could be floated for infrastructure in transportation and related fields if the banks had the cash to purchase the bonds. What was needed was a central bank policy of guaranteeing the banks that they could always discount infrastructure bonds with the central bank. Accordingly, Lautenbach urged a Reichsbank discount guarantee ("Rediskontogarantie") for such infrastructure bonds. The projects financed would increase employment and help expand credit, while increasing the real capital stock of the whole economy. Such measures would provide a goal for national production as a whole, said Lautenbach. He noted in conclusion that failure to proceed in this way would engender a total collapse and utter ruin of the German economy.[110] But there was not sufficient political will to put the Lautenbach Plan into action. [Borchardt and Schötz, 307-325]

Instead, the emergence of a mark zone under Schachtian auspices was assisted by Hoover's Secretary of State, the notorious Anglophile Henry Stimson – the ego ideal of the youthful George Bush. It was in fact Stimson who, while attending the London Conference of July 1931 on the German crisis, proposed the so-called Standstill Agreements, which stated that creditors owed money by the German government or by German banks and businesses would be obliged to refrain from demanding payment, and in any case not to take their money out of Germany. This gambit was found especially appalling by French government economist Jacques Rueff, who was in attendance. A debt moratorium for the duration of the crisis would have been simpler and far more effective. As it was, the ability of German residents to buy and spend abroad was thoroughly curtailed. Soon all trade was restricted, and frozen and blocked accounts were instituted. The Reichsbank rediscount rate went to a strangling 10%, and the rate on collateral loans went to 15%. In the domestic economy, deflation and austerity were the order of the day. All of this played into the hands of Hitler and the Nazis, which was precisely the intention of Montagu Norman.

STANDSTILL = GRIDLOCK

At the London financial conference of July 1931, Germany began to press for a so-called stand-still agreement ("Stillhalte-Abkommen") with her creditors. In the days that followed, these negotiations were carried forward by Melchior and Schmitz for the German side in talks with Tiarks for the United Kingdom and Cannon for the United States. In these talks, a preliminary agreement was reached for a six-month grace period, during which Germany would not be expected to make foreign debt payments. Germany also wanted to transform short-term foreign debt into long-term instruments, and for this question and others another conference was called for August 8, 1931 at

---

[110] Lautenbach was also confident that his stimulus package would be highly effective. He wrote: "Das Gesamtergebnis der angestellten kredittheoretischen Überlegungen läßt sich in den Satz zusammenfassen, daß eine Kreditexpansion in Verbindung mit großzügigen Investitionen nicht zu einer weiteren Illiquidisierung, sondern vielmehr zur Liquidisierung und Konsolidierung unserer Kreditwirtschaft beiträgt." (325)

the Basel headquarters of the new Bank for International Settlements. This special committee of the BIS was known as the Wiggin Committee after its chairman, the Wall Street banker Albert H. Wiggin. It was composed of Beneduce for Italy, Bindschedler for Switzerland, Francqui for Belgium, Hofstede de Groot for the Netherlands, Walter T. Layton for Britain, Melchior for Germany, Moreau for France, Rydbeck for Sweden, and Tanaka for Japan. The committee's report, drafted by Layton, was ready on August 18. The report noted that Germany had felt the effects of "the economic crisis called the depression" in exceptionally severe form, especially because so much of the German debt (like South Korea's in 1997) was in short-term maturities. The Wiggin Committee produced an agreement that froze payment on 6 billion Reichsmarks of German foreign debt, but did so for only six months. This short surcease was totally inadequate, and could never have permitted a German economic recovery and a return to solvency. The one-year pause granted by the Hoover Moratorium was insufficient, but the Wiggin Committee's six months of debt relief was a cruel hoax. In addition, the Wiggin Committee's stand-still agreement did not include a whole series of debt service and payment categories. During the time of the stand-still agreement, Schacht and others worked overtime to set up a system of foreign exchange conservation by Germany which effectively cut the country off from normal world trade, which had provided the sole means for Germany's survival. A Germany which could not export goods would soon begin exporting invasion armies. In retrospect, the stand-still agreements appear as the mirage of a solution. They were in effect a political trick to prevent a timely, unilateral, open-ended, across-the-board debt moratorium which would have given the German economy a real breathing space, and which might have forced the governments of the world to face the issue of permanent debt relief and international monetary reform. Standstill agreements utterly failed to promote a German comeback during 1931-32. Instead, the depression got worse, with the 1933 political consequences which are well known. The Wiggin Committee was also a means for foreign debtors to pressure Germany to adopt the austerity policies they wanted, in an equivalent of the IMF's later conditionality regime.

LONDON'S SINGAPORE DEFENSE OF THE BRITISH POUND, 1931

The surrender to Japan of the British naval base and fortress of Singapore on February 15, 1941 was the culmination of one of the most absurd military farces in the history of Britain. The story told to school children was that the British guns were pointing the wrong way. This was the result of a long-term, conscious and deliberate commitment to surrender Singapore as soon as possible if attacked by Japan, combined with the need to make a sham of defending the place so as not unduly to arouse the suspicions of the bloody Yanks. The British were looking ahead to the postwar world. They wanted to cut and run, to concentrate their resources on the defense of their home islands. They cared little if the Japanese had plenty of time to attain and fortify their Pacific defense perimeter, so that the US losses in rolling back Nippon would be nothing short of catastrophic. At the same time, the British wanted to hide this treachery from the US public. It had to look as if they were caving in to overwhelmingly superior forces.

At the time, every schoolboy knew that the British had fortified their coast defense artillery so that the guns could only point out to sea, and not to the land approaches, which were the axis of attack chosen by the Japanese. The British troops present, mainly imperial conscripts, were more or less overtly told not to fight. Once the needs of dramaturgy for the US market had been satisfied, General Percival, the British commander, surrendered with all deliberate speed.

The feeble efforts to save the pound mounted by Montagu Norman's Bank of England and by Ramsay MacDonald's national unity cabinet in the summer of 1931 can be usefully summed up as a "Singapore defense" *avant la lettre* – a bungling bogus sham that was deliberately designed to fail.

NORMAN INTENDED TO DEFAULT ALL ALONG

There is sold evidence that Montagu Norman's decision to provoke a British default on gold payment dated back at least to mid-July 1931. The following is an account of Montagu Norman's meeting with the German delegation during the London Conference of July 1931, which had been called together to deal with the crisis of the German banks and currency. Norman's preferred recipe for Germany was default on gold payment, standstill agreements, and a possible debt moratorium. As we see here, Norman told German State Secretary Schaeffer that in a few weeks it would be clear what he was driving at – which in retrospect was understood by all concerned as an allusion to Norman's own coming British default on gold payment:

> Zur für die ganze Konferenz entscheidenden internen Sitzung kam es am 21. [Juli 1931] in der britischen Treasury, an der Reichskanzler Brüning, Ministerialdirektor Schwerin-Krosigk, Staatssekretaer Schäffer und Geheimrat Vocke auf deutscher und Montague Norman, Sir William Leith-Ross und Waley auf britischer Seite teilnahmen. In dieser Sitzung erklärte Montague Norman mit aller Offenheit, dass er bei vollem Verständinis fuer die deutsche Lage nicht imstande sei, ueber die Bank von England zu helfen, da diese selbst durch die anhaltende Geldabzüge der letzten Tage (täglich bis zu 2 Mill. Pfund) unter schwerstem Druck stehe. Sein einziger - und unter den gegebenen Verhältnissen auch einzig möglicher - Rat wäre, die Konferenz schnell zu beenden, deutscherseits selbst private Stillhalte-vereinbarungen mit den Auslandsglaübigern zu treffen, gegebenfalls ein Auslandsmoratorium - und im Inneren Suspendierung der Goldeinlösungs- und Golddeckungspflicht, mit anderen Worten genau das, was England acht Wochen später selbst zu tun gezwungen war. Daß Norman dabei bereits an diese spätere eigene Politik dachte, geht daraus hervor, dass er im Anschluss an die Sitzung Staatssekretär Schäffer persönlich erklärte, dass Schäffer ihn in wenigen Wochen wohl verstehen würde." [Lüke 319]

As we see, Norman told the German government in July 1931 that the Bank of England could do nothing to help Germany. Instead, Norman suggested that Germany seek stand-still agreements with its creditors, declare a debt moratorium, and suspend all gold payments. Norman told the Germans that they would understand him better after a few weeks – evidently a reference to the British intention to do the same thing quite soon. This report not only illuminates the timing of Norman's decision to default. It also shows how explicitly Norman pushed Germany into the status of an autarkic currency bloc, with all international payments subject to strict government controls.

On August 23, 1931 Norman (who was nursing one of his periodic nervous breakdowns in Canada) talked by telephone with Governor Harrison of the New York Fed, Benjamin Strong's successor. Harrison asked Norman if he thought that the austerity program proposed by the new British National Government was adequate. Norman replied that he believed that the austerity program was not adequate, and that any inadequate program was bound to cause trouble within a year or so. Norman recommended exploiting the current crisis to force through an economic adjustment featuring a drastic reduction in wages and in the cost of production, so as to make British goods competitive again. If this were done, Norman thought, there would be no need for any loans. Harrison objected that it might be risky to rely exclusively on a balanced budget.

THE BANK OF ENGLAND LIES TO THE CABINET

The Deputy Governor of the Bank of England, Sir Ernest Harvey - the man who actually terminated the British gold standard - was uniformly defeatist throughout the crisis. At a cabinet meeting on September 3, 1931 Harvey expressed his conviction that "the future course of events depended largely upon the attitude of the British public towards the Government's proposals." This view, expressed at the height of the crisis, was at odds with the entire Bank of England and postwar central bank ideology, which stressed the autonomy and power of the central banks over the flailing of the politicians and governments. For three centuries the Bank of England had considered itself responsible for the fate of the pound; now Harvey was talking out of the other side of his mouth. This reversal of attitude was also expressed in Lord Norman's constant refrain that the crisis of the pound had to be solved by a balanced budget on the part of the British government, and not by an increase in the Bank Rate or other measures that only the Bank of England itself could take.

As contemporary observer Melchior Palyi writes, "several 'eyewitnesses' have told this writer that both those in the Treasury and in the Bank had convinced themselves that Britain's house could not be brought into order without first 'teaching a lesson' to a public which was either indifferent or indolent." [Palyi, 269] But that was a cover story for deliberately scuttling the pound. At that same cabinet meeting of September 3, 1931 Sir Ernest Harvey told the cabinet that total losses by the Bank of England since the beginning of the crisis amounted so far to 130 million pounds in gold and foreign exchange. Harvey then deliberately lied to the cabinet, stating that since the loans made to London by the foreign central banks would have to be repaid in gold if they could not be paid any other way, this "amounted in effect to a lien on a portion of their existing gold holding and reduced their actual free holding to little more than 80 million pounds or about the equivalent of the new government credit." As one historian comments, "This alarming exposition of the credit agreements was...seriously misleading. They did not provide for a lien on the Bank of England's gold or anything close to it. Rather they contained a gold payment clause which required that payment be made in gold." [Kunz, 122]

LONDON REFUSES TO RAISE BANK RATE TO CRISIS LEVEL

As Robbins notes, the monetarist orthodoxy of British financial experts between the two world wars was that if a country got into economic trouble, "You must put up your bank rate and you must limit your fiduciary issue [of unbacked paper money]. Anything else is bad finance." Curiously, when the terminal crisis of Montagu Norman's much-vaunted gold standard finally arrived, the British did neither of these things. British monetarist ideology featured the faith that an increase in the Bank of England's bank rate could "pull gold up out of the ground," or even attract gold to London "from the moon." The bank rate was at the heart of the entire British fetish of usury.

Fiduciary issue of currency was a means used to regulate the supply of credit. These were extra bank notes issued by the central bank. Cutting the fiduciary issue would have meant a credit contraction – tight money. In the midst of the summer, 1931 pound and gold crisis, the British actually increased their fiduciary issue, printing new pound notes when their own orthodoxy would have dictated a sharp cut.

NORMAN'S REFUSAL TO HIKE THE BANK RATE

As for the Bank Rate, the Bank of England acted in violent contradiction to its own monetarist orthodoxy. As one scholar later summed up:

On May 14 [1931], immediately after the collapse of the Kredit-Anstalt, the Bank Rate was actually lowered, from 3 to 2 1/2 per cent. It was not changed until July 23rd, when at last it was raised to 3 1/2 per cent. During the last week or so of July the Bank of England lost over 25 million pounds in gold. On July 30th the Bank Rate was again raised, but only to 4 1/2 per cent, and there it remained until September 21st. Great Britain had always advocated a high

Bank Rate as the remedy for a financial crisis and a drain of gold. She had been on the gold standard, in effect, for over two hundred years, with only two breaks – one during the Napoleonic wars and one during the last war [1914-1925]. Now for the first time in her history she suspended gold payments in time of peace and with a Bank Rate of 4 1/2 per cent! Does it follow that the British monetary authorities were secretly glad to leave the gold standard? ... why was the Bank Rate not raised but actually lowered after the Kredit Anstalt closed? Why was it not raised to 8 per cent or perhaps 10 per cent in July or even in August? [Benham, 9-11]

These are good questions.

Back in 1929, when Montagu Norman had been scheming to precipitate the New York stock market panic, 6.5% had not seemed too high a Bank rate in view of the desired result. In April 1920, when the Norman had wanted to undercut New York, the Bank Rate reached 7%, and had stayed there for a full year. But now, 4.5% was the absolute upper limit. A worried J.P. Morgan of New York cabled on September 7, 1931 to Morgan Grenfell in London:

> Are the British Treasury and the Bank of England satisfied that the present method of dealing with the sterling exchange is the best that can be devised? In this connection the question naturally arises as to why the Bank of England does not use the classic remedy of Bank Rate instead of apparently pegging the exchange. [Kunz, 126]

Apologists for Norman and his retainers have advanced various lame arguments to explain the treachery of Threadneedle Street. One argument was that the British domestic economy was already too depressed to survive a rise in the Bank Rate. But on September 21, after defaulting on gold, the Bank of England raised the Bank Rate to 6% and left it there for five months, regardless of the impact on the credit-starved domestic British economy.

Then there is the argument of "prestige," which claims that radically to raise the Bank Rate under the pressure of foreign gold demands would have undermined the prestige of the pound sterling. "It had been intimated that the decision to devalue was due to British 'sensitivity': the Treasury and the Bank found it 'undignified' to balance the national budget under pressure of foreign bankers. Was their dignity better served by defaulting?" [Palyi, 294] As the same author sums it up, "the reluctance to use the discount weapon was at the root of the widely disseminated charge that 'perfidious Albion' had intentionally 'trapped its creditors,'" especially given the fact that British foreign obligations were denominated in pounds, not in the currency of the lending country.

THE FRANCO-AMERICAN LOANS

The British judged that their sham defense of the pound required at least some semblance of support operations for their own currency in the international markets. For this purpose, it was decided to procure loans from the United States and France for these support operations. The main effect of these loans was to make the liquidity crisis that followed the British default more acute in both Paris and New York.

British representative H.A. Siepmann arrived in Paris on August 24, 1931 to begin negotiating the French loan. Given the fast pace of the crisis, Siepmann should have been a man in a hurry. But Siepmann "took the approach that the question of a credit was not a top priority matter, a rather surprising one in the circumstances and one that not only confused Governor Moret but diverged totally from the viewpoint held by Morgan's (N.Y.) and Harrison" at the New York Federal Reserve. [Kunz, 113] Morgan's for its part had been reluctant to undertake the British loan. The mood among other American banks was shown by the unprecedented number of refusals to participate in the underwriting of the loan which arrived in response to the offer cable sent out by Morgan. Banks refusing such an offer ran the risk of being excluded from future Morgan loan syndications. The refusals show the extreme liquidity anxieties already besetting the US bankers.

This state of affairs is reflected in the following cable from Morgan in New York to Chancellor of the Exchequer Philip Snowden in London:

> In reference to the proposed interest rate in America we may emphasize that there is not a single institution in our whole banking community which actually desires the British Treasury Notes on any terms either as to commission or interest.... Every institution is probably making strenuous endeavours to get its position more liquid. [Kunz, 116-117]

The British government organized an initial loan of $250 million from the United States. On August 26, the British requested and were granted a further US loan of $400 million. [Hoover, 81-82] The British loan was the biggest made by Morgan between the world wars. The loan took the form of a pledge by Morgan and 109 other American banks to purchase dollar-denominated Treasury Bills of the British government for periods of 30, 60 and 90 days.

AUGUST 4 CRISIS – NO INTERVENTION BY BANK OF ENGLAND

During the first days of August, the British authorities announced that they would use the loans from foreign central banks for the purpose of conducting support operations for the pound sterling. But on August 4, the Bank of England and its agents were inexplicably absent from the currency markets and carried out no support operations. The pound quotation collapsed below the gold export point to New York. Norman and his crew had "forgotten" to defend the pound that day – clearly a conscious decision to sabotage their own pound. The entire confidence-building effect of the central bank loans was completely dissipated. To make matters worse, support operations seem to have been virtually "forgotten" again two days later.

GOLD SOVEREIGNS SUSPENDED

Around the middle of September, the Bank of England suddenly discontinued its habitual practice of paying out gold sovereigns – that is, gold coins – to those who wanted to exchange pound sterling banknotes. This measure came at a time when gold bullion was still freely available for those who wanted to trade in larger sums. This amounted to the transition from the vestiges of a gold coin standard to a gold bullion standard. The effect on market psychology turned out to be catastrophic. The suspension of official payment in gold sovereigns was seen for what it was – the immediate prelude to the default on all gold payment.

AFTERNOON POUND BREAKS IN NEW YORK

On August 29, 1931 Morgan partner Thomas Lamont sent a cable to Grenfell in London commenting on the loss of confidence in the British government that was spreading on Wall Street. A cable two days later stressed the concern felt at Morgan's New York about "the poor handling of the sterling exchange, a symptom of which was the frequent breaks in the value of sterling in the New York market after the London market had closed. It appeared that the Bank of England agents in New York were setting their watches to London time, and knocking off for the day after lunch." When the pound crashed in the afternoon, Norman's minions were already at home.

NO BEAR SQUEEZES

In the same missive, Morgan also suggested better liaison between the Bank of England, the Bank of France and the New York Federal Reserve "so that the credits would become an offensive weapon rather than a sitting duck for rapacious financiers." [Kunz, 120] To be effective in stopping speculation, the monetary resources obtained by the Bank of England had to be employed dynamically. The Bank of England could not just sit there, buying unlimited quantities of pounds at the floor price. Rather, the money had to be used aggressively to buy pound futures so as to drive the pound quotation up, if only temporarily, with the result that some of the speculators who had sold the pound short would have been severely burned. This was later the lesson of Hong Kong in the fall of 1998. The pound would have received additional support through short covering purchases. The Bank of England needed to organize a short squeeze or bear squeeze so as to create genuine doubt about whether shorting the pound was a sure way to lock in profits. Bear squeezes and short squeezes had been actively organized by French Premier Poincaré during his defense of the French franc some years earlier.

ONLY TWO SMALL BANKS USED

Another feature of Norman's Singapore defense was the method used to organize support operations for the pound. All support operations were conduited through two small banks. Support operations against the dollar were done through the British Overseas Bank, and other support operations were done through the Anglo-International Bank. This absurd method guaranteed that everyone in the markets knew exactly when and in what amount the Bank of England was intervening, and that everyone also soon knew exactly how much of the various French and American support loans remained unused. If it had wished to be effective, the Bank of England would have intervened in its own name, and would also have conduited other operations through the big British clearing banks. The small size of the banks actually used also limited the amount of pound futures they could buy, since their credit was so limited.

LOW FORWARD PRICE OF POUNDS

On September 1, Morgan New York cabled their London partners an analysis of the London and New York sterling markets with special focus on the weakness and lack of depth of the forward market. [Kunz, 121] The elementary strategy for defending the pound would have been to keep the price of pound futures above the spot price for pounds in the cash market. If that could be accomplished, arbitrageurs would have been impelled to sell the pound futures and buy the spot pounds, generating an updraft around the pound quotations. But if pound futures were allowed to sink lower than current pounds, financiers would obviously sell pounds and buy pound futures to lock in their profit. Ignoring these elementary points of finance, Norman neglected pound futures altogether.

POUND PEGGED TOO HIGH

Harrison of the New York Federal Reserve cabled the Bank of England's Harvey on September 3, 1931 that in his opinion the British were attempting to peg the pound/dollar rate much too high. The British were attempting to support sterling at $4.86 to $4.86125, which was considerably above British gold export point. In Harrison's view, the artificially high peg only encouraged sales of sterling. Harrison wanted the pound to fluctuate just above that currency's gold export point.

Harvey declined to make this change, saying that although he was in general agreement, this was not the time to change tactics. [Kunz, 121] But by now his tactics were clearly failing.

DUTCH GUILDER RATE NEGLECTED

In yet another deliberate British fiasco, while the pound to dollar and pound to franc rates were supported, the pound to Dutch guilder quotation received no support of all. Given the considerable importance of the Dutch currency at the time, this was folly. The pound/guilder exchange rate went below the gold export point in September, and significant amounts of British gold were shipped to Amsterdam during the final phase of the bogus defense of the pound.

FOREIGN SECURITIES NOT USED

Lord Reading, the Foreign Secretary, suggested to Snowden between September 10 and September 14, 1931 that the Treasury prepare a plan for the mobilization of the large quantities of foreign securities held in Britain for the purpose of defending the pound. Reading thought that this operation could be modeled on the methods used for the same purpose during the First World War. Lord Reading also wanted MacDonald to order the Bank of England to prepare detailed financial data for the use of the Financial Subcommittee of the cabinet, composed of MacDonald, Snowden, Reading, and Neville Chamberlain. [Kunz, 129]

BRITISH SPECULATORS: OWN GOAL

On Monday, September 14, there was the first meeting of the Financial Subcommittee of the cabinet. Lord Reading wanted to determine exactly who it was that was dumping all the pounds on the international markets. Reading thought that many sales appeared to be British-inspired, and that the cabinet ought to consider a method of cracking down on such transactions. Harvey, who was present, expressed pessimism about the ability of the Government or the Bank to halt British flight capital, and "he further made the false statement that the sale of sterling by British citizens was not really an important problem." Harvey himself knew this was nonsense. In reality, "Harvey had been sufficiently alarmed about British sales of sterling to write to various culprits such as Lord Bradbury to ask them not to continue to purchase dollars. Also Fisher had told [US diplomat] Atherton that internal capital flight was one of the causes of Britain's problems. As the Bank of England, not the Treasury, kept track of currency movements, Fisher could only have known this if the Bank so informed him." [Kunz, 143] The London *Daily Star* was upset enough about flight capital to write that if the National Government were really national, "it could act at once against the traitors who are sending their gold abroad...." [*New York Times*, September 18, 1931]

On the fateful Default Day of September 21, 1931, the New York Times related the comments of the London correspondent of *Le Matin* of Paris. This journalist, Stephane Lauzanne, is quoted as saying: "The most recent purchases of foreign exchange were not undertaken for foreigners, as is stated in the official British statement, but in fact by British subjects. There were considerable withdrawals of foreign capital, but these took place mostly several weeks ago. During the past few days I have been assured by one of the most influential representatives of French banking circles in London that to his personal knowledge orders for the sale of sterling and purchases of dollars were given to the London banks by great numbers of British clients. Even as late as Saturday [September 19, 1931] 10,000,000 pounds left the Bank of England's vaults." [*New York Times*, Monday, September 21, 1931] Even on the eve of the default, London was still exporting capital - getting the most out of available pounds to buy up assets around the world.

THE INVERGORDON FARCE

In late September 1929, Norman had used the Hatry bankruptcy as a pretext for raising the Bank Rate, which he had wanted to do for reasons of economic warfare against the USA. In 1931, an indispensable part of the orchestration of the British default was an alleged "mutiny" in the Royal Navy in protest over pay cuts. On Tuesday, September 15, Sir Austen Chamberlain, the First Lord of the Admiralty, informed MacDonald of a trifling incident which had taken place at Invergordon. About 500 sailors of the Royal Navy had assembled for meetings to discuss the pay cut for experienced seamen which the National Government was proposing. The seamen ignored orders to return to their ships until their protest meetings were over. In response, the Admiral of the British Atlantic Fleet announced the postponement of the scheduled naval maneuvers, and also the dispersal of the Atlantic fleet to its various home ports. It was these latter actions which "elevated what might have remained a small incident into a major occurrence. Sensational headlines around the world pointed to the parallels to the Russian revolution of 1905 and 1917 and the German revolution of 1918, both of which had been marked in their early phases by fleet mutinies." The Red Revolution was about to overpower the Royal Navy itself! In addition to this hysterical hype, there was also the sense that the austerity program would have rough sledding from other groups in Britain as well. [Kunz, 131]

THE BANK OF ENGLAND DEMANDS DEFAULT

A dispatch of September 17, 1931 to the *New York Times* reported that Sir Ernest Harvey, Deputy Governor of the Bank of England, and other financial leaders had gone that evening to the House of Commons to convey to Prime Minister Ramsay MacDonald "a grave warning that the stability of the pound was again imperiled." "It is stated that they gave two reasons for this emergency - first, the naval unrest, and, second, the report that a general election was imminent."

Saturday, September 18, 1931 was the day the British cabinet officially decided to default on Britain's gold obligations. MacDonald called it the most solemn conference ever held at 10 Downing Street. True to form, it was the Bank of England that proposed the abrogation of the gold standard through the mouth of its Deputy Governor, who announced that the only course of action left was for Britain to leave the gold standard. [Kunz, 135] Harvey deliberately created the false impression that he had discussed the situation after the close of trading on Friday with Harrison of the New York Fed. This was not true. Harvey, in response to a question from MacDonald, added that he did not think it worthwhile to raise even 100 million pounds ($450 million) if people were only going to withdraw it. MacDonald quickly agreed to default, and the rest of the cabinet meeting was devoted to technical details of how to terminate the gold standard. [Kunz, 135]

It was only on Saturday, September 19, 1931 that Harvey informed Harrison of the New York Fed of what the British government was now doing. Harrison was described as greatly shocked by this decision, which came as a surprise to him. Harrison persisted for a time in exploring possible alternatives to London's default. [Kunz, 137] But the Bank of England remained adamantly committed to immediate default.

THE END OF THE WORLD

At the time the British decided to default, they thus had an offer from George Harrison and the New York Federal Reserve of additional loans to defend the pound. More help could have been obtained from Paris as well. Then there is the embarrassing fact that during the last week of the gold standard, the Bank of England's gold stocks INCREASED from 133,300,000 to 135,600,000 pounds. [Palyi, 277]

On Sunday, September 20, 1931, the British government issued its statements announcing its decision to "suspend for the time being" the clause of the Gold Standard Act of 1925 requiring the Bank of England to sell gold at the fixed price. All the other elements of the official British mythology were also reflected in the statement: "His Majesty's Government have no reason to believe that the present difficulties are due to any substantial extent to the export of capital by British nationals. Undoubtedly the bulk of withdrawals has been for foreign accounts." The bloody wogs, as we see, were once again the root of the problem. Furthermore: "His Majesty's Government have arrived at their decision with the greatest reluctance. But during the last few days international markets have become demoralized and have been liquidating their sterling assets regardless of their intrinsic worth. In these circumstances there was no alternative but to protect the financial position of this country by the only means at our disposal." As we have seen, there were plenty of other means. Finally, there was the obligatory stiff upper lip: "The ultimate resources of this country are enormous and there is no doubt that the present exchange difficulties will prove only temporary." [*New York Times*, September 21, 1931]

The worldwide shock, as we will see, was severe. In the words of Jackson E. Reynolds. then President of the First National Bank of New York, "when England went off gold it was like the end of the world."

THE BANKERS' RAMP

With the help of demagogic headlines in the London afternoon tabloids, the British oligarchy placed the blame for the fall of the mighty pound on a "bankers' ramp" led by foreign central bankers. A favorite target was poor George Harrison of the New York Federal Reserve, who was rewarded with slander and obloquy for his pathetic and servile devotion to the currency of British imperialism. Another favorite fall-guy was the Banque de France. One British chronicler of these times sums up the official line of scapegoating the foreigners as follows: "It was basically the American trade cycle, and not British monetary policy, that made life so wretched for us." [R.S. Sayers, 97]

JACQUES RUEFF ATTACKS BRITISH HANDLING OF CRISIS

During these weeks of the British crisis in the summer of 1931, the economist Jacques Rueff was serving as the Financial Attaché at the French Embassy in London. This meant that Rueff was in practice the manager of the French sterling balances. Palyi cites the "'posthumous' charge by Rueff that the "Bank of England defaulted intentionally in order to damage the creditor central banks, the Bank of France in particular...." [Palyi, 268]

On October 1, 1931, Rueff completed his memorandum entitled "Sur les causes et les enseignements de la crise financière anglaise," which was intended to be read by French Finance Minister P.-E. Flandin and the French Prime Minister, Pierre Laval.

Rueff first described the modes of intervention of the Bank of England: "Elle avait...deux instruments: le taux d'escompte et la politique dite d''open market'....Depuis 1929 la Banque d'Angleterre a constamment utilisé ces deux instruments pour maintenir aussi bas que possible les taux en vigeur sur le marché de Londres. Elle a toujours retardé au maximum les élévations de taux d'escompte qui s'imposaient, cependant qu'elle cherchait à augmenter, par ses achats de valeurs d'Etat, l'abondance monetaire du marché." [Rueff, 301] The Bank of England had been slow to raise the bank rate, and had used open market operations to augment the money supply.

For Rueff, the British were guilty of violating the implicit rules of the gold exchange standard, since they tried to maintain their liquidity despite a gold outflow. "on peut affirmer notamment qu'en 1929 et 1930, presque sans exception, la politique d''open market' de la Banque d'Angleterre a été faite à contresens. Les mouvements d'or, en effet, tendent à se corriger eux-memes, puisque toute sortie de metal tend à provoquer une restriction de credit, qui hausse les taux du marché. Or, en 1929 et 1930, toutes les fois que de l'or sortait de la Banque d'Angleterre, celle-ci achetait des valeurs d'Etat sur le marché, remplacant ainsi les disponibilités qui venaient de disparaitre." [Rueff, 302] The Bank of England, argued Rueff, had artificially inflated the British money supply and had not permitted the gold standard to work.

Because of these policies, Rueff found, the British had weakened themselves even before the German crisis had begun: "Or, en 1931, ces fautes ont été commises, provoquant des mouvements de capitaux qui ont été mortels pour le change anglais. Il est très probable que l'Angleterre aurait pu y resister, si elle n'avait pas été mise préalablement dans un état de paralysie economique et financière, interdisant à son organisme les réactions spontanées d'un marché normal." [Rueff, 303]

Rueff repeatedly condemned Stimson's intervention at the London Conference of July 1931 with the proposal for standstill agreements which immediately created a liquidity crisis and put world banking in difficulty: "Toutes les banques du monde, voyant soudain immobilisé une fraction très importante de leurs capitaux à court terme, ont cherché à recuperer toutes les reserves qu'elles pouvaient rendre disponibles." [Rueff, 304] But the British always blamed the wogs: "...l'opinion britannique ...recherche à l'exterieur la cause de ses difficultés." [Rueff, 305]

The British had been wallowing in a depression since 1918, and that for them made it a world economic crisis: "Il faut d'abord remarquer que, pour l'opinion britannique, la crise economique d'après guerre n'est pas chose nouvelle. Depuis que l'Angleterre souffre du chomage permanent - c'est-à-dire depuis la guerre - l'opinion britannique et les experts anglais affirment que le monde est en état de crise. Depuis la guerre, même lorsque le monde, sauf l'Angleterre, était en pleine prospérité, les représentants britanniques ne cessaient de demander à la Societé des Nations de trouver un remède à la crise economique, qualifiée de mondiale parce qu'elle affectait les intérêts du Royaume-Uni de Grande-Bretagne et d'Irlande." [Rueff, 307]

For Rueff, all British proposals for international monetary cooperation were stratagems designed to shift the crisis from Britain to the rest of the world: "Il reste enfin à évoquer la dernière des formules par lesquelles l'Angleterre pretend que le monde devrait être reconstruit: la cooperation financière internationale. C'est là un programme dont le sens n'a jamais été defini, probablement parce qu'il n'en a aucun....Il n'est pas douteux que tous les plans présentés à Genève ou a Bâle, plan Norman, plan Kindersley, plan Francqui, tendent seulement à realiser le trust des entreprises en faillite et à y investir des capitaux qui sans cela se seraient refusés. Par là ils sont un merveilleux instrument pour transferer les difficultés financières des États qui les ont provoqués, à ceux qui ont été assez sages ou assez prudents pour s'en préserver...Tel est d'ailleurs le sens profond et l'objet veritable de tous les efforts tendant à realiser la solidarité internationale, solidarité que l'on invoque toujours lorsque l'on veut profiter de la prosperité des États voisins, mais jamais lorsque l'on peut leur venir en aide." [Rueff, 318-319] Rueff suggested a Franco-American accord capable of putting an end to the British game.

THE BANK OF ENGLAND'S DUTCH TREAT

By September 20, 1931 most of the sterling balances held by foreigners who were disposed to liquidate them had already been liquidated. The exception were sterling balances held by foreign central banks, like the Dutch, and these would be loyal to London, partly because their estimate was that the crisis was not so severe as to force the British off gold. The little people of the British middle-class public were proving docile enough to make no attempt to turn in their pound notes for gold. The Big Five London clearing banks were undisturbed by panic runs or the specter of insolvency.

There is no doubt that during the weeks before default, the Bank of England practiced the most cynical deception on other central banks. The Bank of England twice assured the Bank of South Africa that it would do everything in its power to maintain gold payments. The Bank of England acted with great treachery towards the Netherlands Bank, the central bank which had shown itself to be the truest friend of the pound, supporting it in crisis after crisis. The president of the Netherlands Bank, Mr. Vissering, telephoned the Bank of England on September 18, 1931 to inquire whether there were any truth to the rumors about a forthcoming sterling devaluation. The Bank of England official who answered the phone emphatically denied that there would be a devaluation, and offered to pay off the Netherlands Bank sterling balances in gold on the spot. Because of these assurances, the Netherlands Bank did not pull its pound holdings out of the Bank of England and convert them into gold. Because of the repeated reassurances, the Netherlands Bank thought that the Bank of England should safeguard the Netherlands Bank against all the sterling losses to which it was subjected. A discussion of this British betrayal is found in the 1931-32 Annual Report of the Netherlands Bank. [Brown, vol. 2, 1170-1172]

A few days after the call summarized above, "Dr. G. Vissering of the Netherlands' Central Bank called Harvey to request that the Dutch gold held by the Bank of England be earmarked [separated from the Bank of England stocks as a preliminary to shipment to the Netherlands]. Harvey huffily refused, saying that the Dutch could either take their gold back to Amsterdam or keep it in London but if they chose the latter course they would not be placed in the position of a preferred creditor. To assuage Vissering's fears Harvey wrote him about the credits and stressed the total commitment of the National Government to the maintenance of the gold standard [Kunz, 119-120] As a result, "the Netherlands Bank felt, and for good reason so, that it had been deceived by the Bank of England, a turn that was scarcely befitting Norman's idea of central bank cooperation, or the 'ethics' of the gold standard." [Palyi, 278]

Montagu Norman claimed that he had personally not been a participant in the decision to default on gold. As we have noted, Norman's cover story was that he had suffered a nervous breakdown, and had taken a vacation at the Chateau Frontenac in Quebec, Canada. When the Bank of England suspended gold payment, Norman was on board ship in the middle of the Atlantic. Norman claims that he knew nothing of the decision to go off gold until he landed at Liverpool on September 23, 1931. Norman was thus able to blame the default on one of his resident whipping-boys, Deputy Governor Sir Ernest Harvey. Harvey himself suffered a nervous breakdown because of the stress of serving under Norman.

When the British stopped paying in gold, they were quickly followed by Denmark, Sweden, Norway, Holland, Bolivia, and India – most candidates for inclusion in the emerging sterling bloc. Other countries, including Greece, Italy, Germany, Austria, and Hungary were already operating under exchange controls and other measures which effectively prevented gold outflow. [Hoover, 82]

The British strategy for saving the golden pound had included histrionic international appeals from Prime Minister Ramsay MacDonald, who pleaded with other countries not to drain off the last of the British gold. After the British had defaulted, MacDonald's perfidy caused much resentment abroad. In the words of an American economist, "Hardly had Ramsay MacDonald stopped sobbing over the international radio that Britannia should not be forced to sacrifice her honor, than he began to smile broadly because the fall of the pound gave her marked advantage in exports." [Mitchell, 14]

THE BRITISH GAME

A British estimate of the London predicament of the early 1930s reads as follows: "...Great Britain is a highly populated industrial country, carrying a terrific burden of internal debt, dependent predominantly for existence on foreign trade, enjoying the benefits of being the world's chief banking centre, possessed of a large net income from long-term investments abroad, but heavily indebted (in her role as world's banker) to other centres on short-term account." [*Economist*, September 26, 1931, 548] The British racket up until September 1931 had been to use a high pound to maximize their buying up of the world's productive assets and resources. After September 1931, a devalued pound meant that pound-denominated foreign claims on the British financial system - and these were the vast majority - were automatically reduced. Five months after the British default, Norman and the British oligarchy embarked on a policy of cheap money. At this time, a series of Bank Rate reductions was started which soon brought the discount to 2.5%, where it stayed for many years. Montagu Norman himself, the former gold addict, became the main theoretician of Cheap Money in the new era of competitive devaluations. The British stock market quickly recovered and kept rising during most of the 1930s. But unemployment hovered around 2.5 million until the beginning of the Second World War.

"For years, Continental opinion had been coming to the view that the British system was dying of ossification," wrote Lionel Robbins. [Robbins, 93] "Now the British had increased their own relative importance compared to their continental rivals, who had joined them in perdition." The post-1931 British strategy also included Imperial Preference and trade war: "Britain entered the lists with the Import Duties Act of March, 1932 (reaching 33 1/3 per cent), and the later Ottawa Agreement establishing empire tariff preferences spurred other countries in the process of retaliation. Sterling losses of so many countries spread deflation through the struggle for liquidity. The contest between economies that remained on gold and those that had left it became acute." [Mitchell, 14] Soon, US exports to the rest of the world had dropped to about one third of their 1929 level. [Hoover, 83] European purchases of American agricultural products ceased almost entirely. US unemployment increased rapidly. Tax revenue fell by 50%. [Hoover, 89]

BRITISH DEFAULT: TEN MORE YEARS OF WORLD DEPRESSION

The Gibraltar of British Empire finance had crashed. The old saying, "as safe as the Bank of England" was now a mockery. "It was only vaguely understood, if at all, that at stake was what is called today the 'world monetary system.' It was still a sterling system. The likely alternative to...the gold standard, at the old sterling parity, may have been the breakdown of that system. That is what happened after September, 1931." [Palyi, 86] "The cooperation of the central banks in the 1920s ended in a breakdown of the entire system, having been essentially a cloak that masked the ultimate purpose of its chief ingredient, the gold exchange standard, which was to maintain Britain's gold standard without obeying the rules of the gold standard." [Palyi, 146] During the 18-month period after the British default, most world currencies also terminated gold payments through external default. Until March 1933, the US dollar and its satellite currencies in central and South America were able to keep up payments on gold. Otherwise, the gold standard was maintained – often with exchange controls – by a group of countries called the "gold bloc," comprehending France, Holland, Belgium, Switzerland, Italy, Poland, and Estonia. Estonia was forced off gold, and Italy and Poland imposed gold export controls. The Belgian franc was devalued in March 1935. France imposed a gold embargo in September 1936. Switzerland and Holland announced devaluations immediately thereafter.

COUNTRIES LEAVING THE GOLD STANDARD APRIL 1929 - APRIL 1933

1929

APRIL, URUGUAY

NOVEMBER, ARGENTINA

DECEMBER, BRAZIL

1930

MARCH, AUSTRALIA

APRIL, NEW ZEALAND

SEPTEMBER, VENEZUELA

1931

AUGUST, MEXICO

SEPTEMBER, UNITED KINGDOM, CANADA, INDIA, SWEDEN, DENMARK, NORWAY, EGYPT, IRISH FREE STATE, BRITISH MALAYA, PALESTINE

OCTOBER, AUSTRIA, PORTUGAL, FINLAND, BOLIVIA, SALVADOR

DECEMBER, JAPAN

1932

JANUARY, COLOMBIA, NICARAGUA, COSTA RICA

APRIL, GREECE , CHILE

MAY, PERU

JUNE, ECUADOR, SIAM

JULY, YUGOSLAVIA

1933

JANUARY, UNION OF SOUTH AFRICA

APRIL, HONDURAS, UNITED STATES

[Brown 1075]

BEYOND BREAKDOWN TO DISINTEGRATION

The year 1931 is thus a turning point in the financial history of Europe analogous to 1914 in political-military history: "...because of the profound influence of the war upon the structure of the world's credit system and upon the economic environment in which it operated, 1914-19 was a period that marked the breakdown, rather than the suspension or modification, of the pre-war international gold standard system ... *when England suspended the convertibility of sterling in 1931 the international gold standard as a world institution entered into an historical phase which must be described by a stronger term than breakdown.* **September 1931 marked the beginning of its disintegration.**" [Brown 1052, emphasis added]

Current historians and economists are fixated on the New York crash of 1929, but there can be no doubt that the British default of September 1931 was the more important watershed by far. "Britain's devaluation in 1931 had a psychological and political impact on Europe, and beyond, that can hardly be overestimated. In final analysis, the break-up of the international financial and commercial system was a decisive factor in balkanizing Europe and preparing the ground for World War II." [Palyi, 270] Another writer noted that among the "consequences were an increase of international suspicion and hatred, an inflamed nationalism in Europe and, finally, war." [Giuseppi, *Bank of England*, 164] Indeed.

CURRENCY BLOCS AND THE IMPULSION TOWARDS A NEW WORLD WAR

The scuttling of the pound-based, gold exchange international monetary system of the 1920s was perhaps the most potent underlying factor in the universal renewal of armed conflict that soon followed. When the pound fell, a series of currency blocs emerged according to the prototype of what had emerged under the guidance of Norman and Schacht as the German mark area. These currency blocs included the British pound sterling bloc, the US dollar bloc, the gold bloc (which broke up, leaving a franc bloc along with some other shards), the Soviet ruble area, and the Japanese yen zone. The currency chaos meant that there was no reliable means of settling commercial payments among these blocs. World trade atrophied. The situation was difficult for everyone, but it was worst for those blocs which had the greatest dependency on importing oil, metals, rubber, and strategic raw materials.

The pound sterling, dollar, franc and ruble each had some raw materials backing. But the German mark, Japanese yen and Italian lira had virtually none. Each of these states embarked on an economic regime of autarky so as to conserve foreign exchange. For Germany, Italy, and Japan, aggressive territorial expansion towards possible sources of oil and metals soon appeared as the only available surrogate for foreign trade. The ascendancy of fascism was favored in each case by the penury of world trade, and in each case the British stood ready to promote fascist leaders who would ruthlessly act out this logic, as exemplified by Montagu Norman's role as the premier international patron of Hitler and the Nazis, and as the point man for a pro-Hitler policy which was carried out by Sir Henry Deterding, Averell Harriman, and Prescott Bush.

BEGGAR-MY-NEIGHBOR

The British were aware at the time of the colossal magnitude of what they had wrought, and were certainly aware of how rival states might suffer far greater consequences than the British themselves: "...the disappearance of the pound from the ranks of the world's stable currencies threatens to undermine the exchange stability of nearly every nation on earth; ...banking liquidity throughout the world has been seriously impaired... international trade must be temporarily paralysed so long as the future value of many currencies is open to grave uncertainty...there is an obvious risk lest we may have started an international competition in devaluation of currencies motived [sic] by the hope of stimulating exports and leading to a tragic reversion to the chaotic conditions which existed five or six years ago." ["The End of an Epoch," *Economist*, September 26, 1931, 547]

The entire edifice of world trade and world banking had imploded: "The sterling bill enters so deeply into the whole mechanism of international trade, and so many foreign banks, including central banks, have been accustomed to keep a large portion of their reserves in the form of sterling balances in London, that the shock caused by the depreciation of sterling to some 80 per cent. of its value has necessarily been profound....By our action, the value of the legal backing of a number of currencies has suddenly shrunk." [*Economist*, September 26, 1931, pp. 550-551]

By October, the British were noting the massive gold outflow from the United States, which many now considered on the verge of a dollar crisis: "The suspension also of the gold standard in Great Britain had three important results. Firstly, it gave a further shock to confidence. Secondly, it prevented foreign banks from drawing upon their sterling balances except at a heavy loss, and so drove them back on their dollar balances. Finally, it destroyed all faith in the safety and efficacy of the gold exchange standard, for foreign central banks found that the sterling exchange which they had legitimately held as part of their legal reserve had lost part of its value, thereby undermining their own stability, and inflicting upon them losses in many cases commensurate with their own capital." [*Economist*, "America's Money Problems," October 10, 1931, 646] In other words, London's planned default had bankrupted or weakened a series of central banks which had deposited their reserves in the Bank of England. A few weeks later, the *Economist* commented further: "It was inevitable that the suspension of gold payments in England should have a profound effect upon the position of leading central banks.... All these central banks have had to face a 20 per cent. depreciation of their holdings of sterling, which for many of them means a substantial proportion of their legal currency reserves.... Central banks have begun hurriedly to convert their *devisen* into gold. The general tendency has been to leave their sterling holdings intact, but to exchange their dollar balances and bills for gold; and this is a major cause of the recent efflux of gold from the United States. Again, commercial banks ...have had to face the immobilisation under the 'standstill' agreement of such part of their assets as they had ventured in Germany and central Europe; they have suffered, in common with the central banks, a 20 per cent. depreciation of their sterling holdings; and, last but not least, they have had to deal with the widespread dislocation to trade caused by the depreciation of sterling, which is the currency of world commerce...." ["The Gold Rush," *Economist*, October 24, 1931, p. 746]

BRITISH DEFAULT PRECIPITATES US BANKING PANIC OF 1932-33

By August of 1931, Keynes estimated that commodity prices on the world market had fallen since 1929 by an average of 25%, with some commodities falling as much as 40% to 50%. Common stock shares had fallen worldwide by 40% to 50%, he reckoned. Investment-grade bonds were down by only 5%, but lower rated bonds were down by 10% to 15%, and the bonds of many governments had "suffered prodigious falls." When it came to real estate, the picture was more differentiated. Great Britain and France had been able to maintain relative firmness in real estate values, with the result that "mortgage business is sound and the multitude of loans granted on the security of real estate are unimpaired." The worst crash of real estate prices had occurred in the United States, Keynes found. Farm values had suffered a great decline, and newly developed urban commercial real estate was depressed to 60% to 70% of its cost of construction, and often less. Finally, Keynes estimated that the commercial loan portfolios held by banks were in the worst shape of all. Keynes evaluated this 2-year collapse as the worst world-wide deflation in the money values of real assets in history. [Keynes 172-175]

Keynes pointed especially to something far worse yet to come, namely the potential world banking crisis that was implicit in the price collapses he had summed up. He concluded that in most of the non-British world, if bank assets were conservatively re-evaluated, "quite a significant proportion of the banks of the world would be found to be insolvent; and with the further progress of Deflation this proportion will grow rapidly." London had the least to worry about, since "fortunately our own domestic British Banks are probably at present - for various reasons - among the strongest." Once again, the Americans would bear the brunt of the crisis:

> ...in the United States, the position of the banks, though partly concealed from the public eye, may be in fact the weakest element in the whole situation. It is obvious that the present trend of events cannot go much further without something breaking. If nothing is done, it will be amongst the world's banks that the really critical breakages will occur. ["The Consequences to the Banks of the Collapse of Money Values," (August 1931) in Keynes, 177]

During October 1931, the British default had provoked a flurry of bank failures worldwide: the Comptoir Lyon-Alemand closed; Handels Bank of Denmark needed to be bailed out by its central bank; and the Bank für Handel und Gewerbe, Leipzig, suspended payment, as did the Dresden Volksbank, the Franklin Trust Company of Philadelphia and 18 smaller US banks. The central banks were so strapped for cash that there was a run on the Bank for International Settlements, which had to sell great masses of its own assets in order to meet the cash demands of its members, the central banks.

KEYNES: THE CURSE OF MIDAS

Keynes was very explicit that the most destructive consequences of the British default were going to be visited upon the United States, which was still on the gold standard:

> ...the competitive disadvantage will be concentrated on those few countries which remain on the gold standard. **On these will fall the curse of Midas.** As a result of their unwillingness to exchange their exports except for gold their export trade will dry up and disappear until they no longer have either a favourable trade balance or foreign deposits to repatriate. This means in the main France and the United States. Their loss of export trade will be an inevitable, a predictable, outcome of their own action.... For the appreciation of French and American money in terms of the money of other countries makes it impossible for French and American exporters to sell their goods.... They have willed the destruction of their own export industries, and only they can take the steps necessary to restore them. The appreciation of their currencies must also gravely embarrass their banking systems. ["The End of the Gold Standard," (September 27, 1931) in Keynes, 292-293, emphasis added]

One possible outcome contemplated with eager anticipation by London was that the gold outflow experienced by the United States after the British default would lead to the short-term collapse of the US dollar. By law, the Federal Reserve in those days had to have sufficient gold to cover 40% of the value of all outstanding Federal Reserve dollar notes. At first glance, that 40% of Federal Reserve notes might have seemed to set the minimum gold stock necessary for the survival of the dollar in its then-current form. But in reality the gold requirements of the US were far greater, precisely because of the ongoing economic depression. The remaining 60% of the US currency had to be covered in practice by either gold or commercial paper, including bankers' acceptances. But because of the collapse of trade, these trade-based instruments had become very scarce. So even more gold was needed to take up the slack.

THE BRITISH CAST THE CURSE OF MIDAS ON AMERICA

In the event, the impact of the British gold default of September 21, 1931 on the United States banking system was nothing short of catastrophic. Within six weeks, the United States was drained of about $700,000,000 worth of gold. "The rush from abroad to convert dollar balances into gold frightened American depositors, and they began to withdraw currency from their banks." [Kennedy 30] Bank withdrawals were $400,000,000 during these same six weeks. [Mitchell 128] By November, "almost half a billion dollars had gone into hiding."-- meaning hoarding, with individuals putting their cash in a safety deposit box, mattress, or an old sock. [Kennedy, 30] The *Economist* was busy calculating the point at which financial necrosis would set in: "...the United States could, at last gasp, part with $1,700 millions of gold, though the National City Bank very pertinently calls this a theoretical maximum." "A rough calculation, however, shows that European central banks together still hold foreign exchange equal to some $1,400 millions." [*Economist*, October 10, 1931, 646]

In 1928, there had been 491 US bank failures. In 1929, the figure had risen to 642. By 1930, as the collapse of the domestic real estate bubble began to take its toll, bank failures had risen to 1,345. In the wake of the British default, American "bank runs and failures increased spectacularly: 522 commercial banks with $471 million in deposits suspended during October 1931; 1,860 institutions with deposits of $1.45 billion closed between August 1931 and January 1, 1932. At the same time, holdings by the 19,000 banks still open dropped appreciably through hoarding and deterioration of their securities." [Kennedy 30] Thus, the disintegration of the London gold standard represented a qualitative turning point in the development of the US banking panic. In terms of individual bank failures, 1931, the year of the British default, was the worst year in American banking history.

2,298 US BANK FAILURES IN 1931

The decisive role of the pound sterling crisis in detonating the domestic US banking panic is stressed by another chronicler of the Great Depression: "...in all of 1931, a peak number of 2,298 banks with deposits of $1.692 billion succumbed to insolvency. As we have seen, about three quarters of these failures came during or after the British crisis, and the vast majority of the damage to the depositors ($1.45 billion out of $1.692 billion) was inflicted during and after the London default." [Mitchell, 128] The shock waves from the London default were felt first and most severely among the banks of Chicago, Ohio, and other parts of the Midwest, followed by Pennsylvania, New York, and then New England. The US banking system was now being subjected to the kind of speculative attack foreshadowed by the analysis of Lord Keynes. While some of the demands for gold were coming from France, it is evident that a very large proportion were coming from London, whether directly or indirectly. This was an attack which Hoover, disoriented by his superficially cordial personal meeting with Ramsay MacDonald during the British Prime Minister's visit to the US, was ideologically incapable of understanding.

It was in October 1931 that Hoover broke his long immobilism on the banking question and launched the ill-starred National Credit Corporation, his unsuccessful public-private partnership to bail out the banks. This timing suggests that in Hoover's view as well, the London default had been a major milestone on the road to US banking panic. On the evening of October 6, 1931, Hoover met with 32 Congressional leaders of both parties at the White House. Hoover summarized the world economic situation in the wake of the British default:

> The British... are suffering deeply from the shocks of the financial collapse on the Continent. Their abandonment of the gold standard and of payment of their external obligations has

struck a blow at the foundations of the world economy. The procession of countries which followed Britain off the gold standard has left the United States and France as the only major countries still holding to it without modification. The instability of currencies, the now almost world-wide restrictions on exchange, the rationing of imports to protect these currencies and the default of bad debts, have cut deeper and deeper into world trade.

HOOVER: WE ARE FACED WITH SAVING OURSELVES

Hoover was forced to concede that the once-prosperous US had been dragged down to the same level as the chronically depressed British:

> We are finding ourselves in much the same position as the British, but in lesser degree. Long-term loans which we made to Europe and the mass of kited bills bought from them are affecting us sadly with each new default. Like the British, we too are increasingly unable to collect moneys due us from abroad. Extensive deposits in our banks owned by foreigners are demand liabilities on our gold reserves and are becoming increasingly dangerous. After the British abandoned the gold standard, even the dollar came under suspicion. Out of an unreasoning fear, gold is being withdrawn from our monetary stocks and bank reserves. These devitalizing drains and the threat of them hang like a Damoclean sword over our credit structure. Banks, fearing the worst, called in industrial and commercial loans, and beyond all this the dwindling European consumption of goods has decreased purchases of our farm products and other commodities and demoralized our prices, production, and employment. We are now faced with the problem, not of saving Germany or Britain, but of saving ourselves. [Hoover 90]

A day earlier, in a letter to George Harrison at the New York Federal Reserve, Hoover had described the problems created by the British crisis from the point of view of the individual American banker:

> There have been in some localities foolish alarms over the stability of our credit structure and considerable withdrawals of currency. In consequence, bankers in many other parts of the country in fear of such unreasoning demands of depositors have deemed it necessary to place their assets in such liquid form as to enable them to meet drains and runs. To do this they sell securities and restrict credit. The sale of securities demoralizes their price and jeopardizes other banks. The restriction on credit has grown greatly in the past few weeks. There are a multitude of complaints that farmers cannot secure loans for their livestock feeding or to carry their commodities until the markets improve. There are a multitude of complaints of business men that they cannot secure the usual credit to carry their operations on a normal basis and must discharge labor. There are complaints of manufacturers who use agricultural and other raw materials that they cannot secure credits beyond day to day needs with which to lay in their customary seasonal supplies. The effect of this is to thrust on the back of the farmer the load of carrying the nation's stocks. The whole cumulative effect is today to decrease prices of commodities and securities and to spread the relations of the debtor and the creditor. [Hoover 87]

FEBRUARY 7, 1932: US TWO WEEKS AWAY FROM GOLD DEFAULT

On February 7, 1932, Secretary of the Treasury Ogden Mills informed Hoover that the United States was about two weeks away from defaulting on gold payment because of the continued flow of gold out of this country. To this had to be added the dwindling gold stocks of banks, which generally stood ready to convert paper money into gold when depositors asked for it. This gold disappeared domestically as it was added to private hoards. In principle, there was every reason at this time for the United States to abandon the wrecked gold standard, which the British were using for economic warfare. This is what Roosevelt did just a couple of years later. But this had to be done in a well-planned, effective fashion, within the context of some kind of a recovery program like that of Roosevelt's Hundred Days. For the US to make a chaotic retreat from gold would have been a rout. Given the *laissez-faire* obsessions of the Hoover administration, it is likely that such a move, especially if carried out in isolation from a general policy reversal, would have engendered chaos. Hoover dodged the main issues by getting the Congress to allow the commercial banks to use US Treasury securities in place of commercial paper as backing for the dollar. With this, the immediate US gold shortage was eased.

Hoover at first attempted to organize the bankers to take care of their own. This attempt was called the National Credit Corporation, a private Delaware firm launched in October 1931. Upon joining, member banks subscribed 2% of their assets, in return for which they could obtain loans on their sound assets which were not eligible for rediscount at the Federal Reserve branches. But the bankers in charge of this venture were so reluctant to make loans that the National Credit Corporation proved to be an exercise in futility. Despite new waves of bank failures in December 1931 and January 1932, the NCC lent out only one third of its available funds.

JUNE 1932: CHICAGO BANKS IN CRISIS

Next, Hoover tried the Reconstruction Finance Corporation, a creature of the federal government which had been set up by Congress with $3.5 billion of stock and cash in January 1931. In June 1932, the banking crisis again struck Chicago in the wake of the bankruptcy of the Insull group, with 25 suburban banks and 15 downtown institutions closing their doors in the face of panic withdrawals. Only 5 big banks in the Loop remained. To complicate matters, the Democratic National Convention was about to convene in Chicago. The closure of all Chicago banks would have undermined Hoover's claim that prosperity was just around the corner, and given the Democrats a political windfall. The RFC quickly provided a loan, which temporarily saved the Central Republic National Bank; this rescue prevented panic runs which would have submerged the other four surviving Loop banks.

The Federal Reserve Board took the attitude that it had no responsibility at all for banks that were not members of the Fed system. From 1929 to 1932, the Fed did virtually nothing to stem the depression. In 1932 Hoover wanted the Federal Reserve banks to start providing the economy with credit in the form of direct lending to businesses, as practiced by most European central banks. The Federal Reserve Board feared that issuing such loans would open the door to panic runs on the Federal Reserve banks. The Fed finally agreed to make direct loans, but the new law carried the proviso that this could be done only in an emergency. In July 1932, as soon as the direct loan facility had been legalized, Hoover asked the Fed to declare a state of emergency so as to enable the direct loans. But the Fed refused to declare the state of emergency. Senator Carter Glass wanted to prevent Fed credit and loans from being used for speculation, but the New York Fed indignantly rejected the idea that the Fed could regulate the uses of the credit it issued. A good summary of the Fed's Catch-22 immobilism and impotence, verging on outright sabotage was offered by one student of the banking crisis:

> The Federal Reserve stipulated that borrowers must prove they could not receive credit elsewhere but also decided that borrowers did not deserve loans which they would not get elsewhere. [Kennedy 49]

OCTOBER 1932: NEVADA BANKING CRISIS

In the last days of the 1932 presidential campaign, the first shutdown of the banking system of an entire state occurred. This was detonated by the insolvency of the Wingfield group, which controlled almost all of the banks in Nevada. Wingfield was done in by an endless series of bankruptcies among cattle and sheep ranchers, whose assets usually brought about 25 cents on the dollar when put up for auction. On October 31, the lieutenant governor of Nevada declared a 12-day bank holiday during which all state banks could remain closed. It was hoped that during this lapse of time, some solution could be found to permit business to resume. In reality, the Nevada banks remained closed for about four months, until the end of the Hoover administration, and re-opened only in the aftermath of Franklin D. Roosevelt's bank holiday of March 1933.

Many schemes were tried to revive the Nevada banks. One plan was based on the depositors' takeover of ownership of some banks. Wingfield tried several times to get loans from the Reconstruction Finance Corporation, but these never came to fruition. There were attempts to mobilize the "private sector" through loans from California investors and Nevada industrialists, but these proved equally vain. Nevada as a state was unable to re-open its banks. And as it turned out, no state was able permanently to re-open its banks after they had been closed. The Nevada banking crisis was a small episode in terms of the dollar values involved, but its modest dimension only made it loom larger as public proof of the impotence of all levels of government to act.

In late 1932, increasing numbers of rural banks came under the intense pressure of panic runs by depositors. The RFC was able to stem the tide for a while, and made loans to banks in Wisconsin, Pennsylvania, Minnesota, and Tennessee. During December 1932, and during the first six weeks of 1933, numerous banks with large aggregate deposits closed their doors in New Jersey, the District of Columbia, Tennessee, Illinois, Iowa, Missouri, and California. Internal documents of the Hoover administration made public later show that lame duck Hoover had also been concerned about fighting off imminent panic in such larger cities as Cleveland, Chattanooga, Little Rock, Mobile, St. Louis, and Memphis.

FEBRUARY 1933: LOUISIANA

The beginning of the end came in Louisiana in early February 1933. Here a large insurance company had succumbed in January, despite some support from the RFC. The key banking institution in trouble was the Hibernia Bank and Trust Company. US Senator from Louisiana Huey Long tried to raise cash from other bankers to prevent banks from closing because of depositor panic during the morning of Saturday, February 4, 1933. Long hurriedly consulted with Governor Allen of Louisiana, his political ally. Sen. Long decided that a bank holiday was in order, and got the New Orleans city librarian to search the history books for some momentous event that had occurred on February 4. The librarian could find nothing on February 4, but did determine that the United States had broken diplomatic relations with Germany on February 3, 1917. Long proclaimed that such a momentous event deserved two days of commemoration, and not just one. Gov. Allen signed the appropriate order, making February 4 a legal holiday across the state. Many people had no idea why the new holiday had been created; one newspaper which did reveal the link to the banking crisis was seized by the state militia under Senator Long's orders. Thanks to this surcease, the Hibernia Bank was able to announce $24 million in loans on Sunday morning, heading off the panic that might have broken out on Monday.

MICHIGAN: DON'T BANK WITH HANK

The final disintegration of the American banking system began with the explosion of a banking panic in Detroit, Michigan. The 1920s had seen the powerful emergence of automobile production as the leading sector of the US economy, and the Motor City was widely viewed as the most successful, dynamic, and forward-looking metropolis of American capitalism. The shock was all the greater when, at 1:32 AM of February 14, 1933, Governor William A. Comstock signed an order imposing an 8-day bank holiday for all of Michigan. The epicenter of the Detroit crisis was the Guardian banking group, which was personally dominated by celebrated automobile tycoon Henry Ford, with some help from his son Edsel. But if Guardian was rotten, its larger rival, the Detroit Bankers Company, which at the time was the third largest US bank outside of New York City, was putrid. When the Reconstruction Finance Corporation was brought in to save Guardian, the RFC board pronounced itself willing to offer loan assistance – but only if Henry Ford lent Guardian some millions of his own money, and agreed to keep the Ford Motor Company's deposits at Guardian at their current level.

Walter P. Chrysler of Chrysler Motors, Alfred P. Sloan, Jr. of General Motors, and Hudson Department Stores were ready to lend money to Guardian, but Henry Ford started feuding with the RFC and with his estranged business partner, millionaire US Senator James Couzens. After much haggling, Ford agreed to provide $8.25 million in new capital for a merged Guardian-Detroit Bankers. Banners appeared on the streets of Detroit attempting to build confidence in the proposed merger with the slogan "Bank with Hank."

But this Ford loan was contingent on an RFC loan, and the RFC now refused to make their loan because Wall Street banks had refused to renew their outstanding loans to a component of the Detroit Bankers group. So this entire scheme fell apart around February 28, 1933. Starting on March 1, Senator Couzens tried to get Michigan bankers to propose a plan under which the state's banks might re-open. But the bankers were unable to agree on any plan before the state legislature in Lansing had adjourned. Therefore the Michigan banks also stayed closed through the end of Herbert Hoover's term in office. Now the hammer-blows of panic fell thick and fast on the reeling US banks. The RFC was forced by a meddling and impotent Congress to publish the names of the banks that had received RFC loans, most of which were quickly driven out of business by panic runs.

WALL STREET EXPOSED: THE PECORA HEARINGS

The Wall Street banks and especially their stock dealings were during this period subjected to an investigation by the Senate Banking and Currency Committee, chaired by Senator Peter Norbeck, with Sen. Frederick Walcott as ranking Republican. This probe was a political move requested by President Hoover to show that the Wall Street crowd, and not the President, was responsible for the 1929 crash and was now obstructing necessary reforms. Hoover also thought that, unless Congress launched an investigation, bear raids might be launched on the stock exchange by pro-Democratic financiers to get Hoover out of office.

This committee came to be known as the Pecora committee because of the prominent role played by Ferdinand Pecora, a former New York City assistant district attorney in Manhattan, who became the counsel for the committee. Very damaging to bankers in general was the testimony of Charles E. Mitchell, chairman of the board of National City Bank, the ancestor of today's Citibank. Mitchell's testimony documented a series of unscrupulous stockjobbing practices carried out at the expense of a gullible public. The testimony also suggested that the greedy Mitchell was guilty of federal tax evasion, although he was later acquitted in his criminal trial – but convicted in a 1938 civil suit and forced to pay about $1.4 million in back taxes and interest. As one observer put it, these hearings marked the eclipse of the financier as a folk hero in American life. Confidence in the banking system and its managers had received another crushing blow.

Bankers began flailing in desperation. In New Jersey, Maryland, New York, and the District of Columbia, they reduced the interest rates paid on savings account deposits. A number of states allowed banks to limit the amount of money that could be withdrawn from accounts. Even individual cities declared bank holidays to stave off further panic: this was the case in Huntington, Indiana, and Mt. Carmel, Illinois. In other states, some cities began allowing the local banks to issue scrip; paper certificates to be used in lieu of money during the crisis, or, more bluntly, funny money. Indiana declared a bank holiday on February 23; Maryland followed suit on February 25, followed by Arkansas on February 27, and Ohio on February 28.

THE NEW YORK FED ON THE VERGE OF DEFAULT

The chaos in the hinterland increased the pressure on Chicago, and even more on the pre-eminent money center of New York City. Local bankers, strapped for cash, pulled half a billion dollars of their deposits out of New York, undermining the liquidity of the largest commercial banks and even of the flagship New York Federal Reserve Bank.

On March 1, Alabama and Louisiana imposed obligatory bank holidays, while Kentucky and West Virginia left it up to individual banks to decide whether they would open or not. Idaho empowered its governor to declare bank holidays, and Minnesota allowed the commissioner of banking to suspend banking for 15 days when he deemed it necessary. March 2 brought a new harvest of bank holidays across the west, with Arizona, California, Mississippi, Oklahoma, Oregon, and Nevada ordering their banks to close. In Baltimore, the bank holiday was being extended day by day. In the District of Columbia and in several states, savings banks began enforcing the rule that 60 days' advanced notice had to be given by depositors if they wanted to withdraw money.

It was also on March 2 that the Federal Reserve Board in Washington finally advised Hoover to declare a federal bank holiday. This advice was long overdue, but the Federal Reserve Board did not want to share responsibility for a bank holiday or for other measures that might still be considered drastic; they wanted Hoover to take the fall for them in the area of their own responsibility. Now the Federal Reserve banks themselves were on the verge of general default, and they had to strong-arm the Chicago Fed to make a loan to the hard-pressed New York branch. The Fed Board now suggested a bank holiday covering March 3, 4, and 6, 1933. Their assumption was that emergency enabling legislation ratifying the closure would be in place before March 7.

On March 3, 1933 – Hoover's last full day in office – state governors in Georgia, New Mexico, Utah, and Wisconsin declared bank holidays. North Carolina, Virginia, and Wyoming limited withdrawals. By the end of the day 5.504 banks with deposits of $3.4 billion had shut down.

NEW YORK GOVERNOR LEHMAN THROWS IN THE TOWEL

Attention was now concentrated on the battered banks of New York and Chicago, which had kept serving customers until the close of the business day on Friday, March 3. It was now clear that the last currency and gold reserves of these two money centers would inevitably be cleaned out during the Saturday morning banking hours of March 4, 1933, Inauguration Day. At 11:30 PM on Friday evening, Hoover called Roosevelt and repeated his demand that the President-elect act together with him and endorse the actions they might agree to take. (Hoover had that pig-headed stubbornness of which Quakers seem to be capable; all through the crisis, he had ignored urgings and advice, and followed his own Inner Light.) Roosevelt repeated his refusal of such an approach. Hoover went to bed at midnight. At 1 AM Saturday, a courier arrived from the Federal Reserve Board with the draft of an executive order for a nation-wide banking holiday, and a formal letter urging Hoover to take this step at once. But Hoover slept.

During the early hours of Saturday, March 4, Governor Herbert Lehman of New York, himself a Wall Street investment banker, met with representatives of the banking establishment at his Manhattan apartment. Present were the New York State superintendent of banks, executives from the Morgan group and from the other big clearinghouse banks, with George Harrison, boss of the New York Federal Reserve Bank. Harrison had been in touch with Hoover during the day to request a nationwide holiday, but Hoover had replied by shifting the responsibility to Governor Lehman. Lehman wanted a formal request for bank closure from the clearinghouse banks, but these bankers stalled, hoping to escape responsibility. Lehman refused to act until the big banks had signed a petition asking for the bank holiday. With this request in hand, Gov. Lehman at 2:30 AM signed an order suspending banking in New York State through Monday, March 6.

ILLINOIS BANK HOLIDAY: US BANKING SYSTEM PARALYZED

The Chicago bankers had undergone large withdrawals on March 3. They were hoping that Illinois Governor Horner would act alone to impose a bank holiday. But when news of Lehman's action arrived, the Chicago bankers joined in asking Governor Horner for a bank holiday. Horner signed the bank closure order at 3:22 AM local time. Herbert Hoover still had more than seven hours left in his term in office, but the economic heart of the United States, the credit system, had stopped beating. Financial disintegration and economic depression gripped the land. If Hoover's paralysis had been continued under his successor, the very fabric of civilization might have torn to pieces in this country within a few more weeks.

It is instructive today to recall which institutions and economic groups had tried and failed to deal with the banking panic of 1932-33:

* The private sector failed in a spectacular way to stop the banks from closing and to re-open them after they were shut down by the state bank holidays. Bankers were unable to form consortia to help their brethren banks. They were unable to provide credit for the recovery of agricultural and industrial production. They were impotent both as ad hoc groups of private bankers, and also when they acted under the aegis of a government-initiated, private corporation like the National Credit Corporation. The Michigan crisis proved to be the epiphany of the private sector's failure: here men with names like Ford, Chrysler, and Sloan were unable to save the banks they themselves controlled and relied on. **In short, there was no private sector, free-market solution to the disintegration of 1931-33.**

* The Federal Reserve System was one of the principal guilty parties in the Coolidge-Hoover speculative bubble, and in the Crash of 1929. The Fed virtually disowned all banks that were not members of its own system, and was unable to do anything to help the larger banks that were members. The Fed refused to recommend that Hoover declare a nationwide bank holiday until the Federal Reserve banks themselves faced default and bankruptcy, on March 2 – very late in the day. There is clear evidence that the Fed recommended a national bank holiday at this time because its own flagship New York branch was about to fail. The Fed thus protected itself, and not the banking system or the nation. The Fed attempted at every turn to duck its responsibilities, trying to shunt them off on Hoover - as in the Fed's 1932 refusal to declare a state of emergency to permit Fed

loans to nonbank institutions. Under Chairman Eugene Meyer, the father of Katherine Meyer Graham of today's *Washington Post*, the Federal Reserve System displayed an inertia that was the practical equivalent of sabotage. This abysmal record contrasts most vividly with the extravagant claims of pro-Fed lobbyists cited above: that the Fed would make panics and bank failures impossible, that depressions no longer need be feared, and so forth. **Private central banking as exemplified by the Fed, was an accomplice in both collapse and disintegration.**

* The states were tragic in their impotence to save the banks. State governors were able to prevent bank insolvencies by shutting down all banks with a bank holiday. **But no state was ever able permanently to re-open its banks.**

* **Congress acting by itself also failed**. A lame duck Congress was in session for many weeks in January and February 1933, and produced no measures capable of keeping the banks open nor of re-opening the ones that were shut. Senator Borah said that he had never seen a Congress spend so much time on trivialities during a crisis. That was before the Monica Lewinsky era. According to Senator Hiram Johnson: "We're milling around here utterly unable to accomplish anything of real consequence." [Leuchtenburg, 27-28] This inaction generated a widespread public disgust with the legislative branch that was almost as great as the popular hatred of Hoover. Pro-fascist ideologues seized on the impotence of the Congress to make the argument that dictatorship on the Mussolini model was needed to deal with the crisis.

* **Federal agencies were unable to save the banks and fight the depression by themselves**. This included the Reconstruction Finance Corporation, which had been specifically designed to do this. The RFC's piecemeal efforts staved off the demise of a bank here and there, but in the end it proved unable to hold off panic. The RFC's failure in Michigan, refusing to act unless Henry Ford made pledges of loans and deposits, was abysmal.

* **The Hoover cabinet was unable to stop the crisis**. The overall tone was set by Secretary of the Treasury Andrew Mellon, who wanted to liquidate everything in sight. "Liquidate labor, liquidate stocks, liquidate real estate ... values will be adjusted, and enterprising people will pick up the wreck from less-competent people," raved Mellon. This devil-may-care view of the lives of working people was later theorized by Schumpeter as so-called "creative destruction," a doctrine which appeals mainly to those who have never had to wonder where there next meal was coming from. Mellon was no better in his capacity as a leading banker. In September 1931 President Hoover had turned to Mellon and asked him to contribute $1 million to an effort to bail out the Bank of Pittsburgh. Mellon had rejected President Hoover's request. Mellon's successor Ogden Mills and especially Treasury Undersecretary Arthur Ballantine provided plans which Roosevelt used to stop the disintegration, but these could only be executed by Presidential leadership.

* **President Herbert Hoover was the most obvious failure of all**. This was due to Hoover's narrow construction of the powers and responsibilities of the presidency, and his refusal to use the implied emergency powers of the office. Hoover first tried voluntary corporatism among bankers. When this failed, he mustered the feeble activism of the RFC. After his election defeat, Hoover refused to take any action that had not been approved in advance by Roosevelt. Roosevelt neither refused nor agreed, but did nothing until he had taken office, when he acted quickly with a nationwide bank holiday and other measures.

In sum, the only institution able to combat the banking panic and the disintegration effectively proved to be the activist presidency of Roosevelt. This brief overview refutes as absurd the various theories of weak government, free market supremacy, states' rights, government by the permanent Washington bureaucracy, and Congressional primacy that have circulated in

Washington in recent years, especially during the Newt Gingrich Speakership. ***When the new crisis comes, it will take an activist president to deal with it.***

STATUS OF US BANKING BY STATE, INAUGURATION DAY, MARCH 4, 1933

Alabama - closed indefinitely
Arizona - closed until March 13
Arkansas - closed until March 7
California - most closed until March 9
Colorado - closed until March 8
Connecticut - closed until March 7
Delaware - closed indefinitely
District of Columbia - 3 banks limit withdrawals to 5%; 9 savings banks invoke 60 days' notice
Florida - withdrawals restricted to 5% plus $10 until March 8
Georgia - closed on banks' option until March 7
Idaho - closed on banks' option until March 18
Illinois - closed until March 8, then 5% limit for 7 days
Indiana - half restricted to 5% withdrawals indefinitely
Iowa - closed 'temporarily'
Kansas - 5% withdrawals indefinitely
Kentucky - most on 5% withdrawals until March 11
Louisiana - mandatory closing until March 7
Maine - closed until March 7
Maryland - closed until March 6
Massachusetts - closed until March 7
Michigan - closed indefinitely
Minnesota - closed 'temporarily'
Mississippi - 5% withdrawals indefinitely
Missouri - closed until March 7
Montana - closed indefinitely
Nebraska - closed until March 8
Nevada - closed until March 8
New Hampshire - closed indefinitely
New Jersey - closed until March 7
New Mexico - most closed until March 8
New York - closed until March 7
North Carolina - some on 5% withdrawals
North Dakota - closed 'temporarily'
Ohio - most on 5% withdrawals indefinitely
Oklahoma - closed until March 8
Oregon - closed until March 7
Pennsylvania - closed until March 7 (except for Pittsburgh Mellon banks)
Rhode Island - closed March 4
South Carolina - some closed, some restricted on banks' own option
Tennessee - some closed, some restricted until March 9
Texas - most closed; some restricted to $10 per day until March 8
Utah - most closed until March 8
Vermont - closed until March 7

Virginia - closed until March 8
Washington - some closed until March 7
West Virginia - 5% monthly withdrawals indefinitely
Wisconsin - closed until March 17
Wyoming - 5% withdrawals indefinitely
[see Kennedy 155-156]

LORD NORMAN

If Herbert Hoover was hated in the United States, the Mephisthophelean Lord Montagu Norman was hated all over Europe and all over the world with even better reason. Something of the feelings of the normal working bloke of the Clyde or the Midlands comes through in this summation by a British academic, made a quarter century ago: "[Norman's] career must surely rank as one of the most complete failures in public life in this century. His often-stated aim was to make London a successful, leading and powerful financial centre; to keep the pound sterling strong and stable; and to maintain the independence of the Bank, if possible in a leading role in an association with other similarly constituted central banks." [Sidney Pollard, 19]

But this partakes too much of the superficiality of the man in the street. If we compare Norman's achievements to his real goals in economic and financial warfare against the United States, France, and the rest of the world, Norman was highly successful. He was able to drag the rest of the world down to the same depressed level as the British economy, which then enjoyed a purely financial recovery. The British Establishment and the finance oligarchy of the City of London left no doubt that they were well pleased with Norman. Norman was Governor of the Bank of England from 1920 until 1944. His was the longest tenure in office during the twentieth century. Notice that more than half of Norman's tenure at the Bank of England came AFTER the British default of September 1931. It was in fact in 1931 that Norman was named Governor of the Bank of England with an open ended term of office, without time limit. In practice, Norman might have stayed on as Governor for life. After 1939, according to various accounts, the British oligarchy considered Norman's services even more indispensable in wartime because of his matchless expertise in economic and financial warfare. As it turned out, Norman voluntarily retired from the Bank of England in 1944 on medical advice after he had injured himself in a fall.

But there was no doubt at all of the oligarchy's glowing approval of Norman. His highest honor came when he was inducted into the House of Lords as the first Baron of St. Clere in 1944. The hereditary peerage thus given to Norman was an accolade bestowed for his service in orchestrating the Crash of 1929 and the 1931 Disintegration of the world financial system. After Lord Norman's death, his marble bust was unveiled in one of the courtyards of the fortress on Threadneedle Street. So Norman's plotting was never disowned, only lionized, by those who counted most in Great Britain.

VIII. USURY AND NATURAL LAW

Puossi far forza ne la Deitade,
Col cuor negando e bestemmiando quella,
E spregiando natura e sua bontade:
E però lo minor giron sugella
Del segno suo e Soddoma e Caorsa....
—— Dante, *Inferno*, XI.46 ff.

As we have suggested in earlier chapters, one aspect of the current breakdown crisis of civilization involves the greatest orgy of usury ever seen in human history. From the Versailles reparations to the yuppie quants of today, usury has been the scourge of the twentieth century. No attempt to salvage human civilization can succeed it is based on a clear perception of the dangers of usury.

Usury means the charging of interest for loans. In some cases it refers to exorbitant interest rates; in other cases it means taking any interest at all on loans. In pre-Volcker America, the legal definition of usury was often an interest rate higher than 10% on loans to a person or company. Before Volcker, more than 10% was thought a crime. Volcker raised interest rates to double that and well beyond for most borrowers, causing the virtual extinction of the United States as a modern industrial power. Derivatives represent the worst usury, on the largest scale, in history. Trying to float over $200 trillion of financial paper on the basis of a mere $10 trillion or less of commodity production is the most insane exercise in usury that humankind has ever attempted. As we have seen, this colossal folly is doomed to fail.

In the wake of Volcker, usury became embedded among the implicit mental axioms of the average American. What is the rate of return on my investment? What is my bottom line? These became the questions that Americans instinctively asked. Some states wrote into law that money managers are required to invest where they can get the highest rate of return, irrespective of the risk of default. Usury became an integral part of the legal system and the tax system as well. Credit card interest rates went to Volcker levels, and have never come down.

Modern American has forgotten that usury has been a key factor in the destruction of whole civilizations over the past millennia. Usury helped to undermine the Roman and Byzantine Empires. The usury practiced by Genoese bankers of St. George's bank was a cause of the repeated bankruptcies of the Spanish Empire. Usury sapped the economic power of the British Empire at its zenith during the nineteenth century. Venetian-directed usury was a cause of the crisis of the French monarchical state towards the end of the eighteenth century. Usury was a critical factor in the decline of the Ottoman Empire. Usury is the gravedigger of civilizations, even though it tends to be ignored by Paul Kennedy and the entire "collapse of empires" school of historiography.

The question of usury goes back thousands of years, and is worth some attention here. Many of the earliest and most powerful condemnations of usury contained in the holy books of the three monotheistic religions, and we should not remain indifferent to these documents. Those who are indifferent to the spiritual authority of Judaism, Christianity, and Islam as established religions, or who are skeptical about claims of divine inspiration, are invited to consider these writings from a cultural-historical rather than from a theological point of view: they represent the accumulated wisdom of centuries of human civilization. The monotheistic religions are seconded in their condemnation of usury by the Platonists, and to some by the Confucian school of philosophy.

THE BIBLE ON USURY

We read about usury in the Old Testament, where we find strong suggestions that usury is incompatible with the survival of a civilized community. The 15th Psalm had a clear-cut position on the immorality of usury:

> Lord, who shall abide in thy tabernacle? who shall dwell in thy holy hill?....
>
> He that putteth not out his money to usury, nor taketh reward against the innocent. He that doeth these things shall never be moved.

The prophet Ezekiel also had a clear conception of the evil of usury. In the middle of a list of sins and abominations of which men have been guilty, Ezekiel includes usury:

> In thee have they taken gifts to shed blood; thou hast taken usury and increase, and thou hast greedily gained of thy neighbors by extortion, and hast forgotten me, saith the Lord God. [Ezekiel 22:12]

Then there is the famous passage from Deuteronomy 23:19-20, which appears to forbid usury among the Jews, although allowing it against other, usually hostile, peoples:

> Thou shalt not lend upon usury to thy brother; usury of money, usury of victuals, usury of any thing that is lent upon usury:
>
> Unto a stranger thou mayest lend upon usury; but unto thy brother thou shalt not lend upon usury: that the Lord they God may bless thee in all that thou settest thine hand to in the land whither thou goest to possess it.

This implies that usury is a destructive force which cannot be allowed within one's own community, although it may be admissible as a virtual war measure against external enemies. Anyone who perceives the world economy as a global unit cannot, according to this teaching, propose to base it one usury. For the survival of modern civilization, it will be important to follow the teachings of Ezekiel and of the Psalmist. This would allow us to conclude from Deuteronomy that, given today's global interdependency, we cannot inflict usury on any inhabitant of this small planet.

Plato specifies in his *Laws* that usury should normally be illegal:

> Let there be... no lending on usury, the law permitting the borrower to withhold both interest and capital. [*Laws*, V.742c]

Even Aristotle, whose heart was never in the right place, could not afford openly to endorse usury. He limited himself to commenting that money per se "is barren," and that taking interest was "a gain against nature", with the implication that this was unjustified. But this is far from being an explicit condemnation of usury. Oligarchs have generally not allowed this quibble to lower their rates.

For Christians, there can be no doubt that usury is expressly condemned. Here are the words of Jesus Christ from Luke 6:35:

> But love ye your enemies, and do good, and lend, hoping for nothing again; and your reward shall be great, and ye shall be the children of the Highest: for he is kind unto the unthankful and to the evil.

God has thus commanded us to repudiate usury. If you are a coherent fundamentalist Christian, you cannot be a monetarist. Based on this, St. Jerome (340-420) argued during the late Roman Empire that since Christ had made all men brothers and founded a universal church, the ban on usury had been extended to all persons of whatever nationality or faith.

THE ISLAMIC VIEW

The Holy Koran contains explicit and vehement condemnations of usury. Moslems are exhorted to abandon the practice of taking usury, which is portrayed with admirable clarity and in considerable detail. Usury is presented as the antithesis of charity, which is alone pleasing in the sight of Allah. The Prophet writes:

> Those who swallow usury cannot rise up save as he ariseth whom the devil hath prostrated by (his) touch. That is because they say: Trade is just like usury; whereas Allah permitteth trading and forbiddeth usury. He unto whom an admonition from his Lord cometh, and (he) refraineth (in obedience thereto), he shall keep (the profits of) that which is past, and his affair (henceforth) is with Allah. As for him who returneth (to usury) – Such are the rightful owners of the Fire. They will abide therein. [QS: 2:275-5]

> Allah hath blighted usury and made almsgiving fruitful. Allah loveth not the impious and guilty. [QS: 2:276]

> Lo! those who believe and do good works and establish worship and pay the poor-due, their reward is with their Lord and there shall no fear come upon them neither shall they grieve. [QS: 2:277]

> O ye who believe! Observe your duty to Allah, and give up what remaineth (due to you) from usury, if ye are (in truth) believers. [QS: 2:278]

> And if ye do not, then be warned of war (against you) from Allah and his messenger. And if ye repent, then ye have your principal (without interest). Wrong not, and ye shall not be wronged. [QS: 2:279]

> And if the debtor is in straitened circumstances, then (let there be) postponement to (the time of) ease; and that ye remit the debt as almsgiving would be better for you if ye did but know. [QS: 2:280]

> O ye who believe! Devour not usury, doubling and quadrupling (the sum lent). Observe your duty to Allah, that ye may be successful. [QS: 3:130]

> And of their taking usury when they were forbidden it, and of their devouring people's wealth by false pretences, We have prepared for those of them who disbelieve a painful doom. [QS: 4:161]

> That which ye give in usury in order that it may increase on (other) people's property hath no increase with Allah; but that which ye give in charity, seeking Allah's Countenance, hath increase manifold. [QS: 30:39]

The Holy Koran has the great merit of clearly distinguishing between merchandise trade on the one hand, and usury on the other. Trade brings goods where they are needed for production and consumption, while usury simply pyramids debt. Here is implicit one of the basic ideas of natural law, namely that the wealth of an entire society cannot be founded on usurious financial dealings, since these activities do not generate new net wealth. Notice also that debt forgiveness and debt moratoria are explicitly recommended.

ST. AMBROSE AND ST. THOMAS AQUINAS

St. Ambrose of Milan (340-397) one of the most influential fathers of the Latin Church and the person who converted St. Augustine to Christianity, furnished in his *De Tobia* a depiction of usury as a deadly weapon of fearful devastation. Starting from the lines in Deuteronomy quoted above, Ambrose writes:

> From him, it says there, demand usury, whom you rightly desire to harm, against whom weapons are lawfully carried. Upon him usury is legally imposed. On him whom you cannot easily conquer in war, you can quickly take vengeance with the hundredth [i.e., high percentage rates of interest]. From him exact usury whom it would not be a crime to kill. He fights without a weapon who demands usury: he who revenges himself upon an enemy, who is an interest collector from his foe, fights without a sword. Therefore, where there is the right of war, there is also the right of usury. [Nelson 14]

Ambrose's starting point is clearly that under the New Law of Christ, we cannot treat any person in this way in peacetime.

When Charlemagne and his advisor Alcuin of York made their great effort to lift Europe out of the horrors of the Dark Ages, one of their great achievements was a general ban on usury among Charlemagne's Christian subjects. Some of the ideas that motivated this ban were expressed by the scholar Rabanus Maurus (784-856).

In the Middle Ages, William of Auxerre (1160-1229) expressed the idea that the usurer violates natural law by appropriating time, which is part of the world process that belongs to all creatures and to God. The usurer steals time and collects money for it. This is the celebrated argument against the monetization of time, which is taken over later by St. Thomas Aquinas (1225-1274), who comments: "...if those who accept money with usury wish to recover that usury by selling cloth at more than its worth on account of the aforesaid delay, there is no doubt that this is usury since time is clearly sold." [Padelford 6]

The usurer assumes that the money he has lent will bring in a return in the double digits, no matter what is done with the money. But in the real world of commodity production and social reproduction, only certain kinds of activities bring any return at all. These are the productive activities of industry, agriculture, mining, construction, scientific research, and others. And even productive activities of this sort can very seldom generate a real profit beyond 10%. This means that the debt service demanded by the usurer is a net detraction from the productive power of the entire society whenever it is collected from non-productive activity, and whenever it exceeds the real rate of profit earned in production.

St. Thomas Aquinas sums up the medieval Christian view of usury as a sin in and of itself:

> The Jews were forbidden to take usury from their brethren, i.e., from other Jews. By this we are given to understand that to take usury from any man is simply evil, because we ought to treat every man as our neighbor and brother, especially in the state of the Gospel, whereto all are called. [*Summa Theologica*, II.78.1]

St. Thomas thought that it was unlawful to take payment for lending a material good like a bottle of wine. We may justly ask for the bottle of wine to be replaced, but anything more is sinful usury. Franklin D. Roosevelt was speaking in the same spirit when he developed the famous "garden hose" comparison in his late 1940 speech asking the Congress to approve what became the lend-lease program. If you have to lend your neighbor your garden hose so he can stop his own house from burning down, probably saving your own house in the process, you don't ask for payment. All you can reasonably ask for is to get your garden hose back. And if you let a dollar sign prevent or even delay this transaction, you are a fool.

Underlying these attacks on the monetization of time is the notion that the usurer is contributing nothing to society, but only looting something from social reproduction. The usurer thus steals from everybody. This is also the view of the Italian poet Dante Alighieri in his *Divine Comedy*, one of the world's great classics.

As Dante and Vergil descend into Hell, they pause for some moments to become accustomed to the noxious air of the underworld. Vergil, who is guiding Dante through the nether regions, uses the time to give a quick overview of the various categories of sinners who are being punished in the circles of Hell. Usury is presented as a sub-category of violence, and as a form of behavior that is abhorrent to God.

For Dante, usury is specifically violence against God, denial of God, and blasphemy against God. It is also contempt of nature and of the bounty of nature. According to Dante, usury and sodomy are related, and are punished together. To identify usury for his contemporaries, Dante refers to Cahors, a city in southern France which had been a hotbed of the Albigensian heresy of the so-called Cathars, who were also notorious sodomists. St. Thomas also refers in his writings to usurers as "people from Cahors" or "Caorsini" in Latin. [111]

After listening to Vergil's exposition, Dante asks a couple of questions. One of them regards usury. Dante asks Vergil to go back to where he said that usury offends God's goodness, and to please explain that point again. Here is Vergil's answer:

> Philosophy, to him who hears it, points out, not in one place alone, how Nature takes her course
> from the Divine intellect, and from its art; and if you note well the Physics [of Aristotle], you will find, not many pages from the first,
> that your art, as far as it can, follows her, as the scholar does his master; so that your art is, as it were, the grandchild of the Deity.
> By these two, if you recall to your memory Genesis at the beginning, it behooves man to gain his bread and to prosper.
> And because the usurer takes another way, he contemns Nature in herself and in her follower, placing elsewhere his hope. [*Inferno*, XI.94 ff., Carlyle-Okey-Wicksteed]

From Dante's point of view, the sin and crime of the usurer is to violate God's instruction to humanity contained in Genesis 1:28:

> And God blessed them, and God said unto them, Be fruitful, and multiply, and replenish the earth, and subdue it: and have dominion over the fish of the sea, and over the fowl of the air, and over every living thing that moveth upon the earth.

This is the imperative of increased population and economic development, which the usurer does not accept.

When Dante and Vergil finally reach the seventh circle of the Inferno, they find a plain of burning sand on which eternally showers a rain of fire, suggesting the brimstone of God's vengeance upon the cities of Sodom and Gomorrah in Genesis 19:24. Upon this burning sand the blasphemers against God lie prostrate, while the sodomites are forced to run. The usurers sit

---

[111] St. Thomas Aquinas, *Summa Theologiae*, Secunda Secundae, Qu. lxxviii, where reference is made to "fautores et defensores qui fovent usurarios qui dicuntur Caorsini."

crouching, tormented by the burning sand and the flakes of fire. Their human faces have been distorted beyond all recognition; they can only be known by the coats of arms on the purses they wear around their necks:

> Thus also, on the utmost limit of the seventh circle, all alone I went to where the woeful folk are seated.
>
> Through the eyes their grief was bursting forth; on this side, on that, they with their hands kept warding off, sometimes the flames, sometimes the burning soil.
>
> Not otherwise the dogs in summer do, now with snout, now with paw, when they are bitten by fleas, or flies, or breezes.
>
> After I had set my eyes upon the visages of several on whom the dolorous fire falls, I knew not any of them; but I observed
>
> that from the neck of each there hung a pouch, which had a certain color and a certain impress, and thereon it seems their eye is feasting. [*Inferno*, XVII.43 ff., Carlyle-Okey-Wicksteed]

The usurers are compared to dogs, and then to oxen. Their brand of violence is the lowest and the worst, since they are located on the brink of the abyss, wherein fraud is punished.

Dante also considered misers and spendthrifts as mortal sinners. They are confined in the fourth circle of the Inferno, which is guarded by the monster Pluto, the god of riches. Misers are the worse of the two. In the fourth circle, the misers and spendthrifts are divided into two groups who are condemned to push heavy weights around the circle. When they meet, they exchange insults like "Why squander?" and "Why hoard?" Then they turn around, only to meet at the other extreme of the circle, where the ritual is repeated. Both misers and spendthrifts have blotted out their individuality through their incontinence, and none can be recognized as individuals. Vergil warns Dante that the misers will come out of their tombs on Judgment Day with clenched fists (the sign of avarice) and the high rollers with cropped hair (the medieval sign of lavishness and prodigality). Misers and spendthrifts together make up two of the largest groups of sinners in the entire Inferno.

As Vergil points out, these sinners have made themselves slaves to the pagan goddess Fortuna, much worshipped today in Las Vegas and Atlantic City, as well as in Wall Street and the Chicago pits. But all the gold beneath the moon could not buy a minute of rest for these rollers of the heavy weights. The Inferno is the abode of the damned, where sinners are eternally punished for specific acts of usury. In the Purgatory, sinners who have escaped damnation through repentance are purged of the tendency to commit evil acts. In the Purgatory, the punishment is made to fit the crime. The basis for usury and monetarism in the psychology of the human individual is of course greed, long known to western civilization as one of the seven deadly sins. A stay in Purgatory was designed to remove the temptation of these sins.

The greedy sinners are forced to lie face down in the dust, with their hands and feet securely tied up. They must weep and pray until greed has been distilled out of them through their own tears. Greed is considered the worst of the sins of the flesh, and the most widespread. Dante calls greed the "old wolf", and prays that God might put an end to its dominance among humans.

The sinners in Purgatory also repeat examples of greed and rapacity. One of the most memorably of these is Marcus Licinius Crassus, one of the greediest and richest men of the ancient world. Crassus divided the world with Julius Caesar and Pompey the Great in 60 BC, with Crassus taking the east because he thought that was where the money was. But Crassus was killed in a battle with the forces of the Parthian Empire. Since the Parthians hated Crassus because of his opulence, they poured molten gold down the throat of his corpse. Therefore in Dante's Purgatory the sinners chant:

"Tell us, Crassus, since you know, what is the taste of gold?" Here again Dante is pointing toward the basic fact that gold and money cannot be eaten, and are not wealth in and of themselves.

Dante was convinced that economic factors had been very important in the corruption of his native city, Florence. His verdict on Florence was that "the nouveaux riches and the fast buck have created pride and excess." Not a bad summary for the social effects of globaloney today.

CONFUCIUS ON ECONOMICS

Chinese civilization broadly shares the view of natural law and the emphasis on broad-based real economic production and prosperity which has been seen in the other world cultures. Here the most important figure is of course Confucius (551-479 BC). The *Analects of Confucius* contain the following important dialogue, which establishes the overall framework for Confucian economics:

> When Confucius visited the Kingdom of Wei, Jang Yiu drove for him. "What a teeming population," said Confucius. "What do you think that the government should do for such a teeming population?" asked Jang Yiu. "Enrich them," answered Confucius. "What then should be done after its people become rich?" asked Jang Yiu. "Give them education," replied Confucius." [*Analects*, Chapter 13]

It is evident that a Confucian state will be dirigistic, and pursue the general welfare by enhancing the level of moral and material culture of its population. This theme is developed in the Confucian classic called *The Great Learning*:

> The head of state who seeks personal wealth will hire greedy persons to serve him because greedy persons are experts in collecting unjust profits. As soon as greedy persons are hired, abuse of power and economic disaster will become the order of the day. When such a day comes, the availability of capable and virtuous persons will not help it at all. This means that a government must act for the public good instead of collecting unjust profits. [*The Great Learning*, Book X]

Particularly significant is the fact that Confucianism establishes the category of unjust profits. "Unjust profits" refer here primarily to exactions by government, but it is also clear that exorbitant and exploitative practices by private persons would also come under this heading. Confucius himself specifically addressed the problem of excessive taxation, repudiating a former student who had taken part in tax gouging:

> Chi Shih, one of the officials of the Kingdom of Loo, was richer than the Duke of Chou. As one of the ministers to Chi Shih, Jang Chiu assisted Chi Shih in collecting wealth by unjustifiable means, in order that Chi Shih might become richer. Jang Chiu does not seem to be like a disciple of mine. You may denounce him. [*Analects*, Chapter II]

The later Chinese philosopher Mencius, who was also of the Confucian school, commented on this episode in the following terms:

> Confucius felt repugnance towards a state ruler who, instead of executing decent public policies, tried in every way to dig for private profit. (*Book of Mencius*, Chapter IV-A)

Mencius was adamant in his condemnation of such extortion by government officials:

> Nowadays it is generally believed that a servant to a king will be deemed an excellent servant so long as he can help expand the territorial confines of his state or amass a greater fortune for the national treasury. In fact, servants of this kind were held as public embezzlers in the old days. Anyone who conceives ways and means to collect wealth for a king who has neither

public interests nor sensible public policies in mind is actually pursuing personal wealth for a tyrannical ruler. (*Mencius*, Chapter VI-B)

Most contemporary governments, including the American one, are wanting from this point of view. American law and government practice increasingly assume that usury is the order of the day, and engage in it. Tax arrears, for example, accrue interest at the exorbitant market rate. William Bennett, the resident pontificator of the Reagan-Bush faction, has strangely neglected this moral dimension.

THE PROTESTANT VIEW

The Protestant Reformation unfortunately tended to rehabilitate usury. The decisive figure in this regard is John Calvin, the theocratic dictator of Geneva. Calvin broke with the entire tradition of European civilization and Latin Christianity by endorsing usury. His views are expressed very plainly in one of his letters. Calvin is a draconian moralist, insisting on ideas like the absolute depravity of humankind and God's total and eternal predestination of most people to damnation for reasons that have nothing to do with their own conduct. But when he comes to usury, Calvin's heart softens. "If all usury is condemned," he wrote, "tighter fetters are imposed on the conscience than the Lord himself would wish.... I am certain that by no testimony of Scripture is usury wholly condemned." Calvin is usually contemptuous of history, since for him everything depends on Scripture. But when it comes to usury, he is willing to throw out the Bible in the name of a very vague historical analysis. After getting into deep trouble with the Biblical texts given above, Calvin writes:

> ...when it is said that since [our situation] is the same [as in the Bible] the same prohibition of usury should be retained, that there is some difference in what pertains to the civil state. Because the surroundings of the place in which the Lord placed the Jews, as well as other circumstances, tended to this, that it might be easy for them to deal among themselves without usury, while our situation today is a very difference one in many respects. Therefore usury is not wholly forbidden among us....

This is one of Calvin's very few appeals to history. If we needed murder or fraud more than the people of Biblical times, would it be any less a sin? But it is clear that the legalization of usury was one of the great imperatives of the Protestant reformation.

> Calvin also attempted to blur the distinction between the production of tangible physical wealth on the one hand and the circulation of paper promises to pay on the other. He mocks those who say that "money does not...beget money." For Calvin, money production is just as good as food production: "If therefore more profit can be derived from trading through the employment of money, than from the produce of a farm, the purpose of which is subsistence, should one who lets some barren farm to a farmer, receiving in return a price, or part of the produce, be approved, and one who loans money to be used for producing profit, be condemned?" [Usury Laws, 33-35] Part of the answer has to do with what kind of profit is produced: is it merely monetary, or has commodity production been increased?

Another powerful voice in favor of usury in the Anglo-American world was the poet John Milton. Milton was the son of what was called a scrivener. Scriveners were the seventeenth-century equivalent of a finance company. According to all of Milton's writings, he was a staunch defender of usury. In Milton's pamphlet *The Doctrine and Discipline of Divorce* we find: "...usury, so much as is permitted by the Magistrate, and demanded with common equity, is neither against the word of God, nor the rule of charity, as hath been often discussed by men of eminent learning and judgement." [Milton, *Complete Prose Works*, V.322]

In Milton's theological treatise *On Christian Doctrine* we read: "Most people agree that usury is not always illicit, and that in judging it we should take into account the usurer's motives, the rate of interest, and the borrower.... As for the borrower, they agree that it is legitimate to take interest from anyone who is well enough off to pay it.... Given these conditions, no fault can be found with usury.... Usury, then, is no more reprehensible in itself than any other kind of lawful commerce... if we may make a profit out of cattle, land, houses, and the like, why should we not out of money ?" [Milton, *Christian Doctrine* in *CPW* VI.776-777]

> The most ruthless endorsement of usury comes from Jeremy Bentham, the official philosopher of the British Empire. Bentham was an agent of Lord Shelburne and one of the founders of the modern British intelligence services. He developed the slogan of the greatest good for the greatest number in an attempt to justify his doctrine of utilitarianism. His argument for the total unleashing of deregulated usury is contained in his "Usury Laws: or, An Exposition of the Impolicy of Legal Restraints on the Terms of Pecuniary Bargains," often known simply as "Bentham's Defense of Usury." [Usury Laws 7 ff.]

For Bentham, there is no law of God or natural law to prohibit usury. Everything is left up to the two parties to the contract, and the public be damned, so to speak. Bentham takes his stand for the individual liberty of "making one's own terms in money bargains." In Bentham's opinion, this means that "no man of ripe years and of sound mind, acting freely, and with his eyes open, ought to be hindered, with a view to his advantage, from making such bargain, in the way of obtaining money, as he thinks fit; nor (what is a necessary consequence), anybody hindered from supplying him, upon any terms he thinks proper to accede to." This is extreme legal positivism, an important component of British liberalism.

Bentham disposes of Aristotle's comments on usury in the following mocking fashion: "...that great philosopher ... notwithstanding the great number of pieces of money that had passed through his hands (more perhaps than ever passed through the hands of a philosopher before or since)...had never been able to discover, in any one piece of money, any organs for generating any other such piece. Emboldened by so strong a body of negative proof, he ventured at last to usher into the world the result of his observations, in the form of a universal proposition, that all money is in its nature barren." But none of that prevents us from taking as much as the traffic will bear, concludes Bentham. Here we are not far from Michael Milken's paean to greed, which reportedly furnished the basis for the speech put into the mouth of insider speculator and stockjobber Gordon Gekko in Oliver Stone's 1987 movie *Wall Street*: "Greed is good. Greed works."

Bentham discusses at length how the general public sympathizes with bankrupts and spendthrifts, while resenting those provident persons who practice thrift, thus prompting politicians to interfere with the freedom of contracts. So anything goes. And for Bentham, usury is a good thing, which expresses the superiority of usurers "who have the resolution to sacrifice the present to the future," to prodigals "who have sacrificed the future to the present." But what if usury is destructive to the society as a whole? What if usury threatens to cripple world civilization as a whole?

Although it is unknown to most people today, Franklin D. Roosevelt developed an excellent attack on usury which he delivered in his First Inaugural Address, on Saturday, March 4, 1933, in the midst of the worst banking panic this country had known up to that time. These were not simply the throw-away lines of the modern politician; this statement is in line with the wisdom which has sustained western civilization. Roosevelt said on that occasion:

> ...the rulers of the exchange of mankind's goods have failed, through their own stubbornness and their own incompetence, have admitted their failure, and have abdicated. Practices of unscrupulous money changers stand indicted in the court of public opinion, rejected by the hearts and minds of men...

Faced by the failure of credit they have proposed only the lending of more money. Stripped of the lure of profit by which to induce our people to follow their false leadership, they have resorted to exhortations, pleading tearfully for restored confidence. They know only the rules of a generation of self-seekers. They have no vision, and when there is no vision the people perish.

The money changers have fled from their high seats in the temple of our civilization. We may now restore that temple to the ancient truths. The measure of the restoration lies in the extent to which we apply social values more noble than mere monetary profit.

Happiness lies not in the mere possession of money; it lies in the joy of achievement, in the thrill of creative effort. The joy and moral stimulation of work must be forgotten no longer in the mad chase of evanescent profits. These dark days will be worth all they cost us if they teach us that our true destiny is not to be ministered unto but to minister to ourselves and to our fellow men.

Compare that now with St. Thomas Aquinas, the pre-eminent medieval philosopher:

The desire for natural wealth is not infinite because at a certain point the needs of nature are satisfied. But the desire for artificial wealth is infinite because it is subject to disordered concupiscence which observes no measure, as the Philosopher shows. There is a difference, however, between the infinite desire for wealth and the infinite desire for the ultimate good, since the more perfectly the ultimate good is possessed the more it is loved and other things despised, for the more it is possessed the more it is known." [*Commentary on the Nichomachean Ethics*, I.2.1]

The values of natural law, and not greed and usury, represent the values on which a viable civilization can be based.

MONETARISM

The pro-usury and oligarchical view has flourished during the second half of the twentieth century in the form of monetarism, be it the snobbish Viennese monetarism of Friedrich von Hayek or the vulgar monetarism of Milton Friedman and his infamous Chicago school of economics. Thatcher preferred von Hayek, while Nixon and Carter (through Volcker) made the fatal mistake of following Friedman. Both variants are united in the Mount Pelerin society, a group of oligarchs and related power-brokers founded on the mountain of the same name in Switzerland in 1947. Mount Pelerin is located above Lake Geneva, near the town of Vevey, the headquarters of the sinister Nestlé international food cartel.

Milton Friedman's version of monetarism stands out for its crudeness and stupidity. It is an extreme version of the man-in-the-street's illusion that money is the very essence of wealth. Money is all that matters, is what Friedman literally proclaims:

We have always tried to qualify our statements about the importance of changes in M [the money supply] by referring to their effect on nominal income. But this qualification appeared meaningless to economists who implicitly identified nominal and real magnitudes. Hence they have misunderstood our conclusions.

We have accepted the quantity-theory presumption, and have found it supported by the evidence we examined, that changes in the quantity of money as such in the long run have a negligible effect on real income, so that non-monetary forces are 'all that matter' for changes in real income over the decades and money 'does not matter'.... I regard the description of our position as 'money is all that matters for changes in nominal income and for short-run changes in real income' as an exaggeration but one that gives the right flavor of our conclusions." [*Friedman's Framework*, 27]

"Money is all that matters," rant the monetarists at the IMF, the Fed, and the Treasury. "World history shows that inflation is a monetary phenomenon," said a Treasury official to this writer one day in 1993. Back in the 1950s, even schoolboys used to know that the nature of inflation is to have too much money chasing too few goods. In a modern economy, this cannot be solved by reducing the quantity of money, since that will lead straight to depression – although even this folly has been tried recently by ultra-monetarists in Latin America. The answer to inflation is always to increase industrial and agricultural production. This can be done by way of low-interest government lending to companies and other agencies that propose to produce the commodities which we know will promote an economic recovery. Milton Friedman has no idea of the ABCs of real economics.

Money is not what matters. What matters is the long-term increase in the cognitive and productive powers of human labor, an increase that is always mediated by improvements in production technology and in the general level of infrastructure in a society. As Alexander Hamilton knew very well, "mental capital" is what ultimately counts in the productive potential of any nation. Money is simply our best available means for circulating and distributing the products that the society is able to produce.

Friedman is also an admirer of Nazi austerity measures for the purpose of controlling inflation. The following is a passage from Friedman's *Studies in the Quantity Theory of Money*:

> Germany [under Hitler] did not choose to pay for its increased expenditures by taxation. Nor did it urge individuals to invest in government securities. It did, however, borrow heavily from the German banking system. To avoid a price boom, and simultaneously to have ready access to the credit market, the German government imposed economic controls. First wage, price and credit controls and then rationing. Eventually Germany became a directed economy.

> The objective of such controls is the restriction of spending on the part of individuals, so that individual spending will increase less rapidly than the quantity of money. Such a policy, if rigorously enforced, should restrain a rise in the price level. As indicated earlier, this policy appears to have been successful in Nazi Germany. [137]

But notice that in Nazi Germany the inflation was still there. It was simply being gouged out of the hides of workers, pensioners, and the victims of the concentration camps.

In late April 1997, the Mount Pelerin Society celebrated its fiftieth anniversary. In a commentary on this occasion, columnist Walter Williams claimed that the ideas of the Mont Pelerin Society have taken over not just the economics profession, but also politics around the world. In 1947, Williams said, there was a "growing love affair with socialism in Western nations, including the United States," which included a denial that government regulation was inherently totalitarian. Today, wrote Williams, it doesn't take much courage to criticize government growth and control, high taxes, and government infringement on private property. "But back in 1947, it was a different matter." "The entire intellectual climate was in favor of government micro-management of the economy, through fiscal and monetary policy, regulatory agencies, and price controls." At that time, he adds, arguing for transportation deregulation, free trade, school choice, or the balanced budget "were seen as ideas bordering on lunacy." The late New Deal was indeed a much better and saner time.

"Except for a few skirmishes here and there, the ideas of human liberty have triumphed over those of government coercion," Williams concluded. "Much of that victory is a result of a half-century's work by my distinguished colleagues of the Mont Pelerin Society." The worldwide membership of the Mont Pelerin Society is about 500, of whom six have won Nobel prizes in economics. "Several have earned titles of nobility," enthuses Williams, who loves "lords, knights and dames." [*Washington Times*, April 28, 1997] The real target of Mount Pelerin was not communism or socialism, but rather the triumphant US model of dirigistic, regulated, New Deal industrial capitalism which had emerged in the US with the Federal Reserve's submission to Roosevelt. Hayek's 1944 *Road to Serfdom* did not dare to attack President Roosevelt in wartime, but does mount an assault on the Tennessee Valley Authority. Hayek wanted above all to prevent an application of TVA principles to his ancestral homeland in the Danube Valley. "One cannot," argued Hayek, "create a kind of Tennessee Valley Authority for the Danube Basin without thereby determining beforehand for many years to come the relative rate of progress of the different races inhabiting this area or without subordinating all their individual aspirations and wishes to this task." [Hayek 247-8]

A TVA for the Danube was a proposal raised by FDR personally during the wartime conferences with Churchill and Stalin. Hayek argued that, since no TVA plan would please everybody, nothing could be done. And since Hayek talks so much about serfdom, we must recall that Austro-Hungarian feudal aristocrats like the von Hayeks had actually held serfs until 1781-82, and had only given them up when they were forced to by the reforming Emperor Joseph II. Hayek's book became a best seller not because of spontaneous public demand, but rather because groups of reactionary, anti-New Deal businessmen placed bulk orders and then handed out copies. Later, these same businessmen would fund endowed chairs at colleges and universities, and set up think tanks, to spew out monetarism, bringing this fringe doctrine into the mainstream parlor.

Hayek was the disciple of another Viennese monetarist ideologue, Ludwig von Mises, who had made his name defending the Newtonian (or Ortesian) timeless objectivity of economic laws against the German school of historical economics. These two Viennese eccentrics loom large as founders of the self-styled conservative intellectual movement after World War II. Their prominence has gone hand in hand with the increased scientific and moral imbecility, as well as the increased cruelty, of western culture.

The Mount Pelerin Society is the ideological headquarters for today's legions of greed. Well, says the modern reader, what does all that mean today? The point is that usury and the monetarism which it inspires are prime causes of the collapse and disintegration of the world economy looming today.

USURY AND THE FOURTEENTH-CENTURY DISINTEGRATION OF EUROPE

During the thirteenth century, the center of world usury was unquestionably Venice. Between 1250 and 1350, the Venetians controlled the gold and silver markets, and thus controlled the currency trade of the entire world. That included the currency dealings of the entire Mongol Empire of Gengis Khan, which dominated China and parts of India. Marco Polo and his family had sealed a close alliance between the Great Khan and the Venetian Republic. Frederic C. Lane pointed out some years ago that "Venice's rulers were less concerned with profits from industries than with profits from trade between regions that valued gold and silver differently." In other words, arbitrage. The Venetian racket was similar to Montagu Norman's concept for the City of London, or to today's $1.5 trillion per day market in currency arbitrage and derivatives. And the result may well turn out to be similar.

At this time there sat on the English throne a series of Plantagenet kings who are best seen as bankrupt wards of northern Italian bankers in the Venetian orbit like the Bardi, Peruzzi, and Frescobaldi. These bankrupt borrowers included Henry III (1216-1272), Edward I (1272-1307), Edward II (1307-1327), and Edward III (1327-1377). During this time the power of Italian financiers in England was very great. The Genoese galley fleet began visiting England in 1278, and the Venetian state galleys first appeared off the English coast in 1319. British historians like to write about King Edward I as "the English Justinian"; the Italian banker Amerigo dei Frescobaldi called King Edward I "my yeoman."

The main source of wealth for England at this time was wool production. Miriam Beard tells what happened next: "Many Italian firms joined in the great shearing of England. The Frescobaldi, for instance, advanced a few thousand pounds and won the right to collect dues at English and Irish ports. They also supplied wines at fancy prices to the inordinately thirsty English Court. But the chief exploiters remained the Bardi and the Peruzzi. The latter, in return for helping Henry III with running expenses, asked 120% interest and charged 60% more when he was not prompt. They took a lien on the state income and set two merchants as guards to supervise his household accounts...Soon the bankers loaned to the English abbeys and took the sheep as well as the wool for security. Before long, the bankers took the pastures, too." [Beard, 139]

King Edward III, was the madman who in 1338-9 started the Hundred Years' War against France, partly in order to secure loot and booty to stabilize his own financial situation. But sufficient booty proved hard to come by, and total English default became official in 1345. The Bardi and Peruzzi banking houses went bankrupt and closed their doors. According to a chronicler of the age, "all credit vanished together." The backdrop to these events was the arrival of the bubonic plague in Europe. The plague was itself the by-product of a century of Venetian-led speculative loans, which had driven down the standards of living, nutrition levels, and sanitary conditions of peasants and townspeople from England to China. Then came Edward III's Hunded Years' War, and the overall financial crash. The final outcome of the 1345 usury crisis was a decline in the European population over the next century by about a third, from 90 million to about 60 million. This is a prime example of a collapse into financial disintegration. And that is how European civilization had learned that usury was very dangerous indeed.

A recent study has examined the social and political as well as economic effects of the growing debt burden borne by the United States in the late twentieth century. The authors conclude that we are now an "Indebted Society." One of their findings is that, as the power of lenders has grown, the policies of the society as a whole have shifted in favor of the interests of lenders, often to the detriment of other groups. As this study comments, "People who make their living by lending money have, in principle, two overriding concerns. First, they want to receive the highest interest rates they can. Second, they want to make sure that their money retains its purchasing power – which is to say, they want inflation to be as low as possible. To the extent that public policy fosters these two objectives, it is working to the benefit of lenders... the lender's two objectives can be consolidated into one objective: to obtain the highest possible real interest rate." [Medoff and Harless 68]

Among the results of this state of affairs is the shocking prejudice against full employment which dominates the Federal Reserve and Wall Street. Professional economists, generally serving the interests of the lenders, talk of "NAIRU", the "non-accelerating inflation rate of employment" or the "natural rate of employment." The consensus of the academic economists is that 6% constitutes the "natural" jobless rate. Anything less than that is inflationary and bad for bondholders. Today's ruling humbug is thus a paraphrase Eisenhower's Secretary of Defense Charles Wilson: "What's bad for the bondholders is bad for America." If the jobless rate threatens to fall below 6%, the anti-inflation phobia of the Federal Reserve dictates an immediate increase in interest rates to strangle nascent inflation before it becomes irreversible. Unless, of course, the banking system is about to blow. More precisely, we can state that Fed policy aims at a general climate of deflation, so as to permit periodic central bank financial bailouts and rescue operations for speculators which otherwise might have hyperinflationary implications. Producers and working families are squeezed out of existence so that hedge fund bandits and incompetent bankers may be saved.

Medoff and Harless show how many cultural and social characteristics of modern America – summarized under the heading of the "debt culture" – owe their prominence to the coming of the "Indebted Society." These authors see the rising rate of unemployment among middle-aged men as the result of preferential firing of older, better-paid industrial workers to save money for debt service. The same goes for the preference for bringing in temps instead of hiring permanent personnel. With deteriorating jobs offering substandard earnings, we observe the rise of the two-income or multiple-income family. The government tends, as it becomes more and more indebted, to spend less and less on scientific research and development. This has an adverse impact on industrial productivity.

Taken together, Medoff and Harless argue, all this leads to that increasing "alienation" of the increasingly unemployed population which they call "the Paranoid Society:" "The alienation found in a society in which the power of debt has come to exceed the power of humanity leads to another vicious circle – the circle of mistrust. When people feel they have no power, when people see the expectations they had taken for granted dashed to the ground, they are apt to begin viewing most institutions with suspicion.... Outside the government, the circle of mistrust operates as well. Cooperation among workers, and between workers and management, becomes difficult or impossible. Management and stockholders find themselves at odds. Everyone expects the worst from everyone else. As government becomes ineffective, civil lawsuits abound." [Medoff and Harless, 159]

IN THE CLUTCHES OF THE BOND MARKET

After the orgy of debt that characterized the Reagan-Bush era, it could not be surprising that the balance of political power in America had shifted in favor of Treasury bond and junk bond holders, and in favor of their *sanctum sanctorum*, the Federal Reserve. The supremacy of bondholders and borrowers was a new political fact that Bill Clinton, in particular, was forced to deal with. Domestic and international hot-money lenders now had the ability to bring down the government if they did not get their way.

A stunning recent example of the power of lenders is President Clinton's first year in office in 1993. Clinton had pledged to make substantial investments ($231 billion in 4 years) in the future of the United States, including investments in education, job training, and infrastructure. Clinton had also promised a middle-class tax cut. But as soon as he entered the White House, he found himself surrounded by advisers who demanded that he give first priority to the conflicting program of deficit reduction. The pro-debt advisers included Vice President Gore, Treasury Secretary Bentsen, OMB director Leon Panetta, Alice Rivlin, and others. Clinton was also influenced by Greenspan of the Federal Reserve, the chief ideologue and enforcer for the lenders. In December 1992 Greenspan visited President-elect Clinton in Little Rock, Arkansas, and argued for an economic policy guided by usury:

> So Greenspan gave his economics lesson... The long-term interest rates for 10-year, 20-year, and 30-year securities, Greenspan said, were an unusual 3 to 4 percent higher than the short-term rates. Historically, the rates had been closer. The large current gap was basically an inflation premium. Bondholders and traders were sophisticated and anticipated that the federal budget deficit would continue to explode for many years. The anticipated cumulative growth of the deficit over those years was so large that it was perceived to be unstable. History showed, Greenspan said, that with such vast federal expenditures, inflation would inevitably soar at some point.... Investors were now wary and demanding a higher long-term return because of the expectations on the federal deficit.... Greenspan added that if the new administration removed or altered that expectation by exerting some control on the deficit, the

market expectations would change. Bond traders would have more faith that inflation would stay under control. Long-term rates would drop, galvanizing demand for new mortgages.... Addressing the long-term deficit was essential.... it was impossible to jump-start the economy with a short-term stimulus package." [Woodward, 67-68]

The Greenspan "economics lesson" of December 1992 is a condensed catechism of the lenders' creed in an economy in which lenders have triumphed over owners and producers. When Greenspan was put on display between Hillary Clinton and Tipper Gore during Clinton's February 1993 initial State of the Union address, it was a signal that the lenders' lobby was increasing its influence over the new administration. It was Greenspan's thinking that led Clinton to adopt a deficit reduction plan that the President himself repeatedly called "a turkey." And once Clinton had followed his advice, Greenspan turned around and applied his Chinese water-torture of interest rate hikes, leading to the worst bond-market crisis since the Great Depression, with interest rates much higher than they had been in 1993.

Clinton was not immediately converted to the cult of the bond market. On one occasion, Clinton was informed by his advisers during a White House meeting of the skepticism with which he was likely to be viewed by the bond market. Clinton replied with anger and disbelief, "You mean to tell me that the success of the program and my re-election hinges on the Federal Reserve and a bunch of f**king bond traders?" Clinton's advisers were unanimous that this was exactly his predicament. [Woodward, 84]

In another instance, Clinton rejected an attempt by Gore to compare him to Franklin D. Roosevelt, saying: "Roosevelt was trying to help people. Here we help the bond market and we hurt the people who voted us in."[Woodward, 93] A more turbulent moment in Clinton's first term came in April-May, 1993, when the President's investment program had been defeated by the GOP's Dole-led filibuster in the Senate, and he was falling back on deficit reduction. This is an extraordinary document of the forces that are shaping modern American history: "Where are all the Democrats?" Clinton bellowed. "I hope you're all aware we're all Eisenhower Republicans," he said, his voice dripping with sarcasm. "We're Eisenhower Republicans here, and we're fighting the Reagan Republicans. We stand for lower deficits and free trade and the bond market. Isn't that great?" [Woodward, 185] These insights imbue Clinton with a quality of tragic humanity, even in defeat.

In the first Clinton administration, the dominant group of officials were pleased that Treasury bond yields were at their lowest level in 6 years, and then in 16 years. Others thought that the bond market thrived on bad news for the middle class, and that deficit reduction was synonymous with looting the middle class. There was a long debate over whether $140 billion in deficit reduction (the figure specified by Greenspan) would convince "the bond market" that Clinton was serious about austerity. At one point during those early months Clinton admonished reporters who were asking him about a dip in the stock market, that the bond market was actually a much more reliable guide to the state of economy. The Federal Reserve serves the bondholders, the Congress serves the bondholders, and the President is also forced to serve the bondholders. The Supreme Court also serves the bondholders. If the spirit of usury prevails and dominates the regime, who can be astonished if depression is the result?

To sum up, usury is a violation of natural law, and of the most fundamental imperatives of the human condition. The medieval and early modern attacks on usury cited above are not obsolete; they are more accurate than most editorial comments published in newspapers and newsmagazines today. Whatever the economic ideologues of today might imagine, no society based on the rule of usury can long endure. Indeed, history is strewn with the wrecks of civilizations that attempted to build their house on usury. Nobody but nobody can consistently violate natural law with impunity.

CHAPTER
IX. THE AGE OF OLIGARCHY

Aborriti patrizi!
– Verdi/Piave-Boito, *Simon Boccanegra.*

The Twentieth Century is widely regarded as the Age of Dictators – Hitler, Stalin, Mussolini, Mao, and many more. The mass media have exhaustively educated the popular consciousness about the dangers of tyranny. While tyrants are execrated, the evils of oligarchy usually pass unmentioned. But a deeper look into real history reveals that the truly great economic and financial calamities of this century, such as October 1929, September 1931, and August 1971, were the work of oligarchical forces, frequently the City of London and their Wall Street and Washington allies (see Chapters VI and VII). And by the close of the Twentieth Century and the Second Millennium, the principal threat to human progress and to be stability of world civilization comes from oligarchy. An important thesis of this book is that the current disintegration of the world financial system in the wake of the collapse of the greatest speculative bubble of all time is a by-product of the oligarchical domination of world society, especially by an oligarchy of bankers and financiers who control the International Monetary Fund, the Federal Reserve, the Bank for International Settlements, the new European Central Bank (ECB), and the various (private) central banks.

It has been estimated that the true beneficiaries of globaloney number about 500,000 persons worldwide. These are financiers, bankers, top government officials, international civil servants, university and foundation presidents, economics professors, computer magnates, religious leaders, and members of the boards of multinational corporations. It has been suggested that the surest sign of belonging to the emerging oligarchy is the ability to hire household servants; many Americans were surprised to learn how typical this practice is among US elitists during the Zoe Baird scandal at the beginning of the Clinton Administration. More and more, the United States is evolving towards the elite/mass polarity typical of oligarchies and empires, with the atrophy of the middle class. "The general course of recent history no longer favors the leveling of social distinctions but runs more and more in the direction of a two-class society in which the favored few monopolize the advantages of money, education, and power." [Lasch, 29-30]

The famous oligarchies of history have included Sparta in ancient Greece, the Roman Republic (and very often the Roman Empire as well), the Venetian Republic, and Great Britain after 1688. Schiller portrayed Lycurgus of Sparta and Solon as Athens as the protagonists of two opposed and lasting principles of human civilization; the conflict between oligarchs and nation builders (or Platonists or republicans, as the anti-oligarchical faction may be labeled) has been central to world history, and continues to this very day. [112]

Although he acknowledged tyranny as "the extremist pestilence a city can have," Plato also pointed out that oligarchy was "a constitution teeming with many ills," a defective species of constitution for a state. [*Republic* 544c, Rouse 342] This is the regime "based on a property qualification... wherein the rich hold office and the poor man is excluded." [Plato, *Republic* 550c, Hamilton/Cairns 779] Plato also discusses oligarchy as one of the five states of mind or condition of

---

[112] See Friedrich Schiller, "The Legislation of Lycurgus and Solon," in *Friedrich Schiller: Poet of Freedom* (Washington: EIR, 1988), 273-305.

the soul of private individuals. Among the inferior human types Plato mentions "the member of a ruling class – oligarchy." [*Republic* 545a, Rouse 343]

The ruling passion of the oligarchic spirit is **greed** – the concupiscence of wealth. We read in Plato of the oligarch: "Covetous again, such men will be, ... covetous of riches as those in oligarchies are, with a fierce love in the darkness for gold and silver, now they are possessed of storehouses and private treasuries to store and hide these things in; they will build habitations about them to dwell in, nothing less than little nests for themselves, in which they can spend fortunes lavishing money on their women and any others they may wish." [*Republic* 548a, Rouse 346] The transition to oligarchy from other forms of rule is shaped by the inordinate accumulation of great private fortunes amidst a context of general immiseration:

> That storehouse full of gold... which every man has, destroys [the earlier constitution]. First they invent ways of spending for themselves, and neither they nor their wives obey the laws, but they pervert them to support this.... After that, they observe each other and rival each other, and make the whole body of the people like themselves." [*Republic* 550d, Rouse 348]

Oligarchy is thus not just domination by a group of oligarchs over an otherwise sane society. It is an organizing principle that penetrates into every aspect of the social organism, as it has in the United States and most of the world after about 1968-70. Oligarchy as the organizing principle of society is not "over there" in London or Wall Street or Washington; it is the here and now in schools, businesses, and communities in every part of the United States. To consolidate their rule, the oligarchs attempt to anchor the exclusion of the destitute in the basic law, as Plato shows:

> Thus in the end they have become lovers of money and moneymaking and no longer aim at honor and ambition; they praise the rich man and admire him and bring him into places of government, and the poor man they dishonor .... So then they lay down a law of limitation in the constitution; they fix a sum of money, greater or less, according as the oligarchy is more or less complete, and proclaim that no one may share in the government unless his property comes up to the assessment. This they carry out by force of arms, or they have used terror before this to establish such a constitution. [*Republic* 551b, Rouse 349]

In Plato's typology, the oligarchic state passes into a state of mob rule called democracy. This process, which we cannot recapitulate in detail here, may begin when a poor farmer finds himself serving in the army alongside oligarchs in the moment of some national emergency:

> Often enough a sinewy sun-browned poor man may be posted in battle beside a rich man fostered in shady places, encumbered with alien fat, and sees him panting and helpless. Don't you suppose he reflects that his own cowardice has allowed such men to be rich? Will not one pass the word to another, when they meet in private, "We can take these guys! They're a big nothing!" [*Republic* 556d-e, cfr. Rouse 355]

The American oligarchy has taken precautions against just such an eventuality, one might argue: they have created an all-volunteer army so oligarchs and plebeians will not serve together, they are wiping out farmers, and they have instituted a cult of physical fitness for themselves. But the current oligarchy cannot escape calamitous instability, as the financial markets illustrate. Although Plato generally considers tyranny the worst state of affairs, he also points out an important way in which oligarchy is even worse than tyranny: it is harder to reform. In tyranny or autocracy, one can either liquidate the tyrant, or convince him to reform. Plato develops this idea in his *Laws*:

> Clinias: The best state, as I understand you, might arise out of an autocracy, provided, that is, there were a consummate legislator and an autocrat of disciplined character, and the transition

to it would be particularly easy and rapid in that case, less so from an oligarchy – is not that your meaning – and still less from a democracy?

Athenian: By no means. The readiest starting point would be autocracy, the next-best, constitutional monarchy, the next best again, democracy of a kind; oligarchy would come fourth, and only admits of such a development with great difficulty, for there the number of persons of influence is greatest. [*Laws* IV, 710e, Hamilton/Cairns 1302]

So it is better not to fall into oligarchy, since it then becomes very hard to get out of its before one's civilization collapses. The only way to overturn an oligarchy is to create a factional struggle within it, as we read in Plato, where we find that "in every form of government revolution takes its start from the ruling class itself, when dissension arises in that, but so long as it is at one with itself, however small it be, innovation is impossible." [*Republic* 545d,e, Hamilton/Cairns 774] Recent years have shown us the spectacle of an entrenched oligarchy, the nomenklatura of the USSR and its satellites, which willingly jettisoned an ideology, a form of government, and an economic system, but still managed to preserve itself as an oligarchy.

PLATONIC CLASS CONSCIOUSNESS

The oligarchic system is characterized by a small number of rich plutocrats, and a great number of impoverished persons, with very little in between. We read the following exchange in Plato:

Well then, in oligarchic cities do you not see beggars?

Nearly all are such... except the ruling class. [*Republic* 552d, Hamilton/Cairns 781]

The frequent use of the term "ruling class" [*Republic* 552b, Hamilton/Cairns 781] by Plato reminds us that the issue of class and sociological analysis according to class are much older than Marx. Marx hijacked these concepts, and thoroughly discredited them. Marx is the originator of the idea of class just as little as Theodore Roosevelt is the originator of the Grand Canyon; the reality had been there for a long time before it was appropriated in each of these cases. It is time to revive class analysis from the standpoint of Plato, developing what might be seen as **Platonic class consciousness**, no longer materialistic, no longer deterministic, no longer empiricist, no longer atheistic, but concerned with human freedom and with the invincible power of ideas and the human spirit.

CONFUCIUS REJECTS OLIGARCHY

The other great tradition of anti-oligarchical thinking to be found in world culture stems from the influence of Confucius (551-479 BC). Confucianism can perhaps best be understood as a movement to save Chinese civilization from oligarchical depredations which might otherwise have proven fatal. Confucius starts from a standpoint very much like that of Plato: the need to secure good government capable of promoting the general welfare. Confucius recognized that most governments in the divided and balkanized China of his time (called the Spring and Autumn period by modern scholars so as to underline the pervasiveness of change it experienced, or the Warring States period to stress the climate of constant warfare) were unacceptable. The main political issue confronting China in these times was the incessant private warfare of the Chou dynasty military nobility, which served no useful purpose, but kept the country weak and divided, with no effective central government. This situation may be compared to France at the end of the Hundred Years' War, before the accession of Louis XI in 1461. According to Confucius, bad government derived from the fact that rulers and high officials lacked the character and qualifications to serve the general welfare. Confucius thought that the main reason for this incompetence was that the status of the rulers and of the aristocrats around them was hereditary. Confucius had learned to hold hereditary aristocrats in very low esteem. Confucius regarded many of the nobility as parasites, and wrote of them in the *Analects*:

> It is difficult to expect anything from men who stuff themselves with food the whole day, while never using their minds in any way at all. Even gamblers do *something*, and to that degree are better than these idlers. [Creel 1953, 30]

In any age when to be a gentleman meant to be a member of the nobility, Confucius asserted that anyone might be a gentleman if his conduct were characterized by justice and benevolence, and this is what he wanted from his own students. Confucius therefore argued that government needed to be placed in the hands of the most capable and competent persons who could be found. He pointed out that ability has nothing to do with birth, nobility, or wealth, but depends on character and knowledge, which in turn are the results of education. It was therefore necessary to promote and diffuse education as much as possible, and then to recruit the most promising individuals for government posts. Confucius called for the career open to talent, in which appointment and advancement would be based on ability, and not on hereditary rank or titles. Confucius did not call for the overthrow of hereditary rulers, but rather recommended that they accept the best advice they could procure from ministers chosen exclusively according to ability. This last point, one feels, did not represent what Confucius considered the optimum solution, but rather the best outcome that could be realistically hoped for in the Chinese society of his time. Confucius took it upon himself to train the future government officials; one of the cardinal points in his program was that his students had to be ready to give honest advice to the rulers they served, even if such honesty were to mean a horrible death at the hand of a ruler enraged by the proposals offered. In the Confucian view, people must live by loyalty to moral principles, not by feudal loyalty to overlords. Confucius explicitly accepted students according to ability only, not according to wealth or patents of nobility. As we read in the *Analects*:

> In education, there should be no class distinctions.... I have never refused to teach anyone, even though he came to me on foot, with nothing more to offer as tuition than a package of dried meat. [Creel 1953, 32]

It was a great innovation to offer education to persons of all social backgrounds, since at this time education tended to be the monopoly of wealthy aristocrats who could afford expensive private tutors. Confucius asserted that one of his disciples, although not of royal birth, was suitable to occupy a throne. The heart of the Confucian argument against oligarchy is that it represents an irrational principle of domination, which can justify itself neither by the merit and ability of those who rule, nor by the results achieved. The only arguments in favor of oligarchy are custom, and the brute force of repression. The academy of Confucius can be regarded as a training school for anti-oligarchical activists in the China of his time, and ever since. The teaching and example of Confucius amount to a powerful attack on any entrenched and hereditary privilege which cannot be justified by reason. The Confucian teaching is thus a precious resource for humanity in the current Age of Oligarchy.[113]

MACHIAVELLI'S CLASS ANALYSIS

In case anyone still thinks that Marx invented the issue of class, we should also recall the case of Niccolò Machiavelli (1469-1527), the founder of modern political science and sociology.

---

[113] For Confucius, see the works of H.G. Creel.

Machiavelli was willing to see Italy unified under a prince if that were the only way, but his own preference was for a broad-based, middle class republic. Machiavelli is a classic of bourgeois class-consciousness, of what we should today call the middle class outlook. In his fundamental work, the *Discorsi* (discourses on the first ten books of the *History of the Roman Republic* by Titus Livius), Machiavelli was adamant that the presence of an hereditary feudal aristocracy of landowners was a grave disadvantage to any body politic: of these he writes that "the term 'nobility' [*gentiluomini*] is used of those who live in idleness on the abundant revenue derived from their estates, without having anything to do either with their cultivation or with other forms of labor essential to life. Such men are a pest in any republic and in any province .... " [*Discorsi* I.55, cfr. Machiavelli 245-6] Where there are nobles, says Machiavelli, there can be no republic, since the pre-condition for a republic is equality. These observations represented the organic Florentine tradition. Machiavelli, wishing to show that hereditary regimes generally tend to fail, quotes Dante's "rade volte risurge per li rami/ L'umana probitate," "rarely to the branches does human worth ascend" [*Purgatorio* VII, 121-2].

Nobles thus had to be gotten rid of. This left the more wealthy city-dwellers, which he variously calls *grandi* or *ottimati* – something like the *grande bourgeoisie*. These had to be held in check by the people in general. Machiavelli was also of the opinion that class conflict between the rich few and the have-not many was a good thing for political development, provided that it did not become excessive. "Those who condemn the quarrels between the nobles and the plebs," he writes in the *Discorsi*, "seem to me to be criticizing the very things which were the primary cause of Rome's retention of her freedom." (I.4) Oligarchs will always be oligarchs, Machiavelli has no doubt, "perché i pochi sempre fanno a modo de' pochi" ("the few always act like the few"). "And unquestionably if we ask what it is the nobility are after and what it is the common people are after, it will be seen that the nobles desire to dominate and the common people merely desire not to be dominated." (I.5) The safeguarding of liberty is therefore more the task of the have-nots than of the wealthy. For Machiavelli, a stable republic requires a very substantial degree of political and social equality. He argues for incorporating elements of monarchy, aristocracy, and democracy into the constitution of the state so that "each would keep watch over the other" – a view not far from that of the US Constitution of 1787. Machiavelli's three-class analysis, in which the feudal aristocrats must be suppressed as the most dangerous enemies, while the urban rich need to be checked by an aroused citizenry, is even today a much more accurate picture of social reality than Marx's later construct. Indeed, Machiavelli looks forward to Madison's comments on political strife in *The Federalist* No. 10.

A very influential American theoretician of a three-branch government on the Machiavelli model was John Adams, who contributed much to the Constitutional Convention despite the fact that he was away in Europe at the time. Adams had been the prime mover behind the Massachusetts Constitution of 1779, in which the three branches are clearly delineated, and which served as a model for other states during the Articles of Confederation period. Adams was an avid reader of Machiavelli and translated several hundred pages of the Florentine secretary's work, publishing long selections in his *Defense of the Constitution of Government of the United States* (1787-1789). Benjamin Franklin read Machiavelli in the original Italian, and used the format of one of the Florentine's minor works to satirize British ineptitude. Alexander Hamilton had Machiavelli's books in his boyhood home of St. Croix, and brought these books with him when he emigrated to New York. Machiavelli developed the idea of a three-branch government long before Montesquieu, who was largely a creation of the Venetian Antonio Conti. Machiavelli thus emerges as one of the most important influences on the US Constitution, far more so than John Locke, who wanted to import feudalism into South Carolina.

Machiavelli's class analysis distinguishes feudal nobility (*gentiluomini*), wealthy urban bankers and merchants (*ottimati*), the middle and lower bourgeoisie (*popolo*), the poorer urban masses (*plebe*), and the peasants of the surrounding countryside (*contrada*). Among these, Machiavelli views the feudal nobility as incorrigible, while the *ottimati* need to be held in check by the relative have-nots of the *popolo* through a kind of constructive class tension which by implication can yield a harmony of interest if it is done right. For Machiavelli, the *popolo* is the group which is most likely to secure the liberty and progress of all. Machiavelli regards the *plebe* with great suspicion, partly because of its tendency to become a tool of the feudals, and then of the patrician *ottimati*. The popolo needs to be able to rely on the help of the *contrada* in arms.

This is an excellent class analysis of the early modern and modern world, and it has much to teach us today. Marxist analysis, which is discussed in more detail below, appears as a deliberate attempt to impose confusion where Machiavelli had achieved such clarity. In the simplest terms, for Machiavelli the bourgeoisie were the good guys, the feudal nobility were the really bad guys, and the finance oligarchs were the bad guys, who often had the proletariat in their service. The peasants could be good if they supported the bourgeoisie against the feudals and the finance oligarchs. Marxism sees the bourgeoisie as the bad guys, indistinguishable from the finance oligarchs, while the proletariat are the good guys. The peasants are regarded with suspicion because of their potential to support the bourgeoisie, while the feudal aristocrats get a free ride. The result of this is that the proletariat is told to attack the bourgeoisie, for the greater glory of the modernized feudal aristocracy. Marx is thus an example of the very tendency that made Machiavelli distrust the *plebe*. Marx, as we will see below, may be regarded as the ultimate anti-Machiavelli to be brought forward by Anglo-Venetian intelligence.

THE FEDERALIST ON OLIGARCHY

The Founding Fathers of the United States were concerned with the threat of tyranny (often identified with Cromwell), but they were also exceptionally alert to the insidious danger of oligarchy. In No. 57 of *The Federalist*, Madison defended the proposed House of Representatives against the charge that it was projected as an oligarchy, a form which he described as "the elevation of the few on the ruins of the many." In *The Federalist*, No. 58, Madison warned that very large assemblies tended to be dominated in practice by very small groups, and formulated the paradox that as the number of representatives in an elected body increases, "the countenance of the government may become more democratic, but the soul that animates it will be more oligarchic." In No. 63, Madison also deals with the objection that the Senate is likely to act as a "tyrannical aristocracy." In *The Federalist* No. 77, Hamilton defends the vesting of the power to appoint federal officers in the President alone by showing that the proposed alternative of conducting appointments by means of a council "would occasion a monopoly of all the principal employments of the government in a few families and would lead more directly to an aristocracy or an oligarchy than any measure that could be contrived." It is thus clear that the framers of the Constitution knew very well what an oligarchy was, rejected it unequivocally as a form of government, and designed safeguards to prevent the United States from falling prey to this defective regime.

The Confucian tradition and the Platonic tradition, always cognates, have come together during the twentieth century in Dr. Sun Yat-sen's Three Principles of the people, the basis of the Chinese revolution of 1911, which sought to create the first republic in Asia. Dr. Sun often explained that the Three Principles were equivalent to the "of the people, by the people, and for the people" in

Lincoln's Gettysburg Address of November 1863.[114] The Three Principles of the People can be broadly rendered as national sovereignty, a democratic republic, and economic development. The Lincoln-Sun Yat-sen link provides the basis for cooperation in an anti-oligarchical effort between the United States and China, the two most important countries on earth, into the third millennium.

A DISTANT MIRROR: THE ROMAN OLIGARCHY AND THE GRACCHI

The defeat of the attempted land reform of the Gracchi marks the point of no return in the degeneration of the Roman world from a society of independent farmers in which slavery played a marginal role to a society ruled by wealthy oligarchs and made up of parasitical urban populations supported by the labor of vast armies of slaves. After the Roman victories in the Punic Wars over Carthage, vast areas of the Mediterranean came under Roman rule. Would these new domains be distributed to the Roman and allied soldiers who had fought in the wars, thus creating large numbers of new independent farmers, capable in the future of bearing arms against foreign invaders? Or, would the new lands be privatized into the hands of Roman aristocrats, and then farmed for exorbitant profits by gangs of slaves?

The Gracchus brothers or Gracchi were both members of the senatorial nobility; their father had helped to consolidate Roman rule in the Iberian peninsula. The mother of the Gracchi was Cornelia, the daughter of Scipio Africanus, winner over Hannibal and conqueror of Carthage. There is a legend about Cornelia that on one occasion a wealthy patrician lady visited Cornelia's house to show off her jewels, and asked to see Cornelia's jewelry. Cornelia brought out her two sons and replied, "These are my jewels." Tiberius' brother Gaius wrote in a political pamphlet that while Tiberius was travelling through "Etruria on his way to [Spain], he saw for himself how the country had been deserted by its native inhabitants, and how those who tilled the soil or tended the flocks were barbarian slaves introduced from abroad; and that it was this experience which inspired the policy that later brought so many misfortunes upon the two brothers. But it was the people themselves who did most to arouse Tiberius' energy and ambitions by inscribing slogans and appeals on porticoes, monuments, and the walls of houses, calling upon him to recover the public lands for the poor." [115] Tiberius began to agitate for Roman citizenship for Rome's Italian allies, and against the dominance of slave labor: "Tiberius Sempronius Gracchus as tribune spoke at length about the Italians, about their bravery in war and their kinship with the Romans, and about how they were being reduced to poverty and declining in numbers without any hope of revival. And he complained about the slave population, about how it was no use in war and was no longer loyal to its masters, citing the recent disaster which had befallen the masters in Sicily at the hands of their slaves, who had there also been increased in numbers in order to exploit the land; he cited also the war fought against the slaves by the Romans, neither easily nor quickly won, but long-drawn out and involving many different hazards. [116] Soon Tiberius Gracchus proposed a series of measures designed to increase the number of independent farmers and limit the growth of the slave economy.

LAND REFORM OF TIBERIUS GRACCHUS, 133 BC

1. Upon his election as Tribune of the People, Tiberius Gracchus proposed first of all to limit the expropriation or privatization of the public lands, the *ager publicus,* by individual oligarchs. He

---

[114] The Gettysburg Address was itself the American answer to British leader Lord Palmerston's "Civis Romanus Sum" speech of 1850, which had asserted the British Empire as a ruling universal oligarchy.

[115] Plutarch, *Life of Tiberius Gracchus.*

[116] Appian, *Civil Wars,* 35-36.

sought to restore an earlier law that prohibited any person from holding more than 500 iugera (312.5 acres) of the public lands. The impact of this would have been to break up latifundia that had been created by enclosure (or privatization) of public property.

2. At the same time, a commission with three members was set up to supervise the distribution of plots of land in the public lands to future small farmers.

3. There was also a provision for cash grants to those setting out on their careers as family farmers. King Attalus III of Pergamum died during the time that Tiberius Gracchus was Tribune of the People. The will of King Attalus left his kingdom and his state treasury to the Roman people. According to Plutarch's biography, "Tiberius Gracchus at once as leader of the people introduced a bill which provided that the royal treasure should be brought to Rome and be available to those citizens receiving land in the distributions, for equipment and stock for their farmers."

4. Pending their transfer to their new farms, the prospective farmers were to be assisted by grants of public grain.

5. Roman citizenship was to be granted to farmers from certain other Italian states involved in the program.

The farm bill or *lex agraria* and related reforms of Tiberius Gracchus excited the hostility of the wealthy slaveholding latifundists, who saw that they would be deprived of some of the public property they had illegally privatized. Tiberius Gracchus sought to be re-elected as tribune for the year 132. But he was set upon and killed by a group of Roman senators under the leadership of Scipio Nascia during an election tumult.

GAIUS GRACCHUS

In 124 Gaius Gracchus was elected Tribune of the people for the year 123, and attempted to broaden the work begun by his brother. Gaius reaffirmed the *lex agraria* or farm law enacted under Tiberius. Gaius passed a grain law that aimed at providing Rome with an adequate supply at stable prices. The price set by law was a comparatively high one, but needy citizens were still able to acquire grain at a subsidized price. Here is a distant ancestor of the concept of parity price. Gracchus also amended the *Lex Calpurnia* of 149 BC; this law had specified that only Roman Senators could serve on juries in court cases involving abuses of power by Roman provincial governors. With his new *Lex Acilia,* Gaius Gracchus excluded senators from serving on these juries. He turned instead to the Roman knights or *Equites*, a less exalted social grouping, to provide jurors.

Gaius also sought to give all the Latins (that is, all the peoples of west-central Italy) full Roman citizenship, while all Roman *foederati* or *socii* (allies) were to be given the right to trade in Rome and to marry Romans. This measure, if it had been enacted, would have spared Rome and Italy the trauma of the later Social War, during which the Roman allies waged war against Rome in order to obtain the citizenship, which finally had to be granted.

Gaius was a city-builder. He wanted to found a new Roman city on the site of annihilated Carthage. He was also interested in creating new cities at Capua and a number of other sites in Italy. Gaius' opposition accused him of scheming to create colonies that would soon be able to challenge the power of Rome itself. Gracchus was re-elected tribune for 122. He made a trip to Carthage to supervise the building of the new city planned there. But during his absence his enemies were able to undermine his political support, including by the cynical tactic of offering the Roman city mob more generous provisions than Gaius himself had recommended. In 121 a *senatus consultum ultimum* was passed against Gaius and his followers, and he and many others were killed. Opimius, the consul, is reported to have offered the weight of Gaius's head in gold to whoever brought it in. There is also a tradition that Opimius was swindled when the killers hollowed out the head and filled it with lead to increase their reward. The defeat of the Gracchi set the stage for almost 1,000 years of decline by European civilization; despite repeated efforts, the effects of this reverse were not fully overcome until about 1400 AD with the rise of the Italian Renaissance.

KARL MARX: ANGLO-VENETIAN OPERATIVE

The collapse of organized Marxism in most of the world, although welcome in itself, has had the regrettable side effect of suppressing most class-based analysis of late twentieth century society. The world centers of academic Marxism may be found in Great Britain and the United States, but Anglo-American Marxists have ironically been far more interested in race, ethnicity, and gender than in class. The secret of Marxism is that it was from its very beginnings a concoction of the oligarchy. To explain the genesis of Marxism requires some historical background. The world center of oligarchism and monetarism from about 1100 until 1700 was the Venetian Republic. The link between the Venetian Republic and modern communism may seem obscure, but it is made evident by a study of the history involved. In his book on Petrarch, Yale professor Thomas G. Bergin makes a few relevant points about Venice in the course of a survey of fourteenth-century Italy. Bergin shows that Venice was a totalitarian state characterized by state ownership of the means of production (i.e., communism) and dominated by an oligarchy. These are the essential features of twentieth-century communism. Bergin writes: "For Venice was in truth in the *trecento* something of an anomaly. It had never gone through the conventional development of the Italian city-state from feudal fief to commune to despotism. It had never, therefore, been obliged to undergo the anti-feudal bourgeois thrusts that elsewhere were the basis of the communes; in 1310 it had fixed once and for all the status of its citizens before the law with the famous *libro d'oro*, and as a result of an uprising against such definitive regimentation it had established the Council of Ten, all-powerful, secret, and dedicated. It was in effect a totalitarian state and as it had strangled the beginnings of the commune, so in 1355 with equal severity it frustrated the attempt of the Doge Marin Faliero to make himself a despot." Bergin adds that "The power was in the hands of an oligarchy, to be sure, but individuals within the oligarchy were subject, like any other citizen, to the law of the state." He also points out that "In spite of the sharp distinction between the elite and the disenfranchised the *Serenissima* was a united state, one not without a kind of primitive communism; among other things that belonged to the state were the very ships which were the source of its wealth; merchants could sail and trade, but they were leased the ships, which were the property of the Republic." (Bergin 29-30) The shipyard where these vessels were built, known as the arsenal, was for centuries the largest factory in the world, and it was also the property of the Venetian state.

Out of this singular matrix came the founder of modern empiricism, materialism, and determinism, the Venetian Paolo Sarpi (1552-1623), one of the most influential but least appreciated thinkers and operatives in world history. Sarpi was the dominant figure in the intelligence establishment of the Republic of Venice between about 1590 and his death in 1623. Sarpi followed the traditional Venetian-Paduan Aristotelians in their view that human beings have no souls, which was also his way of denying the existence of a human faculty of creative reason and concept formation. This view had been exemplified by Pietro Pomponazzi (1462-1525), who had taught that since there was nothing in the human mind but sense impressions, no human soul could exist. This view was taught at Padua during Sarpi's time by Cesare Cremonini. Here is Sarpi's own summary of his empiricism:

There are four modes of philosophizing: the first with reason alone, the second with sense alone, the third with reason first and then sense, the fourth beginning with sense and ending with reason. The first is the worst, because from it we know what we would like to be, not what is. The third is bad because we many times distort what is into what we would like, rather than adjusting what we would like to what is. The second is true but crude, permitting us to know little and that rather of things than their causes. The fourth is the best we can have in this miserable life. [117]

Sarpi turns out to have been one of the most important influences on English and British philosophy – the philosophy of the emerging British Empire, to which the Venetian banks were transferring their assets during the 1600s. Sarpi was in direct correspondence with Sir Francis Bacon and Thomas Hobbes, who both reflect his ideas. Sarpi procured the telescope which made Galileo famous, and Galileo made his 1609 observations of the Moon and the satellites of Jupiter from Sarpi's monastery in downtown Venice. Galileo called Sarpi "my father" and considered him the greatest mathematician in Europe; Sarpi called Galileo "our mathematician." Sarpi was idolized by King James I, John Donne, John Milton, Izaak Walton, David Hume, Dr. Samuel Johnson, and many more.

Sarpi's method was to dump the formalism and terminology of Aristotle's system, but to preserve the essence of Aristotle's method – the dominance of sense impressions over the concept-forming activity and ideas of the human mind. This was then seasoned with a strong dose of nominalism drawn from William of Ockham. Sarpi portrayed himself as a modern experimental scientist in physics, astronomy, and biology, not a scholastic or Aristotelian. Sarpi dealt with Plato less by direct attack than by shifting all the attention to the figure of Socrates, who was portrayed as a skeptic and scoffer, of great utility in Sarpi's attack on religion.

All of Hobbes' work is little more than an elaboration on the theme of Sarpi's *Pensiero* 405, which asserts; "From the weakness of man derives his characteristic of living in society, but from man's depravity derives the need to live under a supreme authority." The plan for much of Hobbes' career emerged from his 1636 meeting with Galileo, who told him to write a book of ethics on a mathematical-geometrical model, which became the famous *Leviathan*. Hobbes was most impressed by Galileo's idea that motion was the most important question, and this became the standpoint of his sociology. When Hobbes visited Venice in 1614, he probably met Sarpi. According to Marco Foscarini, who later became the Doge of Venice, Sarpi's then-unpublished writings represent "the original from which Locke copied." In France, Descartes and Gassendi also reflect the influence of Sarpi and the Venetian school.

A successor of Sarpi was the Venetian Antonio Conti (1677- 1749), the great architect of the myth of Sir Isaac Newton as the founder of modern mathematical physics. Conti's commentary on Plato's *Parmenides* is an attack on the method of making ideas themselves the center of philosophical attention. Elsewhere Conti wrote that the great error of Plato was to attribute real existence to human ideas. All our ideas are simply the by-product of sense impressions, says Conti. Conti was a friend of Montesquieu, the sponsor of Voltaire, and a major influence on Diderot, Buffon, and the entire school of the French Encyclopedia, including Holbach and Helvétius. A member of Conti's Venetian circle was the economist Giammaria Ortes (1713-1790), the original from which Malthus, Bentham and the English utilitarians later drew upon. Ortes had been schooled in Newton by Conti personally. In 1790, Ortes published his assertion that 3 billion persons represented the insuperable upper limit for the human population of the earth, the absolute

---

[117] Sarpi, *Pensieri* No. 146; see Bouwsma 519-520.

maximum carrying capacity of the planet. Malthus published his "Essay on the Principle of Population" in 1798, and its main ideas are a bowdlerization of Ortes. The influence of Malthus lives on, in turn, through that of Keynes and his school, who regard capitalist depressions as crises of overproduction which can be increased by boosting consumption, whether it be productive or not. Ortes had the mania of quantification, and wrote works with titles like "Calculation on the Truth of History", "Calculation on the Value of Human Opinions" and "Calculation of the Pleasures and Pains of Human Life" (1757), as well as calculations on probability in card games. Ortes is the originator of the notion of a zero-sum game, and thus of modern game theory. He argued that economics was such a zero-sum game, and that a general improvement in the standard of living of the world is impossible, since any nation's gain will always be another nation's loss. Ortes thus furnished the main ideas spun out by Jeremy Bentham (1748-1832) in his hedonistic calculus or felicific calculus with its crude notion of "the greatest good for the greatest number," the centerpiece of the utilitarianism sponsored by the British East India Company.

Pomponazzi, Cremonini, Sarpi, Conti and other leading figures of Venetian philosophy and politics were atheists, materialists, and determinists. We can call them the no-soul brotherhood, since the view shared by all of them was that humans have no soul. This idea was important for the Venetian oligarchy, since it served them as an argument against the dignity of mankind and the notion of inalienable rights. The Venetians also asserted determinism, meaning that human beings are not free, but rather the playthings of fate, history, nature, or other mysterious forces. This Venetian school was the source of British empiricism, utilitarianism, and of the economics of figures like Adam Smith and the Mill family, associated with Lord Shelburne and the British East India Company. The Venetian project was to create social sciences on a mechanistic, materialistic, and deterministic basis borrowed from Newton's physics.

Marx emerges in retrospect as a continuation of the celebrated materialistic and atheist school of Venice and Padua, by way of England.

Karl Marx had a strong Venetian influence in his family tree. One of his most prominent ancestors was Meier Ben Isaac Katzenellenbogen (1482-1565), who was the grand rabbi of Venice and Padua, and the head of the Padua talmudic school. This personage would appear to have been the most important and successful figure among Marx's ancestors. Marx's grandfather was Mordechai Halevi Marx Levy (ca. 1740-1804), a supporter of Voltaire and Rousseau. As a recent biographer of Karl Marx points out, the name "Marx is a German form of Mark, the New Testament Apostle." [Padover 5] In other words, Marx = Mark's. St. Mark is of course the patron saint and symbol of Venice. It is not known whether the name of Karl Marx's grandfather was inspired by admiration for Venice, but in any case Karl Marx came into the world with Venice written all over him.

Marx's distorted and misleading class analysis was dictated by his profound allegiance to the Anglo-Venetian philosophical tradition of British materialism, empiricism, and utilitarianism: in his *Die Heilige Familie* of 1845, Marx portrays Bacon, Locke, Pierre Bayle, Hobbes, Bentham, and even the satanic Mandeville as precursors of modern materialism and socialism. Most of these are English followers of the Venetian Paolo Sarpi; all of them are supporters of Venice, the classic oligarchical state of early modern times, and the model of the post-1688 British constitution. "Der Materialismus ist der eingeborene Sohn Großbritaniens" materialism is the native son of Great Britain, wrote Marx. Taken together with the support received by Marx from David Urquhart of the British Foreign Office, this evidence suggests that Marx's method of playing the working class against the bourgeoisie was a stratagem of the British finance oligarchy, itself a modernized feudal aristocracy.

The Holy Family was written in Paris in the autumn of 1844. This was the first book Marx co-authored along with the British businessman Frederick Engels. The official view of the now-defunct Institute for Marxism-Leninism of the Soviet Communist Party was that *The Holy Family* "reflects the progress in the formation of Marx and Engels' revolutionary materialistic world outlook." [118] The book is largely devoted to an attack on Bruno Bauer and certain other representatives of the Young Hegelian school of philosophy. Most significant for understanding what Marx really was attempting is the section entitled "Critical battle Against French Materialism," to which the Institute for Marxism-Leninism directs our attention in its preface, noting that this part of the book, "briefly outlining the development of materialism in West European philosophy, shows that communism is the logical conclusion of materialist philosophy."

According to Marx and Engels, socialism comes from materialism, and materialism is, as we have seen, "the *natural-born* son of Great Britain." [119] They take this all the way back to the materialism and nominalism in the work of Duns Scotus and his issue of whether matter can think: "Nominalism, the *first form* of materialism, is chiefly found among the English schoolmen," presumably including William of Ockham. They then go on to Sir Francis Bacon, who is lauded as "the real progenitor of *English materialism* and all *modern experimental* science." Marx and Engels are especially enthralled by Bacon's dogma that "the *senses* are infallible and the *source* of all knowledge." Then comes Thomas Hobbes, who continues and systematizes Bacon, falling short only when he failed "to furnish a proof for Bacon's fundamental principle, the origin of all human knowledge and ideas from the world of sensation." This proof was promptly supplied by John Locke, who thus became the starting point for a trend in French materialism which "leads directly to *socialism* and *communism*." Locke's great achievement, according to the classics of Marxism, was to have shown that "the whole development of man ... depends on *education* and *external circumstances*. (The other trends in France include the one that starts with Descartes, whom Marx and Engels regard as a metaphysician, and also the French followers of Sir Isaac Newton.) Locke's influence was mediated into France by Condillac, who – according to Marx and Engels – was able to refute not just Descartes, but Spinoza, Malebranche, and even Leibniz as well. But the great adversary of metaphysics, say Marx and Engels, was Pierre Bayle, another pro-Venetian writer, who proved "that a society consisting only of atheists is *possible*." (Actually, this idea comes from Sarpi.) Next in the Marxist pantheon are Helvétius, with the great discovery that personal interest is the basis of all morality, La Mettrie (with his mechanistic-materialistic *L'Homme machine*), Holbach and Robinet.

Marx and Engels focus on the immediate linkage of this materialism with socialism and communism:

> There is no need for any great penetration to see from the teaching of materialism on the original goodness and equal intellectual endowment of men, the omnipotence of experience, habit, and education, and the influence of environment on man, the great significance of industry, the justification of enjoyment, etc., how necessarily materialism is connected with communism and socialism. If man draws all his knowledge, sensation, etc., from the world of the senses and the experience gained in it, then what has to be done is to arrange the empirical world in such a way that man experiences and becomes accustomed to what is truly human in it and that he becomes aware of himself as man. If correctly understood interest is the principle of all morality, man's private interest must be made to coincide with the interest of humanity. **If man is unfree in the materialistic sense, i.e., is free** not through the negative

---

[118] *Holy Family*, preface, p. 7.

[119] "Der Materialismus ist der eingeborene Sohn Grossbritanniens."

power to avoid this or that, but through the positive power to assert his true individuality, crime must not be punished in the individual, but the anti-social sources of crime must be destroyed, and each man must be given social scope for the vital manifestation of his being. [120] If man is shaped by environment, his environment must be made human. If man is social by nature, he will develop his true nature only in society, and the power of his nature must be measured not by the power of the separate individual, but by the power of society. [Marx and Engels, 154, emphasis added]

The main precursor of the materialist-communist argument cited by Marx and Engels is none other than the satanic British aristocrat Mandeville, the author of *The Fable of the Bees*, whose argument was that private vices and depravities turn into public benefits because they stimulate economic activity in the marketplace: "The apologia of vices by Mandeville, one of Locke's early English followers, is typical of the socialist tendencies of materialism. He proves that in modern society vice is *indispensable* and *useful*." Then we get Gracchus Babeuf, after which the Marxists lay their cards on the table with an endorsement of Jeremy Bentham, the chief of the British intelligence establishment of his era: "Bentham based his system of correctly understood interest on Helvétius' morality, and *Owen* proceeded from *Bentham*'s system to found English communism." Note that communism, according to this, comes from Bentham and the British.[121] From here Bentham's socialist influence returned to France, and that brings us up to 1844 and the tradition in which Marx and Engels locate themselves: "Exiled to England, the Frenchman Cabet came under the influence of communist ideas there and on his return to France become the most popular, if the most superficial, representative of communism. Like Owen, the more scientific French communists, Dézamy, Gay, and others, developed the teaching of materialism as the teaching of *real humanism* and the *logical* basis of *communism*." [Marx and Engels, 155]

For Marx, the precursors of modern materialism and communism are generally members of the Venetian parties of France and England; most of the proto-communists turn out upon closer examination to be direct or indirect disciples of Paolo Sarpi. Sarpi and Marx are thus very close in matters of epistemology. Sarpi and Marx are materialists, and both deny the central importance of the human mind. They are both empiricists and sensationalists, addicts of sense certainty, and committed to belittling human reason. They are both determinists for whom the freedom of the human will does not exist. They are both mortalists, denying the immortality of the human soul in any form. They are both indifferentists, turning away from the rigorous investigation of causality. They are both atheists, attempting to preen themselves as radicals through their attacks on religion. They are both pragmatists. They are both collectivists, with Sarpi representing a system which suppressed individuality rather successfully among the oligarchy. They are both, in short, oligarchs.

---

[120] This means that if you are not free, but subject to determinism, you should feel free to express your individuality in whatever way you wish, however pathological – a favorite theme of modern writers who try to show that various forms of aberrant behavior are genetically determined. In the original text: "**Wenn der Mensch unfrei im materialistischen Sinne, d.h. frei ist,** nicht durch die negative Kraft, dies und jenes zu meiden, sondern durch die positive Macht, seine wahre Individualität geltend zu machen, so muß man nicht das Verbrechen am Einzelnen strafen, sondern die antisozialen Geburtsstätten des Verbrechens zerstören und jedem den sozialen Raum für seine wesentliche Lebensäußerung geben" (138, emphasis added)

[121] Other rather obvious English and British sources for communism not mentioned by Marx and Engels would include the Diggers, Ranters, Quakers, Fifth Monarchists, True Levelers, and some other fanatical sects of the 1640s-1650s, during the English Revolution. These primitive communist doctrines had roots going back to Wycliff and Wat Tyler's rebellion of 1381.

David Urquhart was Marx's patron, and his own career was sponsored by Jeremy Bentham, who lavishly praised "our David" in his letters. Urquhart belonged to a Scottish clan which was notorious for its personal eccentricity. Urquhart's positive contribution to civilization was his popularization of the Turkish bath. He also kept a harem for some time. Urquhart also thought that late Ottoman feudalism was a model of what civilization ought to be. In Turkey, Urquhart was convinced that all the evil in the world had a single root: Russia, through the machinations of the court of St. Petersburg. It was a very convenient view for Palmerston's Britain, which was always on the verge of war with Russia. For Urquhart, the unification of Italy was a Russian plot. He once met Mazzini, and concluded after ten minutes that Mazzini was a Russian agent! (In reality, Mazzini was in the pay of the British Admiralty.)

For this Russophobe, the problem of Great Britain was that Palmerston was a Russian agent, having been recruited by one of his many mistresses, the Russian Countess Lieven. During the years of Chartist agitation, Urquhart bought up working class leaders and drilled them in the litany that all of the problems of the English working man came from Russia via Lord Palmerston. To these workers Urquhart taught something he called *dialectics*, which then came to occupy a place of honor in Marx's theory. Urquhart was a member of Parliament and controlled a weekly paper, *The Free Press*, to which Marx contributed. Urquhart was a fierce opponent of modern capitalism; his remedy was to go back to the simplicity of character of Merrie England, in the sense of retrogression to an organic, bucolic, medieval myth. "The people of England were better clothed and fed when there was no commerce and when there were no factories," wrote Urquhart. Urquhart emerges as a precursor of the radical environmental Green parties of today.

Marx cited Urquhart frequently as an authority, and it would appear that Urquhart significantly influenced the writing of *Das Kapital*. Marx was a professed admirer of Urquhart – acknowledging his influence more than that of most other living persons. Marx even composed a violently Russophobic *Life of Lord Palmerston*, based on Urquhart's obsession that Palmerston was a Russian agent of influence. This says enough about Marx's acumen as a political analyst. Marx and Urquhart agreed that there is no real absolute profit in capitalism, and that technological progress causes a falling rate of profit. Another of Urquhart's operatives was Lothar Bäucher, a confidant of the German labor leader Ferdinand Lassalle, and later of German Chancellor Otto von Bismarck.

MARX AND GIAMMARIA ORTES

Given the fact that he provided the main ideas for the English philosophical radicals, it is not surprising that the Venetian Giammaria Ortes also received high praise from Karl Marx. The samples of Ortes's theorizing provided here may cast some light on the reasons for this affinity. Ortes provides a class analysis imbued with class conflict according to the shifting alliances of the various strata of Venetian patricians to which he was attached. In volume I of *Capital* Marx praised "the Venetian monk, Ortes" as "an original and clever writer." For Marx, Ortes was "one of the great economic writers of the 18th century [who] regards the antagonism of capitalist production as a general natural law of social wealth." [*Capital*, I, 646] Marx quotes Ortes's remark at the opening of his book *On National Economy* that "instead of projecting useless systems for the happiness of the peoples, I will limit myself to investigating the cause of their unhappiness." In Marx's view, Ortes was distinguished by his steady contemplation of "...the fatal destiny that makes misery eternal...." Marx railed against Malthus as a reactionary plagiarist, but summoned only respect for the Venetian Ortes.

MARX VS. LIST

Marx admired Ortes, but stridently attacked the two contemporary economists who were most closely associated with the American System of protectionism and industrial development – Friedrich List and Henry Carey. Marx attacked Friedrich List in his 1859 *Contribution of the Critique of Political Economy*, claiming that "Friedrich List has never been able to grasp the difference between labor as a producer of something useful, a use-value, and labor as a producer of exchange-value, a specific social form of wealth (since his mind being occupied with practical matters was not concerned with understanding); he therefore regarded the modern English economists as mere plagiarists of Moses of Egypt." [*Contribution* 37] What List did understand rather well was that free trade was an ideology propagated by the British Empire for the purpose of world economic and political domination, including a strategy for maintaining the rest of the world in pre-industrial backwardness relative to Britain. List's ideas have been exceptionally successful whenever they have been given a real opportunity to work, such as in 19th century America and Germany, and 20th century Japan. Marx's recipe for class struggle included supporting free trade, the central economic strategy of the British, the dominant oligarchical world empire of his time, and Marx's patrons and hosts.

MARX VS. HENRY CAREY

Marx's attacks on Henry Carey are numerous. Marx, the apostle of class struggle as the motor force of world history, was enraged by Carey's idea of the possibility of attaining a harmony of interest between labor and capital, which would allow the standard of living to be improved even as improved productivity and legitimate profits were realized through technological and infrastructural improvements. In volume one of *Capital,* Marx takes special pains to attack Carey's idea that (as Marx summarizes the issue), the "wages of the different nations are directly proportional to the degree of productivity of the national working days." It is indeed an economic fact that the real productivity of labor (as distinguished from speedup, etc.) is the most important determinant of national wealth, but not for Marx. "The whole of our analysis of the production of surplus-value shows the absurdity of this conclusion," rails Marx. Carey is then vilified as "the man who first declared the relations of capitalist production to be the eternal laws of Nature and reason, whose free, harmonious working is only disturbed by the intervention of the State, in order afterwards to discover that the diabolical influence of England on the world market ... necessitates State intervention, ... i.e., the System of Protection." In Marx's opinion, Carey demonstrated an "atrocious want of the critical faculty" and "spurious erudition." [*Capital* I, 563]

Marx thus defends free trade and the British Empire against the objections of the man who influenced the thinking of Abraham Lincoln. Part of Marx's rage is occasioned by Carey's proposals for constructively resolving class struggle, which Marx was concerned to direct against the industrial bourgeoisie in American and elsewhere, a strategy which meshed perfectly with British geopolitics. Elsewhere, Marx defends his patron Urquhart against Carey, whom he stigmatized as "a great Russophile"; the issue was of course that the Russian Empire and the United States were aligned together against Britain and France from the 1850s through the American Civil War. Marx ridiculed Carey for asserting that "Urquhart himself is one of the chief agents of the ruin of Turkey, where he had made free trade propaganda in the English interest." [*Capital*, I, 749] Karl Marx thus turns out to have been a rather obvious British agent, whose work is based on the soulless Venetian materialism-determinism of Paolo Sarpi. The main enemies of human progress in Marx's time were not the capitalists but the feudal oligarchs, especially those who had made the transition from latifundism to banking and high finance, above all in the City of London, the center of world finance.

THE IRON LAW OF OLIGARCHY

Marxism is thus revealed an anti-Platonic, profoundly oligarchical philosophy – a combined distillation of Venice and the British Empire. The impact of Marxism on the Twentieth Century has been to promote oligarchical thinking in general. The parties, trade unions, countries and regimes which have employed Marxism or versions of Marxism as their official doctrine have thus acquired a built-in tendency towards oligarchy. This fact has played an important role in the creation of modern sociology in Germany before World War I by the group around Max Weber, Edgar Jaffé, Werner Sombart, and Robert Michels.

Michels especially is known for his Iron Law of Oligarchy, which posits an inherent tendency for every human social formation and institution towards the domination of a restricted group. Michel focused his attention almost exclusively on the socialist and democratic parties of central Europe, especially the German SPD, but also the Italian PSI. He ignored American political parties. He also disregarded liberal and conservative parties in Germany and Italy, perhaps feeling that it was clear that these would be dominated by entrenched privilege. He took the socialist parties, suggesting that if true democracy were to be found anywhere, it could be found here; but he discovered that the internal organization of the socialist parties was thoroughly oligarchical, and used this to formulate his celebrated Iron Law of Oligarchy: if you say organization, you are also saying oligarchy. The party is the mother of the dominance of the elected leaders over their voters and supporters. For Michels, the creation of oligarchies is an organic tendency which any and every organization necessarily experiences. [122]

The same dynamic was observed in Soviet Russia, the mass parties of the Second and Third Internationals, the Soviet satellites in eastern Europe and elsewhere, and in Mao's China. But before making such cosmic generalizations about man's oligarchical destiny, Michels should have taken a moment to ask whether the Marxist theory which all these organizations professed were not itself a factor in promoting oligarchy, which it unquestionably was. Whether or not there is an organized oligarchic tendency in recorded human history is not an object of contention: the oligarchical track record is massive. But oligarchy, like evil itself, has no ontological status, is not metaphysically necessary, and we would all be better off without it. During the European Renaissance of the 1400s, for example, Platonic ideas and socioeconomic development combined to produce an historical climate which was increasingly uncongenial for oligarchs.

A fascinating case study is provided by the fortunes of Marxism in India, a country long characterized by a caste system which arbitrarily assigned human individuals to the status of Brahmin, untouchable, or the various ranks in between. Caste is theoretically fixed once and for all at birth, and it thus even more rigid than the types of oligarchy with which we are confronted in Europe and North America. According to Dilip Simeon, an historian of the University of Delhi, Marxism was congenial to the Indian caste system. He described Marx's theory of knowledge as a "brahmanical epistemology," based on the notion that important truths are the monopoly of a priesthood. Simeon points out that the Indian Communist Party was never very egalitarian, since "rank and file workers have rarely enjoyed much standing in any of the main marxist parties" of India. [123]

---

[122] "... die Organisation ist die Mutter der Herrschaft der Gewählten über die Wähler.... Die Bildung von Oligarchien im Schoße der mannigfaltigen Formen der Demokratien ist eine organische, also eine Tendenz, der jede Organisation, auch die sozialistische, selbst die libertäre, notwendigerweise unterliegt." (Michels, 370-1). Michels viewed his own theory as complementary to Marxism; he later moved to Italy and supported Mussolini's fascism.

[123] Edward Tenner, "The Once and Future Marx," *Princeton Alumni Weekly*, October 25, 1995.

RENAISSANCE NEW MONARCHY AND THE MIDDLE CLASS

In France, Louis XI had forged an alliance of the bourgeoisie and the king against the feudal nobility, who organized themselves as the League of the Public Good under Charles the Bold, Duke of Burgundy. The decisive defeat of Charles and the feudal aristocrats came during the siege of Paris, when the city bourgeoisie fought for the king and kept the feudal predators out. Without a middle class, the modern state cannot exist. As Lasch points out, "The decline of nations is closely linked, in turn, to the global decline of the middle class. Ever since the sixteenth and seventeenth centuries, the fortunes of the nation-state have been bound up with those of the trading and manufacturing classes. The founders of modern nations ... turned to this class for support in their struggle against the feudal nobility. A large part of the appeal of nationalism lay in the state's ability to establish a common market within its boundaries, to enforce a uniform system of justice, and to extend citizenship both to petty proprietors and to rich merchants, alike excluded from power under the old regime. The middle class understandably became the most patriotic, not to say jingoistic and militaristic, element in society .... Whatever its faults, middle-class nationalism provided a common ground, common standards, a common frame of reference without which society dissolves into nothing more than contending factions – as the Founding Fathers of America understood so well – a war of all against all." (Lasch, 48-49)

Less than a hundred years after supporting Louis XI, the people of Paris were supporting the Catholic Duke of Guise, one of the most repulsive and murderous of feudal oligarchs, against King Henry IV. By 1600, the general tendency was clear: kings no longer allied with the bourgeoisie against the feudals – the kings now entered into partnerships with the great nobility, or with the landed magnates east of the Elbe. This was the advent of absolutism, however enlightened. After about a quarter century of oligarchical leadership, the United States is beginning to resemble a museum in which the devices of the benighted past are inflicted on the suffering inhabitants. A few examples:

A lasting obsession of the nobility of Castile was that trade and industry were ignoble and abhorrent; they preferred honors. The absolute monarchy of Philip II was not so absolute, since it was based on a pact between the King and the feudal oligarchs: the oligarchs were not taxed, and in exchange refrained from rebelling against the King, at least in Castile after about 1520. In effect, the monarch and the nobility agreed to prey together on the most numerous class, the peasants. These prejudices were seen as "Spanish ideas" in conquered territories like Naples and Milan, and they did much damage wherever they were imitated. The modern American preference for the Malthusian low-growth information society and the repudiation of heavy industry since the Volcker period (1979 ff.) is a close replica of these old and oligarchical "Spanish ideas." Such Spanish ideas doomed the Spanish Empire, despite attempts at reform.

OLIGARCHICAL TAX POLICY

France of the *ancien regime* also had a highly regressive tax structure, deriving proceeds from the *gabelle*, a salt tax, and the *taille*, an income tax which was levied mainly on peasants. Henry IV's finance minister Sully was a bit like Reagan, who lowered the income tax but raised the social security tax: Sully lowered the *taille*, but raised the *gabelle*. Louis XIV's finance minister Colbert tried to impose a real estate tax on all property owners, including the nobles, but he never succeeded. The nobles argued that taxation was a dishonor. France, like Spain, insisted on taxing mainly the peasants and mainly the poor until the French revolution.

Another area where the US is imitating the collapsed empires of the past is tax policy. It is a truism that since the Reagan era, the upper 20% of US incomes have been paying a sharply reduced share of the overall tax burden, while the lowest 20% is paying much more, partly – as we have seen – as a result of the greater bite extracted by the regressive Social Security payroll tax (FICA). In Spain, the upper nobility of grandees as well as the lower nobility or hidalgos were exempted from taxation. In the sixteenth-century Spain of Philip II, one of the most onerous taxes was a national sales tax called the *alcabala*; this amounted to 14% of every transaction carried out in the country. Strangely enough, a favorite Republican plan for tax reform in the US today, the national sales tax, boils down to a close imitation of this very regressive Spanish tax of 400 years ago.

The Austrian Hapsburgs appear as the source of the modern American policy of multiculturalism. The Vienna Hapsburgs cultivated heterogeneity; they were horrified at any plan or project that might allow their subject nationalities to make common cause against the crown. This meant accepting a permanent structural weakness that was masked for a time by the sheer size of their domains. But when a great national effort was finally required in World War I, the Hapsburg armies fragmented along national lines. Today's American oligarchy could presumably know this if it wanted to, but it prefers to talk of "many nations" and to promote multiculturalism as one of its main counter-insurgency strategies. Evidently the American oligarchy feels that the future has no more emergencies in store for this country, which is not a prudent approach to securing a decent future. The absurdities of political correctness are also nothing new. They are typical of past attempts by oligarchs to stifle original thinking according to their needs. The system of elaborate euphemism and circumlocution that does everything possible to avoid plain speaking, known today as political correctness, is also nothing new. There was an epidemic of such doubletalk around 1600 which was called *marinismo* in Italy, *gongorismo* in Spain, and *preciosité* in France; in England it inspired the work of John Lyly, the father of the euphemism. Another good model for the kind of oligarchy now emerging in the United States is the old Kingdom of Poland, which was ruled by an oligarchy of the petty nobility that amounted to about 8% or even 10% of the total population, roughly corresponding to those enjoying the so-called culture of contentment under Reagan-Bush.

THE BRITISH OLIGARCHY

Great Britain, the acknowledged flagship of patrician rule in the late twentieth century, has been an oligarchy since no later than the Glorious Revolution of 1688 and the 1689 Bill of Rights – for oligarchs. The Magna Carta, which naïve Americans still associate with some vague idea of democracy, was in fact an earlier bill of rights for feudal oligarchs – authorizing among other things their recourse to civil war if their oligarchical privileges did not receive adequate deference from the king.

A perceptive student of this issue was the now-forgotten American writer, Louis Bromfield, who offered the following sketch in his 1939 study, *England: A Dying Oligarchy*:

> For centuries England has been ruled by an oligarchy. There were times when strong and shrewd or virtuous rulers like the Tudors or Cromwell broke up the gang rule and built the greatness of England... . The barons at Runnymede were medieval gangsters and the Magna Charta which they wrested from King John provided the foundation of the delusion that England is a democratic nation. This document gave all sorts of rights and powers to the barons, it took care of them very prettily, but it hadn't much to say of the people. The Oligarchy was founded at Runnymede; it has persisted through several centuries, changing its name and its class, sometimes even changing its color, but it has remained essentially the same oligarchy. The Barons of Runnymede have become translated in the Twentieth Century [i.e., 1939] into the National Government and its supporters. Its leaders are Baldwin and Chamberlain, Samuel Hoare, and Sir John Simon, Lord Halifax, et al. The Barons of

Runnymede, savage, vigorous, and primitive, have turned into a clique of undecided elderly politicians, decadent and full of cant, as easily terrified by the prospect of a general election as by the face-making of the dictators. Among them there is no one equipped or worthy to lead the British people. They are not leaders: they are only followers, with one eye always on the ballot box.

Remember that one of the rights acquired by the barons at Runnymede was the right to wage civil war against the king if he were to fail to respect the freedoms (meaning special privileges and prerogatives) of the feudal oligarchs. Bromfield went on to describe British society as dominated by a caste system which "is and has been for centuries as rigid as the caste system of India' but which showed signs of breaking up during the 1930s. But the British caste system, Bromfield was quick to point out, was not based exclusively or even primarily on birth: it was based most of all on money, just as Plato would have expected: "In a considerable experience of life in many nations, I have never witnessed so profound a respect for money, money for money's sake, as in England. That is one of the fundamental reasons for the long and prosperous existence of the oligarchy." The second aspect of the British system which Bromfield stressed was "English hypocrisy." "Anglo-Saxon hypocrisy," he wrote, "is something unique; it is not the cynical double-dealing of a Talleyrand, nor the unbalanced, illogical madness of men like Hitler and Goebbels; it is calculated but uncynical, and very often it deceives its perpetrator far more profoundly than it deceives those at whom it is aimed." These were the qualities being summed up in the figure of Sir Neville Chamberlain during the time Bromfield was writing. Bromfield's prognosis for the British Oligarchy was grim. The only achievement the Oligarchy could point to was "a dubious prosperity benefiting principally one small class in England." Bromfield concluded that "it just may be that the Oligarchy has pushed its intrigue and its hypocrisy too far." [Bromfield, 2-24]

Today the average American still may think of Britain was the Mother of Parliaments, but the post-Thatcher UK is a very sinister police state. A realistic evaluation of the modern British oligarchical state was offered by Paddy Hillyard:

> It is our contention that the contemporary British state falls a long way short of democracy... Rather it is better characterized as 'coercive.' By this we mean that decision-making and administration are exclusive, providing few opportunities for popular participation and where such opportunities do exist, then participation for the majority takes place on highly unequal terms. The workings of the state are so shrouded in secrecy that access to information is at best very limited. Formal provision for scrutiny of the work of those with power is inadequate so, as a consequence, accountability is weak.... and whereas the majority can obtain very little information about the internal workings of the state, the state itself collects vast amounts of information about its 'clients.' While decision-makers are barely accountable for their actions, ordinary people may be subjected to an array of sanctions, many of which are punitive, that are meted out not only by the police, courts, and penal system, but also by supposedly benign welfare state agencies like social services departments and social security offices. In addition, these agencies will sometimes make use of compulsion, surveillance, and threats.... it is difficult to write about the state's coercive machinery without risking accusations of paranoia or belief in a 'conspiracy theory.' [Hillyard 15-17]

THE EUROGARCHS OF THE 1990s

Today's European Union is the scene of one of the greatest orgies of oligarchical power in recent history, with the creation of the European Monetary Union and its common currency, the euro. Today two thousand years of European civilization are being dissolved in the corrosive acid of monetarism. Some have called it a monetary revolution, but it is feudal counter-revolution in its most sinister form. Atop the EMU sits the sinister European Central Bank, which is established by the Maastricht Treaty as a permanent oligarchy of financiers who are to disregard the wishes of the elected national governments which make up the European Union. During the 1920s, Montagu Norman, Hjalmar Schacht, and other central bankers set themselves up as the currency dictators of Europe through means which can only be described as conspiratorial; today European political conditions have deteriorated so much that similar functions have been legitimized by treaty. Monetary and credit policy are to be controlled forever by this autonomous and self-perpetuating oligarchical creation. The squalor of the entire procedure was pointed up at the summit meeting of European heads of government and finance ministers at Brussels on May 2-3, 1998. By this time the European Monetary Union was on its way to its launching on January 1, 1999, and it was clear that eleven countries would attempt to participate.

The European Central Bank (ECB) was about to come into existence on July 1, 1998. The issue was now to choose the first governor of the ECB. Who would take over as the currency dictator of Europe? German Chancellor Helmut Kohl was backing Wim Duisenberg, the former governor of the Netherlands Central Bank, and expected this candidacy to be successful. But French president Jacques Chirac insisted on his own candidate, Banque de France governor Jean-Claude Trichet. The issue was important, because the ECB leadership is destined to renew itself by co-optation, ignoring more and more the national governments and the voters who elect them. The ECB will set interest rates and monetary policy for every business person in Europe. The resulting conflict produced an 11-hour standoff. Out of this long and acrimonious haggling there came a sleazy compromise: Duisenberg would become the first head of the ECB, but would leave office after about four years; he would then be succeeded by Trichet, who would serve out a full 8-year term. There was allegedly no written agreement to this effect. What actually will happen is anybody's guess, meaning that we have entered the realm of total, lawless, oligarchical caprice. It was an illegal, surreptitious, backroom deal of the worst sort - typical of the moral standards of the oligarchy which is the European Union and its component governments. President Chirac was forced to browbeat reporters with the order, "Do not laugh!" French Finance Minister Strauss-Kahn was asked by a reporter, "How is anyone supposed to believe these lies?"

Individual European countries have also gone far down the road towards oligarchical transformation. In Italy, this process has been accelerated by the deliberate scuttling of Christian Democratic and Socialist Parties (for decades the pillars of the governing coalition) by a series of scandals starting in 1992 and speaheaded by prosecuting judges of the "Mani pulite" (clean hands) pool in Milan, including DiPietro, Borelli, and others, whose actions appeared coordinated with the British intelligence services. Sergio Fabbrini, in his recent study *The Rules of Democracy*, approaches Italian politics as now subject to an oligarchical power structure. For Fabbrini, the basic cause of the Italian political crisis of the 1990s is oligarchy: "...la causa fonda ha un nome preciso: l'oligarchia.... il modello di democrazia (che io definisco consociativo) ha generato una struttura oligarchica, non solo nella politica e nei partiti."

Like many Italian writers, Fabbrini attributes great importance to the question of alternation in office between government and opposition forces, and sees in the lack of this a contributing cause of oligarchy: "La tendenza alla oligarchia.... è propria di ogni democrazia che non prevede l'alternanza." In this view, Italy "si è trasformata in un vero e proprio regime politico: la democrazia oligarchica." [Fabbrini 3]

Fabbrini makes the important distinction between oligarchy and elite: an oligarchy is an elite which is able to reproduce itself in power, while an elite is merely a group which carries out a certain function at a given moment in time. Oligarchy is a position, while an elite is a function:

"Insomma, l'una è una posizione, mentre l'altra è una funzione.... in Italia, il pluralismo fisiologico delgi interessi si è transformato in un patologico corporativismo a direzione oligarchica." [Fabbrini 4-5]

But in Italy, oligarchy is not without its apologists. One of these is, not suprisingly, Norberto Bobbio, who, as Fabbrini shows, has attempted to remove the negative connotation of oligarchy, since it is clear that this is the only term that can be adequately applied to the social and political system of Italy (and of most of today's Europe). For Bobbio, oligarchy should no longer be the term of opprobrium it has been since Plato; for Bobbio, it is simply a neutral descriptive term (it is "assiologicament neutrale"). Bobbio has also tried to widen the gulf between democratic and non-democratic oligarchy. Democratic oligarchy, Bobbio has argued, is better because of the source of power and of the way in which it is exercised ("sia per la fonte che per l'esercizio del potere.") Democratic oligarchy, Bobbio has written, obtains legtimacy from formally free elections and from a public opinion which is free within certain limits (the legitimacy of democratic oligarchy comes "da un voto popolare periodico e formalmente libero" and accepts the existence "entro certi limiti della libertà della pubblica opinione.") [Fabbrini 3]

LENIN ON BOLSHEVISM: "THIS IS A FULL-FLEDGED 'OLIGARCHY'"

During much of its history, the USSR was dominated by oligarchy. The most impressive testimony that this was true even in the early phases comes from V. I. Lenin himself, who described the structure of the ruling Bolshevik Party in his 1920 book, *'Left-Wing' Communism, an Infantile Disorder*. Lenin illustrated the way the Bolshevik Party was run by a central committee of 19 persons and a politburo of just five, who concentrated all power in their own hands. Lenin's conclusion: "This is a full-fledged 'oligarchy.'" As Soviet expert Darrell P. Hammer writes,

> During most of its history, the Soviet political system has been an oligarchy in which political power has been concentrated in the small group of party leaders who sit on the Politburo. In theory, the Politburo is accountable to the Central Committee, but the Central Committee is also a small group. Even if the Central Committee were the main source of power rather than the Politburo, the Soviet system would still be an oligarchy. During one period in Soviet history, from the mid-1930s until 1953, the oligarchy was replaced by an autocracy, and the system was ruled by the dictator Joseph Stalin (1879-1953). Stalin was one of the original oligarchs in Lenin's government.... This period of personal dictatorship, or autocracy, came to an end with Stalin's death. The political system then reverted to its earlier oligarchical structure. Within the Politburo, one man has usually been recognized as the leader, but there has been no dictator. [124]

The Union of Soviet Socialist Republics was dominated from the 1950s on by an oligarchy which is generally designated as the *nomenklatura*; a name which refers to certain lists of officials which were maintained as early as the time of Peter the Great. Nikita S. Khrushchev was the leading figure of an oligarchy, not an autocratic dictator in the Stalin mode. The Brezhnev-Suslov-Kossygin-Mikoyan palace coup of August 1964 which ousted Khrushchev brought to power a collective leadership or collegial leadership which was even more evidently an oligarchy. [125]

Yeltsin's Russia is the country where the oligarchy most brazenly proclaims its own dominance of government and society. During the last several years, it has become a journalistic commonplace

---

[124] Darrell P. Hammer, *The USSR: The Politics of Oligarchy* (Boulder: Westview, 1990), pp. 1-2.
[125] For the Soviet oligarchy see Bruno Rizzi, *La bureaucratisation du monde* (1939) and Mikhail Voslensky, *Nomenklatura: The Ruling Class of the Soviet Union* (1984).

(even for the *Washington Post*) that Russia's economic life is now under the control of a group of bankers including Potanin, Berezovsky, Smolensky, Gusinsky, Friedman, and others. Politicians like Yegor Gaidar, Anatoly Chubais and Boris Nemtsov are simply lawyers for these finance oligarchs. This group met at Davos, Switzerland in January 1996 and came to the conclusion that their interests required the re-election of Yeltsin to another term as president of Russia, a decision which they proved capable of imposing on the country despite Yeltsin's very low popularity at the time the oligarchs met.

Chubais customarily refers to the Russian people as the "lumpen" and "marginals" who make up the mass of what he views as the oriental, "Scythian" Russian population. Like the Russian aristocrats of the eighteenth century who spoke French to underline the distance that separated them from their own serfs, today's Russian oligarchy holds its own country in contempt. Igor Chubais, the brother of IMF operative Anatoly, has written that "Russia... is of absolutely no interest to the present elite." The elite is concerned only with "power, money, and privileges." The Russian finance oligarchs see the Russian people as "simply an annoying, tiresome nuisance, which, moreover, for some reason has to be paid wages."[126]

According to the Russian democratic opposition leader Grigory Yavlinsky, Berezovsky has been known to call Russian politicians on the phone and attempt to order them around in the name of "the oligarchy." Aleksandr Solzhenitsyn, the most celebrated Russian author, formally informed the State Duma in a major address on October 28, 1994 that Russian had become a full-blown oligarchical society. The fact that Russia is ruled by an oligarchy is now so common that no politician, whatever his or her real beliefs and intentions, can afford to neglect this theme. Take the example of Gen. Aleksandr Lebed, the former director of the Russian national security apparatus, who recently commented:

> Russia is evolving toward oligarchy. Power is based on a merger between government institutions and financial capital.... about half the economy is controlled by a small group of banks and financial-industrial groups, while the other half is controlled by criminal clans.... Reforms are now being implemented at the expense of the people. Ordinary Russians are now as far from the real levers of power as during the rule of the Communist Party. [127]

LATIN AMERICA: THE HEGEMONY OF THE *NEOBANQUEROS*

Most countries of Latin American have been under various forms of oligarchical rule since they attained their independence from Spain and Portugal. After the Napoleonic wars, the creole latifundist class (Spanish-speaking planters born in the new world) drove out the overseas colonialists from Spain and Portugal, and set up governments subservient to their interests. In post-1815 Latin America, liberalism meant Anglophile oligarchy, as it so often does. In Argentina, the post-independence Rivadavia government, like Boris Yeltsin in Russia, announced that its goal was "establishing a modern system of private property," and began privatizing vast amounts of public lands which had once belonged to the Spanish crown. "The grand irony of this design was that these lands were, naturally, bought up by a small group of ranchers, who concentrated power over vast landholdings, or *estancias*. By 1827, when Rivadavia was forced to resign, 21 million acres of public lands in Argentina had been transferred to only five hundred individuals, and the *estancia*

---

[126] *Nezavisimaya Gazeta*, September 19, 1998.
[127] Associated Press, January 5, 1997.

system was established for a long time to come." [128] (Anatoly Chubais, who made Russian privatization lucrative for the tiny nomenklatura elite, was in the same oligarchical tradition.) Although the form of these regimes has been reorganized, oligarchical domination by latifundists, joined later by bankers and financiers, has been a constant.

> Latin American society is a traditional one; it is a society opposed to being transformed into a nation. The Latin American states are not nation-states but oligarchies. Therein lies the key to the whole problem. The Latin American countries are not nations, because the oligarchies have always systematically opposed any move toward nationhood, any evolution that would be conducive to the emergence of national characteristics. For any development of these characteristics would mean the end of oligarchy. But, as we live in an era in which nationalism is the rule and in which mass means of communication rule out intellectual or ideological isolation, the oligarchies have encouraged a special type of nationalism, one that will serve as a substitute for nationhood. [Alba 16]

This analysis is of course too sweeping, and does not do justice to serious nation-building efforts in Mexico, in Argentina, in Brazil, and in several other Latin American countries. But it does identify the greatest single problem of Latin American civilization. Later in the nineteenth century, the Latin American oligarchic elites developed new systems for ensuring their continued domination. The literature on oligarchical domination in Latin American is so vast and explicit that its outlines cannot even be sketched in this brief overview. Suffice it to say that in the less economically backward and more European-oriented countries like Argentina and Chile, according to most accounts, these elites assumed direct control of government through a kind of democracy, the analysis of which can contribute to our understanding of the modern US political process. As two present-day historians of the phase in question have written that "in both Argentina and Chile there was mild competition between political parties that tended, at least in this early phase, to represent competing factions of the aristocracy. But there was more agreement than disagreement about basic policy issues, and little serious opposition to the wisdom of pursuing export-oriented economic growth. Competition was restricted and voting was often a sham. One might think of such regimes as expressions of 'oligarchic democracy.'" [Skidmore and Smith 46][129]

In the age of post-1991 globalism, a situation obtains which is not so different. The labor movement and the left-wing opposition political parties have been weakened, and the permissible range of issues has been narrowed out of fear of the ever-present military coup waiting the wings. Issues of economic justice, land reform, and other questions of basic economic policy have no chance of being implemented, as long as globalization prevails: "Middle-class standards of living can be expected to decline throughout what is all too hopefully referred to as the developing world. In a country like Peru, once a prosperous nation with reasonable prospects of evolving parliamentary institutions, the middle class for all practical purposes has ceased to exist. A middle class, as Walter Russell Mead reminds us in his study of the declining American empire *Mortal Splendor,* 'does not appear out of thin air.' Its power and numbers 'depend on the overall wealth of the domestic economy,' and in countries, accordingly, where 'wealth is concentrated in the hands of a tiny oligarchy and the rest of the population is desperately poor, the middle class can grow to only a limited extent.... [It] never escapes its primary role as a servant class to the oligarchy.'

---

[128] Carlos Fuentes, *The Buried Mirror: Reflections on Spain in the New World* (New York: Houghton Mifflin, 1992), p. 263.

[129] For a recent left-wing view of this issue, see the proceedings of North American Committee on Latin America (NACLA) conference, "The Concentration of Wealth and Class Structure in the Americas in the Neoliberal Age," held at the University of South Florida, February 21-23, 1997.

Unfortunately this description now applies to a growing list of nations that have prematurely reached the limits of economic development, countries in which a rising 'share of their own national product goes to foreign investors or creditors.' Such a fate may well await unlucky nations, including the United States, even in the industrial world." (Lasch 31)

AFRICA

The problems of the nations and societies of sub-Saharan Africa are attributable in large measure to the destructive effects of colonialism and neo-colonialism, to the distortions of the globalized financial system, and to the dictates of the IMF and World Bank. Nevertheless, these problems have been made worse by the fact that many of these societies are clearly oligarchic in nature. This is the conclusion of Robert H. Jackson, who uses the terms "personal rule" or "princely rule" as an equivalent to oligarchy. After discussing the instability and corruption of Africa in the post-colonial era, Jackson writes: "Personal rule is a system of relations linking rulers not with the 'public" or even with the ruled (at least not directly), but with patrons, associates, clients, supporters, and rivals, who constitute 'the system.'.... The system is 'structured,' so to speak, not by institutions, but by the politicians themselves. When rulers are related to the ruled, it is indirectly by patron-client means.... An effective ruler may be a political policeman with sufficient power and authority to preside over the game and keep it orderly – in a regime we shall term 'princely rule.'" [Jackson 19-20] Such a system has great difficulty in providing for economic progress in the present international environment.

JAPAN: THE PARALYSIS OF OLIGARCHY

The reforms carried out under the Emperor Mutsuhito in the time known as the Meiji era of the latter nineteenth century were largely influenced by the United States and western Europe, and enjoyed important successes, but they did not succeed in altering the basic feudal/oligarchical nature of Japanese society. The reforms themselves were carried out by the oligarchy, and this fact turned out to constitute an insuperable barrier to further success.[130] The Japanese tradition included a weak, almost absent, Emperor and the preponderant power of about a dozen great industrial and financier families, known as the *zaibatsu* and including such names as Mitsubishi, Mitsui, Sumitomo, Yasuda, and others. There were important differences of orientation among these families, but the structure was that of an oligarchy. There was a distinct military oligarchy, which had seized control of the country during the 1930s, and which was called the *gumbatsu*. General MacArthur wrote of the Japanese society he found before him at the beginning of the American occupation of the country in 1945:

> Supposedly, the Japanese were a twentieth-century civilization. In reality, they were more nearly a feudal society, of the type discarded by Western nations some four centuries ago.... Indeed, an American viewing Japan would be inclined to class it as more nearly akin to ancient Sparta than to any modern nation. [MacArthur 284]

MacArthur's reforms were a concerted attempt to eradicate oligarchism from Japanese society, including:

> an attempt to end feudalism, drastic curtailment of ancient privilege, land reform, liberation of women, extremely advanced labor legislation, education for the masses, 'bookmobiles' out in the villages, abolition of the nobility, wide extension of social service, birth control, public

---

[130] See J. Mark Ramseyer and Frances M. Rosenbluth, *The Politics of Oligarchy: Institutional Choice in Imperial Japan* (Cambridge, 1998).

health, steep taxation of the unconverted rich, discredit of the former military, and, embracing almost everything in every field, reform, *reform*, REFORM. [131]

Reform included specifically the abolition in MacArthur's Japanese Constitution of the House of Lords, which had played an important role in the Meiji-era constitution. Ironically, despite MacArthur's right-wing political coloration, it was one of the last, best fruits of the American New Deal. MacArthur's handbook during the occupation years was Plato's *Republic*, including the sections referred to above.[132] MacArthur's policies were very consciously anti-oligarchical in inspiration. The great success story of postwar Japan is in significant measure a tribute to their success: all other things being equal, a Platonic state will always be more successful than an oligarchical one. But although MacArthur's smiting of the Japanese oligarchs laid them low for almost two generations, the cultural tendency towards oligarchy persisted. This tendency was revived under the influence of British and American oligarchs, specifically of people like Volcker, Bush, Baker, Shultz, Don Regan, and others, with the Plaza accords of 1985 and the launching of the Japanese bubble economy. Oligarchical tendencies in Japan have been made worse by the Anglophilia of the Imperial family, notably the fact that Akahito, the present Emperor, was educated in Great Britain. During the 1990s, the Japanese political system was been systematically gutted by an interminable series of scandals piloted by British and American intelligence circles with the eager cooperation of Japanese oligarchs. Present-day Japan displays the tragic spectacle of a modern society hampered by oligarchy in its attempts to deal with the reality of the world economic disintegration.

CHINA

The party-army system consolidated by Mao and the Communists in China after 1949 was unquestionably an oligarchy, but it has experienced great changes, and in its current form it may be one of a very few ruling elites in today's world which are evolving in a positive direction. To understand why, we must first recall that the past century and a half of Chinese history since the British Opium Wars and the 1850s Celestial Kingdom of the Tai Ping has been as tumultuous as that experienced by any part of the world, bar none. To limit our consideration to the twentieth century alone, we see that Dr. Sun Yat-sen's Chinese Revolution of 1911 was followed by the ascendancy of Yuan Shih-Kai and other Chinese military men who carved the country up into petty warlord dukedoms with foreign encouragement during the 1920s. Most of China was re-united by Chiang Kai-Shek's Northern Expedition of 1928, which set up a central government at Nanking. But in 1932, Japan seized the important Chinese province of Manchuria, and in 1937 Japan began a war with China which lasted until 1945. The Japanese defeat was followed by a civil war between Nationalists and Communists, which ended with Mao's victory in 1949. Mao, acting on British assurances, intervened in the Korean War against the United States, and suffered heavy losses between 1950 and 1953, but the communist regime was secured.

The extremism, utopianism, repression and incompetence of the Mao regime were amply demonstrated in fiascos like the Great Leap Forward, the Hundred Flowers (or Bloom and Contend) campaign, and the Great Proletarian Cultural Revolution of 1966. In 1962, China and India engaged in a brief border war in the Himalayas. In 1969 China and the USSR came to the brink of war over their common border along the Ussuri River, and tension remained high for a number of years.

---

[131] John Gunther, *The Riddle of MacArthur: Japan, Korea, and the Far East* (New York, 1951), 121.

[132] William Manchester writes in his biography of MacArthur that "those who were with him in Tokyo recall that he often quoted Plato's *Republic*." See Manchester, *American Cæsar* (New York: Dell, 1978), p. 562.

Bloody faction fights broke out over the Lin Piao challenge to Mao, and Mao's death was followed by the failed coup attempt of the Gang of Four. After 1978, China under Deng and his successors had enjoyed the longest single period of national unity, peace, relative stability and economic development it has known for over a century,[133] and substantial progress has been made, although the futile Tien An Men repressions of 1989 created notable difficulties.

The Chinese Communist Party leadership which had emerged from the wars and civil wars of the 1930s and 1940s formed a gerontocracy which exerted power well into the 1990s. The elder-led command structures of the field armies of 1945-49 lived on as informal factional networks based on "guanxi," or personal affiliations among the commanders. (Something similar was observable among Guomindang [KMT] veterans on Taiwan through the late 1980s.) But, although Chinese leadership appeared as militarized over decades after 1949, this situation was not typical of Chinese history and culture, and seems to have represented an aberration, which was not destined to last.

General MacArthur, in his address to Congress of April 16, 1951, made two important points about China, whose culture he knew better than any academic. The first was that military dominance was alien to the tradition of Chinese civilization: "The war-making tendency was almost non-existent, as they still followed the Confucian ideal of pacifist culture." The second was that recent events had overturned the tradition: "Through these past fifty years, the Chinese people have thus become militarized in their concepts and ideals." [MacArthur 402] This contrast left open the possibility of a future reversion to the Confucian tradition, which is what seems to have happened by the late 1990s. A recent RAND Corporation analysis of China attempted to obfuscate this possible alternative by observing that "...during most dynastic reigns, the notion of bureaucratic rule through a select elite of scholar officials steeped in a Confucian moral and ethical doctrine that denigrated the soldier usually concealed a pattern of power politics founded upon a keen appreciation of personal control over armed forces." [Swaine 3] The hopes of people like Chris Patten, the last British Governor of Hong Kong, that the death of Deng might open a new warlord era in China, have been frustrated. We must therefore conclude that China is now evolving away from a military oligarchy professing Marxist ideology and towards new forms of government more harmonious with Confucian tradition, in which the oligarchical elements may be attenuated. That is the promise held out by current Chinese economic policy.

WORLD GOVERNMENT BY OLIGARCHY

The United Nations has always been a thoroughly oligarchical institution in practice. Diplomats in many countries, especially in Europe, tend to be drawn from the ranks of the hereditary feudal aristocrats. The UN was a favorite alternative for British civil servants who were being downsized as a result of the loss of their empire. European aristocrats like the UN because, with its pose of being superior to the nation states, it reminds them of entities like the Hapsburg Empire, or the old Holy Roman Empire. This tendency has become more pronounced over the past 30 years through the rise of the NGOs (non-governmental organizations), who have come to play a more and more important role in the UN's routine operations and in special events like international conferences on themes like population, pollution, and so forth. The NGOs, usually funded by foundations (or by intelligence agencies), arrogate to themselves the role of world public opinion. The result is that the intellectual and cultural atmosphere of the United Nations is pervaded by oligarchical styles and values. In this atmosphere, at circus-like international conferences in Cairo, Rio, and Kyoto, the UN purports to legislate for mankind, with predictably disastrous results.

---

[133] Only the 1928-1937 interval under Chiang Kai-Shek comes close, and during this time China's progress was hobbled by the post-1931 disintegration of the world financial system.

AMERICAN OLIGARCHY

Oligarchical tendencies have always been present in American life. They have tended to become stronger during those periods in which the Anglophile financial community has been more powerful, and in which mass organizations and movements of protests have been weak. The last quarter of the twentieth century has fulfilled both requirements. But the roots of the current problem go deep. After the death of Roosevelt and the coming of Truman, revived oligarchical tendencies were observable in many aspects of society. The research of C. Wright Mills on the question of a power elite dates back to this time. Mills saw the top levels of US society becoming more organized, even as the lower levels were losing such organization as the momentum of industrial unions ebbed:

> What I am asserting is that in this particular epoch a conjunction of historical circumstances has led to the rise of an elite of power; that the men of the circles composing this elite, severally and collectively, now make such key decisions as are made; and that, given the enlargement and centralization of the means of power now available, the decisions they make and fail to make carry more consequences for more people than has ever been the case in the world history of mankind. I am also asserting that there has developed on the middle levels of power, a semi-organized stalemate, and that on the bottom level there has come into being a mass-like society which has little resemblance to the image of a society in which voluntary associations and classic publics hold the keys to power. The top of the American system of power is much more unified and much more powerful, the bottom is much more fragmented, and in truth, impotent, than is generally supposed by those who are distracted by the middling units of power which neither express such will as exists at the bottom nor determine the decisions at the top. [Mills 1956, 29]

Mills also chronicled the mid-century decline of the older, more autonomous middle class figures of the doctor, lawyer, small entrepreneur, family farmer, and others, as they were supplanted by the far less independent-minded white collar employees of large companies.

At the end of the century, awareness of oligarchy as an accomplished fact in America is growing. Robert D. Kaplan, writing in the *Atlantic Monthly* of December 1997, found that "democracy in the United States is at greater risk than ever before, and from obscure sources; and that many future regimes, ours especially, could resemble the oligarchies of ancient Athens and Sparta more than they do the current government in Washington." The emerging oligarchy of the United States holds the vast majority of the American population in deep contempt, considering them as Okies, bubbas, ghetto-dwellers, white trash, wetbacks, Appalachians, crackers, red-necks, losers, rubes, and hicks.

American oligarchs have been an important presence since the emergence of the Boston Brahmins, best understood as American satellites of the British East India Company: these included the Cabots, Lowells, Saltonstalls, Perkins, Cushings, Forbes, etc. The current American oligarchy goes back specifically to the Peabody and Morgan counting houses in the mid-nineteenth century. The House of Morgan was the principal US agent for the City of London. This group of families provided a key point of coagulation of the US Establishment, more precisely termed the Eastern Anglophile Liberal Establishment, or Eastern Establishment for short. The "eastern" should not be allowed to occasion any needless confusion: this Establishment is no longer a regional faction in any sense, has absorbed all competing regional groupings of any importance, and represents the united front of the finance oligarchs of the entire country. "Liberal" should also not be interpreted as meaning left-wing. This liberalism goes back to the Venetian and British liberalism of the Enlightenment, which might best be described as the oligarchy's delphic response to the Italian Renaissance.

The core tenets of this liberalism are that human reason is weak and unreliable, that there is no verifiable difference between right and wrong, that there are no objective goals which human society must attain in order to survive, and that human society should therefore be ruled by opinion – so long as opinion does not attempt to interfere with oligarchical rule.

The ruling elite of the United States, the tiny group that has been the beneficiary of recent changes, has been enjoying one of the longest free rides in its history. It has not been subjected to any significant restrictions since the 1930s, and lately has been spared even the scrutiny of muckraking journalists. The plutocrats who reap the benefits of the globaloney economy are very restricted in number. Inside the United States, an oligarchical ruling elite has entrenched itself and is consolidating its power. The Eastern Anglophile Liberal Establishment, national and not regional in scope, controls local affairs through its emanations in every part of the United States. This Anglophile elite borrows tries to borrow its cultural ethos from the British aristocracy and the City of London, whose cynical and nihilistic cunning it admires, but does not possess. The center of gravity of the American ruling elite is composed of the chiefs of the largest commercial and investment banks, insurance and investment companies, and the top administrators of foundations and pension funds. Among the retainers of these financiers we find the members of the Federal Reserve Board and the Federal Reserve district presidents, the CEOs of the other Fortune 500 companies, media, broadcasting and publishing moguls, university presidents and trustees, chiefs of the leading law firms and HMOs, and top elected and bureaucratic officials.

This ruling elite is somewhat larger than the 400 families that dominated America around 1900, or Lundberg's 60 families of the 1930s, and it is somewhat more restricted than the richest 1% of the population – the 932,000 families who together own more property than the lower 90% of Americans. The mass of these American oligarchs are not really capitalists, certainly not entrepreneurs, and do not represent a national bourgeoisie. They are financial administrators who serve the institutionalized family fortunes (*fondi*) and the agglomerations of finance capital which are at the heart of every bank, merchant bank, and insurance company. They are intellectually mediocre, blandly conformist in relation to the norms observed by their oligarchical confreres, and almost collectivist in outlook. They are still plagued by the personal psychological insecurity which the British and other self-assured continental oligarchs have always noticed among would-be American patricians. They are prepared to live with immorality and stupidity, but they fear "inappropriate" conduct.

As Michael Lind and others have pointed out, the American ruling elite is canny enough as to prefer anonymity to celebrity. For three decades and more questions like "Who rules America?" have generally not been posed. Lind's *The Next American Nation* made a rare attempt to identify the emerging American elite, which he presents under the heading of "Portrait of an Oligarchy." As Lind notes, "no ruling class wants the scandalous details of its maintenance and recruitment policies discussed in public. No secrets are more jealously guarded in any society than the truth about how power and wealth are actually handed on. The British establishment does not appear on TV with charts and graphs, detailing old school ties. The Soviet Academy of Sciences did not publish studies of nepotism in the nomenklatura. Knowledge of the inner workings of the Mexican oligarchy is limited to rumor, mixed with fantasy. The dominant class in every country would prefer to pass in silence over its own workings, and focus on the shortcomings of other classes...." [Lind 140]

The US Establishment combines the old Southern planter latifundists with the northeastern financiers. It is Anglophile to the core, a condition which is exacerbated by its nagging feelings of inferiority and illegitimacy. It is not self-assured, and it is not very bright. The Establishment cannot be simply identified with organisms like the New York Council on Foreign Relations, the Bohemian Grove meeting, or the Trilateral Commission, which it rather uses as a means for distributing its political directives. For a number of decades after World War II, the US Eastern Liberal Establishment was compact enough to thrust forward a person who was generally identified as its informal or *de facto* spokesman. Mark well that to be the spokesman does not mean that one is the dominant figure in policy making. During the late 1930s and early 1940s, the Establishment spokesman may well have been Col. Henry Stimson, the Republican who had served as Taft's Secretary of War and Hoover's Secretary of State, and who in 1940 became Secretary of War in the Franklin D. Roosevelt cabinet. George C. Marshall was in many ways the chief Establishment spokesman for the crucial half-decade after 1945.

The columnist Richard Rovere wrote in the *American Scholar* in 1961 that he had tried in 1958 to determine the identity of the Chairman of the Establishment. Rovere says that the economist John Kenneth Galbraith told him in that year that he knew who the chairman was, and challenged Rovere to guess the name. Rovere recounts that he considered answering that it was Arthur Hays Sulzberger of the *New York Times*, but then decided to guess that it was John J. McCloy, the Wall Street lawyer who had been the US High Commissioner for the occupation of postwar Germany, who was then serving as the chairman of the board of the Chase Manhattan Bank, of the Ford Foundation, and of the Council on Foreign Relations. Galbraith confirmed that his conclusion was also that McCloy was the man.

Again, this does not mean that McCloy was by any stretch of the imagination the secret dictator of the United States. We are talking about the public spokesman of an oligarchy. Averell Harriman was perhaps more powerful behind the scenes, and Dean Acheson and the Dulles brothers may have had just as much influence on foreign policy matters. When Lyndon B. Johnson wanted to curry favor with the Establishment a few years later, he asked National Security Council Director McGeorge Bundy for advice. Bundy replied with a memo in which he sketched the outlines of the Wall Street group, and concluded with the annotation: "The key to these people is McCloy." (Isaacson 28) This was authoritative advice, since McGeorge Bundy himself later became the generally recognized spokesman of the Eastern Liberal Establishment. Bundy was a central figure in the GI generation of the American oligarchy, the generation described by David Halberstam in his book *The Best and the Brightest*. The Best and the Brightest were a new generation of the Wise Men, down to details like the fact that McGeorge Bundy's brother William, a top government official and one of the architects of Vietnam intervention, had married the daughter of former Secretary of State Dean Acheson, one of Truman's most active controllers. Unfortunately for the United States, the Best and the Brightest turned out to be a gaggle of mediocre bunglers who managed to wreck the dollar and cook up the Vietnam debacle, even as they squandered most of the formidable advantages this country had possessed at the close of World War II.

Since Bundy's death, no clear successor has emerged. One contender might have been David Rockefeller, who, as recently as the fall of 1993, repeatedly expressed the consensus of the entire financier oligarchy that a failure to approve President Clinton's request for fast-track authority for NAFTA would lead to an economic collapse and a depression. But David Rockefeller may not have possessed the mental capacity necessary for this demanding role. Volcker might have been a candidate, but even retired central bankers are traditionally too obsessed with secrecy to become public spokesmen. They may also be too widely resented. In any case, the post of spokesman would currently appear to be vacant. Whatever else this may mean, it is not a sign of health for the Eastern Anglophile Liberal establishment. If the policy making of the US Establishment has broken down, as this seems to indicate, we can be sure that the much better organized London finance oligarchy will make every effort to fill the void, as they have done increasingly since the end of the USSR through figures like Bush's governess, Margaret Thatcher, and Clinton's would-be Svengali, Tony Blair.

If McCloy and Bundy were spokesmen for the Board, who were (or are) the other members who might shift in and out of the "board" according to their prestige and ascendancy? Twenty or thirty years ago one or two dozen fairly obvious names would have been the starting point for a plausible answer, but today any answer would be highly speculative until more research can be done. If the US oligarchy is the leaderless and fragmented group that it seems to be, that would be another symptom of breakdown. In these matters, we must recall a celebrated speech made by Doge Marco Foscarini of the Venetian Republic. This speech was made in 1761 to defend the infamous Council of Ten and its steering committee, the Council of Three. Despite the mystifications contained in his remarks, Foscarini made important points about the nature of oligarchy and the indispensable conditions for its survival. Foscarini is reported to have told his fellow members of the Council of Ten:

> This tribunal has frequently saved the State from dangerous conspiracies. Its impartiality is above suspicion if we remember that office lasts for one year only, and that its members can easily be removed by a decree of the Great Council. It is certain from the universal testimony of all statesmen that no Oligarchy can last for long unless it provide some corrective for its defects. Those defects are the lack of secrecy and rapidity. In some corner of the State we must place a rapid and secret authority. Thanks to the Great Council the State has been able to preserve in efficiency such a tribunal, while preventing it from affecting in the smallest degree the fundamental constitution of the republic. (Horatio Brown 172)

By 1761 the Great Council was a mockery, full of impoverished patricians whose votes were readily bought and sold by the half-dozen richest families in the city. The Council of Ten's hegemony had meant a constant narrowing of the base of actual oligarchical power. But Foscarini's comment about the need of an oligarchy for quick and secret action remains valid, suggesting that the US oligarchy is at the close of the 20th century a very imperfect oligarchical specimen, probably destined increasingly to undergo the influence of the London financiers, that is to say of an oligarchy which has shown itself more alert to the imperatives mentioned by Doge Foscarini.

FDR AGAINST THE OLIGARCHS

To trace the origins of the American oligarchy of today, we start with the wealthy circles which hated President Roosevelt. The American finance oligarchy hated Franklin D. Roosevelt because he was skillful and determined enough actually to exercise the powers ascribed by the Constitution to the President. He refused to be a doge, refused to be a puppet. Those who thought they controlled him soon thought that he had many controllers, and then realized that he was actually President in his own right. Roosevelt resembles in many respects a Louis XI or Henry VII of twentieth-century America, a head of state and government who allied with the broad middle class to oppose the new feudalism of the finance oligarchs. The New Deal immensely strengthened the white collar and blue collar middle class with innovations such as the Wagner Act to guarantee the rights of labor to organize, and the Social Security Act to provide unemployment insurance, pensions for sickness and old age, and welfare payments to prevent the poor from starving to death – all as a matter of right pertaining to the inherent dignity of each and every American citizen, indeed of each and every person subject to US jurisdiction. Farmers were helped to survive by means of parity prices, an idea developed by the populists of the 1890s. Today's neo-feudal oligarchs spit out the word entitlement as if it were a curse, attempting to obscure the fact that the so-called entitlements are nothing but the economic rights of the American people, finally recognized thanks to the political genius and moral commitments of Franklin Roosevelt. The gutting of the Social Security Act by Gingrich and the craven failure of Clinton to veto this outrageous step is a barometer of how far public morality has declined in this oligarchic *fin de siècle*.

The essence of FDR's New Deal was the national constituency coalition which supported it. This was a combination of big city Democratic machines, Southern Democrats, AFL and CIO labor unions, black voters, urban ethnic blocs, farmers, small businessmen, intellectuals, and soldiers. It was an expression of the American Middle Class: of those who were in it and those who wanted to join it. It was nationalist and enlightened; the New Deal American state saved world civilization from Hitler, Stalin and Mao, split the atom, put the first man on the moon, conquered polio, and gave industrial capitalism a new lease on life at Bretton Woods. If Roosevelt had lived, the cruel relics of colonialism, imperialism, and racism could have been further weakened. (The worldwide post-1945 New Deal coalition for world economic development would have started with Roosevelt, Stalin, and Chiang Kai-shek, and would have gone on from there.)

Roosevelt's domestic coalition was a profoundly anti-oligarchical development, the most important one since Lincoln. The function of government was to deliver economic progress and a better life to the voters. The essence of oligarchical politics ever since 1932 has been the attempt to smash this coalition, a quest which largely succeeded with the breakup of the FDR-era Democratic Party in 1968-1972. But the FDR coalition is deeply rooted in the country, and has continually threatened to spring back to life. Republican wedge-issue ideologues have never forgotten what their enemy image was: in the fall of 1998, the fading Newt Gingrich was still talking about "the ongoing slow-motion collapse of the Democratic majority Franklin Roosevelt created." The wedge issues of the right and the multiculturalism of the left have represented converging attacks by different wings of the oligarchy on this FDR national coalition.

The finance oligarchs bitterly resented Franklin D. Roosevelt because he had "betrayed his class" by going over to nationalism, branding the oligarchy as "money-changers," "economic royalists" and "malefactors of great wealth" in the process. Eugene Meyer, the Federal Reserve chairman who bought the *Washington Post*, left the Fed because he opposed FDR's monetary and financial policies.

There was an attempt to assassinate Roosevelt in Miami in early February 1933, before the President-elect could take office. In August 1934 the finance oligarchs created an anti-Roosevelt, anti-New Deal organization under the name of the Liberty Lobby. Among the leading personalities of the Liberty League were the stockjobber John J. Raskob, who had represented du Pont on the board of General Motors, and who has been chairman of the Democratic National Committee. Here was also Al Smith, the defeated 1928 Democratic presidential candidate who was now motivated by personal animosity towards Roosevelt after having been passed over for the 1932 nomination. There was also John Davis, the Morgan asset who had been the Democrats' standard bearer in 1924. Among those present were also E.F. Hutton, W.R. Perkins of National City Bank, Irénée du Pont, Alfred Sloan of General Motors, and others. Worthy of special mention was J. Howard Pew whose Sun Oil fortune was used to fund a group of American stormtroopers who called themselves the Sentinels of the Republic. Pew money is being used today to promote oligarchy through the so-called Pew Charitable Trusts.

The financiers discussed strategies for deliberately provoking a new financial crash as a way to discredit FDR, something they were accused of doing in 1937. In 1935, Morgan partner Thomas Lamont and Davis were implicated in the attempt to carry out a fascist coup against Roosevelt by creating a mass organization of disgruntled veterans similar to Mussolini's *fasci di combattimento,* Hitler's *Sturmabteilungen* (SA) and the French fascists of the *Croix de Feu*. Davis wanted a US return to the gold standard to be a central demand of such a movement. This plan was exposed by US Marine Gen. Smedley Butler, a World War I hero who was opposed to fascism. Butler was told of the plot by Morgan operatives who were attempting to recruit him to play the role of figurehead leader for the new US fascist movement. Butler related some aspects of the Morgan putsch plot to

Congressmen, including Rep. John McCormack of Massachusetts.[134] The *New York Times* and Henry Luce's *Time* magazine were instrumental in blocking further action against the coup plotters.

FDR appealed explicitly to "the forgotten man" at the bottom of the economic pyramid. It was in Roosevelt's Second Inaugural Address that he said "I see one-third of a nation ill-housed, ill-clad, ill-nourished." Roosevelt's second term was in many ways more radical than his first. The finance oligarchs were outraged by FDR's refusal to use force to break the sit-down strikers, who began their action in Cleveland and in Flint, Michigan on December 28-30, 1936. But on February 11, 1937, General Motors was forced to recognize the United Auto Workers as a bargaining agent for the auto workers. Within a month, United States Steel had recognized the United Steel Workers. But this was followed by the stock market crash of August to October 1937, during which interval the Dow Jones index dropped from 190 to 115.

During the last four months of 1937, 2 million people were thrown out of work. Assistant Attorney General Robert Jackson – later the US prosecutor at the Nuremburg war crimes trials, blamed the downturn on monopolists who "have simply priced themselves out of the market, and priced themselves into a slump." Jackson accused business leaders of having organized a "strike of capital" because of their discontent with the Wagner Act, the ban on interstate movements of strikebreakers, and Roosevelt's other pro-labor policies. FDR himself entertained the idea that the Wall Street powers were deliberately sabotaging the economy in order to embarrass and weaken the President who certified that collective bargaining was an economic right of all the people. Secretary of the Interior Harold Ickes charged that "America's Sixty Families" were pursuing "the old struggle between the power of money and the power of democratic instinct"; he saw a danger of "big business fascism." (Leuchtenburg 247)

During the summer of 1937, a group of mainly Southern conservative Democratic senators broke away from Roosevelt and the Democratic Party and formed a bloc with the Republicans for the purpose of sabotaging the New Deal. A leading figure of this group was Vice President John Nance Garner of Texas, who wanted a balanced budget and vigorous measures to break strikes. The resulting anti-New Deal bloc contained Southern Bourbon oligarchs like Harry Byrd of Virginia, border state senators like Millard Tydings of Maryland, and northern financier spokesmen like Royal Copeland of New York. The anti-New Deal bloc sought to humiliate Roosevelt by rejecting his entire legislative agenda, with the hope that this might also get him out of the White House.

By 1938, the oligarchs had fully regrouped and were fighting Roosevelt to a standstill. The "nine old men" of the Charles Evans Hughes Supreme Court dismantled many of the laws which Roosevelt had rammed through during the Hundred Days, which was the time of the 1933 banking panic. After that, however, the Supreme Court became frightened, and tried to neutralize Roosevelt's bid to name new pro-New Deal justices by upholding the constitutionality of many of his measures, such as the unemployment insurance provisions of the Social Security Act, and the Wagner Act with its right to collective bargaining. By 1939-40, the political situation was thoroughly stalemated, and soon the world war imposed priorities of its own. But the New Deal, understood as the United States government conducted to a significant degree in the service of the country's middle class majority, did not end in 1938. During World War II, Roosevelt successfully engineered a full economic recovery with legislation including Lend-Lease. The full employment made possible by Lend-Lease created labor market conditions which empowered working people to the detriment of oligarchical privilege, quite apart from any further legislation. The ultimate bulwark of the finance oligarchs, the Federal Reserve System, was *de facto* nationalized by

---

[134] See Jules Archer, *The Plot to Seize the White House* (New York: Hawthorne, 1973).

Roosevelt, who used his tremendous political ascendancy and the needs of the emergency simply to dictate monetary and interest rate policy to the Fed, which was reduced to the status of a bureau of the Treasury. (See Chapter IV.) Many of the permanent reforms of the New Deal remained in place for three more decades. However, deep oligarchical traditions also persisted.

THE SOUTHERN BOURBON OLIGARCHY

In addition to the New York, Boston, and Philadelphia finance oligarchs, the descendants of the slave-holding planter aristocracy of the Southern states also deserve special attention. The oligarchical domination of the American South is an established fact of life so well known that it can hardly be denied by any serious investigator. The Southern oligarchy frequently expresses in a naked and blatant form the views and intentions of the rest of the US oligarchy, including the Wall Street financiers. In the South, we can see how oligarchs have used the racial question as a weapon in their efforts to preserve their own power. The South is thus a good place to observe the American oligarchy, provided that we do not let the finance moguls off the hook, or kid ourselves that the Yankees are any less subjugated by oligarchs.

The Southern oligarchy was studied according to the methods of empirical sociology by Yale professor John Dollard in his 1937 book *Caste and Class in a Southern Town*. In the course of his exposition, Dollard noted that "the existence of social classes in the South has been noted by many observers despite the convention that social class is not a feature of our American democratic society. We are not accustomed to think in these terms and, to be sure, the class hierarchy is not so clearly marked in the northern states." [Dollard, 74] According to my own observations, the difference is partly that oligarchical domination in the American South is territorial and personal, with even medium-sized cities being dominated by a few intermarried families who furnish the mayor, the congressman, the newspaper editor, the bank president, and the CEOs of the main local employers. Activities frowned on by this extended family and its hangers-on become taboo for all the respectable citizens, and may be boycotted, or broken up by the police. Southern towns, in short, still tend to have visible territorial masters. Southern oligarchy thus retains a directly feudal-manorial quality by comparison with the more powerful Wall Street variety, which operates more through the impersonal mystifications of "the market." Dollard distinguishes upper, middle and lower classes within the white caste and within the black caste as well. The white upper class were the descendants of the planter aristocracy, while the white middle class were known as the "strainers" because of their struggle to get ahead. The lower class whites were reviled as the white trash, red necks, crackers and sagers.

Other writers on the subject converge on similar views. Paul Lewinson wrote of the *ante bellum* South in his *Race, Class and Party*: "The whole system...stratified Southern society. At the bottom was the slave, a chattel rather than a person; at the top, the plantation-owner and slave-holder. Ground between these two millstones were the proletarian 'poor whites,' 'hill billies,' 'red necks,' and 'clay-eaters,' and a middle class, mostly agricultural, of small farmers and town dwellers, who, – as is usual with middle classes – to some degree looked up with veneration and emulative price to the aristocrats of the system, to some degree bitterly opposed them." [135] In these prewar analyses, the middle class whites are portrayed as having the greatest contempt for the poor whites. It is also the middle class whites who are most militant in enforcing discrimination against blacks. The neo-aristocrats, by contrast, could afford to be relaxed and paternalistic, affecting tolerance and

---

[135] Paul Lewinson, *Race, Class, and Party* (New York: Oxford, 1932), p. 7.

enlightenment towards blacks and poor whites as well. The aristocrats have always been less tradition-bound, more cosmopolitan, one might almost say – more multicultural.

A very perceptive writer on the American South was the North Carolina journalist W.J. Cash, who died young in 1941. Cash's study, *The Mind of the South*, is in part an account of the close interrelation of the Southern social structure and the Southern ideology. He is especially good on the changing attitudes of the Southern oligarchy towards Franklin D. Roosevelt, a lens through which we can see the basic attitudes of the Republican leaders of the late 1990s. The basis of the mentality of the Southern mill owner, Cash shows, is the idea that property rights are absolute, and are not balanced by any social responsibility whatever: "the mills were their owners' to do with wholly as they pleased," he wrote. In economics, the Southern oligarchs are spontaneously and naively Physiocrats, instinctively assuming "the natural right of the man of property to claim all revenues over and above what was required to feed and clothe the workmen after the established standard." (Cash 407)

For the Southern oligarchs, Cash points out, the high cotton price of 20 cents per pound during the 1920s made that period a golden age for plantation owners and textile mill operators. But the 1929 collapse and the 1931 disintegration changed all that, and by 1931 most Southern mills were shut down or operating two or three days per week. By 1932, writes Cash, "everybody was either ruined beyond his wildest previous fears or stood in peril of such ruin." (Cash 371) The planters feared that universal bankruptcy, labor upsurge, and the breakdown of their entire social order was at hand. "And so it fell out that no section of the country greeted Franklin Roosevelt and the New Deal with more intense and unfeigned enthusiasm than did the South." (Cash 373) The upper crust congratulated itself that the Democratic Party has been the right horse after all. "Thus the South, essentially as unanalytical now as it had always been, bothered neither to observe that the New Deal ran counter to its established ideas and values nor to weight it in any wise, but took Mr. Roosevelt and all his purposes to its heart with a great burst of thanksgiving. And in the first glad relief of escape from terror and defeat, even the ruling classes carried, or seemed to carry, that mood of candor and humbleness of spirit which they had begun to show before Roosevelt to greater lengths still." (Cash 377) The Coolidge-era *laissez-faire* excesses had been a terrible mistake, the Southern elite now thought: "... many of them were exhibiting a strange humbleness of spirit – were confessing that it was possible that they, the South, America, the world, had been following false gods all during that long period of speculation in the twenties.... " But, as Cash shows, this mood of self-criticism did not last long. But as soon as the panic had subsided and recovery of a sort had begun in 1933-34, the Southern patricians reverted to their old ways:

> Before long, and while eagerly availing themselves of all opportunities to seize benefits from the government on their own account – loudly demanding more, in fact – they were heartily cursing Mr. Roosevelt for all that they found wrong, and especially for the fact that they could not make money as in the good old days of the twenties, to which they now hankered warmly to return. Nothing could ever be right again, they said in chorus, until That Man was got rid of, the spending stopped and the budget balanced, and the foolishness about wages and hours done away with, so that a man could be made to do an honest day's work for what his employers felt he was worth." (Cash 394-5)

In the harvest of 1937, the Southern patricians mobilized police departments to force farm workers, who wanted to stay on their federally sponsored WPA jobs, to harvest cotton fourteen hours a day at 50 cents per hundred pounds. Here we have the entire program of the 1980 Reagan Revolution and the 1994 Contract with America: forcibly remove the safety net, so that Americans can be forced to work for whatever the plantation owners are willing to pay. What Cash described is the current axiomatic mental map of such spokesmen for the Southern oligarchy as Trent Lott, Tom Delay, Dick Armey, Richard Shelby, and Beauregard Sessions, or of doughface retainers like Newt Gingrich and Henry Hyde. The tragedy of America on the eve of the millennium is that the old, discredited Southern ways of thinking have become so highly influential within the US oligarchy taken as a whole. It amounts to a rollback of Appomattox. The old chiseling on New Deal payments by mill owners and latifundists (who put federal payments destined for workers and sharecroppers into their own pockets) is the precise prototype of the corporate welfare of today. (These ideas were also projected onto the literary plane by the John Crowe Ransom-Allen Tate-Cleanth Brooks-Robert Penn Warren literary clique known variously as the Fugitives or the Agrarians, through whose influence oligarchical tastes and outlooks were incorporated into postwar English departments.)

What has to be grasped is the primacy of oligarchy over all the other interests of such a ruling class. The purpose of the oligarchy is not racism. Rather, racism is employed as a means of perpetuating oligarchical domination. The overriding purpose of an oligarchy is to rule. Racism is a predicate of oligarchy, and not the other way around. In post-1968 America, we have an oligarchy which uses a strange and demagogic pose of anti-racism in order to secure oligarchical power.

During the Kennedy Administration, Lewis W. Jones provided some perceptive comments about a somewhat more recent phase of oligarchical domination in the American South, writing of a "cold rebellion," a kind of prolonged insurrection by the Dixie aristocracy against the formal norms of the US Constitution:

> A cold rebellion has persisted for nearly a century with the Southern rebels participating in the federal government while ruling their domain as an oligarchy – irresponsive to federal authority and contemptuous of federal law.... The dominant few claim legitimacy on the basis of the votes of a small electorate.... Oligarchs in their loud praise of democracy attribute their control of power to the accepted values of 'our way of life,' 'our democratic system.' ...Rule by the oligarchy is shown to rest on a one-party system supported by a narrowly-restricted electorate.... The very existence of the oligarchy and the circumstances that produce it is obviously not a matter of concern only to the people it controls. Its influence extends far beyond its direct control. This influence bears on the fate of the nation and the lives of the people who live in the rest of the United States.... The very rules of the Congress, with their seniority provisions, are hospitable to the accretion of power on the part of the representatives of the oligarchy.... Unfailingly, members of the oligarchy outshout all others in the defense or advancement of democracy – their version.[136]

It is a mistake to think that these neo-Confederates were ever primarily concerned with racism and Jim Crow as their main objective. Their object has always remained the same: oligarchical power. They used slavery, Jim Crow, and segregation as means to preserve oligarchy. But during the past 25 years they have proven remarkably willing to use multiculturalism to pursue the same goal - oligarchy. The Southern Strategy pursued by the Republican Party after 1968 has greatly magnified the importance of the neo-Confederate forces on the national scene; by the late 1990s the center of gravity of the Republicans had definitively shifted to Dixie.

---

[136] See Lewis W. Jones, *Cold Rebellion: The South's Oligarchy in Revolt* (London: MacGibbon and kee, 1962), pp. 7-15. See also William H. Skaggs, *The Southern Oligarchy: An Appeal in Behalf of the Silent Masses of Our Country Against the Despotic Rule of the Few* (1924), and V.O. Key, *Southern Politics*.

THE WISE MEN DIRECT HARRY TRUMAN

The finance oligarchs and their regional allies were determined that there should never again be a president as powerful and effective as Roosevelt. They got their fondest wish in the person of Harry S Truman, a president who was more than willing to be directed by a select committee of oligarchs. This explains the constant praise of Truman today, as for example in the almost hagiographical books of the historian David McCullough. After twelve years of FDR, the oligarchs were simply enchanted to go back to the rule of the few as it has been practiced during the 1920s. Knowing that Roosevelt was ill, in 1944 they secured the choice of Senator Harry Truman, a former member of the Ku Klux Klan who had spent his political career as a cog in the Pendergast political machine of Missouri. Truman knew that he could have been impeached at virtually any time, and he was reminded of his vulnerability when Boss Pendergast was indicted, convicted, and thrown into prison during Truman's presidency. Truman was largely the puppet of an oligarchical grouping that has been called in retrospect "the Wise Men," although wisdom was not their strong suit. This grouping revolved around the Brown Brothers, Harriman investment bank in Wall Street. Among the group's leading figures were Averell Harriman, Dean Acheson, Robert Lovett, John J. McCloy, George Kennan, and Charles Bohlen. The fateful decisions on the part of Truman which brought on the needless Cold War with the USSR were taken under the influence of Harriman, who was practically a member of Sir Winton Churchill's household. Clark Clifford, another member of this circle, managed the domestic affairs of the Truman Administration, and did his level best to bust up the Roosevelt national coalition. (See Chapter IV)

Clark Clifford's memoirs provide one of the frankest statements of how a president's handlers can operate. During Truman's second term, Harriman was joined by Dean Acheson, George Marshall, Dean Rusk and others. Acheson later wrote of how he was "working with and on the president" to obtain the desired results, how he "stepped on the president's foot" during a summit with the British when Truman strayed from the agreed line.[137]

By accepting dictation from the Harriman clique, Truman was hardly upholding his oath of office as president. In the 1951 controversy over the conduct of the Korean War, Truman fired Gen. Douglas MacArthur, the most celebrated American hero of that moment because MacArthur refused to accept the oligarchical way of doing things. Independent, strident, imperious, melodramatic, and egregiously successful, MacArthur demanded that Truman make hard decisions, which the oligarchs preferred to fudge, when China intervened in the Korean War. The Anglo-Harrimanite propaganda of that time insist that the prerogatives of the presidency had to be exercised by Truman alone, but this President was visibly the plaything of the powerful clique that surrounded him.

The ouster of Gen. MacArthur, quite apart from the specific issues of the time, marked a qualitative degeneration of the American character away from courage, intelligence, and independence, and towards conformism and stultification. Truman was also the president who, in 1951-52, allowed the Federal Reserve to break free of the control exercised by Roosevelt and resume its lawless and highly pernicious status as a privately owned and privately managed central bank beyond the control of the American voter. Precisely because of his subservience to the Wall Street oligarchy, Truman has been touted as a model chief executive by numerous historians.

Dwight Eisenhower was anything but a powerful leader. As Allied Supreme Commander in Europe, he had refused to curb the geopolitical sideshows of Churchill and Montgomery, and won the nickname of "chairman of the board." Many important decisions between 1953 and 1961 were made by men like the Dulles brothers, Charles Wilson, Nelson Rockefeller, C. Douglas Dillon,

---

[137] See the Dean Acheson and Clark Clifford memoirs.

George Humphrey, and Ike's favorite golf partner, Senator Prescott Bush of Connecticut, the father of George.

One very lasting feature of the oligarchical reaction against the heritage of Franklin D. Roosevelt is the XXII Amendment, which was passed by the Republican Congress on March 21, 1947, and which was finally ratified on February 27, 1951. This is the amendment which states: "No person shall be elected to the office of President more than twice, and no person who has held the office of President, or acted as President, for more than two years of a term to which some other person was elected President shall be elected to the office of the President more than once." Eisenhower was the first President to which this term limit applied. This ban on the third term has caused a permanent weakening of the office of the Presidency, and an enhancement of the oligarchical tendencies in American life, which is what its sponsors unquestionably wanted. The new President must get everything done in his first hundred days, or he is washed up. After the hundred days, he must concentrate on getting re-elected. But once he has been re-elected, his power is not strengthened for having received a public vote of confidence: he is now a virtual has-been, a lame duck. In the second terms of Eisenhower, Reagan, Nixon, and Clinton, the presidency has been tied in knots by scandals promoted by media forces who evidently have no reason to fear the chief executive. A president who might run for a third, fourth, or fifth term would be far more formidable to his many enemies, and the country might enjoy a more stable government. One of the reasons why the Republicans felt free to support the Starr inquisition against Clinton was that Clinton could not hope to return to the White House in the year 2000, and was thus a spent force in electoral terms.

JOHN F. KENNEDY VS. WALL STREET

The elite knew John F. Kennedy's youthful profile as a dissolute playboy and hedonist, and they were accordingly disagreeably surprised when Kennedy attempted to create a presidency according to the criteria of the Constitution. He attempted to break the Federal Reserve's control of the national currency, attempted to liquidate the Cold War, refused to become committed to Vietnam, and compelled Roger Blough and the other steel executives to roll back the price increase they had attempted in defiance of earlier pledges.[138] Kennedy's success is all the more remarkable because of the wretched quality of his cabinet and other advisers, most of whom had been chosen by Robert Lovett, a Brown Brothers Harriman partner. These were people like Robert McNamara, Dean Rusk, C. Douglas Dillon, the Bundy brothers, and Averell Harriman. Although the precise mechanisms of the Kennedy assassination remain uncertain, British intelligence remains a prime suspect, and it is highly unlikely that any such assassination could have succeeded without the complicity somewhere in this oligarchy. There is little doubt that Kennedy was planning to terminate US involvement in Vietnam as a prelude to his 1964 re-election campaign. Recent evidence also shows that Kennedy was aware of the suspicious role of Averell Harriman, then at the State Department, in orchestrating the murder of South Vietnamese President Diem in a US-backed military coup.

Lyndon B. Johnson had many positive features, which were associated with his personal and family background as a Texas populist and New Deal politician.[139] But Johnson was in awe of the

---

[138] See Gibson, *Battling Wall Street.*

[139] Johnson was inspired in part by "the populist-progressive Texas Governors "Ma" (Miriam Ferguson) and "Pa" (James E. Ferguson), a husband-and-wife team who dominated early twentieth- century Texas politics and, among other things, decimated the Ku Klux Klan. Lyndon Johnson, whose father was a major Ferguson supporter in the Texas legislature, told Wallace the story of the Fergusons at a White House luncheon for governors in 1966." [Lind, 185 n.] Johnson's grandfather had run for office in Texas as a candidate of the Populist Party.

Harvard boutique, and deferred to his foreign policy advisers in precisely the way that Kennedy refused to. Doris Kearns had catalogued the psychological syndromes which made Johnson so suggestible, so unsure of himself in his dealing with the elitists. Since Johnson, most presidents have operated under severe handicaps. The preferred criterion of selection by the Establishment appears to be a psyche that has been so traumatized as to rule out forceful autonomous activity and decisions. Richard Nixon's life was overshadowed by the extreme poverty of his youth and the Quakerism of his family. Nixon had been devastated by the real and imagined snubs of Eisenhower, who had excluded him from his inner circle. Nixon had been defeated for the presidency in 1960, after which he had attempted to get elected governor of California in 1962. His defeat in that bid for a come-back appears to have triggered a kind of nervous breakdown signaled by his famous "You won't have Dick Nixon to kick around any more" press conference of November 1962. Only after this breakdown did Nixon seem to acquire presidential caliber in the eyes of the oligarchs. Nixon proved generally worthy of this confidence by dutifully deferring to such creatures as Nelson Rockefeller's protégé, Henry Kissinger, a close associate of Lord Burke Trend and Lord Eric Roll.

THE FOLLY OF VIETNAM INTERVENTION

The US intervention in Vietnam represented an act of incredible folly. But counter-insurgency had become a fad among the Best and the Brightest circles of the Kennedy Administration. In this clubby Ivy League atmosphere, British theoreticians like Sir Robert Grainger Kerr Thompson convinced McGeorge Bundy, William Bundy and other patricians that it was time for the United States to carry on the cause of European colonialism.[140] President Kennedy rejected this advice, and took seriously the warning coming from Gen. Douglas MacArthur, Gen. Eisenhower, and others that sending American ground troops into a war on the Asian land mass was suicidal lunacy. The tragic flaw of Lyndon Johnson was that he lacked the intellectual and moral fortitude to reject the interventionist demands made by the Bundy brothers right after Kennedy's assassination. The active duty officers of those days were far more craven, and declined to sacrifice their careers by objecting to a strategy which was militarily absurd. The war might have been ended in 1965 or 1966 by building a fortified line across the Ho Chi Minh trail and stopping all infiltration from north to south, but the military leaders were too weak to break with the counterinsurgency fad. They were too weak to insist on a clear choice between staying out or winning the war, and this led to the downfall of the American army.

The Vietnam adventure was not the work of the much-despised Joe Sixpack, but rather of the Harvard geopolitical boutique, unopposed by the Pentagon careerists. However, once the country was engaged, Joe Sixpack and the rest of Middle America believed it was patriotic to support the troops and the war they were fighting. The impulses of World War II, Korea, and the Berlin and Cuban missile crises were still operative among the masses. Soon the Harvard boutique had grown tired of Vietnam, and left Johnson isolated as the chief warmonger fighting for his own political survival. Later, Nixon's successful demagogic appeal to the Silent Majority and the hard hats gave the Harvard boutique the opportunity to assume a posture of horror at the depravity of the American masses, who had always been racists and who were now supporting a war of genocide. It is fair to say that many leftish academics and intellectuals by this time had come to hate the American people. This marked a change from the 1930s, when leftist intellectuals had generally expressed some degree of sympathy with the suffering of the depression-stricken American masses. The change heralded an important split in the old FDR national coalition.

---

[140] See Webster G. Tarpley, *Against Oligarchy*, "The British," online at www.tarpley.net.

ROBERT KENNEDY: URBAN POPULIST, TRIBUNE OF THE UNDERCLASS

A recent and attractive model for modern urban populism with a strong international appeal is provided by the brief 85-day quest for the presidency on the part of New York Senator Robert Kennedy, who had just won the decisive California Democratic primary and was building momentum for the White House when he was assassinated in June 1968. There is every reason to think that he would have been elected, and that his campaign would have focused attention on real issues, especially economic issues. In thirty-year retrospect, the patrician Kennedy appears not just as a successor to FDR, but perhaps also as the Tiberius Gracchus of the postwar US empire, offering a last chance to implement reform and avoid disaster, before being silenced by an assassin. 1968 was a year of upheaval, caused in part by the Johnson administration's policy of waging war in Vietnam. However, there was also an atmosphere of acute racial conflict, which had been expressed in inner-city riots in places like Watts, Newark, and Detroit. The background for this racial discontent was the drought of US productive job creation after 1958. But when the stunning Tet offensive of the Vietcong coincided with the January opening of the presidential primary season, the presidential contest focused initially on Vietnam.

Robert Kennedy knew what the Roosevelt coalition had been, and knew the importance of either preserving it or renovating it to make it more effective. Kennedy's friend and adviser, the *Village Voice* writer Jack Newfield, recalls: "Class, in the economic and sociological sense, was the key to understanding Kennedy's appeal in Indiana, in the country, and what he dreamed of doing if he ever became President. Late one night, near the end of the Indiana primary, Kennedy said to me, 'You know, I've come to the conclusion that poverty is closer to the root of the problem than color. I think there has to be a new kind of coalition to keep the Democratic Party going, and to keep the country together.... We have to write off the unions and the South now, and replace them with Negroes, blue-collar whites, and the kids. If we can do that, we've got a chance to do something. We have to convince the Negroes and poor whites they have common interests. If we can reconcile those two hostile groups, and then add the kids, you can really turn this country around." (Newfield 278-9) This contradicted the strategy which was being elaborated at that time by most sectors of the US ruling class and its operatives. In 1968, figures as ideologically diverse as McGeorge Bundy of the Ford Foundation, Nixon Labor Secretary George Shultz, and black power activists like James Forman and Stokely Carmichael were becoming interested in using the pretext of the fight against racism to mobilize the black ghetto poor to weaken and break up white-dominated unions in the building trades and other sectors.

Harvard historian and Kennedy family ally Arthur Schlesinger portrays the Robert Kennedy of 1968 as "the tribune of the underclass," a patrician acting in the overriding cause of national unity. Kennedy said on March 17, 1968: "We are more divided now than perhaps we have been in a hundred years." He wanted "to heal the deep divisions that exist between the races, between age groups and on the war." Kennedy had opposed the Vietnam War starting in January 1966. According to Schlesinger, Kennedy sought "a coalition of the poor and powerless in the battle to bring the excluded groups into the national community." "I've got every establishment in American against me," said Kennedy on April 2, 1968. "I want to work for all who are not represented. I want to be their President." (Schlesinger 872)

Schlesinger quotes writer Robert Coles: "Kennedy had a unique ability to do the miraculous: attract the support of frightened, impoverished, desperate blacks, and their angry insistent spokesmen, and, as well, working-class white people." (891) Alexander Bickel commented: "His greatest gift to the country would have been the respite these two groups [blacks and ethnic white workers] would have granted him to seek solutions that cannot at anyone's hands come quickly."

(Schlesinger 891) Paul Cowan, a radical activist, observed that Kennedy was "the last liberal politician who could communicate with white working class America." (Schlesinger 891) Kennedy was opposed by Johnson's Vice President, Hubert Humphrey, whose vapid slogan of "the politics of joy" translated into endless war in Vietnam and the status quo on the home front.

OLIGARCHY VS. URBAN ECONOMIC POPULISM: McCARTHY VS. KENNEDY

The first to challenge Johnson in a Democratic primary had been Minnesota Sen. Eugene McCarthy, who had come close to besting the President in New Hampshire. Right after that, Kennedy entered the race. Senator Eugene McCarthy's wife (in whom Norman Mailer saw "a most critical lady of the gentry") described her husband's base of support in the following terms: "The constituency was bigger than the Movement so called, which unites the New Left and the civil rights and peace activists, although they were part of it. It was not just the reformers of politics, although they were part of it. It was more than academia united with the mobile society of scientists, educators, technologists, and the new post-World War II college class. It was more than the coalition of these and the liberals of the suburbs." Here were the beneficiaries of the GI Bill of Rights and populist Senator Ralph Yarborough's National Defense Education Act, now succumbing to cosmopolitan snobbery because ignorant white workers didn't like Rap Brown and thought the Vietnam war was containing communism.

Sen. McCarthy himself referred to his base as "the educated vote." For Norman Mailer, McCarthy was no political leader: "... he seemed more like the dean of the finest English department in the land." McCarthy sniped that Kennedy was running best "among the less intelligent and less educated people in America." One of McCarthy's closest friends was the poet Robert Lowell, of the celebrated Boston Brahmin family. Sen. McCarthy said he wanted to end the war, but on most issues of domestic policy he was well to the right of the Johnson administration. Especially in the California primary, the Humphrey camp pumped money into McCarthy's effort in order to head off the much more serious threat, which came from Kennedy.

McCarthy tried to reach out to churches and suburbs, to civic-minded businessmen and liberal (Rockefeller) Republicans. This was an affluent, elite constituency that objected more to the draft than to the war, and had little sympathy for the economic aspirations of the black and eastern European steelworkers of Gary, Indiana who supported Kennedy. McCarthy's voting record in the Senate included opposition to extending the minimum wage to farm workers and others. As part of the reaction against Johnson 's immense strategic gullibility, the liberal academic intelligentsia began to advocate a weak presidency. If McCarthy had a philosophy, it was that the New Deal, from Roosevelt to Kennedy and Johnson, had excessively expanded the powers of the presidency. McCarthy seriously proposed that the presidency be decentralized. "McCarthy, one felt, was the first liberal candidate in the century to run *against* the Presidency; doing this, moreover, in times of turbulence that seemed to call for a strong Presidency to hold the country together." (Schlesinger 893-4) Barry Stavis, a McCarthy supporter, feared that under a McCarthy administration, "the federal government would lose its power to protect exploited people."

McCarthy's view of the chief executive's job comes down to a critique of the Imperial Presidency, although he does not appear to have used this term, which became common during the Nixon years. McCarthy thought that the presidency had taken power away from the Congress and the Supreme Court, and although the phenomenon he was talking about goes back to FDR, McCarthy argued that it had started with John F. Kennedy. Johnson, said McCarthy, had been "eroding and weakening" the legislative and judicial branches. McCarthy suggested at various times that he wanted to be a one-term president. In sum, McCarthy's view of the presidency closely corresponded to the weak executive, more or less at the mercy of powerful oligarchical forces, which emerged in the post-Watergate era and which is now being subjected to a further turn of the thumbscrews by the Mellon Scaife clique and their point man Starr. McCarthy wanted a weak president who would be a mere first among equals in his own cabinet, a kind of American doge.

Viewed in this light, McCarthy appears as a precursor of the weak and even disastrous presidency of Jimmy Carter, who allowed the Volcker Federal Reserve to wreck the national industrial base in pursuit of monetarist chimeras. More broadly, McCarthy's theory of the weak presidency points towards the sapping of the powers of the presidency by powerful oligarchical forces of finance, banking, and the mass media which is so much in evidence at the end of the 1990s. One theory of the oligarchical presidency originated among the left-wing mandarins of the 1968 McCarthy campaign. Another version has been the notion of Congressional supremacy, as advocated by columnist George Will and others.

McCarthy and Robert Kennedy more or less agreed on one important issue, ending the war in Vietnam. But beyond that there were highly significant differences, which can be best understood by applying an analysis based not on race or on gender, but rather on class. Jack Newfield of the *Village Voice* wrote in May 1968 about "the deep hatred of Kennedy that is now so chic among liberal intellectuals." The patrician Robert Lowell mocked Kennedy for wearing "charisma suits." Richard Harwood of the *Washington Post* attacked Kennedy as a "demagogue." (Schlesinger 864) The haters portrayed themselves as disturbed that Robert Kennedy had engaged in dirty politics, by working on Joe McCarthy's committee staff, by his witch-hunt against Jimmy Hoffa and the Teamsters. Many claimed to resent Kennedy because he had waited until after McCarthy's success in New Hampshire to declare his candidacy. Kennedy was widely accused of being ruthless and vindictive, of unscrupulously grabbing for power. Important issues were involved here, but the ultimate divide between McCarthy and Kennedy was the class nature of their constituencies.

As we have seen, McCarthy appealed to left of center academics and intellectuals. He had traction neither among Joe Sixpacks of the white working class, nor in the black ghetto. This meant that the McCarthy candidacy had insuperable limits. It meant, among other things, that McCarthy would not win the presidency. Since McCarthy's appeal was so limited, there was a grave danger that his candidacy would end up as a demand for more special privilege on the part of those who already had it: this was the year when critical epithets like the "new mandarins" were being applied to well-known professors by Noam Chomsky in the pages of the *New York Review of Books*. Ironically, one group of McCarthy advisors was known among campaign insiders as "the mandarins." Another group, the one that included Robert Lowell, was known as "the astrologers."

Kennedy's appeal was much broader. In the spring of 1968, Robert Kennedy and Martin Luther King were converging on a political enterprise based on a program that included the rejection of the Vietnam war plus effective measures to fight poverty and despair on the home front. King had supplemented his basic program of racial integration, civil rights, and national reconciliation with two other vital points: first, he had come out against the war in Vietnam. Secondly, King had begun to support strikes by predominantly black labor unions, including the Memphis sanitation men. Walter Fauntroy and others close to King were sure that he would have supported Kennedy if he had not been killed. Other civil rights leaders, like the Freedom Rider John Lewis and Charles Evers of Mississippi, campaigned for Kennedy. When Martin Luther King was assassinated, there was every indication that he was preparing to endorse Robert Kennedy for President.

Much of organized labor was initially loyal to the Democratic machine, which generally meant that they supported Hubert Humphrey and the "politics of joy." Walter Reuther, the president of the United Auto Workers – perhaps the most politically aggressive of the industrial unions – delayed endorsing Kennedy because of Humphrey's clout among the apparatchiki, but Reuther's brother Victor was certain that the UAW would have supported Kennedy. Firmly in the Kennedy camp was Cesar Chavez, the founder of the United Farm Workers union. Kennedy had a long association with Chavez and the mostly Hispanic UFW, which was organizing day laborers in the agribusiness of the southwest; Chavez was elected as a Kennedy delegate in the California primary. When McCarthy had been campaigning in New Hampshire, Kennedy had been walking the picket line with Cesar Chavez at the grape strike in Delano, California.

Kennedy also had backing from Michael Harrington, the author of *The Other America*. He had a group of left-wing intellectuals many of whom, as Newfield notes, came from working class backgrounds. He had support from the main American Indian groups. Kennedy showed his appeal among family farmers by handily winning primaries in South Dakota and Nebraska. Kennedy took the Nebraska primary with 51.5% of the vote to 30% for McCarthy. The one primary in which McCarthy defeated Kennedy was in Oregon, a prosperous state with a minority population of less than 2%. In the Indiana primary, the university campuses supported McCarthy, while most of organized labor went for Humphrey. In Gary, Indiana, Kennedy campaigned with "Tony Zale, the former middleweight boxing champion from Gary, who was a saint to the East Europeans who worked in the steel mills" and with "Richard Hatcher, the thirty-four-year-old Negro Mayor of Gary. Together, the three men, in a pose symbolizing the Kennedy alliance that might have been, clung to each other's waists, standing on the back seat of the convertible, waving to the cheering citizens of the city that so recently seemed at the edge of a race war." (Newfield 286-7)

Kennedy thus had a coalition that reached from Abbie Hoffman on the extreme left all the way to hard hats and truckers. It was in reality far more diverse than anything seen over the last thirty years, but it was in no sense a rainbow coalition, and had no multicultural quotas. It was based on an appeal to aspirations to a better life through economic progress and the solution of glaring social problems in a spirit of fairness and equity. It succeeded precisely because it argued that race did not matter, and that poverty and exclusion – which respect no ethnic lines of division – were at the heart of the problem.

The essence of FDR's national constituency machine was the notion that government had an obligation to deliver economic improvement to the individual citizen. The government's duty was to move the economy forward, raise living standards, open up educational opportunity, and create new well-paid jobs. The private sector had often failed to do these things in the past, and it could not be trusted to provide them reliably anytime soon. So government had to intervene, and deliver the goods. McCarthy seemed to regard this elementary idea as reprehensible greed. The expression today might be "pork." McCarthy was in some ways an exponent of asceticism: "Hard was his face, hard as the bones and scourged flesh of incorruptibility, hard as the cold stone floor of a monastery in the North Woods at five in the morning," wrote Norman Mailer of this harbinger of austerity.

On June 4, 1968 Robert Kennedy won the California Democratic primary with 45% to 42% for McCarthy; Humphrey got only 12%. On the same day, he also won the South Dakota primary, getting more votes than Humphrey and McCarthy combined. It now appeared inevitable that McCarthy would drop out of the race, and that the anti-war students would have nowhere to go but to Kennedy. This would have paved the way for the white middle class to join the white ethnic workers, blacks, and farmers in the Kennedy camp. Once it was clear that Kennedy was a winner, the Democratic Party machine would have come around, and the labor bureaucrats would have followed their membership in supporting Kennedy. Here was a new and refurbished version of the FDR national constituency coalition. How much of the south could Kennedy have taken? Perhaps Texas, perhaps more than one might think today, but he could also have won without the South.

Only after Robert Kennedy's death did the South become an indispensable asset in the Electoral College.

Kennedy had quarreled with FBI Director J. Edgar Hoover when he had been Attorney General in his brother's administration. It was a foregone conclusion that Hoover would have been sacked if Robert Kennedy had reached the White House. J. Edgar Hoover, to put it mildly, had no reason to be diligent in protecting the life of his bitter enemy, Robert Kennedy. *Newsweek* correspondent John J. Lindsay and French novelist Romain Gary voiced warnings before the fact that Kennedy was going to be assassinated. The killing was attributed solely to Sirhan Sirhan as a lone assassin, allegedly motivated by the idea that Kennedy was a Zionist tool. The passing of the railroad train that carried Kennedy's body to his burial place occasioned scenes of grief which can only be compared to those which accompanied the railroad funeral cortege of Abraham Lincoln in 1865, that of Roosevelt in 1945, or of John F. Kennedy in 1963.

After the elimination of Robert Kennedy, the outlook typified by Eugene McCarthy has come to dominate the left wing of the US ruling elite, especially among university and foundation presidents, publishing executives, and professors. Kennedy demanded that the economic decay of the society be at least addressed, and something done to assist the victims of stagnation. The pro-McCarthy group argued in effect that political stability could be restored simply by ending the war. This group refused to attack the causes of black ghetto poverty, Appalachian white poverty, Hispanic poverty, inner-city poverty, or other by-products of incipient globalism. The ghetto would remain more or less untouched, while the political problem it posed would be addressed through the tokenism of multicultural preferences, buying off the most talented young black leaders. The profound suspicion of populism on the part of the left wing of the US elite is expressed with the obsessive vehemence which these circles typically mobilize when their arbitrary class privileges are in danger. Their critique of populism is inseparable from their fear of red necks, okies, crackers, and white trash, which is how they seem to view the mass of the US population.

WATERGATE: THE ANGLO-AMERICAN OLIGARCHY OUSTS NIXON

The oligarchs objected to Nixon's authoritarian tendencies, which may have been rooted in his right-wing antinomian Quakerism. (The Quakers are after all the sect most closely identified with Oliver Cromwell, who put England under a weird military-theocratic dictatorship with a phalanx of Major Generals as regional enforcers.) The patrician elitists ridiculed the Haldeman-Ehrlichman Chinese Wall or palace guard around Nixon. The attempt to overthrow Clinton prompts us to inquire once again into the dynamics of the original 1972-74 Watergate coup d'etat. Nixon's counterespionage unit, the Plumbers, were called into existence by the complaints of Henry Kissinger about high-level leaks to Jack Anderson and others. The Plumbers themselves were a joint venture of the Kissinger clique with some Cold War veterans of the CIA. Jim Hougan pointed out years ago that the Democratic National Committee was repeatedly warned of the coming break-in by a certain A. J. "Wooly" Woolston-Smith of the British Secret Intelligence Service, a CIA interface and probable holdover from the British Security Coordination set up in Manhattan by Sir William Stephenson (Intrepid) during World War II. This suggests that MI-5, MI-6, or the City of London was part of Watergate from a very early phase. Whoever Deep Throat turns out to have been, there is no doubt that the *Washington Post* has always been the organ of some very recalcitrant barons of the finance oligarchy, and was run by a daughter of a singularly incompetent Chairman of the Federal Reserve. Watergate was a coup d'etat against a president who had foolishly set himself up for ouster by responding on profile to outside provocations, and who was egged on by elements within his own administration.

Most of all, Watergate was a successful effort radically to diminish the powers of the presidency while enhancing the oligarchical principle. In his efforts at a coverup, Nixon displayed the antinomianism of the original Quaker creed, the belief that the elect are exempt from the Law when they are acting in accordance with revelation of the Inner Light as it is personally manifest to them. This made him an easy target.

On the brief interlude of Gerald Ford, the defining wisdom remains the comment attributed to LBJ that this man was "too dumb to walk and chew gum at the same time." Jimmy Carter had for his part undergone a nervous breakdown, an experience which he later preferred to describe as being born again in Christ. This occurred when Carter was defeated during an attempt to be re-elected as Governor of Georgia. There is an unconfirmed but highly credible report that Carter was feted as the next President of the United States at a meeting of the Trilateral Commission in Kyoto, Japan in 1974. There is no doubt that Carter, after flailing for a while on his own, turned the government over to Volcker and the Federal Reserve.

Ronald Reagan, on the vast majority of his days in office, was indeed the "amiable dunce" he was called by Sen. Moynihan, although the amiability may have been an illusion. Detached and uninterested in detail, Reagan sleepwalked and stumbled through his presidency, reading from index cards, dozing off in the presence of the Pope and obsessively reciting anecdotes about mythical black welfare queens chiseling the public. When he was younger and more energetic, Reagan had shown a decidedly mean and vindictive streak as Governor of California, among other things by doing everything in his power to break the Delano grape strike mounted by Cesar Chavez and his United Farm Workers union. Reagan's profile had been softened into that of a favorite uncle by Michael Deaver's media makeover, which stands as a masterpiece of modern media demagogy.

After the right-wing Reagan loyalists were iced out during the first year or two, and the clique around Al Haig had been eliminated, the country was run in the interests of George Bush by the Princeton trio of Bushman James Baker in the White House (and later at the Treasury), George Shultz at the State Department, and, still most powerful of all, Paul Volcker at the Federal Reserve. In the Kemp-Roth tax cuts, the 1985 Rostenkowski tax reform, the Gramm-Rudman law, and the increased reliance for revenue on the regressive Social Security tax, the "princes of privilege" got what they wanted: a massive shift of the tax burden from the rich to the backs of the poor, even as the de-industrialization of the United States was being completed. During Reagan's second term, Reagan's mental decomposition was played up by the Bushmen who wanted the aging actor to abdicate in favor of Bush. But there was plenty for them to work with, including the presidential couple's reliance on an astrologer, as Don Regan revealed in his memoir.

George Bush was by birth an Anglo-American oligarch of some standing, a descendant of the pro-Venetian Herbert family and the Dukes of Pembroke. His administration thought of itself as the most consummate assemblage of experienced professional bureaucrats since the beginning of time. Bush had obediently functioned as Henry Kissinger's messenger at the United Nations, leaving no doubt about his own servility. The Bush foreign policy team was packed with partners from Kissinger Associates, including Brent Scowcroft and Lawrence Eagleburger. By 1991, the stress of the presidency had left Bush a very sick man, with his psychosomatic thyroid disorder and convulsive collapse in the presence of the Japanese prime minister pointing to deeper and more systematic disorders. [141]

---

[141] See Tarpley and Chaitkin, *George Bush: The Unauthorized Biography*, online at www.tarpley.net.

THE ALSO-RANS

We should also notice also that persons who have come close to the presidency have also exhibited strong elements of psychopathology. Michael Dukakis appears to have suffered from depression after being defeated for re-election as governor in 1984. His wife Kitty introduced herself as an alcoholic and substance abuser in her later autobiography. Walter Mondale had a notorious dependency on tranquilizers. Bob Dole also appears to have suffered some kind of mental breakdown in the wake of the 1980 New Hampshire primary, when he came in last among the Republicans despite having been his party's vice presidential candidate in 1976. This brief summary leaves no doubt as to a perennial preference of the oligarchical king-makers and economic royalists for an impacted, weak and compliant president, a person lacking the psychological prerequisites for independent and forceful action.

THE OLIGARCHS VS. CLINTON

1992 marked the first time since 1928 that a presidential election had been conducted in the absence of either an officially recognized economic depression or an acute external threat to national security. Oligarchical heteronomy, which had accepted restraints because of the need to deal with a powerful foreign enemy, now felt free to run amok. Bill Clinton was not the oligarchy's first choice for president, but there was a widespread elite awareness that Bush was politically not viable, and in any case very ill. On the Democratic side, Tsongas appeared as a masochistic parody of Dukakis, and he was also very sick. Clinton was grudgingly accepted by the oligarchy, partly because it was believed that his syndrome of being the adult child of an alcoholic father would render him pliable enough to accept the dictation of the oligarchy, and also because his pedigree as a Rhodes scholar reassured the Anglophile element. But as in the case of John F. Kennedy, the complacent expectation that Clinton would fulfill all the wishes of the oligarchy was not fulfilled.

THE CLINTON CRISIS: ECONOMIC POPULISM OR GLOBALONEY?

The 1992 Clinton campaign and the policy conflict of the first Clinton administration can also be seen as a conflict between populists and elitists, both among Clinton's advisers and within his personality. Among the populists was Stanley J. Greenberg, a former Yale political science professor who became Clinton's 1992 campaign pollster. Bob Woodward writes in his study of the economic policies of the Clinton regime that Greenberg, in a 1991 article for *The American Prospect*, had called Clinton's attention to "the Democrats' perceived indifference to the value of work and the interests of working people." Greenberg was trying to account for the defection of middle-class and working-class whites, the so-called Reagan Democrats, to Reagan and Bush. Greenberg urged Clinton to focus on these strata, and to offer them tax relief. [Woodward 10-11]

Other consultants to the 1992 Clinton campaign included chief strategist James Carville (a lawyer from Louisiana, where the Democratic Party was still dominated by the heritage of the populist Huey Long and by the Huey Long machine) and Carville's partner Paul Begala, who later became a White House counselor. Woodward reported that Carville and Begala had written an important speech for Georgia Governor Zell Miller, which caught Clinton's attention. "For too many presidential elections, we have had things backwards,' Miller had admonished his party. "We have chosen to fight on social issues rather than to run on the economic issues that shape the daily lives of American families." Miller had recommended that the Democrats turn away from elitist social issues like gay rights, school prayer, abortion, etc., and emphasize "economic populism." Zell Miller also called for a tax cut for the middle class, an idea which he thought might provide a unifying theme to address their economic insecurity. Clinton read Miller's speech and devoted a marathon late-night session at the Georgia Governor's Mansion to discussing it and the future of the Democratic party. But Clinton remained reluctant to accept a populist label. Clinton thought that populism was too anti-business. He wanted to chart his course without relying on old labels.

Carville developed the theory that the lower middle class working people are the key to any American presidential election, not the country club set. This was the origin of "It's the economy, stupid!" – the slogan of the highly effective 1992 Clinton campaign against Bush. Woodward writes, based on his interviews, that Begala told Clinton that "'middle-class' or 'kitchen-table economic' issues, as he called them, shaped, dominated, and even destroyed families. A good job, a college education for their kids, owning a home, affordable health care, and retirement with economic security – these were the issues voters cared about." Begala had studied the strategies of Republican operative Lee Atwater, and agreed with Atwater's analysis that politics was divided into populist and elitist issues. He had further concluded that Democrats tended to take elitist positions and Republicans populist ones on social issues, while on economic issues, it was the reverse. Both 1988 candidates, Dukakis and Bush, had been elitists. Neither Dukakis nor Bush had had real popular appeal. Begala urged Clinton to force Bush to fight the 1992 campaign on the terrain of economic issues, "where the Democrats could brandish the populist sword."[Woodward 14-15]

This accounted for a populist complexion in the Clinton campaign, which the economic royalists of Wall Street and London found threatening: When Clinton announced his presidential candidacy in Little Rock on October 3, 1991, he said that his central goal was "restoring the hopes of the forgotten middle class." Clinton made ten references to the middle class in his seven-page announcement, and specifically promised a middle-class tax cut. "Middle-class people are spending more hours on the job, less time with their children, and bringing home a smaller paycheck to pay more for health care and housing," said Clinton." [Woodward 15] Begala saw that Clinton had two sides to his character: "A Southern, populist, religious side that connected with the average hardworking middle class; and a Northern, elitist, Yale Law School side that craved approval from liberal intellectuals and the journalists at *The New York Times* and *The Washington Post....* Now, on the deficit issue, the elitist Clinton seemed to be overpowering the populist Clinton." [Woodward 136]

A different tendency in the Democratic Party was typified by Leon Panetta, the California Congressman from a wealthy suburban district who became budget director and then White House chief of staff for Clinton: Panetta represented the 17th Congressional district of California, which included the well-to do areas of Pacific grove, Monterey, and Big Sur, noted for its palatial seaside homes. Begala told Woodward that "of all 435 congressional districts, Panetta's was the least representative of America – the pure, elitist unreal world of California dreaming. Panetta seemed to love talking about nothing more than deficit reduction and all the truth-in-budgeting discipline he was imposing...." [Woodward, 136] Panetta was a prime example of the tendency cited by Lind: "Although the Democratic Party has more middle-class and working class voters, the power of organized labor has radically declined as suburban activists, more interested in race and gender quotas and environmentalism than bread-and-butter populist issues, have replaced labor leaders in the inner circles of the party." (Lind, 187)

The composition of the Clinton cabinet bears out this analysis. As of September 1998, at least 6 of 14 of the officers in Clinton's cabinet were millionaires. The clear-cut millionaires were Treasury Secretary Rubin (net worth between $57 million and $81 million), Secretary of State Albright, Commerce Secretary Daley, Interior Secretary Babbitt (heir among other things to a supermarket fortune in Arizona), Housing and Urban Development Secretary Cuomo, and Education Secretary Riley. Health and Human Resources Secretary Shalala was also a likely millionaire, but this could not be exactly determined because of the vagueness of federal disclosure forms. The same was true of Labor Secretary Alexis Herman and Veterans' Affairs Secretary Togo West. Languishing in relative penury in such a company were Energy Secretary Richardson (who put his net worth above $500,000), Transportation Secretary Slater (above $167,000), and Attorney General Reno (above $184,000). [142] Despite Clinton's efforts to have a cabinet that was diverse in ethnicity and gender, there was little socioeconomic or class diversity. It was a cabinet of rich people who could and did hire servants, not a cabinet that looked like America.

PRESIDENT OR DOGE: THE VENETIAN EXAMPLE

One of the great historical preoccupations of the Venetian oligarchy was its desire to prevent the elected head of state, the Doge (or duke) of the Venetian Republic, from asserting himself as a strong executive in his dealings with the ruling oligarchy. If the doge had asserted a personal dictatorship, the oligarchy would have been terminated. The city of Venice had 110,000 inhabitants during the sixteenth century, in addition to extensive territory in northern Italy and a far-flung ocean empire. But Venice was ruled by an oligarchical caste of patrician families. In 1527, there were about 2,700 patricians entitled to a vote in the Grand Council. Many of these were minor government officials, many were poor, and some were destitute, forced to live on the income derived from selling their vote, the only commodity they possessed. (There was also an estimated one prostitute for every ten persons.)

From time to time, the oligarchy asserted its collective domination over the Doge. In 1355, the Doge Marin Faliero was deposed and executed by the Council of Ten (the chiefs of the secret political police, and comparable to the ephors of Sparta) on the charge of attempting to overthrow the oligarchical constitution in favor of a personal autocracy of the type which was then common among the Italian states. Faliero was accused of preparing to mobilize the common people on his side, a charge made plausible by the fact that the vast majority hated Venice's stifling aristocratic rule. Another oligarchical maritime city state, Genoa, experienced numerous coups and insurrections of this type, but the Council of Ten always succeeded in preserving the continuity of oligarchy in Venice. This was an important and long-lasting precedent: in 1505 a political poster was found near the Rialto in which Doge Leonardo Loredan was accused of tyranny and threatened with beheading, the fate suffered by Faliero.

Doge Francesco Foscari was ousted from office by the Council of Ten in 1457, providing another key example of the domination of the oligarchy over its elected head of state. The Loredan family had waged a three-decade vendetta against Foscari, and they finally succeeded in organizing enough patrician support in the Council of Ten and the other top organs of the Venetian government to – in today's parlance – impeach and convict Doge Foscari. In those days, much state business was conducted by patricians meeting near the Doge's Palace in the *piazza del broglio,* which took its name from an orchard that has once stood there. Here votes were bought and sold, candidacies hatched, and deals made, giving rise to the term *imbroglio,* which has migrated into English as well. The *broglio* was very powerful, often more powerful than the Doge. The Venetian oligarchs never tired of repeating that their Doge was not above the law – indeed, he was no better than any other noble. Gasparo Contarini wrote in his treatise on Venetian government and institutions that the Doge "only has the power of a single ballot" in the Grand Council. [Finlay 63] A Venetian diarist of the 1500s asserted that the Doge was merely the first among equals, forced to pay taxes just "like any other Venetian citizen." [Finlay 123]

---

[142] *Washington Post,* September 21, 1998.

The Doge was not allowed to display his own coat of arms at the Doge's Palace. One Doge in the 1400s had put his own likeness on a coin, but this practice was quickly outlawed. The Doge could not by law be depicted as a sovereign ruler in mosaics displayed in the churches and basilicas of Venice. His sons were forbidden to hold public office – a major sacrifice for poorer patrician clans, who needed the income provided by elective government posts. The Doge's use of public money was audited with great care. The Doge could not open his own mail by himself. Any conversations or written communications the Doge carried on were closely supervised by his advisers, who could always report him to the Council of Ten (whose meetings the Doge often attended). The Doge was not permitted to move about the city or travel without permission from the Senate or the Council of Ten. The saying went that the Doge was allowed to leave his palace without his advisors only when he was demonstrably dead. Minute details of the Doge's life were subject to intrusive regulation. After the death of a Doge, the oligarchy often introduced changes into the Doge's oath of office, seeking to rule out specific practices which they had found obnoxious during the ducal tenure in office just ended. One merciful aspect of the Venetian system in comparison with the modern American one is that it was illegal under normal circumstances to sue a Doge or put him on trial during his lifetime. Instead, a new government bureau was created, called the Investigators of the Dead Doge.. This was a kind of posthumous special prosecutor or independent counsel. The task of this office was especially to probe cases of the misuse of public funds and, if the dead Doge were found guilty, to collect damages from the late Doge's family and heirs.

In 1521 the Doge's oath specified that he was not allowed to enter into detailed negotiations with the representatives of foreign states. He had to limit himself to generalities, and leave the detailed talks to his advisors. This was a response to alleged excesses by Doge Loredan. In his talks with the ambassador of Mantua on September 21, 1519, Doge Loredan had dared to offer his personal opinion concerning a debt owed by Mantua to Venice. As soon as he did so, three of his advisers interrupted him to protest, admonishing him that he should not respond categorically without consulting them first. Loredan was accused of being soft on Mantua.

There was a great fear that a Doge might build a dynasty which could become powerful enough to challenge the power of the oligarchy. The Grand Council looked for candidates for Doge who were as old as possible – the average age of the newly elected Doge was 72 over the period between 1400 and 1600. The ideal candidate was one who was practically moribund, like Nicolò da Ponte, who came from a modest patrician house but who was 87 years old when elected This was at a time when the average Pope was elected at age 54 and died at age 64. [Finlay 125] The average Doge thus started his tenure in office at an age when most Popes were already long dead. This arrangement gave the entire Venetian government the character of a gerontocracy, with doddering, decrepit, and even senile men at the top. The Doge was usually so old that he had no time to consolidate a strong executive power, and this suited the oligarchy. The reality of the gerontocracy meant that the most visible internal squabbles of the Venetian Republic tended to take the form of a generational conflict between young patricians and older patricians. In this conflict of generations, there were few real political differences, and the main issue was power. The fight for public posts was a strong endorsement of the oligarchical system itself.

In modern America, as the society has become more oligarchical, public interest in generational questions has rapidly grown. A leading theorist of generational analysis in modern America has been Landon Y. Jones, the founder of *People Magazine*, who is said to have coined the term "baby boomer." A sociological analysis that centers on GIs, baby boomers, Xers, etc., is very convenient for the oligarchy because it tends to divide the population, while neatly dodging the central issue, which is the oligarchical transformation of the entire society in depth.

It was also a great advantage for a candidate for Doge to have no living children – in this case, there could be no question of creating a ruling house. Members of the Doge's family were forbidden to make special pleas to the government in the presence of the Doge, since it was feared that this might foster conflict of interest. The Venetians had an inordinate fear that members of the Doge's family would become powerful enough to challenge the oligarchical principle; members of the Doge's immediate family were this regarded with great suspicion if they became prominent. In modern America, the resentment directed against figures as diverse as Eleanor Roosevelt, Margaret Truman, Billy Carter, Nancy Reagan, and Hillary Clinton seems to partake in some way of a similar attitude by members of the power elite.

The Doge was expected to provide symbolic leadership and comforting cliches in times of crisis and national disaster, which tended to come more frequently. One thinks again of Reagan, who acted these parts so well. The Doge was expected to project a façade of public morality, to be reassuring, to be conciliatory and unifying. He was a kind of ombudsman or expediter, mediating conflicts among the various organs of government. The Doge was supposed to function like an American Vice President presiding over the Senate, usually very passive but occasionally called upon to break a tie between two equally matched factions of oligarchs. The Dogeship was thus no bed of roses. Doge Agostino Barbarigo was an exhausted and embittered man towards the end of his career, worn out by internecine political strife. Barbarigo complained in 1495 that "everyone persecuted him, that he has been made old and can no longer bear the weight of the dogeship." [Finlay 124]

Oligarchies are always very much concerned with conformity and consensus. To be influential in an oligarchy means to represent its *mainstream*. The virtues cultivated by the Venetian oligarchy included stability, compromise, self-effacement, and deference to convention. Conformity meant stability and survival, and those were the paramount interests of the state. The Venetian oligarchy thus tended toward a cultural collectivism of the ruling class. It was important not to be offensive, and not to engage in *inappropriate* conduct. In modern America, conduct is very rarely condemned for immorality or stupidity, but it is often condemned for being **inappropriate**.

Finally, we must always recall that the ruling passion the Venetian patriciate taken was greed – greed for wealth, which was always mixed together with the lust for power. Donald E. Queller has called attention to the fact that, in at least one prominent statue, the open book carried by the winged lion of Venice, the official symbol of the Republic, is actually a palimpsest, and that underneath the official public motto of *PAX TIBI MARCE EVANGELISTA MEUS* (peace be with you, St, Mark, my evangelist) we can read the real maxim of the Venetians, which was "*Dayla, dayla*" – meaning roughly, "Gimme ! Gimme!" Queller's perceptive book is a fascinating exposé of the sleaze, corruption, irresponsibility, and greed which marked the everyday life of the Venetian oligarchy. Many of these tendencies are all too evident in the United States in the late twentieth century. The American Constitution calls for a strong Executive power in the form of the Presidency, and is wholly incompatible with the oligarchic notion of a Doge. But powerful oligarchical forces are striving to weaken the US Presidency.

OLIGARCHY AND OSTRACISM

One of the most powerful weapons in the oligarchical armory has been, from time immemorial, the mobilization of a mob against those who seek to challenge the oligarchs. This process was illuminated by David Riesman in his 1950 classic of modern American sociology, *The Lonely Crowd*. Riesman was concerned to investigate the lack of personal autonomy and moral backbone of the modern American character. This led to his formulation of the "other-directed" type, the person who lacks any internal moral gyroscope and instead reacts to signals of approval or disapproval as they are imparted to him by the shifting fads and opinions of shifting peer groups. The other-directed person is the conformist: "What is common to all other-directeds is that their contemporaries are the source of direction for the individual – either those known to him or those with whom he is indirectly acquainted, through friends and through the mass media." [Riesman 22]

The older middle class of doctors, lawyers, small businessmen and farmers had been inner-directed, concerned with living up to a moral code which had been implanted in them in childhood. As these older middle classes yielded to the new middle class of office workers, white collar employees, and salaried functionaries of large firms, the other-directed type has prevailed more and more. The other-directed type is associated with a period of declining population growth, and also with the loss of industrial dynamism. As part of his investigation, Riesman also inquired into the prevalence of other-directed, inner-directed, and tradition-directed character types in various epochs of world history. In the course of this, he turned his attention to Athens between 500 and 400 BC, and the phenomenon of ostracism. His finding was that at this time in Athens

> ...we see the rise of social forms that seem to indicate the presence of the other-directed mode of conformity. For example, the institution of ostracism, introduced as a means of preventing tyranny, became in the fifth century a formidable weapon of public opinion, wielded capriciously as a means of insuring conformity of taste and "cutting down to size" those statesmen, playwrights, and orators of markedly superior ability. In addition, the common people produced a numerous breed of informers "who were constantly accusing the better and most influential men in the State, with a view to subjecting them to the envy of the multitude."[143] In *The Jealousy of the Gods and Criminal Law in Athens* Svend Ranulf has meticulously traced the incidence and development of the "disinterested tendency to inflict punishment" which, based upon a diffuse characterological anxiety, could perhaps be described as the ascendancy of an omnipotent "peer-group." [Riesman 29]

Ostracism involved a public trial of prominent person accused of threatening the stability of the state by some egregious behavior. The charges were thus very vague; often there were no charges at all. The trial was conducted in public before an assembly of the whole people, often meaning any idlers who had time to sit in. The arguments were demagogic, and were made by sophists, the talking heads of that age. Each juror voted on a piece of broken pottery; the Greek word for these shards is *ostrakon*. If convicted, the defendant could be sent into exile for a decade or more; capital punishment was also possible. The most famous ostracism was the trial of Socrates in 399 BD; he was accused of corrupting the youth with his questions. Modern American ostracism is not limited to the obvious obsession with impeaching the elected President. Similar dynamics are observable at many levels of society. Another interesting parallel to ancient Athens in the institution of the roast, the mock ostracism, which is practiced in jest in social clubs and elsewhere. Beneath the surface of the ribbing and teasing is the unmistakable idea that the roast and the public lynching of impeachment have many similarities.

NEO-MCCARTHYISM

Modern America has seen three waves of ostracism, including the McCarthy anti-communist witch hunt, the Watergate scandal, and the Clintongate campaign. (The firing of Gen. MacArthur, itself a landmark case of attempted ostracism of an outstanding individual by a group of oligarchs,

---

[143] Cfr. Paula Jones, Linda Tripp, Monica Lewinsky, the Arkansas state troopers, Luciane Goldberg, and many others.

stands in the midst of the McCarthy episode.) Each of these had deep and long-lasting effects, partly because of the fear they inspired in all quarters of society and the terrible examples they produced, and partly because each tended to be imitated on a smaller scale at the lower levels of government and society. It is certainly not a coincidence that a book about the other-directed character should have such a perceptive analysis of ostracism. As the modern world has become more and more oligarchical in social structure – and this is the universal tendency fostered by globalization – modern approximations of ostracism have become more and more prevalent in many countries. Examples are Japan and Italy, where the political parties which had prevailed since the end of World War II were virtually destroyed by scandals during the 1990s. Certainly the role of British intelligence in these scandals needs to be recognized. But the scandals would not succeed (and might never have been attempted) without an oligarchical social structure and mass political psychology conducive to such outbursts of ostracism.

This background puts into perspective the campaign against Clinton by elitist editors, Congressmen, federal judges, former federal prosecutors, and television pundits. Whatever else it is, the anti-Clinton hysteria certainly reflects the desire of oligarchical groupings permanently to weaken the Constitutional powers of the Presidency, since this is a process of which these oligarchs imagine that they will be the principal beneficiaries. Pompous editors and pundits demanded that Clinton take a leaf from the sermons of televangelist Jimmy Swaggart and grovel in public, parading contrition and begging for forgiveness. Gerald Ford wanted Clinton to submit to degradation in the House chamber, a procedure which would symbolize a wholly unconstitutional shift to British-style parliamentary government, in which the legislature feels free to topple the prime minister whenever they feel like it. The American Presidency was designed to be and has generally been a much stronger office than that of any prime minister.

THE ORGANIZATION MAN

During the 1950s, Riesman's other-directed personalities of the American middle class were molded into William H. Whyte's Organization Men in the corporate and government bureaucracies of the era. Whyte wrote in 1956 of a generation of bureaucratic conformists who believed in what he called the Social Ethic-- a quasi-collectivist way of life based on submerging one's individuality in loyalty and dedication to the company. Whyte saw that the pressures for stultification and conformity inherent in the Social Ethic were pushing America in a deleterious cultural and social direction. "The fault is not in organization, in short; it is in our worship of it," wrote Whyte. One symptom Whyte cited for the changing climate in the United States was the fact that in 1954 the number of students majoring in business administration for the first time exceeded any other undergraduate field except teacher training.

Whyte saw the components of the Social Ethic as "belongingness," "togetherness," and "scientism." Whyte pointed out that the emphasis on belongingness reflected the influence of Elton Mayo, professor of industrial research at the Harvard Business School and the founder of the human relations tendency in social science. According to human relations, in order to build an effective organization it is necessary to re-create in the minds of the organization people "the belongingness of the Middle Ages" in "an *adaptive* society."[Whyte 36] The rhetoric about organic cooperation, harmony, security, acceptance, and association cannot hide the obvious program of rolling back history to the time before Louis XI and Henry VII, the era of feudal oligarchy and domination by petty aristocrats in countries like France and England. Ironically, American companies (like Western Electric, at whose Hawthorne, Illinois plant Mayo did surveys in 1927) became centers for neo-feudal indoctrination.

CLINTONGATE

A key role in every phase of the scandal was played by Federal judges. There are presently about 1200 Federal judges, all of whom serve for life, and whose salaries cannot be reduced. Almost all come from law schools and/or law careers. Given the criteria of selection and the overall political-cultural climate, it should come as no surprise that the federal judiciary operates as a very class-conscious oligarchy indeed. The Alliance for Justice estimated in 1998 that out of 238 persons appointed by Clinton to the federal bench, 86 were millionaires – 36% of Clinton's total.[144] By contrast, just 3.9% of Jimmy Carter's appointee to the federal bench were millionaires. Reagan managed to name millionaires as federal judges in 21.4% of his appointments, and Bush attained 32.5%. Even allowing for the erosion of the dollar, the federal judiciary as a moneyed oligarchy has solidified under Clinton. The federal bench does not look like America. The Federal judiciary has been a witting party to the campaign to whittle the Presidency down to size so as to assert oligarchical supremacy by the legislative and judicial branches, among other baronial fiefdoms.

The Supreme Court's December 1997 opinion that allowed Paula Corbin Jones to proceed with her frivolous and harassing lawsuit against Clinton belongs in the same dustbin with Roger Taney's Dred Scott decision and other judicial monstrosities. One of Clinton's lawyers had tried to show that in the past, even enlisted soldiers on active duty had been protected from lawsuits while they were serving, but the Republicans and the media set up a hue and cry that this was an attempt to put draft-dodger Clinton above the law. The President needs to be above the law during his or her term in office, to the extent that the chief executive must be temporarily immune from civil lawsuits, which must be held in abeyance until the President leaves office. Otherwise, any rich oligarch who cares to hire a shyster lawyer can indulge in the hobby of harassing and perhaps toppling the one official who is elected by all the people. Congressmen who rant that the President should not be above the law need to be reminded that they themselves a free to indulge in unlimited criminal libel and slander from the floor of Congress, thanks to the speech and debate clause of the Constitution.

Judge David Sentelle bears grave responsibility for his insistence on replacing Robert Fisk, the earlier Whitewater special prosecutor, with the highly partisan, ambitious, and unscrupulous adventurer Kenneth Starr. Judge Norma Holloway Johnson, who was supposed to supervise Starr, is responsible for allowing him to run amok, attempting to entrap the President with the help of the intelligence community asset Linda Tripp and the unstable mythomaniac Monica Lewinsky. Other judges could have taken action to protect the Constitution, but most failed to do so. Judge Lawrence Silberman and some of his colleagues in the federal circuit court of appeals which handles the District of Columbia were virtually a cheering section for their former colleague, Kenneth Starr. Attorney General Janet Reno, who talked so much about the criteria of professionalism, failed to exercise oversight over Starr. We must also recall that New York Democratic Senator Daniel P. Moynihan was the first leading Democrat to call for a special prosecutor in the first place, despite the fact that the legal prerequisites for naming an independent counsel had not been fulfilled.

The Clinton scandals have been fomented by a small clique of persons supported by the wealthy financier Richard Mellon Scaife. This group includes former prosecutors Theodore B. Olson and his wife Barbara Olson (a television talk show fixture), Supreme Court Justice Clarence Thomas, defeated Supreme Court candidate, former Justice official and former federal appeals judge Robert Bork, federal appeals judge Lawrence Silberman, *Wall Street Journal* editor Robert Bartley, *American Spectator* editor Emmet Tyrell, former Bush White House counsel C. Boyden Gray, and

---

[144] *Washington Post*, September 21, 1998.

former federal judge and Justice Department official Kenneth Starr.[145] This cabal has worked in synergy with the Jesse Helms-Lauch Faircloth Congressional Club of North Carolina; a client of this group is Federal appeals judge David Sentelle, who appointed Starr as special prosecutor. Starr's fanatical chief assistants, Hickman Ewing and Jackie Bennett, had records as prosecutors and were found congenial to this grouping. The techniques of overreaching, overzealous, selective and vindictive prosecution were applied with a vengeance to the President of the United States.

The Executive branch has proven too weak to resist these assaults. The Presidency has been stripped of a large part of its economic and financial power, which has been transferred to the Federal Reserve, an independent barony controlled by private-sector plutocrats. The Presidency has also been weakened by the fact that the Department of Justice and the FBI each regard themselves as independent fiefdoms, not subject to the orders of the President elected by all the people, but rather baronies operating according to their own self-generated criteria of "professionalism" – a thin veil for oligarchical ideology and interest. The entrenched career prosecutors of the Department of Justice, in particular, regard their agency as no longer responsible to the President. Although Clinton fired all United States Attorneys at the beginning of his first term, he failed to follow through with a thorough house-cleaning at main Justice in Washington, where some top officials have been on the job since the days of Truman and Johnson. As the Presidency has weakened, firings of and forced resignations by cabinet officers have become less frequent.

The mass media, although they exploit airwaves which are the property of all the people, constitute an evident case of oligopoly, and are increasingly controlled from abroad. NBC and CNBC are owned by General Electric, now more a financial corporation than an industrial producer. CBS is owned by the gutted shell of what used to be Westinghouse. ABC is the property of Disney, a firm which has inflicted incalculable damage on American culture. The risqué Fox network is the barony of Australian Rupert Murdoch and his Newscorp. The Public Broadcasting System (radio) and the Corporation for Public Broadcasting (television) speak for the left wing of the oligarchy. The CPB's original flagship was WGBH of Boston (whose call letters were interpreted as God Bless Harvard), a station dominated by Ralph Lowell of the Boston Brahmin family; the money came from the Rockefellers and others. Add in the *Washington Post*, the *New York Times*, and the Associated Press, and we get an oligarchical phalanx which might be called the 1998 version of the Duke of Burgundy's 1465 *Ligue du bien public*, an insurrection of the leading feudal aristocrats against King Louis XI of France. W also cannot forget Pat Robertson, Jerry Falwell, and the rest of our television Savonarolas, who are all just as militantly faithful to the oligarchical program as that original book burner.

On the day before the 1998 general elections, the *Washington Post* printed the bitter recriminations from top Washington insiders who resented Clinton, as compiled by influential reporter Sally Quinn. "He came in here and he trashed the place, and it's not his place," sniffed columnist David Broder about Clinton. "This is a company town," said former Senator and Reagan chief of staff during Iran-contra Howard Baker. "This is our town," growled Connecticut Democratic Senator Joseph Lieberman, one of the first right-wing Democrats to pontificate against Clinton. Added NBC reporter Andrea Mitchell (the wife of Greenspan), "We all know people who have been terribly damaged personally by this." Well, why not blame Starr and his cabal of wealthy backers? Quinn explains: "Starr is a Washington insider, too. He has lived and worked here for years. He had a reputation as a fair and honest judge. He has many friends in both parties. Their wives are friendly with one another and their children go to the same schools." It looks like Starr has more clout in the Washington hierarchy than Clinton does, despite the fact that the latter was

---

[145] See article by David Brock, *Esquire*, July 1997.

elected President by all the people. Quinn concludes that "Bill Clinton has essentially lost the Washington Establishment for good."[146] If we replace terms like "establishment," "lobby," and "insider" with "oligarchy" and "oligarch," articles like this one become more readily understandable. Other common synonyms for the modern US oligarchy or parts thereof include "the Street" (meaning the financial community), "inside the Beltway," "the elite," "this town" (usually meaning Washington DC), etc. The US oligarchy usually does not like to characterize or refer to itself in any way, but when it attempts to package its system for export, it is likely to speak of "market democracy" or, as we have seen, "globalization."

AMERICAN NEO-FEUDALISM

The systematic crushing over recent decades of the American family – one of the classic forms of middle class property – has given some of the victims of this process a clarity of analysis which goes far beyond the insights of which comfortable and complacent professors are capable. 300,000 American farmers have been wiped out during the last 20 years by the joint efforts of the grain cartels and the US Department of Agriculture, and in early 1999 the hog price of 15 cents a pound was about one half of what a hog producer needed to break even, meaning that hog farmers were going bankrupt.

The latest variation on this theme is the fad of "contract feeding" operations, under which an agribusiness corporation (usually based in the former CSA) encourages a hapless farmer in the Dakotas to go $500,000 into debt to build confinement feeding barns on his property. The agribusiness corporation the provides the farmer with baby pigs and feed. The farmer contributes his labor, pays for water, electricity and heating, and takes care of taxes, overhead, and environmental regulations. This last point is significant, since it means that if the Environmental Protection Agency decides to launch a lawsuit because of pig manure pollution, it is the farmer and not the corporation which will be left holding the bag for all kinds of liability. Farmer Don Hoogestraat of Hurley, South Dakota told a reporter: "The feed comes from out of state, the hogs come from out of state, and the hogs are shipped out of state for the slaughter. That leaves us with nothing but the manure, and the farmer becomes a hired hand on his own farm."

Another comment, this one from farmer Charlie Johnson of Madison. South Dakota, summed up the essence of the process: "It's ironic when you consider our heritage here in South Dakota. Our ancestors left the landlords and kings in Europe to come here for their economic freedom, and now we're making the big corporations the new feudal rulers. Sometimes I think nobody is paying attention while the big corporations are just taking over the whole farm economy and destroying an American way of life."[147] This neo-feudalism is typical of the current Age of Oligarchy.

This perception is by no means limited to rural America. A similar awareness of neo-feudalism was voiced by Kenneth T. Lyons, president of the National Association of Government Employees, when he said: "For more than 40 years I have fought – and this organization has fought – to remove favoritism and patronage from the Federal civil service system, and now once again under the guise of meritocracy, the Vice President proposes sending us back to the Dark Ages where if you don't genuflect when your boss walks by, you won't get a raise." Lyons, who made these remarks on January 15, 1999, was speaking out against Al Gore's scheme to re-invent the federal government.

---

[146] Sally Quinn, "Not in Their Back Yard," *Washington Post*, November 2, 1998.
[147] *Washington Post*, January 3, 1999.

MODERN OLIGARCHY

In recent years, a very few writers have around the world have called attention to the reality of oligarchical domination, and many of them have been from Europe, where the Brussels eurogarchy and its virtual property qualification for entrance into the new European Monetary Union have been a matter of open controversy. This has been especially so in France, which had the benefit of a strongly nationalist and anti-oligarchical government until 1970, although France then reverted by stages to the same oligarchical misrule which she had suffered under the Fourth Republic. Michael Harsgor is the author of *Un très petit nombre*, a study of the much-neglected factor of oligarchy in history. Harsgor points out that any oligarchy invariably has only one program: the establishment and perpetuation of its own power. He calls this "le but inavouable de l'oligarchie," and adds: "...oligarchies et oligarques n'aiment jamais avouer que leur but majeur est, purement et simplement, l'acquisition du pouvoir. Une fois celui-ci en leur possession, leur nouveau but majeur sera sa conservation indéfinie." [Harsgor 503]

Harsgor's great merit is to call for greater attention to oligarchy, which is often referred to euphemistically as an elite nowadays; he issues an eloquent call for a revival, now at the close of the century, of the classic Greek interest in social analysis in the form of a new discipline, which he calls "oligarchology": "L'oligarchie, appelée pudiquement 'élite' par certains chercheurs, doit être étudiée en profondeur. Il s'agit donc de l'identifier précisément dans le magma de la population extra-oligarchique, et pas seulement du point du vue financier.... L'étude systématique des groupes dirigeants et des oligarchies n'a pas encore commencée dans le monde occidental.... Nous pensons qu'une réflexion sereine sur le siècle qui s'achève montre, dans toute son ampleur, l'importance non seulement des personnalités se trouvant à la tête des entités étatiques et politiques, mais aussi des équipes sans lesquelles l'action des chefs se serait révélée impossible – donc des groupes dirigeants.... l'étude des oligarchies ayant été quelque peu negligée depuis que certains Grecs subtils et pénétrants s'en sont occupés, il y a de cela un certain temps, il serait temps d'établir les bases d'une 'oligarchologie', une étude comparée des groupes dirigeants et oligarchies des différents lieux et époques." [Harsgor 503-510]

OLIGARCHICAL POWER: THE FOUNDATIONS

The family fortune of the old-line oligarchical family is sometimes referred to with the Italian term of *fondo*, since it was in Venice that these self-perpetuating patrimonies were most highly developed during the late Middle Ages and early modern times. The family *fondo* is an enduring source of oligarchical power. It can do something that individual oligarchs cannot do: make itself immortal. Through the magic of compound usury, the *fondo* can defy biology and mortality, and exert the influence of the noble family over centuries and beyond.

The so-called charitable foundations are key vehicles for the increasing oligarchical control of American society. In early 1998, a survey conducted by the *Chronicle of Philanthropy* among 121 of this country's largest private foundations found that they possessed endowments amounting to more than $126 billion, an increase of 22% over the previous year. These foundations receive generous tax breaks from the federal government in exchange for meeting the requirement that they give away about 5% of their investment assets each year. This means that in 1998, these 121 selected foundations alone will have more than $6 billion to spend on shaping the culture and politics of the United States. [148]

---

[148] *Washington Post*, February 28, 1998.

It is a safe bet that very little of this money will be spent on fighting oligarchical domination. A great deal will be spent on fostering diversity, that is to say on finding new ways to fragment and divide the American people so as the promote the oligarchical ascendancy.

If a society chooses oligarchy as its ordering principle, certain constant features of the oligarchical outlook will tend to predominate. Oligarchs cannot imagine a shared interest of humanity as a whole, since they represent a ruling class which deliberately sets itself against most people. Oligarchical ideology must therefore express a general contempt for humanity, with exceptions granted only for those of special wealth, prestige, or status – in other words, for oligarchs. Much of modern American intellectual production expresses this contempt for humanity. Because people in general are regarded with disdain, an oligarchy must always be preoccupied with overpopulation and overdevelopment, as we see in the cases of Ortes, Malthus, and modern American radical environmentalism. Theories of overpopulation have no basis in fact, but express the same impulse as that which moved some Greeks of long ago to argue that the Trojan war had been a necessary means of depleting the masses of people who were oppressing the breast of Mother Earth. Oligarchs furthermore cannot escape irrationality, because their very existence as a ruling class depends on an irrational discrimination. Why should oligarchs rule, if they cannot justify their predominance on the basis of greater ability or better results for the society as a whole? The oligarchs can only launch appeals to tradition, precedent, custom, power, divine right, or other irrational arguments.

Oligarchy represents an irrational principle of domination, and any society which accepts it will be more and more pervaded by astrology, gambling, determinism of all sorts, Nostradamus, channeling, End Time prophecy, meteorites, and entertainment.

Oligarchs do not like arenas of human activity in which individual and collective ability can be objectively tested. On such arena is the production of industrial commodities. Another is space travel. In such fields, whether you succeed or not is not a matter of opinion. You either produce the steel, and come back safely from Mars, or you do not.

Oligarchs prefer areas in which authoritative opinion can provide the ultimate test. Thus, they like politics, the law, and academia. Oligarchs tend not to like science, technology, and industry, although they will tolerate them for military purposes. Science, technology, and industry tend to create channels of upward mobility, for individuals and for nations, which the oligarchy cannot control. Oligarchy, in a word, is green. Environmentalist and ecological organizations like the Club of Rome, the World Wildlife Fund, the Sierra Club, and the Nature Conservancy display strong oligarchical dominance. The oligarchical idea of wealth resides in money; oligarchs are instinctively monetarists. They cannot see wealth in the scientific culture of a population, since this threatens the discrimination upon which oligarchy depends. Oligarchs like very much the idea that money can reproduce itself based on human opinions, which is called usury. Oligarchs cannot be nationalists, since nations have to do something for each of the many groups which make them up. Oligarchs will generally pursue an oligarchical interest at the expense of a national interest, ignoring the consequences. Finally, oligarchs tend toward intellectual and moral mediocrity. The genius or the hero is motivated by the sacred fury of patriotism or the passion of discovery, but the oligarch must be concerned about the norms of group acceptance and the appropriateness of conduct. Oligarchs make rather bad scientists and bad generals.

Ronnie Dugger, the founding editor of *The Texas Observer* and one of the few acute critics of the public career of George Bush, noted some years ago that "the oligarchy, tut-tutting against 'class warfare' at every hint of a politics that might threaten its wealth and privileges, has declared its own class war against the poor." [149]

ACADEMIC MANDARINS

This state of affairs at the foundations has much to do with the deterioration of the quality of scholarship and academic life. As the late Christopher Lasch put it, "The academic left, which claims to speak for the common people, might be expected to resist a restructuring of higher education that effectively leaves them to their own fate. But academic radicals, these days, are more interested in the defense of their professional privileges against criticism from outside." Lasch quoted Joan Scott of the Institute for Advanced Study in Princeton, New Jersey, who dismissed such criticism as the complaint of "disaffected scholars" and "marginal intellectuals." Lasch pointed out that "Left-wing academics cannot be bothered to argue with opponents or enter into their point of view. They speak, with irritating complacency, as members of a professional establishment that has given up the attempt to communicate with a broader audience, either as teachers or writers." (Lasch, 177-8)

Branding your opponent as "marginal" (i.e., not affluent, but impoverished) appears to be a favorite code of the modern oligarchy all over the world. In Russia, to be an intellectual also means accepting social responsibility for those sectors of society which have not been given the opportunity of higher education. In modern America, such an attitude is almost unheard of, as Lind points out: "American intellectuals tend to be snobs, deeply disdainful of the culture of middle-class and working-class Americans and hostile to their moral values." Lind also finds the American intelligentsia "colonial in its attitudes," and "communicating with one another in an impenetrable scholastic patois." (Lind, 340)

The snob as the archetype of the American intellectual can be illustrated by the pervasive Anglophilia of college campuses. One case study is the critical acclaim accorded to the British writer D. H. Lawrence. Lawrence was idolized during the 1950s and 1960s mainly for his prurient novels, but there was also more at work. As the son of a coal miner, Lawrence condemned the English working class for its slave mentality, and for a long time idolized the British aristocracy, which he tried to join by marrying a German aristocrat. Lawrence's hatred of the United States its Constitutional government was informed by his devotion to oligarchy. Some critics were lucid enough to point out that Lawrence was an insufferable, social-climbing snob. Characteristic of the postwar, post-New Deal American academic view is the defense of Lawrence offered in 1946 by Diana Trilling, a central figure of the New York literary establishment, who wrote: "All artists are snobs, whatever the social group with which they make common cause, if only to the extent that they live by discriminations. Since all art represents a privileged view of life, all artists are privileged members of society by assumption." [150]

Lasch also notes the important role of class prejudice in forming elite attitudes in this country today. He describes how well-to-do liberals, when confronted with resistance to their ideas of social engineering, "betray the venomous hatred that lies not far beneath the smiling face of upper-middle-class benevolence," and turn on those who "just don't get it." (Lasch, 28) The result is an academic culture which appears to be contemptuous of the human potential of vast strata of the American population.

---

[149] *The Nation*, August 14/21, 1995.
[150] Diana Trilling's introduction to *The Portable D. H. Lawrence* (New York: Viking, 1961), p. 26.

THE CONGRESS AS OLIGARCHY

Today, the American political landscape is largely dominated by oligarchy. Winning a seat in the Congress entails meeting a very exacting qualification in terms of wealth: the ability to spend (for television and other advertising) between $500,000 and $1,000,000 for a seat in House of Representatives, and between $5 million and $20 million for a seat in the Senate, depending on the state involved. During the first half of the 1980s, the property qualification for the House was stringent enough so that House members who chose to run for re-election had a better chance of staying in office than their counterparts in the Supreme Soviet in Moscow, a watchword for immobilism at that time. The upper limit of the Senate figure has been pushed up in recent years by the extravagant expenditures of figures like Oliver North of Virginia, Michael Huffington of California, and others. The Congress is for plutocrats, a millionaires' club. This essential case has been conceded by Rep. Jim Leach (R-Iowa), who, as chairman of the House Banking Committee, is admirably situated to study this matter. Leach recently told columnist Mark Shields: "Campaign finance reform is the most pressing issue facing the nation. Any political system where money is dominant means, simply, that the few control the many and not that the many control the few. That is not a democracy...It is an oligarchy." [151]

The same estimate was confirmed by spokesmen for the other body. The Senate Democratic Party majority leader George Mitchell summed it up late in 1994, shortly before he chose to leave the Senate: "This system stinks. This system is money." [152]   Oligarchy breeds more oligarchy, including in the halls of Congress. On October 18, 1998, during the last phase of budget negotiations between the Clinton White House and the Congressional leaders, Sen. Moynihan of New York complained on CNN *Late Edition* of the "breakdown of legislative procedures" which had led to "century-old rules" being "wiped out." The traditional House-Senate conference committees, where the differences between two versions of a bill had traditionally been ironed out, were now virtually paralyzed. Moynihan lamented that the deliberative activity of Congress had come to a standstill, and that all important decisions were being made by "a very small group of people" which included Clinton's chief of staff Erskine Bowles, along with Speaker Gingrich, House Minority Leader Gephardt, Senate Majority Leader Lott, and Senate Minority Leader Daschle. Moynihan described this as a "bastard parliamentary system" in which ability of each senator to vote for the best interests of his or her constituents had been fatally weakened by a top-down party discipline. A week later, Sen. Bob Kerry (D-Nebraska) reacted to the same situation by noting that what we had in the Congress was no longer government of, by, and for the people, but rather "government by four people."[153] This means oligarchy.

Over recent years, American politics has taken on a decidedly hereditary tone. In a recent gubernatorial primary, Minnesota Democrats were offered a choice among candidates named Humphrey, Freeman, and Mondale, each one the son of a leading official of the previous generation. In California during the same year, the Republican senate candidate was Matt Fong, the son of California's former Democratic Secretary of State. In Pennsylvania, where Robert Casey had been governor, there was a Casey running for Congress. In Ohio, there was a Taft on the ballot. George Bush was himself the son of a US senator, and his fondest hope had been to found a dynasty to rival the Roosevelt and Kennedy clans. By late 1998, Bush had one son serving as governor of Florida, and one as governor of Texas, with a bid for the White House in the offing. If a state

---

[151] Mark Shields, "The Politician Who Won't Wobble," *Washington Post*, May 22, 1998.
[152] *The Nation*, August 14/21, 1995.
[153] *This Week*, ABC television network, October 25, 1998.

governorship, for example, were to be held by the same family of oligarchs over several generations, it might well come to resemble an hereditary dukedom. Ceauşescu of Romania had tried but failed to establish what amounted to an hereditary communist monarchy with his son Nicu, while Kim il Sung of North Korea had been succeeded by his son as dictator of that country, and now the notion of political office as a quasi- hereditary family possession was beginning to take root in the United States.

American television is the property of a very aggressive oligopoly, and its programming is the product of an oligarchy of script-writers and producers. William Baker, the author of *Down the Tube*, a study of the failure of American commercial television, has stated that most programming seen in this country is purchased for broadcast by a very small group of "fewer than one hundred people." The creative side of the enterprise is almost as restricted: Baker reports that "fewer than four hundred writers are responsible for most of what is seen on prime time in the course of a season." Ideas for television series "come from a variety of sources, most of them within a few miles of Sunset Boulevard." Political discussion on American television is similarly dominated by 100 or so sophists who interview each other endlessly, sometimes appearing on two or three programs each week, incessantly repeating the same threadbare clichés, and doing great damage to the American language in the process. We are reminded that Renaissance civilization tended to jettison oligarchy precisely because it produced shoddy results, it still does.

LOOKING FORWARD

If current trends continue unabated, the perspective for American society is for greater polarization between a wealthy elite and an impoverished mass, with not much middle class in between. Lind calls this Brazilianization, meaning under this heading " not the separation of cultures by race, but the separation of races by class. As in Brazil, a common American culture could be indefinitely compatible with a blurry, informal caste system in which most of those at the top of the social hierarchy are white, and most brown and black Americans are at the bottom – *forever*" (Lind 188-216) But we should beware of the pessimism which might be occasioned by simply extrapolating current trends. For whatever else social development may be, it is certainly not linear.

In the midst of the gathering gloom of the Age of Oligarchy, it may still be possible to advance a conjunctural perspective on how this state of affairs might be altered in the direction of a return to a New Deal on the scale required by the twenty-first century. Political scientists have long identified certain presidential elections as landmark turning points. Among these they have enumerated the coming of Jackson in 1824, the Lincoln victory in 1860, McKinley's defeat of Bryan in 1896, Roosevelt's 1932 win, and Nixon's triumph of 1968. Each of these was a sea-change which established the winning party as the dominant force in national politics for a period of several decades into the future. Related to these turning points are a series of fundamental watersheds.

Samuel Huntington, in his 1981 study entitled *American Politics*, described these as explosions of the "American Creed," which he saw as a mixture of liberty, equality, individualism, and democracy." He viewed American history as punctuated by a series of periods of heightened political awareness and activity which he called "creedal passion periods." His forecast was that "if the periodicity of the past prevails, a major sustained creedal passion period will occur in the second and third decades of the twenty-first century." However, blurred any attempt to look into the future by excluding from consideration social and economic upheavals like the Populists of the 1890s and the mass strikes of the 1930s.

American history has indeed been marked by economic, social, and political upheavals which have created at least the potential for social change; sometimes these moments have tragically backfired. Among these moments have been the Great Awakening of the 1740s, the American Revolution of 1776, the Great Revival of about 1800, the Jacksonian upsurge of 1828, the Civil War of 1861-65, the Populist heyday of the 1890s, the New Deal, including the mass strikes of the early 1930s, and the civil rights movement and anti-war movement culminating in the assassinations and repressions of 1968. It is very likely that this series will not end here. Given Huntington's commitments as spokesman for the right-wing academic mandarin point of view, it is not surprising that he was looking forward to the next "creedal passion period" as the possible point of emergence of an authoritarian state. In the next creedal ferment explosion, he wrote, "the oscillations among the responses could intensify in such a way as to threaten to destroy both ideals and institutions" in this country. This might include "the replacement of the weakened and ineffective institutions by more authoritarian structures more effectively designed to meet historical needs."

Totalitarian dictatorship would indeed be worse than what prevails today, although the current oligarchical regime is already bad enough, and is deteriorating quickly. On a world scale, the final defeat of the Soviet Union and its satellites has set the stage for the world-wide triumph of the Anglo-American finance oligarchy and its clients. But there can be no doubt that the crisis-ridden world system of economic globaloney has everywhere sent human progress into reverse, and cannot represent a viable way of organizing human affairs. As we argue throughout this book, the extreme lability of the current global financial arrangements is evident, and there is every reason to believe that a systemic crisis or disintegration of globalized world finance is historically imminent. Huntington's estimate of a new political upheaval on the scale of the 1960s to be expected between 2010 and 2030 may be overtaken by an upsurge growing out of the Millennium Meltdown in the same way that the mass strikes of the 1930s grew out of the economic breakdown of those years.

Economic programs are indispensable, but they are not enough by themselves. They require among other things a bearer who is not hopelessly discredited. During the interval between the November 1932 presidential election and the March inauguration, Franklin D. Roosevelt repeatedly refused to take action on the economic and financial crisis in association with the lame duck Hoover. And these were precisely the months during which the entire US banking system became insolvent and was forced to shut down. New Deal insiders have suggested that Roosevelt refused to join with Hoover in doing anything because the outgoing president was so thoroughly hated and discredited that any program with his name on it or even supported by him would have been seen as hopeless and doomed to fail. So despite the desperate situation, Roosevelt felt he had to wait until he could act in his own name; to do otherwise would have been to squander the most precious resource of all: public confidence. President Yeltsin of Russia had by 1997 reached a similar point of political bankruptcy: in his faltering hands, any economic program, no matter how dirigist, and would have been likely to fail. We must therefore face the fact that certain politicians and governments are structurally incapable of carrying out the necessary economic measures. The imperative today is to prepare for the reform of the US economy. Because of the connection among mass education, scientific discovery, and economic progress, reforms that make the best sense economically will tend to be anti-oligarchic in their social and political impact. American history itself offers abundant examples of this connection.

AMERICAN IDEOLOGY: CLASS DISMISSED

The United States is in its own way one of the most acutely class conscious societies on earth, but American ideology vehemently asserts that social classes do not exist here. No account of economic and productive decline would be complete without a discussion, however brief, of social class and the class war waged by the international finance oligarchy against American working people and the American middle class. Over the three decades of the world monetary crisis, a number of developments have combined to obscure the public awareness of issues of class and social stratification so much that these questions are now more neglected and ignored than they have been in many years. This has been the case especially since the USSR, the Warsaw Pact, the Comecon, and the world communist movement collapsed. Ironically, while most people have forgotten about class altogether, class-based interests have been running wild, breaking the postwar social contract with middle class working people, revamping the tax system along regressive lines, driving down the standard of living, rending the social safety net, gouging wages, busting unions, and promoting the runaway shop. It has been a very one-sided class war.

We argue here for a frank recognition of conflicting class interests in the spirit of Plato and Machiavelli, and for the need to resolve such conflicts in ways that promote genuine scientific, technological, and economic development through energy-intensive capital investment in technology and broad enhancement in standards of living coherent with the need to prepare the next generation for the technology of the coming century. These criteria of the general welfare, and not the immediate greed of a group of parasitical plutocrats, must become the dominant ones in making national policy. Recognizing class conflicts does not mean the advocacy of class warfare. The main exponents of the American System, from the *Federalist* to Carey and Lincoln to Franklin D. Roosevelt, never lost sight of the fact that labor and capital represent different social forces. Let us recall that it was Lincoln who observed that "labor is prior to, and independent of capital. Capital is only the fruit of labor, and could never have existed if labor had not first existed. Labor is the superior of capital, and deserves much the higher consideration."

Let us recall that the social doctrine of the Roman Catholic Church also clearly distinguishes between labor and ownership, and seeks to guarantee for labor the right to form unions for the assertion of its legitimate interests, and posits the right of labor to a living wage sufficient to raise a family on a single paycheck. Many of these points have been stressed in the encyclicals and homilies of John Paul II, who has criticized "wild capitalism" with its "structures of sin." So it would be idiotic to argue that the notion of social and economic class is a Marxist notion or was discovered by Marx. Class is simply a fact of life, which the American System seeks rationally to deal with by means of a national policy founded on the potential harmony of interests between labor and capital. In a healthy situation, labor would articulate the requirement of raising the standard of living, while capital would assert the need for productive investment. But the American System has no patience with the free-trade, anti-labor, derivatives-speculating policies of the rentier financiers who claim to stand for capital today. After almost three decades of headlong rout of the labor movement, we require urgent steps to restore balance between labor and capital, and today this can only mean shifting the policy terrain very substantially in favor of labor.

RACE OR CLASS?

Lind correctly notes that post-1968 multiculturalism represents a demagogic and successful form of tokenism applied as a counterinsurgency strategy; for Lind, "identity politics is merely America's version of the oldest oligarchic trick in the book: divide and rule." (141) The atrophy of class analysis in modern American is partly the fault of the 1960s New Left, which was much more interested in race and gender than in class. The New Left was interested in community control for the black community, which happened to be the main domestic counterinsurgency tactic of the Sargent Shriver Office of Economic Opportunity and the Ford Foundation. This was the apparatus of so-called "poverty pimps" who regarded black ghetto victims as a readily salable political commodity. During the late 1960s, the various factions of the US ruling elite converged on a strategy of divide and rule which involved playing the black ghetto against the Joe Sixpack or hardhat layers of the white lower middle class. McGeorge Bundy, at that time widely seen as the spokesman for the ruling elite in its totality, expressed this in his November 1977 article in the *Atlantic Monthly* in which he argued for race preferences in college admissions with the words, "To get past racism, we must here take account of race." This is the classic divide and conquer approach to ethnic groups which has been assumed by imperial ruling classes from time immemorial, from the Ottoman *milliyet-bachi* (or ethnark) system to the British Raj in India to the Soviet autonomous republics set up by Stalin.

The basic problems of black ghetto victims by 1970 (or 1997) were in reality largely economic – jobs, wages, health care, education, mass transit, housing, and related issues. The same was true of black rural poor. To even begin to address these problems would have required a domestic Marshall Plan, a second New Deal on a vast scale. The post-1957 stagnation of productive employment and industrial investment would have had to be reversed. Such an approach would necessarily have treated the disadvantaged layers of all ethnic groups, and would have required very substantial investments and other expenditures. The US financial elite, fixated on its new runaway shop opportunities in the globaloney economy, was not interested in such a domestic Marshall Plan.

The finance oligarchs also had reason to fear a multiracial coalition from below, which had been attempted during the Detroit mass strikes of the 1930s and 1940s, as documented in the section "Black and White, Unite" of Maurice Zeitlin's *Talking Union*. These mass strikes had forced the finance oligarchs to accept the existence of unions. A program of domestic counterinsurgency based on racial tokenism and "shucks" for the oppressed ethnic groups now seemed far more attractive to them. The basic mentality involved is subtly hinted at by Albert Blumrosen, who as a 1970 functionary of the Equal Employment Opportunity Commission helped to lay the groundwork for the current system. Blumrosen wrote in his book on *Black Employment and the Law*: "If discrimination is narrowly defined, for example, by requiring an evil intent to injure minorities, then it will be difficult to prove that it exists. If it does not exist, then the plight of racial and ethnic minorities must be attributable to some more generalized failures in society, in the fields of basic education, housing, family relations, and the like. The search for efforts to improve the condition of minorities must then focus in these general and difficult areas, and the answers can come only gradually as basic institutions, attitudes, customs and practices are changed."

This same outlook had been expressed a little earlier by George Shultz. Over the years Shultz has been Secretary of Labor, of the Treasury, and of State, and is said to have a Princeton tiger tattooed on his posterior. During Nixon's first term, Shultz revived the so-called Philadelphia Plan, a system of racial quotas for hiring in the then largely white construction trades which had been developed by Labor Secretary Willard Wirtz of the Johnson administration. John Ehrlichman of Nixon's palace guard later commented that Tricky Dick "thought that Secretary of Labor George Shultz had shown great style constructing a political dilemma for the labor union leaders and civil rights groups....Before long, the AFL-CIO and the NAACP were locked in combat over the passionate issues of the day." [Ehrlichman, 228-229] Later, the McGovern group in the Democratic party would inscribe racial and gender quotas on their own banner so prominently that Nixon in 1972 could get away with attacking McGovern as "the quota candidate."

The Democratic Party and the unions should at this point have adopted a plank calling for expanded production and productive jobs for all Americans, rather than accept the logic of quotas, which amount to quarreling over the distribution of the shrinking pie. The decline of the Democratic Party and of the labor movement over the reactionary quarter century after 1970 is the result of the failure to advocate economic expansion, and not quotas, during Nixon's first term. Quotas and associated practices like school busing have become lightning rods for white backlash and resentment, which in turn made possible the successful Republican southern strategy in the Electoral College and the long night of Reagan, Bush, and Gingrich. [154]

According to one account, in a meeting with Republican Congressional leaders "Nixon emphasized the importance of exploiting the Philadelphia Plan to split the Democratic constituency and drive a wedge between the civil rights groups and organized labor." [Graham] Civil rights leader Bayard Rustin told a 1969 AFL-CIO gathering that Nixon's successful playing off of black groups against the unions was "a source of tremendous satisfaction to powerful enemies of the labor movement." To underline the consensus in the ruling elite, the blue-ribbon commission chaired by former Illinois Governor Otto Kerner which studied the causes of the ghetto riots of the mid-1960s concluded that "white racism" was the cause of black discontent and of the race problem in America – white racism alone, and not slums, low wages, wretched schools, nonexistent health care, and unemployment. The Kerner Commission report was the voice of the white and inept US ruling elite scapegoating white workers and the white middle class for its own sorry record.

Martin Luther King was opposed to racial quotas all his life, as were Robert Kennedy and King's civil rights ally Bayard Rustin. Rustin wrote later that "any preferential approach postulated on racial, ethnic, religious, or sexual lines will only disrupt a multicultural society and lead to backlash. However, special treatment can be provided to those who have been exploited or denied opportunities if solutions are predicated on class lines, precisely because all religious, ethnic, and racial groups have a depressed class who would benefit."

The supporters of race quotas included Floyd McKissick of the Congress of Racial Equality (CORE), Stokely Carmichael of the Student Non-Violent Coordinating Committee (SNCC), and the incendiary H. Rap Brown. Not as well known but very influential were activists like James Farmer of CORE and James Forman. Quotas were the stock in trade of the so-called cultural nationalists, whose main goal appeared to be not the social progress of their people, but rather procuring well-endowed tenured professorships for themselves.

Originally, racial quotas and affirmative action were supposed to represent redress for past discrimination. After a decade or two that was transformed into the need to enhance diversity among a series of artificial, bureaucratically defined "cultures", including African-Americans, Asians and Pacific islanders, Hispanics, native Americans, and whites as the five official variants. Women, no matter how affluent, are also the recipients of quotas and set-asides, and one suspects that in practice homosexuals are too.

Race quotas, preferences, set-asides, offsets and the rest of the dismal apparatus of multiculturalism amount to a sophisticated and insidious counterinsurgency strategy which fosters the co-opting of talented black, Hispanic and other organic leaders into an artificial stratum of clients of the ruling elite. Multiculturalism, it must be stressed again, has not lead to economic development or to broad-front improvement in the condition of any ethnic group. Multiculturalism is tokenism. Black and Hispanic ghetto victims have not been helped by this approach. Multiculturalism has delivered material advantages for the few, and has betrayed the hopes of the

---

[154] Incredibly enough, historian Herbert Parmet wrote of Richard Nixon that "It would do a great injustice to deny [Nixon's] intellectual and spiritual commitment to racial equality." As Michael Lind comments, "In fact, Nixon's purpose in reviving and implementing the Philadelphia Plan was to split the Democratic coalition by pitting white labor against the black civil rights movement." Later, an authorized biography of Bush was published by Parmet, a professor at the City University of New York with a background as an apologist for Republican politicians. Parmet simply ignored most of the wealth of documentation cited in the Tarpley-Chaitkin biography of Bush, and based his work largely on superficial interviews. The result is a whitewash. See Lind, *Up From Conservatism* (New York: The Free Press, 1996), p. 192.

many. In the world of education, the irrationalist attempt to justify quotas and discrimination has debased the quality of intellectual and cultural life, which cannot escape the fact that the hopes of the majority of all ethnic origins have been betrayed.

One of the most durable villains of the Washington bureaucracy of recent decades was Stanley Pottinger, an asset of the George Bush machine. Pottinger was in 1976 the assistant Attorney General in charge of the Civil Rights division of the Justice Department (a post he held from 1973-77) who sabotaged the investigation of the Letelier-Moffit murders on Washington's Embassy Row.[155] Later Pottinger was involved in the 1979-80 arms-for hostages dealings between the Carter administration and Cyrus Hashemi of Iran. Pottinger was also the head of affirmative action at the old Department of Health, Education, and Welfare (HEW). When someone commented to Pottinger that affirmative action is a form of discrimination against whites, Pottinger replied with the following outburst of elemental class-consciousness: "That is the biggest crock I have ever heard. It is the kind of argument one expects to hear from a backwoods cracker farmer."[156]

The wealth of the ruling elite and its most immediate clients has been enhanced by the scandalous pay differentials which the tax code and other factors have allowed to open up between top executives and production workers. In 1993, the average American company president received compensation that was 157 times the salary made by the worker on the shop floor. Back in 1960, this differential was 41 times in the US. In today's Japan, the typical CEO makes 17 times the wages of the worker, and in Britain 35 times as much.

Class-based quotas would be just as impossible as race-based ones. The only sane policy is to reject all quotas in favor of merit within the framework of expanded productive employment and the revolution this would create in the American labor market for all concerned, with a program of infrastructural investment as described in the final chapter of this book. It was folly to institute quotas in the first place, and it would be folly simply to abolish them today without providing full employment and an economic bill of rights for all Americans in the context of a broad-based industrial recovery. By the late 1990s, a number of state referenda abolishing racial preferences were approved, including those in California and Washington state. These referenda were acts of desperation by voters, and took place in the face of a refusal of political leaders to respond to the economic crisis. Because of the failure of the politicians, the termination of preferences and minority outreach programs appeared as a tragic retrogression, with vindictive and reactionary overtones. The better way to defuse the issue of quotas is to submerge them and make them meaningless through color-blind and need-based measures which would help the poor, the lower middle class, and the broadest strata of the middle class. A greater percentage of blacks, Hispanics, and other minorities than of whites would benefit from such programs, but at the same time the absolute majority of those befitting would be white. In other words, programs aimed at building the middle class would enjoy a broad national constituency. The outline for such a strategy is given at the end of the final chapter.

MIDDLE CLASS BUBBLE PEOPLE

On no account should the ruling elite of aspiring oligarchs be confused with such broader generalizations as the upper middle class or the "achievers" of market demographics. The fact that even the upper reaches of the middle class per se have little to do with the ruling elite was underlined in the Rostenkowski-Packwood-Bradley tax reform law of 1985-86, which relegated the

---

[155] Chaitkin and Tarpley, 318 ff.
[156] Paul Seabury, "HEW and the Universities," *Commentary*, February 1972, 44.

upper middle class to the status of "bubble people." The bubble in question was the 33% tax rate assessed on incomes between $74,850 and $155,320. This was a bubble because while the bracket immediately below the bubble (for middle-class incomes between $30,950 and $74,850) paid 28%, the wealthier bracket immediately above the bubble (incomes over $155,320) reverted to a top rate of 28%. So the bubble people were singled out for a tax rate that was 5% higher than the one reserved for the very rich, the true princes of privilege. Under the 1986 tax code, a hard-working suburban doctor or was paying 33%, while Michael Millken and David Rockefeller only had to pay 28% on whatever income their accountants could not shelter for them in some other way. This singular anomaly remained in force for a number of years.

A CLASS STRATEGY

Max Lerner suggested a functional definition of class for Americans – "a stratum with similar economic opportunities, similar access to education, health, courtship, and the other major elements that fit a man for the voyage of life.... Seen in this frame, the idea of class is neither narrowly economic in the Marxist sense of income and power nor narrowly subjective in the [Lloyd] Warner sense of prestige and status, but is broadened to include the total strategic situation of the personality in the culture – the sum of the chances he gets at life and the preconditionings to life which flow not from his heredity or personality but from his location in the society." [Lerner 537]

Popular ideology is pervaded by elements of social Darwinism, which suggest that the struggle to get ahead is governed by the survival of the fittest, implying that the winners constitute a meritocracy. If a classless society was always an illusion, Americans could at least hope for a system of great mobility and interpenetration among the social strata. These have declined as the society has fragmented into a series of subdivisions. One of the great agencies of intermingling was compulsory military service, which is now a quarter of a century in the past. Writing in the mid-1950s, Lerner already found that upward social mobility was becoming constricted, with an "increasing closure of the top power and income positions to the sons of workers and farmers...." [Lerner 474] With the waning of the New Deal, there were "evidences that the class reality of America is moving steadily away from the classless ideal." [Lerner 470] Already under Eisenhower, "one of the striking facts about the whole American status system is exactly its high degree of insecurity." [Lerner 475]

Benjamin DeMott, in a very perceptive analysis, argues that US public life is distorted by the dichotomy between a society which is emphatically divided into classes and a popular mythology which claims that class distinctions either do not exist or are irrelevant. For Demott America is "a nation in shackles" because of an ideology (the chains of illusion on the heart) which claims that class barriers do not matter, when in practical everyday life they turn out to matter very much indeed. America is one of the most class-ridden societies in the world, and one reason for this is the hysterical denial of class in the general political debate.

DeMott demonstrated the central importance of the "icon of classlessness – the myth asserting, as President George Bush puts it, that class is 'for European democracies or something else – it isn't for the United States of America. We are not going to be divided by class.'" [DeMott, 9-10] DeMott called attention to the fact that "social wrong is accepted in American partly because differences in knowledge about class help to obscure it, and the key to those differences is the degree of acceptance of the myth of classlessness." [DeMott, 10-11]

The myth of "class dismissed" is the key to understanding a political climate in which Ronald Reagan could bust unions, remove minimal safeguards on health and safety in many industries, preside over the worst recession since 1945, sign a tax bill that soaked the poor to provide a bonanza for the rich, and still keep a relatively high popularity rating as America's favorite uncle. The myth of classlessness also provides the reason why such trash as the writings of Charles Murray (author of the racist *The Bell Curve*, and earlier tracts calling for the abolition of welfare), could be seriously debated. Here is Demott's ironic critique of Murphy:

> All welfare programs fail because character is all and class is nothing – hence Murray's proposal to scrap "the entire federal welfare and income support structure for working-aged persons, including AFDC, Medicaid, Food Stamps, Unemployed Insurance, Worker's Compensation, subsidized housing, disability insurance, and the rest" .... Reagan assumed a stance of doubt – of instant incredulity – when told of poverty and suffering. He observed that the Sunday newspaper listed thousands of jobs for which there were no takers, and that some homeless people slept on grates "by choice." Edwin Meese insisted that "some people are going to soup kitchens voluntarily...because the food is free and that's easier than paying for it." The voice of political sophistication intimated that the sense of shame or pity for the miserable and the unlucky reflected an absurd "passion of compassion" .... [DeMott 208]

This resurgence of social Darwinism reached an interim culmination in the Gingrich Contract on America of 1994 and in the reactionary mood of the Congress elected that year: the Republicans wanted to put poor children into orphanages, they wanted to chisel the kids' school lunches, they wanted to abolish welfare. Gingrich and company liked building prisons much more than they liked hiring police officers, and anyone could see that their goal was to create a large pool of slave laborers. Their push to abolish the Social Security entitlement went in the same direction. As the depression grew worse, it was easy to see how the Gingrich mind set would tend to converge on that of someone like Heinrich Himmler. Clinton resisted the Gingrich Congress on some points, but gave in on others: he capitulated on Medicaid and on welfare "reform." The welfare reform act was Clinton's great sellout of 1996. Fortunately, when Clinton in 1997 tried to sell out for the third time (after NAFTA and GATT) to the free trade demands of the finance oligarchs via the so-called fast track authority, he was prevented from doing so by his own Democratic party in the House of Representatives, which feared the wrath of a reawakening labor movement. By 1998, Clinton was fighting impeachment. As he did so, he found that his pals among the crypto-Republican New Democrats had run for cover, leaving him in the lurch, while the New Deal Democrats were fighting to save the Presidency. If Clinton did survive 1998, there was a chance that he might be pulled considerably to the left by the New Dealers.

The traditional American system of economics always preferred cooperation between labor and capital for the good of the nation and the quest for a harmony of interest between the two sides. Class struggle in itself was a blind alley; the central role of the labor movement in the FDR war mobilization was a model of how such problems could be solved. But over the past 30 years, the finance oligarchs and the corporate executives who serve them have repudiated the social contract on which decades of progress had been based: they have welshed on the commitment to a decent and rising standard of living for labor, with a social safety net to take care of those who are hurt by economic dislocations. The pendulum has swung much too far in the direction of the financiers. What the United States needs today is a powerful dose of class consciousness on the part of working people. The vast majority of the American population are either in the middle class, or trying to get into it. That sets them apart from the economic royalists and princes of privilege, paper-thin top stratum who are the immediate beneficiaries of globaloney.

CHAPTER

X. THE AMERICAN SYSTEM

There can be no understanding of economics without an awareness of its history. Galbraith, *Economics in Perspective*, 1987.

The most successful school of economics in the modern world is the one exemplified by Alexander Hamilton. Despite the claims of his detractors, Hamilton's economic theory is anti-oligarchical, and aims at building a strong nation around a prosperous and well-educated middle class. Recovery from the millennium meltdown will require a return to Hamiltonian economics, which have been virtually expunged from the curriculum of most colleges and universities in favor of Viennese and Chicago *laissez-faire*, free trade nostrums.

HAMILTON'S AMERICAN SYSTEM

Alexander Hamilton stated the doctrines of the American System by in his "Report on Public Credit," "Report on a National Bank," and "Report on the Subject of Manufacturers," which informed his work as George Washington's Secretary of the Treasury between 1789 and 1795. Hamilton's reports are among the greatest classics of economic writing, and contain every important principle necessary to the fight for the American System. Hamilton reflects not only the lessons of Colbert, but also of colonial New England, where the son of Governor Winthrop was a correspondent of Leibniz, plus the contributions of Benjamin Franklin, William Penn, and many others. Hamilton's argument was that the industrial development of the United States is both possible and historically imperative. His goal was to create an economically and militarily powerful nation state capable of resisting and defeating the British Empire. He polemicized with the *laissez-faire* school, with the Physiocrats, agrarians, with Adam Smith in favor of his own dirigistic approach. It was clear to Hamilton that an agrarian economy would be in constant peril of economic warfare and military assault, and that the terms of trade in a world economy dominated by the British were hopelessly stacked against those who could only offer raw materials. It was therefore necessary, in his words, "to promote the adoption of machines using fire and water to perform the labor of many human beings." This was the capital-intensive, energy-intensive program of Leibniz.

Priority undertakings in this context were for Hamilton iron foundries and other phases of metallurgy, coal mining, steel, copper, lead, textiles, gunpowder, and other commodities. These new industries the United States must protect and stimulate above all by a system of protective duties and tariffs, the indispensable means of shielding the new industries from British commercial warfare (the British had openly announced their intention of strangling these new industries). Hamilton discussed protective duties as part of an array of protectionist measures that include the outright embargo of the importation of certain manufactures, the payment of pecuniary bounties (which we would call subsidies), and premiums or prices paid to the producers of export products. Of these he especially recommended the bounty or subsidy, since this is a way that sale in foreign markets, as well as sale in the home market, can be obtained. This amounted to a kind of export subsidy which since has been imitated in various countries. Under GATT/WTO rules, Alexander Hamilton would be an outlaw.

NATIONALISM AND INDUSTRIALISM

Hamilton was adamant that the interest in developing new industries is a national and not a regional interest. He attempted to show the southern states, who thought they were capable only of agriculture with the use of slaves, that industrialization anywhere in the United States would do them the great service of providing a guaranteed and stable market for their produce, while foreign markets were politically and commercially uncertain. Protectionism might initially raise the price of manufactured articles that farmers bought, but in the medium and long term it would lower it, making possible a high-technology, energy-intensive farming of the type that has since been established. In addition, he hinted that the southern states could derive enormous benefits from the development of their mineral wealth of coal and iron.

Industrialization, in Hamilton's view, would increase the division of labor and therefore the diversification of risks in case of the collapse of this or that commodity. Industry would provide a rapid increase in the number of available jobs, and would provide these jobs at higher wages. Hamilton told American "undertakers" as he called the entrepreneurs, that they "can afford to pay the price" of more expensive American labor, thus foreshadowing the successful high-wage economy of later years. Industry would also expand the base of taxation. Hamilton asked for public funds to pay for a Board for the promotion of advanced industry and agriculture through the stimulation of immigration, the buying of foreign machines, and prizes.

HAMILTON'S THEORY OF VALUE

The theoretical basis of these recommendations is to be found in Hamilton's celebrated theory of value, which locates the source of national wealth in the increase of the productivity of labor. The introduction of Artificers (or workers) in addition to farmers, he argues, "has the effect of augmenting the productive powers of labor, and with them, the total mass of the produce or revenue of a country. In this single view of the subject, therefore, the utility of Artificers or Manufacturers, towards promoting an increase of productive industry, is apparent." To which he adds: "To cherish and stimulate the activity of the human mind, by multiplying the objects of enterprise, is not among the least considerable of the expedients, by which the wealth of a nation may be promoted." To stimulate industrialization, Hamilton called for a comprehensive system of internal improvements, including roads and canals, to be built at the expense of the federal government. He wanted to stimulate immigration to bring new skilled workers, and indeed foreign capitalists, into the new country. He wanted to build a navy to protect foreign commerce.

A FUNDED NATIONAL DEBT

All of these plans, however, had above all to be buttressed by a solution to the overwhelming monetary and credit problems of the new-born United States. The preceding period of the Articles of Confederation had created financial chaos, with the government not empowered to levy taxes except through appeals to the states. Now the new Constitution had given the power to tax, as well as the power to borrow, to the federal government. But the credit rating of the government was uncertain, since there was a great deal of debt left over from the Revolution, the future payment of which was quite problematic. The federal government had borrowed 12 million dollars abroad and 42 million dollars at home to fight the revolution. In addition, the thirteen states had a total of 18 million dollars of war debts whose payment was wholly conjectural. Some of this debt was selling for as little as 25 cents on the dollar in the open market, but Hamilton argued that the public credit of the United States at home and especially abroad demanded that the debt be funded at par, that is, at 100% of its face value. All of the state debt left outstanding was taken over by the federal government. The old debt was re-issued in a number of new high-quality US government obligations, which were paid using customs duties. By the end of 1794, the United States had the highest credit rating in Europe, and these bonds were selling at 10% above par. An investment counselor and stockjobber of the day in France, whose name happened to be Talleyrand, told his clients and friends that the US bonds were "safe and free from reverses. They have been funded in such a sound manner and the prosperity of the country is growing so rapidly that there can be no doubt of their solvency." Talleyrand was in awe of Hamilton. By 1801, Europeans had bought some 33 million dollars' worth of the country's $80 million public debt. As Hamilton had predicted, the US funds were so solid that they served as money — an uncertain debt instrument is but a fluctuation commodity, he said, but a funded debt is capital and money. This idea of monetizing the public debt, which monetarists oppose, later came up with Franklin D. Roosevelt. More money in circulation meant lower interest rates, another of Hamilton's goals.

HAMILTON'S FIRST BANK OF THE UNITED STATES

At a time when there were only three banks in the entire country, Hamilton recommended the creation of the First Bank of the United States, the crowning achievement of his work. This issue is relevant at a time when three banks, or no banks at all, might prove to be solvent in the wake of a derivatives panic. The new BUS was chartered by the Federal government as a private corporation, with the shares being sold to the public and paid for one fourth in specie (coin), and three fourths in the new US government debt instruments, with a six percent return. Into the bank went all the deposits of the US government. The bank could issue paper money, which the government at that time did not do. With its capital of ten million dollars, a very large sum for that time, the bank was able to generate a large amount of credit at reasonable interest rates for a country in which, as Franklin had pointed out, the simple lack of money was one of the greatest barriers to expansion.

The BUS proved to be a massive bulwark in defense of the national economy, defending the national credit by making loans to the government when required, and also by policing the state-chartered banks that soon appeared. By acting as collection agent for payments to the federal government made by the state banks, the BUS demanded coin from them in exchange for their bank-notes and was thus well placed to judge their solvency. This function limited fictitious expansions of bank notes by the state banks and had the effect of establishing a sound paper circulation. Thus the BUS fought land speculators and other types of speculators by cutting off their sources of wildcat liquidity – the opposite of what the Federal Reserve was doing in the late 1990s.

In proposing the BUS, Hamilton was bitterly opposed by Thomas Jefferson and by James Madison, both democratically capitulating to strong anti-centralist backwardness in their home state of Virginia. Jefferson, who was sometimes an ideologue of rural backwardness in the Rousseau tradition, offered his objections on Constitutional grounds in his "Opinion on the Bank," the wellspring of the restrictive exegesis of the Constitution. President Washington, however, approved the bill setting up the Bank, which was in existence until 1811, when it was allowed to lapse under the Madison administration.

THE WAR HAWKS AND POST-1815 US NATIONALISM

The failures of the Jefferson administration, such as the Embargo on all foreign trade, and the shocking defeats of American military forces in the War of 1812, combined to catalyze a revival of Hamiltonian nationalism, especially among a group of western politicians known as the War Hawks, who urged pre-emptive attack on the British to head off British-induced Indian warfare, and wanted to proceed to the conquest of Canada. Except for the spectacular exploits of the American navy on the lakes and the high seas, where the British were dealt some of their most stinging defeats in centuries, the progress of American arms was a lamentable fiasco, only slightly retrieved by General Jackson's victory over the British at New Orleans when the war was already over. Chief among US reverses was the capture and burning of Washington by a British expeditionary force that was narrowly defeated when it attempted to do the same thing to Baltimore. The assault on Canada broke down with loss. The oligarchy of the New England states openly took the side of the British, and threatened to secede, which pointed up the grave dangers of sectionalism, fomented from London. The extinction of the BUS forced the government to borrow abroad, at exorbitant interest rates.

The War of 1812 thus ushered in a period of resurgent nationalism, marked also by the first landmark decisions of Chief Justice John Marshall of the Supreme Court. The most prominent of the War Hawks was Henry Clay, from the western state of Kentucky, the best available spokesman and political operative of a group of American system supporters which included Mathew Carey, the Philadelphia economist and publicist. Clay was also acquainted with Friedrich List, whom he met in Washington in 1825 when the latter was visiting there with the Marquis Gilbert de Lafayette. Clay's program, as laid out for example in his unsuccessful Presidential campaign of 1824, he called the American System, a phrase borrowed from Alexander Hamilton. The American System was Clay's programmatic platform in the election contest. The adversary of the American System he referred to as "the foreign policy."

HENRY CLAY'S AMERICAN SYSTEM

Clay's program was designed to become the platform of a new political party that would be nation in scope and nationalist in character. This party turned out to be the Whig party, which achieved only limited success in its mission of nation-building. Clay was determined to fight sectionalism by re-establishing the pre-eminence of the national economic interest, also in order to build the country's military strength. This meant the institution of a strongly protective tariff, of the type that Hamilton had recommended but been unable to obtain. "There is a remedy," said Clay, "and that remedy consists in modifying our foreign policy and in adopting a genuine American system. We must naturalize the arts in our country, and we must naturalize them by the only means which the wisdom of nations has yet discovered to be effectual – by adequate protection against the overwhelming influence of foreigners."

Clay also demanded a vigorous policy of new road and canal building to link up regional markets and reduce the costs of transportation of goods. As he knew as a congressman from Kentucky, the frontier had now advanced to the trans-Appalachian west, beyond the mountains, and transportation was an urgent issue, although it had been neglected by Jefferson and Madison. Clay favored the creation of an inter-American development block, joining with the newly independent republics of former Spanish and Portuguese America. In this, he strongly supported the Monroe Doctrine, and agitated for the immediate recognition of the new states as they acquired their independence. As the Secretary of State under John Quincy Adams, Clay intended to use a conference of Latin American states held in Panama in 1826 as a vehicle for these plans, but this was not successful, and he was later disappointed by Bolivar's lust for power at any price. Clay exhorted his fellow citizens to support the revolt against colonialism in Ibero-America: "Let us break these commercial and political fetters; let us no longer watch the nod of any European politician; let us become the real and true Americans, and place ourselves at the head of the American system." Clay at one time proposed the building of the Pan-American highway, a road that would link all the Americas in defiance of British sea power.

Clay, as Speaker of the House of Representatives, was later instrumental in obtaining the approval of the bill re-creating the Bank of the United States. Here he was aided by John C. Calhoun of South Carolina, a War Hawk who later turned pro-states rights over the slavery issue. The second BUS was set up in 1816, with a twenty year charter. This time the capital of the bank was made 35 million dollars, which made it the largest corporation in the world, with one fifth of the stock being bought by the government. The Bank survived an initial round of financial warfare and went on to become even more successful than the first BUS. The Constitutionality of the Second BUS was affirmed by Chief Justice Marshall in the 1819 opinion in the case of McCulloch vs. Maryland. Clay was also a partisan of a standing army and a powerful navy. His two main points were a protective tariff and internal improvements. As he told the House after returning from a trip abroad, the lessons of his trip "were lessons that satisfied me that national independence was only to be maintained by national resistance against foreign encroachments, by cherishing the interests of the people, and giving the whole physical power of the country an interest in the preservation of the nation." He urged the House to "commence the great work, too long delayed, of internal improvement." He desired to see a "chain of turnpike roads and canals from Passamoquoddy to New Orleans; and other similar roads intersecting the mountains, to facilitate intercourse between all parts of the country, and to bind and connect us together." He spoke out for the protection of domestic manufacturing, "not so much for the sake of the manufacturers themselves, as for the general interest." "We should thus have our wants supplied when foreign resources are cut off; and we should also lay the basis of a system of taxation, to be resorted to when the revenue from imports is stopped by war," argued Clay.

The Whig program was summed up by Pennsylvania Senator Andrew Stewart: "The true policy of this country... was to make New England instead of Old England, the great theatre of our manufactures. They had the capital and their population had become sufficiently dense to justify its employment in this way. We will thus create in our own country an ample market for the consumption of the cotton and the sugar of the south, and the wool and flour of the middle and western states, which no longer found a market abroad. It will make the great sections of our confederacy mutually dependent on each other. It will bind and unite them together by the strong ties of interest and intercourse, combining all the elements of national prosperity – agriculture, manufactures, commerce. These, with a good system of internal communications, would render our prosperity perfect, and our Union indissoluble." This constituted what was properly and emphatically called the 'American system of policy.'"

THE PROTECTIVE TARIFF

Support for these views was strong enough to permit the passage, in the aftermath of the war of 1812, of the first truly protective tariff, the tariff of 1816. This inaugurated a tendency for further protectionism that lasted until 1833, in the midst of the Jackson years. 1816 thus emerges as a watershed year, with the Second BUS and a protective tariff levy going through in the same year. The twenty years after 1816 were accordingly ones of unprecedented growth. This was the case also because of the Presidency of John Quincy Adams, a strong pro-development dirigist who defeated Clay for the Presidency in the contested election of 1824. Clay, as we have seen, became Quincy Adam's Secretary of State. In Adam's inaugural address, he stunned the crabbed states' rights exegetes of the Constitution by announcing that "the great object of the institution of civil government is the improvement of those who are parties to the social compact", and enumerated the impressive powers that the Constitution afforded to do just that, going on to say that "if these powers may be effectually brought into action by laws promoting the improvement of agriculture, commerce, and manufactures, the cultivation of the mechanic and the elegant arts, the advancement of literature, and the progress of the sciences, ornamental and profound, then to refrain from exercising them for the benefit of the people themselves would be to hide in the earth the talent committed to our charge - would be treachery to the most sacred of trusts." Adams recommended a national university, astronomical observatories, and a whole array of scientific enterprises. He ridiculed the narrow-minded sectionalism of most opportunist politicians, asking if they were "palsied by the will of their constituents." Adams here was out far in advance of Clay, who did not have the same personal authority of independent intellectual accomplishments.

Adams pressed hard for internal improvements, instructing the army engineers to survey prospective transportation routes. Under Adam's leadership the Congress regularly voted substantial financial aid to interstate roads and canals. The prime improvement carried out by the federal government itself was the Cumberland Road, or National Road, from Cumberland, Maryland to Jefferson City, Missouri, although only Vandalia, Illinois had been reached when the project collapsed in the panic of 1837. This turned out to be the only wholly-owned federal project of this type in the pre-Jackson period. Adams' term in office was the height of the canal-building epoch, highlighted by the 1825 Erie Canal from the Hudson River in New York state to Lake Erie, which radically cut the time and cost for shipments to the west, since the Great Lakes were linked up with the Atlantic. The Erie was later supplemented by the Pennsylvania Canal, and other canals.

FRIEDRICH LIST: AMERICAN POLITICAL ECONOMY

It was during the term of Adams that Friedrich List published his 1827 *Outlines of American Political Economy* in Philadelphia, addressing the book to Charles Ingersoll, vice president of the Pennsylvania Society. List was against those who wished to limit the role of the central government: "... it is questioned whether government has the right to restrict individual industry in order to bring to harmony the three component parts of national industry and, secondly, it is questioned whether government does well or has it in its power to produce this harmony by laws and restrictions. Government, sir, not only has the right, but it is its duty, to promote every thing which may increase the wealth and power of the nation, if this object cannot be effected by individuals. So it is its duty to guard commerce by a navy, because merchants cannot protect themselves; so it is its duty to protect the carrying trade by navigation laws, because carrying trade supports naval power, as naval power protects carrying trade; so the shipping interest and commerce must be supported by breakwaters – agriculture and every other industry by turnpikes, bridges, canals and railroads – inventions by patent laws – so manufactures must be raised by protective duties, if foreign capital and skill prevent individuals from undertaking them." Some pages on, List draws up his celebrated contrast of the British system with the American system:

> American national economy, according to the different conditions of the nations, is quite different from English national economy. English national economy has for its object to manufacture for the whole world, to monopolize all the manufacturing power, even at the expense of the lives of the citizens, to keep the world and especially her colonies in a state of infancy and vassalage by political management as well as by the superiority of her capital, her skill, and her navy. American economy has for its object to bring into harmony the three branches of industry, without which no national industry can attain perfection. It has for its object to supply its own wants, by its own materials and its own industry – to people an unsettled country – to attract foreign populations, foreign capital, and skill – to increase its power and its means of defense, in order to secure the independence and future growth of the nation. It has for its object lastly to be free and independent and powerful, and to let everyone else enjoy freedom, power, and wealth as he pleases. English national economy is

predominant; American national economy aspires only to become independent. As there is no similarity in these two systems, there is no similarity in the consequences of it.

List polemicized fiercely against Adam Smith whose free trade he branded a "Cosmopolitical" doctrine, alien to national economy. List was also the author of the *National System of Political Economy* (1840). List was a founder of the historical school of economics, which later had to endure the attacks of the Austrian school of von Mises and von Hayek.

Unfortunately, John Quincy Adams and Henry Clay went down to crushing defeat at the hands of Andrew Jackson, the general whom Adams had kept out of the White House four years earlier. Aided by the almost universal manhood suffrage doctrines coming out of the western states, Jackson rode into the White House on a rising tide of frontiersmen, poor farmers, and a class of New York city radical Jacobins called the loco-focos. Jackson won thanks to King Numbers, or, in the words Marshall's friend Justice Joseph Story, King Mob. Jackson postured at being a great friend of the common man against the aristocratic J. Q. Adams, but Jackson's banking policy worked great hardship on common men and their families. Jackson was allied with Martin Van Buren, the New York party boss, who kept in touch with the world of the Astors and the New York financial community. Another member of the Jackson kitchen cabinet was Amos Kendall, who had made a fortune in the telegraph business, gave the following expression to the synthetic ideology which the Jackson group professed: "The world is governed too much. Our countrymen are beginning to demand" that the government limit itself to "protecting their persons and property, leaving them to direct their labor and capital as they please, within the moral law; getting rich or remaining poor as may result from their own management or fortune." This was *laissez-faire* camouflaged as a backwoods attack on the eastern plutocrats. Most of the kitchen cabinet were in fact wealthy business men of the monetarist-rentier type, who wanted more freedom for speculation, and in this they facilitated the destabilization of the United States by the British.

JACKSON AND VAN BUREN CREATE THE PANIC OF 1837

In the eight years of Jackson and the four of Van Buren that followed, the entire Hamiltonian apparatus was destroyed by a Tory counter-revolution: this included the BUS, the protective tariff, and the internal improvements policy, all of which were dismantled, with consequences which lasted all the way until the outbreak of the Civil War, a conflict which Jackson's policies alone made irrepressible.

"Relief, sir! Come not to me Sir! Go to the monster. It is folly to talk to Andrew Jackson. The government will not bow to the monster. Andrew Jackson yet lives to put his foot upon the head of the monster and crush him to the dust. Andrew Jackson would never recharter that monster of corruption. Sooner than live in a country in which such a power prevailed, he would seek asylum in the wilds of Arabia." This was Jackson talking to a delegation of businessmen come to the White House to protest his measures against what the Jacksonians branded that "hydra of corruption," the Second BUS. Jackson vetoed the new charter of the bank when it was renewed by Congress in 1832, and then in the spring of 1834, withdrew all the US government deposits from the bank, even though its federal charter still had two years to go. Jackson personally affected to believe that banks were evil and should be outlawed. He shared this view with the president of the BUS, Nicholas Biddle of Philadelphia, to whom he said: "I do not dislike your bank more than all banks, but ever since I read the history of the south Sea Bubble, I have been afraid of all banks." In his veto message, Jackson argued that the bank was un-American because of the large number of foreign stock-holders, and "undemocratic" because it placed too much "power in the hands of a few men irresponsible to the people." It was also, according to his construction, unconstitutional.

Jackson's western base of land speculators and wildcat bankers had good reason to resent the BUS, which was always calling on the state-chartered banks to provide gold and silver coin, or specie, to make good their bank notes received by the federal government for taxes. This tended to restrain land speculation and real estate swindles. The termination of the BUS was the prelude to the most colossal financial crisis of the US economy in the first half of the nineteenth century, a crisis of the worldwide pound sterling system to be sure, but one which the British, in the absence of a US national bank, were able to turn against the US, with tragic and long-lasting consequences.

The US funds taken out of the BUS were placed in state banks, such as the one owned by Roger Taney, Jackson's Secretary of the Treasury. These were called the "pet" banks. With the decline of BUS, the pet banks and state banks expanded their lending massively and also rapidly proliferated in their numbers. This led to a land boom, especially in the sale of government lands. The phrase "doing a land-office business" became a permanent part of the language. At the same time, the state and pet banks were using their new freedom to issue paper money far in excess of a normal reserve ratio, in relation to the gold and silver coin they kept. At the height of the bubble, two events converged to produce a panic of tremendous proportions. The Bank of England, seizing as a pretext the fact that the US balance of trade was collapsing, raised its discount rate, which cut off credit by British traders to American merchants. Those American merchants now needed gold and silver coin to buy from Britain, and had to pull all their bank deposits to get them.

At about this time, Jackson, ever the foe of all banks, became alarmed by the western land bubble, and decided that the federal government must no longer accept paper money from banks for the purchase of western lands, but only silver and gold coin, or specie. This was the Specie Circular of 1836. Since the state banks in the west had little or no precious metal coins, the land boom was brought to a catastrophic halt, collapsing into panic. Since at the same time another law was passed which distributed the federal budget surplus (which had been deposited in state banks) to the state governments, there was no hard money left for the state banks, and the entire US banking system came crashing down. By May 1837, every bank in the United States had suspended specie payment. Paper money was worthless. The states of Mississippi, Louisiana, Maryland, Pennsylvania, Indiana, and Michigan defaulted on their public debts, undermining US foreign credit for a very long time. There were calls for the federal government to assume the state debts, as under Hamilton, but these were ignored by Jackson. The states dropped out the internal improvements business for the relevant historical future.

On the tariff front, the protectionist forces were successfully judoed into an unlikely trap. A tariff bill was proposed that added counter-productive duties on the import of raw materials, not manufactured products. This bill might have been rejected, except for the change in vote of Senator Daniel Webster of Massachusetts. The new law quickly became known as the Tariff of Abominations of 1828. South Carolina, the center of British trade and influence in the south, reacted some time later by declaring this law null and void, not binding upon the state and her citizens, with the Nullification Ordinance of 1832. The state threatened to secede from the Union if Washington attempted to coerce South Carolina to observe the tariff. Henry Clay immediately proposed the Compromise Tariff of 1833, which avoided the outbreak of armed hostilities in Charleston Harbor, but this was a step away from protection and, worse, the beginning of a long decline in the protective tariff, which reached its low point in the tariff of 1857, which restored free trade on the eve of the Civil War. From 1833 to 1861, the tendency was to abandon protectionism.

With the BUS and the protective tariff fatally weakened and the nation's finances ruined, it only remained for Jackson to end the policy of federal support for internal improvements. This he did in 1830 with the veto of the Maysville Road bill. This set a strong precedent against federal financing of roads, canals, and railroads. The destruction of the American System under Jackson was thus complete. The end of the Second BUS ushered in an entire generation of banking anarchy and monetary disorder, with rapid depreciation and with total confusion about what money itself was. Swarms of state banks emitted a debased paper currency, and were at times joined in this by cities, stores, and railroad companies. Hard money was gold and silver coin, and this specie remained very scarce. President Van Buren added the coup de grace to this situation with his independent Treasury Act, which established the principle that the US government should have no dealings with banks of any type, but rather maintain vaults or sub-treasuries under Treasury officials, who would take in and pay out only gold and silver coin. This meant that the federal government could not regulate or otherwise control the banks, so chaos and periodic panics were made a constant feature of economic life. The divorce from the banks was applauded by the loco-focos, who also hated banks. The government collected no interest on these funds. A bill to create a Third Bank of the United States was passed by the Congress that had been elected along with William Henry Harrison in 1840, but by the time it reached the White House Harrison was dead and the atrocious John Tyler was in power, and Tyler twice vetoed the Third BUS. His entire Whig cabinet resigned in protest, except for Daniel Webster, who stayed on in order to avoid serious trouble with the British over the Maine border, after which he also resigned.

IRREPRESSIBLE CONFLICT ?

All of this set the stage for the fatal slide toward the Civil War. The lack of a national bank and the uncertainty about money meant that while there might be some credit found for railroad building, there would be no credit for the industrial development of the slave-holding south, and no protective tariff to make such development feasible. The best to procure the end of slavery without civil war was to create in the south an industrial counter-weight against the slave power. The key to this was the mineral wealth of coal and iron which later, in this century, made Birmingham, Alabama a great center of steel production. As Henry Carey wrote in 1861: "If Henry Clay's tariff views had been carried out sooner there would have been no secession because the southern mineral region would long since have obtained control of the planting area." In 1853, well before the war, Carey had written: "Let the people of Maryland and Virginia, Carolina, Kentucky and Tennessee be enabled to bring into activity their vast treasures of coal and iron ore, and to render useful their immense water-powers..." At another point, Carey referred to the hill region of the south as "one of the richest, if not absolutely the richest in the world" which with protection "would long since have been filled with furnaces and factories, and the laborers in which would have been free men, women, and children, white and black, and the several parts of the Union would have been linked together by hooks of steel that would have set at defiance every effort of the 'wealthy capitalists' of England for bringing about a separation." But Henry Clay's last-ditch attempt to create the Third BUS and return to protectionism under William Henry Harrison failed when that president died in 1841 after a month in office, under most suspicious circumstances, and the Civil War came.

It is worth stressing that while slavery was a grave problem, it could have been solved without civil war in a setting of economic development. But free trade made rebellion inevitable. As Carey wrote after the Civil War: "Slavery did not make the rebellion. British free trade gave us sectionalism, and promoted the growth of slavery, and thus led to rebellion. Had Mr. Clay been elected in 1844, all the horrors of the past few years would have been avoided." With industrialization, the southern slaveocrat power would have been forced to contend with a southern industrial-based interest. In addition, the price of food, land, and labor would have increased, and this was what the slavery men were determined to prevent.

The logic of slavery, with backing from Wall Street and the city of London, was to prevent not only the industrialization of the south but of the north as well. The goal was to stop labor from entering manufacturing, and rather to force people back to the land, with a minimum of capital, to grow food at the cheapest possible rates for the consumption of the slaves. All of this meant free trade, and no internal improvements. In addition, the peculiarity of growing cotton with gangs of slaves as a staple export crop, year in, year out, was that cotton monoculture rapidly exhausted the land, and this depreciation caused by the primitive quality of slave agriculture itself meant that cotton growing on a fixed amount of land could not be profitable in the long run, quite apart from the violent ups and downs of the world cotton market. Thus, the supporters of King Cotton had to promote the cancerous expansion of slavery not only into the territories, but also into the Caribbean and Central America. As the *Trenton Gazette* wrote in 1861, at the outbreak of the rebellion: "Their aim is to found a Southern Empire, which shall be composed on the southern states, Mexico, Central America, and Cuba, of which the arch-conspirators are to be the rulers."

Thus, when a cotton boom developed in the world market during the late forties and fifties, the British, the New York financiers who were the financial middle men for the cotton crop, and the slave-holder planters themselves took advantage of the impotence of the federal government, itself the product of treason and corruption, to launch the foolhardy adventure of secession.

DIRIGISM OF ABRAHAM LINCOLN

Lincoln's Civil War dirigism consisted in a very substantial re-introduction of the Hamiltonian program, begun as soon as the secessionist states had left the Union. Just as Lincoln was taking office, a strong protective tariff was enacted under the guidance of Representative Justin S. Morrill of Vermont, the chairman of the House Committee on Agriculture. The new protectionist Morrill tariff was repeatedly revised upward during the course of the Civil War, until in 1864 it reached an average import levy of 47%, the highest in the history of the nation. This permitted the gearing up of the northern heavy industries that were to produce the world's largest fleet of ironclad warships, masses of cannon balls and armor plate, rifles and all of the other sinews of war. The high tariff was here to stay, and remained a permanent feature of US economic life, guaranteeing at least some progress of industrialization even when other points in the Hamilton program had been removed.

In terms of internal improvements, Lincoln and the Congress launched one of the great enterprises of the day, the transcontinental railroad, begun during the war. In 1862 the Congress chartered the Union Pacific and Central Pacific Railroads, awarding them grants of land along the track that they laid down and loans in government bonds for each mile of track laid. The immense project was completed in 1869, and was soon followed by the Northern Pacific, and the Texas and Pacific lines, built under similar dirigist schemes.

In 1861, Lincoln proposed the building of rail lines into the loyal or reconquered parts of Kentucky, North Carolina, and Tennessee, to permit reconstruction and mineral development to begin there. Carey was behind the proposal for a great north-south railway to supplement the transcontinental one. Thus., the basic American System stress on internal improvements was given new life by Lincoln. A key role was played by the United States military railroad building agency under the German-born engineer Hermann Haupt.

LINCOLN'S GREENBACKS

In finance, despite the presence of the incompetent Secretary of the Treasury Salmon P. Chase, Lincoln was able to undo at least some of the chaos of the post 1837 period. He took the country off the gold standard in the first year of the war, and for the first time issued a paper currency of the federal government which was to be legal tender for all public and private debts (except the payment of import duties and interest on the national debt). These were the famous greenbacks, which were issued inside the country when it became impractical to obtain further loans from the British-dominated foreign capital markets. This policy, if maintained, would have been the key for liberating the country from the baleful effects of the deflationary, monetarist, anti-development nineteenth century gold standard administered by the City of London. Even as it was, the north's ability to finance its own expenses with impunity against the financial warfare forays of London was much increased. The Philadelphia financier Jay Cooke took the lead in organizing war loan drives in a way that provided the model used ever since. At the same time, a national banking system was created which, although it was qualitatively inferior to the BUS, at least remedied the "Independent Treasury" folly of previous decades, gave the government a source of credit.

Federal regulation of bank notes was handled through the National Bank Act, which created the office of the Comptroller of the Currency, who was authorized to charter national banks, which held one third of their capital as US bonds deposited with the Treasury. The greenback national bank notes were issued against these US bonds, up to a value of 90% of their market value. The result of this was to end the era of state bank notes, the funny money that had proliferated after 1837. It is interesting to note that this Act again amounted to a partial monetization of the national debt, making government bonds into a form of money.

Other key dirigist measures of the period included the vast land reform of the Homestead Act of 1862, which gave any person who wanted to become a farmer a quarter of a square mile of land without cost. The Morrill Land Grant Act made grants of public lands to the states to be sold to build up funds for education in agriculture, the mechanic arts, and military training. This led to the establishment of state agricultural colleges which contributed to a high-technology approach to farming. Progress was favored by the growth of domestic heavy industry, and by wartime manpower needs: by 1865, there were about 250,000 of the new McCormick reapers in the US, and King Wheat showed greater international power than King Cotton. The tragedy of the post-war period is that Lincoln was not alive to extend this dirigistic approach to include the rapid industrial development into the devastated south.

POST-1865 DECLINE OF AMERICAN SYSTEM ECONOMICS

The period after the Civil War, in the wake of the assassination of Lincoln, was marked by a great economic boom, but also by a rapid degeneration in the quality of national policy. The war had been won, but the peace was increasingly lost. In retrospect it became clearer that the fatal flaw of the Civil War had been the failure to create a Third BUS to make the greenbacks into the basis for a dirigistic national currency, which could have opened horizons of development superior to those actually attained. The British began their epistemological and financial counter-attack well before Lee's surrender to Grant at Appomattox. Their task was facilitated by the mediocrity of the Union leaders after the war. Grant in particular was susceptible to the Seligman counting house of Wall Street, one of whom was his long-time friend. Otherwise the British-Belmont interest acted through such assets as Treasury Secretary McCulloch and the Treasury's special commissioner on revenue, David A. Wells. Both were free trade advocates.

Incompetent Salmon P. Chase, now chief justice of the supreme court, declared that the greenbacks were illegal as legal tender for debts, and the "sound money" men set up a howl for the return to a hard currency, which meant the dumping of the greenbacks and a return to the British gold standard. Since about 450 million greenback dollars were in circulation, the return to gold could only be accomplished by drastic reduction of the greenbacks, equivalent to a sharp contraction of the overall supply of money and credit. Preparations for a return to the gold standard were thus marked by a severe domestic deflation, guaranteeing that there would be no credit left over for southern reconstruction and southern industrialization, as Lincoln and Carey had planned. The deflation of the sixties and seventies also induced a thirty-year decline in farm prices, manipulated through British control of the world markets. The return to the gold standard did indeed place large parts of the US on a British "cross of gold" as the populist orator William Jennings Bryan later alleged.

AMERICAN POPULISM

The rise of the American Populist movement of the 1890s was influenced by a number of economic, social, and political factors. These included the abrupt truncation of Reconstruction in the former Confederate States of America, the abandonment of Lincoln's successful Civil War dirigism, the return of the United States to a *laissez-faire* regime, and protracted economic crisis. Especially as a result of the ill-considered return to the British gold standard, the US internal market was subjected to the pronounced and sometimes violent fluctuations of the London-centered pound sterling system, which created dislocations and hardships for American farmers in particular. A principal form of middle class property in late nineteenth-century America was the family farm, and it was the family farm that was directly exposed to the depredations of Wall Street and City of London financiers. The populist epoch thus offers striking parallels to the current waning years of the twentieth century, when the middle class household is buffeted by the shifting gales of market globalization, global hot money, and the worldwide runaway shop. The comparison between the "cross of gold" of the 1870s-1890s and the present era of globalization has been made by observers of our contemporary scene. To take just one example, Robert D. Kaplan, a contributing editor of the *Atlantic*, has observed in a recent article that "... there are strong similarities between now and a century ago. In the 1880s and 1890s America experienced great social and economic upheaval." [Kaplan 73]

GREENBACKS OR GOLD ?

Early in the American Civil War, as we have seen, the Lincoln Administration had suspended the redemption of US paper currency in gold and silver, thus terminating the practice known as "specie payment" and taking the country off the gold standard. The gold standard of that time was not a value-neutral, technical arrangement to expedite world trade and development. It was rather the monetary expression of the world supremacy of the British Empire and the British fleet. The removal of the golden fetters was accompanied in February 1862 by the issuance of the United States notes or greenbacks. The greenbacks were legal tender secured by the full faith and credit of the United States government, but not by any specific cache of precious metals. The greenbacks, despite many technical imperfections, provided the US for the first time with a national currency subject to the dirigistic control of the federal government, and not at the mercy of British bankers. The greenbacks were denounced as fiat money by some financiers, and they underwent significant depreciation. But the great virtue of the greenbacks was that they provided abundant capital for investment and production. The Lincoln greenbacks permitted the US victoriously to prosecute the Civil War, and also made possible the highest rates of economic expansion the country had ever known. By the end of the Civil War, the US was well on the way to becoming the greatest industrial power on earth.

The mighty wartime boom that began in 1861 continued undiminished until 1873. The financial panic of that year subsumed a joint effort by rival banks on both sides of the Atlantic to eliminate the firm of Jay Cooke of Philadelphia, the patriotic bankers who had financed Lincoln's war effort and had thus functioned for a time as the de facto national bank. After 1873, the US economy remained depressed for most of the rest of the decade.

POST-1873 GLOBALIZATION

The study of American history later co-authored by John D. Hicks, one of the first great chroniclers of American populism, comments on the Panic of 1873: "Conditions in Europe had much to do with bringing on the depression of 1873. Long before the United States had lost its political isolation, it was very closely tied to the Old World commercially. In this 'one world of finance and trade,' a large-scale reverse abroad was soon reflected in the Western Hemisphere. A sharp panic on the Vienna Bourse in May 1873 inaugurated a general European depression that could not long be kept from America." [Hicks and Mowry 411] This globalization of the late nineteenth century was to a large degree a matter of world export markets, where wheat from Minnesota competed with wheat from the Russian Ukraine, Argentina, or western Europe. The staple market for many of these commodities was London. The gold standard also permitted large-scale international financial flows, including flight capital and speculative hot money.

In the midst of the 1873 depression, a plutocratic backlash against Lincoln's dirigist heritage began to develop. Its centerpiece was the Resumption Act (sometimes called the Specie Resumption Act), which was passed by a Republican-dominated Congress early in 1875. This law, which was signed by President Grant, directed the Secretary of the Treasury to build up the government's gold reserve in order to prepare for a return to gold convertibility of greenbacks on January 1, 1879. This measure had been sponsored by Senator John Sherman of Ohio, the brother of the celebrated general.

In 1877, John Sherman became Secretary of the Treasury in the Republican Hayes administration, and thus received the task of carrying out the legislation he himself had authored. Hayes and Sherman came to power in the wake of the disputed election of 1876, in which neither Republican Hayes nor the Democratic governor of New York, Samuel J. Tilden, had received a majority. The election was accordingly thrown into the House of Representatives and then referred to a special Electoral Commission. The resolution of this constitutional crisis in favor of Hayes entailed as an evident *quid pro quo* the withdrawal of federal troops from the southern states, allowing a full restoration of the pro-Confederate local oligarchs, who quickly proceeded to exploit sharecroppers and tenant farmers irrespective of race, deny black voting rights, institute Jim Crow segregation and otherwise violate the XIV and XV amendments to the Constitution. The Republicans kept power in Washington, but only by betraying the ideals of the cause which Lincoln had championed. From this point on, oligarchical tendencies in the Washington government steadily increased. One example of this was the brutal crushing by federal troops of the railroad strike during the summer of 1877 – a turning point on the order of Reagan's destruction of the air traffic controllers' union.

GOLD RESUMPTION

The main result of the Resumption Act was a period of prolonged deflation. Dollars, in other words, got more and more expensive, and would buy more and more goods. This was a secular trend, with the dollar rising from an index value of 100 in 1865, through various peaks and valleys, to 300 by 1895. This severe and relentless deflation, which has definite parallels in our own epoch of globalization, was probably the biggest single factor in the genesis of populism. For the bondholder, the lender, and the rentier, the long deflation was a colossal bonanza. At one moment of Union defeatism during 1864, the value of a paper greenback had fallen to 39 cents of a dollar gold piece. When Lee surrendered at Appomattox, a greenback had risen to 67 gold cents. By the close of the war, some $2 billion in US government securities were outstanding, which of course had been purchased at prices reflecting these greenback discounts. Bankers who had bought government bonds with 50 cent dollars could now exact payment in dollars worth 100 cents, or later 150 cents. The bankers claimed that they bought Union bonds on the unspoken assumption that they would be redeemed at "par," meaning in gold. British and New York financial circles discovered deep ethical and moral issues at stake in the proposed return to "sound money." Their propaganda stressed that the nation's long-term financial stability hinged on the return to "honest money." They also elevated the expected windfall to a matter of national honor. Naturally, it was the American taxpayer who would be called upon to make good the difference between the cheap dollars lent and the gold dollars to be repaid.

FARM DEPRESSION

The impact of Resumption on the American farmer was devastating. One of the great achievements of the Lincoln era had been the Homestead Act of 1862, sponsored by Rep. Justin S. Morrill of Vermont. This law, a classic example of dirigistic economic development and one of the high points of the American spirit, provided that any person over 21 years of age or the head of a household, be they alien or citizen, could receive title to a farm of 160 acres free of charge out of the public lands of the United States, if they were prepared to reside upon it and carry on cultivation for five years. This law had been blocked for years by the pro-slavery party, but secession had removed this impediment. The Homestead Act stimulated immigration from Europe and helped increase wheat production. It was the key to promoting settlement in the arid areas of the high plains west of the 100th meridian - the American steppe. Gold resumption effectively betrayed the aspirations of the pioneers who had braved poverty and hardship to push back the frontier by building their little huts on the prairie.

The farmer who had mortgaged his farm to buy one of the new McCormick reapers or carry out other capital improvements found that the dollars he was required to pay back were worth far more in terms of head of livestock or bushels of grain or corn than the dollars he had borrowed. Debts became dearer and farm prices declined, and the farmer was crushed in between. If farmers tried to borrow more to avoid bankruptcy, they found that interest rates that were impossibly high. Many farmers succumbed to what was in effect a process of primitive accumulation carried out by finance capital at their expense. Soon there were efforts to use political means to halt the implacable march of deflation. The Greenback Party advocated a further issue of paper currency, and in 1878 it polled over a million votes and elected 15 members of Congress. Others tried to agitate for bimetallism, meaning an increase in the money supply through increased silver coinage. But pro-silver and anti-deflation forces discovered that the Coinage Act of 1873 had terminated US minting of silver coins. Proto-populist sentiment was aroused by denunciations of this "Crime of '73" on the part of the "international gold ring" or "Anglo-American gold trust" and the "money power." Opponents of free silver assailed the silverites for their alleged appeal to dishonesty and cheating.

GROVER CLEVELAND SELLS OUT TO WALL STREET

A very severe US depression under conditions of gold convertibility began with the Panic of 1893, which was set off by a rapid fall in the unprotected US gold reserves. The Panic of 1893, which came at the beginning of Democrat Grover Cleveland's second term, was in turn a by product of a financial crash in Europe: "From 1889, and particularly after the so-called 'Baring panic' of 1890 in England, all Europe had recorded subnormal business conditions; indeed, one reason for the depletion of the American gold reserve was the withdrawal of foreign capital from investment in America in order to bolster up the waning fortunes of European enterprise." [Hicks and Mowry 524] US gold stocks kept falling during all of 1893 and 1894, posing the threat that the country would be forced into default. In 1894 Secretary of the Treasury Carlisle made a journey to New

York to beg a group of Wall Street Bankers - Stillman, Woodward, Stuart, and King - to buy Treasury bonds for gold. Faced with a similar crisis in 1933, Franklin D. Roosevelt unhesitatingly assumed sovereign control of the monetary destiny of the country by abandoning the gold standard, and by resisting efforts to re-impose it.

Grover Cleveland did the opposite: he sacrificed the national economy to monetarist ideology and oligarchical interest. He secured the repeal of a law which had allowed some small-scale silver coinage. August Belmont, dean of British Wall Street agents, then brokered the government's surrender to J.P. Morgan. Morgan met with President Cleveland and demanded that, in return for his procuring of gold from Britain in order to replenish the Treasury reserves, the Treasury make a private contract with the British-backed Morgan syndicate. Cleveland accepted Morgan's offer, which was yielded windfall profits for the Morgan syndicate. In February 1895, by the terms of Cleveland's deal with the two dominant Wall Street firms of Belmont and J.P. Morgan, these financiers received the astounding privilege of buying a large issues of US Treasury securities at a price well below the market. The essence of Morgan's service was that he would prevent increased demand for payment from New York, including demands for gold. It was a kind of private stand-still agreement. "In return for a handsome profit, the bankers agreed to procure half the needed gold from abroad, and to use their influence to prevent further withdrawal of gold from the Treasury. By thus 'selling out to Wall Street,' as the enraged silverites described the deal, Cleveland was able to maintain the gold standard, but his popularity with the debtor South and West dropped completely out of sight." [Hicks and Mowry 525]

Cleveland huddling with Belmont and Morgan partners, lining their pockets out of the public till, and urging them to use their influence in London to prevent a run on Treasury gold stocks – all that would appear to fulfill the definition of conspiracy under the United States Code. The answer to this crisis would have been greenbacks and the Fourth BUS, but by this time the Hamiltonian party had virtually ceased to exist. Cleveland's capitulation to Morgan and thus to London set the stage for the Federal Reserve Act of 1913, when the desires for the British banking oligarchy were codified as US law by Paul Warburg.

CLEVELAND CAFÉS

The same Cleveland who rewarded the Belmont and Morgan counting houses with public funds and the control of the US public debt was simultaneously opposed to measures of relief for stricken farmers and workers. Cleveland, like Jackson, provides a small sample of what can happen when a US President responds to a crisis in a disastrous fashion. In 1894, when Kansas farmers were literally starving to death, Cleveland's Secretary of Agriculture pontificated that "the intelligent, practical, and successful farmer needs no aid from the Government. The ignorant, impractical, and indolent farmer deserves none." [McMath 182] In the 1930s the shantytowns built by destitute and homeless men were known as "Hoovervilles." After the Panic of 1893, California unemployed began to call the soup kitchens where charity was dispensed to them "Cleveland cafes." Just as Hoover was blamed for the depression of the 1930s, Cleveland was justly held responsible for the debacle of the 1890s. The Hoover depression kept the Republicans out of the White House for twenty years; the Cleveland depression made the Democrats the party of economic calamity and kept them out of the White House for 40 years, except for the 1912 and 1916 victories of Woodrow Wilson, each of which was made possible by extraordinary circumstances, including a split in the Republican Party and an unprecedented World War.

ATTACKS ON THE POPULISTS

Populism has been slandered first of all by discontented reactionaries seeking to find ways of attacking the Roosevelt New Deal at its roots. Their argument was that populism was a precursor of fascism. More serious was the attack on populism by Richard Hofstadter, which appears in retrospect as an artifact of the Cold War backlash against agitation and protest. In his *Age of Reform: From Bryan to FDR* (1955), Hofstadter leveled a series of less than substantiated charges against the populists. Hofstadter wrote: "By 'Populism' I do not mean only the People's (or Populist) Party of the 1890's; for I consider the Populist Party to be merely a heightened expression, at a particular moment in time, of a kind of popular impulse that is endemic in American political culture." [Hofstadter 4] Hofstadter presented samples of populist rhetoric and analysis which he did not prove to be representative. He taxed the populists with xenophobia and racism, although he did not attempt to show that the populists were any more racist in practice than Republicans, Democrats, or the American society of that era in general. He tended to suggest that the populists expanded into something resembling an atomized mass society, despite that fact that late nineteenth century America was permeated by voluntary associations from the husking bee to the Grange. Decades before Chubais, Hofstadter tried to suggest that the populists were somehow "dysfunctional," marginal losers who might have protested any financial system. Hofstadter seemed to depend on theoretical constructs from Émile Durkheim, including the assumption that the natural state of society is harmony and that protest is an irrational response to change. In effect, he stigmatized the victims. Hofstadter attempted to account for populism not on the grounds of economic distress and the demand for economic justice, nor of farmbelt culture and politics, but rather of status panic and status envy:

> Rank in society! That was close to the heart of the matter, for the farmer was beginning to realize acutely not merely that the best of the world's goods were to be had in the city...but also that he was losing in status and self-respect as compared with [urbanites]. [Hofstadter cited by McMath, 12)

"There was in fact a widespread idea," commented Hofstadter, "that all American history since the Civil War could be understood as a sustained conspiracy of the international money power." [Hofstadter 70] Hofstadter treated the populists as *prima facie* paranoids because they some of them alleged that the Bank of England or certain London financiers had acted conjointly and covertly to secure a return of the US to the unalloyed gold standard, both for personal profit and for the larger strategic goal of preventing the economic power of the US from outstripping that of England. He liquidated the issues posed by the "Crime of '73" issue as the "standard greenback-silverite myth concerning that event." [Hofstadter 76] He implied that all of these charges are simply too fantastic to be seriously examined, and he certainly did nothing to examine them. Today's student of these matters, knowing something of the escapades of Lord Montagu Norman, Benjamin Strong, Hjalmar Schacht, and the central bankers' cabal of the 1920s, as well as of George Soros in the 1990s, is hardly likely to be so dismissive in this regard. Hofstadter thus neatly ducked the main issues of the time he was describing.

With his frequent recourse to charges of "paranoia," Hofstadter opened wide the door for subsequent neo-conservatives who prefer to vilify protest movements rather than debate them, especially when arbitrary class privilege is called into question. Hofstadter nevertheless conceded: "Populism was the first modern political movement of practical importance in the United States to insist that the federal government has some importance for the common weal; ... Most of the 'radical' reforms in the Populist program proved in later years to be either harmless or useful. In at least one important area of American life, a few Populist leaders in the South attempted something profoundly humane – to build a popular movement that would cut across the old barriers of race – until persistent use of the Negro bogy [by rival Democrats] distracted their following." [Hofstadter 61]

Andrew Jackson had campaigned on the slogan "equal rights to all, special privilege to none," which remained a populist byword. A more important populist source was Henry J. Carey. Carey's school was sometimes called "producerism," since it saw a harmony of interest between labor and productive capital against their common adversary, the finance capitalist. The work of Bruce Laurie has attempted to show that Carey's producerism, also known as radical republicanism, "remained the most powerful organizing principle of working-class consciousness in American throughout most of the nineteenth century." [McMath 53] American family farmers of the late nineteenth century were no longer on the same high level of literacy and even of classical education which had been enjoyed by the revolutionary "Latin farmers" of Massachusetts in 1775-6, but these were also not by any stretch of the imagination illiterate and benighted peasants gathering for a *jacquerie*. Although the Populist movement never produced a Lincoln, many populists came from the same type of environment which had produced a Lincoln.

THE FARMERS' ALLIANCE OF 1886: OUTLAW DERIVATIVES

Populism as an organized movement and political party can be traced to the 1877 Texas founding of the Farmers' Alliance, which emerged from earlier strongholds of the declining Greenback Party, with some anti-monopoly influences also coming from the Knights of Labor, the first large-scale American labor union. The first annual meeting of the Farmers' Alliance was held in Cleburne Texas in August 1886. A political platform approved at Cleburne included: support for cooperatives; the issuance of greenbacks; equal protection for labor and capital; reserving land for settlers, not speculators; the establishment of a National Bureau of Labor Statistics; payment of wages in legal tender; mechanics' and laborers' liens; prohibition of prison contract labor; banning futures trading in farm commodities; the removal of illegal fences; an Interstate Commerce Commission to regulate the railroads; and bimetallic reflation through the "minting of silver and gold to full capacity and offering both without discrimination." [McMath 79-80] The BLS and ICC later became reality; the ban on farm futures was partially enacted in 1936 and remained in place until the Reagan era.

PLATO: POPULIST

The term "populist" derives from the People's Party of the United States, the organizing committee for which may be considered as having been formally constituted at Cincinnati, Ohio in May 1891. During their long train ride home, some members of the Kansas delegation discussed the need for a more succinct label for their movement. Recalling the Latin word *populus*, meaning people, they coined the term "populist" which became the characteristic adjective for the new movement. So perhaps there were still Latin farmers in 1890s America after all.

Those who supported greenbacks and reflation reached all the way back to Plato, whom they portrayed as a supporter of fiat money. This economic school was called cartalism. ("Cartalism, which dates back at least to Plato, is the antithesis of metallism, asserting that the value of money is not derived from the commodity value of metals (or other commodities) into which it is convertible." [Goodwyn 698] The relevant passage is from Plato's *Laws:* "With these injunctions goes also a further law by which no possession of gold or silver is permitted to any private man, but only a currency for the purpose of daily exchange, such as is hardly to be avoided by craftsmen or any whose business it is to pay wages in such a kind to wage earners, whether slaves or alien settlers; whence we shall lay it down that they must have an internal currency, of value at home but worthless abroad." (V, 742) This may qualify Plato as the first populist.

Western wheat growers were exploited in particular by the railroads. These railroads had been built with the dirigistic help of the states and the federal government, including extensive land grants along their right of way which the rail companies then sold to farmers at exorbitant prices. The railroads, turning their back on any notion of social responsibility, gouged the farmers mercilessly to transport their goods to market: short-haul freight, where the railroad held a monopoly position, was often more expensive than longer-haul freight over the same tracks in the same direction, since here some competition might be operative. Southern farmers were often sharecroppers who worked all year to turn part of their harvest over to the landlord, only to be told that their debt had increased because of low prices and high interest.

To all of these groups the Farmers' Alliance had undoubted appeal. When Kansas and Dakota groupings joined the original Texas-centered group, the name was changed to National Farmers' Alliance and Industrial Union. The platform of the expanded group called for the nationalization and public ownership of the railroads, not just their regulation. (This demand was later fulfilled under Richard Nixon.) There was also a demand, proposed by Charles Macune, for federal sub-treasuries. This was a plan to fight the power of agricultural cartels, bankers, brokers, and middlemen with the help of government intervention. It also aimed at saving the farm cooperatives from being strangled by lack of affordable credit, something that was already putting many of the cooperatives into bankruptcy liquidation. The plan called for warehouses to be created by the federal government in numerous localities, including virtually every important farm county. In these sub-treasuries non-perishable farm commodities might be deposited by farmers, and become the collateral for 12 month, 1% interest loans equivalent to 80% of the momentary market price or "local current value" of these goods. The populists referred to 1% interest as "money at cost," meaning that 1% was seen as the basic cost of administering a loan. The loans would be made in US Treasury notes, thus creating a new source of currency creation independent of the workings of the gold market. This was expected to provide a modest reflation. Later, land loans were included among the functions demanded of the sub-treasuries. Land loans were credit lines equal to 80% of the value of holdings of 200 acres or less, up to a ceiling of $3,000, payable over as much as 50 years at interest of 2%.

POPULIST REFLATION DEMANDS

The land loan plan was advanced with the announced policy goal of fostering an expansion of the circulating currency outside banks by $50 per person. The actual levels of currency per capita during the 1890s generally ranged between $14 and $15, with a low of $12 in 1896 and a high of $16 in 1900, possibly reflecting the war with Spain. In the event, US currency in circulation did not reach $50 per capita until 1940. The sub-treasury plan would thus have engendered a currency expansion of 300% to 400%. According to the appraisal offered by Duke University economics professor William P. Yohe, such a currency growth might have produced a one-shot inflationary surge of almost 250%, followed by 10 years of downward drift in prices. Yohe found that the populists could have attained their goal of significant reflation with a per capita currency issue smaller than the one they were stipulating. Activating the printing press to get to $50 at once he called "overkill." Yohe sums up his evaluation of Macune's sub-treasury plan as follows: "Theoretically sound as it was, however, the sub-treasury concept constituted a working basis for the monetary system, even considering the unnecessary margin of inflation its advocates were willing to tolerate. It would have achieved what its supporters claimed – real income distribution in favor of 'the producing classes.' " [Goodwyn 580]

THE POPULIST ORIGIN OF PARITY PRICES: MACUNE

Charles Macune was "America's foremost agrarian monetary theorist of the nineteenth century, the father of large-scale cooperation, commodity credit, delayed commodity marketing, and thus, of a number of the eventual doctrines of farm parity." [Goodwyn 567] Farm parity refers to the concept, embodied in New Deal and later farm legislation, that the government must maintain a support price for farm commodities which will permit the producer to realize sufficient income to cover the costs of production, plus ideally a profit to be re-invested in capital improvements and modernization. Farm parity is based on the simple idea that future supply of farm products cannot be guaranteed if the market price is allowed to fall permanently below the costs of production. During World War II, when food was needed for the war effort, farm prices were sometimes raised to 110% of parity in a successful effort to stimulate production. According to a recent appreciation of Macune's work, his

> sub-treasury system achieved something the Federal Reserve Act of 1913 utterly failed to achieve – a system whereby the government could serve as the lender of last resort as a means of maintaining a flexible and workable monetary system. Above all, Macune's plan brought the nation's monetary system under democratic control and gave millions of citizens access to capital at low interest – an achievement that promised to expand the human possibilities of the entire society. The sub-treasury system was the ideological culmination both of nineteenth-century greenback theory and of the cooperative crusade of the National Alliance. It offered 'the whole class' of farmers a way out of peonage .... the sub-treasury system was a culturally inadmissible idea – in the 1890's, as today. Any system involving the termination of the gold standard was unthinkable to the nation's financial and political elites of the 1890's .... Indeed, the very idea of democratic influence over interest rates through a central bank of sufficient capital and currency issuing power is one that points to an important loss of economic privilege by those very financial elites who consolidated their political and cultural power in the 1890's and retain it with augmented authority today.... This causal relationship is, of course, completely outside the received intellectual transactions dominant in American graduate schools in both history and economics. [Goodwyn 567-8]

Goodwyn also commented that "culturally, it has not been considered good manners in the American academy to draw critical attention to bankers." [569] Discussing the failure of the populists to force though the sub-treasury system, he comments that

> to implement such a plan, however, its political supporters in the capitalist world would have to overcome the received culture of mass deference to bankers and the lobbying power of bankers themselves, both in American and in Europe.... The last politically active theorists who were culturally autonomous enough to grapple, as an intellectual challenge, directly with organic monetary problems and theory, were politically defeated and culturally isolated eighty years ago. Their names were Charles Macune and Harry Tracy." [Goodwyn 570]

Even so, a part of the sub-treasury idea became reality with the creation of the Federal Farm Loan Act and the Warehouse Act of 1916. This was when Woodrow Wilson was interested not just in getting re-elected, but also in procuring the support of the anti-war farmers for intervention into the European war on the side of the despised British. Wilson also knew that he needed vast food resources in order to wage war. The Southerner Macune always refused to break with the Democratic Party because he supported racial segregation. This racism proved to be his fatal flaw. But this made him no more of a racist than Grover Cleveland, Woodrow Wilson, or Ku Klux Klan member Harry Truman, to all of whom a different standard is applied.

Another important populist gathering too place in February 1892 in St. Louis. Here the keynote speech was provided by Ignatius Donnelly of Minnesota, a leading populist orator and intellectual. Donnelly evoked a serious crisis in the national life of the United States:

> We meet in the midst of a nation brought to the verge of moral, political, and material ruin. Corruption dominates the ballot box, the legislatures, the Congress, and touches even the ermine of the bench. The people are demoralized. Many of the States have been compelled to isolate the voters at the polling places in order to prevent universal intimidation or bribery. The newspapers are subsidized or muzzled; public opinion silenced; business prostrate; our homes covered with mortgages, labor impoverished, and the land concentrating in the hands of capitalists. The urban workmen are denied the right of organization for self-protection; imported pauperized labor beats down their wages; a hireling standing army, unrecognized by our laws, is established to shoot them down, and they are rapidly disintegrating to European conditions. The fruits of the toil of millions are boldly stolen to build up colossal fortunes, unprecedented in the history of the world, while their possessors despise the republic and endanger liberty. From the same prolific womb of government injustice we breed two great classes – paupers and millionaires. In this crisis of human affairs the intelligent working people of the United States have come together in the name of justice, order, and society, to defend liberty, prosperity, and justice. We declare our union and our independence. We assert one purpose to support the political organization which represents our principles. We charge that the controlling influences dominating the old political parties have allowed the existing dreadful conditions to develop without serious effort to restrain or prevent them. They have agreed together to ignore in the coming campaign every issue but one. They propose to drown the cries of a plundered people with the uproar of a sham battle over the tariff, so that corporations, national banks, rings, trusts, 'watered stocks,' the demonetization of silver, and the oppression of usurers, may all be lost sight of...."[Goodwyn 265-6, McMath 161-2]

Donnelly was adamant that the government had to be the instrument of popular action against abuses by private interests. He emphatically endorsed an activist government: "We believe that the powers of government – in other words, of the people – should be expanded... as rapidly and as far as the good sense of an intelligent people and the teachings of experience shall justify, to the end that oppression, injustice, and poverty shall eventually cease in the land." [McMath 168]

POPULIST PRECURSORS OF THE NEW DEAL

In June 1892, the Democratic National Convention refused to reflect any farmers' demands in its platform, and then went on to nominate former President Grover Cleveland for the presidency. The People's Party thereupon convoked its own national convention in Omaha, Nebraska on July 4, 1892. James B. Weaver of Iowa, a former Union general and the 1880 Greenback presidential candidate, was nominated for the presidency, with Confederate veteran James G. Field for vice president. Neither man had any long- standing connection to the populist movement. The 1892 Populist platform included:

* reflation, through a combination of "free and unlimited coinage of silver at the ratio of sixteen to one" plus paper issue so that the money supply could "be speedily increased to not less than fifty dollars per capita."

* government ownership and management of railroads and telephone and telegraph systems.

* return to the governments of public lands granted to railroads and other corporations "in excess of their actual needs," with these lands being distributed for homesteads.

* prohibition of land ownership by foreigners.

* introduction of the sub-treasury system.

* Australian or secret ballot in elections. This was accomplished.

*graduated income tax. This became the XVI Amendment to the Constitution, ratified in 1913.

*postal savings banks. These were created, but abolished during the 1970s. Postal savings is a big issue in Japan today, with the financiers demanding that it be abolished.

* government regulation of the working day. Laws of this type were later passed in many states.

*legislative initiative and referendum for voters. Together with the primary election, these became a part of the "Wisconsin idea" of Republican Senator Robert La Follette and were widely enacted, for example in California.

*Direct election of US Senators, which at this time were still chosen by state legislatures. This was enacted with the XVII Amendment to the Constitution, ratified in 1913.

*A one-term limit for President and Vice President. A two-term limit was enacted with the XXII Amendment to the Constitution, enacted in 1947.

In the southern states, the Populists were mercilessly race-baited by the Democrats, who accused the new party of threatening to put an end to white supremacy by weakening or toppling the Democratic Party. Vote fraud was frequently used by Democratic machines to quell populist opposition.

In the 1892 presidential vote, the Democrat Cleveland swept the Solid South. Populists made limited inroads among eastern workers and small proprietors, averaging only about 5%. The Populist Weaver received more than a million votes and carried Kansas, Colorado, Nevada, and Idaho, and received a share of the electoral votes of North Dakota and Oregon. This made 22 electoral votes, and a third party had broken into the Electoral College for the first time since 1860. Populist governors were elected in Kansas and Colorado. A handful of Populists joined the House and the Senate in Washington.

RACISM: ACHILLES HEEL OF THE 1890s POPULISTS

The problem which the Populists were never able to resolve was racism, especially in the Old South and Texas. The Democratic Party was the bulwark of white supremacy and racial segregation. If the southern populists were to desert the Democrats, then racial equality might follow. This issue, as noted, was the main weapon of the oligarchical Bourbon Democrats against the Populists. It was clear that even if the Populists succeeded in taking control of the Democratic Party in the Southern states, this would not suffice to seize power in the national Democratic party. Many Southern Populists stayed inside the Democratic Party despite this blind alley. In the end, this proved to be an insuperable obstacle for further Populist growth. [157]

As economic depression deepened under Cleveland in 1994, a wealthy pro-greenback Ohio businessman named Jacob Coxey organized a march of the unemployed on Washington DC. Coxey demanded that the federal government fight the depression by launching a massive program of public works, hiring the unemployed to build roads and infrastructure at a wage rate of $1.50 per day, to be financed by an issue of $500 million in greenbacks. Coxey initially received much favorable publicity, but when his group reached Washington, they were brutally dispersed by the Cleveland regime. When he got out of jail, Coxey went home to run for Congress as a Populist. But here again, the populist movement can be seen as the incubator for the later New Deal and for what would be seen today as Keynesian counter-cyclical measures.

---

[157] Some of the most racist populist leaders, like Tom Watson, had started off supporting black and white cross-racial political alliances.

In the 1894 elections, the total Populist vote was 40% larger than it had been in 1892. In the decisive presidential year of 1896, the Republican platform adamantly rejected free silver coinage "except by international agreement with the leading commercial nations of the world," another anticipation of supernational globalization. The Republican nominee was William McKinley, a supporter of the high protective tariff. A group of "Silver Republicans" defected. The Democratic Party, universally execrated because of the Cleveland depression, experienced a profound internal crisis. Powerful silver mining interests used their wealth to assume power, and they dictated the nomination of William Jennings Bryan of Nebraska, who had borrowed much of the Populist rhetoric along with the demand for free silver. Donnelly said of Bryan: "We put him to school, and he wound up by stealing the schoolbooks." Bryan's stock speech included the classic peroration: "You shall not press down upon the brow of labor this crown of thorns, you shall not crucify mankind upon a cross of gold." The Democratic platform also protested the "absorption of wealth by the few," and demanded increased federal regulation of railroads and trusts.

Many veteran Populist leaders protested against the degradation of the movement's program to the single issue of silver, but the Populist Party convention nominated Bryan for President, plus the Georgia Populist landowner Tom Watson for Vice President. In the crucial election of 1896, Bryan won the farm and mountain states along with the Solid South, but McKinley triumphed in the northeast and California, thus winning the electoral college 271-176. The wave of jingoism around the Spanish-American War effectively terminated the presidential hopes of the Populist Party, which had ceased to exist before World War I started. Bryan went on to become Secretary of State for Woodrow Wilson; he was dumped when he opposed war with Germany.

The Populists offer the classic case of a much vituperated third party which failed to upset the power monopoly of the two-party system, but whose ideas later become reality. Many Populist ideas came to full fruition with the New Deal of Franklin D. Roosevelt. The Populist movement proved to be a decisive source for ideas about economic reform, at a time when pro-business academic economists tended to act as sterile apologists for the abuses of the status quo.

THE DEMAGOGY OF CULTURAL POPULISM: THE LEE ATWATER WEDGE ISSUE THEORY

Some modern critics of populism attempt to blame this movement for a series of disparate and unrelated phenomena ranging from the anti-communist witch hunt of Senator Joe McCarthy to the Bush asset Rush Limbaugh. There is little resemblance, and what resemblance there is based on political counter-insurgency strategies which depend on the cynical appropriation of populist rhetoric. The McCarthy red scare was a top-down bureaucratic-authoritarian campaign of ostracism and intimidation that was carried out by the FBI, Congressional investigating committees, Manhattan lawyers, press and radio barons, parts of the Catholic and Protestant clergy, union bosses, and other elite circles. Public opinion went along with the witch-hunt, which simply showed that the planned intimidation of the public had succeeded. McCarthyism was an artificial ingredient in a general campaign to break the postwar US strike wave, while eroding the FDR national political coalition. To use the category of populism to attempt to analyze 1890s farm economists together with 1950s wealthy urban red-baiting and union-busting lawyers reduces the whole notion of populism to an absurdity.

A ruling class like the American one, which has delivered a quarter century of declining real wages, de-industrialization, and permanent racial ghettoes, is inevitably going to be the target of widespread criticism and discontent. One way to deflect this discontent is to sponsor a series of domesticated populist-sounding spokesmen. The right-wing Moral Majority of the 1980s, with Jerry

Falwell and Pat Robertson, took advantage of Democratic elitism to portray itself as populist. Ronald Reagan sounded many cultural populist themes, but he also presided over the rout of the US labor movement and the greatest government-promoted upward redistribution of wealth in recent American history. Ross Perot's speeches borrowed much from the young Mussolini, and he had a Texarkana populist twang, but his economic nostrums reflected the interests of the rich rentiers and bondholders, and were no different than the recommendations of the Federal Reserve.

The crucial distinction turns out to be the one between cultural or social issues populism on the one hand, and economic populism on the other. The authenticity of economic populism is easy to determine. Cultural and social populism easily lends itself to counter-insurgency and demagogy, as we have seen in the case of the racist Southern Democrats. Bush's election strategist Lee Atwater is responsible for the most coherent formulation of demagogic cultural populism, which he developed in his theory of the *wedge issue*. Working as an adviser to the South Carolina Republican Senator Strom Thurmond, Atwater was confronted again and again with the task of winning elections in the face of a dominant Democratic Party coalition. Atwater's preferred weapon was the wedge issue (or "hot button social issue") which could be demagogically exploited in order to split the Democrats and allow the Republicans to prevail. This strategy depended on keeping economics off the table as much as possible, while attacking the Democrats for the upper-class cultural tendencies (such as those of "limousine liberals") which have became pronounced since 1968, and which are emphatically rejected by most Americans.

Examples of successful wedge issues include: jingoistic patriotism (used by Nixon in 1972 ("the Silent Majority," plus the 1970 Agnew "effete snobs" and "nattering nabobs of negativism" speeches, written by Buchanan and Safire) and by Bush in 1988, whose campaign was based on the pledge of allegiance to the flag); abortion; school prayer; gun control; anti-government and pro-business rhetoric; strikes by public employees or by those providing public services (from the Taft-Hartley Act to Reagan's union-busting); special dispensations for homosexuals, lesbians, and others; multiculturalism; and many more. The most basic wedge issue in America involves skin color and race, playing blacks against whites while oligarchs and plutocrats exploit workers of both races and feed at the public trough. Cultural populist wedge issues have been the primary tool for breaking up the FDR national interest coalition of big city machines, Southern Democrats, labor unions, blacks and racial minorities, senior citizens, defense contractors, intellectuals, farmers, and small businessmen. As Atwater said, "Populists have always been liberal on economics. So long as the crucial issues were generally confined to economics – as during the New Deal – the liberal candidate would expect to get most of the populist vote. But populists are conservatives on most social issues.... When social and cultural issues died down, the populists were left with no compelling reason to vote Republican." [158]

Owing to the effects of the wedge issues and of multiculturalism, US public awareness of the rudiments of the American System of economics reached a new low during the Reagan-Bush years.

---

[158] Lee Atwater, "The South in 1984," unpublished memo for the Reagan-Bush campaign, quoted in Thomas Byrne Edsall and Mary D. Edsall, *Chain Reaction: The Impact of Race, Rights, and Taxes on American Politics* (New York: Norton, 1990), p. 221, cited by Lind, 185.

XI. SELF-DEFENSE IN THE CRISIS

Rocco: Hat man nicht auch Gold beineben, Kann man nicht ganz glücklich sein.
-Beethoven, *Fidelio*, Act I.[159]

Before you decide to do anything, there is one thing that you must realize: your broker or banker and the lawyers that may work with them cannot be trusted to safeguard your interests. They may be expected to attempt to load you with exactly the kind of paper, including mutual funds and other derivatives, that will become worthless most rapidly when the final panic starts.

CAVEAT: NEVER TRUST A BROKER

Take for example Bankers Trust, the Morgan-controlled bank which is no longer a bank making loans to agriculture and industry, but rather resembles a bucket shop interested in selling its own proprietary products – especially designer derivatives – to money managers for governments and corporations. Let us examine, as a case study, the "culture" of Bankers Trust when dealing with *Fortune* 500-class clients which can command a much better deal than a small investor ever could. It was back in November 1993 that Bankers Trust sold a leveraged and complex derivative product to Procter & Gamble Co., which supposedly makes soap. Two Bankers Trust managers were discussing whether P&G had walked into the deal with their eyes open. "They would never know," says one BT woman on the tape. "They would never be able to know how much money was taken out of that." The money in question was the big profit BT stood to rake in. "Never, no way, no way," says another BT officer. "That's the beauty of Bankers Trust." This conversation was recorded by an internal taping system installed at the bank, whose employees apparently did not learn the lesson of the Nixon White House. After being billed by Bankers Trust for almost $200 million in losses, P&G decided to sue Bankers Trust. In court papers alleging a "culture of greed and duplicity" on the part of BT, P&G quoted other passages from the now-notorious Bankers Trust tapes.

In one discussion, a BT employee talks about a possible derivatives transaction among BT, IBM, and Sony, announcing that "what Bankers Trust can do for Sony and IBM is get in the middle and rip them off – take a little money." An internal BT document discussing a derivatives deal with Federal Paper Board Co. allegedly says that BT would get a $1.6 million profit, including a "7 [basis point] rip-off factor." In another discussion, two BT bankers talk about a client's loss, and one suggests that the other "Pad the number a little bit." In another confab, one BT banker says to the other, "Funny business, you know? Lure people into that calm and then just totally f**k 'em."

Yet another BT banker describes the investment portfolio of one of his clients: "If this ever comes out in the press, it is the most insane mess of trading I've ever, ever seen....they just kept trying to trade them out of losses...Everything they put in [the client's portfolio] lost." When things began to go wrong, P&G was told by Bankers Trust that its profit or loss on the derivatives deal would be determined by a proprietary computer model for determining price which Bankers Trust would not disclose. P&G would have to take their word for it, and pay whatever loss Bankers Trust chose to pull out of its hat.

In February 1994 P&G bought a second derivative "product." The tell-tale tapes recorded a post-deal exchange between two BT bankers: "Do they [P&G] understand that? What they did?" asks

---

[159] From the libretto by Joseph Sonnleithner and Friedrich Treitschke, 1804.

one. The second banker: "No. They understand what they did but they don't understand the leverage, no." Later this second banker appears as paying P&G only half of what an option transaction is really worth. "This could be a massive future gravy train. This is a wet dream," gloats the Bankers Trust officer. In dealing with another firm, a taped segment has one BT banker planning for a presentation to a client: "...what we show them is gonna be kind of baloney." [160]

Now, if this is the kind of treatment given to large and well-known companies like Procter & Gamble, Federal Paper Board, and Gibson Greeting Cards, what hope could a mere small investor have for fair treatment? You might also take advice from an insurance salesman. If you do, you had better recall the "misleading and improper" sales practices of the Prudential Life Insurance Company. Under the decision of a New Jersey federal court made on March 7, 1997 and later published in various newspapers, persons who bought so-called "whole life insurance policies" from Prudential are entitled to a Remediation Plan if they feel they were misled regarding "the use of policy values to purchase a new policy, sales of life insurance as an investment product (and not primarily as life insurance), the number of premium payments you would have to make, or the use of the policy's dividends or policy values to reduce out-of-pocket premium payments." As we approach the breakdown crisis, listening to advice like this could very well wipe out all your assets, with scant hope of a class action suit later on.

Back in 1929, insolvent brokers were reputed to end it all by jumping from skyscrapers. At the end of the century, troubled brokers are more likely to abscond, and less willing to lose their lives. Jack Burlbaugh of Rockville, Maryland ran Currency Management Inc., a small financial firm specializing in foreign currency futures. In July 1998 he became insolvent, left his wife, flew to Europe, and disappeared. Burlbaugh had given an interview to *Futures* magazine some time before, recounting that he was engaged in defensive hedging or overlay strategies involving the dollar and the South Korean won. Like Marc Rich, Burlbaugh was apparently hiding out in Switzerland. He wrote a letter saying, "I am sorry" to his office manager, who was suing him. Burlbaugh's clients were left holding the bag to the tune of $3 million. His wife began selling his 8 Argentinian polo ponies to pay the bills. Many other brokers will be going over the hill in the weeks and months to come. Many will be holding reunions in the bars of Geneva and Lausanne, if their money holds up. The atmosphere may be reminiscent of the Ritz Bar in the F. Scott Fitzgerald's "The Crack-Up." But it is better not to join the ranks of Jack Burlbaugh's clients. [161]

As the storm clouds gather and the skies darken, **the only way to lower risk is to get out of the stock market, and stay out**. Staying out may prove to be just as important as getting out. The legendary hedge fund operator Jesse Livermore survived October 1929 more or less intact, but began moving his cash into stocks during the short-lived mugs' rally of the spring of 1930. He believed that the post-crash rally was real, and this put him on the course to ruin and suicide. The lesson is, **stay out**. Brokers will be sending everyone on their sucker list brochures recommending "Buy when everyone else is selling." "Buy when there's blood in the streets." "You have to be greedy when everyone else is fearful." And so forth. Don't listen.

A STRATEGY FOR SHORT-TERM PERSONAL SURVIVAL

Based on our analysis of the collapse phases and disintegrations of the twentieth century so far, the best strategy is to flee from all forms of paper investment. Instead of holding paper that is likely to become worthless, your approach must be to control those use values upon which your daily life

---

[160] *Business Week*, October 16, 1995, pp. 106-111.
[161] *Washington Post*, July 31, 1998.

depends. By "use values" we mean above all your home with your appliances for cooking, heating, water treatment and air conditioning, your car, your computer, and the tools of your trade. We mean your dwelling, with the roof over your head and the kitchen where you cook your meals. We mean your car and other means of personal transportation. If sports are a vital necessity for you, then by all means include sporting equipment in this category. Include a decent wardrobe of clothing and shoes to get through the crisis, especially since you may be going to more job interviews than you think.

Today, over 40% of American families have money in the stock market. Our basic strategic premise is that, given the unacceptable risk or holding stocks during the closing years of the second millennium, most of these families would be far wiser to convert those stocks into cash and use the proceeds to pay down their existing debts, which are often costing them more in interest than the stocks can yield. The hope of capital gains which lured them into stocks has become less and less realistic during 1997 and 1998. Paying down debt delivers a guaranteed, risk-free and tax-free return, while holding stocks is now fraught with colossal risk.

OWNING MEANS OWNING - NOT BORROWING

The trick is to OWN all this, and to own it free and clear. In recent years the very idea of ownership has been clouded by the usury that has penetrated all aspects of life. Debt-free ownership sounds old-fashioned, even scandalous. So let us make it absolutely clear: by ownership we mean just that in the old sense - you should strive to be the sole proprietor of these use values. There should be no mortgage, no second mortgage, no home equity loan, no lien, no hypothecation of any kind. There must be no encumbrance to your clear title as sole owner. The things you need most you must own free and clear. There must be no bank, mortgage company, finance company, or credit card in the picture.

OWN YOUR OWN HOME

For many families, the central point of this strategy will involve paying off the mortgage on their principal residence. This may appear to involve an unacceptable sacrifice, but it must be stressed that whatever sacrifices you may have to make today cannot be compared with the horror of finding yourself out on the street, with your furniture and belongings at the curb, in the middle of the worst world depression of all time. You should therefore liquidate stocks, bonds, options, futures, mutual funds, and other paper investments and use the proceeds to pay down your mortgage as far as you can.

Don't be surprised if your banker or other investment counselor tries to discourage you from taking this course of action. Many bankers are perfectly aware of how fast the promissory notes and commercial paper they hold can turn into waste paper in a world financial panic. These bankers and mortgage company officers regard your house as a form of tangible wealth which they will be able to foreclose on and seize when you are unable to keep up the payments. Your banker, in other words, has become accustomed to viewing your home as HIS own hedge against a collapse of paper values. Lawyers beholden to these bankers and mortgage operatives will be offering the same advice. "Wes Brot ich eß, des Lied ich sing'", as the German proverb has it - I sing the song of the one who gives me bread.

"Why give up your ability to deduct the mortgage interest on your tax return ?" they will ask. Hopefully you will remember that the question is now not the amount of your tax bill, but whether or not you will become homeless in the depression. The size of Uncle Sam's tax bite is the least of your worries by comparison. "Why sell that stock when it's going to go up?" they will ask, despite price/earnings ratios which are stratospheric by historical standards. You will remember that no rate of return on your money - not even 50% or 75% or even 100% per year - could offset the risk of staying in today's market, which is a virtual 100% certainty of grievous losses or annihilation. Remember that the longer you dabble in stocks, bonds, or derivatives, the more likely it becomes that you will lose everything. So your first priority has to be to own your home free and clear. Your problem is no longer return *on* capital; your problem is return *of* capital.

PAY OFF YOUR HOME MORTGAGE

Owning your home free and clear is the most effective single measure of self-defense you can take during the runup to the crash. Between now and the crash, paying off the home mortgage will improve anyone's situation. What would you say if you were offered an investment that would you pay 7, 8, or 9% guaranteed annual return after taxes, with absolutely no risk to you, that will actually REDUCE your overall financial risk? Well, that is what you obtain when you pay off your home mortgage early by making additional payments each month.

The indispensable source book for freeing yourself from mortgage usury is Marc Eisenson's *The Banker's Secret*, which comes complete with numerous tables that allow you to calculate your pre-payment so as to pay off your mortgage in what is the optimum time for you. Making these calculations can be an important part of motivating yourself to use money to pay down that mortgage. In a world where many claim to be consumer advocates, Eisenson actually is one, offering help in fighting one of the worst scourges of the modern American family – debt in all its forms.

A of this writing, a 30-year fixed rate mortgage in most areas of the US came quipped with an annual interest rate of 7- 8%, plus points and other charges. Eisenson uses as a model a 30-year $75,000 mortgage paying 10% interest. He stresses from the outset that paying off such a mortgage month by month over 30 years will require payments of $237,000, meaning that the homeowner will have paid $162,000 to hire the initial $75,000. The interest is twice the principal, and the home buyer gets one house for the price of three. In this hypothetical case, the monthly mortgage payment would be $658.18. This monthly payment is made up at the beginning of the loan of $625 in interest and $33.18 in principal. As Eisenson shows, simply by sending in an extra $33.46 with the first payment, the homeowner automatically saves $624.72 in interest that will never have to be paid, and also reduces the term of the loan from 359 months to 358 months. By sending in $101.22, about $1,873 in interest is saved, and you will be rid of the mortgage three whole months sooner.

As Eisenson's tables also show, if you want to cut a 30-year, $75,000 mortgage at 10% down to 15 years, you must pay $147.78 extra each month - and many people spend more than that on the lottery for no return at all. By prepaying $147.78 per month, you will obtain an interest savings of a cool $91,871. Why writhe in the bonds of usury when a modest effort will give you a perspective on being debt-free?

The sooner in the life of the loan that pre-payment is begun, the greater the interest savings will be and the sooner the homeowner will be free from mortgage slavery. Make sure that the pre-payment goes only for the principal, since pre-paying interest gets you nowhere. At the end of the process you will receive a letter of satisfaction from the mortgage lender, which should be filed with the county clerk. This will guarantee that, come hell or high water, your home will not be foreclosed upon.

Every time you make a pre-payment, you increase your equity in your home. This means that if you are faced with a life-or-death emergency, you can borrow that money back with a home equity loan, which you should always regard as a last-ditch alternative. The higher your mortgage interest rate, the more you will save by pre-payment. ANY amount you are able to add to your monthly mortgage payment can count as a pre-payment to reduce the principal, and will thus cut the debt service you will pay over the life of the loan. Even if there is a penalty of 5% or some similar figure on pre-payment, go ahead and do it anyway. The savings are so substantial that you will come out ahead in any case. Don't let some loud-mouthed bank officer tell you that you can't pre-pay.

The only serious barrier to reaping huge savings by pre-payment is the so-called "rule of the seventy-eighths" or the "sum of the digits." These punish consumers by front-loading the interest payments so that the principal remains intact longer. Never sign any mortgage or loan without being absolutely sure that it is not governed by the "rule of seventy-eighths." In many states, the rule of seventy-eighths has been outlawed. If it is illegal in your state, make sure you do not pay it. If it is not illegal in your state, it should be outlawed at once.

Know the interest rate on your home mortgage. Look then at any assets you may have - mutual funds, stock, bonds, CDs, and the like. Does any of them offer an *after-tax* rate of return greater than the interest rate on you home mortgage? It is highly unlikely that any actually does. Brokers and bankers may attempt to argue that by using assets to pre-pay a mortgage loan, you are giving up your tax deduction for mortgage interest. This is pure sophistry. Whatever your tax bracket may be, you will save more by not making a mortgage interest payment at all than you could ever hope to gain by deducting the same amount from your gross income.

Rather than risk your money in the mutual fund casino by picking one of the controlled choices in your employer's 401 (k) plan, you are better off building up equity and personal net worth by paying down your mortgage on the fast track. Your increased equity in the house will not be subjected to capital gains tax. If you ever do make a capital gain on your house, you may be able to benefit from the $125,000 one-time capital gains exclusion extended to taxpayers over 55.

Still, this is necessary but not sufficient. There is of course the matter of property tax, that is to say of the tax imposed by your state government on your house and lot. Clearly it will not do you very much good to own your home if you cannot pay the property tax. If that happens, you may have escaped the shark at your local bank or mortgage company only to fall victim to the county sheriff, who will pitilessly auction off your home to the highest bidder.

Your problem is therefore how to pay property tax on your principal residence. In states where this is possible, you should pre-pay a year or more of property tax. If you have the money and if it is administratively feasible, go ahead and pre-pay as many years as you can. Do this long enough before the crash hits, and you will also be increasing your deductions on your pre-crisis income tax return, while your income is higher than it is likely to be later on.

Some states, like Maryland, have "circuit breaker" provisions built into their property tax codes. The Maryland circuit breaker was introduced in 1975 in order to prevent elderly persons from losing their homes if their income were drastically reduced as a result of retirement, illness, or other factors. As of this writing, this program is available to all homeowners regardless of age. In the Maryland law, the level of your gross household income from all sources determines a maximum property tax. If your income is $4000, for example, your property tax is zero. At $10,000 of income, your maximum tax is $210. At $20,000 your maximum tax is $980, and at $25,000 it is $1430, and so forth. A circuit breaker program of this type could save you from homelessness in the coming depression. If your state has one, make damn sure that the Republican phalanxes of greed don't remove just when it will be needed most. If your options are still open, note that whether a state has a circuit breaker or not becomes a ponderable factor in your decision as to whether or not to buy a home there. If your state has no such law and you can't move out, try getting the AARP and other senior citizen groups interested in adding this to their legislative agenda. Don't be pessimistic - the American people may not be willing to take this depression lying down.

If you cannot prepay your property tax, then you must put some cash aside. As always in this book, cash means, optimally, *cash* - dollar bills stored for safekeeping in your safe deposit box. Don 't be tempted by the interest on a savings account, money market, or certificate of deposit (CD), whether they are insured by the FDIC or not. Again, the interest rate will never be high enough to offset the colossal risk of holding paper instruments as we go in to collapse and then disintegration. You may also decide to hold you savings in gold, as we will discuss shortly.

Skeptics may argue that if we get into the abyss via the hyperinflationary route, then your mortgage debt will be wiped out overnight anyway, so why struggle now to pay it off. That may sound plausible, but we must stress again that there is absolutely no certainty that the crash will be hyperinflationary. The issue involves political factors which have not yet been finally decided. It is still perfectly possible that the road to the crash may take us through a period of hyperdeflation. If hyperdeflation comes, then those who still must make house payments will be ruined. In line with our general maxim of doing whatever is necessary now in order to increase chances for short-term survival later on, our advice must be to pay off that mortgage at all costs.

AVOID CREDIT CARD DEBT

Twenty years ago, anyone demanding an interest rate of 20% or even more on the unpaid balances carried forward from month to month on a credit card would have gone to jail for violation of the usury laws, and would have richly deserved their jail term. It is an index of the depravity of this age that such usurious interest rates are now accepted by so many, even including the victims who have to pay such exorbitant rates.

If you have a $2000 balance on a credit card charging interest of 19.8% and exacting a $20 annual fee, it will take you 31 years to pay off your balance. During that endless process, if the interest rate does not vary, you will pay a total of $7,700 to the credit card company, and a whopping $5,700 of that will be interest. In other words, you will pay for your credit card purchases nearly four times over. This stunning pillage means that you must carefully examine any savings accounts, stocks, bonds, or other investments you may have. Is their rate of return superior to the interest rate charged on your credit card debt? If not, you should promptly liquidate these other accounts and investments, and apply the entire sum to reducing your credit card balance. Otherwise you are in effect borrowing money at 19.8% in order to invest in a risky mutual fund that pays perhaps 8% or 10% after taxes, or in any case most likely less than the credit card rate. Don't worry about being caught short of cash later. By paying off your balance, you will begin to attract credit card offers featuring lower interest rates. You will acquire some leverage in trying to push your credit card company to give you a lower rate right now. So you will be able to reduce your interest payments towards zero right now, and pay a lower rate if you need to buy something on credit between now and the disintegration. Use at least part of the money you save to start pre-payments on your home mortgage so you can be free of that usury, too.

AVOID CAR LOANS

What has been said about hanging on to your home applies also to your car. Since public transportation is either primitive or nonexistent in most parts of the United States, your ability to improvise an income may well depend on you ability to get around on your own. For most people this priority will be second on the list after they have secured their principal dwelling place. Pay off your car note, and get that finance company out of your life for good. If your resources permit, you may be able to purchase a slightly newer model, or make repairs and other improvements on the car you have. Try to guarantee your mobility three to five years into the future. The last US depression lasted for about ten years, and that was only a collapse, not the kind of disintegration waiting for us around the bend.

Obviously, the argument that is valid against home mortgages and credit-card debt also applies to car loans. Some may respond that they need a car to get to work and thus have no choice but to go on paying. But now you must factor in the question of the coming collapse-disintegration. If you default on your car loan, your auto will be repossessed by the bank or finance company. If you lease and cannot maintain the payments, you will have your car repossessed and be assessed outrageous penalties. Where will that leave you? You are much better off being the real owner of a much older and less stylish car, provided it keeps running and you can really own it. Stay away from car loans, liens, leases, and other encumbrances. Crash risk shifts the balance towards an ugly duckling that is 100% your property.

If you have cash and space, buy that extra set of tires, air and oil filter, belts, spark plugs, and whatever else wears out fastest on your car. Since this advice will not reach all holders of car notes, and some will ignore this advice even if they hear it, it is clear that many cars will be repossessed in the coming depression. There are already parts of the Arizona desert which are used for parking jet aircraft which have been repossessed by the bondholders and creditors of bankrupt airlines in the post-Frank Lorenzo and post-Elizabeth Dole era. These parking lots for jets cover many acres. Think of how many more acres will be needed to accommodate all the cars that will be repossessed by banks and finance companies! The entire Great Basin may not be large enough. Before things get to that point, of course, someone may have the sense to pass a uniform federal law to halt all repossession of motor vehicles for reasons of default on car notes. That would be the rational thing to do, since otherwise not many workers are going to make it to whatever jobs remain. But that is uncertain. So make sure your car remains in your possession by paying off your note as soon as possible.

THE TOOLS OF YOUR TRADE

The same general principle applies to the tools with which you earn your living. For some people this means the tools of a plumber, electrician, mechanic, or photographer. For others, it means a computer, a fax, or a photocopier. Whatever equipment or apparatus you need to earn a living, make sure you own it free and clear so that no finance company can repossess it.

A MORMON PANTRY

South Korea, Indonesia, and Russia have all experienced panic buying of food and household staples. In order to avoid problems ranging from serious inconvenience to real privation, it will be prudent to keep a very well-stocked pantry. Without falling into the delusions of survivalism, common sense suggests that you will fare better if you can keep a one or two month supply of items like rice, sugar, tea, coffee, pasta, canned or freeze-dried foods, laundry and dishwashing detergent, light bulbs, razor blades, matches, batteries, bottled water, and other indispensable items in the house. Remember that whatever is imported may be in short supply, be it because of the crisis already raging out there, or the crisis which is likely to strike over here. It is a Mormon tradition to maintain a very well-stocked larder; because of world depression, we should all be Mormons now, in this regard.

SAVINGS BONDS

We have warned repeatedly that all paper financial instruments are inherently risky today, and will become even riskier as the world economy lurches from collapse to disintegration. But we also realize that for many people, the optimum course of putting your cash in a safe deposit box may seem too extreme. Such people may also feel that the timing of the collapse and disintegration may prove to be highly uncertain. Because of their personal circumstances, they may feel that the need to hold interest-bearing paper in order to make it. Although "no paper" remains the best policy, we want to offer some advice to this category.

If you must hold paper, there is only one type of paper that a sane person would even consider. This is United States Treasury paper, backed by the full faith and credit of the United States Government, the most powerful institution on the face of the earth. Treasury paper means Treasury paper physically in your hands, not in the hands of some mutual fund. The so-called hillbilly cousins of the Treasury – Fanny Mae, Ginnie Mae, Freddie Mac, Sally Mae, and the rest – are just not in the same league. For this paper, the pledge of the full faith and credit of the government is far less emphatic, and the risk of default is consequently much higher. Even when you acquire Treasury paper, you are taking a gamble on both politics and economics. The gamble is that the government will have the political will not to default.

Although the US government has never defaulted, there is always the danger that it might some day do so. During the autumn of 1995, Speaker Gingrich and Senator Domenici loudly stated that they thought that default through a confrontation with President Clinton over the budget impasse of that year was preferable to accepting future deficits. Another risk comes from speculative manipulation of the Treasury market. During the late 1980s, John Gutfreund of Salomon Brothers was accused of manipulating the Treasury market in this way.

UNITED STATES SAVINGS BONDS

These are backed by the full faith and credit of the US government, with the added plus that they are offered as a vehicle for the average person, the small saver. Series EE bonds can be bought in denominations as small as $25 for a $50 bond. On bonds purchased before May 1, 1997, the interest rate is based on the New York secondary market in Treasury securities. For the first five years, an EE bond earns what is called the Treasury's short-term rate. The short-term rate is equal to 85% of the average yield of six-month Treasury bills over the three months before the rate is announced. These announcements take place every six months, on May 1 and November 1. After five years, EE bonds earn the Treasury's long-term rate. The long term rate is calculated as 85% of the average yield of a five-year Treasury note over the six-month period before the announcement. Announcements are made on May 1 and November 1. As of April 1997, the short-term savings bond rate was 4.56%, and the long-term rate was 5.53%. Consider the risk of other bonds and the fact that savings bonds are free of state income tax before turning your nose up at these rates.

An EE bond must be held for six months before it can be redeemed, during which time it earns interest at the short-term rate. As of September 1998, the average interest rate across the country is 4.63% for a six-month CD, and 5.10% for a five-year CD. So if you think of an EE savings bond as a 6-month CD, you are getting an interest rate from the Treasury that is only 29 basis points lower than that offered by your bank. Now, which is more likely to go belly up in the meltdown, a derivative-laden bank or the United States Government? The reduced risk of dealing directly with the Treasury is more than worth the 29 basis points of interest differential. An EE bond will beat a money market bank account every time. In September 1998 the national average for a money market account was 2.53%.

EE bonds formally mature in 17 years after issue date. If the interest earned in seventeen years has not been enough to bring the bond to maturity, the Treasury will make a one-time payment to bring them to full face value at the 17-year mark. This affords an extra measure of protection against deflation. In other words, there is a 4% minimum rate of interest guaranteed. As an added plus, all interest earned on US Savings Bonds is exempt from city, county, and state taxes, although federal income tax must be paid. This can make a big difference in high-tax states.

Interest on these bonds is compounded and credited twice a year, on December 1 and June 1. EE bonds cannot be redeemed until six months after purchase. Everyone can buy $15,000 worth of EE bonds per calendar year. Under certain circumstances, the interest on EE bonds may be freed of federal income tax if the proceeds are used to pay for education.

On May 1, 1997, the Treasury announced a series improvements designed to make US Savings bonds more attractive. Series EE savings bonds purchased on or after May 1, 1997 immediately start earning interest equal to 90% of the average yield on the Treasury's marketable 5-year notes. The EE bonds increase in value every 6 months, with interest compounded semi-annually. Bonds cannot be cashed in during the first six months. However, the Treasury will now exact a penalty equal to 3 months of interest if the bonds are cashed in before five years have elapsed. Rates are still announced in May and November. Savings bonds earn interest for thirty years. Interest on EE bonds is exempt from state, county, and city income taxes, and there are tax breaks for those who redeem their bonds to pay for education expenses. Denominations now range from $50 to $10,000, and maturity to full face value is guaranteed after 17 years. The result is that EE bonds issued after May 1997 were paying 5.06% interest in September 1998.

I-BONDS: INFLATION-PROTECTED SAVINGS BONDS

During 1998, the Treasury for the first time offered its new I-Bonds, special inflation-protected savings bonds, in denominations of $50 and up. Inflation-protection savings bonds are available either directly from the Treasury or from banks. With these inflation-protection savings bonds, both interest and principal will fluctuate up and down according to the rate of inflation or deflation. Given the tremendous instability of world finance, one possible strategy would be to acquire equal amounts of EE savings bonds and inflation-protection bonds to acquire protection against both inflation and deflation. The interest rate paid on Inflation-Protection Savings Bonds is based on the rate on marketable TIPS (see below). In September 1998, the I-Bond rate was 4.66%, reflecting a basic rate of 3.60% plus the inflation adjustment.

HH BONDS

The Treasury also offers series HH bonds, which are current income bonds paying interest twice a year at a fixed rate. HH bonds are issued in denominations between $500 and $10,000.The rate is set for the first 10 years the bonds are held, and is then adjusted for another ten years. The rate is currently 4%. The Treasury will transform EE bonds into HH bonds in multiples of $500. The idea is that retirees may want to hold EE bonds until they retire, and then switch into HH bonds to collect the current interest as income. Although the interest rates on savings bonds go up and down with the interest rates on Treasury securities, savings bonds still leave the holder vulnerable to inflation, which can erode or wipe out the value of the principal. In order to hedge against inflation, it will be prudent to hold balance US savings bonds with comparable amounts of Inflation-Protection Savings Bonds (see below).

TREASURY DIRECT

In addition to US savings bonds, which the government stands ready to redeem based on the amount paid and interest accrued, there are also the Treasury bills, bonds and notes that fluctuate in market value every day on the secondary Treasury market in lower Manhattan. The average person seldom considers marketable Treasury securities when planning an individual investment strategy.

This is most unfortunate since Treasury securities, while certainly not risk-free, represent the safest marketable paper in the world. Brokers and bankers will very seldom tell their average customer about Treasuries because they have very low commissions even when bought from a bank, and of course are not the proprietary products of any bank, mutual fund, brokerage, etc. You can buy Treasuries direct from the government by mail with no commissions at all. Payments are always by direct deposit, meaning that you will never need to worry about checks stolen or lost in the mail. The Treasury will even keep your securities in your own private account, which is free up to $100,000 and costs a nominal $25 per year above that.

The Treasury's marketable securities that are bought and sold on the secondary market can be purchased through banks, financial institutions, and bond dealers. But here you are likely to pay commissions, although not always. The other method for buying Treasury securities is to purchase them when they are first issued directly from the Treasury at one of its regular auctions. This is not as complicated as it sounds; in fact, it is simpler than dealing with a broker.

For the small investor's purposes, there are three kinds of Treasury securities to be considered. These are bills, notes, and bonds. Treasury bills are short-term obligations issued with a term of one year or less. Treasury bills are sold for a price less than their face value (also called par value) and do not pay interest until they mature. When they mature, they are paid back at face value. So the difference between the purchase price of the bill and the face value paid at maturity is the interest earned on the bill. Treasury bills, often referred to as T-bills, come in 13-week, 26-week, and 52-week maturities. You can buy Treasury bills direct from the government for a minimum of $10,000, and in multiples of $1,000 beyond that.

Finance insiders sometimes say "cash" when they are actually talking about T-bills. This is because T-bills have generally been the most liquid and easy to sell form of interest-bearing paper. If you hold T-bills in a Treasury Direct account, you can request automatic multiple reinvestment, meaning that your maturing T-bills will automatically be used to buy new T-bills at the next auction. Once requested, this process will go on for 2 years after the first maturity date. Treasury notes bear a stated interest rate, and you are paid interest twice a year by direct deposit into your bank account. Treasury notes have maturities of more than one year, but not more than 10 years. At this time the Treasury regularly issues notes in 2-year, 3-year, 5-year, and 10-year maturities. You can buy Treasury notes with maturities of 2 years and 3 years from the government for a minimum of $5,000, and in multiples of $1,000 beyond that. Notes with maturities of 5 years and 10 years can be bought for a minimum of $1,000 and in multiples of $1,000 beyond that.

Treasury bonds have a maturity of more than 10 years. Right now there is only one kind of bond being issues, and that is the 30-year bond, often referred to as the "long bond" or "bellwether long bond", because its price is so important for the setting of long-term interest rates. Interest on the long bond is paid twice a year via direct deposit into your bank account. The 30-year Treasury bond can be bought from the government for a minimum of $1,000 and in multiples of $1,000 beyond that. If you want to re-invest a note or bond, you must order the Treasury to re-invest it at least 20 days before maturity. Otherwise, redemption and reimbursement are automatic.

Treasury notes and bonds are fixed-income securities. When they are issued by the Treasury, they come equipped with a face value and an interest rate which do not change for the life of the bond. If the face value of the bond is $1,000, and the stated interest rate is 7%, then the holder will receive two interest payments per year totaling $70. Confusion about these bonds often arises because when the Treasury auction is held (or when a trade is made on the secondary market), these notes and bonds very often do not sell at their exact face value, but at some figure above or below face value.

The $70 yearly interest payment on the bond mentioned will never vary, but your rate of return will be determined by what you actually pay for the bond.

If you buy a 30-year bond with a 7% stated interest rate for $1100, for example, you will be earning less than 7% – you will be earning about 6.36%. If you buy the same bond for $800, you will not be earning 7% – you will be earning 8.75%. The $70 total yearly payment will not change, but the percentage return will vary according to how much money you had to put down to get the Treasury's guarantee to pay you $70 a year for the next 30 years.

You may notice that if the purchase price of the bond goes up, the interest rate goes down. Conversely, if the purchase price of the bond goes down, then the interest rate goes up. Once you buy the bond, you have locked in the momentary interest rate and that will be your rate of return until you sell the bond or until it matures. This is the source of the famous bond-market axiom, printed virtually every day in the *New York Times*, that the market price and the yield of bonds move in the opposite direction. So if inflation and higher interest rates come, bonds with their fixed rates of return become less desirable, and their prices will go down. Buy them when they are down, and you will get a better rate of return. If deflation comes, bonds become very attractive, and their prices go up. If you want to buy them after the prices have risen, you will have to pay more to get the same fixed rate of return.

In addition to the periodic interest payments, Treasury notes and bonds pay back their face value when they mature. That may be more or less than what you paid for the bond. If you paid 90 for the bond, or if you paid 110, you will get 100 at maturity – again assuming that Rep. Gingrich and Sen. Domenici have not driven the country into default. What if you buy any of these Treasury securities from the government but then find you need to convert them into ready cash? Under normal conditions, you can readily sell any bill, note or bond through a broker (or many banks) on the secondary market in New York. You will get a market price which may be more or less than what you paid, and can also be more or less than the face value of the bond.

BUYING TREASURY SECURITIES BY MAIL WITH NO COMMISSION

Buying Treasury securities when they are first auctioned off by the government is as simple as dropping a check in the mail, and there is no broker's commission to pay. There are about 150 Treasury auctions of various kinds during the year, including weekly auctions of 13-week bills and 26-week bills. The Treasury issues press releases about a week before each auction announcing the amount of securities to be sold, the maturity, and other details. These notices are usually carried by the *New York Times*, *Wall Street Journal*, and other business papers. You can also call the Bureau of the Public Debt or your local Federal Reserve office.

When you send in a bid to buy Treasury securities, you must state the total face value of the securities you want to buy. This is the only slightly tricky part of the process. If you tell the Treasury you want to buy $1,000 of the next thirty-year bond, and send them a check in that amount, you may end up having to pay more than $1,000. This is because, if the bond is in demand, the auction price may to 103 or 105. If the auction price for the bond you want is greater than the face value that you have ordered, then the Treasury will require you to pay a premium, which is the difference between the par price and the purchase price. But if the auction attracts less interest, it can very well be that the selling price of the securities will be less than their face value. In that case, the Treasury will send you a refund or discount, which will again be the difference between the purchase price and par. This is the element of unpredictability in buying Treasury securities. In practice, small investors should keep a cash cushion of about 5% of the face value of the securities they want to buy.

As a small investor, you will want to make what is called a non-competitive bid when buying Treasury securities. Banks and brokers make competitive bids, but this arena is too unpredictable for the average person. The average person cannot know market conditions as well as the Wall Street insiders do. When you make a non-competitive bid, you do not specify an exact price at which you will buy. You let the Treasury calculate the average selling price of that day's auction.

By making a non-competitive bid, you agree to buy the amount of securities you request at a price determined by averaging all bids at the auction that were accepted by the Treasury. At the computerized bureaucratic procedure known as the auction, the Treasury tries to cover its borrowing requirements by selling its securities to the highest bidders, thus getting the best deal it can for the government. If you send in a low bid, it may be rejected. If you send in a high bid, it will be eagerly accepted, and you will pay a price higher than that paid by Wall Street. To avoid these two unpleasant alternatives, send in a non-competitive bid that will always put you squarely in the middle of the pack. If you make a non-competitive bid, the Treasury guarantees that you will receive a security.

Treasury securities these days are all electronic book-entry securities stored in computers. What the buyer gets is a receipt, which should be carefully conserved. If you put your electronic book-entry securities in a Treasury Direct Account, you will also receive a Treasury Direct statement each time there is a change in your account. Older Treasury bonds are still in what is "definitive" form – meaning that you get a handsomely engraved certificate on thick bank note paper that you can put in the safe deposit box. If you prefer owning your securities in the form of definitive certificates, you will have to go to your bank's T-bond trading department and specify that you want to buy definitive long bonds issued years ago, back in the era before electronic book-entry became the rule.

If you want to buy Treasuries by mail, tender forms and payment may be submitted to the nearest Federal Reserve Bank or to the Bureau of the Public Debt in Washington. Tenders must be received by the time stated in the offering announcement. Generally, the deadlines are prior to 12:00 noon Eastern time for hand-delivered noncompetitive bids. If you send in a non-competitive bids through the mail, it must be postmarked by the day before the auction is held and must be received by the issue date of the security.

If you want to buy T-bills, then you must send a cashier's check or have you personal check certified by your bank. No two-party checks will be accepted. For notes and bonds, your personal check is entirely sufficient. Another question is where you want to keep your securities. This depends on what you plan to do with them. If you think you may have to sell them before maturity, one possibility is the commercial book-entry system maintained by the Federal Reserve banks in their capacity as fiscal agents of the Treasury. But here you face the added risk of the insolvency of the Federal Reserve, a privately-owned and privately managed institution which is not a part of the US government.

Much better, especially if you plan to hold your securities to maturity, is the Treasury Direct system. Anyone can open a Treasury Direct account at any time, even if you do not yet own any Treasury securities. You send in an application, and you receive the number which corresponds to your personal account. All bills, notes, and bonds can be held together in this account, with a statement issued to the owner whenever there is a change in the account. The trick is that securities cannot be sold out of Treasury Direct. If you need to sell, you must shift your securities from Treasury Direct to the Federal Reserve commercial book-entry system, whence they can be sold on the secondary market.

TREASURY INFLATION-PROTECTION BONDS

In January 1997 the Treasury for the first time issued marketable Treasury Inflation-Protection Securities (TIPS). With these bonds ,the value of the principal is adjusted for inflation (or deflation), and every six months the securities pay interest equal to a fixed percentage of the inflation-adjusted value of the principal. When the security matures, the principal paid back will be increased to adjust for inflation, but in any case will not be less than the original par value of the security. The inflation rate used in adjusting the security is the non-seasonally-adjusted Department of Labor Consumer Price Index. The CPI is an imperfect index, and is even less accurate now than before it was tampered with by a certain Mr. Boskin, but it still provides some indication of the level of inflation. TIPS are available in multiples of $1000 and the plan is to auction them quarterly. The first issue of TIPS came in the form of a 10-year note. These are book-entry securities, with ownership recorded in the Treasury computers, and no bond certificate to be held by the owner.

With TIPS, if inflation goes up, so does the interest on the bond, and so does the par value of the bond paid back at maturity. That makes TIPS a bond protected against inflation, which is the nemesis of all bonds. The problem is that TIPS are subject to declining interest payments in a period of deflation. Deflation would be shown by a substantial fall in the Consumer Price Index, and TIPS interest payments would go down with it. But no matter how severe deflation were to become, the principal would be paid back at par value.

As the Treasury stated: "If at maturity the inflation-adjusted principal is less than the original principal value of the security, an additional amount will be paid at maturity so that the additional amount plus the inflation-adjusted principal equals the original principal amount." Mindful that tinkering with the Consumer Price Index by Boskin and his ilk might scare off investors with the specter of more bogus reductions in the CPI in the future, the Treasury pledges that once TIPS have been sold, no revisions in the CPI will be used in calculating the inflation adjustments for those TIPS.

More information on US Treasury securities and US savings bonds is available from a number of sources. For more about savings bonds, write:

Bureau of the Public Debt
Savings Bond Operations Office,
Parkersburg, West Virginia 26106-1328

Current interest rate information on savings bonds can be obtained by phone from 1-800-4US BOND (1-800-487-2663). Their web site is www.savingsbonds.gov.

The Bureau of the Public Debt has a highly informative Internet web site. The URL is http://www.publicdebt.treas.gov, and offers downloadable forms for tender offers on marketable Treasury securities. Every regional Federal Reserve bank and branch office has a department that handles inquiries about marketable Treasury securities. The Federal Reserve also receives bids for Treasury auctions. The technicalities of how to bid on Treasury securities are summed up in the booklet *Buying Treasury Securities*, available from the Bureau of the Public Debt, Washington, DC 20239-0001. Tender forms for making bids are available from the same address.

BANK ACCOUNTS AND CERTIFICATES OF DEPOSIT

If you have to choose between a Treasury security on the one hand, and a bank account or certificate of deposit insured by the Federal Deposit Insurance Corporation, you should choose the Treasury security every time. The risk of general banking panic has always been great, and with the failure of Long Term Capital Management, it has become overwhelming. Don't take our word for it. On the pleasant early autumn Sunday of September 27, 1998, readers of the Jim Hoagland column in the *Washington Post* were regaled with the mid-September words of the managing director of "one of New York's most successful investment firms," who commented: ...for the first time in my life I hear serious people worrying about the survival of their banks.... Fortunately they are not doing this worrying in public and spooking everybody. But the concern is there."

It is the Federal Deposit Insurance Corporation (FDIC) that insures $100,000 per person in checking accounts, money market accounts, and certificates of deposits. The Savings Association Insurance Fund, administered by the FDIC, has replaced the old FSLIC (Federal Savings and Loan Insurance Corporation) in insuring the deposits of savings banks and savings and loan institutions, also called thrifts. As of the last day of 1996, the 11,452 commercial banks insured by the FDIC held insured deposits of just over $2 trillion. (Total deposits, including non-insured deposits, came in at just under $3.2 trillion.) Against these $2 trillion in insured deposits, the FDIC's Bank Insurance Fund held a total of about $26.9 billion. The ratio of total deposits to the money in the insurance fund that is expected to insure these deposits come to 1.34%, the highest in many years. The FDIC is very proud that the Bank Insurance Fund has now exceeded its target ratio of covering 1.25% of total deposits. And indeed, the situation is now much better than it was back at the end of 1991, when the BIF was more than $7 billion in the red, and the percentage of insured deposits covered by the fund was under water by a minus 0.36% ratio. Over at the Savings Insurance Fund, things are slightly more shaky. The SAIF has $8.9 billion in the till to deal with $683 billion in deposits, meaning that 1.30% of current deposits could be covered by cash on hand. Factor in against all this that the total derivatives exposure of Chase Manhattan Bank was more than $7.7 trillion, well above the total public debt of the United States, which was a mere $5.5 trillion as of late September 1998. Ponder that Chase Manhattan's derivatives exposure is sufficient to wipe out its equity capital 356 times.

The same issue of the FDIC Quarterly Banking Profile [First Quarter 1998] that reported this information given also announced that "Off-balance-sheet-derivatives" of the FDIC member banks amounted to $27 trillion. These derivatives represent 54 times the capital of all US commercial banks. So it's official: the US banking system will be bankrupt 54 times over when the derivatives panic gets going in earnest. If the FDIC Bank Insurance Fund were to be cleaned out by bank failures, there is the strong assumption that the Congress and the President would approve laws authorizing and appropriating the funds necessary to pay off the depositors of the banks – hopefully not the stockholders, not the bondholders, not the executives, not the holders of debentures and commercial paper, but the small depositors with balances up to $100,000. Such measures to indemnify the small depositors would have to come in the context of an effective anti-depression program.

Now, it is surely to be hoped that the US Government will honor its commitment to the small depositors. Decades ago, or even more recently, it might have been possible to state that the US Government would probably do the right thing. But in the post-Newt Gingrich era in the Congress, the moral imperative to honor the most essential public commitments might be blocked if Newt's successors were to decide that betraying the small depositors were the next step in the never-ending battle against Big Government. After all, the FDIC was part of FDR's New Deal program of creeping socialism! All of this means that the bill providing the money for the small depositors may be a long time in coming, even under extreme depression conditions. Or it may never come. There are endless possibilities for stalling, chiseling, and red tape. And this means that bank deposits and certificates of deposit have become a very risky affair at best. A default on Treasury securities, by contrast, would be a high-profile and explosive event, and those denied payments would be the biggest financial interests in the world. Small bank depositors might prove politically easier to sacrifice than the great counting houses and foreign interests that hold Treasury bonds. So, as far as it is possible to see in the murky future of collapse into disintegration, we can conclude that while both Treasury securities and FDIC-insured bank accounts are both at risk, the government's own Treasury transactions are likely to be more reliable and more prompt than those of private banks, even with their last-resort government guarantee.

GOLD

Gold still represents a strong defense against hyperinflation, and hyperinflation has been in the air during the past several months. According to Adrian Van Eck, Alan Greenspan told an off-the-record meeting of G-7 central bankers to print money in case of a financial panic. In Van Eck's view, Greenspan "may not care whether <u>foreign</u> countries suffer inflation." According to this account, in 1987 Greenspan, "working through the New York Fed," told US mutual funds, "'When hit by waves of redemptions, do not sell any stocks or bonds to raise cash. *Pay them Money, on demand.*' The Funds said, 'We don't have enough cash in reserve to handle redemptions. Our bank will bounce our checks!' "Don't worry,' said the Federal Reserve. 'We have told banks to send all such dishonored checks to us.' The Fed cleared them using money from their bottomless 'magic' check book." [Van Eck-Tillman Advisories, c1998] Apart from the details, such practices by the Fed are notorious, and create the prospect that, at some point, the central bank lender of last resort may use its printing presses to stoke the furnaces of hyperinflation. This is where gold comes in.

If you have succeeded in owning your home, car and the tools of your trade, are debt free, have a well-stocked pantry, plus enough cash in a safe deposit box to pay the property tax on your home for a number of years, you may also want to think about a gold hedge as a last-ditch defense against hyperinflation and related monetary disasters. How much gold should you buy? These are parlous times, so 10% of your personal net worth might be a suitable amount, if you can afford it. Of course, you can never have too much gold.

American Eagle and other gold coins can be purchased from many dealers. Here it pays to shop around very carefully, since many dealers charge outrageous service charges on gold sales. Brace yourself for the realization that many dealers also want to charge you an exorbitant service charge to buy the gold back. Look in the newspaper to see the rates of gold coins like American Eagle, Canadian Maple Leaf, South African Krugerrand, Chinese Panda, and other coins issued by governments. Do not consider gold commemorative medals or medallions of the type advertised in the magazines that come with the Sunday papers. Stick to standard, government-issue gold coins currently minted by the great powers of the world. The selling prices for one-ounce gold coins are listed in the *New York Times, Wall Street Journal*, and other financial papers. Notice that the one-ounce gold coin costs more than a generic ounce of gold as determined by the daily fixing at the London Metals Exchange. That is because one-ounce gold coins are more liquid and more negotiable than the equivalent weight in a bar of gold which does not bear the stamp of a government. Gold bullion, gold ingots, gold dust, gold nuggets are so forth are highly inconvenient and should not be the choice of the average person. In order to sell these non-standardized forms of gold, you must pay an expert to weight them and even conduct as assay to determine the purity of the gold. These tests represent needless and useless additions to your costs.

American Eagle gold coins are issued by the United States government. Their weight and the purity of the gold they contain are standardized and well-known to dealers. They will not require costly and time-consuming tests. Do not buy gold coins that are valued above the market price for historical, artistic, or numismatic qualities. Never pay extra for an antique $20 or $50 gold piece. The pricing for these is too complicated, and their value as collectible antiquarian objects of speculation will always fluctuate too much.

If you buy gold from a dealer, your gold will often be sent to you a week or two later by registered mail. This can make a small investor nervous, but it is generally quite safe. The gold will be delivered to you personally. If you are not home when the US Postal Service attempts to deliver your gold, you will find a notice to that effect in your mail box asking you to come to the local post office with your driver's license to take delivery of the gold in person. Take the gold to your bank at once and put it in your safety deposit box. Along with the gold you will get a receipt, which you should keep for possible future use in determining future capital gains.

The only way to buy gold is to pay cash and then take personal, physical possession of the gold. Never, never, never leave the gold on deposit in somebody else's bank vault or brokerage. Never play around with gold options or gold futures. You face the risk of an unpleasant surprise when the exchange clearinghouses go bankrupt at the critical moment, and your money is trapped in the shambles. Gold stocks are also an enormous risk, as the case of Bre-X minerals and that notorious Indonesian gold mine remind us. Bre-X stock collapsed, but the price of gold barely rippled. The way to buy gold is to keep standard gold coins in a safe deposit box.

Never, never, never attempt to buy gold using futures, options, or borrowed funds. The British finance oligarchs who control most of the gold in the world periodically organize shake-outs of the gold market. The price dips 20% or 30% or even more, and this is enough to wipe out the little people who have attempted with their options and futures to muscle in on a racket the British want reserved for oligarchs.

The most cogent objection that can be made against this analysis involves the stagnant gold price. For years now gold was locked in a very narrow trading range, hovering between $350 and $385 per troy ounce. In the late 1990s, gold has generally stayed even lower, below $300 per ounce. This trading range has prevailed during the Gulf war and various financial shocks. If the family fortunes of the aristocrats are being transferred into commodities, the skeptic might argue, the classic way to do that is by buying and holding gold coins and gold bullion. If the oligarchs are turning to speculative hoarding, there ought to be a rise in the gold price to reflect that. Fair enough.

The answer to this apparent riddle is a concerted effort to control the price of gold carried out by a consortium of central banks. This central bank interest in setting the price of gold goes back to the Montagu Norman - Benjamin Strong clique of the 1920s, when the issue was American support for Sir Winston Churchill's desire to return to the gold standard at the impossibly high parity of $4.86 gold-backed dollars to the pound. The Bretton Woods system of 1944 handled the gold parities of the various currencies by giving them a narrow band of fluctuation against the US dollar, while setting gold at $35 dollars per ounce. The story of the 1960s gold pool is told in Chapter IV; this was an explicit effort by the central banks to control the gold price.

Since Nixon and Kissinger destroyed the Bretton Woods gold convertibility of the dollar in 1971, the central banks have evolved a method for managing this problem informally. The City of London and Wall Street have traditionally been hostile to a monetary role for gold, since gold tends to act as a reality principle which limits the scope of their desired swindles. The last phase of the dollar's gold convertibility was marked by a running battle on this issue between the Fed and the Bank of England, on the one hand, and French President Charles de Gaulle and his chief economist, Jacques Rueff, on the other. De Gaulle's argument was that "only gold is imperishable."

In recent years it is clear that the central banks, meeting for example at the privately owned Bank for International Settlements in Switzerland, are conniving to make sure that the gold price stays below a certain level. For a number of the years during the 1980s, this task was facilitated by Soviet gold sales. Gorbachev's moribund Union of Soviet Socialist Republics, because of its economic chaos and stagnation, was obliged to sell vast quantities of gold to procure foreign exchange for such needs as grain purchases. The gold was shipped to Switzerland by air and quietly placed on the market.

More recently, the Belgian and Netherlands central banks have attracted attention as prime selling agents for the central bank cartel. Gold bugs noticed that any rise of gold beyond the $400 level was soon followed by orchestrated selling which continued until the $385 level was reached once again. Establishment market commentators tried to use this pattern to argue that gold is a dead end and that no combination of stock market crashes and inflationary commodity shortages will ever cause gold to break above $400-$500.

Those who are still skeptical can look at the matter in this way. It is routine for central banks to conduct support operations for national currencies which are in trouble. In recent years. a number of central banks conducted this kind of support operation for the dollar, the yen, and other currencies. Since gold is traditionally perceived as the main alternative to paper financial instruments, including currencies, operations to keep down the price of gold are essentially support operations for paper instruments of all kinds. During the rapid fall of the US dollar in the spring of 1995, knowledgeable observers in Europe pointed out that the central bank anti-gold cartel was fully mobilized to prevent a general loss of confidence in paper holdings. Coming in the wake of Orange County, Mexico, and Barings, the nosedive of the dollar carried with it a danger of precisely this type. Therefore the central bankers dumped gold in order to prevent a panic flight out of paper.

Some inkling of these realities seeped into John Dizard's "Gekko" column in the *National Review* of September 11, 1995. This piece quotes gold bug Frank Veneroso, who comments that "a big hand is over the gold market. For the past two years, whenever the gold price penetrates $390 an ounce, large sellers have come into the market. I assume that represents one or more central banks liquidating their holdings." Specifically, Veneroso reports that "there is a flow of about 40 tons a month from the US, most of which is coming from the foreign central-bank holdings at the New York Federal Reserve Bank."

For those interested in gold, the artificially low price of gold provides them with an opportunity to stock up on American Eagles at bargain basement prices, and to do so right up to the prelude to the final cataclysm, when this system will inevitably be torn apart by economic reality. A realistic price for gold today would be at least $1000 per ounce, almost four times the current level. And that could go up rapidly, depending on what happens to the dollar.

In January 1997, *Neue Zürcher Zeitung*, *Handelsblatt* and the *Wall Street Journal* reported that the Netherlands central bank had officially admitted to having sold 300 tons of gold during 1996. That represented 20% of the Netherlands' overall gold reserves. Only days before, the Belgian central bank had stated that it had sold 200 tons of gold in 1996, equal 20% of all the Belgian central bank gold reserves. According to the German economic daily *Handelsblatt*, the 1996 Netherlands gold sales alone amounted to two thirds of South Africa's entire yearly gold production.

Several other European Union central banks were also believed to have sold considerable amounts of gold recently, thereby driving the gold price down in spite of a sharp rise in global gold demand. During 1997, despite the southeast Asian crisis, gold lost more than 15% of its price. By November 1997, the yellow metal was hovering around $290, a 12-year low. In addition to the central banks already named, the Australian central bank had helped organize this bear stampede by selling 167 tons of monetary gold. It also turned out that the central bank of Argentina had sold off all its monetary gold during the first half of 1997. There were rumors in the market that central banks had sold some 500 tons during September 1997 alone. One central bank was said to have sold off 220 tons in November 1997. Soon the central banks would have little gold left, and the oligarchs would have most of it.

The Belgian and Netherlands central bank announcements also expose most available statistics about the international gold trade as deliberate lies. The London-based consulting firm Gold Fields Mineral Services had estimated the total central bank gold selling in the second half of 1996 at 213 tons, including an estimated 90 tons by Russian and Chinese authorities. While the Netherlands gold sales are believed to have been occurred in the last quarter of 1996, these figures are obviously absurd. The Gold Fields Mineral Services estimate for sales by all Western central banks for the full year 1996 was 208 tons, far less than the Dutch sold by themselves.

WHERE THE GOLD IS

The United States in 1998 still had about 260 million ounces of gold, most of which is kept in vaults at Fort Knox, Kentucky, West Point, New York, and Denver, Colorado. This is approximately one fifth of all gold held by governments in the world, and the proportion tends to rise as other central banks sell off their gold. The US government must retain these gold stocks at all costs, and should certainly not sell them off with the argument that gold does not earn interest. This gold is an important national asset, and will be a key component in our sponsorship of a new monetary system. The New York Federal Reserve Bank is thought to represent the largest single gold storehouse in the world. The New York Fed holds 10,000 tons of bullion and coins on behalf of 60 governments. [162] A great power in the world of gold is the International Monetary Fund. The IMF has $120 billion in capital, and about $40 billion of that is estimated to be in the form of gold. Speaking at a conference sponsored by the Jerome Levy Economics Institute of Bard College in the spring of 1998, IMF Executive Director Lissaker put the IMF's current gold holdings at 100 million ounces.

---

[162] See *National Geographic*, January 1993.

CHAPTER

XII. POLICIES FOR WORLD ECONOMIC RECOVERY

> This criterion is the *end*, to which the measure relates as a *mean*. If the *end* be clearly comprehended within any of the specified powers, collecting taxes and regulating the currency, and if the measure have an obvious relation to that *end*, and is not forbidden by any particular provision of the Constitution, it may safely be deemed to come within the compass of the national authority. Alexander Hamilton, *Report on the Bank*, 1791.

History suggests that federal government action, and especially Presidential action, will be required to deal with the coming collapse into disintegration of the world financial system and of the world economy. Much will depend upon the actions that the President will take in response to the manifest and palpable outbreak of an overwhelming crisis. The first task of the President is to provide moral leadership. He must officially inform the people of the existence of an economic emergency of unprecedented gravity. He must make the people understand that the federal government knows that this is a life-and-death situation, and that there can be no question of continuing business as usual. The President must provide assurance that he knows what to do and is fully prepared to act in order to preserve the nation. When the interplay of private interests and market forces has brought on a breakdown crisis, it is up to the President to assert the common interest, the public interest, the general welfare, against chaos and crisis. This is something that only the President can do. If the President should fail, then Hell gapes literally under the feet of humankind. Let us appeal to Almighty God that on this day of all days, there be no uncertain trumpet.

It is the American President who must act, not just in the name of the national interest, but with measures worthy of being promulgated in the name of human civilization. The world believes that American is the dominant power of the world and the only remaining superpower. The United States thus remains the cynosure of humanity. Whether or not American wisdom and power have thus far merited this reputation will be beside the point; the universal perception of American world leadership will be a priceless asset to be used with the greatest responsibility, and never to be dissipated by petty chauvinist greed, or by abuse or treachery. Of all the institutions on this planet, it is only the American Presidency that retains the ability to promote, in response to the economic breakdown, a workable solution that the nations of the world can readily accept.

FROM DEPRESSION TO GLOBAL BOOM

The first requirement is to reassure the American people and let them know that the Executive power is taking seriously the mandate to promote the general welfare. The task to be accomplished is the one carried out so masterfully by Franklin D. Roosevelt in his First Inaugural Address of March 4, 1933, spoken on the day the nation's financial heart had stopped beating with the closure of the New York and Illinois banks, leaving the entire banking system paralyzed. On that occasion, Roosevelt did much to restore confidence simply by making the following statement:

> This is preeminently the time to speak the truth, the whole truth, frankly and boldly. Nor need we shrink from honestly facing conditions in our country today. This great Nation will endure as it has endured, will revive and will prosper. So, first of all, let me assert my firm belief that

the only thing we have to fear is fear itself - nameless, unreasoning, unjustified terror which paralyzes our needed efforts to turn retreat into advance. In every dark hour of our national life a leadership of frankness and vigor has met with that understanding and support of the people themselves which is essential to victory. I am convinced that you will again give that support to leadership in these critical days.

Values have shrunk to fantastic levels, taxes have risen, our ability to pay has fallen; government of all kinds is faced by a serious curtailment of income; the means of exchange are frozen in the currents of trade; the withered leaves of industrial enterprise lie on every side; farmers find no market for their produce; the savings of many years in thousands of families are gone. More important, a host of unemployed citizens face the grim problem of existence, and an equally great number toil with little return. Only a foolish optimist can deny the dark realities of the moment.

This reassurance was a physiological necessity for the American people. This is what they had never heard from the do-nothing Hoover Administration, which was expert only in producing explanations of why it could do nothing to stop the depression. Here resounded the determination to fight and to win. And here was a moment of historic drama which no joint resolution by Congress could ever hope to evoke.

EMERGENCY ECONOMIC POWERS OF THE PRESIDENCY

But Roosevelt knew that reassurance and new-found confidence, if not followed by effective measures, would soon wither: "Restoration calls, however, not for changes in ethics alone. This Nation asks for action, and action now." What is then the special duty and ability of the President to act in a crisis? The general purpose of the government of the United States is summed up in the Preamble to the Constitution:

We the people of the United States, in order to form a more perfect union, establish justice, insure domestic tranquillity, provide for the common defense, promote the general welfare, and secure the blessings of liberty for ourselves and our posterity, do ordain and establish this Constitution for the United States of America.

These are the goals for which the government has been instituted. Under all normal circumstances, it is a government of laws. Since we are now approaching the most acute crisis in the history of the United States, we must examine what powers the United States government possesses to deal with the imminent emergency. As we have seen, there will be no private sector solution to the coming emergency. Banks, corporations, and individuals will be overwhelmed by bankruptcy and financial chaos. At this point we will need every ounce of the power wielded by the United States Government, still the most powerful institution on the face of this planet, and even more powerful if it is properly run. Under these circumstances, *laissez-faire* and free trade mean defeat and failure, and a narrow interpretation of the function of government will be a death warrant.

During the US-USSR Cold War, the President's entourage always kept near him a briefcase called The Football, which contained the codes needed to launch a thermonuclear attack. By the end of the Cold War, the likely warning for an all-out Soviet first strike was down to 10 or 15 minutes. Because of this horrible reality, no role remained for Congress in the fateful question of war and peace, including planetary destruction. There would have been no time for a Congressional debate followed by a formal declaration of war. During four decades of de facto thermonuclear emergency, it was clear to most people that the finger on the button could only be the President's. It was not an ideal or desirable situation, but it was the uncontestable reality.

The coming collapse into disintegration of the world financial system under conditions of world economic depression will pose a similar problem. It will probably not be a matter of 10 or 15 minutes, but it is possible that the President will have to make decisions within days or weeks which will spell the difference between economic recovery and utter national bankruptcy, ruin, and famine. These decisions will include measures to restore a functioning banking system to provide credit for vital production, decisions to protect government solvency and insured savings, international negotiations to create a new world monetary system, and the like.

The good news is that under the US Constitution and the various statute laws, the President has all the powers he needs to deal with the crisis in ways that are incontestably legal and firmly anchored in the traditional leading role of the President in time of national emergency. The function of the President is defined in the Constitution as follows: "The executive power shall be vested in a President of the United States of America." (III.1.1) And further: "The President shall be the commander in chief of the army and navy of the United States, and of the militia of the several States, when called into the actual service of the United States ...."(III.2.1) The President is also required to "take care that the laws be faithfully executed."

The Constitution specifies in great detail what the Congress can do and cannot do. But when it comes to the powers of the Presidency, the Constitution is vague, generic, even silent. The broad grant of executive, law enforcement and military command powers given to the President is the basis of the doctrine of implied powers. Since the President is given these tasks, he must also have the flexibility to take whatever actions are necessary to carry them out. The doctrine of implied powers pioneered by Hamilton has become institutionalized in the form of Executive Orders, the directives issued by the President which are nowhere mentioned in the Constitution.

Related to the **implied powers,** we also find the **inherent powers** of the Presidency. The inherent powers also derive directly from the Constitution and are beyond the ability of Congress to limit by any statute. The inherent powers involve the duty of the President to do what is necessary to preserve the nation in the most dire emergencies, when speedy action is necessary for survival, or in situations that cannot be foreseen or have not been foreseen by Congress.

In addition to the implied and inherent powers of the Presidency derived from the Constitution, we also have a series of statutes passed by Congress which specifically authorize the President to do certain things by himself under exceptional conditions that under normal circumstances are done by laws which have to be passed by the Congress and signed by the President. These statutes are by their nature far more narrow and far more specific than the vast panoply of implied and inherent powers, but even so they already grant the President many of the economic emergency powers needed to deal with the coming financial meltdown.

This is the reality behind the brief but lucid sketch of Presidential powers offered by Roosevelt in his First Inaugural and that day of crisis and hope:

> ...our Constitution is so simple and practical that it is possible always to meet extraordinary needs by changes in emphasis and arrangement without loss of essential form. That is why our constitutional system has proved itself the most superbly enduring political mechanism the modern world has produced. It has met every stress of the vast expansion of territory, of foreign wars, of bitter internal strife, of world relations.

> It is to be hoped that the normal balance of executive and legislative authority may be wholly adequate to meet the unprecedented task before us. But it may be that an unprecedented demand and need for undelayed action may call for temporary departure from that normal balance of public procedure.

I am prepared under my constitutional duty to recommend the measures that a stricken nation in the midst of a stricken world may require. These measures, or such other measures as the Congress may build out of its experience and wisdom, I shall seek, within my constitutional authority, to bring to speedy adoption.

But in the event that the Congress shall fail to take one of these two courses, and in the event that the national emergency is still critical, I shall not evade the clear course of duty that will then confront me. I shall ask the Congress for the one remaining instrument to meet the crisis – broad Executive power to wage a war against the emergency, as great as the power that would be given to me if we were in fact invaded by a foreign foe.

An important difference between Roosevelt's situation in 1933 and that of the President called upon by destiny to deal with the disintegration of the world financial system during the next few years is, we stress again, that today's President in many cases no longer needs to request that Congress grant him "broad Executive power to wage a war against the emergency." The brutal crises of the middle twentieth century have already impelled the Congress to delegate to the President, at one time or another, vast powers which fortunately include just about everything that will be needed to begin rolling back the disintegration. Some of these delegations are still in force, while others have been abrogated or allowed to lapse. But they can and must be revived to deal with the emergency. The implied and inherent powers are still there, instantly to be called on in some future unforeseeable circumstance. But in many cases they will not even need to be called on. For today the President's armory is full of sweeping emergency economic powers already granted by the Congress which will facilitate the first and most urgent steps towards recovery.

The exercise by the Executive of these delegated powers generally involves the proclamation of a state of economic emergency, with which the President triggers the emergency provisions of certain laws. For a long time, there was no up-to-date central compilation of the various statutes that delegated emergency powers to the President. At the outset of hearings into questions concerning emergency powers on April 11, 1973, Senator Frank Church, then the co-chair of the Senate Special Committee on the Termination of the National Emergency, noted that there "580 separate sections of the United States Code delegating extraordinary powers to the President in time of war or national emergency. These more than 580 Code sections delegate to the President a vast range of powers, which taken all together, confer the power to rule this country without reference to normal constitutional processes. Emergency powers laws embrace every aspect of American life. Under the powers delegated by these statutes, the President may seize properties, mobilize production, seize commodities, institute martial law, seize control of all transportation and communications, regulate private capital, restrict travel...."

Presidents have also exercised powers to order the stockpiling of strategic materials, such as uranium and other fuels. They have imposed export controls, such as embargoes against selling modern supercomputers to the Soviet bloc, according to the so-called COCOM list. Presidents have been able to order the production of any product deemed necessary for defense, by requiring industries to give priority to government contracts, and by seizing, if necessary, industries that failed to comply with such orders. Presidents have also had the power to fix wages and prices, and to control credit.

Senator Church in 1973 later summed up the delegated powers as follows: "We have a compendium now of 470 significant, separate provisions of law delegating to the President emergency powers. We have selected the 470 out of several thousand provisions of law as the most significant delegation of authority. Taken all together, if the President were to choose to exercise all of these powers, they would seem to me to be plenary. These powers, if exercised, would confer upon the President total authority to do anything he pleased." The compilation directed by Senator Church updated an earlier collection of emergency laws that had been made in November 1962.

The collected emergency provisions were shown to the Congress as Senate Report 93-459 and published by the Church committee under the title *Provisions of Federal Law Now in Effect Delegating to the Executive Extraordinary Authority in Time of National Emergency.*[163] Many of these laws delegating powers to the President are still in force. Some of them have been repealed. In some cases, the Executive branch has condemned the attempted repeal as itself unconstitutional. But even those provisions that have been formally repealed can still readily be revived by the President under the doctrine of implied powers and inherent powers. The powers delegated in the past were delegated to meet crisis situations. Now we have the greatest crisis of them all, much more serious than World War I or World War II, comparable perhaps only to the Civil War in gravity. *ANY emergency power delegated to the President in the past MUST therefore be available to meet the unprecedented rigors of the coming emergency.*

With Nixon in the White House, Church was worried about the extent of these powers, but today the full panoply of President powers must be available to fight an unprecedented emergency. The Church-Mathias Committee found that the state of emergency declared by Franklin D. Roosevelt as a result of the banking panic of 1933 still remained in force in 1973, more than forty years later. It also found that President Truman's state of national emergency, proclaimed on December 16, 1950 in response to the entry of the People's Republic of China into the Korean War, was also still in force. During the twentieth century, states of emergency were declared in 1933, 1939, 1941, 1950, 1970, and 1971. The 1939 and 1941 wartime emergencies were terminated in 1952. (The 1970 emergency was declared by Nixon as an abusive, strike-breaking exercise against Moe Biller's postal workers' union, which was attempting to block the New York City General Post Office. We have examined Nixon's August 15, 1971 emergency in detail in Chapter IV.) The 1933, 1950, 1970 and 1971 emergencies were terminated with the passage of the National Emergencies Act and its signature by President Ford on September 14, 1976.

When he signed the National Emergencies Act, Ford endorsed the termination of the 1933, 1950, 1970, and 1971 states of emergency, but objected to the provision in this bill which stated that the Congress could terminate a state of emergency declared by the President with a concurrent resolution passed by a majority of both houses, but not needing the President's signature. Ford rightly pointed out that this provision was clearly unconstitutional. As former US Solicitor General Erwin Griswold repeatedly asserted in hearings before the Church-Mathias Committee on National Emergencies, once the President has exercised his uncontested right to declare a state of emergency, a full-fledged public law, meaning an act of Congress signed by the President or passed by a two thirds supermajority over the President's veto, is the only way that state of emergency can be terminated. Concurrent resolutions by the two Houses of Congress attempting to terminate a declared state of emergency would have no legal status under the US Constitution.

POWERS DELEGATED TO THE PRESIDENT BY STATUTE

Sweeping economic powers were granted to the President by the Trading with the Enemy Act (TEA), passed by Congress in 1917 as part of US participation in World War I. These powers are centered in the famous section 5-b of the TRA, which states "that the President may investigate, regulate, or prohibit, under such rules and regulations as he may prescribe, by means of licenses or otherwise, any transactions in foreign exchange, export, or earmarking of gold or silver coin or

---

[163] Washington, DC: Government Printing Office, 1973.

bullion or currency, transfers of credit in any form (other than credits relating solely to transactions to be executed wholly with the United States), and transfer of evidences of indebtedness or of the ownership of property between the United States and any foreign country, whether enemy, ally of enemy, or otherwise, or between residents of one or more foreign countries, by any person within the United States; and he may require any such person engaged in any such transaction to furnish, under oath, complete information relative thereto, including the production of any books of account, contracts, letters, or other papers, in connection therewith in the custody or control of such person, either before or after such transaction is completed."

The idea here is that the President was able to regulate and restrict trade between Americans and foreigners, either in wartime, or under a Presidentially-declared state of emergency. We note in passing that this provision allows the President to outlaw derivatives by Executive Order.

ROOSEVELT'S 1933 BANK HOLIDAY

Franklin D. Roosevelt was inaugurated as President of the United States a little after 1 PM on Saturday, March 4, 1933. At this time, virtually all American banks were shut down, either through their own insolvency of through state bank holidays and closure orders. On Monday, March 6, Roosevelt declared his famous bank holiday. Roosevelt acted with an emergency proclamation ordering the suspension of "all banking transactions" in all US states and territories. At the same time that the banks were closed, all gold payments and transfers were suspended: banks were told not to "pay out, export, earmark, or permit the withdrawal or transfer in any manner or by any device whatsoever, of any gold or silver coin or bullion or currency, or take any other action which might facilitate the hoarding thereof." Banks were also ordered not to "pay out deposits, make loans or discounts, deal in foreign exchange, transfer credits from the United States to any place abroad, or transact any other banking business whatsoever." [S. E. Kennedy, 158-159] This proclamation spoke of "all banking institutions," meaning that they Federal Reserve banks were explicitly included and thus indisputably subjected to the legal authority of the President. The Federal Reserve Board had promised to issue an order closing down its own member banks, but it characteristically had failed to deliver on this commitment.

This proclamation was based the authority given to the President under the Trading with the Enemy Act of 1917. The Roosevelt bank holiday avoided the chaos which otherwise must have ensued on the morning of Monday, March 6, 1933. Starting on the morning of Sunday, March 6, FDR's new Secretary of the Treasury William Woodin held meetings with representatives of the New York and Chicago banking communities in the presence of Raymond Moley and Adolf Berle of the new administration's so-called Brain Trust. The bankers were invited to draw up a plan for saving the banking system, but they were able to agree on precisely nothing. After a fruitless first day, these meetings continued fewer participants on March 7, after which they ended with no results. Once again, the bankers had proven impotent to do anything to save their own system.

After the failure of the bankers to make any constructive suggestions, Roosevelt gravitated towards a simple plan presented by the outgoing Secretary of the Treasury, Ogden Mills. This provided for a triage of the banks: a first group of banks were solvent and could be opened almost immediately; a second group needed capital infusions and other help, but could eventually open; and a third group was hopelessly bankrupt and would have to be liquidated, paying the depositors as much as possible on each dollar of deposits. Secretary Woodin added the idea of amending the Federal Reserve Act of 1913 to allow the use Federal Reserve notes to provide banks with enough currency to pay off depositors if needed. All this was to be accomplished under a temporary seizure of the banks by the President to protect the interests of the depositors.

At that time, there were proposals in the air for the nationalization of all banks, including the Federal Reserve System itself. Economists from the University of Chicago proposed to Secretary of Agriculture Henry A. Wallace that the United States government be given the ownership and management of the Federal Reserve System. This would have been a very wise measure, and we face suffered immeasurably ever since because it was not carried out. Given the magnitude of the crisis, it is very likely that any program that Roosevelt had endorsed would have had been virtually assured immediate approval. It was one of those rare moments where the subjective quality of leadership meant everything.

According to the legislative calendar of those days, the new session of Congress convened on March 9, after the inauguration recess. The Senate convened at noon, and Roosevelt's emergency banking bill was submitted to the Banking Committee at 1:40 PM, where the provisions were explained to the committee members by Senator Carter Glass of Virginia, the co-author of the Federal Reserve Act of 1913. By 4:10 the bill was reported out of committee, and by 4:30 it had reached the floor of the Senate. An amendment offered by Senator Huey Long of Louisiana to protect smaller rural banks by making them members of the Federal Reserve System was defeated by voice vote. The bill passed the Senate at 7:23 in the evening by a roll-call vote of 73 to 7. Voting against were Senators Borah, Carey, Costigan, Cale, LaFollette, Nye and Shipstead.

The House convened that same afternoon of March 9, 1933 and at 2:55 PM began to consider the Emergency Banking bill. "Members did not even have copies of the bill – at one point it was represented by a folded newspaper – and the majority leader forbade amendments. The minority leader noted that such procedures were 'entirely out of the ordinary' but saw no practical choice. 'There is only one answer to this question,' he said, 'and that is to give the President what he demands and says is necessary to meet the situation.'" [S. E. Kennedy] That was a very sensible attitude at that time. The Emergency Banking bill passed the House at 4:05 PM.

When the Speaker of the House was informed that the Senate had passed an identical bill, he signed the House copy and sent it to the White House. President Roosevelt signed the Emergency Banking Act of 1933 at 8:36 PM that evening. Two hours later he issued a proclamation which extended the bank holiday indefinitely.

Title I of the new law gave retroactive Congressional approval to the original Roosevelt bank holiday, which had been in force on March 6, 7, 8, and 9 on the basis of Executive Orders. The Congress concurred that this suspension of all banking activity had been the right thing to do, and also found that the legal authority of the Trading with the Enemy Act was sufficient basis for FDR's actions. In addition, the President was here given additional powers in time of national emergency to regulate and prohibit various operations by member banks of the Federal Reserve System, including gold operations. Title II enabled the Ogden Mills triage plan, which required new provisions that allowed national banks with impaired assets to be reorganized by a conservator rather than subjected to compulsory liquidation. Title III allowed banks to rebuild their capital by issuing preferred stock. Title IV allowed Federal Reserve banks to make cash advances to member banks using any acceptable assets as collateral.

Roosevelt explained these provisions to a radio audience estimated at 60 million people on the evening of Sunday, March 12, 1933: it was the first of the celebrated fireside chats. On Monday, March 13, banking operations resumed at many banks. There was at least one bank open in each of the 12 Federal Reserve district cities; all but 9 banks in New York City opened the first day. Banks representing 97% of Chicago's banking resources were reopened, as was the Bank of American with its 410 branches around San Francisco. By March 29, a majority of American banks was functioning. By the last day of March, 5,387 Federal Reserve member banks were open, while

1,307 remained shut down. A new bank created by federal regulators opened in Detroit on March 24. During the first month after the bank holiday, 12,817 banks with about $31 billion in deposits resumed operations. By the middle of 1934, about 1,000 banks with deposits worth some $1.8 billion had been liquidated.

Hoover had been able to halt neither the collapse of financial markets nor the disintegration of the US banking system. Roosevelt's program had halted the banking panic and currency crisis. The US banking system was preserved. But because of flaws in Roosevelt's plans, the private and banker-dominated Federal Reserve System was also preserved when it should have been abolished, and that same Fed is now the scourge of the 1990s. Although Roosevelt was able to stop disintegration, he was unable to put an immediate end to economic depression per se, because the Federal Reserve continued to control credit allocation. The result was that the US economy remained depressed, with high unemployment, until the defense mobilization got under way in 1940. It was finally the Lend-Lease program that put an end to mass unemployment during 1941. These two mistakes by FDR are related: the failure to nationalize the Federal Reserve meant that there continued to be insufficient credit to generate economic recovery until the defense mobilization became imperative.

NIXON'S WAGE AND PRICE CONTROLS

In 1970, Congress passed the Economic Stabilization Act, which authorized the President to "issue such orders as he may deem appropriate to stabilize prices, rents, wages, and salaries," in addition to delegating further powers for national defense. This was the authority used by Nixon on August 15, 1971 to declare the 90-day wage and price freeze that history knows as Phase I. On August 15, 1971, President Nixon also cited the Tariff Act and the Trading with the Enemy Act in imposing a 10% import surcharge. On the same occasion, Nixon ordered the US Treasury to cease gold payment to foreign central banks seeking to exchange paper dollars, thus defaulting on US commitments under the Bretton Woods Treaty.

The Tariff Act and the Trading with the Enemy Act are precisely the traditional provisions that the President will need to employ to reverse decades of free trade insanity with a single strike of the pen. Nixon voided the gold convertibility of the dollar as required by the Bretton Woods Treaty of 1944 (which had been ratified, and thus incorporated into US public law) with a single executive order. In the coming crisis, the President will need to abolish the North American Free Trade Agreement, the General Agreement on Tariffs and Trade, and US participation in the World Trade Organization. He will use an Executive Order citing the precedent of the Trading with the Enemy Act to render NAFTA, GATT, and WTO null and void in just a few minutes. He will terminate US participation in the International Monetary Fund, World Bank, and related organizations, and cancel the membership of the New York Federal Reserve Bank in the Swiss Bank for International Settlements under the same Trading with the Enemy Act.

In 1977, more fearful of the Watergate abuses of the Nixon Administration than concerned about the future, Congress attempted to limit the power of the President to institute economic controls during states of emergency declared by him. By PL 94-412 Congress sought to restrict the President's more far-reaching powers under the TEA to times of declared war. But this overreaction to the excesses of Watergate was plainly unconstitutional.

There are other laws which have provided emergency powers in time of need. The Defense Production Act of September 1950 gives the President the power to impose wage and price controls, to control and order the production of materials needed for national defense and to ration strategic materials by a priority system. In 1979, the Congress passed the Credit Control Act, with provisions that were later used by President Carter to regulate credit issuance. Another important set of economic powers is made available to the President by the International Emergency Economic Powers Act.

FREE TRADE, FREE MARKET, DEREGULATION NOT MANDATED BY GOD

The initiation of a long-overdue antitrust action by the Justice Department against the notorious monopolistic practices of Microsoft in October 1998 occasioned a series of television statements in defense of Microsoft by a parade of self-righteous philistines who happened to own companies in Silicon Valley. These CEOs were sincerely indignant because they though that the Justice Department was violating the sacred laws of free market. Their vehemence was of the kind that is mobilized when a taboo is violated, or when a fetish is not respected. Some of them expressed the belief that a free market means anything which economic royalists have the power and determination to impose, including monopoly, oligopoly, cartels, restraint of trade, dumping, driving competitors out of business, and so forth. We must remind these true believers in *laissez-faire* of a few relevant facts.

Free trade and the free market are not mentioned among the Ten Commandments. They figure neither in the Sermon on the Mount nor in the two great commandments enunciated by Jesus Christ. They are not prescribed by the Confucian *Analects*, nor by the Holy *Koran*. There is nothing about free trade in the Nicene Creed. Indeed, the holy books of the three great monotheistic faiths and of many leading world religions include financial and economic regulations, which makes it impossible to argue that a regulated economy is abhorrent in the sight of God.

As Americans, we need to point out that free trade and the free market are not mandated by the Declaration of Independence. The general welfare is listed as an imperative in the preamble to the US Constitution, but free trade and the free market are not, and they are not mentioned in any of the articles. Free trade is not part of Lincoln's Gettysburg Address, but government of the people, by the people, and for the people is strongly endorsed. Freedom from want is one of the Four Freedoms included in the Atlantic Charter, but free trade is not. There is, in short, no basis in fact for the contention that free trade and the free market somehow enjoy the status of cosmic imperatives in human affairs. Only for the venal speechwriters of such figures as Margaret Thatcher and her current Labour Party imitators has this been so.

PROVEN MEASURES, NOT MONETARIST UTOPIA

This chapter discusses a number of the policies required for national and world economic survival. Monetarist and oligarchical spokesmen can be expected to assail measures like these with epithets like radical, extreme, socialistic, communistic, corporatist, fascist, totalitarian, and an array of other choice adjectives. In reality, every policy or measure advocated here has already been successfully put into practice in some form at some time by the United States Government. The policies included here are not simply copies of what has been done in the past, but improvements and refinements of the mechanisms already employed. The policies advocated here are time-tested. They are proven. They are reliable. They are tried and true. Their track record in enviable, and their success in predictable. They have worked before and they will work again. They are sure-fire. They are old friends for anyone who knows anything about American history. The reflexes, procedures, and plans they represent are still latent in file cabinets and data banks in the nooks and crannies of the various bureaus of the US government. Most of them can be taken off the shelf and dusted off for quick use. By contrast, it is the deregulated, stateless, hot-money, hedge fund regime of the globaloney advocates which represents an unattainable and unworkable pie-in-the-sky Utopia.

THE RETURN TO DIRIGISM

The United States and the world must therefore turn away from the destructive and discredited recipes of financial globalization and globaloney, and return to the great traditions of constructive government action. What is required has nothing to do with the failed methods of the twentieth-century totalitarian states. We must draw from the great tradition of government-supported economic growth and modernization represented by Plato, the Florentine Medici, Louis XI of France, Henry VII of England, Cardinal Richelieu and Jean-Baptiste Colbert of France, Gustavus Adolphus of Sweden, the Great Elector of Brandenburg, Charles III of Spain, Gottfried Leibniz and Friedrich List of Germany, Cavour of Italy, Count Witte of Russia, Sun Yat-sen and Chiang Kai-Shek of China, Mustafa Kemal Ataturk of Turkey, and Benjamin Franklin, Alexander Hamilton, John Quincy Adams, Friedrich List, Henry Clay, Abraham Lincoln, Matthew and Henry Carey, Franklin D. Roosevelt, Douglas MacArthur, and John F. Kennedy in our own country. This is the tradition of mercantilism, protectionism, and dirigism. Dirigism is the American way, as American as apple pie. It is the tradition of positive, humanitarian nationalism and nation-building. It is the tradition which has built the modern nations and the modern world. This is the tradition which corresponds best to the outlook and interests of the great American middle class, which is now called upon once more to lift the world out of the economic depression and financial disintegration in which the finance oligarchs have landed us.

One of the most eminent recent practitioners of economic dirigism was a great nation builder of our own century, French President Charles De Gaulle. When he came to power in 1958, De Gaulle found France as a financial derelict, locked in the coils of the IMF and on the brink of national collapse. De Gaulle's economic policies of currency reform and indicative planning, developed in cooperation with the economist Jacques Rueff, saved the French nation and restored its dignity and economic growth. Thanks to this dirigism, France was able to develop its own independent nuclear industry for independent defense during the period of the Soviet threat, while endowing the country with the most modern and best-developed nuclear-powered electricity grid in the world. French aerospace boasts achievements like fast railroads and a supersonic transport which the United States cannot match. And as we will see, French trains are currently the fastest in the world. Here is De Gaulle's quick overview of economic dirigism as formulated for his memoirs:

> For us, then, the task of the State was not to force the nation under a yoke, but to guide its progress. However, though freedom remained an essential lever in economic action, this action was none the less collective, it directly controlled the nation's destiny, and it continually involved social relations. It thus required an impetus, a harmonizing influence, a set of rules, which could only emanate from the State. In short, what was needed was State direction (*dirigisme*). [De Gaulle, 150-151]

A little further on General de Gaulle ably summed up the tools which the nation-state must mobilize to protect the general welfare and advance the public interest of all its citizens:

> In practical terms, what it primarily amounted to was drawing up the national plan, in other words deciding on the goals, the priorities, the rates of growth and the conditions that must be observed in the national economy, and determining the extent of the financial outlay which the State must make, the fields of development in which it must intervene, and the measures to be taken in consequence through its decrees, its laws, and its budgets. It is within this framework that the State increases or reduces taxation, eases or restricts credit, regulates customs duties; that it develops the national infrastructure – roads, railways, waterways, harbors, airports, communications, new towns, housing, etc., harnesses the sources of energy – electricity, gas, coal, oil, atomic power; initiates research in the public sector and fosters it in

the private; that it encourages the rational distribution of economic activity over the whole country, and by means of social security, education, and vocational training, facilitates the changes of employment forced on many Frenchmen by modernization. In order that our country's structures should be remolded and its appearance rejuvenated, my government, fortified by the new-found stability of the State, was to engage in manifold and vigorous interventions. [De Gaulle 151]

Dirigism is also the Japanese system, which derives from the American and European tradition indicated above. The reforms of the Emperor Mutsuhito (or Meiji, 1867-1912) stand as the beginning of one of the most successful modernizations of all time. In this effort, American models were second to none, and some of the most important anti-oligarchical reforms were actually completed under MacArthur's US occupation government after World War II. One of the best-known American students of the post-1945 Japanese economic miracle had this to say about the viability of the Japanese model as it existed in the early 1980s, before the excesses of the bubble economy urged by Don Regan and James Baker III: "...in Japan the state's role in the economy is shared with the private sector, and both the public and private sectors have perfected means to make the market work for developmental goals. This pattern has proved to be the most successful strategy of intentional development among the historic cases. It is being repeated today in newly industrializing states of East Asia – Taiwan and South Korea – and in Singapore and other South and Southeast Asian countries. As a response to the original beneficiaries of the industrial revolution, the Japanese pattern has proved to be incomparably more successful than the purely state-dominated command economies of the communist world. Since the death of Mao Tse-tung even China has come to acknowledge, if not yet emulate, the achievements of the capitalist developmental state." [Johnson, viii]

In short, the cataclysm must be embraced as an opportunity, since it affords to enact, in the course of a week, a day, or a single afternoon, more progressive legislation than has been implemented in the past three decades.

FIVE STEPS TO LAUNCH AN ECONOMIC RECOVERY

I. THE PRESIDENT DECLARES A STATE OF EMERGENCY

It should be clear by now that there is no private sector cure for a world economic and financial collapse into disintegration. Rescuing the national and the world economy will require not just government action, and not just federal government action: it will require Presidential action of the most courageous and decisive kind. Even under the less extreme circumstances of 1932-1933, historical experience proved that even the most powerful commercial bankers were unable to stop the disintegration, whether they were acting individually or in groups. Other business leaders, including Henry Ford, were impotent to save the banks. The Federal Reserve was the cause of the problem, and was not part of the solution – the Fed brought forward no meaningful initiatives. State governments were pathetic in their weakness: states could and did close their banks, but not one state was able to re-open its banks. Between January and March 1933, the Congress provided the strongest proof of its utter inability to act swiftly and decisively in a crisis. The few things Congress was able to do only made the panic worse. Within the Executive Branch cabinet departments and cabinet officers were by themselves ineffective.

The first step to economic recovery will therefore be a formal declaration by the President of a state of economic emergency. Part of this speech would be authoritatively to inform the citizens of this republic of the existence of a world economic depression of unprecedented severity. The President would pose to the country the irreversible breakdown of the old System, and the urgency of measures to promote a broad-based economic recovery.

The Defense Production Act allows the President to order the production of any commodity in any quantity that the President deems necessary for the national defense. Under the Defense Production Act, the President can seize any bank, and run it as a ward of the federal government. Regional and local banks must be kept open and running, whatever their level of insolvency. The local bankers, with their valuable knowledge of local economic conditions and of the capabilities of local entrepreneurs, will be needed to help administer R-loan credit (see below) in all parts of the country. Manufacturing companies, shipping lines, railroads, mines, public utilities, communications firms and any other business enterprise which is threatened by bankruptcy or foreclosure can be seized by Presidential order and directed to continue production of specified commodities at specified levels of employment under the Defense Production Act.

Part of the initial declaration of a state of economic emergency must be the extension of protection from creditors to the entire United States economy. The logic of Chapter XI bankruptcy is that we have before us a potentially viable enterprise which finds itself insolvent for contingent reasons. The idea is that the bankrupt company could be reorganized with the help of an outside agency (in the case of a single bankrupt enterprise, a court) and become a going concern once again. In the kind of economic breakdown crisis that awaits us at the end of the twentieth century, all levels of government, companies and firms of all kinds, farmers, businessmen, families and individuals will tend to find themselves insolvent, often through no fault of their own. Insolvency means that they will lack the liquid funds to meet debt payments that they are legally obligated to pay. From the point of view of statutory law, such people might be declared bankrupt and their goods seized for auction. But if this were to happen, so much economic activity would come to a halt that and mass starvation would result. At this point natural law intervenes, asserting the priority of national survival and human life over the debt contract.

We will require, first by Executive Order and later by public laws passed by Congress and signed by the President, uniform federal directives halting the shutting down of production or the foreclosure on personal property for reasons of non-payment of debt. All foreclosures on private homes must be halted by such uniform and orderly federal dispositions. No cars must be repossessed for non-payment, for the duration of the crisis. No business or farm, large or small, which can produce something that is needed must be interfered with for reasons of debt. During Roosevelt's Hundred Days of 1933, a federal law was signed which stopped farm foreclosures: this was the Emergency Farm Mortgage Act, which went into effect on May 12, 1933. This law halted foreclosures until farm prices had returned to normal levels. This time, it must be for the whole economy and for the entire duration of the economic emergency.

The federal government must assert the sanctity of life over the fetish of debt, and it must practice what it preaches. A blanket tax amnesty must be swiftly declared, wiping the slate clean for all individuals, families, farms, and small businesses. The Internal Revenue Service must be ordered to remove and suspend all tax seizures, liens, attachments and garnishes for the duration of the crisis. The Farmers Home Administration and other components of the farm credit system must extend a moratorium on all debts and debt service, for the duration of the crisis. The Student Loan Marketing Association (Sally Mae), Freddie Mac and Fannie Mae must be ordered to extend comprehensive debt moratoria covering interest and principal on all sums owned to them, again for the duration of the state of emergency. The Congress, corrupted by credit card companies, has recently been trying to place bankruptcy beyond the reach of the struggling working family. In the cataclysm, new laws must be passed that will make it easy for individuals to declare personal bankruptcy and start afresh with a clean slate. Under normal circumstances, personal bankruptcy and debt cancellation should be streamlined so as to take no more than one working day, and the laws must be designed to make this possible. The national interest requires that precious man-days of productive work not be lost on protracted litigation, and that the resources of depleted families not be squandered on exorbitant lawyers' fees. This country has been tormented by debt long enough.

Certain promises to pay, however, must be scrupulously respected. As the number one strategic priority, the United States Treasury must not default on any of its payment obligations. United States Savings Bonds must be regarded as a sacred trust to the small saver. The FDIC Bank Insurance Fund must be fully funded so as to pay back savings accounts, certificates of deposit and checking accounts up to the full insured level of $100,000 per person. The President must use Executive Orders to direct the Office of Thrift Supervision and National Credit Union Administration to guarantee and disburse as required the deposits of all S&L and credit union account holders up to the full legal limit. Not one penny of federally insured deposits can be allowed to go lost. The Pension Benefit Guarantee Corporation must be given the means to protect retired persons from losing their means of existence. Every effort must be made to prevent default by the states and municipalities on their bonds and other payment obligations. In general, government commitments must be honored, since credit generated by government will be the key to recovery. Any HMOs, insurance companies, or other medical insurance providers which are in distress must be seized and operated by the federal government for the sole purpose of maintaining benefit payments to the subscribers, without regard to the outcome for the stock or bondholders or corporate officers. The President must also see to it that there be no interruptions in the activities of the Social Security Administration.

WIPE OUT DERIVATIVES BY EXECUTIVE ORDER

On the other hand, no attempt must be made by government to shore up stock prices. The Brady system of drugged markets described above must be brought to an end. No special loans should be issued to mutual funds in order to facilitate their redemptions. Nothing can be done to save mutual fund investors from the consequences of their own folly. Commercial paper and money markets will be left to their own devices. Derivatives must be swiftly and finally outlawed, and all derivatives contracts made null and void. Attempts to continue derivatives markets in any guise must be dispersed by armed force if necessary, and stiff criminal penalties applied in exemplary cases. The holders of futures, options, swaps, index options, index futures, structured notes, over-the-counter derivatives and all other derivatives are beyond human assistance, and any attempt to bail them out would doom the hopes for recovery. Banks will be shorn of their derivatives and will be kept open as wards of the Treasury, but bank stocks, bonds, and commercial paper will not be supported. Real estate prices will have to find their own level. Those who worshipped at the altar of the free market may now find themselves sacrificed on that same altar. There is not enough money on the planet, much less in the coffers of the US government, to shore up so much worthless speculative paper. There must be no attempt to monetize this debt.

We must operate in the spirit of Franklin D. Roosevelt's First Inaugural, when he stated:

> ...there must be an end to a conduct in banking and in business which too often has given to a sacred trust the likeness of callous and selfish wrongdoing. Small wonder that confidence languishes, for it thrives only on honesty, on honor, on the sacredness of obligations, on faithful protection, on unselfish performance; without them it cannot live.

> Finally, in our progress toward a resumption of work we require two safeguards against a return of the evils of the old order; there must be a strict supervision of all banking and credits

and investments; there must be an end to speculation with other people's money, and there must be provision for an adequate but sound currency.

The same criteria must be employed in the international arena. Leaders of the International Monetary Fund and other supernational financial entities have been blunt about their desire to become bankruptcy receiver in case of the bankruptcy of national states, including the United States. The notion here is that the IMF would unlawfully place itself over the government in Washington in the same way that the Municipal Assistance Corporation extended its authority over the elected government of New York City and New York State in 1975, or in the same way that the Financial Control Board has illegally usurped the authority of the elected government of the District of Columbia during the last few years. The President must make clear that all of the powers of the United States government, including military force, will be employed to prevent the IMF, World Bank, United Nations, Bank for International Settlements, or any other foreign entity from extinguishing the national sovereignty of this country. If the IMF attempts to declare the United States of America bankrupt, the United States government will have no choice but to take note of the bankruptcy of the International Monetary Fund and take charge of its gold reserves, cash balances, premises, offices, computers, and so forth, pending the final liquidation of the IMF. In this process, the IMF could be subjected to a serious audit for the first time. At the same time, the US Treasury must stop counting the IMF's Special Drawing Rights (SDRs) as money, and write them off as a total loss, pending US efforts to collect on them in the course of the liquidation of the IMF.

As has been shown elsewhere in this book, one of the greatest barriers to world economic recovery has been the crushing burden of debt service and amortization of principal that has been heaped on the poorest countries of the world. No economic recovery can take place unless this debt can be neutralized. The President must therefore take the lead in promoting a blanket worldwide moratorium of interest and principal payments on international financial debt. In other words, all such international payments must be frozen. They must be frozen, not in some do-it-yourself standstill gridlock of dubious legality, and not for some arbitrary short-term period such as a year or two years. They must be **FROZEN 100% AND FOR THE DURATION OF THE CRISIS**. (One of the great defects of the Hoover Moratorium of 1931 was that its duration was far too short to help world recovery.) Only when the world economy is safely back on the track and world economic recovery well underway, will it be time to even discuss what should ever happen with this debt. Every nation on earth, without exception, must enjoy the benefits of a comprehensive debt moratorium. The United States should have nothing further to do with the London and Paris Clubs of creditors.

Debt moratorium is not the same thing as debt cancellation. The debt remains on the books, and the obligation to negotiate a solution to the debt problem at some future time remains. But during the time the debt moratorium is in force, no interest accrues on the account of the debtor; the debt is literally frozen, placed in suspended animation. The most likely outcome of the debt moratorium process is that part of the principal will eventually be partially repaid by way a series of installments over many years. Short-term debt will eventually be transformed into long-term debt. Another likely result of repayment negotiations will be a drastic lowering of interest rates.

The international financial debt owed by the poorest countries to governments and private lenders should be placed in a different category, and should permanently and unconditionally cancelled. In the wake of the killer hurricane Mitch, French President Chirac and former US President Carter recommended that the entire foreign debt of Honduras and Nicaragua be expunged. Mitch was a category five hurricane; a financial hurricane of far greater destructive power is about to lash the world, making debt forgiveness the only way out for dozens of countries across the globe. The

United States should take the lead in facilitating the expunging of such debt, which is unpayable in any case.

Another key part of the recovery effort will be the lowering of interest rates. There is no natural level for interest rates. It is certain, however, that US interest rates have been far too high since Harry Truman allowed the Federal Reserve to escape from the control of the President and the Treasury Department which had been established under Franklin D. Roosevelt. The tradition of excessive interest rates was carried forward with a vengeance by McChesney Martin, by Volcker, and then by Greenspan. The optimum rate of interest for loans granted by the government in a non-usury economy is almost always the costs of administering the loan. In other words, granting and supervising any loan always entails a lending officer, an office staff, research, and the like. The expense of these services, generally in the range of 1% to 2%, is the only reason for charging interest on a government loan. No longer must the federal government give any legitimacy to interest rates prevailing in the so-called "market." No agency of the United States government must ever again be a party to exacting interest rates on farmers, businessmen, students, or any other persons or entities in excess of the 1-2% level justified to defray administrative expense.

EXCHANGE AND CAPITAL CONTROLS

At the same time that chapter XI bankruptcy and international debt moratorium are declared, it will be prudent to insulate the dollar from speculative attack by imposing comprehensive capital and exchange controls. Controls mean in practice that persons and corporations wishing to transfer sums of money above a specified minimum in or out of the country must obtain a license from the Treasury Department to do so. They are required to disclose the nature of their business. The license can be issued only if the purpose of the fund transfer meets the criteria specified by law. It must be made impossible electronically to transfer large sums for derivatives, speculation, or hedge fund purposes. Controls like these were most recently in place under Lyndon B. Johnson, and were most unwisely removed by the Nixon Administration on the eve of the collapse of Bretton Woods. No funds originating in the United States must be allowed to flee the country for purposes of overseas speculation. Foreign hot money steered by sociopaths like George Soros must not be allowed to create wild gyrations by entering and leaving US markets.

EMERGENCY RELIEF

Another area requiring emergency intervention by the President will be emergency poor relief – saving lives threatened by starvation, destitution, homelessness, and exposure. The President will need to direct and assist state and local agencies to furnish emergency poor relief in adequate quantities to prevent hardship and starvation. The model here is the experience of the Federal Emergency Relief Administration, created by Harry Hopkins starting in May 1933. Hopkins and FERA had to face hysterical attacks from businessmen, especially in the south, who complained that federal relief payments were higher than the coolie wages they were offering for long days of backbreaking work. Local oligarchs, confident they could control state relief programs, screamed that there should be no federal welfare program at all. Businessmen in all parts of the country saw federal relief as interfering with their efforts further to drive down wages. A farmer wrote to Governor Eugene Talmadge of Georgia to complain that federal work relief was paying $1.30 per day, making it impossible for him to exploit day laborers at his accustomed rate of fifty cents per day. When Talmadge forwarded this to Roosevelt, the President calculated that fifty cents per day in seasonal farm work might come to an annual income of $60 to $75 per year. Roosevelt wrote in reply: "Somehow I cannot get it into my head that wages on such a scale make possible a reasonable American standard of living." [Schlesinger 1959, 274] Businessmen can be expected to be as blind to the need for federal emergency poor relief in this depression as they were in the last one. But to allow their narrow-minded views to control the national agenda would be to violate the Nuremburg standard of 1945. Recovery from depression will entail a transition from the current low-wage economy to a high wage economy in the best American traditions.

Today's guideline must be that every person under US jurisdiction has the inalienable human right not to die of hunger or exposure. Persons and families who are unemployed and destitute must be provided with emergency food, clothing, and shelter as a reflection of that right. By contrast, there is no right to be homeless. Large homeless populations living in the streets or in makeshift Hoovervilles, persons living in cars, tunnels, or other makeshift dwellings, and seeking food in today's Cleveland cafes, constitute breeding grounds for tuberculosis, typhus, typhoid, hepatitis, cholera, AIDS, and other communicable diseases, and thus represent an intolerable risk of epidemics. No one has the right to choose to be a vehicle for tuberculosis or typhus. Vagrancy laws must thus be enforced by providing homeless persons with a heated and sanitary dwelling place and fully adequate food, clothing, and medical care. This is the elementary self-interest of society as a whole, since any substantial group of persons living in unsanitary and depressed conditions constitutes a dangerous breach in the epidemiological defense line of the community. Unoccupied apartments, office buildings, and other emergency dwelling places must be speedily requisitioned for these homeless persons. For food aid, we will doubtless require a massive increase in the availability of federal food stamps. Medical care can be delivered under the aegis of the national health care program. Job training must be offered free of charge, as it was during the New Deal, to qualify destitute persons for the job opportunities which will be opening up in economic development projects financed by federal R-loans.

The United States should expand its Food for Peace humanitarian relief to other countries on the part of the Agency for International Development and other agencies. One elementary step which is long overdue is the cancellation of every economic sanction, general or selective trade embargo, economic blockade, or economic warfare measure presently pursued or imposed by the United States against any country. It is well past time to normalize economic relations with countries like Cuba, North Korea, Iraq, Iran, Libya, Sudan, Serbia, and all other states, making them eligible for emergency assistance.

II. THE NATIONALIZATION OF THE FEDERAL RESERVE SYSTEM

The Federal Reserve Act of 1913 is manifestly unconstitutional. In the US Constitution Article II Section 8 clause 5 that Congress shall have the power "to coin money, regulate the value thereof, and of foreign coin, and fix the standard of weights and measures." If the Constitution specifies that coining money is a function of the Congress with the concurrence of the President, that function cannot be abdicated to a private agency without a Constitutional amendment. Since the Constitution has not been amended on this point, the arrogation of these powers by bodies of private bankers calling themselves "Federal Reserve Board of Governors" and "Open Market Committee" is illegal and unconstitutional. Given the vast powers accumulated by the Federal Reserve, the resulting state of affairs is the equivalent of an open insurrection against the legal government of the United States.

The President must therefore, as an integral and indispensable part of his program to fight the depression, seize and nationalize the Federal Reserve System. He must do this speedily in order to prevent the Federal Reserve from destroying all hope of recovery and restoration of business confidence by monetizing tens of trillions of dollars of derivative instruments which private commercial bankers will seek to fob off on the Federal Reserve and the taxpayers, to the great detriment of the national economy.

The Federal Reserve is a private institution operating with an illegal government charter. Federal Reserve stock is not held by the government, but is owned by banks. The vast majority of the top Federal Reserve officials, especially in the outlying regions,   are chosen by bankers without reference to Presidential appointment or to confirmation by the Senate. This illegality must be brought to a halt. The average voter will be inclined to support the nationalization of the Federal Reserve. Indeed, the average voter has always been of the mistaken belief that the Federal Reserve is a government institution. The decisive factor in the eyes of the average person will be the simple fact that the Federal Reserve not only has failed to avoid depression, but rather has caused it. Most voters will know that. Many voters will also remember that it was the Volcker Federal Reserve whose ill-conceived monetarist policies de-industrialized this country and brought on depression conditions in 1982-83. A few, especially readers of this book, will remember that the Federal Reserve was responsible for the 1929 bubble and proved totally impotent to save the banking system in 1931-33. The record of Greenspan in fomenting the derivatives plague and in refusing to curb the hedge funds is evident to all.

The Federal Reserve is a private institution. As we have seen, the emergency powers of the President indisputably give the President the power to seize private property if this should prove necessary for the protection of the general welfare in a national emergency. The Federal Reserve's assets, buildings, communications systems, and other property will be transferred to the custody of the United States Treasury. The President formally declare, and should ask Congress to establish by law, that matters of money supply and interest rates will henceforth be determined by means of public laws of the United States, passed by a majority of both Houses of Congress, and signed into law by the President – the only legal way we have of doing things in this country. Politicians who are ambitious enough to seek public office will have to accept the power and the responsibility for making these most basic economic decisions, and must be held accountable for what they do. No longer will they be able to blame the uncontrollable, unaccountable Federal Reserve.

As part of the process of nationalization, the secretive Federal Reserve, which has in practice seen itself as beyond the law, must be subjected for the very first time in history to a thorough outside audit. Federal Reserve officials who prove to have been responsible for abuses must be punished according to law. In particular, investigators must search for evidence of deliberate collusion on the part of Federal reserve authorities in covering up the laundering by Federal Reserve member banks of cash proceeds from illegal drug trading.

On January 22, 1996 *New York Magazine* published an exposé of the close relations among the New York Federal Reserve, the Republic National Bank of New York of Lebanese financier Edmond Safra (linked by the US Customs in 1989 to illegal money laundering), and the Russian Mafia. The issue involved a weekly traffic of between $100 million and $1 billion in US hundred dollar bills which were shipped from New York's Kennedy airport to Moscow. In addition, scandals around the crime-family dealings of former Mexican President Carlos Salinas de Gortari and his relatives indicate a high degree of collusion between the Federal Reserve and Citibank's Private Bank, an elite insider financial institution with $80 billion in assets. This involves the relationship between the Mexican President's brother, Raul Salinas de Gortari, who has been indicted in Mexico for theft and conspiracy to commit murder, and Amelia Grovas Eliot of Citibank. Citibank and Eliot between 1989 and 1993 moved tens of millions of dollars of hot money around the world for Raul Salinas, whose personal wealth may have approached $1 billion. Much of this activity was illegal. Said illegal activity went on during the years when, as we have seen, when Citibank was under the day to day control of the New York Fed, one of whose officers at that time was Maurice "Hank" Greenberg of American International Group, an insurance company. A thorough audit by outside investigators is long overdue. Congressional hearings on Citibank and the Salinas de Gortari family have every potential to explode into the Pecora hearings of the 1990s, profoundly changing the climate of public opinion.

The former Federal Reserve as re-constituted under the Treasury could be designated as the "Fourth Bank of the United States" to stress its continuity with Alexander Hamilton's First Bank of the United States, Henry Clay's Second Bank of the United States, and William Henry Harrison's and Daniel Webster's stillborn Third Bank of the United States. The board, president, and officers of the Fourth Bank of the United States must be appointed by the President and confirmed by the Senate, since the BUS will be a wholly owned federal agency carrying out a series of functions prescribed by public law. Especially in times of war or economic emergency, the Bank of the United States must stand ready to float Treasury debt issues at the prices prescribed by the Secretary of the Treasury and approved by the President. This was the system implemented by Franklin D. Roosevelt during World War II, which allowed interest rates to be held at historically low levels during the most destructive international conflict in human history. The Fourth Bank of the United States would also function as a national development bank.

The Treasury and the BUS will take over operations of the existing Fedwire system for interbank transfers of payments and government securities. It will be necessary in all probability to bring existing interbank netting and settlement systems, such as CHIPS, under BUS management. Treasury and other government computer experts will be mobilized to restore service at automatic teller machines and other automatic cash dispensers, which are likely to have ceased functioning at some point in the crisis. These problems may prove far more intractable than the much-touted Y2K computer software issues, but they must be solved if recovery is to begin.

To guarantee the integrity of the United States dollar, the issue of eurodollars and other so-called xenodollars will have to be addressed. Over the past four decades, masses of US dollars have been allowed to accumulate in foreign countries, especially in London. The presence of untold trillions of eurodollars beyond the reach of US law constitutes a weakness and vulnerability which should no longer be accepted. An important goal of the US recovery program should be to repatriate the eurodollars as quickly as possible by running a sustained US balance of payments surplus, gradually bringing the eurodollars home in the form of payments to US exporters for high-technology capital goods. At the same time, the US Export-Import Bank, Commodity Credit Corporation and other agencies should stand ready to finance foreign projects and purchases which are sound from a developmental point of view. In the meantime, the Comptroller of the Currency must become far more intrusive in supervising and regulating banks and other institutions which are active in the eurodollar market. Any foreign bank which maintains branch offices on US territory, or which habitually does business in US financial markets, must be subjected to a regime of complete transparency by US regulators, in the sense that US authorities must have access to that bank's entire worldwide bookkeeping. Banks which turn out to be hedge funds in disguise must be prevented from operating anywhere under US jurisdiction. Banks which engage in the laundering of monies from activities which would be illegal under US law must also be stopped from doing business here.

III. FEDERAL CREDIT ISSUANCE FOR ECONOMIC RECOVERY

The Treasury and the Bank of the United States, acting under the supervision of the President and the Secretary of the Treasury, will become the lead agencies for a program of credit issuance for promote economic recovery. The Treasury will issue the currency, and the Bank of the United States will mobilize the inherent capacity of the United States Government to function as its own bank, especially important at a time when most private banks will be paralyzed by bankruptcy. The mandate of the Bank of the United States will be to bring about general economic recovery through full employment at union pay scales in modern, capital-intensive and energy-intensive commodity production, while avoiding inflation and preserving the value of the dollar as a leading currency of international trade and development. This latter task will require a special effort to promote US high-technology exports of modern capital goods. The outcome of these policies will be an elevation of the overall US standard of living for the first time since 1973. All these tasks are directly pursuant to the general welfare clause of the Constitution.

As mentioned before, the United States Government, if properly run, is without question the most powerful institution on the planet. The US Government can send men to the moon, reach the depths of the oceans, dispatch probes into interstellar space, and solve the riddles of the atom. How is it possible that an institution equipped with these awesome powers cannot function as its own bank? The US Government has no intrinsic need of a private central bank, nor of private commercial banks. Indeed, these banks and all corporations are creatures which exist only under the laws the government has established.

In the coming crisis, the indispensable role of the US Government as the source of credit will be dramatically underlined by the insolvency of the banking system. Even now, banks have increasingly abandoned their past role as lenders to corporations for trade and acquisitions of capital equipment. Banks today are mainly interested in selling their proprietary derivative "products." They are more hedge funds than banks. In the depths of the crisis, things will be much worse. Most banks will be dependent on US Government assistance for their survival, and will be in no position to provide credit for a recovery from their own decimated reserves. The US Treasury was, is, and will be more credit-worthy than any bank.

ONE TRILLION DOLLARS IN FEDERAL LENDING PER YEAR

Pursuant to a public law, the Treasury will accordingly issue one trillion dollars of United States Treasury notes. This sum will be placed on deposit with the Bank of the United States and made available for lending through local commercial banks. The older "Federal Reserve Notes" will continue to circulate for the time being at their full face value, but they will gradually be withdrawn from circulation and replaced by the new United States Treasury Notes.

Federal loans in the form of United States Treasury Notes will be made available to borrowers engaged in productive activities and other necessary activities in the public interest. These loans might be called Recovery Loans or R-Loans, perhaps recalling to some the Victory Loans or V-Loans of the World War II national defense mobilization.

R-Loans will carry rates of interest much lower than have been customary in the post-Volcker world. The standard rate of interest on an R-Loan will be about 2%, in conformity with the general principle that interest rates ought to converge on the administrative cost of the loan. Loans for certain projects can be interest free. The maturity of an R-loan will depend on the nature of the project to be financed and the needs of the borrower, meaning that maturities of 5, 10, 15, or 25 years and longer will be routine.

Even during the period of monetarist ascendancy, the notion of low-interest or no-interest federal lending to promote national goals was never completely lost. In 1985, a bill submitted for House consideration through the Public Works and Transportation Committee sought to establish a "National Infrastructure Fund to provide funds for *interest-free* loans to State and local governments for construction and improvement of highways, bridges, water supply and distribution systems, mass transportation facilities and equipment, and waste water treatment facilities, and for other purposes." These interest-free loans were to be paid back over a period of 20 years. [W. Peterson 209] This is the spirit which must inform national efforts for economic recovery and reconstruction.

THE TREASURY CATALOGUE

The basis of effective credit policy is a rigorous scientific distinction between what is productive and what is not productive. Productive workers are those who are engaged in carrying out progressive changes in the physical order of nature – changes beneficial to society. The changes made by productive workers have the effect of increasing the power of mankind and of the human individual over the physical universe. The physical changes made through production must facilitate the self-reproduction of humanity at higher population levels and higher standards of living, including culture. This is what human progress has been all about. Infrastructure is socially necessary because it increases the productive power of society, and because it increases the productivity of human labor.

Some services are socially necessary because they allow productive workers to do their job of being productive. For every 1,000 productive workers, we will require the backup of determinable numbers of doctors, nurses, health technicians, teachers, librarians, and other service providers. But there should be no confusion: the basis of the economy is production, and not the services that are indispensable to production. The notion of a service-based economy is absurd.

Many aspects of today's "service economy" are unnecessary and parasitical. These include most advertising agencies, public relations firms, and "image consultants." Financial speculators and their financial services firms are parasitical and destructive. So are the various dimensions of organized crime, such as drug trading. Hollywood is much bigger than it needs to be, and the quality is abysmal. The growth of jobs in hamburger sales and pizza home delivery has gone too far in recent decades. We can do without the services provided by croupiers and bouncers in gambling casinos, and of pimps and prostitutes in brothels. This point needs to be emphasized, since in the credit climate of the 1980s and 1990s the parasitical and illegal activities were given *de facto* preference for whatever credit existed, since these activities have much higher rates of profit than can be obtained in normal production. In effect, productive activities and their more modest profits have been discriminated against by the high-interest policies of bankers and brokers. We have been experiencing dirigism in reverse. This situation must now be redressed. In recent years we have heard about the "motion picture industry", the "securities industry", the "banking industry", the "mutual fund industry", and the "entertainment industry." We have even witnessed the protests of the "sex workers". None of these are industries, and their employees cannot be regarded as productive workers in their present occupations. Industry, for purposes of law, must mean the manufacturing of commodities.

When it comes to organizing a recovery, these are not theoretical or semantic questions. The US Treasury Department will have to prepare, within guidelines specified by law and/or Executive Orders, an exhaustive catalogue of the forms of business activity that can be classed as productive. The general guideline is that productive activities produce hard-commodity, physical wealth. We must channel the available credit, manpower, and resources into productive activity because we have the scientific certainty that these will help economic recovery from depression.

The Treasury Catalogue will have hundreds of thousands, ultimately millions of entries. Here are some activities that will generally be classed as either productive or socially necessary:

Farming
Industry (production of commodities)
Mining
Construction (stressing industrial plant, housing, and hospitals, rather than malls and office buildings)
Scientific Research
Transportation
Infrastructure building and maintenance (including highways and bridges)
Commerce (buying and selling, import and export of physical commodities)
Defense Production
Nuclear Reactors
Electric Power
Water Projects
Mechanical Repairs
Machine Tools
Railroad Equipment
Health Care and Hospitals

Businessmen and entrepreneurs, along with state, county, and city officials will be able to apply to their local bankers for long-term, low-interest R-loans to re-start business activity. If the projects they propose to undertake are listed in the Treasury Catalogue, and if the local banker can certify that they have the wherewithal to undertake the project with a reasonable perspective for success, they should be granted the R-loan they desire. The main thing is to make sure that the R-loans go only to productive business activity, as well as to certain urgent socially necessary categories.

Financial services operators and speculators need not apply for R-loans. The same goes for mafia bosses, drug smugglers, image consultants, ad agencies, public relations gurus, psychic networks, pornographers, pimps, and others who are not productive and not socially necessary. Although some of these activities are clearly illegal, not all are outlawed. The ones that are legal can take their chances procuring credit on their much-admired free market, if they can find it. But not one penny of R-loan credit should go for parasitical or criminal activities.

The companies, executives, and managers who receive the R-loans will be able to draw on their checking accounts at their local banks, which will be operating in cooperation with the Bank of the United States. From these checking balances they will begin to purchase raw materials and semi-finished commodities, while also beginning to hire workers and pay the weekly payroll. They will place orders for steel, concrete, construction equipment, scientific apparatus, turbines, and the like. The workers and their families will head for supermarkets, car dealerships, furniture and department stores. Economic recovery will thus begin. "But all that will cause inflation!" may object someone who has been disoriented by decades of economic illiteracy in public life. (As if inflation were the most urgent problem facing this average Joe, who is on the average $50,000 in debt, and who has not been clipping very many bond coupons lately!) "And what about the budget deficit!"

Notice once again that we are talking here about **federal LENDING**, and not federal *spending*. The only way that industrial capitalism has worked for the past 500 years has been because money lent to a businessman and spent on productive plant and equipment plus fair wages for productive workers will, when the goods produced are brought to market, fetch a selling price that will be enough to cover the original expenditure and at the same time produce a profit. Industrial capitalism is not based on looting or theft; it depends upon the production of real surplus value by dint of technology and labor, and it allows this surplus to be re-invested. Otherwise industrial capitalism would have folded several centuries ago. R-loans are not soft loans; they are hard-headed business propositions, designed to be paid back to the Bank of the United States and the Treasury out of the profits of successful production.

R-loans issued by the Bank of the United States according to the strict criteria indicated above will never be inflationary. If anything, the longer-term effect of R-loans for production will be mildly deflationary, since they will revive the long-term tendency for the prices of manufactured goods and farm goods to decline, both in absolute terms and as a percentage of the average paycheck. Oranges, ball point pens, roasting chickens, and quartz watches with silicon chips were once rather expensive. They are all relatively cheap these days because of the long-term deflationary effect of industrial progress under capitalism. According to historian Rudolph Bell of Rutgers, during the 1300s, the average western European peasant had to work as many hours for a single one-pound loaf of white bread (a delicacy) as a modern worker puts in to buy groceries for a week. During the 1400s, a skilled Flemish mason had to work half a day to buy a pound of sugar, which a modern skilled worker can purchase with one minute of labor. [164]

JOBS

Our main priority must be to raise levels of productive employment as rapidly as possible. In 1945, about half of all working Americans were working in productive occupations today the proportion is well below 20%. Wall Street commentators habitually estimate that two thirds of the entire US economy is devoted to consumer goods production and sales; this kind of economy cannot survive. (An economy totally devoted to consumer goods would be one made up of subsistence farmers only.) The portion devoted to the production of modern capital goods must become much larger very fast, even as employment rates and standards of living rise. As Roosevelt said in his First Inaugural:

> Our greatest problem is to put people to work. This is no unsolvable problem if we face it wisely and courageously. It can be accomplished in part by direct recruiting by the Government itself, treating the task as we would treat the emergency of a war, but at the same time, through this employment, accomplishing greatly needed projects to stimulate and reorganize the use of our natural resources.

The most obvious recipients for R-loans are federal agencies, along with state, county, and municipal governments and such regional consortia as they states may set up. Federal agencies taking a leading role would include the Department of Transportation's Federal Railroad Administration, which would go from its present status as a sleepy little bureaucracy with no money to a bustling powerhouse overseeing multi-billion dollar maglev projects. Amtrak would also be given the capital it has always needed for modernization. Commuter railroads need R-loan credit to modernize rights of way, and to buy new rolling stock. The surviving freight railways would be invited to participate in the modernization program with the help of R-loans. If they cooperate wholeheartedly, they will prosper. But if they persist in regarding the existing freight lines as cash cows to be used for asset-stripping, they must be speedily nationalized by Presidential Executive Order under the Defense Production Act and other legislation.

The Federal Highway Administration would receive funding for a thorough rebuilding and modernization of the interstates. The Department of Energy will promptly and expeditiously process applications from public utilities for R-loan financing for new high-temperature nuclear reactors. The Federal Aviation Administration will see to the modernization of airports. The US Army Corps of Engineers would be the lead agency for a vast series of water projects. Interstate or multi-city

---

[164] See "Medieval Sticker Shock," *Washington Post*, April 19, 1998.

consortia stepping up to apply for R-loan credit would typically include the Port of New York Authority, a joint venture of the state of New Jersey and New York, the Metropolitan Washington Area Council of Governments, or the Bay Area Rapid Transit authority of California. More of these regional authorities can be expected to emerge.

As stated, the federal credit issue during the first year of the recovery will amount to about $1 trillion. In the first year of a recovery policy, we can expect the Bank of the United States to approve more than $300 to $400 billion in infrastructure loans to governments at all levels. This money will go for maglev lines, nuclear reactors, water projects, highway repairs, schools, hospitals, and the like. As a rule of thumb, we can expect that $100,000 invested in machinery, materials, benefits, and wages will create one modern construction job in infrastructure. Because of the role of the Bank of the United States in providing the loans, all these jobs, no matter where they are located, will be covered by the Davis-Bacon Act, which requires union pay scales for government contracts. The gross take-home pay for construction workers employed on R-loan infrastructure projects will range between $50,000 and $60,000 per year. That is, they will receive an acceptable middle-class income that ought to permit family formation and allow their wives to stay home, if they like, with their infants and young children.

$300 to $400 billion invested will give us between 3 and 4 million jobs the first year with the prime contractors of a broad array of infrastructure projects. (Implicit here is again the notion that it takes about $100,000 per year to create and maintain a decent, modern job. Worthwhile employment is capital-intensive employment, and $100,000 should be only the beginning. As soon as possible, the capital investment per worker must be increased.) But the infrastructure jobs themselves are not the end of the story. Canals, maglev lines, HTR power grids, and hospitals will require millions of tons of steel, concrete, bricks, high-tension cables, and other materials. All of these must be produced by sub-contractors, vendors, and upstream factories. About $300 to $400 billion of R-loan credit must be channeled into these activities, which will generate another 3 to 4 million modern jobs at union wages. So, in the first year of recovery, between 6 and 8 million wage-earners and their families will enter the consumer market, and their purchases will assist the revival of the consumer products business.

This leaves us with between $200 billion and $400 in R-loan credit. Every farmer will need credit to buy the seed for spring planting. Consumer goods and light industry will need credit. Every steel mill will need working capital. Every auto assembly line will need bank loans to keep the wheels turning. Every importer and exporter will need financing and credit guarantees. Many of these companies will have been forced to close their downs in the chaotic last phase of the twilight of the gods of usury. New businesses will require startup capital. The Bank of the United States must stand ready to provide ample R-loan credit for all these needs.

If we think of the economic recovery program as lasting for the four years of a Presidential term, we can estimate that one trillion dollars in R-loans each year will produce between 24 million and 32 million new productive jobs over the four-year effort. The 15% to 20% of American wage-earners who are today actually unemployed will be re-absorbed into the labor force, and vast legions of those who had given up in despair will find their way back to factories, construction sites, and industrial parks. Unemployment rates among black and Hispanic youth will be reduced to below 5%, and will soon be lower than the prevailing rate today among the population in general. Social tensions in the inner cities will ease as high-wage factory jobs return to metropolitan areas, after having been increasingly scarce since the 1958 recession.

Before the four years are over, there is every reason to believe that a labor shortage will begin to be visible in some areas. This is exactly what we should expect from the history of twentieth-century economic recoveries. Starting in 1951-53, the German *Wirtschaftswunder* attracted Italian, Spanish, and Turkish workers into German plants. The Italian *miracolo economico*, starting a few years later, drew workers from Calabria, Sicily, and the Venice region into Milan and Turin. In the Republic of China on Taiwan, the successful economic dirigism of Chiang Ching-Kuo during the late 1970s and early 1980s pulled the labor market as tight as a drum, and attracted immigrants from all over southeast Asia. The Japanese boom attracted workers from the Philippines, Korea, and other countries. There is every reason to expect that something similar will happen in the United States under conditions of sustained economic recovery.

FULL EMPLOYMENT

Sometime between the fourth and the eighth year of economic recovery, the country will approach full employment for the first time since 1944-45. At this point, certain adjustments will need to be made in the granting of R-loans by the Bank of the United States. Once full employment has been attained, certain types of credit expansion might indeed produce inflation and economic dislocation. If the labor market is saturated, it will make no sense to grant R-loans to more and more entrepreneurs who will bid against each other for the same vanishing pool of unemployed persons or young people seeking jobs for the first time. At this point, horizontal expansion will be replaced by the more interesting phase of vertical expansion, in which emphasis will shift towards the introduction of new industries, such as mining and other production in the nearby solar system, which will have to be preceded and accompanied by large-scale educational efforts to upgrade whole sectors of the work force for their new, better paid occupations. One feature of this transition will be a very marked increase in the capital investment per worker. During this phase, we will be going towards a $150,000 to $200,000 average investment per job, and beyond. Education, training, and research will absorb a larger and larger portion of the federal budget, and will absorb significant amounts of R-loan credit as well.

If wages are low, labor is cheap and life is cheap. Three decades of low wages have caused a secular demoralization of the American spirit, which is the only way to explain most current television programming and election results. America's successful years were achieved when we were a high-wage, high-technology nation. An emphatic goal of economic recovery is to make the United States once again a country of highly-skilled, highly-paid workers, technicians, scientists, researchers, and engineers, producing very high value added products. Wages must rise so that one paycheck will allow a family of four the material and intellectual culture needed to prepare them for the new technologies emerging on the horizon of the mid-twenty-first century. Vigorous demand for labor transmits the notion that people, specific individuals, are valuable and important; pessimism will decline and optimism will grow.

32 million new productive jobs will also restore the American tax base, which was destroyed by the Volcker 22% prime rate with some help from the oil shocks and the deregulation pioneered by Jimmy Carter. Thanks to the new jobs, new corporate profits, and recovering real estate values, federal, state, and local governments will reach or exceed the break even point of tax revenue as against expenditures. Revenue will increase, even as unemployment compensation and welfare payments gradually decline. Budget deficits will shrink and vanish, and governments will return to budget surplus.

As a by-product, the standard of living of the average American will increase by between 20% and 30%, reversing the post-1967 fall in real wages and making the American way of life once again a byword for solid economic and cultural substance. Specifically, the goal must be to raise average weekly earnings, according to the Labor Department's current definition, by at least 5% per year during the coming years. This means that an effective President will be one who has improved average weekly earnings by 20%. An extraordinary President will be one who can raise average weekly earnings by 25% or more during a four-year term. Infrastructure investments will need to go forward at high levels for a long time. Even at $300 to $400 billion per year, it will take many years to pay back today's accumulated $10 trillion infrastructure deficit. But long before the infrastructure deficit is paid off, we will need to meet the need for multiple science drivers to enhance the thermodynamic efficiency of the entire US and world economies.

IV. ECONOMIC RECONSTRUCTION AND DEVELOPMENT

THREE SCIENCE DRIVERS: BIOMEDICAL, LASERS, AND AEROSPACE

A science driver means a large-scale research, development, and engineering project capable of providing new technological innovations and energy sources to keep an entire economy moving forward with high rates of modernization. The science driver is the leaven of the national economy. The 3 science drivers needed for the early 21st century will include biomedical research, high-energy physics for modern production and national defense, and a moon-Mars space exploration and colonization program.

1. AN OFFENSIVE IN BIOMEDICAL RESEARCH

More than a quarter century after President Nixon declared a national war on cancer, and almost 40 years after French President Charles De Gaulle urged the wealthier nations to shift their resources from the futility of the arms race to a peaceful effort in biomedical research, cancer remains the scourge of mankind. The US has spent a little more than $30 billion on cancer research over the last 26 years; the cancer research budget enjoys a special status in the budget process, but progress has still been far too slow. As of 1998, cancer costs the United States $107 billion per year in direct medical costs and lost productivity. 1.5 million Americans are diagnosed with cancer every year. Breast cancer has assumed epidemic proportions among young women. Prostate cancer is the terror of elderly men. But only one cent out of every $10 in taxes the federal government collects goes for cancer research. It is the same in other areas: Heart disease continues to strike down more men and women in the prime of life than any other killer, and AIDS continues to resist our efforts at prevention and cure. Tropical diseases like Ebola virus, Dengue fever, and new forms of tuberculosis threaten to sweep over the globe and overwhelm our frail antibiotic lines of defense. Because of the Asian economic decline, we must reckon with the danger of new and virulent forms of influenza, perhaps as dangerous as the killer Spanish flu after World War I. Surely the time has come to declare a serious, all-out war on these savage killers. We must also put an end to the heart-rending competition among cancer victims, heart patients, AIDS sufferers, diabetics, and paraplegics for the shrinking pie of health research and health care dollars.

The American people are more than ready for such a great national effort. That much was evident to anyone who attended the March on Washington organized by a coalition of anti-cancer organizations on September 25-26, 1998 under the slogan "No More Cancer." Here speakers that ranged from Jesse Jackson to Gen. Norman Schwartzkopf called on the voters to force politicians of both parties radically to increase the budget allocations for cancer research. The tone of the speeches was decidedly militant, with outbursts of frustration and frustration overt the government's non-feasance and inertia. Many speakers lamented the precious national time lost because of the Starr witch-hunt. There were appeals to traditional American optimism as exemplified by the 1969 moon shot, appeals made vivid by military metaphors of the necessity for victory drawn from the world wars, and the Cold War. This mobilization, which was held at many sites around the country, was instrumental in obtaining an increase of some $400 million in the federal budget finally approved in October 1998. When the Cold War ended, no politician had the vision to propose a great national purpose. Surely the conquest of killer diseases would represent a crusade worthy of America. Here is an issue of sure-fire political resonance.

Taking the Manhattan District Project of World War II as the starting point, we must accordingly launch a crash program to find the means of prevention and cure for these dread diseases. This must be a comprehensive effort in depth. We must reverse the alarming decline in the numbers of American college graduates going to medical school, and we must provide generous scholarships and fellowships to medical students to accomplish this. This is the new front line of national defense. Training facilities for registered nurses have been disappearing, although they should be within walking distance of every larger hospital. Part of the biomedical research budget can come directly from federal outlays, but R-loans will also be extensively used to purchase the laboratory equipment and pay the technicians and physicians that will vanquish the old tormentors of mankind.

The price tag for such a crash program starts at $25 billion per year, and we should be delighted to pay it. This is a fraction of what Bush wasted on bankrupt S&Ls, or about what the Clinton administration is giving to the IMF in 1998. Our real problem is that we cannot spend nearly as much as this problem deserves. In fact, our goal should be to spend as much as we can today in order to increase our ability meaningfully to spend tomorrow, by expanding the laboratories and research programs beyond what we can put into the field in the near future. The time has come to create a new biomedical science city, perhaps somewhere in the Great Plains, and make that the Oak Ridge of this effort.

Lost on all sides in the deplorable health care debate of 1994, and lost in the cost-accounting of the HMOs and insurance companies thereafter, is the basic fact that the only way to save money in health care is to find cheap and reliable preventions and cures for the most widespread diseases. If you don't want to pay $200,000 per year to treat an AIDS patient, the answer is not to kill the victim through "managed care." The answer is to find a $50 cure for AIDS that will give the victim a passport back to many decades of normal, healthy productive life. Or, better yet, find a vaccine that will stop AIDS from ever gaining a foothold.

Another example: caring for people suffering from diabetes now absorbs $100 billion per year, or about 15% of US health care costs. Want to save $100 billion? It's easy: find a prevention and a cure for diabetes of all types. Any other logic leads towards violations of the Nuremburg Code. Without an approach based on scientific discovery, there can be no morality in medicine. In the meantime, we must wage a determined struggle to save each life, even for the seemingly hopeless cases – especially for the hopeless cases. We know that the harder we fight for each life using special experimental protocols and the like, the more likely we are to gain the experience and the insights that will make a final cure possible. With a crash program, there will be more than enough experimental protocols to go around. Even losing battles waged against imminent death can teach us something which can save other lives later on. At this point in history, life may well be the only absolute value we can get the world to agree on. Although individual life is fragile and ephemeral, the life of humanity goes on, and no person is too sick or too old to contribute.

NATIONAL HEALTH INSURANCE

The crash program in biomedical research is above and beyond the basic effort to restore the availability of top-quality medical care to all persons under US jurisdiction. Given the decimation of medical care outlined in a previous chapter, that availability will require the construction of about 1000 completely equipped modern hospitals, along with the training of doctors, nurses, technicians, orderlies, and other personnel. The results of the great effort in biomedical research will make it easier to face the long-overdue obligations to offer health care for all Americans, especially the 40 million who are uninsured. Now that the millennium is upon us, we must bow at length to necessity and humanity by instituting a comprehensive national health insurance program in which the best available care, including catastrophic and long-term care, is available to all persons free of charge. The benefits of such a system should be extended to all persons under US jurisdiction, if only for the simple reason that any person afflicted by a contagious disease can easily infect others if quick treatment is not provided. Such a system should start from the well-established and successful German model, which has accumulated more than a century of experience. The German national health insurance system reached its high point about 1970, and this should be used as the reference for the American plan. One important difference is that health insurance coverage should be granted to all persons, whether employed or not. The German system has allowed numerous private insurance companies to operate, and does not involve monolithic government control.[165] The British and Canadian systems, by contrast, are what the average American thinks of under the heading of socialized medicine. They are inadequate because of their woefully insufficient provision of medical technology, long waiting periods, and other shortfalls and abuses. Under no circumstances should the British or Canadian models be duplicated here. US national; health insurance should incorporate the provisions contained in the Patient's Bill of Rights which was killed by the Republican leadership in the 1998. It should also outlaw the rationing of modern technology, or decisions made on the basis of what accountants call cost/benefit analysis. The right of every patient – the entitlement – to the most modern form of treatment available should be anchored in law. The national plan must not force general practitioners into the degrading and corrupting role of gatekeeper, forcing family doctors to sacrifice the health of their patients to enhance the windfall profits of management and investors. Patients must have direct access to specialists. No longer must middle class families face financial annihilation because profit-oriented insurance companies refuse to pay up. No longer must millions of man hours be wasted in efforts to get the HMOs to honor their responsibilities.

The existence of a national health insurance program will not rule out private health plans for those with the ability and the desire to pay. But even here, problems will inevitably be generated by for-profit health plans which will always seek to economize on forms of care upon which human lives depend. Therefore, thorough federal regulation, including binding definitions of the minimum benefits which must be offered, will be indispensable.

Ten to twenty billion dollars per year for a crash program in research is only a starting point. We need not only to increase the rate of expenditure on medical research, we need to increase the possible rate of expansion of our research budget. Polio was the last dread disease to be vanquished; in recent times tuberculosis and other scourges which had been thought close to extinction have come back in new and more virulent forms. Our medical war machine is obviously inadequate. We will need more doctors and researchers, new laboratories, and a vast park of the most modern equipment. To finance these things, we need R-loans for the biomedical effort, tax breaks, and every other dirigistic instrument that can be brought to bear.

2. HIGH ENERGY PHYSICS

Lasers and other devices employing the principles of high energy physics represent a readily available means of modernizing US production technologies and the US machine tool park so as to

---

[165] The present writer had his tonsils out under the German system while working in Hanover in 1972, so this endorsement is based on first-hand experience.

make them the most modern in the world. This will be a separate crash program in its own right, with extensive research in fields of high-energy physics, plasma physics, and particle physics. Laser research will produce valuable progress in the area of laser machine tools for the cutting, perforation and milling of the hardest and most resistant industrial materials. We will be able to reverse the current backwardness of the US machine tool park by making the leap to laser machine tools at the start of the new century. Laser machine tools will give the production worker the ability to alter the molecular structure of matter at the work bench, opening new perspectives in high technology output. New lasers will also find extensive applications for surgery and other medical procedures.

National defense must not remain neglected. An important undertaking in this regard will be the revival of the Strategic Defense Initiative announced by President Reagan on March 23, 1983. Out of this research will come x-ray lasers, electron beams, particle beams, chemical lasers, and other anti-missile defense systems based on relativistic new physical principles. These new systems will help make the world safe for economic development by suppressing once and for all the specter of nuclear and thermonuclear attack using airplanes and missiles. They will also help us to preserve the few truly modern production teams which have survived the lethal aftermath of 1989-91 defense downsizing. These new systems should be developed first in conjunction with Russia, and this cooperation then extended to China and other nuclear powers. It is likely that the program of plasma physics research carried out for the revived Strategic Defense Initiative will also give us the first commercially viable thermonuclear fusion reactor. This will give us a follow-on to the nuclear fission power reactors of today, and assure that our energy needs will be covered well beyond the end of the 21st century.

During 1998, both India and Pakistan conducted nuclear tests, while North Korea lobbed a medium-range missile over Japanese territory. Right-wing columnists pointed with alarm to mysterious Iraqi threats, and to the Chinese Long March ICBMs capable of reaching US territory. A blue-ribbon commission chaired by former Defense Secretary Donald Rumsfeld concluded that the United States would have "little or no warning" of merging threats from hostile powers equipped with Intercontinental Ballistic Missiles. But, 15 years after Reagan's speech of March 23, 1983, the US still had no anti-missile shield, and no defense whatsoever against even the accidental launch of a single missile. Rep. Jim Courter (R-NJ) wrote on this occasion that although $50 billion had spent on the programs suggested by Reagan in 1983, nothing had been deployed. He noted that there were now 30 countries with ballistic missiles, for a total of 10,000 launchers capable of carrying chemical and bacteriological, as well as nuclear, weapons. Courter called for the development of directed energy weapons, especially the Airborne Laser, a chemical laser mounted on a 747 jumbo jet and capable of destroying a missile at a distance of 500 kilometers. Courter spoke of spending $11 billion to equip 8 of these Airborne Lasers, which within two to three years could begin to provide an anti-missile defense where now there is none.[166] $100 billion should be allocated over a number of years for anti-missile measures, which would have the highly desirable effect of sustaining the aerospace production lines of the US defense sector, now threatened by the collapse of aircraft orders from Asia. There is every reason to contemplate joint development of such defensive weapons in cooperation with Russia, China, Japan, Israel, the European nations, and other friendly powers.

All in all, the crash program in high-energy physics will increase our mastery of the micro-world of physics in the very small, and open the way to anti-matter research and other issues that will engage the centuries to come. The spinoffs of a plasma physics crash program for comprehensive anti-missile defense will generate patents whose sale and licensing fees will go very far towards

---

[166] *Aviation Week*, April 13, 1998.

paying back the research and development costs of the entire program. Part of this program can be covered by the federal defense budget, while the rest can be financed by R-loan credit.

Outside of and beyond the directed energy research, development, and deployment programs, the United States requires a defense establishment powerful enough to meet any conceivable emergency, a power so preponderant that its very existence will tend to prevent political and ethnic conflicts from becoming military, and which will thus represent an important factor of world pacification. The much-discussed hollowing of the US military is real enough; it was begun very openly and deliberately under Bush and Cheney during the Gulf War. Before globalization came along, the United States could afford an Army of 18 divisions, with two paratroops divisions and an adequate number of armored divisions. We had a Navy which exceeded five hundred ships, with a dozen or more aircraft carrier battle groups. We had several Marine divisions for rapid deployment. We had over 1000 MIRVed ICBMs, and 38 Air Force wings, enough to keep the Strategic Air Command and Tactical Air Command at satisfactory levels. The levels of the late Cold War period must again become the targets for current readiness. In addition, all units must be equipped with the most modern directed energy, radio frequency, and other modern weapons systems. We will need a new strategic bomber for the twenty-first century, and a full array of space weapons. Since it appears that we will have an all-volunteer army for the foreseeable future, we must significantly increase the rates of pay for enlisted personnel and officers. Just as elsewhere in society, the standard here must be that nobody who has less than a bachelor's degree can be considered employable, and the necessary public resources must be allocated to upgrade the US work force to this level.

3. COLONIZE THE MOON AND MARS

The third in our trio of science drivers is space exploration and colonization. Here we must look far beyond the Space Shuttle and the International Space Station, which have been and will be indispensable stepping stones along the way. We must consider a program which includes the dimension of space colonization as well as exploration. We must look forward to placing a permanent colony on the moon as the prelude to establishing a permanent colony on Mars over the period of the next 35 to 40 years. Permanent colonies on the moon and Mars will take much more than contemporary rocket science. We will need energy sources of the type which only thermonuclear fusion power can provide. We will need nuclear fission and fusion propulsion systems. We will need an inventory of advanced lasers. We will need biological breakthroughs in space medicine regarding the problems posed by zero gravity and other issues. We will need lightning-fast supercomputers built on a miniature scale. Part of the colonization effort will involve setting up new cities, mines and factories on the moon and eventually on Mars. Space mining and manufacturing as well as zero-gravity environments offer important economic advantages that will come to defray more and more of the costs of the colonization program itself.

In the meantime, the benefits of a space colonization program will be felt on earth right away. Studies of the 1960s Apollo Program show that every dollar spent in the Moon program was returned ten times over to the civilian economy. This included US world leadership in semiconductors (silicon chips), computers, and airframes, plus some renewal of machine tools.

The cultural and psychological impact of a rebirth of the space program on a grand scale is of vital importance even though it is impossible to quantify. At present mankind is living through a decadent and pessimistic *fin-de-siècle*. This could readily be transformed into a new upsurge in positive scientific and technological ferment. The spirit of the age could shift from designer drugs and rave dances for burned-out youth to new interest in interplanetary travel and cosmological problems. Such a shift would represent a sudden jump in the general intelligence level of the American population.

INFRASTRUCTURE

Naturally, it will be important for the Bank of the United States to get the biggest bang for the buck when tackling the huge task of economic recovery. As a matter of priority, we must start with a list of the most important and urgent national goals. This does not mean national economic planning in the old, discredited sense of the Soviet Gosplan, which tried to steer every transaction down to the last bolt and washer. An anti-depression plan is simply a strategy to put people back to work in the most effective way.

President Clinton has shown a commendable understanding of the importance of infrastructure investment. During his first year in office, Clinton came forward with a modest $20 billion economic stimulus package of forward-looking investments in infrastructure and education. This stimulus package was jawboned to death in the Senate by a Republic filibuster lead by Senator Dole. Beyond this, Clinton had espoused a series of longer-term investments in job training, education, and rebuilding infrastructure amounting initially to about $90 billion. At the beginning of his first term, Clinton referred to these programs as "the things I got elected for." [Woodward, 91]

THE MODEL: TENNESSEE VALLEY AUTHORITY

Private companies have never excelled at building infrastructure because of the titanic capital outlays involved, and because it sometimes takes many years for the projects to become profitable. If we look back at American history, we can readily see that great works of infrastructure like the National Road, the Erie Canal, the Transcontinental Railroad, the Panama Canal, the Tennessee Valley Authority, the Interstate Highway System and the nation's airports have generally been carried out by government at some level. Looking around the world, we see that many great projects like the Trans-Siberian Railway were built in the same way – by governments.

One of the most successful and popular recent examples of government-promoted infrastructure is the Tennessee Valley Authority, which was created by legislation co-sponsored by Senator George Norris of Nebraska and Representative Lister Hill of Alabama which was signed by Franklin D. Roosevelt on May 18, 1933, at the very nadir of the world depression, and it the midst of the epic Hundred Days. The TVA was a regional agency of the United States Government, and was set up as a public corporation. Its constitutionality was upheld by the Supreme Court in the case of Ashwander v. TVA in 1936. The TVA was charged with flood control, navigation, and the generation of electric power.

Navigation on the Tennessee River was blocked by some 20 miles of rapids at Muscle Shoals, Alabama, and efforts by states and by private business to solve this problem had not been successful. During World War I the federal government began building 2 nitrate factories at Muscle Shoals, and also started construction on a hydroelectric dam and a steam power plant to provide the electricity necessary in producing nitrate. The original goal was national self-sufficiency in nitrates, which were otherwise imported from Chile and Germany. But with the end of World War I, the need for nitrates was viewed as less acute. Despite an investment of $100 million, none of the nitrate projects had been completed, and the government decided to suspend them. For the next 15 years construction ceased, but there were a number of attempts to terminate and privatize the unfinished project by free enterprise fanatics eager to seize and loot what the taxpayers had begun to construct.

Roosevelt regarded Muscle Shoals as the leading edge of a regional recovery program for the impoverished and backward southern Appalachian area. Soon the TVA had become the motor for jobs and business in Mississippi, Alabama, Georgia, North Carolina, Virginia, Kentucky, and Tennessee. TVA itself provided about 15,000 jobs. The TVA eventually came to operate 48 dams, which added up to a comprehensive river control system. All dams in the system were operated as a single unitary system, with flood control as the first priority. No major flood damage has occurred on the Tennessee River since the TVA was completed – in sharp contrast to the flood-plagued upper Mississippi and Missouri Rivers, which have never gotten the complete TVA treatment. River traffic increased from 33 million ton-miles in 1933 to 600 million ton-miles in 1950, and exceeded 2 billion ton-miles during the 1960s. Between 1933 and 1945, TVA was the biggest construction project anywhere in the world.

Electrical power produced by the TVA rose to the level of 12 million kilowatts by the time the system was virtually complete in the 1960s. This electric power was of vast strategic significance. When the Manhattan District Project created the atomic laboratories at Oak Ridge, Tennessee during World War II, this single facility was able to command more electrical energy than the entire German war economy was capable of producing at that time. This energy was the key to the gaseous diffusion process, which produced the first atomic pile and the first atomic bombs. TVA also logged one of the great victories in the history of public health. The Tennessee Valley was until the 1930s a region of endemic malaria. Because of the vigorous mosquito control program carried out on the TVA reservoirs, malaria became virtually extinct, with not one case of malaria traceable to the Tennessee River being reported after 1948. The TVA thus combined flood control, river navigation, electric power, and much more. If we add potable water systems and irrigation, we have the method required for water projects to help defeat the present economic depression. The lessons of the heroic phase of TVA were summed up in 1944 by the project's director, David Lilienthal, in his book *TVA: Democracy on the March*, which must rank as one of the great documents of American optimism. "No longer do men look upon poverty as inevitable, or think that drudgery, disease, filth, famine, floods, and physical exhaustion are visitations of the devil or punishment by a deity," Lilienthal wrote.

By the 1990s, self-styled ecologists were proposing that the flood control system along the Mississippi, Missouri and other rivers be simply abandoned, and that the flood plains be abandoned to desolation. This is cultural pessimism worse than Oswald Spengler. In lines that need to be studied by present-day environmentalists, Lilienthal observed: "The basic objection to all efforts to use the machine for human betterment lies in an attitude of absolute pessimism: that life is an evil in itself; that therefore anything which seeks to mitigate its inescapable pain and utter dullness is misdirected and futile." This book was translated into German, French, Italian and Danish as a kind of manual of New Deal thinking. Projects modeled on the TVA have brought great benefit to the Columbia River basin in Washington and Oregon. The Boulder Dam on the Colorado River is one of the greatest engineering and construction epics of humankind, and a great economic asset today. The Arkansas River water projects promoted by Sen. Robert Kerr have been an important part of postwar development in Oklahoma and neighboring states. In August 1962, President Kennedy dedicated the Oahe Dam north of Pierre, South Dakota, which at the time was the largest earthen dam in the world.

This method must now be applied to water resources and water needs on a continental scale. During the Yalta Conference, Roosevelt told Stalin and Churchill that he was thinking of a TVA approach to the development of the Danube River basin, from which half a dozen central European countries would have directly benefited. In 1998, Chinese leaders spoke of the TVA as a model for what they were trying to begin with the Three Gorges Dam and other measures designed to prevent a recurrence of the disastrous floods on the Yangtze River.

NORTH AMERICAN WATER AND POWER ALLIANCE

NAWAPA was first proposed in 1964 by the Ralph Parsons Engineering Company of Pasadena, California. This project essentially applies the lessons of the Tennessee Valley Authority and of similar water projects on the Mississippi, Missouri, Arkansas, Columbia, and other rivers to the water systems of the entire North American continent. From the very beginning it represented a far-sighted approach to water needs over the course of a century or more. NAWAPA starts from the reality that the majority of the fresh water reserves of the North American continent are located in far northwest Canada and Alaska. Almost all of this water flows into the Arctic Ocean and is simply wasted. The great water deficit areas are located in the southern part of the American Great Basin and related desert areas in the American southwest and northern Mexico. The basic notion of NAWAPA is therefore to transfer water from northwest Canada and Alaska to the southwestern United States and northern Mexico. In the process the aquifers and water tables of much of the continent would be replenished and restored. Under NAWAPA, the main rivers of northern Alaska and northern British Columbia would be dammed. Chief among these is the mighty MacKenzie River. The Yukon, Susitna, Tanana, Skeena, Peace, Churchill, and Fraser Rivers would all be extensively engineered. A part of this fresh water would then be diverted southward along the 500-mile Rocky Mountain Trench that runs southward through British Columbia and into the United States. The Rocky Mountain Trench would become an immense reservoir holding 400 million acre feet of water.

A minor portion of this water would be diverted towards the Great Lakes and the Mississippi River to raise the level of the Great Lakes, resulting in greater hydroelectric generation at Niagara Falls by the New York State Power Authority, and also on the Canadian side. The level of the Mississippi would rise sufficiently for ocean-going vessels to proceed as far north as St. Louis – resulting in a kind of St. Lawrence Seaway for the American south. Some water would also be transferred to the Columbia River in the American northwest. But the majority of the fresh water in the system would travel south. Idaho would receive 2.3 million acre-feet per year, Texas would get 11.7 million, California, 13.9 million, and Mexico 20 million acre-feet. Without this water, not just agriculture and industry but human habitation in general will become untenable at some point during the 21st century. NAWAPA is the only way places like Los Angeles, San Diego, and Dallas-Fort Worth will have a future.

The cost of NAWAPA was originally estimated at $100 billion to $200 billion, and would have been a bargain at those prices. Today the costs have risen, but the imperative remains the same. California and Texas are now our two largest states. Will we keep them viable or not? And if we cannot provide fresh water for homes, farms, and industries in Texas and California, what *can* we do? Other parts of the US are also threatened by lack of water. One of our greatest national resources is the Ogallala aquifer, which lies under the key farm states of Nebraska, Kansas, Oklahoma and Texas. The groundwater of the Ogallala aquifer is being rapidly depleted. NAWAPA would provide the key to re-hydrating and restoring the Ogallala and other vital aquifers. Existing laws forbidding any interbasin transfer of water must be voided by the President using the emergency powers by the Trading with the Enemy Act, the Defense Production Act, and the inherent powers that pertain to the Presidency under the Constitution.

A further Canadian dimension of NAWAPA is the Great Replenishment and Northern Development Canal (GRAND Canal), which was first outlined by Thomas Kierans during the

1950s. This involves a huge dike across the northern end of James Bay, which is an arm of the larger Hudson Bay. Because of the dike, the runoff from the rivers emptying into James Bay would cause it to rise. Part of this water would go into the Great Lakes, with some of it ending up in Lake Diefenbaker in Saskatchewan and points further west. R-loan financing would permit US firms to take part in these desirable Canadian efforts. The impact of NAWAPA in northern Mexico would also be highly beneficial. Obviously, Mexican agriculture would benefit. Modern industry is water-intensive, and the availability of sufficient water would accelerate the industrialization of northern Mexico.

The other aspect of American water systems that requires special attention is that of canal transportation. The European Community has recently completed its Rhein-Main-Danube canal, which finally carries out a plan that dates from the time of Charlemagne around 800 AD. Romania has built a very modern canal which provides a shortcut to the Black Sea, bypassing the Danube Delta. Bulk transport on canals is highly developed and flourishing in continental Europe and also appears to have a bright future in China. During the first half of the nineteenth century, the United States, by virtue of the Erie Canal and related efforts, was the world leader in canal building. It is time for this country to reclaim its status as a canal builder and operator of the first rank.

Since the completion of the successful Tennessee-Tombigbee (Tenn/Tom) barge canal, which had had beneficial consequences for the Port of Mobile, Alabama, very little has been done in the way of American canal building. Jimmy Carter was responsible for canceling dozens of urgently necessary water projects. Now it is time to catch up. One obvious place to start is the modernization of the New York State Barge Canal, the successor to the Erie Canal. When the St. Lawrence Seaway was completed, pessimists argued that the New York State Barge Canal was obsolete. But the barge canal's decline had more to do with the permanent US industrial downturn after 1958 than it did with the alleged competition of the Seaway, which could of course accommodate larger ships. In the framework of economic recovery, modern barge canal traffic including oil and construction materials could quickly to return to profitability on along the industrial corridor of Albany-Utica-Syracuse-Rochester-Lockport-Buffalo, and in many other similar areas, not just in the northeast. The St. Lawrence Seaway is itself obsolete, and needs an urgent upgrade to be able to handle the much larger vessels of today. The same goes for the Sault St. Marie canals, the busiest in the world. A very obvious improvement would be to build a canal from the western end of Lake Superior to the Pacific Ocean, allowing ocean-going vessels to travel straight across the continent for the first time. A related effort would be the construction of at least one completely new sea-level isthmian canal in central America, given the present overloading of the Panama Canal and its inability to handle the largest modern bulk carriers and supertankers.

Oligarchs do not like Great Projects. In the fifth century BC, the survival of Athens depended upon building what was a Great project for those times – the Long Walls from Athens to the port of Piræus. These walls gave Athens safe access to the closest major port, and were the foundation of Athenian sea trade, sea power and thus of the greatness of the Athenian city-state. Each of the two Long Walls was about four miles long, and they were twelve feet thick, being constructed of large blocks of stone. They were begun about 460 BC. The historian Thucydides points out that the oligarchical party of Athens opposed the building of the Long Walls, and was even prepared to enter into treasonous collaboration with Sparta in order to sabotage this vital building project. The oligarchs feared that trade and sea power would undermine the power of oligarchy. Aspects of this problem are also treated by the anonymous contemporary source usually referred to as the "Old Oligarch."[167] Oligarchs oppose Great Projects nationalism because they contradict oligarchy. We

---

[167] See David Stockton, *The Classical Athenian Democracy* (New York: Oxford, 1990), 141.

can expect them to oppose the projects necessary for world economic recovery today, probably by citing ecological or budget considerations. Such objections will have no merit.

RAIL TRANSPORTATION

American railroads have been in decline since just after World War II. Railroads were used as cash cows by corporate management intent only on loot. The World War II wartime federal excise tax on railroad travel was absurdly maintained until 1962, by which time many US railroads were hopelessly obsolete. The highway lobby and the airline lobby, both recipients of generous federal subsidies, had literally killed off their most formidable competitor. In 1970-1971, after the bankruptcy of Penn-Central (what was left of the Pennsylvania Railroad and the New York Central) the Nixon Administration "nationalized" passenger rail services in the form of Amtrak. Amtrak has historically had very few resources, and has had to depend on obsolete equipment several decades old. Even so, Amtrak has scored some important successes, and still offers the basis on which to build the future. But losses have also been severe. During the Amtrak era, some large railway stations, like St. Louis or the Jersey Central terminal on the New York waterfront, ceased rail operations altogether and were turned into museums, meeting halls, or boutiques. Even more wretched were railroad stations like Detroit's, which stands today as a gutted and abandoned ruin, mutely testifying to the tragic shortsightedness and greed which have shaped the American economy in the oligarchical era.

Nixon's two sinister advisors, Haldeman and Ehrlichman, schemed to kill Amtrak altogether. Ford's Secretary of Transportation, William T. Coleman, called Amtrak "outmoded outhouses." In one of the greatest recent acts of pure folly by an American President, Ford in 1975 eliminated all funding for high-speed ground transportation research. This move killed plans to build a magnetic levitation test track at China Lake, California, which could have guaranteed US world leadership in this critical field. President Carter showed an ineptitude just as great as Ford's. During the second oil shock of 1979, when gas lines were forming at service stations across the country, Carter and his Transportation Secretary Brock Adams insisted on abolishing some of Amtrak's most popular trains. Reagan and Bush attempted to abolish Amtrak every year from 1986 to 1991. Reagan's Secretary of Transportation, Drew Lewis, wrote that his "department is opposed to expanding rail corridor service." [Vranich 255] The best that Amtrak has been able to manage are the 1970s vintage, now-obsolete 125-mile per hour New York to Washington DC Metroliners. But apart from these premium trains, Amtrak's technology is still back in the 1930s.

An obvious place to accelerate modernization is the line linking Boston, New York, Philadelphia, Baltimore, Washington DC, and Richmond, potentially the biggest rail market in the world. There are 776 bridges along this line, and one fourth of them were built before 1895. The 231-mile right of way between New York and Boston is completely obsolete: there are numerous grade crossings where roads and highways cross the tracks, and there are so many curves that the top speed of normal passenger trains cannot exceed 90 miles per hour, although innovations like the Italian *pendolino* and Swedish X2000 tilt trains will be of some help here. For these to be brought in, the New York to Boston line will have to be electrified, something that is only now being done. The old Metroliners can cover the 224 miles from Washington to New York in 2 hours 25 minutes, but the current F40PH diesel locomotives require 4 hours 30 minutes to travel the 230 miles between New York and Boston. Amtrak plans to cut that to about 3 hours by introducing the X2000 tilt train by 1999. Michigan, Illinois, Southern California and the Pacific Northwest are all asking for high speed tilt trains.

One example of successful investment in rail infrastructure comes from France, which has developed the *Train à Grande Vitesse* (TGV). These modern high-speed trains require a special roadbed and right-of-way that must be built expressly for them, starting from scratch. TGV trains do not use existing rails, which had to be designed with the needs of heavy freight trains in mind. Using separate rails also avoids interference from freight trains and local short-range commuter trains. The TGV first began operating in 1981 on a line between Paris and Lyon; the top speed on that line in routine operations is now 168 mph. Another TGV line, called *Atlantique* and reaching from Paris to the seaport of Brest, was begun in 1985 and finished by September 1989. The total cost of the TGV *Atlantique*, including trains and roadbeds, was about $3.3 billion. The line is host to about 25 million passengers per year.

On May 18, 1990 a special train running with no passengers on the TGV *Atlantique* line set a world rail speed record of just over 320 miles per hour. The French have also tested two trains crossing each other in opposite directions at a closing speed of 483 miles per hour, with no problems. The top speed of the TGV passenger trains in normal service on this line is now almost 190 mph. Between Paris and the new Chunnel (the tunnel under the English Channel), the average speed of trains is almost 200 miles per hour. Another TGV line from Paris to the French Riviera will shortly be cruising at almost 220 mph in routine service. All French TGV lines have a perfect safety record; not one passenger or crew member has ever been killed because of an accident.

The TGV was built using off-the-shelf, readily available, existing technology, with no exotic materials or experimental techniques. This fact was stressed in Congressional testimony by Dagobert Scher, a vice-president of the French national railroad company SNCF. In fact, most of the technology used in the TGV was already available back in the 1955, when a French test train broke the 200 mph barrier. This underlines the admirable achievement of the French, but also suggests that the cutting edge in rail technology for the twenty-first century may be elsewhere.

Spain, Italy, Germany, Great Britain, and the smaller European countries already have or will shortly possess trains more or less comparable to the TGV. A general upgrade of transport infrastructure costing 220 billion European Currency Units (or about 35 billion ECU per year) was contemplated by Jacques Delors' European Commission white paper of June 1993. [European Commission 77] Australia and Russia also plan high-speed rail initiatives. So do the Japanese, who began the modern era of high-speed trains with their celebrated *Shinkansen* bullet train in 1964. The series 300 bullet train known as the Super Hikari set a bullet train speed record of 202 mph in 1991.

MAGLEV: AN AMERICAN IDEA

Even more attractive than the TGV-style steel wheel on steel rail trains are the magnetic levitation trains (maglevs) which are now ready for large-scale application in both German and Japanese variants. As of right now, there is no American version. This is ironic, since the most promising type of maglev train, the superconducting or electrodynamic maglev, was invented in the United States. One of the earliest references to what has become the maglev technology of today came from American rocket pioneer Robert Goddard. In the November 1909 issue of *Scientific American*, Goddard outlined how a tunnel could be built between Boston and New York City in which "the cars might be held in suspension by the repulsion of opposing magnets. When thus isolated, they could be propelled by the gigantic power of magnetism."

A breakthrough came in 1961, when James Powell, a nuclear engineer at the Brookhaven National Laboratory on New York's Long Island, was caught for several hours in a traffic jam on his way from New York City to Boston. Powell conceived of a train that would be suspended by electromagnetic forces over a special electromagnetic right of way. The train would float on an air cushion, with no mechanical contact with the ground. Such a train could reach velocities higher than anything possible by steel wheels running along steel rails. The magnetic suspension would involve superconductors. Powell developed this idea with the help of his friend, the physicist Gordon Danby.

Before too long, the idea had attracted the interest of a host of US firms and research institutes, including Stanford Research Institute, North American Rockwell, Sandia National Laboratories, Ford, General Motors, Mitre Corporation, and TRW Systems. MIT developed a maglev vehicle called the Magneplane, which had a practical top speed of about 220 mph and used superconducting coils. But the entire American maglev program was destroyed by Ford's 1975 cutoff of all federal funding for high-speed ground transportation research. As a result of Ford's tragic 1975 blunder, it was the Germans and the Japanese who took the lead in maglev.

The German maglev is called the Transrapid, whose first model started at 55 mph back in 1970. By 1992, the Transrapid-07 had reached a speed of 310 mph while carrying passengers. Since 1983, Transrapids have operated on a special test facility near Emsland in northern Germany. The Transrapids glide swiftly and silently over the heads of grazing cows, who pay no attention. The lower part of the Transrapid literally wraps around the train's guideway. Magnets are located on the underside of the guideway pull up on the train's wrap-around component, allowing the vehicle to float about a centimeter above the top surface of the guideway.

One of the two Japanese maglev models uses an approach similar to that of the Transrapid. This is the High Speed Surface Transport or HSST, which was started by Japan Airlines. The HSST was clocked at 191 mph in an early test in 1978. HSSTs have operated at expositions in Tsukuba, Japan, in Vancouver, Canada in 1989, and in 1988 near Tokyo. A total of 1.25 million people have ridden on these HSSTs. At present the backers of the HSST are offering a 62-mph urban rail system and a 205 mph express train.

The other approach to maglev is the one pioneered by Powell: this is the electrodynamic or repulsive method. Here the electromagnets are located on the upper surface of the guideway and push up on the bottom of the train so that it floats about 6 inches above the surface of the guideway. Propulsion in both cases comes from a series of electromagnets along the sides of the guideway which are controlled by computers. These magnets rapidly change their polarity so as to exert a combined push-pull effect on the train, permitting high speeds. Up to one train per minute can be accommodated on each guideway, greatly increasing the ability to carry passengers. The Japanese superconductor maglev is the 250-mph MLU-001/002, known as the Linear Motor Car. An early MLU-type vehicle travelling without passengers reached 323 mph back in December 1979. The MLU trains are not as thoroughly tested as the Transrapid, but there are indications that their technology would ultimately be capable of greater speeds.

In 1989, the Argonne National Laboratory recommended that 300 mph maglev trains could be used to replace airplanes for most trips of 600 miles or less. The Argonne report recommended building a 2000-mile network at a cost of $30 billion. Argonne came out in favor of maglev service in the Boston-New York-Washington corridor, the San Diego-Los Angeles-San Francisco corridor, and for links between Chicago and the main cities of the Midwest. Much of the needed maglev network could be constructed along the median strips of existing interstate highways. But because of budget constraints and the non-availability of capital, this good idea has gone essentially nowhere.

Many US localities desire maglev or TGV service and have tried to obtain it. These include Orlando, Florida, Pittsburgh-Philadelphia, Las Vegas, Nevada, the northeast corridor, New York City, Buffalo, Georgia, Minneapolis-Chicago, Cleveland-Cincinnati, St. Louis-Topeka, Rockford, Illinois, Kansas City, Louisville, Colorado, Houston-Dallas/Fort Worth-Tulsa, Houston-New

Orleans, Santa Fe-Albuquerque, Portland-Seattle-Spokane, and California-Arizona-Nevada. The national interest and good economics will require that these local, state and regional projects be united into a single seamless continental grid. This would include international links such as New York-Montreal-Quebec, Detroit-Toronto, Buffalo-Toronto-Ottawa-Montreal and Seattle-Vancouver BC segments, as well as connections to Mexico and points south. *Popular Mechanics* magazine has performed a public service over the years by campaigning for the installation of modern rail technology in this country. [168]

A 300 mph plus maglev train could complete the 900-mile trip from New York to Chicago in about three hours. Since this is city center to city center, no existing airliner and airport combination could come close to this rapidity. The 450-mile Boston to New York run could be covered in about 90 minutes. There would be no delays caused by weather, air traffic problems, or traffic jams. Politicians should note that states that have expressed interest in high speed rail and/or maglev construction represent a majority of the seats in both houses of Congress, and an overwhelming majority of the Electoral College. So obtaining political support to launch the program might be easier than most politicians believe.

Speaking at Princeton University in 1990, Yoshihiro Kyotani, the retired head of the Japanese maglev program, put forth the perspective that advanced maglev trains operating in air-evacuated tubes could reach speeds of Mach 3. Kyotani produced maps depicting train trips from Tokyo to London in 3 hours 50 minutes; and from Montreal to Buenos Aires in 5 hours 45 minutes. American maglev inventor Powell was there to support Kyotani's thinking.

American has not given up on railroads. On September 28, 1998, Secretary of Transportation Rodney E. Slater and representatives of the Federal Railway Administration marked the ninetieth anniversary of Washington's Union Station, and the tenth anniversary of its renovation. Slater spoke of Amtrak's commitment to introduce fast rail service for the New York-Washington rail corridor starting in November 1999. The transportation bill signed into law during the summer of 1998 included $950 million in federal funding authorizations (but not yet appropriations) to help build the first US maglev line. Five proposals will be selected in the spring of 1999 to take part in the final phase of the competition, after which one will be chosen. A leading contender is the project to build a 240-mile per hour maglev train along the Washington to Baltimore corridor. The new line, with a total cost of some $2 billion, would go from Union Station to Baltimore's Camden Station, with a possible stop for some trains at Baltimore-Washington International Airport. Maryland Delegate Carol Petzold predicted that the maglev train might help attract the Olympics of 2012, since it "would have a lot of pizzazz." [169] If built swiftly, this could still be the first functioning maglev line for the general traveling and commuting public anywhere in the world.

FREIGHT TRAINS

The issue of freight railways must be addressed. As of 1998, the Union Pacific railroad had lost much of its former capability of moving grain from the farm states to consumer markets and to dockside for export. This included the inability of Union Pacific to ship sufficient grain from the plains states to California feed grain suppliers. American rail freight is now an oligopoly dominated by the Union Pacific-Southern Pacific combine, CSX (the old Chesapeake and Ohio), Norfolk Southern, Burlington Northern Santa Fe, and Conrail, which is in the process of being carved up. Most of these roads were in the hands of asset strippers. The nationalization of all existing freight

---

[168] See "Ride America' First Bullet Train," *Popular Mechanics*, March 1993.
[169] *Montgomery Gazette*, October 23, 1998.

lines may prove the only way to stop the systematic looting of the capital investment represented by the nation's rail lines. The management of the freight railroads must be ready to launch imaginative and aggressive programs of expansion, modernization and improvement of service using R-loans. Otherwise, their ouster will be unavoidable. Further looting of the capital embodied in US railways threatens to make any future recovery impossible.

URBAN MASS TRANSIT

By the late 1990s, there was a belated revival of interest in mass transit systems for urban areas. The greater Washington DC area became aware of the problem when it was found that the average local commuter who drove to work was spending more time in traffic jams than anywhere else in the country, with the sole exception of Los Angeles. The Capital Beltway, now over thirty years old, was wholly obsolete, and the Woodrow Wilson bridge across the Potomac south of the capital urgently needed to be replaced. The Washington Metrorail system needed a circle line parallel to the Beltway to facilitate the increasingly common suburb-to-suburb commuting. Washington needed light rail reaching north to southern Pennsylvania, south to Richmond, and west to Harper's Ferry, West Virginia. But railroad links along these axes were either non-existent or rudimentary.

In the case of New York City, subway construction for all intents and purposes ground to a halt when the New Deal ran out of steam. There has been no expansion of the New York subway since 1940, when the Interborough Rapid Transit reached Main Street, Flushing. The cars are now air-conditioned, but the tunnels and rights of way are as much as a century old, and the technology is thoroughly obsolete because of the false economies made by the metropolitan Transit Authority in order to keep up payments to the bondholders. Decades ago, New York city planners assumed that growth was a given, and that their task was to manage such growth. The most recent study of New York's future suggests that growth has ended, and that the city has gone into a decline which may prove irreversible unless large-scale investments in modernization are made. The same considerations apply to dozens of US metropolitan areas.

Even a city like Paris, which is certainly no paradise, possesses relatively modern, high-speed RER rail links which take commuters from the city center to suburbs from ten to fifty miles away at speeds which are far greater than those attained by the conventional Paris Metro trains. The entire American debate on urban mass transit is vitiated by narrow-minded provincialism and ignorance about promising and interesting things which are being done in other parts of the world, even under today's difficult conditions. American expectations regarding urban mass transit and infrastructure are tragically low, and it is time to ratchet them up, or our cities will not survive.

BUILD 200 NUCLEAR REACTORS IMMEDIATELY

The US electrical power grid is now approaching the point of breakdown. Deregulation ideologues deny this, pointing to excess capacity. Bernard Cohen notes that an average of 14% of the generating capacity of the typical utility is shut down at any given time for purposes of maintenance and repairs. Because of this, a reserve capacity of 20% has traditionally been considered advisable, and a reserve of capacity of 17.5% has been viewed as the irreducible minimum to avoid catastrophic blackouts. The East Coast of the United States dipped below 15% reserve capacity in 1993, and the rest of the nation east of the Rockies went below 17.5% that same year. There is every reason to believe that the situation has been worsening. [Cohen 10-11]

American utility companies placed orders for a total of 231 nuclear power plants through the end of 1974, but only 15 additional orders were placed after that, and none at all after 1978. (1978 was of course the year of the highly suspicious Three Mile Island incident, a likely case of deliberate sabotage which furnished the trigger for public hysteria stoked by the news media.) Between 1974 and 1982, orders for more than one hundred nuclear plants were cancelled. Canceling orders in many cases meant abandoning reactors that were already under construction, which inflicted about $10 billion in useless costs on the national economy. [Campbell 3-4] Not a single plant ordered after 1973 was successfully completed and brought on line. [McCaffrey 10] The most astounding case of such wanton and self-inflicted carnage has been the Shoreham nuclear reactor on Long Island, which was torn down when it had been fully completed, and which thus became probably "the largest engineering project in all history that ever was completed and then abandoned without every being used." [Aron xiii]

The track record still holds that not one person has ever been killed by a nuclear reactor accident in any nuclear facility designed in western Europe, the United States, or Japan. The Chernobyl reactor which blew up in 1986 was at bottom a military facility designed to maximize plutonium production for weapons purposes. (If Soviet inability to make a technology work properly were grounds for its abandonment elsewhere, color television would be extinct, since Soviet color television sets also had a notorious tendency to explode.) By 1988 France was deriving 70% of her energy from nuclear plants, and no catastrophes have ensued. As we observe the highly successful operation of the nuclear power industry in France and other modern countries which had more stable governments than we did during the late 1970s, we are forced to the conclusion that such collective insanity, a figment of the nightmare presidency of Jimmy Carter, must now be relegated to the past. As Bernard Cohen sums up the case, "As we face up to our growing need for more power plants, the only real choice in most cases is between nuclear and coal burning. Nuclear power will be substantially less expensive and thousands of times less harmful to our health and our environment. The time truly seems ripe for a resurgence of nuclear power in the United States." [Cohen 296]

US nuclear reactor construction needs clearly start with the 100 reactors ordered during the 1970s, but never built. The last good years for nuclear reactor construction were 1966, when 16 reactors were ordered which eventually came on line, 1967, with 24 new reactors, and 1968, with 10 new reactors. After that, best year was 1970, with 9 such reactors. In all, 97 reactors were ordered during the 1960s and 1970s and eventually came on line. By 1988, the US had 110 operating nuclear facilities. All of these reactors must be considered obsolete or obsolescent as of 2000. Therefore, the initial nuclear reactor construction mandatory for the economic survival of this country amounts to more than 200 reactors of the most modern type. That would put us where we ought already to be today. But a program of 200 reactors is already far beyond the existing depleted capabilities of the moribund nuclear industry, which will have to be rebuilt to handle the tasks at hand. In the near future, additional reactors can and should be ordered as economic recovery takes off, and demand for electric power increases. Returning to the nuclear option now would allow the US to transform its backwardness into an advantage by leaping ahead of France, Japan, and other powers in building the most modern, efficient, and safest reactor types in sizes of 1000 megawatts and up. This might include the High Temperature Nuclear Reactor or other recent designs.

1000 HOSPITALS, 50,000 SCHOOLS, 200,000 BRIDGES, 40,000 MILES OF INTERSTATE, 20 AIRPORTS

Other areas of infrastructure will also require attention, including rural and inner city hospitals, schools, and libraries. We recall that 675 US hospitals were shut down between 1980 and 1993 alone. If we add in the replacement of obsolete facilities and of numerous hospitals closed since 1993, we can see that providing adequate medical care – including accessible emergency medical care – to the people of this country will require a hospital building program of not less than 1000 fully equipped and modern hospitals, together with the training of the doctors and nurses needed to staff them.

Tackling the accumulated infrastructure deficit will also require the construction of some 50,000 new schools and 200,000 bridges. The entire 40,000 miles of the Eisenhower-era interstate highway system need to be rebuilt, at least to the standards of the high-speed German *Autobahn*, which are beyond most Americans' wildest dreams. These measures would simply restore assets that are now obsolete.

Former Secretary of Transportation Samuel Skinner estimated that the United States required twenty new airports by the year 2000. So far, the country managed to modernize one during the 1980s (Atlanta) and build one during the 1990s (Denver). Even though economic recovery must emphasize modern maglev and high-speed rail transport where possible, there is no question that the twenty airports, including the reconstruction of obsolete relics from the 1930s, are urgently needed. Since a modern airport costs between $4 and $5 billion, here is an area where $100 billion of R-loan credit can be well invested. [W. Peterson 221]

Many of the most urgent projects for national economic recovery would be impossible to initiate because of the jungle of federal environmental regulations. If left intact, these laws and regulations might constitute an insuperable barrier to national economic survival. Many of these misguided laws, the fruit of the pessimism of the floating-rate era, must be suspended by the President's emergency order. This would include the Endangered Species Act, the Wilderness Act, many provisions of the Clean Air Act, and those dispositions regarding so-called wetlands which block the draining of swamps. The criterion here is the constitutional imperative of promoting the general welfare: the environmental rules we need to respect and indeed strengthen are the ones which protect the American people from pollution, toxicity, and other abuses. But it is *people* we are defending. The extinction of animal and plant species is a process which occurs constantly in nature, and the attempt to interfere with it represents an unwarranted and unnecessary meddling in this natural process. We should do what we reasonably can for the spotted owl or the snail darter, but we cannot allow human beings to be hungry, homeless, and unemployed under the pretext of protecting these creatures. The Wilderness Act tries to establish the wilderness as a value in and of itself. But the Grand Canyon is not the Grand Canyon for itself, but rather for the recreation and education of the American people. It must be there as a vacation destination for the slum child from Harlem or South Central Los Angeles who needs to be given a taste of the great outdoors. So the point of preserving wilderness sites is to make them available for the American people. As for draining swamps, it has been part of the elementary progress of civilization from Rome to medieval Holland on down to the present day. We must also recall that there is no compelling scientific evidence of global warming or for a deterioration of the ozone layer, and that attempts to limit greenhouse gases and hydrofluorocarbons reflects little more than an oligarchical hysteria. Any treaties dealing these issues which might hobble economic recovery must be simply rendered inoperative by Executive Order.

NEW CITIES AND PORTS

It has been a long time since the United States has successfully created any new cities. Oak Ridge, Tennessee was largely a creation of the TVA, and the Richland-Pasco area grew up around the Hanford nuclear facility. Alamogordo, New Mexico and Cape Canaveral, Florida might also qualify, but just barely. In the near future, maglev transportation will make it highly economical to create whole new cities, planned from the ground up, in areas which are very sparsely populated today. The Soviet Union created science cities in Siberia, and the Japanese government has also created science cities. With maglev, it becomes feasible to locate American science cities in regions like the High Plains, the Great Basin, and the desert Southwest. These cities can and should be organized around areas of research, as for example biotech, astrophysics, high energy physics, and the like.

Another vital issue involves US port facilities. Today, the most important export of the once-great Port of New York is garbage. The East Coast and Gulf Coast of this country presently have no facilities capable of accommodating freighters of 100,000 tons, despite the fact that vessels of this size have been prevalent on the high seas since about 1980. Only Long Beach, California and Puget Sound, Washington can handle bulk carriers up to 150,000 tons. The Louisiana Offshore Oil Port (LOOP) can handle supertankers, but the country requires other facilities of this size. To redress this ominous and tragic situation, we must create new port facilities and expand existing ones in places like Boston, New York-New Jersey, Baltimore, Norfolk, Charleston SC, Mobile, New Orleans, Galveston, San Diego, Long Beach, San Francisco, Puget Sound, Anchorage, and Hawaii. Parallel to this, we must begin a national effort to rebuild a US-flag merchant marine, with American-built ships of the most modern type.

V. A NEW WORLD MONETARY SYSTEM - BRETTON WOODS II

No domestic recovery program can succeed without a general world economic recovery. World trade is the lifeblood of each national economy, and the health of world trade now dictates sweeping monetary reform. World economic recovery requires the short-term activation of a new world monetary system to facilitate a boom in the physical volume as well as the dollar value of world trade. The original Bretton Woods Conference of 1944 put an end to a harrowing 13-year ordeal of depression and world war which had followed the British default of September 1931, which had swept away the old pound-centered monetary system. We must now gird ourselves for the task of normalizing world trade after an equally harrowing quarter-century in which the world economy has attempted to operate without a world monetary system, with disastrous results.

The three key elements of the Second Bretton Woods System are obvious from our earlier observations on the rise and fall of the original Bretton Woods (see Chapter IV). It will be necessary to return to the obligatory practice of gold settlement of international trade imbalances. Not just the dollar, but most of the main trading currencies of the world will require their own direct gold parity. The dollar/gold parity might initially be set in the neighborhood of $1000 per troy ounce, but this needs to be calculated very carefully based on the real economic conditions obtaining at the moment these measures are taken. Every national currency will have its own fixed-parity relation with every other national currency, with bands of permissible fluctuation of plus or minus 1%. Most important, the technical features of the system must be accompanied by the political commitment of the developed countries of North America, Europe, and Japan to promote the export of modern capital goods, especially to the traditional developing countries and the newly independent successor states of the USSR.

Like the original Bretton Woods of 1944, the new system must use gold for yearly settlement of balance of payments discrepancies. At the end of each year, the national banks of the various countries would net and clear their international transactions, and deficits would be paid in gold at $1000 per ounce. The obligation for gold payment would be limited to foreign national banks or sovereign nations. This would not be a pre-1914 gold coin standard, under which paper dollars and gold coins would circulate side by side, and under which any person could ask for gold in exchange for paper. The amount of gold in the possession of a country would in no way limit the amount of credit that country might issue, for such limitation would court permanent deflation and depression.

The new system should be what has been called in the past a gold bullion standard, with each country obligated to ship gold ingots to buy back sums of its own currency remaining in the hands of other nations at the end of a year or other suitable accounting period. Countries would be encouraged to protect their gold stocks and their general international solvency by using capital controls, exchange controls, and credit controls as needed, and in regulating their international trade through measures designed to secure a healthy balance of payments profile, notably by encouraging high-technology exports and by expanding their own domestic consumer goods industries.

Gold has no magic powers. The strength of the new system will reside in the dynamism of exports and in the related development programs, which must guarantee a strong demand for the principal currencies for purposes of capital investment and working capital in the infinite variety of commodity production. The system will stand or fall according to its dedication to full employment, rising standards of living, and scientific, technological, and industrial progress. The sole but indispensable purpose of gold settlement is to provide a universally recognized reality principle for the economic policies of each sovereign state. Gold is not the basis of the health of the system, but rather the needed barometer of the system's well-being. A system of gold settlement will restore national sovereignty to all states, and prevent any nation from flooding the world with a depreciated paper currency which others are obliged to accept. Any such system, like the dollar after 1971, leads the authorities of the country so privileged to neglect the solvency of their own financial system, creates uncontrolled offshore markets, and so forth. But no country has a monopoly on gold, and this is why gold is indispensable.

The technical aspects of returning to fixed exchange rates can be facilitated through the existence, even inside the present-day Federal Reserve System, of a school of economic thought which supports fixed exchange rates. One of these economists is Arthur J. Rolnick, Senior Vice President and Director of Research of the Federal Reserve Bank of Minneapolis, Minnesota. In articles like "The Case of Fixed Exchange Rates" and "In Order to Form a More Perfect Monetary Union," Rolnick has over the years argued that post-1971 currency fluctuations tend not to reflect economic fundamentals, but tend to vary on the random walk model. Rolnick is convinced that fixed exchange rates stimulate foreign investment, and that a fixed-rate system would be economically more efficient for the world. In his view, the dollar, the yen, and the D-mark would be the three indispensable components of a fixed rate structure.[170] It is not surprising that this point of view comes from the farm belt, which is among the most export-dependent areas of the United States. Every sector of the US economy would benefit from the general economic betterment which fixed rates would bring. Gold convertibility is also indispensable to obtain the full beneficial effect.

In one of his worst moments, President Reagan once told the United Nations General Assembly that there is no inherent right to national development. In order to guarantee a long-lasting and hopefully permanent world economic recovery, the treaty establishing the new world monetary system must emphatically posit the inalienable and imperative right of every nation under natural law and the law of nations to the fullest possible degree of scientific, technological, cultural and economic development, rising labor productivity, rising standards of living, and full employment.

This program of universal dignity and pacification through economic development and rising standards of living has a very powerful appeal to the less developed countries, the former Soviet bloc, and ultimately to all nations. However, there are those who regard such a perspective with revulsion. Foremost among these adversaries are the British finance oligarchy in the City of London, who regard themselves as the most powerful single financial force within the existing

---

[170] *Minneapolis Star-Tribune*, June 20, 1998.

System. The City of London exerts formidable control over that approximate quarter of the world's land area and quarter of the world population which was once officially the British Empire. The so-called British Commonwealth of Nations has lost much of the national autonomy which the British were forced to grant their former colonies during the quarter-century after 1945, and is now once again an Empire in fact, although it is now conducted more subtly through financial, political, and cultural control than was the pre-1948 form.

This British finance oligarchy will always be the adversary of any world monetary reform tending towards world economic development and scientific advancement. In financial and strategic terms, London hit bottom shortly after the Suez debacle of 1956, but soon began its comeback with the emergence of the London-based Eurodollar market. Today, in a world ravaged by free trade and globaloney, the mummified City of London can more and more successfully assert its claim to be the leading "centre" of world finance. But the capacity of the British isles for hard-commodity production is virtually nil, and, given the mentality of the ruling elite, there is no visible way that it could be restored. So London will always try to sabotage any shift of the definition of economic power away from rentier-style finance and asset stripping towards the export of high-technology, modern capital goods. Accordingly, London's demands must receive no consideration and no political weight in formulating the American plan for world recovery. The British system is a barbarous relic, and must be treated as such. Herbert Hoover thought that Ramsay McDonald was his friend, but McDonald's gold default of September 1931 torpedoed the US banking system. Clinton must not repeat the same kind of blunder with the grinning neo-Thatcherite Tony Blair.

Fortunately, the cultural landscape in a number of other countries is far more favorable to a community of principle based on economic development. In China, first of all, we are experiencing a kind of neo-Confucian reaction against the horrors of the Mao era, itself rooted in the heritage of legalism. In the post-Deng period, the Chinese leaders have appeared to seek a return to the spirit of Dr. Sun Yat-sen, the 1911 founder of the Republic of China and one of the very few truly great figures of the twentieth century. Dr. Sun, after the close of World War I, urged that the main industrial powers cooperate in a program of development and modernization for China. Dr. Sun explicitly proposed this cooperation as an alternative to economic depression. Sun wanted to build 1 million miles of roads, 100,000 miles of modern rails, and three great ports, each one comparable to the Port of New York (at that time). Sun wanted to connect China to Europe via the Russian rail grid, and also via a projected Indo-European rail line. Sun favored extensive water projects and reforestation to prevent the Yellow and Yangtze Rivers from silting up. [171] At a May 1991 University of Hong Kong conference of delegates from China, Hong Kong and Taiwan on the importance of Dr. Sun for the future unification of China, this writer had the honor of recommending exactly this course of action as they way to solve China's main national problems. The end of the twentieth century provides what we must hope will be the first fair chance to realize Dr. Sun's program.

The Chinese government today is prepared to spend $1 trillion on railroad building and such megaprojects as the Three Gorges Dam. The Chinese government is pointing with pride to its New Euro-Asian Land Bridge, which is the new 11,000 kilometer rail line from Lianyungang on the Yellow Sea through Sinkiang province, Kazakhstan, Moscow, Warsaw, and Berlin to Rotterdam, the largest port of continental Europe. This line was completed through the addition of some small missing pieces, and was opened on December 1, 1992. Many parts of the New Euro-Asian Land Bridge are obsolete, but the Chinese government has double-tracked 2,000 km of the line on its territory while electrifying and otherwise modernizing significant portions.

---

[171] See Sun Yat-sen, *The International Development of China.*

Other Eurasian rail developments have included efforts to provide convenient access to the world ocean for the new republics of central Asia, which have yielded a rail line from Turkmenistan to Iran and through Iran to the Gulf. There is also a project to build fiber optic telecommunications links from Europe across Asia to the Pacific. The apt generic name for Eurasian infrastructure development is the New Silk Road, a name which hearkens back to the caravan route which brought Chinese silks across Asia to the ports of the eastern Mediterranean. Every right-of-way of the Chinese rail network can be considered as the axis of a development corridor providing optimal locations for factories, housing, power plants, communication centers, and new cities. Canals, communications, electricity, and transport can all be the objects of integrated planning in connection with these corridors.

The old sterile contrapositions of the Cold War, which froze world political development for half a century, have now become obsolete. The old opposition between China and India has shown some signs of being replaced by cooperation. China and Russia have put aside their absurd enmity, as signaled by the spring 1997 and November 1998 visits of Chinese President Jiang Zemin with Russian President Yeltsin. Iran and Turkey have joined in plans for the large-scale building of oil pipelines. The five former Soviet central Asian republics are eager to participate, and Russian Prime Minister Primakov is highly intrigued by the inherent possibilities of Russia as the rail hub of Eurasia.

The diplomacy of a new world monetary system will require the United States to reach a quick understanding with China, and then with Russia, on the basics of a system. The United States must take the lead. Once China is convinced, Russia – especially under a Eurasian thinker like Primakov – will likely follow suit. A US-Russia-China bloc could be supported by Japan, as well as by the bigger developing countries like India, Brazil, Mexico, Indonesia, South Africa, and others. The poorer countries will be easier to mobilize for recovery than the rich ones. Resistance can be expected from the pro-British element in the European Commission, as well as from the pro-British governments of continental Europe. But this resistance can be outflanked and overcome. Finally, we should concentrate on detaching Canada and especially Australia (which has a strong dirigist tradition) from the hard-core British camp.

A Eurasian rail network could also include Southeast Asia, with Malaysia, Singapore and parts of Indonesia. Japan could be linked to the continent through Sakhalin in the north, and across the Tshushima Strait to Korea in the south. There are obvious connections to Africa through Palestine and across the Straits of Gibraltar, and possibly from Sicily to Tunisia. A modern rail link from Cairo to the Cape is long overdue, as is an east-west rail line from Senegal to Djibouti. Of great interest to Americans is the evident possibility of crossing the Bering Strait with a rail tunnel somewhat longer than the British-French Channel Tunnel. This would connect North and South America with Eurasia/Africa, covering the entire world with a seamless railroad net. If maglev is chosen for freight and high-priority package express, a direct-mail computer manufacturer in South Dakota could ship a package via smooth-as-silk maglev express for second-day delivery virtually anywhere on the land surface of the earth.

THE PACIFICATION OF THE WORLD

The Landbridge/Silk Road is concept embraced by many Asian governments. First, it is the biggest business opportunity of all time. United States diplomacy should aim at getting this country in on the ground floor. Secondly, the Landbridge can accomplish an unprecedented pacification of the Eurasian landmass. If the present moment of universal rapprochement were to be lost, hostile coalitions might emerge involving such gigantic chess-pieces as Russia, China, India, Iran, Turkey,

Kazakhstan, and others. The strategic potentials in play would be so immense that not just Japan and Europe, but the United States as well, could hardly resist the logic of such new blocs. So choosing the Landbridge is also the best war-avoidance strategy that lies to hand.

During the Second World War, one of the finest moments of the Pacific theatre was furnished by SACO – the Sino-American Cooperation Organization, which pooled the resources of the United States and the Chinese nationalists. This might be a good name for a new Chinese-American bilateral economic development authority to facilitate and finance Chinese purchase of US capital goods for economic development purposes.

Geopolitics is inherently immoral and does not work beyond the short run. Geopolitics always involves balance of power coalitions which are inherently unstable. The Venetians and the British were the acknowledged masters of geopolitics, but despite their cunning each was confronted at least once with a united front of its dupes and victims, and narrowly escaped destruction. A community of principle based on national independence and economic development has a far greater war avoidance potential than geopolitical scheming doomed to backfire sooner or later.

Economic development needs to be the central consideration of American foreign policy. After the fall of the Berlin Wall in 1989 and the collapse of the Soviet Union in 1989, an unprecedented opportunity for world pacification was squandered by the Bush administration. Under the foolish slogans of the New World Order and the End of History, the United States forced Russia and other countries to submit to Herbert Hoover economics as expounded by the IMF. This phase produced speculative bonanzas for a few financiers, but ruined the Russian economy. Short-sighted and complacent government officials like Warren Christopher, Madeleine Albright, Anthony Lake, Sandy Berger, Richard Holbrooke, Lloyd Bentsen, Robert Rubin, Larry Summers, and others left the international economic policy of the Bush years on automatic pilot. American diplomacy offered no Grand Design of world economic cooperation, but left world economic arrangements to the gouging monetarists of the IMF. Instead, the US concentrated on vindictive campaigns against Iraq, Iran, Sudan, and a few others. The plan to pacify North Korea by delivering peaceful nuclear energy and food aid was highly promising, but it remained an isolated feature within the general framework of globaloney, and was undermined by Asian economic decline. So the US won the Cold War, but then turned the world over to the IMF. By August 1998, Russia had defaulted, and a rising tide of resistance against the IMF's incompetent economics was visible in the world. The United States needed a foreign policy based on some greater ideal than "market democracy," a hollow slogan that generally meant dollar diplomacy in search of a fast buck. The promise of the 1990s had been to mobilize the energies tragically wasted in the four decades of the Cold War for something better. It was time to wage war on the real enemies of mankind – hunger, poverty, disease, misery, illiteracy, ignorance, exploitation, backwardness and despair. If these could be vanquished, the pacification of the planet would be within reach. After the Cold War, the entire world needed a New Deal.

Bretton Woods II must therefore be a world monetary system with gold settlement, fixed parities, AND development projects on the largest scale built in from the very beginning. The monetary system and projects the Landbridge go hand in hand. The American experience under Bretton Woods proves that if you do not commit to a permanently high volume of capital-goods exports, your currency is accumulated abroad and you ultimately face devaluation and default. The prevention for that is to guarantee a high demand for your currency by aggressively producing and exporting capital goods which countries want to buy for use in their own economic development. Projects like the Landbridge are thus the key to the long-term solvency of the US dollar and of the world.

It may be that the first phases of an international commitment to the projects like the Landbridge and the Bering Strait bridge-tunnel can be accomplished by production and export credits generated by the individual exporting countries that have switched over to Hamiltonian national banking practices. But it is very likely that before long the need will be felt to supplement the various national Export-Import Banks, German Hermes guarantees, and French COFAS credits with an international financing authority.

MULTILATERAL DEVELOPMENT BANK

Because of the destructive practices of the International Monetary Fund, the post-crash world will be deeply distrustful of international organizations. But the advantages and profits of multilateral financing would be considerable. The institution required sooner or later to attain the highest levels of world prosperity through development exports is a Multilateral Development Bank (MDB). Such a bank would function as a purely technical facility for the purpose of expediting economic development projects agreed on by the governments of the sovereign member states. The development projects would be negotiated among the participating governments. The MDB would be a creature and servant of the governments which had created it, and would not be empowered to issues directives of any sort to any government. Its chief function would be as a rediscount agency for letters of credit, bills of exchange, and other commercial paper issued for international commodity transfers in connection with development projects authorized by treaty agreements.

The MDB member states would buy capital shares in the bank and take up their seats on the board. The capital of the MDB would then be used for financing international development projects. In other words, if France, Germany, Poland, Belarus, Russia, China, and Japan agree to build a maglev line from Paris to Beijing and Tokyo with inputs from the United States and Italy, this treaty is forwarded to the International Development Bank. If the MDB is financing the entire project, the MDB will issue a master letter of credit that implicitly covers the entire outlay of the project - say, $100 billion. The master letter of credit guarantees the availability of funds for all the specific letters of credit that will go to make up the project. A building contractor who needs to meet a payroll on the Omsk to Krasnoyarsk segment can take his letter of credit to a local bank and get the funds he needs for wages in a given week. The same goes for the machine tool company in Milan, Italy which is a sub-contractor for part of the rolling stock.

The momentum for infrastructural development is now strongest in Asia. But Europe also has an immense infrastructure deficit, much of its attributable to the Iron Curtain, which severed numerous east-west transportation links. The 1989-1991 collapse of the communist regimes in the satellite states, followed by the dissolution of the Warsaw Pact and the dismemberment of the USSR, opened an exceptional opportunity for building infrastructure in newly united Germany and in the area of Europe's greatest density of industrial capacity, the Paris-Berlin-Vienna triangle. The opportunities of 1990-91 were largely wasted, because of the sabotage of figures like Bush, Thatcher, and Mitterrand, as well as by the ineptitude of leaders like Helmut Kohl. A negative role was also played by the various "free trade" and "market economy" ideologues in Warsaw, Prague, Budapest, and elsewhere – often Marxist retreads – who were more interested in opening derivatives markets than in opening rail links. Currently the Hamburg to Berlin maglev line is still alive as a project, but many other urgently needed initiatives have fallen by the wayside. But there is every reason to believe that European interest in infrastructure building could revive if the international climate changes.

In the area of foreign policy, we would do well to recall Franklin D. Roosevelt's admonition in his First Inaugural: "In the field of world policy I would dedicate this Nation to the policy of the good neighbor – the neighbor who resolutely respects himself and, because he does so, respects the rights of others – the neighbor who respects his obligations and respects the sanctity of his agreements in and with a world of neighbors." This hearkens back to John Quincy Adams' community of principle among independent states, and to Henry Clay's desire to win over the Latin American countries as equal partners in the American System.

NEW LEND-LEASE FOR RUSSIA

In December 1940, Franklin D. Roosevelt had just been re-elected President for an unprecedented fourth term. At this point the British were facing Hitler alone, and they were reaching the bottom of the barrel of financial resources which they could use to buy war materiel from the US under the "cash and carry" policy which the US was following at that time. American interest required that the British not be allowed to succumb. So Roosevelt's problem was to convince a skeptical Congress that US government should ship the British (and later the Soviets) war equipment which they could not pay for. Roosevelt needed totally to divorce military shipments from issues of payment and financing. He accomplished this feat with his masterful "garden hose" press conference of December 1940. How he did this is an object lesson for the strategic vision and political skill which are required today.

At this landmark press conference, the optimistic FDR told reporters: "Now what I am trying to do is to eliminate the dollar sign. That is something brand new in the thoughts of practically everybody in this room, I think – get rid of that silly, foolish old dollar sign."

Today, when Tony Blair's British Libor Party (London Interbank Offered Rate) regime is trying to extract derivatives payments from a bankrupt Russian banking system, the task is once again getting rid of that silly, foolish old dollar sign. FDR went on:

> Well, let me give you an illustration. Suppose my neighbor's house catches fire, and I have a length if garden hose four or five hundred feet away. If he can take my garden hose and connect it up with his hydrant, I may help him put out his fire. Now, what do I do? I don't say to him before that operation, "Neighbor, my garden hose cost me 15 dollars, you have to pay me fifteen dollars for it.' What is the transaction that goes on? I don't want 15 dollars – I want my garden hose back after the fire is over. All right.

FDR showed the reporters that by letting the neighbor use our hose, we can probably stop the fire from spreading from his house to ours. It was the consummate appeal to enlightened self-interest. It was politically risky, but it worked. A few days later, in a fireside chat, FDR declared that "no pessimistic policy about the future of America shall delay the immediate expansion of those industries essential to defense. We need them.... We must be the great arsenal of democracy." Out of this grew HR 1776, the $50 billion Lend-Lease program, the greatest single component of the FDR defense mobilization, and the basis of all US strategy in World War II. In addition to helping to win the war abroad, Lend-Lease also vanquished unemployment here at home. Sir Winston Churchill called the passage of Lend-Lease in early 1941 one of the great turning points of World War II. At the 1943 Teheran Conference, Stalin formally acknowledged that without Lend-Lease, the USSR could not have survived. Lend-Lease aid to the Soviets amounted to some $11 billion, including 12,000 tanks, 8200 anti-aircraft guns, and 75% of all the Red Army's jeeps, trucks, and tractors.

Naturally, there was opposition in those days from the Republicans, who were pretty then much what they always have been in this century. They denounced Lend-Lease as the "blank-check bill," and the "Dictator, War, and Bankruptcy Bill." GOP leader Sen. Robert Taft quipped that "Lending war equipment is a good deal like lending chewing gum. You don't want it back." This kind of narrow-minded thinking would have lost the shooting war back then, and it will lose the economic war today.

Today, we need once again to get rid of that silly old dollar sign. Like FDR, we want to wage war against today's world economic depression. If Russia does not receive timely aid, the results may be tragic for Russians, and they may be incalculable for the United States as well. There is a little matter of over 10,000 nuclear weapons. Russians believe that the US government deliberately unleashed Harvard professor Jeffrey Sachs and his infamous shock therapy on them as a weapon more destructive than any number of nuclear bombs, and it must be said they have a compelling case. But there may still be time for that misguided policy, begun under the Bush administration, to be reversed. First, the United States must grant Russia a full moratorium on all debts and payment commitments, and persuade the other leading countries to do the same. This can be the leading edge of the general international debt moratorium for the entire duration of the crisis which all countries should receive. Generous emergency food aid under the Food for Peace program must be expedited. The United States must then begin to produce capital goods for the reconstruction and development of Russia as a top priority. Just as in 1941-45, producing for the Russian front will be the most effective weapon against the depression here at home. The issue of how and whether Russia can pay for all this is a tertiary matter, which must not be allowed to interfere with rapid action.

Economist Wallace Peterson has reported on the proposals of the Chicago businessman Warren G. Brockmeier to set up a new agency with a federal charter but with private capital (along the lines of the present Ginnie Mae) to finance capital goods exports to eastern Europe and the USSR successor states. This new Lend-Lease Ginnie Mae would "raise money by selling bonds to the investing public" and would then play "a middleman role between American manufacturers and foreign governments and companies that need the equipment. Once the latter parties had reached a tentative agreement on equipment needs, they would turn to the federal agency, which would actually purchase the equipment and arrange for its shipment to the appropriate country." [W. Peterson 225-6] The overseas purchasers of US capital goods would not be expected to pay in dollars, but would pay in their own currencies. This approach would allow private capital to get back into the world of productive investment in plant and equipment, instead of chasing the chimeras of arbitrage and derivatives. Ideas like this deserve to be promoted by government, since they would give private investors the chance to piggy-back on the overall Lend-Lease effort, and make money by doing something to promote the general welfare, which is what industrial capitalism is all about.

A NEW AMERICAN SOCIAL CONTRACT

Above and beyond the five leading points for immediate emergency action, we must turn our attention to rebuilding the American standard of living, in the context of a general improvement of the conditions of life in this world. We have seen that the average weekly earnings provided by the typical American job are now about where they were when Dwight D. Eisenhower left office in 1961, some four decades ago. Forty years on the road to nowhere are far too many. Issues like reform of the world monetary system may seem bewildering to many citizens, which is one reason why the new world monetary system needs to be presented as inseparable from a series of measures designed to improve wages, working conditions, and the climate for collective bargaining in ways that favor working families, and redress the anti-labor policies of government over the past decades. Here is one area where pervasive and often justified mistrust of government as a hostile and alien entity needs to be dissipated by timely reform and timely action.

During and after World War II, most American companies and unions respected the terms of an implicit social contract. This social contract mandated a rising standard of living, decent working conditions, improved standards of health and welfare, and a secure retirement for working families. In exchange, corporate executives received peace on the labor front, and the loyal and diligent service of what was then the best-educated and most talented work force in the world, allowing them to realize growing profits for their stockholders and themselves. As we have seen, this social contract was torn up by the finance oligarchs and their clerks in government during the Carter and Reagan administrations, when America made its tragic U-turn on the road of progress. Since then, wages, job security, fringe benefits, health care, retirement pensions, and a host of other requirements have sharply deteriorated. With Carter, Reagan, and Bush, the federal and state governments appeared in the guise of willing henchmen in the junking of the social contract.

As indicated above, an acceptable level for the new jobs created under the R-loan program would be between $50,000 and $60,000 per year. We must take immediate action to assist the 30 million plus working poor in this country. Thanks to the efforts of Senator Kennedy and others, the minimum wage was raised to $5.15 per hour on September 1, 1997, and while this is an improvement from the pitiful levels prevailing before that, it is still far from sufficient. The current minimum wage yields an annual income of just over $10,700 before taxes – not enough to allow even one person to purchase the barest necessities. In an economy that values productive labor over speculation, an effective minimum wage would have to be at least double the current figure. In November 1998, voters in the state of Washington took a step in the right direction by approving a referendum question establishing a state minimum wage of $6.50 per hour, indexed for inflation – better, but still not enough. Over a 52-week year of 40-hour weeks, a $10 minimum wage would provide an income of just over $20,000 before taxes. Simple humanity and economic survival dictate that no person under US jurisdiction be forced to get by with less. Indeed, it is materially impossible in most areas to work for less.

In addition, a whole array of labor legislation is long overdue. The prevalence of low-wage, no benefit temps in the workforce has been a cause of driving down the standard of living. In 1996, the International Brotherhood of Teamsters went out on strike against United Parcel Service because of the company's excessive reliance on low-paid, no-benefit temps. More than a year later, it appeared that UPS was reneging on its pledge; the need for federal regulation was evident. Federal law must restore the prevalence of permanent, full-time jobs with full health care, vacation, pension, and other benefits. Federal legislation must mandate that no more than 25% of the employees of a company operating in interstate commerce be temps, and that no person who has been on the payroll for 6 months be classified as a temp. The Federal government also has to put its own house in order by ending its own scandalous reliance on low-paid, no-benefit temps in the US Postal Service and many other federal and quasi-federal agencies. We must return to the primacy of the 8-hour day, with a perspective for future shortening of the working day as soon as real productivity increases through technological investment. Overtime must be paid time and a half, and night and holiday work at double time. Americans also deserve a European-style (three to four week) summer vacation and time off policy. A two-week paid vacation per year should be the absolute minimum, with increments for seniority. These are all measures that will enhance the stability and integrity of American families, and even Republican supporters of family values must be made to see the light on these issues.

We need to return to the spirit of the famous section 7 (a) of the National Recovery Act of June 16, 1933, a late fruit of Roosevelt's Hundred Days. Section 7 (a) guaranteed the right of labor to organize and bargain collectively, without "interference, restraint, or coercion" by employers. It outlawed company unions. It required employers to "comply with the maximum hours of labor, minimum rates of pay, and other conditions of employment approved or prescribed by the President." Under the Wagner-Connery Labor Relations Act of May 1936, which was signed in to law after the Nine Old Men of the Supreme Court had declared the NRA unconstitutional, the National Labor Relations Board was authorized to halt unfair practices by employers and to seek relief and remedies in the form of injunctions and restraining orders from the federal courts.

The Taft-Hartley law, passed by the Republican Congress over Truman's veto in June 1947, rolled back much of the progress made during the New Deal by outlawing the closed shop, and permitting harassing lawsuits by employers against unions. The heart of Truman's Fair Deal, such as it was, was the repeal of Taft-Hartley, and this was part of the Democratic platform Adlai Stevenson ran on in 1952. It is high time that the federal government repeal Taft-Hartley, and be empowered to protect the rights of labor. There is no reason why the federal government should deny workers a closed shop if they want it and can win it against employer resistance. The Davis-Bacon law mandating union pay scales for federal contracts anywhere in the country must be strengthened by extending its provisions to cover all projects financed by R-loans. Businessmen who want cheap federal credit for production must be obliged to pay a living family wage. The use of replacement workers or scabs for strikebreaking purposes should be made illegal, along with the transporting of such replacements across state lines. Lockouts should also be made illegal. Federal law should also be aggressively used to override and neutralize the effects of the so-called "right to work" laws imposed by local oligarchs in some states to ban the union shop, at least as far as interstate commerce is concerned. These right-to-work laws operate under a provision of Taft-Hartley, which should be repealed. Witch-hunts against labor leaders by the Department of Justice while monopolists like Bill Gates are allowed to run wild for years contradict any notion of fairness in labor-management relations.

TAX REFORM FOR RECOVERY: TAX RELIEF FOR WORKING FAMILIES

A tax code must not represent a series of more or less plausible expedients to generate income for politicians who have seized control of the government for a period of time. The tax code must embody the fundamental morality of a nation. It must also embody the most advanced insights of modern science. It must impel and sometimes compel individuals to make their sense of self-interest coherent with the national interest. The tax code must aim at providing full employment and a standard of living under which the emerging generation can be educated to assimilate technologies now only faintly discernible on the horizon. So we need a dirigistic tax code in the spirit of Alexander Hamilton or Abraham Lincoln.

When Justice John Marshall of the US Supreme Court pointed out that "the power to tax is the power to destroy," he was communicating an important truth. In general, activities that are to be taxed the most are activities that the national interest wishes to discourage. Activities that society wishes to encourage should be taxed as little as possible. Profiting from illegal narcotics, speculating in stocks, collecting rent from undeveloped land, or gambling in riverboat casinos or with derivatives – all these must be taxed with the intent to discourage. Corporate management must be discouraged from hoarding corporate profits, paying them all out in dividends, squandering them in hostile takeovers or poison pill defenses, or using them to give each other pay raises while ordering mass layoffs. Here the goal of the tax code must be to encourage the re-investment of most of the profits at the highest technological level possible, using the specter of taxation as a goad. Conversely, personal income up to a quite substantial middle class level should not be taxed at all, unless there is some compelling emergency reason.

The current problem is that the middle class, including farmers and small and medium industrialists, which is the most numerous and the most important class in modern society, is being systematically crushed. We are headed back towards a pre-modern and basically feudal two-class society with a tiny elite and a very large impoverished mass and little or nothing in between. It is a well-known historical fact that such a two-class is not viable and cannot survive very long. In addition, a society like the United States cannot allow, as a long-term fixture of society, a permanent underclass of unemployable persons tending to resemble Marx's *Lumpenproletariat* or unemployed working class in rags.

It is the shrinking pie that is the problem, and no amount of distributive justice will fix the problem as long as the pie continues to shrink. So tax policy should aim at increased production of cultural and material wealth. We need the rising tide that will lift all boats. However, it is also true that poorer Americans, who will be very numerous at the end of the 1990s, require more assistance from the government than wealthy ones might. Therefore, the social service programs that serve the poor and the unemployed must be treated as entitlements and kept fully funded under all circumstances. Help must be given on the basis of economic need. Racial identity may be hard to determine, but annual income is eminently knowable. Entitlements are economic rights granted to all persons, and none must be taken away. Otherwise, what might appear to some as attempts at income redistribution are simply efforts to return to fairness and pro-production dirigism after so many years of income redistribution in favor of the very wealthy and of bias in favor of parasitical activities.

The federal personal income tax is thus a very dubious and contradictory way to secure funding for the national government. A personal income tax is inherently a tax that leads us in the wrong direction, namely towards attacking the hard-earned income of wage earners. The personal income tax, along with the Federal Reserve, is part of the bitter heritage of the Woodrow Wilson regime. The really necessary reform is the phasing out of the personal income tax, starting from the lowest incomes and working up. Tariffs, capital gains taxes, estate taxes, and corporate income taxes are good candidates to provide any missing revenue. In the meantime, we will have to persist with the personal income tax for a while longer, but hopefully not too much longer.

The worst possible idea for tax reform is the Steve Forbes "flat tax" fraud, which would put the entire tax burden on wage earners and give rich fat-cats with interest, dividend, and capital-gains income – unearned income – a completely free ride. Finance oligarchs love the flat tax. A flat tax would be a brutally regressive tax and a recipe for class war not far down the road. It is hard to imagine anything worse than a flat tax, but a national sales tax probably qualifies as even more horrendous. A national sales tax of the Lugar variety appears to be a proportional tax, but is of course highly regressive in its own right, since it hits the poorer population much harder than the wealthy. Value-added taxes are destructive because they tax and thus discourage something that a sane society wants to promote. A consumption tax is a diabolical tax on the need of wage-earners and their family to feed, clothe, and house themselves.

Frederick R. Strobel has raised the alarm about the lobbying efforts of the American Council for Capital Formation and its leading light, Charles "Mr. VAT" Walker. According to Strobel, this group "is currently trying to convince the American electorate that it would be better off paying a national sales tax (a value-added tax, or VAT) and eliminating the corporate income tax .... But most economists agree that a value-added (VAT) type of sales tax would be shifted forward to the consumer in the short run. Thus, substituting a VAT for the corporate income tax would most likely further increase the tax burden on the already overtaxed consumer and middle class. It would further lighten the tax load on capital, again adding to its power. And a VAT is regressive, hurting lower-income persons proportionately more than the wealthy. The corporate income tax is just the opposite, that is, progressive." [Strobel 83-84]

The sleight of hand involved in these "tax reform" proposals is obvious enough as to be widely recognized. Another commentator notes that "a strategy of reducing the deficit by means of regressive excise and consumption taxes like a federal sales tax, which would hit poor and working-class Americans the hardest... is favored by many members of the American political and financial establishment as an alternative to higher progressive taxation...Having relieved the top by shifting tax burdens to the lower-middle and working classes in the 1980s by means of the payroll tax, the bipartisan establishment ...may try to balance the budget on the backs of the lower three-fourths in the 1990s by means of regressive consumption taxes." [Lind 194]

A tax on energy (such as a carbon tax, or the British Thermal Unit or BTU tax floated by Vice President Gore at the beginning of the first Clinton Administration) is utter folly, since it would discourage high-technology, capital-intensive, energy-intensive investment, which is exactly the kind of modern investment we need to get out of this depression. Higher excise taxes on gasoline punish wage workers for the government's failure to provide decent infrastructure. Most of these sociopathic tax schemes simply remind us once again how degraded the economics profession has become. In a sane society, any politician daring to advocate flat tax, national sales tax, energy tax, or VAT schemes would be tarred and feathered.

THE 1956 MODEL: A FIRST APPROXIMATION

The US was much better off with a more progressive income tax. In the relatively prosperous and stable year of 1956, for example, the average family of four paid no tax at all on approximately their first $3000 of income; this income was protected by personal exemptions and by a 10% standard deduction. The first $4,000 in income above and beyond the exemptions and deductions was taxed at 20%, and the next $4,000 of income beyond that was taxed at 22%. Income over $32,000 was taxed at 50%, and income over $400,000 was taxed at the top rate of 91%. [Bach 679 ff.]

In the initial enthusiasm of the Clinton transition of 1992-93, the Progressive Policy Institute explored the shrinking ability of dependent exemptions to protect income from taxation. Their finding was that "since 1945, the real value of the dependent exemption has been allowed to erode by three-quarters." The 1948 dependent exemption amounted to $600. To restore the postwar value of these exemptions, Elaine Ciulla Kamarck and William A. Galston suggested either a tax credit of $800 per child (which they preferred), or a total of $5330 in exemptions for the average family. But these estimates had clearly already been adjusted for what the authors estimated the political traffic would bear. These authors noted that in 1958 the dependent exemption of about $800 was close to the estimated extra cost of caring for an infant during its first year. They estimated that by 1990 the cost of providing for a newborn baby would be between $6,000 and $7,500. They also estimated that the 1990 equivalent of a 1948 personal exemption would be between $6,000 and $7,500. According to our own estimate based on experience as a parent, exemptions would by 1998 have to be raised to $10,000 per child in order to restore the income-protecting power of the postwar exemptions. By comparison, the child tax credit finally delivered by Clinton in 1997 starts at $400 in 1998 and goes to $500 thereafter – one of Clinton's finest achievements, but still too little. [Marshall and Schram 166, 372]

To get an approximate current dollar value for these figures, multiply the 1956 dollars by 12. For comparison, note that today (1998) a family of four pays no federal income tax on their first $17,500 in income, and after that they pay 15%. For a rather wealthy 1997 family of four, income between about $150,000 and $270,000 is taxed at 36%, and income over about $270,000 is taxed at the top rate of just 39.6%. So the income tax has become far less progressive.

To restore a progressive tax structure today, it will be necessary to protect a substantial level of family earnings from any federal income tax whatsoever. Given our 12:1 dollar deflator, we can see that if we want to simply return to the tax fairness and equity of 1956 – not of the New Deal or even the Fair Deal, but of the middle of the very moderate Republican Eisenhower Administration! – we would need to provide a family of four with exemptions and deductions amounting to about $36,000. Above that figure, taxation at a level of about 10% could begin. At the other end of the scale, a simple return to Eisenhower-era equity would mandate a 50% tax rate on income over about $385,000. The 91% top rate would kick in for income above over $4.8 million. This would be a tax code designed to protect impoverished low-income families, provide substantial tax relief for the depleted middle class, and impose a rule of reason and fairness on top corporate and bank executives whose exorbitant compensation has become a national and world-wide scandal.

Income can be taxed in different ways depending on the sources from which it is derived. The wages of farm, factory and office workers should be taxed at the lowest rates. During the aftermath of the 1980s S&L fiasco, there were proposals that the moneyed interests who had profited from S&L excess be invited by the federal government to defray the expense of the bailout. This could easily have taken the form of a 10% tax on unearned income such as dividends from stocks and interest from corporate and junk bonds. But this idea was rejected by the Bush administration, which preferred to loot the middle class while protecting the opulence of the super-rich.

In order to promote recovery and insure against a comeback by the speculators, it will be prudent to enact as a recovery measure an unearned income surtax of 10%. But we must also provide ways of avoiding this tax, especially through the Investment Tax Credit (see below). Taxpayers who choose to invest their money in companies that pursue productive activity as defined by the Treasury's catalogue will find that this 10% surtax is more than offset the tax deductions and tax credits available to investors in the firm engaged in real physical production, which will add far more than 10% to the company's dividends. Bondholders will also enjoy this enhancement on their unearned income.

Ground-rent and rent in general represents a form of economic activity which a sane tax code will always require to pay its full fair share. If interest and dividends are taxed an extra 10%, then unearned income in the form of rent for land, apartments, office buildings and other real estate should be taxed at about 15% over above the standard rate. Landlords wishing to escape that levy should be offered a 5% to 8% tax break for maintenance, improvements and modernizations made in the real estate from which their income is derived. In this way landlords will be impelled to keep their buildings in decent condition, instead of regarding them merely as objects of looting. Unimproved land will not be eligible for any of these deductions.

The tax code should also offer a tax credit for savings that are kept for at least three years in federally insured bank accounts, certificates of deposit, Treasury bills, notes, or bonds, state bonds, or the bonds of counties, cities, and localities. However, the tax code should differentiate between stock dividend income and the interest that is paid on corporate bonds. It is time to begin restoring the role of equity ownership via stocks, while cutting the importance of bonded corporate debt down to size. Therefore interest on corporate bonds should be taxed at a rate starting 5% higher than stock dividends.

CAPITAL GAINS TAX

The top capital gains tax rate in the mid-1950s was 25%. In 1956, many wealthy persons avoided the 91% top rate because they got their money through capital gains. In other words, the relatively low capital gains tax was already a notorious tax loophole. At the same time, buying stock in 1956 was far more likely to channel capital to an industrial corporation than buying derivatives in 1997. In those days, there might have been a serious argument to be made in favor of forms of investment which still provided some jobs and some new plant and equipment. Today productive investment is a tiny percentage of financial flows, and derivatives and other speculation are the order of the day. So the relatively low capital gains tax rate of 1956 should not be imitated in the future. After the 1950s, the capital gains tax was increased. Until 1979, the capital gains tax rate was 49%. In that year Congress passed and President Carter signed into law the Steiger Act, sponsored by Rep. William Steiger (R-Wisc), which reduced the capital gains tax to 28%. This was a mighty encouragement to speculators. The Kemp-Roth tax law of 1981 reduced the capital gains tax even further, to 20%. The Tax Reform Act of 1985 restored the 28% capital gains rate. Newt Gingrich has even promised to abolish the capital gains tax. Jack Kemp wants the capital gains tax to be indexed for inflation. These proposals would move the American economy away from productive investment, and even further down the road to speculation and gambling.

Based on the historic evidence, the current capital gains tax needs to be increased. The capital gains tax should be set at 75% for the duration of the state of emergency declared by the President. Once the emergency is over, this rate can be gradually lowered to about 50%. The initial high rate is required to break the speculative habit which has caused so much destruction and suffering in this country. The cold turkey of a 75% capital gains tax is the basis of an effective detox treatment against the speculative contagion. To this must be added other measures to suppress speculation. The capital gains tax on assets held less than a year should be increased by 3%. If the assets are held less than a month, the capital gains tax should increase by 6%. If the assets held for less than a week, the capital gains surtax tax should go to 9%. This would bring us to the level of the wartime rate of taxation of excess corporate profits, under which the country did quite nicely – and here we are talking about capital gains. A higher capital gains tax will protect society from speculative manias of the type we have just been living through. The only reductions we can offer in capital gains taxation would be a 10% rebate for capital gains realized on stocks or bonds belonging to companies which are designated as productive in the Treasury catalogue.

Thus, if you buy stock in a steel mill at an initial public offering and you then sell that stock after it doubles in price, you should pay 65% in capital gains-- provided you have held the stock for more than 12 months. But if the stock of a gambling casino doubles, stockholders cashing in at the new higher price will pay the full 75% capital gains, and more if they sell their stock before a year is out.

CORPORATE INCOME TAX

The second-largest source of government income in 1956 was the corporate income tax. For most corporations, this tax was set at a 52% rate. During the years of World War II, the government had levied an excess corporate profits tax of an additional 30%, which added up to a total tax rate of 82% on all corporate profits in the "excess" category, meaning profits higher than the company's average earnings for 1936-1939 and then for 1946-1949. The excess profits tax was dropped only in 1954. As we have seen, the corporate income tax, which once provided over 28% of all federal revenue, by the 1990s was providing less than 9%. One of our tasks will be to eliminate the loopholes that have allowed corporate American to evade its responsibilities so flagrantly. Corporations must not be allowed to lower their tax by paying what amounts to a large part of their profits to top executives. In order to take the pressure off middle class families, the goal should be to secure 25% to 30% of federal revenue from corporations – especially banks, investment banks, insurance companies, and other financial corporations.

Let us start with a baseline Eisenhower-era corporate income tax of 52%. Given the fact that today's largest corporations, according to many informed estimates, pay little or no corporate income tax, the impulse of most corporate executives will be to seek ways to reduce their tax load. For gambling casinos, stock brokers (if any survive), "entertainment companies" like Walt Disney, and public relations firms, there will be little hope of avoiding the full 52%.

But for firms engaged in producing tangible physical commodities, there will be a number of opportunities to change their conduct and thus pay less tax. First, adequate deductions should be offered for depreciation, amortization and depletion for investments in productive plant and equipment for farms and industries. These deductions apply to almost any purchase of new equipment for hard-commodity production. The tax code should allow the price of capital equipment to be written off within 3-4 years in order to encourage fast technological attrition and the early replacement of obsolete equipment. Part of the depreciation can be deducted from tax owed every year.

Payroll taxes, especially those related to Social Security, brought in $10 billion in revenue in 1956. Payroll taxes are always regressive taxes, falling more heavily on the wage-earner who must work for a living, and sparing the rich coupon-clipper who lounges at home all day. Since about 1980, as we have seen, payroll taxes have been one of the fastest-growing forms of taxation. This tendency must be reversed and rolled back. To the extent that increased revenue from capital gains, unearned income, corporate income tax, transfer taxes, and tariffs permits, payroll taxes should be abolished, and Social Security should be financed from these alternative sources.

Estate and gift taxes in 1956 were markedly progressive. Federal estate tax in those days kicked in for estates exceeding $60,000 and reached a rate of 77% for the portion of estates in excess of $10 million. Today, a generous exemption is in order for family farms and small businesses. But estates consisting of real estate and financial paper should no longer escape a tax of about 40% Part of this would reflect an effort to recapture windfall profits which accrued under the misguided tax policies of Carter, Reagan, and Bush. An important tax reform will also be to close the loophole by which large family fortunes can escape the estate tax by being transferred to foundations or charitable trusts. Over the past half century, few forces have been so contrary to the public interest as groups like the Ford Foundation, the Carnegie Foundation, the Pew Charitable Trust, the Rockefeller Foundation, and MacArthur Foundation, and their myriad of clones. These foundations avoid the federal estate tax, and then constitute themselves as tax-exempt mouthpieces for the oligarchical point of view in every area of human endeavor. The general welfare is damaged twice: once because the family fortune escapes taxation, and secondly because the money is now used to spew out ideological poisons favorable to oligarchism. Foundations by the end of the 1990s possess assets in the neighborhood of $150 billion. These assets should be taxed at 10% per year for the duration of the crisis, and 5% per year thereafter. The additional $15 billion in revenue thus obtained will be important for replacing the proceeds of the onerous payroll tax on wage earners, thus helping to guarantee the future of Social Security.

INVESTMENT TAX CREDIT

The other ready and easy way for corporations to reduce their 52% tax rate is to take advantage of the investment tax credit. In order to receive this extra benefit, the company in question must be primarily dedicated to activity certified as productive on the Treasury catalogue. If a productive company is willing to transform its entire mode of production, shifting from steel wheel to maglev, it should receive 30% of those costs in the form of a tax credit, which may be spread over several years. If a steel concern modernizes its production methods with continuous casting, 30% of that investment should be subtracted from its corporate income tax. New types of machine tools should always be eligible for the investment tax credit. This tax credit can also be offered for smaller-scale technological improvements. Plant and equipment expenditures by companies engaged in scientific research in any potentially productive area should be eligible for the investment tax credit, providing a strong incentive for new companies to be founded in this area, or for established companies to become involved. The point is that scientific research is an indispensable part of the national interest.

The company which carries out the investment in new technology should receive 30% of its investment as a tax credit. Stockholders and bondholders of the company investing in new technology should also enjoy a tax break on their unearned income, as suggested above. Banks providing corporate financing to the company in question should also enjoy a tax break. Finally, even small depositors with savings accounts at banks that provide bank loans for companies installing new technology should have their interest taxed at a lower rate. Their bank statements should tell them the tax credit they are getting and why. Stockholders and bondholders of such banks should also know exactly why they will be paying a slightly lower tax on their dividends and interest payments than they had otherwise. The goal here is equity, and also to foster the greatest possible public awareness that the way to generate real wealth is through scientific research incorporated in new machine tools and other capital goods based on the technology which scientific research can provide.

The coming crisis will be the right time to close several notorious tax loopholes whose ill effects have been amply documented during the years of the speculative boom. First, corporations, including banks and investment banks, must be prohibited from deducting for tax purposes the interest and principal on bonds (usually junk bonds) used in takeovers of other companies, mergers, and acquisitions. The taxpayers must no longer subsidize leveraged buy-outs like the takeover of RJR Nabisco by Kohlberg-Kravis-Roberts or other dubious transactions based on the issuance of junk bonds. Second, companies like sports teams and others must no longer have the ability to deduct the astronomical salaries paid to sports and entertainment figures. Again, the taxpayer can no longer be asked to subsidize the astronomical multi-year contracts of these stars. Companies wishing to pay astronomical compensation to sports stars must do so with their own means, not by withholding the money from the public till.

NO MORE RACE TO THE BOTTOM

In recent years, states and localities have been pressured by corporations to offer these corporations special tax incentives in order to attract new plants and jobs, or to prevent the plants and jobs from relocating to other states or to foreign countries. This had led to a bidding war among depression-strapped localities, which have desperately sacrificed large parts of their tax revenues in order to secure some low-paid jobs for the community. We need a uniform federal law outlawing such state and local tax incentives for individual firms, since they deprive all citizens of the equal protection of the law and are thus unconstitutional. Such a law will deprive these companies of the ability cynically to play one depressed locality against another.

TAX ADVANTAGES FOR SMALL AND MEDIUM INDUSTRY

An important factor of weakness in the American economy of the last quarter of the twentieth century has been the decline of small and medium industry. As the banking system has become more and more focussed on selling proprietary derivatives, and as the stock markets have become more and more the arena of hostile, junk-bond leveraged takeovers, more and more small and medium industrial companies have been swallowed up or have ceased to exist. Small and medium industrial repair and engineering companies are essential for a successful economy because they often provide the link between the scientific laboratory, on the one hand, and the factory production line, on the other. Small and medium industry is where the scientific breakthrough takes shape in the form of a machine tool ready to improve the efficiency of mass production.

Small and medium industrialists were an excellent leaven for politics and for society as a whole, primarily because of the spirit of independence informed by technical knowledge that the small and medium entrepreneur represented. The human type of the entrepreneur steeped in science and engineering has far more innovative and productive potential than the bureaucrat-manager the of the giant, oligopolistic firm.

Criteria can be developed to determine what kind of firm qualifies as a small or medium industrial concern. This can embrace the maximum number of employees, the products, and the relative weight of research and development in the corporate budget. The end result should be that small and medium industrial companies will pay a corporate income tax of 30%, as compared with the overall corporate income tax of 52%. The companies that qualify for this advantage will continue to be eligible for the Investment Tax Credit if their degree of technological innovation qualifies them for that.

PROTECTIVE TARIFFS

As already mentioned, there will be no US recovery from depression without the abrogation of NAFTA, GATT, WTO, and the related "free trade" and runaway shop agreements of the past two decades. Free trade has failed. But the alternative to free trade is not trade war. The alternative to free trade is protectionism designed to secure orderly and prosperous domestic and international markets for all kinds of production.

The key concept that needs to be assimilated is that of the parity price. Parity price calculation starts by studying the average well-managed farm, mine or factory that produces a given commodity in the areas of grains, meats, basic metals, etc. What needs to be calculated is the average cost of production of the commodity in this average well-run firm. This average cost of production needs to reflect labor costs, plant and equipment, transportation, pensions for retired workers, and all other facets of the productive process. This is the price which the company needs to sell its product in order to stay in business on what amounts to a breakeven basis.

In addition to the figure obtained so far, we must add an additional 10% to 20%. This addition is required to provide money for the company to self-finance technological improvements, new plant and equipment, the expansion of production, and other modernization. Part of the addition should also represent the profit of the company of farm.

The basic principle of the parity price is that it will be impossible to remain well-supplied with sufficient quantities of basic commodities at reasonable prices if we insist on keeping the price of those commodities below their actual average cost of production. If we pay less than it costs to produce, then sooner or later the producers go bankrupt and the supply runs out. This is just common sense.

So the national interest requires that no imported commodities reach the US market at prices which are less than parity. This is dumping, and will destroy our domestic production unless the government takes action. Similarly, we need to support our domestic prices in such a way as to ensure that prices not fall below 100% of parity. The US agricultural sector has abundant experience with parity prices – good results when parity prices were maintained, and disastrous experiences when prices were allowed to decline to 50% or 60% of parity. Parity was a vital part of the war effort in World War II. At that time the country's armies needed larger amounts of food than ever before to be produced by fewer farm workers than previously. The answer was to set parity at 110% or even higher

Following the repudiation of NAFTA, GATT and WTO, the US government must work out parity agreements with as many foreign governments as possible. By these agreements, the US and other governments will agree to buy and sell a whole list of uniform basic commodities from farms, forests, and mines at parity prices. Since the new monetary system will already incorporate parity prices for gold as well as for the national currencies, the extension of the same principle to the list of key commodities should appear as self-evident to governments of good will.

Manufactured goods require a specific and differentiated tariff treatment. Whatever cannot be produced in the United States should be free of duty, unless Congress and the Executive branch decide that we want to initiate production . Some items should have duties of 100% of their original value, and some even more. In 1956, tariffs averaged about 40%, although this varied greatly from one item to another. For most imported consumer goods, including cars, consumer electronics, and textiles, an *ad valorem* tariff of 40% would be reasonable today. Imported capital goods need to be treated in a more differentiated manner, partly because the US ability to produce some of them has atrophied so much. Imported steel should pay at least 20% or whatever is necessary to prevent the cutthroat dumping seen during 1998. Imported capital goods might pay 5%, or nothing in other cases. Import duties are an indispensable component in the re-industrialization of America; they will afford a first measure of protection against the runaway shop and the sweatshop on a world scale. They will also provide an important source of revenue.

A 40% tariff has been endorsed by Professor Ravi Batra of Southern Methodist University in his book, *The Myth of Free Trade*. Batra starts from the sound premise that "*manufacturing, not trade, is the main source of prosperity.*" Noting that "throughout its history, at least until 1970, America was practically a closed economy," he recommends that

> as a practical matter, average tariffs should be raised from the current 5 percent rate to 40 percent in order to reduce the import share of GNP to the 1972 level of roughly 6 percent. Today, this share is about 13 percent. Tariffs ... should be phased in over five years so that foreign producers have time to adjust to the new policy.... The main sectors to be protected are automobiles, consumer electronics, heavy industrial machinery, farm equipment, household appliances, photographic equipment, primary metals, computers, semiconductors, tires, telephone and telegraph apparatus, light machine tools, robotics, and facsimile machines, among others." [Batra 1993, 37, 196-7]

This approach needs to be supplemented by the awareness that there is absolutely no need to import most consumer goods, which can readily be produced here with the help of R-loan credit. In the future, we cannot afford to waste foreign exchange on such consumer goods. But if there are capital goods which cannot be produced domestically to service the recovery, these will have to be imported. Such vital capital goods will not initially be candidates for tariffs.

OIL IMPORT TAX

Another key commodity which needs a parity price is oil. When the oil price descended into single digits during the 1980s and again in 1998, US states whose economies depend on oil were thrown into a severe economic downturn which also resulted in the 1980s regional banking crisis. Here we must be concerned with preventing the price of oil on the US domestic market from dropping below the minimum price at which oil can be produced. Oil is still quite abundant in the earth's crust, but today it is often found further underground and further underwater. It may also be harder to bring to the surface. The parity price must reflect these increased expenses.

If we assume a parity price for oil at $30 per barrel for US domestic producers, this parity price becomes the trigger price below which an oil import tax kicks in. If the world market price stays above $30, then such oil can freely enter this country. But if the world price dips below $30, an import tax is imposed which amounts to the difference between $30 and per barrel price of the foreign oil being brought into this country. This tax is imposed at the border or port of entry. The result is that the domestic price of oil cannot dip below $30. Domestic producers are thus protected, and can base their planning and investment on a stable and predictable oil price.

DERIVATIVES ILLEGAL UNDER SEVERE CRIMINAL PENALTIES

After the 1932-33 banking panic in the depths of the last depression, the Senate hearings known as the Pecora hearings focussed public rage on top executives of the largest New York money center banks for a long catalogue of sleazy practices. If the nation survives the coming depression, it is likely that hearings on the proliferation of derivatives will provide the same kind of dramatic focus. As we have stated above, many "derivative financial products" are already illegal under securities laws, gambling laws, bucket shop laws, and other existing legislation. Since many of these laws have been egregiously flaunted over recent years, we will require emergency action by the President to re-assert the illegality of derivatives. Futures trading must be illegal. In particular, anyone caught trading futures contracts based on United States Treasury bills, notes, or bonds is *ipso facto* fostering speculative excesses in those securities and should be very severely punished. There must be no more T-bond futures sold in Chicago. Financial options and commodity options must also be made illegal; options traders must be prosecuted with great vigor. Currency swaps and structured notes are *prima facie* illegal even under existing law, since they almost always include buying and selling futures outside of the officially recognized exchanges.

SECURITIES TRANSFER TAX (TOBIN TAX)

Today, most American states impose a sales tax, a highly regressive and undesirable way of gathering revenue. In many states, the sales tax reaches 5%, 6%, or even 7%. In some states, like Virginia, even basic household groceries are taxed in this way. Some cities add an additional sales tax of their own. These taxes are often approved by state legislatures which are beholden to local oligarchs who refuse to accept the proper progressive structure of their state income tax, and prefer to finance their own opulence on the backs of poor wage earners. These sales taxes are thoroughly un-American, a nuisance for all and a tragic hardship for many. An important part of revamping the tax code to restore progressivity and remove the extremely unfair regressive elements will accordingly be to encourage state legislatures and city councils to abolish these sales taxes.

But there is another area where sales taxes urgently need to be introduced – the area of financial transactions. There are between 1.5 and 2 billion stock transactions in the United States every business day, and not one penny of tax is paid on any of these transfers. The same goes for the markets in options, futures, indexes, commodities, and other financial instruments. Since the average working family has been taxed for so long on their purchases of everyday necessities, surely banks, brokerages, and hedge funds can now be called upon to contribute to the general welfare. We therefore recommend a tax on all sales of financial instruments (stocks, bonds, option, futures, securities, foreign exchange, REITs, indexes, commercial paper, and over-the counter derivatives contracts, etc.). This tax should be set at 5 mills on the dollar, or half a cent for every dollar of turnover. As a sales tax, it would be payable to the Treasury by the seller.

This tax would be similar to, but much broader than, the kind of transfer tax which has been advocated by Professor James Tobin of Yale University, and which has been called the Tobin tax. Professor Tobin's proposed levy would be payable on foreign exchange transactions only. With an estimated $1.5 trillion churning through the forex markets every business day, the narrower Tobin tax would be highly useful, and would constitute a step in the right direction.

Tobin is a professed follower of Lord Keynes, who in 1936 pointed out that a transactions tax could strengthen the weight of long-range fundamentals in determining stock market prices, as against speculators' guesses of the short-range behaviors of other speculators. Tobin formulated his plan as follows:

> An international uniform tax would be levied on spot transactions in foreign exchange (including, of course, deliveries pursuant to futures contracts and options). The proposal has two major motivations. One purpose is to increase the weight market participants give to long-range fundamentals relative to immediate speculative opportunities. The second is to allow greater autonomy to national monetary policies, by creating a larger wedge between short interest rates in different currencies. [Tobin 222]

Tobin hoped that his tax idea would "discourage short-horizon speculations and create a wedge between interest rates in different currencies within which central banks could pursue policies appropriate to their different circumstances." [Tobin 168] He also sought to "diminish speculation in foreign exchange markets and allow larger differences among currencies in short-term interest rates, permitting somewhat greater autonomy in national monetary policies." [Tobin 175] It is worth noting that Tobin saw such a tax as a means of enhancing the ability of different countries, including small ones, to pursue their own national economic policies, by affording a measure of protection against the typhoons of speculative hot money which today sweep across the globe at relativistic speeds, leaving immense destruction in their wake. Up to now, these hot money flows have had a free ride, and have been exempt from any taxation in the vast majority of countries. Even a very small tax would have the power to exert considerable braking power on such hot money flows. Tobin explained that a 5 mill on the dollar or 0.5 per cent tax on foreign exchange transactions in both directions would be the equivalent of a 4 per cent difference in annual interest rates on three-month bills. Even such a small tax would represent a considerable deterrent to speculators considering a quick arbitrage play involving another currency. At the same time, the tax would have very little impact on long-term long term portfolio or direct investment in another economy. Tobin's intent was to slow down capital movements, not commodity trade. "It is important," he wrote, "even for small countries to maintain some degree of autonomy in monetary policy, so that local interest rates are not wholly determined by foreign markets. The foreign exchange transactions tax is one way to do that." [Tobin 176] Tobin especially deplored the inability of the smaller European states to conduct their own monetary policies because of the pervasive influence of the very doctrinaire German Bundesbank. The idea of slowing down the mad pace of international capital flows is what Tobin referred to as the "sand in the wheels" aspect of his proposal.[172]

In addition to making speculation less attractive, the STT would also produce considerable revenue if it were enacted today. Pre-crash levels of turnover in financial markets have been so colossal that very significant revenues would be generated by taxes that will appear very modest in percentage terms. And if the average family is paying a sales tax of 5% or more, why can't Merrill Lynch and Schwab pay a few mills on the dollar as well? The other great advantage is that the STT would guarantee that all financial transactions be reported to the Treasury under penalty of law. For those who claim to want transparency, here it is. Right now the federal government has no means of knowing how many derivatives are held by hedge funds, and is thus unable to quantify the size of the threat derivatives pose to the economy. Hedge funds of course need to be outlawed, but making all financial transactions taxable and thus reportable will prevent new threats from reaching critical mass in the future. The legal obligation to report all sales would go far in the fight to wipe out the cancer of derivatives, especially in the form of structured notes, designer derivatives, and other monsters not traded on exchanges but lurking in the laptops of yuppy quants. Bills for Securities Transfer Taxes to be instituted by state governments have been considered in Pennsylvania, New Hampshire, Alabama, Louisiana, and other states.

RESTORE ANTI-USURY LAWS

Before the disastrous tenure of Volcker at the Federal Reserve, most American states had comprehensive laws forbidding usury. Generally, any rate of interest above 10% was considered a violation of the usury laws. Not only the states, but the federal government as well should, once the smithereens of the collapse/disintegration have been swept away, enact tough anti-usury statutes to assert this fundamental point of natural law. If 10% had seemed a reasonable ceiling in the past, perhaps the painful experiences the collapse-disintegration will prompt some to demand a lower cap – 8% or 5%, for example – on interest rates for the future. Some, especially those with religious scruples, may want both a lower rate and the anchoring of the prohibition in a Constitutional amendment.

The federal usury laws will facilitate a uniform lowering of the interest rate paid on Treasury securities of all types. As the old Treasury securities mature, the new auctions of bills, notes, and bonds will be required to respect the usury caps. All callable securities should be called as soon as possible, to take advantage of the lower rates. If the other measures outlined here are fully implemented, there will be no conflict between the interest rates at auction and the usury caps. In fact, the measures in this book were adopted, they would probably produce an interest rate structure like that of the World War II years, with a top rate of 2.5% on the 20-year long bond of that era.

EXPORT STIMULUS AND THE US EXPORT-IMPORT BANK

Concerning exports, the tax system must be amended to encourage those companies which are willing to do the extra work needed to sell US goods abroad. The post-1944 experience shows that the dollar cannot be stable unless there is a constant and growing demand in other countries for the capital goods which Americans know how to produce. The United States can no longer expect to run astronomical balance of trade deficits with impunity. The new Bretton Woods system will be

---

[172] See "A Proposal for International Monetary Reform," *Eastern Economic Journal* 4, July-October 1978, 153-159, reprinted in Tobin, *Essays in Economics*, Volume 3: Theory and Policy (Cambridge, Mass: MIT Press, 1982), chapter 20.

eminently fair, but precisely for that reason it will no longer oblige other countries to accept non-convertible US dollars *ad infinitum*. Without growing exports of manufactured goods, there can be no financial or economic stability in the long run. This requirement will be reflected in a number of ways in the new dirigistic tax system. A significant percentage, 25% for example, of the final profit from export transactions involving the shipment of tangible physical commodities must be exempted from corporate income tax – another way to lower that 52% top rate. After the Second World War, US exports were allowed to stagnate for a number of decades, resulting in a dollar glut and the instability of a system that finally succumbed to British speculative attack. It is therefore in the national interest to stimulate exports in order to assure a healthy demand for the US dollar around the world, so that dollars earned by foreign companies on goods sent to the US will be speedily repatriated as part of merchandise transactions. Otherwise dollars might build up abroad once again, in a replay of the parasitic and unregulated Eurodollar market of the post-1958 era. All this is of course illegal under the globaloney philosophy of NAFTA, GATT, and WTO – but they will have been abolished.

The United States Export-Import Bank was established by Franklin D. Roosevelt in 1934 to provide financing for export and import transactions between the United States and other nations in those instances in which it was not possible to finance such trade through private banking channels at reasonable cost. In the post-crash world, with most private banks flattened by the derivatives blowout, almost any international commodity transactions will be virtually impossible to finance through normal banks. That will give a revived Ex-Im Bank an immense new field of activity. We should turn to the Ex-Im Bank at once to re-start US exports and thus help stabilize the dollar, without waiting for what other nations might or might not do. The original Ex-Im Bank mandate was to borrow funds from the Treasury to finance trade, which means that Ex-Im should now receive a very large infusion, perhaps $100 billion right off the bat, in the form of no-interest R-loans. Exports financed with these resources will represent the life blood of the US recovery. Loans to producers in other countries who have something to sell us which we vitally need can also help to stimulate economic recovery abroad. The World Bank, despite its generally destructive record of appropriate technology and technological apartheid, also managed to finance a small number of useful projects around the world, although these almost always were distorted by the prevailing monetarist ideology. After the liquidation of the World Bank, the Ex-Im Bank should stand ready to finance development projects around the world, giving preference to American exports of capital goods and other materials destined for those projects. From its beginnings, the Ex-Im Bank also provided guarantees for the repayment of private loans used in trade. To the extent that private capital survives the cataclysm, it should be encouraged to enter this vital area of new economic growth.

Under international monetary arrangements which no longer encourage the United States to import foreign goods without having to pay for them, it will become important to cut down on needless imports in order to avoid wasting foreign exchange. This is a kind of discipline which all other countries have had to face in one way or another, but which has been forgotten here. Among other things, it will be advisable to develop domestic energy sources, including oil, during the period in which the economy is in transition to nuclear power generation. When the free ride of dollar inconvertibility reaches its inevitable end, domestic oil will be in demand. Blanket bans on developing oil resources for reasons of extremist environmentalist ideology will have to yield to the imperatives of national survival. This will include a rational policy for the development of oil deposits such as those in northeast Alaska and elsewhere.

ANTI-CARTEL LEGISLATION

Over the past 40 years, extensive damage has been done to the American economy by a series of international cartels and oligopolies, including some which are headquartered abroad, either in London, Switzerland or in some off-shore banking center. The Organization of Petroleum Exporting Countries (OPEC) is the cartel the US public may know best, but it hardly qualifies as a serious cartel. OPEC has rather almost always served as a cat's paw of the real oil cartel, once known as the seven sisters, today composed of Royal Dutch Shell, British Petroleum, Exxon, Mobil, Texaco, and Compagnie Française des Petroles. This oil cartel is the force responsible for the two great oil shocks of the 1970s. The oil cartel attempted to regroup with meetings in September 1998. There is also an international grain cartel, which has generally been more powerful in practice than the US Department of Agriculture; indeed, the grain cartel has generally been in control of the USDA. Members of the grain cartel include Dreyfuss, Cargill, Continental Grain, Archer-Daniels Midland, Bunge, Ralston-Purina, and a few British firms. ADM was recently found guilty of illegal price-fixing in a case which involved Dwayne Andreas' son. There is also a food cartel in the generic sense, centered on companies like Nestlé, Cadbury-Frye, Rowntree, Grand Met-Guinness, and Tate and Lyle. Production of sugar, coffee, cocoa, and related products is organized by this cartel. British interests have been attempting to foster a gold cartel centered on Barrick Gold and a few other companies. One of the most famous of all cartels is the diamond cartel, controlled by DeBeers Consolidated Mines of South Africa. Here in the United States, we have a very harmful oligopoly in the mass media, which are dominated by giants like Disney-ABC, Westinghouse-CBS, General Electric-NBC, Rupert Murdoch's Newscorp-Fox, CNN/Time Warner, and a few others. Anti-trust legislation and enforcement must be made powerful enough to break the power of these cartels on the US and world markets. US regulators must aggressively seek confrontations with each of these cartels on terms favorable to the national interest so as to dismantle the machinery of the cartel's market domination.

FOOD FOR PEACE: A FARM BILL

The battered US farm sector provides an excellent case study of how dirigistic measures can be used to revive a production sector which was once highly successful, but which has been profoundly damaged by cartel practices operating under the ideological cover of "free trade." The American family farm has proven itself repeatedly as the most effective approach to agricultural production. For the past several decades, US government policies have favored the rapacity of the international cartels at the expense of the family farm. In 1998, the farm sector was leading the rest of the US economy towards qualitatively new levels of economic depression. These failed policies must be rolled back. Just like every other businessman, the farmer will benefit from the Presidential Chapter XI protection accorded the entire US economy when the anti-depression program is instituted. Farm, farmhouse, barn, tractors, combines, livestock land, and all other farm assets will be invulnerable to seizure and foreclosure for the duration of the economic emergency. The farmer will also receive a debt moratorium under which all interest and principle payments will be frozen and suspended for the duration of the crisis. The farmer will be eligible for R-loan credit for the working capital needed for the spring planting and for the harvest, as well as for fertilizer, machinery and capital improvements to expand farm production. Every farmer will be guaranteed a minimum of 100% parity on his farm products, with the US government prepared to intervene with unlimited purchases at the support price. The US Government will need large quantities of farm produce for domestic reserves and above all for an aggressive foreign policy of famine relief to protect world public health standards, ward off the emergence of new plagues and exotic diseases, and to ensure political and military stability in famine areas. Because of the need for abundant food resources, all programs of set asides or other artificial limits on production will be summarily terminated, with compensation to farmers who have been injured. In particular, Newt Gingrich's misguided and dangerous "Freedom to Farm" law must be overriden by emergency executive order, and swiftly repealed. Environmental laws based on junk science and ideological hysteria whose provisions are inimical to expanded farm and forestry production will be rendered inoperative by Presidential emergency actions and later formally repealed by the Congress.

RE-REGULATION

The dismantling of government regulations time-tested over many decades and pertaining to a whole array of economic activities has proven a disastrous failure. This applies to truck transportation, natural gas, banks, airlines, securities markets, telecommunication, electric power utilities, and other fields. We must swiftly re-regulate these areas of economic activity, using Eisenhower-Kennedy era standards as a benchmark unless a different approach is clearly indicated by present-day conditions.

PEACE DIVIDEND FOR EDUCATION

In 1944, the GI Bill of Rights guaranteed returning servicemen one full year of unemployment compensation at $20 per week, plus a $2000 loan for buying a home or starting a small business, plus college education or vocational job training for up to four years, with generous payments for tuition, books, and living expenses. Senator Ralph Yarborough, the Texas populist, fought to get similar benefits for Korean and later Cold War veterans. The GI Bill was one of the most powerful laws ever passed for building up the American middle class. It established that home ownership and a college education would henceforth be hallmarks of belonging to or joining the middle class, the bedrock of social stability and representative government. When the East German communist regime, the Warsaw Pact, the Comecon and the Soviet Union itself collapsed between 1989 and 1991, the American people had every reason to expect a Peace Dividend in the form of new federal programs to give the threatened middle class Roosevelt had created a new lease on life. Instead, the oligarch George Bush, notorious for his lack of historical vision, offered nothing except new taxes on the middle class to finance the S&L bailout made necessary by the financial excesses of his own social circles and power base during the 1980s. There was no Peace Dividend, and no new GI Bill. Clinton's plan for a middle class tax cut was dropped.

It is time for government to deliver a belated Peace Dividend to the American people in recognition of their achievements and sacrifices in saving civilization from Hitler, Stalin, Mao, and their heirs. During this process, the American people paid defense bills ranging between $5 trillion and $10 trillion, depending on how these expenditures are calculated. The Peace Dividend must at the same time represent a measure designed to prepare the country for the economic life of the twenty-first century. The Peace Dividend should assume the form of a comprehensive commitment to high-quality free, universal, public education for all persons, from preschool through a full four-year college diploma. This translates into 16+ years of high quality education for every young American. This commitment must take into account not just classroom education per se, but all phases of human development from conception on.

PRENATAL CARE AND FAMILY ALLOWANCES

For the welfare of expectant mothers, we must provide comprehensive pre-natal benefits within the framework of the national health insurance plan discussed above. This will include an adequate number of visits to the doctor during pregnancy, and free maternity services as needed, with federal guarantees of an adequate number of days in the hospital after delivery to safeguard the life and health of both mother and child. A mandatory paid maternity leave of 6 months, long established in many European countries, must be offered to American mothers as a matter of right. To encourage the stability of young families, the US federal government must follow the lead of a number of progressive European countries which provide family allowances, direct cash payments to expectant parents which continue through age 18. Such payments might start between $5,000 and $7,000 per year, depending on income and whether or not the mother and father are unemployed, and ought to be indexed for inflation. Such payments must be tax-exempt.

WIC

One of the most successful federal programs of recent years is WIC (Women-Infants-Children), which provides a subsidy for high-protein and other nutritionally valuable foods as components of the diet of expectant mothers and children. Childhood nutrition is unquestionably one of the most important factors in developing early cognitive ability. WIC coupons must therefore be available to all mothers who request them.

HEAD START

Many experts have pointed to the great benefits which can be derived from investing resources in improving the preschool years from zero to three. The centerpiece of this should be funding Head Start to an extent never before contemplated by making this highly successful program available to every parent who requests it for their child, without exception. Head Start provides a nutritious breakfast, since it is clear that hungry children cannot learn and develop. It also provides various forms of pre-school education. Head Start should be organized as an extended day program, in effect providing free federal day care from early morning into well into the evening for all working parents who ask for it.

FREE SCHOOL BREAKFASTS AND LUNCHES FOR ALL

The problems of kindergarten through grade 12 will be addressed by the classroom construction program addressed above. One important area of federal activity ought to be the provision of a free school breakfast and a free school lunch to every child who requests it, without regard to means. The federal government can also help finance the construction and stocking of school libraries, the provision of computers, scientific and laboratory equipment, and the renovation of existing school buildings.

A FREE FEDERAL COLLEGE EDUCATION

To be a productive worker in the twenty-first century, it is evident that a college degree or advanced vocational training will be the irreducible minimum qualification for the kinds of highly skilled, high-wage jobs we want to create and which will restore the prosperity of America. A college education means membership in the middle class, which is the overall social goal towards which America must tend. Every student who has demonstrated qualification by attaining and maintaining a C average or above must be provided with federal vouchers and/or cash payments covering the entire cost of tuition, room, board, books, and an allowance for living expenses at a four-year public college or state university. Such vouchers could be used at private institutions of higher learning, although they might need to be supplemented by additional payments or scholarships. For those who cannot make a C average, free remedial programs must be available to help them to qualify. For young people from disadvantaged circumstances, these remedial programs should be offered free of charge in the context of a new Civilian Conservation Corps. The education program should also be automatically applicable to any combination of up to four years of community college training, advanced vocational training, and other courses. Special provision must be made for attracting students into physics, chemistry, biology, and other basic science. It should no longer be necessary for college students to stagger across the stage to receive their diplomas because they are groaning under tens of thousands of dollars of high-interest debt.

Back in the 1930s, the College of the City of New York (CCNY) was famous far and wide because the excellent education it offered was absolutely free to qualified applicants who were given admission. In the early 1960s, the entire City University of New York, including CCNY, Brooklyn College, Queens College and related institutions, was still absolutely free of charge. Many distinguished careers were made possible by this free education. This is the model towards which our nation must now tend.

The American System of economics has always seen the overall level of education as the most accurate barometer of national wealth. This idea was stated by Alexander Hamilton, and repeated by Friedrich List and Henry Carey. This same point was made more recently by the late Edward Denison, who was a senior fellow with the Brookings Institution in Washington, in his landmark study, *Trends in American Economic Growth*, published by Brookings in 1985. Denison's central finding was that 63% of the substantial gains in productivity achieved by the United States were attributable to increased knowledge and expertise. [Peterson 233-4] The policy of guaranteeing a college education to every qualified young person (and indeed to any qualified person of any age who wants it) is the key to reversing the productivity slide discussed in Chapter V, and to securing the economic future of the United States in the new century.

A NEW NATIONAL DEFENSE EDUCATION ACT FOR GRADUATE STUDY

For postgraduate study, we need to reactive the National Defense Education Act of 1958, which was passed because of the untiring efforts of Sen. Ralph Yarborough of Texas. The NDEA offered three-year fellowships, including tuition and a stipend, in various academic disciplines. A new NDEA should be geared especially to revive the number of American Ph. D.s in physics and the other hard sciences, while providing strong support for history, languages, and other components of a classical education. The NDEA grants should also be available to medical students. There is no need for further federal subsidies for lawyers.

FOR AN ECONOMIC BILL OF RIGHTS

To crown the edifice of economic reconstruction, we should refurbish Franklin D. Roosevelt's proposal for an Economic Bill of Rights for all Americans, irrespective of race, creed, color, class, and national origin. We should formulate the economic rights which our achieved level of civilization permits us to discern and codify, leaving the list open, as Roosevelt did, for the addition of others at such time as the God-given light of Reason and Progress allow us to recognize them. We want to create a series of new entitlements. And we want to anchor them in the Constitution, in the form of a second or economic Bill of Rights to complement and buttress the original political Bill of Rights. In doing this, we will be spelling out our expanded and improved understanding of the concept of the General Welfare enshrined in the preamble. For Roosevelt, the Economic Bill of Rights was the essential domestic platform for the conduct of the Second World War, as well as the blueprint for a better America in the future. The measures outlined would have gone a long way toward permanently eradicating oligarchy from American society, and might well have generated a century-long economic expansion. The voice you will now hear is that of the most powerful man in the world at that time speaking on *your* behalf, and it will remind you why the oligarchs hate the office of the presidency as defined in the Constitution. Here are Roosevelt's remarks, signed by him at the White House on January 11, 1944:

It is our duty now to begin to lay plans and determine the strategy for the winning of a lasting peace and the establishment of an American standard of living higher than ever before known. We cannot be content, no matter how high the general standard of living may be, if some fraction of our people, whether it be one-third or one-fifth or one-tenth – is ill-fed, ill-clothed, ill-housed and insecure.

This Republic had its beginning, and grew to its present strength, under the protection of certain inalienable political rights – among them the right of free speech, free press, free worship, trial by jury, freedom from unreasonable searches and seizures. They were our rights to life and liberty.

As our nation has grown in size and stature, however – as our industrial economy expanded – these political rights proved inadequate to assure us equality in the pursuit of happiness.

We have come to a clear realization of the fact that true individual freedom cannot exist without economic security and independence. "Necessitous men are not free men." People who are hungry and out of a job are the stuff of which dictatorships are made.

In our day these economic truths have become accepted as self-evident. We have accepted, so to speak, a second Bill of Rights under which a new basis of security and prosperity can be established for all, regardless of station, race, or creed.

Among these are:

The right to a useful and remunerative job in the industries or shops or farms or mines of the nation;

The right to earn enough to provide adequate food and clothing and recreation;

The right of every farmer to raise and sell his products at a return which will give him and his family a decent living;

The right of every business man, large and small, to trade in an atmosphere of freedom from unfair competition and domination by monopolies at home and abroad;

The right of every family to a decent home;

The right to adequate medical care and the opportunity to achieve and enjoy good health;

The right to adequate protection from the economic fears of old age, sickness, accident, and unemployment;

The right to a good education.

All of these rights spell security. And after this war is won we must be prepared to move forward, in the implementation of these rights, to new goals of human happiness and well-being.

America's own rightful place in the world depends in large part upon how fully these and similar rights have been carried into practice for our citizens. For unless there is security here at home there cannot be lasting peace in the world.

One of the great American industrialists of our day – a man who has rendered yeoman service to his country in this crisis – recently emphasized the grave dangers of "rightist reaction" in this nation. All clear-thinking business men share his concern. Indeed, if such reaction should develop – if history were to repeat itself and we were to return to the so-called "normalcy" of the 1920s – then it is certain that even though we shall have conquered our enemies on the battlefields abroad, we shall have yielded to the spirit of fascism here at home.

I ask the Congress to explore the means for implementing this economic Bill of Rights, for it is definitely the responsibility of Congress to do so. Many of these problems are already before committees of the Congress in the form of proposed legislation. I shall from time to time communicate with the Congress with respect to these and further proposals. In the event that no adequate program of progress is evolved, I am certain that the nation will be conscious of the fact.

Our fighting men abroad, and their families at home, expect such a program and have the right to insist upon it. It is to their demands that this Government should pay heed, rather than to the whining demands of selfish pressure groups, who seek to feather their nests while young Americans are dying.

The foreign policy we have been following – a policy that guided us to Moscow, Cairo, and Teheran – is based on the common sense principle which was best expressed by Benjamin Franklin on July 4, 1776: "We must all hang together, or assuredly we will all hang separately."

I have often said that there are no two fronts for America in this war. There is only one front. There is one line of duty, which extends from the hearts of the people at home to the men of our attacking forces in our farthest outposts. When we speak of our total effort we speak of the factory and the field and the mine as well as the battlefield – we speak of the soldier and the civilian, the citizen and his government.

Each and every one of us has a solemn obligation under God to serve this nation in its most critical hour, to keep this nation great, to make this nation greater in a better world.

Today, after three decades of rightist reaction and free market "normalcy," these tasks remain the great unfinished business of the United States and of humanity.

APPENDIX:
SHADOWS OF THINGS THAT MIGHT BE

It is 2 o'clock on a hypothetical Monday afternoon, and the Dow Jones industrial average has plummeted 664 points, on top of an 847-point slide the previous week. The chairman of the New York Stock Exchange has called the White House chief of staff and asked permission to close the world's most important stock market. By law, only the president can authorize a shutdown of US financial markets. In the Oval Office, the president confers with the members of his Working Group on Financial Markets – the secretary of the treasury and the chairmen of the Federal Reserve Board, the Securities and Exchange Commission and the Commodity Futures Trading Commission. The officials conclude that a presidential order to close the NYSE would only add to the market's panic, so they decide to ride out the storm. The Working Group struggles to keep financial markets open so that trading can continue. By the closing bell, a modest rally is underway.

According to the Washington Post, *this tame little story is one of the "nightmare scenarios" that have been reviewed by top financial policymakers in Washington during the ten years that have passed since the October, 1987 stock market crash. It is an anodyne scenario, a bedtime story in which we see that if the government has the sense to do nothing, the magic of the marketplace (as Uncle Ron used to say) will guarantee a happy ending. [*Washington Post, *February 23, 1997]*

But there are other scenarios which might be imagined. Here are just two of them.

1. EUROPE 2001

In January 1999, the countries of the European Union faced their deadline for the launching of the Euro, the joint European currency unit. The European Union countries had agreed to the euro several years before as part of their supernational -oligarchical Maastricht Treaty. The world would soon say good-bye to francs, marks, lire, and gulden, and being paying for the groceries with euros. Atop the new edifice of monetary Europe was the European Central Bank, the unelected and unaccountable currency dictators of the old continent. From Gibraltar to the Bug, from Sicily to North Cape, monetarism reigned over 400 million thralls.

THE MILL ON THE MEUSE

Maastricht was a Dutch town located on a river which Americans, if they have heard of it at all, probably know as the Meuse. The river Meuse seemed destined to bracket the tragic fall of European civilization during the twentieth century. The year-long battle of Verdun in 1916, by bleeding white both France and Germany, marked the end of five centuries of the world supremacy of European civilization; after Verdun, the United States assumed primacy. Now, at the end of a century of wars, depressions, dictators, and disasters, it was in Maastricht, a couple of hundred kilometers north of Verdun on the same river Meuse, that the European states had signed their collective suicide pact. This time the issue was not world supremacy; that was long gone. This time around the question was whether civilization of any kind could endure in Europe very far into the twenty-first century.

Joining the Euro zone was dependent on fulfillment of what were called the Maastricht convergence criteria. These criteria were monetarist in inspiration. Everything had to be based on extreme free-market, laissez-faire, free-trade, liberalism, a tradition foreign to the mixed economies of postwar Europe, but very much in tune with what Margaret Thatcher had done to Britain after 1979. The Pope in Rome attacked this as "wild capitalism," and had condemned the Maastricht dismantling of the social welfare safety net. To join the Euro, for example, a country had to reduce its budget deficit to no more than 3% of its gross domestic product. There was a draconian upper limit on inflation. These were hard to attain, since Europe had been in full-fledged economic depression since about 1982-1983. By 1999, real unemployment in Germany (as distinct from the doctored official figures) was somewhere between 8 and 8.5 million persons. By contrast, the country had had 6.5 million unemployed in 1933, at the time that Hitler seized power. In Italy in the same year, there were only 2.7 million officially unemployed, but there were untold millions languishing in the illegal submerged economy. For British farmers, things were about where they had been in 1931.

The Maastricht convergence criteria had been written by central bankers and monetarist ideologues, not by trade unionists or small businessmen – nor by businessmen of any kind. If the central bankers had been open and honest – which they never are – the preamble to Maastricht would have read something like this: "We the central bankers and usurers of Europe, worshipping at the altar of speculation, asset-stripping, hostile takeovers, globaloney, outsourcing, and the runaway shop, in order to pump up the derivatives bubble, bust unions, gouge wages, reduce the living standard, demolish the social safety net, fight the demon inflation, increase unemployment, glorify debt, mortify equity and initiative, gut the power of national governments, strangle economic growth, make economic depression permanent and irreversible for ourselves and our posterity, and institutionalize the power of our own degenerate finance oligarchy from now until the end of time, do hereby ordain and establish the following Diktat for the subject populations of Europe. And by the way – let 'em eat cake."

This would have been no hollow rhetoric. Maastricht Europe would be under the virtual monetary dictatorship of a super-national central bank that would be beyond the authority of any of the elected European governments. Once the edifice was in place, only a revolutionary civil war could topple the money-changers from their exalted thrones. Once that central bank was in place, the arm of criticism would become impotent, and only the critique of arms would avail.

Maastricht was therefore very controversial. The European labor movement had been moribund in the early 1990s, but Maastricht worked the miracle of reviving it. As the various countries strove to reduce their deficits in order to clear the Maastricht hurdle, they began to chip away at the underpinnings of European social welfare capitalism. They began to chisel national health insurance programs, by requiring extra fees, and by degrading the quality of care. They began to tamper with cost of living escalator clauses for pensioners and retirees. They began to hack at social conquests that Americans have never even heard of – maternity benefits, family allowances, and job guarantees. They began to constrict wage increases for government and public sector employees. And at a time when unemployment insurance was the last line of defense for many families who would otherwise have ended up homeless on the sidewalk, the governments began to cut, or shorten, or block access to jobless payments.

During 1995 and 1996 virtually every country in Europe experienced large-scale labor actions aimed at beating back the Maastricht-inspired austerity and deflation. Sometimes these mass protests overstepped the bounds of usual business unionism and ventured into the hyperspace of the political mass strike – in short, of revolution. Late in 1995, when Prime Minister Juppé took out his pen and started to slash away at the social safety net, France was gripped for several weeks by a mass strike of this type. The Italian labor movement also began to go on the offensive, but the Dini-Ciampi Bank of Italy clique brought the camouflaged Italian Communist Party into the government for the first time to help with strikebreaking, with a pro-British academic technocrat, Romano Prodi, as figurehead. After a couple of years, the Italian neo-communist took power directly, in the person of Prime Minister Massimo Dilemma. It was the old scenario always advocated by the British agent Ugo LaMalfa: use the communists to impose austerity for the bankers, and then thrown them on the scrap heap once they had become discredited.

In Belgium, the same government and political class that was wielding the Maastricht scalpel turned out to be a nest of pedophiles and child-murderers that used NATO headquarters as one of their hide-outs. Here the protest demonstrations were colossal. There were protests in Spain, Greece, Denmark, and virtually everywhere else.

In Germany, the first big explosion came during the spring of 2000. A group of British and American financial freebooters had been brought in to take over the running of the country's biggest bank, the Teutonische Bank. In past decades, the Teutonische Bank, which was also the biggest in continental Europe, had cultivated a tradition of investing in German industry to make profits by expanding production. Teutonische Bank took over Financiers Trust, in reality completing the takeover of Teutonische bank by the mentality of the J. P Forgan faction. Now the Anglo-Saxon freebooters decided that Germany needed to experience the wonders of the junk-bond-leveraged, asset-stripping hostile takeover. Teutonische Bank decided to engage Michael Millken to direct an attempt by Krupp to take over Thyssen, a larger rival in steel manufacturing and metal-working. It was clear from the start that many thousands of jobs would be lost in the German industrial heartland of the Ruhr if the Krupp takeover attempt were to succeed.

With their backs to the wall, the German workers and even their unions went into action, marching through Cologne and Essen and Duesseldorf, marching on the Teutonische Bank headquarters in Frankfurt, marching on the capital in Bonn. Teutonische Bank backed down for the moment.

The summer of 2000 brought better weather, and a spurt in construction and farming jobs drained off some of the tensions on the labor market. But then came the terrible winter of 2000-2001.

Germany was still, at least in per capita terms, the largest exporter in the world. So it was much more sensitive than a country like the US to the violent contraction in world demand that started when the leaves began to fall in the autumn of 2000. Part of the problem was the collapse of Brazil, where the currency and the stock market began to melt away in October. The US responded along the lines of what it had done during the Mexican crisis of 1994-1995, this time dragooning the IMF, the BIS, and a few others to put up $100 billion to save Brazil. The quick fix worked – almost, and Brazil limped towards Christmas 2000 hemorrhaging flight capital and hot money. The government's austerity program was the most brutal that had ever been seen in Latin America. Sensing their own vulnerability, Mexico and every other "emerging market" in the developing sector launched its own austerity program pre-emptively, hoping to preserve confidence before a local panic could even begin. The result was that from Indonesia to Malaysia to Argentina, factories closed, demand contracted, and exports were cut in half.

Back in Germany, the number of those out of work began to climb from the estimated 8 million of February 2000 to nine million plus by St. Nicholas's day in early December. January 2001 brought 1.5 million layoffs. February brought the carnival, but also another 1.25 million pink slips. Then came March 2001, with an unheard of 2 million firings. This cruelest winter of German discontent had inflicted almost five million new unemployed on the staggering German economy, bringing the grand total to almost 13 million. It was almost as bad as the final days of Hitler. Then people had blamed the Allied armies and the bombs. Now they began to blame Chancellor Schröder, the Brussels eurocrats, and the deflation freaks at the Bundesbank.

By late winter, Chancellor Schröder and Finance Minister LaFontaine were thoroughly alarmed as they watched the statistics roll in. In a pathetic attempt to lie their way out of the worst crisis in half a century, they ordered the Federal Labor Office to report only a fifth of the lost jobs in the official statistics. But they fooled very few.

Schröder and LaFontaine, both thoroughly out of touch with social reality, paid most of their attention to the growing gap between falling tax contributions on the one hand, and skyrocketing unemployment insurance benefits paid out, on the other. The German deficit was growing exponentially. The Maastricht ratio of deficit to DGP, which had once seemed within their grasp, was now a million miles away.

Schroeder now repeated the fateful mistake of Chancellor Heinrich Brüning in 1930. At the height of the crisis, he decided to cut the average unemployment check by about one half. The pro-labor social Catholic wing of the opposition CDU tried a no-confidence vote, but it failed because there was no agreement on a successor to Schröder, as required by the German constitution. But Schröder, although he retained the chaotic Green Party on his side, lost the support of the neo-communist PDS, and the Schröder government no longer had a majority in parliament.

Schröder now committed his second fateful error, again in imitation of Bruening. On March 1, 2001 Schröder declared a state of emergency, citing the Notstandgesetze or emergency laws of the late 1960s. Giving the reason that the European Central Bank and its chief Düsentrieb were demanding that all governments observe the universally hated Maastricht criteria no matter how bad the depression might get, Schröder used emergency decrees to slash away half of the unemployment compensation that was the lifeline for 13 million unemployed and their families. What the east-Elbian Prussian Junker nobleman Bismarck had found just and affordable more than a century before, the Third Way Social Democrat Schröder was tearing down as extravagant and excessive. Such was the magic of globaloney.

With this, Schröder had jettisoned the social contract that underlay Germany's postwar institutions. He was now in effect a bankers' bonapartist, setting the government and the moneyed power above the society and in deadly opposition to the survival needs of most of the population. The riposte of the notoriously passive German workers took Schröder breath away: by the end of the day on March 1 he was facing a general strike of classical German thoroughness that succeeded in shutting down the country down to the most minute detail. Barricades went up in the pedestrian shopping zones at the heart of every major city. Trains and buses were halted; airplanes did not take off. Even electrical plants shut down. All stores were closed. Demonstrators massed in Bonn before the government offices, and before the banks in Frankfurt. The Hamburg dockyards closed down. In parts of what had been the Soviet East German puppet state, there were calls for the re-institution of communism, since under communism there had been no unemployment and no mass starvation. Local committees of public safety began to emerge with programs like the repudiation of Maastricht, exit from the European Union, debt cancellation for the jubilee, no foreclosures on homes, farms, and businesses, an increase in jobless pay, a halt to firings, and guaranteed food, apartments and jobs for everyone.

Even before Schröder was able to think of calling out the police and the army, they had melted away. The police trade union became one of the most aggressive components of the mass strike. The military, the Bundeswehr, seeing no enemy but the Schröder government, simply dissolved and went home, often walking long distances to reach their families. Public employees almost without exception shut down their offices and joined the general strike.

There were still significant numbers of US, British, and French troops stationed in Germany, and by March 3 Schröder began to think of pinning Maastricht back together with foreign bayonets. Washington declined, but Paris and London were ready to talk about the plan. An emergency summit of the European Union was called at 3 hours' notice. Since it was the Italians' turn to play host, they got to pick the site; it was an out-of-the-way village of called Canossa.

Here Schröder was joined by Lionel Jospin of France, Tony Flair of Great Britain, and the neo-communist Massimo Dilemma of Italy, plus the leaders of the smaller countries of Scandinavia and Iberia.

Despite the fact that they were nominally pro-labor politicians, the Labourite Flair and the neo-communist Dilemma turned out to be fanatical strikebreakers – and trigger happy, too. Each promised to use his own army to put down strikes if the German unrest were to spill over the border into their countries. Flair said he was also willing to use the British army on the Rhein to break strikes in the Ruhr region. Flair also put pressure on Jospin to use the French forces stationed in Germany around Baden-Baden to do the same.

Jospin was hesitant. He was a socialist, but his loyalty to Maastricht had then turned him into an austerity fanatic. In late 1995 and early 1996, Jospin had seen Juppé, his predecessor as prime minister, almost toppled by a mass strike against Maastricht austerity. Jospin knew how dangerous it could be to appear as anti-labor. But Jospin, fatefully inspired by the spirit of the 1956 Anglo-French Suez suicide pact, decided to join Dilemma in following Flair. France, thought Jospin, could never survive without the British. Flair and Jospin issued orders to their contingents in Germany to put down rioting, break strikes, and restore order. For Jospin in particular, the gesture was homicidal and impotent at the same time. On March 4, the specter of class warfare stalked Europe.

For France, the debacle was almost instantaneous. As soon as the French labor unions heard of Jospin's declaration of war against the German strikers, they called their own unlimited general strike in protest. Within hours, France was shut down more thoroughly than it had ever been in 1968. When they received their orders to attack the German strikers, the French forces in Baden mutinied and refused to attack anybody. Some of them departed in armored vehicles the direction of Paris, saying that they wanted to clean up the mess in the Elysée Palace. Everywhere the French army melted away, apart from a few elite divisions of paratroopers. It was worse than the great mutinies of the French army of 1917.

General strikes were called by the unions and professional associations in Belgium, the Netherlands, Italy, Spain, Portugal Greece, Denmark, Sweden, Norway, and Finland. Polish workers, desiring to show that they were in step with Europe, also walked off the job, as did those in Hungary, the Czech Republic, and Slovakia. Trains, planes, and trucks were halted all over Europe, and there was no force visible that had any motivation to break the strikes.

For the moment, globalism and globaloney seemed dead. Terrified governments offered the labor leaders sweeping concessions to end the strike. The offers included wage increases, job guarantees, better pensions, more medical benefits, an end to outsourcing, protective tariffs against low-wage foreign competition, and more. In the twinkling of an eye, the entire grim apparatus of dog-eat-dog free trade was in danger of being dismantled.

The Canossa group of Flair, Jospin, Dilemma, Schöder, and their smaller colleagues was stunned and panicked by the response. The would-be strikebreakers now decided to save themselves by offering the most sweeping concessions: to repudiate Maastricht and the single currency, with the promise that the convergence criteria were a dead letter, and would be replaced by a bill of economic rights. Now the labor leaders were interested, and the mood of the strikers became less ominous.

But at this point, on March 8, the finance oligarchy of Europe lost all confidence in the impotent politicians. The politicians were giving away Maastricht, the single currency, the "independent" central bank above all politics, their "competitiveness" – everything. The finance oligarchs panicked, and were followed by the money managers, the institutional investors, the bankers, the concern bosses, insurance companies, and the rest of the moneyed power.

The European banking panic broke out with the bank whose survival had depended most on politics – the government-owned Credit Charolais, the largest in France, and not so long ago the largest in Europe. In the fall of 1996, a French newsmagazine had referred to the Credit Charolais failure as "the biggest banking crash in history, without precedent in the entire world." Credit Charolais had gone bankrupt in 1993 (when the Paris real estate bubble had burst), in 1994, and again in 1996. It was kept going by an unlimited government pledge to cover its losses, which translated into looting every French taxpayer of $1000. It was like making every French taxpayer work for a month at the minimum wage, and give the proceeds to bail out Credit Charolais.

Now the political climate had changed, and such largesse for the bankrupt institution was extremely doubtful. The world now witnessed an electronic panic run on one of the largest banks in the world. Everybody in the world wanted to get their funds out of Credit Charolais. The bank tellers in the local branches were all on strike, but the executives and traders continued to operate, keeping in touch with the main money markets and exchanges of the world. They would have been smarter to have stayed home. Bigger depositors used electronic transfer orders and electronic bank drafts, and smaller depositors whipped out their Automatic Teller Machine cards. A giant sucking sound was heard as the cash departed from Credit Charolais at over a billion dollars an hour, and the money exodus was accelerating exponentially.

But this was only the beginning. If the French government could not save the Credit Charolais, the country's biggest, and "too big to fail" by any usurer's standard, could the Paris government be relied on to save any bank? The answer was uncertain, meaning that all funds had to be withdrawn at once. The Paris banks were whipped by the hurricane of electronic banking panic.

And where did the money go? The French petite bourgeoisie reverted to its age-old habits: they bought gold coins as long as the supply lasted, and kept the rest as bank notes in a sock under the mattress. But soon there were no bank notes left. Banking panic had led, as it always must, to a full-fledged currency crisis.

Twenty-four hours after the panic run began, Credit Charolais and most of the other large French banks had been cleaned out of reserves and especially currency. The government did virtually nothing. But that was also because most public employees were out of their offices, striking against Maastricht. It was 6 PM in the evening of Monday, March 9, 2001. The French banking system had been bankrupted and liquidated, swept away in one business day. Many French bank executives were seen that evening heading for the airports to take their private jets to Switzerland or destinations outside Europe to avoid imminent indictments.

Nowhere were these events more closely observed on that same day than in Italy, where the Banco di Milano, the Banca Privata Anonima, and the Banca Nazionale del Turismo – to name only the biggest – had been limping along for some time as de facto wards of the government. Here the fate of the French banks raised the obvious pertinent questions. Given that Italy was also paralyzed by an anti-Maastricht general strike which Dilemma had been unable to prevent, big depositors began to pull their money out, hoping to buy gold, platinum, or diamonds. At the European closing, gold had jumped from the pre-crisis norm of $300 per ounce to almost $1000. By dusk on March 9, most of the Italian banks had succumbed as well. The last gurgle of the Italian banks came when the Banca Finanziaria closed its doors. At the Mezzabanca investment bank in Via Filodrammatici behind the La Scala opera house, old Enrico Muccia, the dean of Italian bankers, blew his brains out with a 1942 Luger pistol, standard SS issue, when he was told of his own insolvency.

The banking panic had spread all over Europe that day. As the business day ended with the sun sinking into the Atlantic, the central banks – the Banque de France and the Banca d'Italia – made the horrifying discovery that they, too, were insolvent and facing formal bankruptcy the very next morning. In their final agony, the commercial banks of the two countries had pulled their last reserves out of the central banks, and had also drawn on existing lines of credit to the utmost in order to procure cash. Now most of these banks had failed, leaving the central banks holding the bag.

The French and Italian central banks thereupon tried to withdraw the reserves they had deposited with Bank for International Settlements in Basel, the legendary central bank of central banks. Members of the BIS board like Fritz Lautweiner and Alexandre Lammphallus were thunderstruck. Other central banks like the Germans, the Dutch, the Belgians, the Spanish and all the rest were also clamoring to get reserves and loans from the BIS. The BIS had case-by-case contingency plans to bail out its member central banks and even some of the largest commercial banks. But it had to adequate plan to bail itself out, and no way of printing money of its own. The Bank for International Settlements became the target of a panic run and was declared bankrupt by an emergency decree of the Swiss government slightly before midnight, March 9, 2001. "BIZ GAU," screamed the headline of the Bild Zeitung *extra the following morning. This meant that the BIS had blown. At this point the Swiss government activated its own emergency plan designed to save its three largest banks. This amounted to the pre-emptive shutting down of these banks, which already been battered by a long day of panic withdrawals.*

The news of the demise of the BIS set off wild rumors in Frankfurt that the German big three, Teutonische Bank, Leipziger Bank, and Finanzbank had failed to get their money out of France, Italy, and the BIS, and that the trio of German biggies would could not to survive until noon on March 10.

Now a true miracle happened: there was a panic run on the European Central Bank. The central banks of the individual countries and the national governments decided that since Maastricht was a dead duck, they wanted their money back. They announced that they were taking back their deposits and going home; they would nothing further to do with the European Central Bank. A short but intense firefight broke out at the bank's Brussels branch between armed guards and Belgian army paratroopers who arrived to take charge of the bank's gold and other reserves. The armed guards surrendered, and the European Central Bank went the way of so many New Orders.

When New York, Boston, and Philadelphia bankers reached their offices on the morning of March 9, the European banking crisis was already approaching its climax. Naturally Wall Street had been disturbed to see the European labor movement rise from the dead and challenge the governments of the Canossa group. But the panic run that had closed or bankrupted so many of the largest banks in Europe in a single business day posed a very concrete problem for the Wall Street and east coast bankers.

The secret of the Wall Street banks was that they were no longer banks, that is, institutions that made loans to businesses. That world was long gone. Wall Street had given up on corporate lending during the 1970s. After that, the New York money center banks had tried Latin American loans, junk bonds, real estate, and finally derivatives. Just one New York bank, Pace Manhattan, had a derivatives exposure that was almost twice the entire public debt of the United States. For Pace, Financiers Trust, and the rest, banking now meant selling the bank's proprietary derivative "products" to other banks, corporate money managers and others. Derivatives had taken over banking; banking was derivatives. And the US banks' total derivatives exposure was approaching $100 trillion dollars out of a world total of some $250 trillion.

Those who lived by derivatives would now perish by derivatives, the banks discovered. The derivative business, logically enough, depended on getting paid by one's "counterparties." The counterparties included prominently Credit Charolais, Banco di Milano, Banca Finanziaria, the shut-down Swiss big three and the threatened German big three, plus some key Dutch players. In other words, the name of the game was now counterparty default due to counterparty bankruptcy. Bankers had blathered about using derivatives for hedging in order to manage risk, but everybody knew that most derivatives were wild speculative side bets of the type one would have made sixty years ago in a bucket shop.

The bigger the bank, the more derivatives it had. So the old policy of "too big to fail" was in gravest danger. The banks knew it. The corporations knew it. The brokers knew it. The mutual fund managers and institutional investors knew it. Before too long even the public knew it.

The result, during the morning of March 9, 2001, was a panic run on virtually all American banks. This banking panic gathered up all the panic potential of every bank failure of 1932-33 (when all US banks had shut down), and raised it to the tenth power. Every corporation on the Fortune 500, remembering how Financiers Trust had ripped off Procter and Gamble, wanted its money out, today, right now, in cash. Fiber optic lines sizzled with electronic bank drafts all marked "withdrawal." Virtually every corporate executive spent the morning firing off wires and e-mail demanding prompt disbursement. Brinks and the other armored car companies with overwhelmed urgent cash deliveries ordered by corporate customers. Then these same executives ran to bank branches and automatic teller machines to try to retrieve whatever funds they personally had on deposit. By the middle of the morning, it was impossible to find an ATM that had not been drained of every dollar of cash by panicked depositors determined to become former depositors. A few executives who had slept late hired computer hackers to try to get their withdrawal orders honored.

That morning Pace tried to hold a regularly scheduled auction of its commercial paper, but not one bidder appeared. The auction was quickly shut down in the hope of avoiding adverse publicity, but the word was soon out on Wall Street. Bank stocks became penny stocks within minutes, and soon joined the category of non-negotiable paper. Everyone wanted to sell stocks and bonds, and get their hands on cash. The stock markets panicked, and long lines of people seeking redemption formed in mutual fund offices. But mutual fund offices turned out to be the wrong place to find redemption.

The New York Federal Reserve and the rest of the Fed did everything they could to keep the banks from running out of cash. The federal funds overnight interbank lending rate was pushed down as close to zero as it could get, and the open market trading desk was buying Treasury bonds at warp speed to keep the holders flush with cash. But the problem was that, after the day's events in Europe, everybody but everybody wanted cash – actual greenbacks on the barrel-head. An estimated $150 trillion in US financial paper was chasing just $500 billion in US bank notes. What good did it do to move balances from one electronic book-entry to another? Everybody wanted the certainty they imagined that only cash payment could bring.

Urgent orders were placed with the Bureau of Engraving and Printing to bring the printing presses up to full throttle. Even so, the banks were hemorrhaging cash much faster than it could be printed. There were after all only about $500 billion worth of Federal Reserve notes in the entire world, and about half of them were Eurodollars, Asia dollars, zenodollars, which circulated outside of the United States.

At J.P. Forgan & Co. in Wall Street, a few top bankers met among the highly polished mahogany desks of a bygone era. These men were in the advanced stages of mental disintegration that panic, despair, and dry martinis can combine to produce. It was late afternoon, well past lunchtime, but they did not care to eat. The top bankers found that, at the current rate of withdrawals, their banks were on average about two hours away from insolvency and failure; they might have enough green dollars to get through the day to the normal closing time, but what would they do tomorrow?

The bankers needed dollars. Who had dollars? The New York Fed. So the bankers, escorted by their plainclothes security men, trooped out of Forgan's and down Wall Street to the New York Federal Reserve. There they demanded to see MacDuff, the president, whom most of them knew as part of the same opulent social circle. The bankers told MacDuff that they were facing a currency crisis, a liquidity crunch, and that nothing would save them but a massive infusion of large-denomination dollar bills. Otherwise they could not collectively last more than a couple of hours.

MacDuff replied that he, too, had run out of cash for the moment; he had cancelled the weekly shipment of $1 billion in hundred-dollar bills to Moscow, and that had been given to the banks, but was already all gone. MacDuff had a plan to procure more: he had heard that the Bank for International Settlements was under heavy attack, so he was terminating the New York Fed's membership in the BIS with immediate effect, and demanding immediate repayment of the New York Fed's BIS deposits plus the New York Fed's paid-up share of the BIS's capital. He was instructing the BIS to pay him off using the dollar cash balances held by Swiss and other European BIS member banks in the United States, much of which was minutes away in lower and central Manhattan. The New York Fed was in a position to go to the head of the line of depositors seeking to get their hands on these dollars. With the help of some US Marshals and a fleet of commandeered armored cars, the cash of the ex-BIS could save the day for the embattled Wall Street giants, *enabling them to meet depositor demand until closing time. This was the best news the bank presidents had heard all day; their hysteria eased a few notches.*

But now, a little after 6 PM eastern standard time, there arrived the crushing news wire that the BIS was already bankrupt, and was seeking a chapter XI bankruptcy decree in the Foley Square federal district court to protect its assets from being seized by its creditors – among them, the New York Fed. The bankers, in their professional capacity, were stunned and speechless. The BIS, the keystone of the entire privately-owned central bank system, of the world, had been knocked out in little more than a day! MacDuff began talking about calling the White House to get an executive order seizing the BIS cash and putting it at the disposal of the New York Fed. But now the bank presidents had lost confidence in the central bankers. The knew that the if the BIS was gone, other central banks might follow, including the Fed. In that very instant, the fall of the BIS had detonated a panic run on the Federal Reserve itself.

The Federal Reserve System of which the New York Fed was a part was, after all, only a bank. Its depositors were the member banks. It was also member banks who owned the shares of stock that represented ownership of the Fed. For the Fed was emphatically not, as most people believed, an agency of the US government. It was a privately owned and privately managed company that had successfully usurped powers of the Executive Branch and the Congress.

The bank presidents turned on MacDuff and proclaimed that they had lost confidence in him and in his institution. They were quitting the Fed system. Secession was a popular idea: well, they were seceding from the Fed! They wanted their cash bank reserves, which were on deposit with the New York Fed, to be repaid to them instantly. They wanted to divest themselves of the Fed stock they owned; they suspected that by now it would be worthless, and in that case they wanted the Fed Board of Governors in Washington to indemnify them – to buy the stock back from them at the price they had originally paid – today, before the hour was out! The New York Fed president began to protest. The commercial bankers cut him off. If he didn't have currency, they wanted gold coins and gold bullion – right that very minute! They would quell the panic by paying their depositors in gold! (Forty years of Anglo-American scheming to demonetize gold went out the window with that one.) MacDuff was apoplectic: did his panicked confreres realize that this meant the end of the whole world System? They understood the stakes all too well, shot back the commercial bankers, who were now trooping out of the office and into the hallway. Each one had already drawn a cellular phone and was barking out orders to their office staffs that would set into motion a swift panic run against the New York Fed and the entire Federal Reserve System.

Soon Pacific Rimbank knew what had happened, and joined the panic, as did Penultimate Chicago, and the rest of the top twenty. These were people who knew how to collect. They were not interested any more in the ideology of an independent central bank. They wanted to escape liquidation by getting their reserves back. They though that Chairman Greenstreet of the Fed was responsible in some ways for the crisis, since he had endorsed derivatives and refused to rein in the hedge funds. Irrational ebullience of speculation indeed! The bankers fought for their reserves with a vengeance.

President MacDuff of the New York Fed called Chairman Greenstreet in Washington and told him of the desperate resolve of the New York bankers, which he thought was sure to be imitated by the vast majority of the banking community. Greenstreet was alarmed: a panic run on the Fed itself was at hand! Greenstreet said first that he was issuing his supersecret "launch on warning" order, meaning that a Boeing 747 loaded with several billion dollars in cash kept in a fortress-like hangar would take off from Dulles airport in the direction of New York's JFK. He would call out the media and hope that the hoopla might take the edge off the crisis. Greenstreet said he would call his wife

at MDB News and tell her to put out the line: "Fed acts to quell New York currency crisis."
MacDuff said that was fine, but that much more cash was needed, and fast. Did Greenstreet have a
100,000 ton bulk carrier loaded with thousand dollars bills to send his way? No, but Greenstreet
promised that all his vaults would disgorge the long green. Still not enough, objected MacDuff.

Greenstreet was sweating. In reality, because of the pre-eminent position of the New York Fed,
MacDuff and not Greenstreet was the more powerful figure. Greenstreet got the publicity, but
MacDuff had the real power. Greenstreet's specialty was talking out of both sides of his mouth
without being understood by anyone; it was said that he had studied with the famous comedian Al
Kelley, the champion of doubletalk. Now Greenstreet recalled that he had heard that the
International Monetary Fund, warned by the British that a great crisis was about to erupt, had been
hoarding dollar bills in various stashes including in secret underground vaults at IMF
headquarters not far from the White House.

"I've got it!", exclaimed Greenstreet. We have $38 billion on deposit with the IMF! We can get
that back in cash and gold and pay off the depositors that way!" MacDuff told him to get moving,
and to make sure that Federal Reserves notes were shipped to New York by the end of the day.

The Presidents of the Federal Reserve Banks of Minneapolis, Richmond, Kansas City, and
Cleveland had called in and were now waiting on the line to talk to him, but Greenstreet had no
time for them now. He would not have any cash for them that day, either. Instead, Greenstreet
placed a call to Jacques Àrebours, the Managing Director of the International Monetary Fund,
whose office was about half a mile away.

Àrebours was a French civil service bureaucrat who had moved up to be the head dun of the
Paris Club, the creditors' cartel and debt collection agency for governments and official lenders.
Àrebours was a dyed-in-the-wool Cartesian. The IMF and its inhuman austerity policies, as
President Mubarak of Egypt had once said, were responsible for the needless deaths of half a
billion people, 50 million a year over ten years. Now it was more like twenty years, and the majority
of the deaths had occurred under Àrebours' tenure. Àrebours kept himself well splashed with his
favorite couturier's brand of effete French eau-de-cologne.

Àrebours had also felt the icy breath of panic on his own neck. He had been horrified by the
sudden panic liquidation of the Bank for International Settlements, and even more by the fall of the
European Central Bank. Àrebours, a fanatical Anglomaniac, had thought of Admiral Beatty, the
British commander at the battle of Jutland in 1916, who had seen three of his best battle cruisers
blow up under German fire during the first 10 minutes of fighting and commented, "What's wrong
with our bloody ships today?" "What's wrong with our bloody banks today?" mused Àrebours,
with all the panache of a man who fancied himself the Beau Brummel of international bankers.

Àrebours had been getting calls from European governments about the status and even the
location of the IMF reserves of these countries. Àrebours, although reeking of cologne himself, was
astute enough to smell a panic run brewing up. The Europeans had been afraid to pull their funds
out of the IMF first, because they feared the wrath of the United States. Now it was Greenstreet
calling in the name of the United States.

"Hello, Jacques?," said Greenstreet. "We have a currency crisis going on. We've got panic runs
hitting our biggest banks. They can't hold out for more than a few more hours. We need all the
dollars and gold we can get this evening at the latest. I have to ask you for our $38 billion in
reserves, as much as possible in greenbacks, the rest in gold. With instantaneous delivery!"

"Hélas, mon President," sighed Àrebours. "You know that this means the end of le Système, our
whole world System!"

Greenstreet's reply was a heated mixture of short-term pragmatism and unprintable obscenity. He was not a philosopher. He was a servant of Wall Street. Greenstreet was suddenly not talking in the riddles and circumlocutions that he usually used for public statements.

"OK, OK, I understand," replied the intimidated Àrebours. "First of all, can I give you part of your reserves in Special Drawing Rights?" The allusion was to the IMF's "paper gold" based on a "basket of world currencies."

*"Take your SDRs and shove them up your ****," roared Greenstreet with uncharacteristic clarity. "They're worthless! Nobody in his right mind wants that toilet paper now!"*

Àrebours had the last laugh. "Then I am desolated to tell you, Monsieur, that I cannot pay. Almost all our dollars and gold are in London, in the vaults of the Bank of England. We have moved them during the last six months, and somehow I neglected to tell you. They are too far away to help you this afternoon. And, since the British government of M. Flair has frozen all international capital movements during the night, they are beyond our reach. I cannot deliver the funds you ask."

Àrebours heard no articulated reply, but rather an inchoate sound, a mixture of a scream and a gurgle, which was emitted by Greenstreet as he collapsed to the floor of his office in an apoplectic fit. There was malicious gossip that he had been found foaming at the mouth and chewing the carpet, but this was surely unfounded. Greenstreet was quickly hospitalized and diagnosed as having undergone a mild heart attack along with a severe nervous breakdown; Greenstreet's doctors told him to get six months of rest in a sanatorium. By the morning of March 10, 1998, most US banks had quit their memberships in the Federal Reserve System, cleaning out the Fed's reserves and forcing it into receivership. Ironically, the US central bank, which had so long arrogated to itself the most important powers of the Federal government, was forced to seek chapter XI bankruptcy protection from a mere US magistrate in the Federal court at the foot of Capitol Hill.

The story of the dollars shipped to London would be recorded by the historians of future centuries as the "fantastic imbroglio of M. Àrebours." But on that fateful day of March 9, 2001, Àrebours' ploy had guaranteed the final bankruptcy of the New York banks, and, as the sun moved westward across North America, of most American banks with them. With their derivative counterparties in Europe bankrupt or unable to pay, with all their depositors clamoring for cash, and with the Federal Reserve itself insolvent and unable to come to their aid, the banks defaulted.

Nor had Àrebours saved the IMF. Once news of the US demand for the restitution of reserves had leaked out to the press, every Congressman tried to pin the blame for the crisis on Àrebours.

There remained only the tragedy of the little people, of the poor trusting citizens who had kept their money in commercial banks and savings banks because they thought their accounts were insured by the Federal government. They had put their trust in the Federal Deposit Insurance Corporation. But most of them had not imagined that the FDIC had funds sufficient to cover less than one and one half per cent of insured deposits. The FDIC's Bank Insurance Fund had been theoretically exhausted at 11:49 AM on the morning of March 9, when three commercial banks in North Carolina, upstate New York, and Philadelphia were seized as insolvent. These depositors could be paid off. But what of the other 98.5% of deposits?

That would be a question of political will. All eyes turned to President George Bush, the Republican who had replaced President Gore in January 2001. He was known as George II to his followers. President Bush solemnly announced that as a committed freemarketeer and opponent of big government, he had always regarded federal bank deposit insurance as one of the most misguided excesses of the F.D. Roosevelt's New Deal. The government had no business insuring bank deposits in the first place, George II confided. It was an unwarranted interference in the private sector. He proclaimed that he would veto any bill proposing new funding for the FDIC in order to enable it to meet the long-standing guarantee to depositors. He rather called on the Congress to allow the FDIC, now a bankrupt and needless institution, to be allowed to expire. And so the small depositors were left with nothing but their eyes to cry with.

While all this was going on, the banking panic had wiped out most of the financial institutions of Latin America. But the American banks, ironically, had preceded them in their descent into the underworld. The planet pitilessly continued to turn. The bankers of Japan knew that they were next. All of their derivatives counterparties across the world had defaulted through outright bankruptcy or seizure by governments. The BIS was gone, the European Central Bank was gone, the Fed was gone, the IMF was gone. The full tidal wave of the world banking panic was about to break on Tokyo. The Japanese Ministry of Finance and the Bank of Japan abruptly decided that free trade and economic liberalism had gone far enough. They decided to declare a bank holiday, shut down the Tokyo and Osaka bourses and all the other exchanges, and develop a program for self-defense before re-opening. So all the Japanese banks were nationalized. The world called it protectionism, but Japan and its new co-prosperity sphere fared relatively better.

Asia was divided between those who shut down and took cover, like the Japanese, and those who choose to go down with their free-trade colors flying. The suicidal group included, New Zealand, Australia, Singapore, and Thailand. Those who put survival before fealty to the ideology of a dead international system included South Korea, Taiwan, and Malaysia, who were soon joined by India.

By the time Tuesday dawned over central Europe, the international financial and banking system was a smoldering ruin. The main institutions of international finance had ceased to exist. The process of interbank netting and settlement had come to a halt. Most stock markets and derivatives exchanges were shut down, either because their clearinghouses had failed, or because of government decree. There were not more than a hundred small commercial banks and savings banks left open in the world, and most of them were destined to succumb before the end of the week. Currency trading had declined by over 90%, in part because of exchange controls imposed by a number of countries. Options, futures, stock indices, and the rest of the derivatives were worthless, or better, had negative value. You had to pay someone to come and unwind them before carting them away.

In short, some $250 trillion in paper values had been destroyed in a day or two. It was the greatest breakdown crisis of civilization since the end of the Roman Empire. The entire house of cards had come down. The deregulated post-1971 finance structures based on stateless, supernational hot money flows, deregulated markets and free trade had given the final lesson of their instability and impracticality.

Average Americans were stunned. Their stocks and mutual funds were simply wiped out. President Bush had left the small depositors in the lurch. The Treasury was still solvent, but nobody thought that it could hold out much longer. Most insurance companies were gone, so most annuities and Guaranteed Income Contracts were a bitter joke.

Social security recipients did rather well, until President Bush allowed the government to default rather than print the dollars necessary to keep up monthly payments. Corporate bonds, even of the best investment grade, stopped paying even sooner. Before the crash, the bond market had always rejoiced over data showing a weak economy, and had reacted with hysteria if unemployment were falling or nominal wages rising. The bond market had thought that as stagnant economy meant good bond prices. This time around, many in the bond market were cheering right up to the point of general default.

So when the smoke had cleared, the immediate problems were means of payment, and food. Banks were shut, although some kept their safe-deposit departments open. Automatic Teller Machines were drained of cash and paralyzed. There were no more credit cards, no more debit cards, smart cards, or plastic money of any kind. Checks were not negotiable. The average person was left with about $25 in purse or wallet, and, if they were lucky, a pocketful of change.

What people really wanted in payment now was gold, which increased its buying power about fifty-fold, but who had gold? Because there were no other means of payment, the battered paper dollar went through an interlude of massive deflation. Paper dollars could suddenly buy more – more of what there was, at least. A single dollar could suddenly buy dinner for two with wine at a nice restaurant. Since coins were now even more desirable, eight quarters could buy the same dinner for four or five. People were pleasantly surprised when they saw how far their pocket change would go.

The pleasant surprise ended when they realized that they were going to have to pay their rent or mortgage payment, and their consumer debt with these deflated dollars. Everyone defaulted on credit cards and consumer loans, which seemed hopeless propositions. Credit cards in the most prestigious denominations of gold, silver, and platinum were to be found in every trash basket downtown. People tried to keep up their mortgage payments, but it proved impossible for the vast majority. There were fifty million personal and family bankruptcies during the first 10 weeks after the crash. Home foreclosures were soon running at almost 10 million per week. At that rate, the entire United States was destined to end up on the street by the end of the year.

But the mortgage bankers did not fare well, either. They could seize the houses through foreclosures, but what then? Nobody was prepared to purchase those houses at more than about 10% of their pre-crash values. The mortgage bankers tried renting, but nobody would or could pay more than a pittance. Within a month or two the mortgage bankers, despite their impressive inventory of assets, were themselves bankrupt. But a large part of the nation's housing stock continued to stand empty, even as the numbers of the homeless grew past all imagination.

Appeals were made to President Bush to promote legislation to mandate the immediate selling or renting of forty million empty homes and apartments to the 20 to 30 million homeless persons, but President Bush refused, citing the need to let the infallible forces of the free market work out the depression in their own way, undisturbed, until recovery should come through the magic of the marketplace itself. This stubborn refusal was one of the main factors in the final breakdown of public order during the harsh winter of 2001-2002, when the fabric of civilization itself began to dissolve.

Squatters, often middle class families with children, would break into empty homes and try to set up housekeeping. Spurred on by the demands of the mortgage bankers, the police would arrive to evict the squatters. Before too long, the police found that the squatters were armed, and determined in many cases to fight to the death. The police thereupon found that evicting squatters was their lowest priority in an atmosphere of increasing crime. The mortgage bankers reacted by bringing in bounty hunters and hired guns to carry out the court-ordered evictions. But there were now whole ex-middle class communities of squatters, who soon organized themselves into armed militias to deal with the bounty hunters. Many previously peaceful and law-abiding suburban communities where the squatters were the majority made a point of hanging the decomposing corpse of a bounty hunter on a tree or lamppost along their access roads. The financial meltdown thus transformed normal communities into armed camps. More ominously still, each suburb and indeed each neighborhood soon had its petty warlord, and these warlords were seeking to form state-wide and even regional alliances, allegedly to protect themselves against the itinerant armed gangs which were also growing rapidly. And these were not the only signs of a return to the dark ages.

The same incredible process led to the de-motorization of the United States, taking away America's wheels for the first time since the 1920s. No matter how much they needed their cars, people simply could not meet their car payments. The finance companies came to repossess the cars. Soon the finance companies had their lots full of cars which they could not resell at the prices they wanted. Not long after, some of these repossessed cars began to disappear during the night, followed by even more thefts. The alarmed finance companies then thought of the fleets of used aircraft left over from recent airline bankruptcies that were sitting in the Arizona desert. Soon hundreds of square miles of the Arizona desert were parking lots for repossessed cars, encircled by barbed wire and patrols of armed guards.

Now large parts of the American economy were crippled simply because nobody could get to work. Some of the companies that were still operating tried organizing bus service for their workers, but for many even this solution was out of reach. Urban mass transit, what there was of it, was now more and more crippled by breakdowns, since many of the cars had been manufactured overseas, and world trade was at a virtual standstill for lack of a system of payment. Domestic producers had mostly gone bankrupt and closed down. Appeals to President Bush were met once again with paeans to the free market and the iniquity of any government interference. The depression had to be allowed to work itself out "through the natural market mechanisms," repeated George II.

Globaloney and free trade had turned out to be pure folly. "Why produce it here when you can buy it abroad much cheaper?" had ranted the proponents of free trade and global sourcing. Now, just when they were most needed, a myriad of minerals, technologies, spare parts, and high-tech specialty products became almost impossible to procure. The globaloney merchants had neglected the possibility of a general collapse of world trade, and that was precisely what was now going on.

Electric utilities had been privatized during the year before the crash, and reserve production capacity had been sold off. Now there was no money for maintenance and repairs, and electric power was soon available for about four hours per day.

But the cruelest problem of all was food. Most Americans had thought that their country was self-sufficient in food. Now they realized that there was still a small grain surplus in theory, but in fact a shortfall because of the increasing difficulty of transporting the grain. But as far as meat, fish, dairy products, fruits, and vegetables were concerned, the US had become a heavy net importer by 2001. Now all that was over. As the world had learned after 1931, if you want to have orderly world trade, you have to have a functioning world monetary system. By late March 2002, the post-Bretton Woods monetary and financial order was in ruins. Many Americans had forgotten what pellagra, scurvy, rickets, beriberi, and night-blindness were; they now received a cruel reminder of vitamin deficiencies. Death rates, especially for children and old people, quickly reached astronomical levels.

By the end of the millennium, the United States was a thoroughly impoverished post-industrial wreck, with organized crime so pervasive as to reach the threshold of civil war. President Bush was increasingly embattled. Bush, for his part, urged continued staunch faith that the invisible hand of the free market would soon restore business confidence and prosperity. But there were rumors that a loose coalition of suburban warlords was planning a coup d'etat against George II, who had lost the confidence of the wretched and impoverished populace.

2. JAPAN 2000

At 9 o'clock in the morning of March 30, 2002, a group of terrorists from the Aum sect assassinated the Emperor of Japan. Akahito died in a series of explosions when dozens of members of the sect wearing explosive charges and poison gas dispensers overpowered security forces in a suicide charge on the Emperor's motorcade as it approached one of the bridge entrances to the Imperial Palace in downtown Tokyo. Although a number of the Aum sect members were shot down by imperial guards, several of the fanatics were able to reach the imperial limousine, where they detonated an undetermined number of explosive and poison gas back packs. Because of the poison gas, almost everyone in the vicinity was killed. The Japanese Prime Minister at once declared a state of emergency, imposed martial law, and announced his intention to rule by decree.

The flash bulletin from GiGi Press telling of the tragic event flickered across the computer screens of the world, causing consternation and a whiff of panic everywhere - everywhere except London, where the dominant feeling was one of Schadenfreude. Key players in the City of London seemed to have known in advance the general lines of what occurred. Later it would be found that the London merchant banks and clearing banks had taken very large short positions in Japanese stocks and currency futures before the fact. What had London known?

Mr. Eisuke Sakakibara, the legendary "Mr. Yen" of the Japanese Finance Ministry (MOF), was informed of the terrorist hecatomb in his office at the ministry. By the time he was told, the Nikkei stock average, which had stood at a little over 12,000 before the terrorist attack, had collapsed into a free fall. Not a single buyer was found until prices had reached about 8,000. The only available spot quote put the US dollar at 255 yen, almost double the pre-assassination exchange rate. Mr. Sakakibara was quickly on the telephone with the Finance Minister and the Prime Minster, and they decided to close all financial exchanges at once. They also ordered the closing of all banks, finance companies, and credit unions for a one-week period of official mourning. The Japanese officials were relieved that they could save face by citing the official mourning, for they knew that otherwise they would have been obliged to close the banks and exchanges simply to quell the financial panic.

In his MOF office, Mr. Sakakibara sadly contemplated the events of the previous twelve months. The system had been forced to absorb many bankruptcies. The bubble economy of 1986-91 had left Japanese banks with $1.5 trillion of bad real estate loans. During 1995 the discount rate had been lowered to almost nothing, and the banks had been encouraged to rebuild their balance sheets by speculating abroad. They had done so, and in the process had shored up the New York stocks and bonds. In 1997, some big Japanese banks had barely survived the end of the fiscal year on March 31, the day when Japanese banks must mark their securities holdings to market, cutting the old values down to the current sale price. It had been a Herculean effort to bring some very large banks over the hurdle, but it had been done.

In late 1997, important banks had begun to succumb anyway. Despite government support, Nippon Credit Bank had failed, followed by Hokkaido Takushoku, and then by Yasuda Trust, and Chuo Trust. Other large banks had been kept going by taxpayer-funded bailouts. During late 1999 and early 2000, Mr. Sakakibara had been working to pull the banking system through the end of yet another fiscal year. Now, with the assassination and the ensuing panic, he saw that this could not be done in the normal way. His thoughts wandered to a little blue lake and a bamboo hut where, like a good Confucian civil servant, he loved to go to fishing.

But soon Sakakibara was placing phone calls. The first was to the US Treasury Secretary Topaz, the second to Governor Greenstreet at the Federal Reserve in Washington. He told the Americans that the Japanese stock markets and currency markets had collapsed in panic, and that they would be kept shut indefinitely – far beyond the official mourning period. He told Topaz that it was time to *activate the $500 billion fund that had been set up in the late summer of 1995 to help Japanese banks sell their US Treasury bonds under the table – directly to the Federal Reserve, without the embarrassing need to dump them on the New York secondary Treasury market, where so much selling would lead to uncontrollable panic. Sakakibara added that the Japanese government would find a way use the state of emergency to finesse the end of the fiscal year on March 31, since virtually every Japanese bank was now technically bankrupt because of stock and currency losses and would have to be seized under normal conditions. Sakakibara finished up each call with a warning to the Americans that it was time to activate their emergency anti-collapse plans. Even though it was 3 AM in Washington, Topaz called President Bush and asked him to convoke the White House crisis staff for financial emergencies.*

But in the meantime the Japanese panic began to work its way across Eurasia. In Taipei, the stock market went down by one third during the first hour after the new from Japan hit. Then the markets were closed by government order. In Hong Kong, the shock was even greater, and the order soon came from Beijing to suspend trading. China then proceeded to freeze all financial transactions, especially international ones, for the duration of the crisis. And China, it turned out, was the large country best able to insulate itself from some of the early effects of the crash. Bangkok and Kuala Lumpur both crashed, and then shut down as well.

In Singapore, the local regime was determined to stay open in order to assert the free-market philosophy of which senior statesman Lee Kwan Yew was a fanatic supporter. The Singapore regime contained London-style Jap bashers who wanted to see the Tokyo crisis play out to its final extremes. So while the Straits Times index crashed by an average 25%, the futures of a number of Japanese stocks fell by almost 50%. And then there was the action over at SIMEX, the Singapore International Monetary Exchange, which had been the bailiwick of Nick Leeson of Barings. Now, SIMEX trembled as the tsunami of the Japanese crash come rolling in.

The Singapore chaps also inaugurated a trend that would often be seen around the world during the following days. They concluded that since the Japanese banks were in the biggest trouble, Tokyo would have to liquidate their estimated $700 billion in US Treasury paper, and a trillion or two of other investments besides. The Singapore chaps decided to sell US Treasury bonds short, sell the dollar short, sell America short up and down the line. Their short orders poured into London, and into Wall Street later in the day.

Panic next touched India, where stock markets fell by one fourth, and Japanese tourists at the Taj Mahal suddenly found that their yen were no longer being accepted as legal tender.

When the panic reached Russia, a large secondary explosion developed. The post-1992 Russian banking system had always been a speculative house of cards, based on laundering the cash proceeds of the Russian mafia, the great beneficiary of the organized crime counterrevolution which had followed the fall of communism. The Russian banks were based on drug money, flight capital, and Albanian-style Ponzi schemes like MMM.

Now the ramshackle Russian banking structure failed to withstand the wind that blew across the steppes of Asia from Japan. The Russian people had not had very much time to become familiar with the new "free market" financial structures, and what they had seen certainly did not inspire confidence. Ironically, the Russians had fewer illusions than most other peoples. At the first dispatches from Tokyo, lines formed at the offices of many Russian banks. The Russian banking panic started in the Far East, where it was only an hour or two earlier than in Tokyo. Small riots broke out here and there when bank officials tried to shut their lobbies. The mood of the crowds was ugly but realistic: they wanted the banks kept open as long as there were depositors who wanted their money. When the police were called, they usually fraternized with the depositors, and often joined them in demanding their money back once they realized what was happening. Most of the time the crowds got their way, and by the time the clocks in western Russia pointed to midnight, most Russian bank branches had been cleaned out. More than a few branches were burned when it turned out that cash reserves were inadequate to satisfy even the first wave of panicked depositors.

The wave of panic lapped around Turkey, where it tipped the Turkish pound and the banking system into crisis. On the Arabian peninsula, the Saudi Arabian Monetary Authority officials were reading their telexes about the carnage in the Japanese markets shortly after they reached their desks. Within minutes they had seen the exceptional gravity of the situation, and by the end of the hour they had lost their heads. Whole legions of Saudi princes called their personal brokers and placed sell orders to liquidate their European and American assets. Some of the more cunning princes placed their orders on GLOBEX, the round-the-clock financial market that allows many kinds of trading from anywhere in the world at any hour of the day or night. GLOBEX prices had been falling continuously, not just on Japanese, but on European and American securities as well. The wave of Saudi sell orders was the last straw; there were no buyers, so the GLOBEX did what it was never supposed to do: it closed down, citing the impossibility of keeping an orderly market.

By now the panic was eight hours old, and it was time for the banks and businesses of Europe to open their doors. The arrival of the panic in such neophyte markets as Warsaw, Budapest, and Prague is quickly told: in each of these cities, the markets became chaotic during the first few minutes of trading; most stocks never opened, and the markets had to be closed before the end of the first hour. There were no buyers for yen or Japanese stocks, and very few buyers for anything. Here and there appeared signs of banking panic on the Russian model.

Then came Frankfurt. The DAX index had closed the previous evening at 3625, despite the wretched state of the German economy and society in general.

 The DAX had been pulled down during late 1998 and early 1999 by the great decline in German exports. Braun razors, Krups coffeemakers, Mercedes Benz, Audi and BMW cars, Grundig radios and Köckner-Humboldt-Deutz engines had once been in demand around the world because of their superior quality. But now that all the parts came from Thailand and Malaysia, why pay more for Germany's wares? It was the final triumph of Alonzo de Caudillo – otherwise know as El Cheapo – whom Volkwagen had lured from General Motors in order to obtain his matchless expertise in global sourcing, the process of buying cheap, low-quality parts from impoverished third-world workers. Volkwagen had paid fabulous sums to learn El Cheapo's fabled secret, and that secret was: "The Cheapest is Always The Best." In the end the DAX had been propped up by the mass importation of Anglo-American stockjobbing methods.

And what hit Germany that morning was not just the impact of the Japanese events; it was also the news of the banking panic in Russia. With these shocks, all the wonderful leverage that had been built into the market by the years-long orgy of junk bonds turned into reverse leverage. Within a couple of hours Frankfurt had lost 35%. German bonds, like the government's Bund, were equally hammered. Finance Minister LaFontaine ordered the exchanges shut. At the Teutonische Bank, the expatriate Englishmen, Americans, and New Zealanders who ran the bank congratulated themselves that they had sold off their German stocks, and had bought derivatives. But their moment of truth was not far off. In the grey shadows of after-hours trading, there were no buyers, and it was clear that the bottom had fallen out.

The Bahnhofstrasse in Zuerich, Switzerland fared much better-- at least for the moment. As soon as the initial news bulletins from Japan had been received, The Confoederatio Helvetica – that is to say, the Swiss government – implemented its own secret wartime crisis plan, pre-emptively closing all exchanges and imposing capital and exchange controls, while holding price controls in ready reserve. The government authorities knew that their goal was to save the three biggest banks in Zürich. An unlimited line of credit was opened by the Swiss National Bank – the central bank – to each of these giants of the Bahnhofstrasse. All other banks faced the strictest triage. Swiss stocks gave up about 15%, the Swiss franc about a third of that. Many gullible investors around the world still thought of the Swiss franc as being as good as gold. In the coming days many would discover that the Swiss franc had more derivatives behind it than bullion. But that realization would take a little time.

For many years the central banks of the world had conducted a little operation which was far from secret, but which had been treated as a taboo by compliant reporters. Back in the 1960s there had been a gold pool, designed to suppress the price of gold in order to make the depreciated paper of the central banks look good by comparison. The gold pool had long since been officially disbanded, but in reality it had lived on and if anything become more active than it had been, as the financial fragility of the System had increased. For much of the nineties, the central banks had joined in dumping enough gold on the market to keep the price near a target of $290 per ounce. Sometimes they would take the price down fifty dollars or so to put the squeeze on any gold bugs who had been accumulating gold on margin.

But on this day the gold pool strove in vain to keep gold below $500. The pool employed its whole panoply of tactics, including dumping gold, selling gold stocks, plus all the permutations of futures, options, and all manner of other derivative contracts. But the frenzy of gold buying from small nations' governments, wealthy Arabs, prosperous Chinese, and German dentists overwhelmed all their ploys.

Gold rocketed up from $285 to about $685, but that, thought the Swiss, was an American problem. The Swiss considered themselves impregnable in their Alpine fortress. But they were wrong. The Swiss banks were carried trillions of dollars of swaps, structured notes, and other derivatives on their off-balance sheet ledgers. In the following days, more and more of the counterparties to these derivatives contracts were destined to go under. Each derivative default added to the overall derivative gridlock, and each default gnawed away at the capital base of the banks. But the full impact of derivative default would not be obvious for a week or more.

Then came the agony of the Paris Bourse and the marché à terme – the futures exchange. The French were facing the combined momentum just of the Japanese crash, but of the Russian crash and the German crash as well. The French banking and financial system had a plausible facade of stability, but in essence the French banks of the late twentieth century were as hollow as the French army of May-June 1940.

When the panic wave inundated Paris, the French financial operators proved to be impressionable and excitable. The CAC 40 dropped 35% in the first hour – worse than Germany, and worse than the US October crash of 1987. At that point rumors developed according to which one or more large banks was in trouble and might have to close. The government of Prime Minister Lionel Jospin dithered for more than an hour, attempting to balance prestige, confidence, and their commitment to Anglo-Saxon liberalism against the need for quick government action to stop the panic. They finally were obliged to accept the reality and close the markets. By that time the CAC had shed 45%.

In London, the story was different, at least initially. Through some strange mechanism, the British seemed to have been aware that a big shock had been about to hit Japan. Many of the merchant banks and hedge funds had shorted Japanese securities, both stocks and bonds. The Bank of England, now in its second year of periodic, incremental increases in its discount rate, had just taken the bank rate up another quarter of a percent the previous week. So at least part of the City was prepared to accept the Japanese tragedy with the attitude of Dickens' Mr. Pecksniff in Martin Chuzzlewit – *a mask of genteel condolences hiding the self-satisfied grin of perfidy.*

For the Japanese, there was no mercy. Because he wanted to stem the panic, the mercurial Eddie George, the Governor of the Bank of England, simply banned any market transactions involving Japanese stocks or bonds. He did not mention over-the-counter derivatives, for there was nothing he could do about those. A couple of brokerages specializing in Japanese securities ceased to exist, and there was a police line and bobbies in front of the closed doors of every Japanese bank branch in the City.

At the opening, the stocks of some of the merchant banks that were known to have shorted Japanese instruments got a modest boost. But at the same time an undertow began to develop. Traders surveyed the carnage in Japan, the Russian banking panic, the German losses, the debacle across the Channel in Paris. This was already the worst panic since 1929, and was already far worse than 1929 for countries like France. Exporters and companies committed to the European Community began to falter, and then to decline. The euro was plummeting, although not as fast as the yen or dollar.

A big panic factor in London was also provided by the fate of the American companies whose shares on the Exchange. By 2002, the American economy was a giant with feet of clay, threadbare and depleted from junk bonds, derivatives, and speculative bubbles. If a world panic was now in progress, the stockjobbers of the world were reasoning, then the full force of that panic was likely to hit the dominant world currency, the overextended and battered US dollar, which retained only the faintest residue of its own strength of three decades before, when the monetary crises had started. Yes, the dollar was very vulnerable, nodded the stockjobbers, and so were American stocks.

When London opened, piles of sell orders had built up against all the American issues. These came from Japan, Singapore, from Saudi Arabia, from Switzerland, and above all from the United States itself. When the Tokyo panic had started, it had been the middle of the evening in New York and Boston, and dinner time in Los Angeles. The mutual fund managers and pension fund directors who remembered 1987 recalled that Wall Street had dissolved into chaos right from the opening bell, with no chance for the orderly execution of sell orders. So, taking a leaf from the book of some of the cleverest mutual fund managers in 1987, the American mutual funds took the lead in placing as many of their sell orders as possible in London. They would have tried GLOBEX too, but GLOBEX had already shut down. The mutual fund managers were themselves already panicked, since their phone circuits were tied up with Sunday-night calls demanding redemptions.

The downward slide was accelerated by the hedge funds, which were all over the floor of the stock exchange, where they were shorting everything, especially everything American. At the London Metals Exchange, the hedge funds were buying gold heavily in the cash market for immediately delivery to their own warehouses, with platinum also in demand. Gold was soon up to $700 per troy ounce, and headed higher. With all forms of paper suddenly in disrepute, gold was back in vogue after a quarter-century in eclipse because of central bank dumping. Then there was LIFFE, the London futures market. The hedge funds and the merchant banks pounded US Treasury futures, dollar futures, S&P 500 futures, selling them all short on LIFFE. At one point George Spurious, whom everybody knew was the Queen's banker, appeared near the exchange, as if he were taking a stroll. Some were reminded of the Forgan group's "organized support" personified by Richard Whitney of the New York Stock Exchange, who had appeared at the height of the Crash of 1929 and ostentatiously placed some orders for US Steel. Spurious, on the other hand, embodied organized short-selling.

When the reporters asked Spurious where he was going, he said that he was on his way to the LIFFE to short the dollar with every penny in his possession. Soon the derelict British pound sterling was good for almost three American dollars, a price not seen since the Union Jack had disappeared from east of Suez in the long twilight of empire.

So the London morning trading of the American stocks was itself already chaos, with an avalanche of sell orders and no buyers to be found at any price. Most of the American stocks never opened, for want of buyers; the few that did open had to be suspended after less than an hour, with losses of between one third and one half. This already implied a 40% decline in the Dow Jones Industrial Average at the New York opening.

By early afternoon, the panic had become so pervasive that British Treasury bonds, the so-called gilts, had been hammered down by 25% The Footsie index had lost more, almost a third of its value. But the British congratulated themselves that they had lost less than Japan and less than the continent, except for the Gnomes of Zürich, and that they were consequently more powerful than they had been before the crash started.

Elsewhere in Europe the destruction was appalling. The Italian Prime Minister Frodi thought that he had been very clever in issuing a midnight order pre-emptively closing the Milan stock exchange and slapping on exchange controls to prevent flight capital – all before any panic could develop. Italian Treasury paper also stood up better than expected. But all the more pitilessly did the international markets punish the lira on the international markets; by the end of the day the Italian currency was down almost 50%.

Scandinavia had been in a very evident economic depression for a couple of years before the panic. So traders in Copenhagen, Stockholm and Oslo were surprised to see their stocks, which they thought had come to rest at all-time lows, gather up enough energy to fall another 30%. The same pattern held true in Belgium and the Netherlands. In Luxemburg, there was the usual story of losses, spiced up with rumors that one of two of the banks had been seized. Spain fared very badly, with about 50% losses across the board.

The sun was now well above the horizon on the coast of Maine. Stammering television and radio commentators read out news bulletins featuring the grim details of what was already the greatest stock market collapse in the history of the world. The American public had seen the newsfilm of the death of Akahito late in the previous evening. Now that horror was crowded out by the bank riots in Russia, and scenes of despair outside the stock exchanges of Paris, London, and Frankfurt.

Further west, dawn was breaking over Chicago and its famous futures markets. Ever since the days of the Brady Report of January 1988, a system had existed between New York and Chicago for the purpose of injecting frequent shots of adrenaline into the Dow and of thus maintaining public confidence in markets in general. A group of yuppie quants had studied the relation between the S&P futures contract in Chicago – a derivative – and the price of the underlying stocks bought and sold in the cash market in New York. The quants had found that a few tens of millions of buying of the Chicago futures could generate billions of buying updraft for the New York exchange blue chips. The trick was simply to keep the Chicago future above the implied price of the underlying New York stock. If that were the case, the index arbitrageurs with their computerized buy and sell programs would sell the Chicago futures, and buy the New York stocks, for the reason that the latter were cheaper. Especially since 1987, the Federal Reserve and the Chicago Fed in particular had channeled much of the new liquidity for the whole country through these drugged-market operations.

But today the determined attempt to generate an updraft of buying was simply swept away by a hurricane of selling.

The stockjobbers of the world knew that the pandemonium of the Chicago trading pits would now set the stage for the New York opening. When the S&P 500 futures contract began trading on the Chicago Mercantile Exchange, it went limit down and was halted after the first minute. Experienced traders estimated a New York opening with the Dow Jones down almost 50%.

Stock trading is supposed to have been conducted since 1792 in the approximate area of lower Manhattan now occupied by the New York Stock Exchange. There had been many ups and downs on the way to 7,654, which is where the Dow Industrials had closed the previous afternoon. But never had the specialists and officers faced a day like this. The officers of the New York exchange agreed before the bell that a 50-point loss during the 15 seconds was a foregone conclusion, so the imposed program trading curbs even before the opening, to mitigate the avalanche of computer-driven sell programs by the index arbitrageurs. All stop-loss orders were summarily banned, including those of institutional investors and of small individual investors as well. The little people who thought they could get to the exit automatically when things got rough were thus cruelly disappointed. Some of the American stocks that had been slaughtered in London were halted by the floor governors before they ever opened. Many companies called the New York exchange to ask that their stocks be halted before the opening bell.

Of the 3400-odd stocks listed on the New York exchange, only a few dozen of the biggest actually opened when trading began. Of the ones that did actually open, the specialists charged with maintaining an orderly market found themselves swamped with sell orders, but could see no buyers. These specialists therefore turned to the floor governors, who agreed without exception on non-regulatory halts, meaning that trading in these stocks had to be halted for at least thirty minutes. The thirty minutes were purely a formality, and many of these stocks did not open all day.

But even a few minutes of trading by a few stocks from the Dow thirty produced a Dow Jones Industrials decline of 800 points, thus fulfilling the pre-conditions for an across-the-board trading halt for the entire New York exchange, as well as for the American stock exchange, the over-the-counter computer market, and the exchanges in Philadelphia, Los Angeles, and other cities - in short, of all stock trading in the United States.

After that came the mandatory 60-minute cooling-off period, which served only to heighten the tension. When the market re-opened, even fewer stocks were still trading. But these were still enough to sink the Dow by 800 additional points in just a few more minutes for a total decline of 1600, making this the worst point loss in recorded history. The fall of 1600 points brought prices to just above 6000. At this point a mandatory pause of two hours took effect, with the panic once again increasing rather than dissipating. When trading resumed, the market soon accomplished the task of wiping out the existing record for percentage decline as well. When the total loss exceeded 2400 points, the market shut down for the day. The Dow closed at 4943, a drop of more than 30%, worse than the worst day of the crash of 1987.

Famous brokerage houses were brought to the brink of insolvency very quickly. Many of the brokers' customers had bought their stock on margin, using loan money from the call market. The brokers kept the stock in their office vaults as collateral. Now the stock prices had fallen so much that the stock certificates were no long enough to serve as collateral for the amount borrowed. The stock market clearinghouse duly noted that fact, and called upon the brokers to post more margin. The brokers got on the telephone and the Internet as quickly as they could and informed them that unless they paid cash as collateral, their shares would be sold at once.

Many customers simply did not understand; the brokers had never told any of them what might happen in the unlikely eventuality that the market would ever move down. Some customers were able to organize the money needed to meet the margin calls, often just in time to be told that the brokers needed still more margin because of a further deterioration in the stock prices.

It was the classic 1929 routine all over again. But with so many shares being dumped on the market because of insufficient margin, downward pressure on the market became even more irresistible. More threatening than that was the fact that many of the biggest brokers were now insolvent. The market circuit-breakers had proven inadequate; the market's fall was more rapid than in 1987 despite the periodic trading pauses.

Much to the chagrin of bond market traders, there was no flight to Treasury bond quality that day. Sell orders from the Japanese banks overwhelmed the buy orders of investors fleeing the stock market. The big Japanese banks, desperate for liquidity, were placing their orders directly with the New York Federal Reserve; otherwise the panic on the Treasury market would have been even greater.

At about four in the afternoon, the Governors of the New York exchange met and decided to appeal to the President to shut down all the markets for several days until the panic had subsided. President Bush came on the line and told the stunned and exhausted market officials that such a closure would constitute a violation of the rules of the free market to which he had dedicated his entire political career. For him to order a closure was thus out of the question. But he said that Chairman Greenstreet of the Federal Reserve was with him, and wanted to give them assurances.

Greenstreet then came on the line and promised that the Fed would stand ready as a lender of last resort to provide banks and brokerages with abundant liquid cash to prevent failures. But even that still left the exchange men on the spot, but George II promised that the first signs of stabilization would be evident by the next day, once it became clear to the public that the Fed was going to open the cash spigot as it had never been opened before. Greenstreet, Bush said, had convinced him that a panic could always be stopped by a determined lender of last resort.

One or two of the exchange men piped up, urging Greenstreet to extend credit to three big banks and about half a dozen brokerage firms that they knew were on the verge of failing. They also reminded the two men in the Oval Office that the clearinghouse of the Chicago options exchange, always a weak point, was about half an hour away from going bankrupt. And there might be other problems in Chicago as well. A few fairly substantial regional brokers were though to be unsalvageable. Greenstreet told the exchange officials to arrange takeovers of those brokers by surviving ones, and he would guarantee the financing. George II announced that he would address the nation within the hour with a promise of unlimited liquidity to stem the tide. Then the call ended and the meeting broke up.

When Greenstreet left the White House, he returned to his own office at the Federal Reserve on the north side of the Mall. He knew the entire System was thoroughly bankrupt by any traditional criteria, but he was confident that the System could be saved. The System, thought Greenstreet, had been to the brink three dozen times or more in the past thirty years. To anybody else, that might have seemed an argument that the System was totally unstable and ought to be junked. But for Greenstreet, it was a proof of resilience and durability.

Now, thought Greenstreet, it was time to unleash what he called his Money Machine. It was time to flood the gutters of Wall Street with green liquid lucre. He was soon in touch with the Federal Reserve Bank of New York, the keystone of the entire System. MacDuff, the President of the New York Fed, was meeting in his office with the manager of the open market desk, who joined the call with Greenstreet. The three began to go down the list of what banks, brokerages, and insurance companies, and mutual funds were in trouble after the unprecedented losses of the day. The list was long, and the famous names were many. Greenstreet had said that he was ready to act as lender of last resort. Now the Fed had to deliver the money.

The manager of the open market desk reported on what his office two floors below was already doing. The open market desk, acting as an agent of the entire Federal Reserve system, had entered the Treasury market an hour before the close and had begun buying unlimited quantities of Treasury bills, notes, bonds, strips, plus any and all agency securities, including Ginnie Maes, Sallie Maes, Freddie Macs, and so forth. The Fed was also buying derivatives – structured notes, swaps, floaters, and the rest. The purchases were being made at artificial support prices in order to maximize the amount of cash going into circulation. The Fed was carrying out the biggest coupon passes of its history, and was offering unlimited system repos or repurchase agreements on sweetheart terms. The tone of the Treasury market had improved noticeably. The rate of fall had slowed and the market had become almost stationary at its lows; and the manager hoped that the market would begin to gain back some losses the following day. Greenstreet reminded the New York Fed to make sure they sent an official to the evening meeting of the plumbers – his joking name for the interbank computerized clearing system. The New York Fed had already thought of that.

As a result of all these measures, the US M1 money supply was already growing at an impulse rate of 25% per day.

Other Fed officials were on the phones with the top fifty banks in the country. The commercial bankers were given the instruction – or strong encouragement, as the bankers preferred to say – not to cut any credit lines to financial institutions, but rather to lend them whatever they needed. The big banks were invited simply to tell the Federal Reserve how much they needed. In the gathering gloom of twilight that terrible day the Federal Reserve Board in Washington issued a communiqué stating that the discount rate was being lowered immediately by four and a half points, from 5% to 0.5%.

The banks were strongly encouraged to borrow all they needed to be ready for short-term emergencies. It was soon an open secret that the Federal funds rate, the interest charged among banks for overnight lending, would soon be at 0.1%. The Fed also lowered the margin requirement for buying stocks on credit from 20% to 1%. All of these Fed benchmarks were destined to fall even further during the following days.

And what were the little people thinking that day? Over the years, the average person had deserted savings accounts and certificates of deposit in favor of mutual funds, especially stock mutual funds, and most particularly the so called "aggressive growth," "leveraged growth," and "maximum capital appreciation" category of mutual funds. The little people had taken their nest eggs, their life savings, their retirement money, the tuition money for their children's college education, and invested them in a speculative and overbought stock market in the middle of a world economic decline that had been going on for longer than any of the little people could remember.

By 2002, more than half of American households were holders of mutual fund shares, for a total of almost $6 trillion dollars. Back in the crash of 1987, the total of shareholding households was a fraction of that amount. Mutual fund managers were surprised that more shareholders had not demanded their money back in 1987, since the fund management is pledged to redeem their own fund shares for cash. But now, in 2002, the mutual fund phenomenon had roots in the population that had not existed in 1987.

The average American, much more likely now to be an owner of stock or mutual funds, was much more attuned to stock market quotations than he or she had been in 1987. Many families regarded their mutual fund investment as the great wager which would determine whether they would be able to retire in comfort, or whether they would be able to retire at all. So it took very little in the way of turbulence to fixate their attention on how that critical wager was faring. For decades the pundits had told these little people to buy and hold, oblivious of the fluctuations of the market – even as the hedge funds moved billions across the globe every few seconds to snap up a fast buck.

Shortly after the Wall Street opening word of the crash began to spread like a prairie fire through the million offices in a thousand cities that were the habitat of the old-fashioned American white-collar middle class. The workers in home offices heard the news on the radio, or saw it displayed on the innumerable news tickers of the Internet or on the cable financial news stations, of which there were by now five. It could be seen that if the average blue-chip stock had fallen by one third, the net asset values of the average mutual fund had fallen by more than half. The closed-end funds had fared even worse.

How many dreams of a comfortable old age of leisure and contentment vanished that day, yielding to a grim vision of grinding want! The tired and desperate Baby Boomers were transfixed by horror as they watched their life savings being decimated minute by minute. Now all the sugar-coated sales pitches of the news media about buying and holding for the long term were exposed as absurd lies. Middle America knew what it wanted, and it wanted out. Americans ran for the exit in the electronic equivalent of the great migrations of human history. The Baby Boomers wanted to be short; they did not want to rely on anybody's paper promises to pay.

Hapless Middle America had been told that their mutual fund investment would give them not only the capital gains and dividend income of a choice portfolio of stocks. They would also get something more: the expert judgment of the fund manager, purified and hardened to reliability in the crucible of market euphoria and despair. The genius of the manager was the greatest asset of every fund, from Peter Cinch to his epigones. But now angry and betrayed Middle America did not want to hear about the genius of the fund managers; they considered those reputations to be the equivalent of garbage which has no value, or more precisely a negative value, because you had to hire Waste Management or Laidlaw to take the nuisance away.

The telephones in the offices of the mutual fund companies began to ring like never before. One word was in every caller's mouth: redemption. That meant the shareholders wanted cash, and they wanted it now. Even on Sunday night the fund managers had foreseen this wave of redemptions, and they had realized that they had to avoid payment in full or else they would be swept away.

But unfortunately, most of the poor shareholders had failed to read to fine print of the mutual fund prospectus they had been given when they turned their money over to the professionals. The attention of the would-be redeemers was now directed to those fine-print clauses that governed the process of redemption. Here it emerged that the mutual funds in many cases had the right to delay repayment for the shares turned in for seven full business days. Another shocking detail in almost as many fund brochures was that payment could be made in kind, that is to say, not in money, but in the form of stocks or other securities whose market price on the day the redemption was initiated was the equivalent of the cash owed by the fund to the departing shareholder.

After waiting for hours to have their calls answered by the mutual funds, Middle America was beside itself in rage to learn that it were not to receive the proverbial cash on the barrel-head, but a dubious security to be handed over a week hence, after its value had been mercilessly eroded by the panic collapse of the markets. A great rage was conceived in the minds of the American Middle Class.

A few days later, the consternation of Middle America became complete when the Securities and Exchange Commission issued a blanket order, approved by President Bush, permitting all mutual funds to cease redemptions until further notice.

But the feelings of Middle America Baby Boomers counted little for the moment. What did count that first night was a meeting being conducted in a meeting room of the New York Federal Reserve. The issue here was the final evening settlement of the interbank payment system, that is to say of the netting and clearing system among the big money-center banks doing business primarily in US dollars. Here, as the now-extinct Marxists might have said, was indeed the heart of world finance capital.

The work of the clearinghouse had been done in past decades by couriers carrying envelopes full of checks and documents from place to place in Manhattan. Back in the days of the policy racket, the numbers game had worked off the last few digits of the clearing statistics, which were printed in the newspaper every day. But lately this work had been increasingly done by means of computers. The New York Fed officials referred to the netting and settlement men as the plumbers because they were the guardians of the system of money transfers that linked banks and other financial institutions. And nobody played the numbers any more; now there were derivatives.

All during the business day, over a hundred of the largest New York and other banks, and more than a hundred associated banks, had been wiring payments back and forth to each other by means of the settlement system. Each of the hundred associated banks represented other banks around the world, or even whole countries, like Brazil. Normally, the total daily turnover was well in excess of one and a half trillion dollars. This time it was more than eleven times that sum.

Every day the debits and credits of each bank had to be added up; this was called the netting phase, since it resulted in a single net plus or minus position for each bank. If a bank had a surplus vis-a-vis all other banks, it would receive a cash payment from a settlement account at the New York Federal Reserve by way of Fedwire, the Federal Reserve wire transfer system. If the bank had run a deficit that day, then it would be obliged to make a payment into the New York Fed settlement account by way of Fedwire. Most often these end-of-the-day payments were made to and from the bank's reserve account at the New York Fed.

The dicey moment arrived at the end of each day when it came time to proceed to settlement. Every day a settlement account was created at the New York Fed into which all the banks with a net debit paid in what they owed, and from which the banks with a net credit withdrew what was coming to them. At the very end of the day, the settlement account was emptied out and shut down.

The trick was that before the settlement account could be drawn down, the books had to balance up and down the line. The big hitch in the system was that unless all transactions balanced, no settlement could be paid out. This feature of the clearing system had threatened the jam-up and meltdown of the system during great financial crises like Brazil, Conti Illinois, Mexico, and so on. In some of those crises, the Fed had been brought into the final phase of settlement; the Fed had anted up the payments that certain cash-strapped banks had been unwilling or unable to make. In that way the Fed had saved the system from immediate meltdown. The danger was that the plumbing of the interbank system would freeze, and the System would be brought to a standstill.

The bankers thought that they had solved this problem and achieved what they called settlement finality in 1990 with the binding provision that if one or more banks went bankrupt or otherwise failed to settle, the surviving members would be obliged to pay a pro-rated share of the settlement payments of the fallen banks. Each bank was forced to deposit cash collateral with the settlement system equal to 5% of the amount of exposure it was willing to accept vis-a-vis all the other banks combined.

It had also been made illegal for a bank on the brink of insolvency to take in payments during the day, and then renege on the net settlement payment due in the evening. With these measures the bankers thought that they had reduced the netting, clearing, and settlement risk to the lowest possible level.

But this was no ordinary settlement hour. The clearinghouse men brought their printout to the New York Fed office on Wall Street. Many Japanese banks, they saw, had taken advantage of the state of emergency to suspend all payments to the outside world, although they had continued to collect their own accounts receivable. The whole Russian banking system had virtually ceased to exist. A number of European banks had succumbed. Some banks that were officially still solvent had simply not checked in with their payments. All in all, the shortfall in the settlement system was approaching $145 billion.

The clearinghouse men had been joined at the Fed by a number of bank officials, as well as by some Fed officers. The $145 billion shortfall was stunning to all of them – it was simply the biggest financial hole they had ever seen, enough money to run the whole US government for a month. According to the rules, it was now time to pass the hat among the gasping bankers, the idea being that they should cough up the missing 145 gigabucks, or else their whole System was a dead duck.

Each of the elegantly dressed bankers offered to pay the standard 5% of his own bank's daily outward exposure. But that amounted to much less than the sum required. All eyes turned to MacDuff, the New York Fed president. After some seconds of great tension MacDuff left the room and called Washington, informing Greenstreet that he was about to jump into the breach and save the settlement system with $145 billion of what most people would have considered public money. (But since the Fed was privately owned and privately managed, most people, once again, were wrong.)

No President or Congressman or any other federal official could legally have done this under normal conditions, but a Fed district president, not appointed by the President and who had never undergone Senate confirmation, could. MacDuff also asked Greenstreet to please tell the boys at Engraving and Printing to crank up the presses that night.

MacDuff returned to his meeting room of bankers and told them that the Fed would guarantee the integrity of the settlement process, that evening and every evening for the duration of the crisis. The public credit of the United States had been committed to sustain a congeries of bankrupt wastrels, and the elected President and the public had not even been informed – although they hastened to agree when they were.

In other rooms in other buildings, foreign central bankers made other decisions. A few decided to save the three or the ten largest banks in their countries, while triaging the others. A few central banks opted for mass liquidation of everything, while attempting to save themselves.

On the following day, all financial business in Japan remained shut down. But otherwise the wave of panic selling went on, around the world and around the clock, albeit in slightly smaller percentage terms. Frankfurt and Paris lost another 15% before the second day was over, and London was surprised to lose 20%. The Swiss were displeased to see their exchanges shed a fifth or more of their value. This had something to do with wild rumors about derivatives default that buzzed through the trading rooms and the coffee shops of the Bahnhofstrasse.

Now it was no longer the panic of the exchanges that undermined the banks, but the panic of the banks that kept the exchanges in mortal fear. For the long-ticking derivatives time bombs were now in the process of detonating.

The $250 trillion of derivative contracts in existence in 2002 had in the main embodied certain basic assumptions about the structure of world leverage and interest rates. One assumption had been the continued role of Japanese hot money as the lubrication of the entire System. Now that *premise had been overturned by the Aum sect. The System gyrated wildly out of kilter. Banks and brokerages sucked up any cash they could find. Currency rates had broken all the usual patterns. All the currencies of the world were in decline, with the dollar leading the pack into the abyss. All of this meant that the derivatives had entered uncharted territory, with levels never seen in the post-1971 derivatives era. Half of the counterparties in the world were big losers and would soon default, and half of them were big winners who would never collect; and the result was that all were bankrupt.*

Now it was time for Greenstreet to step up to the plate once again. Derivatives were illegal under a whole series of laws, including under the 60-year old prohibitions against bucket shops. But Greenstreet had fostered derivatives anyway.

But out of the general chaos at least one clear tendency had emerged: the dollar could be relied on to fall. Despite an attempt at stringent secrecy by the Fed concerning its open market and discount window operations, rumors had begun to filter out about the prodigious output of Greenstreet's Money Machine. It was a giant snow blower of greenbacks. Everyone knew that the Fed's money supply figures were now an even bigger fake than usual. The prudent thing now, it seemed, was to short the dollar without mercy.

In New York, the second day of the panic was very similar to the first. It was the same routine of limit down selling, 60 and then 120 minutes of "cooling off" that only served to load the sell orders onto the floor brokers, and then a few minutes of free-fall selling. They day closed with another loss of over 35%. But day two was mostly a matter of clearing away the piles of sell orders that had been accumulated on day one. With the market down two thirds, it appeared that the panic was abating somewhat. There were even signs here and there of some plungers re-entering the market. While that seemed incredible, it was clear that the bottom fishers were relying on their 1987 experience, and believed that the market would always make a comeback. But mostly it reflected mutual funds who were borrowing money from the Fed to cover their redemptions while continuing to hold their stocks – for holding all shares was the pre-condition for getting the Fed loans. It could have been much worse, the exhausted brokers agreed, and now the Dow stood at about 2500.

For the second day in a row, Greenstreet's Money Machine, joined by all its auxiliaries in the district Federal Reserve banks, raced ahead at full speed, like an immense vacuum cleaner that was determined to suck every stray T-bill and every Ginnie Mae out of the forgotten crevices of every small-town bank in America. With every passing hour, the Fed was the holder of a larger and larger proportion of the entire $6 trillion dollar public debt of the United States. On this second afternoon there was a regular weekly auction of t-bills, and the Fed was taking no chances. The San Francisco Fed put in a bid for the entire issue at a price that went beyond generosity into prodigality, so determined were the Fedmen to support the price of all paper.

It was just what the Fed had so often loudly refused to do, since this was an alleged violation of the free market fetish and the independence of the central bank. But now the Fedmen were T-bill buyers with a vengeance.

The New York Fed appeared that second evening at the clearinghouse settlement meeting, confirming what was now an obligatory routine. This time there were fewer formalities: after the debits and credits had been added up, the shortfall was almost $250 billion, largely because of a couple of foreign banks which had failed during the day. The Fed representative, now a middle level bureaucrat, did not even blink as he reassured the bankers that meltdown was going to be avoided at all costs. The money supply quietly jumped.

And it seemed to be working: By the morning of the third day, the rush of sell orders had subsided. Every broker knew that he could borrow from the Fed to buy for his company account any shares of stock that a client wanted to dispose of. Indeed, bank regulators were now suspicious of any banker, broker, or insurance man who was NOT borrowing like there was no tomorrow. To be a bear was momentarily as bad as being a communist had been, once upon a time.

Late in the afternoon on the third day, the stock market ventured a small rally, up 15 points to 2265. That evening, more Fed liquidity sloshed into Wall Street, and by morning the Chicago futures, suitably injected with $25 billion in buy orders, were pointing towards a recovery. At the Wall Street opening the market leapt forward by around a hundred points, and had passed the 3000-point milestone on the upside by the end of the day.

But near-fatal damage had already been done. In the early evening of the third day, the Chairman of Pace Manhattan Bank showed up at MacDuff's office and asked for a conference call with Greenstreet. MacDuff and Greenstreet were happy to oblige: Pace Manhattan had the largest derivatives exposure in the world, by now amounting to over $8 trillion, 135% of the entire public debt of the United States. Pace had also invested heavily in the hedge funds of George Spurious, which had now been wiped out.

"Mr. Greenstreet," said the banker, "I can't wait to get funding in the usual ways. My counterparties all over the world have been defaulting for several days. Supporting the stock market is all well and good, but we all know what has really been keeping the stock market going for the last dozen years – derivatives! Without derivatives, there would be no stock market today. Stock market panic is bad, but the derivatives panic is so much worse, as you must know! You have got to take high-profile steps to reassure the derivatives markets. I am asking you here and now to discount my derivatives for me!"

Greenstreet paused for a second. Pace Manhattan was asking him to buy up their derivatives as if they were Treasury notes or commercial paper. It was a lot of trillions. If he discounted the Pace Manhattan derivatives, he could restore confidence with one colossal gesture. But then all the other banks and hedge funds would come forward with their own worthless derivatives and demand cash. The total hit on the Fed would be $50 trillion, and soon $100 trillion. But if Greenstreet refused, the panic might resume and go out of control. Greenstreet weighed his words well.

"The Federal Reserve will discount unlimited quantities of derivative instruments for any member bank that asks for that service," intoned Greenstreet with his best institutional modulations. That was the verbal contract that sealed the biggest transaction in human history – although in dollar terms, it did not remain so for long. In one stroke, $50 trillion was added to the money supply – more than the total value of all stocks, bonds, real estate, buildings and factories in the United States. It would take a little while before the results of that promise showed up in the money supply statistics, which were now becoming quite fictitious.

Confidence was miraculously reborn.

A glow of reassurance and relief was detectable up and down the streets of lower Manhattan. The System had overcome the most dangerous crisis ever. After a few more days, the Dow had crossed above 4,000. No banks or brokers went bankrupt in public, although a number were absorbed. Shell-shocked editorial writers came out of their survival bunkers in Arizona and started churning out propaganda that the System was indeed the summation of all previous civilization, and thus invincible.

But the deeper reality was less reassuring. Central bankers were supposed to be fanatically opposed to inflation, but now they were deliberately creating the greatest worldwide hyperinflation of all time. For three decades, the central bankers had tacked and zigzagged between the two reefs *of dollar collapse on the one hand, and internal bankruptcy on the other. Now the reefs were joined together dead ahead, and there was no where to turn. The System was indeed at an end.*

Every evening the clearinghouse men met with the New York Fed at the settlement hour, and every evening the Fed had to provide a hundred billion or two to wrap up the day's business. The Money Machine continued to hum along at what was now cruising speed, and the money supply was doubling every 9 to 10 days.

For the average person in the United States, the beginning of hyperinflation was both mildly pleasant and unreal at the same time. It was living in a dream, or walking down the street in a trance. One day the public feared the market crash and the confused alarms of worldwide deflation. But suddenly, the great fear had dissipated. The stock market was climbing again. There was relief in the air, and it was springtime.

But before too many days went by, people began top notice that other prices were climbing, too. The meat at the supermarket, which was largely imported, began to go up, first by a quarter every day or two, and then by dollars per pound. Fruits and vegetables also began to rise. Then all types of food were going up, with breadstuffs rising a little slower than the rest. When it was time to gas up the car, it turned out that gasoline was $2 a gallon, then $5, and then $50.

The post-collapse relief gave way to irritation, and then anger. It was worst for those who had put most of their money in mutual funds, since many of these had given up the ghost on the second day of the crash, and were not around to enjoy the drugged revival. All of a sudden it was clear that prices were rising faster than they ever had, much faster than in the days of malaise under the Jimmy Carter administration.

It took almost four weeks before one of the economic pundits put the word HYPERINFLATION for the first time on the cover of a newsmagazine. But hyperinflation it was. The Fed had pumped astronomical quantities of dollars into bankrupt banks, brokers, insurance companies, and clearinghouses. The same thing had been done on a more modest scale during previous crashes, although only for limited periods. In those days it had been enough to open the liquidity spigot full blast for a week or two, until the momentary panic had abated. But this time it was different. Now it was not a spigot; it was a monetary Niagara Falls! This time the banks were demanding more and more loans, even after the panic had been drowned in money. The banks were hemorrhaging cash through the myriad cuts of their derivative exposure. The bankers had touted derivatives as the ultimate answer to risk, and they had brought $250 trillion or more of them into the world. Now it was those derivatives that made a "normal" post-1971 bank bailout impossible. There was not enough money in the world to pay off the derivatives losses, although the Fed and some other central banks were trying as hard as they could. The US money supply was now growing at a 5000% yearly rate, and that rate of growth, bad as it was, was itself doubling every three to four weeks.

A number of large corporations became troubled when they saw how much the hyperinflation was disrupting the daily lives of their workers. Some hired a private economic research firm and told the statisticians there that this time they wanted to know the truth about inflation. When the terrible answer came back, the companies, in order to keep going, decided to begin indexing their wages to the figures from the private economic researchers. They disregarded the Bureau of Labor Statistics report of a doubling of inflation from 3% to 6%, since they knew that was simply a trick to keep down the rise in social security payments. The whole US economy quickly divided into two camps: on the one hand, the smarter corporate managements who kept their companies going for the moment by means of indexing wages to inflation, and, on the other, the short-sighted and vindictive company bosses who held to their creed that pay raises had to be fought to the death.

The employees of the non-indexed companies saw that they could not survive the impact of the hyperinflation on their wages. In small companies they simply walked out the door. In some larger firms there were epic strikes which had the net effect of shutting down those companies too, sometimes with violent outbursts along the way. The labor market became chaotic, with workers deserting the non-indexed companies and lining up by the hundreds for any job openings announced by an indexed concern.

As the lucky workers of the wage-indexed companies began to receive their indexed paychecks, they succumbed to the momentary illusion that they had it made. These employees had spent most of their adult lives writhing under a burden of grinding debt – mortgage debt, consumer debt, home equity debt, auto loans, and all the rest. They had been bled white by usury. Now they gloated as they saw that their fixed debt payments were taking a smaller and smaller bite out of their weekly indexed paychecks. Soon the smarter ones were paying off their mortgages with the new, depreciated dollars. As hyperinflation gathered momentum, some of the more daring began to buy homes, luxury cars, and furniture on credit, wagering that hyperinflation would eat up those new debts so rapidly that they could be paid off in just a few months with even more depreciated, hyperinflated dollars.

Bond holders fared very poorly, as did those with fixed incomes, guaranteed investment contracts, annuities, and any kind of bonds. The stock market rose, but it trailed the hyperinflation at an increasing distance. The Bodkin Board, established to prevent the Social Security cost of living escalator from "overstating" inflation, soon discredited itself and became the object of limitless rage among retired persons because of its habit of keeping the official inflation estimate down to about 10% of the real inflation figure. One of the inflation fighters was actually lynched to a lamppost by a commando of men and women who, according to an eyewitness, were all white-haired and probably over 75 years old.

Every day began to revolve around the fixing of the gold price in London, which took place at noon local time. That meant, for inhabitants of the American eastern seaboard, that each day their clock-radios set for 7 AM local time would lead off the hourly news broadcast with the new price of gold as expressed in dollars. From this the newsmen and bankers calculated how much the dollar had depreciated overnight and the dollar price that would be in force for the new day.

In the third month after the crash, hyperinflation accelerated by one order of magnitude. At one point inflation reached 60% per day. Then it rocketed upward six HUNDRED per cent per day, which came out to 25% per hour. Restaurants began to pro-rate their lunch and dinner prices to their estimate of the following day's dollar-gold fixing in London, meaning that the same item would cost more for lunch than for breakfast, and far more for dinner than for lunch. Those who came for a lengthy luncheon meeting found when they asked for the check that they were being charged dinner prices, and that a $100,000,000 hamburger cost $400,000,000 a few hours later.

With money depreciating so rapidly, there was a tendency to spend it as fast as possible after it was received. The old proverb that money would burn a hole in your pocket was revisited with a vengeance. Bond markets went on a reduced schedule, and most soon closed entirely. As soon as people received dollar bills, they customarily ran to buy the first physical objects they could find, even if they had no need of the merchandise in question. They would barter their acquisition later for some object they actually needed; anything was better than holding cash, a wasting asset.

While hyperinflation gripped the United States, the rest of the world presented a mixed picture. The Bank of England had responded to the panic and liquidity crisis in much the same way as the Federal Reserve had, and soon the United Kingdom was experiencing a hyperinflation along American lines. The finance oligarchs of the City of London were content to let the hyperinflation play out. For a number of years they had been transferring their own assets – the assets that really counted, the assets that made up their own family fortunes – into gold, other precious metals, real estate, and the like. By the time of the crash, the gold, diamonds, platinum, and so forth were secure in fortress-like personal warehouses in the burned-out centers of Midlands industrial towns and along the rivers of England. The finance oligarchs had gone short on paper long ago, and long on high-value commodities. They thought that hyperinflation was jolly good fun, since it drove the prices of their commodities into the ionosphere and underlined how smart they had been to take up speculative hoarding in the first place. And at the same time they had the pleasure of seeing everyone else's assets first eroded, and then destroyed, by hyperinflation. And if Barings had gone belly-up, why should these bloody little upstarts complain, snorted the new age, third way Colonel Blimps in their country houses.

The press lords of Cheat Street packaged the world disaster according to the needs of the oligarchy. The crisis was the fault of that American, George Spurious, and his ilk, they railed. The nation of bankrupt shopkeepers was ruined, and of all the bloody wogs it was the bloody Yanks that had to take the blame.

On the continent, reactions varied. The Banque de France had churned out liquidity at an epic pace in order to save what was left of the French banking system after the Credit Charolais had definitively gone under. The French petty bourgeoisie were great savers, and their legendary thrift had supported a series of rentier-type investments. So French politicians were quick to thunder against the "American hyperinflation" which was robbing the thrifty French middle class of all its accumulated wealth.

Germany was a different story. The Bundesbank had always been dominated by a clique of fanatical neo-Schachtian monetarists on its board. These monetarist fanatics sincerely believed their own propaganda about the need to avoid a new bout of Weimar-style hyperinflation as seen in 1922-23. A few days after the panic, the Bundesbank demanded that the liquidity spigot be closed, and that non-viable banks and brokers be allowed to go bust. The weakened Schröder government collapsed at this demand, and was replaced under an all-party government led by a faceless Green Party yuppy. The new government obeyed the dictates of the Bundesbank, and the Germany economy, bucking the general trend, collapsed into hyperdeflation, with attendant mass layoffs, collapsing production, and immediate immiseration. The little burger with his sleeping cap, the symbol for the average German in the cartoons of the editorial pages, blamed the United States.

Countries like Italy and Spain were swept along willy-nilly with the hyperinflationary tide. Saudi Arabia found itself suddenly penniless as all its dollar assets vaporized, even as it was still selling oil for disappearing dollars. The former holders of savings accounts in Russia bewailed their wretched state, and joined in blaming the United States for their losses.

In Japan, the first instinct was to attune to the US policies because of the exceptional degree of economic integration via the consumer market. The Japanese banks were fascinated with the idea of hyperinflation, since it finally offered a way to get rid of the $2 trillion of bad real estate debts in the banking system. Japan joined in hyperinflation, and the $2 trillion were soon about the price of an office building in Tokyo, and then of a new Toyota, and finally of a daily newspaper, and were thus forgotten. But soon this elation was replaced by the decided feeling that something was wrong. Japanese imports to the United States were now being repaid with dollars that literally vanished before one's eyes, that could never be spent fast enough to avoid colossal foreign exchange losses. The one-night stand with hyperinflation left a thoroughly unpleasant hangover which got worse and worse, and not better.

Something similar took place in Latin America. Debtor nations like Mexico, Brazil, and Argentina watched with delight as their crushing international debt exposure to New York, London, and the international institutions melted away in the hyperinflation heat wave. Then came the realization that raw materials export were being recompensed in dollars that melted away even faster. African countries saw their foreign debts removed, and their foreign exchange devalued. But there were not many functioning governments left in sub-Saharan Africa by this time. The only thing that everyone could agree on was that the United States dollar and thus the United States government were at fault. Americans increasingly found that it was very dangerous to appear in the poverty-ridden streets of foreign cities.

Ever since the Bretton Woods treaty of 1944, the American dollar had been the principal trading and reserve currency of the world. This had not always been so. Before 1931, the British pound sterling had been the unrivalled vehicle for the vast majority of the world's trade, a position the pound had occupied since the Napoleonic wars and even earlier. For a time after 1931, the world had been divided into currency zones, groups of countries in which the pound, the dollar, the yen, the mark, the French franc, and the Soviet ruble had ruled to the exclusion of all others. This had led to the collapse of world trade. But when merchandise cannot cross borders, soldiers will, and so the system of currency zones had led directly to the Second World War. In 1944, the dollar became the premier currency of the world.

The only exceptions to the post-1944 general rule of dollar hegemony had been the Soviet Union, its satellites, and China. When the Soviet empire collapsed between 1989 and 1991, all the satellites and all the Soviet successor states were herded into the dollar zone, meaning that there was no game left in town but the dollar. The Chinese, for their part, were more reticent about betting the ranch on the dollar, and tended to remain on the sidelines except for some limited dabbling in stock markets and the like in a few special economic zones around the largest cities. Since 1944, oil prices had been posted in dollars, and collected in dollars. Dollars could be exchanged everywhere, and in many places they were preferred to the local currency.

The fall of the Eurodollar market had been a lurid and sensational affair, especially as followed through the British tabloids. When the American hyperinflation got going, Eurodollar loans, bonds and futures became worthless practically overnight. London Eurodollar brokers, much to the amusement of the bank-benchers of the House of Lords, were ruined to a man. One of them used US Treasury bonds in six-figure amounts to paper his living room, and then invited in the television cameras. Five hundred Eurodollar brokers chained themselves in protest to the wrought-iron fence outside Number Ten Downing Street, the Prime Minister's residence. The euro was by now completely worthless as well, used to stuff mattresses in homeless shelters. The Labor Premier Tony Flair and his Chancellor of the Exchequer Gordon Brown regarded this as a turning point.

Flair and Brown began meeting with a group of British senior statesmen that included Lord Barrington and Lord Fromer. Flair announced with much fanfare that the United Kingdom was repudiating what remained of the Bretton Woods Treaty, and intended from that day forth to refuse dollars in settlement for international transactions. Since Britain controlled the vast majority of the gold in the world (having most recently taken over the best gold mines in Africa with the help of Mouseveni and Kagame), the British government and the Bank of England were launching a new reserve currency called the golden pound, which would be available at some undetermined future time for settlement purposes among central banks of the new golden pound zone.

The British golden pound would once again make available to the governments of the world all the wonderful advantages that had been enjoyed during the good old days of the nineteenth century, said the mellifluous Flair. The countries of the European Union had accepted the invitation to join the golden pound area, said Flair, as had Australia, South Africa, and many other Commonwealth states. Russia was considering an invitation to join, and China was interested but non-committal. How about the United States, asked a journalist. "As for them," snarled Flair, "they had better get their house in order and stop exporting hyperinflation and chaos around the world." Only when the Americans got their inflation under control could they be even considered for membership in the new sterling area, added the Chancellor of the Exchequer curtly. "The Americans have to learn to live within their means!" And that was the end of the American century.

Most of Flair's speech was double-talk, and his golden pound was largely a demagogic ploy, but countries all around the world began to follow the British and European Union lead, and refused dollars in payment for their products and commodities. When Japan did so, it experienced the biggest wave of mass layoffs in a century. All the Asian Tigers collapsed into ruins. Latin American exporters were wiped out, as were those of the few remaining African states. Arab oil producers and OPEC nations in general offered a crazy quilt of pricing systems: some switched to gold, others to Swiss francs, some to British pounds; a few, fearing US invasion, stayed with a gold-indexed dollar price.

With the world clearing system in ruins, all means of international payment became much riskier than they had been, and world trade, already in decline, began to contract at an even faster pace. The dollar era was over. But at the same time, there was no substitute for the dollar. After the fall of the yen, the euro, and the dollar, nobody wanted pounds, even if they claimed to be golden pound, which nobody believed they were. So chaos ensued.

There was no confidence left anywhere in the world in any financial institution. Everyone was deathly afraid of paper assets of any kind. If the dollar was worthless outside of the United States, what were the currencies of the various petty states of the world then supposed to be worth? The really serious problems involved foreign trade. Oil supplies were subjected to cruel shortages. Superhighways were deserted simply because the average person could no longer afford to pay for gasoline, and there was no mass transit able to take up the slack. Heating oil became astronomically expensive. Electricity, which most people thought came out of the wall, was now available only if assets were pledged in advance to cover the expected monthly bills, which were enormous. Electric lights, an electric range, or even an electric shaver, which had been taken for granted as the essentials of civilization a few years before, were now something people thought long and hard about turning on. Computers were less and less reliable; paper made a comeback, especially for interbank transfers. Bicycle courier now became a growth occupation on the streets of Manhattan, where many a fifty-year old unemployed mutual fund salesman could be seen huffing and puffing as he pedaled along Broadway.

By Christmas, 2002 the United States population sat shivering and hungry in the dark. But the Americans were the lucky ones. In Europe and Japan the drop in the standard of living had been even more extreme, and food riots had destroyed public order. And apart from these industrialized areas, it was not clear how human civilization would survive to the end of the first decade of the twenty-first century. World trade had dropped to about 5% of its 1997 level. Industrial production was down 90%, and food production was down about 80%. Mortality rates were skyrocketing, not just for children and old people, but for young adults. It made the Great Depression of 1932-33 look like a picnic.

BIBLIOGRAPHY

Dean Acheson, *Present at the Creation: My Years in the State Department* (New York: Norton, 1969).

John Adams, *Defence of the Constitutions of Government of the United States of America* in The Works of John Adams (Boston: Little Brown, 1865), vol. IV-V. For an extensive discussion of Machiavelli.

Victor Alba, *Nationalists Without Nations: The Oligarchy Versus the People in Latin America* (New York: Praeger, 1968).

George Anders, *Merchants of Debt: KKR and the Mortgaging of American Business* (New York: Basic Books, 1992).

Jules Archer, *The Plot to Seize the White House* (New York: Hawthorne, 1973).

Joan B. Aron, *Licensed to Kill? : The Nuclear Regulatory Commission and the Shoreham Power Plant* (Pittsburgh: University of Pittsburgh Press, 1997).

Ken Auletta, *The Underclass* (New York: Random House, 1982).

George Leland Bach, *Economics: An Introduction to Analysis and Policy* (Englewood Cliffs, New Jersey: Prentice-Hall, 1958).

Bank for International Settlements, *Recent Developments in International Interbank Relations* (Basel: BIS, 1992).

Ravi Batra, *The Myth of Fee Trade: A Plan for America's Economic Revival* (New York: Scribner, 1993).

Ravi Batra, *Surviving the Great Depression of 1990* (New York: Simon and Shuster, 1988).

Miriam Beard, *A History of the Business Man* (New York: MacMillan, 1938).

Steven K. Beckner, *Back from the Brink: the Greenspan Years* (New York: Wiley, c1996).

Tanya Styblo Beder, "Updating Risk Management to Control Losses," in Lederman and Klein, *Financial Engineering with Derivatives* (Burr Ridge, Illinois: Irwin, 1995), pp. 167-182.

Frederic Benham, *British Monetary Policy* (London: King, 1932).

Thomas G. Bergin, *Petrarch* (Boston: Twayne, 1970).

Kai Bird, *The Chairman* (New York: Simon and Shuster, 1992).

Barry Bluestone and Bennett Harrison, *The Deindustrialization of America* (New York: Basic Books, 1982).

Barry Bluestone and Bennett Harrison, *The Great U-Turn: Corporate Restructuring and the Polarizing of America* (New York: Basic Books, 1988).

Albert Blumrosen, *Black Employment and the Law* (New Brunswick: Rutgers University Press, 1971).

William J. Bouwsma, *Venice and the Defense of Republican Liberty* (Berkeley: University of California, 1968). A celebration of Sarpi.

Andrew Boyle, *Montague Norman* (London: Cassell, 1967).

Nicholas Brady and others, *Report of the Presidential Task Force on Market Mechanisms* (Washington, DC: Superintendent of Documents, 1988).

William Baker, *Down the Tube* (New York: Basicbooks, 1998).

Michael Binstein and Charles Bowden, *Trust me: Charles Keating and the Missing Millions* (New York: Random House, 1993).

Henry Brandon, *The Retreat of American Power* (Garden City: Doubleday, 1973).

Costantino Bresciani-Turroni, *The Economics of Inflation* (London, 1937).

Bretton Woods Commission, *Bretton Woods: Looking to the Future* (Washington DC: Bretton Woods Commission, 1994).

John Brooks, *Business Adventures* (New York: Weybright and Talley, 1969).

John Brooks, *Once in Golconda* (New York: Harper and Row, 1969).

Louis Bromfield, *England: A Dying Oligarchy* (New York: Harper, 1939).

Horatio Brown, *The Venetian Republic* (London: Dent, 1902).

W. A. Brown, Jr., *The International Gold Standard Reinterpreted*, 1914-1934 (New York: National Bureau of Economic Research, 1940).

Connie Bruck, *The Predators' Ball* (New York: Simon and Shuster, 1988).

R. Dan Brumbaugh, *Thrifts Under Siege* (Cambridge MA: Ballinger, 1988).

Pearl Buck, *How it Happens*; *Talk About the German People* (New York: John Day, 1947).

Hugh Bullock, *The Story of Investment Companies* (New York: Columbia University Press, 1959).

Alec Cairncross and Barry Eichengreen, *Sterling in Decline* (Oxford: Blackwell, 1983).

John Campbell, *Edward Heath: A Biography* (London: Jonathan Cape, 1993).

John L. Campbell, *Collapse of an Industry: Nuclear Power and the Contradictions of US Policy* (Ithaca: Cornell University Press, 1988).

Douglas Casey, *Crisis Investing* (New York: Pocket Books, 1980).

Douglas Casey, *Crisis Investing for the Rest of the '90s* (New York: Birch Lane Press, 1993).

W.J. Cash, *The Mind of the South* (New York: Vintage, 1969).

Lester V. Chandler, *Inflation in the US, 1940-1948* (New York: Harper, 1951, 1983).

Lester V. Chandler, *Benjamin Strong, Central Banker* (Washington, DC: Brookings Institute, 1958).

Pat Choate, *America in Ruins: The Decaying Infrastructure* (Durham, North Carolina: Duke University Press, 1983, c1981).

Pat Choate, *Bad Roads: the Hidden Costs of Neglect* (Riverdale, Maryland: National Asphalt Paving Association, c1983).

Pat Choate, *Rebuilding America's Infrastructure: An Agenda for the 1980s* (Durham, North Carolina: Duke University Press, 1983).

Dimitris N. Chorafas, *Chaos Theory in the Financial Markets* (Chicago: Probus, 1994).

Michael Chossudovsky, *The Globalization of Poverty* (Halifax: Fernwood, 1998).

Donald Christensen, *Surviving the Coming Mutual Fund Crisis* (Boston: Little, Brown, 1994).

Stephen V.O. Clarke, *Central Bank Cooperation, 1922-1931* (New York: Federal Reserve Bank of New York, 1967).

Sir Henry Clay, *Lord Norman* (London: Macmillan; 1957).

Clark Clifford and Richard Holbrooke, *Counsel to the President* (New York: Random House, 1991).

Bernard L. Cohen, *The Nuclear Energy Option: an Alternative for the 90s* (New York: Plenum, 1990).

Stephen S. Cohen and John Zysman, *Manufacturing Matters: The Myth of the Post-Industrial Economy* (New York: Basic Books, 1987).

Commission of the European Communities, "Growth, Competitiveness, Employment: The Challenges and Ways Forward into the 21st Century," *Bulletin of the European Communities*, Brussels, June 1993.

John Connally, *In History's Shadow: An American Odyssey* (New York: Hyperion, 1993).

H.G. Creel, *Chinese Thought: From Confucius to Mao Tse-tung* (New York: Mentor, 1953).

H.G. Creel, *Confucius, the Man and the Myth* (New York, 1949).

Dante Alighieri, *The Divine Comedy: Dante's Divine Comedy: The Inferno*, translated by John Aitken Carlyle (New York: Harper, 1849); *The Purgatorio of Dante Alighieri* translated by Philip Henry Wicksteed (London: Dent, 1900).

James Dale Davidson & Lord William Rees-Mogg, *The Great Reckoning* (New York: Simon & Schuster, 1993).

Greg Daugherty, *The Consumer Reports Mutual Funds Book* (Yonkers, New York: Consumer Reports Books, 1994).

Lester and Irene David, *Bobby Kennedy: The Making of a Folk Hero* (New York: Dodd, Mead, 1986).

Kathleen Day, *S&L Hell* (New York: Norton, 1993).

W. Davis Dechert (ed.), *Chaos Theory in Economics: Methods, Models, and Evidence* (Cheltenham, UK: Elgar, 1996).

Darrell Delmaide, *Debt Shock* (Garden City: Doubleday, 1984).

Benjamin DeMott, *The Imperial Middle: Why Americans Can't Think Straight About Class* (New York: William Morrow, 1990).

Derivatives Week, *Learning Curves* (New York: Institutional Investor, 1994).

John Dollard, *Caste and Class in a Southern Town* (New York: Doubleday, 1957).

Economic Report of the President (Washington: Government Printing Office), recent editions.

Franklin R. Edwards, "Will Derivatives Cause the Next Financial Crisis?" American Enterprise Institute Conference Paper, November 7, 1994.

Judith Ramsey Ehrlich and Barry J. Rehfeld, *The New Crowd* (Boston: Little, Brown, 1989).

John D. Ehrlichmann, *Witness to Power*, (New York: Simon and Shuster, 1982).

Barry Eichengreen, *Golden Fetters: The Gold Standard and the Depression, 1919- 1939* (New York: Oxford University Press, 1992).

Marc Eisenson, *The Banker's Secret* (New York: Villard Books, 1990; previous edition Elizaville, New York: Good Advice Press, 1989).

Paul Einzig, *The Tragedy of the Pound* (London: Kegan Paul, 1932).

Paul Erdman, *Tug of War: Today's Global Currency Crisis* (New York: St. Martin's, 1996).

Sergio Fabbrini, *Le regole della democrazia: guida alle riforme* (Bari: Laterza, 1997).

Hans Fallada, *Wolf Among Wolves* (New York: G. P. Putnam, 1938).

Harry E. Figgie, Jr., *Bankruptcy 1995* (Boston: Little, Brown, 1992).

Robert Finlay, *Politics in Renaissance Venice* (New Brunswick: Rutgers, 1980).

John T. Flynn, *Investment Trusts Gone Wrong!* (New York, 1930).

Viviane Forrester, *L'Horreur economique* (Paris; Fayard, 1996).

Tenney Frank, *An Economic Survey of Ancient Rome* (New York: Pageant Books, 1959).

Albert J. Fredman and George Cole Scott, *Investing in Closed-End Funds* (New York: New York Institute of Finance, 1991).

Benjamin M. Friedman, *Day of Reckoning: The Consequences of American Economic Policy under Reagan and After* (New York: Random House, 1988).

Milton Friedman's Monetary Framework: A Debate with His Critics (Chicago: University of Chicago Press, 1974).

Uriel Frisch, *The Legacy of A.N. Kolmogorov* (Cambridge University Press, 1995).

Carlos Fuentes, *The Buried Mirror: Reflections on Spain and the New World* (New York: Houghton Mifflin, 1992).

John Kenneth Galbraith, *The Great Crash 1929* (Boston: Houghton Mifflin, 1979).

John Kenneth Galbraith, *A Short History of Financial Euphoria* (New York: Viking Penguin, 1990).

Charles de Gaulle, *Memoirs of Hope: Renewal and Endeavor* (New York: Simon and Shuster, 1971).

General Accounting Office, *Financial Derivatives: Actions Needed to Protect the Financial System* (Washington, DC: General Accounting Office, May 1994).

Donald Gibson, *Battling Wall Street: The Kennedy Presidency* (1994).

George Gilder, *Wealth and Poverty* (New York: Basic Books, 1981).

Lawrence Goodwyn, *Democratic Promise: The Populist Moment in America* (New York: Oxford University Press, 1976).

Stanislav Govorukhin, *Velikaya Kriminal'naya Revolutsia* (Moscow, Andreyevsky Flag, 1993).

Carole Gould, *The New York Times Guide to Mutual Funds* (New York: Random House, 1992).

Hugh Davis Graham, *The Civil Rights Era* (New York: Oxford, 1990).

Stanley B. Greenberg, *Middle Class Dreams: The Politics and Power of the New American Majority* (New York: Random House, 1995).

William Greider, *Secrets of the Temple: How the Federal Reserve Runs the Country* (New York: Simon and Shuster, 1987).

William Greider, *One World, Ready or Not: The Manic Logic of Global Capitalism* (New York: Simon and Shuster, 1997).

John Gray, *False Dawn: The Delusions of Global Capitalism* (London: Granta, 1998).

William Guttman, *The Great Inflation* (London: Gordon and Cremonesi, 1975).

David Halberstam, *The Best and the Brightest* (New York: Fawcett, 1972).

Alexander Hamilton, James Madison, and John Jay, *The Federalist Papers,* ed. Clinton Rossiter (New York: Mentor, 1961).

John Hargrave, *Montagu Norman* (New York: The Greystone Press, 1942).

Michael Harsgor, *Un très petit nombre* (Paris: Fayard, 1994).

Stefan Hedlund and Niclas Sundstrom, "The Russian Economy After Systemic Change," *Europe-Asia Studies*, vol. 48 no. 6, 1996, 887-914.

Diana B. Henriques, *Fidelity's World* (New York: Scribner, 1995).

John D. Hicks and George E. Mowry, *A Short History of American Democracy.* (Boston: Houghton Mifflin, 1956).

Paddy Hillyard, *The Coercive State* (London: Pinter, 1988).

Fred Hirsch, *Alternatives to Monetary Disorder* (New York: McGraw-Hill, c1977). Contains discussion on controlled disintegration.

Richard Hofstadter, *The Age of Reform: From Bryan to F.D.R* (New York: Knopf, 1955).

Jim Hougan, *Secret Agenda* (New York: Ballantine, 1984).

Herbert Hoover, *The Memoirs of Herbert Hoover* (New York: MacMillan, 1951).

Samuel Huntington, *American Politics: The Promise of Disharmony* (Cambridge: Harvard University Press, 1981).

International Monetary Fund, *Report on the Measurement of International Capital Flows* (Washington: IMF, December 1992).

Walter Isaacson and Evan Thomas, *The Wise Men* (New York: Simon and Shuster, 1986).

Robert H. Jackson and Carl G. Rosberg, *Personal Rule in Black Africa* (Berkeley: University of California, 1982).

Harold James, *International Monetary Cooperation Since Bretton Woods* (Washington DC: International Monetary Fund, 1996).

Christopher Jencks and Paul E. Peterson, *The Urban Underclass* (Washington, DC: Brookings Institution, 1991).

Roy Jenkins, *Truman* (New York: Harper and Row, 1986).

Chalmers Johnson, *MITI and the Japanese Economic Miracle* (Stanford: Stanford University Press, 1982).

Lewis W. Jones, *Cold Rebellion: The South's Oligarchy in Revolt* (London: MacGibbon and Kee, 1962).

Philippe Jorion, *Big Bets Gone Bad* (San Diego: Academic Press, 1995).

Richard D. Kahlenberg, *The Remedy: Class, Race, and Affirmative Action* (New York: HarperCollins, 1997).

Robert D. Kaplan, "Was Democracy Just a Moment?" *Atlantic Monthly*, December 1997, pp. 55 ff.

Ethan B. Kapstein, "Shockproof: The End of the Financial Crisis," *Foreign Affairs*, January-February 1996.

Jane Holtz Kay, *Asphalt Nation* (Berkeley: University of California Press, 1997).

Michael Kazin, *The Populist Persuasion* (New York: Basic Books, 1995).

Doris Kearns, *LBJ and the American Dream* (New York: Signet, 1976).

Susan Estabrook Kennedy, *The Banking Crisis of 1933* (Lexington: University Press of Kentucky, 1973). The best account of the banking panic.

Kerner Commission, *Report of the National Advisory Commission on Civil Disorders* (New York: Bantam, 1968).

John Maynard Keynes, *Essays in Persuasion* (New York: Norton, 1963).

Charles P. Kindleberger, *Manias, Panics, and Crashes: A History of Financial Crises* (New York: Wiley, 1996). Third edition.

Henry A. Kissinger, *White House Years* (New York, 1979).

David C. Korten, *When Corporations Rule the World* (West Hartford, Connecticut: Berrett-Koehler Publishers and Kumarian Press, 1995).

Robert Kuttner, *The Life of the Party: Democratic Prospects in 1988 and Beyond* (New York: Viking Penguin, 1987).

Kung Te-cheng, *Confucius: His Life, Thought, and Influence* (Taipei: Government Printing Office, 1986). (Prof. Kung is the 77th lineal descendent of the philosopher Kung fu-tzu, known in the West as Confucius.)

Diane B. Kunz, *The Battle for Britain's Gold Standard in 1931* (Bechenham, UK: Croom Helm, 1987).

Andrew Krieger, *The Money Bazaar* (New York: Times Books, 1992).

Alexandre Lamfalussy, "The Restructuring of the Financial Industry: A Central Banking Perspective," SUERF lecture, City University, London, March 5, 1994.

David Folkerts-Landau, Peter Garber, and Dirk Schoenmaker, "The Reform of Wholesale Payment Systems" (online).

David Folkerts-Landau and Takatoshi Ito, *International Capital Markets: Developments, Prospects, and Policy Issues* (Washington: IMF, 1995).

Frederick C. Lane, *Money and Banking in Medieval and Renaissance Venice* (Baltimore: Johns Hopkins, 1985).

Lyndon H. LaRouche, *How the International Development Bank Will Work* (New York, 1975).

Christopher Lasch, *The Revolt of the Elites and the Betrayal of Democracy* (New York: Norton, 1995).

Wilhelm Lautenbach, "Möglichkeiten einer Konjunkturbelebung durch Investitionen und Kreditausweitung," in Knut Borchardt and Hans Otto Schötz eds., *Wirtschaftspolitik in der Krise: Die Geheimkonferenz der Friedrich-List-Gesellschaft vom September 1931 über Möglichkeiten und Folgen einer Kreditausweitung* (Baden-Baden: Nomos, 1991), 307-325.

Jess Lederman and Robert A. Klein (eds), *Financial Engineering with Derivatives: cutting-edge innovations and real-world applications* (New York: Irwin, 1995).

V.I. Lenin, *"Left-Wing" Communism, an Infantile Disorder* (Peking: Foreign Languages Press, 1965).

Max Lerner, *America as a Civilization* (New York, Simon and Shuster, 1957). 2 vols.

William E. Leuchtenburg, *Franklin D. Roosevelt and the New Deal* (New York, Harper, 1965).

David Lilienthal, *TVA: Democracy on the March* (New York: Harper, 1953).

Michael Lind, *The Next American Nation: The New Nationalism and the Fourth American Revolution* (New York: The Free Press, 1995).

Friedrich List, *Outlines of American Political Economy*, ed. Michael Liebig (Wiesbaden: Boettiger, c1996).

Phillip Longman, *The Return of Thrift: How the Collapse of the Middle Class Welfare State will Reawaken Values in America* (New York: The Free Press, 1996).

Rolf E. Lüke, *Von der Stabilisierung zur Krise* (Zürich: Polygraphischer Verlag, 1958).

Rolf E. Lüke, *13. Juli 1931: Das Geheimnis der deutschen Bankenkrise* (Frankfurt am Main: Knapp, c1981).

Ferdinand Lundberg, *America's Sixty Families* (New York: Vanguard, 1937).

Douglas MacArthur, *Reminiscences* (New York: McGraw-Hill, 1964).

Niccolò Machiavelli, *The Discourses* (London: Penguin, 1983).

Jeffrey Madrick, *The End of Affluence* (New York: Random House, 1995).

Burton G. Malkiel, *A Random Walk Down Wall Street*, (New York: Norton, 1996).

John F. Marshall and Kenneth R. Kapner, *Understanding Swaps* (New York: Wiley, 1993).

Will Marshall and Martin Schram, *Mandate for Change* (New York: Berkeley Books, 1993).

Hans Peter Martin and Harold Schumann, *The Global Trap: Globalization and the Assault on Democracy and Prosperity* (New York: St. Martins, 1998).

Karl Marx, *Capital: A Critique of Political Economy* (New York: International Publishers, 1967). 3 vols.

Karl Marx, *A Contribution to the Critique of Political Economy* (Moscow: Progress Publishers, 1970).

Karl Marx and Friedrich Engels, *Die Heilige Familie oder Kritik der Kritischen Kritik Gegen Bruno Bauer und Konsorten* (Berlin: Dietz, 1971).

Karl Marx and Friedrich Engels, *The Holy Family, or Critique of Critical Criticism Against Bruno Bauer and Company* (Moscow: Progress Publishers, 1975).

Martin Mayer, *Nightmare on Wall Street: Salomon Brothers and the Corruption of the Marketplace* (New York: Simon & Schuster, 1993).

David P. McCaffrey, *The Politics of Nuclear Power: A History of the Shoreham Nuclear Power Plant* (Dordrecht-Boston: Kluwer, 1991).

George McJimsey, *Harry Hopkins: Ally of the Poor and Defender of Democracy* (Cambridge: Harvard University Press, 1987).

Robert C. McMath, Jr., *American Populism: A Social History, 1877-1898* (New York: Hill and Wang, 1993).

James Medoff and Andrew Harless, *The Indebted Society* (Boston: Little, Brown, 1996).

Ronald L. Meek, *Marx and Engels on Malthus* (London: Lawrence and Wishart, 1953).

Richard Meese, *Exchange Rate Instability: Determinants and Predictability* (San Francisco: Center for Pacific Basin Monetary and Economic Studies, Economic Research Department, Federal Reserve Bank of San Francisco, 1997).

Seymour Melman, *Our Depleted Society* (New York: Dell, 1965).

Seymour Melman, *Profits Without Production* (New York: Knopf, 1983).

Robert Michels, *Zur Soziologie des Parteiwesens in der modernen Demokratie: Untersuchungen über die Oligarchischen Tendenzen des Gruppenlebens* (Stuttgart: Alfred Kröner, 1970).

C. Wright Mills, *White Collar* (New York: Oxford, 1951).

C. Wright Mills, *The Power Elite* (New York: Oxford, 1956).

C. Wright Mills, *Power, Politics, and People: The Collected Essays* (New York: Oxford, 1967).

Broadus Mitchell, *Depression Decade* (White Plains, New York: M. E. Sharpe, 1947).

J.M. Moore, *Aristotle and Xenophon on Democracy and Oligarchy* (University of California Press, 1975).

Roger Moore, *Downsize This! Random Threats from an Unarmed American* (London: Boxtree, 1997). By the maker of *Roger and Me*, the film exposé of GM's managerial incompetence.

Henry R. Nau, *The Myth of America's Decline* (New York: Oxford University Press, 1990).

William R. Neikirk, *Volcker: Portrait of the Money Man* (New York: Congdon and Weed, 1987).

Benjamin Nelson, *The Idea of Usury* (Chicago: University of Chicago Press, 1969).

Jack Newfield, *Robert Kennedy: A Memoir* (New York: Dutton, 1969).

Richard Nixon, *R.N.: The Memoirs of Richard Nixon* (New York: Grosset and Dunlap, 1978).

Alexander Dana Noyes, *The Market Place: Reminiscences of a Financial Editor* (Boston: Little, Brown, 1938).

John S. Odell, *U.S. International Monetary Policy* (Princeton, 1982)

Chris Ogden, *Maggie* (New York: Simon & Schuster, 1990).

Kenichi Ohno, "The Case for a New System," in *Bretton Woods: Looking to the Future* (Washington DC: Bretton Woods Commission, July, 1994).

Giammaria Ortes, *Calcolo sopra i giuochi della bassetta e del faraone* (Venezia: Pasquali, 1757).

Giammaria Ortes, *Della Economia Nazionale* (Milano: Marzorati, 1971).

Giammaria Ortes, *Riflessioni sulla Popolazione delle Nazioni per Rapporto all'Economia Nazionale* (1790), reprinted in Custodi, *Scrittori Classici Italiani di Economia Politica* (Milan, 1804), vols. XXIV and XLII.

Walton M. Padelford, "The Scholastics on Just Price and Usury," *The Northwest Missouri State University Studies* (XXXVI, number 2, May 1976).

Thomas I. Palley, "The Forces Making for an Economic Collapse," *Atlantic Monthly*, July 1996, 44-58.

Melchior Palyi, *The Twilight of Gold 1914 - 1936* (Chicago: Regnery, 1972).

Anthony J. Pansini, *Niccolò Machiavelli and the United States of America* (Greenvale, NY: Greenvale Press, 1969).

Maurizio Parasassi, *Cospirazioni economiche* (Firenze: Sansoni, 1974).

Alain Parguez, "Debts and Savings or the Scourge of the Search for Sound Finance," in *Economies et Societés: le Rôle de la Dette dans l'Economie Capitaliste* (Paris: Cahiers de l'ISMEA, 1994).

Peter G. Peterson, *Facing Up* (New York: Simon & Schuster, 1993).

Wallace C. Peterson, *Silent Depression: Twenty-five Years of Wage Squeeze and Middle-Class Decline* (New York: Norton, 1994).

Thomas Petzinger, Jr., *Oil and Honor: The Texaco-Pennzoil Wars* (New York: Putnam, 1987).

Kevin Phillips, *Boiling Point* (New York: Random House, 1993).

Kevin Phillips, *Arrogant Capital* (Boston: Little, Brown, 1994.)

Stephen Pizzo, Mary Fricker, and Paul Muolo, *Inside Job: The Looting of America's Savings and Loans* (New York: Harper, 1989).

Plato, *Collected Dialogues*, ed. Edith Hamilton and Huntington Cairns (Princeton University Press, 1989).

Sidney Pollard (ed.), *The Gold Standard and Employment Between the Wars* (London: Methuen, 1970).

Robert R. Prechter, Jr., *At the Crest of the Tidal Wave: a Forecast for the Great Bear Market* (Gainesville, Georgia: New Classics Library, 1995).

Donald E. Queller, *The Venetian Patriciate: Reality versus Myth* (Urbana: University of Illinois, 1986).

William J. Quirk, *The Betrayal of the Middle Class* (Lanham, Maryland: Madison Books, c. 1992).

J. Mark Ramseyer and Frances M. Rosenbluth, *The Politics of Oligarchy: Institutional Choice in Imperial Japan* (Cambridge University Press, 1995).

Judith H. Rawnsley, *Total Risk* (New York: HarperBusiness, 1995).

Robert B. Reich, *The Work of Nations* (New York: Knopf, 1991).

James Reston, Jr., *The Lone Star: The Life of John Connally* (New York: Harper and Row, 1989).

David Riesman, *The Lonely Crowd; A Study of the Changing American Character* (New Haven: Yale University Press, 1950).

Lawrence S. Ritter (ed.), *Money and Economic Activity* (Boston: Houghton Mifflin, 1961).

Lionel Robbins, *The Great Depression* (London, 1934).

Arthur J. Rolnik, "The Case for Fixed Exchange Rates," in *Annual Report of the Federal Reserve Bank of Minneapolis*, 1989.

Arthur J. Rolnik, "In Order to Form a More Perfect Monetary Union," 1993.

Robert Rowthorn and Ramana Ramaswamy, "Deindustrialization: Causes and Implications," IMF Working Paper, April 1997.

Jacques Rueff, *De L'Aube au Crépuscule* (Paris: Plon, 1977).

David Ruelle, *Chance and Chaos* (New Jersey: Princeton University Press, 1991).

William Safire, *Before the Fall: an Inside View of the pre-Watergate White House* (New York: Da Capo Press, 1988, 1975).

Paul Samuelson, *Economics* (New York: McGraw-Hill, 1980). Eleventh edition.

Robert J. Samuelson, *The Good Life and its Discontents* (New York: Random House, 1995).

Paolo Sarpi, *Pensieri naturali, metafisici e matematici*. ed. Luisa Cozzi and Libero Sosio (Milano:Ricciardi, 1996).

R.S. Sayers, "The Return to Gold, 1925" in Pollard (ed.), *The Gold Standard and Employment Between the Wars* (London: Methuen, 1970).

US Senate Report 93-459: Provisions of Federal Law Now in Effect Delegating to the Executive Extraordinary Authority in Time of National Emergency (Washington, DC: Government Printing Office, 1973).

Jean-Jacques Servan-Schreiber, *The American Challenge* (New York: Avon, 1969).

Mary Schiavo, *Flying Blind, Flying Safe* (New York: Avon, 1997).

Friedrich Schiller, "The Legislation of Lycurgus and Solon,", in *Poet of Freedom* (Washington DC: Schiller Institute, 1988), vol. III, pp. 273-305.

Arthur M. Schlesinger, Jr., *The Coming of the New Deal* (Boston: Houghton Mifflin, 1959).

Arthur M. Schlesinger, Jr., *Robert Kennedy and His Times* (Boston: Houghton Mifflin, 1978).

Steven Schlosstein, *The End of the American Century* (New York: Congdon and Weed, 1989).

Juliet B. Schor, *The Overspent American: Upscaling, Downshifting, and the New Consumer* (New York: Basic Books, 1998).

Juliet B. Schor, *The Overworked American: the Unexpected Decline of Leisure* (Basic Books, 1991).

John E. Schwartz and Thomas J. Volgy, *The Forgotten Americans* (New York: Norton, 1992).

Securities and Exchange Commission, *Investment Trusts and Investment Companies* (Washington, 1939).

Max Shapiro, *The Penniless Billionaires* (New York: Truman Talley, 1980).

Judy Shelton, *Money Meltdown: Restoring Order to the Global Currency System* (New York: The Free Press, 1994).

Robert E. Sherwood, *Roosevelt and Hopkins* (New York: Harper, 1948).

Morton Shulman, *How to Invest Your Money and Profit from Inflation* (New York: Ballantine, 1981).

George P. Shultz and Kenneth W. Dam, *Economic Policy Beyond the Headlines* (New York: Norton, 1977).

Thomas E. Skidmore and Peter H. Smith, *Modern Latin America* (New York: Oxford, 1997).

Robert Slater, *Soros* (Burr Ridge, Illinois: Irwin Professional Publishing, 1995).

Robert Sobel, *Panic on Wall Street* (New York: General American Investors , 1977).

Robert Solomon, *The International Monetary System 1945-1976* and *The International Monetary System 1945-1981* (New York: Harper & Row, 1977, 1982).

Stephen Solomon, *The Confidence Game* (New York: Simon and Shuster, 1995).

Irvine H. Sprague, *Bailout: An Insider's Account of Bank Failures and Rescues* (New York: Basic Books, 1986).

Herbert Stein, *The Fiscal Revolution in America* (Washington, DC: AEI Press, 1996).

Walter Stewart, *Too Big To Fail* (Toronto: McClelland & Stewart, 1993).

Susan Strange, *Casino Capitalism* (Oxford: Blackwell, 1986).

Susan Strange, *The Retreat of the State: the Diffusion of Power in the World Economy* (New York: Cambridge University Press, 1996).

Susan Strange, *Mad Money: When Markets Outgrow Governments* (Ann Arbor: University of Michigan Press, 1998).

Frederick Strobel, *Upward Dreams, Downward Mobility: The Economic Decline of the American Middle Class* (Lanham, Maryland: Rowman and Littlefield, 1993).

Bruce J. Summers and Akinari Horii, "Large-Value Transfer Systems," in *The Payment System: Design, Management, and Supervision,* (Washington: International Monetary Fund, 1994).

William Graham Sumner, *On Plutocracy: Political Writings* (Washington DC: Plutarch Press, 1991).

Sun Yat-sen, *The International Development of China* (New York: Da Capo, 1975). Probably the best national development strategy produced in the twentieth century.

Anthony C. Sutton, *The War on Gold* (Seal Beach, California: '76 Press, 1977).

Michael D. Swaine, *The Military and Political Succession in China* (Santa Monica: RAND, 1992).

John J. Sweeney, *American Needs a Raise* (Boston: Houghton Mifflin, 1996).

Webster Griffin Tarpley and Anton Chaitkin, *George Bush: The Unauthorized Biography* (Washington DC: Executive Intelligence Review, 1992), online at www.tarpley.net.

Webster Griffin Tarpley, *Against Oligarchy: Essays and Speeches, 1970-1996* (Gaithersburg, Maryland: Washington Grove Books, 1997), online at www.tarpley.net.

Gordon Thomas and Max Morgan-Witts, *The Day the Bubble Burst* (Garden City: Doubleday, 1979).

James Tobin, *Full Employment and Growth: Further Essays on Keynesian Policy* (Cheltenham, UK: Edward Elgar, 1996).

John Train, *The Craft of Investing* (New York: HarperBusiness, 1994).

Margaret Truman, *Harry S. Truman* (New York: Morrow, 1973).

United States Department of State, *Proceedings and Documents of the United Nations Monetary and Financial Conference, Bretton Woods, New Hampshire, July 1-22, 1944* (Washington DC: Government Printing Office, 1948), 2 vols.

Usury Laws, (New York: The Society for Political Education, 1881).

Tonis Vaga, *Profiting from Chaos: Using Chaos Theory for Market Timing, Stock Selection, Option Valuation* (New York: McGraw-Hill, 1994).

Frank A. Vanderlip, "From Farm Boy to Financier" in *The Saturday Evening Post*, 1934-35.

Natalya M. Vitrenko, *Sotsial'naya Infrastruktura Ukrainy* (Kiev: Naukova Dumka, 1993).

Paul Volcker and Toyoo Gyohten, *Changing Fortunes: The World's Money and the Threat to American Leadership* (New York: Times Books, 1992).

Joseph Vranich, *Supertrains* (New York: St. Martin's, 1991).

E. Wandel, *Hans Schäffer, Steuermann in wirtschaftlichen und politischen Krisen* (Stuttgart: Deutsche Verlags-Anstalt, 1974).

Russell R. Wasendorf and Thomas A. McCafferty, *All About Options* (Chicago: Probus, 1993).

John Weitz, *Hitler's Banker: Hjalmar Horace Greeley Schacht* (Boston: Little, Brown, 1997).

Byron Wien and Krisztina Koenen, *Soros on Soros* (New York: Wiley, 1995).

Jules Witcover, *85 Days: The Last Campaign of Robert Kennedy* (New York: Putnam, 1969).

Christopher Wood, *The Bubble Economy* (New York: Atlantic Monthly Press, 1992).

Bob Woodward, *The Agenda: Inside the Clinton White House* (New York: Pocket Books, 1995).

Maurice Zeitlin, *Talking Union* (Urbana: University of Illinois Press, 1996).

Stefan Zweig, *Die Welt von Gestern* (Frankfurt: Fischer, 1993). English translation: *The World of Yesterday*, (New York: Viking, 1943).

Devastating Critique of Wall St. Financiers
by WEBSTER GRIFFIN TARPLEY

9/11 Synthetic Terror: Made in USA provides *answers*, not just questions, and *purpose:* the way to stop endless war. A masterpiece and a "Bible of 9/11 Truth," with the only working model of the 9/11 plot: a rogue network of moles, patsies, and professional killer cells, operating in privatized paramilitary settings, and covered by corrupt politicians and corporate media. With a penetrating, insightful world view of geopolitics and history. 512 pages, only $17.95.

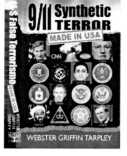

Tarpley's groundbreaking classic exposé of the Bush dynasty and their New World Order, *George Bush: The Unauthorized Biography*. Exhaustively documents how the Bushes and their Skull & Bones brethren made fortunes on financing the Nazi death camps. 700 pages, 19.95

In 2008, Webster Tarpley scoops the big shift at the top of the US-UK empire. The Trilaterals are pushing aside the neo-cons, taking power, and their chosen puppet is Barack Obama. *Obama – The Postmodern Coup: Making of a Manchurian Candidate* exposes his handlers as enemies of the people. Foreign policy vizier Brzezinski, instigator of Al-Qaeda and the Afghan-Soviet war, is gunning for a global showdown with Russia and China. Regressive Skull & Bones advisors will plunder the people for Wall Street. In this and his second book on Obama, Tarpley draws on an unparalleled store of erudition, independent insight, historical precedents and inside knowledge of today's political players, the essentials you need to know about US and world politics. 320 pages, $15.95.

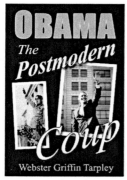

Barack H. Obama: The Unauthorized Biography, is a massive, devastating exposé. Obama, creature of the Ford Foundation, classic existentialist anti-hero, is utterly without principles – perfect for a career in the most corrupt turf in the USA, the Chicago political machine. Fraud and graft reach dizzy heights – his close cronies, the felons Al-Samarrae, Auchi and Rezko, have stolen countless millions. Zbig and Obama will take us to the cleaners like we've never been before. 595 pp., $19.95.

Listen anytime to Tarpley's weekly talk show, World Crisis Radio, at http://www.gcnlive.com. He has appeared on CNN, Fox News Channel, C-SPAN, Charlie Rose, and numerous talk radio programs in the United States and around the world.

Barack H. Obama
The Unauthorized Biography

Webster Griffin Tarpley
author of *George Bush: The Unauthorized Biography*

Printed in the United States
153499LV00001B/2/P